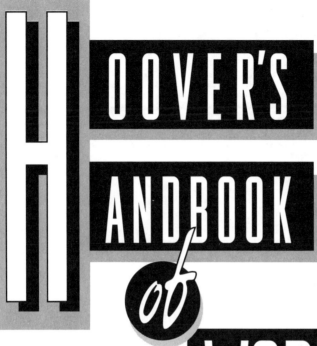

HOOVER'S HANDBOOK of WORLD BUSINESS 1995-1996

EDITED BY
PATRICK J. SPAIN
& JAMES R. TALBOT

^{TM}

The Reference Press, Inc.

Copyright © 1995 by The Reference Press, Inc. All rights reserved. No part of this book may be reproduced or transmitted in any form or by any means, electronic or mechanical, including by photocopying, facsimile transmission, recording, rekeying, or using any information storage and retrieval system, without permission in writing from The Reference Press, Inc., except that brief passages may be quoted by a reviewer in a magazine, in a newspaper, on-line, or in a broadcast review.

10   9   8   7   6   5   4   3   2   1

Publisher Cataloging-In-Publication Data

Hoover's Handbook of World Business 1995. Edited by Patrick J. Spain and James R. Talbot

   Includes indexes.
   1. Business enterprises — Directories.   2. Corporations — Directories.
HF3010   338.7

The complete *Hoover's Company Database* is available on-line on America Online, CompuServe, eWorld, LEXIS/NEXIS, Bloomberg Business Network, NlightN, and on the Internet on Quotecom (e-mail: info@quote.com), Farcast (e-mail: info@farcast.com), and InfoSeek (http://www.infoseek.com). A catalog of Reference Press products is available on the World Wide Web **(http://www.hoovers.com)** and Gopher (gopher.hoovers.com).

ISBN 1-878753-44-4 clothbound
ISSN 1055-7199

This book was produced by The Reference Press on Apple Macintosh computers using Aldus Corporation's PageMaker 4.2 software and Adobe System, Inc.'s fonts from the Clearface and Futura families. Graphs were created using DeltaGraph, a product of DeltaPoint, Inc. Cover design is by Kristin M. Jackson, of Austin, Texas. Electronic prepress and printing were done by Quebecor Printing, Fairfield, Inc., in Fairfield, Pennsylvania. Text paper is 60# Postmark Bright White (manufactured by Union Camp). Cover stock is 80#, coated two sides, text weight.

US AND WORLD (EXCEPT EUROPE)
The Reference Press, Inc.
6448 Highway 290 E., Suite E-104
Austin, Texas 78723
Phone: 512-454-7778
Fax: 512-454-9401
e-mail: refpress6@aol.com

EUROPE
William Snyder Publishing Associates
5, Five Mile Drive,
Oxford OX2 8HT,
England
Phone & fax: +44 (01)865-513186
e-mail: 100072.2511@compuserve.com

THE REFERENCE PRESS

Founder: Gary Hoover
Chairman, President, CEO, and Senior Editor: Patrick J. Spain
Vice President of Sales and Marketing: Dana L. Smith
Senior Managing Editor: James R. Talbot
Director of Sales and Marketing for Electronic Products: Tom Linehan
Senior Editor of Online Publishing: Matt Manning
Controller: Deborah L. Dunlap
Desktop Publishing Manager: Holly Hans Jackson
Advertising and Publicity Manager: Angela J. Schoolar
Senior Researcher: Laraine Johnston
Office Manager: Tammy Fisher
Customer Service Manager: Rhonda T. Mitchell
Sales Assistant: Lisa Treviño

The Reference Press Mission Statement

1. To produce business information products and services of the highest quality, accuracy, and readability.
2. To make that information available whenever, wherever, and however our customers want it through mass distribution at affordable prices.
3. To continually expand our range of products and services and our markets for those products and services.
4. To reward our employees, suppliers, and shareholders based on their contributions to the success of our enterprise.
5. To hold to the highest ethical business standards, erring on the side of generosity when in doubt.

ABBREVIATIONS

AB – Aktiebolaget (Swedish)*

ADR – American Depository Receipts

AG – Aktiengesellschaft (German)*

AMEX – American Stock Exchange

AS – Aksje Selskap (Norwegian)*

ASEAN – Association of South East Asian Nations

ATM – automated teller machines

CAD-CAM – computer-aided design – computer-aided manufacturing

CD-ROM – compact disc – read-only memory

CEO – Chief Executive Officer

CFO – Chief Financial Officer

COMECON – Council for Mutual Economic Assistance

COO – Chief Operating Officer

DAT – digital audio tape

DOD – Department of Defense (US)

DRAM – dynamic random-access memory

EC – European Community

ECU – European Currency Unit

EEC – European Economic Community

EFTA – European Free Trade Association

EPS – earnings per share

EVP – Executive Vice-President

FCC – Federal Communications Commission (US)

FDA – Food and Drug Administration (US)

FTC – Federal Trade Commission (US)

FY – fiscal year

GATT – General Agreement on Tariffs and Trade

GDP – gross domestic product

GmbH – Gesellschaft mit beschränkter Haftung (German)*

GNP – gross national product

HDTV – high-definition television

HMO – health maintenance organization

IMF – International Monetary Fund

LAN – local-area network

LBO – leveraged buyout

LCD – liquid crystal display

LD – laser disc

LDC – less-developed country

LP – limited partnership

Ltd. – limited*

MFN – Most Favored Nation

MITI – Ministry of International Trade and Industry (Japan)

NAFTA – North American Free Trade Agreement

Nasdaq – National Association of Securities Dealers Automated Quotations

NATO – North Atlantic Treaty Organization

NV – Naamlose Vennootschap (Dutch)*

NYSE – New York Stock Exchange

OAS – Organization of American States

OECD – Organization of Economic Cooperation and Development

OEM – original equipment manufacturer

OPEC – Organization of Petroleum Exporting Countries

OTC – over the counter

P/E – price per earnings

PLC – public limited company*

R&D – research and development

RISC – reduced instruction set computer

ROA – return on assets

ROE – return on equity

ROI – return on investment

SA – Société Anonyme (French)*; Sociedad Anónima (Spanish and Portuguese)*

SA de CV – Sociedad Anónima de Capital Variable (Spanish)*

SEC – Securities and Exchange Commission (US)

SEVP – Senior Executive Vice-President

SIC – Standard Industrial Classification

SpA – Società per Azioni (Italian)*

SPARC – scalable processor architecture

SVP – Senior Vice-President

VAT – value-added tax

VC – Vice-Chairman

VP – Vice-President

WAN – wide-area network

* These abbreviations are used in companies' names to convey that the companies are limited liability enterprises; the meanings are usually the equivalent of *corporation* or *incorporated*.

Contents

List of Lists

Companies Profiled

* Companies added to *Hoover's Handbook of World Business 1995–1996*

ABOUT HOOVER'S HANDBOOK
OF WORLD BUSINESS

I n 1990 we at The Reference Press broke new ground with the first annual publication of *Hoover's Handbook*. This book was the first widely distributed, reasonably priced, easy-to-use annual reference book on major companies and was an immediate success. This book has since been split into 2 volumes: this volume, *Hoover's Handbook of World Business*, and a companion volume, *Hoover's Handbook of American Business*. We have also added a number of new titles to the *Hoover's* series in the past 5 years, including *Hoover's Handbook of Emerging Companies, Hoover's MasterList of Major US Companies, The Texas 500: Hoover's Guide to the Top Texas Companies, The Bay Area 500: Hoover's Guide to the Top San Francisco Area Companies*, and, most recently, *Hoover's Guide to Private Companies*. We have also migrated the *Hoover's* products from print to various electronic media, including CD-ROM, floppy diskette, on-line, and personal digital assistant (PDA) formats.

The book you hold in your hand profiles 227 of the largest and most influential companies based outside the United States. It is founded on the belief that these days, more than ever, the world of business really does involve the whole world. In the 1950s giant corporations were largely an American and European phenomenon. Today the idea of the large profit-driven business enterprise is accepted globally. While it is obvious to anyone with open eyes that world politics are changing, it may be less obvious that world economics are changing just as fast.

These changes have manifested themselves in various ways. For example, the number of foreign companies with equities listed on American stock exchanges has skyrocketed in the last few years to over 1,250. Also, the fall of Communism in eastern Europe and the economic liberalization in China have resulted in for-profit, publicly traded companies springing up in the unlikeliest of places, for example, China-based Shanghai Petrochemical (profiled on page 468 of this book).

Clearly anyone with a need for business information also has a need for *international* business information. If you are looking for a job, you may be missing great opportunities if you are unwilling to talk to foreign-owned firms such as News Corp. (Fox Broadcasting), Matsushita (MCA and Universal Pictures), and Grand Metropolitan (Pillsbury and Burger King). If you sell products but fail to call on Toyota, Siemens, or Hudson's Bay, you may be missing the boat. If you're buying stocks but not considering foreign companies, you may be cheating yourself out of opportunities in Sony, Cifra, Nestlé, and Teléfonos de Chile equities.

We believe that *Hoover's Handbook of World Business* represents the most complete source of in-depth information on large, non-US-based business enterprises readily available to the general public. We have gone to great effort and expense to provide you with a concise, accurate, and timely guide to business.

Hoover's Handbook of World Business 1995–1996 consists of the following 4 components:

1. The first section, "Using the Company Profiles," explains how to get the most out of the company profiles. It details the information contained in each section and the styles and conventions we have used in presenting the data.

2. The next section, "A List-Lover's Compendium," contains numerous lists covering, among other things, the largest companies in the book, the largest companies in key industries, and the companies that are included in the world's major stock market indexes.

3. The third and most important section of the book contains the profiles themselves —
   227 profiles of business enterprises of global importance.

4. The book concludes with 3 indexes: (1) an index of profiles by industry, (2) an index of
   companies by headquarters location, and (3) the main index of the book, containing the
   names of all brands, companies, and people mentioned in the profiles.

Longtime readers of the book will notice that we have streamlined the front materials and removed the country profiles that were included in previous editions. Although those features
were popular with many of our readers, your calls and comments clearly indicated that you
would prefer seeing more company profiles in the book. We've obliged by adding 42 new companies to this edition ranging from a rising UK-based cosmetic retailer (The Body Shop) to an
African mining concern (Zambia Consolidated Copper Mines).

As always, we hope you find our books useful; we invite your comments: by phone
(512-454-7778), fax (512-454-9401), e-mail (refpress3@aol.com), or mail.

The Editors
Austin, Texas
February 8, 1995

USING THE PROFILES

Selection of the Companies Profiled

The 227 business enterprises profiled here include numerous publicly traded companies, from Accor to Zambia Copper, several private businesses (e.g., Bertelsmann and The Body Shop), and a selection of government-owned (e.g., PEMEX and Qantas) entities. The companies selected represent a cross section of the largest, most influential, and most interesting companies based outside the United States.

In selecting these companies our foremost question was "What companies will our readers be most interested in?" Our goal was to answer as many questions as we could in one book, in effect trying to anticipate your curiosity. This approach resulted in the selection of 7 types of companies:

1. The global giants with whom each of us, no matter where we live, has contact (e.g., Daimler-Benz, Toyota, and British Petroleum).

2. Companies with substantial activity in the United States, either exporting their products to the states or making products (or providing services) here.

3. Businesses that either dominate big industries or lead the industry in their country (e.g., Rhône-Poulenc, France's biggest chemical company).

4. Representative companies from around the world (one Indian company, Tata; one Malaysian company, Sime Darby; one Chinese company, Shanghai Petrochemical; etc.).

5. Companies representing virtually every major industry, from steel to hotels, brewing to publishing.

6. Companies that have high profiles with consumers (e.g., The Body Shop and Club Mediteranee) or interesting stories (e.g., Virgin Group).

7. The Big Six accounting firms. Though all are headquartered or co-headquartered in the United States, they have truly global reach. These enterprises include the only US-headquartered firms contained in this book.

Organization of the Profiles

The 227 company profiles are presented in alphabetical order. We have shown the full name of the enterprise at the top of the page, unless it is too long, in which case you will find it above the address in the Where section of the profile. If a company name starts with a person's first name, like Arthur Andersen, it is alphabetized under the first name. We've also tried to alphabetize companies where you would expect to find them — for example, Deutsche Lufthansa is in the L's and Groupe Schneider can be found under S. All company names (past and present) used in the profiles are indexed in the main index of the book.

Certain pieces of basic data are listed at the top left of the second page of each profile: where the stock is traded (if the stock is available in the US the ticker symbol is listed as well) and when the company's fiscal year ends.

Overview

In this section we have tried to give a thumbnail description of the company and what it does. The description will usually include information on the company's strategy, reputation, and ownership. We recommend that you read this section first.

When

This longer section reflects our belief that every enterprise is the sum of its history, and that you have to know where you came from in order to know where you are going. While some companies have very little historical awareness and were unable to help us much, and other companies are just plain boring, we think the vast majority of the enterprises in the book have colorful backgrounds. When we could find information, we tried to focus on the people who made the enterprise what it is today. We have found these histories to be full of twists and ironies; they can make for some fascinating and quick reading.

Who

Here we list the names of the people who run the company, insofar as space allows. We have shown age and pay information when available, although most non-US companies are not required to report the level of detail revealed in the US.

While companies are free to structure their management titles any way they please, most modern corporations follow standard practices. The ultimate power in any corporation lies with the shareholders, who elect a board of directors, usually including officers or "insiders" as well as individuals from outside the company. The chief officer, the person on whose desk the buck stops, is usually called the chief executive officer (CEO) in the US. In other countries practices vary widely. In the UK, traditionally, the Managing Director performs the functions of the CEO without the title, although the use of the term "CEO" is on the rise in the UK. In Germany it is customary to have 2 boards of directors: a managing board populated by the top executives of the company and a higher-level supervisory board consisting of outsiders.

We have tried to list each company's most important officers, including the chief financial officer (CFO) and chief personnel (human resources) officer. For companies with US operations, we have included the names of the US CEO, CFO, and top human resources executive, where this information was available. The Who section also includes the name of the company's auditing (accounting) firm. The people named in the profiles are indexed in the book's main index by their last names.

Where

Here we included the company's headquarters address and phone and fax numbers as available. We also list the same information for

the main US office of each company, if one exists. Telephone numbers of foreign companies are shown using standardized conventions of international dialing. In most countries callers will have to dial a prefix to make an international call (e.g., 011 in the US). In some countries it is necessary to dial an additional digit if the call is made within the country (e.g., 1 before the area code in the US). This digit is not dialed from abroad. We have indicated such local calling digits by using parentheses [e.g., (0)].

We have also included as much information as we could gather and fit on the geographical distribution of the company's business, including sales and profit data. Note that these profit numbers, like those in the What section below, are usually operating profits rather than net profits. Operating profits are generally those before financing costs (interest payments) and taxes, which are considered costs attributable to the whole company rather than to one division or part of the world. For this reason, the net income figures (in the How Much section) are usually much lower, since they are after interest and taxes. Pretax profits are after interest but before taxes.

What

This section lists as many of the company's products, services, brand names, divisions, subsidiaries, and joint ventures as we could fit. We have tried to include all its major lines and all familiar brand names. The nature of this section varies by industry, company, and the amount of information available. If the company publishes sales and profit information by type of business, we have included it. The brand and division names are listed in the last index in the book, with past and present company names.

Key Competitors

In this section we have listed those other companies that compete with the profiled company. This feature is included as a quick way to locate similar companies and compare them. For this edition of the book, we have broadened the scope of the Key Competitors section from just those in *Hoover's Handbooks* to the entire universe of business enterprises. Due to the difficulty in identifying companies that only compete in foreign markets, the lists of competitors are still weighted heavily to large international companies with a strong US presence. Whenever the company or another source identified a company's primary competitors, we have tried to incorporate that information into our lists.

How Much

Here we have tried to present as much data about each enterprise's financial performance as we could compile in the allocated space. While the information varies somewhat from industry to industry, and is less complete in the case of private companies that do not release these data (though we have always tried to provide annual sales and employment), the following information is generally present.

A ten-year table, with relevant annualized compound growth rates, covering:

- Fiscal year sales (year-end assets for most financial companies)

- Fiscal year net income (before extraordinary items and after minority interests, wherever possible)

- Fiscal year earnings per share (EPS) (fully diluted if available)

- Calendar year stock price high, low, and close

- Calendar year high and low price/earnings ration (P/E)

- Fiscal year dividends per share for US$-denominated ADRs and share dividends as declared for most other shares (in many countries it is customary to pay dividends out of the prior year's earnings)

- Fiscal year-end book value (shareholders' equity per share)

- Fiscal year-end or average number of employees

Key year-end statistics that generally show the financial strength of the enterprise, including:

- Debt ratio (total debt as a percentage of combined total debt and shareholders' equity)

- Return on average equity (net income divided by the average of beginning shareholders' equity and ending shareholders's equity) for the fiscal year

- Cash and marketable securities on hand at the end of the fiscal year

- Current ratio at fiscal year-end (ration of current assets to current liabilities) for those profiles with US$-denominated How Much tables

- Total long-term debt (excluding capital lease obligations) at fiscal year-end

- Number of shares of common stock outstanding at fiscal year-end

- Dividend yield (fiscal year dividends per share divided by the calendar year-end closing stock price)

- Dividend payout (fiscal year dividends divided by fiscal year EPS)

- Market value at calendar year-end (calendar year-end closing stock price multiplied by fiscal year-end number of shares outstanding) in US$

- Sales (or assets, where applicable) translated into US$ for those profiles with foreign currency–denominated How Much tables

A Note on The Numbers

Since the last edition of the book, we've changed the way we assemble some of our financial information. For example, we no longer attempt to modify reported sales by deducting interest income, sales, excise tax, and similar items. All revenue numbers are as reported by the company in its annual report. Also, the year at the top of each column in the How Much is now the year in which the company's fiscal year actually ends. Thus, information for a company with a February 28,

1994, year-end is shown in the 1994 column. Stock price information for companies with year-ends between January and June is for the last trading day of the prior calendar year and is so footnoted on the chart.

We include ten-year information on number of employees in order to aid readers interested in knowing whether a company has a long-term trend of increasing or decreasing employment. As far as we know, we are the only company that publishes this information in print format.

Note that, throughout the How Much section, per-share data are adjusted for stock splits. Some of the data for US-listed companies has been provided to us by Media General Financial Services, Inc. All other data were generated by The Reference Press based on information provided by the companies and other publicly available sources.

In many countries it is common for companies to raise capital through rights issues. Companies usually try to entice shareholders to exercise rights to buy new shares by offering them at below-market prices. A large, low-priced rights issue can be very dilutive and can cause a sharp drop in the price of a company's shares. Although they may be beneficial to the shareholders, rights issues can make stock performance appear weak. Because there is no truly satisfactory way to account for rights, the share information in this book has not been adjusted for rights issues.

We have shown data in US dollars wherever available since this is the currency most familiar to our readers. This approach allows some trends to be seen more clearly. For example, if a country is experiencing hyperinflation (100%, 1,000%, or even more per year), the sales and earnings of a company based in that country might seem to have skyrocketed when viewed in the local currency. However, when the results are converted to a more stable currency, like the US dollar, the trend could be revealed as flat or even down, depending on how much the foreign currency was devalued. On the other hand, converting foreign currency into US dollars can sometimes distort trends due to exchange-rate fluctuations. This problem is particularly evident in the case of certain Japanese companies due to the dramatic fluctuations in the yen-dollar exchange rate in recent years. By contrast, however, the US dollar and the French franc have remained remarkably stable for a number of years.

Throughout this book we have tried our best to present data that are accurate and comparable. However, the world of business will have to become much more standardized before we can confidently promise accurate comparability.

Major Currency Symbols

Country	Currency	Symbol
Argentina	peso	Ps
Australia	dollar	A$
Belgium	franc	BF
Brazil	cruzeiro real	CR$
Canada	dollar	C$
Chile	peso	P
China	renminbi yuan	RMB
Denmark	krone	DK
Finland	markka	FIM
France	franc	FF
Germany	deutsche mark	DM
Hong Kong	dollar	HK$
India	rupee	Rs
Ireland	pound, pence	IR£, p
Israel	shekel	NIS
Italy	lira	Lit
Japan	yen	¥
Malaysia	ringgit	M$

Country	Currency	Symbol
Mexico	new peso	peso
The Netherlands	florin (guilder)	F1
New Zealand	dollar	NZ$
Norway	krone	NOK
Philippines	peso	P
Portugal	Escudo	Esc
Singapore	dollar	S$
South Africa	rand	R
South Korea	won	Won
Spain	peseta	Pta
Sweden	krona	SEK
Switzerland	franc	SF
Taiwan	dollar	NT$
Turkey	lira	Lt
UK	pound, pence	£, p
US	dollar	$
Venezuela	bolivar	B
Zambia	kwacha	K

A LIST-LOVER'S
COMPENDIUM

Top 100 Companies in *Hoover's Handbook of World Business* 1995–1996 Ranked by Sales

Rank	Company	Sales ($ mil.)	Rank	Company	Sales ($ mil.)
1	Mitsui Group	172,237	51	Carrefour	20,847
2	Mitsubishi Group	154,250	52	British Telecommunications plc	20,307
3	Sumitomo Group	151,786	53	Petróleo Brasileiro S.A.	20,244
4	ITOCHU Corporation	149,482	54	National Westminster Bank Plc	19,877
5	Marubeni Corporation	139,214	55	Mazda Motor Corporation	19,536
6	Toyota Motor Corporation	95,032	56	Robert Bosch GmbH	18,698
7	Royal Dutch/Shell Group	92,482	57	STET	17,396
8	Hitachi, Ltd.	72,174	58	Bayerische Motoren Werke AG	16,676
9	Matsushita Electric	64,307	59	Samsung Group	16,486
10	Nippon Telegraph and Telephone	59,705	60	Canon Inc.	16,452
11	Nissan Motor Co., Ltd.	56,319	61	Mannesmann AG	16,071
12	Daimler-Benz Aktiengesellschaft	56,171	62	British Aerospace PLC	15,917
13	The British Petroleum Co. p.l.c.	52,580	63	Imperial Chemical Industries PLC	15,728
14	Thyssen AG	49,082	64	J Sainsbury plc	15,656
15	Siemens AG	46,924	65	Repsol, S.A.	15,485
16	IRI Group	46,577	66	Ciba-Geigy Limited	15,199
17	Volkswagen AG	44,015	67	BCE Inc.	14,977
18	The Tokyo Electric Power Co., Inc.	42,152	68	Hanson PLC	14,467
19	Unilever	41,878	69	BTR plc	14,463
20	Toshiba Corporation	41,348	70	Koç Holding A.S.	14,406
21	Allianz AG Holding	40,302	71	The General Electric Company p.l.c.	14,351
22	Nestlé Ltd.	38,581	72	Bridgestone Corporation	14,328
23	Honda Motor Co., Ltd.	37,448	73	Sanyo Electric Co., Ltd.	14,153
24	Sony Corporation	36,250	74	Kirin Brewery Company, Ltd.	14,061
25	Elf Aquitaine	35,478	75	Union Bank of Switzerland	14,042
26	RWE Aktiengesellschaft	35,185	76	Royal Ahold nv	13,973
27	NEC Corporation	35,096	77	Isuzu Motors Limited	13,946
28	Deutsche Bank AG	31,747	78	Hyundai Group	13,671
29	Fiat S.p.A.	31,693	79	Rhône-Poulenc S.A.	13,632
30	Philips Electronics N.V.	31,626	80	AB Volvo	13,339
31	Ente Nazionale Idrocarburi S.p.A.	31,619	81	Sharp Corporation	13,304
32	B.A.T Industries p.l.c.	30,725	82	AB Electrolux	13,033
33	Renault	28,734	83	The Broken Hill Proprietary Co.	12,201
34	ABB Asea Brown Boveri Ltd	28,315	84	Compagnie de Saint-Gobain SA	12,105
35	Fujitsu Limited	28,128	85	Grand Metropolitan PLC	12,012
36	Ito-Yokado Co., Ltd.	27,735	86	Tokio Marine and Fire	11,900
37	Industrial Bank of Japan, Limited	27,352	87	Groupe Danone	11,863
38	Petróleos Mexicanos	26,686	88	Fried. Krupp AG Hoesch-Krupp	11,808
39	Hoechst AG	26,464	89	Daewoo Group	11,799
40	Alcatel Alsthom	26,452	90	Coles Myer Ltd.	11,782
41	BASF Group	24,783	91	Thomson S.A.	11,422
42	The Dai-Ichi Kangyo Bank, Limited	24,703	92	Suzuki Motor Corporation	10,955
43	PSA Peugeot Citroën	24,608	93	Michelin	10,710
44	Nippon Steel Corporation	24,545	94	Bertelsmann AG	10,599
45	The Daiei, Inc.	23,972	95	Deutsche Lufthansa AG	10,190
46	Bayer AG	23,567	96	Fuji Photo Film Co., Ltd.	10,157
47	TOTAL	22,924	97	Sandoz Ltd.	10,134
48	Barclays PLC	21,879	98	Petrofina S.A.	9,881
49	HSBC Holdings plc	21,560	99	Marks and Spencer p.l.c.	9,676
50	Petróleos de Venezuela, S.A.	21,275	100	Roche Group	9,607

Top 100 Companies in *Hoover's Handbook of World Business* 1995–1996 Ranked by Profits

Rank	Company	Net Income ($ mil.)	Rank	Company	Net Income ($ mil.)
1	Unilever	2,912	51	Repsol, S.A.	560
2	Teléfonos de México, S.A. de C.V.	2,900	52	Ito-Yokado Co., Ltd.	556
3	HSBC Holdings plc	2,672	53	The Tokyo Electric Power Co., Inc.	554
4	Royal Dutch/Shell Group	2,664	54	Allianz AG Holding	554
5	British Telecommunications plc	2,624	55	Koç Holding A.S.	536
6	Glaxo p.l.c.	2,011	56	Bass PLC	517
7	Nestlé Ltd.	1,938	57	Nintendo Co., Ltd.	514
8	Tokio Marine and Fire	1,768	58	TOTAL	502
9	B.A.T Industries p.l.c.	1,691	59	Singapore Airlines Limited	501
10	Roche Group	1,663	60	BASF Group	493
11	Union Bank of Switzerland	1,522	61	The Nomura Securities Co., Ltd.	485
12	CS Holding	1,338	62	Allied Domecq PLC	480
13	Toyota Motor Corporation	1,277	63	Barclays PLC	463
14	Deutsche Bank AG	1,246	64	The Toronto-Dominion Bank	459
15	SmithKline Beecham plc	1,220	65	Reuters Holdings PLC	442
16	Ciba-Geigy Limited	1,194	66	L'Oréal SA	437
17	BTR plc	1,194	67	Bertelsmann AG	436
18	Alcatel Alsthom	1,182	68	The Boots Company PLC	426
19	Sandoz Ltd.	1,145	69	British Airways PLC	425
20	Hanson PLC	1,098	70	The RTZ Corporation PLC	425
21	Petróleos de Venezuela, S.A.	1,089	71	Jardine Matheson Holdings Ltd.	424
22	Philips Electronics N.V.	1,050	72	Anglo American	401
23	Siemens AG	1,036	73	Norsk Hydro A.S	399
24	Hong Kong Telecommunications	979	74	Kirin Brewery Company, Ltd.	384
25	Petróleos Mexicanos	959	75	The Seagram Company Ltd.	379
26	The Broken Hill Proprietary Co.	947	76	Fletcher Challenge Limited	377
27	The British Petroleum Company p.l.c.	910	77	Cadbury Schweppes plc	360
28	STET	898	78	Kyocera Corporation	359
29	The News Corporation Limited	883	79	Daimler-Benz Aktiengesellschaft	346
30	National Westminster Bank Plc	863	80	LM Ericsson Telephone Company	340
31	Marks and Spencer p.l.c.	855	81	Cifra, S.A. de C.V.	333
32	Hutchison Whampoa Limited	817	82	Thorn EMI plc	330
33	The General Electric Company p.l.c.	799	83	Hoechst AG	328
34	Cable and Wireless PLC	764	84	Hopewell Holdings Limited	316
35	Nippon Telegraph and Telephone	741	85	Coles Myer Ltd.	314
36	YPF Sociedad Anonima	707	86	Royal Bank of Canada	300
37	Petróleo Brasileiro S.A.	687	87	Bayerische Motoren Werke AG	297
38	Canadian Imperial Bank	674	88	Sharp Corporation	286
39	Telefónica de España, S.A.	673	89	Akzo Nobel N.V.	283
40	Hitachi, Ltd.	666	90	Carrefour	282
41	Guinness PLC	641	91	Imperial Oil Limited	279
42	Grand Metropolitan PLC	611	92	The Thomson Corporation	277
43	Bank of Montreal	611	93	Heineken N.V.	268
44	LVMH Moët Hennessy Louis Vuitton	604	94	Bridgestone Corporation	250
45	Swire Pacific Limited	603	95	Reckitt & Colman plc	250
46	Peninsular and Oriental	596	96	Tate & Lyle PLC	249
47	Groupe Danone	588	97	Robert Bosch GmbH	245
48	RWE Aktiengesellschaft	584	98	Matsushita Electric	238
49	Fuji Photo Film Co., Ltd.	569	99	Honda Motor Co., Ltd.	230
50	Reed Elsevier PLC	562	100	Sega Enterprises, Ltd.	225

Top 100 Companies in *Hoover's Handbook of World Business* 1995–1996 Ranked by Market Value

Rank	Company	Market Value ($ mil.)	Rank	Company	Market Value ($ mil.)
1	Nippon Telegraph and Telephone	103,629	51	Guinness PLC	14,213
2	Industrial Bank of Japan, Limited	80,412	52	Reed Elsevier PLC	13,981
3	Toyota Motor Corporation	78,648	53	The General Electric Co., p.l.c.	13,847
4	Royal Dutch/Shell Group	55,955	54	Fujitsu Limited	13,757
5	The Dai-Ichi Kangyo Bank, Limited	49,318	55	All Nippon Airways Co., Ltd.	13,657
6	British Telecommunications plc	44,182	56	Honda Motor Co., Ltd.	13,266
7	HSBC Holdings plc	37,660	57	L'Oréal SA	12,849
8	The Tokyo Electric Power Co., Inc.	36,823	58	The RTZ Corporation PLC	12,781
9	Roche Group	36,530	59	Telefónica de España, S.A.	12,213
10	Teléfonos de México, S.A. de C.V.	35,845	60	Anglo American	12,196
11	Nestlé Ltd.	34,746	61	TOTAL	11,991
12	Allianz AG Holding	33,038	62	STET	11,824
13	Glaxo p.l.c.	31,814	63	J Sainsbury plc	11,757
14	The Nomura Securities Co., Ltd.	31,364	64	NEC Corporation	11,740
15	The British Petroleum Co., p.l.c.	29,072	65	Fuji Photo Film Co., Ltd.	11,590
16	Matsushita Electric	28,292	66	RWE Aktiengesellschaft	11,154
17	Siemens AG	26,766	67	Canon Inc.	10,959
18	B.A.T Industries p.l.c.	25,019	68	Reuters Holdings PLC	10,922
19	Hitachi, Ltd.	24,960	69	Singapore Airlines Limited	10,821
20	Deutsche Bank AG	24,029	70	BCE Inc.	10,749
21	Hong Kong Telecommunications	23,466	71	Hoechst AG	10,746
22	Union Bank of Switzerland	23,227	72	Groupe Danone	10,741
23	Daimler-Benz Aktiengesellschaft	22,900	73	Kirin Brewery Company, Ltd.	10,656
24	Sandoz Ltd.	22,163	74	Fiat S.p.A.	10,434
25	The Broken Hill Proprietary Co.	21,321	75	BASF Group	10,200
26	Alcatel Alsthom	20,439	76	LVMH Moët Hennessy	10,070
27	Toshiba Corporation	19,514	77	Cifra, S.A. de C.V.	9,990
28	BTR plc	19,205	78	Kyocera Corporation	9,823
29	Japan Airlines Company, Ltd.	19,124	79	Mitsui Group	9,779
30	Nippon Steel Corporation	18,883	80	The Thomson Corporation	9,775
31	Ito-Yokado Co., Ltd.	18,829	81	Nintendo Co., Ltd.	9,766
32	Marks and Spencer p.l.c.	18,664	82	The Seagram Company Ltd.	9,731
33	Sony Corporation	18,642	83	Carrefour	9,322
34	Ciba-Geigy Limited	18,517	84	Repsol, S.A.	9,263
35	Hanson PLC	18,468	85	Allied Domecq PLC	9,214
36	Hutchison Whampoa Limited	18,038	86	The Boots Company PLC	9,209
37	Cable and Wireless PLC	17,454	87	YPF Sociedad Anonima	9,178
38	The News Corporation Limited	16,692	88	Mannesmann AG	8,871
39	CS Holding	16,471	89	Bridgestone Corporation	8,854
40	Elf Aquitaine	15,771	90	Swire Pacific Limited	8,737
41	Nissan Motor Co., Ltd.	15,488	91	LM Ericsson Telephone Company	8,694
42	Barclays PLC	15,318	92	Imperial Chemical Industries PLC	8,544
43	National Westminster Bank Plc	15,243	93	Volkswagen AG	8,446
44	Sharp Corporation	14,996	94	Sumitomo Group	8,246
45	Mitsubishi Group	14,951	95	Sega Enterprises, Ltd.	7,939
46	SmithKline Beecham plc	14,675	96	Northern Telecom Limited	7,759
47	Grand Metropolitan PLC	14,569	97	Kubota Corporation	7,607
48	Tokio Marine and Fire	14,503	98	Bayerische Motoren Werke AG	7,469
49	Unilever	14,356	99	Komatsu Ltd.	7,295
50	Bayer AG	14,247	100	The Daiei, Inc.	7,274

Top 100 Companies in *Hoover's Handbook of World Business* 1995–1996 Ranked by Number of Employees

Rank	Company	Employees	Rank	Company	Employees
1	Siemens AG	391,000	51	Elf Aquitaine	94,300
2	Daimler-Benz Aktiengesellschaft	366,736	52	Ito-Yokado Co., Ltd.	93,529
3	IRI Group	333,958	53	Compagnie de Saint-Gobain SA	92,348
4	Hitachi, Ltd.	330,637	54	Groupe Schneider	91,458
5	Unilever	294,000	55	National Westminster Bank Plc	91,400
6	Volkswagen AG	280,137	56	Honda Motor Co., Ltd.	91,300
7	Fiat S.p.A.	260,951	57	Ciba-Geigy Limited	87,480
8	Matsushita Electric	254,059	58	British Aerospace PLC	87,400
9	Philips Electronics N.V.	252,214	59	Bridgestone Corporation	87,332
10	Tata Group	250,000	60	Grand Metropolitan PLC	87,163
11	Nippon Telegraph and Telephone	248,000	61	Carrefour	85,200
12	Reuters Holdings PLC	223,700	62	The British Petroleum Co., p.l.c.	84,000
13	Nestlé Ltd.	209,755	63	Rhône-Poulenc S.A.	81,678
14	ABB Asea Brown Boveri Ltd	206,490	64	Vendex International N.V.	80,200
15	Jardine Matheson Holdings Ltd.	200,000	65	The Boots Company PLC	80,099
16	Alcatel Alsthom	196,500	66	Fried. Krupp AG Hoesch-Krupp	78,376
17	B.A.T Industries p.l.c.	190,308	67	Ladbroke Group PLC	78,000
18	Toshiba Corporation	175,000	68	Daewoo Group	76,986
19	Hoechst AG	172,483	69	KPMG Peat Marwick	76,200
20	Robert Bosch GmbH	164,506	70	Bass PLC	75,845
21	Fujitsu Limited	163,990	71	Telefónica de España, S.A.	74,340
22	British Telecommunications plc	156,000	72	Hanson PLC	74,000
23	Bayer AG	153,866	73	AB Volvo	73,641
24	NEC Corporation	147,910	74	Akzo Nobel N.V.	73,400
25	PSA Peugeot Citroën	143,900	75	Deutsche Bank AG	73,176
26	Accor SA	143,740	76	Arthur Andersen & Co, SC	72,722
27	Nissan Motor Co., Ltd.	143,310	77	Allied Domecq PLC	71,824
28	Thyssen AG	141,009	78	Crédit Lyonnais	71,351
29	Renault	139,733	79	Allianz AG Holding	69,859
30	STET	136,184	80	George Weston Limited	69,600
31	Coles Myer Ltd.	135,365	81	LM Ericsson Telephone Company	69,597
32	The General Electric Company p.l.c.	134,000	82	Imperial Chemical Industries PLC	67,000
33	Sony Corporation	130,000	83	Coopers & Lybrand L.L.P.	66,300
34	BTR plc	129,814	84	Bayerische Motoren Werke AG	66,201
35	Mannesmann AG	127,695	85	Canon Inc.	64,535
36	J Sainsbury plc	124,841	86	Teléfonos de México, S.A. de C.V.	62,977
37	Michelin	124,575	87	Marks and Spencer p.l.c.	62,120
38	Royal Ahold nv	119,027	88	Ernst & Young LLP	61,287
39	BCE Inc.	118,000	89	Northern Telecom Limited	60,293
40	RWE Aktiengesellschaft	117,958	90	Zambia Consolidated Copper Mines	60,259
41	Royal Dutch/Shell Group	117,000	91	The RTZ Corporation PLC	59,975
42	BASF Group	112,020	92	Sanyo Electric Co., Ltd.	59,264
43	Toyota Motor Corporation	110,534	93	Petróleo Brasileiro S.A.	56,900
44	AB Electrolux	109,400	94	CS Holding	56,804
45	Petróleos Mexicanos	106,951	95	Groupe Danone	56,419
46	Ente Nazionale Idrocarburi S.p.A.	106,391	96	Roche Group	56,082
47	Thomson S.A.	99,895	97	Royal Bank of Canada	52,745
48	Lonrho Plc	99,309	98	Sandoz Ltd.	52,550
49	HSBC Holdings plc	98,396	99	SmithKline Beecham plc	51,900
50	Barclays PLC	97,800	100	Bertelsmann AG	51,767

World's 100 Largest Public Companies

Rank	Company	Country	Market Value ($ mil.)
1	NTT	Japan	130,344
2	Royal Dutch/Shell	Netherlands/U.K.	97,170
3	General Electric	U.S.	86,005
4	Toyota Motor	Japan	78,788
5	Mitsubishi Bank	Japan	75,029
6	Exxon	U.S.	73,899
7	AT&T	U.S.	73,875
8	Industrial Bank of Japan	Japan	70,890
9	Fuji Bank	Japan	65,354
10	Sumitomo Bank	Japan	63,339
11	Sanwa Bank	Japan	62,542
12	Dai-Ichi Kangyo Bank	Japan	59,190
13	Coca-Cola Co.	U.S.	57,575
14	Wal-Mart Stores	U.S.	57,469
15	Philip Morris	U.S.	48,235
16	Sakura Bank	Japan	47,363
17	Nomura Securities	Japan	43,295
18	Tokyo Electric Power	Japan	40,515
19	Roche Holding	Switzerland	40,459
20	DuPont	U.S.	40,231
21	Procter & Gamble	U.S.	38,008
22	Merck	U.S.	37,148
23	General Motors	U.S.	36,990
24	IBM	U.S.	36,018
25	Singapore Telecom	Singapore	35,723
26	British Telecom	U.K.	35,170
27	British Petroleum	U.K.	34,576
28	Matsushita Electric Industrial	Japan	34,311
29	Nestle	Switzerland	33,564
30	Mobil	U.S.	33,396
31	Allianz Holding	Germany	32,009
32	Ford Motor	U.S.	31,811
33	Hitachi	Japan	31,613
34	Bank of Tokyo	Japan	31,331
35	HSBC Holdings	U.K.	31,265
36	BellSouth	U.S.	31,005
37	GTE	U.S.	30,345
38	Johnson & Johnson	U.S.	30,220
39	American International Group	U.S.	29,919
40	Amoco	U.S.	29,722
41	Motorola	U.S.	29,601
42	Unilever	Netherlands/U.K.	29,599
43	Microsoft	U.S.	29,232
44	Chevron	U.S.	28,909
45	Asahi Bank	Japan	28,496
46	Seven-Eleven	Japan	28,344
47	Long-Term Credit Bank	Japan	27,948
48	Bristol-Myers Squibb	U.S.	27,260
49	Glaxo Holdings	U.K.	26,637
50	Tokai Bank	Japan	26,331

Note: Companies are ranked by market value as of July 31, 1994.

World's 100 Largest Public Companies (continued)

Rank	Company	Country	Market Value ($ mil.)
51	Mitsubishi Heavy Industries	Japan	26,111
52	Daimler-Benz	Germany	25,791
53	Southwestern Bell	U.S.	25,210
54	Kansai Electric Power	Japan	25,149
55	Intel	U.S.	24,767
56	PepsiCo	U.S.	24,363
57	Bell Atlantic	U.S.	24,292
58	Siemens	Germany	23,939
59	Federal National Mortgage	U.S.	23,635
60	Toshiba	Japan	23,517
61	Broken Hill Proprietary	Australia	23,373
62	Schweiz Bankgesellschaft	Switzerland	23,136
63	Abbott Laboratories	U.S.	23,094
64	Nippon Steel	Japan	22,972
65	Minnesota Mining & Mfg.	U.S.	22,738
66	Walt Disney	U.S.	22,713
67	Ameritech	U.S.	22,412
68	Hong Kong Telecom	Hong Kong	22,232
69	Sony	Japan	21,900
70	Ito-Yokado	Japan	21,791
71	Deutsche Bank	Germany	21,740
72	Daiwa Securities	Japan	21,455
73	B.A.T Industries	U.K.	20,889
74	Mitsubishi Trust & Banking	Japan	20,800
75	East Japan Railway	Japan	20,564
76	BTR	U.K.	20,350
77	Hanson	U.K.	19,977
78	Pfizer	U.S.	19,897
79	Tokio Marine & Fire	Japan	19,766
80	Elf Aquitaine	France	19,684
81	Hewlett-Packard	U.S.	19,639
82	Sharp	Japan	19,438
83	Chubu Electric Power	Japan	19,376
84	Assicurazioni Generali	Italy	19,336
85	Nissan Motor	Japan	19,309
86	McDonald's	U.S.	19,161
87	Fujitsu Ltd.	Japan	19,041
88	Dow Chemical	U.S.	18,974
89	Mitsubishi	Japan	18,769
90	Sumitomo Trust & Banking	Japan	18,750
91	Sandoz	Switzerland	18,443
92	Nikko Securities	Japan	18,175
93	Home Depot	U.S.	18,132
94	Marks & Spencer	U.K.	18,026
95	British Gas	U.K.	17,852
96	U S West	U.S.	17,821
97	Seibu Railway	Japan	17,821
98	American Home Products	U.S.	17,791
99	NEC	Japan	17,529
100	BankAmerica	U.S.	17,269

Source: *The Wall Street Journal*; September 30, 1994

World's Largest Publicly Traded Non-US Companies by Country

Country	Company	Industry	1993 Sales ($ mil.)
Argentina	YPF	Energy	3,962
Australia	Broken Hill Proprietary	Energy	11,310
Austria	OMV	Energy	5,738
Belgium	Petrofina	Energy	10,930
Brazil	Petrobras	Energy	15,029
Canada	BCE	Telecommunications	15,369
Denmark	Den Danske Bank	Banking	4,819
Finland	Kesko Group	Trading	4,520
France	UAP-Union des Assurances	Insurance	40,284
Germany	Daimler-Benz Group	Automobiles	59,116
Hong Kong	Jardine Matheson Holdings	Multi-industry	8,425
India	Steel Authority of India	Metals - steel	3,853
Italy	Fiat Group	Automobiles	34,668
Japan	Mitsui & Co	Trading	163,529
Korea	Samsung Corp	Trading	16,595
Mexico	Grupo Financiero Bancomer	Banking	8,264
Netherlands	Royal Dutch/Shell Group	Energy	95,153
New Zealand	Fletcher Challenge	Forest products	5,049
Norway	Norsk Hydro	Energy	8,789
Singapore	Singapore Airlines	Airlines	3,893
South Africa	Barlow Rand Group	Multi-industry	11,507
Spain	Repsol	Energy	17,418
Sweden	Volvo Group	Automobiles	14,281
Switzerland	Nestle	Food, household	38,904
United Kingdom	British Petroleum	Energy	52,496

Source: *Forbes*; July 18, 1994

World's Largest Nonpublic Non-US Companies

Rank	Company	Country	1993 Sales ($ mil.)
1	Nippon Life Insurance	Japan	59,551
2	Samsung Group	Korea	51,534
3	Sumitomo Life Insurance	Japan	37,940
4	ENI-Ente Naz Idrocarburi	Italy	34,309
5	Electricite de France	France	32,420
6	Meiji Mutual Life Insurance	Japan	31,949
7	Tengelmann Group	Germany	31,135
8	Daewoo Group	Korea	31,007
9	Renault Group	France	29,981
10	Credit Agricole	France	29,464
11	Pemex-Petroleos Mexicanos	Mexico	26,573
12	France Telecom	France	25,098
13	Petroleos de Venezuela	Venezuela	21,469
14	Norinchukin Bank	Japan	21,076
15	Mitsui Mutual Life Insurance	Japan	19,920
16	Robert Bosch Group	Germany	19,639
17	Asahi Mutual Life Insurace	Japan	19,444
18	Westdeutsche Landesbank	Germany	16,535
19	Idemitsu Kosan	Japan	15,587
20	Franz Haniel & Cie	Germany	14,768

Source: *Forbes*; July 18, 1994

35 Wealthiest Non-US Individuals and Families

Rank	Who	Where	What	How Much 1993 ($ bil.)
1	Rausing, Hans and Gad	Sweden	Packaging	9.0
2	Tsutsumi, Yoshiaki	Japan	Real estate, resorts	8.5
3	Sacher, Paul, and Hoffmann family	Switzerland	Pharmaceuticals	7.8
4	Tsai family	Taiwan	Insurance, construction	7.5
5	Albrecht, Theo and Karl	Germany	Retailing	7.3
6	Slim Helu, Carlos	Mexico	Conglomerator	6.6
7	Lee Shau Kee	Hong Kong	Real estate	6.5
8	Kwok brothers	Hong Kong	Real estate	6.4
9	Quandt, Johanna, Susanne and Stefan	Germany	Automobiles	6.3
10	Henkel family	Germany	Chemicals, consumer products	6.3
11	Mori, Minoru and Akira and family	Japan	Property development	6.2
12	Haniel family	Germany	Food wholesaling, retailing	6.0
13	Haub, Erivan	Germany	Supermarkets	5.8
14	Li Ka-shing	Hong Kong	Real estate, diversified	5.8
15	Azcárraga Milmo, Emilio and family	Mexico	Media	5.4
16	Chearavanont, Dhanin and family	Thailand	Agribusiness	5.3
17	Thomson, Kenneth	Canada	Publishing, retailing, real estate	5.2
18	Takei, Yasuo and family	Japan	Consumer finance	5.0
19	Sainsbury, David and family	U.K.	Supermarkets	4.4
20	Bettencourt, Liliane	France	Cosmetics	4.2
21	Otto family	Germany	Mail order	4.2
22	Brenninkmeyer family	Netherlands	Retailing	4.0
23	Irving family	Canada	Forest products, shipbuilding, oil, media	4.0
24	Kadoorie family	Hong Kong	Utilities, hotels	4.0
25	Kinoshita family	Japan	Consumer finance	4.0
26	Shin Kyuk-ho	Korea	Food, beverage, real estate	4.0
27	Agnelli family	Italy	Automobiles, etc.	3.9
28	Ito, Masatoshi and family	Japan	Retailing	3.8
29	Schickedanz family	Germany	Mail order	3.8
30	Chung Ju-yung and family	Korea	Automobiles, heavy industry	3.6
31	Iwasaki family	Japan	Logging, property, resorts	3.5
32	Flick, Friedrich Karl Jr.	Germany	Investments	3.3
33	Pao family	Hong Kong	Shipping, property development, etc.	3.3
34	Cheng Yu-tung and family	Hong Kong	Real estate, telecommunications	3.3
35	Finck, Wilhelm and August, von	Germany	Banking, real estate	3.2

Source: *Forbes*; July 18, 1994

World's 500 Largest Industrial Corporations

Rank	Company	Country	1993 Sales ($ mil.)
1	General Motors	U.S.	133,622
2	Ford Motor	U.S.	108,521
3	Exxon	U.S.	97,825
4	Royal Dutch/Shell Group	Britain/Netherlands	95,134
5	Toyota Motor	Japan	85,283
6	Hitachi	Japan	68,582
7	International Business Machines	U.S.	62,716
8	Matsushita Electric Industrial	Japan	61,385
9	General Electric	U.S.	60,823
10	Daimler-Benz	Germany	59,102
11	Mobil	U.S.	56,576
12	Nissan Motor	Japan	53,760
13	British Petroleum	Britain	52,485
14	Samsung	South Korea	51,345
15	Philip Morris	U.S.	50,621
16	IRI	Italy	50,488
17	Siemens	Germany	50,381
18	Volkswagen	Germany	46,312
19	Chrysler	U.S.	43,600
20	Toshiba	Japan	42,917
21	Unilever	Britain/Netherlands	41,843
22	Nestlé	Switzerland	38,895
23	Elf Aquitaine	France	37,016
24	Honda Motor	Japan	35,798
25	ENI	Italy	34,791
26	Fiat	Italy	34,707
27	Sony	Japan	34,603
28	Texaco	U.S.	34,359
29	NEC	Japan	33,176
30	E.I. du Pont de Nemours	U.S.	32,621
31	Chevron	U.S.	32,123
32	Philips Electronics	Netherlands	31,666
33	Daewoo	South Korea	30,893
34	Procter & Gamble	U.S.	30,433
35	Renault	France	29,975
36	Fujitsu	Japan	29,094
37	Mitsubishi Electric	Japan	28,780
38	ABB Asea Brown Boveri	Switzerland	28,315
39	Hoechst	Germany	27,845
40	Alcatel Alsthom	France	27,599
41	Mitsubishi Motors	Japan	27,311
42	Pemex (Petróleos Mexicanos)	Mexico	26,573
43	Mitsubishi Heavy Industries	Japan	25,804
44	Peugeot	France	25,669
45	Nippon Steel	Japan	25,481
46	Amoco	U.S.	25,336
47	Boeing	U.S.	25,285
48	PepsiCo	U.S.	25,021
49	Bayer	Germany	24,797
50	BASF	Germany	24,532

World's 500 Largest Industrial Corporations (continued)

Rank	Company	Country	1993 Sales ($ mil.)
51	TOTAL	Germany	23,917
52	Conagra	U.S.	21,519
53	PDVSA	Venezuela	21,275
54	United Technologies	U.S.	20,736
55	Thyssen	Germany	20,673
56	Hewlett-Packard	U.S.	20,317
57	Mazda Motor	Japan	20,279
58	Eastman Kodak	U.S.	20,059
59	Robert Bosch	Germany	19,634
60	Nippon Oil	Japan	19,585
61	INI	Spain	18,639
62	Dow Chemical	U.S.	18,060
63	Xerox	U.S.	17,790
64	BMW (Bayerische Motoren Werke)	Germany	17,546
65	Repsol	Spain	17,411
66	Atlantic Richfield	U.S.	17,189
67	Motorola	U.S.	16,963
68	Mannesmann	Germany	16,909
69	Canon	Japan	16,507
70	British Aerospace	Britain	16,159
71	USX	U.S.	16,137
72	Metallgesellchaft	Germany	16,102
73	Imperial Chemical Industries	Britain	15,966
74	Sunkyong	South Korea	15,912
75	Ciba-Geigy	Switzerland	15,323
76	RJR Nabisco Holdings	U.S.	15,104
77	Petrobrás	Brazil	15,029
78	NKK	Japan	14,891
79	BTR	Britain	14,675
80	Sara Lee	U.S.	14,580
81	Ferruzzi Finanziaria	Italy	14,507
82	Ssangyong	South Korea	14,480
83	McDonnell Douglas	U.S.	14,474
84	Koç Holding	Turkey	14,409
85	Bridgestone	Japan	14,377
86	Digital Equipment	U.S.	14,371
87	Preussag	Germany	14,371
88	VIAG	Germany	14,352
89	Volvo	Sweden	14,272
90	Rhône-Poulenc	France	14,223
91	Ruhrkohle	Germany	14,155
92	Johnson & Johnson	U.S.	14,138
93	Minnesota Mining & Mfg.	U.S.	14,020
94	Coca-Cola	U.S.	13,957
95	Sanyo Electric	Japan	13,850
96	Sharp	Japan	13,810
97	Japan Energy	Japan	13,736
98	Isuzu Motors	Japan	13,731
99	International Paper	U.S.	13,685
100	Sumitomo Metal Industries	Japan	13,521

World's 500 Largest Industrial Corporations (continued)

Rank	Company	Country	1993 Sales ($ mil.)
101	Usinor-Sacilor	France	13,295
102	Tenneco	U.S.	13,255
103	Lockheed	U.S.	13,071
104	Idemitsu Kosan	Japan	12,857
105	Electrolux	Sweden	12,856
106	Nippondenso	Japan	12,835
107	Saint-Gobain	France	12,630
108	Fried. Krupp	Germany	13,399
109	Danone Group	France	12,377
110	Georgia-Pacific	U.S.	12,330
111	Phillips Petroleum	U.S.	12,309
112	MAN	Germany	12,107
113	Thomson	France	11,917
114	AlliedSignal	U.S.	11,827
115	IBP	U.S.	11,671
116	Goodyear Tire & Rubber	U.S.	11,643
117	Caterpillar	U.S.	11,615
118	Kobe Steel	Japan	11,575
119	Westinghouse Electric	U.S.	11,564
120	Anheuser-Busch	U.S.	11,505
121	Cosmo Oil	Japan	11,484
122	Barlow Rand	South Africa	11,468
123	Statoil	Norway	11,425
124	Bristol-Myers Squibb	U.S.	11,413
125	Suzuki Motor	Japan	11,371
126	Broken Hill Proprietary	Australia	11,308
127	Hanson	Britain	11,211
128	Michelin	France	11,175
129	Grand Metropolitan	Britain	11,164
130	Pechiney	France	11,127
131	Asahi Glass	Japan	11,034
132	Kawasaki Steel	Japan	10,983
133	Bertelsmann	Germany	10,957
134	Petrofina	Belgium	10,937
135	Rockwell International	U.S.	10,840
136	Showa Shell Sekiyu	Japan	10,717
137	Asahi Chemical Industry	Japan	10,672
138	Dai Nippon Printing	Japan	10,616
139	Merck	U.S.	10,498
140	Snow Brand Milk Products	Japan	10,283
141	Sandoz	Switzerland	10,217
142	Sumitomo Electric Industries	Japan	10,209
143	Japan Tobacco	Japan	10,151
144	Coastal	U.S.	10,136
145	Toppan Printing	Japan	10,101
146	Ishikawajima-Harima Heavy Ind.	Japan	10,018
147	Mitsubishi Kasei	Japan	9,982
148	Schneider	France	9,953
149	Kawasaki Heavy Industries	Japan	9,919
150	Mitsubishi Materials	Japan	9,864

World's 500 Largest Industrial Corporations (continued)

Rank	Company	Country	1993 Sales ($ mil.)
151	Archer Daniels Midland	U.S.	9,811
152	Roche	Switzerland	9,685
153	Fuji Photo Film	Japan	9,555
154	Ashland Oil	U.S.	9,554
155	Weyerhaeuser	U.S.	9,545
156	Lagardère Groupe	France	9,530
157	GEC (General Electric Co.)	Britain	9,491
158	Martin Marietta	U.S.	9,436
159	Fuji Heavy Industries	Japan	9,414
160	SmithKline Beecham	Britain	9,257
161	Hyundai Motor	South Korea	9,204
162	Raytheon	U.S.	9,201
163	Degussa	Germany	9,195
164	Matsushita Electric Works	Japan	9,182
165	Kubota	Japan	9,078
166	Alcoa	U.S.	9,056
167	Aérospatiale	France	8,977
168	Ricoh	Japan	8,974
169	Nippon Paper Industries	Japan	8,911
170	Akzo	Netherlands	8,887
171	Baxter International	U.S.	8,879
172	Sekisui Chemical	Japan	8,841
173	Maruha	Japan	8,833
174	Norsk Hydro	Norway	8,814
175	Intel	U.S.	8,782
176	Textron	U.S.	8,669
177	Pohang Iron & Steel	South Korea	8,591
178	Texas Instruments	U.S.	8,523
179	Sumitomo Chemical	Japan	8,419
180	Abbott Laboratories	U.S.	8,408
181	Henkel	Germany	8,385
182	American Home Products	U.S.	8,305
183	American Brands	U.S.	8,288
184	Toray Industries	Japan	8,193
185	Emerson Electric	U.S.	8,174
186	Chinese Petroleum	Taiwan	8,169
187	Northern Telecom	Canada	8,148
188	General Mills	U.S.	8,135
189	Occidental Petroleum	U.S.	8,116
190	L.M. Ericsson	Sweden	8,083
191	Unocal	U.S.	8,077
192	Glaxo Holdings	Britain	8,001
193	Apple Computer	U.S.	7,977
194	TRW	U.S.	7,948
195	CEA-Industrie	France	7,945
196	Ralston Purina	U.S.	7,902
197	Monsanto	U.S.	7,902
198	Dainippon Ink & Chemicals	Japan	7,861
199	Komatsu	Japan	7,839
200	Kirin Brewery	Japan	7,760

World's 500 Largest Industrial Corporations (continued)

Rank	Company	Country	1993 Sales ($ mil.)
201	Unisys	U.S.	7,743
202	Mitsubishi Oil	Japan	7,739
203	Fuji Electric	Japan	7,729
204	Deere	U.S.	7,694
205	Indian Oil	India	7,658
206	Daihatsu Motor	Japan	7,568
207	Whirlpool	U.S.	7,533
208	News Corp.	Australia	7,511
209	Pfizer	U.S.	7,478
210	Sun	U.S.	7,297
211	Aisin Seiki	Japan	7,294
212	Alcan Aluminium	Canada	7,232
213	Allied-Lyons	Britain	7,231
214	Compaq Computer	U.S.	7,191
215	Kao	Japan	7,172
216	Colgate-Palmolive	U.S.	7,141
217	H.J. Heinz	U.S.	7,103
218	Suntory	Japan	7,100
219	L'Oréal	France	7,090
220	Solvay	Belgium	7,063
221	Guinness	Britain	7,003
222	Kimberly-Clark	U.S.	6,973
223	Hillsdown Holdings	Britain	6,901
224	Nippon Meat Packers	Japan	6,821
225	Associated British Foods	Britain	6,798
226	Takeda Chemical Industries	Japan	6,745
227	CPC International	U.S.	6,738
228	Hyundai Heavy Industries	South Korea	6,735
229	Borden	U.S.	6,700
230	Zeneca	Britain	6,668
231	Campbell Soup	U.S.	6,586
232	South African Breweries	South Africa	6,564
233	British Coal	Britain	6,560
234	Stora	Sweden	6,476
235	Eli Lilly	U.S.	6,452
236	Hyosung	South Korea	6,332
237	British Steel	Britain	6,304
238	Kellogg	U.S.	6,295
239	Cooper Industries	U.S.	6,274
240	Haci Ömer Sabanci Holding	Turkey	6,272
241	Ajinomoto	Japan	6,255
242	Veba Oel	Germany	6,246
243	New Oji Paper	Japan	6,239
244	Johnson Controls	U.S.	6,182
245	Toyo Seikan	Japan	6,170
246	Hüls	Germany	6,144
247	Furukawa Electric	Japan	6,115
248	Saint Louis	France	6,056
249	Yamaha Motor	Japan	6,050
250	Oki Electric Industry	Japan	6,038

World's 500 Largest Industrial Corporations (continued)

Rank	Company	Country	1993 Sales ($ mil.)
251	Petronas	Malaysia	6,022
252	Honeywell	U.S.	5,963
253	Levi Strauss Associates	U.S.	5,893
254	Pirelli	Italy	5,883
255	Amerada Hess	U.S.	5,852
256	Thomson Corp.	Canada	5,849
257	Warner-Lambert	U.S.	5,794
258	PPG Industries	U.S.	5,754
259	ÖMV Group	Austria	5,737
260	W.R. Grace	U.S.	5,737
261	Quaker Oats	U.S.	5,731
262	Holderbank	Switzerland	5,702
263	Continental	Germany	5,666
264	Tate & Lyle	Britain	5,633
265	Cadbury Schweppes	Britain	5,594
266	Tonen	Japan	5,565
267	Arbed	Luxembourg	5,550
268	Litton Industries	U.S.	5,480
269	Olivetti	Italy	5,479
270	Coca-Cola Enterprises	U.S.	5,465
271	Yamazaki Baking	Japan	5,463
272	Dana	U.S.	5,460
273	BICC	Britain	5,427
274	UBE Industries	Japan	5,426
275	Nippon Light Metal	Japan	5,414
276	Gillette	U.S.	5,411
277	Kanebo	Japan	5,409
278	Lafarge Coppée	France	5,372
279	Goldstar	South Korea	5,367
280	L'Air Liquide	France	5,363
281	American Cyanamid	U.S.	5,306
282	Asahi Breweries	Japan	5,300
283	Rolls-Royce	Britain	5,283
284	Reynolds Metals	U.S.	5,269
285	Seagram	Canada	5,227
286	Teijin	Japan	5,215
287	United Biscuits (Holdings)	Britain	5,174
288	Kia Motors	South Korea	5,105
289	Shiseido	Japan	5,090
290	Champion International	U.S.	5,069
291	Northrop	U.S.	5,063
292	Deutsche Babcock	Germany	5,062
293	Stone Container	U.S.	5,060
294	Fletcher Challenge	New Zealand	5,046
295	Bull	France	4,987
296	Hino Motors	Japan	4,963
297	Toyota Auto Body	Japan	4,912
298	Black & Decker	U.S.	4,882
299	Hitachi Zosen	Japan	4,861
300	Tostem	Japan	4,859

World's 500 Largest Industrial Corporations (continued)

Rank	Company	Country	1993 Sales ($ mil.)
301	Cepsa (Española de Petróleos)	Spain	4,822
302	Mead	U.S.	4,790
303	Sankyo	Japan	4,789
304	RTZ	Britain	4,782
305	RMC Group	Britain	4,760
306	Scott Paper	U.S.	4,749
307	Pioneer Electronic	Japan	4,725
308	Farmland Industries	U.S.	4,723
309	Tyson Foods	U.S.	4,707
310	Navistar International	U.S.	4,694
311	BOC Group	Britain	4,673
312	General Dynamics	U.S.	4,661
313	James River Corp. of Va.	U.S.	4,650
314	Union Carbide	U.S.	4,640
315	Toyobo	Japan	4,607
316	Toyoda Automatic Loom Works	Japan	4,579
317	Showa Denko	Japan	4,572
318	Pharmacia	Sweden	4,571
319	Konica	Japan	4,568
320	Onoda Cement	Japan	4,554
321	De Beers Consolidated Mines	South Africa	4,533
322	Sumitomo Rubber Industries	Japan	4,526
323	Sulzer	Switzerland	4,504
324	Nintendo	Japan	4,500
325	Meiji Milk Products	Japan	4,471
326	Sumitomo Heavy Industries	Japan	4,467
327	Pacific Dunlop	Australia	4,432
328	Repola	Finland	4,427
329	Foster's Brewing	Australia	4,409
330	Eaton	U.S.	4,401
331	R.R. Donnelley & Sons	U.S.	4,388
332	Schering-Plough	U.S.	4,341
333	Linde	Germany	4,337
334	DSM	Netherlands	4,328
335	Bethlehem Steel	U.S.	4,323
336	VF	U.S.	4,320
337	Sun Microsystems	U.S.	4,309
338	Shin-Etsu Chemical	Japan	4,304
339	Carnaudmetalbox	France	4,297
340	SCA (Svenska Cellulosa)	Sweden	4,291
341	Itoham Foods	Japan	4,291
342	Omron	Japan	4,271
343	Honam Oil Refinery	South Korea	4,267
344	Cockerill Sambre	Belgium	4,264
345	Cummins Engine	U.S.	4,248
346	Nippon Suisan	Japan	4,241
347	TDK	Japan	4,239
348	Heineken	Netherlands	4,226
349	Mitsui Toatsu Chemicals	Japan	4,217
350	Dresser Industries	U.S.	4,216

World's 500 Largest Industrial Corporations (continued)

Rank	Company	Country	1993 Sales ($ mil.)
351	Mitsubishi Petrochemical	Japan	4,216
352	LVMH	France	4,205
353	Reed Elsevier	Britain/Netherlands	4,199
354	Alusuisse-Lonza	Switzerland	4,187
355	LTV	U.S.	4,163
356	Crown Cork & Seal	U.S.	4,163
357	Honshu Paper	Japan	4,147
358	Nokia	Finland	4,142
359	Burmah Castrol	Britain	4,142
360	Sumitomo Metal Mining	Japan	4,140
361	Yamaha	Japan	4,130
362	Pilkington	Britain	4,118
363	Besnier	France	4,103
364	Ebara	Japan	4,085
365	Doosan	South Korea	4,078
366	Noranda	Canada	4,073
367	Chiquita Brands International	U.S.	4,033
368	CRA	Australia	4,028
369	Ingersoll-Rand	U.S.	4,021
370	Loral	U.S.	4,009
371	Avon Products	U.S.	4,008
372	Corning	U.S.	4,005
373	Kyocera	Japan	3,964
374	YPF	Argentina	3,962
375	Toto	Japan	3,959
376	Boise Cascade	U.S.	3,958
377	Inland Steel Industries	U.S.	3,888
378	Masco	U.S.	3,886
379	Hoogovens Group	Netherlands	3,886
380	Lucas Industries	Britain	3,864
381	Lyondell Petrochemical	U.S.	3,850
382	American Standard	U.S.	3,831
383	Times Mirror	U.S.	3,809
384	Morinaga Milk Industry	Japan	3,773
385	Klöckner-Werke	Germany	3,765
386	FMC	U.S.	3,754
387	SKF	Sweden	3,749
388	Rothmans International	Britain/Netherlands	3,738
389	Bombardier	Canada	3,687
390	Nissan Shatai	Japan	3,676
391	Coats Viyella	Britain	3,670
392	Alps Electric	Japan	3,651
393	Gannett	U.S.	3,642
394	Petrogal	Portugal	3,628
395	Upjohn	U.S.	3,611
396	Yokohama Rubber	Japan	3,598
397	Valeo	France	3,572
398	Tosco	U.S.	3,559
399	Casio Computer	Japan	3,557
400	Investor	Sweden	3,551

World's 500 Largest Industrial Corporations (continued)

Rank	Company	Country	1993 Sales ($ mil.)
401	Pitney Bowes	U.S.	3,543
402	Nisshin Steel	Japan	3,538
403	Owens-Illinois	U.S.	3,535
404	NSK	Japan	3,522
405	Vitro	Mexico	3,507
406	Citizen Watch	Japan	3,501
407	Petro-Canada	Canada	3,493
408	Hershey Foods	U.S.	3,488
409	Kanto Auto Works	Japan	3,474
410	Kværner	Norway	3,465
411	AMP	U.S.	3,451
412	Tomkins	Britain	3,447
413	Boehringer Ingelheim	Germany	3,445
414	Snecma	France	3,443
415	Daikin Industries	Japan	3,436
416	Yamanouchi Pharmaceutical	Japan	3,417
417	Hindustan Petroleum	India	3,414
418	Amcor	Australia	3,391
419	PACCAR	U.S.	3,379
420	Nisshin Flour Milling	Japan	3,379
421	CSR	Australia	3,375
422	Petroleum Authority of Thailand	Thailand	3,332
423	Redland	Britain	3,328
424	Air Products & Chemicals	U.S.	3,328
425	Harrisons & Crossfield	Britain	3,319
426	Italcementi	Italy	3,283
427	Kerr-McGee	U.S.	3,281
428	Rohm & Haas	U.S.	3,269
429	Daido Steel	Japan	3,266
430	Tüpras	Turkey	3,266
431	Schering	Germany	3,243
432	Grumman	U.S.	3,225
433	Mitsui Engineering & Shipbldg.	Japan	3,220
434	E. Merck	Germany	3,211
435	Shionogi	Japan	3,193
436	Bowater	Britain	3,172
437	ZF Friedrichshafen	Germany	3,167
438	Wellcome	Britain	3,163
439	General Sekiyu	Japan	3,161
440	Illinois Tool Works	U.S.	3,159
441	Agway	U.S.	3,149
442	Reckitt & Colman	Britain	3,147
443	Südzucker	Germany	3,131
444	Union Camp	U.S.	3,120
445	Tyco International	U.S.	3,115
446	Seiko	Japan	3,102
447	Harris	U.S.	3,099
448	Berkshire Hathaway	U.S.	3,099
449	Premark International	U.S.	3,097
450	Union Minière	Belgium	3,095

World's 500 Largest Industrial Corporations (continued)

Rank	Company	Country	1993 Sales ($ mil.)
451	Campina Melkunie	Netherlands	3,089
452	Northern Foods	Britain	3,082
453	Mitsui Petrochemical Industries	Japan	3,079
454	McDermott International	Panama	3,060
455	Schindler Holding	Switzerland	3,056
456	Astra	Sweden	3,050
457	Universal	U.S.	3,047
458	Seagate Technology	U.S.	3,044
459	Unitika	Japan	3,042
460	GKN	Britain	3,037
461	Meiji Seika	Japan	3,032
462	Tosoh	Japan	3,029
463	Kuraray	Japan	3,029
464	Voest-Alpine Stahl	Austria	3,005
465	Sapporo Breweries	Japan	3,003
466	Courtaulds	Britain	3,001
467	Maytag	U.S.	2,987
468	Unigate	Britain	2,978
469	Minolta	Japan	2,976
470	Cemex	Mexico	2,966
471	Boral	Australia	2,963
472	Sherwin-Williams	U.S.	2,949
473	Jefferson Smurfit	U.S.	2,948
474	Owens-Corning	U.S.	2,944
475	Johnson Matthey	Britain	2,941
476	Mitsui Mining & Smelting	Japan	2,939
477	Pioneer International	Australia	2,928
478	Carl-Zeiss-Stiftung	Germany	2,928
479	Nobel Industries	Sweden	2,927
480	Iscor	South Africa	2,925
481	Fujikura	Japan	2,920
482	Kyowa Hakko Kogyo	Japan	2,906
483	Lion	Japan	2,891
484	Beiersdorf	Germany	2,881
485	Dell Computer	U.S.	2,873
486	Reader's Digest Association	U.S.	2,869
487	Hormel Foods	U.S.	2,854
488	Mitsubishi Rayon	Japan	2,849
489	Kymmene	Finland	2,849
490	Oil & Natural Gas Corp.	India	2,845
491	Steel Authority of India	India	2,813
492	Trelleborg	Sweden	2,811
493	Pearson	Britain	2,808
494	Siebe	Britain	2,804
495	Goodman Fielder	Australia	2,800
496	Sandvik	Sweden	2,795
497	Nihon Cement	Japan	2,779
498	Aichi Machine Industry	Japan	2,775
499	Bolswessanen	Netherlands	2,774
500	Hercules	U.S.	2,773

Source: *FORTUNE*; July 25, 1994

Japanese Auto Sales

Rank	Manufacturer	No. Cars Sold (mil.)	% Market Share
1	Toyota	2,057	31.8
2	Nissan	1,098	17.0
3	Mitsubishi	717	11.1
4	Honda	552	8.5
5	Suzuki	530	8.2
6	Mazda	405	6.3
7	Daihatsu	397	6.2
8	Fuji Heavy	310	4.8
9	Imports	201	3.1
10	Isuzu	129	2.0
11	Hino	38	0.6
12	Nissan Diesel	28	0.4

Source: Japan Automobile Dealers Assoc., Japan Mini-Vehicle Dealers Assoc.; *Nikkei Weekly*, January 17, 1994

World's Top 12 Vehicle Producers

Rank	Manufacturer	1993 Production
1	General Motors	7,299,000
2	Ford Motor Co.	5,700,000
3	Toyota Motor Corp.	4,450,309
4	Volkswagen AG	3,000,000
5	Nissan Motor Co.	2,818,017
6	Chrysler Corp.	2,348,030
7	Mitsubishi Motors Corp.	1,875,000
8	Honda Motor Co.	1,827,800
9	Renault SA	1,761,306
10	Peugeot-Citroen PSA	1,751,600
11	Fiat Group	1,600,000
12	Mazda Motor Corp.	1,241,564

Source: *Automotive News*, 1994 Market Data Book issue

European Auto Sales

Rank	Manufacturer	No. of Cars Sold
1	Volkswagen	1,846,300
2	Peugeot SA	1,527,800
3	General Motors	1,512,500
4	Ford	1,397,700
5	Renault	1,305,400
6	Fiat Auto	1,286,900
7	Mercedes-Benz	422,400
8	BMW	389,000
9	Rover	385,900
10	Nissan	384,000
11	Toyota	312,700
12	Volvo	200,300
13	Mazda	177,600
14	Honda	167,800
15	Mitsubishi	119,100
16	Suzuki	74,000
17	Chrysler	65,500
18	Skoda	58,200
19	Saab	52,600
20	Lada	38,400
21	Subaru	37,600
22	Daihatsu	25,000
23	Jaguar	10,900

Source: *Automotive News*; January 23, 1995

10 Best-Selling Imported Models in the US

Rank	Make	Model	No. of Imports Sold (1993)*
1	Toyota	Tercel	93,820
2	Toyota	Camry	89,791
3	Nissan	Maxima	87,602
4	Honda	Civic/del Sol	86,699
5	Mazda	Protege	81,642
6	Honda	Accord	80,982
7	Acura	Integra	58,757
8	Nissan	Sentra	52,545
9	Mercury	Tracer	45,754
10	BMW	3-Series	45,590

*Excluding vehicles assembled in the US

Source: *Automotive News*, 1994 Market Data Book issue

100 Largest Information Technology Companies

Rank	Company	1993 Information Science Revenue ($ mil.)	Rank	Company	1993 Information Science Revenue ($ mil.)
1	IBM	62,716.0	51	Packard Bell	1,250.0
2	Fujitsu	21,871.9	52	Maxtor	1,237.8
3	NEC	16,674.8	53	Silicon Graphics	1,159.2
4	Hewlett-Packard	15,600.0	54	Novell	1,123.0
5	Digital	13,637.0	55	Memorex Telex	1,070.9
6	Hitachi	12,629.1	56	Data General	1,059.5
7	AT&T	9,860.0	57	Intergraph	1,050.0
8	Toshiba	8,819.7	58	Motorola	1,029.0
9	EDS	8,507.3	59	Finsiel	1,027.5
10	Apple	7,900.0	60	Lockheed	994.0
11	Siemens Nixdorf	7,225.5	61	3M	981.4
12	Unisys	7,200.5	62	Lotus	981.2
13	Compaq	7,200.0	63	Cisco*	928.0
14	Olivetti	5,070.2	64	Nomura	907.2
15	Matsushita	5,050.7	65	Wang	904.2
16	Canon	5,033.0	66	Cray	894.9
17	Groupe Bull	5,000.0	67	Ceridian	886.1
18	Sun Microsystems	4,493.0	68	Science Applications	870.0
19	Microsoft	4,110.0	69	Tatung	867.0
20	ICL	3,915.7	70	Price Waterhouse	860.0
21	NTT	3,905.6	71	Texas Instruments	852.3
22	Xerox	3,330.0	72	Computervision	827.3
23	Seagate	3,114.0	73	Bell Atlantic	818.4
24	Mitsubishi	3,042.5	74	Martin Marietta	792.6
25	Andersen Consulting	2,876.3	75	EMC*	782.6
26	Dell	2,870.0	76	Sema Group	749.3
27	Nihon Unisys	2,697.8	77	Comparex	736.4
28	Computer Sciences	2,502.0	78	British Telecom	731.3
29	ADP	2,339.1	79	SHL Systemhouse	707.7
30	Ricoh	2,290.0	80	WordPerfect	707.0
31	TRW	2,251.0	81	SynOptics*	704.5
32	Northern Telecom	2,250.0	82	Getronics	703.8
33	Oki	2,245.6	83	3Com	696.0
34	Conner Peripherals	2,200.0	84	General Electric	684.0
35	Computer Associates	2,054.8	85	Systematics	677.8
36	Tandem	2,023.0	86	Sligos	675.2
37	Quantum	2,002.0	87	PRC	667.0
38	AST Research	1,971.0	88	SAP	665.0
39	Cap Gemini	1,946.9	89	CSK	638.3
40	Acer	1,898.0	90	Ernst & Young	637.0
41	Intel	1,844.2	91	Mitac	626.4
42	Seiko Epson	1,768.6	92	Sony	611.4
43	Gateway 2000	1,731.7	93	Racal	583.6
44	Oracle	1,692.9	94	Cabletron*	568.0
45	Amdahl	1,680.5	95	Intec	546.2
46	First Data	1,500.0	96	Stratus*	513.7
47	Samsung	1,494.4	97	Shared Medical Systems*	501.3
48	StorageTek	1,405.0	98	Software AG*	497.0
49	Lexmark	1,350.0	99	Wyse*	481.6
50	Western Digital	1,267.0	100	D&B Software	476.0

Source: *DATAMATION*, June 15, 1994

*New in 1993

Japan's Top 50 Electronics Companies

Rank	Company	1993 Electronics Sales ($ mil.)	Rank	Company	1993 Electronics Sales ($ mil.)
1	Matsushita	41,882	26	Minolta	2,900
2	NEC	34,755	27	Murata	2,711
3	Toshiba	32,200	28	Seiko	2,700
4	Fujitsu	30,479	29	Yokogawa Electric	2,352
5	Sony	28,585	30	Yamaha	2,300
6	Hitachi	28,400	31	Kenwood	2,197
7	NTT	23,900	32	Japan Radio	2,161
8	Canon	17,800	33	Ryosan	2,133
9	Mitsubishi Electric	17,100	34	Nikon	1,950
10	Sharp	12,122	35	Matsushita Elec Works	1,950
11	Ricoh	8,800	36	Rohm	1,942
12	Sanyo	7,631	37	Olympus	1,900
13	Oki Electric	6,325	38	Nissan	1,850
14	Pioneer	4,950	39	Tokyo Electron	1,842
15	Nintendo	4,715	40	Mitsumi Electric	1,807
16	Omron	4,474	41	Clarion	1,695
17	TDK	4,441	42	Konica	1,660
18	Nippondenso	4,400	43	Shimadzu	1,600
19	Alps	3,824	44	Shin-Etsu Chemical	1,400
20	Casio	3,726	45	Sanshin Electronics	1,309
21	Kyocera	3,600	46	Yaskawa Electric	1,274
22	Toyota	3,400	47	Kokusai	1,254
23	Sega	3,300	48	Minebea	1,230
24	Citizen	3,139	49	Brother Industries	1,223
25	Fuji Electric	3,100	50	Honda	1,200

Source: *Electronic Business Asia*, September 1994

Europe's Top 20 Electronics Companies

Rank	Company	Country	Market Value ($ mil.)
1	Siemens AG	Germany	20,388
2	Alcatel Alsthom Cie Generale d'Elec. SA	France	16,980
3	General Electric Company Plc	UK	13,703
4	Telefonaktiebolaget LM Ericsson	Sweden	9,802
5	Thorn EMI plc	UK	5,485
6	SMH Schw. Ges. f. Mikroelektronik. u. Uhrenindustrie	Switzerland	5,116
7	Philips Electronics N.V.	Netherlands	5,050
8	Thomson-CSF SA	France	3,460
9	Siebe PLC	UK	2,814
10	OY Nokia AB	Finland	1,901
11	Rheinelektra AG	Germany	1,689
12	SAP AG Syst., Anwend., Prod. i. d. Datenverarbeitung	Germany	1,614
13	Smiths Industries Plc	UK	1,591
14	Cap Gemini Sogeti SA	France	1,463
15	AEG AG	Germany	1,233
16	Olivetti Group-Ing C. Olivetti & C. SPA	Italy	1,001
17	SAGEM - Ste d'Applic. Gen. d'Elec. & de Mec.	France	938
18	Compagnie des Machines Bull SA	France	911
19	Racal Electronics Plc	UK	909
20	Philips Kommunikations Industrie AG	Germany	907

Source: *The European 5000*, 1994/95 Edition Indices

Asia's Top 100 Electronics Companies

Rank	Company	1993 Electronics Sales ($ mil.)	Rank	Company	1993 Electronics Sales ($ mil.)
1	Samsung Electronics	10,093	51	Star Light Electronics	169
2	Goldstar Company	5,405	52	National Electronics	167
3	Daewoo Electronics	2,505	53	Ocean Information	156
4	Acer	1,859	54	Giken Sakata	150
5	Hyundai Electronics Industries	1,572	55	Daewoo Electronic Components	146
6	Samsung Display Devices	1,523	56	Hon Hai Precision Industrial Co.	145
7	Goldstar Electron	1,096	57	Goldstar Instrument & Electric	145
8	Samsung Electro-Mechanics	915	58	General Electronics	144
9	Anam Industrial	779	59	Compeq Manufacturing Company	142
10	Mitac Group	626	60	Elec & Eltek International	136
11	Orion Electric	596	61	ASM Pacific Technology	133
12	Daewoo Telecom	592	62	Sam Young Electronics	132
13	Tatung Co.	589	63	Dae Ryung Industrial	128
14	VTech Group	532	64	Goldstar Electric Machinery	124
15	Indian Telephone Industries	492	65	GSS/Array Technology	121
16	First International Computer	438	66	Orient Power	114
17	Trigem Computer	382	67	Advanced Semiconductor Eng	114
18	United Microelectronics	378	68	S. Megga International	110
19	Kinpo Electronics	364	69	Tri-M Technologies	109
20	IPC	360	70	Dae Young Electronics Industrial	102
21	Wearne Brothers	343	71	Kumho Electric	96
22	Compal Electronics	336	72	Korea Computer	94
23	Korea Electronics	333	73	Luks Industrial	94
24	Tomei International	322	74	Aztech Systems	91
25	ADI	319	75	PCI	91
26	Alphatec Electronics	317	76	Microtek International	89
27	Delta Electronics	314	77	Sam Wha Electric	87
28	Chuntex Electronic Company	308	78	Termbray Industries Int	82
29	Anam Electronics	303	79	IDT International	82
30	Maxon Electronics	300	80	Microelectronics Technology	82
31	Samsung Aerospace Industries	298	81	Dae Duck Electronics	80
32	Goldstar Telecommunications	296	82	Newmax	78
33	Creative Technology	292	83	Sam Hwa Electronics	77
34	Inkel	291	84	Picvue Electronics	77
35	Videocon International	288	85	Team Concepts	74
36	Bharat Electronics	271	86	Electronic Resources	73
37	Wong's International	257	87	Modi Xerox	72
38	Taiwan Kolin Company	251	88	Titan Industries	72
39	Nan Ya Plastics	236	89	Mirc Electronics	72
40	GVC	235	90	Dae Duck Industries	71
41	NatSteel	219	91	Singatronics	70
42	Sampo	207	92	Precision Siliconware	69
43	Goldtron	206	93	HB International	67
44	Tae Il Media	205	94	Kin Son Electronic	67
45	Teco Electric	204	95	Hana Microelectronics	66
46	Johnson Electric	195	96	Venture Manufacturing	65
47	Hai Tai Electronics	192	97	Amtek Engineering	64
48	BPL	177	98	JCT Electronics	63
49	QPL International	176	99	Eltech Electronics	63
50	Liton Electronics	172	100	Gold Peak Industries	61

Source: *Electronic Business Asia*, September 1994

World's Top 30 Oil & Gas Companies

Rank	Company	Country	Liquids Output (1000 bbl/day)	Total Revenues ($ mil.)
1	Saudi Aramco*	Saudi Arabia	8,047	—
2	NIOC*	Iran	3,425	—
3	Pemex*	Mexico	3,140	26,686
4	CNPC*	China	2,829	—
5	PDV*	Venezuela	2,563	21,275
6	RD/Shell	Netherlands/UK	2,133	125,814
7	KPC*	Kuwait	1,881	—
8	Exxon	US	1,667	111,211
9	NNPC*	Nigeria	1,524	—
10	Luk Oil*	Russia	1,374	—
11	Libya NOC*	Libya	1,361	—
12	BP	UK	1,242	52,425
13	Sonatrach*	Algeria	1,147	—
14	Adnoc*	UAE	1,055	—
15	Chevron	US	950	33,014
16	Mobil	US	838	63,975
17	Texaco	US	728	34,071
18	Pertamina*	Indonesia	708	—
19	Arco	US	684	19,183
20	Amoco	US	678	28,617
21	Petrobras*	Brazil	668	18,029
22	Elf Aquitaine*	France	619	39,916
22	INOC*	Iraq	619	—
24	ENI*	Italy	536	34,760
25	ONGC*	India	534	—
26	EGPC*	Egypt	502	—
27	PDO*	Oman	466	—
28	Statoil*	Norway	449	11,579
29	Conoco	US	434	15,771
30	Total	France	430	24,112

Source: *Petroleum Intelligence Weekly*; December 12, 1994

*State-owned company

World's Top 10 Upstream Companies

Rank	Company	Country	Output (1000 boe/day)
1	Gazprom*	Russia	10,608
2	Saudi Aramco*	Saudi Arabia	8,694
3	NIOC*	Iran	3,913
4	Pemex*	Mexico	3,609
5	RD/Shell	Netherlands/UK	3,486
6	PDV*	Venezuela	3,322
7	CNPC*	China	3,093
8	Exxon	US	2,756
9	Sonatrach*	Algeria	2,117
10	KPC*	Kuwait	1,960

Source: *Petroleum Intelligence Weekly*; December 12, 1994

*State-owned company

Note: boe equals barrels of oil equivalent

World's Top 10 Downstream Companies

Rank	Company	Country	Sales (1000 bbl/day)
1	RD/Shell	Netherlands/UK	5,374
2	Exxon	US	4,925
3	BP	UK	3,019
4	Mobil	US	2,934
5	Chevron	US	2,594
6	Texaco	US	2,334
7	PDV*	Venezuela	2,073
8	Saudi Aramco*	Saudi Arabia	1,800
9	Pemex*	Mexico	1,442
10	Amoco	US	1,312

Source: *Petroleum Intelligence Weekly*; December 12, 1994

*State-owned company

Note: bbl equals barrels

World's 50 Largest Utilities

Rank	Company	Country	1993 Sales ($ mil.)
1	Tokyo Electric Power	Japan	125,961
2	Électricité de France	France	112,824
3	Deutsche Bundespost Telekom	Germany	88,649
4	Enel	Italy	83,179
5	Kansai Electric Power	Japan	60,586
6	Chubu Electric Power	Japan	53,480
7	France Telecom	France	45,790
8	British Gas	Britain	44,614
9	GTE	U.S.	41,575
10	STET	Italy	41,429
11	Kyushu Electric Power	Japan	36,960
12	Hydro-Québec	Canada	36,122
13	Ontario Hydro	Canada	33,728
14	BT	Britain	33,579
15	BellSouth	U.S.	32,873
16	Tohoku Electric Power	Japan	31,886
17	Bell Atlantic	U.S.	29,544
18	NYNEX	U.S.	29,458
19	Telefónica de España	Spain	28,654
20	Pacific Gas & Electric	U.S.	27,163
21	Southern	U.S.	25,911
22	Taiwan Power	Taiwan	25,556
23	Southwestern Bell	U.S.	24,308
24	Commonwealth Edison	U.S.	23,963
25	Iberdrola	Spain	23,451
26	Pacific Telesis Group	U.S.	23,437
27	Ameritech	U.S.	23,428
28	Chugoku Electric Power	Japan	23,273
29	Entergy	U.S.	22,877
30	Telebrás	Brazil	21,589
31	Texas Utilities	U.S.	21,518
32	SCEcorp	U.S.	21,379
33	US West	U.S.	20,680
34	Teléfonos de México	Mexico	17,033
35	PTT Suisses	Switzerland	16,797
36	Public Service Enterprise Group	U.S.	16,305
37	Electric Power Development	Japan	16,218
38	American Electric Power	U.S.	15,341
39	Peco	U.S.	15,032
40	Tokyo Gas	Japan	14,776
41	Shikoku Electric Power	Japan	14,385
42	Bell Canada	Canada	14,292
43	Hokuriku Electric Power	Japan	13,617
44	Consolidated Edison of New York	U.S.	13,484
45	Long Island Lighting	U.S.	13,456
46	Dominion Resources	U.S.	13,350
47	Royal PTT Nederland	Netherlands	13,124
48	FPL Group	U.S.	13,078
49	Eskom	South Africa	13,057
50	Hokkaido Electric Power	Japan	12,838

Source: *FORTUNE*; August 22, 1994

World's 100 Largest Commercial Banking Companies

Rank	Company	Country	1993 Assets ($ mil.)
1	Fuji Bank	Japan	538,243
2	Dai-Ichi Kangyo Bank	Japan	535,357
3	Sumitomo Bank	Japan	531,835
4	Sanwa Bank	Japan	525,127
5	Sakura Bank	Japan	523,731
6	Mitsubishi Bank	Japan	487,547
7	Norinchukin Bank	Japan	435,599
8	Industrial Bank of Japan	Japan	414,926
9	Crédit Lyonnais	France	337,503
10	Bank of China	China	334,753
11	Mitsubishi Trust & Banking	Japan	330,479
12	Tokai Bank	Japan	328,685
13	Deutsche Bank	Germany	319,998
14	Long-Term Credit Bank of Japan	Japan	315,026
15	Sumitomo Trust & Banking	Japan	305,347
16	HSBC Holdings	Britain	304,521
17	Mitsui Trust & Banking	Japan	296,911
18	Crédit Agricole	France	281,787
19	Asahi Bank	Japan	277,688
20	Bank of Tokyo	Japan	273,884
21	Daiwa Bank	Japan	262,567
22	Société Générale	France	259,129
23	ABN AMRO Holding	Netherlands	252,168
24	Banque Nationale de Paris	France	249,110
25	Barclays Bank	Britain	245,284
26	Yasuda Trust & Banking	Japan	235,528
27	Cie Financière de Paribas	France	229,025
28	National Westminster Bank	Britain	225,860
29	Dresdner Bank	Germany	218,888
30	Citicorp	United States	216,574
31	Union Bank of Switzerland	Switzerland	209,177
32	Toyo Trust & Banking	Japan	204,003
33	Westdeutsche Landesbank	Germany	191,213
34	Bankamerica Corp.	United States	186,933
35	Nippon Credit Bank	Japan	168,052
36	Bayerische Vereinsbank	Germany	166,262
37	Commerzbank	Germany	164,058
38	Shoko Chukin Bank	Japan	160,861
39	NationsBank Corp	United States	157,686
40	Crédit Suisse	Switzerland	156,042
41	Groupe des Caisses d'Épargne	France	155,972
42	Bayerische Hypotheken & Wechsel	Germany	152,657
43	Chemical Banking Corporation	United States	149,888
44	Bayerische Landesbank	Germany	149,591
45	Istituto Banc. San Paolo di Torino	Italy	145,916
46	Banca di Roma	Italy	141,761
47	Swiss Bank Corporation	Switzerland	139,091
48	Zenshinren Bank	Japan	137,431
49	J.P. Morgan & Co.	United States	133,888
50	Rabobank	Netherlands	130,049

World's 100 Largest Commercial Banking Companies (continued)

Rank	Company	Country	1993 Assets ($ mil.)
51	Deutsche Genossenschaftsbank	Germany	127,196
52	Royal Bank of Canada	Canada	124,766
53	Bank of Yokohama	Japan	124,317
54	Chuo Trust & Banking	Japan	120,109
55	Lloyds Bank	Britain	117,844
56	Hokkaido Takushoku Bank	Japan	107,025
57	Canadian Imperial Bank of Commerce	Canada	106,883
58	Norddeutsche Landesbank	Germany	102,660
59	Chase Manhattan Corporation	United States	102,103
60	Generale Bank	Belgium	101,547
61	Bankers Trust New York Corp.	United States	92,082
62	Banca Nazionale del Lavoro	Italy	90,632
63	Banco Central Hispano Americano	Spain	90,466
64	Bank of Montreal	Canada	88,403
65	Cariplo	Italy	87,856
66	Südwestdeutsche Landesbank	Germany	84,393
67	Chiba Bank	Japan	83,598
68	Union Européenne de Cic	France	83,262
69	Crédit Communal de Belgique	Belgium	81,574
70	Bank of Nova Scotia	Canada	81,407
71	Banco Bilbao Vizcaya	Spain	81,281
72	Monte Dei Paschi di Siena	Italy	81,243
73	Banc One Corp.	United States	79,919
74	Banca Commerciale Italiana	Italy	78,082
75	Hokuriku Bank	Japan	77,641
76	Argentaria	Spain	75,868
77	National Australia Bank	Australia	75,617
78	Groupe des Banques Populaires	France	75,423
79	Landesbank Hessen-Thüringen	Germany	74,820
80	Shizuoka Bank	Japan	74,813
81	Banque Bruxelles Lambert	Belgium	73,891
82	Banco di Napoli	Italy	73,518
83	Banco de Santander	Spain	72,948
84	Banco do Brasil	Brazil	71,199
85	Joyo Bank	Japan	71,066
86	First Union Corp.	United States	70,787
87	Credito Italiano	Italy	69,542
88	Kredietbank	Belgium	69,047
89	Crédit Mutuel	France	68,424
90	Westpac Banking	Australia	67,530
91	Ashikaga Bank	Japan	65,752
92	Banque Indosuez	France	65,355
93	Australia & New Zealand Banking	Australia	64,448
94	Toronto-Dominion Bank	Canada	64,305
95	Bank of Fukuoka	Japan	63,966
96	Hiroshima Bank	Japan	63,907
97	PNC Bank Corporation	United States	62,080
98	Commonwealth Bank	Australia	60,631
99	Swedbank	Sweden	58,385
100	ASLK-CGER	Belgium	56,606

Source: *FORTUNE*; August 22, 1994

Europe's 20 Largest Banks

Rank	Company	1993 Assets ($ mil.)
1	Crédit Lyonnais	338,848
2	Deutsche Bank	322,445
3	HSBC Holdings	305,214
4	Crédit Agricole	282,911
5	Société Générale	260,162
6	ABN-AMRO Bank	252,986
7	Banque Nationale de Paris	250,443
8	Barclays Bank	245,901
9	CS Holding (Credit Suisse)	234,190
10	Compagnie Financière de Paribas	229,938
11	National Westminster Bank	226,429
12	Dresdner Bank	220,562
13	Union Bank of Switzerland	210,379
14	Westdeutsche Landesbank Giro.	192,675
15	Bayerische Vereinsbank AG	167,256
16	Commerzbank	164,898
17	Groupe Caisse d'Epargne	161,858
18	Bayerische Hypo- & Wechsel-Bank	153,630
19	San Paolo Bank Holding	147,072
20	Bayerische Landesbank Girozentrale	140,502

Source: *The Banker*, September 1994

Latin America's 20 Largest Banks

Rank	Company	1993 Assets ($ mil.)
1	Banco do Brasil	71,199
2	Banamex	43,012
3	Bancomer	36,134
4	Banco do Estado de São Paulo	22,876
5	Banca Serfin	21,390
6	Banco Bradesco	17,954
7	Banco Mexicano	13,969
8	Banco de la Nacion	13,058
9	Banco Itaú	12,528
10	Multibanco Comermex	12,188
11	Banco Internacional	11,703
12	Banco Bamerindus do Brasil	9,244
13	Banco Nacional	9,088
14	Banpais	8,601
15	Unibanco	7,909
16	Banco del Atlantico	7,899
17	Banco Real	7,556
18	Banco de la Provincia de Buenos Aires	7,119
19	Banco del Estado de Chile	6,060
20	Banco Economico	5,683

Source: *The Banker*, August 1994

Japan's 20 Largest Banks

Rank	Company	1993 Assets ($ mil.)
1	Fuji Bank	507,218
2	Dai-Ichi Kangyo Bank	506,563
3	Sumitomo Bank	497,781
4	Sakura Bank	495,975
5	Sanwa Bank	493,588
6	Mitsubishi Bank	458,906
7	Norinchukin Bank	429,258
8	Industrial Bank of Japan	386,916
9	Tokai Bank	311,451
10	Long-Term Credit Bank of Japan	302,185
11	Asahi Bank	261,963
12	Bank of Tokyo	242,445
13	Daiwa Bank	170,622
14	Nippon Credit Bank	166,831
15	Shoko Chukin Bank	159,218
16	Mitsubishi Trust & Banking Corp.	156,840
17	Mitsui Trust & Banking	143,615
18	Sumitomo Trust & Banking	142,657
19	Zenshinren Bank	136,249
20	Bank of Yokohama	119,134

Source: *The Banker*, July 1994

Asia's 20 Largest Banks

Rank	Company	1993 Assets ($ mil.)
1	Industrial & Comm. Bank of China	337,769
2	Bank of China	234,026
3	People's Construction Bank of China	183,737
4	Agricultural Bank of China	177,498
5	National Australia Bank	66,603
6	Westpac Banking Corporation	59,277
7	ANZ Banking Group	56,201
8	Commonwealth Bank Group	54,663
9	Taiwan Cooperative Bank	50,033
10	Bank of Taiwan	45,625
11	Korea Exchange Bank	39,065
12	Korea Development Bank	34,541
13	Cho Hung Bank	32,379
14	State Bank of India	32,186
15	Land Bank of Taiwan	31,805
16	Bank of Communications	31,387
17	First Commercial Bank	31,202
18	Bangkok Bank	30,433
19	Hua Nan Commercial Bank	29,308
20	Chang Hwa Commercial Bank	28,291

Source: *The Banker*, July 1994

World's 50 Largest Savings Institutions

Rank	Company	Country	1993 Assets ($ mil.)
1	Abbey National	Britain	123,821
2	Halifax Building Society	Britain	100,776
3	La Caixa	Spain	54,829
4	Nationwide Building Society	Britain	52,506
5	H.F. Ahmanson	U.S.	50,871
6	Confédération Desjardins	Canada	44,162
7	Great Western Financial Corp.	U.S.	38,348
8	Woolwich Building Society	Britain	37,284
9	CT Financial Services	Canada	34,804
10	Caixa Geral de Depósitos	Portugal	31,860
11	Alliance & Leicester Bldg. Society	Britain	31,156
12	Grupo Caja de Madrid	Spain	30,875
13	Leeds Permanent Bldg. Society	Britain	29,163
14	Golden West Financial Corp.	U.S.	28,829
15	Raiffeisenbanken	Switzerland	28,461
16	Nederlandse Spaarbankbond	Netherlands	27,614
17	Girocredit Bank AG der Spark.	Austria	27,154
18	Cheltenham & Gloucester Bldg.	Britain	26,133
19	Wüstenrot Holding	Germany	25,354
20	BHW Holding	Germany	23,994
21	Bradford & Bingley Bldg. Society	Britain	20,485
22	Hamburger Sparkasse	Germany	20,113
23	Britannia Building Society	Britain	19,068
24	Natl. & Provincial Bldg. Society	Britain	18,794
25	Glendale Federal	U.S.	17,905
26	Landesgirokasse	Germany	17,256
27	California Federal Bank	U.S.	16,326
28	Washington Mutual Savings Bank	U.S.	15,827
29	Frankfurter Sparkasse	Germany	12,758
30	Sparebanken Nor	Norway	12,638
31	Stadtsparkasse Köln	Germany	12,478
32	Bristol & West Building Society	Britain	12,028
33	National Trustco	Canada	11,971
34	Standard Federal Bank	U.S.	10,905
35	Northern Rock Building Society	Britain	10,756
36	Caixa D'Estalvis de Catalunya	Spain	10,663
37	Nassauische Sparkasse	Germany	10,499
38	Stadtsparkasse München	Germany	9,752
39	Dime Savings Bank of New York	U.S.	9,276
40	Firstfed Michigan Corp.	U.S.	9,264
41	Bilbao Bizkaia Kutxa	Spain	8,858
42	Kreissparkasse Köln	Germany	8,706
43	Caixa Galicia	Spain	8,265
44	Coast Savings Financial	U.S.	8,095
45	Sparkasse In Bremen	Germany	7,953
46	Anchor Bancorp	U.S.	7,917
47	Yorkshire Building Society	Britain	7,900
48	Ibercaja	Spain	7,887
49	Metropolitan Financial Corp.	U.S.	7,007
50	People's Bank	U.S.	6,400

Source: *FORTUNE*; August 22, 1994

World's 50 Largest Diversified Financial Companies

Rank	Company	Country	1993 Assets ($ mil.)
1	Federal National Mortgage Association	U.S.	216,979
2	Salomon	U.S.	184,835
3	ING Group	Netherlands	174,323
4	Merrill Lynch	U.S.	152,910
5	AXA	France	141,214
6	Union des Assurances de Paris	France	141,074
7	Allianz Holding	Germany	128,057
8	GAN	France	124,713
9	Cie de Suez	France	120,009
10	Fortis	Belgium/Netherlands	108,595
11	Travelers Inc.	U.S.	101,360
12	American International Group	U.S.	101,015
13	Aetna Life & Casualty	U.S.	100,037
14	Morgan Stanley Group	U.S.	97,242
15	American Express	U.S.	94,132
16	CIGNA	U.S.	84,975
17	Federal Home Loan Mortgage	U.S.	83,880
18	Nomura Securities	Japan	80,530
19	Nippon Shinpan	Japan	72,505
20	Orient	Japan	71,213
21	ITT	U.S.	70,560
22	AEGON	Netherlands	65,843
23	Assurances Générales de France	France	64,243
24	Nykredit	Denmark	61,501
25	Zurich Insurance	Switzerland	60,059
26	BAT Industries	Britain	58,028
27	Bear Stearns	U.S.	57,440
28	Münchener Rück	Germany	56,592
29	Daiwa Securities	Japan	52,665
30	Assicurazioni Generali	Italy	51,104
31	Student Loan Marketing Association	U.S.	46,509
32	Tokio Marine & Fire Insurance	Japan	46,253
33	Loews	U.S.	45,850
34	Istituto Mobiliare Italiano	Italy	45,223
35	American General	U.S.	43,982
36	Orix	Japan	42,693
37	Swiss Reinsurance	Switzerland	40,120
38	Japan Securities Finance	Japan	39,602
39	Winterthur Group	Switzerland	38,660
40	Yamaichi Securities	Japan	37,123
41	Paine Webber Group	U.S.	37,027
42	Transamerica	U.S.	36,051
43	Nikko Securities	Japan	35,122
44	S.G. Warburg Group	Britain	33,607
45	Yasuda Fire & Marine Insurance	Japan	33,270
46	Japan Leasing	Japan	32,994
47	Household International	U.S.	32,962
48	APLUS	Japan	31,689
49	Crediop	Italy	30,299
50	Skandia Group	Sweden	27,732

Source: *FORTUNE*; August 22, 1994

25 Largest Investments in US Companies by Foreign Companies in 1993

Rank	Acquirer	1993 Acquisition	Industry	Price ($ mil.)
1	Hanson PLC (U.K.)	Quantum Chemical Corp.	Polyethylene	3,219.7
2	Seagram Co. Ltd. (Canada)	8.1% of Time Warner Inc.	Periodicals and book publishing	1,189.0
3	RTZ Corp. PLC (U.K.)	NERCO Inc.	Coal, gold, silver mining	1,161.9
4	Schlumberger Ltd. (France)	Remaining 50% of Dowell Schlumberger Inc.	Chemicals	1,124.6
5	Siemens AG (Germany)	Electrical products business of GTE Corp.	Light bulbs	1,000.0
6	British Telecommunications PLC (U.K.)	4.9% of MCI Communications Corp.	Telecommunications services	830.0
7	Aurora National Life Assurance (France)	Executive Life Insurance Co.	Life insurance	800.0
8	Hoechst AG (Germany)	51% of Copley Pharmaceutical Inc.	Pharmaceuticals	546.0
9	CITGO Petroleum Corp. (Venezuela)	Houston refinery of Lyondell Petrochemical Co.	Petroleum refining	500.0
10	Bowater Industries PLC (U.K.)	Specialty Coatings International Inc.	Laminated paper products	434.0
11	Cisneros Group of Cos. (Venezuela)	Pueblo International Inc.	Supermarkets	420.0
12	Fukutake Publishing Co. Ltd. (Japan)	Berlitz International Inc.	Language schools	419.5
13	Reed Elsevier PLC (U.K.)	Official Airline Guides Inc.	Travel magazine publishing	417.0
14	C.K. Acquisitions Corp. (Bahrain)	The Circle K Corp.	Convenience stores	399.5
15	Axa SA (France)	17.6% of Equitable Cos. Inc.	Life insurance	382.0
16	MEPC PLC (U.K.)	American Property Trust	Real estate	346.0
17	United Dominion Industries Ltd. (Canada)	Marley Co.	Pumps	340.0
18	Cadbury Schweppes PLC (U.K.)	A&W Brands Inc.	Beverages	334.0
19	ECC Group PLC (U.K.)	Calgon Water Management unit of Merck & Co.	Water management services	307.5
20	Philips Electronics NV (Netherlands)	Motown Record Co. LP	Records, tapes, CDs	301.0
21	British Airways PLC (U.K.)	20% of USAir Group Inc.	Airline	300.0
22	Unilever NV (Netherlands)	Ice cream business of Kraft General Foods Inc.	Ice cream	300.0
23	ECI Telecom Ltd. (Israel)	Telematics International Inc.	Communications products	278.5
24	Cadbury Schweppes PLC (U.K.)	20.2% of Dr Pepper/Seven-Up Cos. Inc.	Soft drinks	231.3
25	Sumitomo Metal Industries Ltd. (Japan)	10% of LTV Corp.	Steel, aerospace	200.0

Source: *Mergers & Acquisitions*, May/June 1994

15 Largest Acquisitions of Foreign Businesses by US Companies

Rank	Acquirer	1993 Acquisition	Industry	Price ($ mil.)
1	Philip Morris Cos. Inc.	Freia Marabou A/S (Norway)	Candy and chocolates	1,493.3
2	General Electric Co.	43 planes of GPA Group PLC (Ireland)	Airplanes	1,350.0
3	General Electric Co., Ingersoll-Rand Co., Dresser Industries Inc., et al	69% of Nuovo Pignone Industrie Meccaniche E Fondaria (Italy)	Machinery, fluid meters	662.2
4	Gillette Co.	Parker Pen Holdings Ltd. (U.K.)	Writing instruments	589.7
5	Cyprus Amax Minerals Co.	Cerro Verde copper mine of Minero Peru (Peru)	Copper mining	522.0
6	Bell Atlantic Corp.	23% of Iusacell SA de CV (Mexico)	Cellular communications services	520.0
7	Anheuser Busch Cos. Inc.	17.7% of Grupo Modelo (Mexico)	Brewing	477.0
8	IBM Corp.	Cie. Generale d'Informatique (France)	Computer Services	457.9
9	Raytheon Co.	Corporate Jets Ltd. (U.K.)	Corporate jets	387.1
10	General Electric Co.	Finax (Sweden)	Credit card services	385.6
11	Harsco Corp.	MultiServ International NV (Netherlands)	Metal recovery services	384.5
12	DuPont Co.	Fibers division of Imperial Chemical Industries PLC (U.K.)	Nylon fibers	355.9
13	Southern Co. Inc.	59% of Hidroelectrica Alicura SA (Argentina)	Electric utility	352.9
14	Sara Lee Corp.	Personal products unit of SmithKline Beecham PLC (U.K.)	Personal care products	319.8
15	Philip Morris Cos. Inc.	Terry's Group unit of United Biscuits PLC (U.K.)	Confectionary products	319.0

Source: *Mergers & Acquistions*, May/June 1994

15 Biggest Deals of 1994

Buyer	Acquisition	Transaction Type	Value ($ bil.)
AT&T	McCaw Cellular Comm.	Stock swap	18.92
Viacom	Paramount Communications	Cash and securities acquisition	9.60
American Home Products	American Cyanamid	Cash acquisition	9.27
Pacific Telesis shareholders	PacTel (Airtouch Comm.)	Spinoff	8.64
Viacom	Blockbuster	Stock swap	7.97
Columbia Healthcare	HCA-Hospital Corp. of America	Stock swap	5.60
Roche Holding	Syntex	Cash acquisition	5.31
Eastman Kodak shareholders	Eastman Chemical	Spinoff	4.03
Eli Lilly	PCS Health Systems	Cash acquisition	4.00
Society Corp.	KeyCorp	Stock swap	3.92
Sandoz	Gerber	Cash acquisition	3.67
United Airlines workers	UAL (55%)	Labor contract concessions	3.47
Federated Dept. Stores	R.H. Macy	Bought out of bankruptcy	3.45
Tele-Communications	Liberty Media	Stock swap	3.41
SmithKline Beecham	Sterling Winthrop	Cash acquisition	2.92

Source: Securities Data Co.; *The Wall Street Journal*, January 3, 1995

10 Largest Mergers and Acquisitions Involving Canadian Companies

Acquirer	Target	Industry	Price ($ mil.)
Royal Bank of Canada	Canadian and international assets of Genira Inc.	Finance	1,328
Seagram Co. Ltd.	8.1% of Time Warner Inc.	Media, entertainment	1,189
Methanex Corp.	Fletcher Challenge Methanol (New Zealand)	Methanol	934
Semi-Tech Microelectronics Ltd.	15% of Singer Co. NV (Hong Kong)	Sewing machines	848
Fletcher Challenge Ltd. (New Zealand)	Forest products of Crown Forest Industries Ltd.	Forest products	704
BCE Inc.	20% of Mercury Communications Ltd. (U.K.)	Telecommunications services	682
Talisman Energy Inc.	Encor Inc.	Oil and gas	376
United Dominion Industries Ltd.	Marley Co. (U.S.)	Pumps	340
Philip Morris Cos. Inc. (U.S.)	20% of Molson Breweries of Canada	Brewing	273
Shaw Cablesystems Ltd.	CL Systems Ltd.	Cable television	258

Source: *Mergers & Acquisitions*, May/June 1994

Major European Deals

Acquirer	Target	Industry	Price ($ mil.)
Rothmans International PLC (U.K.)	Tobacco business of Rothmans International PLC (U.K.)	Cigarettes	4,729
Vendome Group PLC (U.K.)	Cartier Monde S.A.(France)	Watches, perfumes	3,446
Sydkraft A/B (Sweden)	Bakab Energi (Sweden)	Electric utility	1,900
Kingfisher PLC (U.K)	Financière Darty S.A.(France)	Appliance stores	1,506
MB-Caradon PLC (U.K.)	Pillar division of RTZ Corp. PLC (U.K.)	Building, electrical products	1,184
Procordia AM (Sweden)	51% interest in Erbamont Inc. and Farmitalia Carlo Erba SRL (Italy)	Pharmaceuticals	1,126
GS Holding AG (Switzerland)	Swiss Volkshank (Switzerland)	Banking	1,101
Scottish & Newcastle Breweries (U.K.)	Chef and Brewer chains of Grand Metropolitan PLC (U.K.)	Pubs	1,072
Tejo Energia (Portugal)	Pego Power Station (Portugal)	Electric and gas utility	1,004
Magyar Com (Germany)	30% interest in Hungarian Telecommunications (Hungary)	Telecommunications services	875

Source: SDC Merger & Corporate Transactions Database; *Mergers & Acquisitions*, May/June 1994

World's Top 10 Underwriters of Non-US Securities 1994

Manager	Amount ($ bil.)	1994 % Market Share
Goldman Sachs	21.2	6.1
CS First Boston	20.0	5.8
Merrill Lynch	19.0	5.5
Morgan Stanley	15.2	4.4
J.P. Morgan	14.4	4.2
Swiss Bank	14.3	4.1
Nomura Securities	13.2	3.8
Deutsche Bank	13.0	3.8
UBS	12.3	3.6
Daiwa Securities	11.6	3.4

Source: Securities Data Co./*Bond Buyer; The Wall Street Journal*, January 3, 1995

World's 10 Largest Securities Firms

Rank	Company	Capital ($ mil.)
1	Nomura Securities (Japan)	18,119
2	Goldman Sachs (US)	15,732
3	Salomon (US)	14,597
4	Merrill Lynch (US)	13,262
5	Daiwa Securities (Japan)	11,031
6	Nikko Securities (Japan)	10,225
7	Morgan Stanley (US)	9,813
8	Lehman Brothers Holdings Inc. (US)	9,418
9	Yamaichi Securities (Japan)	9,172
10	Dean Witter, Discover (US)	6,617

Source: *The Wall Street Journal*; September 30, 1994

World's 50 Largest Life Insurance Companies

Rank	Company	Country	1993 Assets ($ mil.)
1	Nippon Life	Japan	339,053
2	Dai-Ichi Mutual Life	Japan	239,205
3	Sumitomo Life	Japan	208,964
4	Prudential Of America	U.S.	165,742
5	Meiji Mutual Life	Japan	144,773
6	Metropolitan Life	U.S.	128,225
7	Asahi Mutual Life	Japan	109,074
8	Prudential	Britain	95,785
9	Mitsui Mutual Life	Japan	90,384
10	Yasuda Mutual Life	Japan	79,898
11	Teachers Insurance & Annuity	U.S.	67,483
12	Chiyoda Mutual Life	Japan	61,686
13	Taiyo Mutual Life	Japan	56,918
14	Allianz	Germany	55,602
15	New York Life	U.S.	53,571
16	Standard Life	Britain	53,341
17	Toho Mutual Life	Japan	52,280
18	Aetna Life	U.S.	51,535
19	Australian Mutual Provident	Australia	50,734
20	Kyoei Life	Japan	49,454
21	Connecticut General Life	U.S.	48,372
22	Equitable Life Assurance	U.S.	47,309
23	Legal & General	Britain	44,917
24	Northwestern Mutual Life	U.S.	44,058
25	John Hancock Mutual Life	U.S.	43,694
26	Daido Mutual Life	Japan	41,728
27	Swiss Life	Switzerland	41,288
28	CNP Assurances	France	40,611
29	Principal Mutual Life	U.S.	40,072
30	Norwich Union	Britain	39,943
31	Commercial Union	Britain	38,397
32	Nippon Dantai Life	Japan	36,481
33	Massachusetts Mutual Life	U.S.	34,314
34	Lincoln National Life	U.S.	34,040
35	Fukoku Mutual	Japan	33,825
36	Sun Life Assurance of Canada	Canada	33,712
37	Daihyaku Mutual Life	Japan	32,843
38	Travelers	U.S.	32,672
39	Scottish Widows' Fund & Life	Britain	29,718
40	Manufacturers Life	Canada	29,041
41	Hartford Life	U.S.	28,971
42	IDS Life	U.S.	28,041
43	Old Mutual	South Africa	24,716
44	Sun Life	Britain	23,172
45	Nationwide Life	U.S.	23,050
46	Hamburg-Mannheimer	Germany	22,233
47	Allstate Life	U.S.	21,234
48	Sanlam	South Africa	20,943
49	Volksfürsorge Holding	Germany	20,918
50	Nissan Mutual Life	Japan	20,536

Source: *FORTUNE*; August 22, 1994

World's 50 Largest Transportation Companies

Rank	Company	Country	1993 Sales ($ mil.)
1	East Japan Railway	Japan	21,717
2	United Parcel Service	U.S.	17,782
3	AMR	U.S.	15,816
4	Nippon Express	Japan	15,352
5	UAL	U.S.	14,511
6	Delta Air Lines	U.S.	11,997
7	Japan Airlines	Japan	11,646
8	Air France Group	France	11,087
9	Lufthansa Group	Germany	10,722
10	Central Japan Railway	Japan	10,322
11	West Japan Railway	Japan	10,282
12	SNAM	Italy	9,543
13	British Airways	Britain	9,481
14	SNCF	France	9,348
15	CSX	U.S.	8,940
16	Deutsche Bundesbahn	Germany	8,695
17	Northwest Airlines	U.S.	8,649
18	Peninsular & Oriental Steam Navigation	Britain	8,629
19	Kinki Nippon Railway	Japan	8,070
20	Nippon Yusen	Japan	7,950
21	All Nippon Airways	Japan	7,944
22	Federal Express	U.S.	7,808
23	Union Pacific	U.S.	7,561
24	USAir Group	U.S.	7,083
25	Canadian Pacific	Canada	6,048
26	Continental Airlines	U.S.	5,775
27	Mitsui O.S.K. Lines	Japan	5,641
28	Ryder System	U.S.	5,304
29	Swire Pacific	Hong Kong	5,270
30	Yamato Transport	Japan	5,234
31	SAS Group	Sweden	5,023
32	Odakyu Electric Railway	Japan	4,992
33	Seibu Railway	Japan	4,874
34	Alitalia	Italy	4,753
35	Burlington Northern	U.S.	4,699
36	British Railways Board	Britain	4,664
37	Transnet	South Africa	4,616
38	KLM Royal Dutch Airlines	Netherlands	4,609
39	Norfolk Southern	U.S.	4,460
40	Swissair Group	Switzerland	4,332
41	Tokyu	Japan	4,251
42	Schweizerische Bundesbahnen	Switzerland	4,248
43	Consolidated Freightways	U.S.	4,192
44	Roadway Services	U.S.	4,156
45	Kawasaki Kisen	Japan	4,116
46	Qantas Airways	Australia	4,081
47	Keio Teito Electric Railway	Japan	3,967
48	Singapore Airlines	Singapore	3,894
49	Nedlloyd Group	Netherlands	3,563
50	Iberia Airlines	Spain	3,497

Source: *FORTUNE*; August 22, 1994

World's Top 20 Airlines — Sales

Rank	Airline	1993 Sales ($ mil.)
1	American	14,785
2	United	14,511
3	Delta	12,295
4	Japan Airlines	8,890
5	Lufthansa	8,800
6	Northwest	8,649
7	British Airways	8,460
8	Federal Express	8,152
9	All Nippon	7,200
10	USAir	7,083
11	Continental	5,775
12	SAS Group	4,968
13	Swissair Group	4,420
14	KLM	4,327
15	Qantas	4,173
16	Singapore	3,737
17	Korean	3,371
18	TWA	3,157
19	Cathay Pacific	3,078
20	Air Canada	2,726

Source: *Air Transport World*, June 1994

World's Top 20 Airlines — Revenue Passenger Miles

Rank	Airline	1993 No. of Miles (mil.)
1	United	97,772
2	American	93,798
3	Delta	79,992
4	Northwest	56,669
5	British Airways	47,584
6	Continental	40,859
7	USAir	34,003
8	Japan Airlines	33,130
9	Lufthansa	30,820
10	Qantas	26,822
11	Air France	26,185
12	Singapore	24,759
13	KLM	22,473
14	TWA	21,880
15	All Nippon	20,580
16	Cathay Pacific	17,451
17	Alitalia Group	17,032
18	Southwest	16,136
19	Korean	15,544
20	Iberia	13,961

Source: *Air Transport World*, June 1994

World's Top 20 Airlines — No. of Passengers

Rank	Airline	1993 Passengers (thou.)
1	Delta	85,032
2	American	82,567
3	United	69,816
4	USAir	53,678
5	Northwest	44,201
6	Continental	38,628
7	All Nippon	33,722
8	Southwest	33,509
9	Lufthansa	28,439
10	British Airways	28,134
11	Japan Airlines	23,590
12	Alitalia Group	19,570
13	TWA	18,976
14	SAS	18,600
15	Air Inter	16,583
16	Korean	16,487
17	Japan Air System	15,018
18	America West	14,740
19	Iberia	14,383
20	Air France	14,374

Source: *Air Transport World*, June 1994

World's Top 20 Airlines — No. of Aircraft

Rank	Airline	1993 Aircraft
1	American	667
2	Delta	550
3	United	544
4	Federal Express	456
5	USAir	441
6	Northwest	358
7	Continental	316
8	British Airways	244
9	Krasnoyarskavia	229
10	Lufthansa	206
11	TWA	191
12	Southwest	157
13	SAS	153
14	Far Eastern	150
15	UPS	148
16	Iberia	142
17	Air France	140
18	Alitalia Group	138
18	Flagship	138
20	All Nippon	129

Source: *Air Transport World*, June 1994

15 Top Ranking Container Shipping Operators

Operator	1000 dwt	1000 teu
Maersk	1,917.7	114.4
Evergreen	1,837.7	114.1
Sea-Land	1,436.3	107.3
Nippon Yusen Kaisha	1,338.1	83.3
Mitsui-OSK Lines	1,073.2	62.8
American President Lines	848.9	58.4
P & O Container Ltd.	944.3	58.1
Hapag-Lloyd	932.1	57.0
Hanjin	928.9	56.9
Yangming	777.1	56.8
Orient Overseas Container Line	768.5	51.2
Nedlloyd	842.5	50.9
Kawasaki Kisen Kaisha	799.0	48.8
Zim Israel Navigation Co. Ltd.	802.3	41.8
Neptun Orient Lines	590.9	37.8

Source: *World Export Services Handbook 1994*

Note: dwt equals deadweight tons; teu equals twenty-foot equivalent units

Existing World Container Fleet by Leading Yards

Ship Builder	1987–92 Total (1000 teu)
China SB	133.7
Howaldt	122.3
Ishikawajima	111.1
Vulkan	96.5
Hyundai	91.5
Mitsubishi	89.6
Odense	86.8
Daewoo	86.5
Samsung	59.6
Mitsui	44.1
Tsuneishi	40.4
Kawasaki	37.2
Flender	31.5
Onomichi	34.3
Imabari	32.7
Hitachi	29.1
Warnow	28.7
Koyo	26.9
Alsthom	23.9
Blohm	22.6
Others	646.5

Source: *World Export Services Handbook 1994*

Note: teu equals twenty-foot equivalent units

World Airliner Fleet

Jets	Aircraft in Service 1993	On Order Year-end 1993	Other Aircraft	Aircraft in Service 1993	On Order Year-end 1993
Boeing	5,300	901	Turboprops	3,936	163
McDonnell Douglas	2,288	134	Piston-engines	521	0
Lockheed	193	0	Helicopters	59	0
Other U.S.	35	0	Other	19	0
Canadair	13	57	**Total other aircraft**	**4,535**	**163**
Airbus	977	243	**Total aircraft**	**15,378**	**1,738**
Other European	2,037	240			
Total Jets	**10,843**	**1,575**			

Source: *Air Transport World*, June 1994

World's 100 Largest Diversified Service Companies

Rank	Company	Country	1993 Sales ($ mil.)
1	Mitsui	Japan	163,453
2	Mitsubishi	Japan	160,109
3	Sumitomo	Japan	157,551
4	ITOCHU	Japan	155,162
5	Marubeni	Japan	144,503
6	Nissho Iwai	Japan	95,463
7	American Telephone & Telegraph	United States	67,156
8	Tomen	Japan	64,631
9	Nippon Telegraph & Telephone	Japan	61,651
10	Nichimen	Japan	53,483
11	Kanematsu	Japan	52,747
12	Veba Group	Germany	37,065
13	RWE Group	Germany	28,786
14	CIE Générale des Eaux	France	25,573
15	Shimizu	Japan	21,359
16	Taisei	Japan	21,126
17	Kajima	Japan	18,300
18	BCE	Canada	16,256
19	SUPERVALU	United States	15,937
20	Toyota Tsusho	Japan	15,757
21	Takenaka	Japan	15,665
22	Obayashi	Japan	15,318
23	Franz Haniel	Germany	14,771
24	Hyundai	South Korea	13,739
25	Kawasho	Japan	13,303
26	SINOCHEM	China	13,241
27	Fleming	United States	13,092
28	McKesson	United States	12,428
29	Mitsui Fudosan	Japan	12,065
30	MCI Communications	United States	11,921
31	SHV Holdings	Netherlands	11,897
32	Sekisui House	Japan	11,756
33	Sprint	United States	11,368
34	Neste	Finland	11,027
35	Dentsu	Japan	10,990
36	Bouygues	France	10,801
37	Columbia/HCA Healthcare	United States	10,775
38	SYSCO	United States	10,022
39	Nittetsu Shoji	Japan	10,014
40	Sumikin Bussan	Japan	9,954
41	George Weston	Canada	9,247
42	WMX Technologies	United States	9,136
43	Inchcape	Britain	8,826
44	Daiwa House Industry	Japan	8,741
45	Thyssen Handelsunion	Germany	8,698
46	Kumagai Gumi	Japan	8,612
47	Walt Disney	United States	8,529
48	Electronic Data Systems	United States	8,507
49	Jardine Matheson	Hong Kong	8,425
50	Edeka Zentrale	Germany	8,197

World's 100 Largest Diversified Service Companies (continued)

Rank	Company	Country	1991 Sales ($ mil.)
51	Enron	United States	7,973
52	Fluor	United States	7,971
53	Toshoku	Japan	7,832
54	Marriott International	United States	7,430
55	Dalgety	Britain	7,255
56	Fujita	Japan	7,024
57	Philipp Holzmann	Germany	7,017
58	Ladbroke Group	Britain	6,951
59	Bergen Brunswig	United States	6,824
60	Toda	Japan	6,800
61	Bass	Britain	6,780
62	Schlumberger	Netherlands	6,706
63	Alco Standard	United States	6,591
64	Time Warner	United States	6,581
65	Tohan	Japan	6,573
66	Eiffage	France	6,482
67	Thorn EMI	Britain	6,456
68	Halliburton	United States	6,351
69	Tokyu Construction	Japan	6,343
70	Nippon Shuppan Hanbai	Japan	6,334
71	Sato Kogyo	Japan	6,194
72	Sumitomo Forestry	Japan	6,005
73	Nissei Sangyo	Japan	5,965
74	Trafalgar House	Britain	5,909
75	Capital Cities/ABC	United States	5,674
76	Chori	Japan	5,656
77	Hyundai Eng. & Construction	South Korea	5,597
78	Klöckner	Germany	5,546
79	Yuasa Trading	Japan	5,545
80	Hazama	Japan	5,502
81	AGIV	Germany	5,446
82	National Intergroup	United States	5,409
83	Kandenko	Japan	5,376
84	Booker	Britain	5,359
85	Hitachi Sales	Japan	5,267
86	Nishimatsu Construction	Japan	5,204
87	ICA Handlarnas	Sweden	5,176
88	Accor	France	5,140
89	Iwatani International	Japan	5,111
90	Lucky-Goldstar International	South Korea	5,097
91	GTM-Entrepose	France	5,081
92	Hanwa	Japan	5,038
93	Nagase	Japan	4,964
94	Provigo	Canada	4,948
95	Maeda	Japan	4,938
96	ARA Group	United States	4,891
97	Daikyo	Japan	4,862
98	Nichirei	Japan	4,851
99	Dun & Bradstreet	United States	4,710
100	Hakuhodo	Japan	4,682

Source: *FORTUNE*; August 22, 1994

World's 50 Largest Retailing Companies

Rank	Company	Country	1993 Sales ($ mil.)
1	Wal-Mart Stores	U.S.	67,345
2	Sears Roebuck	U.S.	54,873
3	Kmart	U.S.	34,156
4	Ito-Yokado	Japan	26,488
5	Daiei	Japan	24,369
6	Kroger	U.S.	22,384
7	Carrefour	France	21,751
8	J. C. Penney	U.S.	19,578
9	Dayton Hudson	U.S.	19,233
10	American Stores	U.S.	18,763
11	Jusco	Japan	16,130
12	Promodès	France	15,998
13	J Sainsbury	Britain	15,919
14	Safeway	U.S.	15,215
15	Price/Costco	U.S.	15,155
16	Koninklijke Ahold	Netherlands	14,588
17	Nichii	Japan	13,034
18	Tesco	Britain	12,915
19	Seiyu	Japan	11,990
20	Kaufhof	Germany	11,558
21	Karstadt	Germany	11,316
22	Albertson's	U.S.	11,284
23	Groupe Pinault-Printemps	France	11,175
24	Groupe Casino	France	11,124
25	Asko Deutsches Kaufhaus	Germany	11,102
26	Takashimaya	Japan	11,059
27	May Department Stores	U.S.	11,020
28	Winn-Dixie Stores	U.S.	10,832
29	Delhaize "Le Lion"	Belgium	10,746
30	Coles Myer	Australia	10,578
31	Migros	Switzerland	10,462
32	Melville	U.S.	10,435
33	Great Atlantic & Pacific Tea	U.S.	10,384
34	Otto Versand	Germany	10,190
35	Marks & Spencer	Britain	9,839
36	Woolworth	U.S.	9,626
37	Mitsukoshi	Japan	9,504
38	Corte Inglés	Spain	9,471
39	Home Depot	U.S.	9,239
40	Argyll Group	Britain	8,435
41	Kooperativa Förbundet	Sweden	8,351
42	Walgreen	U.S.	8,295
43	Toys "R" Us	U.S.	7,946
44	Quelle Group	Germany	7,901
45	Spar Handels	Germany	7,810
46	Asda Group	Britain	7,722
47	UNY	Japan	7,571
48	Publix Super Markets	U.S.	7,473
49	Daimaru	Japan	7,443
50	McDonald's	U.S.	7,408

Source: *FORTUNE*; August 22, 1994

World's 25 Largest Accounting Practices

Rank	Company	1993 Revenues ($ mil.)
1	Arthur Andersen & Co., SC	6,017
2	KPMG	6,000
3	Ernst & Young	5,839
4	Coopers & Lybrand	5,220
5	Deloitte Touche Tomahtsu International	5,022
6	Price Waterhouse	3,887
7	BDO Binder	1,150
8	Grant Thornton International	1,080
9	Moores Rowland International	732
10	RSM International	686
11	Summit International Associates	619
12	Nexia International	603
13	Horwath International	519
14	Accounting Firms Associated, Inc.	462
15	HLB International	436
16	Clark Kenneth Leventhal	435
17	Moore Stephens	381
18	TGI	334
19	International Group of Accounting Firms	327
20	BKR International	284
21	The European Group	273
22	DFK International	257
23	Associated Accounting Firms International	245
24	Independent Accountants International	217
25	Kreston International	212

Source: *Bowman's Accounting Report*; December 7, 1994

World's 25 Largest Management Consulting Firms

Rank	Company	1993 Management Consulting Revenues ($ mil.)
1	McKinsey & Co.	1,274
2	Cooper's & Lybrand	1,002
3	Ernst & Young	922
4	Price Waterhouse	876
5	Andersen Consulting	858
6	Deloitte & Touche	792
7	KPMG Peat Marwick	769
8	William M. Mercer Cos.	600
9	Gemini Consulting	516
10	Towers Perrin	450
11	Booz-Allen & Hamilton	400
12	Arthur Andersen	395
13	The Wyatt Co.	349
14	The Boston Consulting Group	340
15	CSC Consulting Group	312
16	Arthur D. Little	301
17	Hewitt Associates	296
17	Sedgwick Noble Lowndes	296
19	A.T. Kearney	278
20	American Management Systems	218
21	PA Consulting	214
22	Bain & Co.	213
23	Grant Thornton	212
24	Proudfoot PLC	210
25	Woodrow Milliman	203

Source: *Consultants News*, July 1994

World's 50 Largest Advertising Organizations

Rank	Organization	HQ	1993 Sales
1	WPP Group	U.K.	2,634
2	Interpublic Group of Cos.	U.S.	2,079
3	Omnicom Group	U. S.	1,876
4	Dentsu Inc.	Japan	1,403
5	Saatchi & Saatchi Co.	UK/US	1,355
6	Young & Rubicam	U.S.	1,009
7	Euro RSCG Worldwide	France	865
8	Grey Advertising	U.S.	766
9	Hakuhodo Inc.	Japan	668
10	Foote, Cone & Belding Communications	U.S.	634
11	Leo Burnett Co.	U.S.	622
12	Publicis Communication/Pulicis-FCB	France	572
13	D'Arcy Masius Benton & Bowles	U.S.	554
14	BDDP Group	France	279
15	Bozell Worldwide	U.S.	270
16	Tokyu Agency	Japan	182
17	Daiko Advertising	Japan	182
18	Asatsu Inc.	Japan	171
19	Ketchum Communications	U.S.	140
20	Dai-Ichi Kikaku	Japan	135
21	Dentsu, Y&R Partnerships	U.S./Japan	125
22	Chiat/Day	U.S.	122
23	N W Ayer	U.S.	109
24	Yomiko Advertising	Japan	108
25	Cheil Communications	Korea	107
26	I&S Corp.	Japan	105
27	Gold Greenlees Trott	U.K.	100
28	Ayer Europe	U.K.	96
29	TMP Worldwide	U.S.	92
30	Asahi Advertising	Japan	92
31	Lopex	U.K.	90
32	Man Nen Sha	Japan	84
33	Ross Roy Communications	U.S.	81
34	Gage Marketing Group	U.S.	79
35	Oricom Co.	Japan	74
36	DIMAC Direct	U.S.	64
37	Clemenger/BBDO	Australia	62
38	Armando Testa International	Italy	61
39	Sogel Inc.	Japan	59
40	Kyodo Advertising Co.	Japan	55
41	Hal Riney & Partners	U.S.	53
42	Earle Palmer Brown Cos.	U.S.	53
43	Chuo Senko Advertising	Japan	52
44	Oricom Inc.	South Korea	50
45	W.B. Doner & Co.	U.S.	49
46	Ally & Gargano	U.S.	48
47	Jordan, McGrath, Case & Taylor	U.S.	47
48	Bronner Slosberg Humphrey	U.S.	46
49	Duailibi Petit Zaragoza	Brazil	44
50	Springer & Jacoby	Germany	43

Source: *Advertising Age*; April 13, 1994

World's Largest Non-US Advertising Agencies by Country

Country	Agency	1993 Sales ($ mil.)
Argentina	Ayer Vasquez	14,746
Australia	George Patterson Pty.	59,046
Austria	Demner & Merlicek	12,366
Belgium	McCann-Erickson	18,487
Brazil	McCann-Erickson Publicidade	70,327
Canada	BBDO Canada	31,611
Chile	BBDO de Chile	7,429
China	Saatchi & Saatchi	3,500
Colombia	Young & Rubicam Colombia	13,592
Costa Rica	Alberto H. Garnier	2,963
Czech Republic	Mark/BBDO	3,564
Denmark	Grey Communications Group	30,650
Dominican Republic	Young & Rubicam Damaris	2,127
Ecuador	Norlop Thompson Asociados	3,047
Egypt	Americana Advertising	4,411
Finland	AS & Grey	18,731
France	Euro RSCG	318,973
Germany	BBDO Group Germany	93,570
Greece	Spot Thompson Group	24,204
Guatemala	Communica Publicidad	1,887
Hong Kong	JWT-Hong Kong	19,389
Hungary	McCann-Erickson	3,223
India	Hindustan Thompson Associates	13,332
Indonesia	Lintas Indonesia	7,055
Ireland	Wilson Hartnell Group	8,826
Israel	Dahaf	4,801
Italy	Armando Testa Group	57,776
Japan	Dentsu Inc.	1,260,510
Malaysia	Ogilvy & Mather	6,545
Mexico	McCann-Erickson Mexico	25,158
Netherlands	BBDO Nederland	39,997
New Zealand	Colenso Communications	10,014
Norway	BSB Bates Gruppen	21,650
Pakistan	Orient/McCann	1,144
Panama	Campagnani Pulicidad	1,964
Philippines	McCann-Erickson Philippines	8,611
Poland	BSB/S&S Marco	5,576
Portugal	McCann-Erickson/Hora	17,385
Puerto Rico	Badillo/SSA	8,793
Russia	D'Arcy Masius Benton & Bowles	1,162
Saudi Arabia	Saatchi & Saatchi Advertising	2,900
Singapore	Batey Communications Group	23,016
South Africa	Ogilvy & Mather Rightford	18,064
South Korea	Cheil Communications	95,000
Spain	Bassat, Ogilvy & Mather	36,500
Sweden	McCann-Erickson	19,265
Switzerland	Young & Rubicam Switzerland	20,207
Taiwan	Ogilvy & Mather	12,182
Thailand	Lintas Thailand	16,598
Turkey	Cenajans Grey	20,668
United Arab Emirates	Madco Group Advertising	6,535
United Kingdom	Saatchi & Saatchi Advertising	126,514
Uruguay	Empresas Punto Ogilvy & Mather	3,521
Venezuela	Corpa	13,382

Source: *Advertising Age*; April 13, 1994

Brand Value: Product Lines

Brand	Company	Brand Value ($ mil.)	Brand Sales ($ mil.)
Coca-Cola	Coca-Cola	35,950	9,687
Marlboro	Philip Morris	33,045	9,782
Nescafe	Nestle	11,549	5,710
Kodak	Eastman Kodak	10,020	6,510
Microsoft	Microsoft	9,842	3,753
Budweiser	Anheuser Busch	9,724	5,960
Kellogg's	Kellogg	9,372	5,477
Motorola	Motorola	9,293	16,309
Gillette	Gillette	8,218	2,118
Bacardi	Bacardi	7,163	1,505
Hewlett-Packard	Hewlett-Packard	6,996	20,117
Intel	Intel	6,480	6,720
Frito-Lay	PepsiCo	5,907	4,365
Pampers	Procter & Gamble	5,732	4,141
GE	General Electric	5,710	7,450
Nintendo	Nintendo	5,224	4,779
Levi's	Levi Strauss	5,142	3,533
Pepsi	PepsiCo	4,939	4,340
Campbell's	Campbell Soup	4,633	3,413
Newport	Loews, BAT Industries	4,287	1,094
Compaq	Compaq Computer	4,033	7,191
Kraft	Philip Morris	3,940	4,993
Nike	Nike	3,591	2,942
Colgate	Colgate-Palmolive	3,442	1,700
Benson & Hedges	BAT, Am. Brands, P. Morris	3,353	2,326
Heinz	HJ Heinz	3,325	1,691
General Mills	General Mills	3,281	2,220
Louis Vuitton	LVMH	3,117	912
Goodyear	Goodyear Tire & Rubber	2,866	6,905
Duracell	Duracell	2,693	1,742
Fanta	Coca-Cola	2,676	1,316
Hennessey	LVMH	2,566	753
Nestle	Nestle	2,522	4,369
Avon	Avon Products	2,439	3,504
Chivas Regal	Seagram	2,382	455
Wrigley's	Wm Wrigley Jr	2,309	1,340
Hershey's	Hershey Foods	2,298	2,000
Winston	RJR Nabisco	2,272	2,388
Martini	Bacardi	2,262	1,024
Johnnie Walker Black	Guinness	2,233	457
Nabisco	RJR Nabisco	2,223	3,100
Fruit of the Loom	Fruit of the Loom	2,140	1,788
Johnnie Walker Red	Guinness	2,086	497
L'Oreal	L'Oreal	2,084	2,792
Guinness	Guinness	2,067	1,032
Quaker Oats	Quaker Oats	1,981	1,769
Tylenol	Johnson & Johnson	1,976	1,023
Purina	Ralston-Purina	1,974	1,687
Kirin	Kirin Brewery	1,970	3,641
Sprite	Coca-Cola	1,955	858

Source: *FW*; August 2, 1994

Stock Market Capitalization

Rank	Country	1993 Total Market Capitalization ($ mil.)	Rank	Country	1993 Total Market Capitalization ($ mil.)
1	U.S.	5,223,768	21	Brazil	99,430
2	Japan	2,999,756	22	India	97,976
3	U.K.	1,151,646	23	Belgium	78,067
4	Germany	463,476	24	Israel	50,773
5	France	456,111	25	Chile	44,622
6	Hong Kong	385,247	26	Argentina	43,967
7	Canada	326,524	27	Denmark	41,785
8	Switzerland	271,713	28	China	40,567
9	Malaysia	220,328	29	Philippines	40,327
10	South Africa	217,110	30	Turkey	37,496
11	Australia	203,964	31	Indonesia	32,953
12	Mexico	200,671	32	Austria	28,437
13	Taiwan, China	195,198	33	Norway	27,380
14	Netherlands	181,876	34	New Zealand	25,597
15	Korea	139,420	35	Finland	23,562
16	Italy	136,153	36	Luxembourg	19,337
17	Singapore	132,742	37	Portugal	12,417
18	Thailand	130,510	38	Greece	12,319
19	Spain	119,264	39	Pakistan	11,602
20	Sweden	107,376	40	Kuwait	10,103

Source: *Emerging Stock Markets Factbook 1994*

Total Value Traded

Rank	Country	1993 Total Value Traded ($ mil.)	Rank	Country	1993 Total Value Traded ($ mil.)
1	U.S.	3,507,223	21	China	43,395
2	Japan	954,341	22	Israel	30,327
3	U.K.	423,526	23	Turkey	23,242
4	Taiwan, China	346,487	24	India	21,879
5	Germany	302,985	25	Denmark	20,989
6	Korea	211,710	26	South Africa	13,049
7	France	174,283	27	Belgium	11,199
8	Switzerland	167,880	28	Argentina	10,339
9	Malaysia	153,661	29	Indonesia	9,158
10	Canada	142,222	30	Norway	8,751
11	Hong Kong	131,550	31	Finland	8,112
12	Thailand	86,934	32	New Zealand	6,785
13	Singapore	81,623	33	Philippines	6,785
14	Australia	67,711	34	Austria	6,561
15	Netherlands	67,185	35	Portugal	4,835
16	Italy	65,770	36	Chile	2,797
17	Mexico	62,454	37	Greece	2,713
18	Brazil	57,409	38	Kuwait	2,612
19	Spain	47,156	39	Poland	2,170
20	Sweden	43,593	40	Venezuela	1,874

Source: *Emerging Stock Markets Factbook 1994*

Listed Domestic Companies

Rank	Country	1993 No. of Listed Domestic Cos.	Rank	Country	1993 No. of Listed Domestic Cos.
1	U.S.	7,607	21	Netherlands	245
2	India	6,800	22	Peru	233
3	Japan	2,155	23	Switzerland	215
4	U.K.	1,646	24	Italy	210
5	Canada	1,124	25	Sri Lanka	200
6	Australia	1,070	26	Mexico	190
7	Korea	693	27	China	183
8	Pakistan	653	28	Portugal	183
9	South Africa	647	29	Argentina	180
10	Israel	558	30	Philippines	180
11	Brazil	550	31	Singapore	178
12	France	472	32	Indonesia	174
13	Hong Kong	450	33	Nigeria	174
14	Germany	426	34	Belgium	165
15	Malaysia	410	35	Bangladesh	153
16	Spain	376	36	Turkey	152
17	Thailand	347	37	Greece	143
18	Taiwan, China	285	38	Ecuador	142
19	Chile	263	39	New Zealand	136
20	Denmark	257	40	Iran	124

Source: *Emerging Stock Markets Factbook 1994*

Nikkei Index

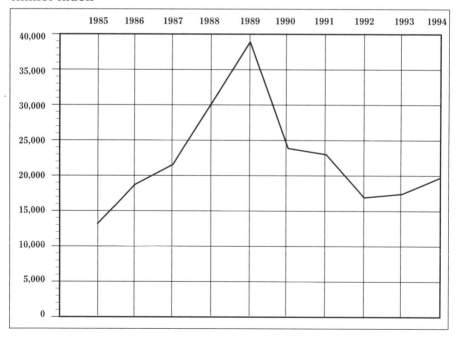

DAX Index

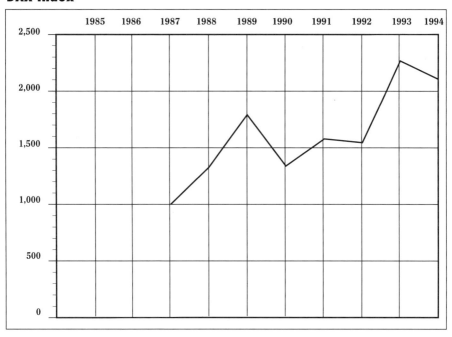

FT-SE Index

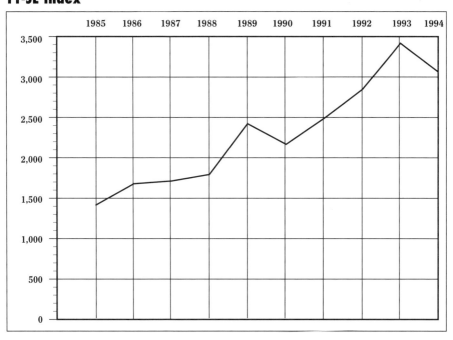

CAC Index

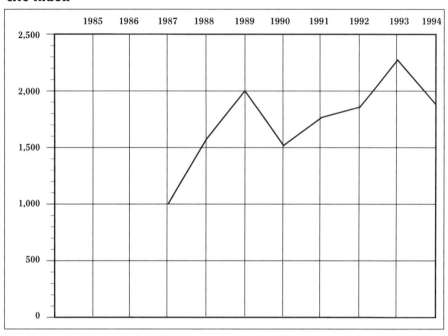

Hang Seng Index

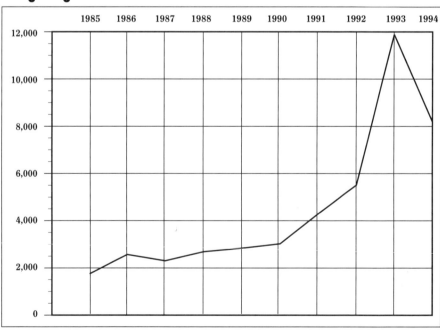

Straits Times Index

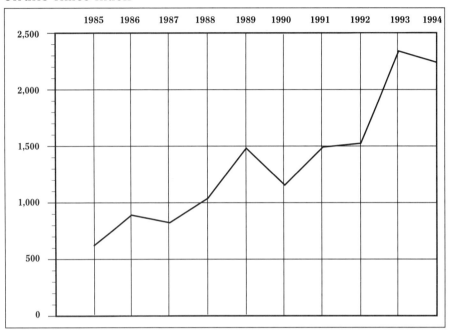

All Ordinaries Index

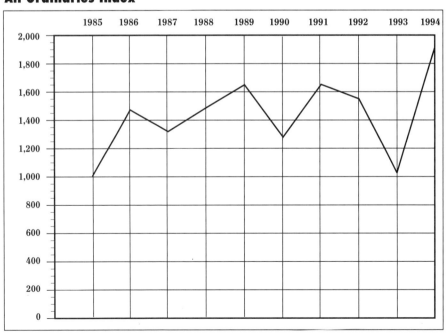

Australian Companies in the Australian Stock Exchange All Ordinaries Index

AAPC
Aberfoyle
Adelaide Bank
Adelaide Brighton Cement
  Holdings
Adridian Consolidated
Advance Bank Australia
Advance Property (Combined)
Advance Property (Growth)
Advance Property (Income)
Airboss
Alcan Australia
Amalgamated Holdings
Amcor
Ampolex
Aqua Vital Australia
Argo Investments
Armstrong Jones Off.
Armstrong Jones Ret.
Arnotts
Ashton Mining
Atkins Carlyle
Atlas Steels
Aurora Gold
Ausdoc
Ausdrill
Australia & New Zealand
  Banking Group
Australian Chemical Holdings
Australian Foundation
  Investment
Australian Gas Light
Australian Med. Ent.
Australian National Industries
Australian Oil and Gas
Australian Provincial
  Newspaper Holdings
Australian RBS.
Australis Media
AWA
Azon
Ballarat Brewing
Bank of Melbourne
Bank of Queensland
Bendigo Building Soc.
Bendigo Mining
Biota
Blackmores
Boral
Bougainville Copper
Brambles Industries
Brierley Investments
BRL Hardy (CTG)
BRL Hardy (FPO)
Broken Hill
  Proprietary
BT Australian Equity
  Management
BT Global Asset Man.
BT Property Trust (Growth)
BT Property Trust (Income)
BT Property Trust (ORD Units)

BT Resources Management
BTR Nylex
Burns, Philp & Company
Burmine
Burswood Property Trust
BZW-Mirvac Property (Growth)
BZW-Mirvac Property (Income)
BZW-Mirvac Property (ORD Unit)
Caltex Australia
Capcount Property Trust
Cape Range
Capital Property (New)
Capital Property (UNT)
Carlton Investments (BNS)
Carlton Investments (FPO)
Central Equity
Central Norseman Gold
Centro Properties (CTG)
Centro Properties (FPO)
Challenge Bank
Charles Davis
Climax Mining
Clyde Industries
Coca-Cola Amatil
Coles Myer
Colonial Mutual Australian
  Property Fund
Comalco
Command Petroleum Holdings
Commonwealth Bank
Computershare
Computer Power Group
Consolidated Paper
Consolidated Rutile
Coolgardie Gold
Coplex Resources
Cortecs International
Country Road
Coventry Group
CRA
G.E. Crane Holdings
Crown
Crusader
CSL
CSR
CUC Australasia
Cudgen RZ
Cultus Petroleum NL
Datacraft
Davids
Defiance Mills
Delta Gold
Denehurst
Devex
Diversified United Investment
Dominion Mining
Eastern Aluminum
Elders Australia
Eltin
Email
Emerging Markets
Emperor Mines

Energy Developments
Energy Equity Corp.
Energy Resources of Australia
Equatorial Mining NL
Equitilink
ERG
Evans Deakin Industries
Exicom
FAI Insurances
FAI Life
Finemore Holdings
F.H. Faulding & Company
Five Arrows Australia Fund
Fletcher Challenge (Forests)
Fletcher Challenge (ORD DIV)
Foodland Associated
Forrestania Gold
Foster's Brewing
Franked Income Fund
Futuris
Galore Group
Gandel Retail Trust
GEM Commercial (Growth)
GEM Commercial (Income)
GEM Commercial (ORD Units)
GEM Retail Property (Growth)
GEM Retail Property (Income)
GEM Retail Property (ORD Units)
General Property Trust
George Weston Foods
Gibson Chemical Industries
GIO Australia
Golden Shamrock
Gold Mines of Australia (FPO)
Gold Mines of Australia (RTS)
Gold Mines of Kalgoorlie
Goodman Fielder
Gowing Bros.
Great Central Mines
Green's Foods
Grosvenor Trust
G.U.D. Holdings
Guinness Peat Group
GWA International
Gwalia Consolidated
Hamilton Island
Harvey Norman (FPO)
Harvey Norman (DEP)
HDC Group Ltd.
Healthscope
C.E. Heath International Holdings
Heine Industrial (Capital)
Heine Industrial (Income)
Heine Industrial (New)
Heine Industrial (ORD Units)
Henry Walker Group
Highlands Gold
Hills Industries
Homestake Gold of Australia
Howard Smith
Hudson Conway
Hydromet Corp. Ltd.

Australian Companies in the Australian Stock Exchange
All Ordinaries Index (continued)

ICI Australia
Incitec
ISR Group
James Hardie Industries
Jardine Fleming China
Jennings Group
J.N.A. Telecommmunications
John Fairfax Holdings
Jupiters
Just Jeans Holdings
Kalamazoo Holdings
Keycorp
Kidston Gold Mines
Lanes
Lang
Leighton Holdings
Lend Lease
Lion Nathan
Macraes Mining
Matrix Telecomm.
Mayne Nickless
McIntosh Securities
McPherson's
Memtec
Metal Manufactures
Metway Bank
Mildara Blass
Milton Corporation
M.I.M. Holdings
Mineral Resources
Minproc Holdings
Mirvac
MMI Ltd.
Mount Edon Gold Mines (Aust)
Mt. Leyshon Gold Mine
National Australia Bank
National Can Industries
National Consolidated
National Foods
National Industrial
National Mutual Property Trust
Newcrest Mining
News Corporation
Niugini
Normandy Poseidon
North Limited
Northern Build. Soc.
North Flinders Mines
Oil Search
OPSM Protector
Orbital Engine
Orion Resources N.L.
Oroton International
Pacific BBA
Pacific Dunlop

Pacific Magazines & Printing
Pacific Mutual Australia
Pancontinental Mining
Parbury
Pasminco
Peptide Technology
Perilya Mines N.L.
Permanent Trustee
Perpetual Trustees Australia
Peter Kurts Properties
Petrol N.L.
Petroleum Securities
Pirelli Cables Aust.
Pioneer International
Placer Pacific
Platinum Capital
Plutonic Resources
Portman Mining
Poseidon Gold
Premier Investments
Prime Credit Prop.
Prime Television
Property Income
Publishing and Broadcasting (FPO)
Publishing and Broadcasting
    (PREFORD)
QBE Insurance Group
QCT Resources
QDL
Queensland Metals
QNI Ltd.
QIW
Q.U.F. Industries
Ranger Minerals NL
Reinsurance Aust
Resolute Resources
Renison Goldfields
    Consolidated
Ridley
Ross Mining N.L.
Rothmans Holdings
Rural Press
S.A. Brewing Holdings
S.E.A.S.
Sagasco Holdings
St. Barbara Mines
St. George Bank
Samantha Gold
Santos
Savage Resources
Schroders IPF NV
Schroders Property Fund
Scott
Sea World Property Trust
Seven Network

SGIO Insurance
Shomega Ltd.
Siddons Ramset
Simsmetal
Sons of Gwalia
Southcorp Hodlings
Spicers Paper
Spotless Group
Spotless Services
Stanilite Pacific
Star Mining
Stockland Trust Group
Sunbeam Victa
Sunraysia Television
Sunshine Broadcasting Network
Tassal
TNT
Templeton Global Growth Fund
Thakral Holdings Group
Ticor
Toll Holdings
Tubemakers of Australia
Tyndall Australia
Union Gold Mining
Valdora Minerals NL
Venture Exploration
Villa World
Village Roadshow
Vision Systems
Walker
Washington H. Soul
    Pattinson & Co.
Wattyl
Wesfarmers
Wesgo
West Australian Newspapers
    Holdings
Western Mining Corporation
    Holdings
Westfield Holdings
Westfield Trust (CTG)
Westfield Trust (New)
Westfield Trust (Unt)
Westpac Banking Corp.
Westpac Property Trust
Westralian Forest Industries
Westralian Sands
W.H. Wills Holdings Ltd.
Wiluna Mines Ltd.
Woodside Petroleum
Woolworths
Arthur Yates & Co
Zapopan

Source: Australian Stock Exchange; List current as of December 5, 1994.

The 225 Japanese Companies in the Nikkei Index

All Nippon Airways	Kyokuyo	Nippon Steel
Ajinomoto	Kyowa Hakko Kogyo	Nippon Suisan
Aoki	Marubeni	Nippon Synthetic
Asahi Breweries	Maruzen	Nippon Yakin Kogyo
Asahi Chemical Ind.	Matsushita Elect. I	Nippon Yusen
Asahi Denka Kogyo	Mazda Motor	Nippondenso
Asahi Glass	Meidensha	Nissan Chemical Ind.
Bank of Tokyo	Meiji Milk Products	Nissan Motor
Bridgestone	Meiji Seika	Nisshin Flour Mills
Canon	Mercian	Nisshin Oil Mills
Chiyoda	Minebea	Nisshinbo Industries
Citizen Watch	Mitsubishi	Nissho Iwai
Dainippon Pharmaceut	Mitsubishi Bank	Nitto Boseki
Dai Nippon Printing	Mitsubishi Electric	NKK
Dai-Ichi Kangyo Bank	Mitsubishi Estate	NOF
Daiwa House Industry	Mitsubishi Heavy Ind.	Nomura Securities
Denki Kagaku Kogyo	Mitsubishi Kasei	Noritake
Dowa Mining	Mitsubishi Materials	NSK
Ebara	Mitsubishi Oil	NTN
Fuji Bank	Mitsubishi Paper	NTT
Fuji Electric	Mitsubishi Rayon	Obayashi
Fuji Photo Film	Mitsubishi Steel Mfg	Odakyu Electric Rail
Fuji Spinning	Mitsubishi Trust & Banking	Oki Electric Ind.
Fujikura	Mitsubishi Warehouse	Okuma
Fujita	Mitsui	Onoda Cement
Fujitsu	Mitsui Engin & Ship	Osaka Gas
Furukawa	Mitsui Fudosan	Pioneer Electric
Furukawa Electric	Mitsui Marine & Fire	Rasa Industries
Hazama	Mitsui Mining	Ricoh
Heiwa Real Estate	Mitsui Mining & Smelt	Sakura Bank
Hino Motors	Mitsui O.S.K. Lines	Sankyo
Hitachi	Mitsui-Soko	Sankyu
Hitachi Zosen	Mitsui Toatsu Chemic.	Sanyo Electric
Honen	Mitsui Trust & Banking	Sapporo Breweries
Hokuetsu Paper Mills	Mitsukoshi	Sato Kogyo
Honda Motor	Morinaga	Seika
Honshu Paper	Nachi-Fujikoshi	Sharp
IHI	Navix Line	Shimizu
Iseki	NEC	Shimura Kako
Isuzu Motors	New Oji Paper	Shin-Etsu Chemical
ITOCHU	NGK Insulators	Shinagawa Refractory
Iwatani	Nichirei	Shionogi
Japan Energy	Nichiro	Showa Denko
Japan Secur. Finance	Nihon Cement	Showa Electric Wire
Japan Steel Works	Niigata Engineering	Showa Line
Japan Wool Textile	Nikko Securities	Showa Shell Sekiyu
Kajima	Nikon	Sony
Kanebo	Nippon Beet Sugar	Sumitomo
Kansai Elec. Power	Nippon Carbide Ind.	Sumitomo Bank
Kawasaki Heavy Ind.	Nippon Carbon	Sumitomo Cement
Kawasaki Kisen	Nippon Chemical Ind.	Sumitomo Chemical
Kawasaki Steel	Nippon Denko	Sumitomo Coal Mining
Keihin Electric Rail	Nippon Express	Sumitomo Electric
Keio Teito Railway	Nippon Flour Mills	Sumitomo Heavy Ind.
Keisei Electric Railway	Nippon Kayaku	Sumitomo Metal Ind.
Kikkoman	Nippon Light Metal	Sumitomo Metalmining
Kirin Brewery	Nippon Metal Ind.	Suzuki Motor
Kobe Steel	Nippon Oil	Taisei
Komatsu	Nippon Paper Inds.	Takara Shuzo
Konica	Nippon Piston Ring	Takeda Chemical Ind.
Koyo Seiko	Nippon Sharyo	Teijin
Kubota	Nippon Sheet Glass	Teikoku Oil
Kumagai Gumi	Nippon Shinpan	Tekken
Kuraray	Nippon Soda	Toa

The 225 Japanese Companies in the Nikkei Index (continued)

Toagosei	Tokyo Rope Mfg.	Toyo Seikan
Tobishima	Tokyu	Toyobo
Tobu Railway	Tokyu Department	Toyota Motor
Toei	Tomen	Ube Industries
Toho Rayon	Tonen	Unitika
Toho Zinc	Toppan Printing	Yamaha
Tokai Carbon	Topy Industries	Yamanouchi Pharmaceu
Tokio Marine & Fire	Toray Industries	Yasuda Fire & Marine
Tokyo Dome	Toshiba	Yokogawa Electric
Tokyo Electric Power	Tosoh	Yokohama Rubber
Tokyo Gas	Toto	Yuasa

Source: Nihon Keizai Shimbun America, Inc.; List current as of June 30, 1994.

Straits Times Industrial Index

Avimo Singapore	Keppel Corporation	Singapore Petroleum Company
Cerebos Pacific	Lum Chang Holdings	Singapore Press Holdings
CWT Distribution	Metro Holdings	Singapore Tech Industries
Cycle & Carriage	NatSteel	Singapore Telecom
Fraser & Neave	Neptune Orient Lines	Singatronics
General Magnetics	Sembawang Corporation	Times Publishing
Haw Par Brothers Intl.	Sime Singapore	United Industrial Corp.
Inchacape BHD	Singapore Aerospace	WBL Corporation
Intraco	Singapore Airlines	Wing Tai Holdings
IPC Corporation	Singapore Bus Service 500	Yeo Hiap Seng

Source: Stock Exchange of Singapore, Ltd.; List current as of December 21, 1994.

The 33 Hong Kong Companies in the Hang Seng Index

Amoy Properties	Henderson Land Development	Johnson Electric Holdings
Bank of East Asia	Hong Kong Aircraft Engineering	Mandarin Oriental International
Cathay Pacific Airways	Hong Kong & China Gas	Miramar Hotel & Investment
Cheung Kong (Holdings)	Hong Kong Telecommunications	New World Development
China Light & Power	Hongkong Electric Holdings	Oriental Press Group
Citic Pacific	Hongkong Land Holdings	Shun Tak Holdings
Dairy Farm International Holdings	Hongkong & Shanghai Hotels	Sun Hung Kai Properties
Great Eagle Holdings	Hopewell Holdings	Swire Pacific
Guangdong Investment	HSBC Holdings	Television Broadcasts
Hang Lung Development	Hutchison Whampoa	Wharf (Holdings)
Hang Seng Bank	Hysan Development	Wheelock and Co.

Source: HSI Services Ltd.; List current as of November 30, 1994.

The 30 German Companies in the DAX

Allianz	Deutsche Babcock	Mannesmann
BASF	Deutsche Bank	Metallgesellschaft
Bayer	Dresdner Bank	Preussag
Bayerische Hypotheken und	Henkel	RWE
Wechselbank	Hoechst	Schering
Bayerische Vereinsbank	Karstadt	Siemens
BMW	Kaufhof	Thyssen
Commerzbank	Linde	VEBA
Continental	Lufthansa	VIAG
Daimler-Benz	MAN	Volkswagen
Degussa		

Source: Deutsche Börse AG; October 10, 1994

UK Companies in the FT-SE 100 Index

ASDA Group	General Elect.	Ryl Bk Scotland
Abbey National	Glaxo	Royal Insurance
Allied Domecq	Granada	RTZ
Argyll Group	Grand Met.	Sainsbury
Arjo Wiggins	GUS	Schroders
Assoc. Brit. Foods	GRE	Scottish & New.
BAA	GKN	Scottish Power
Bank of Scotland	Guinness	Sears
Barclays	Hanson	Severn Trent
Bass	HSBC	Shell Transport
BAT Inds.	ICI	Siebe
Blue Circle	Inchcape	Smith & Nephew
BOC	Kingfisher	SmKl Beecham "A"
Boots	Ladbroke	SmKl Beecham Units
Bowater	Land Securities	Southern Elect.
BP	Legal & General	Standard Chartd
Brit. Aerospace	Lloyds Bank	Sun Alliance
British Airways	Marks and Spencer	Tesco
British Gas	MEPC	Thames Water
British Steel	NatWest Bank	Thorn EMI
BT	National Power	TI Group
BTR	North West Water	Tomkins
Burmah Castrol	Northern Foods	TSB
Cable & Wire	Pearson	Unilever
Cadbury Schweppes	PowerGen	United Biscuits
Caradon	Prudential	Vodafone
Carlton Comms.	Rank Org.	Warburg (SG)
Comm. Union	Reckitt & Colman	Wellcome
Courtaulds	Redland	Whitbread
De la Rue	Reed Intl.	Williams Hldgs.
Eastern Elect.	Rentokil	Wolseley
Enterprise Oil	Reuters	Zeneca
Forte	RMC	
Gen. Accident	Rolls Royce	

Source: *Financial Times*; December 2, 1994.

French Companies in the CAC 40 Index

Accor	Compagnie Générale des Eaux	Michelin
Air Liquide	Crédit Commercial de France	Paribas
Alcatel Alsthom	Crédit Foncier de France	Pernod Ricard
AXA	Crédit local de France	Peugeot S.A.
Banque Nationale de Paris–BNP	Groupe Danone	Rhône-Poulenc
Bouygues	Docks de France	Saint-Gobain
Canal+	Elf Aquitaine	Saint Louis
Cap Gemini Sogeti	Euro Disney	Sanofi (ex-Elf Sanofi)
Carrefour	Havas	Schneider S.A.
Casino	Lafarge Coppée	Société Générale
CGIP	Legrand	Suez
Chargeurs	L'Oréal	Thomson-CSF
Club Méditerranée	LVMH Moët Hennessy Louis Vuitton	Total
Compagnie Bancaire	Lyonnaise des Eaux-Dumez	UAP

Source: *French Company Handbook 1994*, 14th Edition

French Companies in the SBF 120

Accor	Elf Aquitaine	Poliet
AGF	Eridania Béghin-Say	Primagaz
Air Liquide	Essilor	Promodès
Alcatel Alsthom	Esso	La Redoute
Alcatel Cable	Eurafrance	Rémy Cointreau
AXA	Euro Disney	Rexel
Bail Investissement	Euro RSCG	Rhône-Poulenc
Bic	Europe 1 Communication	Roussel Uclaf
Banque Nationale de Paris	Eurotunnel S.A.	Sagem
Bolloré Technologies	Filipacchi Medias	Saint-Gobain
Bongrain	GAN	Saint Louis
Bouygues	Gaz et Eaux	Salomon S.A.
Canal+	GTM-Entrepose	Sanofi
Cap Gemini Sogeti	Guyenne et Gascogne	Schneider S.A.
CarnaudMetalbox	Havas	SEB S.A.
Carrefour	Idia	Sefimeg
Casino	Imétal	SGE (Société Générale
Castorama-Dubois Investissements	Institut Mérieux	d'Entreprise)
Crédit Commercial de France	Interbail	Sidel
Cetelem	Jean Lefebvre	SIMCO
CGIP	Lafarge Coppée	SITA
Chargeurs	Lagardère Groupe	Skis Rossignol
Clarins	Lapeyre	Sligos
Club Méditerranée	Legrand	Société Générale
Colas	Legris Industries	Sodexho
Compagnie Bancaire	LVMH-Moët Hennessy Louis Vuitton	Sommer Allibert
Compagnie Générale des Faux	Lyonnaise des Eaux-Dumez	Sovac
Comptoirs Modernes	Michelin	Spie Batignolles
CPR (Compagnie Parisienne	Moulinex	Strafor Facom
de Réescompte	Naf Naf	Suez
Crédit Agricole d'Ile-de-France	Navigation Mixte	Synthélabo
Crédit Foncier de France	Nord Est	TF1
Crédit local de France	L'Oréal	Thomson-CSF
Crédit Lyonnais	Paribas (Compagnie Financière de	Total
Crédit National	Paribas)	UAP
Groupe Danone	Pechiney CIP	UIC (Union Industrielle de Crédit)
Degremont	Pechiney International	Unibail
DMC (Dollfus-Mieg)	Pernod Ricard	Valeo
Docks de France	Peugeot S.A.	Vallourec
Ecco	Pinault-Printemps Redoute	Worms et Cie
Eiffage	Plastic Omnium	Zodiac

Source: *French Company Handbook 1994*, 14th Edition

Non-US Company Stocks Available Through US Stock Markets

Company	Exchange	Symbol
Argentina		
Alpargatas S.A.I.C.	OTC	ALPAY
Banco de Galicia y Buenos Aires	Nasdaq	BGALY
Banco Frances del Rio de la Plata	NYSE	BFR
Buenos Aires Embotelladora S.A.	NYSE	BAE
Compania Naviera Perez		
Compance S.A.	OTC	CNPZY
Irsa Inversiones		
y Representaciones S.A.	OTC	IRSAY
Nortel Invesora S.A.		
Series "A" GDR	None	NOIAG
Nortel Invesora S.A.		
Series "B" GDR	None	NOIBG
Sol Petroleo, S.A.	OTC	SOLPY
Telecom Argentina - STET		
GDR B	None	TASG
Telefonica de Argentina, S.A.	None	TEAGDR
Telefonica de Argentina S.A. GDR	NYSE	TAR
YPF Sociedad Anonima	NYSE	YPF
Australia		
Accor Asia Pacific	OTC	AAPCY
Agen Ltd.	OTC	AGLTY
Airboss Ltd.	OTC	ABOSY
Amadeus Oil N.L.	OTC	AMDOY
Amcor Ltd.	Nasdaq	AMCRY
Ampolex Ltd.	OTC	APLXY
Ashton Mining Ltd.	OTC	ASHMY
Asia Oil and Minerals Ltd.	OTC	AOMLY
Astro Mining NL	OTC	ATRMY
Auridiam Condolidated N.L.	OTC	AURAY
Australia & New Zealand		
Banking Group	OTC	ANEWY
Australian Consolidated		
Investments Ltd.	OTC	ACIEY
Australian Consolidated Press Ltd.	OTC	ACPLOTC
Australian Hydrocarbons N.L.	OTC	AUSHY
Australian National		
Industries Ltd.	OTC	ANNDY
Australian Oil And Gas Corp Ltd	OTC	AUOGY
Barrack Energy Ltd.	OTC	BAENY
Barrack Mines Ltd.	OTC	BACKY
Barrack Technology Ltd.	OTC	BATEY
Biota Holdings Ltd.	OTC	BTAHY
Black Hill Minerals	OTC	BLKMY
Bond Corporation Holdings	OTC	BCHFY
Boral Ltd.	Nasdaq	BORAY
Boulder Gold	OTC	BDRGY
Bridge Oil Ltd.	OTC	BROLY
Broken Hill Proprietary Company	NYSE	BHP
Brunswick N.L.	OTC	BWIKY
Burns, Philip and Company Ltd.	OTC	BPHCY
Cape Range Ltd.	OTC	CPRNY
Centaur Mining and		
Exploration Ltd.	OTC	CEMGY
Central Norseman Gold		
Corporation	OTC	CNOGY
Central Pacific Minerals N.L.	Nasdaq	CPMNY
Charter Mining N.L.	OTC	CMNGY
City Resources Ltd.	OTC	CYRSY
Claremont Petroleum N.L.	OTC	CLPTY
Clyde Industries Ltd.	OTC	CYDNY

Company	Exchange	Symbol
Coca-Cola Amatil Ltd.	OTC	CCLAY
Coles Myer Ltd.	NYSE	CM
Comalco Ltd. "A" Shares	OTC	COMOTC
Consolidated Gold Mining Areas	OTC	CGGOTC
Coopers Resources N.L.	OTC	COROTC
Cord Holdings Ltd.	OTC	CRDOTC
Cortecs International Ltd.	Nasdaq	DLVRY
CRA Ltd.	OTC	CRADY
Cracow Gold Ltd.	OTC	CRWOTC
Crystal Mining N.L.	OTC	CRYOTC
CSR Limited	OTC	CSRLY
Delta Gold N.L.	OTC	DLGOTC
Denehurst Ltd.	OTC	DENOTC
Dioro Exploration N.L.	OTC	DIOOTC
Dominion Mining Ltd.	OTC	DMNOF
East West Minerals N.L.	OTC	EWMOTC
Eastern Group Ltd.	OTC	EPAOTC
EMail Ltd.	OTC	EMLOTC
Emperor Mines Ltd.	OTC	EMROTC
Enterprise Gold Mines N.L.	OTC	ENTOTC
ERG Australia Ltd.	OTC	ERGAY
Euralba Mining Ltd.	OTC	EUROTC
Expo Ltd.	OTC	EXPOTC
F.H. Faulding & Co. Ltd.	OTC	FAFHY
FAI Insurances Ltd.	NYSE	FAI
Federation Resources N.L.	OTC	FEDOTC
First Australian Resources N.L.	OTC	FAUSY
Firstpac Ltd.	OTC	FIROTC
Forsayth N.L.	OTC	FORNY
Foster's Brewing Group Ltd.	OTC	FBWGY
Golconda Minerals N.L.	OTC	GOLOTC
Gold & Minerals Exploration N.L.	OTC	GLDOTC
Gold Mines of Kalgoorlie Ltd	OTC	GMKGY
Golden Valley Mines N.L.	OTC	GVMOTC
Goodman Fielder Ltd.	OTC	GDMOTC
Great Central Mines N.L.	Nasdaq	GTCMY
Great Eastern Mines Ltd.	OTC	GOLDY
Great Fingall Mining Co. NL	OTC	GFMOTC
Greenvale Mining N.L.	OTC	GEEOTC
Gwalia International Ltd.	OTC	GWAOTC
Gwalia Resources Ltd.	OTC	GWBOTC
Hallmark Gold N.L.	OTC	HGLOTC
Haoma Northwest N.L.	OTC	HAOOTC
Hardman Resources N.L.	OTC	HMNRY
Hartogen Energy Ltd.	OTC	HTGOTC
HMC Australasia	OTC	HNCOTC
Hooker Corporation	OTC	HOKOTC
Hoyts Entertainment Ltd.	OTC	HELOTC
Hydromet Corporation Ltd.	OTC	HYDOTC
Independent Resources Ltd.	OTC	IRLOTC
Indonesian Diamond Corporation		
Ltd.	OTC	IDOOY
International Mining Corporation	OTC	IMCOTC
James Hardie Industries Ltd.	OTC	JHINY
Jason Mining Ltd.	OTC	JASOTC
Jimberlana Minerals N.L.	OTC	JIMOTC
Jingellic Minerals N.L.	OTC	JINGY
Jones David, Ltd.	OTC	DAJOTC
Julia Mines N.L.	OTC	JMNOTC
Kern Corporatoin	OTC	KCTOTC
Kidston Gold Mines Ltd.	OTC	KSGMY
Kitchener Mining N.L.	OTC	KITOTC

Non-US Company Stocks Available Through US Stock Markets (continued)

Company	Exchange	Symbol
Lennard Oil N.L.	OTC	LENOY
Lightning Jack Film Trust	OTC	LJFTY
M.I.M. Holdings Ltd.	OTC	MIMOY
Magellan Petroleum Australia Ltd.	OTC	MAGOTC
Magnet Group Ltd.	OTC	MMTLY
Matrix Telecommunications Ltd.	OTC	MRXTY
Mayne Nickless Ltd.	OTC	MAYNY
McPherson's Ltd.	OTC	MCPOTC
Memtec Ltd.	Nasdaq	MMTCY
Meridian Oil N.L.	OTC	MEOLY
Merlin Mining N.L.	OTC	MNNOTC
Metana Minerals N.L.	OTC	METOTC
Mid-East Minerals N.L.	OTC	MIDOTC
Mincorp Petroleum N.L.	OTC	MRTOTC
Minefields Exploration N.L.	OTC	MNEOTC
Mintaro Slate & Flagstone Co., Ltd.	OTC	MSFOTC
Monarch N.L.	OTC	MONOTC
Mount Burgess Gold Mines N.L.	OTC	MBGOTC
Mt. Kersey Mining N.L.	OTC	MTKRY
Mt. Leyshon Gold Mines Ltd.	OTC	MLGOTC
National Australia Bank Ltd.	NYSE	NAB
Network Media Ltd.	OTC	NWOOTC
New Australia Resources	OTC	NAROTC
Newcrest Mining Ltd.	OTC	NWCMY
News Corporation Ltd., The	NYSE	NWS
Normandy Poseidon Ltd.	OTC	NPLOTC
North Broken Hill-Peko Ltd.	OTC	NBHKY
North Queensland Resources N.L.	OTC	NQROTC
Orbital Engine Corporation Ltd.	NYSE	OE
Pacific Dunlop Ltd.	Nasdaq	PDLPY
Pact Resources, N.L.	OTC	PACOTC
Palmer Tube Mills Ltd.	Nasdaq	PTMLY
Pancontinental Mining Ltd.	OTC	PANOTC
Pelsart Resources N.L.	Nasdaq	PELRY
Petrogulf Resources Ltd.	OTC	PRLOTC
Pioneer Int'l. Ltd. Preferred Series A1	OTC	PA1
Pioneer Int'l. Ltd. Preferred Series A2	OTC	PA2
Pioneer Int'l. Ltd. Preferred Series B1	OTC	PB1
Pioneer Int'l. Ltd. Preferred Series B2	OTC	PB2
Pioneer International Ltd.	OTC	PONNY
Placer Pacific Ltd.	OTC	PLCAY
Poseidon Gold Ltd.	OTC	PSGLY
Range Resources Ltd.	OTC	RRLOTC
Regent Mining Ltd.	OTC	REGOTC
Roycol Ltd.	OTC	RYLOTC
Samantha Gold N.L.	OTC	SMGOY
Samson Exploration N.L.	OTC	SAENY
Santos Ltd.	Nasdaq	STOSY
Sapphire Mines N.L.	OTC	SAPOTC
Shomega Ltd.	OTC	SEGAY
Smith (Howard) Ltd.	OTC	SMHOTC
Sons of Gwalia N.L.	OTC	SOGAY
Southcorp Holding Ltd.	OTC	STHHY
Southern Goldfields Ltd.	OTC	SGFOTC
Southern Pacific Petroleum	Nasdaq	SPPTY
Southern Resources Ltd.	OTC	SRLOTC
Southern Ventures N.L.	OTC	SVNOTC

Company	Exchange	Symbol
Southwest Gold Mines	OTC	SGLOTC
Sovereign Oil Australia Ltd.	OTC	SOVOTC
Spargos Mining N.L.	OTC	SPAOTC
St. Barbara Mines Ltd.	OTC	STBRY
Striker Resources N.L.	OTC	SKRRY
Tennyson Holdings Ltd.	OTC	TNYOTC
Terrex Resources N.L.	OTC	TRXRY
TNT Ltd.	OTC	TNTMY
Tolltreck Systems, Ltd.	OTC	TOLRY
Trans-Global Resources N.L.	Nasdaq	TGBRY
Transcontinental Holdings	OTC	THLOTC
Triad Minerals N.L.	OTC	TRDOTC
Trust Company of Australia Ltd.	OTC	TCAOTC
Vam Ltd.	OTC	VAMOTC
Victoria Petroleum N.L.	OTC	VICEY
Walhalla Mining Co. N.L.	OTC	WMNOTC
Wattle Gully Gold Mines N.L.	OTC	WGGOTC
Western Mining Corporation Holdings Ltd.	NYSE	WMC
Westpac Banking Corporation	NYSE	WBK
Westpac Banking Corporation Preferred	NYSE	WBK+
Woodside Petroleum Ltd.	OTC	WOPEY
Zanex N.L.	OTC	ZANXY
Austria		
EVN AG	OTC	EVNVY
Lauda Air Luftfahrt AG	OTC	LAUOTC
Lenzing AG	OTC	LNZNY
OMV AG	OTC	OMVAY
Veitsch - Radex A.G.	OTC	VMAOTC
Z-Landerbank Austria AG	OTC	ZLAEY
Belgium		
Gevaert Photo-Production N.V.	OTC	GPPOTC
Petrofina S.A.	OTC	PTRFY
Bermuda		
Fairhaven International Ltd.	Nasdaq	NIMSY
London and Overseas Freighters Ltd.	Nasdaq	LOFSY
Smedvig Tankships Ltd.	OTC	SVKTY
Zambia Copper Investments Ltd.	OTC	ZAPOTC
Botswana		
Botswana RST Ltd.	OTC	BOTWY
Brazil		
Acesita-Cia. Acos Especias Itabir	OTC	ACEOTC
Aracruz Celulose S.A.	NYSE	ARA
Bombril S.A.	OTC	BMBBY
Celesc-Centrais Ele. da Santa Catarina	OTC	CELEOTC
Celesc-Centrais Ele. da Santa Catarina A	OTC	CELEA
Celesc-Centrais Ele. da Santa Catarina B	OTC	CELEB
Ceval Alimentos, S.A. Common	OTC	CEVALO
Ceval Alimentos, S.A. Preferred	OTC	CEVALY
Companhia Energetica de Minas Gerais	None	CEMGDR

Non-US Company Stocks Available Through US Stock Markets (continued)

Company	Exchange	Symbol
Companhia Energetica de Minas Gerais - CEMIG	OTC	CEMCY
Companhia Energetica de Sao Paulo	OTC	CESPY
Companhia Siderurgica de Turbarao GDR	None	CSTGDR
Companhia Siderurgica Nacional-CSN	OTC	CSNMY
Companhia Suzano de Papel e Celulose	OTC	CSZPY
Companhia Vale do Rio Doce	OTC	CVROY
Copene - Petroquimica do Nordeste S.A.	OTC	CPEPY
CTM Citrus	OTC	CTMMY
Industrias de Papel Simao S.A.	OTC	IDPSY
Iochpe-Maxion Preferred Shares	OTC	IMAXYP
Refrigeracao Parana	OTC	RFPOTC
Sao Paulo Alpargatas Common Shares	OTC	SPALYC
Sao Paulo Alpargatas Preferred Shares	OTC	SPALYP
Sementes Agroceres S.A.	OTC	SMTAY
Telecomunicacoes Brasileiras, S.A.	OTC	TBRAY
Usinas Siderurgicas de Minas Gerais S.A.	None	USMSRS
Canada		
A & A Foods Ltd.	Nasdaq	ANAFF
Aber Resourses Ltd.	Nasdaq	ABERF
Abitibi-Price Inc.	NYSE	ABY
Agnico-Eagle Mines Ltd.	Nasdaq	AEGGF
Alaska Apollo Resources, Ltd.	Nasdaq	APLOF
Alcan Aluminum Ltd.	NYSE	AL
Alias Research Inc.	Nasdaq	ADDDF
American Barrick Resources Corp.	NYSE	ABX
American Sensors, Inc.	Nasdaq	SNIFF
Andyne Computing Ltd.	Nasdaq	ADYNF
Applied Carbon Technology, Inc.	Nasdaq	ACTYF
Arakis Energy Corp.	Nasdaq	AKSEF
Artagraph Reproduction Technology Inc.	Nasdaq	XARPF
Artagraph Reproduction Technology Inc.	Nasdaq	XARLF
Artagraph Reproduction Technology Inc.	Nasdaq	XAROF
Audrey Resources Inc.	Nasdaq	AUYMF
Battery Technologies, Inc.	Nasdaq	BTIOF
BCE Inc.	NYSE	BCE
Big Rock Brewery Ltd.	Nasdaq	BEERF
Biochem Pharma Inc.	Nasdaq	BCHXF
Biomira Inc.	Nasdaq	BIOMF
Brio Industries Inc.	Nasdaq	BRIOF
BRL Enterprises, Inc.	Nasdaq	BRALF
Caledonia Mining Corp.	Nasdaq	CALVF
Call-Net Enterprises Inc.	Nasdaq	CNEBF
Cam-Net Comm. Network Inc.	Nasdaq	CWKTF
Campbell Resources Inc.	NYSE	CCH
Canada Southern Petroleum Ltd.	Nasdaq	CSPLF
Canadian Pacific Ltd.	NYSE	CP
Canstar Sports Inc.	Nasdaq	HKYIF
Celltech Media, Inc.	Nasdaq	CTMIF

Company	Exchange	Symbol
Chai-Na-Ta Corp.	Nasdaq	CCCFF
CHC Helicopter Corp.	Nasdaq	FLYAF
Cinar Films, Inc.	Nasdaq	CINRF
Cineplex Odeon Corporation	NYSE	CPX
Cirque Energy Ltd.	Nasdaq	CIRQF
Clearly Canadian Beverage Corp.	Nasdaq	CLCDF
Clearnet Communications Inc.	Nasdaq	CLNTF
Cognos Inc.	Nasdaq	COGNF
Computalog Ltd.	Nasdaq	CLTDF
Consolidated Mercantile Corp.	Nasdaq	CSLMF
Consolidated Nevada Goldfields Corp.	Nasdaq	KNVCF
Consolidated Ramrod Gold Corp.	Nasdaq	CYNXF
Consolidated Western and Pacific Resource Corp.	Nasdaq	CWNPF
Conwest Exploration Company Ltd.	Nasdaq	CEXCF
Corel Corporation	Nasdaq	COSFF
Cornucopia Resources Ltd.	Nasdaq	CNPGF
Cott Corporation	Nasdaq	COTTF
Current Technology Corporation	Nasdaq	CRTCF
Cusac Industries Ltd.	Nasdaq	CUSIF
Daleco Resources Corporation	Nasdaq	DLOVF
DeNovo Corp.	Nasdaq	DNVOF
Delrina Corporation	Nasdaq	DENAF
Domtar	NYSE	DTC
Draxis Health Inc.	Nasdaq	DRAXF
Dreco Energy Services Ltd.	Nasdaq	DREAF
Dusty Mac Oil & Gas Ltd.	Nasdaq	DMACF
Dynamic Oil Ltd.	Nasdaq	DYOLF
EMCO Ltd.	Nasdaq	EMLTF
El Condor Resources Ltd.	Nasdaq	ECNCF
Elephant & Castle Group, Inc.	Nasdaq	PUBSF
Enscor Inc.	Nasdaq	ENCRF
Fahnestock Viner Holdings Inc.	Nasdaq	FAHNF
Federal Industries Ltd.	Nasdaq	FILAF
First Dynasty Mines Ltd.	Nasdaq	FDYMF
First Standard Ventures Ltd.	Nasdaq	FSLRF
Frisco Bay Industries Ltd.	Nasdaq	FBAYF
Fulcrum Technologies Inc.	Nasdaq	FULCF
Gandalf Technologies Inc.	Nasdaq	GANDF
Glamis Gold Ltd.	NYSE	GLG
Golden Knight Resources, Inc.	Nasdaq	GKRVF
Golden Quail Resources Ltd.	Nasdaq	GQRVF
Goran Capital, Inc.	Nasdaq	GNCNF
Greenstone Resources Ltd.	Nasdaq	GRERF
Hariston Corp.	Nasdaq	HRSNF
Highwood Resources Ltd.	Nasdaq	HIWDF
Hollinger Inc.	Nasdaq	HLGRF
Horsham Corporation	NYSE	HSM
Hummingbird Communications Ltd.	Nasdaq	HUMCF
Hyal Pharmaceutical Corporation	Nasdaq	HYALF
ID Biomedical Corporation	Nasdaq	IDBEF
IMUTEC Corp.	Nasdaq	IMUTF
Inco Ltd.	NYSE	N
InterTAN Inc.	NYSE	ITN
IPL Energy Inc.	Nasdaq	IPPIF
IPSCO Inc.	Nasdaq	IPSCF
Imax Corporation	Nasdaq	IMAXF
Intera Information Technologies Corporation	Nasdaq	IITCF

Non-US Company Stocks Available Through US Stock Markets (continued)

Company	Exchange	Symbol	Company	Exchange	Symbol
International Absorbents Inc.	Nasdaq	IABSF	Sand Technology Systems		
International Business			International Inc.	Nasdaq	SNDCF
Schools Inc.	Nasdaq	IBSIF	Seagram Company Ltd.	NYSE	VO
International Platinum			Semi-Tech Corp.	Nasdaq	SEMCF
Corporation	Nasdaq	TIPNF	SHL Systemhouse Inc.	Nasdaq	SHKIF
I.S.G. Technologies Inc.	Nasdaq	ISGTF	Silverado Mines Ltd.	Nasdaq	SLVRF
Jannock Ltd.	Nasdaq	JANNF	Spectral Diagnostics Inc.	Nasdaq	DIAGF
JetForm Corporation	Nasdaq	FORMF	Spectrum Signal Processing Inc.	Nasdaq	SSPIF
KWG Resources, Inc.	Nasdaq	KWGDF	Stake Technology Ltd.	Nasdaq	STKLF
LAC Minerals Ltd.	NYSE	LAC	Sunport Medical Corp.	Nasdaq	SMQCF
Laidlaw Inc. (Class A)	NYSE	LDWA	Sutton Resources, Ltd.	Nasdaq	STTZF
Laidlaw Inc. (Class B)	NYSE	LDWB	Taseko Mines Ltd.	Nasdaq	TKOCF
Laser Friendly Inc.	Nasdaq	LFIIF	Technigen Corp.	Nasdaq	TGPAF
La Teko Resources Ltd.	Nasdaq	LAORF	Tee-Comm Electronics Inc.	Nasdaq	TENXF
Leisureways Marketing Ltd.	Nasdaq	LMLAF	Texas Star Resources Corp.	Nasdaq	TEXSF
Loewen Group Inc. (The)	Nasdaq	LWNGF	Tracer Petroleum Corp.	Nasdaq	TCXXF
Mackenzie Financial Corp.	Nasdaq	MKFCF	TransCanada Pipelines Ltd.	NYSE	TRP
MacMillan Bloedel Ltd.	Nasdaq	MMBLF	United Dominion Industries Ltd.	NYSE	UDI
Magna International Inc.	NYSE	MGA	Vengold, Inc.	Nasdaq	VENGF
Methanex Corp.	Nasdaq	MEOHF	Wescast Industries Inc.	Nasdaq	WCSTF
Mitel Corporation	NYSE	MLT	Westcoast Energy Inc.	NYSE	WE
Modatech Systems Inc.	Nasdaq	MODAF	Wharf Resources Ltd.	Nasdaq	WFRAF
Moore Corporation Ltd.	NYSE	MCL	Zoom Telephonics, Inc.	Nasdaq	ZOOM
MTC Electronic Technologies					
Co. Ltd.	Nasdaq	MTCEF	**Chile**		
MTC Electronic Technologies			Banco O'Higgins	NYSE	OHG
Co. Ltd.	Nasdaq	MTCGF	Chilgener S.A.	NYSE	CHR
Multi-Corp, Inc.	Nasdaq	MCUAF	Chilquinta, S.A. GDR	None	CHIGDR
NII Norsat International Inc.	Nasdaq	NSATF	Compania Cervecerias		
Norris Communications Corp.	Nasdaq	NORRF	Unidas S.A.	Nasdaq	CCUUY
North American Palladium Ltd.	Nasdaq	PDLCF	Compania de Telefonos		
Northern Telecom Ltd.	NYSE	NT	de Chile (CTC)	NYSE	CTC
Northgate Exploration Ltd.	NYSE	NGX	Cristalerias de Chile, S.A.	NYSE	CGW
NOVA Corporation of Alberta	NYSE	NVA	Embotelladora Andina, S.A.	NYSE	AKO
Nowsco Well Service Ltd.	Nasdaq	NWSLF	Empresas Telex-Chile S.A.	NYSE	TL
Optima Petroleum Corp.	Nasdaq	OPPCF	Endesa-Empresa Nacional		
Pacific Sentinel Gold Corp.	Nasdaq	PSGVF	de Electricidad	NYSE	ECO
Park Meditech Inc.	Nasdaq	PMDTF	Enersis S.A.	NYSE	ENI
PC DOCS Group International	Nasdaq	DOCSF	Laboratorio Chile S.A. "B"	NYSE	LBC
Perle Systems Ltd.	Nasdaq	PERLF	Madeco S.A.	NYSE	MAD
Petersburg Long Distance Inc.	Nasdaq	PLDIF	Maderas y Sinteticos SA (MASISA)	NYSE	MYS
Petromet Resources Ltd.	Nasdaq	PNTGF	Sociedad Quimica y Minera		
Philip Environmental Inc.	Nasdaq	PENVF	de Chile, S.A.	NYSE	SQM
Placer Dome Inc.	NYSE	PDG	Vina Concho y Toro S.A.	NYSE	VCO
Potash Corporation of					
Saskatchewan Inc.	NYSE	POT	**China**		
Prairie Pacific Energy Corp.	Nasdaq	PRPEF	Qingling Motors Co., Ltd. Reg S	None	QINREGS
Premdor Inc.	NYSE	PI	Shandong Huaneng		
Prime Equities International Corp.	Nasdaq	PEZVF	Power "N" Shares	NYSE	SH
Qsound Labs, Inc.	Nasdaq	QSNDF	Shanghai Chlor-Alkali Chemical		
QSR Ltd.	Nasdaq	QSRTF	Co., Ltd.	OTC	SLLBY
Quadra Logic Technologies Inc.	Nasdaq	QLTIF	Shanghai Erfangji Co. Ltd. "B"	OTC	SHFGY
Quality Dino Entertainment Ltd.	Nasdaq	RCORF	Shanghai Petrochemical		
Ranger Oil Ltd.	NYSE	RGO	Company Ltd.	NYSE	SHI
Rea Gold Corp.	Nasdaq	REOGF	Shanghai Tyre and Rubber		
Repap Enterprises Inc.	Nasdaq	RPAPF	Co. Ltd.	OTC	STRCY
Revenue Properties Co. Ltd.	Nasdaq	RPCLF	Shenzhen S.E.Z. Real Estate		
Rich Coast Resources Ltd.	Nasdaq	KRHCF	and Prop.	OTC	SZPRY
Rogers Cantel Mobile					
Communications Inc.	Nasdaq	RCMIF	**Colombia**		
Sanctuary Woods Multimedia			Cementos Diamante S.A. GDR	None	CEDGDR
Corp.	Nasdaq	SWMCF			

Non-US Company Stocks Available Through US Stock Markets (continued)

Company	Exchange	Symbol
Denmark		
Den Danske Bank	OTC	DDBOTC
Novo Nordisk A/S	NYSE	NVO
Tele Danmark A/S	NYSE	TLD
El Salvador		
Compania de Alumbrado		
Electrico de SS	OTC	CSSOTC
Finland		
Amer Group Ltd.	OTC	AGPDY
Cultor Ltd.	OTC	CTRLY
Cultor Ltd.	OTC	CULTY
Instrumentarium Corporation	Nasdaq	INMRY
Nokia Corporation	OTC	NKAOTC
Repola Corporation	OTC	REPOL
France		
Alcatel Alsthom Cie Generale		
d'Elect	NYSE	ALA
Business Objects S.A.	Nasdaq	BOBJY
Canal Plus	OTC	CNPLY
Ciments Francais	OTC	CIMFY
Clarins	OTC	CRASY
Club Mediterranee	OTC	CLMDY
Coflexip	Nasdaq	CXIPY
Compagnie de Suez	OTC	CSUZY
Compagnie des Machines Bull	OTC	CODMY
Groupe Danone	OTC	GPDNY
Elf Aquitaine	NYSE	ELF
Fiat France S.A. (FFSA)	OTC	FFSSY
France, Oats 8.50% 6/25/97	NYSE	FRZ
France, Oats 9.80% 1/30/96	NYSE	FRA
Havas	OTC	HAVSY
L'Air Liquide	OTC	AIROTC
L'Oreal	OTC	OREOTC
Lafarge Coppee S.A.	OTC	LFCPY
LVMH, Moet Hennessey		
Louis Vuitton	Nasdaq	LVMHY
Pernod Ricard S.A.	OTC	PDRDY
Peugeot Citroen S.A.	OTC	PEUGY
Rhone Poulenc S.A. Series A	NYSE	RP
Rhone-Poulenc "PSSA" ADRS	NYSE	RP+A
Rhone-Poulenc S.A. (CIPS)	OTC	RP.C
Schneider et Cie	OTC	SETOTC
Societe Generale	OTC	SEGLY
Thomson-CSF	Nasdaq	TCSFY
TOTAL "B" Shares	NYSE	TOT
Valeo	OTC	VAEOTC
Germany		
AEG AG	OTC	AEGXY
BASF AG	OTC	BASFY
Bayer AG	OTC	BAYRY
Bayerische Vereinsbank AG	OTC	BAVNY
Berliner Handels-und		
Frankfurter Bank	OTC	BHFFY
Commerzbank AG	OTC	CRZBY
Continental AG	OTC	CTTAY
Daimler-Benz AG	NYSE	DAI
Deutsche Bank AG	OTC	DBKAY
Deutsche Lufthansa AG	OTC	DLHOTC

Company	Exchange	Symbol
Dresdner Bank AG	Nasdaq	DRSDY
Hoechst, AG	OTC	HOEHY
Hoesch, AG	OTC	HOEOTC
Hypo-Bank-Bayerische	OTC	BHYWY
Karstadt AG, Rudolf	OTC	KSTOTC
Kaufhof Holding AG	OTC	KAAGY
Kaufhof Holding AG Preferred	OTC	KAAZY
Kloeckner Werke, A.G.	OTC	KLWOTC
Mannesman AG	OTC	MNSMY
Rosenthal, AG	OTC	RENOTC
RWE AG	OTC	RWAGY
Siemens AG	OTC	SMAWY
Stahl Werke Peine Salzgitter, A.G.	OTC	SPSOTC
Thyssen Huette, AG	OTC	THYOTC
Volkswagen AG	OTC	VLKAY
Volkswagen AG Preferred	OTC	VWBP
Greece		
Boutari & Son, S.A.	OTC	BOUOTC
Boutari & Son, S.A. Preferred	OTC	BJSPY
Credit Bank A.E.	OTC	CBAEY
Globe Group S.A.	OTC	GGSOTC
Hong Kong		
Amoy Properties Ltd.	OTC	AWOZY
Applied International Holdings	OTC	APIHY
Asia Orient Company Ltd.	OTC	AOLOTC
Bank of East Asia, Ltd.	OTC	BKEAY
C.P. Pokphand Co. Ltd.	OTC	CPPKY
Carrian Investments Ltd.	OTC	CANVY
Cathay Pacific Airways Ltd.	OTC	CPARY
Champion Technology Holding		
Ltd.	OTC	CMPLY
Cheung Kong (Holdings) Ltd.	OTC	CHEUY
China Aerospace International		
Hlds. Ltd.	OTC	CNCOTC
China Light and Power	OTC	CHLWY
China Strategic Investment Ltd.	OTC	CSILY
Chuangs Holdings Ltd.	OTC	CHUNY
Dairy Farm International		
Holdings Ltd.	OTC	DFIHY
Evergo Holdings Company Ltd.	OTC	EVEOTC
First Pacific Company Ltd.	OTC	FPCOTC
Frankie Dominion		
International Ltd.	OTC	FKDMY
Giordano Holding Ltd.	OTC	GIOOTC
Gold Peak Industries		
(Holdings) Ltd.	OTC	GPIHL
Grand Hotel Holdings Ltd.	OTC	GHOAY
Great Wall Electronics	Nasdaq	GWALY
Guangdong Investment Ltd.	OTC	GILOTC
Hang Lung Development		
Company, Ltd.	OTC	HANLY
Hang Seng Bank	OTC	HSBOTC
Hanny Magnetics (Holdings) Ltd.	OTC	HMHOTC
Henderson Land Development		
Co., Ltd	OTC	HLDOTC
Hong Kong and China Gas		
Co. Ltd.	OTC	HKCOTC
Hong Kong Telecommunications	NYSE	HKT
Hongkong Electric Holdings Ltd.	OTC	HONGY
Hongkong Land Holdings Ltd	OTC	HKHGY

Non-US Company Stocks Available Through US Stock Markets (continued)

Company	Exchange	Symbol	Company	Exchange	Symbol
Hopewell Holdings Ltd.	OTC	HOWWY	Gujarat Narmada Valley		
Hutchison Whampoa Ltd.	OTC	HUWHY	Reg S GDR	None	GNVFRS
Hysan Development Co., Ltd.	OTC	HYSNY	Hindustan Development		
Jardine Matheson Holdings Ltd.	OTC	JARLY	Corp. Ltd. GDR	None	HDCCYGDR
Jardine Strategic Holdings Ltd.	OTC	JDSHY	I.T.C. Ltd. GDR	None	ITCGDR
Jinhui Holdings Company Ltd.	OTC	JHUHY	JCT Ltd. Reg S GDR	None	JCTREGS
Johnson Electric Holdings Ltd.	OTC	JELCY	Ranbaxy Laboratories GDR	None	RANYGDR
Keng Fong Sin Kee Construction			Tube Investments of India		
and Inves	OTC	KENGOTC	Ltd. Reg S GDR	None	TUBERS
Mandarin Oriental International			United Phosphorus Ltd. GDR	None	UPLGDR
Ltd.	OTC	MAORY			
New World Development Co. Ltd	OTC	NEWDY	**Indonesia**		
Onfem Holdings Ltd.	OTC	ONHLY	P.T. Inti Indorayon Utama	OTC	PTIOTC
Pacific Concord Holdings Ltd.	OTC	PFCHY	P.T. Tri Polyta Indonesia	OTC	PFCHY
Peregrine Investments Holdings					
Ltd.	OTC	PGIQY	**Ireland**		
Playmates International Holdings			Allied Irish Banks, PLC	NYSE	AIB
Ltd.	OTC	PYPHY	Allied Irish Banks, PLC Preferred	NYSE	AIB+
Semi-Tech (Global) Co. Ltd.	OTC	SITGY	Anglo Irish Bankcorp	OTC	AGBKY
Shun Tak Holdings Ltd.	OTC	SHTGY	Aran Energy	Nasdaq	ARANY
Sino Land Company Ltd.	OTC	SINOTC	CRH PLC	Nasdaq	CRHCY
South China Morning Post			Elan Corporation, PLC	AMEX	ELN
(Holdings) Ltd.	OTC	SCHPY	Elan Warrants	AMEX	ELN%
Star Paging International			Elan/ATS Unit	AMEX	ELNE
Holding Ltd.	OTC	STPGY	Glencar Exploration PLC	OTC	GLCOTC
Starlight International			Hibernia Foods PLC ADR	Nasdaq	HIBNY
Holdings Ltd.	OTC	SIHLY	Hibernia Foods PLC Unit	OTC	HIBUF
Sun Hung Kai & Co., Ltd.	OTC	SHKOTC	Hibernia Foods PLC Warr "A"	Nasdaq	HIBWF
Sun Hung Kai Properties Ltd.	OTC	SUHKY	Pharma Patch "Unit"	Nasdaq	SKIUF
Swire Pacific Ltd. "A"	OTC	SWIRY	Pharma Patch Class "A" Warrant	Nasdaq	SKIWF
Swire Pacific Ltd. "A"	OTC	SWRAY	Pharma Patch Class "B" Warrant	Nasdaq	SKIZF
Swire Pacific Ltd. "B"	OTC	SPCBY	Pharma Patch Class "C" Warrant	Nasdaq	SKIMF
Tai Cheung Holdings Ltd.	OTC	TCHOTC	Pharma Patch PLC	Nasdaq	SKINY
Techtronic Industries			Phoenix Shannon PLC	Nasdaq	PHNXY
Company Ltd.	OTC	TTNDY	Power Corporation PLC	OTC	PWRCY
Television Broadcasts Ltd.	OTC	TVBOTC	Trinity Biotech PLC ADR	Nasdaq	HIVSY
Truly International Holdings Ltd.	OTC	TRUCY	Trinity Biotech PLC Unit	OTC	HIVUF
TVE (Holdings) Ltd.	OTC	TVEOTC	Trinity Biotech PLC Warr "A"	Nasdaq	HIVWF
Vtech Holdings Ltd.	OTC	VTKHY	Trinity Biotech PLC Warr "B"	Nasdaq	HIVZF
Wah Kwong Shipping			Waterford Wedgewood PLC	Nasdaq	WATFZ
Holdings Ltd.	OTC	WKSOTC			
Welback Holdings Ltd.	OTC	WELKY	**Israel**		
Wharf Holdings Ltd., The	OTC	WARFY	4th Dimension Software Ltd.	Nasdaq	DDDDF
Wheelock and Company Ltd.	OTC	WHELY	Aladdin Knowledge Systems Ltd.	Nasdaq	ALDNF
Wing Hang Bank, Ltd.	OTC	WGHGY	Aryt Industries Ltd.	Nasdaq	ARYTF
Winsor Industrial			Comet Software International		
Corporation Ltd	OTC	WICOTC	Ltd.	Nasdaq	CMTTF
			ECI Telecom Ltd.	Nasdaq	ECILF
Hungary			Edunetics Ltd.	Nasdaq	EDNTF
Fotex RT	OTC	FOTOTC	EduSoft Ltd.	Nasdaq	EDUSF
			Elbit Ltd.	Nasdaq	ELBTF
India			Elite Industries Ltd. NIS 1	OTC	ELEIY
Bombay Dyeing & Manufacturing			Elite Industries Ltd. NIS 5	OTC	ELEDY
Co. Ltd.	None	BDMGDR	Elron Electronic Industries Ltd.	Nasdaq	ELRNF
CESC Ltd. Reg "S" GDR	None	CESCRS	Eshed Robotec (1982) Ltd.	Nasdaq	ROBOF
CESC Ltd. Reg "S" Warrants	None	CESCRSW	Gilat Satellite Networks Ltd.	Nasdaq	GILTF
Dr. Reddy's Laboratories GDR	None	REDDSY	Healthcare Technologies Ltd.	Nasdaq	HCTLF
The East India Hotels Ltd.			Idan Software Industries-I.S.I. Ltd.	Nasdaq	IDANF
Reg S GDR	None	EIHLRS	IDB Bankholding Corporation	OTC	IDBBY
Garden Silk Mills Ltd.			I.I.S. Intelligent Information		
Reg "S" GDR	None	GSM	Systems Ltd.	Nasdaq	IISLF
Grasim Industries Ltd. "GDR"	None	GILGDR			

Non-US Company Stocks Available Through US Stock Markets (continued)

Company	Exchange	Symbol
ISG International Software Group Ltd.	Nasdaq	SISGF
Israel Land Development Company, Ltd., The	Nasdaq	ILDCY
Isras Investment Company Ltd. NIS 1	OTC	ISIMY1
Istec-Industries & Technologies Ltd.	Nasdaq	ISTEF
Kopel Ltd.	OTC	KOPLY
Lannet Data Communications Ltd.	Nasdaq	LANTF
LanOptics Ltd.	Nasdaq	LNOPF
Laser Industries Ltd.	Nasdaq	LASGF
Magal Security Systems Ltd.	Nasdaq	MAGSF
Magic Software Enterprises Ltd.	Nasdaq	MGICF
Medis El Ltd.	Nasdaq	MDSLF
M-Systems Flash Disk Pioneers Ltd.	Nasdaq	FLSHF
Nexus Telecommunications Systems, Ltd.	Nasdaq	NXUSF
Orbotech, Ltd.	Nasdaq	ORBKF
OSHAP Technologies Ltd.	Nasdaq	OSHSF
Rada Electronics Industries Ltd.	Nasdaq	RADIF
Scitex Corp. Ltd	Nasdaq	SCIXF
Silicom Ltd.	Nasdaq	SILCF
Taro Pharmaceutical Industries Ltd.	Nasdaq	TAROF
TAT Technologies Ltd.	Nasdaq	TATTF
Tecnomatix Technologies Ltd.	Nasdaq	TCNOF
Teledata Communication Ltd.	Nasdaq	TLDCF
Telegraph Communications Ltd.	Nasdaq	TELGF
Teva Pharmaceutical Industries Ltd.	Nasdaq	TEVIY
Tower Semiconductor Ltd.	Nasdaq	TSEMF
T.V.G. Technologies Ltd.	Nasdaq	TVGTF
T.V.G. Technologies Ltd.	Nasdaq	TVGUF
Italy		
Bastogi I.R.B.S.	OTC	BIROTC
Benetton Group S.p.A.	NYSE	BNG
Fiat S.p.A. (Ordinary)	NYSE	FIA
Fiat S.p.A. (Preference)	NYSE	FIA+
Fiat S.p.A. (Savings)	NYSE	FIAA
Fila Holding S.p.A.	NYSE	FLH
Finanziaria Agroindustriale, Non Conv Sav	OTC	FISOTC
Finanziaria Agroindustriale,S.p.A.	OTC	FINOTC
Industrie Natuzzi S.p.A.	NYSE	NTZ
Istituto Nazionale delle Assicurazioni	NYSE	INZ
Italcementi Fabriche Riunite Cemento SpA	OTC	ICFOTC
La Rinascente S.p.A.	OTC	LSCOTC
Luxottica Group S.p.A.	NYSE	LUX
Montedison S.p.A.	NYSE	MNT
Montedison S.p.A. Savings SHS	NYSE	MNT+
Olivetti & C., S.p.A. (Non-Convertible)	OTC	OLSOTC
Olivetti & C., S.p.A. (Ordinary Shares)	OTC	OLIVY
Olivetti & C., S.p.A. (Preference Shares)	OTC	OLIPY

Company	Exchange	Symbol
Pirelli, S.p.A. .	OTC	PIROTC
Simint S.p.A. (Ordinary Shares)	OTC	SIMOTC
Simint S.p.A. (Preferred Shares)	OTC	SIMPTC
SNIA Viscosa	OTC	SVCOTC
Soc. Fin. Siderugica "A"	OTC	SFSOTC
STET - Non Conv. Savings Shares	OTC	SNCS
STET (Soc. Finanziara Telefonica)	OTC	3TFEY
Jamaica		
Caribbean Cement Co. Ltd.	OTC	CACOTC
Ciboney Group Ltd.	OTC	CIBOTC
Jamaica Flour Mills Ltd.	OTC	JFMOTC
Japan		
Aida Engineering	OTC	ADERY
Ajinomoto Company	OTC	AJINY
Akai Electric	OTC	AKELY
All Nippon Airways Co. Ltd	OTC	ALNPY
Alps Electric Co., Ltd	OTC	ALPSY
Amada Co., Ltd	OTC	AMDLY
Amway Japan Ltd.	OTC	AWJNY
Amway Japan Ltd.	NYSE	AJL
Asahi Bank, Ltd (The)	OTC	ASBOTC
Asahi Chemical Industry	OTC	ASHIY
Asahi Glass Company, Ltd.	OTC	ASGLY
Ashikaga Bank Ltd.	OTC	AKGBY
Bank of Fukuoka, Ltd.	OTC	BOFLY
Bank of Tokyo	OTC	BTKYY
Bank of Yokohama	OTC	BKJAY
Banyu Pharmaceutical Co., Ltd	OTC	BNYUY
Bridgestone Corporation	OTC	BROCY
Brother Industries	OTC	BRTRY
Calpis Food Industry Co.,Ltd	OTC	CPISY
Canon Inc	Nasdaq	CANNY
Casio Computer Company Ltd.	OTC	CSIOY
CSK Corp.	Nasdaq	CSKKY
Dai Nippon Printing Co., Ltd.	OTC	DNPOTC
Dai'ei, Inc., The	Nasdaq	DAIEY
The Dai-Ichi Kangyo Bank, Ltd.	OTC	DIKOTC
Daibiru Corporation	OTC	DACOTC
Daiwa Danchi Co., Ltd	OTC	DANOTC
Daiwa House Industry Co., Ltd.	OTC	DHIOTC
The Daiwa Securities Co., Ltd.	OTC	DSCOTC
Daiwa Seiko, Inc.	OTC	DSIOTC
Ebara Corporation	OTC	EBAOTC
Eisai Company	OTC	EISOTC
Fuji Bank, Ltd., The	OTC	FJBOTC
Fuji Heavy Industries Ltd.	OTC	FUHOTC
Fuji Photo Film Co., Ltd.	Nasdaq	FUJIY
Fujita Corporation	OTC	FJAOTC
Fujitsu Ltd.	OTC	FUUOTC
Furukawa Electric Co., Ltd.	OTC	FEKOTC
Hachijuni Bank, Ltd., The	OTC	HJBOTC
Hino Motors, Ltd.	OTC	HIMOTC
Hitachi Cable, Ltd	OTC	HCLOTC
Hitachi Koki Co., Ltd.	OTC	HKKOTC
Hitachi Ltd.	NYSE	HIT
Hitachi Metals, Ltd.	OTC	HMLOTC
Hochiki Corporation	OTC	HOCOTC
Hokuriku Bank, Ltd., The	OTC	HRBOTC
Honda Motor Co., Ltd.	NYSE	HMC
Industrial Bank of Japan	OTC	IBJOTC

Non-US Company Stocks Available Through US Stock Markets (continued)

Company	Exchange	Symbol	Company	Exchange	Symbol
Isuzu Motors Ltd.	OTC	ISUZY	Omron Corporation	OTC	OMROTC
Ito-Yokado Co., Ltd.	Nasdaq	IYCOY	Onoda Cement Company Ltd.	OTC	OCCOTC
ITOCHU Corporation	OTC	ITOOTC	Onward Kashiyama & Co. Ltd.	OTC	ONWOTC
Japan Airlines Co., Ltd.	Nasdaq	JAPNY	Pioneer Electronic Corporation	NYSE	PIO
Japan Steel Works	OTC	JSWOTC	Ricoh Company, Ltd.	OTC	RICOY
JUSCO Co., Ltd.	OTC	JUSOTC	Sakura Bank Ltd., The	OTC	SAKOTC
Kajima Corporatin	OTC	KAJOTC	Sanwa Bank Ltd.	OTC	SBLOTC
Kanebo, Ltd.	OTC	KANOTC	Sanyo Electric Co., Ltd.	Nasdaq	SANYY
Kao Corporation	OTC	KAOOTC	Sanyo Securities Co., Ltd.	OTC	SANSE
Kawasaki Steel Corporation	OTC	KSKSY	Secom Co., Ltd	OTC	SECOTC
Kirin Brewery Co., Ltd	Nasdaq	KNBWY	Sega Enterprise, Ltd.	OTC	SEGNY
Kobe Steel, Ltd.	OTC	KBSTY	Sekisui House, Ltd.	OTC	SEKOTC
Komatsu Ltd.	OTC	KMATY	Seven-Eleven Japan Co., Ltd.	OTC	SEVOTC
Konica Corporation	OTC	KONOTC	Sharp Corporation	OTC	SHCAY
Kubota Ltd.	NYSE	KUB	Shiseido Co., Ltd.	OTC	SSDOY
Kumagai Gumi Co., Ltd.	OTC	KMAOTC	Shizuoka Bank, Ltd., The	OTC	SZUOTC
Kyocera Corporation	NYSE	KYO	Showa Sangyo Co., Ltd.	OTC	SSCOTC
Makita Corporation	Nasdaq	MKTAY	Sony Corporation	NYSE	SNE
Marubeni Corporation	OTC	MAROTC	Sumitomo Bank, Ltd., The	OTC	SMBOTC
Marui Co., Ltd.	OTC	MCLOTC	Sumitomo Electric Industries	OTC	SEIOTC
Matsushita Electric Industrial			Sumitomo Metal Industries, Ltd.	OTC	SMMLY
Co., Ltd.	NYSE	MC	Suruga Bank Ltd.	OTC	SUROTC
Matsushita Electric Works	OTC	MATOTC	Taisei Corporation	OTC	TAIOTC
Meiji Seika Kaisha Ltd.	OTC	MSKOTC	Taiyo Yuden Co., Ltd.	OTC	TYYOTC
Minebea Co., Ltd.	OTC	MBLOTC	TDK Corporation	NYSE	TDK
Mitsubishi Bank, Ltd., The	NYSE	MBK	Teijin Ltd.	OTC	TINOTC
Mitsubishi Chemical Machinery			Teijin Seiki Co. Ltd.	OTC	TESOTC
Mfg., Co.	OTC	MFGOTC	Toa Harbor Works Company Ltd.	OTC	TOAOTC
Mitsubishi Corporation	OTC	MICOTC	Tokai Bank Ltd.	OTC	TKBOTC
Mitsubishi Electric Corp	OTC	MECOTC	Tokio Marine & Fire Insurance		
Mitsubishi Estate Co., Ltd.	OTC	MITOTC	Company	Nasdaq	TKIOY
Mitsubishi Kasei Corporation	OTC	MCIOTC	Tokyo Dome Corporation	OTC	TOKOTC
The Mitsubishi Trust & Banking			Tokyu Land Corporation	OTC	TLCOTC
Corp.	OTC	MBAOTC	Toppan Printing Co., Ltd.	OTC	TPPOTC
Mitsui & Company Ltd.	Nasdaq	MITSY	Toray Industries, Inc.	OTC	TOROTC
Mitsui Marine and Fire Insurance			Toto Ltd.	OTC	TOTOTC
Company	OTC	MMFOTC	Toyo Suisan Kaisha Ltd.	OTC	TOSOTC
Mitsukoshi, Ltd.	OTC	MIKOTC	Toyobo Co., Ltd.	OTC	TYOOTC
Nagoya Railroad Co., Ltd.	OTC	NGYOTC	Toyota Motor Corporation	Nasdaq	TOYOY
NEC Corp.	Nasdaq	NIPNY	Tsubakimoto Precision		
New Japan Securities Co., Ltd	OTC	NJSOTC	Products Co., Ltd.	OTC	TSBOTC
Nifco Inc.	OTC	NIFOTC	Tsugami Corporation	OTC	TSUOTC
The Nikko Securities Co. Ltd.	OTC	NSCOTC	Victor Company of Japan	OTC	VCPOTC
Nikon Corp.	OTC	NIKOTC	Wacoal Corporation	Nasdaq	WACLY
Nintendo Co., Ltd.	OTC	NTDOY	Yamaichi Securities Co. Ltd.	OTC	YAMAY
Nippon Kangyo Kakumaru			Yamazaki Baking Co., Ltd.	OTC	YAMOTC
Securities Co.	OTC	NPPOTC	Yasuda Trust and Banking		
Nippon Seiko K.K.	OTC	NSKOTC	Co. Ltd.	OTC	YASOTC
Nippon Shinpan Co., Ltd.	OTC	NSPOTC			
Nippon Shokubai Co., Ltd.	OTC	NSLOTC	**Luxembourg**		
Nippon Suisan Kaisha, Ltd.	OTC	NSUOTC	Anangel-American		
Nippon Telegraph and			Shipholdings Ltd.	Nasdaq	ASIPY
Telephone Corp.	NYSE	NTT	BT Shipping Ltd.	Nasdaq	BTBTY
Nippon Yusen Kabushiki Kaisha	OTC	NYKOTC	Indosuez Holdings S.C.A.		
Nippondenso Co., Ltd.	OTC	NCLOTC	Pref Series A	None	INHOTC
Nissan Motor Co., Ltd.	Nasdaq	NSANY	Minorco	Nasdaq	MNRCY
Nisshin Steel Co., Ltd.	OTC	NSSOTC			
Nitto Denko Corp.	OTC	NITOTC	**Malaysia**		
NKK Corporation	OTC	NKKOTC	Amalgamated Steel Mills Berhad	OTC	ASMOTC
Nomura Securities Co., Ltd.	OTC	NOMOTC	Angkasa Marketing Berhad	OTC	AMBOTC
Oji Paper Company Ltd.	OTC	OJIOTC	Bandar Raya Developments		
Olympus Optical Co., Ltd.	OTC	OLYOY	Berhad	OTC	BROBY

Non-US Company Stocks Available Through US Stock Markets (continued)

Company	Exchange	Symbol	Company	Exchange	Symbol
Berjaya Corp. Berhad	OTC	BJYAY	Grupo Financiero Mexival		
Boustead Holdings Berhad	OTC	BSTHY	Class "C"	OTC	MEXAY
Genting Berhad	OTC	GEBEY	Grupo Financiero Prime Int'l,		
Inter-Pacific Industrial			S.A. de CV	OTC	GRPOTC
Group Berhad	OTC	IPIGY	Grupo Financiero Probursa "B"	OTC	GRFPY
Kesang Corporation Berhad	OTC	KSGCY	Grupo Financiero Probursa "C"	OTC	GRFNY
Kuala Lumpur Kepong Berhad	OTC	KLKOTC	Grupo Financiero Serfin	NYSE	SFN
Lion Land Berhad	OTC	LONLY	Grupo Industrial Durango	NYSE	GID
Malayan United Industries			Grupo Industrial Maseca		
Berhad	OTC	MUIOTC	S.A. de C.V.	NYSE	MSK
MBf Holdings Berhad	OTC	MBFHY	Grupo Industrial Maseca		
Perlis Plantations Berhad	OTC	PPBOTC	S.A. de C.V. "A"	OTC	GIMAY
Resorts World Berhad	OTC	RSWSY	Grupo Industrial Maseca		
Selangor Properties Berhad	OTC	SELOTC	S.A. de C.V."B"	OTC	GRBMY
Sime Darby Berhad	OTC	SIDBY	Grupo Iusacell, S.A. de C.V.		
Tenaga Nasional Berhad	OTC	TNABY	Series "D"	NYSE	CELD
			Grupo Iusacell, S.A. de C.V.		
Mexico			Series "L"	NYSE	CEL
Abaco Grupo Financiero,			Grupo Mexicano de Desarrollo,		
S.A. de C.V.	OTC	ABGFY	S.A. "B"	NYSE	GMDB
Apasco, SA de CV "A"	OTC	AASAY	Grupo Mexicano de Desarrollo,		
Apasco, SA de CV "B"	OTC	AASBY	S.A. "L"	NYSE	GMD
Banpais, S.A.	NYSE	BPS	Grupo Radio Centro, S.A. de C.V.	NYSE	RC
Bufete Industrial, S.A.	NYSE	GBI	Grupo Sidek, S.A. de C.V.	OTC	GPOSY
Cemex, S.A. B Shares	OTC	CMXBY	Grupo Sidek Series "L"	NYSE	SDK
Cifra, S.A. de C.V.	OTC	CFRAY	Grupo Simec, S.A. de C.V.	AMEX	SIM
Coca-Cola Femsa, S.A. de C.V.	NYSE	KOF	Grupo Situr, S.A. de C.V.	OTC	SITRY
Consorcio G Grupo Dina			Grupo Synkro, S.A. de C.V. "B"	OTC	GPSYY
SA de CV	NYSE	DIN	Grupo Syr, S.A. de C.V.	OTC	GSYOTC
Controladora Commercial			Grupo Televisa, S.A. GDR	NYSE	TV
Mexicana S.A.	OTC	CRRXY	Grupo Tribasa, S.A. de C.V.	NYSE	GTR
Corporacion Geo, S.A. de C.V.			IEM SA (Industria Electrica		
Reg S	None	GEOREGS	de Mexico)	OTC	IEMOTC
Corporacion Industrial SanLuis			Internacional de Ceramica B		
Ser A	OTC	CISAOTC	Shares	OTC	CEROTC
Corporacion Industrial SanLuis			Kimberly Clark	OTC	KCDMY
Ser A-1	OTC	CORSY	Ponderosa Industrial, S.A. de C.V.	OTC	PNDIY
Corporacion Industrial SanLuis			Sears Roebuck de Mexico, S.A.		
Ser A-2	OTC	CILSY	de C.V. GDR	None	SRMGDR
Corporacion Mexicana de Aviacion	OTC	CMXVY	Servicios Financieros Quadrum,		
Desc, Soc. de Fomento Indust.			S.A.	Nasdaq	QDRMY
Series C	OTC	DSFOTC	Telefonos de Mexico S.A. de		
E.P.N., S.A. de C.V.	OTC	EPNSY	C.V. Ser A	Nasdaq	TFONY
El Puerto de Liverpool, SA de			Telefonos de Mexico S.A. de		
CV GDR	None	EPLGDR	C.V. Ser L	NYSE	TMX
Empaques Ponderosa	OTC	EMPOTC	Tolmex, S.A. de C.V. "B" Shares	OTC	TLMXY
Empresas ICA-Sociedad			Transportacion Maritima		
Controladora	NYSE	ICA	Mexicana "A"	NYSE	TMMA
Far-Ben, S.A. de C.V.	OTC	FAROTC	Transportacion Maritima		
Grupo Casa Autrey	NYSE	ATY	Mexicana "L"	NYSE	TMM
Grupo Embotellador de Mexico			Tubos de Acero de Mexico, S.A.	AMEX	TAM
GDR	None	GEMGDR	Vitro, S.A. de C.V.	NYSE	VTO
Grupo Embotellador de Mexico,					
SA de CV	NYSE	GEM	**The Netherlands**		
Grupo Financiero Bancomer,			ABN Amro Holding N.V.	OTC	ARBLY
S.A. de C.V. GDR	None	GRFGDR	Aegon N.V.	NYSE	AEG
Grupo Financiero Inverlat, S.A.			Ahold N.V.	NYSE	AHO
de C.V.	OTC	GFIOTC	Akzo Nobel N.V.	Nasdaq	AKZOY
Grupo Financiero			Amev N.V.	OTC	AMVNY
Invermexico "B"	OTC	GFIMB	DSM N.V.	OTC	DSMKY
Grupo Financiero			Elsevier NV	OTC	ELNVY
Invermexico "C"	OTC	GFIMC	Heineken N.V.	OTC	HINKY

Non-US Company Stocks Available Through US Stock Markets (continued)

Company	Exchange	Symbol	Company	Exchange	Symbol
Hunter Douglas N.V.	OTC	HDOUY	Oil Search Ltd.	OTC	OISHY
Internationale Nederlanden					
Group	OTC	INLGY	**Peru**		
KLM Royal Dutch Airlines	NYSE	KLM	Banco Weise Limitado	NYSE	BWP
Koninklijke Bijenkorf Beheer					
KBB NV	OTC	KBBOTC	**The Philippines**		
Koninklijke Bolfwessanan NV	OTC	KNWSY	Manila Electric Company		
Koninklijke Nederlandsche			(Meralco)	OTC	MELOTC
Hoogovens EN	OTC	KNBOTC	Petron Corporation GDR	None	PETCOGDR
Memorex Telex N.V.	Nasdaq	MEMXY	Philippine Long Distance Tel.		
N.V. Konink. Neder. Vlieg.			GDR Com.	None	PHIGDR
Fokker	OTC	FOKKY	Philippine Long Distance Tel.		
N.V. Koninklijke KNP BT	OTC	NVKJY	GDR Pref.	None	PHLGDR
N.V. Verenigd Bezit	OTC	VNUNY	Philodrill Corporation, The	OTC	PHPOTC
Oce Van der Grinten NV	Nasdaq	OCENY	San Miguel Corp.	OTC	SMGBY
Philips N.V.	NYSE	PHG			
Polygram N.V. "New York Shares"	NYSE	PLG	**Portugal**		
Royal Dutch Petroleum Co.	NYSE	RD	Banco Comercial Portugues	NYSE	BPC
Royal Nedlloyd Group N.V.	OTC	RNGOTC	Espirito Santo Financial Holding		
Unilever N.V.	NYSE	UN	S.A.	NYSE	ESF
Van Ommeren Ceteco NV	OTC	VMMOTC			
Wolters Kluwer NV	OTC	WTKWY	**Singapore**		
			City Developments Ltd.	OTC	CDEVY
New Zealand			Cycle and Carriage Ltd.	OTC	CYCOTC
Brierley Investment Ltd.	OTC	BYILY	The Development Bank of		
Fletcher Challenge Ltd.			Singapore Ltd.	OTC	DEVBY
"Forests Div."	NYSE	FFS	GB Holdings	OTC	GBHLY
Fletcher Challenge Ltd.			Hai Sun Hup Group Ltd.	OTC	HISHF
"Ord. Division"	NYSE	FLC	Inchcape Berhad	OTC	INCOTC
New Zealand Petroleum			Keppel Corporation Ltd.	OTC	KPELY
Company	Nasdaq	NZPCY	Malayan Credit Ltd.	OTC	MLCOTC
Telecom Corporation of			Neptune Orient Lines Ltd.	OTC	NOLOTC
New Zealand Ltd.	NYSE	NZT	Overseas Union Bank, Ltd.	OTC	OUBOTC
			Sembawang Shipyards Ltd.	OTC	SSLOTC
Norway			Singapore Land Ltd.	OTC	SINPY
Bergesen D.Y. A/S (A Shares)	OTC	BEDAY	United Overseas Bank Ltd.	OTC	UOLOTC
Bergesen D.Y. A/S (B Shares)	OTC	BEDBY			
Hafslund Nycomed A/S "A"			**South Africa**		
Shares	OTC	HAFAY	Abercom Group Ltd.	OTC	ABGRY
Hafslund Nycomed A/S "B"			AE and CI Ltd.	OTC	AECLY
Shares	NYSE	HN	Afmin Holdings Ltd.	OTC	AHLOTC
Nora Industries A/S	OTC	NUIOTC	Afrikander Lease Ltd., The	OTC	AFLOTC
Norsk Data A/S	OTC	NORKZ	Anglo American Coal Corporation	OTC	ANAMY
Norsk Hydro A/S	NYSE	NHY	Anglo American Corporation		
Petroleum Geo-Services A/S	Nasdaq	PGSAY	of SA Ltd.	Nasdaq	ANGLY
Saga Petroleum "A"	OTC	SGABY	Anglo American Gold		
Saga Petroleum "B"	OTC	SAGB	Investment Co., Ltd	Nasdaq	AAGIY
Smedvig A.S.	OTC	SMEDY	Anglo American Investment		
Tomra Systems, A/S	OTC	TOMOTC	Trust Ltd	OTC	ANGVY
Unitor Ships Services A.S.	OTC	USSOTC	Anglo-Alpha Cement Ltd.	OTC	ANGAY
Vard A/S Class "A"	OTC	VARDY	Anglovaal Holdings Ltd.	OTC	ANAVY
Viking Media A/S	OTC	VIKOTC	Anglovaal Ltd. "A"	OTC	ANVAY
			Anglovaal Ltd. "Ord"	OTC	ANAVF
Pakistan			Anglovaal Ltd "N" GDR	None	ANAGDR
The Hub Power Company Ltd.			Barlow Ltd.	OTC	BRRAY
Reg S GDR	None	HPCLRS	Beatrix Mines	OTC	BTRXY
Pakistan Telecommunications			Blue Circle Cement Ltd.	OTC	BCLOTC
GDR	None	PKTLYGDR	Blyvooruitzicht Gold Mining		
			Co. Ltd.	Nasdaq	BLYVY
Papua New Guinea			Bracken Mines Ltd.	OTC	BRACY
Bougainville Copper Ltd.	OTC	BOCOY	Buffelsfontein Gold Mining Ltd.	Nasdaq	BFELY
Niugini Mining Ltd.	OTC	NGIMY	C.G. Smith Ltd.	OTC	CGSMY

Non-US Company Stocks Available Through US Stock Markets (continued)

Company	Exchange	Symbol	Company	Exchange	Symbol
Consolidated Modderfontein	OTC	CMDOTC	Randfontein Estates Gold		
Consolidated Murchison Ltd.	OTC	CMROTC	Mining Co. Witw	OTC	RANOTC
De Beers Consolidated Mines	Nasdaq	DBRSY	Rembrandt Group Ltd.	OTC	REMOTC
Deelkraal Gold Mining			Rustenberg Platinum Holdings	OTC	RPATY
Company Ltd.	OTC	DLKOTC	Samancor Ltd.	OTC	SMNCY
Doornfontein Gold Mining			Sasol Ltd.	Nasdaq	SASOY
Company	OTC	DORDY	Simer and Jack Mines Ltd.	OTC	SIJOTC
Driefontein Consolidated Ltd.	Nasdaq	DRFNY	The South African Breweries Ltd.	OTC	SABLY
Duiker Exploration Ltd.	OTC	DKEOTC	South African Land &		
Durban Roodeport Deep Ltd.	OTC	DURBY	Exploration Co., Ltd	OTC	STHAY
East Daggafontein Mines Ltd.	OTC	EDMOTC	South Roodeport Main Reef Areas	OTC	SROOTC
East Rand Gold and Uranium			Southvaal Holdings Ltd.	OTC	STHVY
Company Ltd.	OTC	EASRY	St. Helena Gold Mines Ltd.	Nasdaq	SGOLY
East Rand Proprietary Mines Ltd.	OTC	ERNDY	Stilfontein Gold Mining Company	OTC	STILY
Eastern Transvaal Consolidated			Sub Nigel Gold Mining Co Ltd	OTC	SNGOTC
Mines Ltd	OTC	ETCOTC	Tiger Oats Ltd.	OTC	TIOAY
Egoli Consolidated Mines Ltd.	OTC	EGOOTC	Transnatal Coal	OTC	TNCOTC
Elandsrand Gold Mining Co.	OTC	EGMOTC	Unisel Gold Mines Ltd.	OTC	UNSGY
Engen Ltd.	OTC	ENGNY	Vaal Reefs Exploration & Mining		
Ettington Investments Ltd.	OTC	ETTOTC	Company	Nasdaq	VAALY
Federale Mynbou Beperk	OTC	FMBOTC	Vereeniging Estates Ltd.	OTC	VEEOTC
Fedsure Holdings Ltd. "Ord"	OTC	FHLO	Vlakfontein Gold Mining Co. Ltd.	OTC	VLAKY
Fedsure Holdings Ltd.			Welkom Gold Mining Company		
"Preference"	OTC	FHLP	Ltd.	Nasdaq	WLKMY
Free State Consolidated Gold			West Rand Consolidated Mines		
Mines Ltd	Nasdaq	FSCNY	Ltd.	OTC	WRCOTC
Free State Development &			Western Areas Gold Mining Co.		
Invest Corp.	OTC	FSDOTC	Ltd.	OTC	WARSY
Genbel Investments Ltd.	OTC	GNBOTC	Western Deep Levels Ltd.	Nasdaq	WDEPY
Gencor Ltd.	OTC	GNCLY	Winkelhaak Mines Ltd.	OTC	WINKY
Gold Fields of South Africa	Nasdaq	GLDFY	Witwatersrand Nigel Ltd.	OTC	WWNOTC
Gold Fields Property Company			Zandpan Gold Mining Company		
Ltd.	OTC	GFPOTC	Ltd.	OTC	ZGMOTC
Grootvlei Proprietary Mines	OTC	GTPMY			
Harmony Gold Mining Company	OTC	HYGMY	**Spain**		
Hartebeestfontein Gold Mining	OTC	HBGDY	Banco Bilbao Vizcaya, S.A.	NYSE	BBV
Highveld Steel and Vanadium			Banco Bilbao Vizcaya, S.A.		
Corp.	Nasdaq	HSVLY	Ser "A"	NYSE	BVG+
Impala Platinum Holdings Ltd.	OTC	IMPAY	Banco Bilbao Vizcaya, S.A.		
Iscor Ltd.	OTC	ISCRY	Ser "B"	NYSE	BVGB
Johannesburg Consolidated			Banco Bilbao Vizcaya, S.A.		
Invest Company	OTC	JOHOTC	Ser C	NYSE	BVGC
Kinross Mines Ltd.	OTC	KNRSY	Banco Central		
Kloof Gold Mining Company Ltd.	Nasdaq	KLOFY	Hispanoamericano, S.A.	NYSE	BCM
Leslie Gold Mines Ltd.	OTC	LESGY	Banco de Santander	NYSE	STD
Loraine Gold Mines Ltd.	OTC	LORAY	Banco Espanol de Credito		
Lydenburg Platinum Ltd.	Nasdaq	LYDPY	(BANESTO)	OTC	BNSTY
Malbak Ltd.	OTC	MLBAY	Bankinter S.A.	OTC	BKISY
Messina Ltd.	OTC	MESOTC	Compania Sevillana de		
Middle Witwatersrand			Electricidad S.A.	OTC	COVDY
(Western Areas) Ltd	OTC	MWWOTC	Corporacion Bancaria de		
Modder B Gold Holdings Ltd.	OTC	MOBOTC	Espana S.A.	NYSE	AGR
New Wits Ltd.	OTC	NWLOTC	Corporacion Mapfre	OTC	CRFEY
O'Okiep Copper Company Ltd.	AMEX	OKP	Empresa Nacional de		
Orange Free State			Electricidad, S.A.	NYSE	ELE
Investments Ltd.	Nasdaq	OFSLY	Repsol S.A.	NYSE	REP
Palabora Mining Company Ltd.	OTC	PBOMY	Telefonica de Espana SA	NYSE	TEF
Pepkor Ltd.	None	PEPKYPG			
Rand Mines Ltd.	OTC	RMLOTC	**Sri Lanka**		
Rand Mines Properties Ltd.	OTC	RMPOTC	John Keells Holdings Ltd.	None	JKHGDR
Randex Ltd.	OTC	RNDXY			

Non-US Company Stocks Available Through US Stock Markets (continued)

Company	Exchange	Symbol	Company	Exchange	Symbol
Sweden			Attwoods PLC	NYSE	A
AGA AB "B" Shares	OTC	AGABY	Automated Security (Holdings)		
Asea AB "B" Shares	Nasdaq	ASEAY	PLC	NYSE	ASI
Astra Series "A"	OTC	ARRAY	B.A.T Industries P.L.C.	AMEX	BTI
Astra Series "B"	OTC	ARRBY	BAA PLC	OTC	BAAPY
Atlas Copco AB "A" Shares	OTC	ATLAOTC	Barclays Bank Capital Note		
Atlas Copco AB "B" Shares	OTC	ATLSY	Unit, Ser E	NYSE	BCB+
Electrolux AB	Nasdaq	ELUXY	Barclays Bank PLC	NYSE	BCS
Ericsson Telephone Company			Barclays Bank Preferred		
"B" Shares LM	Nasdaq	ERICY	(Series A)	NYSE	BCBA
Ericsson Telephone (LM)			Barclays Bank Preferred		
Debenture	Nasdaq	ERICZ	(Series B)	NYSE	BCBB
Esselte AB "B" Shares	OTC	EBBOTC	Barclays Bank Preferred		
Gambro AB	Nasdaq	GAMBY	(Series C)	NYSE	BCBC
Pharmacia AB	Nasdaq	PHARY	Barclays Bank Preferred		
Sandvik AB	OTC	SAVKY	(Series D)	NYSE	BCBD
SKF AB	Nasdaq	SKFRY	Bass PLC	NYSE	BAS
Volvo AB "B" Shares	Nasdaq	VOLVY	Bell Cablemedia PLC	Nasdaq	BCMPY
			Bespak PLC	OTC	BSPOTC
Switzerland			BET Public Ltd. Company	NYSE	BEP
BBC Brown Boveri Ltd.	OTC	BBOVY	Bio-Isolates (Holdings) PLC	OTC	BISOY
Ciba-Geigy AG	OTC	CBGXY	Blenheim Exhibitions Group PLC	OTC	BLEOTC
CS Holding	OTC	CSHKY	Blue Circle Industries PLC	OTC	BCLEY
Nestle S.A. Bearer Participation			BOC Group PLC, The	OTC	BOCNY
Cert.	OTC	NESAY	Body Shop International PLC	OTC	BDSPY
Nestle S.A. Registered Shares	OTC	NSRGY	Booker PLC	OTC	BKERY
Roche Holding Ltd.	OTC	ROHHY	Boots Company PLC, The	OTC	BOOTY
Sandoz, Ltd.	OTC	SDOZY	Bowater Industries PLC	Nasdaq	BWTRY
Swiss Bank Corporation	OTC	SWBKY	Brent Walker Group PLC	OTC	BWGOTC
Union Bank of Switzerland	OTC	UBSUY	British Airways PLC	NYSE	BAB
			British Bio-Technology		
Taiwan			Group PLC	Nasdaq	BBIOY
Chia Hsin Cement Corp. GDR	None	CHCGDR	British Gas Public Ltd. Company	NYSE	BRG
China Steel Corporation GDR	None	CHSGDR	British Petroleum P.L.C.	NYSE	BP
Micro-Electronics			British Steel PLC	NYSE	BST
Technology Inc.	None	MELGDR	British Telecommunications PLC	NYSE	BTY
Yageo Corporation GDR	None	YGOCYGDR	British Telecommunications PLC		
			"Interim"	NYSE	BTYP
Thailand			BTR PLC	OTC	BTRUY
Advanced Info Service PLC	OTC	ACITY	Burmah Castrol PLC	Nasdaq	BURMY
Asia Fiber Company Ltd.	OTC	ASFBY	Burton Group PLC	OTC	BURUY
Charoen Pokphand Feedmill			Cable and Wireless PLC	NYSE	CWP
Co., Ltd.	OTC	CPOKY	Cadbury Schweppes P.L.C.	Nasdaq	CADBY
Hana Microelectronics PLC	OTC	HANAY	Cantab Pharmaceuticals PLC	Nasdaq	CNTBY
Shinawatra Computer &			Caradon PLC	OTC	CAROTC
Communications PLC	OTC	SHWCY	Carlton Communications PLC	Nasdaq	CCTVY
Thai Telephone &			Charterhall PLC	OTC	CHALY
Telecommunication Reg S	None	TTTPRS	Chloride Group Ltd.	OTC	CDGPY
			Christian Salvesen PLC	OTC	CSALY
Turkey			Christies International PLC	OTC	CTTDY
Garanti Bankasi	OTC	TURKY	CML Microsystems PLC	OTC	CMLMY
Net Holding Inc.	OTC	NETHY	Coats Viyella PLC	OTC	COATY
Tofas Turk Otomobil Fabrikasi			Corporate Service Group P.L.C.	OTC	CSGOTC
Reg "S"	None	TOFAYPS	Courtaulds PLC	AMEX	COU
Turkiye Garanti Bankasi GDR	None	TURKYPGDR	Crossroads Oil Group PLC	OTC	CRSOY
			Danka Business Systems PLC	Nasdaq	DANKY
United Kingdom			The De la Rue Company P.L.C.	OTC	DLROTC
Airship Industry	OTC	AIRSY	Dixons Group PLC	OTC	DXNOTC
Albert Fisher Group	OTC	AFHGY	East Midlands Electricity PLC	OTC	EMELY
Allied Lyons	OTC	ALLYY	Eastern Electricity PLC	OTC	ESTNY
Associated British Foods	OTC	ASBFY	Egerton Trust PLC	OTC	EGTOTC
Astec (BSR) PLC	OTC	ASTCY			

Non-US Company Stocks Available Through US Stock Markets (continued)

Company	Exchange	Symbol	Company	Exchange	Symbol
Elf Aquitaine UK (Holdings) Series "A"	OTC	ELAOTC	Laura Ashley Holdings PLC	OTC	LARAY
Elf Aquitaine UK (Holdings) Series "B"	OTC	ELBOTC	Legal & General Group PLC	OTC	LGGNY
Elf Aquitaine UK (Holdings) Series "C"	OTC	ELCOTC	LEP Group PLC	Nasdaq	LEPGY
Elf Aquitaine UK (Holdings) Series "D"	OTC	ELDOTC	London Electricity PLC	OTC	LNDNY
Elf Aquitaine UK (Holdings) Series "E"	OTC	ELFEOTC	London Finance and Investment	OTC	LFIOTC
Elf Aquitaine UK (Holdings) Series "F"	OTC	ELFFOTC	London International Group	Nasdaq	LONDY
Elf Aquitaine UK (Holdings) Series "G"	OTC	ELFGOTC	Lonrho PLC	OTC	LNRHY
Elf Aquitaine UK (Holdings) Series "H"	OTC	ELFHOTC	Manweb PLC	OTC	MANWY
Elf Aquitaine UK (Holdings) Series "I"	OTC	ELFIOTC	Marks & Spencer	OTC	MSLOTC
English China Clays PLC	NYSE	ENC	Medeva PLC	AMEX	MDV
English China Clays AMPS Series "A"	OTC	ECAOTC	Micro Focus Group PLC	Nasdaq	MIFGY
Enterprise Oil PLC	NYSE	ETP	Midland Bank PLC Preference "A"	NYSE	MIBA
Enterprise Oil PLC Pref. Series "A"	NYSE	ETP+	Midlands Electricity PLC	OTC	MIDEY
Enterprise Oil PLC Pref. Series "B"	NYSE	ETPB	National Power PLC	OTC	NPWRY
Ethical Holdings PLC	Nasdaq	ETHCY	National Westminster Bank PLC	NYSE	NW
Eurotunnell PLC/Eurotunnel S.A.	OTC	ETNLY	National Westminster Bank PLC Ser A	NYSE	NW+A
Fisons PLC	Nasdaq	FISNY	National Westminster Bank PLC Ser B	NYSE	NW+B
Futuremedia PLC	Nasdaq	FMDAY	Neozyme II Corporation	Nasdaq	NIIUF
Futuremedia PLC Warrant	Nasdaq	FMDYW	NFC PLC	AMEX	NFC
General Electric Company P.L.C., The	OTC	GNELY	NFC PLC Rights	AMEX	NFC$
Gestetner Holdings PLC (Ordinary)	OTC	GEZOTC	NMC Group PLC	OTC	NMCOTC
GKN PLC	OTC	GKNOTC	Northern Electric PLC	OTC	NORLY
Glaxo Holdings P.L.C.	NYSE	GLX	Norweb PLC	OTC	NORWY
Gold Greenlees Trott PLC	OTC	GGTOTC	Pacific Basin Bulk Shipping Ltd.	Nasdaq	PBBUF
Govett & Company Ltd.	Nasdaq	GOVTY	Peninsular and Oriental Steam Navigation	OTC	PIAOTC
Govett Strategic Investment Trust PLC	OTC	GOVOTC	Pentos PLC	OTC	PENOY
Grand Metropolitan PLC	NYSE	GRM	Pittencrieff PLC	OTC	PNCIY
Great Universal Stores PLC	OTC	GUSOTC	Powergen PLC	OTC	PWGNY
Guinness PLC	OTC	GURSY	Premier Consolidated Oilfields PLC	OTC	PCOOTC
Hanson PLC	NYSE	HAN	Prudential Corporation PLC	OTC	PRUOTC
Hanson PLC Warrants	NYSE	HAN%	Racal Electronics PLC	OTC	RCALY
Hanson PLC Wts CLS "B"	AMEX	HANB	Rank Organization PLC, The	Nasdaq	RANKY
The Hartstone Group P.L.C.	OTC	HSTEY	Redland PLC	OTC	REDPY
Hillsdown Holdings PLC	OTC	HDNHY	Redland PLC (Series A)	OTC	REDPYA
Horace Small Apparel PLC	OTC	HSACY	Redland PLC (Series B)	PTC	REDPYB
HSBC Holdings PLC	OTC	HSBHY	Redland PLC (Series C)	OTC	REDPYC
Huntingdon International Holdings	NYSE	HTD	Redland PLC (Series D)	OTC	REDPYD
Imperial Chemical Industries, PLC	NYSE	ICI	Redland PLC (Series E)	OTC	REDPYE
Integrated Micro Products PLC	Nasdaq	IMPTY	Reed International PLC	OTC	RENEY
Invesco PLC	OTC	ISCOY	Regional Elec Co's Unit	OTC	ELCUY
Kingfisher PLC	OTC	KGFIY	Rentokil Group PLC	OTC	RTOKY
Ladbroke Group PLC	OTC	LADGY	Reuters Holdings PLC	Nasdaq	RTRSY
Lasmo PLC	NYSE	LSO	Rodime PLC	OTC	RODMY
Lasmo PLC Cumulative Dollar Pref	NYSE	LSOA	Rolls Royce PLC	OTC	RYCEY
			Rothmans International PLC	OTC	ROTHY
			Royal Bank of Scotland Pref A	NYSE	RBSA
			Royal Bank of Scotland Pref B	NYSE	RBSB
			Royal Bank of Scotland Pref C	NYSE	RBSC
			RTZ Corporation PLC, The	NYSE	RTZ
			Ryan Hotels PLC	OTC	RYHOTC
			Saatchi & Saatchi Company PLC	NYSE	SAA
			Sainsbury PLC, J.	OTC	SAINY
			Scantronic Holdings PLC	OTC	SCHOTC
			Scottish and Universal Investments PLC	OTC	SUIOTC
			Scottish Hydro-Electric PLC	OTC	SHYAY
			Scottish Power PLC	OTC	SPYAY
			Sears PLC	OTC	SEROTC

Non-US Company Stocks Available Through US Stock Markets (continued)

Company	Exchange	Symbol	Company	Exchange	Symbol
Sedgwick Group PLC	OTC	SDWOTC	Trinity International Holdings		
Seeboard PLC	OTC	SEEBY	PLC	OTC	TNYLY
Senetek PLC	Nasdaq	SNTKY	UK of GB and N. Ireland 3.5%		
Senetek PLC Class A Warrants	Nasdaq	SNTWF	War Loan ST	OTC	UKGOTC
Senetek PLC Class B Warrants	Nasdaq	SNTZF	Unigate PLC	OTC	UNLOTC
Shell Transport & Trading			Unilever PLC	NYSE	UL
Company Ltd	NYSE	SC	Unitech PLC	OTC	UNTKY
Siebe PLC	OTC	SIBEY	United Biscuits (Holdings) PLC	OTC	UTBTY
Signet Group PLC	Nasdaq	SIGGY	United Newspapers Public Ltd.		
Signet Group PLC			Company	Nasdaq	UNEWY
Convertible Preferred	Nasdaq	SIGGZ	Vickers Public Ltd. Company	OTC	VPLOTC
Signet Group PLC V.T.P.			Virtuality Group PLC	OTC	VRTGY
Series "A"	OTC	SIGVA	Vodafone Group Public Ltd.		
Signet Group PLC V.T.P.			Company	NYSE	VOD
Series "B"	OTC	SIGVB	Wace Group PLC	OTC	WACE
Signet Group PLC V.T.P.			Waste Management Int'l PLC	NYSE	WME
Series "C"	OTC	SIGVC	Wellcome PLC	NYSE	WEL
Signet Group PLC V.T.P.			Wembley PLC	OTC	WMBOTC
Series "D"	OTC	SIGVD	Williams Holdings	OTC	WODOTC
Signet Group PLC V.T.P.			Willis Corroon Group PLC	NYSE	WCG
Series "E"	OTC	SIGVE	WPP Group PLC	Nasdaq	WPPGY
SmithKline Beecham Group PLC	NYSE	SBH	Xenova Group PLC	NAS	XNVAY
SmithKline Beecham Group PLC			Xenova Group Unit	NAS	XNVAZ
(A Shares)	NYSE	SBE	Yorkshire Electricity Group PLC	OTC	YOREY
South Wales Electricity PLC	OTC	SOWLY	Zeneca Group PLC	NYSE	ZEN
South Western Electricity PLC	OTC	SWSTY			
Southern Electric PLC	OTC	SOELY	**Venezuela**		
System Designer PLC	OTC	SYPOTC	Ceramica Carabobo Series "A"	OTC	CRCAY
Systems Connection Group PLC	OTC	SONOTC	Ceramica Carabobo Series "B"	OTC	CRCBY
T & N PLC	OTC	TANOTC	Corimon C.A. S.A.C.A.	NYSE	CRM
Tarmac PLC (AMPS) Series "A"	OTC	TAAOTC	Dominguez y Cia. Caracas C.A.	OTC	DCIAY
Tarmac PLC (AMPS) Series "B"	OTC	TABOTC	Mantex, S.A.I.C.A. S.A.C.A.	OTC	MTXOTC
Tarmac PLC (AMPS) Series "C"	OTC	TACOTC	Mavesa, S.A.	OTC	MVSAY
Tarmac PLC (AMPS) Series "D"	OTC	TADOTC	Siderurgica Venezolana		
Tate and Lyle P.L.C.	OTC	TATYY	Sivensa (SIVENSA)	OTC	SVNZY
Tesco PLC	OTC	TESOY	Sudamtex de Venezuela, C.A.	OTC	SDPDY
Thorn EMI PLC	OTC	THEOTC	Venprecar C.A. GDR	None	VPCG
TI Group PLC	OTC	TIGUY			
Tiphook PLC	NYSE	TPH	**Zambia**		
Tomkins PLC	Nasdaq	TOMKY	Zambia Consolidated Copper		
Trafalgar House Public Ltd. Co.	OTC	THZOTC	Mines Ltd.	OTC	ZAMOTC
Transport Development					
Group Ltd.	OTC	TDMOTC	**Zimbabwe**		
			Mhangura Copper Mines Ltd.	OTC	MTDOTC

Sources: The Bank of New York (current as of October 1994); The Nasdaq Stock Market (current as of November 1994);
NYSE Fact Book, 1993 Data (current as of December 31, 1993)

Closed-End Country Funds

Fund Name	Stock Exchange	Fund Name	Stock Exchange
Argentina Fund	NYSE	Jakarta Growth Fund	NYSE
Asia Pacific Fund	NYSE	Japan Equity Fund	NYSE
Asia Tigers Fund	NYSE	Japan OTC Equity Fund	NYSE
Austria Fund	NYSE	Jardine FI China	NYSE
Brazil Fund	NYSE	Jardine FI India	NYSE
Brazilian Equity Fund	NYSE	Korea Equity Fund	NYSE
Canadian General Inv. Fund	Toronto	Korea Fund	NYSE
Chile Fund	NYSE	Korean Investment Fund	NYSE
China Fund	NYSE	L. Bros Latin Amer. Growth Fund	NYSE
Czech Republic Fund	NYSE	Latin America Equity Fund	NYSE
Emerging Mexico Fund	NYSE	Latin America Investment Fund	NYSE
Emerging Tigers Fund	NYSE	Malaysia Fund	NYSE
Europe Fund	NYSE	Mexico Fund	NYSE
European Warrant Fund	NYSE	Morgan St Africa Fund	NYSE
F&C Middle East Fund	NYSE	Morgan St Asia Fund	NYSE
Fidelity Emerging Asia Fund	NYSE	Morgan St India Fund	NYSE
Fidelity Ad Korea Fund	NYSE	New Germany Fund	NYSE
First Australia Fund	AMEX	New South Africa Fund	NYSE
First Iberian Fund	AMEX	Pakistan Investment Fund	NYSE
First Israel Fund	NYSE	Portugal Fund	NYSE
First Philippine Fund	NYSE	ROC Taiwan Fund	NYSE
France Growth Fund	NYSE	Schroder Asian Fund	NYSE
Emerging Germany Fund	NYSE	Scudder New Asia Fund	NYSE
Future Germany Fund	NYSE	Scudder New Europe Fund	NYSE
Germany Fund	NYSE	Singapore Fund	NYSE
Greater China Fund	NYSE	Southern Africa Fund	NYSE
Growth Fund of Spain	NYSE	Spain Fund	NYSE
GT Developing Mkts. Fund	NYSE	Swiss Helvetia Fund	NYSE
GT Greater Europe Fund	NYSE	Taiwan Equity Fund	NYSE
Herzfeld Caribbean Fund	Nasdaq	Taiwan Fund	NYSE
India Fund	NYSE	Templeton China Fund	NYSE
India Growth Fund	NYSE	Templeton Dragon Fund	NYSE
Indonesia Fund	NYSE	Templeton Vietnam Fund	NYSE
Irish Investment Fund	NYSE	Thai Capital Fund	NYSE
Italy Fund	NYSE	Thai Fund	NYSE
		Turkish Investment Fund	NYSE
		United Kingdom Fund	NYSE

Source: *The Wall Street Journal*; January 3, 1995

The Largest Initial Public Offerings of 1994

Issuer	Global Amount	Offering Price	Issuer	Global Amount	Offering Price
TeleDanmark	2,975.1	23.53	Morgan Stanley India Invest.	535.5	15.00
Istituto Nazionale Assicur.	2,866.6	15.25	India Fund	510.0	15.00
British Sky Broadcasting	1,374.9	24.05	GT Global Developing Mkts.	480.0	15.00
Pharmacia	1,101.6	15.30	SGS-Thomson Microelec.	467.3	22.25
Indosat	1,053.4	32.05	John Hancock Bank & Thrift	450.0	20.00
Global Privatization Fund	1,050.0	15.00	Nokia	423.9	40.38
Morgan Stanley Asia/Pacific	802.5	15.00	Vastar Resources	420.0	28.00
Templeton Dragon Fund	795.0	15.00	AK Steel Holding	412.9	23.50
OfficeMax	627.0	19.00	Western National	388.2	12.00
Huaneng Power Int'l	625.0	20.00	Liberty Property Trust	365.0	20.00
TeleWest Communications	615.6	28.50	First Indus. Realty Trust	356.6	23.50
DeBartolo Realty	560.5	14.75	RCM Strategic Global	350.1	12.50

Source: Securities Data Company; *The Wall Street Journal*, January 3, 1994

Top 50 Emerging-Market Companies

Rank	Company	Country	Market Value ($ bil.)
1	Telefonos de Mexico (Telmex)	Mexico	32.94
2	Korea Electric Power	Korea	20.76
3	Cathay Life Insurance	Taiwan	14.50
4	Telebras	Brazil	11.22
5	Eletrobras	Brazil	10.26
6	Grupo Financiero Banacci	Mexico	9.89
7	YPF	Argentina	9.29
8	Grupo Carso	Mexico	9.18
9	Hua Nan Bank	Taiwan	8.99
10	Grupo Televisa	Mexico	8.98
11	Cifra	Mexico	8.73
12	Telecomasia	Thailand	8.56
13	Telefonica de Argentina	Argentina	8.51
14	First Commercial Bank	Taiwan	8.09
15	Cemex	Mexico	7.73
16	Pohang Iron & Steel	Korea	7.59
17	Petrobras	Brazil	7.50
18	Bangkok Bank	Thailand	7.06
19	Chang Hwa Bank	Taiwan	7.01
20	Samsung Electronics	Korea	6.79
21	China Steel	Taiwan	6.65
22	Telecom Argentina	Argentina	6.36
23	San Miguel	Philippines	6.01
24	Endesa	Chile	5.91
25	Siam Cement	Thailand	5.05
26	Vale do Rio Doce	Brazil	4.92
27	Grupo Financiero Bancomer	Mexico	4.75
28	Telecomunicacoes de Sao Paulo (Telesp)	Brazil	4.67
29	Tolmex	Mexico	4.58
30	Telefonos de Chile	Chile	4.49
31	COPEC	Chile	4.37
32	Indocement Tunggal Prakarsa	Indonesia	4.34
33	Nan Ya Plastics	Taiwan	4.28
34	Kimberly Clark de Mexico	Mexico	4.21
35	Banco Bradesco	Brazil	4.08
36	Manila Electric	Philippines	3.97
37	Formosa Plastics	Taiwan	3.90
38	Philippine Long Distance Telephone	Philippines	3.78
39	Thai Farmers Bank	Thailand	3.78
40	Int'l Commercial Bank of China	Taiwan	3.76
41	Goldstar	Korea	3.44
42	Shinawatra Computer & Communs.	Thailand	3.41
43	Land & House	Thailand	3.39
44	Empresas La Moderna	Mexico	3.34
45	Reliance Industries	India	3.24
46	Hyundai Motor	Korea	3.24
47	Thai Airways International	Thailand	3.17
48	Advanced Info Service	Thailand	3.10
49	Krung Thai Bank	Thailand	3.09
50	Ayala	Philippines	3.09

Source: Morgan Stanley Capital International; *Business Week*, July 11, 1994

50 US Companies with the Largest Non-US Sales

Rank	Company	Non-US Sales ($ mil.)	Total Sales ($ mil.)	Foreign as % of Total
1	Exxon	75,369	97,825	77.3
2	General Motors	38,646	138,220	28.0
3	Mobil	38,535	57,077	67.5
4	IBM	37,013	62,716	59.0
5	Ford Motor	32,860	108,521	30.3
6	Texaco	24,292	45,395	53.5
7	Citicorp	20,762	32,196	64.5
8	El du Pont de Nemours	16,756	32,621	51.4
9	Chevron	16,601	40,352	41.1
10	Procter & Gamble	15,856	30,433	52.1
11	Philip Morris Cos	15,315	50,621	30.3
12	Hewlett-Packard	10,971	20,317	54.0
13	American Intl Group	10,148	20,135	50.4
14	General Electric	10,036	60,562	16.6
15	Coca-Cola	9,351	13,957	67.0
16	Xerox	9,242	19,434	47.6
17	Digital Equipment	9,152	14,371	63.7
18	Dow Chemical	8,775	18,060	48.6
19	United Technologies	8,148	21,081	38.7
20	Eastman Kodak	7,980	16,364	48.8
21	Motorola	7,450	16,963	43.9
22	ITT	7,411	22,762	32.6
23	Johnson & Johnson	6,935	14,138	49.1
24	Minn Mining & Mfg	6,894	14,020	49.2
25	PepsiCo	6,712	25,021	26.8
26	JP Morgan & Co	6,255	11,941	52.4
27	Chrysler	5,753	43,600	13.2
28	Amoco	5,740	25,793	22.3
29	AT&T	5,576	67,156	8.3
30	UAL	5,560	14,511	38.3
31	Chase Manhattan	5,545	11,417	48.6
32	Sara Lee	5,172	14,580	35.5
33	Bank of Boston	4,962	7,396	67.1
34	Goodyear Tire & Rubber	4,866	11,643	41.8
35	Bankers Trust New York	4,858	7,800	62.3
36	Bristol-Myers Squibb	4,686	11,413	41.1
37	Colgate-Palmolive	4,608	7,141	64.5
38	Merck	4,584	10,498	43.7
39	Atlantic Richfield	4,373	17,189	25.4
40	Intel	4,366	8,782	49.7
41	Salomon	4,361	8,799	49.6
42	CPC International	4,326	6,738	64.2
43	RJR Nabisco	4,200	15,104	27.8
44	American Express	4,180	14,173	29.5
45	Merrill Lynch	4,150	16,588	25.0
46	Aflac	4,127	5,001	82.5
47	Woolworth	4,028	9,626	41.8
48	AMR	3,909	15,816	24.7
49	Alcoa	3,777	9,056	41.7
50	Unisys	3,670	7,743	47.4

Source: *Forbes*, July 18, 1994

Top 25 US Export Markets

Rank	Country	1993 Exports ($ bil.)
1	Canada	100.2
2	Japan	48.0
3	Mexico	41.6
4	United Kingdom	26.4
5	Germany	19.0
6	Taiwan	16.3
7	South Korea	14.8
8	France	13.3
9	Netherlands	12.8
10	Singapore	11.7
11	Hong Kong	9.9
12	Belgium-Luxembourg	9.4
13	China	8.8
14	Australia	8.3
15	Switzerland	6.8
16	Saudi Arabia	6.7
17	Italy	6.5
18	Malaysia	6.1
19	Brazil	6.0
20	Venezuela	4.6
21	Israel	4.4
22	Spain	4.2
23	Argentina	3.8
24	Thailand	3.8
25	Philippines	3.5

Source: *Business America*, April 1994

Top 25 US Supplier Countries

Rank	Country	1993 Imports ($ bil.)
1	Canada	110.9
2	Japan	107.3
3	Mexico	39.9
4	China	31.5
5	Germany	28.6
6	Taiwan	25.1
7	United Kingdom	21.7
8	South Korea	17.1
9	France	15.2
10	Italy	13.2
11	Singapore	12.8
12	Malaysia	10.6
13	Hong Kong	9.6
14	Thailand	8.5
15	Venezuela	8.1
16	Saudi Arabia	7.7
17	Brazil	7.5
18	Switzerland	6.0
19	Netherlands	5.5
20	Indonesia	5.4
21	Belgium-Luxembourg	5.4
22	Nigeria	5.3
23	Philippines	4.9
24	India	4.6
25	Sweden	4.5

Source: *Business America*, April 1994

Top 25 US Trade Surplus Countries

Rank	Country	1993 US Surplus Positions ($ bil.)
1	Netherlands	+7.4
2	Australia	+5.0
3	United Kingdom	+4.6
4	Belgium-Luxembourg	+4.0
5	Argentina	+2.6
6	Turkey	+2.2
7	Egypt	+2.2
8	Mexico	+1.7
9	Russia	+1.2
10	Spain	+1.2
11	Chile	+1.1
12	United Arab Emirates	+1.1
13	Panama	+0.9
14	Switzerland	+0.8
15	Iran	+0.6
16	Bahrain	+0.6
17	Greece	+0.5
18	Paraguay	+0.5
19	Poland	+0.5
20	Brunei	+0.4
21	Morocco	+0.4
22	Jamaica	+0.4
23	El Salvador	+0.4
24	Bahamas	+0.4
25	South Africa	+0.4

Source: *Business America*, April 1994

Top 25 US Trade Deficit Countries

Rank	Country	1993 US Deficit Positions ($ bil.)
1	Japan	-59.3
2	China	-22.8
3	Canada	-10.8
4	Germany	-9.6
5	Taiwan	-8.9
6	Italy	-6.8
7	Thailand	-4.8
8	Malaysia	-4.5
9	Nigeria	-4.4
10	Venezuela	-3.5
11	Indonesia	-2.7
12	South Korea	-2.3
13	Sweden	-2.2
14	France	-2.0
15	Angola	-1.9
16	India	-1.8
17	Brazil	-1.4
18	Philippines	-1.4
19	Singapore	-1.1
20	Saudi Arabia	-1.0
21	Gabon	-0.9
22	Kuwait	-0.8
23	Sri Lanka	-0.8
24	Finland	-0.8
25	Norway	-0.7

Source: *Business America*, April 1994

25 Largest Foreign Investors in the US

Rank	Company	Country	US Investments	% owned	1993 Sales ($ mil.)
1	Seagram Co Ltd	Canada	EI du Pont de Nemours	24	36,516
			JE Seagram	100	
2	Royal/Dutch Shell Group	Netherlands/UK	Shell Oil	100	20,853
3	British Petroleum	UK	BP America	100	16,006
4	Sony Corp.	Japan	Sony Music Entertainment	100	12,195
			Sony Picture Entertainment	100	
			Sony Electronics	100	
5	Grand Metropolitan	UK	Burger King	100	11,775
			Pillsbury	100	
			Heublein	100	
			Pearle Vision	100	
			Other companies	100	
6	Hanson	UK	Hanson Industries	100	10,948
			Quantum Chemical	100	
			Smith Corona	48	
			Ground Round Restaurants	33	
			Marine Harvest International	27	
7	Tengelmann Group	Germany	Great A&P Tea	53	10,384
8	Nestle/L'Oreal	Switzerland/ France	Nestle USA	100	9,993
			Alcon Laboratories	100	
			Cosmair	>50	
9	B.A.T Industries/ Imasco	UK/Canada	Brown & Williamson Tobacco	100	9,440
			Farmers Group	100	
			Hardee's Food Systems	100	
10	Toyota Motor Corp./ Nippondenso	Japan	Toyota Motor Mfg.	100	9,400
			New United Motor Mfg.	50	
			Nippondenso America	100	
11	Petroleos de Venezuela	Venezuela	Citgo Petroleum	100	9,107
12	Unilever	Netherlands/UK	Unilever United States	100	8,970
13	Delhaize "Le Lion"	Belgium	Food Lion	25	7,610
14	Ahold	Netherlands	First National Supermarkets	100	7,269
			BI-LO	100	
			Tops Markets	100	
			Giant Food Stores	100	
			Red Food Stores	100	
15	Philips Electronics NV/ Polygram NV	Netherlands	Philips Electronics NA	100	7,114
			Whittle Communications LP	25	
			PolyGram Records	100	
16	Hoechst AG	Germany	Hoechst Celanese	100	6,899
17	Siemens AG	Germany	Siemens Corp.	100	6,537
			Osram Sylvania	100	
18	AXA	France	Equitable Cos.	49	6,480
19	Bayer	Germany	Miles	100	6,459
20	Matsushita Electric Industrial	Japan	Matsushita Electric Corp. (Am)	100	6,300
			MCA	100	
21	Rhone-Poulenc SA	France	Rhone-Poulenc Rorer	68	6,255
			Rhone Poulenc Inc.	100	
22	Franz Haniel & Cie	Germany	Scrivner	100	6,000
22	Honda Motor Co.	Japan	Honda of America Mfg.	100	6,000
24	Ito-Yokado/Seven-Eleven	Japan	Southland	64	5,781
25	ABB Asea Brown Boveri	Sweden/ Switzerland	Asea Brown Boveri	100	5,600

Source: *Forbes*; July 18, 1994

THE COMPANY PROFILES

ABB ASEA BROWN BOVERI LTD

OVERVIEW

ABB Asea Brown Boveri Ltd is the world's leading electrical engineering joint venture, jointly owned by public companies ASEA AB of Sweden and BBC Brown Boveri of Switzerland. Its main activities are power generation, transmission and distribution, industrial and building systems, and rail transportation. It also operates a financial services unit to support its many construction and engineering projects. ABB is made up of 1,300 companies in 140 countries.

Swedish CEO Percy Barnevik has been a driving force in the globalization of the company. He describes ABB as a "multi-domestic" corporation with a decentralized structure (its Zurich headquarters employs only 176 people, down from 2,000 in 1988), with national subsidiaries closely linked to their local customers and labor force.

ABB is investing heavily in Eastern Europe and China as growth areas, while cutting factories and employees in the US and Western Europe. Barnevik has shelled out over $2 billion in Eastern Europe and China in the 1990s, despite the recession in Europe and the dearth of available capital.

WHEN

Asea Brown Boveri (ABB) was formed in 1988 when 2 competitive giants, ASEA AB of Sweden and BBC Brown Boveri of Switzerland, combined their electrical engineering and equipment businesses. Percy Barnevik, head of ASEA, became CEO of the new company.

Ludwig Fredholm had founded ASEA in Stockholm in 1883 as Electriska Aktiebolaget to manufacture engineer Jonas Wenstrom's electric dynamo. In 1890 he merged his company with Wenstrom's brother's company to form Allmänna Svenska Electriska Aktiebolaget (ASEA), which became a pioneer in industrial electrification. Ailing from the mismanagement of Gustaf de Laval (in control from 1896 to 1903), ASEA turned to J. Sigfrid Edstrom (former manager of Gothenburg Tramways Company), who remained in power until WWII. Under Edstrom the company participated in its first railway electrification project and in the 1920s and 1930s provided locomotives and other equipment for Sweden's national railway. ASEA became one of Sweden's largest electric equipment makers by buying its rival, Elektromekano, in 1933; it entered the US market in 1947, while continuing to expand at home and abroad. In 1962 ASEA bought 20% of electric appliance maker Electrolux and formed Scandinavian Glasfiber with Owens-Corning Fiberglas (US). ASEA formed the nuclear power venture ASEA-ATOM with the Swedish government in 1968, buying full control in 1982.

BBC Brown Boveri had been formed as a partnership, Brown, Boveri, and Company, by Charles Brown and Walter Boveri in Baden, Switzerland, in 1891 to produce electrical generation equipment. It produced the first steam turbines in Europe (1900). BBC estab-lished companies in Germany (1893), France (1894), and Italy (1903) to produce and distribute its steam and gas turbine equipment. After WWII the company diversified into nuclear power generating equipment. Electrical machinery production expanded with the purchase of Maschinenfabrik Oerlikon (1967), a Swiss company that manufactured electrical equipment in France and Spain. In 1979 BBC formed a joint venture with Gould (US) to produce electrical equipment.

In an unusual merger, both ASEA and BBC withheld certain assets, such as ASEA's holdings in Electrolux, from the combination, and each company continues as a separate entity, sharing equal ownership of the new company. ABB formed 2 joint ventures with Westinghouse in 1988, one to produce turbines and generators, the other to make electrical transmission equipment. In 1989 ABB bought Westinghouse's half of the transmission joint venture. The purchase of Cincinnati Milacron in 1990 enhanced ABB's industry automation and environmental control systems segments.

In 1992 ABB led a consortium that was awarded a $1.25 billion contract to build one of the world's largest hydroelectric plants in Iran. In 1993 ABB closed 15 plants around the world and cut its work force by 7,000. It spent 8% ($2.3 billion) of 1993 sales on R&D. Also that year Barnevik announced plans to invest $1 billion in expansion in Asia.

By mid-1994 the company had a total of 12 joint ventures operating in Russia. Restructuring continued in 1994; the total work force was reduced to 200,000 by year end. In 1995 ABB announced it might consolidate its parent and ABB into one company.

Nasdaq symbol: ASEAY (ASEA AB, ADR)
OTC symbol: BBCBY (BBC Brown Boveri, ADR)
Fiscal year ends: December 31

Co-Chairman: Peter Wallenberg, age 68
Co-Chairman: David de Pury, age 51
President and CEO: Percy Barnevik, age 53
**Senior Corporate Officer, Corporate Staff
Coordination:** Thomas Gasser, age 61
Senior Corporate Officer (R&D): Craig Tedmon,
age 55
**EVP; CEO and President, Asea Brown Boveri
(US):** Robert E. Donovan, age 53
CFO, Asea Brown Boveri (US): Timothy Powers
VP Human Resources, Asea Brown Boveri (US):
Richard Walsh
Auditors: KPMG Klynveld Peat Marwick;
Goerdeler SA

HQ: PO Box 8131, CH-8050 Zurich, Switzerland
Phone: +41-1-317-71-11
Fax: +41-1-311-98-17
US HQ: Asea Brown Boveri Inc., 500 Merritt 7,
Norwalk, CT 06856
US Phone: 203-750-2200
US Fax: 203-750-2263

ABB operates through 1,300 companies
worldwide. Major offices are located in Australia,
Austria, Brazil, Canada, Finland, France,
Germany, India, Italy, the Netherlands, Norway,
Spain, Sweden, Switzerland, the UK, and the US.

	1993 Sales	
	$ mil.	% of total
Western Europe	15,533	54
North & South America	5,573	20
Asia/Pacific	3,625	13
Central & Eastern Europe	465	2
Middle East & North Africa	2,130	8
Other countries	989	3
Total	**28,315**	**100**

	1993 Sales		1993 Operating Income	
	$ mil.	% of total	$ mil.	% of total
Industrial & building systems	11,934	36	649	29
Power plants	7,864	24	739	33
Power transmission & distribution	6,597	20	520	24
Transportation	2,757	8	84	4
Financial services	362	1	232	10
Other	3,534	11	(43)	—
Adjustments	(4,733)	—	—	—
Total	**28,315**	**100**	**2,181**	**100**

Selected Products and Services

AC and DC drives	Power plants
Electrical cables and capacitors	Project and trade finance
Indoor climate control systems	Rail systems
Light-rail vehicles	Relays
Locomotives	Robotics
Low- and medium-voltage systems	Rolling stock
Metros	Signaling systems
Monitoring and control instrumentation	Switchgears
Motors	Trains
Power plant control systems	Transformers
	Treasury centers
	Waste handling systems

Alcatel Alsthom	Gerber Scientific	Mitsubishi
Allied Waste	Halliburton	Nippon Steel
Ashland Oil	Hitachi	Peter Kiewit
Bechtel	Honeywell	Sons'
Black and Veatch	Ingersoll-Rand	Rolls-Royce
Broken Hill	International	Siemens
Browning-Ferris	Power	Teledyne
Cooper Industries	Machines	Thyssen
Daimler-Benz	Johnson	Toshiba
Duke Power	Controls	Vanguard
Eaton	LTV	Automation
Fluor	Mannesmann	Westinghouse
GEC	Mark IV	WMX
General Electric	McDermott	Technologies
General Signal	Medar	

	Annual Growth	1984	1985	1986	1987	1988	1989	1990	1991	1992	1993
Sales ($ mil.)	9.7%	—	—	—	—	17,832	20,560	26,688	28,883	29,615	28,315
Net income ($ mil.)	(29.3%)	—	—	—	—	386	589	590	609	505	68
Income as % of sales	—	—	—	—	—	2.2%	2.9%	2.2%	2.1%	1.7%	0.2%
Employees	4.0%	—	—	—	—	169,459	189,493	215,154	214,399	213,407	206,490

1993 Year-end:
Debt ratio: 62.1%
Return on equity: 1.8%
Cash (mil.): $5,700
Current ratio: 1.22
Long-term debt (mil.): $3,195
Assets (mil.): $24,904

Net Income ($ mil.)
1988–93

ACCOR SA

OVERVIEW

Accor, near Paris, offers the world's most comprehensive range of hospitality services, operating restaurants, cruise lines, railroad services, and institutional catering as well as more than 2,000 hotels. It is also part owner (with the US's Carlson Companies) of one of the world's largest travel agency networks. Although Accor has tried to build up its luxury hotel chain Sofitel, its strength lies in moderate- and budget-priced hotels.

But Accor has been feeling growing pains and an identity crisis in recent years. Its fast growth in Europe left it with reduced occupancy rates during the European recession. This hit the company hard because unlike many hotel companies it owns 50% of its hotels, rather than simply managing chains, as many other leading hoteliers do (including its US partner Carlson, with Radisson). Moreover, the performance of its luxury Sofitel chain has been particularly disappointing as travelers become more budget-minded.

Accor has undertaken an aggressive growth program in Asia, where it is strong in developing markets, including Vietnam. It plans to take much less of an ownership role than a developmental and managerial role in these new ventures. In addition, Accor has taken steps to reduce its holdings in Sofitel, sell off other assets, such as most of its restaurant holdings, and simplify its hotel portfolio by merging some of its hotels.

WHEN

Until Gérard Pélisson and Paul Dubrule built their first hotel in 1967, French hotels were generally either quaint old inns or very expensive luxury hotels in cities. Pélisson and Dubrule's Novotel pioneered the development of standardized midprice hotels on the American model. The pair went on to open the Ibis Hotel in 1973 and bought the Mercure chain in 1975. By 1979, when it opened its first US hotel in Minneapolis, Novotel was Europe's #1 hotel chain, operating 184 hotels in Europe, Africa, South America, and the Far East.

Dubrule and Pélisson married their growing hotel business to Jacques Borel International, forming Accor in 1983. Jacques Borel had started out with one restaurant in 1957 and was Europe's #1 restaurateur by 1975, when he took over Belgium's Sofitel luxury hotels. Losses in the hotel game compelled Borel to sell Sofitel to Dubrule and Pélisson in 1980, making the company one of the world's top 10 hotel operators — a list traditionally dominated by American chains. They picked up the rest of Borel's empire in 1983, launching Accor into the restaurant business.

Accor started offering package vacation tours in 1984, after buying a majority stake in Africatours (the largest tour operator to Africa), then expanded its offerings to the South Pacific, Asia, and the Americas by buying Ted Cook's Islands in the Sun (1986), Asietours (1987), and Americatours (1987).

The company opened its first budget hotels (Formule 1) in France in 1985. Accor started marketing Paquet cruises aboard the *Mermoz* cruise ship in 1986. The Hotelia chain, offering senior citizens hotel service with in-house medical care, opened in 1987. That same year Accor opened the Parthenon chain of residential hotels in Brazil.

In 1988 the company and several partners opened Cipal-Parc Astérix, a theme park 20 miles north of Paris, based on a cartoon character living in Gaul. That same year Accor lost out to British bookmaker Cyril Stein in a bidding war for Hilton International.

Faced with a mature European market and taking advantage of a favorable dollar-franc exchange rate, Accor bought Dallas-based budget hotel chain Motel 6 for $1.3 billion in 1990. Accor had been a minor player in the US for more than a decade, but with the purchase of Motel 6 it finally achieved a significant North American presence. However, Accor also acquired Motel 6's heavy debts, which impaired profitability. The next year Accor purchased Regal Inns in the US for $85 million.

Also in 1990 Accor joined Société Générale de Belgique to buy 26.7% of Belgium's Wagons-Lits, owner of about 300 hotels in Europe, Thailand, and Indonesia, and restaurants, caterers, and travel agencies throughout Europe. After a lengthy battle that involved both Belgian and EC antitrust officials, Accor was allowed to purchase a majority stake of Wagons-Lits.

In 1994 Accor's prospects were dimmed when the company lost a bidding war for Air France's luxury hotel chain, Meridien, to the UK's Forte PLC.

Principal exchange: Paris
Fiscal year ends: December 31

WHO

Co-Chairman: Paul Dubrule, age 59
Co-Chairman: Gérard Pélisson, age 61
Group VP Finance and Administration:
Michel Baillon
Group VP Human Resources: Volker Büring
President and CEO, Accor North America:
Patrick Bourguignon
VP Finance (CFO), Accor North America: Larry
Cross
Director Human Resources, Novotel (US):
Kathy Guilbert
Auditors: Deloitte & Touche Tohmatsu

WHERE

HQ: 2, rue de la Mare-Neuve, 91021 Évry Cedex,
France
Phone: +33-1-60-87-43-20
Fax: +33-1-60-77-04-58
US HQ: Accor North America Corp., 2 Overhill
Rd., Ste. 420, Scarsdale, NY 10583-5325
US Phone: 914-725-5055
US Fax: 914-725-5640

	1993 Sales		1993 Operating Income	
	FF mil.	% of total	FF mil.	% of total
France	11,001	38	850	42
South America	2,009	7	416	21
Other Europe	14,971	51	742	36
Other countries	1,134	4	25	1
Adjustments	—	—	(310)	—
Total	**29,115**	**100**	**1,723**	**100**

WHAT

	1993 Sales		1993 Operating Income	
	FF mil.	% of total	FF mil.	% of total
Hotels	9,660	33	886	51
Institutional catering	7,187	25	171	10
Travel agencies	4,313	15	61	4
Restaurants	3,519	12	193	11
Other & adjust.	4,436	15	412	24
Total	**29,115**	**100**	**1,723**	**100**

Selected Hotel Chains
Etap
Formule 1
Marine Hotel
Mercure
Motel 6
Novotel
Parthenon
Sofitel

Restaurants
B. Burger
Caféroute
L'Arche
Le Bœuf Jardinier
Pizza del Arte

Other Activities
Airport and airline catering
Car rentals (Europcar)
Cruises (Croisières Paquet)
Institutional catering
Package tours (Africatours,
Asietours, Americatours)
Theme park (Cipal-Parc
Astérix)
Travel agencies (Carlson
Wagonlit Travel)
Wholesale equipment
suppliers (Devimco)

HOW MUCH

$=FF5.91 (Dec. 31, 1993)	Annual Growth	1984	1985	1986	1987	1988	1989	1990	1991	1992	1993
Sales (FF mil.)	17.6%	6,755	8,053	9,558	11,121	12,337	14,311	13,776	14,038	30,569	29,115
Net income (FF mil.)	12.9%	142	178	232	334	469	606	795	766	582	423
Income as % of sales	—	2.1%	2.2%	2.4%	3.0%	3.8%	4.2%	5.8%	5.5%	1.9%	1.5%
Earnings per share (FF)	5.5%	16	19	21	24	29	35	40	36	36	26
Stock price – high (FF)	—	244	300	593	573	594	910	1,065	836	840	736
Stock price – low (FF)	—	202	235	285	280	272	567	644	585	474	560
Stock price – close (FF)	10.7%	238	285	478	316	594	906	679	649	615	593
P/E – high	—	15	16	28	24	20	26	26	23	23	28
P/E – low	—	13	12	13	12	9	16	16	16	13	22
Dividends per share (FF)	15.6%	4.90	5.80	6.50	8.50	10.50	12.50	15.00	16.00	18.00	18.00
Book value per share (FF)	20.6%	90	116	144	230	313	299	404	434	463	486
Employees	21.3%	—	—	37,182	56,254	61,352	45,630	41,976	45,743	—	143,740[1]

1993 Year-end:
Debt ratio: 59.5%
Return on equity: 5.5%
Cash (mil.): FF3,076
Long-term debt (mil.): FF14,456
No. of shares (mil.): 25
Dividends
  Yield: 3.0%
  Payout: 69.5%
Market value (mil.): $2,478
Sales (mil.): $4,926

Stock Price History
High/Low 1984–93

[1]Includes employees of unconsolidated companies

AIRBUS INDUSTRIE

Airbus is the world's #2 aircraft manufacturer (after Boeing), with 30% to 40% of commercial aircraft sales. The company is a European consortium that pools funds from shareholders Daimler-Benz (37.9%, Germany), British Aerospace (20%, UK), Aerospatiale (37.9%, France), and CASA (4.2%, Spain).

Fighting back from the worldwide slump in aircraft sales, Airbus closed several major deals in 1994, including a 30-airplane order from the International Lease Finance Corporation (US) worth at least $1.5 billion.

For years Airbus has operated behind a veil of fiscal secrecy; it has no reporting requirements and pays no taxes. Some estimates say the company has been given as much as $20 billion in subsidies since 1970. With the US's aerospace industry mired in

recession, the US government has accused Airbus of receiving unfair subsidies, allowing it to undercut prices.

Two projects will drive Airbus's growth into the next century: development of a "super jumbo" commercial airliner, dubbed the A3XX, capable of carrying up to 800 passengers, and production of a European military transport aircraft. In 1994 Airbus Finance Corporation was formed to help arrange financing for projects such as the A3XX and to limit shareholder liability.

A series of accidents, including 4 in the first half of 1994, has raised concerns about Airbus's groundbreaking fly-by-wire flight controller, a computerized system that lets pilots adjust the aircraft's control surfaces on the wings and tail.

By the 1970s, 3 US companies — Boeing, Lockheed, and McDonnell Douglas — dominated the commercial aircraft market. The British and French began discussing an alliance to build a competing jet as early as 1965, but political infighting crushed the spirit of cooperation. Finally, in 1969 the French and West Germans committed to build the Airbus A300. Airbus Industrie was born in France in 1970 as a Groupement d'Intérêt Économique (grouping of economic interest), with no operating capital of its own. Seed money came from Airbus's partners, Aerospatiale and Deutsche Airbus. CASA joined in 1971.

In 1974 the A300 entered service with Air France, but Airbus had trouble selling it outside member countries. In 1975 Bernard Lathière took over as CEO and hired former American Airlines president George Warde to help market the A300 in the US. In 1978 Warde's and Lathière's efforts paid off when Eastern Air Lines decided to buy the A300. That year Airbus launched the A310, a smaller, more fuel-efficient version of the A300. The UK joined the consortium in 1979.

By 1980 it had surpassed McDonnell Douglas and Lockheed, trailing only Boeing among the world's commercial jet makers. In 1984 the A320, with its computer-operated "fly-by-wire" system, was introduced. Orders poured in, making the A320 the fastest-selling jetliner in history.

In 1985 Lathière and Roger Béteille, the chief engineer credited as the father of Air-

bus, retired. Piloted by Jean Pierson, Airbus continued to gain popularity among the world's airlines but drew criticism from US jet makers, who accused the highly subsidized consortium of undercutting competitors by pricing its planes 15% to 25% lower.

In 1987 Airbus launched the A330 and A340, larger planes designed for medium- and long-range flights. Two years later it delivered its 500th airplane and introduced the A321, a stretched version of the A320. Airbus floated its first international bond issue in 1991 to help finance the A320 jet. It received a $6 billion order from Federal Express, one of its largest to date.

In 1992 the German government agreed to sell its 20% stake in Deutsche Airbus to Daimler-Benz, giving Daimler-Benz 100% ownership of the German partner. Also in 1992 Airbus announced plans to develop the A319, a smaller version of its A320.

In March 1993 Airbus delivered its 1,000th plane. The company was scrambling for customers, however, as worldwide sales stalled. Also in 1993 previous Boeing loyalists Virgin Airlines and Cathay Pacific, along with China Aviation Supplies, all placed orders. Meanwhile, Boeing began discussions with Airbus's partners on development of a super jumbo carrier while Airbus began talks with Japan about the same project.

In 1994 Airbus was awarded a 30-plane contract (10 orders, with an option for 20 more planes) from Singapore Airlines.

European consortium
Fiscal year ends: December 31

Supervisory Board Chairman: Edzard Reuter
Executive Board Chairman, CEO, and Managing Director: Jean Pierson
COO: Volker von Tein, age 54
Financial Director: Ian Massey
VP Human Relations: Thierry Schutte
Chairman and CEO, Airbus Industrie of North America: Jonathan M. Schofield
CFO, Airbus Industrie of North America: Robert Hein
VP Human Resources and Administration, Airbus Industrie of North America: Robert N. Ehrenfeld

HQ: One Rond Point Maurice Bellonte, F-31707 Blagnac Cedex, France
Phone: +33-61-93-34-31
Fax: +33-61-93-49-55
US HQ: Airbus Industrie of North America, Inc., 593 Herndon Pkwy., Ste. 300, Herndon, VA 22070
US Phone: 703-834-3400
US Fax: 703-834-3340

Largest Customers

Asia	Middle East
All Nippon Airways	Egyptair
Cathay Pacific	Kuwait Airways
China Airlines	
Indian Airlines	**North America**
Japan Air Systems	Air Canada
Korean Air	America West
Singapore Airlines	American
	Delta
Europe	Federal Express
Air France	ILFC
Alitalia	Mexicana
Iberia	Northwest
Lufthansa	United
Virgin	

	1994 New Aircraft Orders	
	No.	% of total
A319/A320/A321	95	76
A330/A340	30	24
Total	**125**	**100**

	Cumulative Orders	
	No.	% of total
A319/A320/A321	856	46
A300/A310	729	39
A330/A340	263	14
Total	**1,848**	**100**

Subsidiaries
Airbus Industrie of North America, Inc. (AINA, marketing subsidiary targeting the US and Canada)
Airbus Service Company, Inc. (ASCO, after-sales service for US and Canadian customers)

Associates
Belairbus (Belgium)
Fokker (the Netherlands)

Aircraft

Widebody-twins	Single-aisle
A300-600	A319
A300-600F	A320
A300-600R	A321
A300B2	
A300B4	**Four-engine**
A310-200	A340-200
A310-300	A340-300
A330	

Boeing	McDonnell Douglas
FlightSafety	Northrup Grumman
Ilyushin	Raytheon
Lockheed	

	Annual Growth	1985	1986	1987	1988	1989	1990	1991	1992	1993	1994
Sales ($ mil.)	11.6%	—	—	—	—	4,900	4,700	7,500	7,700	8,700	8,500
Aircraft orders	3.5%	92	170	114	167	421	404	101	136	38	125
Aircraft deliveries	12.7%	42	29	32	61	105	95	163	157	138	123
Order backlog	16.8%	152	288	370	470	774	1,038	952	836	667	615
Employees	(0.6%)	—	—	—	—	—	1,400	947	2,700	2,700	1,367

1994 Year-end:
Orders value (mil.): $9,100

Aircraft Deliveries 1985–94

AKZO NOBEL N.V.

OVERVIEW

If Akzo Nobel executives had wanted to paint the town after the merger that created their company was completed in early 1994, they would have had no problem. The marriage of the Netherlands's Akzo N.V. and Sweden's Nobel Industries created the world's largest paint manufacturer. The new company is the 9th largest chemical manufacturer in the world, with combined annual sales of approximately $11.7 billion.

Based in Arnhem, the Netherlands, Akzo Nobel can do more than paint a pretty picture. It is the world's #1 salt producer, selling under the Diamond Crystal and Sterling brand names in the US.

The company also produces basic and specialty chemicals, including polymer and rubber chemicals, catalysts, and detergents; coatings, including finishes and resins; industrial and textile fibers; and health care products, including oral contraceptives, antidepressants, blood testing systems, and veterinary products.

Since the merger Akzo Nobel has concentrated on streamlining its operations, including eliminating duplicated jobs. However, the company has also earmarked nearly $1 billion over the next few years for capital investments as it works to expand geographically, with an eye toward Asia.

WHEN

The merger with Nobel Industries was the latest in a series of combinations for Akzo.

Akzo traces its roots back to a German rayon and coatings producer, Vereinigte Glanzstoff-Fabriken, founded in 1899. The German company merged with Nederlandsche Kunstzijdebariek (known as NK or Enka) in 1929 to create Algemene Kunstzijde-Unie (AKU). NK had been founded in the Netherlands in 1911 to manufacture rayon. In 1928 the company built a plant near Asheville, North Carolina, in an area that later became the town of Enka, North Carolina.

In 1967, 2 Dutch companies, mineral and inorganic chemical producer Kon. Zout-Ketjen and chemical, drug, detergents, and cosmetics producer Kon. Zwanenberg Organon, merged to form Koninkijke Zout-Organon (KZO). In 1969 KZO acquired US-based International Salt. That same year KZO merged with AKU and gave birth to a bouncing baby acronym: Akzo.

Fibers were the company's main business during the 1970s, but when Aarnout Loudon became chairman in 1982, he began to reduce Akzo's reliance on them. In 1985 Akzo sold its largest US fiber business, American Enka, to BASF. Louden concentrated on building Akzo's specialty chemicals, coatings, and pharmaceuticals businesses.

In the late 1980s the company began a major restructuring, reorganizing operations, centralizing management, reducing its work force, and streamlining R&D.

In 1993 Akzo sold its paper and pulp business to Nobel. A few months later it got it back when it merged with Nobel.

Remembered best for the annual prizes that bear his name (which were first awarded in 1901 through a bequest in his will), Alfred Nobel was also the inventor of dynamite. In 1863 Nobel invented the blasting cap, making it possible to control the detonation of nitroglycerin. He then persuaded Stockholm merchant J. W. Smitt to help him finance Nitroglycerin Ltd. to manufacture and sell the volatile fluid (1864). Nobel's ongoing quest to improve nitroglycerin led to the invention of dynamite in 1867. In 1894 Nobel bought the Swedish munitions factory A. B. Bofors-Gullspång.

After Nobel's death in 1896, Bofors continued to produce munitions. Nitroglycerin Ltd. remained an explosives maker and in 1965 changed its name to Nitro Nobel. In 1978 Swedish industrialist Marcus Wallenberg bought Nitro Nobel for his KemaNord chemical group, known afterward as KemaNobel.

Industrialist Erik Penser started buying stakes in Bofors and KemaNobel, and by 1984 he controlled both, bringing the 2 companies together as Nobel Industries.

Heavy, risky investments by Penser led, in the summer of 1991, to financial collapse. All of Penser's holdings, including Nobel, were taken over by a government-owned bank, Nordbanken. In 1992 Nobel spun off its Consumer Goods business area to offset the nearly $1 billion that it lost in 1991.

In 1993 Akzo agreed to acquire Nobel from a Swedish government-owned holding company and in 1994 the merger was completed.

Nasdaq symbol: AKZOY (ADR)
Fiscal year ends: December 31

Chairman: C. J. A. van Lede, age 52
Secretary: E. C. E. van Rossum, age 52
EVP Financial Affairs: Syb Bergsma, age 58
EVP Human Resources: F. L. Vekemans, age 61
President and CEO, Akzo Nobel (US): Piet Provo
  Kluit
Auditors: KPMG Klynveld

HQ: Velperweg 76, PO Box 9300, 6800 SB
  Arnhem, The Netherlands
Phone: +31-85-66-44-33
Fax: +31-85-66-32-50
US HQ: Akzo Nobel Inc., 300 S. Riverside Plaza,
  Chicago, IL 60606
US Phone: 312-906-7500
US Fax: 312-906-7680

Akzo Nobel has operations in more than 50
countries.

	1993 Sales
	% of total
The Netherlands	32
North America	25
Germany	18
Other Europe	17
Other countries	8
Total	**100**

	1993 Sales		1993 Operating Income	
	Fl mil.	% of total	Fl mil.	% of total
Chemicals	5,816	35	351	31
Coatings	4,024	24	199	17
Pharma	3,421	21	590	52
Fibers	3,239	20	(21)	—
Other	9	0	(48)	—
Total	**16,509**	**100**	**1,071**	**100**

Chemicals
Catalysts
Chlorine
Detergents and surfactants
Functional chemicals
Industrial chemicals
Polymer chemicals
Pulp and paper chemicals
Rubber chemicals
Salt

Coatings
Aerospace finishes
Automotive finishes
Decorative coatings
Industrial coatings
Industrial wood finishes
Resins

Pharma
Analgesic cream
Antidepressants
Antipsychotics
Diagnostic systems
Menopause treatments
Oral contraceptives
Raw materials for the
  pharmaceutical industry
Veterinary products
Vitamins

Fibers
High-performance fibers
Industrial fibers
Industrial nonwoven fibers
Membranes
Textile fibers

BASF	Glaxo	PPG
Bayer	Hercules	Rhône-Poulenc
Cargill	Hoechst	Roche
Ciba-Geigy	Imperial Chemical	Samsung
Daimler-Benz	Koor	Sandoz
Dow Chemical	Kyocera	Sherwin-Williams
DuPont	Merck	Siemens
Elf Aquitaine	Monsanto	SmithKline
Fletcher Challenge	Morton	Beecham
Formosa Plastics	Novo Nordisk	Thomson SA

$=Fl1.94 (Dec. 31, 1993)	9-Year Growth	1984	1985	1986	1987	1988	1989	1990	1991	1992	1993
Sales (Fl mil.)	(0.0%)	16,520	18,010	15,615	15,535	16,581	18,736	17,246	16,851	16,713	16,509
Net income (Fl mil.)	(3.4%)	752	843	742	9,422	843	954	663	580	646	549
Income as % of sales	—	4.6%	4.7%	4.8%	60.7%	5.1%	5.1%	3.8%	3.4%	3.9%	3.3%
Earnings per share (Fl)	(6.1%)	20.60	21.36	21.06	23.46	20.96	23.05	15.06	12.89	14.06	11.67
Stock price – high (Fl)	—	123	143	182	178	158	157	141	135	166	201
Stock price – low (Fl)	—	77	101	140	80	85	125	64	75	124	135
Stock price – close (Fl)	7.3%	100	146	168	86	154	142	75	133	140	188
P/E – high	—	6	7	9	8	8	7	9	10	12	17
P/E – low	—	4	5	7	3	4	5	4	6	9	12
Dividends per share (Fl)	0.9%	6.00	6.60	6.60	6.60	7.50	8.00	6.50	6.50	6.50	6.50
Book value per share (Fl)	1.3%	101.80	104.16	107.40	94.80	106.61	103.84	104.50	103.62	110.40	113.99
Employees	1.2%	66,100	65,000	65,000	67,400	71,000	70,900	70,500	65,200	62,500	73,400

1993 Year-end:
Debt ratio: 37.9%
Return on equity: 10.4
Cash (mil.): Fl1,863
L-T debt (mil.): Fl12,339
No. of shares (mil.): 54
Dividends
  Yield: 3.5%
  Payout: 55.7%
Market value (mil.): $5,230
Sales (mil.): $8,510

**Stock Price History
High/Low 1984–93**

Financial information is for Akzo N.V. only.

ALCAN ALUMINIUM LIMITED

OVERVIEW

Alcan Aluminium has had its mettle tested by a flood of cheap Russian aluminum that poured into Western markets following the end of the Cold War, cutting the price of the metal in half. Alcan has been forced to cut costs and improve the efficiency of its operations to counter the Russian flood, and it hopes to bounce back when prices return to normal. Higher exports of its fabricated products lifted Alcan's profitability in 1994.

Based in Montreal, Alcan is one of the world's largest aluminum companies and is the largest North American manufacturer of fabricated aluminum products. The company mines bauxite and is involved in aluminum refining, manufacturing, marketing, and recycling. End-user markets include the container, packaging, transportation, electrical, and construction industries.

The Canadian multinational has operations on 4 continents, with its primary mining and alumina processing plants located in Canada, Ireland, and Jamaica.

In 1992 the company undertook a comprehensive, year-long study of the aluminum market as the basis for restructuring its operations. In 1993 Alcan increased its aluminum rolling capacity by 50% through expansions at its Logan plant in Kentucky and Norf unit in Germany.

WHEN

In 1900 the Aluminum Company of America (Alcoa) established its first Canadian smelter at Shawinigan Falls, Quebec. In 1928 Alcoa organized its Canadian and other foreign operations as a separate company (as mandated by a US antitrust divestment order), which took the name Aluminium Limited (changed to Alcan in 1966). Alcan retained close ties with Alcoa (the Mellon and Davis families held stock in both companies) and appointed Edward K. Davis (brother of former Alcoa chairman Arthur Vining Davis) as first president. At the time of its formation, Alcan existed primarily as a smelter for raw bauxite that came from a company-owned mine in British Guiana (later renamed Guyana).

After narrowly surviving the Great Depression years of the early 1930s, Alcan established a global sales force and a number of overseas plants in Europe, Australia, India, China, and Japan. The company profited tremendously from WWII, when the need for aluminum made it the world's largest smelter. At the end of the war, Alcan was 5 times larger than it had been in 1937.

In 1950 US courts, ruling on an earlier antitrust suit, ordered the Mellon and Davis families to end their joint ownership of Alcoa and Alcan. Both families opted to stay with Alcoa and sold most of their stock in Alcan. In 1954 Alcan opened its giant Kitimat-Kemano power complex in British Columbia.

During the 1960s and 1970s, the company, which had previously supplied aluminum to other companies for fabrication, started fabricating and distributing it themselves. In 1961 the company started fabricating products in the US in Oswego, New York.

In 1971 Alcan had to readjust its supply strategy when Guyana nationalized its raw resources. Six years later Jamaica (another major provider of bauxite) acquired 70% of Alcan's assets, which resulted in the formation of a joint venture (Jamalcan).

In 1979 David Culver became CEO of the company (the first non–Davis family member to hold the position) and led Alcan through an early 1980s recession with a massive cost-cutting campaign. In 1988 the company achieved record profits ($931 million). In 1989 Alcan commissioned the world's largest aluminum beverage can recycling plant in Berea, Kentucky.

The entrance of the countries of the former Soviet Union and other Eastern Bloc countries into the international aluminum market increased the 1991 primary aluminum supply by 25%. This swollen inventory, coupled with flat demand from industrial customers, resulted in a drastic drop worldwide in aluminum prices. Alcan shut down 8.5% of its smelting capacity in 1991 and cut its work force by 7.6% (4,200 workers).

Despite the slump in the aluminum market, Alcan added 497,500 tons of production capacity in 1992. In 1993 Alcan continued to cut costs aggressively in a bid to stay competitive. Costs fell by $387 million, of which $240 million was due to cost-cutting programs.

In 1994 Alcan's sales were up a whopping 21% to $8.3 billion and the company edged into the black for the first time in 4 years with a $96 million profit.

NYSE symbol: AL
Fiscal year ends: December 31

Chairman: David Morton, age 64, C$659,730 pay
President and CEO: Jacques Bougie, age 46,
  C$511,120 pay
VP and CFO: Suresh Thadhani
VP Personnel: Gaston Ouellet
President, Alcan Aluminum (US): David W.
  Hackbirth
Auditors: Price Waterhouse

HQ: 1188 Sherbrooke St. West,
  Montreal, Quebec H3A 3G2, Canada
Phone: 514-848-8000
Fax: 514-848-8115
US HQ: Alcan Aluminum Corporation,
  100 Erieview Plaza, PO Box 6977, Cleveland,
  OH 44101
US Phone: 216-523-6800
US Fax: 216-523-8243

Alcan produces alumina in 9 countries, has
fabricating plants in 18, and mines bauxite in 6.

	1993 Sales		1993 Net Income	
	$ mil.	% of total	$ mil.	% of total
US	2,689	37	(57)	—
Europe	2,432	34	(31)	—
Canada	911	13	(32)	—
Pacific	686	9	(9)	—
Latin America	468	6	(8)	—
Other countries	46	1	28	—
Adjustments	75	—	5	—
Total	**7,307**	**100**	**(104)**	**—**

	1993 Sales	
	$ mil.	% of total
Rolled products	2,732	40
Extruded products	1,199	17
Nonaluminum products	1,147	17
Ingot products	1,105	16
Other fabricated products	709	10
Adjustments	415	—
Total	**7,307**	**100**

Products

Rolled Products
Beverage containers
Building products
Foil
Packaging
Sheet

Extruded Products
Airplane components
Automotive bumpers
Doors
Truck chassis
Windows

Cast and Drawn Products
Electrical wire and cable
Pistons and other engine
  components

Rivets
Welding wire
Zippers

Other Products
Alumina
Aluminum fluoride
Bauxite
Cryolite
Film wrap
Specialty chemicals

ACX Technologies
Alcatel Alsthom
Alcoa
Alumax
Cyprus Amax
Inco
Industrial Aluminum Group
MAXXAM

Mitsui
Norsk Hydro
Ormet
Reynolds Metals
RTZ
Silgan
Thyssen
Tredegar Industries

	9-Year Growth	1984	1985	1986	1987	1988	1989	1990	1991	1992	1993
Sales ($ mil.)	3.0%	5,576	5,831	6,056	6,878	8,626	9,047	8,919	7,830	7,665	7,307
Net income ($ mil.)	—	284	(147)	277	433	931	835	543	(36)	(112)	(104)
Income as % of sales	—	5.1%	—	4.6%	6.3%	10.8%	9.2%	6.1%	—	—	—
Earnings per share ($)	—	1.15	(0.81)	1.09	1.68	3.85	3.58	2.33	(0.25)	(0.60)	(0.54)
Stock price – high ($)	—	18.33	13.89	15.39	25.25	22.25	21.13	24.50	24.00	22.75	22.38
Stock price – low ($)	—	10.44	10.11	12.28	12.61	15.67	20.17	16.63	18.00	15.25	16.88
Stock price – close ($)	5.5%	12.78	12.89	12.55	17.92	21.75	22.88	19.50	20.00	17.63	20.75
P/E – high	—	16	—	14	15	6	6	11	—	—	—
P/E – low	—	9	—	11	8	4	6	7	—	—	—
Dividends per share ($)	(6.1%)	0.53	0.49	0.35	0.39	0.59	1.12	1.12	0.86	0.45	0.30
Book value per share ($)	3.8%	13.08	12.23	13.18	15.05	18.06	20.30	22.19	21.17	19.06	18.28
Employees	(5.1%)	70,000	70,000	67,000	63,000	56,000	56,400	54,100	50,200	46,500	43,900

1993 Year-end:
Debt ratio: 36.7%
Return on equity: (2.5%)
Cash (mil.): $81
Current ratio: 1.80
Long-term debt (mil.): $2,322
Number of shares (mil.): 224
Dividends
  Yield: 1.4%
  Payout: —
Market value (mil.): $4,648

**Stock Price History
High/Low 1984–93**

ALCATEL ALSTHOM

OVERVIEW

Alcatel Alsthom is one of France's largest conglomerates. The company is named after its 2 biggest subsidiaries, Netherlands-registered Alcatel (the world's #1 manufacturer of telecommunications equipment, systems, and cables) and GEC Alsthom (a joint venture with GEC plc of the UK that is one of Europe's leading engineering concerns, specializing in power plants, electrical equipment, ships, and high-speed trains). The company's other major business operations are electrical engineering and batteries, conducted through French subsidiaries Cegelec and Saft.

Société Générale holds 9.1% and Alcatel group employees 4.6% of the company.

The 1993 purchase of STC Submarine Systems of the UK made Alcatel the world's #1 undersea cable manufacturer.

Activities outside France account for around 71% of total sales. Germany is a strong market, and the group also has an active presence in Russia and the former Soviet bloc through joint ventures with local producers. In China, Alcatel has a 40% share of the public telephone network switching market (7 million lines). Alcatel's biggest power plant is being built in Shanghai.

In 1994 Alcatel chairman and CEO Pierre Suard was caught up in a scandal alleging that he had used unpaid-for company materials in renovating his home.

WHEN

In 1898 Pierre Azaria combined his electric generating company with 3 others to form Compagnie Générale d'Electricité (CGE). As one of Europe's pioneer electric power and manufacturing companies, CGE expanded operations in France and abroad through acquisitions. By WWII CGE was making light bulbs and batteries, in addition to power generating equipment. After the French government nationalized electric utilities in 1946, CGE diversified into the production of telecommunications equipment, consumer appliances, and electronics.

In 1969 Thomson-Brandt (French electronics manufacturer, later renamed Thomson) transferred its heavy equipment maker, Alsthom, to CGE in exchange for CGE's data processing and appliance businesses. In 1976 Alsthom acquired Les Chantiers de l'Atlantique, the French shipbuilding giant.

In the meantime, CGE expanded its telecommunications business by buying Alcatel. Founded in 1879, Alcatel was a French communications pioneer that went on to introduce digital switching exchanges (1970). CGE combined its existing telecommunications division, CIT, with Alcatel to form CIT Alcatel.

The Mitterrand government nationalized CGE in 1982. Soon afterward the company traded its defense and consumer electronics units for Thomson's communications businesses, making CGE the 5th largest telephone equipment manufacturer in the world (1983). Later, CGE combined Alcatel with ITT's phone equipment operations, forming Alcatel NV. The newly formed Brussels-based company (55.6% owned by CGE, 37% by ITT, and 7.4%

by French and Belgian partners) started off as the world's 2nd largest telecommunications enterprise, after AT&T.

In 1987 CGE's chairman, Pierre Suard, supervised the government's sale of CGE to the public for $1.9 billion. Later that year the company bought Sir James Goldsmith's 51% stake in Paris-based Générale Occidentale, which included France's 2nd largest book publisher, Groupe de la Cité.

In 1989 CGE and GEC combined their power systems and engineering businesses to create GEC Alsthom NV (equally owned by CGE and GEC). In 1990 CGE agreed to take over Fiat's telecommunications businesses (Telettra) and to buy a 3% stake in Fiat. Fiat, in turn, bought 6% of CGE. By merging Telettra with Face, Alcatel's existing Italian operation, the company created Alcatel Italia to oversee Alcatel's worldwide transmission and equipment operations. After the company adopted its current name in 1991, its Alcatel unit bought Rockwell International's transmission equipment unit and merged it into Alcatel Network Systems, enhancing Alcatel's presence in the US telecom market.

That same year the firm launched its Alcatel 1000 telecommunication system, which provides high-speed data and image transmission and HDTV capability in addition to standard telephone functions. Alcatel began marketing its GSM cellular phone system in 1992. By the end of 1993 it had received GSM orders from France, Indonesia, South Africa, the US, and Vietnam, among others.

In 1994 Alcatel won a contract for $2.1 billion to provide a new high-speed rail line linking Pusan and Seoul in South Korea.

NYSE symbol: ALA (ADR)
Fiscal year ends: December 31

Chairman and CEO: Pierre Suard
President and COO: François de Laage de Meux
EVP and CFO: André Wettstein
EVP Strategy and Development: Jacques Imbert
VP Human Resources: Stéphane Dacquin
Chairman and CEO, Alcatel NA Cable Systems (US): John E. Peterson
President and CFO, Alcatel NA Cable Systems (US): M.S. Edwards, Jr.
Director Human Resources, Alcatel NA Cable Systems (US): Wayne Cole
Auditors: Acer-Cabinet Payer et Associés; Barbier Frinault et Associés

HQ: Alcatel Alsthom Compagnie Générale d'Electricité, 54, rue La Boétie, 75008 Paris, France
Phone: +33-1-40-76-10-10
Fax: +33-1-40-76-14-00
US HQ: Alcatel NA Cable Systems Inc., 39 Second St. NW, Hickory, NC 28601
US Phone: 704-323-1120
US Fax: 704-328-6339

	1993 Sales		1993 Operating Income	
	FF mil.	% of total	FF mil.	% of total
France	46,087	29	4,829	34
Germany	24,482	16	2,923	20
Other Europe	41,679	27	5,243	37
Other countries	44,086	28	1,283	9
Total	**156,334**	**100**	**14,278**	**100**

	1993 Sales		1993 Operating Income	
	FF mil.	% of total	FF mil.	% of total
Telecom. sys.	75,293	49	8,365	58
Telecom. & cables	30,361	19	2,252	16
Energy & transp.	25,388	16	2,084	15
Electrical engin.	15,261	10	468	3
Services	6,506	4	1,023	7
Batteries	3,525	2	138	1
Adjustments	—	—	(52)	—
Total	**156,334**	**100**	**14,278**	**100**

Major Subsidiaries and Associates
Alcatel NV (telecommunications systems, Netherlands)
Cegelec (99.9%, electrical engineering)
Compagnie Financière Alcatel (99.9%)
Electro Banque (99.5%, financial services)
Framatome (44.1%, nuclear plants)
GEC Alsthom NV (47%, power plants and electrical equipment, Netherlands)
Générale Occidentale (84%, publishing/media)
Saft (99.9%, batteries)

ABB	Hitachi
AMSTED	Johnson Controls
AT&T	Lagardère
Bechtel	Lockheed Martin
Black and Veatch	NEC
British Aerospace	Nokia
Cable & Wireless	Northern Telecom
Cooper Industries	Philips
Dana	Ralston Purina Group
Dresser	Raytheon
Duracell	Reed Elsevier
Emerson	Rolls-Royce
Ericsson	Siemens
Fujitsu	Thyssen
General Electric	Toshiba
GTE	Westinghouse

$=FF5.91 (Dec. 31, 1993)	Annual Growth	1984	1985	1986	1987	1988	1989	1990	1991	1992	1993
Sales (FF mil.)	10.9%	—	71,942	80,903	127,461	127,958	143,897	144,053	160,082	161,677	156,334
Net income (FF mil.)	31.9%	—	761	1,159	1,832	1,453	3,161	4,139	5,524	6,607	6,987
Income as % of sales	—	—	1.1%	1.4%	1.4%	1.1%	2.2%	2.9%	3.5%	4.7%	4.5%
Earnings per share (FF)[1]	8.3%	—	—	—	31	32	40	47	51	53	50
Stock price – high (FF)	—	—	—	—	347	430	538	652	630	694	853
Stock price – low (FF)	—	—	—	—	206	182	368	460	486	536	601
Stock price – close (FF)	25.6%	—	—	—	215	403	538	541	571	692	842
P/E – high	—	—	—	—	11	13	13	14	12	13	17
P/E – low	—	—	—	—	7	6	9	10	10	10	12
Dividends per share (FF)	18.0%	3.37	4.40	6.67	7.50	9.00	11.00	12.50	13.50	14.50	15.00
Book value per share (FF)	—	198	208	224	235	257	276	317	364	368	418
Employees	8.7%	—	153,800	149,010	219,460	204,110	210,300	205,500	213,100	203,000	196,500

1993 Year-end:
Debt ratio: 45.0%
Return on equity: 12.7%
Cash (mil.): FF41,782
Long-term debt (bil.): FF24.8
No. of shares (mil.): 143
Dividends
  Yield: 1.8%
  Payout: 30.1%
Market value (mil.): $20,439
Sales (mil.): $26,452

Stock Price History High/Low 1987–93

[1] Including extraordinary items

ALL NIPPON AIRWAYS CO., LTD.

OVERVIEW

Seiji Fukatsu has been studying Zen and the Art of Airline Management lately. Head of All Nippon Airways (Zen Nippon Kuyu in Japanese), he has been taking steps to get his Tokyo-based company, which has posted losses 2 straight years, back on the road to Nirvana. All Nippon (ANA) is Japan's 2nd largest airline, after Japan Air Lines, and the 7th largest in the world (in passenger volume). With its regional airline subsidiary Air Nippon, ANA is Japan's largest domestic carrier, with a market share of more than 50%.

Through its subsidiaries and affiliates, ANA is also involved in ground support, food service, hotels, travel and leisure, air freight, and real estate. Among these is ANA Enterprises, which owns and operates hotels around the world.

The company has had to restructure to counter the effects of a prolonged Japanese recession that has led many of its former customers to take the train instead. ANA plans to cut unprofitable routes and to reduce employment by 10% through attrition.

The company is also working to build its international business by forming alliances with overseas airlines, including Delta and Air Canada.

WHEN

Two domestic Japanese air carriers got started in 1952 — Nippon Helicopter and Aeroplane Transport and Far East Airlines — and consolidated operations in 1958 as All Nippon Airways.

Up through the 1960s ANA developed a domestic route network linking Japan's largest cities — Tokyo, Osaka, Fukuoka, Sapporo — and its leading provincial centers, including Nagoya, Nagasaki, Matzuyama, and Hokodate. During this period traffic grew at an annual rate of 30% to 60%.

In 1970 the Japanese cabinet formulated routes for its major airlines, giving ANA scheduled domestic service and unscheduled international flights. That same year Tokuji Wakasa became ANA's chairman. The airline set up international charters (starting with Hong Kong) in 1971. ANA then diversified, setting up a hotel subsidiary. In 1978 ANA established Nippon Cargo Airlines (set up jointly with 4 steamship lines), a charter service.

The airline carried 19.5 million passengers in 1978 (making it the world's 6th largest airline), but its growth slowed between 1978 and 1980. High jet fuel prices caused a $45.6 million loss in 1979, but ANA rebounded in 1980, earning $13.9 million. In 1982 ANA opened international charter service to Guam.

In 1985 the Japanese government deregulated air routes, allowing ANA to offer scheduled international flights. ANA offered its first regular flight from Tokyo to Guam in 1986 and soon added service to Los Angeles and Washington, DC. Flights to China, Hong Kong, and Sydney began in 1987. That year Akio Kondo took over as ANA's president.

Between 1988 and 1990 ANA added flights to Stockholm, Seoul, Bangkok, Vienna, London, Moscow, and Saipan. Passenger boardings remained high, but the airline slipped to the world's 8th largest when mergers at NWA and USAir pushed them ahead of ANA in the rankings. In 1988 ANA bought 3.5% of Austrian Airlines (it has since raised its stake to 9%) and set up the domestic computer reservation system (CRS), able. The company's international CRS, INFINI (a joint venture with the CRS co-op ABACUS), went on-line in 1990.

A strong domestic base helped ANA see profits during the Persian Gulf War and the recession years of the early 1990s — it was one of the few major airlines to do so. In 1991 ANA started World Air Network Charter (WAC) to serve pleasure travelers from Japan's smaller cities. WAC, based in Singapore and using Australian pilots, flies out of small local airports to avoid the bottlenecks at Narita and Osaka. ANA also opened its first European hotel in Vienna, was listed on the London Stock Exchange, and established a flight school in California for its pilots that year.

In 1992 ANA placed an order for 15 Boeing 737s for $667 million and premiered a hotel in Beijing. Also in 1992 ANA acquired 13.5% of ABACUS, Southeast Asia's largest computer reservation system.

In late 1994 ANA and British Airways began discussions to form an alliance to compete more effectively against Japan Air Lines on the Tokyo-London route.

OTC symbol: ALNPY (ADR)
Fiscal year ends: March 31

Honorary Chairman: Tokuji Wasaka
Chairman: Takaya Sugiura
VC: Akio Kondo
President and CEO: Seiji Fukatsu
SEVP: Akira Hasegawa
EVP Finance and Accounting: Kazuhiko Komiya
SVP and General Manager, the Americas:
   Yoshinobu Nishikawa
Director Administration (Personnel), North
   America: Osamu Kawabata
Auditors: Century Audit Corporation

HQ: Zen Nippon Kuyu Kabushikigaisha, PO Box
   106, Kasumigaseki Bldg., 3-2-5, Kasumigaseki,
   Chiyoda-ku, Tokyo 100, Japan
Phone: +81-3-3592-3065
Fax: +81-3-3592-3069
US HQ: All Nippon Airways, 630 Fifth Ave.,
   Ste. 646, New York, NY 10111
US Phone: 212-956-8200
US Fax: 212-969-9022
Reservations: 800-235-9262

ANA flies to 29 cities in Japan and 20 cities in
Asia, Australia, Europe, and North America.

	1994 Rev. Pass. Miles		1994 Flights	
	No.	% of total	No.	% of total
Japan	5,732	26	163,300	96
Other countries	16,396	74	7,672	4
Total	**22,128**	**100**	**170,972**	**100**

	1994 Sales	
	¥ bil.	% of total
Passenger	730	85
Cargo	41	5
Other	86	10
Adjustment	(127)	—
Total	**730**	**100**

Airline Subsidiaries
Air Nippon Co., Ltd. (regional airline)
All Nippon Helicopter Co., Ltd.
International Flight Training Academy, Inc.
World Air Network Co., Ltd. (international air charters)
Computer Reservation Systems
ABACUS (Asia/Pacific)   INFINI (international)
able (Japan)

Selected Nonairline Subsidiaries and Affiliates
ANA Enterprises, Ltd. (hotel management)
ANA Hotels Hawaii, Inc.
ANA Hotel Foods Co., Ltd.
ANA Hotels & Resorts (USA), Inc.
ANA World Tours Co., Ltd.

Flight Equipment	No.
Boeing 767	57
Boeing 747	38
Airbus 320	15
Lockheed 1011	4
Total	**114**

Accor	FlightSafety	Philippine Airlines
British Airways	Garuda Indonesia	Qantas
Carlson	IRI	SAS
Central Japan	Japan Air System	Singapore Airlines
Railway	JAL	Swire Pacific
China Airlines	KLM	UAL
Continental Airlines	Lufthansa	Virgin Group
East Japan Railway	Northwest Airlines	West Japan Railway

$=¥112 (Dec. 31, 1993)	Annual Growth	1985	1986	1987	1988	1989	1990	1991	1992	1993	1994
Sales (¥ bil.)	4.3%	—	—	—	567	623	723	803	875	763	730
Net income (¥ bil.)	—	—	—	—	6	8	15	12	7	(1)	(9)
Income as % of sales	—	—	—	—	1.0%	1.2%	2.1%	1.4%	0.8%	(0.2%)	(1.3%)
Earnings per share (¥)	—	—	—	—	—	5	11	8	5	(1)	(6)
Stock price – high (¥)[1]	—	—	640	1,013	2,043	1,790	2,095	2,067	1,490	1,400	1,260
Stock price – low (¥)[1]	—	—	342	614	935	1,333	1,629	962	1,181	855	950
Stock price – close (¥)[1]	12.9%	355	637	987	1,403	1,724	2,067	1,219	1,310	960	1,060
P/E – high	—	—	—	—	—	—	199	—	—	—	—
P/E – low	—	—	—	—	—	—	155	—	—	—	—
Dividends per share (¥)	(1.1%)	3.30	3.50	3.50	3.81	3.81	4.76	5.00	5.00	4.00	3.00
Book value per share (¥)	(0.6%)	—	—	—	122	126	131	134	135	128	118
Employees	3.9%	—	—	—	11,950	—	12,790	13,387	13,974	14,829	14,994

1994 Year-end:
Debt ratio: 85.4%
Return on equity: (5.3%)
Cash (bil.): ¥146
Long-term debt (bil.): ¥857
No. of shares (mil.): 1,443
Dividends
   Yield: 0.3%
   Payout: —
Market value (mil.): $13,657
Sales (mil.): $6,518

Stock Price History[1]
High/Low 1986–94

[1] Stock prices are for the prior calendar year.

ALLIANZ AG HOLDING

OVERVIEW

Allianz is the world's 2nd largest insurance company in premium income (behind Japan's Nippon Life) and a German powerhouse. The Munich-based company has significant equity stakes in several major German companies, among them Germany's largest bank (Deutsche Bank), the world's largest reinsurer (Münchener Rückversicherungs-Gesellschaft), and chemical and pharmaceutical giant Bayer A.G. Under the guidance of former chairman Wolfgang Schieren, Allianz become Europe's largest insurance company through a succession of acquisitions in Britain, France, and Italy during the 1980s. The company also positioned itself to

become a major player in the US and Asia. In 1990 Allianz bought California-based Fireman's Fund, a property and casualty insurer with a national presence.

Current chairman Henning Schulte-Noelle is continuing Schieren's aggressive expansion strategy. In 1991 Allianz became the first German insurer licensed to sell insurance in Japan. A wave of disasters, crime, and stiff competition set the company back in 1992, which was the first time in 20 years the company lost money from its German operations. Allianz restructured its operations that year, and in 1993 profits surged, mostly from international business.

WHEN

In 1890, the same year Carl Thieme founded the company in Germany, Allianz took part in the creation of the Calamity Association of Accident Insurance Companies, a consortium of German, Austrian, Swiss, and Russian firms, to insure world commerce. Thieme also established Allianz offices in the UK (1893), Switzerland (1897), and the Netherlands (1898). Thieme's successor, Paul von der Nahmer, expanded Allianz into Scandinavia, the Balkans, the US, Italy, and France. After WWI Allianz returned to foreign markets.

After the German defeat in WWII, the victors seized Allianz's foreign holdings, except for a stake in Spain's Plus Ultra. In the 1950s Allianz repurchased lost holdings in Italian and Austrian companies.

Allianz saturated the German market and began a full-scale return to the international arena in the late 1950s and 1960s. Wolfgang Schieren took the CEO desk in 1971 and immediately began a decades-long program of creating and buying foreign enterprises. Allianz established a subsidiary in Britain (1973), bought a Brazilian company (1974), and, in a major step, plunged into the US, forming Los Angeles–based Allianz Insurance (1977). In 1979 the company added Fidelity Union Life Insurance of Dallas and North American Life and Casualty of Minneapolis.

In 1981 Allianz launched a takeover (which turned hostile) of the UK's Eagle Star insurance company. Allianz managed to gain more than 28% of the firm. Negotiations continued for more than 2 years until Britain's B.A.T entered the fray as a white knight. After a 1983 bidding joust, Allianz withdrew.

Allianz consoled itself by going shopping, paying DM1.14 billion to win control of Riunione Adriatica di Sicurtà (RAS), Italy's 2nd largest insurance company, in 1984. Then the company returned to the UK to buy Cornhill (on its 3rd try) in 1986. In September 1989 Allianz served as a white knight itself when it purchased part (later upped to controlling interest) of the Via/Rhin et Moselle insurance group of French giant Compagnie de Navigation Mixte (CNM). Allianz Via, the name of the new group, is France's 12th largest insurer (#4 in the private sector). Allianz Via is 65% owned by Allianz, 34% by the CNM conglomerate.

Also in 1989 Allianz acquired 49% of Hungária Biztosító, gaining an early entry into Eastern Europe. In 1990 it stormed into what once was East Germany to win control of Deutsche Versicherungs AG, the state's insurance monopoly.

And that was before it blew out the 100 candles on its birthday cake. Also in 1990 Allianz went shopping in the US, purchasing Fireman's Fund Insurance for a net $1.1 billion.

In 1991 Allianz accumulated a 22% stake in Dresdner Bank, Germany's 2nd largest. In October of that year 20-year veteran and chairman Wolfgang Schieren retired and his designated successor abruptly left, leaving the top spot to Henning Schulte-Noelle, former chairman of a life insurance subsidiary, Allianz Lebensversicherungs.

In 1993 international business accounted for 47% of total sales; the Americas accounted for nearly half of all foreign sales.

Principal exchange: Frankfurt
Fiscal year ends: December 31

Chairman: Henning Schulte-Noelle
Deputy Chairman: Uwe Haasen
Member of the Board of Management, Business Administration: Herbert Hansmeyer
Member of the Board of Management, Finance: Diethart Breipohl
Chairman, President, and CEO, Allianz Insurance (US): Wolfgang Schlink
Auditors: KPMG Deutsche Treuhand-Gesellschaft AG, Wirtschaftsprüfungsgesellschaft

HQ: Königinstrasse 28, Postfach 44 01 24, D-80802 Munich, Germany
Phone: +49-89-3-80-00
Fax: +49-89-34-99-41
US HQ: Allianz Insurance Co., 3400 Riverside Dr., Ste. 300, Burbank, CA 91505-4669
US Phone: 818-972-8000
US Fax: 818-972-8455

Allianz operates 224 companies, 38 subsidiaries, and 48 affiliates in 47 countries.

	1993 Premiums Written	
	DM mil.	% of total
Germany	34,398	53
North & South America	15,213	23
Africa & Asia	268	0
Other Europe	15,670	24
Total	**65,549**	**100**

	1993 Assets	
	DM mil.	% of total
Loans, notes & debentures	73,447	31
Real estate & real estate interest	29,348	12
Other investments	89,562	38
Reinsurance contracts	4,372	2
Insurance accounts receivable	6,647	3
Other	33,268	14
Total	**236,644**	**100**

Selected Holdings
Allianz Insurance Co. (US)
Allianz Lebensversicherungs-AG (46.5%)
Aseguradora Cuauhtémoc SA (49%, Mexico)
Bayerische Hypotheken- und Wechsel-Bank AG (23%)
Colón Compañía de Seguros Generales SA (Argentina)
Cornhill Insurance PLC (UK)
Deutsche Lebensversicherungs-AG
Deutsche Versicherungs-AG
Fireman's Fund Insurance Co. (US)
Hungária Biztosító Rt (55.8%, Hungary)
Lambda-Vermögensverwaltungsgesellschaft mbH (71%)
Munich American Reinsurance Co. (40%, US)
P.T. Asuransi Allianz Utama Indonesia (68%, Indonesia)
Rhin et Moselle Assurances Compagnie Générale d'Assurances et de Réassurances (99.8%, France)
Riunione Adriatica di Sicurtà SpA (Italy)

Aetna	ITT	Prudential
AIG	Lloyd's of London	State Farm
B.A.T	Loews	Tokio Marine
Chubb	MassMutual	& Fire
Crédit Lyonnais	MetLife	Travelers
CS Holding	New York Life	USAA
Deutsche Bank	Nippon Life	USF&G
Equitable	Northwestern	
General Re	Mutual	

$=DM1.74 (Dec. 31, 1993)	Annual Growth	1984	1985	1986	1987	1988	1989[1]	1990[1]	1991[1]	1992[1]	1993[1]
Assets (DM mil.)	31.6%	20,049	23,162	26,053	29,503	33,127	133,273	147,543	180,465	207,415	236,644
Net income (DM mil.)	—	290	304	359	325	502	941	673	381	507	964
Income as % of assets	—	1.4%	1.3%	1.4%	1.2%	1.5%	0.7%	0.5%	0.2%	0.2%	0.4%
Earnings per share (DM)	5.7%	25	22	20	22	33	63	37	21	24	41
Stock price – high (DM)	—	980	1,772	2,457	1,976	1,895	2,440	2,963	2,626	2,328	3,080
Stock price – low (DM)	—	620	736	1,017	927	1,035	1,673	1,938	1,954	1,630	1,945
Stock price – close (DM)	15.2%	823	1,772	1,959	1,144	1,870	2,440	2,100	2,142	1,984	2,948
P/E – high	—	40	82	120	91	57	39	80	125	97	75
P/E – low	—	25	34	50	43	31	27	52	93	68	47
Dividends per share (DM)	20.4%	9.4	10.3	10.3	12.0	12.0	12.0	16.0	13.5	13.5	50.0
Book value per share (DM)	10.3%	255	300	284	384	301	548	554	593	569	614
Employees	19.9%	—	16,330	16,523	16,748	17,002	43,117	45,483	61,158	74,263	69,859

1993 Year-end:
Debt ratio: 17.1%
Return on equity: 6.9%
Equity as % of assets: 6.9%
Long-term debt (mil.): DM3,394
No. of shares (mil.): 20
Dividends
  Yield: 1.7%
  Payout: 122.0%
Market value (mil.): $33,038
Assets (mil.): $136,002
Sales (mil.): $40,302

Stock Price History
High/Low 1984–93

[1] Worldwide results — not available for previous years

ALLIED DOMECQ PLC

It looks like it may no longer be "eat, drink, and be merry" at Allied Domecq. No, the London-based company (formerly Allied-Lyons) hasn't taken to brooding, but it is selling off many of its food businesses to focus on distilling and retailing. As part of its focus on core operations, it acquired Spanish distiller Pedro Domecq in 1994, paying more than $1 billion for the 68% of the company that it did not already own. The deal makes Allied the world's 2nd largest distiller (after Grand Metropolitan).

The acquisition of Domecq brought Allied a number of new brands, including Presidente (the world's #1 selling brandy) and Sauza (the 2nd best-selling tequila). Allied's Spirits and Wine unit also makes Kahlua liqueur, Canadian Club whiskey, Courvoisier cognac, and Beefeater gin. Its Brewing and Wholesaling division produces several beer brands, including Tetley Bitter and Skol. It also owns 50% of Carlsberg-Tetley, a joint venture with Danish brewer Carlsberg.

The company's Retailing unit operates about 4,300 pubs and 1,500 liquor stores in the UK. For those with a sweet tooth, Allied also franchises Baskin-Robbins and Dunkin' Donuts around the world.

In late 1994 the company sold its food ingredients businesses, DCA Food Industries and Margetts Foods, to Irish food maker Kerry Group. Also said to be up for sale are the company's tea maker, Tetley, and its European bakery business. With the purchase of Domecq, the company is looking to increase its presence in Latin America and is also looking for expansion opportunities in Asia and Eastern Europe.

Allied-Lyons was formed through the merger of 3 regional breweries. The oldest of these was an Essex brewing facility created by Edward Ind to provide beer for an inn he had bought in 1799. Ind's brewery merged with the Coope Brewery in 1845, and the combined Ind Coope Brewery established a solid position in southern England's beer market.

Central England was the realm of Joseph Ansell, a hops merchant who opened a brewery in 1881. Ansell Brewery ale became popular in Birmingham and the Midlands.

Joshua Tetley entered the business in 1822 by purchasing a Leeds brewery, with a following in northern England, that had been founded by William Sykes.

Beginning in the mid-20th century, as the industry consolidated and distribution channels expanded nationally, it became increasingly difficult for regional breweries to compete. Tetley was the first of the 3 to combine operations with another brewery, merging with Walker Cain in 1960.

In 1961 the 3 combined as Ind Coope Tetley Ansell Limited, taking the name Allied Breweries in 1963. In 1968 the greatly fortified brewing operation purchased SVPW, a wine and spirits company that had also been formed through a 1961 triple merger.

Allied established its Skol lager in 1974. In 1978 it bought its first food company, J. Lyons and Company, which owned the Baskin-Robbins ice cream chain and several food brands. The company changed its name to Allied-Lyons in 1981.

In 1982 Sir Derrick Holden-Brown, a former naval officer and the head of Allied's brewing operations, assumed the helm and steered the company through an unsuccessful takeover attempt by Elders IXL (1985). He later engaged in a successful battle with the Reichmann family of Canada over control of Hiram Walker (founded in 1848), a major Canadian distilling, oil, and gas concern. Allied-Lyons walked away with Hiram Walker's liquor division for C$2.64 billion.

The company entered the Japanese market in 1988 through a partnership with Suntory. In 1989 Allied acquired Dunkin' Donuts and the following year bought Mister Donut. The 1990 acquisition of Whitbread's liquor business brought the company a long-sought-after premium white liquor brand, Beefeater Gin.

In 1992 Allied sold the Grand Macnish, Lauder's, and Islay Mist brands to MacDuff International and sold UK distribution and marketing rights for Three Barrels brandy to Guinness. It also entered a brewing and wholesaling joint venture with Carlsberg, under the name Carlsberg-Tetley.

In 1993 the company bought a chain of 550 Augustus Barnett liquor stores from Bass for $60 million.

In 1994 Allied Domecq became the official sponsor of the Royal Shakespeare Company.

OTC symbol: ALDCY (ADR)
Fiscal year ends: First Saturday in March

Chairman: Michael C. J. Jackaman, age 58
CEO: Tony J. Hales, age 46
Group Finance Director: Peter F. Macfarlane
President, Allied Domecq Spirits & Wine (NA):
George McCarthy
Auditors: KPMG Peat Marwick

HQ: 24 Portland Place, London W1N 4BB, UK
Phone: +44-(01)71-323-9000
Fax: +44-(01)71-323-1742
No. Am. HQ: Allied Domecq Spirits & Wine, PO
Box 2518, Windsor, Ontario N8Y 4S5, Canada
No. Am. Phone: 519-254-5171
No. Am. Fax: 519-971-5710

	1994 Sales	
	£ mil.	% of total
UK	3,374	61
US	1,064	19
Other Europe	818	15
Canada & other countries	270	5
Total	**5,526**	**100**

	1994 Sales		1994 Operating Income	
	£ mil.	% of total	£ mil.	% of total
Spirits & wine	1,931	33	434	52
Retailing	1,716	29	209	25
Brewing & whlsle.	1,187	20	96	12
Food	1,068	18	87	11
Adjustments	(376)	—	(5)	—
Total	**5,526**	**100**	**821**	**100**

Selected Brands and Franchises

Spirits	Retailing
Ballantine's	Ansells (nightclubs)
Beefeater	Baskin-Robbins (ice cream)
Canadian Club	Dunkin' Donuts
Courvoisier	John Bull (pubs)
Frangelico	Victoria Wine (liquor
Hiram Walker	stores)
Kahlua	
Maker's Mark	**Beer**
Presidente	Burton Ale
Sauza	Carlsberg
Tia Maria	Castlemaine XXXX
	Double Diamond
Wines	John Bull Bitter
Altas Peak	Oranjeboom
Callaway	Skol Lager
Calvet Bordeaux	Tetley Bitter
Clos du Bois	
Cockburn's	**Food**
Moreau	Lyons (food and tea)
William Hill	Maryland Cookies
	Tetley (tea)

American Brands	McEwans
Bacardi	Molson
Bass	Nestlé
Brent Walker	PepsiCo
Brown-Forman	Pernod Ricard
Canandaigua Wine	Philip Morris
Courage	RJR Nabisco
Danone	S&P
Foster's Brewing	San Miguel
Gallo	Sara Lee
Grand Metropolitan	Scottish & Newcastle
Guinness	Seagram
Heileman	Stroh
Heineken	TLC Beatrice
John Labatt	Unilever
Kirin	Whitbread
LVMH	

£=$1.48 (Dec. 31, 1993)	9-Year Growth	1985	1986	1987	1988	1989	1990	1991	1992	1993[1]	1994
Sales (£ mil.)	8.6%	2,626	2,719	3,071	3,587	3,863	4,131	4,405	4,588	5,266	5,526
Net income (£ mil.)	10.2%	135	180	233	281	347	385	313	379	259	324
Income as % of sales	—	5.1%	6.6%	7.6%	7.8%	9.0%	9.3%	7.1%	8.3%	4.9%	5.9%
Earnings per share (p)	7.0%	20	26	34	38	44	48	38	43	30	37
Stock price – high (p)[2]	—	178	306	363	471	494	578	520	647	712	697
Stock price – low (p)[2]	—	138	153	252	290	320	427	408	460	526	517
Stock price – close (p)[2]	17.4%	160	267	322	346	438	496	477	619	643	680
P/E – high	—	9	12	11	12	11	12	14	15	24	19
P/E – low	—	7	6	7	8	7	9	11	11	18	14
Dividends per share (p)	12.8%	7.5	9.5	11.4	13.0	15.0	17.0	18.8	20.0	21.0	22.2
Book value per share (p)	3.2%	196	271	240	250	395	331	303	305	294	260
Employees	0.1%	71,448	70,301	77,549	78,128	81,440	87,273	83,243	78,743	71,713	71,824

1994 Year-end:
Debt ratio: 45.1%
Return on equity: 13.2%
Cash (mil.): £135
Long-term debt (mil.): £1,617
No. of shares (mil.): 916
Dividends
  Yield: 3.3%
  Payout: 60.5%
Market value (mil.): $9,214
Sales (mil.): $8,175

Stock Price History[2]
High/Low 1985-94

[1] Accounting change   [2] Stock prices are for the prior calendar year.

HOOVER'S HANDBOOK OF WORLD BUSINESS 1995-1996   **111**

ANGLO AMERICAN CORPORATION

South Africa's largest company and the world's #1 miner, Anglo American is a diverse investment corporation with holdings in gold, diamond, platinum, and coal mining; financial services, such as banking and insurance; and industrial concerns, such as steel, paper, timber, and chemicals.

Anglo American and its subsidiaries own 32.5% of De Beers Consolidated Mines and 29.4% of De Beers Centenary. The world's largest diamond group, De Beers supplies about half of the world's diamonds and controls more than 80% of the rough diamond

market through its management of the Central Selling Organization, an international diamond cartel.

Anglo also owns 20.4% of South African banking group First National Bank Holdings and 39.9% of South African insurer The Southern Life Association. Its operations outside Africa are managed by Minorco, a 45.8%-owned holding company in Luxembourg.

With its diverse holdings in South Africa, Anglo is looking to benefit from the flood of investment into the country following the end of apartheid.

WHEN

In 1905 the Oppenheimers, a German family with major interest in the Premier Diamond Mining Company of South Africa, acquired control of Consolidated Mines Selection, one of the smaller South African gold mining companies, and used it to buy up some of the richest gold-producing land in South Africa by 1917. The family formed Anglo American that year to raise money from J. P. Morgan and other US banking and mining interests for mine development. The name was chosen to disguise the company's German background during WWI and because the original suggestion, African American, was rejected by the US investors.

Under chairman Ernest Oppenheimer, Anglo American acquired diamond fields in German Southwest Africa (now Namibia) in 1920, and the company broke the De Beers hegemony in diamond production. De Beers Consolidated Mines had been formed by Cecil Rhodes in 1888 with the financial help of England's powerful Rothschild family and had since extended its control over the South African diamond industry.

De Beers had been able to reap large profits because of its monopoly position and cheap black labor and had diversified into cattle ranching, agriculture, wine production, coal, railroads, explosives, and other basic industries. The diamond monopoly was reestablished in 1929 when Anglo American took control of De Beers.

After WWII Anglo American and De Beers extended control over the gold industry, becoming the largest producers in South Africa by 1958. They were also major world producers of coal, uranium, and copper. In the

1960s and 1970s, Anglo American expanded through mergers and cross-holdings in industrial and financial companies.

The Oppenheimers have long supported moderate opposition politicians and black labor unions, but in 1987, when black unions went on strike, Anglo American dismissed 60,000 workers, and 7 men died in the ensuing violence.

Minorco sold its interest in Consolidated Gold Fields (1989) for a net gain of $645 million and bought US-based Freeport-McMoRan Gold Company (1990, renamed Independence Mining). Minorco — whose US holdings already included 56% of Inspiration Resources and 49% of Adobe Resources — later created Minorco (U.S.A.) Inc. to oversee North American investments. In mid-1991 Minorco purchased Hudson Bay Mining & Smelting ($87 million) and announced plans to modernize its copper smelter and zinc-treatment plants to meet Canadian emission standards.

In 1993 Minorco paid $1.4 billion in stock and other assets for Anglo American's and De Beers's South American, European, and Australian operations as part of a swap that put all of Anglo American's non-African assets, except diamonds, in Minorco's hands. While Anglo said the swap would improve its ability to develop mining activities outside Africa, some analysts claimed the company moved the assets outside South Africa to keep them from being nationalized by the new, black-controlled government.

In 1994 Anglo spun off insurer African Life to a group of black businesspeople led by Donald Ncube, a former executive with Anglo.

Nasdaq symbol: ANGLY (ADR)
Fiscal year ends: March 31

Chairman: Julian Ogilvie Thompson, age 60
Deputy Chairman; Chairman, Diamond Services Division: E. Peter Gush, age 56
Deputy Chairman; Chairman, Industrial Group: Leslie Boyd, age 57
Deputy Chairman: W. G. Boustred, age 69
Deputy Chairman; Chairman, Central Selling Organization: Nicholas F. Oppenheimer, age 49
Director of Financial Management and Consulting Services and Banking and Insurance: M. W. King, age 57
Finance Manager: G. M. Holford
Manager Manpower Resources: J. F. Drysdale, age 62
VP and General Counsel, Minorco (U.S.A.): Ben Keisler
VP and Controller (CFO), Minorco (U.S.A.): Jim Hall
Auditors: Deloitte & Touche; KPMG Aiken & Peat

HQ: Anglo American Corporation of South Africa Limited, 44 Main St., Johannesburg 2001, South Africa
Phone: +27-11-638-9111
Fax: +27-11-638-2445
US HQ: Minorco (U.S.A.) Inc., 5251 DTC Pkwy., Ste. 700, Englewood, CO 80111
US Phone: 303-889-0700
US Fax: 303-889-0707

Anglo American's subsidiaries and affiliates have operations in 21 countries.

	1994 Net Earnings
	% of total
Mining finance	25
Diamonds	22
Industry & commerce	18
Gold & uranium	13
Financial services & property	10
Coal	5
Platinum, base metals & other mining	4
Other	3
Total	**100**

Selected Affiliates
Anglo American Coal Corp. Ltd. (51.8%, coal mining)
Anglo American Industrial Corp. Ltd. (49.9%; steel, autos, paper, and chemicals)
Anglo American Investment Trust Ltd. (52.2%, diamond mining and trading)
De Beers Consolidated Mines Ltd. (32.5%, diamond mining and marketing)
First National Bank Holdings Ltd. (20.4%, financial services)
Johannesburg Consolidated Investment Co. Ltd. (39.5%, holding company for mining finance)
Minorco (45.8%; mining finance holding company, owns 100% Minorco (U.S.A.) Inc.; Luxembourg)
Rustenburg Platinum Mines Ltd. (23.8%, platinum mining)
The Southern Life Association Ltd. (39.9%)
Vaal Reefs Exploration and Mining Co. Ltd. (29.3%, gold and uranium mining)
Western Deep Levels Ltd. (44.2%, gold and uranium mining)

Amoco	General Electric	Mobil
ASARCO	GFSA	Phelps Dodge
Broken Hill	Hanson	Placer Dome
Cyprus Amax	Homestake Mining	Rembrandt
DuPont	Inco	Group
Fluor	Komdragmet	RTZ
FMC	Lydenburg	Thyssen
Gencor Industries	Platinum	

$=R4.19 (Dec. 31, 1993)	9-Year Growth	1985	1986	1987	1988	1989	1990	1991	1992	1993	1994
Attributable earnings (R mil.)	12.1%	601	806	1,031	1,037	1,254	1,507	1,401	1,680	1,404	1,681
Earnings per share (R)	9.7%	2.64	3.53	4.51	4.53	5.45	6.51	6.04	7.24	7.22	6.05
Stock price – high (R)[1]	—	26.65	39.75	74.00	95.50	66.00	116.25	147.75	128.00	132.00	220.00
Stock price – low (R)[1]	—	19.75	22.00	37.00	51.50	44.10	62.75	89.50	84.00	74.60	86.75
Stock price – close (R)[1]	28.5%	23.00	39.75	65.85	55.50	61.00	108.00	95.00	124.25	86.75	219.50
P/E – high	—	10	11	16	21	12	18	24	18	18	36
P/E – low	—	7	6	8	11	8	10	15	12	10	14
Dividends per share (R)	12.7%	1.35	1.80	2.25	2.25	2.70	3.25	3.25	3.45	3.45	3.95
Net assets per share (R)	19.7%	46.91	70.71	105.39	85.36	124.10	163.39	132.12	152.54	153.00	236.22
Employees	—	—	—	—	—	—	—	—	—	—	—

1994 Year-end:
Debt ratio: 9.9%
Return on equity: 3.1%
Cash (mil.): R2,961
Long-term debt (mil.): R2,398
No. of shares (mil.): 233
Dividends
Yield: 1.8%
Payout: 65.3%
Market value (mil.): $12,196
Earnings (mil.): $401

Stock Price History[1]
High/Low 1985–94

[1] Stock prices are for the prior calendar year.

ARTHUR ANDERSEN & CO, SC

The last 5 years have been a boom time for Arthur Andersen, the world's #1 accounting and management consulting firm. Since 1989 revenues have doubled to $6.7 billion, personnel is up by 41% to nearly 73,000, and offices have mushroomed by 47% to 358.

The company is a worldwide organization that shares assets, costs, and resources on a global basis. It is composed of 2 distinct units (coordinated by a Swiss entity, Arthur Andersen & Co, SC): Arthur Andersen & Co., which provides auditing, business advisory services, tax services, and specialty consulting services; and Andersen Consulting, which provides strategic services and technology consulting.

Andersen Consulting is the world leader in systems integration, hardware configuration, software design, and operator training for clients that include half the FORTUNE 500. It hopes to keep ahead of its consulting firm rivals by providing clients with a "one-stop shop" of integrated services.

Andersen Consulting has tripled its size since 1988. Consumer, industrial, and energy clients account for 40% of its revenues.

Arthur Andersen, an orphan of Norwegian parents, worked in the Chicago office of Price Waterhouse in 1907. In 1908 at 23, after becoming the youngest CPA in Illinois, he began teaching accounting at Northwestern University. Following a brief period in 1911 as controller at Schlitz Brewing, Andersen became head of the accounting department at Northwestern. In 1913 at age 28, he formed a public accounting firm, Andersen, DeLany & Company, with Clarence DeLany.

Establishment of the Federal Reserve and implementation of the federal income tax in 1913 aided the firm's early growth by increasing the demand for accounting services. The company gained large clients, including ITT, Briggs & Stratton, Colgate-Palmolive, and Parker Pen, during the period between 1913 and 1920. In 1915 it opened a branch office in Milwaukee. After DeLany's departure in 1918, the firm adopted its present name.

Andersen grew rapidly during the 1920s and added to its list of services financial investigations, which formed the basis for its future strength in management consulting. The firm opened 6 offices in the 1920s, including ones in New York (1921), Kansas City (1923), and Los Angeles (1926).

When Samuel Insull's empire collapsed in 1932, Andersen was appointed the bankers' representative and guarded the assets during the refinancing. Andersen opened additional offices in Boston and Houston (1937) and in Atlanta and Minneapolis (1940).

Andersen's presence dominated the firm during his life. Upon his death in 1947, it found new leadership in Leonard Spacek. During Spacek's tenure, which continued until 1963, the firm opened 18 new US offices

and began a period of foreign expansion with the establishment of a Mexico City office, followed by 25 more in other countries.

Andersen has been an innovator among the major accounting firms. The company opened Andersen University, its Center for Professional Education, in the early 1970s on a campus in St. Charles, Illinois, and provided the first worldwide annual report in 1973. To broaden its scope, it transferred its headquarters to Geneva in 1977.

During the 1970s Andersen increased its consulting business, which accounted for 21% of revenues by 1979; by 1988 consulting fees made up 40% of revenues, making Andersen the world's largest consulting firm. Tension between the consultants and the auditors eventually forced a 1989 restructuring, which established Arthur Andersen and Andersen Consulting as distinct entities.

A rash of megamergers among the then–Big 8 accounting firms led Andersen and Price Waterhouse to flirt briefly with a merger (1989), but discussions broke down.

In 1992 the RTC sued Arthur Andersen for $400 million, alleging negligence in auditing failed Benjamin Franklin Savings. The firm paid the RTC $65 million in 1993 to settle the case as part of a "global" settlement, exempting it from any possible future government charges for its earlier role as auditor of failed US savings and loans.

In 1994 Arthur Andersen and Deloitte & Touche were named in a $1.1 billion suit brought by investors who claim the 2 firms and Prudential Securities inflated the prices of several limited partnerships. Also that year the #8 UK accounting firm, Binder Hamlyn, was merged into Arthur Andersen.

International partnership
Fiscal year ends: August 31

WHO

Chairman, Managing Partner, and CEO:
Lawrence A. Weinbach
Managing Partner, Arthur Andersen: Richard L.
Measelle
Managing Partner, Andersen Consulting:
George T. Shaheen
CFO: John D. Lewis
General Counsel: Jon N. Ekdahl
Manager Human Resources: Peter Pesce
CEO, Arthur Anderson & Co. (US): James
Kackley

WHERE

HQ: 18, quai Général-Guisan, 1211 Geneva 3,
Switzerland
Phone: +41-22-214444
Fax: +41-22-214418
US HQ: Arthur Andersen & Co., SC, 69 W.
Washington St., Chicago, IL 60602-3094
US Phone: 312-580-0069
US Fax: 312-507-2548

Arthur Andersen & Co, SC, maintains over 350
offices in 74 countries.

Arthur Andersen	1994 Sales	
	$ mil.	% of total
Americas	1,919	55
Europe, India, Africa & Middle East	1,110	31
Asia/Pacific	489	14
Total	**3,518**	**100**

Andersen Consulting	1994 Sales	
	$ mil.	% of total
Americas	1,801	56
Europe, India, Africa & Middle East	1,113	35
Asia/Pacific	306	9
Total	**3,220**	**100**

Worldwide Personnel		
	No.	% of total
Americas	37,382	51
Europe, India, Africa & Middle East	23,676	33
Asia/Pacific	11,664	16
Total	**72,722**	**100**

WHAT

Operating Units

Arthur Andersen
Auditing
Business advisory and corporate specialty services
Tax services

Andersen Consulting
Application software products
Business process management
Change management services
Client/server-based solutions
Object-oriented technology
Strategic services
Systems integration services
Technology services

Selected Representative Clients

American Express
Cadbury Schweppes
Chemical Bank
First Chicago
Inland Steel
KLM
New South Wales Police Service
NYNEX
Pacific Bell

KEY COMPETITORS

Bain & Co.
Booz, Allen
Boston Consulting
Group
Coopers & Lybrand
DEC
Deloitte & Touche
EDS

Ernst & Young
H&R Block
IBM
KPMG
Marsh & McLennan
Perot Systems
Price Waterhouse
SHL Systemhouse

HOW MUCH

	9-Year Growth	1985	1986	1987	1988	1989	1990	1991	1992	1993	1994
Sales ($ mil.)	17.5%	1,574	1,924	2,316	2,820	3,382	4,160	4,948	5,577	6,017	6,738
Offices	5.8%	215	219	226	231	243	299	307	318	324	358
Partners	4.9%	1,630	1,847	1,957	2,016	2,134	2,292	2,393	2,454	2,487	2,517
Employees	11.1%	28,172	36,117	39,645	45,918	51,414	56,801	59,797	62,134	66,478	72,722

1994 Year-end:
Sales per partner:
$2,676,996

BANK OF MONTREAL

OVERVIEW

Bank of Montreal CEO Matthew Barrett is looking south these days, not for a warmer climate but for customers. With more than 1,100 Bank of Montreal branches already saturating Canada, he is looking to the US for expansion opportunities. The company is the 4th largest bank in Canada, with assets of more than $100 billion.

In Canada, Bank of Montreal serves more than 4 million households and over 500,000 commercial accounts, providing a broad range of financial services from personal loans to corporate banking. The company's US operations are headed up by its Chicago-based subsidiary, Harris Bankcorp, which provides personal and commercial banking services to more than 300,000 customers. Barrett wants to triple Harris's presence in the midwestern US by the year 2002; in 1994 Harris acquired Chicago's Suburban Bankcorp, which has 30 branches in the Chicago area.

Bank of Montreal is also expanding its investment banking business. In 1994 it formed Nesbitt Burns, creating Canada's leading investment bank, when it merged its subsidiary Nesbitt Thomson with investment firm Burns Fry.

WHEN

By the early 1800s Montreal had become a key port for fur and agriculture traders. To finance the city's burgeoning trading companies, the Montreal Bank opened for business in 1817. It was Canada's first bank, although it did not receive an official charter until 1822, when its name was changed to Bank of Montreal. The company's ties with the US were strong from the beginning, with nearly 50% of its original capital coming from US investors.

The new bank relied heavily on local trading companies for business, and it also began foreign-exchange and bullion-trading operations. However, when much of Quebec's fur trading activities shifted to Hudson Bay during the 1820s, the bank suffered and began to diversify its lending activities. In 1832 it began financing Canada's first railroad, The Champlain & St. Lawrence.

The bank also began to grow through acquisitions, acquiring the Bank of Canada (1831) and the Bank of the People (1840). The company also expanded outside of Canada, opening a branch in New York in 1859. When Canada was unified in 1867, Bank of Montreal added more branches, following the Canadian Pacific Railroad's expansion to the west. Beginning in the 1860s it became the official bank for the government of Canada, providing financing for government projects, a position it held until 1935 when the Bank of Canada was created. During the early part of the 20th century, Bank of Montreal went on a buying spree, acquiring a number of Canadian banks. By 1914 Bank of Montreal had become Canada's largest bank. The company continued its acquisitions following WWI, buying the British Bank of North America (1918), Merchants Bank of Canada (1922), and Molsons Bank (1925). However, the bank's growth was brought to a grinding halt during the 1930s by the Depression.

WWII pumped up Canada's and the company's economy, and Bank of Montreal enjoyed even greater growth following the war as Canada's economy prospered. The company also began a push for international expansion, particularly in Latin America. However, the company was slow to adapt to changes in the banking industry, failing to capitalize on the growth of consumer and small business lending during the 1960s and becoming the last major Canadian bank to issue a credit card (in 1972). In 1975 Bank of Montreal hired William Mullholland, an American who was a former partner at Morgan Stanley, to run the company. Mullholland closed down unprofitable branches and modernized the company.

In 1984 the bank bought Harris Bankcorp for US$547 million. In 1987, following the deregulation of the Canadian banking industry, Bank of Montreal moved into investment banking, acquiring Nesbitt Thomson, one of Canada's largest brokerage firms.

During the late 1980s Bank of Montreal was hurt by the Latin American debt crisis because of its heavy exposure in Brazil and Mexico. In 1990 Matthew Barrett succeeded Mullholland as chairman. Barrett focused on increasing the bank's mortgage, personal, and commercial lending.

In 1994 Bank of Montreal became the first Canadian bank listed on the NYSE.

NYSE symbol: BMO
Fiscal year ends: October 31

Chairman and CEO: Matthew W. Barrett,
C$1,900,000 pay
President and COO: F. Anthony Comper,
C$1,200,000 pay
EVP and CFO: Robert B. Wells
SVP, Secretary, and General Counsel: Dereck M.
Jones
SVP Human Resources: Harriet Stairs
VC; CEO, Harris Bankcorp (US): Alan G.
McNally, C$934,958 pay
SVP and CFO, Harris Bankcorp (US): Pierre
O. Greffe
SVP Human Resources, Harris Bankcorp (US):
Calvin S. Stowell, Jr.
Auditors: Coopers & Lybrand; KPMG Peat
Marwick Thorne

HQ: PO Box 6002, Postal Station Place d'Armes,
Montreal, Quebec H2Y 3S8, Canada
Phone: 514-877-7110
Fax: 514-877-7525
US HQ: Harris Bankcorp, Inc., 111 W. Monroe
St., Chicago, IL 60603
US Phone: 312-461-2121
US Fax: 312-461-7385

	1994 Assets	
	C$ mil.	% of total
Canada	85,714	62
US	42,811	31
Other countries	9,650	7
Total	**138,175**	**100**

	1994 Assets	
	C$ mil.	% of total
Cash & equivalents	14,659	11
Securities	26,535	19
Loans	88,634	64
Other	8,347	6
Total	**138,175**	**100**

Selected Subsidiaries
Bank of Montreal Asia Ltd. (Singapore)
Bank of Montreal Capital Markets (Holdings) Ltd. (UK)
Bank of Montreal Europe Ltd. (UK)
Bank of Montreal Investment Management Ltd.
Bank of Montreal Investor Services Ltd.
Bank of Montreal Mortgage Corp.
Concordia Financial Corp. (Barbados)
First Canadian Assessoria e Serviços Ltda. (Brazil)
Harris Bankcorp, Inc. (US)
Harris Futures (US)
Harris Nesbitt Thomson Securities Inc. (US)
The Nesbitt Burns Corporation Ltd.
The Trust Company of Bank of Montreal

Banc One	First Chicago
Bank of New York	Imasco
Bank of Nova Scotia	Imperial Bank of Canada
BankAmerica	LaSalle National
Bankers Trust	Lloyds
Barclays	Merrill Lynch
Canadian Imperial	J.P. Morgan
Central Guaranty Trustco	National Bank of Canada
Charles Schwab	NationsBank
Chase Manhattan	NatWest
Chemical Banking	Northern Trust
Citicorp	Paine Webber
CS Holding	Royal Bank of Canada
Dai-Ichi Kangyo	Royal Bank of Scotland
Dean Witter, Discover	Standard Chartered
Deutsche Bank	Toronto-Dominion Bank

$= C$1.35 (Oct. 31, 1994)	9-Year Growth	1985	1986	1987	1988	1989	1990	1991	1992	1993	1994
Assets (C$ mil.)	5.9%	82,420	87,180	84,228	78,909	78,921	87,370	98,725	109,035	116,869	138,175
Net income (C$ mil.)	8.6%	393	310	523	500	(39)	522	595	640	709	825
Income as % of sales	—	0.5%	0.4%	0.6%	0.6%	—	0.6%	0.6%	0.6%	0.6%	0.6%
Earnings per share (C$)	4.9%	2.13	1.56	—	2.16	—	2.10	2.31	2.36	2.55	2.97
Stock price – high (C$)	—	17.25	17.19	19.50	14.88	17.63	16.50	22.13	24.13	28.00	30.75
Stock price – low (C$)	—	13.13	13.50	12.50	12.31	13.88	12.19	14.38	20.63	21.25	22.00
Stock price – close (C$)	5.3%	17.25	16.69	13.13	14.00	17.75	29.13	20.00	22.81	27.88	26.13
P/E – high	—	8	11	—	7	—	8	10	10	11	10
P/E – low	—	6	9	—	6	—	6	6	9	8	7
Dividends per share (C$)	2.3%	0.98	0.98	1.00	1.00	1.06	1.06	1.06	1.06	1.12	1.20
Book value per share (C$)	1.9%	18.10	18.43	14.75	15.61	13.98	15.00	16.05	17.69	19.40	21.39
Employees	0.5%	33,281	32,988	34,482	34,115	33,666	33,580	32,130	32,126	32,067	34,769

1994 Year-end:
Debt ratio: 80.8%
Return on equity: 15.7%
Equity as % of assets: 4.7%
L-T debt (mil.): C$2,218
No. of shares (mil.): 265
Dividends
  Yield: 4.6%
  Payout: 40.4%
Market value (mil.): $5,137
Sales (mil.): $6,747

**Stock Price History
High/Low 1985–94**

BARCLAYS PLC

OVERVIEW

After bad debts resulted in its first-ever unprofitable year (1992), Barclays, the UK's largest bank, has pursued a cautious strategy, backing away from its worldwide loans business in order to build up its UK retail banking segments (whose results were aided by the beginnings of a recovery at home) and its worldwide investment banking businesses.

Barclays has reorganized its operations into 3 major divisions: Banking, Service Businesses, and BZW. BZW (Barclays de Zoete Wedd) handles financial market services, such as money markets, foreign exchange, and trading. In 1993 BZW took over the management of all of Barclays's US banking businesses. Barclays has over 2,000 branches in the UK and operates personal banking services in the UK, France, and Spain. It also issues the Barclaycard credit card, which is used by more than 8 million people. Other services offered include life insurance, pensions, and mortgage banking.

Between 1989 and 1994 the company slashed its UK work force by 25% to 65,100 and cut its branch network in the UK by almost 22%. To appease stockholders upset by Barclays's losses and by the perception of less-than-adequate managerial controls, chairman and CEO Andrew Buxton (a descendant of one of the bank's founding families) split Barclays's traditionally dual executive role in 1993. He hired Martin Taylor (previously CEO of UK textile firm Courtaulds) as CEO while he retains the chairmanship.

WHEN

The eagle that is the symbol of Barclays first spread its wings in 1736 when James Barclay joined a family goldsmithing and banking firm under the sign of a black spread eagle. As other family members joined the London enterprise, it became known as Barclays, Bevan & Tritton (1782).

In the late 19th century, British banking underwent a legislative overhaul, and, as a defensive measure, 20 banks combined to ward off takeovers (1896). The new firm was known as Barclay & Co.

The bank then began to take over other banks. It bought 17 private banks in its first 20 years, including the Colonial Bank, chartered in 1836 to serve the West Indies and British Guiana. The bank renamed itself Barclays Bank Ltd. in 1917. It weathered the Depression as the 2nd largest of the Big 5 London Clearing Banks, after Midland Bank.

Barclays was poised to take advantage of international economic expansion after WWII, and by the late 1950s it had surpassed Midland Bank as the largest London Clearing Bank. Its large branch network was linked by computer (1959), and it introduced the Barclaycard in conjunction with Bank of America's BankAmericard (1966).

In 1968, 3 big London Clearing Banks — Barclays, Martins, and Lloyds — proposed to merge, but the UK's Monopolies Commission barred the combination, fearing an unreasonable reduction of competition. Barclays shifted its aim and bought Martins without any governmental objection.

Barclays entered the US consumer finance market in 1980 when it acquired American Credit. That same year the bank's North American unit, BarclaysAmerican, added 138 finance offices purchased from Beneficial, and Barclays's New York bank added 31 branches with a $26.5 million purchase from Bankers Trust (1982).

During the 1980s London Clearing Banks faced increased challenges from invading overseas banks, from local building and loans, and from the financial markets. After a 1984 act of Parliament, Barclays restructured itself as the holding company for Barclays Bank PLC, its chief operating subsidiary.

To prepare for British financial deregulation in 1986, Barclays formed Barclays de Zoete Wedd (BZW) through a merger of its merchant bank with 2 other London financial firms. To rid itself of unprofitable lines of business in an era of sagging profits, Barclays sold its California bank (to Wells Fargo, 1988) and its US consumer finance outfit (to Primerica's Commercial Credit, 1989).

In 1990 Barclays bought Merck, Finck & Co., a private German bank, and L'Européenne de Banque, a Paris bank. Bad loans, including an estimated $400 million to troubled developer Olympia & York, resulted in a $520 million loss in 1992.

In 1993 Barclaycard created a joint venture with Ford to issue a new credit card. The company sold its Australian retail banking business to St. George's Bank of Australia in 1994.

NYSE symbol: BCS (ADR)
Fiscal year ends: December 31

WHO

Chairman: Andrew R. F. Buxton,
   age 54, £375,000 pay
Deputy Chairman; Chairman, BZW: Sir Peter
   Middleton, age 59
CEO: John Martin Taylor, age 41
CEO, BZW Division: David Band, age 51
Finance Director: Oliver H. J. Stocken, age 52
Director of Personnel: J. W. G. Cotton
Group Secretary: J. M. D. Atterbury
CEO, Barclays Bank PLC (US): Richard M. Webb
Auditors: Price Waterhouse

WHERE

HQ: Johnson Smirke Building,
   4 Royal Mint Court, London EC3N 4HJ, UK
Phone: +44-(0)71-626-1567
Fax: +44-(0)71-696-2811
US HQ: Barclays Bank PLC, 75 Wall St.,
   New York, NY 10265
US Phone: 212-412-4000
US Fax: 212-797-3018

Barclays has over 2,000 branches and offices in
the UK and operates branches around the world.

	1993 Assets	
	$ mil.	% of total
UK	116,362	70
North America	20,725	13
Other European Union	17,005	10
Other countries	11,906	7
Adjustments	79,601	—
Total	**245,609**	**100**

WHAT

	1993 Assets	
	$ mil.	% of total
Cash & equivalents	1,346	1
Treasury securities	8,807	4
Bonds & equities	32,499	13
Loans to customers	138,819	56
Loans to banks	34,403	14
Other	29,735	12
Total	**245,609**	**100**

Major Subsidiaries
Barclays Bank Finance Co. (Jersey) Ltd.
Barclays Bank of Botswana Ltd. (74.9%)
Barclays Bank of Canada
Barclays Bank of Kenya Ltd. (68.5%)
Barclays Bank of Zimbabwe Ltd. (66.2%)
Barclays Bank SA (99.6%, Spain)
Barclays de Zoete Wedd Holdings Ltd.
Barclays Finance Company (Guernsey) Ltd.
Barclays Financial Services Italia SpA (Italy)
Barclays Financial Services Ltd.
Barclays Mercantile Business Finance Ltd.
Barclays Trust and Banking Company (Japan) Ltd.
BarclaysAmericanCorporation (US)

KEY COMPETITORS

Bank of New York	HSBC
Bankers Trust	Imperial Bank of Canada
Canadian Imperial	Industrial Bank of Japan
Chase Manhattan	Lloyds
Chemical Banking	J.P. Morgan
Citicorp	NatWest
Crédit Lyonnais	Royal Bank of Canada
CS Holding	Royal Bank of Scotland
Dai-Ichi Kangyo	Standard Chartered
Deutsche Bank	Union Bank of Switzerland

HOW MUCH

Stock prices are for ADRs ADR = 4 shares	Annual Growth	1984	1985	1986	1987	1988	1989	1990	1991	1992	1993
Assets ($ mil.)	13.7%	77,610	94,217	117,086	165,652	189,251	209,418	260,332	258,193	225,839	245,609
Net income ($ mil.)	3.6%	337	646	908	349	1,604	742	755	452	(520)	463
Income as % of assets	—	0.4%	0.7%	0.8%	0.2%	0.8%	0.4%	0.3%	0.2%	—	0.2%
Earnings per share ($)	(4.7%)	1.77	2.87	3.76	1.39	4.56	1.89	1.91	1.14	(1.30)	1.15
Stock price – high ($)	—	—	—	22.13	30.35	26.78	26.42	30.75	36.00	30.50	39.00
Stock price – low ($)	—	—	—	18.92	20.71	14.99	19.10	22.00	24.00	20.13	22.50
Stock price – close ($)	8.0%	—	—	21.96	24.10	20.88	26.42	28.25	28.00	23.25	37.75
P/E – high	—	—	—	6	22	6	14	16	32	—	34
P/E – low	—	—	—	5	15	3	10	12	21	—	20
Dividends per share ($)	8.4%	—	—	0.46	1.19	1.33	1.28	1.68	1.64	2.00	0.81
Book value per share ($)	5.0%	12.53	19.87	22.80	30.15	26.43	26.03	29.70	26.84	34.05	19.37
Employees	(2.8%)	125,900	105,900	110,000	113,000	118,410	116,500	116,800	111,400	105,000	97,800

1993 Year-end:
Debt ratio: 90.0%
Return on equity: 4.3%
Equity as % of assets: 6.2%
No. of shares (mil.): 406
Dividends
   Yield: 2.1%
   Payout: 70.4%
Market value (mil.): $15,318
Sales (mil.): $21,879

**Stock Price History
High/Low 1986–93**

BASF GROUP

BASF, best known in the US for its audio and video tapes, is the world's 2nd largest chemical manufacturer, after fellow German company Hoechst. The company had one of its poorest sales performance in years in 1993, but its situation appears to be improving owing in part to cost-cutting measures.

The conglomerate has 6 sectors: oil and gas, chemicals, agricultural products, plastics and fibers, dyestuffs and finishing products, and consumer products. BASF is now concentrating on expanding its natural gas business and has finished 2 European pipelines.

BASF, to counter high domestic labor costs, has reduced its payroll by 22,000 since 1990 and plans further reductions. Slow consumer demand and a strong deutsche mark also contributed to its recent difficulties. The company plans major expansion in Asia and claims to be the biggest foreign chemical industry investor in China. Also, its drug division, Knoll, has recently diversified into the German generic drug market.

WHEN

Originally known as Badische Anilin & Soda-Fabrik, BASF was founded in Mannheim, Germany, by jeweler Frederick Englehorn in 1861. Unable to find enough land for expansion in Mannheim, BASF moved to nearby Ludwigshafen in 1865. The company was a pioneer in coal tar dyes, developing a very successful synthetic indigo in 1897. BASF's synthetic dyes rapidly replaced more expensive, inconvenient organic dyes.

BASF scientist Fritz Haber synthesized ammonia in 1909, allowing the company to enter the nitrogenous fertilizers market (1913). Haber received a Nobel Prize in 1919 but later was charged with war crimes for his work with poison gases. BASF grew and concentrated its production at a sprawling manufacturing complex in Ludwigshafen.

Managed by Carl Bosch, another Nobel Prize winner, BASF joined the I.G. Farben cartel with Bayer, Hoechst, and others in 1925, creating a German chemical colossus. Within the cartel BASF developed polystyrene, PVC, and magnetic tape. Part of the Nazi war machine, I.G. Farben manufactured synthetic rubber, using labor from the Auschwitz concentration camp during WWII.

After the war I.G. Farben was dismantled, and in 1952 BASF regained its independence and began rebuilding its war-ravaged factories. Strong postwar domestic demand for basic chemicals aided BASF's recovery. In the late 1950s BASF began joint ventures abroad, including one in the US with Dow Chemical in 1958 (BASF bought out Dow's half in 1978). The company moved away from coal-based products and into petrochemicals, even acquiring German oil and gas producer Wintershall (1969), and became a leading plastic and synthetic fiber manufacturer.

Acquisitions figured prominently in BASF's global expansion and diversification into related businesses. In the US the company purchased Wyandotte Chemicals (1969), Chemetron (pigments, 1979), and Inmont (paint, ink; 1985), among others. Despite its acquisitions and new products, BASF remains largely dependent on sales of basic chemicals.

In 1990 BASF became the first outsider to buy a major chemical company in eastern Germany when it purchased Synthesewerk Schwarzheide (SYS). BASF hoped to take advantage of tax incentives and cheaper labor in the eastern states, but modernizing SYS's facilities has proved expensive. Also in 1990 Jürgen Strube became the board chair.

To expand its natural gas business in Europe, in 1991 the company concluded an agreement with Russia's Gazprom for Russian natural gas and a contract with France's Elf Aquitaine for North Sea gas. BASF also began restructuring its magnetic media sector in 1991, closing a videocassette production plant in Berlin. In 1992 it moved an audiotape manufacturing operation from Massachusetts to Europe. Also in 1992 BASF paid $300 million for Mobil's polystyrene-resin business, giving it almost 10% of the US market. In 1993 the company suffered from an uncertain US health care market and European agriculture policy reform.

In early 1994, after a year of negotiations, BASF bought Imperial Chemical's polypropylene business for $90 million, making BASF Europe's 2nd largest producer of this plastic after the Himont-Royal Dutch/Shell conglomerate. Late in 1994 the company agreed to buy the pharmaceutical arm of Boots (UK) for $1.4 billion in order to expand into the UK and Commonwealth countries.

OTC symbol: BASFY (ADR)
Fiscal year ends: December 31

Chairman of the Supervisory Board: Hans Albers
Chairman of the Board of Executive Directors:
Jürgen Strube
**Deputy Chairman of the Board of Executive
Directors:** Wolfgang Jentzsch
Division Head Finance: Harald Grunert
Division Head Human Resources: Helmut
Glassen
**Chairman, President, and CEO, BASF Corp.
(US):** J. Dieter Stein
Auditors: Schitag, Deloitte & Touche GmbH

HQ: Carl-Bosch St. 38, 67056 Ludwigshafen,
Germany
Phone: +49-621-600
Fax: +49-621-604-2525
US HQ: BASF Corporation, 3000 Continental Dr.
North, Mt. Olive, NJ 07828-1234
US Phone: 201-426-2600
US Fax: 201-426-2610

	1993 Sales	
	DM mil.	% of total
Europe	25,378	63
North America	8,523	21
Asia, Australia & Africa	4,172	10
Latin America	2,495	6
Adjustments	2,555	—
Total	**43,123**	**100**

	1993 Sales	
	DM mil.	% of total
Plastics & fibers	9,811	24
Consumer products	8,740	22
Dyestuffs & finishing products	7,572	19
Chemicals	5,371	13
Oil & gas	4,352	11
Products for agriculture	3,781	9
Other	942	2
Adjustments	2,554	—
Total	**43,123**	**100**

Plastics and Fibers
Engineering plastics
Nylon products
Polyolefins
Polypropylene
Polyurethane

Chemicals
Basic and industrial
chemicals
Color and process chemicals
Fertilizers
Fungicides and herbicides
Pigments

Consumer Products
Audio- and videotapes
Carpet yarns
Coatings and paints
Pharmaceuticals (Knoll)
Printing inks and plates
Vitamins

Other Products
Crude oil
Flavors and fragrances
Natural gas (WINGAS)
Petroleum coke

Akzo Nobel	FMC	Monsanto
AlliedSignal	Formosa Plastics	Novo Nordisk
Bayer	Fuji Photo	Pfizer
Bristol-Myers	Hanson	Polaroid
Squibb	Hercules	Rhône-Poulenc
Ciba-Geigy	Hoechst	Roche
Dow Chemical	Huntsman	Royal Dutch/Shell
DuPont	Chemical	Sandoz
Eastman Chemical	Marion Merrell	Sony
Eli Lilly	Dow	Union Carbide
ENI	Merck	Warner-Lambert
Exxon	3M	Wellcome

$=DM1.74 (Dec. 31,1993)	9-Year Growth	1984	1985	1986	1987	1988	1989	1990	1991	1992	1993
Sales (DM mil.)	0.7%	40,400	44,377	40,471	40,238	43,868	47,617	46,623	46,626	44,522	43,123
Net income (DM mil.)	—	895	998	910	1,051	1,410	2,015	1,107	1,039	615	858
Income as % of sales	—	2.2%	2.2%	2.2%	2.6%	3.2%	4.2%	2.4%	2.3%	1.4%	2.0%
Earnings per share (DM)	(3.4)%	20	19	17	19	25	35	19	18	11	15
Stock price – high (DM)	—	186	275	332	347	287	315	319	260	255	308
Stock price – low (DM)	—	147	177	239	237	223	256	184	194	199	207
Stock price – close (DM)	5.7%	186	271	276	256	280	300	195	220	210	306
P/E – high	—	9	14	20	18	11	9	17	14	24	14
P/E – low	—	7	9	14	12	9	7	10	12	18	21
Dividends per share (DM)[1]	1.5%	7.0	9.0	10.0	10.0	10.0	12.0	14.0	13.0	10.0	8.0
Book value per share (DM)	3.0%	194	207	217	214	219	243	250	257	253	254
Employees	(0.4)%	115,816	130,173	131,468	133,759	134,834	136,990	134,647	129,434	123,254	112,020

1993 Year-end:
Debt ratio: 29.6%
Return on equity: 5.8%
Cash (mil.): DM5,239
Long-term debt (mil.): DM2,223
No. of shares (mil.): 58
Dividends
Yield: 2.6%
Payout: 54.5%
Market value (mil.): $10,200
Sales (mil.): $24,783

**Stock Price History
High/Low 1984–93**

[1] Not including rights offerings

BASS PLC

OVERVIEW

Beer sales for Bass, Britain's leading brewer, are as flat as 2-day-old ale, but revenues from its hotel interests are picking up the slack caused by Britain's shrinking beer market. The company brews and distributes brands such as Bass Ale, Caffrey's Irish Ale, Carling Black Label (Britain's best selling beer), and Worthington Best Bitter. Its Britvic Soft Drinks subsidiary is the 2nd largest UK soft drink maker (after Cadbury Schweppes's venture with Coca-Cola). Bass also operates nearly 3,000 pubs and restaurants and 900 betting shops in the UK.

The 1989 acquisition of Holiday Inn from Promus for $2.8 billion made Bass the world's #1 global hotel operator, with 1,925 hotels in more than 60 countries.

While bemoaning the heavy taxation of British beer and 2% per year decline in beer consumption in the UK, Bass is striking out with an ambitious strategy to expand and upgrade its Holiday Inn hotel chain. After a review of 1,080 Holiday Inn hotels in the US, the Atlanta-based Bass subsidiary, Holiday Inn Worldwide, ordered its US franchisees in 1994 to either come up with $500 million for repairs and upgrading or leave the system. Holiday Inn plans to add 1,205 new hotels worldwide by 1998. The company plans to add 70 hotels in India in the next 10 years.

WHEN

In 1777 William Bass decided to switch from transporting beer to brewing it in Burton-on-Trent in England. Burton's pure water supply allowed Bass to brew lighter ales than were being produced in London. During 1827, when Bass's grandson Michael took charge, the company produced 10,000 barrels. In 1876 Bass became the first company to gain trademark protection (for its red triangle) under the British Trademark Registration Act of 1875. By the time of Michael Bass's death in 1884, the 145-acre Bass brewery was the largest ale and bitter brewery in the world.

Most British brewers employed the tied-house system (where breweries controlled and supplied beer to their own pubs), which limited distribution but assured them of a market for their beer. Bass instead opted for the free-trade system, selling its beer through distributors and relying for expansion on consumers' growing demand for Bass beer. The temperance movement and WWI hurt all brewers, and consumers increasingly turned to movies and other diversions instead of evenings at the local pub. The tied-house pubs responded by upgrading and improving their facilities to lure customers back, and Bass's sales suffered when the pubs serving its beer failed to follow suit. During the 1920s the company acquired several breweries, including rival Worthington & Company in 1926.

When Sir James Grigg, age 70, took over in 1959, he began looking for a merger partner. Bass merged with efficient regional brewer Mitchells & Butler in 1961. Under Sir Alan Walker the company merged with Charrington United (Carling Black Label lager, pubs; 1967) to form a nationwide network of breweries and pubs. By 1970 Bass's British market share approached 25%. Led by lager, sales boomed.

When growth slowed in the 1980s, Bass sold its less profitable pubs and diversified. The rapid growth of the company's Crest Hotel chain (started in 1969) encouraged Bass to buy Coral Leisure (hotels, gambling; 1980). Bass acquired Horizon Travel (packaged holidays) in 1987 and bought the Holiday Inn chain in a series of steps beginning in 1987 and ending in 1990 with the purchase of all North American Holiday Inns.

Named after the Bing Crosby/Fred Astaire movie, Holiday Inns had been founded in Memphis in 1952 by Kemmons Wilson. Franchises rapidly emerged along US highways, creating one of the world's largest lodging chains. The company bought Harrah's (casinos, 1979) and Granada Royale Hometel (later renamed Embassy Suites, 1984) and started Homewood Suites (1988), all of which were spun off to shareholders as Promus Companies when Bass bought Holiday Inn.

In 1990 Bass began a $1 billion renovation of Holiday Inns. But after discovering that many of the hotels didn't meet zoning laws and fell below minimal standards, Bass sued Promus for unspecified damages. The trial was still pending in 1994.

Bass closed 2 UK breweries in 1991. In 1993 the company sold its Augustus Barnett liquor retailer to Allied-Lyons for $60 million. Sales of Bass beers by volume declined by 0.8% in 1994 over 1993 sales.

NYSE symbol: BAS (ADR)
Fiscal year ends: September 30

Chairman and CEO: Ian M. G. Prosser, age 51,
£593,000 pay
Chairman and CEO, Bass Taverns: Philip
Bowman, age 41
**Chairman and CEO, Holiday Inn Worldwide
(US):** Bryan D. Langton, age 57
EVP Finance, Holiday Inn Worldwide (US):
Graham Staley
**SVP Human Resources, Holiday Inn Worldwide
(US):** Michael J. Rumke
Auditors: Ernst & Young

HQ: 20 N. Audley St., London W1Y 1WE, UK
Phone: +44-(0)71-409-1919
Fax: +44-(0)71-409-8503
US HQ: Holiday Inn Worldwide, 3 Ravinia Dr.,
Ste. 2000, Atlanta, GA 30346-2149
US Phone: 404-604-2000
US Fax: 404-604-2009

Bass runs nearly 3,000 pubs in the UK and 1,925
hotels in over 60 countries.

	1994 Sales		1994 Operating Income	
	£ mil.	% of total	£ mil.	% of total
UK	3,753	84	474	75
United States	406	9	127	20
Other Europe, M. East & Africa	213	5	7	1
Other countries	80	2	22	4
Total	**4,452**	**100**	**630**	**100**

	1994 Sales		1994 Operating Income	
	£ mil.	% of total	£ mil.	% of total
Brewing	1,295	29	138	22
Pub retailing	1,079	25	220	35
Leisure	1,027	23	72	12
Hotels	626	14	153	24
Soft drinks	416	9	40	6
Other activities	9	0	7	1
Total	**4,452**	**100**	**630**	**100**

Beer Brands (UK)	Soft Drink Bottling (UK)	Other
Carling Black Label	7-Up	Bass Developments Ltd. (property)
Draught Bass	Britvic	Société Viticole de Château Lascombes SA (95%, wines, France)
Tennent's	Pepsi	
Worthington	Tango	
Hotels and Restaurants	**Leisure**	
Crowne Plaza	Cafe bars	White Shield Insurance Co. Ltd. (Gibraltar)
Holiday Inns	Coral betting	
Toby Restaurants	Gala bingo clubs	
	Hollywood Bowl	

Accor	Foster's Brewing	Ladbroke Group
Adolph Coors	Grand Metropolitan	LVMH
Allied Domecq	Guinness	Manor Care
Anheuser-Busch	Heineken	Marriott
Bally Entertainment	Helmsley	International
Cadbury Schweppes	Hilton Hospitality Franchise	Molson
Carlsberg	Hyatt	Nestlé
Carlson	ITT	Promus
Coca-Cola	J Sainsbury	Rank
Cott	John Labatt	San Miguel
Danone	Kirin	Triarc
		Virgin Group

£=$1.48 (Dec. 31, 1993)	9-Year Growth	1985	1986	1987	1988	1989	1990	1991	1992[1]	1993	1994
Sales (£ mil.)	7.1%	2,411	2,710	3,213	3,734	4,036	4,461	4,383	4,307	4,451	4,452
Net income (£ mil.)	8.7%	165	199	244	307	382	470	452	304	314	349
Income as % of sales	—	6.8%	7.3%	9.0%	8.2%	9.5%	10.5%	10.3%	7.1%	7.1%	7.8%
Earnings per share (p)	5.4%	0.25	0.29	0.35	0.43	0.53	0.54	0.46	0.35	0.36	0.40
Stock price – high (p)	—	336	410	513	423	560	547	527	658	647	619
Stock price – low (p)	—	231	305	358	360	388	438	443	472	441	485
Stock price – close (p)	5.4%	321	360	400	389	514	513	493	635	536	515
P/E – high	—	14	14	15	10	11	10	11	19	18	15
P/E – low	—	9	11	10	8	7	8	10	13	12	12
Dividends per share (p)	12.5%	7.3	8.5	9.8	11.8	14.1	16.2	17.8	18.9	19.8	21.1
Book value per share (p)	8.1%	205	214	352	358	387	404	421	387	393	413
Employees	0.7%	71,260	76,922	79,348	84,843	90,138	98,345	90,104	84,095	81,105	75,845

1994 Year-end:
Debt ratio: 43.0%
Return on equity: 10.0%
Cash (mil.): £851
Long-term debt (mil.): £1,268
No. of shares (mil.): 868
Dividends
  Yield: 4.1%
  Payout: 52.6%
Market value (mil.): $6,613
Sales (mil.): $6,586

**Stock Price History
High/Low 1985–94**

[1] Accounting change

B.A.T INDUSTRIES P.L.C.

OVERVIEW

What goes around comes around. B.A.T Industries, the London-based cigarette giant, celebrated the end of 1994 by acquiring its one-time parent, American Tobacco, for $1 billion. The move brings B.A.T a number of well-known brand names, like Carlton, to add to its own stable, which includes Barclay, Capri, and Kool.

Although the US government initially opposed the acquisition, B.A.T reached a settlement with it by agreeing to sell a manufacturing plant and 7 cigarette brands. Once the deal closed, B.A.T moved quickly to incorporate American Tobacco into its US subsidiary Brown & Williamson, announcing plans

to cut more than half of American Tobacco's workforce.

The company's secondary business lines are insurance and financial services through Allied Dunbar (life assurance and pensions) and Eagle Star (life and general insurance) in the UK and Farmers Group (property and casualty insurance) in the US. B.A.T had legal troubles in the UK in 1994 over misrepresentations made regarding private pensions sold by its insurance subsidiaries.

B.A.T also owns 40% of Canada's Imasco, which includes Imperial Tobacco (Canada's #1 cigarette maker) and Hardee's, a US-based fast food chain.

WHEN

The British-American Tobacco Company was created to end a cigarette price war in Britain between Imperial Tobacco (UK) and American Tobacco. James Buchanan Duke, creator of American Tobacco and owner of exclusive rights to the best cigarette manufacturing technology of the times, had set his sights on the British market after attaining a 90% share in the US. After a year of vicious price cutting in Britain, Imperial counterattacked in America. The companies called a truce and created a cartel in 1902. The deal granted Imperial the British market, American the US market, and jointly owned British-American the rest of the world, with rights to the brand names of its founders.

With Duke in control, British-American began spreading throughout the world. Duke had his greatest early success in China, where a massive billboard campaign in 1907 and the distribution of millions of free samples in 1909 generated annual sales of 25 billion cigarettes by 1920. When the Communist Revolution ended British-American's operations in China, the company lost over 25% of its sales.

A 1911 US antitrust action forced American to sell its interest in British-American and opened the US market to the company. The company purchased an American cigarette manufacturer, Brown & Williamson, in 1927 and continued to grow through geographical expansion until the 1960s. Modest diversification efforts in the 1960s included packaging, paper, and cosmetics.

The 1902 agreement was terminated in Britain in 1972 with the advent of the EC.

British-American's subsequent efforts to penetrate the British market proved unsuccessful, and it withdrew from the market in 1984.

As public concern over smoking mounted, British-American acquired nontobacco businesses and changed its name to B.A.T Industries in 1976. The company bought food retailers in the early 1970s but sold them in the 1980s. The acquisitions of retailers Saks (1973), Argos (UK, 1979), Marshall Field (1982), and numerous others significantly diversified the company's sales base. B.A.T then developed a taste for insurance firms, buying Eagle Star (UK, 1984), Allied Dunbar (UK, 1985), and Farmers Group (US, 1988).

Responding to a 1989 hostile takeover bid from Sir James Goldsmith, B.A.T announced a restructuring plan calling for the spinoff of its British retailers and the sale of all other retail and paper operations, leaving the company with tobacco and financial services. In 1990, after California insurance regulators blocked Goldsmith's attempt to force B.A.T to sell Farmers Group to Axa-Midi (France), Goldsmith abandoned his bid. Meanwhile, B.A.T sold Marshall Field to Dayton Hudson for just over $1 billion and Saks to Investcorp, an Arabian partnership, for $1.5 billion. That same year B.A.T spun off its Wiggins Teape Appleton paper operations.

In 1992 Eagle Star sold its Australian Eagle life and general insurance subsidiary. B.A.T and American Brands swapped brands in some European markets in 1993. In 1994 B.A.T paid $200 million for control of Uzbekistan's tobacco processing industry and also bought a Ukrainian cigarette plant.

AMEX symbol: BTI (ADR)
Fiscal year ends: December 31

WHO

Chairman: Sir Patrick Sheehy, age 63,
£620,181 pay
Deputy Chairman and Group CEO: Martin F.
Broughton, age 46
Group Finance Director: David P. Allvey, age 48
**Chairman and CEO, Brown & Williamson
Tobacco (US):** Thomas E. Sandefur, Jr.
CFO, Brown & Williamson Tobacco (US): Carl
Schoenbachler
**VP Human Resources, Brown & Williamson
Tobacco (US):** Henry Frick
Auditors: Coopers & Lybrand

WHERE

HQ: Windsor House, 50 Victoria St.,
London SW1H 0NL, UK
Phone: +44-(01)71-222-7979
Fax: +44-(01)71-222-0122
US HQ: Brown & Williamson Tobacco Corp.,
PO Box 35090, Louisville, KY 40232
US Phone: 502-568-7000
US Fax: 502-568-7107

	1993 Sales		1993 Operating Income	
	$ mil.	% of total	$ mil.	% of total
UK	8,572	28	1,112	33
Latin America	6,544	21	419	13
Other Europe	6,345	21	1,263	39
North America	5,312	17	160	5
Asia	1,627	5	167	5
Other countries	2,325	8	160	5
Total	**30,725**	**100**	**3,281**	**100**

WHAT

	1993 Sales		1993 Operating Income	
	$ mil.	% of total	$ mil.	% of total
Commercial activities	20,240	66	1,794	55
General insurance	5,341	17	935	28
Life insurance	5,144	17	552	17
Total	**30,725**	**100**	**3,281**	**100**

Selected Cigarette Brands

Benson & Hedges	Barclay
Derby	Belair
Free	Capri
Hollywood	GPC Approved
John Player Gold Leaf	Kool
Kent	Raleigh
Lucky Strike	Richland
Pall Mall	Savannah
Plaza	Viceroy
State Express 555	

Major Subsidiaries and Affiliates
Allied Dunbar (insurance, UK)
B.A.T Cigarettenfabriken (tobacco, Germany)
British-American Tobacco Co. Ltd. (UK)
Brown & Williamson Tobacco Corp. (US)
Eagle Star (insurance, UK)
Farmers Group, Inc. (insurance, US)
Imasco Ltd. (40%; financial services, restaurants,
retailing, and tobacco; Canada)
Investors Guaranty Life Insurance Co. (US)

KEY COMPETITORS

Allianz	Loews	State Farm
Brooke Group	MetLife	Tokio Marine
CIGNA	Philip Morris	and Fire
GEICO	RJR Nabisco	Ultratech Corp.
Hanson	Standard	Universal Corp.
Japan Monopoly Corp.	Commercial	UST Inc.
Liggett		

HOW MUCH

	9-Year Growth	1984	1985	1986	1987	1988	1989	1990	1991	1992	1993
Sales ($ mil.)	10.1%	12,932	15,529	17,519	20,485	20,100	23,176	34,493	30,809	28,314	30,725
Net income ($ mil.)	7.1%	909	974	1,176	1,485	1,716	1,923	685	770	1,316	1,691
Income as % of sales	—	7.0%	6.3%	6.7%	7.2%	8.5%	8.3%	2.0%	2.5%	4.6%	5.5%
Earnings per share ($)	6.6%	0.64	0.68	0.80	0.72	0.88	1.04	0.36	0.44	1.04	1.14
Stock price – high ($)	—	4.25	4.56	7.00	11.56	8.81	15.00	13.88	13.56	15.63	17.25
Stock price – low ($)	—	2.50	3.56	4.19	6.69	6.75	8.00	9.56	10.44	10.50	12.13
Stock price – close ($)	16.4%	4.13	4.50	6.81	8.25	8.06	13.31	10.94	11.50	14.75	16.25
P/E – high	—	7	7	9	16	10	14	39	31	15	15
P/E – low	—	4	5	5	9	8	8	27	24	10	11
Dividends per share ($)	25.7%	0.12	0.16	0.20	0.28	0.36	0.36	2.40	0.60	0.72	0.94
Book value per share ($)	4.0%	3.38	3.59	4.15	4.98	4.35	5.49	3.90	4.11	4.06	4.80
Employees	(2.2%)	212,822	185,503	176,370	168,949	172,715	188,492	217,373	212,316	197,989	190,308

1993 Year-end:
Debt ratio: 87.3%
Return on equity: 25.2%
Cash (mil.): $1,623
Assets (mil.): $1.35
Long-term debt (mil.): $36,266
No. of shares (mil.): 1,540
Dividends
Yield: 5.8%
Payout: 82.5%
Market value (mil.): $25,019

**Stock Price History
High/Low 1984–93**

BAYER AG

Bayer paid $1 billion to end a big headache in 1994. That was the price to regain American rights to the Bayer brand name. Bayer paid SmithKline Beecham for the North American business of Sterling Winthrop, which had owned the Bayer label since it was confiscated by US authorities during WWI. (Only weeks before, SmithKline had purchased Sterling from Eastman Kodak.) In this purchase Bayer also gained big over-the-counter sellers such as Midol and Phillips Milk of Magnesia.

With product breakthroughs a Bayer hallmark, in 1993 the company increased its R&D budget to 7.8% of sales, the largest of any chemical and pharmaceutical company. That year it introduced its first genetically engineered product, the hemophilia treatment Kogenate. Bayer also signed an agreement with Viagene (US) to develop a gene therapy for hemophiliacs.

In 1994 Bayer's US subsidiary, Miles Inc., purchased a minority interest in privately held Schein Pharmaceutical (US), maker of over 350 generic drugs. Miles also signed a 5-year pact with ONYX Pharmaceuticals (US) to develop new drugs for cancer.

Bayer, founded by Friedrich Bayer in 1863, was among the pioneers of the modern German chemical industry. Prolific research labs fueled Bayer's growth beyond its original synthetic dye business, leading to the introduction of such breakthrough compounds as Antinonin (first synthetic pesticide, 1892), aspirin (1899), and synthetic rubber (1915).

Bayer's German heritage figured prominently in its history. Under Carl Duisberg, Bayer was alleged to be the source of the first poison gas, used by Germany in WWI. The US seized Bayer's American operations and trademark rights, selling them to Sterling Drug (US).

In 1925 Duisberg's desire to eliminate competition led to the merger of Bayer, BASF, Hoechst, and other German chemical concerns into the I.G. Farben Trust. The photography businesses of Bayer and the other I.G. Farben firms were combined as Agfa and folded into the trust. Between the wars Bayer's labs developed a treatment for African sleeping sickness (Germanin, 1921) and the first sulfa drug (Prontosil, 1935), while pioneering the development of polyurethanes.

The outbreak of WWII found I.G. Farben solidly and profitably in the Nazi camp. The trust took over chemical plants of Nazi-occupied countries and established factories near Auschwitz to take advantage of slave labor. At the end of the war, Bayer lost its 50% interest in Winthrop Laboratories (US) and Bayer of Canada, again to Sterling Drug. The Potsdam Agreement (1945) called for the breakup of I.G. Farben, and in 1951 Bayer emerged as an independent company consisting of many of its original operations, as well as Agfa.

After quickly rebuilding in Germany, Bayer entered into a US joint venture with Monsanto (Mobay, 1954) and later bought Monsanto's share (1967). Rapid postwar economic expansion in Germany and an expanding US economy bolstered Bayer's businesses. In the 1960s Bayer's labs continued to broaden the company's offerings in dyes, plastics, and polyurethanes, and the company built production facilities internationally. Agfa merged with Gevaert (photography, Belgium) in 1964. Bayer retained 60% ownership in Agfa-Gevaert.

Bayer acquired Cutter Labs (drugs, US, 1974), Metzeler (rubber, Germany, 1974), Miles Labs (Alka-Seltzer, One-A-Day vitamins; US; 1978), the rest of Agfa-Gevaert (1981), and Compugraphic and Matrix (electronic imaging, US, 1989). The acquisition of the Polysar rubber division of Nova Corporation of Alberta (1990) made Bayer a world leader in the synthetic rubber market.

In 1992 the weak world economy and the strong deutsche mark hampered exports, cutting Bayer's revenues. The company integrated its US holdings under the name Miles Inc., merging Miles, Mobay, Agfa, and management holding company Bayer USA.

In 1993 Bayer turned to Asia for new markets, signing an agreement with the Eisai Company to market nonprescription drugs in Japan. In 1994 the company announced plans to develop Bayer and Agfa-Gevaert production facilities in China.

Bayer, which had spent a decade developing solar energy cells from silicon, purchased 2 German manufacturing facilities in 1994. A new subsidiary, Bayer Solar, will oversee production of the photovoltaic wafers.

OTC symbol: BAYRY (ADR)
Fiscal year ends: December 31

Chairman: Manfred Schneider
**VC; Chairman, Investment and Technology
  Committee:** Hermann Wunderlich
Chairman, Finance Committee: Helmut Loehr
Chairman, Human Resources Committee: Klaus
  Kleine-Weischede
CEO, Bayer Corp. (US): Helge H. Wehmeier
EVP and CFO, Bayer Corp. (US): Gerd D.
  Mueller
SVP Human Resources, Bayer Corp. (US):
  Howard W. Reed
Auditors: Treuhand-Vereinigung AG
  Wirtschaftsprüfungsgesellschaft
  Steuerberatungsgesellschaft

HQ: Bayerwerk, 51368 Leverkusen, Germany
Phone: +49-214-301
Fax: +49-214-303-620
US HQ: Bayer Corporation, One Mellon Center,
  500 Grant St., Pittsburgh, PA 15219-2502
US Phone: 412-394-5500
US Fax: 412-394-5578

Bayer operates in 150 countries.

	1993 Sales	
	DM mil.	% of total
Europe	21,072	51
North America	9,719	24
Asia/Africa/Australia	7,570	19
Latin America	2,646	6
Total	**41,007**	**100**

	1993 Sales		1993 Operating Income	
	DM mil.	% of total	DM mil.	% of total
Health care	9,570	23	1,785	71
Industrial products	7,223	18	191	8
Polymers	6,839	17	(115)	—
Imaging technology	6,727	16	221	9
Organic products	5,455	13	(28)	—
Agrochemicals	5,193	13	293	12
Total	**41,007**	**100**	**2,347**	**100**

Health Care
Diagnostics
Pharmaceuticals
Self-medication

Industrial Products
Coating raw materials and
  specialty products
Inorganics
Pigments and ceramics
Polyurethanes
H.C. Starck

Polymers
Fibers
Plastics
Rhein Chemie Rheinau

Rubber
Wolff Walsrode

Imaging Technologies
Graphic systems
Photographic products
Technical imaging systems

Organic Products
Dyes and pigments
E.C. Erdölchemie (50%)
Haarmann & Reimer
Organic chemicals

Agrochemicals
Animal health
Consumer products
Crop protection

Akzo Nobel
American Home Products
BASF
Bristol-Myers Squibb
Ciba-Geigy
Dow Chemical
DuPont
Eastman Chemical
ENI
Fuji Photo

Hercules
Hoechst
Imperial Chemical
ITOCHU
3M
Pfizer
Polaroid
Rhône-Poulenc
Roche
SmithKline Beecham

$=DM1.74 (Dec. 31, 1993)	9-Year Growth	1984	1985	1986	1987	1988	1989	1990	1991	1992	1993
Sales (DM mil.)	(0.5%)	43,032	45,926	38,284	37,143	40,468	43,299	41,643	42,401	41,195	41,007
Net income (DM mil.)	—	1,339	1,259	1,322	1,498	1,855	2,083	1,881	1,824	0	0
Income as % of sales	—	3.1%	2.7%	3.5%	4.0%	4.6%	4.8%	4.5%	4.3%	0.0%	0.0%
Earnings per share (DM)	(3.0%)	26	27	24	24	29	33	29	28	23	20
Stock price – high (DM)	—	193	276	350	377	311	322	334	294	255	536
Stock price – low (DM)	—	152	185	263	247	237	275	195	213	199	253
Stock price – close (DM)	7.5%	193	276	317	264	307	316	216	278	268	370
P/E – high	—	7	10	15	16	11	10	12	10	11	27
P/E – low	—	6	7	11	10	8	8	7	8	9	13
Dividends per share (DM)[1]	5.2%	7.0	9.0	10.0	10.0	11.0	12.0	13.0	13.0	11.0	11.0
Book value per share (DM)	5.6%	161	191	214	219	233	244	246	253	260	264
Employees	(1.4%)	174,755	176,080	173,000	164,400	165,700	170,200	171,100	164,200	156,400	153,866

1993 Year-end:
Debt ratio: 21.1%
Return on equity: 7.6%
Cash (mil.): DM5,242
Long-term debt (mil.): DM2,376
No. of shares (mil.): 67
Dividends
  Yield: 3.0%
  Payout: 55.6%
Market value (mil.): $14,247
Sales (mil.): $23,567

Stock Price History
High/Low 1984–93

[1] Not including rights offerings

BAYERISCHE MOTOREN WERKE AG

OVERVIEW

BMW is rolling in success. In 1993 the maker of the "Yuppiemobile" became Europe's #1 auto exporter. Growing sales in Australia and the US upped the German company's share of the world auto market to 5%. Sales of BMW motorcycles grew 10%. BMW Rolls-Royce, the company's aircraft engine subsidiary, also scored new contracts.

By 1994 BMW was selling cars faster than it could make them. In July its Munich plant assembled its 5 millionth car. Its US plant began making cars in September, with production of 300 cars a day expected by late

1996. BMW also bought Rover from British Aerospace and Honda and introduced a lower-priced Rover (less than $30,000), the 4-wheel-drive Discovery, to strong sales.

Nonvehicle subsidiaries account for 18% of BMW's sales, including softlab (information systems), Axicon Mobilfunkdienste (telephone network equipment and service), and Kontron Elektronik (industrial computers).

Around 60% of BMW is owned by the Quandt family, allowing the company to make large, long-term investments in automobile technology.

WHEN

Traces of BMW's origin may be found in its logo: a rotating propeller in blue and white, the colors of Bavaria. In 1913 Karl Rapp opened an aircraft engine design shop near a Munich airfield. Rapp named his organization Bayerische Motoren Werke (BMW) in 1917. Following WWI the Treaty of Versailles brought German aircraft production to a halt, and BMW was forced to make railway brakes.

After BMW was permitted to resume aircraft engine production, sales took off in the 1930s. In 1923 BMW introduced its first motorcycle, the R32, which held world speed records from 1929 to 1937. BMW entered automaking in 1928 by buying struggling Fahrzeugwerke Eisenach, a company making a small car under license from Austin (UK).

Beginning in 1933 BMW launched a successful series of larger, sportier cars. Hitler forced BMW to build aircraft engines for the Luftwaffe in the 1930s and stopped all auto and motorcycle production in 1941. BMW leader Josef Popp resisted and was forced to resign. In support of the Nazis, BMW operated plants in occupied countries, developed the world's first production jet engine, and built rockets.

With its factories dismantled following WWII, BMW survived by making kitchen and garden equipment. In 1948 the company introduced a one-cylinder motorcycle built from dealer-supplied parts; it sold well as cheap transportation in postwar Germany. BMW autos offered in the 1950s were too large and expensive for the postwar economy and sold poorly. Motorcycle sales declined, and BMW barely escaped extinction by launching the modestly successful Isetta, a 7 1/2-foot-long "bubble car," in the late 1950s.

In 1959 Herbert Quandt bailed out BMW by buying control of it for $1 million. Quandt's BMW concentrated on sports sedans, releasing the first of the "New Range" of BMWs in 1961. Success of the niche strategy enabled BMW to expand production by purchasing ailing automaker Hans Glas in 1966.

In the 1970s BMW's European exports soared, and the company set up its own distribution subsidiary in the US. The release of the larger 5 Series cars placed BMW more squarely in competition with Mercedes-Benz.

Rapid auto export growth continued in the 1980s, particularly in the US, Asia, and Australia, but motorcycle sales fell victim to Japanese competition and lower demand. The launch of the luxury 7 Series autos in 1986 intensified the BMW-Mercedes rivalry. BMW's US sales peaked in 1986 but had fallen 45% by 1991, partly because of Japanese competition. However, in 1992 BMW outsold Mercedes in Europe for the first time.

In 1990 BMW combined with Britain's Rolls-Royce aerospace company to produce a new family of jet-aircraft engines.

In 1992 BMW announced it would become the first European car maker to build a US plant since Volkswagen closed its Pennsylvania factory in 1988. BMW is not building at home because of Germany's high business taxes, short workweeks, and long vacations.

In 1993 BMW Rolls-Royce won a contract to provide engines for Canadian manufacturer Bombardier's Global Express airplanes. In 1994 the subsidiary added an agreement with McDonnell Douglas.

The company announced plans to add supplementary natural gas fuel systems to its 316i and 518i models in 1995.

OTC symbol: BYMTF
Fiscal year ends: December 31

Chairman, Supervisory Board: Eberhard
v. Kuenheim
Chairman, Board of Management: Bernd
Pischetsrieder, age 45
CFO: Volker Doppelfeld
General Counsel: Dieter Löchelt
Chairman and CEO, BMW (US): Helmut Panke
EVP Finance (CFO) BMW (US): Karl Sommer,
age 39
**Manager Human Relations, BMW of North
America:** John F. Cagnina
Auditors: KPMG Deutsche Treuhand-Gesellschaft

HQ: Petuelring 130, BMW Haus, Postfach
40 02 40, W-8000 Munich 40, Germany
Phone: +49-89-38-95-53-87
Fax: +49-89-3-59-36-22
US HQ: BMW (US) Holding Corp.,
300 Chestnut Ridge Rd., Woodcliff, NJ 07675
US Phone: 201-307-3605
US Fax: 201-307-4004 (Corporate Comm.)

BMW manufactures and sells aircraft engines,
automobiles, and motorcycles. It has sales and
customer services in more than 130 countries.

	1993 Sales	
	DM mil.	**% of total**
Germany	11,883	41
Other Europe	8,268	28
Other countries	8,865	31
Total	**29,016**	**100**

	1993 Sales	
	DM mil.	**% of total**
Automobiles	19,859	68
Leasing	3,442	12
Motorcycles	462	2
Other	5,253	18
Total	**29,016**	**100**

Selected Subsidiaries

Axicon Mobilfunkdienste GmbH (mobile telephone
service)
BMW Financial Services (vehicle leasing, sales
financing, and insurance)
BMW Rolls-Royce GmbH (50.5%, aircraft engines)
Kontron Elektronik GmbH (scientific electronic
equipment)
softlab GmbH für Systementwicklung und EDV-
Anwendung (computer information system
development tools; data processing automation)

Allison Engine	Isuzu
Apple	Mazda
Arthur Andersen	Mitsubishi
Chrysler	Nissan
Daewoo	Peugeot
Daimler-Benz	Porsche
Deutsche Telekom	Renault
Fiat	Saab-Scania
Ford	Siemens
General Electric	Suzuki
General Motors	Toyota
Harley-Davidson	United Technologies
Hewlett-Packard	Vickers
Hitachi	Volkswagen
Honda	Volvo
Hyundai	Yamaha
IBM	

$=DM1.74 (Dec. 31, 1993)	Annual Growth	1984	1985	1986	1987	1988	1989	1990	1991	1992	1993
Sales (DM mil.)	8.9%	13,428	14,741	15,559	18,303	20,673	26,515	27,178	29,839	31,241	29,016
Net income (DM mil.)	5.3%	324	301	347	376	379	557	691	754	726	516
Income as % of sales	—	2.4%	2.0%	2.2%	2.1%	1.8%	2.1%	2.5%	2.5%	2.3%	1.8%
Earnings per share (DM)	1.9%	—	—	—	—	26	32	39	46	40	29
Stock price – high (DM)	—	396	464	576	700	492	566	584	530	619	725
Stock price – low (DM)	—	255	272	376	336	391	442	335	319	443	446
Stock price – close (DM)	10.8%	287	437	520	404	466	500	344	474	488	722
P/E – high	—	—	—	—	—	19	18	15	10	15	25
P/E – low	—	—	—	—	—	15	14	9	6	11	16
Dividends per share (DM)	2.0%	10.5	11.1	11.1	11.1	11.1	11.1	11.1	12.5	12.5	12.5
Book value per share (DM)	6.2%	—	—	—	—	283	305	324	351	367	383
Employees	4.2%	45,540	47,777	51,583	55,769	57,691	66,267	70,948	74,385	69,106	66,201

1993 Year-end:
Debt ratio: 46.3%
Return on equity: 7.6%
Cash (mil.): DM4,772
Long-term debt (mil.): DM5,957
No. of shares (mil.): 18
Dividends
  Yield: 1.7%
  Payout: 43.7%
Market value (mil.): $7,469
Sales (mil.): $16,676

Stock Price History
High/Low 1984–93

BCE INC.

OVERVIEW

BCE is trying to get into the fast lane on the "information superhighway." To get up to speed, Canada's largest telecommunications company has tossed ballast, in the form of noncore assets, over the side. BCE is a holding company for an array of telecommunications businesses, including Bell Canada and its sister phone companies, which serve about 70% of Canada's population. Other BCE subsidiaries offer mobile telephone service, design and develop advanced telecommunications equipment, publish directories, and perform telecommunications consulting.

BCE owns 52.1% of Northern Telecom (NT), one of the largest telecommunications

manufacturers in the world. However, NT has been a major drag on BCE's earnings lately. Looking to add more bells and whistles to its switching software, NT ended up with a complicated and unreliable system that had to be rewritten.

While NT is working to right itself, BCE is expanding into other areas of the telecommunications business. The company is developing networking and multimedia services and has also invested in cable television companies in the US and the UK. As part of its concentration on telecommunications, BCE has sold off its financial services and real estate investments.

WHEN

Bell Telephone Company of Canada traces its history to Alexander Graham Bell's father, who took his son's invention north. Bell of Canada was created by Parliament in 1880 to consolidate several smaller companies. Bell interests in the US originally owned part of the company, but AT&T, successor to the Bell companies, severed all ties in 1975. Bell Canada performed its role as a regional provider of telephone service for many years, and mergers with smaller telephone exchanges beginning in 1954 increased its presence in Canada.

Bell acquired a 90% interest in Northern Electric (small equipment, 1957) from AT&T's Western Electric, completing the buyout in 1964. As Canada's telecommunications needs grew and the technology became more complex, Bell branched out into related areas, including investment in a satellite joint venture (Telesat, 1970) and the formation of Bell-Northern Research (1971) to direct R&D. Tele-Direct, established in 1971, consolidated the company's directory publishing operations. Bell reduced its ownership in Northern Electric to 69% (1975) and changed the manufacturer's name to Northern Telecom (1976). Also in 1976 Bell formed Bell Canada International to provide international telecommunications consulting.

In response to proposed legislation that would have calculated manufacturing profits in phone rate formulas, Bell Canada in 1983 created Bell Canada Enterprises (renamed BCE Inc., 1988) to act as a parent company and to separate unregulated businesses from the local regulated telephone carriers.

BCE bought 42% of TransCanada PipeLines (natural gas transmission, 1983, later increased to 49%) and branched into real estate with the purchase of 68% of Daon Development (1985, renamed BCE Development). CEO Raymond Cyr reversed course when the real estate operation hemorrhaged money. BCE took a $440 million loss when it wrote off its investment (1989).

In 1990 BCE sold half its stake in TransCanada to underwriters; and issued warrants to sell the other half. That same year Unitel, a joint venture of Rogers Communications and Canadian Pacific, applied to Canadian regulators for permission to compete with BCE in providing message toll service, WATS, and 800 Service.

In 1991 Northern Telecom spent $2.6 billion to purchase the UK's STC, the world's 12th largest telecommunications equipment manufacturer.

In 1992 Bell Canada agreed to cooperate with GTE, the biggest local telephone company in the US, in selling billing and other information services to telephone utilities in foreign countries, especially those that have been recently privatized. Also in 1992 the Canadian federal government extended for 5 years BCE's Teleglobe subsidiary's monopoly on overseas telecommunications to give it an opportunity to compete with AT&T.

In 1994 BCE sold Montreal Trustco to the Bank of Nova Scotia and acquired 30% of Denver-based Jones Intercable, one of the largest cable TV companies in the US. BCE finished 1994 with sales of $15.4 billion and profits of nearly $837 million.

NYSE symbol: BCE
Fiscal year ends: December 31

Chairman, President, and CEO: Lynton Ronald
Wilson, C$749,578 pay
EVP International: Derek H. Burney,
C$434,799 pay
EVP and CFO: Gerald T. McGoey, C$360,745 pay
SVP Corporate Strategy: J. Derek M. Davies,
C$478,621 pay
Group VP Directories: Thomas J. Bourke,
C$311,000 pay
President and CEO, Northern Telecom (US):
Jean C. Monty
SVP and CFO, Northern Telecom (US): Peter
Currie
**SVP Human Resources, Northern Telecom
(US):** Donald S. McCreesh
Auditors: Deloitte & Touche

HQ: 1000, rue de La Gauchetière Ouest, Bureau
3700, Montreal, Quebec H3B 4Y7, Canada
Phone: 514-397-7000
Fax: 514-397-7223
US HQ: Northern Telecom Limited, 2010
Corporate Ridge Dr., McLean, VA 22102-7838
Phone: 703-712-8000
Fax: 703-712-8603

	1993 Sales		1993 Operating Income	
	$ mil.	% of total	$ mil.	% of total
Canada	8,704	58	2,292	74
US	4,377	29	638	20
Europe	1,585	11	175	6
Other countries	311	2	(25)	—
Total	**14,977**	**100**	**3,080**	**100**

	1993 Sales	
	$ mil.	% of total
Telecomm. equipment	7,969	53
Canadian telecomm.	6,507	43
Directories	397	3
International telecomm.	104	1
Total	**14,977**	**100**

Selected Subsidiaries and Affiliates
BCE Mobile Communications Inc. (65.4%)
Bell Canada
Bell Canada International
Bell-Northern Research Ltd. (owned 30% by Bell Canada
and 70% by Northern Telecom)
Jones Intercable, Inc. (30%, cable television, US)
Maritime Telegraph and Telephone Company, Ltd. (35.2%,
Canadian carrier)
Mercury Communications Ltd. (20%, telecommunications
services, UK)
The New Brunswick Telephone Company, Ltd. (40.5%,
Canadian carrier)
Newfoundland Telephone Company Ltd. (55%, Canadian
carrier)
Northern Telecom Ltd. (52.1%, telecommunications
equipment)
Northern Telephone Ltd. (99.9%, Canadian carrier)
Northwestel Inc. (Canadian carrier)
Télébec Ltée (Canadian carrier)
Tele-Direct (Publications) Inc. (directories)
Teleglobe Inc. (22.5%, overseas communications)

Alcatel Alsthom	Fujitsu	Philips
Anglo-Canadian	GTE	Rogers
Telephone	Kyocera	Communications
AT&T	MCI	Siemens
Bell Atlantic	Mitel	Sprint
BellSouth	Motorola	TCI
BT	NEC	TELUS
Canadian Pacific	Nokia	Time Warner
Ericsson	Oki	Toshiba

$ = C$1.32 (Dec. 31, 1993)	9-Year Growth	1984	1985	1986	1987	1988	1989	1990	1991	1992	1993
Sales ($ mil.)	7.2%	8,014	9,483	10,089	11,272	12,785	14,404	15,839	17,208	16,347	14,977
Net income ($ mil.)	—	712	752	741	836	744	657	989	1,150	1,093	(496)
Income as % of sales	—	8.9%	7.9%	7.3%	7.4%	5.8%	4.6%	6.2%	6.7%	6.7%	—
Earnings per share ($)	—	2.97	2.95	2.73	2.96	2.59	2.10	3.02	3.47	3.31	(1.84)
Stock price – high ($)	—	27.13	33.00	30.00	33.38	32.63	39.38	40.00	42.63	43.25	38.00
Stock price – low ($)	—	22.38	26.00	24.88	23.50	28.13	30.50	30.25	33.38	32.13	32.00
Stock price – close ($)	2.9%	26.88	30.13	27.00	28.50	31.25	39.25	34.13	41.25	32.50	34.88
P/E – high	—	9	11	11	11	13	19	13	12	13	—
P/E – low	—	8	9	9	8	11	15	10	10	10	—
Dividends per share ($)	(0.7%)	2.18	1.69	1.70	1.81	1.99	2.10	2.16	2.23	2.18	2.05
Book value per share ($)	1.7%	20.50	21.25	23.51	25.36	27.08	27.30	28.48	29.92	28.53	23.76
Employees	1.0%	108,100	108,300	109,900	117,000	116,000	120,000	119,000	124,000	124,000	118,000

1993 Year-end:
Debt ratio: 73.6%
Return on equity: —
Cash (mil.): $91
Long-term debt (mil.): $7,893
No. of shares (mil.): 308
Dividends
  Yield: 5.9%
  Payout: —
Market value (mil.): $10,749

**Stock Price History
High/Low 1984–93**

BENETTON GROUP S.P.A.

OVERVIEW

They don't call it the United Colors of Benetton for nothing. Benetton, based in Ponzano Veneto, Italy, is a truly global enterprise, selling its United Colors of Benetton, Sisley, and other brand-name products in 120 countries. Although most of the company's sales come from clothing, Benetton also markets cosmetics, toys, eyewear, and watches. Benetton's more than 7,000 stores are independently owned. Licensees must agree to sell only Benetton products. Benetton family–controlled Edizione Holding owns 71.3% of Benetton Group S.p.A.

Advertising has fueled the company's growth, but has also brought controversy. Benetton ads have included photographs of a priest kissing a nun and body parts labeled HIV positive for which the company was fined $32,000 by a French court in 1995. A 1994 ad, which featured a photo of the blood-soaked clothing of a Croat soldier, drew heated reactions, including bans in several countries.

The company continues to expand, with a particular eye toward Asia. It has announced plans to have 500 stores in China by 1999.

However, its US store count has dropped to below 200 from 600 a few years ago because of stiff competition and the company's failure to keep up with US fashion trends. In response, Benetton plans to switch to megastores, retail outlets 3 to 5 times larger than its normal stores.

WHEN

Luciano Benetton, of Treviso, Italy, began selling men's clothing while still in his teens. His younger, artistic sister, Giuliana, knitted colorful and striking sweaters for a small, local clientele. In 1955 the 2 pooled skills. Giuliana sold Luciano's accordion and a younger brother's bicycle, raising enough money to purchase a knitting machine. Her moderately priced sweaters were then marketed by Luciano.

Demand for the clothes grew, and the pair did so well that 10 years later a factory was built in Ponzano, near Treviso. Siblings Gilberto and bicycle-less Carlo joined the business, and the first Benetton store opened in Belluno, in the Alps, in 1968. Three stores quickly followed; the company went abroad in 1969 with a store in Paris. By 1975 Benetton had 200 stores in Italy and had set up headquarters in a 17th-century villa. In 1979 the company opened 5 stores in the US and in 1982 bought 49% of Italian fashion house Fiorucci.

A highly efficient distribution system helped Benetton keep abreast of fashion trends in the 1980s, a period of huge growth for the company. Through the early- to mid-1980s the company averaged one store opening a day; Benetton was the first Western retailer to enter Eastern Europe.

When it went public in 1986, the company had almost 600 stores in the US. That same year Benetton established a factory in the US. Benetton diversified in 1987 when it set up In Holding, a financial services firm. In the late 1980s the company also acquired a hotel chain, an insurance business, a department store, and ski boot maker Nordica.

The company began losing US market share in the late 1980s. Luciano believes that the company misread American styles, wrongly taking for granted that the sweaters selling so well in Paris would sell as well in New York. Competition from The Gap and The Limited hurt sales also, and store owners began complaining about competition from other Benetton stores. In New York City there were 7 stores on Fifth Avenue alone. In the early 1990s The Gap established stores in the already-mature European market, and Benetton began looking for new markets.

Also in the early 1990s Edizione Holding acquired 80% of Prince Manufacturing, a US maker of tennis equipment, and purchased a 50% interest in the TWR group, a racing car manufacturer.

In 1991 the company set up its first Beijing and Warsaw stores, signed agreements with local manufacturers in Turkey and Brazil to make its clothes, and entered into a joint venture with an Indian company to produce and market its products. The company also formed Benetton Legs to produce and sell pantyhose in Europe and announced it would produce a magazine, *Colors*, to be distributed from its stores. In 1992 Benetton reorganized its growing sports sector under the name Sportsystem.

In 1994 Benetton signed a joint venture agreement with Chinese textile company Lion to build a clothing factory in China. Sales in 1994 were up 4%.

NYSE symbol: BNG (ADR)
Fiscal year ends: December 31

Chairman (CEO): Luciano Benetton, age 59
VC and Managing Director: Gilberto Benetton, age 53
General Manager Finance and Control (CFO): Marco Polo, age 40
General Manager Human Resources, Organization, and International Business: Giovanni Cantagalli, age 53
VP and General Manager, Benetton Services (US): Carlo Tunioli
Controller (Personnel), Benetton Services (US): Paulyne Wang
Auditors: Arthur Andersen & Co. S.a.S.

WHERE

HQ: Via Villa Minelli 1, 31050 Ponzano Veneto, Italy
Phone: +39-(0)422-4491
Fax: +39-(0)422-9695-01
US HQ: Benetton Services Corp., 55 E. 59th St., 24th Fl., New York, NY 10022
US Phone: 212-593-0290
US Fax: 212-371-1438

	1993 Sales		1993 Operating Profit	
	$ mil.	% of total	$ mil.	% of total
Italy	495	31	96	37
The Americas	157	10	(13)	—
Other Europe	619	38	119	46
Other countries	331	21	43	17
Adjustments	—	—	(7)	—
Total	**1,602**	**100**	**238**	**100**

WHAT

	1993 Sales % of total
United Colors of Benetton	81
Sisley	13
Other products	6
Total	**100**

Major Trademarks
012 Benetton (children's clothing)
Sisley (higher-fashion clothing)
  999 (higher-fashion children's clothes)
United Colors of Benetton
  Benetton Donna (women's clothing)
  Benetton Uomo (men's clothing)
  Blue Family (denim products)
  Zerotondo (infant and toddler clothing)

Selected Products

Belts	Jackets	Sunglasses
Cosmetics	Knitwear	Sweatsuits
Dresses	Scarves	Toys
Eyeglass frames	Shirts	Umbrellas
Fragrances	Shoes	Underwear
Golf equipment	Socks	Watches
Household linens		

KEY COMPETITORS

Anne Klein	Ito-Yokado	Montgomery
AnnTaylor	J. Crew	Ward
Bausch & Lomb	J Sainsbury	Nordstrom
Calvin Klein	Lands' End	J. C. Penney
Carrefour	Levi Strauss	Polo/Ralph
Dayton Hudson	The Limited	Lauren
Dillard	Liz Claiborne	Sara Lee
Edison Brothers	Loews	Sears
Federated	Marks and	SMH
The Gap	Spencer	U.S. Shoe
Geoffrey Beene	May	Vendex
Gymboree	Melville	V. F.
Hudson's Bay		

HOW MUCH

	Annual Growth	1984	1985	1986	1987	1988	1989	1990	1991	1992	1993
Sales ($ mil.)	16.7%	—	467	730	980	1,130	1,308	1,805	2,008	1,704	1,602
Net income ($ mil.)	12.0%	—	49	77	101	90	91	118	144	125	121
Income as % of sales	—	—	10.6%	10.5%	10.3%	7.9%	7.0%	6.6%	7.2%	7.3%	7.6%
Earnings per share ($)	56.3%	—	—	—	—	—	0.28	1.26	1.64	1.65	1.67
Stock price – high ($)	—	—	—	—	—	—	14.75	18.13	18.38	23.13	32.50
Stock price – low ($)	—	—	—	—	—	—	12.75	11.50	12.75	17.75	18.25
Stock price – close ($)	23.8%	—	—	—	—	—	13.50	15.13	18.25	19.13	31.75
P/E – high	—	—	—	—	—	—	53	14	11	14	20
P/E – low	—	—	—	—	—	—	46	9	8	11	11
Dividends per share ($)	3.4%	—	—	—	—	—	0.28	0.66	0.26	0.34	0.32
Book value per share ($)	6.4%	—	—	—	—	—	5.90	6.36	7.64	7.65	7.57
Employees	28.0%	—	—	—	—	—	—	—	3,600	5,800	5,900

1993 Year-end:
Debt ratio: 68.7%
Return on equity: 19.5%
Cash (mil.): $473
Long-term debt (mil.): $387
No. of shares (mil.): 82
Dividends
  Yield: 1.0%
  Payout: 19.2%
Market value (mil.): $2,596

Stock Price History
High/Low 1989–93

BERTELSMANN AG

Bertelsmann, based in Gütersloh, Germany, is Europe's leading media company and is #2 in the world after Time Warner. It owns the large US publisher Bantam Doubleday Dell and has 474 subsidiaries around the world. The German entity also owns about 75% of Gruner + Jahr, which publishes magazines in Europe and the US.

The company also publishes religious works and sheet music and has interests in video, radio, and film companies. It manufactures electronic media storage, makes paper, and has printing plants in Europe, the US, and South America. Bertelsmann is one of the world's largest book club operators, with more than 16 million members. Of the company's English-speaking book clubs, Doubleday grew the most in 1993.

Bertelsmann's record labels include RCA and Arista in the US, BMG Ariola in Europe, and BMG Victor in Japan. The company has moved into television, with stakes in the RTL plus network (Germany, Luxembourg) and the pay channel Premiere (Germany).

Bertelsmann's priorities include new magazines, improving and starting new television channels, and expanding in China, eastern Europe and the US. In 1993 former chairman Reinhard Mohn transferred enough voting shares in the company to the nonprofit Bertelsmann Foundation so that the foundation now controls about 70% of stock.

Carl Bertelsmann founded the company that bears his name in Gütersloh, Germany, in 1835. One of his first books, a hymnal, was successful enough to allow the company to grow despite the poverty and low literacy rate of the time. Bertelsmann continued to thrive primarily as a religious publisher until WWII, when the Nazis shut it down.

Reinhard Mohn, whose grandfather had married Bertelsmann's granddaughter, was captured by the Allies in North Africa. He spent the rest of the war in a Kansas POW camp, returning to Germany to find Bertelsmann's Gütersloh plant destroyed. Mohn rebuilt the plant and began publishing in 1948.

Bertelsmann started Lesering, Germany's first book club, in 1950, followed by a record club in the late 1950s. The company bought Germany's UFA (TV and film production, 1964) and 25% of Gruner + Jahr (publisher of *Stern* and *Der Spiegel*, 1969; raised to a controlling interest, 1973). In the US, Bertelsmann bought 51% of Bantam Books in 1977 (and the remaining stock in 1981) and Arista Records in 1979, using these companies in 1980 to launch its US club, American Circle, which folded after 4 years of losses.

In 1981 Mark Wössner succeeded Mohn as CEO. Under Wössner, Bertelsmann increased its US presence in 1986 when it bought RCA Records and control of Doubleday Publishing. Founded in 1897 by Frank Doubleday, Doubleday was one of America's largest publishers, mainly through its strength in hardbacks, Dell paperbacks, and book clubs. Doubleday also owned the New York Mets, which the family, descendants of Abner Doubleday, bought in 1980. Bertelsmann did not buy the Mets, and was criticized for paying too much for the publisher, which had had quality problems in the early 1980s.

Bertelsmann's US operations were less successful than had been hoped. The book clubs that had once provided Doubleday with 35% of its profits lost thousands of members, prompting Bertelsmann to develop new activities in the US through joint ventures rather than large acquisitions.

In 1990 Bertelsmann sold Doubleday Book Shops to B. Dalton and shut down its UK book club, Leisure Circle, leaving a near market monopoly to another Bertelsmann affiliate, Book Club Associates. Also in 1990 Bertelsmann bought eastern Germany's largest book printer, Pössneck. That same year Gruner + Jahr, with Robert Maxwell, agreed to buy the eastern German magazine and newspaper publisher Berliner Verlag (full ownership was assumed after Maxwell's death in 1991). Bertelsmann restructured the company in 1993 into 4 divisions with separate boards of directors, including one for books and one for a new entertainment division.

In 1994 the company absorbed losses from the collapse of German television station Vox, in which it was a major shareholder. Also in 1994 subsidiary T1 News Media announced an exclusive collaboration with Novell to develop multimedia applications for Novell's WordPerfect Main Street consumer software.

Private company
Fiscal year ends: June 30

Chairman of the Supervisory Board: Dieter Vogel
President and CEO: Mark Wössner
CFO: Siegfried Luther
Chairman and CEO, Bertelsmann Music Group: Michael Dornemann
President, Bertelsmann Publishing Group International: Bernhard von Minckwitz
President and CEO, Bantam Doubleday Dell Publishing Group (US): Jack Hoeft
EVP and COO, Bantam Doubleday Dell Publishing Group (US): Erik Engstrom
Auditors: KPMG Deutsche Treuhand-Gesellschaft Aktiengesellschaft, Wirtschaft-prüfungsgesellschaft

HQ: Bertelsmann Aktiengesellschaft, Carl-Bertelsmann-Strasse 270, Postfach 111 D-33311, Gütersloh, Germany
Phone: +49-52-41-80-0
Fax: +49-52-41-7-51-66
US HQ: Bantam Doubleday Dell Publishing Group Inc., 1540 Broadway, New York, NY 10036
US Phone: 212-354-6500
US Fax: 212-782-9698

Bertelsmann has operations in 40 countries. Core businesses include book and music clubs, book and music publishing, electronic media, magazines, printing, and record labels.

	1994 Sales	
	DM mil.	% of total
Germany	6,682	36
Other countries	11,723	64
Total	**18,405**	**100**

	1994 Sales	
	DM mil.	% of total
Books	6,294	33
BMG Entertainment	5,944	31
Gruner + Jahr	3,848	20
Bertelsmann Industry	3,103	16
Adjustments	(784)	—
Total	**18,405**	**100**

Selected Operations

Gruner + Jahr Magazines
Brigitte
Claudia (Poland)
Femme Actuelle (France)
muy INTERESANTE (Spain)
Parents (US)
Prima (UK)
TéLé Loisirs (France)
Vera (Italy)
YM (US)

Music and Video
Arista Records (US)
BMG Ariola (worldwide)
BMG Victor (90%, Japan)
BMG Video (UK and US)
RCA Records (US)
UFA Werbefilm
Zoo Entertainment (US)

Book and Record Clubs
Bertelsmann Club

BCA (50%, UK)
Circulo de Lectores (Spain)
Doubleday Book & Music Clubs (US; 30% Canada)
Euroclub Italia (51%, Italy)
France Loisirs (50%)

Publishing
Bantam Doubleday Dell Publishing Group (US)
Doubleday Canada (30%)
Transworld Publishers (Australia, UK, New Zealand)

Film, Radio, and Television
FPS Funk-Programm-Service (75%)
Klassik Radio (70%)
RTL plus (39%, Luxembourg)
Ufa Filmproduktion

Advance Publications
Axel Springer Verlag
Canal+
Capital Cities/ABC
Commerce Clearing House
R. R. Donnelley
Dorling Kindersley
Harcourt General
Hearst

Houghton Mifflin
John Wiley
Knight-Ridder
Lagardère
Matsushita
McGraw-Hill
News Corp.
Pearson
Philips
Reader's Digest

Reed Elsevier
Sony
Thomas Nelson
Thomson Corp.
Thorn EMI
Time Warner
Viacom
Virgin Group
VNU
Walt Disney

$=DM1.74 (Dec. 31, 1993)	9-Year Growth	1985	1986	1987	1988	1989	1990	1991	1992	1993	1994
Sales (DM mil.)	10.6%	7,441	7,602	9,160	11,299	12,483	13,313	14,483	15,955	17,170	18,405
Net income (DM mil.)	9.4%	337	329	207	362	402	510	540	569	662	759
Income as % of sales	—	4.5%	4.3%	2.3%	3.2%	3.2%	3.8%	3.7%	3.6%	3.9%	4.1%
Employees	5.6%	31,835	31,593	42,013	41,961	43,702	43,509	45,110	48,781	50,437	51,767

1994 Year-end:
Debt ratio: 16.3%
Return on equity: 33.3%
Cash (mil.): DM1,036
Current ratio: —
Debt (mil.): DM464
Sales (mil.): $10,599

Net Income (DM mil.) 1985–94

THE BODY SHOP

Instead of a hammer, a buffer, or an acetylene torch, The Body Shop uses pineapple, rice bran, and seaweed to smooth out the dents. The Littlehampton, England–based company is a pioneer in "natural" cosmetics, selling products such as Banana Shampoo, Honeyed Beeswax and Almond Oil Cleanser, and Peppermint Foot Lotion.

Founded by Anita Roddick, who is credited with pioneering the recent wave of natural cosmetics, The Body Shop has more than 1,000 stores in 45 countries, most of which are franchised. The Body Shop has grown rapidly, thanks to its emphasis on all-natural products and Roddick's ability to generate interest in the company through commitments to a wide variety of causes. Stores at various times have sponsored voter registration drives, Amnesty International signups,

and AIDS awareness campaigns. The company is also committed to various "green" causes, including recycling. Stores offer 25 cents a bottle to customers who return their cosmetics containers.

However, a 1994 article in the journal *Business Ethics* tarnished the company's socially conscious image, claiming that the company uses nonrenewable petrochemicals and that it has increased the use of ingredients that have been tested on animals. The Body Shop has denied the article's charges.

The company is focusing on expanding in the US, Japan, and Europe. It is also facing challenges from a number of big competitors, including Esteé Lauder, that have introduced their own lines of natural cosmetics. Anita Roddick and her husband, Gordon, who is chairman, own 25.4% of the company.

Anita Roddick founded The Body Shop in 1976. She hoped to earn enough money to support herself and her 2 children while her husband, Gordon, went on a 2-year horseback trip through the Americas. Her idea was to provide a small number of cosmetics using natural ingredients that she had learned about in her world travels.

Roddick approached several large cosmetics makers, but none would agree to manufacture her strange concoctions. So she turned to the Yellow Pages and found a herbalist who agreed to make her products. Looking for the cheapest packaging she could find, Roddick chose urine sample bottles, and, to save money, offered to refill customers' bottles if they brought them back in.

Roddick opened her shop in the seaside town of Brighton, England, during one of the hottest summers on record. Brighton was full of tourists, and the business took off as soon as it was opened. Within the year she opened a 2nd shop in Chichester. To raise the money to open the shop, she sold half the business to a local garage owner, Ian McGlinn, for $8,000.

Gordon returned from his trip, after his horse died in Peru, to find that his wife had a thriving business. He suggested they begin franchising, and in 1978 The Body Shop's first franchises were awarded, including one for its first foreign shop in Brussels, Belgium. In 1979 the company continued its overseas

expansion, opening stores in Sweden and Greece.

The company's rapid growth brought the attention of the financial markets, and in 1984 The Body Shop went public on the London Stock Exchange. A year later The Body Shop began the first of its tie-ins with environmental causes when it sponsored posters for Greenpeace's protest of hazardous-waste dumping in the North Sea.

The company continued to grow and gain notoriety. In 1986 Princess Diana presided over the opening of the company's headquarters in Littlehampton, England. In 1987 The Body Shop was named Company of the Year by the Confederation of British Industries. That same year the company paid $3.5 million to 2 families in the US who held the rights to the name The Body Shop in the US and Japan.

The company opened its first US store in New York City in 1988, and in 1990 it opened its first shop in Japan. In 1991 it began publishing *Big Issue* in the UK, a newspaper sold by the homeless.

In 1993 Anita and Gordon Roddick were awarded about $400,000 in a libel suit they brought against a British television station that had broadcast a report challenging the company's socially conscious image.

In 1994 the company began testing Body Shop Direct, a "home-party" marketing business, in the UK.

OTC symbol: BDSPY
Fiscal year ends: March 1

	1994 Sales	
	£ mil.	% of total
UK	91	47
US	50	25
Other Europe	31	16
Other countries	23	12
	195	100

WHO

Chairman: T. Gordon Roddick, £135,000 pay
CEO: Anita Roddick, £138,000 pay
CFO: Jeremy Katt
Secretary: Jane Reid
President, The Body Shop (US): David Edward
VP Finance and CFO, The Body Shop (US): Paul
Crawley
VP Human Resources, The Body Shop (US):
Kathy Schwartz
Auditors: Stoy Hayward

WHERE

HQ: The Body Shop International PLC,
Watersmead, Littlehampton, West Sussex,
BN17 6LS UK
Phone: +44-(01)90-373-1500
Fax: +44-(01)90-372-6250
US HQ: The Body Shop Incorporated, One World
Way, Wake Forest, NC 27587
US Phone: 919-554-4900
US Fax: 919-554-4361

	1994 Stores	
	No.	% of total
UK	239	23
US	170	16
Asia	88	8
Australia & New Zealand	57	5
Other Europe	385	37
Other countries	114	11
Total	**1,053**	**100**

WHAT

Selected Products
Body lotions
Cleansing masks
Facial cleansers and
moisturizers
Hair shampoos and
conditioners
Lip care
Massage oils
Natural oils
Perfume oils
Soaps

Selected Subsidiaries
The Body Shop Inc (90%,
retailing, US)

The Body Shop Norway A/S
(retailing)
The Body Shop (Singapore)
Pte Ltd (retailing)
The Body Shop UK Retail
Company Ltd
The Body Shop Worldwide
Ltd (retailing)
Cos-tec Ltd (color
cosmetics, skin care, and
toiletry products
manufacturing)
Colourings Ltd (color
cosmetics marketing)
Soapworks Ltd (soap
products manufacturing)

KEY COMPETITORS

Alberto-Culver	Eckerd	Mary Kay
Amway	Estée Lauder	May
Avon	Federted	Maybelline
Benetton	Gillette	Mercantile Stores
Boots	Helene Curtis	Neutrogena
Caswell Massey	Henkel	Nordstrom
Coles Myer	Kingfisher	Procter & Gamble
Colgate-Palmolive	The Limited	Shiseido
Dayton Hudson	Lloyds	Thrifty PayLess
Dial	Chemists	Unilever
Dillard	Longs	Vendex
Dr. Bronner	L'Oréal	Walgreen

HOW MUCH

£ = $1.48 (Dec. 31, 1993)	Annual Growth	1985	1986	1987	1988	1989	1990	1991	1992	1993	1994
Sales (£ mil.)	50.6%	5	9	17	28	73	84	116	147	168	195
Net income (£ mil.)	47.4%	1	1	2	4	9	9	12	16	14	19
Income as % of sales	—	12.1%	10.9%	11.9%	13.1%	11.7%	10.1%	10.5%	11.1%	8.2%	9.9%
Earnings per share (p)	(1.7%)	12.0	20.4	20.6	18.6	20.4	10.0	6.7	8.8	7.4	10.3
Stock price – high (p)[1]	—	480	853	765	890	643	604	326	366	371	229
Stock price – low (p)[1]	—	145	440	390	359	230	240	125	178	138	133
Stock price – close (p)[1]	(7.5%)	455	828	765	695	520	501	180	343	192	225
P/E – high	—	40	42	37	48	32	60	49	42	50	22
P/E – low	—	12	22	19	19	11	24	19	20	19	13
Dividends per share ($)	21.7%	—	—	—	—	—	0.9	1.2	1.6	1.7	2.0
Book value per share ($)	16.9%	—	—	—	—	—	—	—	—	44	51
Employees	15.6%	—	—	—	—	—	—	—	—	2,124	2,456

1994 Year-end:
Debt ratio: 27.5%
Return on equity: 21.5%
Cash (mil.): 25
Long-term debt (mil.): 32
No. of shares (mil.): 189
Dividends
   Yield: 0.9%
   Payout: 19.4%
Market value (mil.): $628
Sales (mil.): $289

Stock Price History[1]
High/Low 1985–94

[1] Stock prices are for the prior calendar year.

BOMBARDIER INC.

Not content to hit one industry, Laurent Beaudoin, CEO of Bombardier, is taking aim at a variety of businesses. The Montréal-based company is Canada's largest aerospace company, the leading maker of rail transit equipment in North America, and the North American market leader in the "sit down" segment of the personal watercraft industry.

Bombardier's aerospace and defense units manufacture business aircraft (Challenger, Learjet), commuter aircraft (Canadair, de Havilland), amphibious aircraft, airborne surveillance systems, military aircraft, and missile systems (with France's Thomson). In 1993 the company announced plans to build a long-range business jet capable of flying nonstop from Montréal to Tokyo.

The company's transportation equipment units make subway cars, light rail vehicles, TGV high-speed train equipment, and shuttle train cars for the English Channel tunnel train. Bombardier's Motorized Consumer Products Group makes Ski-Doo and Lynx snowmobiles, Sea-Doo watercraft, and tracked vehicles for utility and maintenance work in snow-covered areas.

Beaudoin's focus on diversification and geographic expansion has helped triple Bombardier's sales since 1989. Bombardier's latest push is into Asia. In late 1994 it signed a deal to manage China's largest passenger-rail factory. The Bombardier family, including Beaudoin (the founder's son-in-law), owns 62.2% of the company's stock.

One would think a company with the name Bombardier had always been an aerospace company, but Joseph Armand Bombardier founded L'Auto-Neige Bombardier Limited in 1942 to build snow vehicles. The company manufactured commercial vehicles at first, but in 1959 Bombardier introduced the first personal snowmobile, the Ski-Doo.

In 1966 Laurent Beaudoin became president of the company at the age of 27. Bombardier went public in 1969. When the bottom dropped out of the snowmobile business because of the energy crisis in 1973, Beaudoin began to diversify the company's operations. Bombardier won its first mass transit contract, to build 423 subway cars for the Montréal Transit Authority, and created its Mass Transit Division in 1974.

As part of its expansion into the mass transportation business, Bombardier merged with MLW-Worthington Limited in 1976. Founded in 1902, MLW-Worthington manufactured diesel engines and diesel-electric locomotives. In 1976 the company's first subway car rolled out of the assembly plant. In 1978 the company became Bombardier Inc.

During the 1980s Bombardier continued to diversify. It expanded into logistic vehicles for the military market. The company became the leading supplier to the North American rail transit industry when it won a contract to build 825 subway cars for New York City.

Beaudoin diversified the company's operations even further in 1986 when he acquired

Canada's largest aerospace company, Canadair, from the Canadian government. Founded in 1920 as the aircraft division of Canadian Vickers, Canadair became a separate company in 1944, producing military and civilian aircraft. The company was acquired by Electric Boat (later General Dynamics) in 1947. The Canadian government nationalized Canadair in 1976. In 1978 Canadair introduced its Challenger 600 business jet, which became a major seller.

In 1989 the company began development of a commuter aircraft, the Canadian Regional Jet, a 50-seat derivative of the Challenger. Also in 1989 Bombardier continued its expansion into the aviation business when it acquired Northern Ireland's Short Brothers PLC, a manufacturer of civil and military aircraft, defense systems, and aircraft components.

A year later the company bought US-based Learjet from Integrated Resources for $75 million. The acquisition gave Bombardier Learjet's service centers, which improved its ability to market its planes to US customers. In 1992 the company acquired regional aircraft maker de Havilland, which it jointly owns with the Province of Ontario. In 1993 Bombardier settled a suit it brought against the Eurotunnel construction consortium to recover cost overruns related to design changes.

In 1994 the company won a $400 million contract to build a 20-mile light rail system in Kuala Lumpur, Malaysia.

Principal exchange: Toronto
Fiscal year ends: January 31

WHO

Chairman and CEO: Laurent Beaudoin, age 56,
C$1,136,000 pay
VC: J.R. André Bombardier
VC: Jean-Louis Fontaine, C$325,000 pay
President and COO: Raymond Royer,
C$680,000 pay
VP Finance: Paul H. Larose, C$266,500 pay
**VP Human Resources and Organizational
Development:** Carroll L'Italien
CEO and President, Learjet (US): Brian Barents
Auditors: Caron Bélanger Ernst & Young

WHERE

HQ: 800 René-Lévesque Blvd. West, Montreal,
Quebec, Canada H3B 1Y8
Phone: 514-861-9481
Fax: 514-861-7053
US HQ: Learjet Inc., One Learjet Way,
Wichita, KS 67277
US Phone: 316-946-2000
US Fax: 316-946-2220

Bombardier has production facilities in Austria,
Belgium, Canada, Finland, France, Mexico, the
UK, and the US.

	1994 Sales	
	C$ mil.	% of total
US & Mexico	2,064	43
Europe	1,946	41
Canada	460	10
Other countries	299	6
Total	**4,769**	**100**

WHAT

	1994 Sales	
	C$ mil.	% of total
Aerospace	2,243	47
Transportation equipment	1,312	27
Motorized consumer products	791	17
Defense	326	7
Financial & real estate services	97	2
Total	**4,769**	**100**

Aerospace
Amphibious aircraft
  CL-215T turboprop
  CL-415 turboprop
Business aircraft
  Bombardier Global
    Express
  Canadair Challenger
  Learjet
Component manufacturing
Regional aircraft
  Canadair Regional Jet
  de Havilland Dash 8

Transportation Equipment
Engine-block machining
Light rail vehicles
Single-level and bi-level
  commuter cars
Subway cars
TGV high-speed train
  equipment

**Motorized Consumer
Products**
Engines
Industrial equipment
Lynx and Ski-Doo
  snowmobiles
Sea-Doo watercraft
Speedster jet boats

Defense
Airborne surveillance
  systems
Missiles (with Thomson-
  CSF)
Support and technical
  services

**Financial and Real Estate
Services**
Aircraft and industrial
  equipment financing
Dealer inventory financing
Real estate development

KEY COMPETITORS

Arctco	Kawasaki	Raytheon
Boeing	Lockheed Martin	Siemens
British Aerospace	McDonnell Douglas	Suzuki
Brunswick	Mitsubishi	Textron
Fiat	Northrop Grumman	Yamaha
Gulfstream	Polaris Industries	

HOW MUCH

$ = C$1.32 (Dec. 31, 1993)	Annual Growth	1985	1986	1987	1988	1989	1990	1991	1992	1993	1994
Sales (C$ mil.)	31.5%	405	555	999	1,406	1,426	2,143	2,892	3,059	4,448	4,769
Net income (C$ mil.)	37.3%	10	16	46	67	68	92	100	108	133	176
Income as % of sales	—	2.5%	2.9%	4.6%	4.8%	4.8%	4.3%	3.5%	3.5%	3.0%	3.7%
Earnings per share (C$)[1]	28.2%	0.11	0.17	0.41	0.50	0.52	0.68	0.71	0.73	0.83	1.03
Stock price – high (C$)[1]	—	1.58	2.42	4.41	7.00	6.69	8.94	10.31	14.25	17.25	21.00
Stock price – low (C$)[1]	—	1.31	1.02	1.81	3.50	3.56	5.56	5.56	6.63	10.38	9.63
Stock price – close (C$)[1]	33.9%	1.52	1.23	4.41	3.63	6.44	8.25	7.63	14.00	11.75	21.00
P/E – high	—	14	14	11	14	13	13	15	20	21	20
P/E – low	—	12	6	4	7	7	8	8	9	13	9
Dividends per share (C$)	28.7%	0.02	0.04	0.05	0.09	0.12	0.14	0.17	0.17	0.21	0.21
Book value per share (C$)	20.7%	1.50	1.63	2.26	2.66	2.92	3.54	4.64	5.67	6.16	8.18
Employees	—	—	—	—	—	—	—	—	—	—	36,500

1994 Year-end:
Debt ratio: 47.7%
Return on equity: 12.6%
Cash (mil.): C$633
Long-term debt (mil.): C$1,035
No. of shares (mil.): 154
Dividends
  Yield: 1.0%
  Payout: 20.6%
Market value (mil.): C$3,244
Sales (mil.): US$3,602

**Stock Price History[1]
High/Low 1985–94**

[1] Stock prices are for the prior calendar year.

THE BOOTS COMPANY PLC

OVERVIEW

These Boots are made for retailing. Based in Nottingham, England, The Boots Company operates some of the UK's largest retailers.

Boots The Chemists is the UK's largest drugstore chain, operating more than 1,100 stores. The company also operates the UK's #1 auto parts chain (Halfords), its #1 home decorating retailer (A. G. Stanley), and its 2nd largest chain of opticians (Boots Opticians). Other Boots retail operations include Childrens World (toys, clothes, and other children's products) and Do It All (do-it-

yourself home products), a joint venture with W. H. Smith.

The company hasn't been sitting back on its heels. It is walking out of the pharmaceutical business in order to concentrate on its drugstore business. In late 1994 it agreed to sell its pharmaceutical division (which licenses Advil in the US) to Germany's BASF for $1.4 billion. The move follows the company's sale of its baby food business, Farley's Health Products, to H. J. Heinz for $140 million in mid-1994.

WHEN

Following his father's death in 1860, Jesse Boot, age 10, began helping his mother run the family's herbal medicine shop in Nottingham, England. In 1863 Boot quit school to work full time, and in 1871 he became a full partner with his mother. They diversified out of herbal remedies, adding basic medications, such as Epsom salts and castor oil, and household goods, such as soap.

In 1874 Boot decided to focus on discount retailing, buying products in bulk directly from the manufacturer and selling at considerably lower prices than his competitors, who had agreements among themselves that kept prices high. Boot, a staunch Liberal, advertised his shop as "The People's Store" and "The Trade Reformer."

Boot began to expand, using the same strategy: low prices, narrow profit margins, and extensive advertising. In 1885 the company added a manufacturing department. A year later Boot married Florence Rowe, the daughter of a bookseller. She helped diversify the company's retail operations into new product lines, including stationery and gifts.

By 1900 the company had 180 stores, more than twice the number of its nearest rival. Boots moved into London in 1901 when it acquired Day's Drug Stores, a chain of 65 shops in London and southeast England. Expansion continued, and by 1914 Boots had 560 stores.

During WWI the company's manufacturing business expanded rapidly as it geared up to supply soldiers with a variety of products, including water sterilizers and pocket stoves. Boots also began to make synthetic drugs, such as aspirin, which had previously been supplied by German drug companies.

In 1920, rather than pass the business on to his son John (who enjoyed drinking and dancing), Jesse (a teetotaler) sold the company to Louis Liggett, head of US drug group Rexall. However, much to the chagrin of Jesse, Liggett made John a director of the company. In 1933 Boots was sold to a group of British investors, and John was named managing director.

During the 1930s and 1940s, Boots expanded overseas, adding shops in Asia, Australia, and Africa. Even after John Boot retired in 1954, the company's managing director maintained an autocratic control, just as the Boots had, that wasn't broken until the 1960s when the company reorganized, setting up a divisional structure.

In 1969 Boots launched the prescription painkiller ibuprofen in the UK, and in the early 1970s it signed a deal with Upjohn to market the drug in the US under the name Motrin. The FDA approved ibuprofen for over-the-counter sales in the US in 1983, and Boots signed a deal with American Home Products to market the drug as Advil.

Christopher Benson became chairman in 1989. That same year the company bought Ward White, which included Halfords, A.G. Stanley, and home repair retailer Payless. In 1990 Boots merged Payless with W. H. Smith's Do It All in a joint venture.

Boots received approval to market heart drug Manoplax in the UK in 1992, but it pulled it from the market a year later after tests indicated higher mortality rates with large doses of the drug and increased hospitalization with lower doses.

In 1994 Michael Angus, former chairman of brewer Whitbread, succeeded Benson as chairman of Boots.

OTC symbol: BOOOY
Fiscal year ends: March 31

Chairman: Sir Michael Angus, age 64
Deputy Chairman and CEO: Sir James Blyth,
age 54
Managing Director, Boots The Chemists:
Gordon M. Hourston, age 59
Finance Director: David A. R. Thompson, age 51
**President and CEO, Boots Pharmaceuticals
(US):** Carter H. Eckert
VP Finance, Boots Pharmaceuticals (US): Steve
Koehler
**VP Human Resources, Boots Pharmaceuticals
(US):** Larry Deans
Auditors: KPMG Peat Marwick

WHERE

HQ: One Thane Rd., Nottingham NG2 3AA, UK
Phone: +44-(0)602-506111
Fax: +44-(0)602-592727
US HQ: Boots Pharmaceuticals Inc., 300 Tri-
State International Center, Ste. 200,
Lincolnshire, IL 60069-4415
US Phone: 708-405-7400
US Fax: 708-405-7505

	1994 Sales	
	£ mil.	% of total
UK	3,724	89
US	181	4
Other Europe	184	4
Other countries	118	3
Adjustments	(40)	—
Total	**4,167**	**100**

WHAT

	1994 Sales	
	£ mil.	% of total
Boots The Chemists	2,808	64
Retail Division	873	20
Boots Pharmaceuticals	492	11
Boots Healthcare International	134	3
Other	61	2
Adjustments	(201)	—
Total	**4,167**	**100**

Boots The Chemists
Large stores (health and beauty products, cooking
utensils, vision products, gift merchandise)
Small stores (health and beauty products)

Retail Division
Boots Opticians
Childrens World (clothing, toys)
Do It All (50%, do-it-yourself home centers)
Halfords (auto parts and service)
A. G. Stanley (home decorating)

**Boots Pharmaceuticals (pharmaceutical
manufacturing)**
Antidepressant (Prothiaden)
Anti-inflammatory/analgesic (Brufen/Advil)
Synthetic thyroid replacement (Synthroid)

Boots Healthcare International
Consumer healthcare product marketing

KEY COMPETITORS

Argos	Lloyds Chemists
Body Shop	Price/Costco
Burton Group	Tesco
J Sainsbury	Toys "R" Us
Johnson & Johnson	Vendex
Kingfisher	Woolworth
Kmart	

HOW MUCH

$ = £1.48 (Dec. 31, 1993)	Annual Growth	1985	1986	1987	1988	1989	1990	1991	1992	1993	1994
Sales (£ mil.)	8.8%	—	2,126	2,352	2,697	2,704	3,385	3,567	3,660	3,962	4,167
Net income (£ mil.)	8.4%	—	—	164	190	203	233	245	230	279	288
Income as % of sales	—	—	—	7.0%	7.0%	7.5%	6.9%	6.9%	6.3%	7.0%	6.9%
Earnings per share (p)	5.2%	—	—	18.6	19.5	20.4	22.6	24.0	25.0	23.0	27.0	28.0
Stock price – high (p)[1]	—	214	276	256	309	259	322	348	445	571	609
Stock price – low (p)[1]	—	140	162	209	205	197	227	247	304	398	416
Stock price – close (p)[1]	13.2%	196	261	232	294	233	273	322	429	561	598
P/E – high	—	—	15	13	15	11	13	14	19	21	22
P/E – low	—	—	9	11	10	9	9	10	13	15	15
Dividends per share (p)	9.8%	—	7.1	8.0	8.8	10.0	11.0	11.6	12.4	13.4	15.0
Book value per share (p)	3.8%	—	—	—	—	—	—	—	143	142	155
Employees	1.9%	—	67,643	—	72,073	69,967	78,648	83,745	80,847	79,738	80,099

1994 Year-end:
Debt ratio: 21.3%
Return on equity: 18.7%
Cash (mil.): $503
Long-term debt (mil.):$268
No. of shares (mil.): 1,041
Dividends
  Yield: 2.5%
  Payout: 53.6%
Market value (mil.): $9,209
Sales (mil.): $6,165

**Stock Price History[1]
High/Low 1985–94**

(chart values: 700, 600, 500, 400, 300, 200, 100, 0)

[1] Stock prices are for the prior calendar year.

BRIDGESTONE CORPORATION

OVERVIEW

Bridgestone's income may be flat, but there's good news for Japan's top tire maker. US-based Firestone, which Bridgestone purchased in 1988, is finally showing a profit; Firestone brings in 36% of Bridgestone's sales. European revenues are also up, just in time to counter the slump caused by Japan's slow auto sales and the strong yen.

Tires account for 75% of Bridgestone's sales. The company supplies tires to such major auto makers as Ford and GM, as well as Porsche and Lamborghini. Its retail channels include the company's own outlets in the US and Japan, as well as Sears, Montgomery Ward, and Kmart. The company has manufacturing facilities in 16 countries, including 20 plants in the Americas.

Bridgestone is the world's top manufacturer of tires for heavy equipment (US mining companies are major customers) and also makes aircraft tires, with sales to Boeing and Airbus Industrie.

A quarter of Bridgestone's sales derive from the manufacture of building materials, sporting goods, industrial rubber, and automotive components.

WHEN

In 1906 on the Japanese island of Kyushu, Shojiro Ishibashi and his brother Tokujiro assumed control of the family's clothing business. They focused on making *tabi*, traditional Japanese footwear, and in 1923 began working with rubber for soles. In 1931 Shojiro formed Bridgestone (Ishibashi means "stone bridge" in Japanese) to make tires. In the 1930s the company began producing auto tires, airplane tires, and golf balls. Bridgestone followed the Japanese military to occupied territories, where it built plants. The company's headquarters moved to Tokyo in 1937.

Although Bridgestone lost all of its overseas factories in WWII, the Japanese plants escaped damage. The company began making bicycles (1946) and signed a technical assistance pact with Goodyear (1951), enabling Bridgestone to import badly needed technology. In the 1950s and 1960s, Bridgestone started making nylon tires and radials and again set up facilities overseas, mostly in Asia. The company benefited from the rapid growth in Japanese auto sales in the 1970s. Shojiro died at age 87 in 1976.

In 1983 Bridgestone bought a plant in LaVergne, Tennessee, from the venerable US tire maker Firestone. Harvey Firestone had founded his tire business in 1900 and expanded with the auto industry in the US. In the 1920s he leased one million acres in Liberia for rubber plantations and established a chain of auto supply and service outlets. After WWII Firestone started making synthetic rubber and automotive components, expanded overseas, and acquired US tire producers Dayton Tire & Rubber and Seiberling. In the 1980s Firestone chairman John Nevin sought to maximize shareholder return by cutting costs, lowering capital spending, and focusing on retail operations.

In 1988 Bridgestone topped a bid by Pirelli and bought the rest of Firestone for $2.6 billion, valuing the tire maker at a lofty 26 times earnings. At that time General Motors announced that Firestone would be dropped as a supplier. Bridgestone/Firestone has compensated for this loss in volume by selling more tires through mass-market retailers. It also began selling tires to GM's Saturn Corporation in 1990.

To improve its distribution, in 1992 Bridgestone renamed its 1,550 North American MasterCare auto service centers "Tire Zone at Firestone" and took the unheard-of step of selling rival Michelin's tires.

In 1991 new Bridgestone/Firestone chairman Yoichiro Kaizaki moved to cut production costs, alienating union workers. In 1993 Kaizaki became company head.

Bridgestone continues to diversify as well as to expand tire production. It added Colonial Rubber Works, a US roofing-materials manufacturer, and America Off The Road Company, which makes tires for heavy equipment. In 1993 it expanded operations in the US, Mexico, Brazil, Indonesia, and Thailand.

Problems have plagued Bridgestone's US operations. In 1994 the company was fined $7.5 million after a worker died at its Oklahoma City plant. An ongoing dispute with the United Rubber Workers has mushroomed into a major international incident. The company added to the problem in early 1995 by revealing that it had hired 2,300 permanent replacement workers.

OTC symbol: BRDCY
Fiscal year ends: December 31

WHO

President: Yoichiro Kaizaki
EVP Original Equipment Tire Sales: Akihiro Ono
SVP Tire Development: Tadakazu Harada
Director Finance and Purchasing: Hiroshi Kanai
SVP; CEO, Bridgestone/Firestone (US): Masatoshi Ono
Director Human Resources, Bridgestone/ Firestone (US): William R. Phillips
Auditors: Asahi & Co.

WHERE

HQ: 10-1, Kyobashi 1-chome, Chuo-ku, Tokyo 104, Japan
Phone: +81-3-3567-0111
Fax: +81-3-3535-2553
US HQ: Bridgestone/Firestone, Inc., 50 Century Blvd., Nashville, TN 37214-8900
US Phone: 615-872-5000
US Fax: 615-872-1599

Bridgestone has factories on 5 continents and sells its products worldwide. US manufacturing plants are located in Arkansas, Illinois, Iowa, North Carolina, Oklahoma, and Tennessee.

	1993 Sales	
	¥ bil.	% of total
Japan	744	47
Other countries	855	53
Total	**1,599**	**100**

WHAT

	1993 Sales	
	¥ bil.	% of total
Tire operations	1,192	75
Other products	407	25
Total	**1,599**	**100**

Selected Products

Tires	Chemical Products
Aircraft tires	Building materials
Automobile tires (Dayton,	Flexible Everlight products
Bridgestone, Firestone,	Thermal insulating
Road King, Seiberling)	Everlight (polyurethane
Heavy equipment tires	foam) products
Motorcycle tires	
Tire tubes	**Sporting Goods**
	Bicycles
Industrial Rubber	Golf balls and clubs
Products	Scuba diving equipment
Belts	Tennis balls, rackets, and
Hoses	shoes
Marine products	
Multirubber bearings	**Retailing**
Vibration-isolating and	Cockpit (Japan)
noise-insulating	Tire Kan (Japan)
materials	Tire Zone at Firestone auto
Waterproofing materials	service centers (US)

KEY COMPETITORS

Anthony Industries	Goodyear	Rubbermaid
Armstrong World	Huffy	Schwinn
Big O Tires	Masco	Sears
Brunswick	Michelin	Sony
Callaway Golf	3M	Standard
Continental AG	Montgomery Ward	Products
Cooper Tire & Rubber	Owens- Corning	Sumitomo W. L. Gore
Gates	Pirelli	Wal-Mart
	Premark	Whitman
		Wilson

HOW MUCH

$=¥112 (Dec. 31, 1993)	9-Year Growth	1984	1985	1986	1987	1988	1989	1990	1991	1992	1993
Sales (¥ bil.)	8.0%	802	864	793	820	1,191	1,689	1,784	1,764	1,745	1,599
Net income (¥ bil.)	3.4%	16	21	21	36	40	10	5	7	28	28
Income as % of sales	—	2.0%	2.4%	2.6%	4.4%	3.4%	0.6%	0.3%	0.4%	1.6%	1.8%
Earnings per share (¥)	4.7%	24	32	30	54	59	13	6	10	37	37
Stock price – high (¥)	—	544	480	645	1,309	1,436	2,070	1,740	1,200	1,220	1,440
Stock price – low (¥)	—	421	413	423	549	1,036	1,330	990	906	1,040	1,120
Stock price – close (¥)	43.7%	426	431	599	1,045	1,360	1,690	990	1,030	1,150	1,280
P/E – high	—	23	15	22	24	24	159	—	124	33	39
P/E – low	—	18	13	14	10	18	101	—	94	28	30
Dividends per share (¥)	13.3%	8.26	8.26	8.26	8.26	10.00	12.00	14.50	14.50	14.50	12.00
Book value per share (¥)	17.2%	394	417	440	482	527	574	571	569	590	634
Employees	11.6%	32,577	32,834	33,425	34,061	88,148	93,193	95,276	83,081	85,835	87,332

1993 Year-end:
Debt ratio: 59.0%
Return on equity: 6.0%
Cash (bil.): ¥66
Long-term debt (bil.): ¥289
No. of shares (mil.): 772
Dividends
  Yield: 0.9%
  Payout: 32.6%
Market value (mil.): $8,854
Sales (mil.): $14,328

Stock Price History High/Low 1984–93

(chart axis values: 2,500 / 2,000 / 1,500 / 1,000 / 500 / 0)

BRITISH AEROSPACE PLC

OVERVIEW

British Aerospace (BAe) has had difficulty trying to turn its swords into plowshares. Europe's largest defense contractor has dabbled with diversification in recent years, expanding into such areas as civil aviation, automobiles (Rover), construction, civil engineering, and property development (Arlington Securities). BAe is also a 20% partner in Airbus Industrie, the European aerospace consortium.

The end of the Cold War has meant decreased demand for BAe's core defense products, and the company's problems have been compounded by depressed property and car markets as well. Following a huge loss for BAe in 1992 chairman John Cahill set about a major restructuring of the company's troubled regional aircraft division, including laying off several thousand workers and closing a major plant.

A much publicized joint venture with Taiwan Aerospace to make regional jetliners fell through in 1993, as did a proposed merger with Britain's General Electric, the UK's #2 defense contractor.

As part of BAe's corporate refocusing on the defense and aerospace industries and on debt reduction strategies, the company sold its construction (Ballast Nedam) and corporate jet businesses in 1993. In 1994 BAe sold its 80% interest in its Rover car unit to German auto giant BMW for $1.2 billion.

WHEN

In the years between the Wright brothers and WWII, a host of aviation companies sprang up to serve the military and transportation needs of the British Empire — too many to survive after the war when the empire had dissolved. Parliament in 1960 took action to save the UK's aviation industry by merging smaller companies to form larger (and, ostensibly, stronger) entities — Hawker-Siddeley Aviation and British Aircraft Corporation (BAC).

Hawker-Siddeley, made up of aircraft (Hawker-Siddeley Aviation) and missiles (Hawker-Siddeley Dynamics) divisions, was created through the combination of A.V. Roe (founded 1910), Gloster Aircraft (founded 1915), Hawker Aircraft (founded 1920), Armstrong Whitworth (founded 1921), and Folland Aircraft (founded 1935). It attained fame in the 1960s for developing the Harrier fighter.

BAC was created through the merger of Bristol Aeroplane (founded 1910), English Electric (founded 1918), and Vicker-Armstrong (founded 1928). In 1962 it joined Aerospatiale to build the supersonic Concorde and later became a partner in ventures to develop the Tornado and the Jaguar fighters. Combined with the commercial failure of the Concorde, the costs of these ventures became more than the company could bear. Realizing British aviation was once again in trouble, the British government nationalized BAC and Hawker-Siddeley in 1976, merging them in 1977 with Scottish Aviation (founded 1935) to form BAe.

British Aerospace joined the Airbus consortium as a 20% equity partner in 1979. That year the government announced plans to privatize BAe. A partial privatization was finally carried out in 1981 when the government sold 51.57% of BAe to the public; the government's remaining shares in the company were sold to the public in 1985.

The late 1980s saw a period of diversification. In 1987 BAe bought Steinheil Optronik (optical equipment), Ballast Nedam Groep (a Dutch civil and marine engineering firm), and 24% of System Designers (computer software and systems; renamed SD-Scicon). In 1988 BAe bought state-owned Rover Group.

In 1990 Honda Motor Company bought a 20% stake in Rover, which received in return a 20% interest in Honda's UK manufacturing activities. Also in 1990 BAe bought 76% of Liverpool Airport and formed Ballast Nedam Construction. In 1991 Rover signed a deal with Honda to develop 3 new car models for the UK market.

BAe sold its corporate jet division to Raytheon in 1993. The clinching of a $7.5 billion contract with Saudi Arabia for Tornado jets in 1993 was offset by the surprise cancellation of a commercial jet joint venture with Taiwan.

In the wake of the collapse of long-standing negotiations on the Taiwan deal, Cahill, who was closely involved in the project, resigned as chairman in 1994. In 1994 BAe sold its satellite business to Matra Marconi Space for $87 million.

Principal exchange: London
Fiscal year ends: December 31

Chairman: Robert Bauman
CEO: Richard H. Evans, age 51
Finance Director: Richard D. Lapthorne, age 50
Chairman, British Aerospace Holdings (US):
Robert L. Kirk, age 65
**SVP and General Manager, British Aerospace
Holdings (US):** Paul L. Harris
**Director Human Resources, British Aerospace
Holdings (US):** Frank Sterrett
Auditors: KPMG Peat Marwick

HQ: British Aerospace Public Limited Company,
Warwick House, PO Box 87, Farnborough
Aerospace Centre, Farnborough, Hampshire
GU14 6YU, UK
Phone: +44-(01)252-373-232
Fax: +44-(01)252-383-000
US HQ: British Aerospace Holdings, Inc.,
22070 Broderick Dr., Sterling, VA 20166
US Phone: 703-406-2000
US Fax: 703-406-1313

1993 Sales		
	£ mil.	% of total
UK	3,720	35
Middle East	2,566	24
US & Canada	635	6
Far East	539	5
Australasia & Pacific	169	2
Central & South America	102	1
Africa	66	0
Other Europe	2,963	27
Total	**10,760**	**100**

	1993 Sales		1993 Profit Before Interest	
	£ mil.	% of total	£ mil.	% of total
Motor vehicles	4,301	38	56	—
Defense	3,963	35	345	—
Civil aircraft	1,580	14	(162)	—
Construction	947	8	28	—
Property dev.	166	2	(17)	—
Other	347	3	(13)	—
Adjustments	(544)	—	—	—
Total	**10,760**	**100**	**237**	**—**

Selected Subsidiaries and Affiliates
Airbus Industrie GIE (20%, France)
Arab British Dynamics Co. (30%, defense, Egypt)
Arlington Securities Plc (property development)
Asia Pacific Training and Simulation Pte. Ltd. (63%,
Singapore)
BAe Finance BV (Holland)
British Aerospace Defence Ltd.
British Aerospace Holdings, Inc. (US)
The Burwood House Group Plc (50%, property
development)
Eurofighter Jagdflugzeug GmbH (33%, Germany)
Nanoquest Defence Products Ltd.
Panavia Aircraft GmbH (42.5%, Germany)
Royal Ordnance plc
Spitfire Insurance Ltd.
Steinheil Optronik GmbH (optical and mechanical
equipment, Germany)

Bombardier	McDonnell Douglas
Daimler-Benz	Northrop Grumman
FlightSafety	Raytheon
Fokker	Rockwell
General Dynamics	Textron
GEC	Thiokol
Lagardère	Thomson SA
Lockheed Martin	Vickers
Loral	

£=$1.48 (Dec. 31, 1993)	Annual Growth	1984	1985	1986	1987	1988	1989	1990	1991	1992[1]	1993
Sales (£ mil.)	17.4%	—	—	—	4,108	5,706	9,085	10,540	10,562	9,997	10,760
Net income (£ mil.)	—	—	—	—	(100)	171	238	278	(152)	(888)	(214)
Income as % of sales	—	—	—	—	—	3.0%	2.6%	2.6%	—	—	—
Earnings per share (p)	—	—	—	—	(43)	61	82	91	(27)	(241)	(62)
Stock price – high (p)	—	—	473	598	675	509	729	595	650	379	468
Stock price – low (p)	—	—	290	416	274	324	413	469	298	100	165
Stock price – close (p)	1.4%	363	463	508	323	420	596	515	320	165	413
P/E – high	—	—	—	—	—	8	9	7	—	—	—
P/E – low	—	—	—	—	—	5	5	5	—	—	—
Dividends per share (p)	(12.9%)	—	—	—	19	21	23	25	25	7	8
Book value per share (p)	(0.1%)	—	—	—	401	815	884	938	697	527	399
Employees	1.6%	75,998	75,645	75,480	93,038	131,300	125,600	129,100	115,700	102,500	87,400

1993 Year-end:
Debt ratio: 50.3%
Return on equity: —
Cash (mil.): £1,449
L-T debt (mil.): £1,337
No. of shares (mil.): 378
Dividends
Yield: 2.0%
Payout: —
Market value (mil.): $2,309
Sales (mil.): $15,917

Stock Price History
High/Low 1985–93

[1] Accounting change

BRITISH AIRWAYS PLC

OVERVIEW

It's taken a lot more than a slick advertising campaign to change passengers' interpretation of British Airways' acronym (BA) from "Bloody Awful" to "Bloody Awesome." BA has worked hard at upgrading its services, and through layoffs and restructurings has transformed itself from a bloated, second-rate firm into the world's most profitable airline.

British Airways is the world's largest scheduled international airline. Based at London's Heathrow, the busiest airport in the world for international flights, BA serves 165 destinations in 75 countries and carries 30 million passengers and 600,000 metric tons of cargo a year.

In 1992 BA wanted to buy a 44% stake in USAir. It hoped to set the stage for the creation of the world's first global airline, with a global brand name, since Pan Am. The Big 3 US airlines (American, United, and Delta) strongly objected, demanding equal access to UK markets. The US Transportation Department sided with the US airlines. BA had to settle for a 25% stake in 1993, the maximum foreign ownership allowed under US law. BA also bought 25% of Qantas in that same year.

A dirty tricks campaign by BA aimed at squeezing out rival Virgin from the transatlantic market led to a lawsuit, bad PR, and the embarrassment of a public apology.

WHEN

British Airways was born as Imperial Airways in 1924, when the British government merged 4 private airlines to form a stronger, subsidized airline to link the British Empire. Of the original 4, British Marine Air Navigation operated between Southampton, Guernsey, and northwestern France, while Daimler Airway, Handley Page Transport, and Instone Air Line connected London with Paris, Brussels, Berlin, and Cologne.

Imperial pioneered air routes from London to India (1929), Cape Town (1932), Singapore (1933), and, with Qantas Empire Airways, Australia (1934). European service remained virtually unchanged, and private UK airlines emerged to fill this gap. Three of these (Hillman's Airways, Spartan Air Lines, and United Airways) merged in 1935 to form British Airways, which shared European service with Imperial until 1939, when the 2 were combined to form state-owned British Overseas Airways Corporation (BOAC).

After WWII, BOAC continued as the UK's international airline, but another state-owned company, British European Airways (BEA), took over domestic and European routes. Private airlines survived primarily as charters. In 1972 the government combined BOAC and BEA to form British Airways.

BA and Air France jointly pioneered supersonic passenger service (the Concorde) in 1976. A public relations victory rather than a financial success, the Concorde contributed to soaring costs, which left BA with a loss of $337 million in 1982. Former Avis president Colin Marshall became CEO in 1983, reduced

manpower, sold planes, and pared the airline's route network, building BA into one of the world's most profitable airlines, despite the Concorde's high operating costs.

In 1987, the year the British government sold BA to the public, the airline bought its chief British competitor, British Caledonian. BCal had begun as a charter airline (Airwork, 1928) that merged with 7 other private operators in 1960 to form British United Airways (BUA). Caledonian Airways (founded in Prestwick, Scotland; 1961) bought BUA in 1970, adopting the name British Caledonian Airways in 1971.

BA gained a foothold in the US through a 1988 agreement with United Airlines and bought 11% of Covia Partnership, owner of United's Apollo computer reservation system. The 2-year-old alliance with United ended when United gained service to Heathrow.

In 1990 BA negotiated with the Dutch carrier KLM to buy Belgium's Sabena World Airlines, but the deal collapsed. Then in 1991 it looked like BA and KLM would tie the knot; but in early 1992 an irresolvable dispute arose over how to value the 2 companies. Also that year the company acquired the principal European and domestic routes of Dan-Air.

In 1993 BA made a franchise deal with UK commuter airline CityFlyer Express, charging a fee for the small airline to fly under BA's colors. Increased demand for luxury and business class seats lifted BA's revenues in 1994, but the financial troubles of USAir pose a threat to BA's future profits and its plans to become a global airline.

NYSE symbol: BAB (ADR)
Fiscal year ends: March 31

Chairman: Sir Colin Marshall, age 60,
£788,019 pay
Group Managing Director: Robert Aylin, age 47
CFO: Derek Stevens, age 55
Managing Director Cargo: Kevin Hatton, age 49
Director Human Resources: Valerie Scoular,
age 38
Company Secretary: Gail F. Redwood, age 45
General Manager Bulova Corp. Center (US):
Barbara Cassani
**SVP Human Resources Bulova Corp. Center
(US):** Irv Rudowitz
Auditors: Ernst & Young

HQ: Speedbird House, Heathrow Airport,
Hounslow, Middlesex TW6 2JA, UK
Phone: +44-(01)81-759-5511
Fax: +44-(01)81-897-1889
US HQ: Bulova Corporate Center, 7520 Astoria
Blvd., New York, NY 11370
US Phone: 718-397-4000
US Fax: 718-397-4364

	1994 Sales		1994 Operating Income	
	$ mil.	% of total	$ mil.	% of total
Europe	3,616	39	102	14
The Americas	3,013	32	191	26
Far East & Australasia	1,394	15	141	19
Other	1,337	14	300	41
Total	**9,360**	**100**	**734**	**100**

	1994 Sales	
	$ mil.	% of total
Passenger services	7,685	82
Freight & mail services	684	7
Nonscheduled services	222	3
Other	769	8
Total	**9,360**	**100**

Major Subsidiaries and Affiliates
Air Russia (31%)
British Airways Capital Ltd. (89%, airline finance)
British Airways Finance BV (airline finance, Netherlands)
British Airways Holidays Ltd. (package holidays)
Caledonian Airways Ltd. (charters)
Deutsche BA LmbH (49%, German airline)
Galileo International Partnership (14.6%, computer
reservation system, US)
Qantas Airways Ltd.(25%, Australia)
TAT European Airlines SA (49.9%, France)
USAir Group, Inc. (25%, US)

Flight Equipment	No.	Orders
Boeing 737	73	—
Boeing 747	59	34
Boeing 757	43	2
Boeing 767	26	5
Boeing 777	—	15
Airbus A320	10	—
Concorde	7	—
McDonnell Douglas DC-10	7	—
Other	28	—
Total	**253**	**56**

Air France	JAL	SAS
All Nippon Airways	KLM	Singapore Airlines
AMR	Lufthansa	Swire Pacific
Delta	Northwest	UAL
IRI	Airlines	Virgin Group

Stock prices are for ADRs ADR = 10 shares	Annual Growth	1985	1986	1987	1988	1989	1990	1991	1992	1993	1994
Sales ($ mil.)	18.5%	2,036	4,511	5,245	7,091	7,184	7,971	8,632	9,069	8,421	9,360
Net income ($ mil.)	15.1%	120	280	238	285	295	405	166	443	269	425
Income as % of sales	—	5.9%	6.2%	4.5%	4.0%	4.1%	5.1%	1.9%	4.9%	3.2%	4.5%
Earnings per share ($)	3.7%	—	—	3.30	3.96	4.10	5.62	2.34	5.38	3.37	4.26
Stock price – high ($)[1]	—	—	—	—	37.50	32.50	37.75	39.38	44.38	57.50	69.00
Stock price – low ($)[1]	—	—	—	—	22.13	24.75	27.88	25.00	24.50	37.38	40.00
Stock price – close ($)[1]	15.5%	—	—	—	28.00	29.38	37.63	27.50	44.38	46.50	66.50
P/E – high	—	—	—	—	10	8	7	17	8	17	16
P/E – low	—	—	—	—	6	6	5	11	5	11	9
Dividends per share ($)	—	—	—	—	1.22	1.40	1.63	1.86	1.76	2.09	1.80
Book value per share ($)	14.5%	—	9.66	13.50	16.59	17.54	28.17	23.22	38.27	24.76	28.44
Employees	2.6%	—	39,635	40,440	43,969	50,204	52,054	54,427	50,409	48,960	48,628

1994 Year-end:
Debt ratio: 74.3%
Return on equity: 18.7%
Cash (mil.): $1,102
Current ratio: 1.30
Long-term debt (mil.): $5,582
No. of shares (mil.): 95
Dividends
  Yield: 2.7%
  Payout: 42.3%
Market value (mil.): $6,344

**Stock Price History[1]
High/Low 1988–94**

[1] Stock prices are for the prior calendar year.

THE BRITISH PETROLEUM COMPANY

OVERVIEW

Headquartered in London, British Petroleum (BP) is the UK's largest company and the world's 4th largest oil company (after Exxon, Royal Dutch/Shell, and Mobil).

BP's rich holdings in Alaska produce more than half of the company's annual output; its North Sea holdings account for 1/3. Since 1989 the company has narrowed its exploration activities, focusing particularly on Alaska, the North Sea, Vietnam, and Colombia.

BP markets its petroleum products in more than 50 countries through a network of 16,400 service stations. Although most of its stations are located in the US and Europe, the company is working to expand in Southeast Asia. Its chemical operations have struggled as chemicals prices have fallen. BP Chemicals markets such compounds as petrochemicals, polymers, and specialty chemicals in more than 60 countries.

As part of its plans to concentrate on core businesses, BP sold its animal feed, breeding, and aquaculture operations to CINVen and Baring Capital Investors for $425 million in late 1994.

WHEN

After negotiating an extensive oil concession with the Grand Vizier in Persia, English adventurer William Knox D'Arcy began exploration in 1901. In 1908, with additional capital from Burmah Oil, D'Arcy's company became the first to strike oil in the Middle East. D'Arcy and Burmah Oil formed Anglo-Persian Oil Company in 1909 to exploit the enormous find. At Winston Churchill's urging, the British government purchased a 51% interest in cash-hungry Anglo-Persian in 1914.

Anglo-Persian had interests in the first major oil discoveries in Iraq (1927) and Kuwait (1938). In 1928, facing a potential oil glut, the company and its major competitors entered into a secret "As Is" agreement, fixing world production and prices for 2 decades.

While other oil companies were negotiating "50-50" deals with producer nations, Chairman Sir William Fraser refused to renegotiate the company's lucrative concession with Iran. Following the 1951 seizing of the company's Iranian assets, a coup in 1953 installed the Shah as Iran's leader. An international consortium resumed business, and the company was allowed a 40% interest. In 1954 the company changed its name to British Petroleum. The Khomeini regime severed Iran's ties to foreign oil companies in 1979.

BP made major strikes in Prudhoe Bay, Alaska, in 1969 and in the North Sea in 1970. In 1970 BP swapped its Alaskan reserves for an eventual 55% interest in SOHIO. From 1979 to 1981 SOHIO invested its huge Alaskan oil profits in exploration and nonoil acquisitions, including Kennecott Copper (1981). Declining oil and copper prices in the mid-1980s, in addition to a large interest in a $1.7 billion dry hole in the Beaufort Sea, led to disappointing earnings. In 1986 BP named Robert Horton CEO of SOHIO. Horton ("The Hatchet") cut overhead and sold poorly performing units.

Britain acquired an additional 20.15% of BP in 1975, then reduced its holdings through public offerings in 1977 and 1979, finally selling its remaining shares in 1987.

Under the direction of Sir Peter Walters from 1981 to 1990, BP purchased Purina Mills (domestic livestock feed, 1986); the remaining shares of SOHIO (1987); and Britoil (1988), a large North Sea oil and gas producer. BP sold most of its minerals businesses, including Kennecott, to RTZ and $1.3 billion in oil properties to Oryx in 1989.

Horton, promoted to BP's chairmanship over rival David Simon in 1990, streamlined the company by cutting corporate staff and pushed for exploration in new areas beyond BP's Alaskan and North Sea fields. BP acquired 93% of Petromed in 1991 for $578 million.

In the first half of 1992, BP suffered the first quarterly losses in its history. In a mid-1992 coup company directors axed Horton, and BP's new managers subsequently slashed by 50% shareholder dividends, which had been protected by Horton despite reduced earnings. To boost company profits BP began liquidating assets, including its 57% share of BP Canada and its gas stations in California and Florida.

In 1993 the company agreed to pay the State of Alaska $630 million in back taxes to settle a disputed audit.

In 1994 BP announced the discovery of 5 trillion cubic feet of gas reserves in Colombia.

NYSE symbol: BP (ADR)
Fiscal year ends: December 31

Chairman: Lord Ashburton, age 65
CEO: David A. G. Simon, age 54
Managing Director and CFO; Chairman, BP Nutrition: Steve J. Ahearne, age 54
Managing Director; CEO, BP Exploration: E. J. P. (John) Browne, age 45
Managing Director; CEO, BP Oil: K. R. (Russell) Seal, age 51
Managing Director; Chairman, BP America: Rodney F. Chase, age 50
CFO, BP America: Charles Bowman
VP Human Resources, BP America: Felix Strater
Auditors: Ernst & Young

HQ: The British Petroleum Company p.l.c.,
Britannic House, One Finsbury Circus,
London EC2M 7BA, UK
Phone: +44-(0)71-496-4000
Fax: +44-(0)71-496-4570 (Investor Relations)
US HQ: BP America Inc., 200 Public Sq.,
Cleveland, OH 44114
US Phone: 216-586-4141
US Fax: 216-586-8066 (Investor Relations)

	1993 Sales		1993 Operating Income	
	$ mil.	% of total	$ mil.	% of total
UK	15,803	30	786	23
US	15,608	30	1,301	39
Other Europe	15,263	29	558	16
Other countries	5,906	11	747	22
Total	**52,580**	**100**	**3,392**	**100**

	1993 Sales		1993 Operating Income	
	$ mil.	% of total	$ mil.	% of total
Refining & marketing	38,431	73	1,116	—
Exploration & production	6,163	12	2,916	—
Chemicals	4,239	8	(361)	—
Nutrition	3,668	7	89	—
Other & corporate	78	0	(368)	—
Total	**52,580**	**100**	**3,392**	**—**

Products and Services

BP Oil	Pipelines and
Marketing	transportation
Refining	Production
Shipping	
Supply and trading	BP Chemicals
Transportation	Advanced materials and
	carborundum
BP Exploration	Bulk chemicals
Gas processing and	Nitriles
marketing	Petrochemicals
Oil and gas exploration	Polymers

Amoco	ENI	Pennzoil
Ashland, Inc.	Exxon	Petrobrás
Atlantic Richfield	Hoechst	Petrofina
BASF	Imperial Chemical	Phillips
Broken Hill	Imperial Oil	Petroleum
Cargill	Ito-Yokado	Repsol
Chevron	Koch	Royal Dutch/
Circle K	Kroger	Shell
Coastal	Mobil	Sun Company
Continental Grain	Norsk Hydro	Texaco
Diamond Shamrock	Occidental	Total
Dow	Oryx	Unocal
DuPont	PDVSA	USX–Marathon
Elf Aquitaine	PEMEX	YPF

Stock prices are for ADRs ADR = 1 share	9-Year Growth	1984	1985	1986	1987	1988	1989	1990	1991	1992	1993
Sales ($ mil.)	1.2%	47,374	63,259	41,278	53,740	47,904	50,679	66,367	62,841	51,864	52,580
Net income ($ mil.)	(6.2%)	1,625	2,309	1,212	2,625	2,188	2,862	3,235	776	(694)	910
Income as % of sales	—	3.4%	3.7%	2.9%	4.9%	4.6%	5.6%	4.9%	1.2%	—	1.7%
Earnings per share ($)	(6.2%)	3.56	5.05	2.65	4.92	4.32	6.47	6.24	1.73	(1.54)	2.01
Stock price – high ($)	—	30.00	35.13	43.75	80.38	63.75	65.88	86.25	77.50	66.38	65.38
Stock price – low ($)	—	21.75	21.38	30.13	43.25	43.25	53.63	59.63	61.88	41.13	42.13
Stock price – close ($)	12.2%	22.63	32.38	43.50	55.88	53.75	65.38	76.88	65.75	45.75	64.00
P/E – high	—	8	7	17	16	15	10	14	45	—	33
P/E – low	—	6	4	11	9	11	8	10	36	—	21
Dividends per share ($)	(0.7%)	1.76	2.01	2.44	2.90	3.28	3.45	3.60	4.16	3.61	1.65
Book value per share ($)	0.9%	29.30	31.29	32.25	40.83	40.97	40.03	47.49	44.27	33.43	31.71
Employees	(4.7%)	130,100	129,450	126,700	126,400	128,450	119,600	116,750	111,900	97,650	84,000

1993 Year-end:
Debt ratio: 68.2%
Return on equity: 6.2%
Cash (mil.): $315
Current ratio: 0.99
Long-term debt (mil.): $10,570
No. of shares (mil.): 454
Dividends
  Yield: 2.6%
  Payout: 82.1%
Market value (mil.): $29,072

Stock Price History
High/Low 1984–93

BRITISH TELECOMMUNICATIONS PLC

OVERVIEW

The UK's largest company, British Telecommunications (BT) is fighting invaders at home by going abroad. Although the London-based company is still the main provider of local and long distance telephone service in the UK, its share of the residential market has dropped from 99% to 94% since 1991. BT has been particularly hurt by Cable and Wireless–owned Mercury Communications, which has cut BT's market share of top business accounts from 94% in 1991 to 88%.

BT's chairman, Iain Vallance, continues to work to make BT one of the world's leading telecommunications companies. As part of his plan to create a global communications network, he paid $4.3 billion for 20% of MCI, the US's 2nd largest long-distance carrier, in 1994. The 2 companies plan to spend $1 billion on a joint venture offering worldwide networking services to corporations.

While it's thinking globally, BT must still put its home in order. The UK is the first country to allow competition for local phone service, so BT continues to work to improve productivity to compete with the dozens of upstarts that analysts say could take away 35% of the UK residential market by 2000. The company continues to shed employees. It has cut its work force by nearly 100,000 people since 1990 and plans to cut another 50,000.

WHEN

In 1879 the government granted the British Post Office an exclusive right to operate telegraph systems. When private companies tried to offer telephone service, the government objected, arguing in court that its telegraph monopoly was imperiled. The courts agreed, and the Post Office was empowered to license private telephone companies, collect a 10% royalty, and operate its own systems.

The National Telephone Company, a private firm, emerged as the leading telephone outfit, competing with the Post Office. When the company's license expired in 1911, the Post Office took over National Telephone's system and became the monopoly telephone company.

In 1936 the phone system introduced its familiar red "public call offices" (known as "phone booths" in the US). The kiosks were designed by Sir Giles Gilbert Scott for the jubilee of King George V.

Under a 1981 law, telecommunication activities were split from the Post Office and placed under the new British Telecommunications Corporation. The government also allowed, for the first time, a competitor — Mercury Communications, formed in 1981 in a joint effort by Cable and Wireless, British Petroleum, and Barclays Merchant Bank (C&W bought out BP and Barclays in 1984). Within a year the Thatcher government called for the privatization of British Telecom.

The Telecommunications Act of 1984 set up the sale of a majority stake in British Telecom to the public later that year. After a $20 million publicity campaign, British Telecom became a publicly traded company in one of the largest UK stock offering's in history. The Telecommunications Act set up an Office of Telecommunications (OFTEL) to regulate British Telecom and tied rates the company could charge to inflation. To become a multinational communications concern, British Telecom went shopping in North America. It bought control of Mitel (Canada, phone equipment, 1986), ITT Dialcom (US, electronic mail, 1986), and 20% of McCaw (US, cellular telephones, 1989).

In 1990 the British government opened the UK to more phone competition. The company faces challenges from cable companies (many owned by US regional Bell operating companies), cellular service providers, European carriers such as France Télécom, and other large corporations with excess capacity on private networks. In 1991 British Telecom spent more than $106 million to improve its corporate image as a provider of quality service by altering its logo to the blue initials "BT" with a red, white, and blue man blowing a trumpet.

In 1993 the British government sold almost all its remaining shares in the company for $7.43 billion.

In 1994 the company announced major price reductions on many direct-dialed international calls. That same year BT competitor Mercury lost a court battle to force OFTEL, the UK's telecommunications regulatory agency, to change the regulations that relate to the way BT charges competitors such as Mercury to use its network.

NYSE symbol: BTY (ADR)
Fiscal year ends: March 31

Chairman: Sir Iain Vallance, age 51,
£650,000 pay
Deputy Chairman: Paul G. Bosonnet, age 61
Group Director and Secretary: Malcolm Argent,
age 58
Group Managing Director: Michael L. Hepher,
age 50
**Managing Director Development and
Procurement:** Alan W. Rudge, age 56
Group Finance Director: Robert P. Brace,
age 44
Chief of Service Operations, BT North America:
Nick Williams
CFO, BT North America: Martin Traill
Director Human Resources, BT North America:
Dave Brown
Auditors: Coopers & Lybrand

WHERE

HQ: British Telecommunications public limited
company, BT Centre, 81 Newgate St.,
London EC1A 7AJ, UK
Phone: +44-71-356-4008
Fax: +44-71-356-5520 (Financial Relations)
US HQ: BT North America Inc., 40 E. 52nd St.,
14th Fl., New York, NY 10022
US Phone: 212-418-7800
US Fax: 212-418-7788 (Financial Relations)

BT offers telephone service and equipment
internationally, but 98% of its revenues are
derived from operations in the UK.

WHAT

	1994 Sales	
	$ mil.	% of total
UK local & long-distance		
telephone calls	7,738	38
Telephone exchange line rentals	3,579	18
International telephone calls	2,920	14
Customer premises equip. supply	1,494	7
Other sales & services	4,644	23
Adjustments	(68)	
Total	**20,307**	**100**

Selected Subsidiaries and Affiliates
Belize Telecommunications Ltd. (25%,
telecommunication services supplier)
BT France (communication services and products)
BT (Marine) Ltd. (subsea engineering contractor)
BT North America Inc. (communication services and
products)
BT Property Ltd. (real estate)
BT Telecom (Deutschland) GmbH (Germany,
communications services and products)
BT (Worldwide) Ltd. (international networks)
Gibraltar Telecommunications International Ltd. (50%,
telecommunication services)
Manx Telecom Ltd. (Isle of Man, telecommunication
services)
MCI Communications Corp. (20%, US)
Syncordia Corp. (US, specialized network services)
Telecom Securicor/Cellular Radio Ltd. (60%, mobile
cellular telephone systems)
Yellow Pages Sales Ltd. (advertising sales)

KEY COMPETITORS

AT&T	Ericsson
BCE	France Télécom
Cable & Wireless	Hutchison Whampoa
Deutsche Bundespost	Sprint
Telekom	

HOW MUCH

Stock prices are for ADRs. ADR = 10 shares	9-Year Growth	1985	1986	1987	1988	1989	1990	1991	1992	1993	1994
Sales ($ mil.)	8.8%	9,490	12,430	15,149	19,229	18,682	20,209	23,000	23,153	20,035	20,307
Net income ($ mil.)	9.4%	1,172	1,581	2,112	2,747	2,643	2,476	3,637	3,548	1,846	2,624
Income as % of sales	—	12.3%	12.7%	13.9%	14.3%	14.1%	12.3%	15.8%	15.3%	9.2%	12.9%
Earnings per share ($)	9.5%	1.87	2.47	3.36	4.46	4.37	4.10	5.94	5.76	3.00	4.23
Stock price – high ($)[1]	—	12.38	30.38	44.00	55.63	47.75	52.00	57.88	74.00	70.63	74.88
Stock price – low ($)[1]	—	9.50	12.00	26.00	31.50	37.75	39.25	40.75	51.25	53.88	57.50
Stock price – close ($)[1]	21.4%	12.38	28.00	32.63	42.13	45.88	50.50	57.50	62.50	61.38	71.13
P/E – high	—	7	12	13	13	11	13	10	13	24	18
P/E – low	—	5	5	8	7	9	10	7	9	18	14
Dividends per share ($)	—	0.00	1.20	1.39	1.73	1.95	1.98	2.67	2.71	2.88	2.54
Book value per share ($)	11.0%	12.21	15.72	18.87	24.81	24.75	25.02	30.08	33.13	29.89	31.14
Employees	(4.5%)	235,178	235,988	234,397	237,205	244,418	245,665	226,900	210,500	170,700	156,000

1994 Year-end:
Debt ratio: 42.0%
Return on equity: 13.9%
Cash (mil.): $1,561
Current ratio: 1.02
Long-term debt (mil.): $4,751
No. of shares (mil.): 621
Dividends
  Yield: 3.6%
  Payout: 60.0%
Market value (mil.): $44,182

**Stock Price History[1]
High/Low 1985–94**

[1] Stock prices are for the prior calendar year.

BROKEN HILL PROPRIETARY

OVERVIEW

Australia's #1 company in terms of market valuation, Broken Hill Proprietary (BHP) is an international resources company with interests in steel, minerals, and petroleum. It has major operations in over 20 countries.

BHP's mineral division produces copper, iron ore, manganese, and gold, as well as 40 million tons of thermal and metallurgical coal annually. BHP holds around 80% of the Australian steel market, while its petroleum unit has proven oil reserves of over 1.5 billion barrels. The company has oil production operations in Australia, North America, the UK, and Vietnam. BHP also runs transport, information technology, and engineering operations in support of its major business groups.

It provides worldwide sea transport and major road and rail transport in Australia.

The company is increasing its activities in South America and Southeast Asia as areas of rapid growth. In particular, BHP is increasing its exploration activities in China with new oil and mineral ventures.

BHP, the #3 producer of manganese ore worldwide, is working with an Irish exploration company to develop a mineral sands (titanium) project in Mozambique.

The company also owns 33.5% of Australian brewer Foster's, a stake it purchased in 1992 when the brewer was in deep financial trouble. Foster's fortunes improved in the following year, and it is now profitable again.

WHEN

In 1883 Charles Rasp, a boundary rider for the Mt. Gipps sheep station, discovered a massive lode of silver, lead, and zinc in the Broken Hill outcrop in New South Wales, Australia. The Broken Hill Proprietary Company was incorporated in 1885 to mine the ore, and 2 years later the company discovered iron ore deposits in southern Australia. By the early 1890s BHP was paying over £1 million a year in dividends.

Until 1915 the company mined, smelted, and refined iron ore, lead, silver, and zinc. That year BHP began producing steel at its Newcastle, Australia, plant. Aided by the steel demand caused by WWI, BHP soon became the largest steel producer in Australia and opened its own coal and iron ore mines to provide the necessary raw materials. By purchasing Australian Iron and Steel (1935) and a number of other steel companies, BHP had gained a virtual monopoly on the Australian steel industry by 1939. The company closed its exhausted Broken Hill mine in 1939.

In 1940 BHP established an operation to build deep-sea ships at Whyalla and later established its own fleet. During WWII the company produced munitions and led the syndicate that created Commonwealth Aircraft, a Melbourne-based manufacturer of fighters and training planes.

During the 1960s the company entered a partnership with Esso Standard Oil (Australia), a subsidiary of Standard Oil of New Jersey, to explore for offshore oil and gas. In 1965 BHP and its partner found large quantities of natural gas and 2 years later discovered oil in the Bass Strait. The resulting Bass Strait oil and gas field soon supplied 70% of the nation's petroleum. In the 1960s and 1970s, BHP started mining iron ore, manganese, and coal for export. In 1969 the company became joint owner of John Lysaght Ltd., a steel products manufacturer, and in 1979 became 100% owner.

In 1984 BHP bought Utah International's overseas assets from General Electric for $700 million; the acquisition allowed BHP to expand its mining operations in the US, South Africa, Canada, Chile, and Brazil. The company underwent a major reorganization between 1983 and 1987 to adapt to its new role as a global company. Acquisitions during the late 1980s included Energy Reserves Group (petroleum, 1985), Monsanto Oil (1986), Gulf Energy Development (1988), Aquila Steel (1988), and Hawaii-based Pacific Resources (crude oil, 1989). In 1990 BHP bought the remaining 70% interest (it owned 30%) in Mount Goldsworthy (iron ore).

As part of a 1988 capital restructuring, BHP purchased preferred stock in International Brewing Investments (IBI), a holding company that included 33.5% of Carlton Brewing, the world's #4 brewer. In 1992 BHP and Vextin, a banking syndicate, took control of Foster's. BHP had to take a large write-down following a major decline in Foster's stock.

In 1993 BHP teamed up with Norwegian firm Elkem AS to produce and sell manganese alloys. In 1994 BHP signed up Westcoast Energy Corp., of Canada, to help it build a $269 million gas pipeline in Australia.

NYSE symbol: BHP (ADR)
Fiscal year ends: May 31

Chairman: Brian T. Loton, age 65
Managing Director and CEO: John B. Prescott, age 53
Executive General Manager Finance: Geoffrey E. Heeley, age 59
Group General Manager Americas, BHP Petroleum: Dennis W. Loughridge
Executive General Manager and CEO, BHP Minerals (US): Jerry K. Ellis, age 56
General Manager Finance, BHP Minerals (US): D. F. Collins
SVP and Group General Manager Human Resources, BHP Minerals (US): R. N. James
Auditors: Arthur Andersen & Co.

HQ: The Broken Hill Proprietary Company Limited, BHP Tower, 600 Bourke St., Melbourne, Victoria 3000, Australia
Phone: +61-(0)3-609-3333
Fax: +61-(0)3-609-3015
US HQ: BHP Minerals, 550 California St., San Francisco, CA 94104
US Phone: 415-774-2030
US Fax: 415-774-2025

	1994 Sales	
	$ mil.	% of total
Australia	8,081	66
North America	1,847	15
Other countries	2,273	19
Total	**12,201**	**100**

	1994 Sales		1994 Operating Income	
	$ mil.	% of total	$ mil.	% of total
Steel	4,791	39	377	29
Minerals	3,880	32	479	37
Petroleum	3,134	26	351	27
Other	376	3	95	7
Adjustments	20	—	(268)	—
Total	**12,201**	**100**	**1,034**	**100**

Steel	Minerals	Silver
Bar	Coal	Zinc
Coke	Copper	
Iron ore	concentrate	**Petroleum**
Plate	Ferro alloys	Butane
Rail products	Gold	Crude oil
Rod	Iron ore	Ethane
Rolled coil	Lead	Liquefied natural
Slab	Manganese	gas
Structural products	dioxide	Natural gas
Wire products	Nickel	Propane

Alcan	Elf Aquitaine	PEMEX
Alcoa	ENI	Pennzoil
Amoco	Exxon	Petrobrás
Anglo American	Fried. Krupp	Petrofina
ASARCO	Hanson	Phelps Dodge
Ashland Oil	Hyundai	Phillips
Atlantic	Inco	Petroleum
Richfield	Inland Steel	Repsol
Bethlehem Steel	IRI	Royal Dutch/
British Petroleum	Koch	Shell
Cargill	LTV	RTZ
Chevron	Mitsubishi	Texaco
Coastal	Mobil	Thyssen
Codelco	Nippon Steel	TOTAL
Cyprus Amax	Norsk Hydro	Unocal
DuPont	PDVSA	USX–Marathon

Stock prices are for ADRs ADR = 4 shares	9-Year Growth	1985	1986	1987	1988	1989	1990	1991	1992	1993	1994
Sales ($ mil.)	9.1%	5,574	5,936	6,241	7,908	7,885	10,303	11,878	10,933	10,938	12,201
Net income ($ mil.)	5.4%	591	690	584	754	831	847	1,083	390	820	947
Income as % of sales	—	10.6%	11.6%	9.4%	9.5%	10.5%	8.2%	9.1%	3.6%	7.5%	7.8%
Earnings per share ($)	5.3%	1.78	1.52	1.32	1.93	2.32	2.32	2.89	1.27	2.55	2.84
Stock price – high ($)[1]	—	17.38	21.34	29.53	25.91	32.38	37.63	47.50	44.25	48.38	62.38
Stock price – low ($)[1]	—	8.28	13.26	15.00	16.38	20.34	26.38	29.00	28.25	34.00	45.00
Stock price – close ($)[1]	17.0%	14.99	17.61	18.63	21.94	29.38	31.25	40.88	36.63	47.50	61.63
P/E – high	—	10	14	22	13	14	16	16	35	19	22
P/E – low	—	5	9	11	9	9	11	10	22	13	16
Dividends per share ($)	—	0.59	0.86	0.90	0.41	1.27	0.82	1.19	1.25	1.17	1.10
Book value per share ($)	8.2%	10.66	12.51	12.99	10.90	13.93	16.24	13.74	16.36	18.39	21.70
Employees	(2.1%)	58,000	58,000	61,000	61,000	51,000	49,000	52,000	51,000	47,000	48,000

1994 Year-end:
Debt ratio: 63.3%
Return on equity: 13.9%
Cash (mil.): $318
Current ratio: 1.06
Long-term debt (mil.): $4,285
No. of shares (mil.): 346
Dividends
  Yield: 1.8%
  Payout: 38.7%
Market value (mil.): $21,321

Stock Price History[1]
High/Low 1985–94

[1] Stock prices are for the prior calendar year.

BTR PLC

BTR is one of the UK's largest conglomerates, with 138 major holdings and over 1,000 subsidiaries worldwide. Businesses include heavy manufacturing (motors, beltings), transportation (locomotives), control and electric systems (meters, sensors), construction (concrete products), and consumer-related products (sports equipment and packaging).

In the 1980s, when the LBO craze made "conglomerate" a dirty word, BTR's philosophy was to buy low-tech niche companies in major markets or minor companies in niche markets, slash costs, and increase profit margins. BTR prefers running facilities at capacity to making investments to boost volume. This keeps costs low and margins high.

BTR's strategy paid off as the company continued to expand beyond the mature markets of Europe and North America into fast-growing Asia. In 1993 and 1994 sluggish European sales and rising raw materials prices put pressure on the all-important margins, and BTR began modifying its strategy by selling companies that distribute products it does not make and buying more high-tech companies.

BTR's earliest predecessor, Arrowsmith & Silver (its name would change frequently), dates back to 1798. In 1823 the company began making waterproof outerwear (useful as the country colonized areas in the tropics) and went on to specialize in other waterproof products, including undersea cable. By 1892 the company had helped start cable companies across the globe and was a major communications power. Then came radio, and the company switched to bicycle and car tires as the demand for cable waned. In 1933 most of the company was bought by British Goodrich (and quickly divested again the next year). By this time it was named British Tyre and Rubber. The company's plants were bombed in WWII.

After the war the company struggled, leaving the tire business in 1956. It then made rubber and plastic odds and ends, foam packaging, and hoses.

In 1965 the company, by then named British Thermoplastics and Rubber, met its destiny in the person of Owen Green. Conglomeration was a key word in 1960s business, and Green began to make acquisitions, including the 1969 purchase of Leyland & Birmingham Rubber Company. Following his niche strategy, Green built a formidable collection of companies in manufacturing, construction, and transportation and began expanding into Europe, South Africa, the US, and Australia. In 1982 BTR went public.

In the 1980s BTR continued to swallow companies, including some of the UK's major players such as Thomas Tilling (construction materials, 1983), which has been the UK's largest takeover to date. The pace of acquisitions continued in the 1980s.

In 1991 BTR shocked financial circles with a hostile takeover of Hawker Siddeley, whose brightest moment was in producing planes for the RAF in WWII and whose performance was described by BTR management as "lamentable."

Green stepped down from active management in 1993 and was succeeded as chairman by Sir Norman Ireland, while Australian Alan Jackson, who had a good track record in making the company's Nylex subsidiary into one of Australia's premier industrial groups, was CEO. It was an indication of Green's unorthodoxy to have tapped such a relative outsider rather than one of the "old boys." In another departure from business traditions, BTR named Kathleen O'Donovan, who is neither old nor a boy, its CFO, making her one of the UK's highest-ranking female executives.

Although the company continues to be profitable and has pulled off a coup in the form of an agreement to help build plants to make bottles for China's nascent bottled drink industry, it had some problems in 1993 and 1994. One of its US subsidiaries, BAE Automated Systems, built the ill-starred, "flying luggage" system for the new Denver International Airport. The failure of this system cost the company dearly. Other US subsidiaries include Eaton Technologies, Fasco Motors, Bear Medical, PET Technologies, and Aerospace Avionics.

In 1995 it was announced that CEO Jackson would be replaced in 1996 by RTZ's deputy CEO, Ian Strachan. Reportedly, Jackson was not tapped to succeed as chairman because an "old boy" was preferred.

NYSE symbol: BTRUY (ADR)
Fiscal year ends: December 31

WHO

Chairman: Norman Ireland, age 66, £139,241
Managing Director and CEO: Alan Jackson, age 58
Director Finance: Kathleen O'Donovan, age 36
Company Secretary: Casson Brown
Personnel Director: Barry Williams
President, BTR (US): John S. Thompson
VP Finance, BTR (US): William Denninger
VP Human Resources, BTR (US): Robert MacQueen
Auditors: Ernst & Young

WHERE

HQ: Silvertown House, Vincent Square, London SW1P 2PL
Phone: +44-(01)71-834-3848
Fax: +44-(01)71-834-3879
US HQ: BTR Inc, 750 Main St., Stamford, CT 06902
US Phone: 203-352-0060
US Fax: 203-964-8025

	1993 Sales		1993 Pretax Income	
	£ mil.	% of total	£ mil.	% of total
UK	2,389	29	416	32
Other Europe	1,214	14	130	10
The Americas	2,365	28	402	30
Australasia	1,578	19	250	19
Other countries	876	10	119	9
Adjustments	1,350	—	(35)	—
Total	**9,772**	**100**	**1,282**	**100**

WHAT

	1993 Sales		1993 Pretax Income	
	£ mil.	% of total	£ mil.	% of total
Consumer	2,076	21	327	23
Transportation	2,042	21	335	24
Industrial	1,974	20	265	18
Construction	1,251	13	176	12
Controls & elect.	1,079	11	214	15
Corporate	1,350	14	122	8
Adjustments	—	—	(157)	—
Total	**9,772**	**100**	**1,282**	**100**

Selected Subsidiaries
ACI Philippines (construction)
ACI Shanghai Glass Co. (70%, packaging)
Aerospace Avionics (aerospace controls, US)
BAE Automated Systems (conveyor belts, US)
Brook Crompton Motors
BTR Inc (holding company, US)
BTR Nylex, Ltd. (60%, Australia)
Eaton Technologies (motors, US)
Hawker Energy Products (batteries)
Lonstroff-BTR (industrial, Switzerland)
Mesnel (transportation, France)
Metzeler Automotive Profiles (transportation, Germany)
Perfiles (transportation, Spain)

KEY COMPETITORS

ABB	General Electric	Motorola
Adila	General Signal	Samsung
AlliedSignal	Groupe Schneider	Siemens
American Standard	Hanson	Sumitomo
Armstrong	Honeywell	Thomson SA
Bechtel	Ingersoll-Rand	Westinghouse
British Aerospace	Johnson Controls	USG
Callaway Golf	Matsushita	Vulcan
Corning	Morrison Knudsen	Materials
Formosa Plastics		

HOW MUCH

£= $1.48 (Dec. 31, 1993)	Annual Growth	1984	1985	1986	1987	1988	1989	1990	1991	1992	1993
Sales (£ mil.)	12.9%	3,290	4,053	3,979	4,336	5,460	6,904	6,742	6,742	8,841	9,772
Net income (£ mil.)	18.4%	177	275	341	413	485	608	536	554	667	807
Income as % of sales	—	5.4%	6.8%	8.6%	9.5%	8.9%	8.8%	8.0%	8.2%	7.7%	8.3%
Earnings per share (p)	15.2%	6.7	10.1	12.3	14.7	17.2	21.1	18.5	18.9	20.6	24.0
Stock price – high (p)	—	132	135	200	224	181	291	281	258	332	409
Stock price – low (p)	—	88	89	120	137	143	175	158	174	229	318
Stock price – close (p)	12.3%	131	113	165	165	176	280	193	229	330	373
P/E – high	—	20	12	16	15	11	14	15	14	16	17
P/E – low	—	1	9	12	9	8	8	9	9	11	13
Dividends per share (p)	18.8%	2.6	3.5	5.0	5.8	7.2	9.0	9.5	9.9	10.8	12.3
Book value per share (p)	7.7%	32	37	45	46	48	55	55	49	56	62
Employees	5.7%	—	—	—	—	98,620	109,501	105,594	104,950	135,133	129,814

1993 Year-end:
Debt ratio: 57.6%
Return on equity: 40.9%
Cash (mil.): £816
Long-term debt (mil.): £887
No. of shares (mil.): 3,479
Dividends
  Yield: 3.3%
  Payout: 51.0%
Market value (mil.): $19,205
Sales (mil) $14,463

Stock Price History High/Low 1984–93

CABLE AND WIRELESS

Telecommunications giant Cable and Wireless (C&W) has emerged as a leading provider of telecommunications services to niche markets of small and mid-size companies and emerging countries. C&W has formed alliances with about 50 communications companies around the world; its holdings include major stakes in Hong Kong Telecommunications, Telecommunications of Jamaica, Paktel (Pakistan), and Belcel (Belarus).

C&W owns 57.5% of Hong Kong Telecommunications, which has an exclusive franchise to provide local telephone services in Hong Kong until June 30, 1995, and international services until September 30, 2006. Hong Kong sales accounted for 44% of revenues and 64% of operating income in fiscal

1994, and the undeveloped China market promises to be a cash cow for several years.

C&W's Mercury Communications unit is a major challenger to British Telecom's dominance of the UK phone market.

While the bulk of C&W's work is in the provision of basic services to countries lacking reliable telephone systems, it also intends to become a leader in the multimedia field. In this regard C&W recently teamed up with US-based Bell Northern Research.

The company is increasing its investment in the mobile communications market; it recently signed a mobile-phone joint venture deal with U S WEST and has started cellular ventures in Latvia, Bulgaria, Colombia, and South Africa.

In 1872 Britisher John Pender began Eastern Telegraph with financial assistance from his wife, Emma. By Pender's death in 1896, Eastern and associated companies owned one of every 3 miles of telegraph cable on the planet.

As the new century began, the scope of telecommunications expanded to include wireless radio communications promoted by, among others, inventor Guglielmo Marconi, head of the UK's Marconi Wireless Telegraph. After WWI, telecommunications grew in importance, and, partly to counter a threat from a new, US-based company called ITT, UK companies, including Marconi Wireless and Eastern Telegraph, combined to form Cable & Wireless in 1929.

As with the British Empire, the sun never set on C&W, because it provided telegraph and telephone services in Britain's far-flung colonies. In 1947, after WWII, the company was nationalized by Clement Attlee's Labor government, and since the 1950s the company has lost some franchises in former British colonies or has seen local governments strip it of its monopolies.

In 1981 the Thatcher government began the process, completed in 1985, to return C&W to private ownership. The government persuaded Eric Sharp (later Sir Eric Sharp and, still later, the Lord Sharp of Grimsdyke, Kt. CBE), a former Monsanto executive, to delay his retirement to lead C&W.

Over the next decade, as demand for telephone-based services swelled, sales and profits soared. Sharp cut management layers

and decentralized as the company built its Global Digital Highway, a combination of undersea fiber-optic cables and satellites that carries data and voice to and from Japan, Hong Kong, the US, the Caribbean, and the UK. To complete the task, C&W assembled the world's largest commercial fleet of cableships.

In 1982 C&W joined British Petroleum and Barclays Merchant Bank to form Mercury Communications, the government-mandated competitor to giant British Telecom. C&W bought out BP and Barclays in 1984. Mercury made inroads into business-based services and in 1985 won the right to interconnect with British Telecom. Until it has obtained 25% of the UK market, C&W will not be assessed any interconnect or access charges for using British Telecom's network. C&W increased its market share from less than 1% to 5% by concentrating on business customers.

In 1990 C&W, C. Itoh, Toyota, and Pacific Telesis formed a Japan-based consortium called International Digital Communications to compete against KDD, Japan's former overseas communications monopoly.

In 1992 C&W formed Metropolitan Communications, a 50-50 joint venture with state-owned Intertelecom, to operate telecommunication networks in Russia.

In tandem with U S WEST, C&W started a UK digital cellular service, Mercury one2one, in 1993. In 1994 C&W bought 25.1% of Petersburg Long Distance, which owns 59% of the Russian city's #2 phone company.

NYSE symbol: CWP (ADR)
Fiscal year ends: March 31

Executive Chairman: Lord Young of Graffham, age 62
CEO: James H. Ross, age 56
Director of Finance: Rodney J. Olsen, age 48
President, Cable & Wireless Communications (US): C. Alan Peyser
CFO, Cable & Wireless Communications (US): Scott Yancy
VP Human Relations, Cable & Wireless Communications (US): Bill McGrath
Auditors: KPMG Peat Marwick

HQ: Cable and Wireless Public Limited Company, 124 Theobalds Rd., London WC1X 8RX, UK
Phone: +44-(01)71-315-4000
Fax: +44-(01)71-315-5000
US HQ: Cable & Wireless Communications, Inc., 777 Third Ave., 35th Fl., New York, NY 10017
US Phone: 212-593-4770
US Fax: 212-593-9069

	1994 Sales		1994 Operating Income	
	$ mil.	% of total	$ mil.	% of total
Hong Kong	3,090	44	1,131	64
UK	2,189	31	367	21
Caribbean	708	10	228	13
North America	569	8	39	2
Other countries	505	7	(9)	—
Adjustments	(83)	—	—	—
Total	**6,978**	**100**	**1,756**	**100**

	1994 Sales	
	$ mil.	% of total
International telephone services	3,386	49
Domestic telephone services	1,803	26
Equipment sales & rental	523	7
Cableships & contracts	270	4
Other telecommunications services	996	14
Total	**6,978**	**100**

Major Subsidiaries and Affiliates
Barbados Telephone Co. Ltd. (75%)
Cable & Wireless Communications, Inc. (US)
Cable & Wireless North America, Inc.
Cable and Wireless (Far East) Ltd.
Cable and Wireless (Investments) Ltd.
Cable and Wireless (Marine) Ltd.
Cable and Wireless (West Indies) Ltd.
Companhia de Telecomunicaçoes de Macau S.A.R.L. (51%)
Dhivehi Raajjeyge Gulhun Private Ltd. (45%, Maldives)
Eastern Telecommunications Philippines, Inc. (40%)
Grenada Telecommunications Ltd. (70%)
Hong Kong Telecommunications Ltd. (57.5%)
Huaying Nanhai Oil Telecommunication Service Co. Ltd. (49%, China)
International Digital Communications Inc. (Japan)
Mercury Communications Ltd. (80%, UK)
Telecommunications of Jamaica Ltd. (79%)
Yemen International Telecommunications (51%)

Air Touch	Ericsson	NTT
Ameritech	GTE	NYNEX
AT&T	Hutchison	Pacific Telesis
Bell Atlantic	Whampoa	SBC
BellSouth	LDDS	Communications
BT	Communications	Sprint
Cincinnati Bell	MCI	U S WEST

	Annual Growth	1985	1986	1987	1988	1989	1990	1991	1992	1993	1994
Sales ($ mil.)	—	1,072	1,263	1,363	2,127	2,589	3,125	4,534	5,514	5,788	6,978
Net income ($ mil.)	—	179	250	334	418	482	540	585	562	778	764
Income as % of sales	—	16.7%	19.8%	24.5%	19.7%	18.6%	17.3%	12.9%	10.2%	13.4%	10.9%
Earnings per share ($)	—	—	—	—	—	0.71	0.51	0.82	0.79	1.08	1.05
Stock price – high ($)[1]	—	—	—	—	—	—	14.25	15.44	16.63	16.81	25.13
Stock price – low ($)[1]	—	—	—	—	—	—	10.88	10.81	12.25	13.38	14.88
Stock price – close ($)[1]	14.8%	—	—	—	—	—	13.81	12.69	16.56	15.81	24.00
P/E – high	—	—	—	—	—	—	28	19	21	16	24
P/E – low	—	—	—	—	—	—	21	13	16	12	14
Dividends per share ($)	—	—	—	—	—	—	0.09	0.34	0.37	0.38	0.36
Book value per share ($)	—	—	—	—	—	3.28	3.41	5.47	5.70	6.31	6.69
Employees	6.3%	23,905	24,161	25,470	26,232	29,320	37,681	39,426	38,835	39,837	41,348

1994 Year-end:
Debt ratio: 31.7%
Return on equity: 16.2%
Cash (mil.): $1,692
Long-term debt (mil.): $1,739
No. of shares (mil.): 727
Dividends
  Yield: 1.5%
  Payout: 34.3%
Market value (mil.): $17,454

**Stock Price History
High/Low 1990–94[1]**

[1] Stock prices are for the prior calendar year.

CADBURY SCHWEPPES PLC

OVERVIEW

"If you can't fight 'em, join 'em" seems to be the philosophy of Cadbury Schweppes. The world's #3 soft drink vendor after Coca-Cola and PepsiCo, London-based Cadbury has only 4% of the market. But a joint venture with Coca-Cola produces Cadbury's soft drinks in the UK, while PepsiCo distributes Cadbury products in Eastern Europe.

In an effort to increase its market share, especially in the US, Cadbury bid $1.3 billion in early 1995 for the 74% of US soft drink maker Dr Pepper/7Up Cos. it did not already own. This acquisition would make it the 3rd largest US soft drink company and follows a number of other recent purchases, including A&W, the US root beer maker, and French chocolatier Banque D'Or.

The company's Schweppes, Canada Dry, Crush, Hires, and other beverages bring in 55% of sales. Candy brands, including Cadbury's and Peter Paul, account for 45%.

Cadbury's next move is the conquest of China . . . with chocolate. Its joint venture plant near Beijing begins production in 1995.

WHEN

Cadbury Schweppes is the product of a 1969 merger of 2 seasoned British firms. The world's first soft drink maker, Schweppes originated in 1783 in London, where Swiss national Jacob Schweppe first sold his artificial mineral water. Schweppe returned to Switzerland in 1799, but the company continued its British operations, introducing a lemonade in 1835 and tonic water (containing antimalarial quinine) and ginger ale in the 1870s. Beginning in the 1880s Schweppes expanded worldwide, particularly in British colonies. In the 1960s the company diversified into food products, acquiring, among others, Chivers (marmalade), Typhoo (tea), and Kenco (coffee).

John Cadbury began making cocoa in Birmingham, England, in 1831 and by 1841 was producing 15 varieties of chocolates. The Cadbury Dairy Milk bar, launched in 1905, became Britain's best-selling candy bar. In 1918 Cadbury bought British candy producer Fry. Cadbury established dominant market positions in the UK, Australia, South Africa, and India in the early 1900s.

Under the direction of Dominic Cadbury, Cadbury Schweppes acquired Peter Paul (Mounds, Almond Joy) in 1978. At the same time Schweppes was increasing beverage sales on the Continent and in Asia. The company's flagging share of the British chocolate market revived with the 1982 introduction of the Wispa bar. In 1982 Cadbury Schweppes entered the US applesauce and juice market when it acquired Duffy-Mott.

Through 1984 Cadbury Schweppes's businesses appeared to thrive, but by 1985 British candy demand had stopped growing. US candy distributor stockpiling had accounted for much of Cadbury's perceived growth in sales. Schweppes tonic was losing share at home and in the US. The US Wispa introduction was a failure. Apple juice was found to be a low-margin business. Dominic Cadbury invoked what Cadbury Schweppes executives call "the R word" — restructuring.

In 1986 Cadbury Schweppes sold its noncandy, nonbeverage businesses; consolidated divisions; eliminated layers of management; and purchased Canada Dry, rights to Sunkist soda, and 34% of Dr Pepper. The company entered into a joint venture with Coca-Cola in 1987, creating a $1 billion UK bottling enterprise. In 1989 Cadbury Schweppes purchased the Orange Crush and Hires brands from Procter & Gamble. Facing Mars's and Hershey's combined 70% share of US candy bar sales, Cadbury signed a $300 million licensing agreement with Hershey, ending direct involvement in the US candy market in 1988. In 1990 the company acquired candy makers Trebor and Bassett and the noncola soft drink operations of Source Perrier.

Cadbury continued its international expansion in 1993, gaining majority control of Cadbury India and Cadbury Egypt, acquiring 80% of Productos Stani, Argentina's top confectioner, and raising its stake in Dr Pepper/7Up to 25.6%. It also signed an agreement to distribute Perrier mineral waters in the UK.

In 1994 the Camelot Group (UK), a consortium that includes Cadbury, won a fierce contest to operate the UK's national lottery. Also that year Cadbury and Kraft began test-marketing the first "non-carbonated diet soft drink," bottled Crystal Light.

Nasdaq symbol: CADBY (ADR)
Fiscal year ends: Saturday nearest December 31

WHO

Chairman: N. Dominic Cadbury, age 53
Deputy Chairman: T. O. Hutchison, age 63
Group CEO: David G. Wellings, age 53
Group Finance Director: David Jinks, age 58
President, Cadbury Beverages North America:
John Brock
VP Finance, Cadbury Beverages (US): David
Garics
VP Human Resources, Cadbury Beverages (US):
John Soi
Auditors: Arthur Andersen

WHERE

HQ: 25 Berkeley Sq., London W1X 6HT, UK
Phone: +44-(01)71-409-1313
Fax: +44-(01)71-830-5200
US HQ: Cadbury Beverages Inc., 6 High Ridge
Park, PO Box 3800, Stamford, CT 06905-0800
US Phone: 203-329-0911
US Fax: 203-968-7854 (Communications and
Public Affairs)

Cadbury Schweppes products are sold in more
than 170 countries worldwide.

	1993 Sales		1993 Operating Income	
	$ mil.	% of total	$ mil.	% of total
UK	2,387	43	288	43
Americas	952	17	151	23
Pacific Rim	752	14	102	15
Other Europe	1,097	20	74	11
Other countries	323	6	50	8
Total	**5,511**	**100**	**665**	**100**

WHAT

	1993 Sales		1993 Operating Income	
	$ mil.	% of total	$ mil.	% of total
Beverages	3,055	55	352	53
Confectionery	2,456	45	313	47
Total	**5,511**	**100**	**665**	**100**

Major Brand Names

Beverages	Confections
A&W	Barratt
Canada Dry	Bassett
Clamato	Cadbury
Crush	Chapelat Humphries
Dr. Pepper	Crystal
Hires	de Faam
Holland House	Frisia
Mott's	Fry's
Mr & Mrs. T	Hueso
Red Cheek	Jacksons
Rose's	Jamesons
Schweppes	Lion
Seven-Up	MacRobertson
Sun-drop	Molly Bushnell
Sunkist	Peter Paul
TriNa	Red Tulip
Vida	

KEY COMPETITORS

Bass	Ferolito,	Ocean Spray
Berkshire Hathaway	Vultaggio	PepsiCo
Borden	Heineken	Philip Morris
Campbell Soup	Hershey	Quaker Oats
Celestial	Kirin	RJR Nabisco
Seasonings	Mars	San Miguel
Coca-Cola	National Beverage	Seagram
Cott	National Grape	Triarc
Danone	Co-op	Unilever
Dole	Nestlé	Whitman

HOW MUCH

Stock prices are for ADRs ADR = 4 shares	9-Year Growth	1984	1985	1986	1987	1988	1989	1990	1991	1992	1993
Sales ($ mil.)	10.0%	2,337	2,708	2,729	3,833	4,307	4,666	6,072	6,043	5,108	5,511
Net income ($ mil.)	17.5%	84	69	113	206	254	266	346	380	296	360
Income as % of sales	—	3.6%	2.6%	4.1%	5.4%	5.9%	5.7%	5.7%	6.3%	5.8%	6.5%
Earnings per share ($)	10.8%	0.72	0.54	0.85	1.44	1.67	1.67	1.95	2.07	1.62	1.81
Stock price – high ($)	—	7.25	10.35	11.65	19.00	30.90	30.05	26.85	32.25	38.38	31.13
Stock price – low ($)	—	6.75	7.00	8.25	11.15	16.50	21.10	20.05	22.60	26.88	25.38
Stock price – close ($)	16.6%	7.55	9.20	11.10	17.10	24.45	22.45	24.50	32.13	27.38	30.00
P/E – high	—	10	19	14	13	19	18	14	16	24	17
P/E – low	—	9	13	10	8	10	13	10	11	17	14
Dividends per share ($)	—	0.00	0.37	0.43	0.54	0.69	0.68	0.88	0.93	1.00	1.31
Book value per share ($)	8.7%	4.61	5.22	4.89	10.58	5.80	6.49	8.52	9.33	8.85	9.73
Employees	1.2%	35,000	33,797	27,730	27,497	28,874	34,982	35,653	35,372	36,579	39,066

1993 Year-end:
Debt ratio: 58.2%
Return on equity: 19.6%
Cash (mil.): $190
Current ratio: 0.98
Long-term debt (mil.): $572
No. of shares (mil.): 207
Dividends
  Yield: 4.4%
  Payout: 72.4%
Market value (mil.): $6,224

Stock Price History
High/Low 1984–93

CANADIAN IMPERIAL BANK

OVERVIEW

Headquartered in Toronto, Canadian Imperial Bank of Commerce (CIBC) is Canada's 2nd largest bank (after Royal Bank) and the 8th largest bank holding company in North America.

As Canada's financial services industry has become saturated, CIBC has entered the recently deregulated insurance market in Canada and in 1993 acquired The Personal Insurance Company.

Currently about 2/3 of CIBC's revenue comes from traditional lending to private and commercial clients and 1/3 of its revenue is generated from fee-based services. By the year 2000 the bank hopes to generate about half of its revenue from fee-based services

such as insurance and investment banking services.

CIBC's long-term plan is to become one of the top 20 investment banks in the world. It currently has subsidiaries on 4 continents and owns a majority (79.4%) of Canadian brokerage firm Wood Gundy. The CIBC's restructuring in 1992, combining its Corporate Bank division, which served commercial customers, and its Investment Bank division, which offered capital and investment management, has better positioned the bank to grow internationally. This combined concern is now one of Canada's largest institutional investment managers. The bank also has a large trust operation with 26 offices across Canada.

WHEN

Canadian Imperial Bank of Commerce started because another bank didn't. In 1858 a charter was granted to an entity called the Bank of Canada, but its investors could not raise enough money to open the bank. William McMaster, a Toronto financier, bought the charter in 1866 and persuaded the provincial legislature to amend the name to Canadian Bank of Commerce because the previous name was too close to another, soon-to-be-defunct bank.

Canadian Bank of Commerce opened in 1867, acquired the Gore Bank of Hamilton (1870), and expanded within 7 years to 24 branches in Ontario and offices in Montreal and New York. Led by Edmund Walker, the bank spread west of the Great Lakes with the opening of a Winnipeg branch (1893) and joined the Gold Rush with branches in Dawson City, Yukon Territory, and Skagway, Alaska, in 1898. A Dawson City employee, Robert W. Service, was later heralded as the Poet of the Yukon.

As the new century began, the bank's acquisitions spanned the breadth of Canada, from the Bank of British Columbia (1901) to the Halifax Banking Company (1903) and the Merchants Bank of Prince Edward Island (1906). After more acquisitions in the 1920s, Canadian Bank of Commerce's assets peaked in 1929 and then plunged during the Depression. The bank recovered during WWII.

In 1961 Canadian Bank of Commerce merged with Imperial Bank of Canada to become Canadian Imperial Bank of Commerce. Imperial Bank had been founded in

1875 by Henry Stark Howland, a former Canadian Bank of Commerce VP. Imperial went west to Calgary and Edmonton and became known as "The Mining Bank." In 1956 Imperial purchased Barclays Bank (Canada). At the time of the merger with Canadian Bank of Commerce, Imperial boasted assets of more than $1 billion (about 1/3 the assets of Canadian Bank of Commerce) and 343 branches.

In the early 1980s CIBC had trouble with bad debts from 2 big customers, Dome Petroleum and tractor maker Massey-Ferguson. CIBC also wrote down $451 million in loans to developing countries (1987).

CIBC bought controlling interest in Wood Gundy, one of Canada's largest investment dealers, in 1988. In 1990 CIBC added the retail brokerage business of Merrill Lynch Canada Inc. The company joined with 4 other corporations, including Mitsubishi and Hong Kong's Cheung Kong, to form an investment banking company, CEF New Asia, now under the auspices of CEF Holdings Limited.

In 1991 CIBC entered a joint venture to create Commcorp Financial Services, which absorbed CIBC's leasing and equipment finance companies, and won the right to underwrite stocks in the US.

In 1992 CIBC took a C$1 billion loan loss provision, in part to cover losses from its C$860 million in loans to troubled real estate developer Olympia & York.

Insurance was the new field for CIBC in 1993. In 1994 the bank set up a separate entity for its corporate and investment banking efforts and its securities firm, Wood Gundy.

Principal exchange: Toronto
Fiscal year ends: October 31

Chairman and CEO: Al Flood, C$1,633,333 pay
VC: Iain Ronald, C$744,667 pay
President, CIBC Wood Gundy: John Hunkin,
C$1,116,000 pay
President, Personal and Commercial Bank:
Holger Kluge, C$1,168,000 pay
EVP Administration and CFO: John C. Doran
EVP Human Resources: Michelle Darling
EVP; Head of US Operations: Al Keiser
Auditors: Arthur Andersen; Price Waterhouse

WHERE

HQ: Canadian Imperial Bank of Commerce,
Commerce Court, Toronto, Ontario M5L 1A2,
Canada
Phone: 416-980-2211
Fax: 416-980-5026 (Investor Relations)
US HQ: CIBC US Headquarters,
425 Lexington Ave., New York, NY 10017
US Phone: 212-856-4000
US Fax: 212-856-4178

CIBC operates in Canada and 12 other countries.

	1994 Assets	
	C$ mil.	% of total
Canada	111,195	74
US	21,664	14
Europe	6,852	5
Asia/Pacific	5,254	4
Other countries	2,153	1
Adjustments	3,915	2
Total	**151,033**	**100**

WHAT

	1994 Assets	
	C$ mil.	% of total
Cash & equivalents	9,436	6
Securities	28,753	19
Mortgage loans	35,395	23
Other loans	64,543	43
Other	12,906	9
Total	**151,033**	**100**

Major Subsidiaries and Affiliates
Canadian Imperial Bank of Commerce
Canadian Imperial Bank of Commerce (New York)
Canadian Imperial Bank of Commerce (Suisse) SA
CEF Holdings Ltd. (50%, Hong Kong)
CIBC Asia Ltd.
CIBC Australia Holdings Ltd.
CIBC Development Corporation
CIBC Holdings (Cayman) Ltd.
CIBC Holdings GmbH (Germany)
CIBC Leasing Inc. (US)
CIBC Securities Inc.
CIBC (U.K.) Holdings Ltd.
The CIBC Wood Gundy Corp. (79.4%)

KEY COMPETITORS

Bank of Montreal	Dai-Ichi Kangyo	Industrial Bank
Bank of New York	Dean Witter,	of Japan
Bank of Nova Scotia	Discover	Lehman Bros.
BankAmerica	Deutsche Bank	Merrill Lynch
Bankers Trust	E-L Financial	J.P. Morgan
Barclays	First Chicago	NatWest
BCE	First City Trust	Paine Webber
Bear Stearns	General Trustco	Royal Bank of
Canadian Trust	of Canada	Canada
Income Invest.	Goldman Sachs	Salomon
Chase Manhattan	HSBC	Toronto-
Chemical Banking	Imasco	Dominion Bank
Citicorp	Imperial Life	Union Bank of
Crédit Lyonnais	Assurance Co.	Switzerland
CS Holding	of Canada	S. G. Warburg

HOW MUCH

$=C$1.32 (Dec. 31, 1993)	9-Year Growth	1985	1986	1987	1988	1989	1990	1991	1992	1993	1994
Assets (C$ mil.)	8.0%	75,834	80,841	88,375	94,688	100,213	114,196	121,025	132,212	141,299	151,033
Net income (C$ mil.)	11.5%	334	311	432	591	450	802	811	12	730	890
Income as % of assets	—	0.4%	0.4%	0.5%	0.6%	0.4%	0.7%	0.7%	0.0%	0.5%	0.6%
Earnings per share (C$)	3.2%	2.64	2.05	2.74	3.34	2.28	4.03	3.93	(0.59)	2.99	3.52
Stock price – high (C$)	—	19.81	22.00	23.63	25.88	32.50	33.63	34.38	37.00	33.63	36.25
Stock price – low (C$)	—	13.31	16.75	15.75	16.88	22.75	21.63	26.13	25.13	23.63	28.00
Stock price – close (C$)	6.2%	19.56	19.13	17.88	25.13	31.63	22.25	34.38	26.75	33.00	33.75
P/E – high	—	8	11	9	8	14	8	9	—	11	10
P/E – low	—	5	8	6	5	10	5	7	—	8	8
Dividends per share (C$)	2.7%	1.04	1.08	1.08	1.14	1.24	1.32	1.32	1.32	1.32	1.32
Book value per share (C$)	3.0%	23.88	23.16	21.12	23.35	24.31	26.90	29.41	27.44	28.90	31.18
Employees	2.2%	33,587	33,914	33,874	36,194	36,466	35,811	34,593	42,773	41,511	40,807

1994 Year-end:
Debt ratio: 93.8%
Return on equity: 11.7%
Equity as % of assets: 5.6%
No. of shares (mil.): 216
Dividends
  Yield: 3.9%
  Payout: 37.5%
Market value (mil.): $5,530
Assets (mil.): $114,419
Sales (mil.): $8,495

Stock Price History
High/Low 1985–94

CANADIAN PACIFIC LIMITED

OVERVIEW

Canadian Pacific (CP) is a diversified company with operations and holdings in transportation, energy, communications, hotels and real estate, manufacturing, and waste management. The company's CP Rail System (which includes 2 US railways, Soo Line and Delaware & Hudson) is the 7th largest in North America. Energy and railway interests represent 60% of the company's assets. CP's Canadian Pacific Hotels & Resorts is Canada's largest hotel chain. Its Marathon Realty commercial real estate company has 25 shopping malls and 24 office buildings.

CP's revenues have been hurting since 1989. To counteract these problems, in 1992 CP instituted a restructuring program, drop-

ping some product lines, selling a number of cyclical companies, closing facilities, and reducing its work force. The company continued this effort in 1993 by selling its 60.7% stake in Canadian Pacific Forest Products, one of the world's largest producers of newsprint and pulp.

A big challenge for CP is the need to substantially improve revenue growth and efficiency in its rail lines operations. This is especially true in eastern Canada where both CP and the nationalized Canadian National Railways have extensive operations. Discussions of a partial merger of these 2 entities (lines east of Winnipeg) continued throughout 1994; however, no action was taken.

WHEN

Realizing that Canada's future depended upon a railway linking the populous east with the western frontiers, bankers George Stephen and R. B. Angus joined James J. Hill (future president of Great Northern Railway) to found Canadian Pacific Railway Company (CP Rail) in 1881, with Stephen as president.

With a 25-million-acre government land grant, CP Rail planned the railroad in 2 sections: one extending from Lake Nipissing to Lake Superior and the other from Winnipeg to Kamloops Lake in British Columbia. William Cornelius Van Horne, CP Rail's general manager, started construction in 1882, reached the summit of the Rockies in 1883, and saw the railroad completed at Eagle Pass in 1885, nearly 6 years ahead of schedule.

In 1886 a CP Rail passenger train made the first trans-Canadian rail crossing from Montreal to Port Moody — the world's longest scheduled train trip — in 139 hours. That same year CP Rail chartered ships to carry tea and silk from the Far East to the Canadian west coast, thereby laying the foundation for CP steamship services (later CP Ships). CP hotel and telegraph services also developed along with the railroad, providing comfort and convenience for CP Rail's passengers.

CP Rail expanded by buying smaller railroads during the late 1800s and early 1900s. It gained a major competitor in 1917 when the Canadian government combined several railroads to form Canadian National Railways (CN). In 1942 CP Rail united 10 local airlines to form Canadian Pacific Air Lines, which pioneered a polar route from Vancouver to

Amsterdam in 1955. In 1962 CP Rail created Canadian Pacific Investments Ltd. (CP) to run its nonrailroad holdings, and in 1971 the parent company changed its name to Canadian Pacific Ltd. CP Rail and CN became all-freight railroads in 1979 by handing over passenger services to government-operated VIA Rail Canada.

When William Stinson became CEO in 1985, CP was operating a wide range of businesses, including Canadian Pacific Air Lines, the Minneapolis-based Soo Line Railroad, a hotel chain (Canadian Pacific Hotels), oil wells (PanCanadian Petroleum), and pulp and paper manufacturing (Canadian Pacific Forest Products). Stinson refocused the company on its most profitable businesses while selling those more cyclical in nature, including the airline (to Pacific Western Airlines, 1987). In 1988 the company bought 12% of Laidlaw (upped to 20% in 1989). In 1990 CP Hotels spent $62.6 million for 80% of Doubletree Hotels Corporation, the US-based operator of 59 Doubletree and Compri hotels.

CP Rail bought the Delaware & Hudson Railway in 1991, adding 1,500 miles of track to its system. In 1992 Canadian authorities approved an application by Unitel (CP's telecommunications arm) to provide public long distance service. During 1993, in addition to the sale of its forestry unit, CP created a strategic alliance with AT&T to hasten its move into the long-distance telephone market. In 1994 the weak Canadian dollar held sales flat at $4.9 billion. However, profits jumped to $279 million, after 3 years of losses.

HOOVER'S HANDBOOK OF WORLD BUSINESS 1995–1996

NYSE symbol: CP
Fiscal year ends: December 31

Chairman and CEO: William W. Stinson,
C$1,353,911 pay
President and COO: David P. O'Brien, age 53
EVP; Chairman and CEO, CP Rail System:
I. Barry Scott, C$666,549 pay
EVP and CFO: W. R. Fatt, C$419,874 pay
VP Personnel and Administration: K. S. Benson
**Chairman and CEO, United Dominion
Industries (US):** William R. Holland
**VP Human Resources, United Dominion
Industries (US):** Timothy Verhagen
CFO, United Dominion Industries (US):
Robert E. Drury
Auditors: Price Waterhouse

HQ: 910 Peel St., PO Box 6042, Station Centre-
ville, Montreal, Quebec H3C 3E4, Canada
Phone: 514-395-5151
Fax: 514-395-7165
US HQ: United Dominion Industries Limited,
2300 One First Union Center, 301 S. College
St., Charlotte, NC 28202-6039
US Phone: 704-347-6800
US Fax: 704-347-6940

	1993 Sales		1993 Operating Income	
	$ mil.	% of total	$ mil.	% of total
Canada	3,800	77	588	85
US	853	17	68	10
Other countries	317	6	35	5
Total	**4,970**	**100**	**691**	**100**

	1993 Sales		1993 Operating Income	
	$ mil.	% of total	$ mil.	% of total
Transportation	3,063	62	214	31
Energy	1,274	25	301	43
Real estate & hotels	761	15	176	26
Adjustments	(128)	—	—	—
Total	**4,970**	**100**	**691**	**100**

Major Subsidiaries and Affiliates

Canadian Pacific Hotels & Resorts Inc.	PanCanadian Petroleum Ltd. (86.9%)
CP Rail System	Soo Line Corp.
CP Ships	United Dominion Industries
CP Trucks	Ltd. (45.3%)
Fording Coal	Unitel Communications
Laidlaw Inc. (19%)	Holdings Inc. (48%)
Marathon Realty Holdings Inc.	

Accor	CSX	Norfolk
Alcatel Alsthom	Elf Aquitaine	Southern
American	Exxon	Olympia & York
President	FedEx	Promus
Ashland Coal	Fletcher	Roadway
Bass	Challenge	Schlumberger
BCE	Four Seasons	Stone Container
Browning-Ferris	GTE	Sun Company
Burlington	Halliburton	Teleglobe
Northern	Hilton	Texaco
Carlson	Hyatt	Union Pacific
Chevron	Imperial Oil	UPS
Chicago and North	ITT	WMX
Western	Loews	Technologies
Conrail	Marriott Intl.	Yellow
Consolidated	Mobil	Corporation
Freightways	Nestlé	

	9-Year Growth	1984	1985	1986	1987	1988	1989	1990	1991	1992	1993
Sales ($ mil.)	(8.8%)	11,335	11,059	9,411	9,266	10,072	9,516	9,052	8,715	7,050	4,970
Net income ($ mil.)	—	286	177	109	490	649	644	306	(791)	(376)	(144)
Income as % of sales	—	2.5%	1.6%	1.2%	5.3%	6.4%	6.8%	3.4%	—	—	—
Earnings per share ($)	—	1.32	0.79	0.37	1.63	2.10	2.03	0.96	(2.48)	(1.18)	(0.46)
Stock price – high ($)	—	14.31	15.75	14.63	22.88	20.13	24.38	22.88	20.00	16.63	17.63
Stock price – low ($)	—	9.38	11.63	10.00	12.75	15.88	18.00	14.88	14.38	10.50	12.50
Stock price – close ($)	2.8%	12.66	13.50	12.88	15.88	18.50	22.25	17.00	15.38	12.63	16.25
P/E – high	—	11	20	40	14	10	12	24	—	—	—
P/E – low	—	7	15	27	8	8	9	16	—	—	—
Dividends per share ($)	(6.8%)	0.47	0.47	0.48	0.51	0.64	0.68	0.80	0.68	0.27	0.25
Book value per share ($)	(1.2%)	15.83	14.77	13.94	16.38	19.28	21.12	21.16	18.19	15.46	14.23
Employees	(11.7%)	120,000	123,400	93,800	85,400	76,400	75,600	72,200	78,200	63,300	39,300

1993 Year-end:
Debt ratio: 64.8%
Return on equity: —
Cash (mil.): $1,237
Current ratio: 0.90
Long-term debt (mil.): $3,543
No. of shares (mil.): 319
Dividends
  Yield: 1.5%
  Payout: —
Market value (mil.): $5,190

**Stock Price History
High/Low 1984–93**

CANAL+

CANAL+ (Channel Plus) was France's first privately owned television company, and is now the biggest pay-television operator in the world. The company claims that its 1993 revenues of around $1.5 billion has edged the previous market leader, US cable channel giant HBO, into the #2 slot for the first time. Modeled after HBO, the company's 3 core activities are TV channel production, the marketing of pay-TV channels, and the production and distribution of TV programs and movies. It also offers thematic channels such as Canal Jimmy (1960s shows), Planète (documentaries), and MCM Euromusique. CANAL+ has a subscriber base of over 3.7 million in France and a further 1.7 million outside, mainly in Germany and Spain.

Le Studio CANAL+, the film production subsidiary of which the company is 59% co-owner, invests in French and foreign productions. Le Studio CANAL+ owns 17% of Carolco (US) and has helped to finance over 300 films, including *JFK, Cliffhanger,* and *Stargate.*

The company is 41.4% owned by the public. Three institutional investors, Havas (23.5%, an advertising firm), Générale des Eaux (20.1%, a water distributor), and Société Générale (5.1%, a bank) merged their interests in 1994 to give the coalition virtual control of the company. The company's chairman, André Rousselet, resigned in 1994 over the increasing influence of the government in the affairs of the company. The French government has stakes in each of the 3 major shareholders, and it was also putting pressure on CANAL+ to invest heavily in the struggling French cable television industry. Rousselet was replaced as chairman by CEO Pierre Lescure.

André Rousselet had rejected the pay-TV concept when it was pitched to him as he became head of the Havas advertising agency in 1982, but soon after, he agreed that Havas should enter show business and he came on board. Because Havas was under government control, Rousselet went to his golfing partner, President François Mitterrand (Rousselet had been Mitterrand's chief of staff), for approval, and, to skirt the Socialist influence on early-1980s France, Rousselet used his political connections to the new channel's advantage, easing its entry to the airwaves.

After CANAL+ signed on in November 1984 with 186,000 subscribers, it came to be called "Canal Minus" as subscriptions to the pay-TV service flattened out and the company lost money. Rousselet, who had left Havas to become chairman of the channel, kept CANAL+ out of bankruptcy by putting the fall 1985 season's slate of blockbuster movies on in the spring — reasoning that there might not be a CANAL+ over which to air the films if he waited. Subscribers responded, and by the end of 1986, with former journalist Pierre Lescure (an original CANAL+ director) as CEO, the company broke even.

Over the next 5 years CANAL+ was considered to be a cash factory. The company went public in 1987; in spite of a market crash, its shares sold out. In 1988 its profits were higher than the 3 French networks combined, and the company reduced its debt to zero. However, the company made a bad investment that year when it joined with Compagnie Générale des Eaux to buy TVS (UK), which presided over losses of TVS's MTM Entertainment (TV production, US) and later lost its license as an ITV (TV network, UK) franchisee.

In 1990 CANAL+ acquired 5% (later increased to 11.9%) of independent US production company Carolco, investing in a promising movie, *Terminator 2,* and later co-producing *Basic Instinct*. But Carolco soon started losing money.

CANAL+ expanded more successfully into other countries, establishing channels as part owner with others (much like CANAL+ itself is co-owned) in Belgium (1989), Spain (1990), Germany (Premiere, 1991, with Bertelsmann and film supplier Kirch-Beta Taurus), and North Africa (1991).

Thematic channels came on-line as well. CANAL+ and Compagnie Générale des Eaux bought a controlling interest along with ESPN (US) in W. H. Smith Group's (UK) television holdings in 1991. CANAL+ acquired 15% of MCM-Euromusique (music) in 1992.

CANAL+ signed a deal in 1994 with German media giant Bertelsmann to collaborate on the future development of digital technology for pay-TV. CANAL+ finished 1994 with $1.8 billion in sales.

OTC symbol: CNPLY (ADR)
Fiscal year ends: December 31

Chairman and CEO: Pierre Lescure
EVP and General Counsel: Marc-André Feffer
EVP and President of Sales and Marketing:
Bruno Delecour
EVP and CFO: Claude Ravilly
Human Resources: Françoise Provotelle
CEO, Le Studio CANAL+ (US): Olivier Granier
CFO, Le Studio CANAL+ (US): Mike Metzer
**Manager Human Resources, Le Studio CANAL+
(US):** Victoria Waks
Auditors: Guy Barbier & Autres (Arthur
Andersen); Salustro Reydel

HQ: 85/89 Quai Andre Citroen, 75015 Paris,
France
Phone: +33-1-44-25-10-00
Fax: +33-1-44-25-12-34
US HQ: Le Studio CANAL+, 301 N. Canon Dr.,
#228, Beverly Hills, CA 90210
US Phone: 310-247-0994
US Fax: 310-247-0998

CANAL+ is the world's leading pay-TV company.

	1993 Subscribers	
	No. (thou.)	% of total
France	3,708	68
Spain	768	14
Germany	755	14
Belgium	150	3
Africa	29	1
Total	**5,410**	**100**

	1993 Sales		1993 Net Income	
	FF mil.	% of total	FF mil.	% of total
CANAL+	7,444	86	1,462	—
Movie prod. & dist.	384	4	(6)	—
Manufacturing	323	4	32	—
TV prod. & dist.	290	3	(8)	—
Cable & satellite	87	1	(94)	—
Sport	38	1	(42)	—
Foreign channels	37	1	(117)	—
Video prod. & dist.	26	0	(10)	—
Publishing	10	0	(1)	—
Finance	2	0	139	—
Thematic channels	—	—	(76)	—
Real estate	—	—	(85)	—
Other	36	0	6	—
Adjustments	(2)	—	2	—
Total	**8,675**	**100**	**1,202**	**—**

Selected Subsidiaries

Movies	**Foreign CANAL+ Channels**
Le Studio CANAL+ (59%)	Canal Horizons (34.2%)
Sogepac (29.1%)	**Video**
Manufacturing	CANAL+ Vidéo SNC
Antennes Tonna Group (51%)	**Publishing**
Television	CANAL+ Editions SNC (51%)
Docstar SNC	**Finance**
Le Studio Ellipse (61.2%)	CANAL+ Finance
Cable and Satellite	**Thematic Channels**
Canalsatellite SNC (96.7%)	Canal Jimmy SNC (42.5%)
Satellite Service (80%)	**Real Estate**
Sport	CANAL+ Immobilier SNC
Data Sport (37.5%)	

International Family
Entertainment
Japan Satellite
Broadcasting
News Corp.

Société Television
Française
Television
Française 1

Time Warner
Viacom
Walt Disney

$=FF5.91 (Dec. 31, 1993)	Annual Growth	1984	1985	1986	1987	1988	1989	1990	1991	1992	1993
Sales (FF mil.)	78.1%	48	558	1,887	3,402	4,340	5,359	6,130	6,998	7,937	8,675
Net income (FF mil.)	—	(96)	(330)	4	407	619	761	910	1,081	1,104	1,202
Income as % of sales	—	—	—	0.2%	12.0%	14.3%	14.2%	14.8%	15.4%	13.9%	13.9%
Earnings per share (FF)	17.5%	—	—	—	22	33	41	48	57	54	58
Stock price – high (FF)	—	—	—	—	360	659	790	993	1,130	1,329	1,399
Stock price – low (FF)	—	—	—	—	320	350	589	738	794	949	1,028
Stock price – close (FF)	20.9%	—	—	—	357	590	765	823	1,023	1,099	1,116
P/E – high	—	—	—	—	—	20	19	21	20	24	24
P/E – low	—	—	—	—	—	11	14	15	14	17	18
Dividends per share (FF)	11.8%	—	—	—	—	—	16.00	18.00	20.00	25.00	25.00
Book value per share (FF)	39.0%	—	—	—	—	59	85	109	131	259	306
Employees	28.3%	—	—	—	—	584	1,459	1,429	1,550	1,697	2,031

1993 Year-end:
Debt ratio: 31.7%
Return on equity: 20.6%
Cash (mil.): FF3,166
Long-term debt (mil.): FF1,163
No. of shares (mil.): 21
Dividends
Yield: 2.2%
Payout: 43.0%
Market value (mil.): $3,954
Sales (mil.): $1,468

Stock Price History
High/Low 1987–93

CANON INC.

Japanese manufacturer Canon is one of the world's top makers of business machines, cameras, and other precision optical equipment. Major products include facsimile machines, bubble-jet printers, laser printers, telephones, workstations, desktop publishing systems, cameras, and camcorders. Canon holds about 25% of the US photocopier market. The company is more international in orientation than some other Japanese manufacturers. In addition to Canon's president Hajime Mitarai being Stanford and MIT trained, and fluent in English, the company follows a corporate philosophy of *kyosei*, or "responsibility to the communities in which it operates." Canon's revenues reflect its international thrust. Japanese sales, which stood at 52% of total revenues in 1991, accounted for only 31% in 1993.

Canon's business machine products range from desktop calculators to PCs and handy terminals for field processing of sales data. The company's famous cameras, faced with a maturing world camera market, account for only 10% of sales. Canon also makes semiconductor production equipment.

Innovative technology has fueled the company's growth. Canon is among the top corporations holding patents in the US and spent $930 million on R&D in 1993. Among its more important new product efforts is ferroelectric liquid display technology that it is developing for flat high-resolution display screens. This technology is projected to replace cathode ray tubes in computer and TV screens as the industry standard. Canon is also taking on industry leader Hewlett-Packard in the color laser printer market.

Takeshi Mitarai and a friend, Saburo Uchida, formed Seiki Kogaku Kenkyusho (Precision Optical Research Laboratory) in Tokyo in 1933 to build Japan's first 35mm camera. The camera was introduced in 1935 under the brand name Kwanon (the Buddhist goddess of mercy) and later renamed Canon. In response to the military buildup before WWII, the company began building X-ray machines for the Japanese military.

After WWII the company sold its Canon brand cameras to US GIs stationed in Japan and adopted the name Canon Camera Company as the brand name gained popularity (1947). Canon diversified into business equipment, introducing the first 10-key electronic calculator (1964) and a plain-paper photocopier, independent of Xerox's patented technology (1968). Canon dropped "Camera Company" from its name in 1969.

In 1972 Canon invented the "liquid dry" system of copying, using plain paper and liquid developer, but failed to produce any new cameras in the interim and was surpassed by Minolta and Pentax as Japan's leading camera exporter. Sales were sluggish in the early 1970s, and Canon had to suspend its dividend in 1975 for the first time since WWII.

At that time Canon's managing director, Ryuzaburo Kaku, convinced Mitarai that the company's problems stemmed from indecisive leadership and weak marketing practices. Kaku turned Canon around, unleashing the

electronic AE-1 in a media blitz that included the first-ever TV commercials for any 35mm camera (1976). With almost every feature (except focus) automated, the AE-1 made 35mm cameras accessible to even the clumsiest camera buff. Its success catapulted Canon past Minolta as the world's #1 camera maker. Kaku became president in 1977.

In 1979 Canon introduced the highly successful NP-200 (NP for New Process), the first copier to use a dry developer. As the plain-paper copier market matured in the early 1980s, Canon shifted to making other automated office machines, including laser printers and fax machines.

Minolta again replaced Canon as the world's #1 camera maker in 1985, when it introduced the fully automated Maxxum 7000. But Canon came back in 1987, introducing the EOS (electronic optical system) autofocus camera that returned the company to preeminence in 1990.

Canon resells computers in Japan through a half-owned subsidiary, Canon Sales, which saw a big jump in Apple Computer sales in 1991. In 1992 Canon announced a joint venture with IBM to produce portable PCs with built-in bubble-jet printers. Also in 1992 the company launched a line of desktop and laptop computers.

Canon teamed up with IBM again in 1994, agreeing to develop a line of products based on the PowerPC, a chip codeveloped by IBM.

Nasdaq symbol: CANNY (ADR)
Fiscal year ends: December 31

Chairman: Ryuzaburo Kaku
VC: Keizo Yamaji
President: Hajime Mitarai, age 56
VP: Hiroshi Tanaka
Senior Managing Director: Masahiro Tanaka
Senior Managing Director: Giichi Marushima
Senior General Manager Finance and Accounting: Ryozo Hirako
President, Canon U.S.A.: Haruo Murase
CFO, Canon U.S.A.: Seymour Liebman
Director Personnel, Canon U.S.A.: Annette Colarusso
Auditors: KPMG Peat Marwick

WHERE

HQ: 30-2, Shimomaruko 3-chome, Ohta-ku, Tokyo 146, Japan
Phone: +81-3-3758-2111
Fax: +81-3-5482-5130
US HQ: Canon U.S.A., Inc., One Canon Plaza, Lake Success, NY 11042-1113
US Phone: 516-488-6700
US Fax: 516-328-5069

Canon's products are sold in over 140 countries.

	1993 Sales	
	$ mil.	% of total
North America	5,266	32
Japan	5,117	31
Europe	4,688	29
Other countries	1,324	8
Adjustments	57	—
Total	**16,452**	**100**

WHAT

	1993 Sales	
	$ mil.	% of total
Business machines		
Copiers	6,119	37
Computer peripherals	4,892	30
Business systems	2,775	17
Cameras	1,622	10
Optical & other products	985	6
Adjustments	59	—
Total	**16,452**	**100**

Business Machines	Cameras and Accessories
Bubble-jet printers	Cameras
Calculators	Still video systems
Copiers	Video equipment
Desktop calculators	
Desktop publishing systems	**Optical and Other Products**
Electronic typewriters	Broadcast lenses
Fax machines	Electronic components
Laser printers	Medical equipment
Microprocessors	Semiconductor production equipment
Personal computers	
Scanners	
Word processors	

KEY COMPETITORS

Applied Materials	Hitachi	Ricoh
Bausch & Lomb	IBM	Sanyo
Brother	Matsushita	Seiko
Casio	Minolta	Sharp
Copifax	NEC	Siemens
Eastman Kodak	Novellus Systems	Silicon Valley
Fuji Photo	Océ	Group
Fujitsu	Oki	Sony
GEC	Olivetti	Texas
General Signal	Philips	Instruments
Hanson	Pioneer	Toshiba
Harris Corp.	Pitney Bowes	Xerox
Hewlett-Packard	Polaroid	Yamaha

HOW MUCH

Stock prices are for ADRs ADR = 10 shares	9-Year Growth	1984	1985	1986	1987	1988	1989	1990	1991	1992	1993
Sales ($ mil.)	19.5%	3,303	4,775	5,628	8,072	8,849	8,181	12,725	14,976	15,338	16,452
Net income ($ mil.)	3.5%	139	185	68	109	297	232	452	418	288	189
Income as % of sales	—	4.2%	3.9%	1.2%	1.4%	3.4%	2.8%	3.6%	2.8%	1.9%	1.1%
Earnings per share ($)	13.2%	1.05	1.30	0.55	0.80	2.05	1.49	2.88	2.61	1.88	1.20
Stock price – high ($)	—	27.00	27.16	34.19	44.31	56.94	69.50	66.00	60.13	59.00	71.13
Stock price – low ($)	—	16.63	16.59	23.75	21.03	33.06	48.84	45.13	44.25	47.25	53.50
Stock price – close ($)	12.4%	23.97	25.56	28.53	32.84	54.78	64.00	47.00	56.88	55.00	68.75
P/E – high	—	26	21	62	55	28	47	23	23	31	59
P/E – low	—	16	13	43	26	16	33	16	17	25	45
Dividends per share ($)	11.5%	0.18	0.21	0.29	0.30	0.34	0.37	0.36	0.39	0.42	0.48
Book value per share ($)	17.4%	9.56	11.69	17.25	22.43	23.01	22.82	30.45	35.65	36.67	40.55
Employees	8.8%	30,302	34,129	35,498	37,521	40,740	44,401	54,381	62,700	64,512	64,535

1993 Year-end:
Debt ratio: 66.7%
Return on equity: 3.1%
Cash (mil.): $5,141
Current ratio: 1.66
Long-term debt (mil.): $3,855
No. of shares (mil.): 159
Dividends
  Yield: 0.7%
  Payout: 40.0%
Market value (mil.): $10,959

Stock Price History High/Low 1984–93

CARLSBERG A/S

Copenhagen-based Carlsberg is the 3rd largest brewer in Europe and the 7th largest worldwide. It has breweries throughout the world and a large presence in Asia, where it expects most of its growth in the coming years. Although brewing is its primary business, Carlsberg is also engaged in everything from glass art objects to biotechnology to amusement parks.

The company's famous beers, sold primarily under the Carlsberg and Tuborg labels, control Denmark's beer market. Carlsberg is also the best-selling foreign beer brand in Portugal. In addition, the company maintains licensing agreements with such industry leaders as Labatt and Anheuser-Busch.

Although the company is traded on the Copenhagen exchange, at least 51% (required by charter) is owned by the Carlsberg Foundation, a charitable organization that supports the natural sciences and the humanities. The foundation oversees the administration of the Frederiksborg Museum of Natural History and, through a subsidiary, acquires art for Danish museums and institutions.

In late 1992 Carlsberg and Allied-Lyons (now Allied Domecq) combined their UK brewing, distribution, and wholesaling operations under the name Carlsberg-Tetley. The $876-million venture created the UK's 3rd largest brewer (behind Bass and Courage) with 6 breweries and an 18% market share.

The modern Carlsberg A/S stems from the amalgamation of 2 proud Danish brewing concerns. The first of these was founded in Copenhagen by Captain J. C. Jacobsen, whose father had worked as a brewery hand before acquiring a small brewery of his own in 1826. Jacobsen inherited the brewery in 1835. Determined to introduce a higher degree of technical skill to Danish brewing, Jacobsen studied extensively, even testing modern brewing methods in his mother's washtub. In 1847 he opened the Carlsberg Brewery (named for his son Carl) and in 1868 exported his first beer to the UK, establishing a presence outside its tiny home market of Denmark. In 1876 Captain Jacobsen established the Carlsberg Foundation to conduct scientific research and oversee brewer operations.

Carl Jacobsen, who fell into disagreement with his father over brewery operations, opened a new brewery (New Carlsberg) adjacent to his father's in 1881. Both men, operating under the motto *Laboremus pro patria* (Let us work for our country), bestowed rich gifts upon their beloved city, including a church, an art museum (the Glyptothek), the renovation of a royal castle, and the famous statue of the Little Mermaid in Copenhagen Harbor. Both father and son willed their breweries to the foundation, which rejoined them in 1906.

Tuborg, the 2nd great Danish brewing enterprise, was founded as Tuborgs Fabrikker in 1873 by a group of Danish businessmen who wanted to establish a major industrial project (including a brewery, a glass factory,

and a sulfuric acid works) on a piece of land around Tuborg Harbor. Philip Heyman headed the group and in 1880 spun off all operations but the brewery.

Carlsberg and Tuborg became Denmark's 2 leading brewers. After WWII, both launched an intense marketing plan to carry their beers outside Denmark. In the period between 1958 and 1972, they tripled exports and established breweries in Europe and Asia. Indeed, the intense drive of both brewers to establish markets in foreign countries greatly influenced their decision to merge. In 1969 the 2 companies joined as United Breweries.

During the 1980s the company diversified, forming Carlsberg Biotechnology in 1983 to extend elements of its research into other areas. It also strengthened its position in North America through licenses with Anheuser-Busch (1985) and John Labatt (1988). United Breweries reverted to the old Carlsberg name in 1987.

In 1991 Guinness purchased Carlsberg's 60% stake in Spanish brewer Unión Cervecera. The company also bought a majority interest in Portugal's largest brewer, Unicer-União Cervejeira SA.

The Carlsberg Allied-Lyons (now Allied Domecq) partnership in late 1992 was hard on smaller UK brewers; the 3 largest brewers now have about 60% of the UK market. In 1994 Carlsberg and its powerful Thai partner's moves to gain market share for Carlsberg led to a beer glut and a temporary shutdown of one of its local breweries.

Principal exchange: Copenhagen
Fiscal year ends: September 30

WHO

Chairman, Supervisory Board: Poul Matthiessen
President and Group CEO: Poul J. Svanholm
EVP Production Denmark: S. E. Albrethsen
EVP Corporate Affairs: Per Green
EVP Risk Management/Environment: B. Grosen
  Rasmussen
VP Finance: Jesper C. Bærnholdt
VP Personnel: Kurt Israelsen
CEO, Carlsberg Agency (US): Paul Steffensen
Auditors: KPMG C. Jespersen; Price Waterhouse/
  Seier-Petersen

WHERE

HQ: 100 Vesterfælledvej, DK-1799 Copenhagen V,
  Denmark
Phone: +45-33-27-33-27
Fax: +45-33-27-47-11
US HQ: Carlsberg Agency Inc., 27 Holland Ave.,
  White Plains, NY 10603
US Phone: 914-428-8222
US Fax: 914-428-8251

Carlsberg operates about 100 subsidiaries, most
of which are outside Denmark. Its beer is
exported worldwide to 130 markets. In the US,
Carlsberg beer is distributed by Anheuser-Busch.

1994 Beer Sales

	Hectoliters (thou)	% of total
Denmark	5,249	17
Other countries	24,942	83
Total	**30,191**	**100**

WHAT

Major Beverage Brands

Burton Ale	Splügen
Carlsberg	Superbock
Carlsberg Ice	Swan Light
Castlemaine XXXX	Tetley Bitter
Dadeko	Tuborg
Elephant Malt	Tuborg Classic
Kurvand	Tuborg Gold Label
Nuuk Carlsberg	Tuborg Grundl
Royal Danish Stout	Wiibroe
Skol	

Selected Subsidiaries and Affiliates
Carlsberg Brewery Hong Kong Ltd. (40.8%)
Carlsberg Brewery Malaysia Berhad (26%)
Carlsberg Malawi Brewery Ltd. (49%)
Carlsberg Marketing (Singapore) Pte. Ltd. (50%)
Carlsberg-Tetley PLC (50%, UK)
Cruzcampo Group SA (8%, Spain)
Fredericia Bryggeri AS (brewery)
Hannen Brauerei GmbH (97%, Germany)
Industrie Poretti SpA (50%, Italy)
AS Kjøbenhavns Sommer-Tivoli (43%, amusement parks)
Royal Copenhagen AS (79%; porcelain, Georg Jensen
  silverware, Holmegaards glass)
AS Rynkeby Foods A/S (50%, fruit processing)
Vingaarden AS (81%, wine and spirits)

KEY COMPETITORS

Adolph Coors	Grolsch	S&P
Anheuser-Busch	Guinness	San Miguel
Asahi Brewery	Heileman	Scottish &
Bass	Heineken	Newcastle
Brown-Forman	John Labatt	Stroh
Corning	Kirin	Tsingtao
Danone	Lego	Walt Disney
Efes	Molson	Waterford
Foster's Brewing	Philip Morris	Wedgwood
Grand Metropolitan	Royal Doulton	

HOW MUCH

$=DK6.78 (Dec. 31, 1993)	Annual Growth	1985	1986	1987	1988	1989	1990	1991	1992	1993	1994
Sales (DK mil.)	3.6%	12,358	13,022	13,343	14,485	14,902	15,141	14,462	14,957	15,595	16,919
Net income (DK mil.)[1]	9.7%	348	415	485	566	618	768	802	854	910	802
Income as % of sales	—	2.8%	2.8%	3.2%	3.6%	3.9%	4.1%	5.1%	5.5%	5.8%	4.7%
Earnings per share (DK)	6.0%	7	8	10	10	11	13	14	13	14	13
Stock price – high (DK)[2]	—	—	—	—	207	266	275	396	380	302	333
Stock price – low (DK)[2]	—	—	—	—	122	173	240	238	253	238	240
Stock price – close (DK)[2]	6.0%	—	—	—	185	266	250	359	255	295	263
P/E – high	—	—	—	—	22	25	21	29	28	21	27
P/E – low	—	—	—	—	13	16	18	18	26	17	19
Dividends per share (DK)[2]	4.1%	2.08	2.50	2.50	2.50	2.50	3.00	3.00	3.00	3.00	3.00
Book value per share (DK)	8.2%	56	65	74	71	82	87	96	100	111	114
Employees	3.3%	14,941	14,760	14,141	13,595	12,585	12,192	11,494	13,777	17,762	17,481

1994 Year-end:	
Debt ratio: 32.5%	
Return on equity: 11.1%	Stock Price History[2]
Cash (mil.): DK5,129	High/Low 1988–94
Long-term debt (mil.): DK2,721	
No. of shares (mil.): 64	
Dividends	
Yield: 1.1%	
Payout: 23.9%	
Market value (mil.): $2,479	
Sales (mil.): $2,495	

[1] Including extraordinary items   [2] "A" shares

CARREFOUR SA

France's largest retailer, Carrefour is considered the originator of hypermarket stores, which offer produce, groceries, clothing, consumer goods, and household appliances in a large open marketplace atmosphere. While the concept failed to turn heads in the US, the company has prospered in other areas of the world and continues to expand internationally. About 1/3 of Carrefour's $20 billion in sales and more than 1/2 of its profits come from outside France.

Carrefour operates more than 200 hypermarkets in 9 countries, including 114 in France. Its Erteco subsidiary operates

France's largest chain of deep discount stores (Europa Discount) and chains of convenience stores (Ed l'Epicier) and produce shops (Ed le Maraîcher).

Carrefour emphasizes one-stop shopping with convenient parking and discount pricing. Its hypermarkets have worked well in less-developed retail markets in Spain, South America, and Taiwan, where there is less competition, but it gave up on an attempt to open a chain of the large stores in the US. However, Carrefour owns stakes in US retailers Office Depot (16%), Price/Costco (10%), and PETsMART(5%).

Carrefour (which means "crossroads") was founded by Marcel Fournier and Louis Defforey, who started with a supermarket in the basement of Fournier's department store in Annecy, France, in 1960. The store was an instant hit, selling out of its goods in 4 days. Buoyed by the success, Carrefour added another store in the Annecy region in 1963 and opened a vast store, dubbed a "hypermarket" by the media, in Sainte-Geneviève-des-Bois, outside Paris.

The company opened more outlets in France and also moved into Belgium, Italy, Switzerland, and the UK, developing joint ventures with local retailers. During the mid-1970s Carrefour concentrated even more on international expansion after French legislation put a limit on expansion in the company's home country. By 1985 Carrefour had stores in 10 countries.

In 1988 Carrefour transported one of its French-style hypermarkets with a marketplace atmosphere to the US by opening a 330,000-square-foot store in suburban Philadelphia that clerks used roller skates to get around in. Aisles wide enough for 4 shopping carts and 60 checkout lanes greeted American customers, but few bought because of scant advertising and limited selections. Local competitors greeted Carrefour by cutting prices, and a local labor union picketed the store for the first 2 years over the company's wages, benefits, and work rules.

After Carrefour and the union exchanged lawsuits, a peace accord was struck following the intervention of Force Ouvrière, the trade union that represents Carrefour workers in France.

Carrefour opened its first hypermarket in Taiwan in 1989. In the same year the company bought an interest in Office Depot. In 1990 Carrefour and Groupama formed Carma, a 50-50 joint venture to sell insurance through Carrefour outlets.

To cement its hold on the French retail market, Carrefour paid over $1 billion for 2 rival chains in 1991: $175 million for the bankrupt Montlaur chain and $850 million for Euromarché, France's #5 hypermarket chain. These major acquisitions were the only way for Carrefour to grow in France, as it had been granted permission to open only one French store in all of 1991.

Michel Bon, the hard-charging architect of Carrefour's acquisitions of Euromarché and Montlaur, resigned in 1992 after a 50% drop in first half profits. Under Bon's 7-year reign, Carrefour's profits had tripled. That same year Carrefour opened a 2nd US store, near its Philadelphia operation, in Voorhees, New Jersey. Earlier efforts to open a store on Long Island in New York were frustrated by community opposition and zoning changes.

In 1993 the company abandoned its attempts to bring the hypermarket concept to the US, closing both its US stores.

In late 1993 the company opened a hypermarket in Mexico with Mexican retailer Gigante, and in 1994 it signed a deal with Gigante to open a chain of hypermarkets in that country. That same year the company signed a joint venture deal with Chinese retailer Lianhua to open a store in China in 1995.

Carrefour completed 1994 with nearly $29 billion in sales.

Principal exchange: Paris
Fiscal year ends: December 31

Chairman: Daniel Bernard
Member of the Executive Board, Finance:
Jacques Badin
Member of the Executive Board, The Americas:
Michel Pinot
CFO, Office Depot (US): Barry Goldstein
Auditors: Cabinet P. Garcin; Guy Barbier &
Autres; Arthur Andersen & Co.

WHERE

HQ: 6, avenue Raymond Poincaré, 75116 Paris,
France
Phone: +33-1-53-70-19-00
Fax: +33-1-53-70-86-16

Carrefour has operations in Argentina, Brazil,
France, Italy, Malaysia, Portugal, Spain, Taiwan,
and Turkey.

	1993 Sales		1993 Net Income	
	FF mil.	% of total	FF mil.	% of total
France	81,991	67	579	35
Spain	21,226	17	455	27
Brazil	10,191	8	337	20
Argentina	5,545	5	189	12
Other countries	4,251	3	105	6
Total	**123,204**	**100**	**1,665**	**100**

WHAT

Hypermarkets
Brepa (80%, Brazil)
Carcoop (50%)
Carrefour Argentina
Carrefour France
Carrefour Italia
Commerciale (60%,
Italy)
Carrefour Malaysia
Carrefour Monaco
Carrefour Portugal (50%)
Carrefour Ticaret Merkezi
(Turkey)
Euromarché
GML (50%)
Presicarre (59%, Taiwan)
Pryca (69%, Spain)
Sofidis (50%)
Sogara (50%)
Sogramo (61%)
Superest (61%)

Mini-Markets
Erteco

Other Activities
Carfuel (90%, gasoline
wholesaling)

Carma (50%, insurance)
Carrefour Vacances
Providange (51%,
autocenters)

Partnerships/Investments
Carpet Land (29%; carpet
and floor coverings;
Benelux countries,
France, Switzerland)
Comptoirs Modernes (23%,
supermarkets)
Metro (18%, discount
warehouse stores)
Office Depot (16%, office
equipment and supplies,
US)
PETsMART Inc. (5%, pet
supplies, US)
Picard Surgelés (10%,
frozen foods)
Price/Costco (10%,
discount warehouse
stores, US)

KEY COMPETITORS

Benetton
Casino Guichard-Perrachon
Cifra
Docks de France
Etablissments Catteau
Federated
Federation National
Achat Cadres

Galeries Lafayette
Lojas Americanas
Marks and Spencer
Mesbla
Promodes
Royal Ahold
Vacco
Vendex

HOW MUCH

$=FF5.91 (Dec. 31, 1991)	Annual Growth	1984	1985	1986	1987	1988	1989	1990	1991	1992	1993
Sales (FF mil.)	13.5%	39,306	44,169	51,472	56,503	64,831	73,866	75,848	100,377	117,139	123,204
Net income (FF mil.)	16.3%	428	520	675	761	911	1,181	1,352	1,225	1,339	1,665
Income as % of sales	—	1.1%	1.2%	1.3%	1.3%	1.4%	1.6%	1.8%	1.2%	1.1%	1.4%
Earnings per share (FF)	14.4%	39	46	55	60	72	92	106	96	105	130
Stock price – high (FF)	—	532	844	1,421	1,464	1,200	1,856	1,897	2,365	2,825	4,380
Stock price – low (FF)	—	275	503	841	810	761	1,113	1,500	1,552	2,005	2,250
Stock price – close (FF)	26.7%	510	848	1,346	915	1,200	1,815	1,640	2,315	2,364	4,304
P/E – high	—	14	18	26	24	17	20	18	25	27	35
P/E – low	—	7	11	15	14	11	12	14	16	19	17
Dividends per share (FF)	10.4%	17.30	19.69	21.38	22.50	26.25	30.00	32.50	32.50	35.00	42.00
Book value per share (FF)	(5.6%)	—	—	—	682	862	968	1,071	640	535	484
Employees	12.9%	28,700	32,300	37,600	40,400	42,900	46,600	51,300	76,200	79,500	85,200

1993 Year-end:
Debt ratio: 33.8%
Return on equity: 25.5%
Cash (mil.): FF3,329
Long-term debt (mil.): FF4,422
No. of shares (mil.): 13
Dividends
 Yield: 1.0%
 Payout: 32.3%
Market value (mil.): $9,322
Sales (mil.): $20,847

Stock Price History
High/Low 1984–93

CASIO COMPUTER CO., LTD.

OVERVIEW

"In our business the life of a product is only about 1 1/2 years, so you better come up with new product all the time," says John McDonald, the head of Casio's US subsidiary. The Japanese company, best known for its electronic calculators and multifunction watches, does just that. Hot items among its recent gadget offering include a video printer that prints images directly from a television and pagers that send as well as receive.

Casio hopes a lower price and more functions will improve sales of Zoomer, a "personal digital assistant" (PDA) the company developed with Tandy. Zoomer's 2nd generation will include software upgrades, wireless e-mail capabilities, improved ability to interface with PCs, and better handwriting recognition. Meanwhile, Casio has sold over one million of its lower-end "personal organizer,"

an electronic mini–address book and appointment calendar. The company's digital diaries, which can send and receive messages, are so popular with children that 1994 production was increased by 20%. Despite new features, sales of another Casio staple, electronic musical instruments, have fallen sharply.

In 1994 Casio introduced several innovations in LCD screen technology. The company is the world's #5 LCD producer by value.

Strong digital diary and word processor sales boosted Casio's domestic revenues in 1994, but the high yen contributed to a nearly 28% drop in exports. To counter the effects of currency fluctuations, the company has moved much of its production overseas, primarily to Thailand and Malaysia. In 1993 30% of Casio products were made outside Japan; by 1994 that amount was 70%.

WHEN

In 1942 Tadao Kashio started a Tokyo-based machine shop, Kashio Manufacturing. His brother Toshio later joined him. After reading about a 1946 computing contest in which an abacus bested an electric calculator, Toshio, an inventor, wrote a note to himself: "Abacus is human ability, calculator is technology." In 1950 he began development of a calculator. The remaining Kashio brothers — Yukio, a mechanical engineer, and Kazuo, who took over the sales function — joined the company in the 1950s.

The Kashio brothers incorporated in 1957 as Casio, an Anglicization of the family name. That year the company launched its first product, an electric calculator featuring an innovative floating decimal point display; it was the first Japanese-built electric calculator. Casio took advantage of new transistor technology to create electronic calculators and in 1965 introduced the first electronic desktop calculator with memory. The company began exports to the US in 1970.

In the 1970s Casio fought in the fierce "calculator war," from which only Casio and Sharp emerged as significant Japanese survivors. Casio's strategy of putting lots of new functions on a proliferation of small models and selling them at rock-bottom prices worked not only with calculators, but with digital watches as well. The company introduced its first digital watch in 1974 and went on to dominate the market.

Casio expanded its product line into electronic music synthesizers (1980), pocket TVs (1983), and thin, card calculators (1983). In the mid-1980s Casio sales were hurt by a rising yen and stiff price competition at the low end of the calculator market from developing Asian nations. The company responded by beefing up R&D spending and releasing more sophisticated calculators designed for such specialized users as architects and insurance agents. To offset the effects of the heightened value of the yen, Casio moved manufacturing offshore to Taiwan, Hong Kong, Korea, and, in 1990, California and Mexico.

In 1990 Casio established Casio Electronic Devices to exploit the company's technology through the sales of components, principally liquid crystal displays and chip-on-film (tiny electronic circuit) products. In 1991 the company acquired a capital interest in Asahi Corporation, a manufacturer of communications equipment and light electrical appliances.

Casio continues to expand into new markets. In 1993 it established 2 joint ventures to produce pagers and other electronic devices in China. That year the company consolidated its Asahi Industries subsidiary operations into a single plant in Malaysia.

In 1994 Casio signed agreements with Mitsui (Japan) and Bharti Telecom (India) to market pagers in India. Casio will supply 60,000 pagers during the pact's first year.

OTC symbol: CSIOF (ADR)
Fiscal year ends: March 31

Chairman: Toshio Kashio
President: Kazuo Kashio
EVP: Yukio Kashio
Senior Managing Director: Toshio Kohzai
Senior Managing Director: Noriaki Shimura
Senior Managing Director: Shigeki Maeno
President, Casio (US): John J. McDonald
Auditors: Asahi & Co.

HQ: Casio Keisanki, Shinjuku-Sumitomo Bldg.,
2-6-1, Nishi-Shinjuku, Shinjuku-ku, Tokyo
163-02, Japan
Phone: +81-3-3347-4803
Fax: +81-3-3347-4533
US HQ: Casio, Inc., 570 Mount Pleasant Ave.,
Dover, NJ 07801
US Phone: 201-361-5400
US Fax: 201-361-3819

Casio's 60 subsidiaries and affiliates are located in
Canada, China, France, Germany, Hong Kong,
Italy, Malaysia, Mexico, Russia, Singapore, South
Korea, Spain, Taiwan, Thailand, the UK, and the
US, as well as in Japan. The company sells its
products worldwide.

	1994 Sales	
	¥ bil.	% of total
Japan	187	49
Other countries	197	51
Total	**384**	**100**

	1994 Sales	
	¥ bil.	% of total
Electronic calculators & personal data equipment	139	36
Electronic timepieces	85	22
Electronic musical instruments	33	9
Data processing systems & other	127	33
Total	**384**	**100**

Selected Products

Calculators and Personal Data Equipment	Data Processing Systems and Other
Digital diaries	Cash registers
Pagers	Blood pressure
Portable phones	monitors
Personal digital assistants	Label printers
	Liquid crystal displays
Timepieces	(LCDs)
Multifunction watches	Mini-TVs
	Video printers
Musical Instruments	Word processors
Keyboards	

Apple	Hyundai	SMH
AST	Loews	Smith Corona
AT&T	Matsushita	Sony
Brother	Motorola	Swiss Corporation for
Canon	NEC	Microelectronics
Compaq	Oki	and Watchmaking
Daewoo	Pioneer	Tandy
Fossil	Samsung	Texas
Fujitsu	Sanyo	Instruments
Hewlett-	Seiko	Timex
Packard	Sharp	Toshiba
Hitachi	Siemens	Yamaha

$=¥112 (Dec. 31, 1993)	Annual Growth	1985	1986	1987	1988	1989	1990	1991	1992	1993	1994
Sales (¥ bil.)	5.4%	239	267	237	248	271	305	335	338	432	384
Net income (¥ bil.)	(4.5%)	8	5	4	5	7	8	9	11	7	5
Income as % of sales	—	3.9%	3.4%	1.9%	1.5%	1.9%	2.4%	2.7%	3.1%	1.6%	1.4%
Earnings per share (¥)	(7.0%)	38	22	15	20	27	28	34	39	26	20
Stock price – high (¥)[1]	—	1,488	1,630	1,603	1,510	1,650	1,600	1,740	1,520	1,330	1,140
Stock price – low (¥)[1]	—	803	1,147	1,124	810	1,100	1,300	905	921	860	885
Stock price – close (¥)[1]	2.9%	1,385	1,541	1,381	1,140	1,350	1,520	963	1,280	1,060	1,060
P/E – high	—	39	70	148	75	62	57	51	39	51	57
P/E – low	—	21	50	101	43	41	47	27	24	33	45
Dividends per share (¥)	3.8%	8.93	9.84	10.77	11.91	12.50	12.50	12.50	12.50	12.50	12.50
Book value per share (¥)	7.0%	341	375	433	460	472	523	571	600	612	625
Employees	2.8%	—	—	—	3,557	3,614	3,757	4,058	4,412	4,423	4,208

1994 Year-end:
Debt ratio: 52.4%
Return on equity: 3.2%
Cash (bil.): ¥94
Long-term debt (bil.): ¥123
No. of shares (mil.): 273
Dividends
  Yield: 1.2%
  Payout: 62.9%
Market value (mil.): $2,584
Sales (mil.): $3,429

Stock Price History[1]
High/Low 1985–94

[1] Stock prices are for the prior calendar year.

CIBA-GEIGY LIMITED

OVERVIEW

Headquartered in Basel, Switzerland, Ciba-Geigy is one of the world's largest drug and chemical companies, but it is looking to get even stronger with its late 1994 acquisition of nearly half of US biotech company Chiron. Ciba will pay approximately $2.1 billion and exchange its diagnostics business and its stake in the 2 companies' vaccines joint venture for 49.9% of Chiron.

While it has been working to improve its pharmaceutical business, Ciba remains a world leader in many of its other operations. The company is the #1 supplier of agrochemicals, pigments, additives, textile dyes, and scales and balances. In the US the company makes NewVues disposable contact lenses, Habitrol nicotine patches, and Sunkist vitamins.

Ciba's pharmaceutical sector makes a variety of drugs to treat heart disease, cancer, central nervous system disorders, and other diseases. The Chiron deal gives Ciba, which has had trouble developing any blockbuster drugs lately, access to Chiron's portfolio of pharmaceuticals in development, including vaccines for herpes and hepatitis.

WHEN

Johann Geigy began selling organic merchandise (spices, natural dyes, etc.) in Basel in 1758. Successive generations of Geigys continued to produce his products and were still doing so when synthetic dyes were invented a century later. The Geigy family began producing the new dyes in 1859.

Geigy, however, was not the only Basel company to exploit the new technology. Alexander Clavel joined the synthetic dye trade, forming the Gesellschaft für Chemische Industrie im Basle (later shortened to Ciba). By the turn of the century, Ciba was Switzerland's #1 chemical firm.

When the powerful German chemical cartel fell during WWI, the Swiss were quick to fill the gap. After the war the German cartel was reestablished as I. G. Farben. Forced to compete with the Germans, Ciba, Geigy, and Sandoz (another Basel company) formed their own cartel, Basel AG, in 1918. Sharing profits, technology, and markets, Basel AG was soon outperforming its German competitors. It used its profits to diversify into pharmaceuticals and other chemicals and also gained a foothold in the US.

In 1929 the German and Swiss cartels merged and later accepted the French and British as well. This so-called Quadrapartite Cartel lasted until 1939 when it was shattered by WWII, leaving only the Basel AG intact. That same year Paul Müller, a scientist at Geigy, invented DDT, for which he was awarded a Nobel prize. After the war the companies of the Basel AG decided that they no longer needed the protection of the cartel and voluntarily dissolved it in 1951.

Ciba and Geigy continued to diversify. During the 1950s Geigy expanded rapidly, finding new markets in agricultural chemicals. By 1967 it had passed Ciba in sales. Faced again with competition from foreign companies as well as from its Swiss peers, Ciba and Geigy merged in 1970. Following the merger Ciba-Geigy began a series of acquisitions in the US, including Airwick Industries and Funk Seeds, both in 1974.

In 1976 the company admitted to testing its product Galecron by paying 6 Egyptian boys to stand barefoot in a field being sprayed with the insecticide, and in 1978 it was revealed that over 1,000 deaths in Japan had been linked to its diarrhea drug. Also in 1978 Ciba-Geigy bought 80% of the voting stock of the US's ALZA (drug delivery systems) but in 1982 sold most of it in a buyback.

In 1986 the company entered a joint venture with Chiron to produce and market genetically engineered vaccines. It acquired Maag AG (agrochemicals) from Hoffmann-La Roche in 1990. Ciba-Geigy also entered a series of research partnerships, including joint ventures with Isis Pharmaceuticals of Carlsbad, California (1990), to study "antisense" technology and Affymax of Palo Alto, California (1991), to study computer-aided screening of pharmaceutical products.

In 1993 Ciba received FDA approval to market Efidac/24, a 24-hour over-the-counter cold medicine, in the US.

In 1994 Glaxo sued Ciba-Geigy for alleged patent infringement of Glaxo's anti-ulcer drug Zantac. However, many analysts saw the move as a stalling tactic to keep Ciba from producing a generic version of Zantac, which goes off patent in 1995. The company also acquired Maalox antacid from Rhône-Poulenc Rorer in 1994.

OTC symbol: CBGXY (ADR)
Fiscal year ends: December 31

Chairman and CEO: Alex Krauer
Chairman of the Executive Committee and COO: Heini Lippuner
CFO: Rolf A. Meyer
Chairman, President, and CEO, Ciba-Geigy Corporation (US): Richard Barth
VP Finance and Information Services and CFO, Ciba-Geigy Corporation (US): Stanley Sherman
VP Human Resources, Ciba-Geigy Corporation (US): Stanton Goldberg
Auditors: Swiss Auditing and Fiduciary Company; Coopers & Lybrand AG

WHERE

HQ: CH-4002, Basel, Switzerland
Phone: +41-61-696-6580
Fax: +41-61-696-3019
US HQ: Ciba-Geigy Corporation, 444 Saw Mill River Rd., Ardsley, NY 10502-2699
US Phone: 914-479-5000
US Fax: 914-478-1201

Ciba-Geigy has operations in more than 80 countries worldwide.

	1993 Sales	
	SF mil.	% of total
Europe	12,258	47
Western Hemisphere	9,595	37
Eastern Hemisphere	4,139	16
Adjustments	(3,345)	—
Total	**22,647**	**100**

WHAT

	1993 Sales	
	SF mil.	% of total
Health care	9,220	41
Industry	8,614	38
Agriculture	4,813	21
Total	**22,647**	**100**

Health Care
Ciba Vision
  Contact lenses
  Lens care products
  Ophthalmic medicines
Pharma
  Anticancer drugs
  Antirheumatics
  Cardiovascular drugs
  Neurotropics
Self-Medication
  Desenex
  Doan's Pills
  Efidac
  Maalox

Agriculture
Fungicides
Herbicides
Insecticides
Parasiticides
Seeds

Industry
Additives
Chemicals
Composites
Pigments
Polymers
Scales and balances
Textile dyes

US Subsidiaries and Affiliates
Chiron Corp. (49.9%)
Ciba Corning Diagnostics Corp.
Ciba-Geigy Corp.
Ciba Vision Corp.
Geneva Pharmaceuticals Inc.
OCG Microelectronic Materials Inc. (over 50%)
Ohaus Scale Corp.

KEY COMPETITORS

Akzo Nobel
American Home Products
Amgen
BASF
Bausch & Lomb
Bayer
Bristol-Myers Squibb
Carter-Wallace
Dow Chemical
DuPont
Eastman Chemical
Formosa Plastics
Genentech
Glaxo
Hoechst
Imperial Chemical
Johnson & Johnson
Merck
Monsanto
PMC Inc.
Procter & Gamble
Rhône-Poulenc
Roche
Sandoz
SmithKline Beecham
Wilbur-Ellis

HOW MUCH

$=SF1.49 (Dec. 31, 1993)	9-Year Growth	1984	1985	1986	1987	1988	1989	1990	1991	1992	1993[1]
Sales (SF mil.)	2.9%	17,474	18,221	15,955	15,764	17,647	20,608	19,703	21,077	22,204	22,647
Net income (SF mil.)	4.6%	1,187	1,472	1,161	1,100	1,325	1,557	1,033	1,280	1,520	1,779
Income as % of sales	—	6.8%	8.1%	7.3%	7.0%	7.5%	7.6%	5.2%	6.1%	6.8%	7.9%
Earnings per share (SF)	4.1%	44	55	43	41	49	57	37	46	52	64
Stock price – high (SF)[2]	—	512	780	910	844	715	944	764	668	736	940
Stock price – low (SF)[2]	—	417	494	755	488	480	534	454	468	599	612
Stock price – close (SF)[2]	7.4%	494	766	774	540	529	748	494	638	670	940
P/E – high	—	12	14	21	21	15	17	21	15	14	15
P/E – low	—	9	9	17	12	10	9	12	10	12	10
Dividends per share (SF)	7.8%	7.60	7.60	7.60	10.00	13.00	12.00	12.00	13.00	14.00	15.00
Book value per share (SF)	1.3%	518	521	537	529	569	596	555	586	616	582
Employees	0.8%	81,423	81,012	82,231	86,109	88,757	92,553	94,141	91,665	90,554	87,480

1993 Year-end:
Debt ratio: 25.0%
Return on equity: 10.7%
Cash (mil.): SF7,213
Long-term debt (mil.): SF2,238
No. of shares (mil.): 29
Dividends
  Yield: 1.6%
  Payout: 23.5%
Market value (mil.): $18,517
Sales (mil.): $15,199

**Stock Price History[2]
High/Low 1984–93**

[1] Accounting change [2] Bearer shares

CIFRA, S.A. DE C.V.

OVERVIEW

If Cifra, Mexico's largest retailer, can ride out that country's stormy fiscal waters caused by the peso's volatility in late 1994, it should be positioned to prosper. Mexico's population is young, and its middle class is growing. Cifra's balance sheet shows no debt and a strong cash flow — and management efficiency has cut operating costs for 5 consecutive years. Finally, NAFTA, while increasing competition in retail markets, is also expected to increase Mexico's median income level.

Cifra is Mexico's 3rd largest public company, after Grupo Financiero Bancomer and Teléfonos de México. It was the first retail operation in Mexico to offer generic brands, to go public, and to combine clothing, food, and hardware in a single store. The Arango family owns a controlling interest in Cifra.

With pressure from a NAFTA-induced invasion by US retailers, Cifra is girding for combat by expanding an alliance it started in 1991 with Wal-Mart. In 1994 the pact included all Cifra stores and eliminated a clause that would let either company pull out of the agreement in 3 years. The companies already co-own 47 stores. Cifra outlets include Aurrerá department stores, Bodega Aurrerá discount warehouses, Superama supermarkets, and Vips restaurant chains. Cifra also operates 2 El Portón restaurants in the Los Angeles area. In late 1994 Cifra and Wal-Mart signed a joint venture agreement with Dillard to open Dillard's stores in Monterrey, Mexico City, and Guadalajara.

While its stores are traditionally concentrated in Mexico City, Cifra is expanding into small cities such as Queretaro and Villahermosa, where there is less competition. The company's growth plans include increasing floor space 50% by mid-1995.

WHEN

Spanish-born Jerónimo Arango Arias, Jr., studied art and literature at several American universities without graduating. In his 20s he wandered around Spain, Mexico, and the US until he saw a crowd waiting in line at the E. J. Korvette discount department store in New York City. Jerónimo called his 2 brothers, Plácido and Manuel, and convinced them to join him in a new business venture.

With about $250,000 borrowed from their father, a Spanish immigrant to Mexico who had done well in textiles, the 3 brothers opened their first Aurrerá Bolívar discount store in downtown Mexico City in 1958. Offering goods and clothing well below manufacturers' list prices, the store was an immediate hit with consumers but encountered hostility from competing Mexico City retailers. When local retailers threatened to boycott the Arangos' suppliers, alternate sources were developed in Guadalajara and Monterrey.

In 1965 the Arango brothers formed a 50-50 joint venture with Jewel Cos. of Chicago to open new Aurrerás. Jewel bought a 49% interest in the Arangos' business one year later. Plácido and Manuel left the business with their portion of the money, but Jerónimo remained to study modern management. The company went public in 1976.

By 1981 almost 1/3 of Jewel's earnings came from its Mexican operations. The following year the Mexican peso crashed, oblit-erating Jewel's Mexican earnings. American Stores took over Jewel in 1984, and Jerónimo bought back Jewel's stake in the company.

With the Mexican economy staggering from the peso devaluation, weak oil markets, and a huge debt crisis, Jerónimo was taking a major risk. Although no new stores were opened, none were closed. Employees were expected to work longer, and those choosing to leave were not replaced. With Mexico's middle class hurting the most, Jerónimo emphasized the Bodega Aurrerá no-frill warehouse in which all kinds of nonperishable merchandise, from canned chili to VCRs, are stacked to the ceiling and heavily discounted.

Cifra and Wal-Mart signed a joint agreement in 1991 to form Comercializadora México-Americana, a trading company designed to promote trade between Mexico and the US, and Club Aurrerá, a membership store that caters to small businesses.

Cifra began refurbishing all its stores in 1992, with work completed in 1994. Also in 1992 Cifra stores installed electronic price scanners at all points of sale.

In 1993 over 50% of Cifra's employees participated in a company stock option plan.

With information essential to modern retailing and corporate operations, in 1993 Cifra spent $25 million on computer equipment to let it take advantage of Wal-Mart's expertise in data processing.

OTC symbol: CFRAY
Fiscal year ends: December 31

Chairman: Jerónimo Arango Arias, age 68
VC: Henry Davis Signoret
Secretary (Finances): Gilberto Perezalonso
Examiner: Guillermo Gómez-Aguado
Director Human Resources: José María García Pérez
Auditors: Price Waterhouse

WHERE

HQ: José Ma. Castorena 470, Delegación Cuajimalpa, 05200 México, D.F., Mexico
Phone: +52-5-327-9211
Fax: +52-5-327-9259

Cifra operates 264 stores and restaurants throughout Mexico and 2 restaurants in the US.

	1993 Operating Data	
	No. of units	No. of customers (mil.)
Vips	106	44
Bodega Aurrerá	45	64
Superama	37	41
Almacenes Aurrerá	33	72
Suburbia	31	12
Club Aurrerá-Sam's Club	7	—
Gran Bazar	3	12
Supercenter	2	—
Total	**264**	**245**

WHAT

	1993 Sales	
	$ mil.	% of total
Almacenes Aurrerá & Gran Bazar	1,625	35
Bodega Aurrerá	1,193	26
Suburbia	553	12
Superama	541	12
Club Aurrerá-Sam's Club & Supercenter	449	10
Vips	219	5
Total	**4,580**	**100**

Major Subsidiaries

Almacenes Aurrerá and Gran Bazar (department stores and hypermarkets offering clothing, general merchandise, and supermarket goods)
Bodega Aurrerá (discount warehouses selling clothing, general merchandise, and groceries)
Club Aurrerá-Sam's Club and Supercenter (50%, joint venture with Wal-Mart Stores, Inc.; members only, semi-wholesale outlets)
Comercializadora México-Americana (51%, import and export)
El Portón (Mexican restaurants, US)
Sigla (real estate development and administration)
Suburbia (family-oriented department stores)
Superama (supermarkets)
Vips (3 restaurant chains featuring Mexican, Italian, and international foods)

KEY COMPETITORS

Comercial Mexicana	Price/Costco
Dayton Hudson	Restaurant Enterprises
El Palacio de Hierro	Group
El Puerto De Liverpool	Sears
Flagstar	TW Services
Gigante	Woolworth
Kmart	
J. C. Penney	
PepsiCo	

HOW MUCH

	Annual Growth	1984	1985	1986	1987	1988	1989	1990	1991	1992	1993
Sales ($ mil.)	27.9%	—	—	820	705	995	1,723	2,463	2,765	3,690	4,580
Net income ($ mil.)	22.6%	—	—	80	61	56	122	173	211	301	333
Income as % of sales	—	—	—	9.8%	8.7%	5.6%	7.1%	7.0%	7.6%	8.2%	7.3%
Earnings per share (pesos)	60.4%	—	—	—	0.02	0.04	0.11	0.17	0.20	0.29	0.32
Stock price – high (pesos)	—	—	—	—	—	—	—	—	—	—	—
Stock price – low (pesos)	—	—	—	—	—	—	—	—	—	—	—
Stock price – close (pesos)	80.0%	—	—	—	0.29	0.24	0.72	1.95	3.45	6.30	9.70
P/E – high	—	—	—	—	—	—	—	—	—	—	—
P/E – low	—	—	—	—	—	—	—	—	—	—	—
Dividends per share (pesos)	16.8%	—	—	—	—	—	—	0.07	0.06	0.09	0.10
Book value per share (pesos)	51.3%	—	—	—	—	0.25	0.53	0.73	0.91	1.43	1.94
Employees	12.2%	—	—	—	—	—	25,200	31,635	34,178	35,321	39,934

1993 Year-end:
Debt ratio: 0.0%
Return on equity: 19.1%
Cash (mil.): $1,940
Current ratio: 1.22
Long-term debt (mil.): $0
No. of shares (mil.): 3,200
Dividends
Yield: 1.1%
Payout: 32.4%
Market value (mil.): $9,990

Net Income ($ mil.) 1986–93

CLUB MÉDITERRANÉE SA

OVERVIEW

There is trouble in paradise for Club Méditerranée, as an unprecedented number of its "sun, sea, and sex" beauty spots are enmeshed in wars and terrorist activities. Its villages in the former Yugoslavia are closed due to the civil war there, while troubles in Egypt brought about an 88% fall in activities there in 1993. Following the attacks and kidnappings of French tourists in Turkey, Club Méditerranée's occupancy rates dropped by 50%. Political tensions in Senegal forced the company to close its village unit, its Haiti complex remained closed, and political unrest kept the company's 14 villages in Israel operating with lower than normal occupancy.

Club Méditerranée manages 139 resorts in 35 countries and operates tours and cruises. Its resorts do business under the Club Med, Valtur, Club Med Affaires (for business travelers), and Club Aquarius brand names. Club Méditerranée operates 2 cruise liners, Club Med 1, which cruises the Caribbean and the Mediterranean, and Club Med 2, which sails the Pacific. The company also arranges specialized tour packages for children and senior citizens. The company's business operations in North and Central America and Asia are handled by its US subsidiary, Club Med, Inc. In addition to a round of cost-cutting measures, the company is refocusing its marketing campaigns. Like the casinos in Las Vegas, Club Méditerranée is now targeting couples with children as a growth area for vacations and cruises. The family vacation market is estimated at $13 billion. The company is also promoting its sports facilities.

Club Méditerranée's massive losses led to its removal from the CAC 40 Index, the Paris Bourse's bellwether index, in 1993. In 1994 sales jumped 15.6% to $1.69 billion.

WHEN

Belgian diamond cutter Gérard Blitz dreamed up the Club Méditerranée concept as an escape from the post-war doldrums of Europe. He convened a gathering of charter members on the Mediterranean island of Majorca in 1950. The group slept in tents, cooked their own food, cleaned up after themselves, and had a great deal of fun. The Club Méditerranée philosophy was born — vacation villages in exotic locations, combining low price and simple amenities with community spirit and entertainment.

The man who provided the US Army surplus tents for that first gathering, Frenchman Gilbert Trigano, came on board as the managing director of the company in 1954 and took Club Méditerranée on a major expansion drive over the next 39 years. Permanent Polynesian-style huts replaced the tents at the newly opened location in Greece in 1954. In 1956 the company set up its first ski resort in Leysin, Switzerland. Club Méditerranée was incorporated the following year.

The Rothschild Group became the company's main shareholder from 1961 until 1988, and provided the capital for much of its expansion. By 1965 the company had 14 summer villages and 11 winter resorts. Trigano decided to take the Club Méditerranée concept into the cruise line business. Unfortunately, a combination of surly crews on leased French cargo ships (which were doubling as cruise ships) and the outbreak of the Arab-Israeli War in 1967 kept occupancy low and scuppered Trigano's first attempt to take Club Méditerranée to sea. Trigano relaunched the cruise line concept in 1990.

In 1967 Club Méditerranée gained a foothold in the US, opening an office in New York, and in 1968 it located its first hotel site, in Bear Valley in Northern California. In the 1970s the company became one of the biggest leisure groups in France through a series of mergers and acquisitions, including rival travel club Club Européen du Tourisme and Italian travel specialist Valtur. The 1970s and 1980s also saw the company hone its freewheeling, anything-goes image. Aimed at the singles market, each village was staffed by GOs (Gentils Organisateurs, or "kind organizers") in their 20s, who took care of cooking, cleaning, and entertaining.

In 1984 Club Med, Inc., was set up in New York to take care of the company's Americas and Asia businesses; it opened new resorts in the US and Japan in the late 1980s.

In 1991 the company's expansion came to a crashing halt as the company suffered its first-ever loss. Political unrest in its prime tourist locations continued to plague the company, leading in 1993 to a major loss of income and Trigano's resignation. His son Serge took over as chairman in 1993 and set about cutting costs in 1994.

OTC symbol: CLMDY
Fiscal year ends: October 31

Chairman and CEO; CEO, Club Med (US):
Serge Trigano
EVP Asia-Pacific: Alexis Agnello
EVP Development - Mergers and Acquisitions:
Salomon Toledano
EVP Administration - Finance: Hugues Harmel
COO American Zone; EVP, Club Med (US):
Jean-Michel Landau
CFO, Club Med (US): Hoh Koon Au Yeung
Director Human Resources, Club Med (US):
Sylvio de Bortoli
Auditors: Cogerco-Flipo; Ernst & Young

WHERE

HQ: 25 rue Vivienne, Place de la Bourse,
F-75088 Paris Cedex 02, France
Phone: +33-1-42-86-4000
Fax: +33-1-42-86-4616
US HQ: Club Med, Inc., 40 West 57th St.,
New York, NY 10019
US Phone: 212-977-2100
US Fax: 212-315-5392

Club Méditerranée operates 139 resort villages in 35 countries.

	1993 Operating Data	
	Hotel days (thous.)	% of total
Europe/Africa	5,368	62
North America	1,961	23
Asia	1,066	12
South America	263	3
Total	**8,658**	**100**

WHAT

	1993 Sales	
	FF mil.	% of total
Land packages	4,379	54
Transportation	1,566	19
Additional village revenues	1,016	12
Aquarius, TO, Maeva & Club City	905	11
Other	281	3
Total	**8,147**	**100**

Major Services
Cruises
Hotels
Time sharing and real estate
Tours
Vacation apartment rental
Vacation villages

Brand Names
Art Liberté
City Club
Club Aquarius
Clubhotel
Club Junior
Club Med
Club Med 1
Club Med 2
Club Med Découverte
Club Renaissance

Les Villas
Maeva
Valtur

Major Subsidiaries
Club Aquarius (France)
Club Med, Inc. (72%, US)
Groupe Maeva (45%, France)
Valtur (23%, Italy)

KEY COMPETITORS

Accor
American Classic Voyages
Carnival Corp.
Carlson
Club Corp.
Fibreboard
Hilton
Hyatt

ITT
Marriott Intl.
Ralcorp
Royal Caribbean Cruises
Sinclair
S-K-I Ltd.
Thomas Cook
Thomson Corp.

HOW MUCH

	Annual Growth	1984	1985	1986	1987	1988	1989	1990	1991	1992	1993
Sales (FF mil.)	5.0%	—	—	—	—	6,387	7,598	8,181	7,842	8,251	8,147
Net income (FF mil.)	—	—	—	—	—	301	365	395	(17)	161	(296)
Income as % of sales	—	—	—	—	—	4.7%	4.8%	4.8%	—	2.0%	—
Earnings per share	—	—	—	—	—	30.68	37.23	40.32	(1.61)	14.81	(27.03)
Stock price – high (FF)	—	1,145	1,635	728	746	550	710	788	530	548	461
Stock price – low (FF)	—	744	390	458	322	330	493	382	383	341	306
Stock price – close (FF)	(11.5%)	1,059	470	684	350	539	700	441	423	382	352
P/E – high	—	—	—	—	—	18	19	20	—	37	—
P/E – low	—	—	—	—	—	11	13	9	—	23	—
Dividends per share (FF)	(100.0%)	—	—	—	—	—	10.00	10.00	6.00	7.00	—
Book value per share (FF)	(3.6%)	—	—	—	—	—	—	—	335	330	311
Employees	(3.0%)	—	—	—	—	—	—	—	—	9,016	8,744

1993 Year-end:
Debt ratio: 55.4%
Return on equity: —
Cash (mil.): FF681
Long-term debt (mil.): FF2,992
No. of shares (mil.): 11
Dividends
  Yield: —
  Payout: —
Market value (mil.): $633
Sales (mil.): $1,379

**Stock Price History
High/Low 1989–93**

COLES MYER LTD.

OVERVIEW

Coles Myer, Australia's largest retailer, is adjusting its store lineup to counter flat sales. The company operates retail, discount, and specialty stores in Australia and New Zealand.

In 1993 Coles Myer initiated a 5-year, $2.8 billion campaign of store expansion and refurbishment and shopping center construction. That year the company introduced World 4 Kids toy and recreation stores and a chain of office supply stores, Officeworks. It also began closing underperforming stores and reducing excess inventories.

In a show of faith in its own recovery, in 1994 Coles Myer repurchased Kmart's 21.5% stake in the company. An agreement allows Coles Myer to continue to use the Kmart name in Australia and New Zealand. Also that year Coles Myer opened its first Chili's Texas Grill restaurant (licensed from US-based Brinker International).

The company opened the first phase of a major shopping center in Ringwood, Victoria, in 1994. It sold its 50% stakes in 2 other developments, raising $220 million.

WHEN

After studying US and UK chain-store retailing, including the "five and ten" stores of S. S. Kresge, George James Coles opened his first "3d., 6d., and 1/-" discount variety store in 1914 in a working-class neighborhood of Collingwood, Victoria. Emphasizing low prices and a money-back guarantee, Coles expanded to a larger store in 1919. With the formation of G. J. Coles & Coy Limited in 1921, Coles began opening stores in other Australian cities in the 1920s and 1930s.

With the outbreak of WWII, 95% of Coles's male staff enlisted. The company survived by promoting female employees to managerial positions. After the war the company embarked on a major acquisition binge that earned its managing director, E. B. Coles, the moniker, "The Takeover King." Coles bought Selfridges (A'Asia), (New South Wales, 1950), F&G Stores (Victoria, 1951), and Penneys (Queensland, 1956).

In 1958 Coles expanded into food retailing with the purchase of the 54-store John Connell Dickins chain. A year later Coles acquired Beilby's of South Australia and, in 1960, the Matthews Thompson group of 265 outlets in New South Wales. Coles pioneered the concept in Australia of selling different types of food (fresh meat, produce, dairy products, and frozen foods) in a single store with the 1962 opening of its first "New World of Shopping" supermarket in Victoria.

Coles opened its first major discount store, Colmart, in 1967. The following year S.S. Kresge of the US offered Coles a 49% interest in a joint venture to operate Kmart stores in Australia. With the opening of the first Kmart in 1969, Australians took to the US concept of discount department stores. In 1978 Coles absorbed the joint venture into a

wholly owned subsidiary by issuing 36 million K shares to Kmart for its interest.

In 1980 Coles bought several liquor store chains, including Liquorland, Claude Fay Cellars, and Mac the Slasher, which were consolidated into the company's Liquorland division.

Coles opened Australia's first hypermarket in 1982 by combining a Kmart with a grocery store. The company next entered women's quality clothing by buying the Katies chain of 117 specialty stores in 1984.

Coles became Coles Myer Ltd., Australia's largest retailer, in 1985 when it merged with the 84-year-old Myer Emporium chain of Melbourne. At the time of the merger Myer was Australia's 3rd largest retailer and largest department store chain, with 56 department stores, 68 Target stores, 122 Fosseys variety stores, 45 Country Road stores, and the Red Rooster chain. In 1987 the company added Charlton Feedlot, a dairy and beef producer, to supply its supermarkets. That same year it entered discount food retailing with the acquisition of 25 Bi-Lo supermarkets.

With the opening of the first New Zealand Kmart and the purchase of Progressive Enterprises of New Zealand (Foodtown, 3 Guys, and Georgie Pie) in 1988, Coles Myer made its first move outside of Australia.

The company issued 5 new free shares for every 4 held and spun off Progressive Enterprises to its shareholders in 1992.

In 1993 Coles Myer established a wholesale distribution subsidiary, Grocery Holdings, to serve its supermarkets.

In partnership with National Australia Bank and Shell Oil, the company introduced the Fly Buys customer incentive program and issued 2.5 million membership cards in 1994.

NYSE symbol: CM (ADR)
Fiscal year ends: July 31

Chairman: Solomon Lew, age 49
Deputy Chairman: S. Baillieu Myer, age 68
Deputy Chairman: Will J. Bailey, age 61
Managing Director and CEO: Peter T. Bartels, age 53
Director Finance and Administration: John L. Barner, age 55
Group Managing Director, Myer Grace Bros. & Specialty Stores: L. Peter Wilkinson, age 50
Managing Director Specialty Group: Peter E. Morgan, age 50
Director Information Services: Garry Campbell
Director Personnel: Peter Hosking
Auditors: Price Waterhouse

HQ: 800 Toorak Rd., Tooronga, Victoria 3146, Australia
Phone: +61-(0)3-829-3111
Fax: +61-(0)3-829-6787

Coles Myer operates 1,725 retail stores in Australia and New Zealand with over 3 million square meters of selling space.

	1994 Sales		1994 Operating Profit	
	$ mil.	% of total	$ mil.	% of total
Australia	11,652	99	488	99
New Zealand	130	1	3	1
Adjustment	—	—	(2)	—
Total	**11,782**	**100**	**489**	**100**

	1994 Sales		1994 Operating Profit	
	$ mil.	% of total	$ mil.	% of total
Supermarkets	5,015	43	148	30
Department stores	2,491	21	70	14
Kmart	2,136	18	94	19
Target	1,086	9	95	20
Specialty group	808	7	15	3
Fosseys	246	2	4	1
Property	—	—	70	14
Adjustment	—	—	(7)	—
Total	**11,782**	**100**	**489**	**100**

Supermarkets
Bi-Lo (discount food)
Coles Supermarkets (food and general merchandise)

Department Stores
Grace Bros.
Myer

Discount Stores
Fosseys
Kmart
Target

Specialty Group
Chili's Texas Grill (casual restaurants)
Katies (apparel)
Liquorland (beer, wine, spirits)
Officeworks (office supplies)
Red Rooster (barbequed chicken)
World 4 Kids (toys)

Arnotts	Grand Metropolitan
Burns Philp	PepsiCo
David Jones	Toys "R" Us
Davids Holdings	Woolworth
Foodland Associated	

	Annual Growth	1985	1986	1987	1988	1989	1990	1991	1992	1993	1994
Sales ($ mil.)	10.9%	4,631	7,219	7,597	10,247	11,066	11,699	11,635	11,295	10,463	11,782
Net income ($ mil.)	14.3%	94	124	146	263	284	290	254	276	284	314
Income as % of sales	—	2.0%	1.7%	1.9%	2.6%	2.6%	2.5%	2.2%	2.4%	2.7%	2.7%
Earnings per share ($)	(20.3%)	—	—	—	7.10	1.64	1.97	1.91	1.77	1.68	1.82
Stock price – high ($)	—	—	—	—	23.31	24.75	20.25	29.25	29.75	30.00	30.75
Stock price – low ($)	—	—	—	—	21.31	18.13	16.38	18.25	19.50	24.00	23.13
Stock price – close ($)	3.9%	—	—	—	22.00	19.88	18.63	27.50	22.00	30.00	27.63
P/E – high	—	—	—	—	3	15	10	15	17	18	17
P/E – low	—	—	—	—	3	11	8	10	11	14	13
Dividends per share ($)	0.3%	—	—	—	1.08	0.80	1.05	0.84	0.92	0.59	1.10
Book value per share ($)	(20.2%)	—	—	—	—	45.87	11.94	17.00	12.06	13.91	14.80
Employees	6.1%	79,584	139,243	141,214	163,650	166,755	158,707	143,182	132,543	136,195	135,365

1994 Year-end:
Debt ratio: 51.2%
Return on equity: 13.3%
Cash (mil.): $60
Current ratio: 1.66
Long-term debt (mil.): $1,083
No. of shares (mil.): 169
Dividends
  Yield: 4.0%
  Payout: 60.4%
Market value (mil.): $4,663

**Stock Price History
High/Low 1988–94**

COOPERS & LYBRAND L.L.P.

OVERVIEW

One of the Big 6 accounting firms, Coopers & Lybrand is the world's 4th largest accounting company and the 5th largest in the US. Besides auditing and tax preparation, the firm provides a variety of business services, including management consulting and human resource consulting. Coopers led the Big 6 in signing on new clients in 1993 after lagging behind its counterparts in the last few years.

Coopers has recently focused on expanding its Human Resource Advisory Group, acquiring several consulting firms, including Bufete Matemico Actuarial, the largest independent

benefits and actuarial consulting firm in Mexico. The additions make the firm's human resource group the world's 5th largest.

In 1994 Eugene Freedman said he would not seek another term as Cooper & Lybrand's chairman. Freedman, who has reached the firm's mandatory retirement age of 62, made his decision after a poll of the firm's partners showed they were not interested in allowing him to bypass the rules to serve another term. Instead, the firm's partners elected Nicholas Moore to be its new chairman when Freedman's term ends.

WHEN

Coopers & Lybrand, the product of a 1957 transatlantic merger, literally wrote the book on auditing. Lybrand, Ross Bros. & Montgomery, as the US ancestor was known, had been formed in 1898 by 4 partners — William Lybrand, Edward Ross, Adam Ross, and Robert Montgomery. In 1912 Montgomery wrote *Montgomery's Auditing*, termed by many as the "bible" of the accounting profession. The book is now in its 11th edition.

In the early years the accounting firm grew slowly, and the Ross brothers' sister served as secretary, typist, and bookkeeper. In 1902 the company opened a New York office at 25 Broad Street. Other offices across the country followed — Pittsburgh (1908), Chicago (1909), and Boston (1915). WWI focused attention on Washington, DC, and the Lybrand firm opened an office there (1919) and then branched out to the new auto capital of Detroit (1920), to Seattle (1920), and to Baltimore (1924). A merger with the firm of Klink, Bean & Company gave the firm a window on California (1924). Another merger brought the firm into Dallas (1930), with an offshoot office in Houston a year later.

In Europe the Lybrand firm established offices in Berlin (1924, closed in 1938 as WWII loomed), Paris (1926), and London (1929). At the same time the UK firm of Cooper Brothers was also expanding in Europe.

Cooper Brothers had begun in 1854 when William Cooper, the oldest son of a Quaker banker, formed his accountancy at 13 George Street in London. He was quickly joined by his brothers, Arthur, Francis, and Ernest. The firm's name of Cooper Brothers & Company was adopted in 1861. After WWI Cooper

Brothers branched out to Liverpool (1920), Brussels (1921), New York (1926), and Paris (1930). After WWII Cooper Brothers acquired 3 venerable firms — Alfred Tongue & Company; Aspell Dunn & Company; and Rattray Brothers, Alexander & France.

In 1957 Coopers & Lybrand was formed by the amalgamation of the international accounting firms, and by 1973 the affiliated partnerships had gravitated toward the Coopers & Lybrand name. In the 1960s the company expanded into employee benefits consulting and introduced a new auditing method that included evaluating clients' systems of internal control. During the 1970s Coopers focused on integrating computer technology into the auditing process.

During the 1980s Coopers dropped from the top of the Big 8 to 5th in the Big 6 as several of its competitors paired off in a series of mergers. However, the firm unexpectedly became the refuge for partners defecting from other international mergers.

In 1991 Coopers and IBM formed Meritus, a consulting service for the health care and consumer goods industries. In 1992 the firm agreed to pay $95 million to settle claims of defrauded investors in now-defunct disk drive maker MiniScribe. In 1993 it hired former SEC chairman Richard Breeden as vice-chairman of its domestic and foreign financial service groups.

In 1994 Coopers & Lybrand introduced Telesim, a management simulation software package for the telecommunications industry. The software was developed with Pacific Telesis, NYNEX, and software maker Thinking Tools.

International partnership
Fiscal year ends: September 30

Chairman and CEO: Eugene M. Freedman,
age 62 (until October 1, 1994)
Chairman and CEO: Nicholas Moore (after
October 1, 1994)
COO: Vincent M. O'Reilly
VC Coopers & Lybrand Consulting: John M.
Jacobs
VC International: William K. O'Brien
VC Human Resources and Strategy: Anthony J.
Conti
CFO: Frank V. Scalia
General Counsel: Harris J. Amhowitz

WHERE

HQ: 1251 Avenue of the Americas, New York, NY
10020
Phone: 212-536-2000
Fax: 212-536-3145

Coopers & Lybrand has offices in 125 countries.

	1993 Revenues	
	$ mil.	% of total
US	1,640	31
Other countries	3,580	69
Total	**5,220**	**100**

WHAT

	1993 US Revenues
	% of total
Accounting & auditing	56
Tax	19
Consulting & other	25
Total	**100**

Representative Clients

American Brands	Johnson & Johnson
AT&T	The Limited
Glaxo	3M
Ito-Yokado	Telmex

Selected Services

Business Assurance
Accounting and SEC
Auditing
Business investigation services
Litigation and claims
Business reorganization
Business management for entertainers (Gelfand,
Rennert & Feldman)
Emerging business services
Mergers and acquisitions

Coopers & Lybrand Consulting
Information technology
Applications design and implementation
Programming
Technology planning
Resource management
Strategic management services

Human Resource Advisory
Benefit systems
Compliance
Defined benefits
Defined contributions
Executive compensation
Group health
Insurance/risk management

Process Management
Business process assessment
Outsourcing
Process improvement

Tax
International tax
Personal financial services
Tax accounting and compliance
Tax planning
Valuation
Washington policy advisory

KEY COMPETITORS

Arthur Andersen	H&R Block
Bain & Co.	Harcourt General
Booz, Allen & Hamilton	Hewitt
Boston Consulting Group	IBM
Deloitte & Touche	A.T. Kearney
Delta Consulting	KPMG
Electronic Data Systems	Marsh & McLennan
Ernst & Young	McKinsey & Co.
Gemini Consulting	Price Waterhouse

HOW MUCH

	9-Year Growth	1984	1985	1986	1987	1988	1989	1990	1991	1992	1993
Sales($ mil.)	17.3%	1,243	1,414	1,780	2,076	2,520	2,977	4,136	4,959	5,350	5,220
Offices	4.7%	488	518	531	550	580	602	710	735	733	740
Partners	—	—	—	—	—	—	—	—	—	—	5,091
Employees	8.0%	33,055	36,243	38,520	41,134	45,486	50,636	63,300	67,175	66,600	66,300

1993 Year-end:
Sales per partner:
$1,025,339

Sales ($ mil.)
1984–93

CRÉDIT LYONNAIS

OVERVIEW

Crédit Lyonnais keeps going to the well, but it has yet to run dry. Europe's largest bank (ranked by assets), Crédit Lyonnais was bailed out not once but twice in 1994. In early 1994 its biggest shareholders, the French government (55%), Thomson-CSF (22%), and Caisse des Depots & Consignations (4%), gave the bank more than $850 million. Later that year the French government agreed to give the bank even more cash after Crédit Lyonnais's auditors refused to certify its first half financial results unless more coverage was given for the bank's higher-than-expected losses.

The company has been bathing in red ink lately because of rising provisions for a passel of bad loans and the costs of a European expansion. It has expanded rapidly throughout Europe, buying banks, brokerage firms, and financial service companies.

In 1993 former insurance executive Jean Peyrelevade replaced Jean-Yves Haberer as head of the company. To get Crédit Lyonnais back on track, Peyrelevade plans to cut employment by 4,400, focus more on commercial banking, and sell pieces of some of the company's diverse holdings, including software maker Sligos and drug maker Rhône-Poulenc. These moves come as the bank works to primp for investors whom it hopes to court for a planned privatization in the late 1990s.

WHEN

Henri Germain, son of a prosperous Lyons family, had been at times a lawyer, stockbroker, mine manager, and silk merchant before, in 1863, with the support of local businessmen and Swiss bankers, he launched Crédit Lyonnais. The bank added branches in Paris and Marseille in 1865, and, as Germain, a widower, remarried into a Paris family and took a seat in Parliament, the bank shifted its emphasis toward the capital.

In the early 1870s, during war with Germany and the civil war that followed, the bank moved some assets to London for safety, thus creating its first foreign branch. In the late 19th and early 20th centuries, Crédit Lyonnais expanded overseas, with branches from Moscow to Jerusalem, from Madrid to Bombay.

Germain died in 1905. Crédit Lyonnais fell from its perch during WWI. By 1929 the bank returned to its #1 ranking in France, but the Great Depression forced Crédit Lyonnais to cut 18% of its staff in the face of a 20% drop in profits.

During WWII the bank used a 32-car train to evacuate 500 tons of stocks, securities, and bonds for safekeeping. After the war the French government nationalized the bank, and Crédit Lyonnais pushed into international markets. In South America it helped form Banco Francês e Brasileiro in Brazil and other entities in Peru and Venezuela.

In 1970 Crédit Lyonnais formed a consortium with Commerzbank (then Germany's 4th largest bank) and Banco di Roma (then Italy's 3rd largest) to offer medium-term Eurocurrency loans. Spain's Banco Hispano Americano joined the consortium in 1973.

Crédit Lyonnais endured a costly strike (1972), the assassination of its president on the steps of its Paris headquarters (by a labor movement fanatic in 1977), and a series of leaders during the changes of governments in the 1980s. Bank president Jean-Maxime Lévêque guided Crédit Lyonnais into dealing in securities, and Clinvest, the bank's investment arm, was created in 1987. Lévêque ran afoul of French officials by preaching privatization for the bank. Jean-Yves Haberer, formerly head of the Paribas merchant bank, succeeded Lévêque in 1988 and expanded the bank's holdings in French companies.

In 1990, to raise capital, the bank took control of Thomson-CSF's finance operations and gave the state-owned electronics giant a stake in the bank. In 1991 Crédit Lyonnais subsidiary Altus Finance won approval of a $3.5 billion purchase of Executive Life's junk bond portfolio.

In 1992 the company acquired 20% of Aerospatiale from the French government in return for providing capital for the state-owned aerospace company to develop new aircraft and missiles. That same year Crédit Lyonnais took control of stock of Metro Goldwyn Mayer (MGM) after the movie studio foundered under Giancarlo Parretti, whom the bank's Dutch branch had lent nearly $1 billion to buy MGM in 1990.

In 1994 the company sold 49% of its life insurance subsidiary Union des Assurances Fédérales to French and foreign investors.

Principal exchange: Paris
Fiscal year ends: December 31

Chairman and CEO: Jean Peyrelevade
General Manager: Michel Renault
Member Executive Committee: Dominique Bazy
Member Executive Committee: Pascal Lamy
Head of Corporate Finance Division: Claude
  Rubinowicz
Head of Personnel Division: Joseph Musseau
CEO, Crédit Lyonnais (US): Robert Cohen
Auditors: Pavie & Associés (Coopers & Lybrand);
  Ernst & Young

WHERE

HQ: 19, Boulevard des Italiens, 75002 Paris,
  France
Phone: +33-1-42-95-70-00
Fax: +33-1-42-95-30-40
US HQ: Crédit Lyonnais, 1301 Avenue of the
  Americas, New York, NY 10019
US Phone: 212-261-7000
US Fax: 212-459-3170

Crédit Lyonnais operates more than 4,500 offices
in 80 countries around the world.

	1993 Operating Income
	% of total
France	30
Other Europe	50
Other countries	20
Total	**100**

WHAT

	1993 Assets	
	FF bil.	% of total
Interbank & money market items	519	26
Loans & other customer items	920	46
Securities	451	23
Other	108	5
Total	**1,998**	**100**

Selected Subsidiaries and Affiliates
Aerospatiale (17.8%, aerospace)
Altus Finance (99.9%)
Banca Jover (99.6%, Spain)
Banco Francês e Brasileiro SA (53.9%, Brazil)
BfG Bank AG (50%, Germany)
Clinvest (investment banking)
Compagnie Navigation Mixte (14.2%, industrial and
  financial holding company)
Concept (55%, information services)
Crédit Lyonnais Securities (Asia) Ltd. (78.8%, Hong
  Kong)
Crédit Lyonnais Securities USA
Hôtel International Iéna (35.7%)
Metro Goldwyn Mayer Inc. (US, film production)
Sligos (55.1%, software)
Union des Banques Arabes et Françaises (40%)
Woodchester Investment Plc (49.3%, Ireland)

KEY COMPETITORS

Allianz	CS Holding	Société
Bank of New York	Deutsche Bank	Générale
Bankers Trust	First Chicago	Sony
Banque Nationale	HSBC	Time Warner
de Paris	Industrial Bank	Turner
Barclays	of Japan	Broadcasting
Chase Manhattan	Matsushita	Union Bank of
Chemical Banking	J.P. Morgan	Switzerland
Citicorp	NatWest	Viacom
Crédit Commercial	Royal Bank	Walt Disney
de France		

HOW MUCH

$=FF5.91 (Dec. 31, 1993)	Annual Growth	1984	1985[1]	1986	1987	1988	1989	1990	1991	1992	1993
Assets (FF bil.)	9.7%	868	831	837	899	1,084	1,221	1,463	1,587	1,902	1,998
Net income (FF bil.)	—	1.0	1.2	1.8	2.2	2.1	3.1	3.7	3.2	(1.8)	(6.9)
Income as % of assets	—	0.1%	0.1%	0.2%	0.2%	0.2%	0.2%	0.3%	0.2%	—	—
Earnings per share (FF)	—	—	61	70	85	79	118	111	90	(49)	(151)
Stock price – high (FF)	—	—	—	702	897	570	763	898	683	677	795
Stock price – low (FF)	—	—	—	659	505	435	477	501	455	372	456
Stock price – close (FF)	1.9%	—	—	670	520	485	700	561	498	466	765
P/E – high	—	—	—	10	11	7	6	8	8	—	—
P/E – low	—	—	—	9	6	6	4	5	5	—	—
Dividends per share (FF)	(100.0%)	—	—	—	15.00	19.00	23.00	23.00	23.00	10.00	0.00
Book value per share (FF)	—	—	—	—	—	—	—	—	—	—	—
Employees	5.0%	45,894	45,691	54,557	58,181	58,151	61,508	68,486	70,567	71,446	71,351

1993 Year-end:
Debt ratio: 84.3%
Equity as % of assets: 4.0%
L-T debt (bil.): FF170
No. of shares (mil.): 45
Dividends
  Yield: 0.0%
  Payout: —
Market value (mil.): $5,796
Assets (mil.): $338,020
Sales (mil.): $7,802

900
800
700
600
500
400
300
200
100
0

Note: All data presented for nonvoting shares   [1] Accounting change

CS HOLDING

Zurich-based CS Holding — the world's 5th largest banking group — comprises 5 financial institutions: Credit Suisse, CS First Boston (investment banking), Fides Trust, Leu Holding, and Swiss Volksbank. Other interests include life insurance (CS Life), information technology services (Fides Informatik), and electricity and engineering (Electrowatt).

Following a shakeup among top ranks at New York–based First Boston in 1993, the subsidiary reorganized operations and consolidated its worldwide businesses under the name CS First Boston. In 1994 CS Holding upped its stake in the subsidiary to over 63%.

Also in 1994 CS Holding announced that it would join with Swiss Reinsurance to provide both financial and reinsurance services to clients. CS Holding also increased its share of Neue Aargauer Bank, one of Switzerland's largest regional banks, to 88%.

In late 1994 CS Holding followed Union Bank of Switzerland's efforts to restructure the outdated Swiss securities market, including elimination of dual share categories.

Shortly after the creation of the Swiss federal government, Alfred Escher opened the doors of Credit Suisse (CS) in Zurich in 1856. Initially CS operated more as a venture capital company than as a lender. The bank helped start Swiss railroads and other industries while opening banks in Italy and Switzerland, including Swiss Bank Corporation. In 1867 CS suffered the only annual deficit in its history when a cotton price collapse following the American Civil War led to losses on cotton import financing.

CS shifted to conventional commercial banking in 1867 and sold most of its stock holdings. By 1871 CS was Switzerland's largest bank. Rapid Swiss industrialization buoyed the bank's business. In 1895 CS helped create a hydroelectric business, the predecessor of Swiss utility Electrowatt.

CS's foreign activity expanded rapidly in the 1920s. During the Great Depression a run on banks forced CS to sell assets at a loss and dip into its undisclosed reserves (profits from past years hidden on its balance sheet).

Swiss neutrality helped CS survive WWII. The bank's international business took off as Switzerland became a major banking center in the postwar period. Foreign exchange dealing and gold trading became important activities to CS, which acquired Valcambi (gold ingots and coins, 1966), Crédit Foncier Suisse (mortgage financing, 1976), and Alliance Credit (consumer credit, 1976).

In 1978 the bank formed a joint venture with US investment bank First Boston. CS owned 60% of the new, London-based entity called Crédit Suissé-First Boston (CSFB) and took a minority stake in First Boston in the bargain. CSFB almost immediately became the largest Eurobond issuer.

Following management disputes, CS created CS First Boston, a new holding company, to own First Boston, CSFB, and CS First Boston Pacific, based in Tokyo. CS Holding, created as a sister entity to the bank in 1982, took a 44.5% interest in the new company. To restructure its commercial and investment banking activities, CS Holding became the parent company of CS and other operations in 1989.

First Boston continued to bleed red ink from $1 billion in bad bridge loans on mergers and acquisitions. In 1990 CS Holding injected $300 million in equity and shifted $470 million in bad loans off First Boston's books. CS Holding took control of CS First Boston and, after Federal Reserve approval, became the first foreign bank to own a major Wall Street investment bank. Also in 1990 CS Holding gained control of Switzerland's 235-year-old Bank Leu.

As a result of a 1989 Swiss Federal Supreme Court ruling that required CS Holding to meet bank capital requirements for each of its subsidiaries, the company announced it would distribute 20% of its shares before the end of 1992 to raise the necessary reserves.

Contributing to CS Holding profits in 1991 was the turnaround at CS First Boston, which had fully repaid its debts to its parent company by March 1992.

In 1992 the company created Fides Informatik to provide business software and information technology to financial and industrial companies. CS Holding strengthened its core business in 1993 by acquiring Swiss Volksbank and full interest in Leu Holding.

CS Holding announced that it would begin operations in Moscow in 1994 and continue its expansion into Eastern Europe.

WHO

Chairman: Rainer E. Gut, age 62
President, Credit Suisse: Josef Ackermann, age 46
President, Leu Holding Ltd.: Peter Küpfer, age 50
Chief Financial and Administrative Officer: Phillip M. Colebatch
Chairman and CEO, CS First Boston (US): John M. Hennessy
Director Human Resources, CS First Boston (US): Peter Boucher
Auditors: KPMG Klynveld Peat Marwick Goerdeler SA

WHERE

HQ: Nüschelerstrasse 1, PO Box 669, 8021 Zurich, Switzerland
Phone: +41-(0)1-212-1616
Fax: +41-(0)1-212-0669
US HQ: CS First Boston, Inc., 55 E. 52nd St., New York, NY 10005
US Phone: 212-909-2000
US Fax: 212-318-1187

	1993 Assets	
	SF mil.	% of total
Switzerland	124,211	36
US	88,519	26
Japan	13,817	4
Canada	4,913	1
Other Europe	97,970	28
Other industrialized countries	2,545	1
Other countries	14,509	4
Total	**346,484**	**100**

WHAT

	1993 Sales		1993 Net Income	
	SF mil.	% of total	SF mil.	% of total
Credit Suisse	9,189	48	1,460	66
Electrowatt	4,739	25	212	10
CS First Boston	2,666	14	328	15
Swiss Volksbank	1,314	7	2	0
Leu Holding	730	4	190	9
CS Life	484	2	1	0
Fides Trust	113	0	6	0
Fides Informatik	103	0	1	0
Adjustments	(5,525)	—	(207)	—
Total	**13,813**	**100**	**1,993**	**100**

Major Holdings

Credit Suisse (99.9%, banking)
CS First Boston, Inc. (63.2%, investment banking, US)
CS Life (life insurance)
Electrowatt Ltd. (46.3%; utility, manufacturing, engineering services)
Fides Informatik (information technology services)
Fides Trust Ltd. (trust business)
Leu Holding Ltd. (99.8%; banking, financial services)
Neue Aargauer Bank (88%, regional banking)
Swiss Volksbank (99.8%, banking)

KEY COMPETITORS

ABN-Amro Holding	Goldman Sachs	Royal Bank
Allianz	HSBC	of Canada
Bank of Tokyo	Industrial Bank	Sakura Bank
Barclays	of Japan	Salomon
Bear Stearns	Merrill Lynch	Sanwa Bank
Chase Manhattan	Mitsubishi	Société Generalé
Chemical Banking	J.P. Morgan	Sumitomo
Citicorp	Morgan Stanley	Swiss Bank
Crédit Lyonnais	NatWest	Tokai Bank
Dai-Ichi Kangyo	Nomura	Union Bank of
Deutsche Bank	Securities	Switzerland
Dun & Bradstreet	Paine Webber	S. G. Warburg
Fuji Bank		

HOW MUCH

$=SF1.49 (Dec. 31, 1993)	9-Year Growth	1984	1985	1986	1987	1988	1989[1]	1990	1991[1]	1992	1993
Assets (SF mil.)	17.0%	84,028	88,662	103,741	107,240	113,383	—	—	220,487	249,353	346,484
Net income (SF mil.)	19.0%	417	507	566	550	634	861	192	980	1,178	1,993
Income as % of assets	—	0.5%	0.6%	0.5%	0.5%	0.6%	—	—	0.4%	0.4%	0.5%
Earnings per share (SF)[2]	9.3%	26	31	32	31	33	41	9	45	45	58
Stock price – high (SF)[2]	—	420	651	711	698	533	587	548	442	430	756
Stock price – low (SF)[2]	—	359	409	564	423	397	447	295	277	314	372
Stock price – close (SF)[2]	6.8%	409	651	691	443	491	533	298	348	426	737
P/E – high	—	16	21	22	23	16	14	61	10	9	13
P/E – low	—	14	13	18	14	12	11	33	6	7	6
Dividends per share (SF)[2,3]	0.8%	16.72	17.60	18.40	18.40	18.38	22.00	15.00	15.00	15.00	18.00
Book value per share (SF)[2]	3.6%	330	339	360	368	390	413	361	385	391	453
Employees	18.6%	12,204	12,743	14,060	15,020	15,055	—	44,153	44,323	51,787	56,804

1993 Year-end:
Debt ratio: 94.8%
Equity as % of assets: 4.6%
Return on equity: 13.8%
No. of shares (mil.): 33
Dividends
  Yield: 2.4%
  Payout: 30.8%
Market value (mil.): $16,471
Assets (mil.): $232,540
Sales (mil.): $9,271

**Stock Price History
High/Low 1984–93**

Note: 1984–88 results for Credit Suisse only   [1] Accounting change   [2] Bearer shares   [3] Not including rights offerings

DAEWOO GROUP

OVERVIEW

Daewoo is South Korea's 4th largest *chaebol* (industrial group), with 19 member companies, operations in over 100 countries, and group sales of nearly $31 billion. Its range of activities includes trading, construction, automobiles, shipbuilding, electronics and telecommunications, machine tools, financing, and aerospace. The 1994 merger of its shipbuilding division into its heavy industry company made the consolidated subsidiary the #2 listed company in terms of capital on the Korea Stock Exchange, after the KEPCO power utility. Other member firms include Daewoo Corporation, the group's trading and construction arm; Daewoo Securities, the country's #1 brokerage; Daewoo Electronics; Daewoo Motor; and Daewoo Telecom.

The company's primary strategies for growth have been the acquisition and revival of bankrupt companies and aggressive expansion into lesser-developed countries. Daewoo's construction firms, for instance, are building in Vietnam, China, and Libya.

Founding chairman Kim Woo-Choong announced in 1994 that he planned to transform Daewoo Motor Co. (South Korea's #3 car company) from a loss maker into one of the group's top businesses. To this end Daewoo Motor agreed to invest $1 billion in an Indian joint venture and $900 million in a Romanian joint venture. Daewoo plans to quadruple its annual auto output by the year 2000 to 2.2 million vehicles, with 50% of the production located outside of Korea.

WHEN

The Korean character for "risk" combines the characters for crisis and chance, both of which have figured prominently in Kim Woo-Choong's high-rolling career. In 1967 Kim and To Dae Do put together their names and $18,000 (much of it borrowed) to create Daewoo, a textile exporting company. Soon Kim bought out To and used low-cost Korean labor to turn Daewoo into a profitable clothing maker, garnering Sears, J. C. Penney, and Montgomery Ward as accounts. As the Korean economy took off, Daewoo entered construction.

In 1976 Korean President Park Chung Hee asked Kim to take over a government-owned machinery plant that had been unprofitable for 37 years. Kim accepted, lived in the plant for 9 months, and turned the business around. Since then the business, now known as Daewoo Heavy Industries, has been consistently profitable.

At the same time, most Korean construction firms were following the flow of oil money to the Middle East. To avoid competition, Kim sought riskier construction contracts and landed $2 billion worth in Libya. Kim eliminated political and economic risks by requiring Libya to pay in advance.

In the late 1970s Daewoo came to the rescue of 2 more state-owned enterprises. President Park asked Kim to take over the government's 50% share of faltering GM Korea. Kim renamed the auto maker Daewoo Motor Company and turned it into Korea's 3rd largest car producer. However, the "Great

Universe" acquired a black hole when Park announced Daewoo's takeover of a partially built, debt-ridden shipyard while Kim was out of the country. Out of patriotism Kim spent $500 million to build a state-of-the-art shipyard, but it remained unprofitable.

In the 1980s Kim inked a string of big export deals exchanging low-cost goods for technology. Daewoo companies became involved in projects with Caterpillar (forklifts); Northern Telecom (telephone equipment); and Boeing, Lockheed, General Dynamics, Daimler-Benz, and United Technologies (aerospace components). Daewoo Motor began making the Pontiac LeMans in 1986.

Daewoo entered electronics and continued to buy ailing companies. In the mid-1980s the group bought foundering custom chip maker ZyMOS (US), and in 1989 Daewoo purchased Leading Edge, a bankrupt US-based PC marketer. Also in 1989 a government bailout helped to keep the group from collapsing because of the losses from Daewoo Shipbuilding. Kim took charge of the unit.

In 1991 Daewoo's construction arm won a contract for a $957-million highway project in Pakistan, and the group formed a joint venture with an auto maker in Uzbekistan in 1992. In 1993 Daewoo posted a 155% rise in the export of its semiconductors over 1992.

In an ongoing government investigation, Kim Woo-Choong, a national presidential contender in 1992, admitted in 1994 to charges of bribing an official of the state power utility, KEPCO.

Principal exchange: Korea
Fiscal year ends: December 31

WHO

Chairman: Kim Woo-Choong, age 58
Chairman: Kim Joon-Sung
VC: Lee Woo-Bock
VC: Lee Kyung-Hoon
EVP Finance/Accounting: Kim Young-Hwan
President, Daewoo International (America): Kim
Ok-Nyun
EVP Finance, Daewoo International (America):
Y. S. Kim
**General First Manager (Personnel), Daewoo
International (America):** C. H. Pak
Auditors: KPMG San Tong & Co.

WHERE

HQ: Daewoo Corporation, 541 Namdaemunno
5-ga, Chung-gu, Seoul, Korea
Phone: +82-2-759-2114
Fax: +82-2-753-9489
US HQ: Daewoo International (America) Corp.,
85 Challenger Rd., Ridgefield Park, NJ 07660-
2114
US Phone: 201-229-4500
US Fax: 201-440-2244

	1993 Exports
	% of total
Asia	40
North America	19
Europe	17
Middle East	7
Africa	2
Other countries	15
Total	**100**

HOW MUCH

WHAT

	1993 Exports
	% of total
Electric & electronics	26
Vehicles	17
Ships	16
Steel & metal	13
Textiles	10
Machinery	8
Chemicals	6
Other	4
Total	**100**

Group Companies
Daewoo Appian Technology Ltd. (telecommunications)
Daewoo Automotive Components Ltd.
Daewoo Capital Management Co., Ltd.
Daewoo Corporation (trading)
Daewoo Electric Motor Industries Ltd.
Daewoo Electronic Components Co., Ltd.
Daewoo Electronics Co., Ltd.
Daewoo Heavy Industries Ltd.
Daewoo Information Systems Co., Ltd.
Daewoo Motor Co., Ltd.
Daewoo Precision Industries Ltd. (machinery)
Daewoo Research Institute
Daewoo Securities Co., Ltd.
Daewoo Telecom Co., Ltd.
Dongwoo Development Co., Ltd. (hotels)
Keangnam Enterprises, Ltd. (construction)
Kyungnam Metal Co., Ltd. (construction)
Orion Electric Co., Ltd.
Orion Electric Components Co., Ltd.

KEY COMPETITORS

Alcatel Alsthom	LG Group	Nippon Steel
Bechtel	Marubeni	Samsung
General Motors	McDermott	Siemens
Hitachi	Mitsubishi	Ssangyong
Hyundai	Mitsui	Sumitomo
Kia Motors	NEC	Sunkyong

$=Won808 (Dec. 31, 1993)	Annual Growth	1984	1985	1986	1987	1988	1989	1990	1991	1992	1993
Sales (Won bil.)	12.3%	—	3,779	4,215	4,453	4,729	4,790	5,246	6,398	8,151	9,534
Net income (Won bil.)	4.7%	—	34	35	34	32	215	53	30	40	49
Income as % of sales	—	—	0.9%	0.8%	0.8%	0.7%	4.5%	1.0%	0.5%	0.5%	0.5%
Earnings per share (Won)	(10.2%)	—	—	982	794	570	3,151	710	350	444	516
Stock price – high (Won)	—	—	—	—	9,590	23,355	25,190	22,696	21,429	16,476	16,200
Stock price – low (Won)	—	—	—	—	5,743	9,224	18,091	11,835	13,810	7,143	9,800
Stock price – close (Won)	(8.8%)	—	—	6,913	9,017	23,209	20,887	17,596	14,667	12,190	15,000
P/E – high	—	—	—	—	12	41	8	32	61	37	31
P/E – low	—	—	—	—	7	16	6	17	39	16	19
Dividends per share	(24.0%)	—	—	—	340	340	449	41	43	48	50
Book value per share	0.3%	—	—	—	—	—	13,130	13,531	13,770	13,520	13,265
Employees	2.3%	—	—	—	—	—	—	—	—	78,727	76,986

1993 Year-end:
Debt ratio: 72.0%
Return on equity: 3.9%
Cash (bil.): Won644
Long-term debt (bil.):
Won1,475
No. of shares (mil.): 104
Dividend
Yield: 0.3%
Payout: 9.7%
Market value (mil.): $1,931
Sales (mil.): $11,799

**Stock Price History
High/Low 1987–93**

(chart values: 30,000 / 25,000 / 20,000 / 15,000 / 10,000 / 5,000 / 0)

Note: Financial information is for Daewoo Corporation only.

THE DAIEI, INC.

OVERVIEW

Daiei (originally The Housewives' Store Daiei) has, as its name implies, emerged from humble beginnings to become Japan's largest retailer. Although it is best known in Japan for its supermarket chain of over 400 super-stores, it also operates nearly 6,000 convenience and specialty retail stores. Beyond this, the firm has interests in a diverse range of businesses, including hotels, restaurants, real estate, credit cards, and tourist attractions. Daiei markets its own brands of apparel, dry goods, films, and soft drinks.

Although Daiei is based in Kobe, the site of a devastating earthquake in 1995, almost 40% of its sales come from the Osaka area.

In 1994 the company merged with retail affiliates Chujitsuya, Uneed Daiei, and Dainaha, boosting its nationwide network of stores. While less than 10% of Daiei's sales are generated outside Japan, like rivals Yaohan International, Nichii, Seiyu, and Jusco, it has been attracted to the growing consumer markets across Asia, especially China. It is building 2 supermarkets there, one in Beijing and one in Shanghai.

Daiei started a price war with Coca-Cola in 1994 when it imported Canadian generic cola and sold it in Japan for about 1/3 of the price of "the real thing." Coca-Cola was forced to follow suit and cut prices.

WHEN

Daiei founder Isao Nakauchi had some narrow escapes with death and the law before launching his first Daiei corner drugstore. As a Japanese soldier serving in the Philippines in WWII, he came under heavy fire but survived. With a penchant for tweaking the noses of the business establishment, he later was quoted as thanking sloppy American engineering (i.e., the bombs that fell near him did not explode) for his survival.

After the war he and his brother made a fortune in the illegal practice of selling penicillin at above the legal price. His brother was arrested for his part in the dealings.

Isao launched his Housewives' Store Daiei in Osaka in 1957 at the very depth of the post–Korean War depression in Japan. The low prices of a discount store appealed to hard-pressed consumers. The success of the first store prompted Nakauchi to open other stores in the Osaka area. He also took advantage of the depression at the wholesale level, buying up surplus goods from cash-strapped manufacturers.

In 1958 the company opened in Sannomiya and in that year introduced the concept of the discount store chain to Japan. Over the next 3 decades the company diversified the range of goods it offered consumers while staying focused on its philosophy of "For the Customers," i.e., low, low prices.

It expanded into Tokyo in 1964 with the purchase of Ittoku and opened its first suburban store in 1968 near Osaka. By 1972 Daiei was not only a nationwide chain, it was also Japan's #1 supermarket operator (with 75 superstores) and #2 retailer.

In 1974 the company overtook Mitsukoshi to become Japan's top retailer. A year later Daiei opened its first convenience store, Lawson.

Showing an increasing interest in sourcing from international businesses, Daiei teamed up with J. C. Penney in 1976 to sell J. C. Penney's goods in Japan, and in 1978 struck up a similar deal with Marks and Spencer. Joint ventures in the restaurant business followed in 1979 with Daiei opening Wendy's and Victoria Station restaurants. In 1980 the firm became the first retailer in Japan to top ¥1 trillion in sales.

Daiei made its first major inroads into the US market with the 1980 purchase of Holiday Mart, a three-store discount chain in Hawaii, and by setting up its first purchasing office, also in Hawaii. Over the next 14 years the company set up overseas purchasing offices in 12 countries under the names The Daiei, D International, The Emmac, The Hi-Daiei Trading Company, and Printemps Ginza.

In 1988 the company entered the hotel business by winning the contract for a $2.2 billion recreation center in Fukuoka.

In 1992 Daiei opened the first American-style membership warehouse in Japan, Kuo's Wholesale Membership Club, located in Kobe. Also that year Daiei acquired 42% of Chujitsuya, one of Japan's top 10 retailers.

Although Nakavchi is his long-time advocate of free market reform, 1994 private label products have threatened market leaders in Japan, and not just foreign companies such as Coca-Cola. Daiei has teamed up with Germany's Agfa to sell Daiei brand film at 1/3 of Japanese film giant Fuji's prices.

Nasdaq symbol: DAIEY (ADR)
Fiscal year ends: Last day in February

Chairman, President and CEO: Isao Nakauchi
Executive VC: Hiroshi Kawashima
EVP: Jun Nakauchi
VP, Head of China Project: Shigeyuki Tanishima
Senior Managing Director; Advisory Director, Government and Public Relations: Shohei Nomura
Senior Managing Director; Advisory Director, Financial and Accounting Relations: Kazumi Taguchi
Senior Managing Director; Divisional Manager and Advisory Director, General Affairs: Tadashi Inoue
Senior Managing Director; Divisional Manager, Human Resources Development Division: Hiromitsu Kameyama
CEO, Daiei USA: Aiko Tetsu
CFO, Daiei USA: Uno Kazuhiko
Director Human Resources, Daiei USA: Kanrad Sasaki
Auditors: Deloitte Touche Tohmatsu

HQ: 4-1-1, Minatojima, Nakamachi, Chuo-ku, Kobe 650, Japan
Phone: +81-78-302-5001
Fax: +81-78-302-5572
US HQ: Daiei USA, Inc., 801 Kaheka St., Honolulu, HI 96814
US Phone: 808-973-6600
US Fax: 808-941-6457

	1994 Stores
	No.
Convenience stores	4,836
Specialty stores	1,009
Superstores	401
Total	**6246**

	1994 Sales
	% of total
Food	35
Clothing & personal-care products	21
Household items	17
Hobby & sporting goods	6
Other	21
Total	**100**

Selected Subsidiaries

D International, Inc.	Holiday Action Gas, Inc.
Daiei Fusha	Japan Prints Systems
Daiei Photo Enterprise	Kobe Restaurant Systems
Daiei Real Estate	Maruetsu
Daiei Hawaii Investments, Inc.	Naha Meat
Dream Sports	Uneed Foods Systems
The Emmac	World Foods
The Hi-Daiei Trading Co., Ltd.	

Coca-Cola	McDonald's
Daimaru	Mitsui
Fuji Photo	Nichii
Hankyu	PepsiCo
Isetan	Seiyu
Ito-Yokado	Takashimaya
Jusco	Toys "R" Us
Kisoji	Uny
Marui	Xebio
Marukyu	Yaohan Intl.
Matsushita	Yaoko

$=¥112 (Dec. 31, 1993)	Annual Growth	1985	1986	1987	1988	1989	1990	1991	1992	1993	1994
Sales (¥ bil.)	9.8%	1,410	1,498	—	—	—	2,115	2,192	2,387	2,369	2,469
Net income (¥ bil.)	—	(9)	1	—	—	—	9	10	10	7	5
Income as % of sales	—	—	0.1%	—	—	—	0.4%	0.4%	0.4%	0.3%	0.2%
Earnings per share (¥)	—	(308)	36	—	—	—	247	246	249	177	105
Stock price – high (¥)[1]	—	737	750	1,760	1,818	2,340	3,340	3,050	1,530	1,140	1,570[1]
Stock price – low (¥)[1]	—	620	600	715	878	1,410	2,170	1,130	1,060	670	790
Stock price – close (¥)[1]	9.6%	631	715	1,280	1,430	2,180	3,120	1,220	1,090	805	1,440
P/E – high	—	—	21	—	—	—	14	12	6	6	15
P/E – low	—	—	17	—	—	—	9	5	4	4	8
Dividends per share (¥)	1.6%	150	150	—	—	—	165	165	165	165	165
Book value per share (¥)	(4.4%)	—	2,782	—	—	—	3,417	3,538	3,580	3,574	2,225
Employees	3.7%	—	—	—	—	—	16,400	17,000	16,800	19,000	19,000

1994 Year-end:
Debt ratio: 89.3%
Return on equity: 4.2%
Cash (bil.): ¥106
Long-term debt (bil.): ¥477
No. of shares (mil.): 520
Dividends
  Yield: 11.5%
  Payout: 157.6%
Market value (mil.): $7,274
Sales (mil.): $23,972

Stock Price History[1]
High/Low 1985–94

(chart y-axis: 4,000 / 3,500 / 3,000 / 2,500 / 2,000 / 1,500 / 1,000 / 500 / 0)

[1] Stock prices are for the prior calendar year.

THE DAI-ICHI KANGYO BANK, LIMITED

OVERVIEW

The world's largest bank, Dai-Ichi Kangyo Bank (DKB) is involved in a wide range of retail and wholesale banking activities in Japan and throughout the world. DKB also owns an interest in New York–based CIT Group, a commercial lending company.

DKB is the leading member of the Dai-Ichi Kangyo Group, the youngest and least formal of Japan's Big 6 *keiretsu*. As such it has provided financing for its member companies and their affiliates. However, this aspect of business has changed as companies increasingly turn to the capital markets rather than to bank loans, for financing.

In addition to a downturn in loan business, the bank has had to contend with the detritus of Japan's 1980s boom in the form of nonperforming domestic loans, for which new loss reserves must be set aside. The Japanese government has helped banks get these loans off their books by creating an agency similar to the US's RTC, except that the Cooperative Credit Purchasing Company buys the loans at a discount (still creating a loss for the bank). In 1994 DKB also began selling off its portfolio of nonperforming US loans.

DKB is counting on liberalized banking regulations in Japan to allow it to attract deposits by offering higher interest rates and to offer a wider range of services, including securities, which would bring back some of the activities lost to the bond markets.

WHEN

Dai-Ichi Kokuritsu (First National) Bank was founded in 1873 by Eiichi Shibusawa as the first bank organized under the Japanese National Bank Act of 1872. Shibusawa later helped found the Bank of Japan (which took over issuing currency from Dai-Ichi in 1883) and the Tokyo Stock Exchange. Although Shibusawa took Dai-Ichi public, the bank was nevertheless the focus of a minor *zaibatsu* of about 100 interconnected companies founded by Shibusawa. By 1905 Dai-Ichi trailed only Mitsui Bank in financial clout. During WWII Dai-Ichi merged with Mitsui but the 2 were later separated by US occupation forces.

In the face of a postwar capital crunch, Japan reassembled the pre-war *zaibatsu* around their lead banks, the 6 city banks, in order to promote the growth of Japanese business. The new groupings were known as *keiretsu*. Although many of Dai-Ichi's traditionally related companies reaffiliated with the bank, its greatest growth came after the 1971 government-sponsored merger with Nippon Kangyo Bank (founded 1897, administrator of the national lottery). DBK thus became the nation's largest bank.

A merger agreement calling for a strict balance of power between Dai-Ichi and Kangyo executives created a bureaucratic morass and institutionalized a culture clash between the 2 banks. Although merger-induced inertia slowed DKB's expansion overseas, the bank's size and Japan's rapid economic expansion enabled it to prosper.

In 1978 the bank formed the Sankin-kai (3rd Friday) council, whose members included leaders from 47 major Japanese firms. Unlike the other *keiretsu*, DKB includes companies that compete within fields.

In the 1970s DKB chose internal growth over acquisitions. Measured in assets DKB became the world's largest privately owned bank in 1984.

Japan enjoyed an unprecedented boom in the 1980s. As the world beat a path to its door to study its management and industrial methods, the country's commercial institutions embarked on a nationwide building boom and a worldwide shopping spree. By the end of the decade real estate and stock prices were wildly inflated and no one believed it would ever end. When it did, DKB and other banks were left holding bad loans and devalued assets. These cut into profits as interest income fell, loan loss reserves increased, and the value of security assets dropped. DKB tried to offset lower profitability in lending to large corporations by emphasizing consumer credit and services, but Japanese consumers have been seized by a crisis of confidence.

Although conditions in Japan have not improved (and will be further weakened by losses related to the Kobe earthquake of 1995) and European business has also been slow in recent years, the US and the rest of Asia and the Pacific are advancing quickly. The bank has continued to strengthen its position in Asia, establishing P.T. Indonesia Dai-Ichi Kangyo Bank in Jakarta (1991) and opening 4 representative offices (Beijing, Guangzhou, Dalian, and Xiamen) and a branch (Shanghai) in China.

OTC symbol: DAIKY (ADR)
Fiscal year ends: March 31

WHO

Chairman: Kuniji Miyazaki, age 62
President: Tadashi Okuda, age 60
Senior Managing Director: Hisao Kobayashi
Managing Director: Yoshiharu Mani
Managing Director, General Manager, and CFO, New York Branch: Toshiji Tokiwa
Director Human Resources, New York Branch: Edward Zinser
Auditors: Century Audit Corporation

WHERE

HQ: 1-5, Uchisaiwaicho 1-chome, Chiyoda-ku, Tokyo 100, Japan
Phone: +81-3-3596-1111
Fax: +81-3-3596-2179
US HQ: The Dai-Ichi Kangyo Bank, One World Trade Center, Ste. 4911, New York, NY 10048
US Phone: 212-466-5200
US Fax: 212-524-0579

The Dai-Ichi Kangyo Bank has 400 offices in Japan and 77 overseas offices in 30 countries.

	1994 Sales
	% of total
Japan	71
Europe	9
The Americas	9
Other Asia & Pacific	11
Total	**100**

WHAT

	1994 Assets	
	¥ bil.	% of total
Cash & equivalents	8,078	15
Call loans	449	0
Securities	5,671	11
Loans & bills discounted	35,600	65
Other	5,023	9
Total	**54,821**	**100**

	1994 Sales	
	¥ bil.	% of total
Interest on loans	1,606	58
Other interest	678	25
Fees & commissions	115	4
Other	368	13
Total	**2,767**	**100**

Selected Subsidiaries
Asian-American Merchant Bank Ltd. (Singapore)
Chekiang First Bank Ltd. (Hong Kong)
The CIT Group, Inc. (US)
DKB Asia Ltd. (Hong Kong)
DKB Financial Products, Inc. (US)
DKB Investment Management International Ltd. (UK)
P.T. Indonesia Dai-Ichi Kangyo Bank
Unibanco-União de Bancos Brasileiros SA (Brazil)
The Yellow River International Leasing Co., Ltd. (China)

KEY COMPETITORS

Barclays	HSBC
Canadian Imperial	Industrial Bank of Japan
Chase Manhattan	Mitsubishi
Citicorp	NatWest
Commerzbank	Royal Bank of Canada
Crédit Lyonnais	Sakura Bank
CS Holding	Sanwa Bank
Deutsche Bank	Sumitomo
Dresdner Bank	Tokai Bank
Fuji Bank	Union Bank of Switzerland

HOW MUCH

$=¥112 (Dec. 31, 1993)	9-Year Growth	1985	1986	1987	1988	1989	1990	1991	1992	1993	1994
Assets (¥ bil.)	5.7%	33,173	36,890	42,330	47,073	54,778	68,765	64,530	63,248	56,301	54,821
Net income (¥ bil.)	(16.5%)	59	63	102	152	199	145	92	84	47	12
Income as % of assets	—	0.2%	0.2%	0.2%	0.3%	0.4%	0.2%	0.1%	0.1%	0.1%	0.0%
Earnings per share (¥)	(18.3%)	23	25	40	59	75	51	30	27	15	4
Stock price – high (¥)[1]	—	1,291	1,791	1,825	3,223	3,400	3,750	3,180	2,710	2,490	2,440
Stock price – low (¥)[1]	—	456	1,244	1,367	1,796	2,590	3,120	1,600	1,910	1,050	1,630
Stock price – close (¥)[1]	3.6%	1,291	1,527	1,777	2,730	3,380	3,160	1,950	2,410	1,670	1,770
P/E – high	—	59	78	73	81	58	50	62	100	167	—
P/E – low	—	21	54	55	45	44	42	31	71	70	—
Dividends per share (¥)	2.9%	6.60	6.80	7.50	7.50	8.00	8.50	8.50	9.0	8.50	8.50
Book value per share (¥)	11.1%	247	276	309	406	542	640	619	637	642	637
Employees[2]	(1.1%)	21,102	20,226	19,293	18,663	18,441	18,466	18,640	18,703	18,849	19,189

1994 Year-end:
Debt ratio: 47.0%
Return on equity: 0.6%
Equity as % of assets: 3.6%
No. of shares (mil.): 3,121
Dividends
 Yield: 0.5%
 Payout: —
Market value (mil.): $49,318
Assets (mil.): $489,469
Sales (mil.): $24,703

**Stock Price History[1]
High/Low 1985–94**

(chart y-axis: 4,000 / 3,500 / 3,000 / 2,500 / 2,000 / 1,500 / 1,000 / 500 / 0)

[1] Stock prices are for the prior calendar year. [2] Non-consolidated

DAIMLER-BENZ AKTIENGESELLSCHAFT

OVERVIEW

Renowned as a preeminent luxury car manufacturer, Daimler-Benz is the world's oldest auto maker, the world's top truck maker, and Germany's biggest industrial company. Through its 4 core businesses, Daimler is a huge automotive, aerospace, industrial, and technology conglomerate. In 1993 Daimler became the first German company to be listed on the New York Stock Exchange.

During the 1980s CEO Edzard Reuter tried to make Daimler into a diversified global titan, but its fabled cars and trucks still accounted for 62% of 1993 revenues. High price tags, oversized cars, and Japanese competition have caused sales to tumble since 1992, causing its worst performance since World War II. As a result Daimler was forced to go through a painful consolidation, cutting 25,000 jobs and pruning noncore businesses to reduce costs. It also lowered its sights: Daimler now will also produce subcompacts, minivans, and sporty, but upscale, 4-wheel drive vehicles. It also upped the production of autos, its cash cows, and moved some manufacturing outside high-cost Germany. It may also sell off other nonstrategic businesses. Reuter retired early and was replaced in 1995 by Jürgen Schrempp, CEO of Deutsche Aerospace, one of Daimler's core companies. Daimler's chief owners are Deutsche Bank (28.13%), Mercedes Holding (25.23%), and the Emirate of Kuwait (14%).

WHEN

Daimler-Benz is the product of a 1926 merger between companies started by German automobile pioneers Gottlieb Daimler and Karl Benz. Daimler and Wilhelm Maybach had set up an engine workshop near Stuttgart in 1882. In the 1880s they created the first motorcycle and sold their engines to French automakers. In 1890 they incorporated as Daimler Engine. Austro-Hungarian Emil Jellinek arranged to buy 36 racing cars from Daimler in 1900, with the understanding that they would be named after his daughter Mercedes. The cars won a 1901 race, and Daimler registered the Mercedes mark the next year.

Benz & Companies was established in Mannheim in 1883 and by 1886 had patented a 3-wheeled car. Despite crashing into a brick wall in the first public demonstration of his car, Benz enjoyed quick success, and by 1899 his company was the world's #1 automaker.

Ford's Model T and WWI hurt both Daimler and Benz, and the companies merged in 1926. Daimler-Benz recovered in the 1930s as Germany built *autobahns* (highways). The company turned out military vehicles and airplane engines during WWII, but most factories were destroyed by bombing.

In the 1950s Germany's postwar recovery led to strong demand for cars and trucks. Daimler bought Auto Union (Audi) in 1958 (sold to Volkswagen in 1966). Acquisitions in the 1960s strengthened its positions in truck and engine markets.

Mercedes sales expanded worldwide in the 1970s. The luxury car appealed to the growing high end of the car market. The oil crisis spared Mercedes, partly because of the wealth of its car customers.

Fearing increased Japanese competition in the luxury car market, Edzard Reuter, then vice-chairman, sought to diversify the company. In 1981 Daimler bought a US heavy truck maker, Freightliner. In 1985 Daimler bought 65.6% of Dornier, all of MTU, and 56% of AEG (consumer and industrial electrical products), all West German firms.

As chairman from 1987 through 1994, Reuter was the architect behind Daimler's aggressive expansion. In 1991 Daimler bought a 10% stake in Metallgesellschaft (metals) and an indirect stake in Cap Gemini Sogeti (computer services, France).

In 1992 Daimler bought a controlling share in Fokker, a Dutch airplane manufacturer, with which Reuter created DASA (Deutsche Aerospace), one of its core companies. That same year Daimler acquired a 5% stake in Ssangyong Motor, a South Korean automotive company; its AEG subsidiary agreed to share production of appliances and exchange shares with Sweden's Electrolux; and Daimler joined with Siemens and Thyssen to promote plans for a German high-speed railroad, Magnetschnellbahn (magnetic fast train).

In 1993 Daimler chose Tuscaloosa, Alabama, as the site of it first American Mercedes factory and engineered a new C class of Mercedes sedans, its smallest, that is more fuel-efficient and much less expensive than the unpopular S line.

NYSE symbol: DAI (ADR)
Fiscal year ends: December 31

Chairman, Board of Management:
Jürgen E. Schrempp, age 49
Board of Management, Finance and Materials:
Gerhard Liener, age 61
Board of Management, Personnel: Hans-
Wolfgang Hirschbrunn, age 60
**President and CEO, Daimler-Benz North
America:** Timothy R. Pohl
VP Treasury, Daimler-Benz North America:
Harvey Traison
**Director of Human Resources, Mercedes-Benz
North America:** Janice Simonson
Auditors: KPMG Deutsche Treuhand-Gesellschaft

HQ: D-70546 Stuttgart 80, Germany
Phone: +49-711-1-7-22-87
Fax: +49-711-1-79-41-09
US HQ: Daimler-Benz North America Corp., 375
Park Ave., Ste. 3001, New York, NY 10152-3001
US Phone: 212-308-3622
US Fax: 212-826-0356

Daimler-Benz operates in 55 countries.

	1993 Sales	
	DM mil.	% of total
Germany	38,319	39
North America	17,138	18
Latin America	5,238	5
Other Europe	25,303	26
Other regions	11,739	12
Total	**97,737**	**100**

	1993 Sales	
	DM mil.	% of total
Mercedes-Benz	64,696	62
Deutsche Aerospace	18,626	18
AEG	11,012	11
Daimler-Benz InterServices (debis)	9,500	9
Adjustments	(6,097)	—
Total	**97,737**	**100**

Corporate Units
Mercedes-Benz
   Luxury passenger cars, 4-wheel-drive vehicles (Europe
   only), commercial vans, trucks, buses, special purpose
   vehicles (Unimog), and industrial diesel engines
Deutsche Aerospace (DASA, 85.3%)
   Aircraft, space systems, defense and civil systems, and
   propulsion systems
AEG Daimler-Benz Industrie (80.2%)
   Automation, domestic appliances, electrotechnical
   systems, microelectronics, and rail systems
Daimler-Benz InterServices (debis)
   Software, insurance, financial services, trading,
   marketing services, debitel (mobile communications)

Akzo Nobel	Isuzu	Renault
BMW	Koç	Saab-Scania
British Aerospace	Koor	Siemens
Chrysler	Lada	Software AG
Detroit Diesel	Mannesmann	Tata
Dial	Maytag	Thomson SA
Fiat	Mazda	Toyota
Ford	Navistar	Volkswagen
General Motors	Nissan	Volvo
Hino Motors	PACCAR	Whirlpool
Honda	Peugeot	Zil
Hyundai	Porsche	

$=DM1.74 (Dec. 31, 1993)	9-Year Growth	1984	1985	1986	1987	1988	1989[1]	1990	1991	1992	1993
Sales (DM mil.)	9.4%	43,505	52,409	65,498	67,475	73,495	76,392	85,500	95,010	98,549	97,737
Net income (DM mil.)	(6.9%)	1,145	1,735	1,805	1,787	1,675	1,700	1,684	1,872	1,418	602
Income as % of sales	—	2.6%	3.3%	2.8%	2.6%	2.3%	2.2%	2.0%	2.0%	1.4%	0.6%
Earnings per share (DM)[1]	(7.9%)	27	41	43	42	40	36	36	40	30	13
Stock price – high (DM)	—	517	1,041	1,256	1,220	772	831	955	794	817	850
Stock price – low (DM)	—	417	481	896	575	527	626	550	507	501	530
Stock price – close (DM)	6.5%	480	1,009	1,233	575	737	828	554	744	537	846
P/E – high	—	19	25	29	29	19	23	27	20	27	66
P/E – low	—	15	12	21	14	13	17	15	13	16	41
Dividends per share (DM)[2]	(0.7%)	8.5	8.5	11.8	12.0	12.0	12.0	12.0	12.0	13.0	8.0
Book value per share (DM)	7.2%	200	225	233	210	241	348	364	391	394	373
Employees	7.0%	199,872	231,077	319,965	326,288	338,749	368,226	376,785	379,252	376,467	366,736

1993 Year-end:
Debt ratio: 52.3%
Return on equity: 3.4%
Cash (mil.): DM9,843
Long-term debt (mil.): DM10,990
No. of shares (mil.): 47
Dividends
   Yield: 0.9%
   Payout: 61.9%
Market value (mil.): $22,900
Sales (mil.): $56,171

**Stock Price History
High/Low 1984–93**

[1] 1989 results include minority interests.   [2] Not including rights offerings

GROUPE DANONE

OVERVIEW

French diversified food group BSN adopted the name of its leading international brand, renaming itself Groupe Danone in 1994. Danone is one of the world's top 6 food producers. It is the world's #1 producer of fresh dairy products and the #2 producer of mineral water and biscuits. In Europe Danone is #1 in dairy products, mineral water, biscuits, sauces, and condiments; #2 in pasta, beer, and glass containers; and #3 in ready-to-serve dishes. The company was a player in the dramatic 1992 takeover of Source Perrier by Nestlé. By siding with Nestlé it acquired the Volvic mineral water brand, one of Perrier's

largest. Danone and Unilever jointly develop and sell ice cream and yogurt desserts.

The company has been expanding internationally during the 1990s through investments, acquisitions, and joint ventures. In Eastern Europe Danone established its presence in Hungary, the Czech Republic, Slovakia, Poland, and Bulgaria. In Asia the company introduced its Danone products in China and Thailand and acquired Amoy (sauces, Hong Kong) and Best (meat products, New Zealand), as well as Nabisco's Asian subsidiaries. Founder and first chairman Antoine Riboud still runs the company.

WHEN

In 1965 Antoine Riboud replaced his uncle as chairman of family-run Souchon-Neuvesel, a Lyon-based glass bottle maker. Befitting a man whose brothers were Jean, then chairman of Schlumberger, and Marc, an internationally recognized photographer, Antoine quickly made his mark on the company. Riboud's first move was to merge (1966) with Boussois, a major French flat-glass manufacturer, creating BSN. In an audacious attempt to expand the company's glass business, he made a bid in 1968 for Saint-Gobain, a diversified French glass manufacturer 3 times BSN's size. The attempt failed.

Undaunted, Riboud enlarged BSN's glass business and filled the company's bottles by acquiring well-established beverage and food concerns. In 1970 BSN purchased Brasseries Kronenbourg (France's largest brewer), Société Européenne de Brasseries (beer, France), and Evian (mineral water, France). The 1972 acquisition of Glaverbel (Belgium) gave BSN 50% of Europe's flat-glass market. A 1973 merger with Gervais Danone (yogurt, cheese, Panzani pasta; France) put BSN into pan-European brand-name food products for the first time and raised sales to $1.7 billion.

In the 1970s increasing energy costs depressed flat-glass earnings. BSN elected to divest its flat-glass businesses, selling the last of them in 1982. In 1978 and 1979 the company acquired interests in brewers in Belgium, Spain, and Italy. BSN bought Dannon, the leading US yogurt maker, in 1981. The company became a major player in the French champagne industry, taking over Pommery and Lanson in 1984. BSN established a strong presence in the Italian pasta market by buying

a majority ownership of Ponte (1985) and a minority interest in Agnesi (1986).

BSN purchased Generale Biscuit, the 3rd largest biscuit company in the world, in 1986, and RJR Nabisco's European cookie and snack food business for $2.5 billion in 1989, selling Walkers Crisps and Smiths Crisps (snack foods) to PepsiCo for $1.35 billion to help finance the acquisition. The next year BSN sold Mother's Cookies (US).

In a series of acquisitions starting in 1986, BSN took over the largest mineral water companies in Italy and Spain, several European pasta makers, and other food companies throughout Europe. The company has been active in strategic alliances, taking a 20% (now 24.4%) stake in Birra Peroni (beer, Italy, 1988), a 50% (now 84.7%) interest in Alken-Maes (beer, Belgium, 1988), a 50% interest in Guangzhou Dairy (yogurt, China, 1989), and, more recently, 24% of San Miguel (beer, Spain, 1992) and 64% (now 79.2%) of Italaquae (mineral water, Italy, 1992). Also in 1992 BSN and Nestlé formed a partnership to acquire Czechoslovakia's largest food producer, Cokoladovny. BSN began selling its popular Danone yogurt in Czechoslovakia and Hungary that year as well.

The company suffered some adverse publicity in 1993 when Heineken was forced to recall thousands of the company's bottles in 8 countries after a batch was found to contain glass splinters.

In 1994 Riboud promoted his son Franck, previously director of business development, to the #2 slot in the company. In that same year the company adopted its new corporate name, Group Danone.

OTC symbol: GPDNY (ADR)
Fiscal year ends: December 31

Chairman and CEO: Antoine Riboud, age 75
VC and President: Franck Riboud
SEVP: Philippe Lenain
SVP Finance: Christian Laubie
SVP Human Resources: Rose-Marie Van Lerberghe
SVP Containers: Jacques Demarty
SVP Biscuits: Philippe Jaeckin
SVP Dairy Products Europe: Jacques Vincent
President and CEO, The Dannon Co. (US):
Patrick Gournay
CFO, The Dannon Co. (US): Mike Gournay
Director Personnel, The Dannon Co. (US):
Richard Corcoran
Auditors: Guérard Viala PSAudit (Price
Waterhouse)

WHERE

HQ: 7, rue de Téhéran, 75008 Paris, France
Phone: +33-1-44-35-20-20
Fax: +33-1-42-25-67-16
US HQ: The Dannon Co., 120 White Plains Rd.,
Tarrytown, NY 10591
US Phone: 914-366-9700
US Fax: 914-366-2805

	1993 Sales % of total
France	46
Italy	15
Spain	9
Other Europe	21
Other countries	9
Total	**100**

WHAT

	1993 Sales		1993 Operating Income	
	FF mil.	% of total	FF mil.	% of total
Dairy	25,898	36	2,321	36
Grocery	13,142	18	970	15
Biscuits	12,949	18	828	13
Containers	6,663	10	556	8
Beer	6,395	9	808	13
Mineral water	6,353	9	971	15
Adjustments	(1,293)	—	(103)	—
Total	**70,108**	**100**	**6,351**	**100**

Major Brand Names

Dairy Products	Liebig (soup)	Beer
Danone	Maille	Cristal
Delisle	(condiments)	Kanterbräu
Galbani	Panzani (pasta)	Kronenbourg
		Peroni
Grocery Products	**Biscuits**	San Miguel
Agnesi (pasta)	Belin	Tourtel
Amora (condiments)	Jacob's	
Amoy (sauces)	LU	**Mineral Water**
Birkel (pasta)	Saiwa	Badoit
Blédina (baby food)		Evian
HP (sauces)	**Containers**	Ferrarelle
Lea & Perrins	VG	Volvic
(Worcestershire	VMC	
sauce)		

KEY COMPETITORS

Adolph Coors	Clorox	Kirin
Allied Domecq	CPC	Nestlé
Anheuser-Busch	General Mills	Nord Est
Associated Milk	Grand	PepsiCo
Producers	Metropolitan	Philip Morris
Bass	Guinness	RJR Nabisco
Bongrain	Heineken	St.-Gobain
Borden	Heinz	Sandoz
Cadbury Schweppes	Idia	TLC Beatrice
Campbell Soup	John Labatt	Unilever
Carlsberg	Kellogg	

HOW MUCH

$=FF5.82 (Dec. 31, 1993)	9-Year Growth	1984	1985	1986	1987	1988	1989	1990	1991	1992	1993
Sales (FF mil.)	11.1%	27,293	28,475	33,623	37,156	42,177	48,669	52,897	66,069	70,840	70,108
Net income (FF mil.)	18.3%	755	798	1,081	1,550	2,189	2,698	3,091	3,445	3,638	3,422
Income as % of sales	—	2.8%	2.8%	3.2%	4.2%	5.2%	5.5%	5.8%	5.2%	5.1%	4.9%
Earnings per share (FF)	12.0%	18	19	25	31	38	45	49	53	56	51
Stock price – high (FF)	—	263	251	432	493	591	709	825	925	1,085	1,010
Stock price – low (FF)	—	214	179	247	337	342	553	623	635	902	823
Stock price – close (FF)	17.5%	218	250	395	394	589	704	645	925	954	935
P/E – high	—	14	13	18	16	16	16	17	17	20	20
P/E – low	—	12	9	10	11	9	12	13	12	16	16
Dividends per share (FF)	13.5%	5.00	5.45	6.36	7.73	9.09	10.45	11.82	13.18	15.00	15.67
Book value per share (FF)	11.8%	172	178	201	243	275	319	370	424	435	470
Employees	4.7%	37,340	33,447	42,780	41,285	42,234	49,693	45,254	59,158	58,063	56,419

1993 Year-end:
Debt ratio: 38.4%
Return on equity: 11.3%
Cash (mil.): FF3,927
Long-term debt (mil.): FF17,223
No. of shares (mil.): 68
Dividends
  Yield: 1.7%
  Payout: 30.7%
Market value (mil.): $10,741
Sales (mil.): $11,863

Stock Price History High/Low 1984–93

DELOITTE & TOUCHE LLP

The product of a 1989 merger of accounting firms Deloitte Haskins & Sells and Touche Ross, Deloitte & Touche is the 3rd largest of the Big 6 accounting firms in the US. Outside the US the company operates as Deloitte Touche Tohmatsu International, the 5th largest accounting firm in the world.

Deloitte & Touche's worldwide revenues were up in 1993 and 1994. The firm plans to emphasize its specialized service lines, including mergers and acquisitions, information technology, international tax, cost reduction, manufacturing technology, and employee benefits. The firm is also focusing on retaining and promoting more women. In

1993 it created an Advisory Council on the Advancement of Women, chaired by Lynn Martin, former secretary of labor.

Claims against Big 6 accounting firms have reached an estimated $30 billion in recent years. Deloitte, like its counterparts, has faced a continuing stream of lawsuits as plaintiffs' attorneys name the accounting firms in management fraud suits, blaming them for negligence in oversight.

In 1994 Deloitte was named in a $1.1 billion suit, along with Arthur Andersen and Prudential Securities, alleging that Prudential, with the accounting firms' help, inflated the prices of several limited partnerships.

In 1845 — 3 years after the UK initiated an income tax — William Welch Deloitte opened his accounting office in London. Deloitte was the grandson of Count de Loitte, who had fled France during the Reign of Terror (1793–94), abandoned his title, and made a living as a French teacher.

In the early years of his accountancy, William Deloitte, a former staff member of the Official Assignee in Bankruptcy of the City of London, solicited business from bankrupts. During the 1850s and 1860s, Parliament established general rules for forming limited liability companies, which required companies to hire accountants. Deloitte performed accounting for the Great Western Railway and, later, for telegraph companies.

As the firm grew, Deloitte added partners, among them John Griffiths (1869). Griffiths visited the US in 1888, and in 1890 the Deloitte firm opened a branch on Wall Street. Branches followed in Cincinnati (1905), Chicago (1912), Montreal (1912), Boston (1930), and Los Angeles (1945). In 1952 the Deloitte firm formed an alliance with the accounting firm of Haskins & Sells, which operated 34 US offices.

Deloitte developed a reputation as a thorough, and therefore expensive, firm. By the late 1970s a partner proclaimed to Fortune, "We want to be the Cadillac, not the Ford, of the profession." But the firm, which was renamed Deloitte Haskins & Sells in 1978, began to lose its conservatism as competition for auditing contracts and for management consulting clients became more intense.

When government regulators nudged the profession to drop restrictions on advertising, Deloitte Haskins & Sells was the first Big 8 firm with aggressive ads extolling its virtues as an advisor.

In 1984, in a move that foreshadowed the merger mania to come, Deloitte Haskins & Sells tried to merge with Price Waterhouse. However, British partners in Price Waterhouse objected to the deal, and it was dropped.

In the US the Big 8 accounting firms became the Big 6 in 1989. Ernst & Whinney merged with Arthur Young to become Ernst & Young, and Deloitte Haskins & Sells teamed up with Touche Ross & Company to form Deloitte & Touche. Touche Ross had been founded in New York in 1947. Before the merger, it had earned a reputation as the hard-charging, bare-knuckled bad boy of the Big 8, running into controversy for its role in junk-bond deals that turned sour during the 1980s. In 1992 California regulators sued Deloitte & Touche, claiming that it had been the "auditor of choice" of a "daisy chain" linking Drexel Burnham junk-bond king Michael Milken to failed Executive Life.

More legal grief came to Deloitte & Touche the same year. The RTC sued the firm for $150 million in connection with its audits of now-defunct Otero Savings, and in 1994 Deloitte & Touche agreed to pay the US government $312 million to settle lawsuits brought by the RTC, the FDIC, and the Office of Thrift Supervision.

International partnership
Fiscal year ends: May 31

Chairman and CEO: J. Michael Cook
Chairman and CEO, International: Edward A.
Kangas
Managing Partner: James E. Copeland
CFO: Robert W. Pivik
**National Director, Marketing and
Communications:** Gary Gerard
General Counsel: Howard J. Krongard
National Director, Human Resources: James H.
Wall

WHERE

HQ: 10 Westport Rd., Wilton, CT 06897
Phone: 203-761-3000
Fax: 203-834-2200

Deloitte & Touche LLP operates offices in more
than 100 US cities and in more than 108
countries worldwide.

WHAT

	1994 US Sales
	% of total
Accounting & auditing	52
Tax advice & planning	22
Management consulting	26
Total	**100**

Selected Services
Accounting and auditing
Information technology consulting
Management consulting
Mergers and acquisitions consulting
Tax advice and planning

Representative Clients

Bank of New York	Lowes
BASF	Mayo Foundation
Boeing	Merrill Lynch
Bridgestone	MetLife
Chrysler	Mitsubishi
Dow Chemical	Mitsui
Equitable	Monsanto
Federated	PPG
Flagstar	Procter & Gamble
General Motors	RJR Nabisco
Great A&P	Rockwell
Litton Industries	Sears

Affiliated Firms
Actuarial, Benefits, and Compensation Group
(consultation on employee pay and benefits)
Braxton Associates (strategic planning)
Deloitte & Touche Eastern Europe
Deloitte & Touche Valuation Group (business
valuations)
Douglass Group of Deloitte & Touche (health care
facility planning and strategy)
DRT Systems Ltd. (computer consulting)
DTTI International
Garr Consulting Group (consulting to retail and
wholesale industries)
Polaris Consulting Services (database, systems
development)
Tohmatsu & Co. (auditing, Japan)

KEY COMPETITORS

Arthur Andersen	Hewitt
Bain & Co.	H&R Block
Booz Allen & Hamilton	IBM
Boston Consulting Group	A.T. Kearney
Coopers & Lybrand	KPMG
Delta Consulting	Marsh & McLennan
Electronic Data Systems	McKinsey & Co.
Ernst & Young	Price Waterhouse

HOW MUCH

	Annual Growth	1985	1986	1987	1988	1989	1990	1991	1992	1993	1994
Sales ($ mil.)	11.7%	1,926	2,339	2,950	3,760	3,900	4,200	4,500	4,800	5,000	5,200
Deloitte Haskins & Sells	—	953	1,188	1,500	1,920						
Touche Ross	—	973	1,151	1,450	1,840						
Offices (US)[1]	(5.9%)	192	205	195	196	125	125	116	116	113	111
Partners (US)[1]	(1.4%)	1,619	1,600	1,590	1,600	1,652	1,670	1,525	1,472	1,426	1,430
Employees (US)[1]	(0.6%)	17,253	17,521	18,252	19,276	19,668	19,500	16,500	15,300	15,800	16,310

Sales ($ mil.)
1985–94

[1] US only; 1985–1988, combined Deloitte Haskins & Sells, Touche Ross

DENTSU INC.

The world's largest independent advertising agency and the 4th largest among advertising organizations, Dentsu has its eye on Asia these days. The reason, of course, is that the Tokyo-based company's clients have their eyes on Asia. With many Japanese companies expanding their sales activities in the Far East, Dentsu is setting up offices across Asia to grab their business.

Dentsu dominates the Japanese advertising business, with more than twice the sales of its nearest competitor. However, the company has seen its Japanese market share shrink as the style of Japanese advertising has changed. Traditionally, Japanese agencies have had competing clients, but as advertis-ing has become more aggressive (with adver-tisements drawing direct comparisons to ri-vals, a long-time taboo in Japan), Dentsu has lost clients to other agencies, who don't have the clients' rivals on their roster.

Dentsu continues to expand beyond tradi-tional advertising into other areas. It provides film and video production, multimedia devel-opment, market research, graphic design, and print production services. The company is also moving into multimedia software; it has signed a deal with Matsushita to develop game software for the 3DO video game player.

The Kyodo and Jiji news services own 28.3% and 20.1% of Dentsu, respectively.

Sino-Japanese war correspondent Hoshiro Mitsunaga wanted to set up a Japanese wire service for faster reporting from the front lines. In 1901 he founded 2 companies: Tele-graphic Service Company and Japan Advertis-ing Ltd. Mitsunaga's wire service allowed newspapers to pay their bills with advertising space, which was resold through his advertis-ing agency. In 1907 he merged the compa-nies. The company later became known as Dentsu, a contraction of part of the old name, Nihon Denpo-Tsushin Sha (Japan Tele-graphic Communication Company). After gaining Japanese rights to the United Press wire in 1908, Dentsu was able to extract fa-vorable advertising rates from its clients.

In 1936 Japan's government seized and consolidated all news services into Domei, a propaganda machine it controlled, and gave Domei half of Dentsu's stock. The govern-ment forced the consolidation of all advertis-ing agencies into 12 entities in 1943. Future Dentsu president Hideo Yoshida's efforts re-sulted in Dentsu controlling 4 of the 12.

During the postwar occupation Domei was dismantled, and Dentsu stock was trans-ferred to the Kyodo and Jiji news agencies. Yoshida became president in 1947; he hired executives previously purged from their com-panies by occupation forces and employed sons of politicians and business leaders, gain-ing invaluable business connections and es-tablishing Dentsu's successful formula of building personal connections and loyalty.

Yoshida's Dentsu essentially created the Japanese TV broadcasting industry by investing in start-up broadcasters. Gratitude of the broadcasters translated into preferen-tial treatment for Dentsu and led to the agency's dominance of Japanese TV advertis-ing through decades of explosive growth.

In 1973 Dentsu became the world's larg-est advertising agency. But by the early 1980s growth had slowed in parallel with Japan's economy, upon which Dentsu remained de-pendent. Having failed to follow its clients as they expanded overseas, Dentsu derived only 1% of its revenue from foreign advertising in 1980. To expand abroad, the agency teamed with Young & Rubicam (US) in a 1981 joint venture to form DYR. In 1986 foreign billings still amounted to only 7% of revenues, and the next year Saatchi & Saatchi passed Dentsu as the world's #1 advertising group. In the same year Eurocom, a French agency, joined the Young & Rubicam/Dentsu partner-ship — renamed HDM Worldwide after Havas (Eurocom's parent), Dentsu, and Marsteller (a Y&R agency) — and brought with it hopes for expansion in Europe.

In the late 1980s a domestic consumption boom lifted Dentsu's revenue, but the agency continued to struggle abroad as Eurocom pulled out of HDM Worldwide in 1990. The newly named Dentsu, Young & Rubicam Partnerships reorganized to focus on North America, Asia, and Australia, and Dentsu joined with Collett Dickenson Pearce to re-main in Europe after HDM's withdrawal.

In 1994 Dentsu acquired UK agency Travis Dale from Collett Dickenson Pearce and renamed it Travis Sennett Sully Ross.

Private company
Fiscal year ends: March 31

Chairman: Gohei Kogure
President: Yutaka Narita
EVP: Toshiro Toyota
Senior Managing Director: Kaushiko Yamashita
Senior Managing Director: Yuzo Irie
Senior Managing Director: Mutso Fuji
Senior Managing Director: Fumio Suzuki
Senior Managing Director: Shuzo Ishikawa
President and CEO, DCA Advertising (US):
  Kiyoshi Eguchi
Treasurer, DCA Advertising (US): Masaki
  Yaegashi
**SVP and Director Administration (Personnel),
  DCA Advertising (US):** Diane Dennis
Auditors: KPMG Peat Marwick

HQ: 1-11 Tsukiji, Chuo-ku, Tokyo 104, Japan
Phone: +81-3-5551-5599
Fax: +81-3-5551-2013 (Corporate
  Communications)
US HQ: DCA Advertising, 666 Fifth Ave, 9th Fl.,
  New York, NY 10103
US Phone: 212-397-3333
US Fax: 212-397-3322

Dentsu and its subsidiaries have offices in 34
countries.

	1994 Sales
	% of total
Japan	91
Europe	2
US	1
Other countries	6
Total	**100**

	1994 Billings	
	$ mil.	% of total
Television	4,882	42
Newspapers	1,934	17
Promotion	1,666	14
Creative services	1,016	9
Magazines	473	4
Radio	300	3
Other	1,242	11
Total	**11,513**	**100**

Selected Subsidiaries
AD Dentsu Tokyo, Inc. (advertising)
cdp europe (44.8%, advertising, UK)
DCA Advertising (US)
Dentsu Actis Inc. (printing and premium production)
Dentsu Cotec Inc. (typesetting and engraving)
Dentsu Deutschland GMBH (advertising, Germany)
Dentsu EYE Inc. (advertising)
Dentsu Institute for Human Studies (think tank)
Dentsu PR Center Ltd. (public relations)
Dentsu Prox Inc. (media production)
Dentsu Research, Inc. (market research)
Dentsu, Sudler & Hennessy Inc. (advertising)
Dentsu Wunderman Direct Inc. (direct marketing)
Dentsu, Young & Rubicam Inc. (advertising, 50%)
Information Services International-Dentsu, Ltd. (joint
  venture with General Electric, information services)

Representative Advertising Clients

All Nippon Airways	Federal Express
Apple	Hitachi
Bridgestone	Matsushita
Canon	Nestlé
Central Japan	Royal/Dutch Shell
Railway	Sanyo
Colgate-Palmolive	TDK
Dai-Ichi Kangyo	Toshiba
Daimler-Benz	Toyota
Dole	V.F.

N W Ayer	Havas
Bozell	Interpublic Group
D'Arcy Masius	Leo Burnett
Euro RSCG	Omnicom Group
Grey Advertising	Saatchi & Saatchi
Hakuhodo	WPP Group

	9-Year Growth	1985	1986	1987	1988	1989	1990	1991	1992	1993	1994
Sales ($ mil.)	14.7%	472	524	755	1,055	1,274	1,166	1,423	1,481	1,385	1,622
Net income ($ mil.)	(1.3%)	27	30	38	62	102	96	140	134	55	24
Income as % of sales	—	5.7%	5.7%	5.0%	5.9%	8.0%	8.2%	9.9%	9.1%	4.0%	1.5%
Employees	0.3%	5,803	5,759	5,844	5,867	5,896	5,893	6,000	5,811	5,834	5,972

1994 Year-end:
Debt ratio: 31.3%
Return on equity: 1.6%
Cash (mil.): $622
Current ratio: 1.43
Long-term debt (mil.): $442

Net Income
($ mil.) 1985–94

DEUTSCHE BANK AG

OVERVIEW

Deutsche Bank, Germany's largest bank, is one of the largest in the world, with operations in Europe, North America, and Asia. In addition to commercial, retail, and investment banking, the company has insurance, leasing, and real estate operations and is one of Germany's largest investors in private industry.

Deutsche Bank's growth has been slowed by the strains of German reunification and by the recession in Europe and Japan. The company also suffered losses in 1994 when real estate developer Jurgen Schneider disappeared after having fraudulently obtained

DM1.2 billion in loans. The bank's luster was further tarnished by the near collapse of Metallgesellschaft, of which the bank was a major stockholder. In the face of these problems, as well as its investment in derivatives, the bank has been forced to increase its loss reserves, which adversely affects income.

Deutsche Bank, which calls itself a universal bank to reflect the breadth of its services, is in the process of turning itself into what Americans have termed a financial supermarket by increasing the range of services available in branches. Selected branches now offer life and pension insurance.

WHEN

In 1870, as Germany united, Deutsche Bank opened its doors in Berlin under the leadership of Georg von Siemens. The company was quick to branch out in Germany and overseas, opening a London office in 1873. The bank's foreign business allowed it to survive a German financial crisis (1873–75) and to expand by buying other German banks.

In the late 1880s Deutsche Bank helped finance the electrification of Germany (carried out by Siemens AG) and the construction of railroads in the US (Northern Pacific) and the Ottoman Empire. Von Siemens managed the bank until his death in 1901.

In the economic chaos after WWI the bank survived by merging with its largest competitor, Disconto-Gesellschaft. Deutsche Bank helped finance the Nazi war machine by buying government debt. In 1945 Allied authorities split the bank's West German operations into 10 separate institutions and stripped it of its overseas operations. The bank became extinct in the East. Deutsche Bank was reassembled in 1957.

Led by Hermann Abs (who died in 1994), the bank rapidly regained international prominence. After concentrating on commercial banking for a relatively small group of West German companies in the 1940s and 1950s, it began offering a wide array of retail banking services in the 1960s. Between 1957 and 1970 the bank expanded from 345 to 1,100 branches. It introduced Eurochecks (personal checks accepted throughout Western Europe) in 1969 to combat US bank credit cards. In the 1960s and 1970s Deutsche Bank helped finance the West German export boom and became a major

Euromarket dealer. In 1975, with the German government worried about domination by foreign investors, the bank bought a 29% stake (now 24%, which it would like to reduce further) in Daimler-Benz, countering a bid from the Shah of Iran.

Deutsche Bank opened its first US operation in 1971 with an investment banking office and set up its first bank branch in 1978. In the 1980s it continued to diversify geographically, buying Bank of America's Italian subsidiary (1986) and the UK merchant bank Morgan Grenfell (1989), and economically, setting up DB Leben (life insurance, 1989).

Deutsche Bank leader Alfred Herrhausen, a symbol of German big business, was murdered by terrorists in 1989. Successor Hilmar Kopper continued foreign expansion and in 1991 restructured the company along product lines, centralized management, and bolstered customer service.

As the Iron Curtain rose, Deutsche Bank saw opportunities at home (eastern Germany) and in Eastern Europe. But the costs and difficulties of building the region have proven greater than anticipated, and the bank has incurred troublesome debt, particularly in Bulgaria and Russia. In eastern Germany the bank has opened retail branches and made direct investments by buying (and actively managing) companies from Treuhandanstalt, the entity charged with administering eastern Germany's former state properties.

More immediately successful has been Deutsche Bank's 1993 foray into retail banking in Spain, where it has over 400 branches. In 1994 the bank bought a major portion of ITT's commercial finance unit.

OTC symbol: DBKAY (ADR)
Fiscal year ends: December 31

	1993 Assets	
	DM mil.	% of total
Cash	7,522	1
Money markets	124,323	23
Bonds & notes	59,671	12
Mortgages	73,890	13
Public sector loans	38,916	5
Other	252,314	46
Total	**556,636**	**100**

	1993 Sales	
	DM mil.	% of total
Interest	33,506	61
Commissions	6,373	12
Fixed income investments	3,399	6
Equities	1,250	2
Insurance business	5,043	9
Other	5,668	10
Total	**55,239**	**100**

WHO

Spokesman of the Board of Managing Directors: Hilmar Kopper
Chairman of the Supervisory Board: F. Wilhelm Christians
Managing Director Treasury: Ulrich Cartellieri
Managing Director Corporate Banking and Legal: Herbert Zapp
Managing Director Personnel, Compliance, and Auditing: Ulrich Weiss
President and CEO, Deutsche Bank (US): John A. Rolls
CFO, Deutsche Bank (US): Bruce van Saun
Head of Personnel, Deutsche Bank (US): Douglas Byers
Auditors: KPMG Deutsche Treuhand-Gesellschaft Aktiengesellschaft Wirstschaftsprüfungs-gesellschaft

WHERE

HQ: Deutsche Bank Aktiengesellschaft, Taunusanlage 12,D-60262 Frankfurt am Main, Germany
Phone:+49-69-71500
Fax: +49-69-7150-4225
US HQ: Deutsche Bank AG, New York Branch, 31 W. 52nd St., New York, NY 10019
US Phone: 212-474-8000
US Fax: 212-355-5655

The Deutsche Bank Group has 1,718 offices in Germany and 754 foreign offices. Operations include retail, commercial, and investment banking, financing, leasing, and commercial mortgages.

Selected Affiliates
Banca d'America e d'Italia SpA
Banca Popolare di Lecco (Italy)
Deutsche Bank, Sociedad Anónima Española
McLean McCarthy Inc. (investment bank, Canada)
Morgan Grenfell Group PLC (investment banking, UK)

KEY COMPETITORS

Allianz	Commerzbank	Lehman
Banca Nazionale	Crédit Lyonnais	Brothers
de Lavoro	CS Holding	NatWest
Banco Santander	Dai-Ichi Kangyo	Royal Bank of
Bankers Trust	Dresdner Bank	Canada
Barclays	Goldman Sachs	Salomon
Bear Stearns	HSBC	Union Bank of
Canadian Imperial	Industrial Bank	Switzerland
Chase Manhattan	of Japan	S. G. Warburg
Citicorp		

HOW MUCH

$=DM1.74 (Dec. 31, 1993)	9-Year Growth	1984[1]	1985	1986	1987	1988	1989	1990	1991	1992	1993
Assets (DM mil.)	10.2%	232,276	237,227	257,223	268,341	305,295	343,984	400,200	449,100	498,711	556,636
Net income (DM mil.)	14.1%	662	854	1,056	658	1,183	1,315	1,025	1,383	1,794	2,168
Income as % of assets	—	0.3%	0.4%	0.4%	0.2%	0.4%	0.4%	0.3%	0.3%	0.4%	0.4%
Earnings per share (DM)	8.0%	23	27	33	19	33	33	23	30	39	46
Stock price – high (DM)	—	385	935	920	817	569	843	850	684	740	907
Stock price – low (DM)	—	302	384	724	387	357	502	554	557	593	628
Stock price – close (DM)	9.8%	383	925	822	388	563	843	597	670	647	887
P/E – high	—	17	35	28	43	17	26	37	23	19	20
P/E – low	—	13	14	22	20	11	15	24	18	15	14
Dividends per share (DM)	3.6%	12.0	12.0	12.0	12.0	12.0	12.0	14.0	14.0	15.0	16.5
Book value per share (DM)	5.6%	266	281	281	299	318	353	353	386	403	434
Employees	4.8%	47,873	48,851	50,590	54,579	54,769	56,580	68,552	71,400	74,256	73,176

1993 Year-end:
Debt ratio: 91.4%
Return on equity: 11.0%
Equity as % of assets: 3.8%
No. of shares (mil.): 47
Dividends
 Yield: 1.9%
 Payout: 35.9%
Market value (mil.): $24,029
Assets (mil.): $319,906
Sales (mil.): $31,747

Stock Price History
High/Low 1984–93

[1] Accounting change

AB ELECTROLUX

OVERVIEW

Stockholm-based Electrolux is Europe's #1 producer of white goods (household appliances) and through its wholly owned subsidiary, Frigidaire, is #3 in the US (behind Whirlpool and GE). Electrolux is the world's leading producer of floor-care products, including brands Eureka (US) and Electrolux (outside the US). Electrolux is not affiliated with Electrolux Corp., which sells vacuum cleaners in the US. Electrolux's other products include aluminum, forestry and garden equipment, food service equipment, leisure appliances (RV absorption refrigerators and air conditioners), kitchen and bathroom cabinets, sewing machines, and industrial laundry equipment.

Sales increased to approximately $13 billion in 1993. The company is benefiting from the depreciation of the Swedish krona, making its products more affordable for foreign buyers. The situation has been especially favorable for its Husqvarna subsidiary, a maker of chainsaws.

Electrolux is restructuring its operations to concentrate on its core household appliance business. In 1994 the company announced it would sell its entire stake in Autoliv AB, a maker of auto safety equipment.

Electrolux is expanding into central Europe and Asia. The company announced it would invest $100 million over the next 3 years to enhance its operations in China.

WHEN

In 1910 Swedish salesman Axel Wenner-Gren saw an American-made vacuum cleaner in a Vienna store window and envisioned selling the cleaners door-to-door, a technique he had learned in the US. In 1912 he worked with fledgling Swedish vacuum cleaner makers AB Lux and Elektromekaniska to improve their existing designs. In 1919 the 2 companies merged to form Electrolux. When the board of the new company balked at Wenner-Gren's suggestion to mass-produce vacuum cleaners, he guaranteed Electrolux's sales through his own sales company.

In the 1920s the company used the "Every home — an Electrolux home" slogan as Wenner-Gren drove his sales force on and launched new sales companies in Europe, the US, and South America. Company lore has him paying a sales call on the Pope in competition with 4 other vacuum cleaner salesmen. After the others had swept their preassigned portions of the carpet, Wenner-Gren pushed his Electrolux over the area cleaned by the competition, dumped out a large pile of dust, and won the order. He scored another publicity coup by securing the blessing of Pope Pius XI to vacuum the Vatican, gratis, for a year. By the end of the 1920s, Electrolux had purchased most of Wenner-Gren's sales companies (excluding Electrolux US) and had gambled on refrigerator technology and won. By buying vacuum cleaner maker Volta (Sweden, 1934), Electrolux gained retail distribution.

Despite the loss of East European subsidiaries in WWII, the company did well until the 1960s, when Electrolux backed an unpopular refrigeration technology. In 1964 Swedish electrical equipment giant ASEA, controlled by Marcus Wallenberg, bought a large stake in Electrolux. In 1967 Wallenberg installed Hans Werthén as chairman. Werthén slashed overhead and sold the company's minority stake in Electrolux US to Consolidated Foods (the US Electrolux business was taken private in 1987). He also bought troubled appliance makers, updated their plants, and gained global component manufacturing efficiencies.

Since 1970 Electrolux has acquired over 300 companies, including National Union Electric (Eureka vacuum cleaners, US, 1974), Tappan (appliances, US, 1979), Gränges (metals, Sweden, 1981), Zanussi (appliances, industrial products; Italy; 1984), White Consolidated (appliances, industrial products; US; 1986), and the garden products division of Roper (US, 1988).

In 1991 it bought Lehel, Hungary's leading refrigerator maker. In 1992 Electrolux purchased 20% of AEG Hausgerate, a household appliances subsidiary of Daimler-Benz. Electrolux acquired the remaining 80% in 1994 for approximately $437 million.

In 1994 Electrolux acquired a 6% interest in Refrigeracao Parana, Brazil's 2nd largest manufacturer of appliances. Electrolux's presence in Latin America remains small compared to arch competitor Whirlpool.

Electrolux finished 1994 with sales of about $14.5 billion.

Nasdaq symbol: ELUXY (ADR)
Fiscal year ends: December 31

WHO

**Chairman and CEO; Chairman, White
Consolidated Industries (US):** Anders Scharp
**President; President and CEO, White
Consolidated Industries (US):** Leif Johansson
Legal Counsel: Ulf Magnusson
Human Resources and Organization: Per Linder
**SVP Finance and Controller, White Consolidated
Industries (US):** Wayne D. Schierbaum
**SVP Human Resources, White Consolidated
Industries (US):** Roderick K. Bowman
Auditors: Ernst & Young AB

WHERE

HQ: Aktiebolaget Electrolux, Luxbacken 1, S-105
45 Stockholm, Sweden
Phone: +46-8-738-6000
Fax: +46-8-656-4478
US HQ: White Consolidated Industries, Inc.,
11770 Berea Rd., Cleveland, OH 44111-1688
US Phone: 216-252-3700
US Fax: 216-252-8073

Electrolux owns 625 companies in 50 countries.

	1993 Sales	
	$ mil.	% of total
US	3,847	29
Germany	1,667	13
Sweden	1,045	8
Asia	595	5
Canada	335	3
Other Europe	4,983	38
Other countries	561	4
Total	**13,033**	**100**

WHAT

	1993 Sales		1993 Operating Income	
	$ mil.	% of total	$ mil.	% of total
Household appliances	7,666	59	142	33
Commercial appliances	1,371	10	45	11
Outdoor products	1,775	14	176	41
Industrial products	2,221	17	62	15
Adjustments	—	—	—	—
Total	**13,033**	**100**	**425**	**100**

Appliance Brands	Other Products
Outside US	Agricultural equipment
Arthur Martin	Aluminum
Tricity-Bendix	Chainsaws
Electrolux	Commercial cleaning
Husqvarna	equipment
Zanussi	Commercial refrigeration
US	equipment
Eureka	Food service equipment
Frigidaire	Home cabinetry
Gibson	Industrial laundry
Kelvinator	equipment
Poulan	Lawn care equipment
Tappan	Materials-handling
Viking	equipment
Weed Eater	
White-Westinghouse	

KEY COMPETITORS

Actava Group	Ingersoll-Rand	Royal Appliance
AlliedSignal	Masco	Sanyo
Berkshire Hathaway	Matsushita	Sharp
Black & Decker	Maytag	Siemens
Deere	Morton	Textron
Fourlis Bros.	Premark	Thomson SA
GEC	Raytheon	Toshiba
General Electric	Rival	TRW
Gillette	Robert Bosch	Whirlpool

HOW MUCH

	Annual Growth	1984	1985	1986	1987	1988	1989	1990	1991	1992	1993
Sales ($ mil.)	13.5%	4,159	4,677	7,485	10,712	12,051	13,672	14,632	14,280	11,366	13,033
Net income ($ mil.)	7.7%	140	164	287	204	386	415	132	68	26	68
Income as % of sales	—	3.4%	3.4%	3.8%	1.9%	3.2%	3.0%	0.9%	0.5%	0.2%	0.5%
Earnings per share ($)	2.1%	1.14	2.31	2.57	3.27	5.26	5.02	1.79	0.99	0.35	0.94
Stock price – high ($)	—	—	—	—	53.63	49.38	58.75	51.25	47.38	48.88	37.38
Stock price – low ($)	—	—	—	—	31.88	32.63	37.75	17.00	27.38	25.63	26.50
Stock price – close ($)	0.6%	—	—	—	32.88	47.25	45.75	28.50	39.25	33.63	34.00
P/E – high	—	—	—	—	16	9	12	29	48	140	40
P/E – low	—	—	—	—	10	6	8	10	28	73	28
Dividends per share ($)	8.5%	0.39	0.88	1.23	1.59	1.87	1.47	2.11	2.06	1.87	0.81
Book value per share ($)	10.4%	10.91	13.82	20.54	23.70	33.38	37.71	40.27	39.97	32.36	26.64
Employees	2.6%	87,000	91,100	129,900	140,500	147,200	152,900	150,900	134,200	119,200	109,400

1993 Year-end:
Debt ratio: 67.5%
Return on equity: 3.9%
Cash (mil.): $1,087
Current ratio: 1.37
Long-term debt (mil.): $2,925
No. of shares (mil.): 73
Dividends
  Yield: 2.4%
  Payout: 86.2%
Market value (mil.): $2,490

**Stock Price History
High/Low 1987–93**

ELF AQUITAINE

France's largest industrial company, Elf Aquitaine, is out on its own these days. The Paris-based company was cut loose by its parent, the French government, in early 1994 when the government cut its stake in Elf from 51.5% to 13.3%, raising about $6 billion. Elf Aquitaine is a parent company with more than 800 subsidiaries worldwide.

Elf Aquitaine is divided into 3 major segments: hydrocarbons, chemicals, and health and hygiene products. The hydrocarbons group explores for oil worldwide, with major activity in France, the North Sea, and Africa's Gulf of Guinea. Elf operates 5 refineries and sells gasoline through a network of more than 6,500 service stations in Europe and West Africa.

Elf Atochem, Elf Aquitaine's chemical group, produces basic (petrochemicals, fertilizers, and chlorinated chemicals) and specialty (fluorinated products, CFC substitutes, and plastic additives) chemicals.

Elf Sanofi, 52% owned by the Elf group, manufactures pharmaceuticals and diagnostic equipment. It boosted its presence in the US market with the recent acquisition of drug maker Sterling Winthrop from Kodak. Elf Sanofi also makes perfumes and beauty products under such brand names as Yves Saint Laurent and Oscar de la Renta.

Just before the outbreak of WWII, the French government formed Régie Autonome des Pétroles (RAP) to exploit the discovery of natural gas in Saint Marcet in southwest France. During the war the Vichy government created a publicly traded company in which the government held a majority interest. It was called Société Nationale des Pétroles d'Aquitaine (SNPA) in honor of the French region, and its mandate was to find oil. After the war De Gaulle set up the Bureau de Recherches de Pétrole (BRP) to hold RAP and the government's stake in SNPA.

SNPA struck a large gas field in Lacq (1951), and BRP invested in subsidiaries that discovered oil and gas in Algeria (1956), Gabon (1956), and the Congo (1957). In 1966 the government creations were consolidated under Entreprise de Recherches et d'Activités Pétrolières (ERAP) led by Pierre Guillaumat. ERAP oversaw the government's SNPA stake, but SNPA remained separate because of its size and private shareholders.

ERAP launched the Elf tradename to consolidate 7 trademarks in 1967. Company legend holds that the name, with no meaning in French, was generated by a computer. US subsidiary Elf Petroleum Corp. began exploration and production in 1967. SNPA invested in petrochemicals with the formation of ATO, Aquitaine Total Organico (1969).

The French companies lost production from nationalized Algerian fields (1971) but gained gas from the Frigg discovery in the North Sea. SNPA launched Sanofi in 1973 to oversee pharmaceuticals and cosmetics manufacturing.

In 1976 Elf-ERAP and SNPA merged into Société Nationale Elf Aquitaine (SNEA), with the French government initially controlling 70% of the new entity. The company expanded abroad, buying the US-based M&T Chemicals (1977) and Texasgulf, a mining company that produced sulfur and other chemicals (1981).

As the French government grappled with the nation's fractured chemical industry in 1983, Atochem was created from the pieces and placed under Elf Aquitaine. Elf Aquitaine added to its chemical holdings with the $1.05 billion purchase of Philadelphia-based Pennwalt (1989), part of a vigorous company-wide acquisition program that included 25% of Enterprise Oil (UK, 1988); Racon (chemicals, US, 1989); Parfums Stern from Avon (US, 1989); and Continental Flavors & Fragrances (US, 1989). In 1991 the company pursued more acquisitions, paying $1.35 billion for Occidental's North Sea holdings.

In 1992 Elf joined Germany's Thyssen (engineering) in a $4.5 billion contract to build an oil refinery in eastern Germany and take full control and modernize Minol, the country's major service station network (1,000 stations with 74% of the market). In 1993 Elf Sanofi acquired French fashion and perfume company Yves Saint Laurent. That same year the company's profits sank because of a European recession and the costs of a restructuring taken before Elf's privatization.

In 1994 Elf Aquitaine suffered a net loss of $1.03 billion associated with a $1.66 billion charge resulting from a write-down of assets. It was the company's first net income loss.

NYSE symbol: ELF (ADR)
Fiscal year ends: December 31

Chairman, President, and CEO: Philippe Jaffré
EVP Refining, Distribution, International Supply, Trading, and Shipping: Bernard de Combret
SVP and CFO; Chairman and President, Elf Aquitaine (US): Bruno Weymuller
EVP and COO (CFO), Elf Aquitaine (US): Dominique Paret
SVP, Chief Administrative Officer, General Counsel, and Secretary (Personnel), Elf Aquitaine (US): Lowell Williams
Auditors: Ernst & Young Audit; Cailliau Dedouit & Associés

HQ: Tour Elf Cedex 45, 92078 Paris La Défense, France
Phone: +33-1-47-44-45-46
Fax: +33-1-47-44-75-94
US HQ: Elf Aquitaine, Inc., 280 Park Ave., 36th Fl., New York, NY 10017
US Phone: 212-922-3000
US Fax: 212-922-3001

	1993 Sales		1993 Operating Income	
	FF mil.	% of total	FF mil.	% of total
France	121,887	58	1,736	27
North America	15,259	7	488	8
Other Europe	69,404	33	1,309	20
Other countries	3,125	2	2,922	45
Adjustments	—	—	(37)	—
Total	**209,675**	**100**	**6,418**	**100**

	1993 Sales		1993 Operating Income	
	FF mil.	% of total	FF mil.	% of total
Refining, marketing & trading	120,102	58	1,366	19
Chemicals	48,444	23	(780)	—
Health	23,612	11	1,780	25
Exploration & production	17,517	8	4,089	56
Adjustments	—	—	(37)	—
Total	**209,675**	**100**	**6,418**	**100**

Selected Brand Names

Chemicals	Petroleum
Appryl (polypropylene)	Elf
Lucolene (PVC)	Minol (Germany)

Perfume and Beauty	Pharmaceuticals
Nina Ricci	Cordarone
Oscar de la Renta	(antiarrhythmic)
Roger & Gallet	Dépakine (antiseizure)
Van Cleef & Arpels	Ticlid (antiplatelet)
Yves Rocher	Tranxène (tranquilizer)
Yves Saint Laurent	

BASF	Hercules	Petrobrás
Bayer	Hoechst	Petrofina
British Petroleum	Imperial Oil	Phillips
Broken Hill	L'Oréal	Petroleum
Caltex Petroleum	LVMH	Repsol
Canadian Pacific	MacAndrews &	Rhône-Poulenc
Chevron	Forbes	Roche
Ciba-Geigy	Merck	Royal Dutch/Shell
Dow Chemical	Mobil	Shanghai
DuPont	Norsk Hydro	Petrochemical
ENI	Occidental	Sun Company
Estée Lauder	PDVSA	Texaco
Exxon	PEMEX	TOTAL
Formosa Plastics	Pennzoil	Unocal

$=FF5.91 (Dec. 31, 1993)	9-Year Growth	1984	1985	1986	1987	1988	1989	1990	1991	1992	1993
Sales (FF mil.)	1.9%	177,374	180,651	119,727	127,353	126,097	149,802	175,479	200,674	200,563	209,675
Net income (FF mil.)	(21.5%)	6,493	5,250	4,279	4,149	7,205	7,218	10,625	9,796	6,177	737
Income as % of sales	—	3.7%	2.9%	3.6%	3.3%	5.7%	4.8%	6.1%	4.9%	3.1%	0.4%
Earnings per share (FF)	(23.8%)	33.00	25.80	21.34	20.35	35.73	33.50	43.80	39.31	24.40	2.87
Stock price – high (FF)	—	139	126	189	200	195	278	365	435	402	469
Stock price – low (FF)	—	86	89	98	106	110	193	255	251	320	307
Stock price – close (FF)	14.3%	109	101	158	118	195	258	284	389	417	362
P/E – high	—	4	5	9	10	5	8	8	11	16	163
P/E – low	—	3	3	4	5	3	6	6	6	13	107
Dividends per share (FF)	9.0%	6.00	6.75	6.75	6.75	7.50	10.00	10.50	13.00	13.00	13.00
Book value per share (FF)	4.6%	217	242	253	266	292	305	312	339	338	327
Employees	2.4%	76,219	73,377	71,350	73,010	72,183	78,179	90,000	86,900	87,900	94,300

1993 Year-end:
Debt ratio: 12.7%
Return on equity: 0.9%
Cash (mil.): FF19,552
Long-term debt (mil.): FF47,480
No. of shares (mil.): 257
Dividends
  Yield: 3.6%
  Payout: 453.0%
Market value (mil.): $15,771
Sales (mil.): $35,478

**Stock Price History
High/Low 1984–93**

ENTE NAZIONALE IDROCARBURI S.P.A.

OVERVIEW

Franco Bernabé is doing some cleaning at Ente Nazionale Idrocarburi (ENI). As the head of Italy's state-owned petroleum and petrochemical company, he is working to clean out the company's subsidiary-clogged structure and clean up the company's tarnished image. The tidying up comes as Bernabé prepares ENI, Italy's 2nd largest company (after IRI), for privatization in 1995.

Bernabé has reorganized ENI's operations into 3 business units: energy, chemicals, and diversified activities. The company's diversified activities, including fertilizers, manufacturing, metallurgy, textile machinery, and publishing, are to be divested as the company continues to streamline its operations. More than 60 subsidiaries have already been sold. Bernabé has also worked to cut ENI's bureaucracy, getting rid of more than 1,000 top managers.

Bernabé took the helm of ENI following a scandal that shook the entire nation. In 1993 the presidents of ENI's 5 largest business units and its chairman, Gabriele Cagliari, were arrested for bribery. Cagliari, who admitted to paying more than $16 million in bribes to government officials, committed suicide in prison.

WHEN

The Italian parliament formed Ente Nazionale Idrocarburi (National Hydrocarbon Agency) in 1953 by combining state-owned petroleum and petrochemical companies into a single entity, but it was Enrico Mattei who was the true father of ENI. In 1945 Mattei, a former partisan leader during WWII, was appointed Northern Commissioner of Agip, a state-owned petroleum company founded in 1926 by Mussolini's Fascist government. Agip had suffered serious damage during the war, and Mattei had orders to liquidate the company. Mattei, however, ignored his instructions and ordered the exploration of the Po Valley. Mattei's gamble paid off when workers found methane gas deposits there in 1946.

When ENI was created in 1953, Mattei was named president. It was his job to find energy resources for a country that was (and remains) oil-poor, so he began to enter a series of joint ventures (both for exploration rights and refineries) with several Middle Eastern and African nations, giving the host countries more attractive deals than his big oil competitors. When Mattei died in a plane crash in 1962, he left behind an ENI that had expanded far beyond hydrocarbons — thanks to Mattei's loose interpretation of the group's charter. Among ENI's additions during Mattei's reign were Pignone (renamed Nuovo Pignone), a machinery manufacturing operation acquired in 1954; Sofid, a finance company established in 1956; *Il Giorno*, a Milan newspaper that began publishing in 1959; and Lane Rossi, a textile company acquired in 1962.

ENI grew during the 1960s thanks, in part, to a controversial deal made for Soviet crude in 1958 and a joint venture with Esso in 1963. ENI also began to expand its chemical activities. In the early 1970s an oil crisis brought on by events in the Middle East, along with poor performance in chemical and textile operations, pushed ENI toward increasing losses. The Italian government also began using the group as a dumping ground for unprofitable companies, including the mining operations of the EGAM group in 1977 (creating a new sector called Samim). In the early 1980s ENI took on a number of troubled chemical companies, creating another new sector called EniChem.

Former finance minister Franco Reviglio became head of ENI in 1983, and he helped to turn the group around by cutting inefficient operations, reducing employment, and selling stock in some of ENI's more profitable companies, including Saipem (drilling services) and Nuovo Pignone. The group began to show a profit again in 1985. In the late 1980s the group entered into a series of partnerships with private companies, including DuPont in 1987 and ICI and Hoechst in 1988.

EniChem merged with Montedison, Italy's largest private chemical company, in 1988, creating Enimont. However, after clashes between the boards of the public agency and the private company, Montedison sold its stake to ENI in 1990. In 1992, as part of its preparation for privatization, ENI was transformed from a government agency into a joint stock company, although the Italian Treasury remains majority stockholder.

In 1994 ENI sold 69% of Nuovo Pignone to a group including General Electric, Ingersoll-Rand, and Dresser for $690 million.

State-owned company
Fiscal year ends: December 31

Chairman: Luigi Meanti
Managing Director and CEO: Franco Bernabé,
  age 46
Director Finance: Marco Mangiagalli
Chairman, Agip: Gugliemo Moscato
Chairman, Agip Petroli: Angelo Ferrari
Chairman, Saipem: Luciano Sgubini
Chairman, Snam: Vittorio Meazzini
Chairman, EniChem: Marcello Colitti
**Chairman, Agip Petroleum and ENI USA
  Representative:** Enzo Viscusi
President and CEO, Agip Petroleum (US):
  Salvatore Fantini
VP and CFO, Agip Petroleum (US): Reno
  Ferdenzi
**Manager Human Resources, Agip Petroleum
  (US):** Dianne McNeill
Auditors: Arthur Andersen & Co. s.a.s.

HQ: Piazzale Enrico Mattei 1, I-00144 Rome,
  Italy
Phone: +39-6-59001
Fax: +39-6-59002141
US HQ: ENI USA Representative Office,
  666 Fifth Ave., New York, NY 10103
US Phone: 212-887-0330
US Fax: 212-246-0009

ENI's subsidiaries have operations on 6
continents.

	1993 Sales	
	Lit bil.	% of total
Italy	32,988	61
Other countries	20,890	39
Total	**53,878**	**100**

	1993 Revenues	
	Lit. bil.	% of total
Energy	36,702	68
Chemicals	9,831	18
Engineering & services	2,917	5
Finance	174	1
Activities to be divested	4,226	8
Adjustments	28	—
Total	**53,878**	**100**

Group Companies
Agip SpA (oil and gas exploration and production)
AgipPetroli SpA (oil refining and distribution)
EniChem SpA (chemicals, fibers, plastics)
Eniricerche SpA (research)
Saipem SpA (drilling, pipelines, civil engineering)
Snam SpA (natural gas distribution)
Snamprogetti SpA (oil and gas plant and pipeline
  construction)
Sofid SpA (finance)

Selected US Subsidiaries
Agip Petroleum Co. Inc. (oil and gas exploration and
  production)
Agip USA Inc. (petroleum equipment supply)
American Agip Co., Inc. (petroleum marketing)
EniChem America, Inc. (chemical marketing)
Snamprogetti USA Inc. (oil and gas plant and pipeline
  construction)
Sonsub, Inc. (subsea engineering)

Amoco	Hoechst
Atlantic Richfield	Mobil
BASF	Occidental
Bayer	Oryx
British Gas	PDVSA
British Petroleum	Petrofina
Chevron	Phillips Petroleum
Ciba-Geigy	Repsol
Coastal	Rhône-Poulenc
Dow Chemical	Royal Dutch/Shell
DuPont	Texaco
Elf Aquitaine	TOTAL
Enron	Union Carbide
Exxon	Unocal

$= Lit1,713 (Dec. 31, 1993)	Annual Growth	1984	1985	1986	1987	1988	1989	1990	1991	1992	1993
Sales (Lit bil.)	7.0%	—	—	33,520	31,730	32,837	44,503	50,033	50,883	49,826	53,878
Net income (Lit bil.)	(11.0%)	—	—	548	687	1,194	1,544	2,033	1,007	(946)	243
Income as % of sales	—	—	—	1.6%	2.2%	3.6%	3.5%	4.1%	2.0%	—	0.5%
Employees	(2.8%)	—	—	129,903	119,158	116,364	135,462	130,745	131,248	124,032	106,391

1993 Year-end:
Debt ratio: 69.9%
Return on equity: 1.5%
Cash (bil.): Lit1,106
L-T debt (bil.): Lit13,672
Sales (mil.): $31,619

**Net Income (Lit bil.)
1986–93**

(bar chart with scale 2,500 / 2,000 / 1,500 / 1,000 / 500 / 0 / -500 / -1,000)

LM ERICSSON TELEPHONE COMPANY

OVERVIEW

LM Ericsson — the Swedish telecommunications equipment maker — is riding the mobile-communications boom. Radio communications equipment now accounts for more of the firm's sales than its traditional cash cow — wire-based public phone network equipment. Indeed, as the firm maintains its world leadership in analog cellular transmission equipment with a 40% share (ahead of Motorola and AT&T), it has captured an even larger share (60%) of the digital wireless wave that's sweeping Japan, Europe, and the US.

The company has emphasized R&D and partnerships with the likes of Texas Instruments and General Electric to maintain its technological and market edge. Now Ericsson hopes to capitalize on the emerging market for personal communications systems, using low-power transmitters and cheap pocket phones to bring mobile communications to the masses.

In 1994 Ericsson became the #1 supplier of mobile telephone systems in China with a $400 million equipment deal.

WHEN

Lars Magnus Ericsson opened a shop to repair telegraph equipment in Stockholm in 1876, the same year American Alexander Graham Bell applied for a US patent on the telephone. Within 2 years Ericsson began making telephones, and his firm grew rapidly as it supplied equipment, first to Swedish telephone companies and later to other European companies. In 1885 Ericsson crafted a combination receiver-speaker in one handset.

Early in the 20th century, Lars Magnus Ericsson retired, and the company branched out overseas. It joined a consortium to operate the Mexican telephone system (1905), won a contract for phone modernization in Bangkok (1908), and built a factory in Paris (1911). Its Russian holdings were nationalized in 1918.

Also in 1918 Ericsson and SAT, the Stockholm telephone company, merged under the Ericsson banner. The company adopted its present name, Telefonaktiebolaget LM Ericsson, in 1926. In 1930 financier Ivar Kreuger, known as the Match King because his Swedish Match Company was the centerpiece of his international financial empire, won control of Ericsson. But the Match King's plans fizzled. Kreuger committed suicide in 1932, and Sosthenes Behn's ITT, one of Kreuger's creditors, won controlling interest in Ericsson.

After WWII the company's holdings in Mexico were nationalized. When ITT began to diversify in 1960, it sold its interest in Ericsson to the Wallenbergs, the first family of Swedish industry. In 1975 Ericsson introduced its computer-controlled exchange, called the AXE. Buoyed by AXE's success, the company launched, with US partner ARCO, development of the "office of the future" in the early 1980s. It diversified into computer making and the office furniture business.

Ericsson's timing was off: AT&T's breakup and British Telecom's privatization were 2 of the highlights of a telecommunications revolution in the early 1980s. The demand for office automation never materialized, Ericsson profits plunged, and ARCO cashed in (1985). Electrolux chairman Hans Werthén was recruited to split his time between the companies and pull Ericsson out of its nosedive.

Ericsson shed its computer business (to Nokia, 1988) and focused on telephone equipment. An Ericsson joint venture edged out larger rivals AT&T and Siemens in bidding for CGCT, a phone equipment maker with 16% of the French market (1987). Under then-EVP Lars Ramqvist, Ericsson dusted off its aging AXE system for use in the burgeoning cellular market. The concentration paid off, and Ericsson won a cellular contract with NTT.

In 1991 Ericsson bought half of Orbitel Mobile Communications of the UK, the equipment manufacturer for Racal Telecom. In 1992 Ericsson acquired a 51% interest in Fuba Telekom. Ericsson and GE restructured Ericsson GE Mobile Communications, giving Ericsson 80% voting control. Also in 1992 the company won a $120 million order from Tokyo Digital Phone to provide cellular service in Tokyo.

In 1994 Ericsson won a $217 million contact to expand Mercury Communications's one2one network in Britain, the world's first personal-communications system (mobile phoning for the masses).

Sales leaped by 31% in 1994 to just over $11 billion; profits shot up 81%.

Nasdaq symbol: ERICY (ADR)
Fiscal year ends: December 31

Chairman: Björn Svedberg, age 57
President and CEO: Lars Ramqvist, age 56
EVP and CFO: Carl Wilhelm Ros, age 53
SVP and General Counsel: Erling Blommé
SVP Corporate Human Resources : Britt Reigo
President, Ericsson North America: Leif Källén
CFO, Ericsson North America: Joe Hagan
Director of Human Resources, Ericsson North America: Ron Kirchenbauer
Auditors: Price Waterhouse

HQ: Telefonaktiebolaget LM Ericsson, S-126 25, Stockholm, Sweden
Phone: +46-8-719-0000
Fax: +46-8-719-1976 (Investor Relations)
US HQ: Ericsson North America, Inc., 100 Park Ave., Ste. 2705, New York, NY 10017
US Phone: 212-685-4030
US Fax: 212-213-0159

Ericsson operates in more than 100 countries.

	1993 Sales
	% of total
Europe, excluding Sweden	45
Asia	13
US & Canada	12
Latin America	11
Sweden	10
Australia, New Zealand & Oceania	5
Middle East	3
Africa	1
Total	**100**

	1993 Sales	
	$ mil.	% of total
Radio communications	3,081	41
Public telecommunications	2,275	30
Business networks	1,501	20
Components	432	6
Defense systems	228	3
Adjustment	105	—
Total	**7,622**	**100**

Public Telecommunications
Digital telephone switches
Management and operations support systems
Mobile telephones
Power systems for telecommunications equipment and component computers
Radio communications
Transport networks

Business Networks
Corporate networks
Data network products
Data networks and broadband transmission
Digital systems for business communications
Digital telephone systems

Defense Systems
Avionics and airborne electronics
Microwave and satellite communications

Alcatel Alsthom	Fujitsu	Oki
AlliedSignal	GTE	Pirelli
Ascom	IRI	SBI
AT&T	Motorola	Siemens
BICC	NEC	STET
BT	Nokia	Sumitomo
Cable & Wireless	Northern Telecom	

Stock prices are for ADRs ADR = 1 share	9-Year Growth	1984	1985	1986	1987	1988	1989	1990	1991	1992	1993
Sales ($ mil.)	9.0%	3,537	3,830	4,780	5,751	5,188	6,367	8,289	8,275	6,644	7,622
Net income ($ mil.)	22.7%	54	99	83	128	215	297	612	160	68	340
Income as % of sales	—	1.5%	2.6%	1.7%	2.2%	4.1%	4.7%	7.4%	1.9%	1.0%	4.5%
Earnings per share ($)	0.6%	1.45	2.67	0.51	0.60	1.05	1.88	2.53	0.67	0.33	1.53
Stock price – high ($)	—	9.68	7.00	8.43	9.40	11.83	28.73	47.58	40.00	27.25	60.25
Stock price – low ($)	—	5.40	4.63	5.53	5.08	5.35	11.73	25.85	15.38	17.88	23.38
Stock price – close ($)	24.2%	5.75	5.93	6.23	5.30	11.83	28.73	32.25	19.25	26.50	40.38
P/E – high	—	7	3	17	16	11	15	19	60	83	39
P/E – low	—	4	2	11	9	5	6	10	23	54	15
Dividends per share ($)	10.5%	0.22	0.20	0.21	0.25	0.25	0.27	0.39	0.49	0.51	0.54
Book value per share ($)	13.0%	3.95	4.93	5.67	6.79	7.39	8.67	14.45	14.71	11.95	11.87
Employees	(0.8%)	75,116	78,159	72,575	70,893	65,138	69,229	70,238	71,247	66,232	69,597

1993 Year-end:
Debt ratio: 29.1%
Return on equity: 13.6%
Cash (mil.): $1,056
Current ratio: 1.58
Long-term debt (mil.): $593
No. of shares (mil.): 215
Dividends
  Yield: 1.3%
  Payout: 35.3%
Market value (mil.): $8,694

**Stock Price History
High/Low 1984–93**

ERNST & YOUNG LLP

OVERVIEW

The 2nd largest accounting firm in the US after Arthur Andersen, Ernst & Young is the product of the 1989 merger of former Big 8 brethren Ernst & Whinney and Arthur Young. The firm provides accounting and auditing services as well as management consulting, human resources services, regulatory consulting, and other services.

The New York–based firm has been able to attract some hot new clients lately, leading the profession in signing on companies that have recently tendered initial public offerings. However, in recent years it has also led the Big 6 in a dubious category, client defec-

tions. Looking for ways to reduce costs, the firm is cutting its office space by allocating space only when it is specifically needed.

Ernst & Young, like its Big 6 counterparts, has faced mounting legal troubles recently, as investors and the government have brought suit against auditors of failed companies. In an effort to lower its litigation costs, the company continues to shed its riskier clients (such as real estate ventures and financial services companies).

In 1993 Philip Laskawy was picked to replace chairman Ray Groves.

WHEN

While the 1494 publication in Venice of Luca Pacioli's *Summa di Arithmetica* — the first published work dealing with double-entry bookkeeping — boosted the accounting profession, it really wasn't until the Industrial Revolution in England that accountants developed their craft.

Frederick Whinney joined the UK firm of Harding & Pullein in 1849. R. P. Harding reputedly had been a hat maker whose business ended up in court. The ledgers he produced were so well kept that an official advised him to take up accounting.

Whinney's name was added to the firm in 1859, and later his sons also became partners. The firm's name changed to Whinney, Smith & Whinney in 1894. The name became the longest-lived of the firm's many incarnations, not yielding until 1965.

After WWII, Whinney, Smith & Whinney formed an alliance with the American firm of Ernst & Ernst. Ernst & Ernst had been founded in Cleveland in 1903 by brothers Alwin and Theodore Ernst. The alliance, which recognized that the accountants' business clients were getting larger and more international in orientation, provided that each firm would operate in the other's behalf within their respective markets.

In 1965 the Whinney firm merged with Brown, Fleming & Murray to become Whinney Murray. The merger also included the fledgling computer department — the harbinger of electronic accounting systems — set up by Brown, Fleming & Murray to serve British Petroleum. Whinney Murray also formed joint ventures with other

accounting firms to provide consulting services.

In 1979 Whinney Murray and Turquands Barton Mayhew — itself the product of a merger that began with a cricket match — united with Ernst & Ernst to form Ernst & Whinney, a firm with an international scope.

Ernst & Whinney, a merger melting pot, wasn't finished with its combinations. Having grown to the world's 4th largest accounting firm by 1989, it merged with the 5th largest, Arthur Young. Arthur Young had taken its name from the Scottish immigrant who had founded a partnership with C. U. Stuart in Chicago in 1894. When Stuart withdrew, Young took brother Stanley as a partner. Arthur Young — the firm — was long known as the "old reliable" of the accounting giants. In 1984 the spotlight shone on it as vice-presidential candidate Geraldine Ferraro chose the firm to sort out her tax troubles.

The new firm of Ernst & Young faced a rocky start. At the end of 1990, it was forced to defend itself from rumors of collapse. In 1991 it pared back the payroll, thinning the ranks of partners and others. That same year it agreed to pay the RTC $41 million to settle claims stemming from its involvement with Charles Keating's Lincoln Savings and Loan.

The next year Ernst & Young agreed to pay $400 million for allegedly mishandling the audits of 4 failed S&Ls. In 1994 a federal judge in Rhode Island ordered Ernst & Young and the state to negotiate a settlement of a suit brought by Rhode Island, which claimed the firm's faulty audits had helped lead to the failure of Rhode Island's credit union system.

International partnership
Fiscal year ends: September 30

Chairman: Philip A. Laskawy
Co-Chairman: William L. Kimsey
CEO, International: Michael A. Henning
VC Finance and Administration: Hilton Dean
VC Human Resources: Bruce J. Mantia
General Counsel: Kathryn A. Oberly

HQ: 787 Park Ave., New York, NY 10019
Phone: 212-773-3000
Fax: 212-773-1996

Ernst & Young maintains more than 600 offices in over 100 countries.

	1993 Sales	
	$ mil.	% of total
US	2,540	42
Other countries	3,480	58
Total	**6,020**	**100**

	1994 US Sales
	% of total
Accounting & auditing	48
Tax	21
Management consulting	31
Total	**100**

Representative Clients

Apple Computer	Martin Marietta
BankAmerica	McDonald's
Coca-Cola	Mobil
Eli Lilly	Time Warner
Hanson	USF&G
Knight-Ridder	Wal-Mart

US Services
Human resources services
    Actuarial, benefits, and compensation consulting
    Expatriate tax services
    Personal financial counseling
    Relocation services
Industry services
    Accounting and auditing services
    Health care consulting
    Insurance actuarial services
    Tax services
International services
    International tax compliance and consulting services
    Investment services
Management consulting
    Continuous improvement
    Focused process improvement
    Information technology services
    Organization alignment
    Organizational change management
    Performance measurement
Outsourcing services
    Corporate tax functions
    Financial and accounting systems
    Internal audit functions
Regulatory and related services
    Environmental consulting
    Federal and state regulatory risk management
    Government relations and contract services
    Health care legislative services
    Insurance regulatory services
    Tax policy and legislative services
Special services
    Capital markets services
    Cash management services
    Corporate finance services
    Corporate real estate advisory services
    Financial products services
    Litigation services
    Restructuring and reorganization services
    Valuation services

Arthur Andersen	H&R Block
Bain & Co.	Hewitt
Booz, Allen & Hamilton	KPMG
Coopers & Lybrand	Marsh & McLennan
Deloitte & Touche	McKinsey & Co.
Electronic Data Systems	Price Waterhouse

	Annual Growth	1985	1986	1987	1988	1989	1990	1991	1992	1993	1994
Sales ($ mil.)	11.0%	2,345	2,919	3,480	4,244	4,200	5,006	5,406	5,701	5,839	6,020
Arthur Young	—	1,160	1,427	1,702	2,053						
Ernst & Whinney	—	1,185	1,492	1,778	2,191						
Offices	1.4%	—	—	—	—	—	642	673	660	663	680
Partners	(1.7%)	—	—	—	—	—	5,609	5,665	5,300	5,318	5,228
Employees	(0.1%)	—	—	—	—	—	61,591	61,173	58,900	58,377	61,287

1994 Year-end:
Sales per partner:
$1,151,492

Sales ($ mil.)
1985–94

7,000
6,000
5,000
4,000
3,000
2,000
1,000
0

ESPÍRITO SANTO FINANCIAL HOLDING S.A.

Espírito Santo means "Holy Spirit" in Portuguese, and the Espírito Santo family might feel that a touch of divine intervention has helped them regain their status as one of Portugal's premier banking families. It owns 32.7% of Espírito Santo Financial Holdings, a holding company for several financial service businesses with operations primarily in Portugal. The family regained its financial empire after its holdings were nationalized by the Portuguese government in 1975. Albert Frère group (owners of Belgium's Petrofina) owns 6.6% of the company and Italy's Agnelli group (owners of Fiat) owns 2.7%.

The company's holdings include 50% of Banco Espírito Santo e Comercial de Lisboa, Portugal's 3rd largest commercial bank, and 74% of Tranquilidade, the country's 3rd largest insurance company. Espírito Santo also controls an investment bank and an asset management company in Portugal.

The company's overseas operations include commercial banking in Paris and Miami, and an asset management company in Switzerland. However, the company plans to continue to focus most of its activities in Portugal, with a particular concentration on commercial banking.

The Espírito Santo financial empire traces its roots back to a bank founded by José Maria de Espírito Santo Silva in Lisbon in 1884. Following WWI, Portugal underwent a major banking expansion, and in 1920 the Espírito Santo family established Banco Espírito Santo, which grew rapidly thanks to post-war expansion and speculation.

José Maria's oldest son, José, became head of the bank but was forced to leave Catholic Portugal after divorcing and remarrying in 1931. His brother, Ricardo, took over and led the massive growth of both the bank and the family's fortune. During the 1930s the Espírito Santos acquired a major interest in insurance company Tranquilidade, and in 1937 Banco Espírito Santo merged with Banco Comercial de Lisboa (founded in 1875) to create Banco Espírito Santo e Comercial de Lisboa.

The Espírito Santo's prospects were aided by Antonio de Oliveira Salazar, Portugal's dictator who came to power in 1933. During WWII Salazar declared Portugal neutral and the country became a sanctuary for many of Europe's elite, bringing business and contacts to the Espírito Santos.

The family's empire continued to grow after the war thanks to Salazar's protectionist policies, which shut out most competition. Banco Espírito Santo became one of Portugal's largest banks and Tranquilidade became one of the country's largest insurance companies. The family also acquired large coffee, sugar, and palm-oil plantations in Portugal's colonies, Angola and Mozambique. At its peak the family's empire was valued at $4 billion.

However, the family's fortunes came crashing down as Portugal went through political upheaval during the 1970s. In 1974 military officers overthrew Marcelo Caetano (who took over from Salazar in 1968). A year later the leftist government nationalized Portugal's major corporations, including Banco Espírito Santo and Tranquilidade.

The family fled to London, where they lived in a borrowed apartment. They pooled their savings to create a new holding company and began to rebuild. In the late 1970s they got a banking license in Brazil, and later set up a fund management company in Switzerland and banking branches in Miami and Paris. The family name, well known across Europe, brought it business and investors.

In 1986 the Portuguese government passed legislation restoring private ownership of financial services organizations. That year Espírito Santo and France's Credit Agricole opened Banco Internacional de Crédito in Portugal. After raising money on the Eurobond market, Espírito Santo bought back insurance company Tranquilidade in 1990. Two years later the company and a group of investors, including Credit Agricole, reacquired Banco Espírito Santo.

In 1993 Espírito Santo Holdings listed its ADR shares on the New York Stock Exchange. That same year the company restructured, reducing its interest in Banco Internacional de Crédito to 47.4%.

Trying to stimulate the country's economy after a 1993 recession, the Bank of Portugal cut interest rates in 1994, which reduced Espírito Santo's interest income but helped its other financial services businesses.

NYSE symbol: ESF (ADR)
Fiscal year ends: December 31

Chairman, CFO, and Accounting Officer:
Ricardo Espírito Santo Silva Salgado, age 48
VC: José Manuel P. Espírito Santo Silva, age 49
SVP Finance: Mário A. F. Cardoso, age 57
SVP and Secretary: Rui Barros Costa, age 70
SVP Treasury: Erich Dähler, age 42
**EVP and General Manager, Banco Espírito Santo
(US):** Joaquim Garnacho
CFO, Banco Espírito Santo (US): Leon Stark
**Administrative Assistant and Personnel Officer,
Banco Espírito Santo (US):** Christina Oliveira
Auditors: Price Waterhouse

HQ: Banco Espírito Santo e Comercial de Lisboa,
S.A., Av. de Liberdade, 195, 1250 Lisboa,
Portugal
Phone: +351-1-315-8331
Fax: +351-1-574924
US HQ: Banco Espírito Santo, 555 Madison Ave.,
New York, NY 10022
US Phone: 212-418-0320
US Fax: 212-688-7082

	1993 Assets	
	$ mil.	% of total
Portugal	12,446	93
France	226	2
Switzerland	134	1
Other countries	593	4
Adjustments	51	—
Total	**13,451**	**100**

	1993 Sales		1993 Operating Income	
	$ mil.	% of total	$ mil.	% of total
Banking	1,760	83	217	—
Other	357	17	(4)	—
Total	**2,117**	**100**	**213**	**—**

	1993 Assets	
	$ mil.	% of total
Cash & equivalents	2,953	22
Securities	3,847	29
Loans & advances	5,761	43
Interest income	188	1
Other	702	5
Total	**13,451**	**100**

Principal Subsidiaries
Banco Espírito Santo e Comercial de Lisboa, SA (50%,
commercial banking)
Banco ESSI, SA (50.6%, merchant banking)
Cia. de Seguros Tranquilidade, SA (74%, insurance)
Compagnie Financière Espírito Santo SA (asset
management, Switzerland)
Espírito Santo Activos Financeros SA (99.5%, asset
management)

Allianz	Chase Manhattan
AIG	Chemical Banking
Banco Comercial	Crédit Lyonnais
Portugues	CS Holding
Banco Portugues	Deutsche Bank
do Atlantico	Lloyds
Banco Portugues	J.P. Morgan
de Investimento	Prudential
Bank of New York	Royal Bank of Canada
BankAmerica	Société Générale
Bankers Trust	Transamerica
Banque Nationale de Paris	Union Bank of Switzerland
Barclays	

	Annual Growth	1984	1985	1986	1987	1988	1989	1990	1991	1992	1993
Assets ($ mil.)	78.8%	—	—	—	—	—	1,316	2,267	2,971	14,794	13,451
Net income ($ mil.)	12.5%	—	—	—	21	17	21	23	19	38	42
Income as % of assets	—	—	—	—	—	—	1.6%	1.0%	0.6%	0.3%	0.3%
Earnings per share ($)	9.7%	—	—	—	—	—	1.22	1.23	1.00	1.67	1.77
Stock price – high ($)	—	—	—	—	—	—	—	—	—	—	18.06
Stock price – low ($)	—	—	—	—	—	—	—	—	—	—	12.63
Stock price – close ($)	—	—	—	—	—	—	—	—	—	—	17.63
P/E – high	—	—	—	—	—	—	—	—	—	—	10
P/E – low	—	—	—	—	—	—	—	—	—	—	7
Dividends per share ($)	58.3%	—	—	—	0.04	0.38	0.38	0.45	0.50	0.60	0.63
Book value per share ($)	11.0%	—	—	—	7.45	7.99	—	—	11.12	11.43	11.30
Employees	(7.6%)	—	—	—	—	—	—	—	—	8,895	8,215

1993 Year-end:
Debt ratio: 93.1%
Return on equity: 16.6%
Equity as % of assets: 1.9%
Long-term debt (mil.): $726
No. of shares (mil.): 22
Dividends
  Yield: 3.6%
  Payout: 35.6%
Market value (mil.): $391
Sales (mil.): $2,117

Stock Price History
High/Low 1993

EVERGREEN GROUP

The properties of Taiwan-based Evergreen are easy to recognize — its ships, cargo containers, airplanes, employee uniforms, even the company's headquarters, are green.

Evergreen Marine, the Evergreen Group's core business, has grown to 76 modern cargo carriers — the world's largest container shipping fleet and the first with round-the-world routes. Airliner subsidiary EVA Air flies to 4 continents.

Evergreen has also diversified into container manufacturing and terminals, computer software, hotels (in Southeast Asia and the US), and construction. Today there are over 10 Evergreen subsidiaries.

Despite the Taiwanese government's current ban on direct shipping to China, Evergreen is investing $80 million in docks, container terminals, and trucking facilities in an effort to establish the company in China and lay the foundation for direct shipping links (the ban could be lifted as early as 1996). In a joint venture Evergreen and General Electric (US) will build a container yard in China's eastern port city of Zhang Jia. The company is also building a container depot in Shanghai. Subsidiary Uniglory Marine will invest another $30 million in China's primary ports.

To keep pace with Asia's growth, Evergreen will also develop container ports at Batam Island and Java, Indonesia.

Founder Yung-fa Chang and his family are Evergreen's principal shareholders. Eldest son Kuo-Hua Chang is VC of Evergreen Marine.

Former Taiwanese sailor Yung-fa Chang — an eccentric billionaire known as a proponent of the egg-eating Duck Egg sect — founded Evergreen Marine Corporation in 1968 with only a secondhand cargo vessel. Japanese trading group Marubeni loaned Chang $450,000 for the start-up. Chang's crew began working the underserved Middle East sea trade routes. Within 2 decades Evergreen was the world's #1 container shipping line.

Chang's Chinese given name translates as "evergreen" or "prospering." The company's ship names all begin with "Ever": Its first new-built ship was the *Ever Safety* (1972) and its first container ship the *Ever Spring* (1975). In 1975 the company established a subsidiary in Panama to oversee a fleet sailing under the Panamanian flag.

Evergreen's tremendous growth depended on its competitive prices and its dependability. All ships and offices are linked by satellite and fax. The company's modern ships require smaller crews, thus saving on labor costs.

In 1984 Evergreen developed an efficient way to operate both eastward and westward around-the-world routes, revolutionizing the shipping industry. Evergreen International USA (now Evergreen America) was established in 1986 to oversee operations in the US, Canada, and the Caribbbean; a German office was opened to coordinate operations in northern Europe and the Mediterranean.

Under pressure from Taiwan's government, Chang took Evergreen public in 1987.

With market overcapacity, rising oil prices, and shippers worldwide using price cuts to gain market share, Evergreen's net income dropped 37% in 1989. That year the company added refrigerated containers to some routes.

In 1991 Chang's EVA Air ordered nearly $4 billion worth of aircraft and began serving routes from Taipei to Bangkok and Seoul, as well as Vienna. (Chang's airline is named EVA because another was already called Evergreen.)

Before EVA was formed, Taiwan, lacking formal relations with many governments, had ceded many of state-owned China Airlines's routes to foreign carriers. As a private company EVA was given those routes. EVA should be in place to pick up routes to Beijing as soon as relations normalize between Taiwan and the People's Republic of China.

Chang pledged $760,000 to underwrite a permanent gallery on 20th century seapower at the British National Maritime Museum. The gallery opened in 1992.

By 1993 EVA had added routes to Los Angeles and Paris. That year the company opened a branch in Hong Kong and extended shipping services to Thailand. Chang was named a senior advisor to Indonesia's minister of research and technology.

In 1994 Evergreen's US subsidiary was fined nearly $900,000 for illegal campaign contributions to more than 20 California politicians.

Principal exchange: Taiwan
Fiscal year ends: December 31

Chairman, Evergreen Group: Yung-fa Chang,
   age 67
Chairman, Evergreen Marine: Sun-San Lin
VC, Evergreen Marine: Kuo-Hua Chang
VC, Evergreen America: S. Y. Kuo
President, Evergreen America: Marcel Chang
Auditors: J.T. Lai & Co. (HLB International)

HQ: Evergreen Marine Corporation (Taiwan)
   Ltd., 166, Minsheng E. Rd., Sec. 2, 10444
   Taipei, Taiwan
Phone: +886-2-505-7766
Fax: +886-2-505-5255
US HQ: Evergreen America Corp., One Evertrust
   Plaza, Jersey City, NJ 07302
US Phone: 201-915-3200
US Fax: 201-915-3898

Evergreen's 76 container vessels offer global
cargo shipping.

1994 Routes

Australia feeder services
Caribbean feeder services
Eastbound around the world
Far East to Mediterranean
Korea/Japan to Pacific Northwest coast
South Africa feeder services
Southeast Asia feeder services
Taiwan/Hong Kong to US West Coast
West Mediterranean to US East Coast
Westbound around the world

	1993 Sales*	
	NT$ mil.	% of total
Shipping	31,297	99
Other	103	1
Total	**31,400**	**100**

Group Subsidiaries and Affiliates

EVA Air
Evergreen America Corp.
Evergreen Computer Information Corp.
Evergreen Container Terminal Corp.
Evergreen Heavy Industrial Corp.
Evergreen International SA (Panama)
Evergreen Marine Corp.
Evergreen Superior Alloys Corp.
Evergreen Transport Corp.
Evergreen-Konoike Construction Corp.
Uniglory Marine Corp. (Panama)

Air France	Mitsubishi
All Nippon Airways	Mitsui
American President	Northwest Airlines
AMR	Orient Overseas Container
China Airlines	Overseas Shipholding
Delta	Pacific International
Garuda Indonesia	Philippine Air Line
General Steamship	SAS
Hyundai	Sea-Land
International	Singapore Airlines
Shipholding	Swire Pacific
IRI	UAL
JAL	Virgin Group
KLM	Yang Ming Marine
Korean Air Lines	Transport
Maersk Line	Zapata Gulf Marine
Maritrans Partners	

$=NT$26.4 (Dec. 31, 1993)	Annual Growth	1984	1985	1986	1987	1988	1989	1990	1991	1992	1993
Sales (NT$ mil.)	6.3%	—	—	20,463	22,049	26,065	25,825	27,900	31,612	30,159	31,400
Net income (NT$ mil.)	16.6%	—	—	957	2,072	4,209	1,666	1,034	2,258	2,707	2,811
Income as % of sales	—	—	—	4.7%	9.4%	16.1%	6.5%	3.7%	7.1%	9.0%	9.0%
Earnings per share (NT$)	0.1%	—	—	—	2.55	2.86	4.53	1.03	2.26	2.71	2.56
Dividends per share (NT$)	—	—	—	—	0.00	1.50	1.50	1.00	1.50	1.00	1.00
Book value per share (NT$)	5.6%	—	—	—	—	—	18.77	18.29	19.53	20.89	23.30
Employees	1.8%	—	—	—	—	—	1,319	1,488	1,519	—	1,415

1993 Year-end:
Debt ratio: 23.3%
Return on equity: 12.7%
Cash (mil.): NT$3,589
L-T debt (mil.): NT$7,063
No. of shares (mil.): 1,000
Dividends
   Yield: 1.6%
   Payout: 39.1%
Market value (mil.): $2,409
Sales (mil.): $1,191

Net Income ($ mil.)
1986–93

Information is for Evergreen Marine Corp. only.

FIAT S.P.A.

The largest private-sector industrial company in Italy, Turin-based Fiat has been doing some tinkering lately. The company, which accounts for more than 3% of Italy's GNP, has had to take a look under the hood after posting the biggest loss in its history in 1993. Fiat is spending $24 billion on an overhaul: tuning its car product line, selling off assets, and streamlining some businesses.

The company is a diversified industrial giant. Its automaking sector is one of Europe's largest car makers and is #1 in Italy. Its commercial vehicles unit (Iveco) and its agricultural and construction equipment unit are major players in European markets. Fiat is involved in a variety of other enterprises, including railway systems, aviation, civil engineering, chemicals, and financial services.

While every European car maker was hit hard by recession, Fiat got an extra helping because of its aging product line, so it is bringing out 18 new car models. The company is also focusing on expanding its car sales in Eastern Europe and Latin America.

To raise money for its retooling, the company got $3 billion in capital from investors, including Alcatel Alsthom and Deutsche Bank. However, as part of the capital injection, much of Fiat's long-term decision-making powers were shifted to a 9-member board and away from the Agnelli family, which still controls 32% of Fiat's stock.

Ex–cavalry officer Giovanni Agnelli founded Fabbrica Italiana di Automobili Torino (Fiat) in 1899. The auto maker soon expanded into trucks (1903), rail cars (1906), aviation (1908), and tractors (1918). Protected by high import tariffs, Fiat became Italy's dominant auto company. Between WWI and WWII Fiat reduced its dependence on foreign suppliers by manufacturing its own parts.

Mussolini's WWII modernization drive boosted Fiat's fortunes, but bombs damaged many of its plants. With US support Fiat rebuilt its facilities and survived weak postwar domestic demand by exporting and by building plants abroad. In 1950 Fiat licensed its know-how to Spain's SEAT, a state-owned auto maker. As growth resumed in Italy, Fiat began making steel and construction equipment.

When the EC forced Italy to lower import tariffs in 1961, Fiat lost market share and responded with a new mid-range car and an import-bashing campaign in its *La Stampa* newspaper. Fiat's domestic woes were offset by success abroad. In 1965 Fiat agreed to build a USSR plant to produce 600,000 cars annually.

In 1966 Giovanni Agnelli II, the founder's grandson, became chairman. Under Agnelli, Fiat bought high-end Italian car makers Lancia and Ferrari (1969) and diversified into biotechnology and telecommunications. Allis Chalmers and Fiat merged their earthmoving equipment businesses in 1973.

Labor strife and the oil crisis hurt Fiat in the 1970s. By 1979, 27 executives had been wounded by the Red Brigade. Needing cash, Fiat sold a 10% interest to Libya in 1976.

In 1980 Cesare Romiti became managing director. Dubbed "Il Duro" ("the hard one"), Romiti announced the elimination of 23,000 jobs. After a 5-week strike, 40,000 workers marched in support of management, crushing the strike and union influence at Fiat.

In the 1980s factory automation improved Fiat's productivity. The Uno, a small car, was an instant success in 1983. That same year the company ended its chronically unprofitable Fiat auto sales operations in the US.

Merger talks with Ford collapsed in 1985, but Fiat's truck operations and Ford's British truck business were combined in 1986. In the same year Libya sold its holdings, and Fiat outbid Ford for Alfa Romeo, whose dealers accounted for 50% of Fiat's domestic sales. In 1988 Chrysler agreed to sell Alfas in the US.

In 1989 and 1990 Fiat agreed to help build over 1 million cars annually in the USSR and Poland. In 1991 Fiat and Ford merged their farm and construction equipment businesses.

In 1992 Fiat expanded its participation in the earthmoving business with Japan's Hitachi and Sumitomo by supplying roller loaders, dozers, and construction equipment, in addition to the previously supplied hydraulic excavators. Fiat sold its telecommunications business to Alcatel Alsthom and a group of French banks, as well as its 25% interest in Alcatel Italia.

In 1994 Fiat sold its battery-making operations to US battery company Exide for $535 million.

NYSE symbol: FIA (ADR)
Fiscal year ends: December 31

WHO

Chairman: Giovanni Agnelli, age 73
VC: Gianluigi Gabetti, age 70
CEO: Cesare Romiti, age 71
Group COO: Giorgio Garuzzo, age 56
CFO; President, Diversified Activities: Francesco Paolo Mattioli, age 53
President and CEO, Fiat U.S.A.: Vittorio Vellano
VP Human Resources, Fiat U.S.A.: Giovanni Berthod
Auditors: Price Waterhouse S.a.s.

WHERE

HQ: Corso Marconi 10, Turin, Italy
Phone: +39-(0)11-686-1111
Fax: +39-(0)11-686-3400
US HQ: Fiat U.S.A., Inc., 375 Park Ave., New York, NY 10152
US Phone: 212-355-2600
US Fax: 212-308-2968

Fiat has operations in 66 countries.

	1993 Sales		1993 Operating Income	
	Lit bil.	% of total	Lit bil.	% of total
Italy	35,603	65	(1,697)	—
Other Europe	10,816	20	(589)	—
Other countries	8,137	15	1,104	—
Total	**54,556**	**100**	**(1,182)**	**—**

WHAT

	1993 Sales		1993 Operating Income	
	Lit bil.	% of total	Lit bil.	% of total
Automobiles	23,805	44	(1,661)	—
Commercial vehicles	6,696	12	(366)	—
Agri. & constr. equipment	5,568	10	238	—
Services	4,556	8	—	—
Other automotive	5,359	10	316	—
Other industrial	6,995	13	153	—
Other	1,577	3	138	—
Total	**54,556**	**100**	**(1,182)**	**—**

Brand Names

Selected Automobiles	Agricultural and Construction Equipment
Alfa Romeo	
Ferrari	
Fiat	Agrifull
Innocenti	Braud
Lancia	Fiat
Maserati	FiatAllis
	Fiat-Hitachi
Commercial Vehicles	Ford
Iveco (buses, diesel engines, firefighting vehicles, quarry and construction vehicles, trucks)	Hesston
	Laverda
	New Holland
	Versatile

KEY COMPETITORS

AGCO	General Motors	Nissan
BMW	Honda	PACCAR
Case Equipment	Hyundai	Peugeot
Caterpillar	Ingersoll-Rand	Renault
Chrysler	Isuzu	Saab-Scania
Daimler-Benz	Kia Motors	Suzuki
Deere	Kubota	Toyota
Dresser	Mazda	Varity
FMC	Mitsubishi	Volkswagen
Ford	Navistar	Volvo

HOW MUCH

$=Lit1713 (Dec. 31, 1993)	Annual Growth	1984	1985[1]	1986	1987	1988	1989	1990	1991	1992	1993
Sales (Lit bil.)	9.6%	23,813	27,594	29,873	39,644	45,512	52,019	57,209	56,488	59,106	54,556
Net income (Lit bil.)	—	627	1,326	2,162	2,373	3,026	3,306	1,613	1,114	551	(1,783)
Income as % of sales	—	2.6%	4.8%	7.2%	6.0%	6.6%	6.4%	2.8%	2.0%	0.9%	—
Earnings per share (Lit)	—	169	357	554	608	776	860	428	287	148	(455)
Stock price – high (Lit)	—	1,260	3,284	9,519	9,902	6,273	7,313	6,792	3,969	3,300	4,531
Stock price – low (Lit)	—	913	1,125	3,195	4,779	4,561	5,413	3,101	2,646	2,025	2,598
Stock price – close (Lit)	15.7%	1,171	3,241	8,290	4,932	5,888	6,679	3,217	2,829	2,403	4,364
P/E – high	—	7	9	17	16	8	9	16	14	22	—
P/E – low	—	5	3	6	8	6	6	7	9	14	—
Dividends per share (Lit)	2.2%	49	60	86	127	162	192	222	222	78	60
Book value per share (Lit)	11.3%	1,697	1,963	2,569	2,926	3,474	4,069	4,083	4,329	4,280	4,448
Employees	4.2%	230,805	226,222	230,293	270,578	277,353	286,294	303,238	287,957	270,876	260,951

1993 Year-end:
Debt ratio: 60.2%
Return on equity: (10.6%)
Cash (bil.): Lit5,718
Long-term debt (bil.): Lit14,562
No. of shares (mil.): 2,425
Dividends
  Yield: 1.4%
  Payout: —
Market value (mil.): $10,434
Sales (mil.): $31,693

**Stock Price History
High/Low 1984–93**

[1]Accounting change

FLETCHER CHALLENGE LIMITED

OVERVIEW

Fletcher Challenge is New Zealand's largest public company. Based in Auckland, Fletchers (as it is known) is involved in forest products, construction, and petroleum.

The company's Pulp and Paper division has operations in 8 countries and is one of the largest newsprint producers in the world. Its Energy unit is involved in oil and gas exploration, production, and marketing in New Zealand and Canada. Fletchers Building Industries is involved in building materials, wood products, and construction. Fletcher Homes is New Zealand's largest home builder. The company's Forestry Division, which manages its timber holdings, has traded as a separate stock since it was spun off in late 1993. Fletchers maintains a 49.5% stake in the division.

Propelled by a series of acquisitions, in 1981 Fletchers catapulted from a domestic concern to a worldwide enterprise. However, the company's shopping spree brought something else: a whopping debt. The company sold off assets to lower its debt but has announced plans to go shopping again, particularly for forestry and energy investments.

WHEN

Fletchers was created by the coming together of 3 companies — Challenge Corporation, Fletcher Holdings, and Tasman Pulp and Paper — in 1981.

Challenge was a Dunedin-based livestock partnership founded in 1861 by John Wright and Robert Robertson. Christened Wright Stephenson & Co. in 1868, the firm expanded throughout New Zealand, opening its first overseas office (London) in 1906. Wright Stephenson diversified into fertilizers (1920), breeding stock (1922), automobiles (1927), electrical appliances (1937), land development (1945), and bicycle and lawn mower manufacturing (1962). Under the chairmanship of Ronald Trotter, the company merged with NMA Company of New Zealand (founded 1864) to form Challenge Corporation in 1972. A New Zealand livestock broker, NMA had grown to become a major meat and seafood exporter.

Fletchers was founded in Dunedin as a construction company in 1909 by Scottish immigrant James Fletcher. James's brothers William and Andrew later joined the company, named Fletcher Construction Company in 1919. Up through the 1930s the company bought several suppliers, such as marble quarries and brickworks, and in 1939 started producing wood-based building materials. The company was reorganized as Fletcher Holdings in 1940. James's son (also James) ran the company from 1942 to 1980.

Tasman — owned by the public, Fletchers, and the New Zealand government — was formed in 1952. The government sold its stake in 1979, and, after a shuffling of stock, Fletchers wound up with 56% of Tasman, and Challenge with 28%. The marriage of these 3 companies in 1981 created an entity that generated about $2 billion in sales (equal to nearly 8% of New Zealand's total GNP) in its first year.

With Trotter as CEO and Hugh Fletcher (the founder's grandson) as COO, Fletchers moved into the Canadian paper business, buying the Canadian forest products operations of San Francisco–based Crown Zellerbach Corporation (renamed Crown Forest Industries) in 1983 and a majority stake in British Columbia Forest Products in 1987. At home Fletchers bought Petrocorp from the government (oil and gas, 1988) and the government-owned Rural Bank (financial services, 1989).

Fletchers entered the European market in 1990 by buying UK Paper (fine paper manufacturing). In 1991 Fletchers bought 90% of Cape Horn Methanol in Chile, becoming the world's largest methanol producer, and controlling interest in Southern Petroleum (oil and gas, New Zealand).

In mid-1992 Fletchers sold Crown Packaging (part of Crown Forest). Later that year it sold 1/3 of Natural Gas Corp., New Zealand's main gas distributor, to the public. It also sold Rural Bank to National Bank of New Zealand.

In 1993 Fletcher Challenge spun off Wrightson Limited, New Zealand's #1 rural servicing organization (wool brokerage, financial services), to shareholders. Also in 1993 the company sold its 43% stake in Methanex, the world's #1 methanol producer, to Canada's Nova Corporation and underwriter Gordon Capital.

In 1994 workers at Fletcher Challenge Canada went on strike, halting work at both of its sawmills.

NYSE symbol: FLC (ADR, Ordinary),
  FFS (ADR, Forestry)
Fiscal year ends: June 30

Chairman: Sir Ronald Trotter, age 66
CEO: Hugh A. Fletcher, age 46
CFO: Ian Donald, age 54
**President and CEO, Blandin Paper Company
  (US):** Alfred C. Wallace
**SVP Finance and Administration, Blandin Paper
  Company (US):** A. Eugene Radecki
**VP Human Resources, Blandin Paper Company
  (US):** Edward Zabinski
Auditors: Coopers & Lybrand; KPMG Peat Marwick

HQ: Fletcher Challenge House, 810 Great
  South Rd., Penrose, Auckland, New Zealand
Phone: +64-9-525-9000
Fax: +64-9-525-0559
US HQ: Blandin Paper Company,
  115 S.W. First St., Grand Rapids, MN 55744
US Phone: 218-327-6200
US Fax: 218-327-6212

	1994 Sales		1994 Operating Income	
	NZ$ mil.	% of total	NZ$ mil.	% of total
New Zealand	3,258	40	549	81
North America	3,023	37	122	18
UK	637	8	(22)	—
Australia	540	7	8	1
Other	659	8	(11)	—
Adjustments	3,120	—	—	—
Total	**11,237**	**100**	**646**	**100**

	1994 Sales		1994 Operating Income	
	NZ$ mil.	% of total	NZ$ mil.	% of total
Building Industries	4,140	51	396	57
Pulp & Paper	2,787	34	(50)	—
Energy	816	10	256	37
Other	374	5	44	6
Adjustments	3,120	—	—	—
Total	**11,237**	**100**	**646**	**100**

Building Industries
Aggregates, cement, and
  concrete products
Building products
  merchandising
Construction
Forestry
Gypsum plasterboard
Industrial, civil, and
  marine engineering
Lumber and wood panels
Project management,
  design, and
  general contracting
Steel and steel products

Pulp and Paper
Coated and uncoated
  woodfree papers
Lightweight coated
  papers, magazine
  papers, printing
  and writing papers
Market kraft pulp
Newsprint, directory
  papers, specialty papers

Energy
Natural gas treatment and
  transmission
Oil and gas exploration,
  development, pro-
  duction, and marketing

Amcor	James River
ARJO Wiggins Appleton	Kimberly-Clark
Boise Cascade	Macmillan
Broken Hill	Manville
Canadian Pacific	Mead
Carter Holt Harvey	Owens-Corning
Champion International	PPG
Fort Howard	Scott
Georgia-Pacific	Stone Container
Hutchison Whampoa	USG
International Paper	Weyerhaeuser

$=NZ$1.79 (Dec. 31, 1993)	9-Year Growth	1985	1986	1987	1988	1989	1990	1991	1992[2]	1993	1994
Sales (NZ$ mil.)	11.6%	4,184	3,986	5,399	8,188	10,461	12,204	11,985	12,460	12,162	11,237
Net income (NZ$ mil.)[3]	5.7%	181	241	255	532	653	662	555	(158)	382	675
Income as % of sales	—	4.3%	6.0%	4.7%	6.5%	6.2%	5.4%	4.6%	—	3.1%	6.0%
Earnings per share (NZ$)[3]	4.1%	0.30	0.36	0.46	0.56	0.60	0.56	0.40	(0.17)	0.24	0.43
Stock price – high (NZ$)[1,4]	—	2.20	3.73	6.20	7.60	5.40	5.68	4.64	3.90	3.61	3.96
Stock price – low (NZ$)[1,4]	—	1.23	1.79	3.54	3.85	4.16	3.92	2.86	3.00	1.63	2.85
Stock price – close (NZ$)[1]	—	—	—	—	—	—	—	—	—	—	—
P/E – high	—	7	10	13	14	9	10	12	—	15	9
P/E – low	—	4	5	8	7	7	7	7	—	7	7
Dividends per share (NZ$)	0.0%	0.13	0.17	0.21	0.24	0.26	0.27	0.27	0.14	0.14	0.13
Book value per share (NZ$)[5]	4.7%	1.65	1.90	2.83	3.01	3.39	3.68	3.68	3.70	3.03	2.50
Employees	(0.7%)	23,400	22,300	37,000	40,000	37,000	40,000	35,000	31,000	24,000	22,000

1994 Year-end:
Debt ratio: 53.5%
Return on equity: 15.7%
Cash (mil.): NZ$285
Long-term debt (mil.): NZ$2,832
No. of shares (mil.): —
Dividends
  Yield: —
  Payout: 28.9%
Market value (mil.): $2,390[6]
Sales (mil.): $6,278

**Stock Price History[1]
High/Low 1985–94**

[1] Stock prices are for the prior calendar year. [2] Accounting change [3] Includes extraordinary items
[4] Fiscal year basis, Ordinary Division beginning in 1994 [5] Excluding goodwill 1985-1991 [6] 1993 year-end

FORMOSA PLASTICS

OVERVIEW

The world's largest producer of PVC (polyvinyl chloride), Formosa Plastics Group is based in Taipei and is Taiwan's biggest nongovernment company. Chairman and founder Yung-ching Wang, who is one of Taiwan's wealthiest individuals, has built the group into a vertically integrated industrial giant. Formosa Plastics produces PVC resin and acrylic fibers, a large portion of which goes to Nan Ya Plastics, the largest plastics manufacturer in the world. Nan Ya produces PVC film and pipe, plastic leather products, printed circuit boards, and polyester. Another affiliate, Formosa Chemicals & Fibre, is Taiwan's largest fiber maker, producing nylon and rayon.

Wang continues to expand his plastics empire. Formosa Plastics is building the world's largest naphtha cracker in Taiwan's Mailiao industrial zone at a cost of $8.5 to $10 billion. By itself the petrochemical complex is expected to add 1% to Taiwan's GNP.

While plastic has long been the Wang family's bread and butter, Wang's children are bringing some new dishes to the table. The family is expanding rapidly into the computer business. Daughter Charlene heads First International Computer (FIC). The world's #1 maker of computer motherboards, FIC is 55%-owned by the Wangs and Charlene's husband's family, the Chiens. Son Winston, head of Nan Ya, is expanding that company's operations into semiconductors and LCD screens. Also, daughter Cher runs PC maker Everex Systems, which the Wangs and FIC acquired in late 1993.

WHEN

In 1932 Yung-ching Wang borrowed $200 from his father, a Taiwanese tea merchant, to buy a rice mill near the town of Jiayi. The mill was destroyed by Allied bombs in 1944, but Wang went on to make a fortune in timber and founded Formosa Plastics, a small PVC plant, in 1954. He bought the technology from the Japanese and jokes that, when he formed the company, he didn't even know what the P in PVC stood for.

At first Wang had trouble finding buyers for his PVC resins, but in 1958 he set up his own PVC resin processor, Nan Ya Plastics. He formed Formosa Chemicals & Fibre to make rayon backing for PVC leather (1965). For the next 15 years, the company continued to grow exclusively as a Taiwanese enterprise.

Between 1980 and 1988 Wang bought 14 US PVC-related manufacturers, including Imperial Chemical's Baton Rouge vinyl chloride monomer plant (1981), Stauffer Chemical's Delaware City PVC plant (1981), and Manville Corporation's PVC businesses (1983). He started building a PVC plant in Point Comfort, Texas, in 1981, cutting construction costs up to 40% by importing equipment from Taiwan.

When the PVC market reached saturation in the mid-1980s, Wang built plants in Taiwan to make chemicals for semiconductors. Nan Ya enlisted the help of Hewlett-Packard to build a plant capable of producing printed circuit boards and the necessary chemicals.

Wang bought several Texas-based oil and gas properties, including 218 producing wells, a gas processing plant, and a pipeline company from Alcoa in 1988. He continued to expand PVC operations but, faced with stricter pollution controls in Taiwan, announced his intention to build an ethylene plant in Point Comfort (1988). Construction was delayed in 1990, when the EPA began investigating allegations that Formosa had contaminated groundwater near the plant.

Wang then turned to mainland China, where there were no pollution controls, planning to build an ethylene complex there (1990). Taiwan balked at the proposal, suggesting that Formosa Plastics should build at home instead. But rather than accept his homeland's environmental constraints (or perhaps to leverage negotiations with the Taiwanese government), Wang sought Chinese approval of the multibillion-dollar project, negotiating through a US subsidiary, Formosa Plastics Corp., to circumvent a Taiwanese law against direct investment in the mainland. Chinese city and provincial authorities rejected a plan in 1991 that called for them to put up 2/3 of the investment on a $7 billion petrochemical complex, and in 1992 the group had delayed plans for further investment in China's petrochemical sector.

In 1992 Formosa Plastics Corp. completed petrochemical and plastics processing plants in Port Comfort, Texas.

In 1994 the group returned to mainland China when Na Ya Plastics announced plans to build 3 plants along China's Long River.

Principal exchange: Taiwan
Fiscal year ends: December 31

Chairman: Yung-ching Wang, age 78
President, Formosa Chemicals & Fibre: Yung-tsai Wang, age 75
SVP, Nan Ya Plastics: Winston Wang, age 43
President, First International Computer: Charlene Wang, age 45
President, Everex Systems: Cher Wang, age 36
President, Formosa Plastics U.S.A.: Susan Wang
CFO, Formosa Plastics U.S.A.: Robert Ho
Director of Personnel, Formosa Plastics U.S.A.: George Karliss

HQ: Formosa Plastics Corporation, 201 Tun Hwa North Rd., Taipei, Taiwan
Phone: +886-(0)2-712-2211
Fax: +886-(0)2-717-5287
US HQ: Formosa Plastics Corp., U.S.A., 9 Peach Tree Hill Rd., Livingston, NJ 07039
US Phone: 201-992-2090
US Fax: 201-992-9627

	1993 Sales % of total
Taiwan	85
Other countries	15
Total	**100**

	1993 Sales % of total
Polyvinyl chloride (PVC) resins	56
Acrylic staple fibers	14
Acrylic esters	7
High-density polyethylene (HDPE)	6
Calcium carbide products	4
Other	13
Total	**100**

Selected Subsidiaries and Affiliates
Everex Systems (personal computers, US)
First International Computer (computer motherboards)
Formosa Chemicals & Fibre Corp. (rayon, nylon filament, and man-made fiber)
Formosa Heavy Industries Co. Ltd (machinery)
Formosa Petrochemical Co., Ltd. (refinery and utilities)
Formosa Plastics Corp., U.S.A. (PVC products)
J-M Manufacturing Co., Inc. (PVC pipe, US)
Mailao Harbor Administration Co., Ltd. (planning, construction, and administration of harbor facilities)
Nan Ya Plastics Corp. (plastic products marketing)
Nan Ya Technology Co. (memory semiconductors and LCD screens)
Tai Shih Textile Industry Corp. (yarns)
Yungchia Chemical Industries Co., Ltd. (polypropylene)

Akzo Nobel	Hercules	Packard Bell
AMD	Hewlett-Packard	Phillips Petroleum
Apple	IBM	Rhône-Poulenc
Armstrong World	Intel	Rubbermaid
BASF	Lyondell	Samsung
Bayer	Petrochemical	Shanghai
Canon	Masco	Petrochemical
Ciba-Geigy	Matsushita	Sony
Dell	Micron	Texas Instruments
DuPont	Technology	Toshiba
Gateway 2000	Milliken	Union Carbide
Georgia-Pacific	Motorola	USG

$=NT$26.4 (Dec. 31, 1993)	Annual Growth	1984	1985	1986	1987	1988	1989	1990	1991	1992	1993
Sales (NT$ mil.)	1.5%	23,747	24,832	27,973	30,274	33,302	30,426	29,578	31,704	30,911	27,165
Net income (NT$ mil.)	10.5%	1,577	1,562	2,469	3,017	3,809	3,181	3,627	3,222	3,860	3,877
Income as % of sales	—	6.6%	6.3%	8.8%	10.0%	11.4%	10.5%	12.3%	10.2%	12.5%	14.3%
Earnings per share (NT$)	10.3%	0.93	0.92	1.45	1.78	2.26	1.88	2.14	1.85	2.22	2.24
Stock price – high (NT$)	—	12	12	17	51	97	66	88	56	45	58
Stock price – low (NT$)	—	7	7	12	16	26	42	21	26	29	32
Stock price – close (NT$)	21.6%	10	12	16	26	46	57	31	36	30	58
P/E – high	—	13	13	12	29	43	35	42	30	20	26
P/E – low	—	7	8	8	9	12	23	10	14	13	14
Dividends per share (NT$)	22.1%	—	—	—	0.37	0.49	0.58	0.69	0.83	0.9	0.9
Book value per share (NT$)	19.0%	—	—	—	—	—	—	11.64	13.85	16.62	16.66
Employees[1]	10.2%	—	—	—	—	—	5,145	4,650	4,767	—	3,345

1993 Year-end:
Debt ratio: —
Return on equity: 13.5%
Cash (mil.): —
Long-term debt (mil.): NT$0
No. of shares (mil.): 1,728
Dividends
 Yield: 1.6%
 Payout: 40.2%
Market value (mil.): $3,763
Sales (mil.): $1,029

Stock Price History High/Low 1984–93

Information is for Formosa Plastics Corp. only. [1] Parent company

FOSTER'S BREWING GROUP LIMITED

OVERVIEW

According to its ads, Foster's is "Australian for beer," and Ted Kunkel is making sure it's no longer also Australian for real estate or agriculture. CEO of the the world's 4th largest brewer, Kunkel has focused on selling off the company's noncore assets, including its investments in Australia Meat Holdings and financial services company Elders Limited, to concentrate on brewing.

What's left is a brewer with operations around the world. Foster's Carlton and United unit is Australia's #1 brewer, with a 50% market share. It makes Australia's most popular beer, which, despite its ad's linguistic claims, is Victoria Bitter and not Foster's Lager. Courage, the company's UK brewer, is Britain's #2 beer producer (after Bass). In North America, Foster's owns 40% of Molson, Canada's largest brewer and maker of the #2 US import, Molson Ice. Foster's Lager is the #1 selling Australian brand import in the US (although most of it is brewed in Canada).

The company continues to expand internationally, with a particular eye toward Asia, where beer consumption is growing at 15% to 20% in some countries. It has joint ventures with 2 breweries in China.

Australian conglomerate Broken Hill Properties owns 33.5% of Foster's, and Japan's Asahi owns 13.8%.

WHEN

In 1839 Scotsman Alexander Lang Elder arrived at what would become Port Adelaide, Australia, and founded Elder Smith Goldsborough, a trading company to serve local farmers. Over the next 140 years, his enterprise grew into one of Australia's largest commodities trading and farm services companies. But it did not achieve international notoriety until the early 1980s when it became a takeover target for Robert Holmes à Court, reputed to be Australia's richest man.

For help, Elder Smith turned to John Elliott, managing director of Henry Jones (IXL), a Tasmanian jam and food company. (The name *IXL* was coined around the turn of the century by the company's semiliterate founder to mean "I excel.") Elliott suggested that Elder Smith take over Henry Jones (IXL) to thwart Holmes à Court, and the 2 companies were joined as Elders IXL in 1981. Elliott and his management group assumed control of the new company. In 1982 Elders acquired Wood Hall Trust, a British trading operation.

In 1983 Carlton and United Breweries (CUB), which owned 49% of Elders, was also threatened by a takeover, requiring Elders's immediate attention. CUB had been founded near Melbourne in 1888 by brothers W. M. and R. R. Foster. The company had first exported its Foster's Lager in 1901 to serve Australian forces fighting the Boer War and in 1907 had joined with 6 other breweries. By 1986 the lager was sold in 80 countries.

In 2 days Elliott raised $720 million and captured more than half of the brewery (buying the rest in 1984), instantly making Elders one of Australia's largest companies.

Following a failed attempt to acquire Britain's Allied-Lyons, the company bought Courage Breweries (UK) for $3.5 billion (Australia's largest overseas takeover) in 1986 and in 1987 acquired Carling O'Keefe Breweries (Canada) for $413 million. At the same time the company greatly expanded its banking and other operations.

In 1989 Elliott and other Elders executives launched a $4.4 billion management takeover that netted around 50% of Elders. In 1990 Elliott stepped down as CEO and became nonexecutive deputy chairman. Under Elliott's replacement, Peter Bartels, the company launched a major restructuring in which it changed its name to Foster's Brewing Group and put all of its nonbrewing assets up for sale.

In 1991 Foster's purchased the brewing interests of Grand Metropolitan in exchange for Foster's 50% interest in Courage Pubs. However, 1991 and 1992 saw several boardroom brawls over company strategy, which sparked the resignations of Bartels and Elliott, who owned 38% of the company.

Foster's posted a major loss for fiscal 1992 because of asset write-downs occurring from bad property loans made in the 1980s. That year Broken Hill Properties, Australia's huge mineral resources company, acquired a stake in the company from creditors of Elliott's investment group.

In 1993 Foster's sold 10% of its interest in Molson to Philip Morris's Miller Brewing. The next year Foster's sold its stake in Northwest Airlines to KLM Royal Dutch Airlines for $180 million.

OTC symbol: FBWGY (ADR)
Fiscal year ends: June 30

WHO

Chairman: Neil "Nobby" R. Clark, age 65
CEO: E.T. (Ted) Kunkel, age 51
Group Director Corporate Affairs: Peter A. Bobeff
Group Director Strategy and Development:
Keith M. Lambert
Group Director Finance and Investor Relations:
A.C. (Tony) Larkin
**Executive Director Integration and Human
Resources Projects:** Rick E. Beker
President and CEO, Molson (NA): J. Bruce Pope
CFO, Molson (NA): Ian Fraser Smith
SVP Personnel, Molson (NA): Gary Burkett
Auditors: Price Waterhouse

WHERE

HQ: One Garden St., South Yarra, Victoria 3141,
Australia
Phone: +61-3-828-2424
Fax: +61-3-826-9310
No. Am. HQ: Molson Breweries, 175 Bloor St.
East, Toronto, Ontario M4W 3S4, Canada
No. Am. Phone: 416-975-1786
No. Am. Fax: 416-975-4088

	1994 Sales		1994 Operating Income	
	A$ mil.	% of total	A$ mil.	% of total
Europe	2,203	44	(456)	—
Australasia/				
Pacific	2,197	43	653	—
North America	668	13	40	—
Adjustments	2,116	—	—	—
Total	**7,184**	**100**	**237**	**—**

WHAT

	1994 Sales		1994 Operating Income	
	A$ mil.	% of total	A$ mil.	% of total
Brewing	4,291	85	491	—
Finance	132	2	—	—
Investments &				
other	645	13	(29)	—
Adjustments	2,116	—	(225)	—
Total	**7,184**	**100**	**237**	**—**

Brewing Group
Carlton and United
 Breweries
Carlton Cold Filtered
 Bitter
Foster's
Fremantle Bitter Ale
Redback Bitter
Victoria Bitter
Courage Limited (UK)
 Draught Beamish
 Stout
 Foster's
 Holsten Pils
 John Smith's
 Kronenbourg 1664

Molson Breweries
 (40%, Canada)
Carling
Carling Draft
Carling Light
Foster's Lager
Molson Canadian Ice
Molson Ice
Red Dog

Finance Group
Investment management

Real Estate
Inntrepreneur Estates
 (50%, UK, property
 management)

KEY COMPETITORS

Adolph Coors	Carlsberg	Moosehead
Allied	Danone	Breweries
Domecq	Guinness	Philip Morris
Anheuser-Busch	Heileman	Power Brewing
Bass	Heineken	S&P
Big Rock	John Labatt	San Miguel
Brewery	Kirin	Stroh
Boston Beer	Lion Nathan	Tsingtao

HOW MUCH

$=A$1.47 (Dec. 31, 1993)	Annual Growth	1985	1986	1987	1988	1989	1990	1991	1992	1993	1994
Sales (A$ mil.)[1]	0.3%	6,995	7,659	10,560	15,350	17,647	15,406	10,633	10,371	9,094	7,184
Net income (A$ mil.)[2]	10.8%	112	202	350	795	630	(1,264)	(43)	(951)	310	282
Income as % of sales	—	1.6%	2.6%	3.3%	5.2%	3.6%	—	—	(9.2%)	3.4%	3.9%
Earnings per share (A$)[2]	5.1%	0.14	0.21	0.21	0.24	0.29	(0.55)	(0.02)	(0.40)	0.11	0.09
Stock price – high (A$)[3]	—	1.33	1.54	3.20	4.23	2.59	2.73	2.42	1.89	1.95	1.60
Stock price – low (A$)[3]	—	0.88	1.07	1.25	1.78	1.84	2.13	1.10	1.24	1.09	1.11
Stock price – close (A$)[3]	2.6%	1.16	1.44	2.81	1.81	2.38	2.16	1.49	1.89	1.36	1.46
P/E – high	—	10	7	15	18	9	—	—	—	18	18
P/E – low	—	6	5	6	7	6	—	—	—	10	13
Dividends per share (A$)	2.0%	0.05	0.07	0.08	0.10	0.15	0.18	0.20	0.03	0.06	0.06
Book value per share (A$)	3.4%	0.63	0.85	1.35	1.65	1.83	1.19	1.07	1.06	0.77	0.85
Employees	33.1%	—	—	—	—	—	33,702	16,300	14,900	10,083	—

1994 Year-end:
Debt ratio: 50.9%
Return on equity: 10.7%
Cash (mil.): A$17
Long-term debt (mil.): A$1,915
No. of shares (mil.): 3,219
Dividends
Yield: 4.1%
Payout: 69.0%
Market value (mil.): $3,197
Sales (mil.): $4,887

**Stock Price History[3]
High/Low 1985–94**

[1] Including excise taxes   [2] Including extraordinary items   [3] Stock prices are for the prior calendar year.

FRIED. KRUPP AG HOESCH-KRUPP

OVERVIEW

Fried. Krupp AG Hoesch-Krupp is an example of the German steel industry reinventing itself in the face of a united European market. The Krupp group of diversified steel and industrial companies was the product of one of Germany's largest mergers, created in a rare hostile takeover in 1991, that combined 2 Ruhr Valley–based steel and engineering companies: Friedrich Krupp and Hoesch. The merger of these 2 leading steel producers created the 2nd largest German steel company, after Thyssen.

Krupp's expectations of higher revenues were dashed by a severe recession in 1992–93, which lowered orders for steel, and by a flood of inexpensive steel from Eastern Europe when the Iron Curtain lifted. Krupp was forced to permanently close its 103-year-old Rheinhausen steel mill and cut thousands of jobs in the consolidation. The company's steep loss in 1993 stemmed mostly from its troubled steel operations; Krupp's other manufacturing, trade, automotive, and building divisions posted less dramatic declines.

The company's stock was publicly traded for the first time in 1993, but the Krupp family foundation still owns the controlling share (54%); the Islamic Republic of Iran owns 25%, and individual shareholders own the remainder of the stock.

WHEN

Arndt Krupp, penniless when he came to Essen in 1587, used his profits from working as a merchant to buy land holdings at bargain prices from victims of the bubonic plague. He soon was one of the city's richest men.

Krupp's son Anton was equally successful, having entered the gun trade just in time for the Thirty Years' War. Krupp fortunes seemed blessed for several generations, until 1811 when Friedrich Krupp, a 6th generation family member, opened a steel factory. The enterprise was a failure, and in 1826 Krupp died, leaving the near-bankrupt factory in the hands of his 14-year-old son Alfred.

Alfred turned the operation around, introducing steel products for the railroad (including the nonwelded, seamless railroad wheel that he had invented) and, at the first World's Fair in 1851, unveiling Krupp's powerful steel cannon (which was far superior to older bronze models).

When Otto von Bismarck assumed power in Prussia, he used Krupp weapons to defeat the French in the Franco-Prussian War. The "Cannon King," as Alfred became known, died in 1887, leaving what was then the world's largest industrial company in the hands of his son Fritz, an eccentric who killed himself after a sexual scandal in 1902.

Alfred's granddaughter Bertha (after whom Germany's Big Bertha guns were named) and her new husband, Gustav von Bohlen und Halbach (later Gustav Krupp), took over and armed the Kaiser for WWI.

The Treaty of Versailles momentarily shut down the company, but Gustav Krupp was back in time to build U-boats, tanks, battleships, and other weapons for Adolf Hitler. In 1943 the ailing Gustav was replaced by his son Alfried, who was convicted at the 1948 Nuremburg trials for using slave laborers during the war.

Alfried was released from prison in 1951 and quickly rebuilt Krupp into Germany's largest steel and machine conglomerate. In 1967 he passed control of the company to a private foundation and died later that year, ending the long era of Krupp leadership.

Berthold Beitz became chairman and greatly expanded Krupp's overseas presence. In 1974 he orchestrated the sale of 25% of the company to the Shah of Iran. Krupp's fortunes began a slow decline in the early 1970s, owing largely to management quarrels, a stubborn insistence on holding on to unprofitable divisions, and the faltering state of the global steel market.

After weathering a 1987 strike by steelworkers and rejecting a takeover bid by Thyssen in 1988, the Krupp board ousted Beitz and initiated a major restructuring in which loss-producing divisions were spun off. That year the company formed Krupp Lonrho, its trading division. In 1990 Krupp purchased Precision Rolled Products (high-performance aircraft products) and Press-und Stanzwerk (auto parts, Liechtenstein). The company disposed of its holdings in the electronics subsidiary, Krupp Atlas Elektronik, in mid-1992.

After the consolidation with Hoesch, Krupp agreed to 2 joint ventures with Thyssen in 1994 to produce tinplate and stainless steel flat products.

Principal exchange: Frankfurt
Fiscal year ends: December 31

Chairman: Gerhard Cromme
Deputy Chairman: Gerhard Neipp
Head of Corporate Finance: Klaus Hübner
Head of Legal Affairs: Henrik-Michael Ringleb
Head of Energy and Environment: Manfred
  Seeger
Head of Information Policy: Jürgen-Peter Voight
Head of Corporate Personnel and Social Policy:
  Heinrich Kahmeyer
President, Krupp USA: Daniel R. Fritz
VP Finance, Krupp USA: Andreas Penninger
Director Human Resources, Krupp USA: Mike
  Dowell
Auditors: C&L Treuhand-Vereinigung
  Aktiengesellschaft

HQ: D-45117 Essen, Germany
Phone: +49-201-188-1
Fax: +49-201-188-4100
US HQ: Krupp USA Inc., 180 Interstate North
  Pkwy., Atlanta, GA 30339-2194
Phone: 404-955-3660
Fax: 404-955-8789

The Krupp group includes 158 domestic and 140
foreign subsidiaries.

	1993 Sales	
	DM mil.	% of total
Germany	10,384	51
America	2,541	12
Other EC countries	3,955	19
Other Europe	1,272	6
Other countries	2,352	12
Total	**20,504**	**100**

	1993 Sales	
	DM mil.	% of total
Steel	6,853	28
Trading & Services	6,421	26
Fabricating	3,079	13
Mechanical Engineering	2,949	12
Automotive	2,578	11
Plantmaking	1,646	7
Other	655	3
Adjustments	(3,677)	—
Total	**20,504**	**100**

Selected Products

Bridges	Logistic services
Bulk cargo shipping	Mobile cranes
Car bodies	Nonferrous metals
Cement plants	Power plants
Coal gasification and	Precision cold forgings
petrochemical plants	Railway equipment
Coated and uncoated steel	Recycling systems
Coin blanks	Semifinished steel
Coke-oven plants	products
Construction equipment	Stainless steel
Diesel engines	Strip steel
Drivetrains and steering	Tinmill products
Heating systems	Waste disposal systems

Major Subsidiaries
Krupp Anlagenbau (plant marketing)
Krupp Hoesch Automotive
Krupp Hoesch International (trading/services)
Krupp Hoesch Maschinenbau (mechanical engineering)
Krupp Hoesch Stahl (steel)
Krupp Hoesch Verarbeitung (fabricating)

Bechtel	General Electric	Marubeni
Bethlehem Steel	General Signal	Mitsubishi
British Steel	Hitachi	Navistar
Broken Hill	Hyundai	Nippon Steel
Cargill	Ingersoll-Rand	Nucor
Caterpillar	Inland Steel	Raytheon
Cooper Industries	IRI	Siemens
Cummins Engine	Klöckner-Werke	Thyssen
Fiat	LTV	USX–
FMC	Mannesmann	U.S. Steel

$=DM1.52 (Dec. 31, 1993)	Annual Growth	1984	1985	1986	1987	1988	1989	1990	1991	1992	1993
Sales (DM mil.)	1.3%	18,239	18,479	15,847	14,105	14,737	17,684	15,570	15,133	23,157	20,504
Net income (DM mil.)[1]	—	579	358	338	252	209	338	272	383	(250)	(589)
Income as % of sales	—	3.2%	1.9%	2.1%	1.8%	1.4%	1.9%	1.7%	2.5%	—	—
Employees	1.9%	66,320	67,402	68,043	65,205	63,391	60,767	59,044	53,115	88,656	78,376

1993 Year-end:
Debt ratio: 70.9%
Return on equity: —
Cash (mil.): DM311
L-T debt (mil.): DM1,825
No. of shares (mil.): —
Dividends
  Yield: —
  Payout: —
Sales (mil.): $11,808

Net Income (DM mil.)
1984–1993

[1] Estimated 1984

FUJI PHOTO FILM CO., LTD.

OVERVIEW

Fuji Photo Film has evolved from a small cinematic film manufacturer to be Japan's #1 and the world's 2nd largest photographic film producer, after archrival Eastman Kodak. The top maker of photosensitive materials in Japan, Fuji boasts a 70% market share in color films on its home turf. The company has leveraged its technical expertise to branch into other types of imaging, such as cameras, camcorders, audio- and videotapes (which represent 37% of 1993 sales), and photofinishing systems (24%). Fuji's office and medical technology products, which include floppy disks, computer media, color printers, and medical diagnosis systems, represented the largest share (39%) of its 1993 revenues.

In 1994 Fuji was forced to temporarily raise US prices after Kodak alleged illegal dumping of its imported photographic paper. But Fuji expects to skirt the problem by manufacturing the paper at its South Carolina plant in 1995. The company also created a new division in the US to hook up with computer companies to develop digital products, an area with huge growth potential. Hoping to revive picture-taking in the age of camcorders, Kodak recruited rivals Fuji, Canon, Nikon, and Minolta to produce a smaller, thinner camera that may create a new standard. Although Agfa-Gevaert has agreed to license the technology, other camera makers have been noncommittal.

WHEN

Mokichi Morita, president of Japan's leading celluloid maker (Dainippon Celluloid Company, founded in 1919), decided to start making motion picture film in the early 1930s. Movies were becoming popular in Japan, but there was no domestic film supplier. Working with a grant from the government, Dainippon Celluloid established Fuji Photo Film, an independent company, in 1934 in Minami Ashigara Village, near Mount Fuji. At first the company had trouble gaining acceptance in Japan as a quality film producer but, with the help of German emulsion specialist Dr. Emill Mauerhoff, overcame its product deficiencies, producing black-and-white photographic film (1936) and the first Japanese-made color film (1948). In the meantime Fuji added 35mm photographic film, 16mm motion picture film, and X-ray film to its product line.

By the early 1940s Fuji was operating 4 factories and a research laboratory in Japan. Its first overseas office, in Brazil, opened in 1955, followed by offices in the US in 1958 and Europe in 1964.

Fuji continued to expand its product line, adding magnetic tape in 1960. In 1962 the company joined Rank Xerox of the UK (an affiliate of America's Xerox and the UK's Rank Organisation) to form Fuji Xerox, a Japanese-based joint venture to sell copiers. In the US Fuji operated as a private label film supplier and did not market its products under its own brand name until 1972.

International marketing VP Minoru Ohnishi became Fuji's president in 1980. Ohnishi's succession marked a new direction for the company; at 55 he was Fuji's youngest president, chosen over more senior officers. Ohnishi worked to decrease Fuji's dependence on Japanese film sales by building sales in the US and pumping money into the production of videotapes, floppy disks, and medical diagnostic equipment.

In 1987 Fuji introduced Fujicolor Quicksnap, the world's first 35mm disposable camera. Quicksnap appealed to consumers looking for convenience at a rock-bottom price.

In 1990 Fuji created FUJIFILM Microdevices, a Japanese subsidiary to produce image processing semiconductors. In 1991 it acquired several wholesale photofinishing labs to strengthen its lab network. New consumer product offerings in 1991 included the Fujix Digital Still Camera System, which stores images electronically and allows computer image processing and transmission.

In 1992 Fuji scientists announced they had successfully built a crude artificial "eye," which could be a forerunner of more efficient eyes for robots. In 1993 Fuji launched the FUJIX Simple-Hi8 (the world's smallest and lightest camcorder) and the Pictrostat instant print system, which produces in one minute color prints from photos, slides, and objects.

As the official sponsor of the 1994 World Cup, Fuji was the exclusive supplier of on-site photographic film and sole provider of film and film processing services for the press. Fuji finished 1994 with $655 million in profits and nearly $11 billion in sales.

OTC symbol: FUJIY (ADR)
Fiscal year ends: March 31

President: Minoru Ohnishi
Senior Managing Director: Hirozo Ueda
Senior Managing Director: Masayuki Muneyuki
CFO: M. Fujita
Personnel Manager: S. Akaishi
President, Fuji Photo Film U.S.A.:
  Sam Inoue
Treasurer, Fuji Photo Film U.S.A.:
  Noboru Tanaka
Director Human Resources, Fuji Photo Film
  U.S.A.: Joe Convery
Auditors: Price Waterhouse

WHERE

HQ: 26-30, Nishiazabu 2-chome, Minato-ku,
  Tokyo 106, Japan
Phone: +81-3-3406-2844
Fax: +81-3-3406-2193
US HQ: Fuji Photo Film U.S.A., Inc.,
  555 Taxter Rd., Elmsford, NY 10523
US Phone: 914-789-8100
US Fax: 914-789-8295

Fuji has operations in Brazil, Canada, Europe,
Japan, the Pacific Basin, and the US.

| | 1993 Sales | |
	$ mil.	% of total
Japan	6,242	61
Other countries	3,915	39
Total	**10,157**	**100**

WHAT

| | 1993 Sales | |
	$ mil.	% of total
Information	3,933	39
Imaging	3,738	37
Photofinishing	2,486	24
Total	**10,157**	**100**

Major Products

Audiotape	Information file system
Batteries	equipment
Blood analyzer	Instant cameras
Camcorders	Instant print systems
Cameras	Liquid crystal display films
Carbonless copying papers	Medical X-ray imaging
Color printer	equipment
Computer tapes	Microfilm systems
Copiers	Motion picture films
Data cartridge tapes	Overhead projectors
Data management systems	Photofinishing labs
Digital still video cameras	Photographic chemicals
Disposable cameras	Photographic films
Enlargers	Photographic paper
Floppy disks	Printing plates
Graphic arts films	Thermal paper
Industrial chemicals	Video projectors
Industrial plastic films	Videotape

KEY COMPETITORS

3DO	Harris Corp.	Pitney Bowes
Agfa-Gevaert	Hewlett-Packard	Polaroid
Alcatel Alsthom	Hillman	Ralston Purina
Apple	Hitachi	Group
BASF	IBM	Ricoh
Bayer	Matsushita	Sanyo
Canon	3M	Sharp
DuPont	Minolta	Siemens
Duracell	Océ	Sony
Eastman Kodak	Oki	Toshiba
Elscint	PictureTel	Xerox
GEC	Pioneer	

HOW MUCH

Stock prices are for ADRs ADR = 2 shares	9-Year Growth	1984	1985	1986	1987	1988	1989	1990	1991	1992	1993
Sales ($ mil.)	15.8%	2,712	3,739	4,803	5,894	6,978	6,539	8,191	8,543	9,162	10,157
Net income ($ mil.)	10.6%	229	330	394	521	653	587	694	725	607	569
Income as % of sales	—	8.5%	8.8%	8.2%	8.8%	9.4%	9.0%	8.5%	8.5%	6.6%	5.6%
Earnings per share ($)	9.2%	0.99	1.48	1.74	2.28	2.80	2.52	2.98	2.83	2.36	2.18
Stock price – high ($)	—	16.11	17.16	39.14	55.88	56.50	64.31	60.33	56.00	47.75	52.63
Stock price – low ($)	—	9.71	10.03	15.71	27.27	38.32	39.14	42.27	41.75	37.88	39.88
Stock price – close ($)	17.7%	10.23	16.73	37.81	52.47	46.98	56.47	46.75	44.25	42.25	44.38
P/E – high	—	16	12	23	25	20	26	20	20	20	24
P/E – low	—	10	7	9	12	14	16	14	15	16	18
Dividends per share ($)	19.0%	0.05	0.05	0.09	0.11	0.13	0.13	0.13	0.17	0.20	0.24
Book value per share ($)	19.5%	7.97	11.14	15.56	20.15	24.90	24.77	30.19	29.70	33.28	39.50
Employees	4.6%	16,689	16,915	17,180	17,703	18,195	19,677	21,946	23,690	24,868	25,074

1993 Year-end:
Debt ratio: 32.9%
Return on equity: 6.0%
Cash (mil.): $4,675
Current ratio: 2.49
Long-term debt (mil.): $370
No. of shares (mil.): 261
Dividends
  Yield: 0.5%
  Payout: 11.0%
Market value (mil.): $11,590

Stock Price History
High/Low 1984–93

Note: For fiscal years ended October 20.

FUJITSU LIMITED

OVERVIEW

Japan's largest computer manufacturer (with a 25% market share) and #2 in the world (after IBM), Fujitsu has been suffering from the same maladies that have hit a number of computer makers lately: mainframe pneumonia and computer chip flu. The Tokyo-based company's sales have dropped, and it has posted losses the last 2 years.

The shift from mainframes to smaller, networked systems has been Fujitsu's main complaint. Traditionally, half of the company's sales and almost all its profits have come from mainframes, but with that market drying up, the company is shifting to client-server systems, streamlining operations, and cutting expenses.

Fujitsu's semiconductor business has also been hurting. Like many of its Japanese siblings, it has seen US semiconductor companies take away market share. To get back in shape (and to save on R&D costs), it has signed development deals with computer chip companies, including AMD and Hyundai. It is also focusing on building its service, software, and multimedia products businesses.

The company owns substantial interests in mainframe makers ICL (UK, 80%) and Amdahl (US, 45%). Fuji Electric is Fujitsu's largest shareholder, with 13.5% of its stock.

WHEN

In 1923 Siemens and Furukawa Electric created Fuji Electric to produce electrical equipment. Fuji spun off Fujitsu, its communications division, in 1935. Originally a manufacturer of telephone equipment, Fujitsu produced anti-aircraft weapons during WWII. After the war Fujitsu returned to telecommunications, becoming one of 4 major suppliers to state-owned monopoly Nippon Telegraph and Telephone and benefiting from Japan's rapid economic recovery in the 1950s and 1960s.

With encouragement from Japan's Ministry of International Trade and Industry (MITI), Fujitsu entered the data processing industry by developing the country's first commercial computer in 1954. Starting in 1959 MITI erected trade barriers to protect Japan's new computer industry. In the early 1960s MITI sponsored the production of mainframe computers, directing Fujitsu to develop the central processing unit. The company expanded into the related areas of semiconductor production and factory automation in the late 1960s. Fujitsu's factory automation business was spun off as Fujitsu Fanuc in 1972. Now called Fanuc, the company has become an important manufacturer of industrial robots.

In the 1970s Fujitsu sought to gain market share by making IBM-plug-compatible computers that provided superior value to buyers. The company bought 30% of plug-compatible manufacturer Amdahl (1972) and gained badly needed technical information. In 1974 Fujitsu introduced its first plug-compatible computer and the following year began supplying Amdahl with OEM mainframe subassemblies. In 1979 Fujitsu passed IBM to become Japan's #1 computer manufacturer.

In Europe Fujitsu entered into computer marketing ventures with Siemens (1978) and ICL (1981). The company teamed with TRW (US) to sell point-of-sale systems in 1980, assuming full control of the operation in 1983. Fujitsu released its first supercomputer in 1982. The company dropped its 1986 bid for Fairchild Semiconductor when the US government expressed concern over foreign ownership of the chip maker.

In 1985 IBM accused Fujitsu of stealing proprietary operating system software technology. Fujitsu objected, citing a secret 1983 agreement under which Fujitsu had paid IBM for software information. In 1988 an arbitrator awarded IBM $237 million. It also granted Fujitsu the right to inspect certain IBM software for 10 years for a relatively small annual fee of $25 million to $52 million.

In 1990 Fujitsu bought 80% of British mainframe maker ICL (from STC). In 1991 ICL bought 50% of the European computer-maintenance operations of Bell Atlantic and all of Nokia Data Holding, the largest computer company in Scandinavia. In 1992 Fujitsu and Advanced Micro Devices agreed to build a $700-million facility in Japan to build flash memory chips.

In 1993 the company and Siemens announced plans to develop a new generation of less expensive mainframes. In 1994 Fujitsu signed a deal with Sun Microsystems to develop microprocessors for Sun's line of workstations.

OTC symbol: FJTSY (ADR)
Fiscal year ends: March 31

Chairman: Takuma Yamamoto
President: Tadashi Sekizawa
EVP: Mikio Ohtsuki
President and CEO, Fujitsu America:
Yoshio Honda
Auditors: Showa Ota & Co.

WHERE

HQ: 6-1, Marunouchi 1-chome, Chiyoda-ku,
Tokyo 100, Japan
Phone: +81-3-3216-7955
Fax: +81-3-3216-9352
US HQ: Fujitsu America, Inc., 3055 Orchard Dr.,
San Jose, CA 95134-2022
US Phone: 408-432-1300
US Fax: 408-432-1318

Fujitsu operates worldwide, with offices in
Abu Dhabi, Amman, Bangkok, Beijing, Bogota,
Brussels, Hanoi, Harare, Honolulu, Jakarta,
Kuala Lumpur, Mexico City, Munich,
New Delhi, New York, Shanghai, Taipei,
and Washington, D.C.

	1994 Sales	
	¥ bil.	**% of total**
Japan	2,214	70
Europe	459	15
The Americas	261	8
Asia & Oceania	185	6
Africa & the Middle East	20	1
Total	**3,139**	**100**

WHAT

	1994 Sales	
	¥ bil.	**% of total**
Computer systems	2,140	68
Communications systems	488	16
Electronic devices	395	12
Other operations	116	4
Total	**3,139**	**100**

Computer Systems
Peripherals
Personal computers
Servers
Software
Storage products
Supercomputers

Communications Systems
ATM products
Optical transmission
equipment
Switching systems
Teleconferencing
equipment

Electronic Devices
Gate arrays
Semiconductors

KEY COMPETITORS

Advanced Logic	Hitachi	Northern
Research	Hyundai	Telecom
Apple	IBM	Oki
AST	Intel	Philips
AT&T	Kendall Square	Samsung
Canon	Research	Sanyo
Compaq	LSI Logic	Seagate
Computervision	LG Group	Siemens
Conner	Machines Bull	Silicon Graphics
Peripherals	MasPar	Sony
Cray Computer	Mission Research	Sun
Cray Research	Mitsubishi	Microsystems
Data General	Motorola	Tandem
DEC	National	Texas
Dell	Semiconductor	Instruments
Gateway 2000	nCube	Thinking
Hewlett-Packard	NEC	Machines
		Toshiba
		Unisys

HOW MUCH

$ = ¥112 (Dec. 31, 1993)	9-Year Growth	1985	1986	1987	1988	1989	1990	1991	1992	1993	1994
Sales (¥ bil.)	8.1%	1,562	1,692	1,789	2,047	2,387	2,550	2,971	3,442	3,462	3,139
Net income (¥ bil.)	—	89	39	21	42	70	87	83	12	(33)	(38)
Income as % of sales	—	5.7%	2.3%	1.2%	2.1%	2.9%	3.4%	2.8%	0.3%	—	—
Earnings per share (¥)	—	55	24	13	24	37	45	42	6	(18)	(21)
Stock price – high (¥)[1]	—	1,313	1,187	1,250	1,610	1,930	1,690	1,640	1,280	850	897
Stock price – low (¥)[1]	—	884	793	819	700	1,160	1,400	936	785	500	502
Stock price – close (¥)[1]	(9.4%)	1,136	1,000	1,060	1,110	1,510	1,510	980	800	550	844
P/E – high	—	24	49	96	67	52	38	39	—	—	—
P/E – low	—	16	33	63	29	31	31	22	—	—	—
Dividends per share (¥)	1.7%	7.60	7.40	8.00	8.00	9.00	9.00	10.00	10.00	8.00	8.00
Book value per share (¥)	13.9%	394	410	427	484	546	602	640	643	607	582
Employees	9.2%	74,187	84,277	89,293	94,825	104,503	115,012	145,872	155,779	161,974	163,990

1994 Year-end:
Debt ratio: 55.6%
Return on equity:(3.5%)
Cash (bil.): ¥375
Long-term debt (bil.): ¥685
No. of shares (mil.): 1,817
Dividends
  Yield: 0.9%
  Payout: —
Market value (mil.): $13,757
Sales (mil.): $28,128

**Stock Price History[1]
High/Low 1985–94**

[1] Stock prices are for the prior calendar year.

HOOVER'S HANDBOOK OF WORLD BUSINESS 1995–1996   231

THE GENERAL ELECTRIC COMPANY P.L.C.

OVERVIEW

With major holdings in electronics, energy, and defense, London-based General Electric Company (GEC) is the UK's largest manufacturing conglomerate. Through 3 decades of mergers and acquisitions, managing director Lord Weinstock has transformed his father-in-law's electrical-appliance company into a diverse industrial giant that is now the UK's 2nd biggest defense contractor and Europe's 5th largest electronics company. Its products include steam turbines and generators, integrated circuits, defense electronics, warships, weapons, high-speed trains, appliances, office equipment, medical equipment, and telecommunications equipment. GEC derives about half of its revenues from overseas operations. GEC's main US subsidiary is A B Dick Company, a supplier of equipment for offices, printing, and graphics.

With the demise of the Cold War, shrinking defense budgets are causing defense contractors to consolidate. In late 1994 GEC ignited a fierce bidding war with British Aerospace, the UK's largest defense contractor, over Vsel, the maker of nuclear submarines. The outcome could influence which company wins the position as the top contractor in the dwindling defense industry.

Another key issue facing GEC is the replacement of 31-year veteran Weinstock as managing director. While company policy forces him to resign from the board at age 70, Weinstock has announced his intentions to stay on another 2 years until age 72.

WHEN

Hugo Hirst and Gustav Byng went into the electrical equipment wholesale business in London in 1886. By 1889 their company, the General Electric Company, was manufacturing its own products, including bells, switches, and telephones. Before long GEC was making light bulbs (1893) and commercial electric motors (1896). GEC, a pioneer in factory electrification, had expanded to Europe, India, South Africa, and the Pacific by the time it went public in 1900.

GEC formed Peel-Connor Telephone Works to install community telephone exchanges in 1910. Work on television receivers commenced in 1935, and GEC eventually branched into nuclear power, computers, and semiconductors. In 1961 the company bought a small but profitable radio and TV business, Radio & Allied Industries. Former Radio & Allied manager Arnold Weinstock joined GEC as managing director in 1963; under his leadership the company became the UK's leading electronics and electrical products supplier. Weinstock initiated GEC's hostile takeover of rival electrical equipment maker Associated Electrical Industries in 1967 and then merged GEC with English Electric, owner of radio and electronics pioneer Marconi Company, in 1968. In the US, GEC bought office equipment maker A B Dick Company of Chicago in 1979 and RCA's medical diagnostic equipment maker Picker International Holdings in 1981.

In 1985 GEC launched an unsuccessful takeover bid for British defense and telecommunications firm Plessey. The 2 companies formed a joint venture (GEC Plessey Telecommunications, 1988). Soon afterward GEC made another bid for Plessey, this time through GEC Siemens, a joint venture with German electronics giant Siemens (1988). GEC then found itself the target of a hostile takeover from Metsun, a company formed by Plessey and France's Thomson (1989). The Metsun offer fell apart in 1989, after GEC announced a joint venture with the US GE linking their appliance, medical equipment, and electrical products distribution businesses (General Domestic Appliances).

GEC Siemens won British government approval to buy Plessey in 1989. Since then GEC and Siemens have effectively divided Plessey's businesses. GEC entered a joint venture with Alcatel Alsthom of France (formerly CGE), combining their power generation, rail transportation, and electrical distribution businesses in 1989.

In 1990 GEC bought the defense operations of British electronics company Ferranti International. Also that year GEC acquired Ferranti International's defense operations, putting GEC in close competition with French rival Thomson-CSF as Europe's top defense electronics supplier.

British Aerospace abruptly cancelled discussions with GEC in July 1993 over merging their defense operations, when notice was leaked to the press. In 1994 GEC Alsthom's high-speed trains (Eurostar TGV) completed the first rail crossing of the English Channel.

OTC symbol: GNELY (ADR)
Fiscal year ends: March 31

Chairman: The Rt. Hon. Lord Prior, age 66
Vice Chairman: M. Lester, age 54
Managing Director: Lord Weinstock, age 70
Group Finance Director: D. B. Newlands, age 47
Director Employee and Community Relations:
Hon. Sara Morrison, age 59
President, A B Dick (US): R. D. Peterson
CFO, A B Dick (US): Richad Kleys
Human Resources Director, A B Dick (US):
Alan Perry
Auditors: Touche Ross & Co.

WHERE

HQ: One Stanhope Gate, London W1A 1EH, UK
Phone: +44-0171-493-8484
Fax: +44-0171-493-1974
US HQ: A B Dick Company,
5700 W. Touhy Ave., Niles, IL 60714
US Phone: 312-763-1900
US Fax: 312-647-8862

GEC has operations worldwide.

	1994 Sales		1994 Operating Income	
	£ mil.	% of total	£ mil.	% of total
UK	4,425	47	344	50
The Americas	1,884	20	142	21
France	1,846	19	93	13
Australasia	273	3	12	2
Asia	115	1	6	1
Africa	24	—	5	1
Other Europe	976	10	82	12
— Total	**9,701**	**100**	**684**	**100**

WHAT

	1994 Sales		1994 Operating Income	
	£ mil.	% of total	£ mil.	% of total
Power systems	3,103	32	166	24
Electronic systems	2,749	28	252	36
Telecommunications	1,050	11	120	17
Medical equipment	674	7	54	8
Electronic metrology	489	5	30	4
Distribution & trading	351	4	14	2
Industrial apparatus	333	3	6	1
Office equipment & printing	323	3	34	5
Electronic components	291	3	8	1
Consumer goods	259	3	17	2
Other activities	72	1	(17)	—
Adjustments	7	—	—	—
Total	**9,701**	**100**	**684**	**100**

Major Subsidiaries and Associated Companies
A B Dick Company (office equipment and printing, US)
Avery Berkel Group (electronic metrology)
GEC Alsthom NV (50%, power systems, The Netherlands)
GEC-Marconi Ltd. (aerospace, defense, electronics)
General Domestic Appliances Ltd. (50%, joint venture
with US's General Electric)
  Cannon Industries Ltd.   Redring Electric Ltd.
  Creda Ltd.   Xpelair Ltd.
  Hotpoint Ltd.
Gilbarco Group (electronic metrology devices)
Picker International Inc. (medical equipment, US)
Videojet Systems International Inc. (coding equipment,
US)
Plessey Holdings Ltd. (50%, electronics)
Yarrow Shipbuilders Ltd. (warships)

KEY COMPETITORS

British Aerospace	ITT	Raytheon
Daimler-Benz	Lockheed Martin	Siemens
General Dynamics	McDonnell Douglas	Thomson SA
Harris Corp.	Racal	Westinghouse

HOW MUCH

£=$1.48 (Dec. 31, 1993)	9-Year Growth	1985	1986	1987	1988	1989	1990	1991	1992	1993	1994
Sales (£ mil.)	6.3%	5,575	5,560	5,555	5,816	6,664	8,786	9,482	9,435	9,410	9,701
Net income (£ mil.)	3.2%	407	428	450	451	510	543	502	502	536	540
Income as % of sales	—	7.3%	7.7%	8.1%	7.8%	7.7%	6.2%	5.3%	5.3%	5.7%	5.6%
Earnings per share (p)	3.1%	15	16	16	17	19	20	19	19	20	20
Stock price – high (p)[1]	—	238	220	224	251	191	281	245	221	288	368
Stock price – low (p)[1]	—	160	150	160	148	143	187	170	167	183	264
Stock price – close (p)[1]	5.1%	218	164	184	160	189	226	175	200	284	342
P/E – high	—	16	14	14	15	10	14	13	12	15	19
P/E – low	—	11	9	10	9	7	9	9	9	9	13
Dividends per share (p)	11.7%	4.0	4.3	5.3	6.5	7.8	9.3	9.3	9.6	10.3	10.8
Book value per share (p)	3.5%	89	98	109	102	112	87	92	100	114	122
Employees	(2.3%)	165,593	164,536	159,579	157,262	145,029	107,435	118,529	104,995	143,000	134,000

1994 Year-end:
Debt ratio: 6.4%
Return on equity: 16.8%
Cash (mil.): £1,579
Long term debt (mil.): £47
No. of shares (mil.): 2,737
Dividends
  Yield: 3.2%
  Payout: 54.6%
Market value (mil.): $13,847
Sales (mil.): $14,351

Stock Price History[1]
High/Low 1985–94

[1] Stock prices are for the prior calendar year.

GEORGE WESTON LIMITED

OVERVIEW

Toronto-based George Weston has had a few rocky years. Between 1989 (when earnings peaked) and 1992, income slid 68% on stagnant sales. This performance was far short of the company's stated goal of 15% growth in earnings per share. This was because of Canada's persistent recession, fierce competition in the grocery distribution and baked goods fields in Canada and the US (its Loblaw subsidiary is Canada's largest food distributor), and low commodities prices, which affected its fishery and lumber businesses. But results were also adversely affected by several strikes in Canada and the US.

In recent years Weston has made several acquisitions and divestitures to strengthen its position in industries where it is already strong, jettisoning its US supermarket operations, William Neilson ice cream, and flour milling operations in order to concentrate on its core business.

President and chairman Galen Weston controls the company, owning 57% of shares.

In the wake of NAFTA's passage, George Weston has begun to go international, with a distribution agreement in NAFTA partner Mexico and another to supply foods for distribution in Asia in 1993.

WHEN

In 1882 George Weston, 18, a baker's helper, founded his own business when he bought 2 bread delivery routes in Toronto. More routes followed. In 1897 George established a bread and cake bakery.

Upon George's death in 1924, son Garfield took control of the company and 4 years later incorporated it as George Weston Limited.

Weston went international in 1935 when Garfield acquired 7 bakeries in the UK. This modest venture grew into Associated British Foods, a UK-based company also controlled by the Weston family.

Weston bought Inter-City Western Bakeries in 1938. Expansion-minded Garfield led the company into the US with the purchase of Associated Biscuit in 1939. By the late 1930s Weston was making cakes, breads, and almost 500 kinds of candy and biscuits.

Throughout the 1940s, affected little by WWII, the company made a number of acquisitions, including Southern Biscuit (1944), Western Grocers (1944, its first distribution company), Edmonton City Bakery (1945), Dietrich's Bakeries (1946), and William Neilson (1948, chocolate and dairy products). Weston also began buying shares in Loblaw Groceterias, a food distributor, and by 1953 controlled a majority interest. Weston continued its acquisitions binge in the 1960s, diversifying into natural resources (Eddy Paper, 1962) and fisheries (British Columbia Packers, 1967).

By 1970, when Garfield's son Galen became president, the company's holdings were in disarray. Galen brought in new managers, consolidated the food distribution and sales operations under Loblaw, and cut back on National Tea (which shrank from over 900 stores in 1972 to 82 in 1993). When Garfield died in 1978, Galen became chairman.

In 1983 Galen, a polo-playing chum of Charles, the Prince of Wales, was the subject of a failed kidnapping attempt by the IRA. The family has since kept a low public profile.

In the mid-1980s Weston was grouped into 3 segments: Weston Foods (baking, candy, and dairy products), Weston Resources (timber and fish processing), and Loblaw Companies (food distribution and stores). In 1986 the company bought 26 St. Louis stores from Kroger. A 5-year price war began between Weston's National Tea stores, Kroger, and a local grocer. The company stuck it out and in 1993 opened several superstores to try to keep an edge in that highly saturated market. But it was ultimately fruitless and National was dismembered between Schnuck Markets and Schwegmann Giant Super Markets in 1995.

Upon purchasing Cadbury-Schweppes's Canadian assets in 1987, Weston became the #1 chocolate maker in Canada. In 1989 Loblaw garnered media attention when it launched its G·R·E·E·N line of environmentally friendly products. But one of Loblaw's most successful lines is its private label, President's Choice, which is widely carried in US supermarkets. Weston Foods's Interbake division (US) makes Girl Scout cookies.

Weston has combated its recent poor sales by expanding its presence in areas of Canada where it is underrepresented. It is also attempting to improve its fishery and lumber results by adding value to the raw commodities.

Principal exchange: Toronto
Fiscal year ends: December 31

Chairman and President: W. Galen Weston,
C$990,000 pay
SVP and CFO: Robert H. Kidd, C$439,000 pay
President, Weston Foods: David R. Beatty,
C$550,000 pay
President, Loblaw Companies: Richard J. Currie,
C$1,400,000 pay
Director Personnel Services: Judy Robinson
President and CEO, Interbake Foods (US):
Raymond A. Baxter
**VP Finance and Administration, Interbake
Foods (US):** Don Niemeyer
**Director Human Resources, Interbake Foods
(US):** Page Stowers
Auditors: KPMG Peat Marwick Thorne

HQ: 22 St. Clair Ave. East, Toronto,
Ontario M4T 2S7, Canada
Phone: 416-922-2500
Fax: 416-922-4395
US HQ: Interbake Foods, 2220 Edward
Holland Dr., Richmond, VA 23230
US Phone: 314-731-5511
US Fax: 314-731-1252

	1993 Sales		1993 Operating Income	
	C$ mil.	% of total	C$ mil.	% of total
Loblaw				
Eastern Canada	5,136	43	91	38
Western Canada	2,863	24	94	39
US	1,357	11	13	5
Other operations	2,575	22	43	18
Total	**11,931**	**100**	**241**	**100**

	1993 Sales		1993 Operating Income	
	C$ mil.	% of total	C$ mil.	% of total
Loblaw Companies	9,356	75	198	81
Weston Foods				
Baking	1,264	11	8	3
Chocolate & dairy	566	5	14	6
Weston Resources				
Fisheries	584	5	25	10
Forestry	527	4	(4)	—
Adjustments	(366)	—	—	—
Total	**11,931**	**100**	**241**	**100**

Selected Subsidiaries

Loblaw Companies Ltd. (70.2%)	Weston Foods Ltd.
Atlantic Wholesalers Ltd.	Interbake Foods
Fortino's Supermarket Ltd.	William Neilson Ltd.
IPCF Properties Inc..	Ready Bake Foods Inc.
Loblaws Inc.	Stroehmann Bakeries, Inc.
Loblaws Supermarkets Holdings Inc.	Weston Bakeries Ltd.
National Grocers Co. Ltd.	Weston Resources Ltd.
Westfair Foods Ltd.	British Columbia Packers Ltd.
Zehrmart Inc.	Connors Bros. Ltd.
	E.B. Eddy Paper, Inc.

Boise Cascade	Hershey	Mars
Bowater	International	Mead
Campbell Soup	Paper	Nestlé
Champion	Interstate	Norsk Hydro
International	Bakeries	Scott
CPC	James River	Stone
Fleming	John Labatt	Container
Fletcher Challenge	Kimberly-	Unilever
Georgia-Pacific	Clark	Weyerhaeuser
Grand Metropolitan	MacMillan	

$=C$1.32 (Dec. 31, 1993)	9-Year Growth	1984	1985	1986	1987	1988	1989	1990	1991	1992	1993
Sales (C$ mil.)	4.2%	8,255	8,880	10,026	11,035	10,831	10,459	10,856	10,770	11,599	11,931
Net income (C$ mil.)	(4.8%)	89	101	119	134	137	150	125	92	48	57
Income as % of sales	—	1.1%	1.1%	1.2%	1.2%	1.3%	1.4%	1.2%	0.9%	0.4%	0.5%
Earnings per share (C$)	(3.6%)	1.69	1.96	2.31	2.58	2.70	3.00	2.52	1.81	0.85	1.21
Stock price – high (C$)	—	19.06	25.94	36.38	46.50	36.88	45.50	43.75	46.50	40.00	45.50
Stock price – low (C$)	—	15.69	18.00	25.00	28.00	30.00	35.00	36.75	35.50	33.00	34.00
Stock price – close (C$)	8.6%	18.56	25.50	35.50	32.00	35.00	43.25	41.75	36.75	37.00	39.00
P/E – high	—	11	13	16	18	14	15	17	26	47	38
P/E – low	—	9	9	11	11	11	12	15	20	39	28
Dividends per share (C$)	6.4%	0.40	0.44	0.51	0.57	0.61	0.66	0.70	0.70	0.70	0.70
Book value per share (C$)	8.8%	12.84	14.48	16.52	18.23	20.60	23.47	25.35	26.24	27.08	27.42
Employees	2.5%	55,625	57,250	53,700	67,300	61,300	55,800	64,200	63,700	62,600	69,600

1993 Year-end:
Debt ratio: 47.1%
Return on equity: 4.4%
Cash (mil.): C$296
Long-term debt (mil.): C$861
No. of shares (mil.): 47
Dividends
  Yield: 1.8%
  Payout: 57.9%
Market value (mil.): US$1,384
Sales (mil.): US$9,039

Stock Price History
High/Low 1984–93

GLAXO P.L.C.

OVERVIEW

Based in the UK, Glaxo has been getting high on its drugs. It is the #1 drug company in Europe and #2 in the world after Merck. An international group of pharmaceutical companies, Glaxo sells its products in about 150 countries, with the US as its largest market (43% of total revenues in 1994).

The company's big money-spinner is Ranitidine, a peptic ulcer treatment sold under the name Zantac, which holds a 35% share of the world's anti-ulcer market and accounts for about 43% of the company's total revenues. But with its Zantac patent expiring in a few years, and with fierce competition in the anti-ulcer market, Glaxo is spending heavily on R&D and on diversifying its drug offerings.

Other products include anti-asthmatic drugs, cardiovascular and anti-emesis (anti-nausea) drugs, dermatological medicines, nasal decongestants, and migraine medicines.

During 1993 and 1994 Glaxo also established major new manufacturing operations in Argentina, Australia, Egypt, Germany, Japan, Singapore, Spain, and the UK, as part of its strategy of commercial expansion.

WHEN

Englishman Joseph Nathan started an import-export business in New Zealand in 1873. While on a buying trip in London, one of his sons encountered a process for drying milk. Intrigued, Nathan obtained the rights and began producing powdered milk in New Zealand. The product was most successful in its application as a baby food, sold under the Glaxo name.

Nathan's son Alec was dispatched to London to oversee sales of the baby food in Britain. He published the *Glaxo Baby Book*, a guide to child care, introducing the "Builds Bonnie Babies" slogan and leading to the rapid acceptance of Glaxo baby foods in the early 1900s. The company expanded in Britain and, shortly after WWI, began distribution in India and South America.

In the 1920s Glaxo acquired a license to process vitamin D and launched vitamin D–fortified formulations. The company entered the pharmaceutical business with its 1927 introduction of Ostelin, a liquid vitamin D concentrate, and continued to grow globally in the 1930s, successfully introducing Ostermilk (vitamin-fortified milk).

Glaxo produced penicillin and anesthetics during WWII. After the war it stepped up penicillin production and isolated vitamin B_{12}. Following precipitous declines in antibiotic prices in the mid-1950s, Glaxo diversified, acquiring veterinary, medical instrument, and drug distribution firms.

Glaxo was the target of a hostile takeover attempt by Beecham in the 1970s. The company arranged a merger with drug manufacturer and retailer Boots to fend off Beecham's bid. The British Monopolies Commission quashed both transactions.

Paul Girolami became CEO in 1980 (and later chairman), as clinical trials of Zantac, neared completion. At the time the company's sales in Nigeria exceeded those in the US. Armed with Zantac (deemed to have slightly fewer side effects than Tagamet, SmithKline's established blockbuster drug), Girolami mounted a marketing blitzkrieg on Tagamet's lucrative US market.

Negotiating the use of Hoffmann–La Roche's big, underused sales force, Girolami got the US marketing clout he had lacked. The Zantac sales assault stunned a complacent SmithKline, wrenching away leadership in US anti-ulcer drug sales and establishing a 53% share while reducing Tagamet's to 29%.

In the 1980s Glaxo shed its nondrug operations, and concentrated on pharmaceuticals. Girolami turned over his post in 1989 to American Ernest Mario. Glaxo faced difficulties in the US market. In 1991 its patents on Zantac and Zofran were challenged. In 1992 Sandoz said it was testing a cheap rival for Imigran, Glaxo's antimigraine drug.

In the midst of negotiations in 1993 between Glaxo, Warner-Lambert, and Wellcome that resulted in a joint marketing agreement for their OTC drugs, Mario resigned suddenly; he was replaced as CEO by Richard Sykes. In 1994 Girolami retired after 29 years with the company.

In early 1995 Glaxo made a surprise $14 billion bid for British drug company Wellcome. The resulting company — Glaxo Wellcome — would be the world's largest drug maker, with annual revenues of over $12 billion. Wellcome officials have opposed the bid, but Glaxo is pressing forward with the acquisition.

NYSE symbol: GLX (ADR)
Fiscal year ends: June 30

Deputy Chairman and CEO: Sir Richard Sykes, age 52
Managing Director Finance: John D. Coombe, age 49
Managing Director Legal and Corporate Affairs: Jeremy A. W. Strachan
President and CEO, Glaxo Inc. (US): Robert A. Ingram
CFO, Glaxo Inc. (US): Thomas Haber
VP Human Resources, Glaxo Inc. (US): Donald Cashion
Auditors: Coopers & Lybrand

HQ: Landsdowne House, Berkeley Square, London W1X 6BQ, UK
Phone: +44-(01)71-493-4060
Fax: +44-(01)71-408-0228
US HQ: Glaxo Inc., 5 Moore Dr., Research Triangle Park, NC 27709
US Phone: 919-248-2100
US Fax: 919-248-2412

Glaxo medicines are sold in 150 countries and the company has production facilities in 31 of them. Glaxo has subsidiaries located in 70 countries.

	1994 Sales	
	$ mil.	% of total
US	3,795	43
Europe	3,053	35
Other countries	1,882	22
Total	**8,730**	**100**

	1994 Sales	
	$ mil.	% of total
Gastrointestinal drugs	3,769	43
Respiratory drugs	1,897	22
Systemic antibiotics	1,346	16
Anti-emesis drugs	624	7
Antimigraine drugs	375	4
Dermatological drugs	282	3
Cardiovascular drugs	116	1
Other drugs	321	4
Total	**8,730**	**100**

Selected Brand Names

Beclovent/Becotide (respiratory)	Imigran/Imitrex (antimigraine)
Beconase (respiratory)	Serevent (respiratory)
Betnovate (dermatological)	Trandate (cardiovascular)
Ceftin (antibiotic)	Ventolin (respiratory)
Dermovate/Temovate (dermatological)	Volmax (respiratory)
	Zantac (gastrointestinal)
Flixonase (respiratory)	Zinacef (antibiotic)
Fortum (antibiotic)	Zinnat (antibiotic)
	Zofran (anti-emesis)

Abbott Labs	Ciba-Geigy	Monsanto
Akzo Nobel	Copley	Novo Nordisk
American Home Products	Pharmaceuticals	Pfizer
	Dow Chemical	Rhône-Poulenc
Amgen	Elf Aquitaine	Roche
Barr Labs	Eli Lilly	Sandoz
Bayer	Genentech	Schering-Plough
Bristol-Myers Squibb	Hoechst	SmithKline Beecham
Carter-Wallace	Johnson & Johnson	Upjohn
Chiron	Merck	Warner-Lambert

	9-Year Growth	1985	1986	1987	1988	1989	1990	1991	1992	1993	1994
Sales ($ mil.)	18.8%	1,726	2,200	2,816	3,525	3,991	4,992	5,517	7,797	7,353	8,730
Net income ($ mil.)	15.9%	342	616	802	978	1,069	1,387	1,481	1,966	1,800	2,011
Income as % of sales	—	19.8%	28.0%	28.5%	27.7%	26.8%	27.8%	26.8%	25.2%	24.5%	23.0%
Earnings per share ($)	15.4%	0.23	0.42	0.54	0.66	0.72	0.93	0.99	1.31	1.19	1.32
Stock price – high ($)[1]	—	3.28	5.78	8.63	15.31	10.25	13.44	17.31	32.38	35.25	24.25
Stock price – low ($)[1]	—	2.47	3.09	5.44	7.69	7.94	9.25	11.31	15.56	21.75	14.75
Stock price – close ($)[1]	23.3%	3.16	5.53	7.69	9.13	9.63	13.00	16.38	31.75	23.75	20.88
P/E – high	—	14	14	16	23	14	14	17	25	30	18
P/E – low	—	11	7	10	12	11	10	11	12	18	11
Dividends per share ($)	27.1%	0.06	0.11	0.09	0.28	0.28	0.36	0.50	1.03	0.62	0.75
Book value per share ($)	20.8%	0.75	1.13	1.58	2.06	2.39	3.20	3.47	4.52	4.47	5.11
Employees	7.0%	25,634	24,728	24,954	26,423	28,710	33,225	35,640	37,083	40,024	47,189

1994 Year-end:
Debt ratio: 9.7%
Return on equity: 27.6%
Cash (mil.): $3,201
Current ratio: 2.18
Long-term debt (mil.): $143
No. of shares (mil.): 1,524
Dividends
  Yield: 3.6%
  Payout: 56.8%
Market value (mil.): $31,814

Stock Price History[1] High/Low 1985–94

[1] Stock prices are for the prior calendar year.

GRAND METROPOLITAN PLC

OVERVIEW

Spirits are down at Grand Metropolitan, the food, liquor, and retailing giant. GrandMet's International Distillers & Vintners (IDV) division accounts for 54% of profits, but sales of name-brand wines and liquors are down.

In 1993 and 1994 GrandMet spent nearly $700 million to reorganize its operations. The sale of its Alpo pet foods and Chef & Brewer pubs and savings due to restructuring have provided funds to promote GrandMet's top brands: Pillsbury, Green Giant, Burger King (the #2 fast-food retailer), and Häagen-Dazs.

With sales slow, Burger King began overhauling operations in 1993. The 7,120-outlet chain reemphasized its basic menu, cut prices, and reduced overhead. After seeing some initial success from his efforts, Burger

King CEO James Adamson jumped ship in early 1995 to lead rival Flagston Corporation.

GrandMet is fighting its spirits sales slump by expanding into China, Eastern Europe, India, and Russia. In 1993 it bought 25% of Zwack Unicum, Hungary's top spirits distiller, and in 1994 it established distributorships in Hong Kong and Slovakia.

In 1994 GrandMet suffered a heavy blow when its contracts to distribute Absolut vodka and Grand Marnier liqueur were not renewed. The company's food segment has also suffered. Harvest fluctuations prompted the closure of 4 Green Giant processing plants. Price wars, private-label brands, and sluggish economies are all stealing sales from GrandMet's big-name brands.

WHEN

Maxwell Joseph dropped out of school in 1926 to work for a real estate agency in London. Five years later he set off on his own and began acquiring properties for resale, but a weak British economy and WWII slowed his progress. In 1946 he purchased a bomb-damaged hotel in London. Believing that hotels were severely undervalued, he bought progressively larger and more prestigious hotels, including the Mount Royal in London and the Hotel d'Angleterre in Copenhagen. In 1961 Joseph's company, Grand Metropolitan, went public, just before its acquisition of Grand Hotels (Mayfair) Ltd.

Diversification began in 1970 with the purchases of Express Dairy, Berni Inns (catering, restaurants), and Mecca (betting shops). In 1971, in what was the largest British takeover up to that time, GrandMet bought Truman Hanburg, a brewing concern, followed by Watney Mann (which owned International Distillers and Vintners, makers of Baileys, Bombay Gin, and J&B) in 1972.

After pausing for a few years to sell unwanted assets and reduce debt, GrandMet returned to its acquisitive ways. Under the scrutiny of the English Monopolies Commission, the company looked overseas, taking over the Liggett Group, an American cigarette maker whose Paddington unit was the US distributor of J&B Scotch, GrandMet's #1 brand. In his last major acquisition before his death, newly knighted Sir Maxwell engineered the 1981 buyout of Intercontinental Hotels from Pan Am.

After Sir Maxwell died GrandMet's focus shifted. It acquired Pearle Health Services (Pearle Vision, US) in 1985 and sold the last of the Liggett tobacco businesses in 1986.

Under new chairman Allen Sheppard, GrandMet began a restructuring based on its food and drink segments. In 1987 it bought Heublein, picking up such brands as Smirnoff, Lancers, and Cuervo and creating the world's largest wine and spirits company. Sheppard disposed of the Intercontinental chain in 1988 for 52 times earnings and acquired Pillsbury (Burger King, Häagen-Dazs, and Green Giant) in a 1989 hostile takeover.

In 1991 GrandMet sold its UK brewing operations to Foster's Brewing and formed a joint UK real estate venture; GrandMet's EIL subsidiary and Foster's Courage subsidiary now jointly manage more than 6,800 pubs.

GrandMet continued its penchant for buying and selling in 1994. Its Pillsbury subsidiary added US food makers Martha White, which packages baking mixes, and Rudi Foods, which produces partially baked breads. GrandMet sold its interest in the Archer-Daniels-Midland flour mills and is expected to sell its Pearle Vision eye-care chain. Also that year it sold its Alpo pet foods line to Nestlé (maker of Little Friskies pet foods) for $510 million. GrandMet finished 1994 with $12.3 billion in sales.

In early 1995 GrandMet announced a $2.6 billion acquisition of Pet, Inc., including Old El Paso Mexican foods and Progresso soups.

NYSE symbol: GRM (ADR)
Fiscal year ends: September 30

Chairman: Sir Allen J. G. Sheppard, age 61,
£629,584 pay
Group Chief Executive: George J. Bull, age 57
**CFO; Chairman and Chief Executive, Food
Sector:** David P. Nash, age 53
Chairman and Chief Executive, Drinks Sector:
John B. McGrath, age 55
SVP Human Resources: Richard W. Etches
Auditors: KPMG Peat Marwick

HQ: Grand Metropolitan Public Limited
Company, 20 St. James's Square, London
SW1Y 4RR, UK
Phone: +44-(01)71-321-6000
Fax: +44-(01)71-321-6001

Grand Metropolitan sells branded consumer
goods in more than 50 countries. Its food sector
brands include Burger King, Green Giant, and
Pillsbury; its drinks sector operates as
International Distillers & Vintners.

	1993 Sales		1993 Operating Profit	
	£ mil.	% of total	£ mil.	% of total
North America	4,713	58	602	58
UK & Ireland	1,343	17	245	24
Africa & Middle East	182	2	15	1
Other Europe	1,550	19	137	13
Other countries	332	4	36	4
Total	**8,120**	**100**	**1,035**	**100**

	1993 Sales		1993 Operating Profit	
	£ mil.	% of total	£ mil.	% of total
Drinks	3,418	42	561	54
Food	3,092	38	228	22
Retailing	1,610	20	246	24
Total	**8,120**	**100**	**1,035**	**100**

Major Brands

Food	Liquor	Retailing
Aunt Nellie's	Baileys	Burger King
Green Giant	Black Velvet	IEL (tenanted pubs)
Häagen-Dazs	Bombay Gin	Pearle Vision
Hungry Jack	Gilbey's	
Jeno's	J&B	**Wine**
Jim Dandy	Jack Daniel's	Christian Brothers
Joan of Arc	José Cuervo	Glen Ellen
Pillsbury	Popov	Inglenook
Rudi's	Smirnoff	Lancers
Totino's	Wild Turkey	M. G. Vallejo

Accor	Domino's Pizza	Procter &
Allied Domecq	Dreyer's	Gamble
American Brands	Flagstar	Quaker Oats
Anheuser-Busch	Gallo	RJR Nabisco
Bacardi	Guinness	Robert
Bass	Heinz	Mondavi
Ben & Jerry's	Imasco	Sara Lee
Borden	Kendall-	Seagram
Brown-Forman	Jackson	Sebastiani
Campbell Soup	LVMH	Vineyards
Canandaigua Wine	McDonald's	Sutter Home
Carlson	Metromedia	Winery
Cole National	National Vision	U.S. Shoe
ConAgra	Nestlé	Unilever
Danone	PepsiCo	Wendy's
Del Monte	Philip Morris	Whitman

£=$1.48 (Dec. 31, 1993)	9-Year Growth	1984	1985	1986	1987	1988	1989	1990	1991	1992	1993
Sales (£ mil.)	5.4%	5,075	5,590	5,291	5,706	6,029	9,298	9,394	8,748	7,913	8,120
Net income (£ mil.)	4.7%	272	272	261	461	702	1,068	1,069	432	616	413
Income as % of sales	—	5.4%	4.9%	4.9%	8.1%	11.6%	11.5%	11.4%	4.9%	7.8%	5.1%
Earnings per share (p)[1]	7.1%	16	14	16	19	24	28	32	33	28	30
Stock price – high (p)	—	180	202	241	303	261	329	341	441	518	483
Stock price – low (p)	—	135	139	166	174	209	212	257	311	380	373
Stock price – close (p)	13.1%	157	199	228	225	215	314	328	441	465	476
P/E – high	—	11	14	15	16	11	12	11	13	18	16
P/E – low	—	8	10	10	9	9	8	8	9	13	13
Dividends per share (p)[2]	12.2%	4.6	5.0	5.1	6.0	7.5	8.9	10.2	11.4	12.3	13.0
Book value per share (p)	2.3%	—	—	—	—	—	—	—	170	183	180
Employees	30.3%	125,074	137,195	131,493	129,436	89,753	137,379	138,149	122,178	102,405	87,163

1993 Year-end:
Debt ratio: 59.4%
Return on equity: 16.4%
Cash (mil.): £349
Long-term debt (mil.): £3,072
No. of shares (mil.): 2,069
Dividends
   Yield: 2.7%
   Payout: 43.8%
Market value (mil.): $14,569
Sales (mil.): $12,012

**Stock Price History
High/Low 1984–93**

[1] Accounting change   [2] Excludes extraordinary items

GUINNESS PLC

OVERVIEW

Guinness is one of the world's leading alcoholic beverage conglomerates, producing and distributing worldwide a tony portfolio of best-selling spirits and the world's most distinctive beer. Although known for its dark, foamy stout, Guinness produces such premium-name liquors as Johnnie Walker (the world's #1 Scotch whisky); Gordon's Gin (the world's #1 gin); Tanqueray gin (the US's #1 imported gin); Dewar's White Label (the US's best-selling Scotch whiskey); and top brands in Australia, Japan, and the UK. Its spirits subsidiary (United Distillers), which accounts for almost 36% of the world's name-brand Scotch whiskey markets, represents 75% of Guinness's 1993 net profits. Guinness's brewing operations (Guinness

Brewing Worldwide) were built around its core brand, Guinness Stout, and produce several premium brands, including 3 of the top 4 most widely distributed beer brands in the UK (Draught Guinness, Kaliber, and Guinness Original). The company also owns the Gleneagles Hotel, a 5-star golf resort in Scotland, and Guinness Publishing, producer of the famous *Guinness Book of Records*.

In 1994 the company swapped its 24% stake in LVMH Moët Hennessy Louis Vuitton for a 34% stake in LVMH's wines and spirits company, Moët Hennessy. Guinness also sold its stake in Christian Dior and Jacques Rober to the Arnault Group, headed by Guinness director Bernard Arnault, to focus on spirits and beer.

WHEN

Arthur Guinness leased a small brewery in Dublin in 1759. At the brewery Guinness made ales and porters, which were at first sold only in Dublin. In 1799 Guinness began specializing in porters. In 1821 Extra Superior Porter, later named stout, represented 4% of Guinness's sales. By 1840 it represented 82% of sales and was spreading across Ireland to England. Sales growth was greatest in Ireland, which still is a key market.

In 1886, managed by the 3rd generation of Guinnesses, the company went public. For many years Guinness was content to focus on stout, slowly extending its reach internationally and advertising the product's legendary health benefits. In the 1950s managing director Hugh Beaver persuaded company executives to launch Harp, a lager, which today remains a leading brand in a highly fragmented British market. Beaver is also credited with conceiving the remarkably successful *Guinness Book of Records* in 1955.

In the 1970s Guinness bought more than 200 unrelated companies, with disappointing results. In 1981 Guinness appointed Ernest Saunders CEO. He disposed of over 140 companies in 2 years, slashed overhead, and spent heavily on successful advertising of Guinness Stout. In 1984 Saunders began his own shopping spree, buying British newsstands, health spas, 7-Elevens, and Arthur Bell & Sons scotch. With higher earnings Saunders involved Guinness in a takeover battle against Argyll Group for control of Distillers Company (Johnnie Walker, Gordon's, Tanqueray).

He bought Distillers for £2.5 billion in 1986. In the months following the Distillers acquisition, the SEC investigation of Ivan Boesky uncovered records linking Saunders to a stock manipulation scheme. Saunders was subsequently fired in 1987 and convicted on criminal charges in 1990.

Sir Anthony Tennant, earlier passed over for the top job at Grand Metropolitan, became Guinness's chairman. He focused the company on brewing and distilling, selling peripheral businesses and acquiring Schenley (Dewar's) in 1987.

In 1988 and 1989 Guinness bought 24.1% of French cognac, champagne, perfume, and leather goods maker LVMH Moët Hennessy Louis Vuitton. LVMH then raised its own stake in Guinness from 12% to 24.1% in 1990. (LVMH cut its stake to 20% in 1994.)

In 1991 Guinness bought Spanish brewer Cruzcampo for over $900 million, one of the largest foreign investments in Spain's history, and Spain's Unión Cervecera, 61% of which was owned by Carlsberg. Other 1991 acquisitions were Inter-American Holdings (Mexico, distributor); Prestige Beverage (Venezuela, distiller); Asbach (Germany, brandy distiller); and Glenmore Distilleries (US). These acquisitions brought Scoresby and Pampero Especial (the world's #1 golden rum brand) into its product line.

In 1992 Sir Anthony Tennant retired as chairman to head Christie's auction house. In 1994 Guinness obtained the US distribution rights to the French liqueur, Grand Marnier.

OTC symbol: GURSY (ADR)
Fiscal year ends: December 31

Chairman and CEO: Anthony A. Greener, age 53
Deputy Chairman: Brian F. Baldock, age 59
Deputy Chairman: Sir David Plastow, age 61
Finance Director: Philip E. Yea, age 39
President and CEO, Guinness America:
  Ove Sorensen
VP Human Resources Administration, Guinness
  America: Richard Martonchik
Auditors: Price Waterhouse

HQ: 39 Portman Sq., London W1H 9HB, UK
Phone: +44-(0)71-486-0288
Fax: +44-(0)71-486-4968
US HQ: Guinness America, Inc.,
  6 Landmark Sq., Stamford, CT 06901-2704
US Phone: 203-359-7100
US Fax: 203-323-3311

Guinness brands are brewed in 46 countries and beer is sold in over 130 countries. The company's distilled products are made in Australia, Canada, Germany, the UK, the US, and Venezuela.

	1993 Sales		1993 Operating Income	
	£ mil.	% of total	£ mil.	% of total
Europe	1,647	35	255	27
UK	944	20	121	13
North America	883	19	204	22
Asia/Pacific	771	17	174	19
Other countries	418	9	184	19
Total	**4,663**	**100**	**938**	**100**

	1993 Sales		1993 Operating Income	
	£ mil.	% of total	£ mil.	% of total
Spirits	2,773	59	701	75
Brewing	1,890	41	237	25
Total	**4,663**	**100**	**938**	**100**

Selected Spirits

Asbach Uralt	Johnnie Walker
Bell's Extra Special	Old Parr
Black & White	Pampero Rum
Booth's Gin	Pimm's
Bundaberg Rum	Rebel Yell
Classic Malts	Safari
Dewar's	Scoresby
The Dimple	Tanqueray
George Dickel	Usher's Green
Gordon's Gin	Stripe
Haig	VAT 69
Inver House Scotch	White Horse
I.W. Harper	

Selected Beer

Alcazar
Cruzcampo
Draught Guinness
Estrella del Sur
Guinness Stout
Harp
Hoffmans
Kaliber (non-
  alcoholic)
Keler
Kilkenny
Macardle's Ale
Satzenbrau

Selected Holdings
Desnoes & Geddes (51%, brewery, Jamaica)
Gleneagles Hotels PLC
Guinness Publishing Ltd.
LVMH Moët Hennessy SA (34%, champagne, France)
Schieffelin & Somerset (50%, spirits distributor, US)

Adolph Coors	Carlsberg	Kirin
Allied Domecq	Danone	Molson
American Brands	Forte	Pernod Ricard
Anheuser-Busch	Foster's Brewing	Philip Morris
Bacardi	Grand	San Miguel
Bass	Metropolitan	S&P
Brent Walker	Heilemann	Seagram
Group	Heineken	Stroh
Brown-Forman	John Labatt	Tsingtao

£=$1.48 (Dec. 31, 1993)	9-Year Growth	1984	1985	1986[1]	1987	1988	1989	1990	1991	1992	1993
Sales (£ mil.)	19.7%	924	1,188	3,252	2,818	2,776	3,076	3,511	4,067	4,363	4,663
Net income (£ mil.)	31.0%	38	54	230	257	325	440	541	628	524	433
Income as % of sales	—	4.1%	4.5%	7.1%	9.1%	11.7%	14.3%	15.4%	15.4%	12.0%	9.3%
Earnings per share (p)	13.1%	10.5	12.7	18.2	14.8	18.0	23.7	29.2	33.6	33.0	31.7
Stock price – high (p)	—	123	162	178	197	179	345	412	535	644	521
Stock price – low (p)	—	58	113	135	114	131	165	313	359	417	388
Stock price – close (p)	16.4%	122	160	157	145	167	343	382	508	518	478
P/E – high	—	12	13	—	13	10	15	14	16	20	16
P/E – low	—	6	9	—	8	7	7	11	11	13	12
Dividends per share (p)	16.7%	3.2	3.6	5.1	4.6	5.8	7.7	9.9	10.8	11.9	12.8
Book value per share (p)	13.0%	62	44	36	126	145	174	189	178	178	186
Employees	6.5%	13,203	29,300	32,027	30,932	17,934	18,106	18,873	24,788	24,032	23,264

1993 Year-end:
Debt ratio: 37.9%
Return on equity: 17.4%
Cash (mil.): £399
Long-term debt (mil.): £1,366
No. of shares (mil.): 2,010
Dividends
  Yield: 2.7%
  Payout: 40.4%
Market value (mil.): $14,213
Sales (mil.): $6,898

Stock Price History
High/Low 1984–93

[1] 15-month fiscal year

HANSON PLC

OVERVIEW

From cod liver oil to cranes, Hanson PLC, one of the world's largest industrial conglomerates, operates a handsome number of basic enterprises, including chemicals, tobacco, housewares, recreation equipment, building products, and mining. Some of Hanson's US brand names are Jacuzzi whirlpool baths, Universal Gym, and Farberware cookware. Hanson also owns Peabody, the largest coal producer in the US.

Partners Lord Hanson (who heads the UK business) and Lord White (who chairs US operations, Hanson Industries) have reputations as dealmakers, constantly adding and deleting names from their list of subsidiaries.

Hanson's strategy is to increase the size of its major businesses: coal, timber, construction, chemicals, and tobacco, while looking for opportunities in new key industries and new geographical areas. The worldwide recession and a US coal strike hurt Hanson's bottom line in the early 1990s, but profits recovered in 1994.

The appointment of Hanson PLC's chief executive, Derek Bonham, as the conglomerate's deputy chairman and David Clarke's (Hanson Industries) appointment as vice chairman of Hanson PLC strongly suggest the board's succession plans.

WHEN

In the 1950s and 1960s, James Hanson and Gordon White were British bon vivants. Hanson was once engaged to Audrey Hepburn, and White enjoyed the company of Joan Collins. They are now better known as sharp businessmen. Their first venture, Hanson-White Greeting Cards, was sold in 1963. When the buyer demanded £10,000 to sell back the Hanson-White name, White, displaying typical frugality, refused. The company became Hanson Trust Limited in 1969 (changed to Hanson Trust Public Limited Company in 1981 and Hanson PLC in 1987).

From the beginning Hanson and White sought poorly managed companies in mature industries at low prices. Within 10 years Hanson Trust consisted of 24 companies in such businesses as brickmaking, aggregates, and construction equipment, with sales in excess of $120 million.

Tired of England's antibusiness attitudes, White formed a New York subsidiary, Hanson Industries, in 1973. Operating autonomously, he made his first American purchase in 1974, buying Seacoast (animal feed). Others followed: Hygrade (Ball Park Franks, 1976), Interstate United (food service, 1978; sold in 1985 for over 3 times its cost), McDonough (tools, shoes; 1981), and US Industries (conglomerate, 1984). Meanwhile, James Hanson bought Ever Ready (batteries, UK, 1981; sold 1992) and Allders (retail, UK, 1983).

In bitterly fought hostile takeovers in 1986, Hanson acquired SCM (Smith-Corona office equipment, Glidden Paints, Durkee's Famous Foods, SCM Chemicals) and Imperial Group (cigarettes, Courage beer, food, hotels, restaurants). Within a year sales of some SCM units (including Glidden and Durkee) generated $960 million in cash, $30 million more than Hanson had paid.

In 1987 Hanson acquired Kidde (security systems, fire protection, Jacuzzi) and in 1989 bought Consolidated Gold Fields (UK) and, with it, 49% of Newmont Mining (gold, US). That same year Hanson divested Gold Fields's South African investments, Kidde fire protection, Allders, and Lea & Perrins and sold 52% of Smith-Corona to the public.

The company acquired Peabody (a leading US coal mining company) in 1990 from joint owners Boeing, Bechtel Investments, Eastern Enterprises, and Newmont. It sold its 49% stake in Newmont Mining to companies controlled by Sir James Goldsmith, in exchange for Cavenham Industries (forest products) in a deal completed in 1991.

In 1991 Hanson purchased Beazer PLC, a UK construction firm with extensive US holdings. During 1992 the company sold a number of assets, including Weber Aircraft for $85 million. In 1993 the significant US acquisition was Quantum Chemicals (2nd largest US retail propane distributor) for $3.4 billion. Also, Peabody exchanged Gold Fields Mining assets for the largest surface coal mine in New Mexico (Lee Ranch) and purchased coal assets of Australian company Costain PLC, which increased Hanson's Pacific Rim holdings. In 1994 Hanson took Beazer Homes (home-building materials, US) public while retaining 30%. Analysts think Hanson PLC might split into separate US and UK companies to increase US investment.

NYSE symbol: HAN (ADR)
Fiscal year ends: September 30

WHO

Chairman: Lord Hanson, age 71
Chairman, Hanson Industries: Lord White, age 70
Deputy Chairman and CEO : Derek C. Bonham, age 50
VC; Deputy Chairman and CEO, Hanson Industries: David H. Clarke, age 52
VC: Martin G. Taylor, age 58
President and COO, Hanson Industries (US): John G. Raos, age 44
VP and CFO, Hanson Industries (US): Robert E. Lee
VP Administration and Benefits, Hanson Industries (US): Dorothy E. Sander, age 40
Auditors: Ernst & Young

WHERE

HQ: One Grosvenor Place, London SW1X 7JH, UK
Phone: +44-(0)71-245-1245
Fax: +44-(0)71-235-3455
US HQ: Hanson Industries, 99 Wood Ave. South, Iselin, NJ 08830
US Phone: 908-603-6600
US Fax: 908-603-6878

Hanson operates principally in the UK and the US with lesser operations in Australia and South Africa.

	1994 Sales	
	$ mil.	% of total
UK	9,337	55
US	6,747	39
Other countries	999	6
Adjustments	572	—
Total	**17,655**	**100**

WHAT

	1994 Sales	
	$ mil.	% of total
Consumer goods	7,353	44
Industrial	5,491	32
Building products	3,985	24
Adjustments	826	—
Total	**17,655**	**100**

Selected US Consumer Brands
Ames (tools)
Ertl (toys, model kits)
Farberware (cookware)
Georgia (boots)
Jacuzzi (spas)
Tommy Armour (golf supplies)
Universal (fitness equipment)
Valley (pool tables, dart games)

Selected US Subsidiaries
Beazer Homes, Inc.
Cavenham Forest Industries, Inc.
Endicott Johnson Corp. (shoes)
Garden State Tanning (leather for autos)
Grove Worldwide Co. (cranes)
Hanson Housewares

Hanson Lighting
Hanson Recreation and Leisure
Kaiser Cement Corp.
Peabody Holding Company, Inc. (coal mining)
Quantum Chemicals Co.
SCM Chemicals
Smith Corona Corp. (48%)
Suburban Propane Co.

Selected UK Companies
ARC Ltd. (aggregates)
Beazer Homes Ltd.
Butterley Brick Ltd.
Crabtree Electrical
Hanson Amalgamated Industries Ltd. (construction)
Imperial Tobacco Ltd.
London Brick Co. Ltd

Australian Company
Renison Goldfields (40%)

KEY COMPETITORS

B.A.T
Brunswick
CML Group
CONSOL Energy
Corning

Eljer Industries
Exxon
Ferrellgas Partners
Justin Industries
Kerr-McGee

HOW MUCH

	Annual Growth	1985	1986	1987	1988	1989	1990	1991	1992	1993	1994
Sales ($ mil.)	18.7%	3,764	6,244	10,862	12,503	11,484	13,412	13,467	15,638	14,467	17,655
Net income ($ mil.)	22.4%	272	521	930	1,143	1,334	1,875	1,937	1,936	1,098	1,679
Income as % of sales	—	7.2%	8.3%	8.6%	9.1%	11.6%	14.0%	14.4%	12.4%	7.6%	9.5%
Earnings per share ($)	11.4%	0.60	0.83	0.91	1.34	1.21	1.87	1.89	2.01	1.13	1.58
Stock price – high ($)	—	—	11.84	16.00	14.63	19.88	21.88	23.25	22.13	21.13	22.50
Stock price – low ($)	—	—	10.03	7.97	10.88	14.00	17.00	16.50	17.13	16.88	17.63
Stock price – close ($)	6.5%	—	10.88	12.13	14.13	18.50	18.63	20.38	18.25	20.00	18.00
P/E – high	—	—	14	18	11	16	12	12	11	19	14
P/E – low	—	—	12	9	8	12	9	9	9	15	11
Dividends per share ($)	23.3%	0.14	0.22	0.39	0.57	0.81	0.88	1.13	1.11	0.98	0.92
Book value per share ($)	15.6%	1.92	2.92	4.26	4.84	2.18	5.25	6.06	7.79	6.14	7.07
Employees	(2.7%)	—	92,000	88,000	105,000	89,000	80,000	70,000	75,000	80,000	74,000

1994 Year-end:
Debt ratio: 78.6%
Return on equity: 25.5%
Cash (mil.): $10,616
Current ratio: 1.48
Long-term debt (mil.): $7,942
No. of shares (mil.): 1,026
Dividends
  Yield: 5.1%
  Payout: 58.2%
Market value (mil.): $18,468

Stock Price History
High/Low 1986–94

HAVAS S.A.

Havas has its fingers in so many pies it needs to add some extra hands. France's largest media and communications group, Havas is a holding company for a network of subsidiaries in a variety of operations.

IP Groupe is Europe's #1 seller of multimedia advertising, serving radio and TV stations, newspapers, and magazines. Avenir Havas Media operates Europe's #1 outdoor advertising company and provides advertising representation for French newspapers. Office d'Annonces (ODA) is France's leading provider of advertising services for print and videotext and handles advertising in France Télécom's directories. Havas Voyages is the #1 integrated business and leisure travel group in France.

C.E.P Communication is the largest business and trade journal publisher on the Continent, and Groupe de la Cité, a joint venture with Alcatel Alsthom, is the #1 book publisher in France and one of the largest in the world. Havas also owns 38% of EURO RSCG, France's largest advertising agency.

Havas is concentrating on strengthening its position in the growing interactive multimedia industry. Thanks to changes in French law that raised equity limits in TV channels, Havas recently teamed its 23.5% stake in Canal+ with Compagnie Générale des Eaux (20.1%) and Société Générale (5.1%) to gain a 48.7% joint interest in Europe's largest pay-TV channel.

Charles-Louis Havas, a former banker, importer, and newspaper publisher, founded Bureau Havas in 1832, 2 years after King Louis-Philippe allowed freedom of the press in France. Bureau Havas provided French newspapers with translations of foreign publications. In 1835 he also began providing translations of French newspapers for foreign publications and changed the company's name to Agence Havas. The company expanded to become a full-fledged news agency.

In 1851 Havas added France's first publicity agency. When Charles died in 1858, his sons took over the business. To further expand its news gathering abilities, the company signed agreements with news agencies Reuters (whose founder was a former Havas employee) and Wolff to divide up territories and share information.

While it was expanding its reach geographically, Havas also got a solid grip on its home territory. In 1862 it signed a deal with the French minister of the interior to be France's official news agency. Havas began trading on the Paris Stock Exchange in 1879.

Havas continued to grow and increase its powerful position in the French media, thanks to its dual operations of news and publicity. Businessmen and foreign governments hired the company to place favorable news stories to tilt public opinion in their direction. During WWI Havas distributed propaganda for the French government.

Following the war the company formed an advertising unit and began to sign exclusive agreements to place advertising in newspapers. By 1930 Havas had exclusive rights to more than 200 newspapers.

During WWII the Germans took control of Havas, and it became a propagandist for the Vichy government. After the war the company was accused of collaboration with the Germans, and Havas was nationalized by the French government.

The company continued to expand, adding advertising and media buying in 1945. It finally separated its publicity business from its news business in 1959.

Havas also continued to expand into other businesses, including leisure and tourist businesses through Havas Tourisme. In 1973 the company reorganized and placed its advertising operations under a newly formed company, Eurocom.

The company entered the television broadcasting business in 1984 when it launched Canal+, a pay-television service. In 1987 French prime minister Jacques Chirac privatized Havas. That same year Eurocom expanded into management consulting when it acquired Bernard Juilhet.

Eurocom merged with publicity group RSCG in 1992 to form EURO RSCG. During 1993 Havas's multimedia sales group IP strengthened its presence in eastern Europe, opening offices in Belarus, Hungary, the Czech Republic, Poland, and Lithuania.

In 1994 Havas formed a joint venture, NHL Partners, with Turner Broadcasting's New Line Cinema to develop interactive software.

OTC symbol: HAVSY (ADR)
Fiscal year ends: December 31

Chairman and CEO: Pierre Dauzier
EVP: Jean-François Meaudre
Senior Director Financial and Legal Affairs:
Nicolas Duhamel
Director Legal Department: Arnaud Ingen-Houz
Business Development: Anne Lalou
Finance: Guy Saigne
EVP and CFO, EURO RSCG Holdings (US):
Robert W. Parker
**VP Administration (Personnel), EURO RSCG
Holdings (US):** James Fuller
Auditors: Cabinet Constantin; Salustro Reydel;
KPMG Audit

HQ: 136, avenue Charles-de-Gaulle, 92522
Neuilly-sur-Seine Cedex, France
Phone: +33-1-47-47-30-00
Fax: +33-1-47-47-3223
US HQ: EURO RSCG Holdings, 350 Hudson St.,
New York, NY 10014
US Phone: 212-886-2000
US Fax: 212-886-4428

Havas has operations in 30 countries.

	1993 Sales
	% of total
France	65
Other countries	35
Total	**100**

	1993 Sales	
	FF mil.	% of total
Public relations & print advertising	19,119	54
Tourism	6,994	20
Information & publishing	5,544	16
Outdoor advertising	3,098	9
Audiovisual & other	202	1
Total	**34,957**	**100**

Selected Subsidiaries and Affiliates
Audiofina/CLT (30%, broadcasting)
Avenir Havas Media (99%; public relations, print and
outdoor advertising)
Comareg (print advertising)
Havas Régies (local press representation)
Canal+ (24%, broadcasting)
C.E.P Communication (44%, publishing)
Groupe de la Cité (68%, book publishing)
EURO RSCG Worldwide (38%, full-service advertising)
Havas Informatique (consulting)
Havas Tourisme
IP Groupe (international multimedia sales)
Métrobus Publicité (50%, mass transit and airport
advertising)
Office d'Annonces (ODA, 50%, directories)
Télé Images (44%, film production)

N W Ayer	McGraw-Hill	Time Warner
Bertelsmann	News Corp.	Viacom
Bozell	Omnicom Group	VNU
Canal+	Pearson	Wolters Kluwer
Carlson	Reed Elsevier	WPP Group
Interpublic Group	Saatchi & Saatchi	Young & Rubicam
Lagardère	Thomson Corp.	

$=FF5.91 (Dec. 31, 1993)	Annual Growth	1984	1985	1986	1987	1988	1989	1990	1991	1992	1993[1]
Sales (FF mil.)	17.5%	—	—	11,299	13,709	15,796	18,870	23,661	26,497	28,183	34,957
Net income (FF mil.)	6.4%	—	—	458	551	751	975	1,154	1,083	823	708
Income as % of sales	—	—	—	4.1%	4.0%	4.8%	5.2%	4.9%	4.1%	2.9%	2.0%
Earnings per share (FF)	(6.9%)	—	—	—	—	22	28	30	28	19	16
Stock price – high (FF)	—	—	—	221	221	281	555	710	574	552	500
Stock price – low (FF)	—	—	—	78	150	139	259	420	361	355	402
Stock price – close (FF)	12.7%	—	—	193	150	265	527	437	444	433	445
P/E – high	—	—	—	—	—	13	20	24	20	28	32
P/E – low	—	—	—	—	—	6	9	14	13	18	26
Dividends per share ($)	25.9%	—	—	1.6	3.0	4.1	5.8	6.9	8.0	8.0	8.0
Book value per share ($)	24.0%	—	—	43	64	139	148	171	220	190	196
Employees	14.6%	—	—	—	—	9,407	11,383	11,904	12,462	12,430	18,628

1993 Year-end:
Debt ratio: 24.1%
Return on equity: 8.1%
Cash (mil.): $5,164
Long-term debt (mil.): $2,242
No. of shares (mil.): 46
Dividends
Yield: 1.8%
Payout: 51.3%
Market value (mil.): $3,461
Sales (mil.): $5,916

Stock Price History
High/Low 1986–93

[1] Accounting change

HEINEKEN N.V.

OVERVIEW

Although the 2nd largest brewer in the world (after Anheuser-Busch), Amsterdam-based Heineken is the most international. Unlike its American competitor, which is almost 3 times its size but sells mostly in the US, this Old World enterprise sells in over 150 countries. Its top markets are Europe (49% of 1993 sales), the Netherlands (24%), and the Western Hemisphere (13%). Known by its familiar green bottle, Heineken is the #1 imported beer in the US; the company's Amstel Light is the US's #1 imported light beer. Heineken also sells soft drinks but sold its spirits and wine operations in early 1994. The 130-year-old brewer is still family-operated, and over 50% of the publicly traded stock is family-owned. Supervisory chairman and main stockholder Alfred (Freddy) Heineken, age 70, has no designated family successor.

Heineken is having to defend its global standing. In the face of a mature market in Europe, it is vying with Anheuser-Busch and #3 ranked Miller Brewing for growing markets in Asia and Latin America. Heineken is defending its claim by piggybacking sales of its higher-priced brand on top of local brews and by staking out new territory through joint ventures in Asia and equity holdings in local beer producers, such as Fujian Brewery, in China, the world's 2nd largest beer market.

The company also is having to become more efficient. In 1993 Heineken cut over 1,300 jobs and then faced its first-ever labor dispute in 1994.

WHEN

Every Sunday morning, Gerard Heineken's mother was appalled by the crowds of drunken Dutchmen who had consumed too much gin the night before. Heineken, who wanted his mother's financial backing, insisted that drunkenness would decrease if people drank beer instead of gin and pointed out that there were no good beers in Holland. His strategy worked. In 1864 Heineken's mother put up the money to buy the 270-year-old De Hooiberg (The Haystack) brewery in Amsterdam.

Heineken quickly proved his aptitude for brewing and within 10 years had established a brewery in Rotterdam. He is also credited with launching the company's lucrative foreign trade by exporting beer first to France, then across Europe, and eventually to the Far East. During the 1880s and early 1890s, the company perfected the yeast strain (Heineken A-yeast) that it still uses in its beer today.

In 1914 Heineken passed the company down to his son Dr. Henri Pierre Heineken, who decided to expand the company's operations to the US and made the voyage himself. While still at sea, Heineken met Leo van Munching, a ship's bartender who displayed a remarkable knowledge of beer. Recognizing van Munching's talent, Heineken hired him as the company's US importer.

Prohibition killed the US operations, although the company entered new markets elsewhere; after repeal Heineken was the first foreign beer to reenter the US market.

After WWII Heineken sent his son Alfred to learn the business under van Munching.

Alfred mastered the art of advertising and marketing and brought his new skills home in 1948. Meanwhile, in the US, van Munching created a national distribution system.

In 1968 Heineken bought the Amstel Brewery in Holland (founded in 1870). Two years later the company became a producer of stout through the acquisition of James J. Murphy in Cork, Ireland. Heineken entered the soft drink and wine industries and in 1971 bought the Bokma distillery in Holland.

Facing a consolidation of the European market, the company launched a campaign during the 1980s to expand its continental beer operations, purchasing breweries in France, Greece, Ireland, Italy, and Spain. During the 1980s the company was victimized by blackmail and extortion attempts and the kidnapping of Alfred Heineken.

Alfred relinquished day-to-day management in 1989, and in 1991 Heineken bought the Van Munching US import business and a majority interest in Hungarian brewer Komáromi Sörgyár, its first central European investment. In 1991 the company closed an unprofitable Canadian brewery, signed a joint agreement to build several breweries in the Asia Pacific region, and announced plans to build a brewery in Vietnam. The company also launched a draught version of its non-alcoholic beer, Buckler, in the Netherlands.

A strike just before a major Dutch celebration, Queen Beatrix's birthday, in 1994 caused Heineken to juggle its imports to bring in beer from overseas.

OTC symbol: HINKY (ADR)
Fiscal year ends: December 31

Chairman, Supervisory Council: Alfred H.
Heineken, age 70
Chairman, Executive Board: Karel Vuursteen
Corporate Financial Director: Leendert Schouten
Director Corporate Human Resources:
Bernard Sarphati
Head of US Operations: Michael Foley
Auditors: KPMG Klynveld

WHERE

HQ: Tweede Weteringplantsoen 21, 1017 ZD, PO
Box 28, 1000 AA Amsterdam, The Netherlands
Phone: +31-20-5239-239
Fax: +31-20-6263-503
US HQ: Van Munching & Co., Inc.,
1270 Avenue of the Americas,
New York, NY 10020
US Phone: 212-332-8500
US Fax: 212-332-8570

Heineken operates over 90 breweries and sells its
products in over 150 countries.

	1993 Sales	
	Fl mil.	% of total
Europe	6,464	73
Western Hemisphere	1,187	13
Asia/Australia	716	8
Africa	501	6
Adjustments	181	—
Total	**9,049**	**100**

WHAT

	1993 Sales	
	Fl mil.	% of total
Beer	7,400	82
Soft drinks	1,000	11
Spirits & wine	400	5
Other	200	2
Adjustments	49	—
Total	**9,049**	**100**

Selected Products

Beer	Pelforth	Soft Drinks
Aguila	Star	Amigo
Amstel	Tarwebok	Pepsi-Cola
Brand		(The Nether-
Buckler	Shandy (beer and	lands)
Gulder	lemonade)	Royal Club
Heineken	Green Sands	7Up (The
Murphy's Irish	Panach	Netherlands)
Stout	Royal Club	

Selected Subsidiaries and Affiliates
Asia Pacific Breweries Pte. Ltd. (42.5%, Singapore)
Athenian Brewery SA (98.8%, Greece)
Birra Dreher SpA (95.6%, Italy)
Brauerei Haldengut (52.3%, Switzerland)
El Aguila SA (51.2%, Spain)
Komáromi Sörgyár RT (55.3%, Hungary)
Sogebra SA (France)
South Pacific Brewery Ltd. (31.9%, Papua New Guinea)

KEY COMPETITORS

Adolph Coors	Danone	Molson
Allied Domecq	Foster's Brewing	Nestlé
American Brands	Grand Metropolitan	Philip Morris
Anheuser-Busch	Grolsch	S&P
Bass	Guinness	San Miguel
Brown-Forman	Heileman	Seagram
Cadbury Schweppes	John Labatt	Stroh
Carlsberg	Kirin	Tsingtao
Coca-Cola		

HOW MUCH

$=Fl1.94 (Dec. 31, 1993)	9-Year Growth	1984	1985	1986	1987	1988	1989	1990	1991	1992	1993
Sales (Fl mil.)	4.4%	6,135	6,402	6,684	6,659	7,291	7,820	8,210	8,696	8,944	9,049
Net income (Fl mil.)	9.5%	229	265	285	287	291	325	366	410	463	519
Income as % of sales	—	3.7%	4.1%	4.3%	4.3%	4.0%	4.2%	4.5%	4.7%	5.2%	5.7%
Earnings per share (Fl)	9.5%	5.71	6.61	7.11	7.14	7.24	8.11	9.11	10.21	11.53	12.92
Stock price – high (Fl)	—	76	110	122	126	100	114	110	131	176	218
Stock price – low (Fl)	—	56	70	96	70	73	76	82	104	126	163
Stock price – close (Fl)	13.2%	70	110	114	80	91	102	109	126	172	215
P/E – high	—	13	17	17	18	14	14	12	13	15	17
P/E – low	—	10	11	14	10	10	9	9	10	11	13
Dividends per share (Fl)	8.5%	1.68	1.68	2.24	2.24	2.24	2.80	2.80	2.80	3.50	3.50
Book value per share (Fl)	7.4%	51.94	54.81	56.01	61.40	69.06	73.55	78.38	83.88	90.95	98.98
Employees	(0.5%)	25,112	28,410	28,749	28,418	28,719	29,127	28,908	27,502	25,320	23,997

1993 Year-end:
Debt ratio: 18.3%
Return on equity: 12.7%
Cash (mil.): Fl2,256
Long-term debt (mil.): Fl462
No. of shares (mil.): 43
Dividends
  Yield: 1.6%
  Payout: 27.1%
Market value (mil.): $4,718
Sales (mil.): $4,658

**Stock Price History
High/Low 1984–93**

HENKEL KGAA

OVERVIEW

Based in Düsseldorf, Henkel is Germany's 4th largest chemical company and one of the world's leading producers of oleochemicals (fat-based compounds used in soaps, cosmetics, and detergents) and metal surface treatments. The vertically integrated company uses these compounds to produce a variety of consumer and industrial products that have made Henkel the European leader in cosmetics and toiletries, detergents and household cleaners, and industrial hygiene.

Since 1991 Henkel has reorganized along product lines (divesting several noncore businesses such as its confectionery operations), built new facilities in the growing markets of the US and Asia, and trimmed facilities in Germany, where high pay and benefit levels have made production less profitable. It has also launched several joint ventures in Russia and Eastern Europe. The company does not compete in the consumer products market in the US except for its 27.8% ownership interest in Clorox.

Sales dipped in 1993 because of the continuing recession in Europe, and costs rose because of the company's acquisition, construction, and restructuring programs.

The founding Henkel family continues to control the company through its ownership of voting stock.

WHEN

In 1876 Fritz Henkel, a chemical plant worker, combined 2 of Germans' passions—chemistry and cleanliness—by starting Henkel & Cie in Aachen in 1876 to make a "universal detergent." Henkel moved the company to Düsseldorf in 1878 and launched "Henkel's Bleaching Soda," one of Germany's first brand-name products. In the 1880s the company began making water glass, an ingredient of its detergent, which differs from soap in the way it emulsifies dirt. In 1907 Henkel introduced its most important product, Persil, a detergent that eliminated the need for rubbing or bleaching clothes. It soon became a leading detergent in Germany.

Henkel set up an Austrian subsidiary in 1913. During WWI it provided medical care and extra food to its workers. In response to a postwar adhesives shortage, Henkel began making glue for its own packaging and soon became Europe's leading glue maker. Henkel began making cleansers with the newly developed phosphates in the late 1920s.

When Fritz died in 1930, Henkel stock was divided among his 3 children. In the 1930s the company sponsored a whaling fleet that provided fats for its products. By 1939 Henkel had 16 plants in Europe.

During WWII Henkel lost most of its foreign plants and made unbranded soap at home. Allied authorities removed the Henkel family from management, but control was restored to them in 1947. After the war the company retooled its plants, branched out into personal care products, and became embroiled in rivalries with Unilever, Procter & Gamble, and Colgate-Palmolive for control of the German detergent market. By 1968 Henkel dominated the market with nearly a 50% share.

In 1960 Henkel bought its first US company, Standard Chemicals (renamed Henkel, Inc., now Henkel Corp.) in 1971. Konrad Henkel, who took over in 1961, modernized the company's image by retuning management structure and marketing techniques. Henkel patented a substitute for environmentally harmful phosphates and in 1977 bought General Mills's chemical business.

In 1985 Henkel, owned by 66 family members, went public with nonvoting shares. The company bought Nopco (US, specialty chemicals) and Parker Chemical (US, metal surface pretreatment) from Ford Motors in 1987 and Emery, the #1 US oleochemicals maker, in 1989.

In 1991 Henkel formed a partnership with Ecolab (of which it already owned 24%); acquired interests in Russia, Poland, Hungary, and Slovenia; and introduced Persil in Spain and Portugal. In 1992 the company established the world's first APG (an oleochemical) plant in Cincinnati, Ohio, and acquired Barnängen, a personal-care product maker, from Nobel Industries.

These acquisitions left Henkel somewhat bloated, especially during a recession. In recent years the company has closed 10 plants. In 1993 about 1,000 jobs were eliminated and cuts continued into 1994.

Although the European market is mature, Henkel's Asian business continues to grow, and the company views NAFTA as a great opportunity to expand in the Americas.

Principal exchange: Düsseldorf
Fiscal year ends: December 31

Chairman: Albrecht Woeste
President and CEO: Hans-Dietrich Winkhaus
EVP Finance and Logistics: Hans-Günter Grünewald
EVP Personnel: Roland Schulz
President and CEO, Henkel Corp. (US): Harald P. Wulff
CFO, Henkel Corp. (US): John Knudson
Personnel, Henkel Corp. (US): William Jenkins
Auditors: KPMG Deutsche Treuhand-Gesellschaft Aktiengesellschaft Wirtschaftprüfungsgesellschaft

WHERE

HQ: Henkelstrasse 67, D-40191 Düsseldorf, Germany
Phone: +49-2-11-797-0
Fax: +49-2-11-798-4040
US HQ: Henkel Corporation, 2200 Renaissance Blvd., Ste. 200, Gulph Mills, PA 19406
US Phone: 610-270-8100
US Fax: 610-270-8291

Henkel's subsidiaries sell products in 55 nations.

	1993 Sales	
	DM mil.	% of total
Germany	4,069	29
Other Europe	6,705	48
North America	1,606	12
Asia & Australia	781	6
Other countries	706	5
Total	**13,867**	**100**

WHAT

	1993 Sales	
	DM mil.	% of total
Detergents & cleansers	4,333	31
Chemical products	3,803	28
Industrial adhesives & consumer products	2,219	16
Cosmetics & toiletries	1,410	10
Institutional hygiene	1,312	10
Other	790	5
Total	**13,867**	**100**

Selected Products

Personal Care	Cleaning Products
AOK	Megaperls
Diadermine	Persil
Fa	Perwall
Musk	Sil
Poly Color	Somat 2000
Poly Diadem	Super Croix
Poly Kur Hair Care	Vernel
Sergio Tacchini	Wipp Automáticas
Thera-med	Witte Reus

Selected Subsidiaries and Investments

The Clorox Company (27.8%, US)
Ecolab Inc. (23.8%, US)
Loctite Corp. (29.6%, US)

KEY COMPETITORS

Akzo Nobel	Estée Lauder	Procter &
American Home	Hoechst	Gamble
Products	Imperial Chemical	Rhône-Poulenc
Avon	S.C. Johnson	Roche
BASF	Koor	St.-Gobain
Borden	L'Oréal	Shiseido
Colgate-Palmolive	Petrofina	SmithKline
Dial	PPG	Beecham
Dow Chemical		Unilever

HOW MUCH

$=DM1.74 (Dec. 31, 1993)	Annual Growth	1984	1985	1986	1987	1988	1989	1990	1991	1992	1993
Sales (DM mil.)	4.5%	9,343	9,224	8,716	9,256	10,252	11,639	12,017	12,905	14,101	13,867
Net income (DM mil.)	7.8%	—	170	212	272	323	362	389	398	344	311
Income as % of sales	—	—	1.8%	2.4%	2.9%	3.1%	3.1%	3.2%	3.1%	2.4%	2.2%
Earnings per share (DM)[1]	(4.1%)	—	—	—	—	—	26	28	30	24	22
Stock price – high (DM)[1]	—	—	389	458	539	512	581	690	607	638	648
Stock price – low (DM)[1]	—	—	334	329	406	381	470	500	440	526	502
Stock price – close (DM)[1]	7.0%	—	369	448	432	512	560	501	518	555	635
P/E – high	—	—	—	—	—	—	22	25	20	26	29
P/E – low	—	—	—	—	—	—	18	18	15	21	23
Dividends per share (DM)[1]	16.2%	—	3.0	7.5	8.0	8.5	9.0	9.5	10.0	10.0	10.0
Book value per share (DM)	—	—	—	—	—	—	—	—	—	—	—
Employees	2.8%	31,612	30,935	32,038	34,731	35,943	38,145	38,803	41,475	42,244	40,480

1993 Year-end:
Debt ratio: 27.1%
Return on equity: —
Cash (mil.): DM492
Long-term debt (mil.): DM174
No. of shares (mil.): 14
Dividends
　Yield: 1.6%
　Payout: 45.2%
Market value (mil.): US$5,131
Sales: US$7,970

Stock Price History
High/Low 1985–93

[1] Preferred shares

HITACHI, LTD.

Hitachi is the #1 Japanese manufacturer of electrical machinery and is one of the world's largest makers of semiconductors. Its range of activities includes the manufacture of power equipment, information and communication systems, electronic devices, consumer products, industrial and plant machinery, metals, chemicals, and wire and cable. The multinational conglomerate is a major producer of IBM-compatible mainframe computers, heavy machinery, home electronics, and power plants.

Hitachi is the world's #2 maker of DRAMs, behind Korea's Samsung. After losing money in 1991 and 1992, semiconductor results

bounced back in 1993 and 1994. Hitachi is the top 4-Mbit DRAM supplier and is making inroads into the multimedia market.

However, Hitachi's dependency in recent years on its money-losing main frame segment has hurt the company's growth. Its consumer electronics division also continues to be unprofitable.

Hitachi and Mitsubishi agreed in 1994 to pool their development and technological resources to develop flash-memory chips in an attempt to compete with Intel, the market leader. The flash-memory market is expected to grow by 500% by 1997.

Namihei Odaira, an employee of Kuhara Mining in the Japanese coastal city of Hitachi, wanted to prove that Japan did not have to depend on foreigners for technology. In 1910 he began building 5-hp electric motors in Kuhara's engineering and repair shop. Japanese power companies were forced to buy Odaira's generators when WWI made imports scarce. Impressed, they reordered, and in 1920 Hitachi (meaning "rising sun") became an independent company.

During the 1920s acquisitions and growth turned Hitachi into a major manufacturer of electrical equipment and machinery. In the 1930s and 1940s, Hitachi developed vacuum tubes and light bulbs and produced radar and sonar for the Japanese war effort. Postwar occupation forces removed Odaira and closed 19 Hitachi plants. Reeling from the plant closures, war damage, and labor strife, Hitachi was saved from bankruptcy by US military contracts during the Korean War.

In the 1950s Hitachi was designated a supplier to Nippon Telegraph and Telephone (NTT), the state-owned communications monopoly. Japan's economic recovery led to strong demand for the company's communications and electrical equipment. Hitachi began mass-producing home appliances, radios, TVs, and transistors. The company spun off Hitachi Metals and Hitachi Cable in 1956 and Hitachi Chemical in 1963.

With the help of NTT, the Ministry of International Trade and Industry (MITI), and computer technology licensed from RCA, Hitachi produced its first computer in 1965. In the 1960s Hitachi began producing color

TVs, built factories in Southeast Asia, and started manufacturing integrated circuits.

Hitachi launched an IBM-plug-compatible computer in 1974. The company sold its computers in the US through Itel until 1979, and afterward through National Semiconductor's NAS (National Advanced Systems) unit. In the 1980s the company sold plug-compatibles in Europe through Olivetti (Italy) and BASF (Germany). In 1982 FBI agents caught Hitachi staff buying documents allegedly containing IBM software secrets. Hitachi settled a civil case with IBM for around $300 to $500 million and $2 to $3 million per month for 8 years as compensation for the use of IBM's software.

In the late 1980s the rising Japanese yen hurt exports. Hitachi responded by focusing on burgeoning domestic markets and investing heavily in factory automation. In 1988 the company and Texas Instruments agreed to join in the costly development and production of 16 megabit DRAMs. In 1989 Hitachi bought 80% of NAS, giving it direct control of its US distribution. In that same year, Motorola and Hitachi became embroiled in a patent dispute but settled the case in 1990.

Despite their rivalry, in 1991 Hitachi agreed to resell IBM notebook PCs under its own name in Japan; in 1992 the 2 companies agreed to jointly develop high-end printers. In 1993 Hitachi began selling an 8-processor very large mainframe computer. In a major restructuring move to combat sluggish consumer electronics sales, Hitachi announced in 1994 that it would merge with its marketing subsidiary, Hitachi Sales Corp.

NYSE symbol: HIT (ADR)
Fiscal year ends: March 31

Chairman: Katsushige Mita, age 70
President: Tsutomu Kanai, age 65
EVP: Toori Sato
EVP: Takeo Miura
EVP: Kazuo Morita
EVP: Reijiro Fukutomi
President, Hitachi America: Koichi Ueno
VP and CFO, Hitachi America: Shuji Nakanishi
VP and General Manager (Personnel), Hitachi America: Iwao Hara
Auditors: KPMG Peat Marwick

HQ: Kabushiki Kaisha Hitachi Seisakusho, 6, Kanda-Surugadai 4-chome, Chiyoda-ku, Tokyo 101, Japan
Phone: +81-3-3258-1111
Fax: +81-3-3258-2375
US HQ: Hitachi America, Ltd., 50 Prospect Ave., Tarrytown, NY 10591-4698
US Phone: 914-332-5800
US Fax: 914-332-5555

Hitachi operates 62 subsidiaries worldwide.

	1994 Sales	
	$ mil.	% of total
Japan	66,909	85
Other countries	12,119	15
Adjustments	(6,854)	—
Total	**72,174**	**100**

	1994 Sales	
	$ mil.	% of total
Info sys. & electronics	25,155	32
Power & industrial systems	23,235	30
Materials & others	22,140	28
Consumer products	8,122	10
Adjustments	(6,478)	—
Total	**72,174**	**100**

Information Systems and Electronics
Broadcasting equipment
Computers and peripherals
CRT displays
Medical electronics
Semiconductors
Telephone exchanges
Test equipment

Power and Industrial Systems
Auto equipment
Elevators and escalators
HVAC equipment
Industrial robots
Power plants

Materials and Others
Ceramic materials
Copper products
Electric wire and cable
Pipe fittings
Printed circuit boards
Rubber products
Steel and steel products

Consumer Products
Air conditioners
Dry batteries
Kitchen appliances
Microwave ovens
Refrigerators
TVs and VCRs
Vacuum cleaners

Alcatel Alsthom
Amdahl
AT&T
Cray Research
DEC
Ericcson
Fluor
Fujitsu
GEC
IBM
Intel
Matsushita
Micron Technology
Microsoft
Mitsubishi
Motorola
nCUBE
NEC
Nippon Steel
Northern Telecom
Samsung
Siemens
Sony
Tandem
Texas Instruments
Thinking Machines
Toshiba
United Technologies
Whirlpool
Yamaha

Stock prices are for ADRs ADR = 10 shares	9-Year Growth	1985	1986	1987	1988	1989	1990	1991	1992	1993	1994
Sales ($ mil.)	15.3%	20,053	28,204	33,257	40,010	48,496	44,797	55,025	58,388	67,863	72,174
Net income ($ mil.)	(2.5%)	839	846	677	1,100	1,406	1,335	1,637	960	696	666
Income as % of sales	—	4.2%	3.0%	2.0%	2.7%	2.9%	3.0%	3.0%	1.6%	1.0%	2.0%
Earnings per share ($)	(4.2%)	2.88	2.85	2.53	3.34	4.47	3.71	4.69	2.78	2.04	1.96
Stock price – high ($)[1]	—	44.13	38.88	74.00	110.50	152.25	133.75	112.00	100.25	76.38	84.75
Stock price – low ($)[1]	—	31.00	26.50	35.50	59.25	93.13	100.00	76.75	67.50	56.00	55.50
Stock price – close ($)[1]	8.8%	34.38	38.75	69.00	90.75	129.00	105.50	82.00	74.50	59.88	73.50
P/E – high	—	15	14	29	33	34	36	24	36	37	43
P/E – low	—	11	9	14	18	21	27	16	24	28	28
Dividends per share ($)	11.2%	0.33	0.36	0.75	1.12	0.89	0.51	0.71	0.70	0.75	0.86
Book value per share ($)	15.5%	23.32	34.95	44.68	55.56	57.28	52.75	61.07	6.70	80.81	84.99
Employees	8.0%	164,951	164,117	161,325	159,910	274,508	290,811	309,757	324,292	331,505	330,637

1994 Year-end:
Debt ratio: 39.5%
Return on equity: 2.3%
Cash (mil.): $20,760
Current ratio: 1.62
Long-term debt (mil.): $9,954
No. of shares (mil.): 340
Dividends
  Yield: 1.2%
  Payout: 43.9%
Market value (mil.): $24,960

Stock Price History[1]
High/Low 1985–94

[1] Stock prices are for the prior calendar year.

HOOVER'S HANDBOOK OF WORLD BUSINESS 1995–1996   251

HOECHST AG

OVERVIEW

As the world's largest chemicals manufacturer, Hoechst (pronounced "herxt") is involved in the development, production, and marketing of dyes, plastics, pharmaceuticals, agricultural chemicals, fibers, paints, and industrial gases. With operations in over 120 countries, Hoechst is also Europe's biggest chemical concern. Its overseas operations, which include Hoechst Celanese, a major US chemical company, accounted for 38% of 1993 sales. Future growth is expected from Hoechst's international operations.

Like other European industries buffeted by competition and recession, Hoechst has consolidated operations to improve its competi-

tiveness, closing plants and laying off thousands of employees in the process. Hoechst has also embarked on joint ventures and mergers to cut costs and pursue new markets.

In 1993 Hoechst's spotless environmental record was tarnished by a series of freak chemical spills that resulted in a government investigation and the early retirement in 1994 of chairman Wolfgang Hilger, who was replaced by CFO Jürgen Dormann.

Apparently planning another foray into the US drug market, Hoechst announced in early 1995 that it planned to acquire at least a controlling interest in Marion Merrell Dow.

WHEN

Chemist Eugene Lucius founded Hoechst in the German village of the same name in 1863 to make dyes. While successfully developing thousands of dyes, Hoechst chemists moved into the new field of pharmaceutical research, producing diphtheria vaccines and analgesics (1890s) and Salvarsan (a syphilis cure, the first man-made disease-specific medicine; 1910). In 1923 they isolated insulin. Also during this time Hoechst acquired German dye and fertilizer producers.

In 1925 Hoechst joined with Bayer, BASF, and other German chemical firms to form the I.G. Farben cartel. The huge cartel was instrumental in supplying the Nazi war machine and was dismantled following WWII. Hoechst reemerged as an independent company in 1952, most of its plants having survived the war intact.

Expanding rapidly with the postwar boom in Germany, Hoechst moved into fibers, plastics, and petrochemicals in the 1950s. Most of the company's overseas expansion was accomplished by establishing foreign subsidiaries, until the 1970s when Hoechst acquired Berger, Jenson & Nicholson (Britain's largest paint producer), Hystron Fibers (US), and majority control of Roussel Uclaf (pharmaceuticals, perfume; France). The company enjoyed continued success in pharmaceuticals, particularly diuretics, diabetic medications, antibiotics, and polio vaccines.

In 1982 the Kuwaiti government, through Kuwait Petroleum, purchased a 24% interest in Hoechst and gained a seat on the company's board. In the 1980s Hoechst emphasized pharmaceuticals and US expansion. The

company invested in genetic engineering, establishing a joint venture with Massachusetts General Hospital. Hoechst gave $70 million — the largest grant in history at the time — to have first crack at the product of biotechnical research at Harvard's teaching hospital.

The company bought New Jersey–based Celanese in 1987, giving it a strong position in the US in chemical production and marketing. Hoechst strengthened its presence in North America when it took controlling interest in Celanese Mexicana (1990), Mexico's largest private chemical company.

Hoechst has also actively courted the Far East market, reaching an agreement with Teijin in Japan to produce and market flame-retardant fiber (1990). In 1991 the company entered into a joint venture with Mitsubishi Kasei, launching Hoechst Diafoil in Wiesbaden, Germany, to make polyester films for audio and video tape.

In 1992 the company expanded its presence in Europe by buying the powder coatings group of Beckers (Sweden), taking over the fiber activities of Chemiefaser Guben in eastern Germany, and purchasing 2 industrial coating plants from Lacufa. In 1993 it bought a 51% stake in troubled US drug maker Copley Pharmaceutical.

Under increasing environmental pressure Hoechst ended its production of chlorinated solvents in 1993 and started building a plant to produce an alternative to CFCs, called R 134a. In 1994 the company started building a new plant to make water-based paint, considered an environmentally friendly product.

OTC symbol: HOEHY (ADR)
Fiscal year ends: December 31

WHO

Chairman, Board of Management: Jürgen Dormann
VC, Board of Management: Günter Metz
Managing Director Finance and Accounts: Ernest H. Drew, age 57
Director Personnel: Justus Miche
President and CEO, Hoechst Celanese (US): Karl G. Engels, age 50
SVP Finance and CFO, Hoechst Celanese (US): Harry R. Benz
VP Human Resources, Hoechst Celanese (US): Charles M. Langston
Auditors: C&L Treuhand-Vereinigung

WHERE

HQ: D-65926 Frankfurt am Main, Germany
Phone: +49-69-3050
Fax: +49-69-303-665
US HQ: Hoechst Celanese Corp., PO Box 2500, Route 202-206, Somerville, NJ 08876
US Phone: 908-231-2000
US Fax: 908-231-3225

	1993 Sales		1993 Operating Profit	
	DM mil.	% of total	DM mil.	% of total
EC	21,160	46	289	19
North America	10,691	23	660	45
Africa/Asia/ Australasia	7,186	16	256	17
Latin America	3,851	8	186	13
Other Europe	3,159	7	85	6
Total	**46,047**	**100**	**1,476**	**100**

WHAT

	1993 Sales		1993 Operating Profit	
	DM mil.	% of total	DM mil.	% of total
Health	11,262	24	1,136	66
Chemicals & colors	10,666	23	162	9
Polymers	7,260	16	(248)	—
Engineering & technology	7,259	16	85	5
Fibers	6,840	15	220	13
Agriculture	2,760	6	121	7
Total	**46,047**	**100**	**1,476**	**100**

Selected Products
Animal feed additives
Carbon products
Dyes and films
Electronics chemicals
Engineering ceramics
Engineering plastics
Herbicides
Industrial gases
Insecticides
Paints and synthetic resins
Pharmaceuticals
Plant engineering
Plastics and waxes
Printing and copying processes
Surfactants
Technical fibers
Textiles

Major Subsidiaries
Behringweke AG (pharmaceuticals)
Hoechst Celanese (textile fibers, US)
Hoechst Schering AgroEvo (60%, crop protection)
Messer Griesheim GmbH (66.7%, industrial gases)
Roussel Uclaf (56.6%, pharmaceuticals, France)

KEY COMPETITORS

Akzo Nobel	Elf Aquitaine	Occidental
Albemarle	Eli Lilly	PPG
AlliedSignal	Formosa Plastics	Praxair
American Home Products	FoxMeyer Health	Rhône-Poulenc
BASF	Glaxo	Roche
Bayer	W. R. Grace	Sherwin-Williams
Ciba-Geigy	Hercules	SmithKline
Dow Chemical	Imperial Chemical	Beecham
DuPont	Merck	
	Monsanto	

HOW MUCH

$=DM1.74 (Dec. 31, 1993)	9-Year Growth	1984	1985	1986	1987	1988	1989	1990	1991	1992	1993
Sales (DM mil.)	1.2%	41,457	42,722	33,231	36,956	40,964	45,898	44,862	47,186	45,870	46,047
Net income (DM mil.)	(6.1%)	1,077	1,200	1,216	1,378	1,824	1,929	1,573	1,097	1,034	571
Income as % of sales	—	2.6%	2.8%	3.7%	3.7%	4.5%	4.2%	3.5%	2.3%	2.3%	1.2%
Earnings per share (DM)	(8.2%)	21	23	22	25	32	33	26	19	18	10
Stock price – high (DM)	—	196	294	328	347	311	320	319	277	272	320
Stock price – low (DM)	—	156	183	239	227	237	259	177	198	245	229
Stock price – close (DM)	5.8%	191	294	269	251	305	291	210	222	249	318
P/E – high	—	9	13	15	14	10	10	12	15	15	33
P/E – low	—	7	8	11	9	7	8	7	10	14	24
Dividends per share (DM)	(3.9%)	10.00	10.00	10.00	11.00	12.00	13.00	13.00	12.00	9.00	7.00
Book value per share (DM)	2.1%	157	158	190	155	179	196	198	204	202	190
Employees	(0.3%)	177,940	180,561	181,176	167,781	164,527	169,295	172,890	179,332	177,668	172,483

1993 Year-end:
Debt ratio: 38.1%
Return on equity: 5.0%
Cash (mil.): DM1,588
Long-term debt (mil.): DM4,684
No. of shares (mil.): 59
Dividends
  Yield: 2.2%
  Payout: 72.1%
Market value (mil.): $10,746
Sales (mil.): $26,464

Stock Price History
High/Low 1984–93

HONDA MOTOR CO., LTD.

OVERVIEW

Maverick, mechanical genius, and Honda Motor Co. founder Soichiro Honda was the Japanese counterpart to Henry Ford. Honda created a company that became a world leader in automobiles as well as the world's top maker of motorcycles. The Honda Accord was the #1 selling US car model from 1989 to 1991. By 1993 Honda Motor Co. was the 3rd largest seller of cars in the US (after General Motors and Ford), selling 2 cars in the US for each one sold in Japan.

But since then Honda Motor has skidded, hurt by falling sales, stiff competition from both US and other Japanese car makers, and a strong yen, which erodes profits. To recoup, CEO Nobuhiko Kawamoto reorganized the company, slashed costs, and shifted much of its manufacturing operations to North America. Honda is boosting production, reducing the number of parts in its cars, building a new plant in Mexico, and using more American-made parts. The company also is pursuing new markets, with a sport utility vehicle (Passport, made by Isuzu), minivan (Odyssey), and V-6 engine for its Accord.

To strengthen its American credentials and boost advertising, Honda announced in early 1994 that it would build engines for the Indianapolis 500. Booming sales of Honda's motorcycles, especially in China, have bolstered the company's profits, accounting for 63% of operating income in 1994.

WHEN

After 6 years as an apprentice at Art Shokai, a Tokyo auto service station, Soichiro Honda opened his own branch of the repair shop in Hamamatsu (1928). In addition to repairing autos, he raced cars and received a patent for metal spokes that replaced wood in wheels (1931). In a race in 1936 Honda set a long-standing Japanese speed record, then crashed at the finish line but escaped critical injury.

In 1937 Honda started a company to make piston rings. The Sino-Japanese War and WWII increased demand for piston rings, and the company mass-produced metal propellers for Japanese bombers, replacing handmade wooden ones. When bombs and an earthquake destroyed most of his factory, Honda sold it to Toyota (1945) for nearly $800,000. He then installed a large drum of alcohol in his home, drank, and entertained friends.

In 1946 Honda established the Honda Technical Research Institute to motorize bicycles with small, war-surplus engines. This inexpensive form of transportation proved popular amid the scarcity of postwar Japan, and Honda soon began making engines.

The company was renamed Honda Motor in 1948 and began producing motorcycles. To allow himself to focus on engineering, Honda hired Takeo Fujisawa (1949) to take on management tasks. Honda's innovative overhead valve design made the Dream Type E (1951) motorcycle an immediate runaway success. Fujisawa enlisted 13,000 bicycle dealers to launch Honda's smaller F-type Cub (1952), which accounted for 70% of Japan's motorcycle production by the end of the year.

Funded by a public offering (1954) and heavy support from Mitsubishi Bank, Honda expanded capacity and began exporting in the 1950s. The versatile C100 Super Cub, released in 1958, became an international bestseller. American Honda Motor was formed in Los Angeles (1959), accompanied by the slogan "You meet the nicest people on a Honda," created to counter the stereotypical "biker" image. In the 1960s the company added overseas factories and began producing lightweight trucks, sports cars, and minicars.

In 1972, on the eve of the oil crisis, Honda introduced the economical Civic, emphasizing the US market and targeting Volkswagen buyers. Honda released the higher-priced Accord in 1976, as cumulative Civic sales passed one million. In 1982 Accord production started at Honda's Marysville, Ohio, plant, now a source of exports to Japan. Honda successfully launched a more upscale Acura line in the US in 1986 and bought 20% of the Rover Group in 1990.

Soichiro Honda died in 1991. Also that year Honda started selling Chrysler Corp.'s Jeeps in Japan. In 1992 Honda established the first joint venture to manufacture motorcycles in China and agreed to license Daewoo Motor to produce the Legend in South Korea. Later that year the Big Three US auto makers, who wanted trade sanctions against Japanese car makers, threw Honda out of the US car makers trade association. After BMW bought an 80% share of Rover from British Aerospace in 1994, Honda sold its 20% stake in the company for a $130 million profit.

NYSE symbol: HMC (ADR)
Fiscal year ends: March 31

President and CEO: Nobuhiko Kawamoto, age 58
EVP: Yoshihide Munekuni, age 56
EVP: Hiroyuki Yoshino, age 55
President, American Honda Motor Co.: Koichi
  Amemiya, age 54
VP Finance, American Honda Motor Co.:
  Robert Weil
**VP Human Resources, American Honda Motor
  Co.:** Sherry Cameron
Auditors: KPMG Peat Marwick

WHERE

HQ: Honda Giken Kogyo Kabushiki Kaisha,
  No. 1-1, 2-chome, Minami-Aoyama,
  Minato-ku, Tokyo 107, Japan
Phone: +81-3-3423-1111
Fax: +81-3-3423-0511
US HQ: American Honda Motor Co. Inc.,
  1919 Torrance Blvd., Torrance, CA 90501
US Phone: 310-783-2000
US Fax: 310-783-3900

Honda manufactures its products in 40 countries
and has 4 manufacturing plants in the US.

	1994 Sales	
	$ mil.	% of total
North America	16,005	43
Japan	12,437	33
Europe	4,256	11
Other regions	4,750	13
Total	**37,448**	**100**

WHAT

	1994 Sales	
	$ mil.	% of total
Automobiles	29,402	79
Motorcycles	5,302	14
Other	2,744	7
Total	**37,448**	**100**

Automobile Models (US)

Acura	Honda
Integra	Accord
Legend	Civic
NSX	del Sol
Vigor	Passport (sport utility)
	Prelude

Minivan (US)
Odyssey

Motorcycles (US)

Elite (scooter)	Shadow 1100
Gold Wing	TRX

Power Products

All-terrain vehicles (ATVs)	Portable generators
General purpose engines	Power carriers
Lawn mowers	Power sprayers
Lawn tractors	Power tillers
Outboard motors	Snow blowers

KEY COMPETITORS

Actava	Ford	Outboard Marine
Black & Decker	General Motors	Peugeot
BMW	Harley-Davidson	Renault
Brunswick	Hyundai	Saab-Scania
Caterpillar	Isuzu	Suzuki
Chrysler	Kawasaki	Textron
Daewoo	Kia Motors	Toyota
Daimler-Benz	Mazda	Volkswagen
Deere	Mitsubishi	Volvo
Fiat	Nissan	Yamaha

HOW MUCH

Stock prices are for ADRs ADR = 2 shares	9-Year Growth	1985	1986	1987	1988	1989	1990	1991	1992	1993	1994
Sales ($ mil.)	15.6%	10,184	16,151	18,721	27,240	26,434	24,354	30,592	33,084	35,981	37,448
Net income ($ mil.)	(8.1%)	494	813	546	456	737	516	543	489	334	230
Income as % of sales	—	4.8%	5.0%	2.9%	1.7%	2.8%	2.1%	1.8%	1.5%	0.9%	0.6%
Earnings per share ($)	(8.5%)	1.07	1.65	1.12	1.73	1.49	1.05	1.10	1.00	0.68	0.48
Stock price – high ($)[1]	—	12.06	12.75	17.78	25.75	37.56	34.94	26.00	24.75	25.50	31.38
Stock price – low ($)[1]	—	8.31	9.59	11.00	15.59	20.09	24.50	18.50	17.38	17.75	19.88
Stock price – close ($)[1]	12.2%	9.69	11.84	17.16	20.50	33.34	25.13	19.38	23.75	20.75	27.25
P/E – high	—	11	8	16	15	25	33	24	25	38	65
P/E – low	—	8	6	10	9	13	23	17	17	26	41
Dividends per share ($)	11.9%	0.08	0.09	0.12	0.23	0.24	0.17	0.17	0.18	0.19	0.22
Book value per share ($)	13.3%	6.26	9.42	10.74	13.40	14.41	14.19	15.91	17.08	18.56	19.26
Employees	6.8%	50,609	53,730	57,130	58,000	71,200	79,200	85,500	90,500	90,900	91,300

1994 Year-end:
Debt ratio: 66.9%
Return on equity: 2.5%
Cash (mil.): $1,811
Current ratio: 1.14
Long-term debt (mil.): $5,938
No. of shares (mil.): 487
Dividends
  Yield: 0.8%
  Payout: 91.7%
Market value (mil.): $13,266

**Stock Price History[1]
High/Low 1985–94**

[1] Stock prices are for the prior calendar year.

Hong Kong Telecommunications (HKT) has had a lock on providing telecommunications services to the growing city of Hong Kong. It has also established a consultative board with the Chinese telecommunications ministry to oversee the 8–10 projects the company is actively pursuing on the mainland, including the provision of mobile phone services. In addition, HKT is part of the APC Cable system, a collaborative effort of some 40 telecom companies that links Hong Kong with Japan, Singapore, Malaysia, and Taiwan, using the longest fiber-optic cable in Asia.

HKT is one of Hong Kong's largest employers, with over 16,000 on its payroll, and is 57.5%-owned by UK telecom giant Cable and Wireless.

HKT provides over 3 million telephone lines to Hong Kong's population of 6 million. The Hong Kong market is #3 in the world in terms of density of telephone lines. HKT provides free local calls and offers one of the lowest international tariffs in the world. The company has invested heavily in R&D and has maintained a state-of-the-art communications system. HKT achieved full digitization of the Hong Kong phone system in 1993.

To meet the growing Chinese demand for phone services, HKT is installing a 3rd fiber-optic cable in nearby Guangdong province.

In the early 1870s Britisher John Pender formed the China Submarine Telegraph Company. In 1871 the company connected Hong Kong to Singapore and to London by means of an undersea telegraph cable. In 1873 Pender consolidated his Australian, Chinese, and British India companies into the Eastern Extension Australasia and China Telegraph Company (Eastern Telegraph). In 1925 the Hong Kong Telephone Company took over the interests of Pender's China and Japan Telephone and Electric Company.

In the decades following WWI, telecommunications grew in importance, and, partly to counter a threat from a new, US-based company called ITT, UK companies including Marconi Wireless and Eastern Telegraph combined to form Cable and Wireless (C&W) in 1929. As with the British Empire, the sun never set on C&W, because it provided telegraph and telephone services in Britain's far-flung colonies.

Hong Kong Telephone grew with the rapid development of the colony after World War II, as the colony's population increased from one million in 1945 to 6 million in 1994. By 1972 C&W's largest operation worldwide was its Hong Kong subsidiary, which provided 88% of the company's profits. In 1981 C&W was granted a renewal of its franchise to provide international communications for the colony and formed Cable and Wireless Hong Kong (later changed to Hongkong Telecom International) to take care of the subsidiary's international services. In 1984 C&W began to develop a digital telephone system for the territory and adjacent areas. By the end of 1986 the company had linked up 25 cities in Guangdong province in southern China to Hong Kong, a critical step in allowing the expansion of Hong Kong–managed manufacturing operations. In that same year the company opened fax lines linking Hong Kong to Beijing, Guangzhou, Shanghai, and Shenzhen.

Originally the Hong Kong Telephone Company's franchise for services to the colony was scheduled to end in 1975, but that date has been extended to 1995, shortly before the Chinese resumption of sovereignty over the territory. The company's contract for international services does not expire until 2006.

In 1988 Hong Kong Telecommunications Ltd. (HKT) was formed as a holding company to consolidate the activities of Hongkong Telecom and Hong Kong Telephone. C&W (Hong Kong) veteran Mike Gale was appointed CEO.

The opening of the Chinese market in the 1980s became a key factor in HKT's growth. By 1989 China traffic accounted for 38% of HKT's total volume, and in 1990 the Chinese government announced that it would invest $6 billion by 1995 to improve the country's telecommunications network. The company has worked closely with the China Ministry of Post and Telecommunications, and in 1994 the 2 parties agreed to form a joint venture to install undersea cables throughout Asia.

Mike Gale died suddenly in 1994, at the age of 54, only hours before the planned announcement of his promotion to deputy chairman.

NYSE symbol: HKT (ADR)
Fiscal year ends: March 31

Chairman: Lord Young of Graffham, age 62
Deputy Chairman: David K. P. Li
Deputy Chairman: Brian A. Pemberton
Deputy Chairman: James H. Ross, age 56
CEO: Linus W. L. Cheung
**Deputy CEO; Managing Director, Hong Kong
Telephone and HKTI:** Peter D. Howell-Davies
Finance Director: John G. Tonroe
Operations Director: Norman K. T. Yuen
**Company Secretary and Director of Legal
Affairs:** M. Brown
Personnel and Director of Administration:
M. Hayton
**VP Investor Relations, Hong Kong Telecom
(US):** Tom McDonnell
Auditors: KPMG Peat Marwick

WHERE

HQ: Hong Kong Telecommunications Limited,
26th Fl., Office Tower, Convention Plaza,
One Harbour Rd., Wanchai, Hong Kong
Phone: +852-888-2888
Fax: +852-877-8877
US HQ: Hong Kong Telecommunications
Limited, 777 Third Ave., 35th Fl., New York,
NY 10017
US Phone: 212-593-4813
US Fax: 212-593-9069

Hong Kong Telecommunications operates
telephone services in Hong Kong and China.

WHAT

	1994 Sales	
	HK$ mil.	% of total
International telephone service	15,165	63
Other telecommunication services	3,588	15
Local telephone service	3,281	13
Equipment sales & rentals	1,406	6
Computer, engineering & other services	840	3
Total	**24,280**	**100**

Products and Services
Data services
Datapak (public data computer network)
Fax services
International telephone services
Leased circuits
Local telephone services
Mobile telephone
Paging
Telegram
Telex
Voice communications

Major Subsidiaries
Hong Kong Telecom International Ltd. (international services)
Hong Kong Telephone Company Ltd. (local services)

KEY COMPETITORS

Alcatel Alsthom	LDDS Communications
AT&T	MCI
BCE	NTT
BT	NYNEX
GTE	Sprint
Hutchison Whampoa	

HOW MUCH

$=HK$7.72 (Dec. 31, 1993)	Annual Growth	1985	1986	1987	1988	1989	1990	1991	1992	1993	1994
Sales (HK$ bil.)	17.1%	5,855	6,786	8,209	9,915	11,837	14,134	16,266	18,371	21,645	24,280
Net income (HK$ bil.)	21.0%	1,359	1,867	2,369	2,992	3,631	4,360	4,339	5,673	6,430	7,558
Income as % of assets	—	23.2%	27.5%	28.9%	30.2%	30.7%	30.8%	26.7%	30.9%	29.7%	31.1%
Earnings per share (HK$)	16.0%	0.18	0.25	0.27	0.27	0.33	0.39	0.45	0.51	0.58	0.68
Stock price – high (HK$)[1]	—	—	3.37	5.17	6.43	7.80	5.80	6.80	8.30	10.60	18.00
Stock price – low (HK$)[1]	—	—	1.66	3.10	3.37	4.77	4.30	5.20	6.00	7.75	9.00
Stock price – close (HK$[1]	22.0%	—	3.32	4.93	4.17	4.77	5.30	6.25	8.05	9.65	16.25
P/E – high	—	—	14	19	24	24	15	15	16	18	26
P/E – low	—	—	7	11	12	15	11	11	12	13	13
Dividends per share ($)	—	0.00	0.00	0.00	5.00	0.23	0.28	0.33	0.38	0.43	0.51
Book value per share ($)	10.1%	0.59	0.70	0.74	0.65	0.79	0.90	0.96	1.09	1.23	1.40
Employees	0.5%	15,361	15,793	16,201	16,755	17,261	17,800	16,279	15,449	15,888	16,039

1994 Year-end:
Debt ratio: 0.0%
Return on equity: 51.4%
Cash (mil.): $4,251
Long term debt (mil.): $0
No. of shares (mil.): 11,153
Dividends
  Yield: 3.1%
  Payout: 75.0%
Market value (mil.): $23,466
Sales (mil.): $3,144

**Stock Price History[1]
High/Low 1986–94**

(chart values: 18, 16, 14, 12, 10, 8, 6, 4, 2, 0)

[1] Stock prices are for the prior calendar year.

HOPEWELL HOLDINGS LIMITED

Hopewell Holdings is a holding company run by Gordon Wu, Hong Kong's 10th richest man (worth an estimated $1.7 billion). Wu's Hopewell concern has interests in property investment and development, transportation and civic engineering projects, power stations, hotels, and construction. The company (which is 35% owned by Wu) also dabbles in the treasury markets in the US and Europe. Its largest projects include a super-highway connecting Hong Kong with Guangzhou, 122 kms away, and a $3.2 billion road and rail project in Bangkok.

Princeton-educated Wu expanded the company from a simple Hong Kong property developer to the Crown colony's biggest power and civil construction player in China. Hopewell invested heavily in power plants and road projects there in the 1980s.

With his eyes set on becoming an international power magnate in Asia, Wu reorganized Hopewell in 1993, consolidating all his power projects under a new publicly listed subsidiary, Consolidated Electric Power Asia (CEPA). In 1994 Wu negotiated power contracts with India, Pakistan, Indonesia, and the Philippines worth over $25 billion. CEPA is holding off on further China projects until the Chinese government allows greater returns on investments.

Like a number of other successful Hong Kong entrepreneurs, Gordon Wu's Hopewell empire grew from humble beginnings. His father started out as a Hong Kong taxi owner and driver and helped finance Gordon's first-class US education. In the late 1950s he was the only Hong Kong Chinese student in his year to study at Princeton, where he earned an engineering degree.

On his return to Hong Kong in 1962 Wu took up a job in the government's Land Department. He later left to help his father develop a property business. When his father retired in 1969, Chinese family custom forbade Wu Sr. from handing the reins of the company over to Gordon, the 7th of 9 children. Instead, he wound the company up and guaranteed a $2.5 million loan to his son to start a property company of his own.

By 1972 the ambitious engineer had developed a company big enough to gain a listing on the Hong Kong Stockmarket as Hopewell Holdings Limited.

In the early 1980s, while visiting nearby Guangzhou to promote a hotel project, the small-time property developer saw the opportunity to expand his company. Power cuts were a frequent occurrence during his visit. Realizing that the province would boom in the 1980s and 1990s, Wu dropped the hotel idea and persuaded the Chinese authorities to let him build a power plant to upgrade the power grid. By 1987 the $560 million, 700-megawatt plant was on-line.

Wu's success in China was followed by other major infrastructure projects, including contracts for 2 more power stations in Guangdong province and a contract to build China's first modern artery, a 6-lane toll road linking the cities of Guangzhou and Hong Kong.

But Wu's outstanding success in negotiating with the Chinese authorities, which he attributes to 11 years of lobbying and consuming several gallons of mao tai (a very potent liquor served at formal dinners in China), and his American-style "can-do" approach have gained him some enemies among the stuffy colonial types in Hong Kong. He took on the Hong Kong government in 1972 (after it had banned him from building a 65-floor headquarters in central Hong Kong) and won. A vocal advocate of the need for a new airport in 1986, Wu was embarrassed in 1987 when the Royal Hong Kong Jockey Club (the Territory's leading social institution) banned him from racing for 9 months for the not-uncommon practice of infringing betting rules. Hopewell insiders claim that he was singled out for treatment by jealous rivals. The Tiananmen Square episode in 1989 shook Hong Kong and nearly cost Hopewell the $800 million loan for the road project in China. But Wu kept the nervous bankers on track.

Undaunted, in 1990 while visiting Thailand to promote a power station project, Wu changed tack and sold the Thais on a massive road and rail project for Bangkok instead. Work on Hopewell's 2nd Guangdong power plant commenced in 1992.

In 1993 Hopewell spun off its power subsidiary, CEPA. Hopewell opened the highway linking Hong Kong and Guangzhou in 1994.

OTC symbol: HOWWY (ADR)
Fiscal year ends: June 30

WHO

Chairman: James Man-Hon Wu
Deputy Chairman: Douglas Laing
Managing Director: Gordon Ying Sheung Wu, age 58
Deputy Managing Director: Eddie Ping Chang Ho
Finance Controller: Robert Van Jan Nien
Company Secretary: Peter Yip Wah Lee
Executive Director: Henry Hin Moh Lee
Executive Director: Stewart W. G. Elliott
Executive Director: Kevin Ka Yan Yeung
Auditors: Kwan Wong Tan & Fong

WHERE

HQ: 64th Fl., Hopewell Centre, 183 Queen's Rd. East, Hong Kong
Phone: +852-528-4975
Fax: +852-529-8602

Hopewell Holdings develops properties, hotels, power plants, and infrastructure projects across Asia.

	1994 Sales
	% of total
China	46
Hong Kong	28
Philippines	14
Europe	3
North America	3
Other Asian countries	6
Total	**100**

WHAT

	1994 Sales	
	HK$ mil.	% of total
Civil & building construction	917	40
Power stations & infrastructural projects	462	20
Treasury investments	333	14
Property investment & development	312	14
Hotel operations	265	11
Other	16	1
Total	**2,305**	**100**

Selected Subsidiaries and Associates
Art Way Ltd. (securities investment)
Consolidated Electric Power Asia Ltd. (CEPA, 61%)
Fan Wai Properties Ltd. (property investment)
Grand Hotel Excelsior Ltd.
Hopewell China Development (Superhighway) Ltd.
Hopewell Construction Co., Ltd.
Hopewell Credit Ltd. (loan financing)
Hopewell Food Industries Ltd. (50%, restaurants)
Hopewell Housing Ltd. (property agents)
Hopewell Power (Philippines) Corp. (87%)
Kowloon Panda Hotel Ltd.
Nova Taipa Urbanizacoes Ltda. (50%, property development, Macau)
Pangasinan Electric Corp. (power plant, Philippines)

KEY COMPETITORS

ABB	Future Energy	McDermott
AES	General Electric	Peter Kiewit
Alcatel Alsthom	Hang Lung	Sons'
Bechtel	Development	Siemens
Cheung Kong	Hongkong Land	Swire Pacific
Duke Power	Hutchison Whampoa	Westinghouse
Fluor	Jardine Matheson	Wharf
Foster Wheeler	Marriott Intl.	Wing Group

HOW MUCH

$=HK$7.72 (Dec. 31, 1993)	Annual Growth	1985	1986	1987	1988	1989	1990	1991	1992	1993	1994
Sales (HK$ mil.)	16.1%	—	—	—	—	1,094	1,073	982	1,623	2,890	2,305
Net income (HK$mil.)[1]	40.3%	116	120	287	473	517	626	719	1,623	2,028	2,438
Income as % of sales	—	—	—	—	—	47.3%	58.4%	73.2%	100.0%	70.2%	105.8%
Earnings per share ($)	12.2%	—	—	—	—	0.32	0.38	0.41	0.42	0.47	0.57
Stock price – high ($)[2]	—	—	—	—	—	—	4.25	3.92	4.05	5.90	10.25
Stock price – low ($)[2]	—	—	—	—	—	—	2.30	1.56	2.70	3.15	4.25
Stock price – close ($)[2]	32.7%	—	—	—	—	—	3.27	2.52	3.20	4.33	10.13
P/E – high	—	—	—	—	—	—	11	10	10	13	18
P/E – low	—	—	—	—	—	—	6	4	6	7	7
Dividends per share (HK$)	12.5%	—	—	—	—	0.20	0.22	0.24	0.30	0.34	0.36
Book value per share (HK$)	—	—	—	—	—	—	—	—	—	3.99	5.01
Employees	—	—	—	—	—	—	—	—	—	—	—

1994 Year-end:
Debt ratio: 33.7%
Return on equity: 12.6%
Cash (mil.): HK$168
L-T debt (mil.): HK$10,986
No. of shares (mil.): 4,318
Dividends
 Yield: 3.5%
 Payout: 63.1%
Market value (mil.): $5,666
Sales (mil.): $299

Stock Price History[2]
High/Low 1990–94

[1] Includes gains from sales of assets. [2] Stock prices are for the prior calendar year.

HSBC HOLDINGS PLC

For nearly 130 years the development of the Hongkong & Shanghai Banking Corporation (HSBC) has been synonymous with that of Hong Kong itself. As Hong Kong grew, so did HSBC; it now ranks as one of the largest banking organizations in the world.

But with the imminent takeover of Hong Kong by the Chinese government (in 1997), the British-owned and -managed bank has made some bold moves to hedge its bets on its future in Hong Kong. In 1992 HSBC paid $6 billion for Midland Bank, Britain's 3rd largest. This move almost doubled HSBC's assets and profits and gave the bank a financial power base beyond the reach of the Chinese government. In 1993 HSBC shifted its corporate headquarters to London.

HSBC operates some 1,900 offices in 20 countries in Europe and 600 offices in 19 countries in Asia. Its major area of business is commercial banking, but the bank also provides a comprehensive range of financial services, including trade services, pension fund management, capital markets services, and insurance. Major subsidiaries include Hang Seng Bank (Hong Kong) and Marine Midland Bank (US).

HSBC is one of the most strongly capitalized financial institutions in the world, with 170,000 shareholders in over 90 countries.

Founded by Scotsman Thomas Sutherland and a group of businessmen, the Hongkong & Shanghai Bank opened its doors in Hong Kong in 1865. The bank initially financed and promoted British imperial trade in opium, silk, and tea in the East Asian region and quickly established a London office. Hongkong & Shanghai Bank created an international branch network emphasizing China and East Asia, where it claims to have been the first bank in Thailand (1888).

War repeatedly disrupted operations, but the bank managed to survive. When its chief manager, Sir Vandeleur Grayborn, died in a Japanese POW camp during WWII, the bank temporarily relocated its headquarters to London. Following the Communist takeover the bank withdrew from China, and by 1955 only a single Shanghai office remained. The bank played a key role in Hong Kong's explosive postwar growth by financing industrialists who fled there from China.

Hongkong & Shanghai Bank began expanding its East Asian activities in the late 1950s and later executed a strategy of globalization. In 1959 the bank acquired the British Bank of the Middle East, founded in 1889, with branches throughout that region. The bank acquired Mercantile Bank (India, Southeast Asia, 1959) and 61.5% of Hang Seng, Hong Kong's 2nd largest bank (1965). In 1978 the Saudi British Bank assumed control of the Saudi Arabian branches of British Bank of the Middle East. BBME retained a 40% interest in the Saudi bank and managed the new entity.

During the 1980s the bank purchased a controlling interest in Marine Midland Bank (US, 1980), 51% of primary treasury security dealer Carroll McEntee & McGinley (US, 1983), major London stockbroker James Capel & Co. (1986), most of the assets and liabilities of the Bank of British Columbia (1986), and the rest of Marine Midland (1987).

The bank established subsidiaries Wayfoong (mortgage and small business finance, Hong Kong, 1960), Wardley (investment banking, Hong Kong, 1972), Hongkong Bank of Canada (1981), and HongkongBank of Australia (1986). Hongkong & Shanghai Bank's 1981 bid for the Royal Bank of Scotland failed when the British government stopped the transaction, citing the bank's international, rather than Scottish, orientation.

Hongkong Bank of Canada, by acquiring Lloyds Bank Canada in 1990, became the largest foreign-owned bank there. In 1991 HSBC sold most of its long-held stake in Cathay Pacific Airways to Chinese interests. HSBC sold the remaining stake in 1992.

HSBC became a truly "global" bank with the 1992 acquisition of the UK's 3rd largest bank, Midland Bank. The following year an IRA bomb blast in London's financial district severely damaged HSBC's headquarters, and the bankruptcy of Olympia & York's development project in London's East End left HSBC holding $758 million in shaky loans.

In 1994 Hongkong Bank Malaysia Berhad (with 36 HSBC bank branches) became the first foreign bank to be locally incorporated in Malaysia.

OTC symbol: HSBHY (ADR)
Fiscal year ends: December 31

Chairman: Sir William Purves, age 62
Group CEO: John R. H. Bond, age 52
Deputy Chairman: Baronness Lydia Dunn, age 54
Deputy Chairman: Sir Peter Walters, age 63
Executive Director Investment Banking:
Bernard H. Asher, age 58
Group Finance Director: Richard Delbridge,
age 51
General Manager Group Human Resources:
Robert A. Tennant
CEO, Midland Bank: Keith Whitson
Chairman and CEO, HSBC Holdings (US):
Aman Mehta
Auditors: KPMG Peat Marwick

HQ: 10 Lower Thames St., London EC3R 6AE, UK
Phone: +44-(01)71-260-0500
Fax: +44-(01)71-260-0501
US HQ: HSBC Holdings Inc., 140 Broadway,
New York, NY 10005
US Phone: 212-658-5500
US Fax: 212-658-5897

The company operates 3,000 offices worldwide.

	1993 Assets	
	HK$ bil.	% of total
UK	951	40
Hong Kong	693	30
Americas	356	15
Other Asia/Pacific	243	10
Other Europe	110	5
Total	**2,353**	**100**

	1993 Assets	
	HK$ bil.	% of total
Cash/balances at central banks	19	1
Loans/advances to customers	1,123	48
Loans & advances to banks	499	21
Debt securities	298	13
Government securities	81	3
Equity interests	30	1
Other	303	13
Total	**2,353**	**100**

Principal Subsidiaries
The British Bank of the Middle East
Carroll McEntee & McGinley Inc. (securities, US)
The Cyprus Popular Bank Ltd. (22.1%)
Egyptian British Bank SAE (40%)
Hang Seng Bank Ltd. (61.5%, Hong Kong)
The Hongkong and Shanghai Banking Corp. Ltd.
Hongkong Bank of Canada
Hongkong Bank of Australia Ltd.
HSBC Finance (Malaysia) Berhad
James Capel Investment Services Ltd.
Marine Midland Bank (US)
Midland Bank plc
The Saudi British Bank (40%)
Trinkhaus & Burkhardt KGaA (Germany)
UBAF Bank Ltd. (24.8%)
Wardley Ltd. (merchant banking, Hong Kong)
Wayfoong Finance Ltd. (Hong Kong)

BankAmerica	Deutsche Bank
Bank of China	Industrial Bank of Japan
Barclays	Lloyds Bank
Canadian Imperial	J.P. Morgan
Chase Manhattan	NatWest
Citicorp	Royal Bank
Crédit Lyonnais	Standard Chartered
CS Holding	Union Bank of Switzerland
Dai-Ichi Kangyo	Wing Lung Bank

$=HK$7.72 (Dec. 31, 1993)	9-Year Growth	1984	1985	1986	1987	1988	1989	1990	1991	1992	1993
Assets (HK$ bil.)	19.7%	467	537	707	823	884	1,038	1,158	1,249	1,999	2,353
Net income (HK$ bil.)	25.9%	3	3	3	4	4	5	3	6	14	21
Income as % of assets	—	0.6%	0.5%	0.4%	0.4%	0.5%	0.5%	0.3%	0.4%	0.7%	0.9%
Earnings per share (HK$)	18.1%	1.83	1.90	2.15	2.28	2.71	3.00	1.92	3.49	7.28	8.20
Stock price – high (HK$)	—	—	18.80	24.55	33.36	22.94	27.64	28.00	36.00	68.00	117.00
Stock price – low (HK$)	—	—	15.15	15.48	19.38	19.50	18.00	18.10	18.00	34.00	54.50
Stock price – close (HK$)	24.5%	15.99	17.03	24.55	21.79	21.16	26.91	18.90	35.75	55.50	115.00
P/E – high	—	—	10	11	15	8	9	15	10	9	14
P/E – low	—	—	8	7	8	7	6	9	5	5	7
Dividends per share (HK$)	11.0%	1.05	1.02	1.17	1.20	1.29	1.49	1.64	1.58	2.23	2.68
Book value per share (HK$)	12.4%	14.67	15.38	18.64	21.17	22.66	32.93	33.11	34.53	37.46	42.16
Employees	9.1%	45,000	46,000	49,669	51,950	52,414	53,375	54,408	53,770	98,716	98,396

1993 Year-end:
Debt ratio: 94.9%
Equity as % of assets: 4.5%
Return on equity: 20.6%
No. of shares (mil.): 2,528
Dividends
Yield: 2.3%
Payout: 32.7%
Market value (mil.): $37,660
Assets (mil.): $304,793
Sales (mil.): $21,560

Stock Price History
High/Low 1985–93

HUDSON'S BAY COMPANY

OVERVIEW

With a history of trading for over 300 years, Hudson's Bay Company (HBC) is one of Canada's leading retailers and also North America's oldest corporation. Known as a "company of adventurers," HBC opened the Canadian Arctic in the late 1800s by building remote trading posts in Canada's huge Hudson's Bay territory and dominated the world fur trade until the past 15 years. At its peak the company presided over 8% of the world's land surface. Over time and under media baron Kenneth Thomson, who bought a 75% stake in 1979, the company has dwindled to a collection of department and discount stores. The Thomson family recently reduced its stake in HBC to 23%.

HBC has reduced its operating divisions to The Bay (traditional department stores) and Zellers (discount stores), which is modeled after Wal-Mart, the US's largest retailer. Zellers accounts for 68% of company profits. HBC also operates Fields, a general merchandise discounter, whose sales represent less than 2% of the company's total revenues.

In 1993 HBC significantly expanded westward by buying Woodward's, one of Canada's main department store operators in the region. Competition is expected to increase since Wal-Mart's 1994 acquisition of 120 of Woolco's discount stores in Canada. HBC is renovating its stores, upgrading its merchandise, and looking for joint ventures to expand into China.

WHEN

In 1668 the British ketch *Nonsuch* reached the bay named for explorer Henry Hudson. The ship returned to Britain the following year laden with furs, attracting the attention of King Charles II. In 1670 Charles granted a royal trading charter to a party of 18 men and appointed Prince Rupert, a former Royalist cavalry officer, as the company's first governor.

The company built a series of fortifications and engaged in a seesawing battle with French warships for control of Hudson's Bay. This continued until 1713 when the Treaty of Utrecht placed the bay officially in British hands. From HBC's base at York Factory, company explorers began to penetrate Canada's vast interior. In 1774 Samuel Hearne established HBC's first inland post on the Saskatchewan River.

During the late 18th century, the Montreal-based North West Company, a rival fur-trading concern, threatened HBC's fur-trading dominance. Both HBC and NWC organized increasing numbers of inland routes and forts, sparking frequent and often violent clashes between the competing traders.

In 1821 the 2 competitors ceased hostilities by merging under the HBC name, giving the company control over 173 posts throughout 3 million square miles of wilderness. In 1869 the company transferred possession of HBC-chartered land to the Canadian government.

By the turn of the century, HBC had transformed many posts into stores to serve growing Canadian cities. In 1929 the company formed the Hudson's Bay Oil and Gas Company. HBC acquired the Henry Morgan department store chain in 1960 and 5 years later changed its store name to The Bay. In 1970 the company finally moved its headquarters from London (most of the company's governors had never ventured into Canada) to Winnipeg and later to Toronto.

The company expanded its department store holdings in the late 1970s by purchasing Zellers, Fields, and Simpsons. In 1979 newspaper magnate Kenneth Thomson bought 75% of HBC. During the 1980s the company became mired in debt from its prolific acquisitions. To trim the fat the company sold its oil and gas operations, its large fur houses (under pressure from animal rights activists), and, to the horror of many company veterans, 179 of its original northern province stores.

During a steep recession in 1990 the company spun off its Markborough real estate subsidiary to shareholders and purchased the Towers Bonimart chain of discount department stores. In 1991 HBC integrated the Towers stores into its Zellers chain and converted 6 of its Simpsons high fashion stores into The Bay stores, selling the rest to Sears for $37 million.

In 1992–93 shopping on Sunday was legalized in Ontario and Quebec, which boosted sales in 2 key markets. Also in 1993 HBC acquired Linmark, an overseas buying agency with 13 offices in Asia.

In 1994 Donald McGiverin, governor for 12 years, retired. Also that year HBC donated company archives to 2 Manitoba museums.

Principal exchange: Toronto
Fiscal year ends: January 31

Governor: David E. Mitchell, age 67
President and CEO: George J. Kosich
EVP and CFO: Gary J. Lukassen
EVP; President, The Bay: N. R. Peter
EVP; President, Zellers Inc.: Paul S. Walters
VP Human Resources: David J. Crisp
Auditors: KPMG Peat Marwick Thorne

HQ: 401 Bay St., Ste. 500, Toronto, Ontario
M5H 2Y4, Canada
Phone: 416-861-6112
Fax: 416-861-4517

1994 Stores	No.	Sq. ft. thou.
Ontario	144	13,824
Quebec	78	7,307
British Columbia	51	5,449
Alberta	47	4,616
Nova Scotia	19	1,514
Manitoba	12	1,606
Other provinces	35	2,335
Total	**386**	**36,651**

1994 Sales	% of total
Ontario	42
Western Canada	32
Quebec	19
Maritimes	7
Total	**100**

	1994 Sales		1994 Operating Income	
	C$ mil.	% of total	C$ mil.	% of total
Zellers	3,159	58	256	68
The Bay	2,183	40	122	32
Other	100	2	(14)	—
Total	**5,442**	**100**	**364**	**100**

1994 Stores	No.	Sq. ft. thou.
Zellers	285	20,133
The Bay	101	16,518
Total	**386**	**36,651**

Stores
The Bay (department stores)
Fields Stores (discount family stores)
Zellers Inc. (discount stores)

Chateau Stores of Canada	North West Company
Dalmys	J. C. Penney
Dylex	Pennington's
Gendis	Stores
Grafton	Price/Costco
Imasco	Reitmans Canada
Kmart	Sears
Lands' End	Toys "R" Us
Marks and Spencer	Wal-Mart
Montgomery Ward	Woodward's

$=C$1.32 (Dec. 31, 1993)	Annual Growth	1985	1986	1987	1988	1989	1990	1991	1992	1993	1994
Sales (C$ mil.)	1.3%	4,829	5,271	5,692	4,345	4,491	4,604	4,970	5,032	5,152	5,442
Net income (C$ mil.)	—	(107)	(9)	33	13	37	144	158	83	117	148
Income as % of sales	—	0.0%	(0.2%)	0.6%	0.3%	0.8%	3.1%	3.2%	1.6%	2.3%	2.7%
Earnings per share (C$)	—	(5.40)	(1.23)	0.32	(0.51)	0.32	3.64	3.34	1.61	2.32	2.72
Stock price – high (C$)[1]	—	24.00	26.63	33.00	26.50	25.13	37.38	34.00	37.00	33.38	41.13
Stock price – low (C$)[1]	—	17.00	16.25	22.13	18.25	18.38	24.63	15.75	19.50	25.25	29.00
Stock price – close (C$)[1]	9.6%	17.25	24.63	23.25	19.38	25.13	31.00	20.00	34.00	29.25	39.50
P/E – high	—	—	—	103	—	78	10	10	23	14	15
P/E – low	—	—	—	69	—	56	7	5	12	11	11
Dividends per share (C$)	3.2%	0.60	0.60	0.60	0.60	0.60	0.60	0.80	0.80	0.80	0.80
Book value per share (C$)	(1.7%)	33.28	30.49	28.40	16.33	14.41	21.09	25.53	24.43	25.92	28.56
Employees	4.2	42,500	39,000	41,000	—	—	—	55,000	56,500	—	—

1994 Year-end:
Debt ratio: 43.9%
Return on equity: 10.0%
Cash (mil.): C$17
Long-term debt (mil.): C$1,084
No. of shares (mil.): 57
Dividends
  Yield: 2.0%
  Payout: 29.4%
Market value (mil.): $1,691
Sales (mil.): $4,122

**Stock Price History[1]
High/Low 1985–94**

[1] Stock prices are for the prior calendar year.

HUTCHISON WHAMPOA LIMITED

OVERVIEW

In land-hungry Hong Kong it pays to have property, and conglomerate Hutchison Whampoa, one of the oldest *hongs* (colonial trading companies) in Hong Kong, has some prime locations that have become high-rise rental properties in recent years. Hong Kong's buoyant property market enabled Hutchison to bring in $168 million in revenues from its rental properties in 1993. But Hutchison is more than a land bank; it is a major diversified company with interests in property, container terminal operations, retailing, energy, finance and investment, telecommunications, and media. Its Hongkong International Terminals Ltd. (78%-owned) handles 60% of the traffic passing through

Hong Kong's container port, the world's busiest.

Chairman Li Ka-shing (who began his career as a poor, 14-year-old Chinese immigrant selling plastic flowers and is now the richest man in Hong Kong) controls 43% of the company through his Cheung Kong Holdings property company. His sons head up various parts of his business empire.

The company's several overseas holdings include a stake (49%) in Husky Oil, Canada's largest independent integrated oil company, and 75% of the Port of Felixstowe, the UK's leading container port.

Hutchison is building up its property and container businesses in China.

WHEN

In 1977 Hong Kong companies Hutchison International and Hongkong and Whampoa Dock merged to form Hutchison Whampoa. Originally established in 1880 by John Hutchison, Hutchison International became a major Hong Kong consumer goods importer and wholesaler. Managed by Sir Douglas Clague, the company bought controlling interests in Hongkong and Whampoa Dock (dry docks) and A.S. Watson (drugstores, supermarkets, soft drinks) in the midst of a wild acquisition binge in the 1960s. The purchases were accomplished through a complex web of deals that fell apart in the mid-1970s. To save Hutchison International, the Hongkong & Shanghai Bank took a large stake in the company and replaced Clague with Australian turnaround specialist "Dollar" Bill Wyllie. Wyllie slashed expenses, sold 103 companies in 1976, and bought the rest of Hongkong and Whampoa Dock in 1977.

Hongkong and Whampoa Dock, the first registered company in Hong Kong, was established in 1861. The company bought dry docks in Whampoa (port of Canton, China) following the kidnapping and disappearance of their owner, John Couper, during the 2nd Opium War. Hong Kong docks were first purchased in 1865. Hongkong and Whampoa Dock operated shipyards and shipping container terminals at the time of the merger with Hutchison.

Hutchison Whampoa's finances improved vastly under Wyllie. In a surprise move Hongkong & Shanghai Bank sold its 22.8% stake in Hutchison to Li Ka-shing's Cheung

Kong Holdings in 1979 at 50% of its value. Wyllie, thought to have been planning his own bid for Hutchison, left in 1981.

In the 1980s Hutchison developed its former dockyard sites (now prime real estate). The company's International Terminals unit grew with Hong Kong's container traffic and became the world's largest privately owned container terminal operator. Following the appointment of former French foreign legionnaire Simon Murray as managing director in 1984, the company bought large minority stakes in Hongkong Electric (utility, 1985), Husky Oil (Canada, 1987), and Cluff Resources (gold and minerals mining, UK, 1987). It also purchased Australian paging and UK mobile telephone units (1989).

In 1990 the *hong* launched the AsiaSat I satellite in a joint venture with Cable & Wireless and China International Trust & Investment Corp. In 1991 Hutchison bought a 75% interest in the UK's #1 container port and bought the UK cellular telephone operations of Millicom. STAR TV (18%-owned by Hutchison, 63% by News Corp, and 19% by Li) began broadcasting to 38 countries across Asia in 1991 using AsiaSat I. In 1992 it acquired 50% (now 40%) of Shanghai's container port.

In 1993 Chinese officials announced plans to build the largest commercial store in the country (in Chungking); 95% of its funding would be from Hutchison.

Hutchison planned to set up a company with other Hong Kong interests in 1994 to invest with Chinese partners in a $120 million property joint venture in Shanghai.

OTC Symbol: HUWHY (ADR)
Fiscal year ends: December 31

Chairman: Li Ka-shing
Deputy Chairman: Richard T. K. Li
Group Managing Director: Canning K. N. Fok
Group Finance Director: William Shurniak
Company Secretary and Senior Group Legal
Advisor: N. D. McGee
Managing Director, Hutchison Whampoa
(Europe): The Lord Derwent
Auditors: Price Waterhouse

WHERE

HQ: Hutchison House, 22nd Fl., 10 Harcourt Rd.,
Hong Kong
Phone: +852-523-0161
Fax: +852-810-0705
European HQ: Hutchison Whampoa (Europe)
Limited, 9 Queen Street, Mayfair,
London W1X 7PH, UK
Phone: +44-(0)71-499-3353
Fax: +44-(0)71-491-0872

Hutchison Whampoa has operations in 17
countries.

	1993 Sales		1993 Operating Income	
	HK$ mil.	% of total	HK$ mil.	% of total
Hong Kong	18,446	75	4,623	92
Europe	3,589	14	(119)	—
Asia	2,411	10	218	5
North America	302	21	165	3
Total	**24,748**	**100**	**4,887**	**100**

WHAT

	1993 Sales		1993 Operating Income	
	HK$ mil.	% of total	HK$ mil.	% of total
Retail, telecom., media & other services	16,765	68	744	13
Container terminals	5,408	22	2,889	49
Property	1,566	6	1,237	21
Energy, finance & investment	1,009	4	1,034	17
Adjustments	—	—	(1,017)	—
Total	**24,748**	**100**	**4,887**	**100**

Retail, Telecom., and Other Services
Asia Satellite Telecom.
Co. Ltd. (33%)
Hutchison Paging Ltd.
(75%)
Hutchison Telecommun-
ications Ltd.
Hutchison Telephone Co.
Ltd. (70%)
Hutchvision Hong Kong
Ltd. (18.2%)
Procter & Gamble–
Hutchison Ltd. (31%,
investments)
A. S. Watson & Co., Ltd.
(holding company)

Container Terminals
Hongkong International
Terminals Ltd. (78%)

Hongkong United Dockyards
Ltd. (50%)
Port of Felixstowe Ltd. (75%)
Shanghai Container
Terminals Ltd. (40%)

Property
Hongkong and Whampoa
Dock Company, Ltd.
Hutchison Properties Ltd.
International City Holdings
Ltd.

Energy, Finance, and Investment
Cavendish International
Holdings Ltd.
Cluff Resources plc (28%,
mining, UK)
Hongkong Electric Holdings
Ltd. (35%, utility)
Husky Oil Ltd. (49%, Canada)

KEY COMPETITORS

BT
Cable & Wireless
Hopewell Holdings
Jardine Matheson
Swire Pacific

HOW MUCH

$=HK$7.72 (Dec. 31, 1993)	Annual Growth	1984	1985	1986	1987	1988	1989	1990	1991	1992	1993
Sales (HK$ mil.)	18.9%	5,215	5,466	7,529	10,524	12,875	17,685	15,975	19,212	21,030	24,748
Net income (HK$ mil.)	22.3%	1,029	1,194	1,630	1,864	2,340	3,031	3,519	3,328	3,052	6,304
Income as % of sales	—	19.7%	21.8%	21.6%	17.7%	18.2%	17.1%	22.0%	17.3%	14.5%	25.5%
Earnings per share (HK$)	19.9%	0.35	0.42	0.57	0.65	0.77	1.00	1.16	1.09	0.96	1.79
Stock price – high (HK$)	—	3.66	5.60	9.30	15.90	9.70	12.30	13.20	16.50	20.60	40.25
Stock price – low (HK$)	—	1.68	3.70	4.80	5.65	6.65	6.80	7.95	11.90	13.30	14.75
Stock price – close (HK$)	30.0%	3.64	5.50	9.25	7.05	8.60	8.80	12.10	14.60	15.10	38.50
P/E – high	—	10	13	16	24	13	12	11	15	21	22
P/E – low	—	5	9	8	9	9	7	7	11	14	8
Dividends per share (HK$)	17.4%	0.16	0.20	0.25	0.35	0.42	0.54	0.65	0.68	0.55	0.68
Book value per share (HK$)	25.2%	1.8	2.3	3.6	4.7	5.2	7.4	8.1	9.1	10.7	13.6
Employees	11.9%	—	—	—	—	12,500	14,500	13,000	15,000	17,700	22,500

1993 Year-end:
Debt ratio: 31.9%
Return on equity: 14.7%
Cash (mil.): HK$6,153
L-T debt (mil.): HK$14,235
No. of shares (mil.): 3,617
Dividends
Yield: 1.8%
Payout: 38.0%
Market value (mil.): $18,038
Sales (mil.): $3,206

Stock Price History
High/Low 1984–93

HYUNDAI GROUP

OVERVIEW

Hyundai, one of Korea's largest *chaebols* (industrial groups), is evolving from the disciplined, unified heavy industry organization founded and controlled by Chung Ju-Yung into a looser confederation of companies under his brother, sons, and protégés. This metamorphosis is the result of anti-*chaebol* sentiment in Korea (upon which Chung tried to capitalize politically) as well as the changing nature of Korean business. Korea's growth during the 1970s and 1980s was the result of its ability to produce goods in the heavy industry sector more cheaply than could Japan or the US. But rising expectations and a higher standard of living have almost priced Korea out of this market, and its industrial giants, including Hyundai, are trying to diversify into higher-end goods.

The Hyundai Group includes companies involved in everything from shipbuilding to construction to electronics. The company's main new priorities are to become one of the 10 biggest auto makers in the world by the year 2000 and to become a premier maker of computers and such related products as non-memory chips.

Hyundai (pronounced "hi-un-dye" everywhere except in the US, where it rhymes with Sunday) has faced the wrath of the Korean government since Chung Ju-Yung's anti-government campaign for the presidency in 1992. In the ensuing political firestorm, one of Chung's sons was jailed, Chung was sentenced to jail for fraud (the sentence was suspended), and the group suffered because it was denied government development loans.

WHEN

After WWII Chung Ju-Yung went into business repairing trucks for US occupation forces in South Korea. In 1947 Chung started Hyundai Engineering and Construction, the first Korean contractor to win overseas construction projects. Hyundai Motor was formed in 1967 to assemble Fords.

Chung repeatedly gambled on new businesses. When Hyundai won a $1 billion contract in the 1970s to build a port in Jubail, Saudi Arabia, Chung saved money by using Korean parts and not insuring the shipments, risking ruin. The gamble paid off and Hyundai became a major factor in Middle East construction.

In the 1970s Chung enjoyed the support of the militarist Park government, and his Hyundai enterprises multiplied. In 1973 he began building the world's largest shipyard (Hyundai Heavy Industries) despite having no experience in shipbuilding. He succeeded thanks to government backing, near-monopoly conditions, and an extremely hardworking Korean labor force. With help from 15%-owner Mitsubishi Motors, Hyundai Motor built the first Korean car, the Pony, in 1975. Chung created Hyundai Corporation in 1976 and established the Ulsan Institute of Technology in 1977 to increase South Korea's pool of engineering talent.

The Hyundai *chaebol* continued to expand its scope in the 1980s, forming Hyundai Electronics Industries (1983) to produce semiconductors and microcomputer equipment

despite a lack of experience in high-tech industry. Hyundai spent heavily on electronics without apparent success. In 1985 the company closed a plant in Santa Clara, California, when it found that Americans would not regularly work the same hours as Koreans.

Hyundai took advantage of low labor costs to start an export drive in the 1980s, beginning shipments of the Pony to Canada (1984), where it became #4 in auto sales (1985). In the US the company introduced Blue Chip brand PCs (1986) and, in the most successful imported car launch in US history, the inexpensive Excel subcompact (1986).

Then things began to fall apart. When the military government relinquished power, the formerly strictly controlled labor movement reacted with a rash of strikes (which continue into the mid-1990s), which led to wage increases that have resulted in the export of jobs. Moreover, the company suffered from a worldwide slump in shipbuilding and continued difficulties with its electronics ventures. Car exports fell as the won rose and as quality problems with Hyundai cars increased.

Hyundai suffered more in the aftermath of Chung's failed political campaign, as it was forced onto the commercial money markets to raise capital. Besides denying it loans, the Korean government refused the group permission to list some of its subsidiaries in the OTC market and subjected it to retaliatory audits. An abject apology by Chung in 1993 improved the situation.

Principal exchange: Korea
Fiscal year ends: December 31

Group Chairman: Chung Se-Yung
President: Park Se Yong
VP, CFO, and Head of Personnel: Park Won-jin
President, Hyundai Motor America: Y. I. Lee
Director of Finance, Hyundai Motor America:
  Jim Hannefield
VP Administration (Human Resources),
  Hyundai Motor America: Keith Duckworth
Auditors: Anjin Accounting Corp.

WHERE

HQ: Hyundai Corp., PO Box 8943, 140-2, Kye-
  Dong, Chongro-Ku, Seoul, Korea
Phone: +82-2-746-1114
Fax: +82-2-741-2341
US HQ: Hyundai Motor America, 10550 Talbert
  Ave., Fountain Valley, CA 92728-0850
US Phone: 714-965-3000
US Fax: 714-965-3816

Hyundai sells cars and computers and other
electronics, and engages in construction
activities throughout the world.

	1993 Sales % of total
South Korea	40
Other countries	60
Total	**100**

WHAT

	1993 Sales % of total
Electronics & electrical equipment	33
Ships & industrial plants	27
Machinery & transportation	22
Steel & metal	9
Other	9
Total	**100**

Selected Subsidiaries

Aluminum of Korea	Hyundai Marine & Fire
Hyundai Australia Pty.,	Insurance
Ltd.	Hyundai Merchant Marine
Hyundai Construction	Hyundai Mipo Dockyard
Equipment Industries	Hyundai Motor
Hyundai Corp. Europe	Hyundai Precision & Industry
GmbH	Hyundai Robot Industry
Hyundai Corp. U.K. Ltd.	Hyundai Singapore Pte. Ltd.
Hyundai Electrical	Hyundai Steel Tower
Engineering	Industries
Hyundai Electronics	Hyundai Wood Industries
Hyundai Engineering	Inchon Iron & Steel
Hyundai Engineering &	Keumkang Development
Construction	KKBC International Ltd.
Hyundai Heavy	Koryeo Industrial
Industries	Development

KEY COMPETITORS

Bechtel	Hitachi	Motorola
Compaq	Honda	National
Daewoo	IBM	Semiconductor
Deere	IRI	NEC
Fiat	Isuzu	Samsung
Ford	ITOCHU	Siemens
Fujitsu	Kia Motors	Tenneco
General Motors	LG Group	Texas
Groupe	Marubeni	Instruments
Schneider	Mitsubishi	Toyota

HOW MUCH

$=Won808 (Dec. 31, 1993)	Annual Growth	1984	1985	1986	1987	1988	1989	1990	1991	1992	1993
Sales (Won bil.)	24.4%	1,550	2,853	3,876	5,254	5,622	5,703	6,328	9,361	11,220	11,046
Net income (Won bil.)	6.2%	3.2	4.5	4.9	3.7	8.6	4.6	6.6	9.0	5.3	5.5
Income as % of sales	—	0.2%	0.2%	0.1%	0.1%	0.1%	0.1%	0.1%	0.1%	0.0%	0.0%
Earnings per share (Won)[1]	1.4%	1,005	1,394	1,530	761	1,798	966	1,367	1,881	1,095	1,135
Stock price – high (Won)	—	—	13,190	16,350	21,900	30,300	35,200	30,000	26,300	21,000	24,000
Stock price – low (Won)	—	—	8,590	9,210	12,800	17,500	22,700	23,400	18,500	10,300	12,300
Stock price – close (Won)	7.6%	—	—	13,500	20,290	30,300	26,600	25,500	19,700	15,000	22,500
P/E – high	—	—	9	11	29	16	36	21	14	19	21
P/E – low	—	—	6	6	17	10	23	17	10	9	11
Dividends per share (Won)[1]	0.0%	—	500	500	500	500	500	500	500	500	500
Book value per share (Won)	6.3%	—	9,220	10,024	9,380	11,046	11,557	12,381	13,743	15,132	15,000
Employees	—	—	—	—	—	—	—	—	—	—	41,450

1993 Year-end:
Debt ratio: —
Return on equity: 7.5%
Cash (mil.): —
Long-term debt (mil.): —
No. of shares (mil.): 5
Dividends
  Yield: 2.2%
  Payout: 44.1%
Market value (mil.): $134
Sales (mil.): $13,671

Stock Price History
High/Low 1985–93

(chart axis values: 40,000 / 35,000 / 30,000 / 25,000 / 20,000 / 15,000 / 10,000 / 5,000 / 0)

Information is for Hyundai Corporation only. [1] Including minority interests

IMPERIAL CHEMICAL INDUSTRIES PLC

OVERVIEW

Imperial Chemical Industries (ICI) reduced the size of its empire with the 1993 spinoff of Zeneca, a newly listed company encompassing ICI's pharmaceuticals, agrochemicals, and specialty chemicals divisions. Britain's largest manufacturer and the 6th largest chemical company in the world, ICI has decided to focus on its core chemical businesses — paints, materials, industrial chemicals, and explosives — and on cutting costs after years of declining income.

ICI is the largest manufacturer of industrial explosives in the world and Europe's largest producer of titanium dioxide pigments, a key ingredient in the manufacture of ink, paper, and plastic.

The chemical giant also manufactures CFC replacements, catalysts, PVC tubing, and a number of leading-brand coatings and paints (Glidden, Dulux, ICI Autocolor) used for architecture, auto finishing, and domestic and industrial buildings.

The Zeneca spinoff transformed ICI's financial position into one of strength, giving it a robust balance sheet. The company continued cost cutting measures in 1993 and 1994. It disposed of several noncore assets, including the sale of its European polypropylene business to BASF; its Canadian fertilizers business, Nitrogen Products, to the US firm Terra Industries; and its US-based Polyols business to Specialty Products International.

WHEN

Imperial Chemical Industries was created from the 1926 combination of 4 British chemical companies. The companies — Nobel Industries; Brunner, Mond and Company; United Alkali; and British Dyestuffs — joined in reaction to the German amalgamation that created I. G. Farben.

The most famed ICI predecessor, Nobel Industries, had been created as the British arm of Alfred Nobel's explosives empire. Nobel mixed highly explosive, unstable nitroglycerin with porous clay to make dynamite. In 1886 Nobel created the London-based Nobel Dynamite Trust to embrace British and German interests. After Nobel's death in 1896, the empire began to unravel, and WWI severed the German and UK components of the Nobel firm. The British arm became Nobel Industries (1920).

ICI relied on the old Nobel alliance with the premier American chemical company, DuPont. In 1929 ICI and DuPont signed a patents-and-process agreement, sharing research information. ICI also muscled into consortia with I. G. Farben in 1931 and 1932.

ICI, as Britain's representative in the worldwide chemical industry, plunged into research. It recruited skilled chemists, engineers, and managers and formed alliances with universities. Between 1933 and 1935 its Dyestuffs Group laboratory created 87 new products and in 1935 its Alkali Group laboratory invented polyethylene.

After WWII the chummy club of cartels began to disband. The US government won antitrust sanctions against the DuPont-ICI alliance (1952) and ICI faced new competition with the sundered components of I. G. Farben (Bayer, BASF, Hoechst). ICI added operations in Germany, the UK, and the US (a Bayonne, NJ, plant) in the 1960s, but fortunes declined and in 1980 ICI posted losses and cut its dividend for the first time.

The company turned to John Harvey-Jones in 1982. Harvey-Jones cut layers of decision making, reorganized internationally along product lines, and added directors from outside the UK to the board. ICI also shifted production from bulk chemicals such as soda and chlorine to high-margin specialty chemicals (ICI calls them "effect chemicals") such as pharmaceuticals and pesticides.

Harvey-Jones bought 100 companies from 1982 until his retirement in 1987. ICI expanded in the US market by purchasing Beatrice's chemical operations (1985, $750 million), Glidden paints (1986, $580 million), and Stauffer Chemicals (1987, $1.7 billion), of which it sold all but the agricultural chemicals operations. In 1990 ICI paid $310 million for the remaining 50% of Tioxide (from "titanium oxide").

In 1992 ICI agreed to sell its nylon business to DuPont in exchange for DuPont's acrylics business and about $430 million. UK conglomerate Hanson, which had purchased 2.8% of ICI in 1991, sold its stake in 1992.

ICI spun off its specialty chemicals and agricultural operations as Zeneca in 1993. The company pulled out of polypropylene manufacturing in Europe in 1994 and also sold its Indian fertilizer business.

NYSE symbol: ICI (ADR)
Fiscal year ends: December 31

Deputy Chairman and CEO: Ronnie C. Hampel
Executive Director, Research and Technology,
Engineering, and Personnel: R. J. Margetts
Executive Director, Finance: A. G. Spall
Chairman, ICI Americas: John Danzeisen, age 46
VP Finance, ICI Americas: Bruce G. Peters
Director Human Resources, ICI Americas:
D. I. Hartnett
Auditors: KPMG Peat Marwick

WHERE

HQ: Imperial Chemical House, Millbank,
London SW1P 3JF, UK
Phone: +44-(0)71-834-4444
Fax: +44-(0)71-834-2042
US HQ: ICI Americas Inc., Concord Plaza, 3411
Silverside Rd., Wilmington, DE 19850-5391
US Phone: 302-887-3000
US Fax: 302-887-2972

	1993 Sales		1993 Operating Income	
	£ mil.	% of total	£ mil.	% of total
UK	3,493	36	39	12
Americas	2,409	25	127	38
Asia/Pacific	1,871	20	107	32
Other Europe	1,486	15	21	6
Other countries	374	4	40	12
Adjustments	999	—	1	—
Total	**10,632**	**100**	**338**	**100**

WHAT

	1993 Sales		1993 Operating Income	
	£ mil.	% of total	£ mil.	% of total
Industrial chemicals	3,691	35	106	33
Paints	1,691	15	103	31
Materials	1,494	13	18	6
Regional businesses	1,416	13	45	14
Explosives	643	6	52	16
Adjustments	1,697	—	11	—
Total	**10,632**	**100**	**335**	**100**

Selected Products

Industrial Chemicals	Materials
Petrochemicals	Acrylics
Polymers	Polyester film (Melinex)
Polyurethanes	Polyurethanes
Titanium dioxide	Fiberite composite
	materials
Paints	
Architectural coatings	**Explosives**
Automotive refinish (ICI	Industrial explosives
Autocolor)	Initiating systems
Decorative (Dulux,	Sodium azide gas (for air
Glidden)	bags)

KEY COMPETITORS

Akzo Nobel	Fletcher Challenge	PPG
Albemarle	Formosa Plastics	Praxair
AlliedSignal	W. R. Grace	Rhône-Poulenc
American Home	Hercules	Royal/Dutch
Products	Himont	Shell
BASF	Hoechst	Sherwin-
Bayer	Kyocera	Williams
Dai Nippon	Merck	Thomson SA
Dow Chemical	Monsanto	TOTAL
DuPont	Neste	Union Carbide
Elf Aquitaine	Occidental	USG

HOW MUCH

£ = $1.48 (Dec 31, 1993)	9-Year Growth	1984	1985	1986	1987	1988	1989	1990	1991	1992	1993
Sales (£ mil.)	0.8%	9,909	10,725	10,136	11,123	11,699	13,171	12,906	12,488	12,061	10,632
Net income (£ mil.)	(15.1%)	605	552	600	760	881	930	391	542	(570)	138
Income as % of sales	—	6.1%	5.1%	5.9%	6.8%	7.5%	7.1%	3.0%	4.3%	—	1.3%
Earnings per share (p)	(16.6%)	98	86	92	114	130	135	88	76	(80)	19
Stock price – high (p)	—	746	882	1,116	1,645	1,184	1,335	1,251	1,376	1,410	1,289
Stock price – low (p)	—	526	632	727	965	950	1,013	808	852	975	608
Stock price – close (p)	0.9%	736	756	1,086	108	1,013	1,134	866	1,210	1,049	800
P/E – high	—	8	10	12	14	9	10	14	18	—	42
P/E – low	—	5	7	8	8	7	8	9	11	—	32
Dividends per share (p)	(1.0%)	30.0	33.0	36.0	41.0	50.0	55.0	55.0	55.0	55.0	27.5
Book value per share (p)	(1.2%)	617	538	558	510	575	722	660	674	600	552
Employees	(5.9%)	115,600	118,600	121,800	127,800	130,400	133,800	132,100	123,600	114,000	67,000

1993 Year-end:
Debt ratio: 34.3%
Return on equity: 3.3%
Cash (mil.): £1,086
L-T debt (mil.): £1,717
No. of shares (mil.): 722
Dividends
  Yield: 3.4%
  Payout: 143.2%
Market value (mil.): $8,544
Sales: $15,728

Stock Price History
High/Low 1984–93

(chart y-axis: 1,800 / 1,600 / 1,400 / 1,200 / 1,000 / 800 / 600 / 400 / 200 / 0)

IMPERIAL OIL LIMITED

OVERVIEW

Imperial Oil's empire has been shrinking lately. The Toronto-based oil and gas company has sold off assets, reduced employment, and closed down service stations in an effort to control costs. Imperial's bottom line has responded to the austere treatment, rebounding after sinking in the early 1990s.

Imperial, which is 69.6%-owned by Exxon, is Canada's largest oil company, holding about 1/5 of the country's proved reserves. It is one of Canada's largest natural gas producers, its #1 refiner and marketer of petroleum products, and a major supplier of petrochemicals. Imperial sells more than 700 petroleum products, including gasoline, heating oil, and diesel fuel, under the Esso and other brand names.

Most of the company's production comes from fields in Alberta and the Northwest Territories. It also continues to conduct experimental operations at Cold Lake, Alberta, using steam to recover very heavy crude from oil sands deposits.

Imperial plans to continue cutting costs, with a goal of reducing expenses in its natural resources unit by 25%. It also plans to focus on higher-margin, Esso-branded products and to increase natural gas sales.

WHEN

London, Ontario, boomed from the discovery of oil in the 1860s and 1870s, but the market for Canadian kerosene became saturated in 1880, and 16 refiners banded together to form the Imperial Oil Company.

The company refined sulfuric Canadian oil, nicknamed "skunk oil" for its powerful smell. Imperial faced tough competition from America's Standard Oil, which marketed kerosene made from lighter, less odorous Pennsylvania crude. Guided by American expatriate Jacob Englehart, Imperial built a better refinery and hired a chemist to develop a process to clean sulfur from the crude.

By the mid-1890s Imperial had expanded from coast to Canadian coast. Cash-starved from its expansion, the company turned to old nemesis Standard Oil, which bought controlling interest in Imperial in 1898.

After the turn of the century, Imperial began producing gasoline to serve the new automobiles. In 1907 an Imperial manager in Vancouver, to prevent the commotion when horseless carriages spooked workhorses at the warehouse where fuel was sold, opened the first Canadian service station. Imperial marketed its gasoline under the Esso banner borrowed from Standard Oil.

In 1920 an Imperial crew discovered oil at Norman Wells in the remote Northwest Territories. In 1924 a subsidiary sparked a new boom with a gas well discovery in the Turner Valley area northeast of Edmonton. But soon Imperial's luck ran as dry as the holes it was drilling; it came away empty from the next 133 consecutive wells. That string ended in 1947 when it struck oil in Alberta at the Leduc No. 1. To get the oil to market, Imperial invested in the Interprovincial Pipe Line from Alberta to Superior, Wisconsin. The pipeline, later extended to the Toronto area, was the longest crude oil pipeline in the non-Communist world.

In the 1970s, amid the OPEC-spawned oil crisis, Imperial continued to search for oil in northern Canada. It found crude on land near the Beaufort Sea (1970) and dipped its toes into the icy Beaufort, building a gravel island as a drilling base (1972). In 1978 it formed its Esso Resources Canada Ltd. subsidiary to oversee natural resources production.

In 1989 Texaco, still reeling from the Pennzoil court battle and its brief flight into bankruptcy court, sold Texaco Canada to Imperial for C$5 billion. To diminish debt and comply with regulators, Imperial agreed to sell some of Texaco Canada's refining and marketing assets in Atlantic Canada (C$115 million), its interests in Interhome Energy, Inc. (C$500 million), and Western Canada oil and gas properties (C$300 million).

The company reorganized in 1992, centralizing several company units. Also in 1992 CEO Arden R. Haynes retired and was succeeded by COO Robert B. Peterson.

In 1993 the company announced it would close its 44,000-barrel-a-day refinery at Port Moody, British Columbia, in early 1995.

In 1994 Imperial sold most of its fertilizer business, including a production plant in Alberta, to Canadian mining, chemicals, and materials company Sherritt for $282 million. Also in 1994 Imperial posted $255 million in net profits through sales of $6.4 billion.

AMEX symbol: IMO
Fiscal year ends: December 31

WHO

Chairman and CEO: Robert B. Peterson, age 56,
C$837,500 pay
President: Ronald A. Brenneman, age 47,
C$507,083 pay
SVP, Resources Division: Doug D. Baldwin,
C$469,333 pay
SVP, Products and Chemicals Division: Brian J.
Fischer, C$370,000 pay
VP and Treasurer (Principal Financial Officer):
John F. Kyle
Manager of Human Resources Services:
Hugh O'Neill
Auditors: Price Waterhouse

WHERE

HQ: 111 St. Clair Ave. West, Toronto, Ontario
M5W 1K3, Canada
Phone: 416-968-4111
Fax: 416-968-4272 (Investor Relations)

Exploration and Development: Western
provinces of Canada, Northwest Territories, and
the Yukon
Refining and Marketing: 5 Canadian refineries,
3,400 retail outlets throughout Canada
Chemicals: Petrochemical and plastics plants in
Ontario, Nova Scotia, and British Columbia

	1993 Petroleum Products Sales
	% of total
Canada	95
Other countries	5
Total	**100**

HOW MUCH

WHAT

	1993 Sales		1993 Pretax Income	
	$ mil.	% of total	$ mil.	% of total
Petroleum prods.	5,909	80	395	61
Chemicals	813	11	46	7
Natural resources	667	9	208	32
Other	81	—	(27)	—
Total	**7,470**	**100**	**521**	**100**

Petroleum Products
Crude oil purchasing
Marketing
  Gasoline
  Heating, diesel, and jet fuels
  Heavy fuel oils
  Liquid petroleum gas
  Lube oils
Refining
Transportation

Chemicals

Benzene	Resins
Ethylene	Solvents
Plasticizer intermediates	

Natural Resources
Exploration and development
Petroleum and natural gas production

KEY COMPETITORS

Amoco	Horsham	Petrobrás
Ashland, Inc.	Corporation	Petro-Canada
Atlantic Richfield	Hutchison	Petrofina
British Petroleum	Whampoa	Phillips Petroleum
Broken Hill	Koch	Repsol
Canadian Pacific	Mobil	Royal Dutch/Shell
Chevron	Norcen Energy	Sun Company
Coastal	Occidental	Texaco
DuPont	PDVSA	TOTAL
Elf Aquitaine	PEMEX	Unocal
ENI	Pennzoil	USX–Marathon

	9-Year Growth	1984	1985	1986	1987	1988	1989	1990	1991	1992	1993
Sales ($ mil.)	1.9%	6,287	6,006	4,849	5,777	6,763	11,626	12,984	8,846	7,923	7,470
Net income ($ mil.)	(7.0%)	404	489	319	551	420	456	493	140	153	211
Income as % of sales	—	6.4%	8.1%	6.6%	9.5%	6.2%	3.9%	3.8%	1.6%	1.9%	2.8%
Earnings per share ($)	(8.9%)	2.52	3.02	1.95	3.36	2.56	2.54	2.22	0.73	0.79	1.09
Stock price – high ($)	—	34.38	40.25	37.38	61.63	51.25	55.38	59.63	52.75	39.88	39.00
Stock price – low ($)	—	25.38	30.25	25.13	36.50	36.63	40.63	45.88	33.63	31.00	31.25
Stock price – close ($)	0.6%	32.00	36.50	37.13	43.50	41.88	55.13	50.63	34.75	31.75	33.88
P/E – high	—	14	13	19	18	20	22	27	72	51	36
P/E – low	—	10	10	13	11	14	16	21	46	39	29
Dividends per share ($)	(0.4%)	1.45	1.20	1.65	1.60	1.80	1.80	1.53	1.56	1.56	1.51	1.40
Book value per share ($)	1.9%	21.59	22.12	22.52	26.17	29.56	37.86	38.86	30.31	26.93	25.59
Employees	(4.5%)	14,331	14,674	12,516	11,627	12,161	15,248	14,702	11,936	10,152	9,470

1993 Year-end:
Debt ratio: 48.7%
Return on equity: 4.1%
Cash (mil.): $457
Current ratio: 1.82
Long-term debt (mil.): $1,534
No. of shares (mil.): 194
Dividends
  Yield: 4.1%
  Payout: 128.4%
Market value (mil.): $6,567

Stock Price History
High/Low 1984–93

INCO LIMITED

OVERVIEW

The #1 nickel producer in the Western world, with a 25% share of the world market, Inco is working hard to make sure a nickel mined is a nickel (and not a ruble) earned. The Toronto-based company has seen its sales shrink as Russia and other former Eastern bloc countries have pushed the price of nickel down by dumping the mineral on the market in a quest for hard currency.

Nickel is Inco's most important commodity, but the company's primary metals operations also produce copper, platinum, silver, cobalt, sulfuric acid, and liquid sulfur dioxide. Inco's primary mining and processing operations are in Canada and Indonesia.

Other Inco operations include Inco Alloys International (IAI), which produces nickel alloys for the aerospace, chemical, energy, and other industries, and Inco Engineered Products (IEP), which manufactures precision metal components, mainly for use in the aerospace industry. Inco is also involved in the manufacture of mining equipment, metals reclamation, construction materials, and venture capital funding.

Inco is working to lower costs and improve productivity by reducing employment and modernizing its facilities. It also continues to expand internationally, opening a mining equipment plant in Chile.

WHEN

Hundreds of millions of years ago, a meteorite slammed into the earth, punching a hole that allowed molten, mineral-rich material to bubble up to the crust. The mineral treasures just below Canada's landscape were hidden until 1883, when a Canadian Pacific Railway blacksmith noticed copper and nickel deposits in an excavation in the Sudbury Basin.

Two companies — the Orford Nickel and Copper Company and the Canadian Copper Company — tried to exploit the ore but were confounded by the lack of a process to separate nickel, all but worthless at the time, and copper. In 1890 Orford, led by Robert Mearns Thompson, patented a process for separation, just as the US Navy was beginning to use a nickel-steel alloy for armaments.

Enter financier J. P. Morgan, father of the newly formed US Steel. With Morgan's assistance Orford and Canadian Copper combined with 5 smaller companies (Anglo-American Iron; American Nickel Works; Nickel Corporation, Limited; Vermillion Mining of Ontario; and Société Minière Caledonienne) in 1902 to form New Jersey–based International Nickel Company. The company in 1916 formed a Canadian subsidiary, International Nickel Company of Canada.

After WWI, sales plummeted 60% and International Nickel, under President Robert Crooks Stanley, cut costs. In a 1928 restructuring the Canadian subsidiary became the parent company, and in 1929 International Nickel bought Mond Nickel, a British refiner of nickel and copper ores. With the Mond deal International Nickel controlled the world's nickel output. In the 1950s it accounted for 85% of non-Communist production.

Oil crises and inflation decreased demand for metals and battered International Nickel in the 1970s and early 1980s. In 1974 International Nickel launched a successful takeover bid for ESB Ray-O-Vac, the world's largest maker of batteries, and in 1976 International Nickel shortened its name to Inco Limited. The battery operations were sold in the early 1980s.

Inco continued to suffer from lack of demand for its metals until 1986. CEO Donald Phillips cut employment and invested heavily in techniques to boost productivity at Inco's mines and refineries. When demand — especially for stainless steel — began its upswing in the late 1980s and prices rose, Inco results went from dismal to delightful. Sales more than doubled from 1987 to 1989.

Inco merged its gold interests with Consolidated TVX Mining in 1991. That same year Inco sold a 30% interest in its subsidiary Exploraciones y Explotaciones Mineras Izabal in Guatemala to the Guatemalan government.

In 1993 Inco sold its 61.8% interest in TVX Gold to a group of Canadian underwriters for about $300 million. That same year it announced it would suspend nickel production for 8 weeks as part of a plan to reduce the worldwide nickel supply.

In 1994 the company discovered a high-grade nickel deposit in Manitoba, which analysts said could be Inco's richest Canadian deposit. Inco finished 1994 with profits of $22 million on sales of $2.5 billion.

NYSE symbol: N
Fiscal year ends: December 31

WHO

Chairman and CEO: Michael D. Sopko, age 55,
  $348,800 pay
VC: Walter Curlook, age 64, $272,000 pay
VC and CFO: Ian McDougall, age 63,
  $290,000 pay
President: Scott M. Hand, age 51, $328,500 pay
EVP, General Counsel, and Secretary:
  Stuart F. Feiner, age 45, $603,300 pay
VP Human Resources: Lorne M. Ames, age 56
President, Inco Ltd. (US): David J. Anderson
Director HR, Inco Ltd. (US): Ted Vonhoff
Auditors: Price Waterhouse

WHERE

HQ: Royal Trust Tower, Toronto-Dominion
  Centre, Toronto, Ontario M5K 1N4, Canada
Phone: 416-361-7511
Fax: 416-361-7781
US HQ: Inco Ltd., One New York Plaza,
  New York, NY 10004
US Phone: 212-612-5500
US Fax: 212-612-5770

Inco has operations in 21 countries.

	1993 Sales		1993 Operating Income	
	$ mil.	% of total	$ mil.	% of total
US	735	34	(10)	—
Europe	595	28	20	—
Canada	230	11	(65)	—
Other countries	570	27	35	—
Adjustments	206	—	13	—
Total	**2,336**	**100**	**(7)**	**—**

WHAT

	1993 Sales	
	$ mil.	% of total
Primary nickel	1,185	51
Alloys & engineered products	511	22
Refined copper	216	9
Precious metals	97	4
Cobalt	39	2
Other	288	12
Total	**2,336**	**100**

Primary Metals
Cobalt
Copper
Liquid sulfur dioxide
Palladium
Platinum
Primary nickel
Rhodium
Silver
Sulfuric acid

Alloys and Engineered Products
Blades
Castings
Components
Discs
Nickel alloys
Rings
Vanes

Other Businesses
Continuous Mining Systems Ltd. (mining equipment)
Inco Venture Capital Management (venture capital)
International Metals Reclamation Co., Inc. (metals
  reclamation)
LaQue Center for Corrosion Technology, Inc. (corrosion
  testing and consulting)
Western Aggregates, Inc. (construction materials)

KEY COMPETITORS

Alcan	Ingersoll-Rand	RTZ
Anglo American	Inland Steel	Société
ASARCO	Lockheed Martin	Métallurgique le
Broken Hill	New Caledonia	Nickel
Cyprus Amax	and Western	USX–U.S. Steel
Falconbridge	Mining	Vulcan
FMC	Nippon Steel	
Hanson	Phelps Dodge	

HOW MUCH

	9-Year Growth	1984	1985	1986	1987	1988	1989	1990	1991	1992	1993
Sales ($ mil.)	5.3%	1,468	1,491	1,452	1,790	3,263	3,948	3,108	2,999	2,559	2,336
Net income ($ mil.)	—	(77)	52	0	125	691	753	441	83	(18)	28
Income as % of sales	—	—	3.5%	0.0%	7.0%	21.2%	19.1%	14.2%	2.8%	—	1.2%
Earnings per share ($)	—	(1.02)	0.28	(0.16)	1.09	6.50	7.11	4.18	0.74	(0.21)	0.22
Stock price – high ($)	—	15.25	15.38	16.88	24.00	35.13	37.63	31.88	38.00	34.38	27.75
Stock price – low ($)	—	8.63	10.38	10.50	11.75	17.38	25.63	22.13	23.88	19.13	17.38
Stock price – close ($)	9.0%	12.38	13.25	11.75	22.00	25.88	26.88	25.38	30.50	22.38	26.88
P/E – high	—	—	55	—	22	5	5	8	51	—	126
P/E – low	—	—	37	—	11	3	4	5	32	—	79
Dividends per share ($)	—	0.00	0.20	0.20	0.20	0.20	0.70	1.00	1.00	0.85	0.40
Book value per share ($)	5.1%	9.32	9.68	9.75	10.33	6.51	12.33	15.78	15.70	14.71	14.57
Employees	3.5%	22,239	20,828	20,171	18,706	18,658	19,337	19,387	18,369	17,724	16,087

1993 Year-end:
Debt ratio: 58.7%
Return on equity: 1.8%
Cash (mil.): $10
Current ratio: 2.41
Long-term debt (mil.): $946
No. of shares (mil.): 110
Dividends
  Yield: 1.5%
  Payout: 181.8%
Market value (mil.): $2,964

**Stock Price History
High/Low 1984–93**

HOOVER'S HANDBOOK OF WORLD BUSINESS 1995–1996   273

INDUSTRIAL BANK OF JAPAN, LIMITED

OVERVIEW

Industrial Bank of Japan (IBJ) is the largest of Japan's long-term credit banks (primarily for big industry) and ranks #1 worldwide in terms of market capitalization. IBJ boasts that it does business with 90% of Japan's top 200 corporations. It is also the 8th largest commercial bank in the world in terms of assets and a leading manager of Eurobond underwriting.

Its power in Japan is obscured by its relatively few locations. IBJ's profits dipped in the early 1990s because its traditional clients, Japanese heavy-industry companies, have stumbled. However, IBJ is now trying to take advantage of the deregulation of Japan's financial system by entering fields it was previously banned from, such as securities underwriting and trust businesses. The company's securities subsidiary, IBJ Securities Co., ranks 6th in Japan behind 5 traditional brokers in terms of corporate bond issuance. The long-term health of the bank will be influenced by these expansions.

While IBJ's current concentrations overseas is in North America and Europe, IBJ president Yoh Kurosawa expects his bank to have an increasing presence in other Asian countries, including China and Vietnam. However, he suggests that investors in Asia must take care not to dominate local economies; instead they should encourage the localization of their operations in a given area.

WHEN

After Japan met the West in the 19th century, the Meiji Restoration replaced the old ways of the shogunate with a national imperative to modernize (1868). Prince Masayoshi Matsukata, the Meiji finance minister, shaped the country's modern banking system. Out of Matsukata's plan came specialized, government-controlled banks designed to provide long-term financing for commerce.

Industrial Bank of Japan began in 1902. It primarily lent money to the fledgling industries arising from the Meiji reforms. Almost immediately IBJ had to finance Japan's first war against a European power, Russia.

IBJ grew along with Japanese industry. Before WWII it helped finance Japanese incursions into China. During the war the Japanese government leaned on the bank's financing of the war machine. In 1944, faced with defeat, the government assigned 2,000 key companies to the top 4 banks of Japan. Then the government ordered the banks to grant the companies unlimited credit.

After Japan was beaten, US occupiers attempted to "demilitarize" IBJ. One law forced IBJ to write down ¥7.5 billion in war-related loans. IBJ was nearly disbanded, but the Japanese government convinced the Americans to allow the bank to continue. However, its direct links with the government were severed. IBJ, along with its sister long-term banks, prospered during Japan's resurgence in the 1950s and 1960s. In the 1960s IBJ helped create Nippon Steel through a merger.

In 1971 the bank received permission to establish overseas branches. In the 1980s IBJ fell prey to reduced loan demand, both because of the 1970s oil shock and because wealthy Japanese clients could finance growth through cash or by issuing bonds.

IBJ began diversifying its activities in the mid-1980s with successful Eurobond issues, and in 1985 it bought J. Henry Schroder Bank & Trust, a New York–based merchant bank with $5.2 billion in assets. It bought Aubrey G. Lanston & Co., a primary dealer (transacting business directly with the Federal Reserve Bank) in US Treasury securities (1986) and formed an American subsidiary, the Bridgeford Group (1990), to focus on mergers and acquisitions.

In the 1980s deregulation of the banking industry squeezed margins. As a result, lending standards slipped as banks tried to increase earnings, resulting in lower-quality loans. That trend reversed as Japan deregulated its markets. In 1991 new president Yoh Kurosawa declared that the bank would immerse itself in the securities and trust businesses. IBJ purchased stakes in 2 medium-sized securities firms, New Japan Securities and Wako Securities.

In 1992 IBJ set up Krung Thai IBJ Leasing with the Krung Thai Bank Group and International Finance Corporation to meet a demand for leasing services in Thailand. In 1993 IBJ created its own domestic securities subsidiary.

In early 1994, as the Japanese economy appeared to be improving, IBJ moved forward to upgrade its computer systems and marketing efforts both domestically and worldwide.

Principal exchange: Tokyo
Fiscal year ends: March 31

President: Yoh Kurosawa
Deputy President: Tatsuo Yoshida
Deputy President: Masao Nishimura
General Manager (International Finance):
Shoji Noguchi
General Manager (Corporate Banking): Masaaki
Kushida
Managing Director (America Committee):
Isamu Koike
Director and General Manager (International):
Kimizo Shimamura
CEO and President, IBJ Trust (US): Susumu
Yasuma
SVP and Personnel Director, IBJ Trust (US):
Paul Frank
Auditors: Chuo Audit Corporation

HQ: 3-3, Marunouchi 1-chome, Chiyoda-ku,
Tokyo 100, Japan
Phone: +81-3-3214-1111
Fax: +81-3-3213-6066
US HQ: The Industrial Bank of Japan Trust
Company, 245 Park Ave., New York, NY 10167
US Phone: 212-557-3500
US Fax: 212-692-9075

Industrial Bank of Japan operates 30 domestic
branches and 1 securities subsidiary, 17 overseas
branches and agencies, and 13 overseas representative offices. It also owns 17 major overseas
subsidiaries.

	1994 Assets	
	¥ bil.	% of total
Cash & equivalents	4,550	11
Trading account	978	2
Loans & bills discounted	24,024	57
Customers' liabilities for		
acceptances & guarantees	2,578	6
Call loans	929	2
Investment securities	6,382	15
Other	3,047	7
Total	**42,488**	**100**

Major Overseas Subsidiaries
Banque IBJ (France) SA
The Bridgeford Group, Inc. (mergers and acquisitions,
US)
IBJ Asia Ltd. (Hong Kong)
IBJ Australia Bank Ltd.
IBJ International plc (UK)
IBJ Merchant Bank (Singapore) Ltd.
IBJ Schroder Bank & Trust Co. (99.2%, US)
"IBJ-CA Consult" Handels- und
Investitionsberatungsgesellschaft mbH (50%, Austria)
The Industrial Bank of Japan (Canada)
The Industrial Bank of Japan (Luxembourg) SA
The Industrial Bank of Japan (Switzerland) Ltd.
The Industrial Bank of Japan Trust Co. (58.4%, US)
Industriebank von Japan (Deutschland)
Aktiengesellschaft (83.3%)
P.T. Bumi Daya — IBJ Leasing (52%, Indonesia)
P.T. IBJ Indonesia Bank (85%)

Asahi	Citicorp	Deutsche Bank
Bank of Tokyo	Crédit Lyonnais	Fuji
Barclays	CS Holding	HSBC
Chase Manhattan	Dai-Ichi Kangyo	Nomura Securities
Chemical Banking	Daiwa	Sumitomo

$=¥112 (Dec. 31, 1993)	Annual Growth	1985	1986	1987	1988	1989	1990	1991	1992	1993	1994
Assets (¥ bil.)	7.0%	23,121	26,054	29,920	33,869	38,789	45,004	45,062	44,305	42,220	42,488
Net income (¥ bil.)	(7.7%)	45	51	56	65	84	85	66	59	41	22
Income as % of assets	—	0.2%	0.2%	0.2%	0.2%	0.2%	0.2%	0.1%	0.1%	0.1%	0.1%
Earnings per share (¥)[1]	(8.2%)	20	21	24	27	35	41	34	29	17	9
Stock price – high (¥)[2]	—	850	1,640	2,650	5,500	4,500	6,540	6,740	3,930	3,280	3,560
Stock price – low (¥)[2]	—	400	844	1,000	2,480	2,520	4,010	2,090	2,980	1,250	2,220
Stock price – close (¥)[2]	17.4%	—	1,080	2,240	2,700	4,350	6,380	3,300	3,220	2,470	3,830
P/E – high[1]	—	40	68	98	157	110	187	198	136	189	383
P/E – low[1]	—	19	35	37	71	61	115	61	103	72	239
Dividends per share (¥)	2.9%	6.56	6.56	7.02	7.19	8.00	8.50	8.50	9.00	8.50	8.50
Book value per share (¥)	13.1%	196	210	226	246	361	485	570	586	594	595
Employees	1.0%	—	—	—	5,164	—	5,500	5,293	5,151	—	5,466

1994 Year-end:
Debt ratio: 96.4%
Return on equity: 1.6%
Equity as % of assets: 3.3%
No. of shares (mil.): 2,351
Dividends
Yield: 0.2%
Payout: 91.4%
Market value (mil.): $80,412
Assets (mil.): $379,004
Sales (mil.): $27,352

Stock Price History[2]
High/Low 1985–94

[1] Unconsolidated earnings per share 1985–1992 [2] Stock prices are for the prior calendar year.

IRI GROUP

OVERVIEW

Originally set up by Benito Mussolini to rescue the Italian banking industry, Istituto per la Ricostruzione Industriale (IRI), Italy's largest industrial group, has been participating in the privatization trend that has been sweeping through many of Europe's state-owned conglomerates. Through its *finanziarie* (2nd-tier holding companies), IRI controls several hundred companies engaged in everything from TV broadcasting to shipbuilding. IRI's holdings include STET (telecommunications) and ALITALIA (aviation).

In 1991 a new political mood in the Italian electorate, calling for an end to political corruption, brought in a reformist government. The new government pulled the plug on the decades-old policy of financially propping up state-run companies, such as the loss-making but politically influential IRI. In order to raise capital (both for IRI and for the Italian treasury), the government and IRI are privatizing many of the group's companies. In 1993 the group privatized its Credito Italiano and Banca Commerciale Italiana financial institutions and its SME food business, and restructured its ILVA steel concern in preparation for sale. By 1996 IRI plans to dispose of about $10 billion of businesses.

WHEN

The Depression of the 1930s drove many major Italian enterprises to insolvency, in turn threatening their creditor banks. The Italian government established IRI as a temporary, Resolution Trust–style holding company in 1933 to rescue the banks and sell off their unwanted assets. IRI soon controlled many troubled businesses, including Alfa Romeo, 3 regional telephone companies (consolidated as STET), and 3 major Italian banks: Banca Commerciale Italiana, Credito Italiano, and Banco di Roma.

IRI established 2 more *finanziarie*, FINMARE (shipping) and FINSIDER (steel), and was given permanent status by the Mussolini regime in 1937. The Fascist state directed IRI to focus on businesses most useful to the military. In 1939 the company built an aircraft engine plant near Naples.

IRI sustained heavy damage during WWII and experienced difficulty recovering from the war as pressure from labor and political groups limited the organization's ability to reduce the number of employees. IRI began to emerge from its malaise with the construction of its Cornigliano steel mill, which had been started before the war but dismantled by the Nazis. Major expansion in steel production followed. In 1952 the government turned over control of RAI, the national broadcasting company, to IRI.

In 1955 the government had trouble financing road construction and turned to IRI to raise money for and to build and operate *autostrade* (highways). Other government-inspired transactions of the 1950s included the purchases of a large bankrupt textile company, the rest of the regional telephone companies, and control of ALITALIA. In 1957 IRI was instructed to help develop the economy of southern Italy. In the 1960s, when the government nationalized the electric utility operations of IRI unit SME, the *finanziaria* became a food processor instead.

In the early 1970s IRI was, in some quarters, considered to be a model state enterprise, but later in the decade heavy debt, surging interest rates, economic recession, Japanese competition in steel, and a load of failing companies forced on IRI by the government led to mounting losses. In 1982 economics professor Romano Prodi became president and began slashing payroll and selling businesses. He sold Alfa Romeo to Fiat in 1986 and sold shares of IRI companies to the public. In 1986 IRI returned to profitability.

IRI's SGS Microelettronica chipmaking unit merged with a Thomson CSF subsidiary in 1987. The next year the troubled FINSIDER steel unit began restructuring in an effort to trim losses while maintaining an Italian steel industry.

In 1992 IRI opened an office in Moscow and entered into a joint venture to build the southern leg of an optical-fiber cable that will connect Russia with other parts of Europe. Also in 1992 IRI sold its 83.3% stake in software subsidiary FINSIEL to STET.

Reflecting Italy's turbulent politics, IRI's chairman Franco Nobili was arrested on corruption charges in 1993. His replacement, Romano Prodi, resigned in 1994 and was replaced by Michele Tedeschi.

IRI entered into negotiations with McDonnell Douglas in 1994 about acquiring a stake in the US airplane maker.

WHO

Chairman: Michele Tedeschi
General Manager: Enrico Micheli
Deputy General Manager: Franco Simeoni
Secretary: Pierpaolo Dominedo
Head, Secretariat, General Affairs and Public Relations Unit: Fabrizio Antonini
Head, Finance Division: Pietro Ciucci
Head, Internal Audit Division: Marcello Bigi
Head, Labor Policies and Development Division: Vincenzo Dettori
Head, Administration Division: Ezio Lepidi
Head, Internationalization and Innovation Division: Alessandro Ovi
Head, Planning and Control Division: Maurizio Prato
Head, Studies and Research Unit: Duccio Valori
Head, Press Office: Silvio Sircana
Director, US Representative Office: Giuseppe Zampaglione

WHERE

HQ: Istituto per la Ricostruzione Industriale S.p.A., Via V. Veneto 89, I-00187 Rome, Italy
Phone: +39-6-47271
Fax: +39-6-47272308
US HQ: 1101 15th St. NW, Ste. 612, Washington, DC 20005
US Phone: 202-223-5804
US Fax: 202-331-0560

Although the IRI Group holds interests in companies worldwide, most of its operations are in Italy.

WHAT

Major Products and Services
Aerospace
Airport management
Civil aviation
Communications
Defense systems
Energy
Financial services
Industrial automation
Microelectronics
Radio broadcasting
Shipbuilding
Telecommunications
Television broadcasting
Transport
Venture capital

Major Group Holdings
ALITALIA (86.4%, aviation)
Compagnia Finanziamenti e Rifinanziamenti SpA (COFIRI)(financial services)
FINCANTIERI (99.9%, shipbuilding)
FINMARE (99.9%, shipping)
FINMECCANICA (94.4%, high technology and mechanical engineering)
FINTECNA (plant engineering)
RAI (99.6%, broadcasting)
SPI (97.5%, new enterprises)
STET (52.2%, telecommunications)

KEY COMPETITORS

ABB
Alcatel Alsthom
Air France
American Power Conversion
AMR
Bechtel
British Aerospace
British Airways
Cooper Industries
Crédit Lyonnais
Daewoo
Emerson
Evergreen
Fluor
General Electric
Ingersoll-Rand
Johnson Controls
KLM
Lagardère
Lockheed Martin
Lufthansa
Mitsubishi
Mitsui
Morrison Knudsen
News Corp.
P&O
Peter Kiewit Sons'
Raytheon
Rolls-Royce
SAS
Siemens
Toshiba
Westinghouse

HOW MUCH

$=Lit1,713 (Dec. 31, 1993)	9-Year Growth	1984	1985	1986	1987	1988	1989	1990	1991	1992	1993
Sales (Lit bil.)[1]	7.5%	46,585	50,536	52,583	53,006	59,017	66,747	73,547	79,901	82,988	79,786
Net income (Lit bil.)	—	(2,036)	(850)	367	247	1,263	2,021	1,108	(312)	(4,057)	(10,191)
Income as % of sales	—	—	—	0.7%	0.5%	2.1%	3.0%	3.0%	—	—	—
Employees											
Industrial	(3.0%)	442,609	420,096	480,310	360,561	358,235	363,075	366,703	368,267	345,485	327,266
Banking	(22.2%)	63,716	63,235	62,292	61,128	59,646	52,737	52,862	39,799	40,095	6,690
Total	(4.5%)	506,325	483,331	542,602	421,689	417,881	415,912	419,565	408,066	385,580	333,958

1993 Year-end:
Debt ratio: 74.7%
Return on equity: —
Cash (bil.): —
Long-term debt (bil.): —
Sales (mil.): $46,577

Net Income (Lit bil.) 1984–93

[1] Value of production

ISUZU MOTORS LIMITED

OVERVIEW

"Keep on truckin' " is the motto these days at Isuzu. One of the world's leading truck makers and #2 in Japan (after Toyota's Hino Motors), the Tokyo-based company has discontinued its passenger car operations to focus on commercial and recreational vehicles.

Isuzu's products include pickup trucks, light- to heavy-duty trucks and tractor units, and sport-utility vehicles (sold under the Trooper name in the US). The company is also one of the world's most-respected diesel engine makers. While the company has stopped manufacturing passenger cars, it does market the Honda Gemini in Japan.

General Motors owns 37.5% of Isuzu, and the 2 companies continue to strengthen their ties. GM builds light-duty trucks for Isuzu at its Janesville, Wisconsin, plant, and in 1994 it agreed to begin production of Isuzu pickups for the 1996 model year at its Shreveport, Louisiana, plant.

Isuzu continues to work to cut costs. In 1994 the company had sales of $11.5 billion and a net income of approximately $73 million, its first profit since 1989.

WHEN

After collaborating on car and truck production for 21 years, Tokyo Ishikawajima Shipbuilding and Engineering and Tokyo Gas and Electric Industrial formed Tokyo Motors, Inc., in 1937. The partners, Japanese pioneers in automotive manufacturing, had begun by producing the A truck (1918) and the A9 car (1922) under licenses from Wolseley (UK). A lengthy study of diesel technology resulted in the 1937 introduction of the company's first air-cooled diesel motor.

Tokyo Motors produced its first truck under the Isuzu nameplate in 1938 and by 1943 was selling trucks powered by its own diesel engines, mostly to the Japanese military. It spun off Hino Heavy Industries, predecessor of Hino Motors, in 1942.

The company renamed itself Isuzu (Japanese for "50 bells") in 1949. With generous public and private sector financing and truck orders from the US Army during the Korean War, Isuzu survived and established a reputation as a top diesel engine and truck producer. A pact with the Rootes Group (UK) enabled Isuzu to enter automaking. Beginning in 1953 Isuzu built Rootes's Hillman Minx in Japan. The company attempted to marry diesels with autos in 1961 when it introduced a diesel-powered car. A few years later the noisy auto was discontinued.

Despite its strong reputation as a truck builder, Isuzu suffered financially, and by the late 1960s its bankers were shopping the company around to more stable competitors. General Motors, after witnessing rapid Japanese progress in US and Asian auto markets, bought 34.2% of Isuzu in 1971. In the 1970s Isuzu launched the popular Gemini car and gained rapid entry into the US through GM,

exporting such vehicles as the Chevy Luv truck and the Buick Opel.

In 1981, as exports to GM waned, Isuzu set up its own dealer network in the US. In the same year GM CEO Roger Smith told a stunned Isuzu chairman T. Okamoto that, as a foreign partner in auto production, Isuzu lacked the global scale GM sought and asked Okamoto for help in buying a piece of Honda. After Honda declined and GM settled for 5% of Suzuki, Isuzu extended its GM ties, building the Geo Storm and establishing joint production facilities in the UK and Australia.

Despite the widely noticed advertising campaign featuring a lying Joe Isuzu, the company suffered in the 1980s as it failed to retain a significant share of the US passenger car market. Post-1985 yen appreciation hurt exports. Subaru-Isuzu Automotive, a joint venture with Fuji Heavy Industries, started production in Lafayette, Indiana, in 1989.

In 1990 Isuzu announced a linkup with P.T. Gaya Motor to make pickup trucks in Indonesia. After Isuzu lost nearly $500 million in 1991 and continued to lose money in 1992, it called on GM for help. GM responded by sending Donald Sullivan, a strategic business planning expert, to become Isuzu's #2 operations executive.

In 1993 Isuzu signed a joint venture with Jiangxi Automobile Factory and ITOCHU to build light-duty trucks in China.

In 1994 Nissan, its subsidiary Nissan Diesel, and Isuzu agreed to a cross-supply agreement of commercial vehicles, including Nissan's Caravan and Isuzu's 2- and 3-ton Elf trucks. Isuzu's sales were up just 2.3% in 1994, but it turned a profit for the first time in 5 years.

OTC symbol: ISUZY (ADR)
Fiscal year ends: October 31

Chairman: Junji Takahashi
President: Kazuhira Seki
EVP Corporate Planning, Product Planning, Engineering, Production and Engineering Operations: Donald T. Sullivan
EVP Accounting and Finance, Overseas Sales, and International Business Development: Hiromichi Matsuka
President, American Isuzu Motors: Yoshito Mochizuki
SVP and CFO, American Isuzu Motors: Jack Hosoi
Human Resources Manager, American Isuzu Motors: Karen Chan
Auditors: Century Audit Corporation

HQ: Isuzu Jidosha Kabushiki Kaisha, 26-1, Minami-oi 6-chome, Shinagawa-ku, Tokyo 140, Japan
Phone: +81-3-5471-1111
Fax: +81-3-5471-1091
US HQ: American Isuzu Motors Inc., 13181 Crossroads Pkwy. North, 4th Fl., City of Industry, CA 91746
US Phone: 310-699-0500
US Fax: 310-692-7135

	1993 Sales	
	¥ bil.	% of total
Japan	544	46
Other countries	630	54
Adjustments	388	—
Total	**1,562**	**100**

	1993 Sales	
	¥ bil.	% of total
Light-duty vehicles	466	40
Heavy- & medium-duty vehicles	224	19
Passenger cars	40	3
Engines, components & other	444	38
Adjustments	388	—
Total	**1,562**	**100**

Selected Vehicles
4 x 2 and 4 x 4 pickup trucks
Buses
Tractor units
Trooper (sport-utility vehicle)
Trucks
WFR (minivan)

Principal Subsidiaries and Affiliates
American Isuzu Motors Inc.
Automotive Foundry Co., Ltd.
Automotive Manufacturers (Malaysia) Sdn. Bhd.
General Motors Egypt S.A.E.
I.K. Coach Co., Ltd. (buses)
IBC Vehicles Ltd. (UK)

IFCO Inc. (financing and leasing)
Isuzu–General Motors Australia Ltd. (commercial vehicles)
Isuzu Motors America, Inc.
Isuzu Real Estate Co., Ltd.
Jiangling-Isuzu Motors Co., Ltd. (light-duty trucks, China)
P.T. Mesin Isuzu Indonesia (engines and steering systems)
Shatai Kogyo Co., Ltd. (auto bodies)
Subaru-Isuzu Automotive Inc. (US)
TDF Corporation (drop forging and stamping dies)
Zexel Corp. (fuel injectors and air conditoners)

BMW
Caterpillar
Chrysler
Cummins Engine
Daewoo
Daimler-Benz
Fiat
Ford
Hino Motors

Honda
Hyundai
Kubota
Mazda
Mitsubishi
Navistar
Nissan
PACCAR
Penske

Peugeot
Renault
Saab-Scania
Suzuki
Toyota
Volkswagen
Volvo
Zil

$=¥112 (Dec. 31, 1993)	9-Year Growth	1984	1985	1986	1987	1988	1989	1990	1991	1992	1993
Sales (¥ bil.)	6.7%	872	1,139	1,120	1,086	1,212	1,324	1,520	1,523	1,580	1,562
Net income (¥ bil.)[1]	—	(17)	17	12	7	7	17	(8)	(62)	(29)	(4)
Income as % of sales	—	—	1.4%	1.1%	0.6%	0.5%	1.3%	—	—	—	—
Earnings per share (¥)[1]	—	(20)	18	(13)	7	7	16	(8)	(60)	(28)	(4)
Stock price – high (¥)	—	345	445	376	466	982	1,036	1,160	670	448	559
Stock price – low (¥)	—	240	291	282	280	345	782	445	341	226	245
Stock price – close (¥)	0.8%	329	350	315	380	881	975	506	369	332	352
P/E – high	—	—	24	—	65	150	63	—	—	—	—
P/E – low	—	—	16	—	39	53	48	—	—	—	—
Dividends per share (¥)	—	0.00	0.00	0.00	0.00	4.55	4.55	5.00	0.00	0.00	0.00
Book value per share (¥)	(2.3%)	76	115	98	128	140	153	160	96	69	62
Employees	(1.9%)	15,524	15,997	16,064	13,757	13,616	13,382	13,427	13,600	13,299	13,084

1993 Year-end:
Debt ratio: 92.8%
Return on equity: —
Cash (bil.): ¥187
Long-term debt (bil.): ¥465
No. of shares (mil.): 1,031
Dividends
  Yield: —
  Payout: —
Market value (mil.): $3,239
Sales (mil.): $13,946

Stock Price History High/Low 1984–93

[1] Including extraordinary items

ITOCHU CORPORATION

OVERVIEW

Venerable ITOCHU, a Japanese *sogo shosha* (general trading company), has been bumped from #1 to #4 among world companies (after 3 other *sogo shosha*). Company sales dropped 13% in 1994 to $149 billion. ITOCHU operates 5 business groups: textiles; basic industries; food, forest products, and general merchandise; machinery, aerospace, and electronics; and construction. But these divisions scarcely indicate the company's business and geographic diversity. ITOCHU's interests range from textile mills in Italy to steel mills in Australia, from aircraft sales in the US to satellite broadcasting in Asia.

Determined to keep pace with technology, ITOCHU expects to invest over $850 million on multimedia by the end of the decade. The company's telecommunications investments include satellite communications (Japan Satellite Systems) and cable TV (Chofu Cable Television). ITOCHU is the domestic distributor for SPARC workstations made by Sun Microsystems (US).

In response to lower revenues and Japan's continuing recession, in 1994 management reemphasized the company's move toward global integration by increasing imports and overseas production and by improving distribution channels. The company will also expand its involvement in natural resources development and financial services.

ITOCHU has been particularly vigorous in courting business in China, with over 100 joint ventures already established there. The company has also begun to develop business interests in Vietnam.

WHEN

Chubei Itoh organized his own wholesale linen business, C. Itoh & Co., Ltd., in 1858. He was only 18. His retail operations became another leading Japanese trading company, Marubeni. Despite domestic turmoil as Japan opened to foreign trade in the 1860s, the firm prospered and was one of Osaka's largest textile wholesalers by the 1870s. C. Itoh established a representative trade office in San Francisco in 1889.

Upon Itoh's death in 1903, his son, also named Chubei, took over the business. By 1919 C. Itoh trading offices were operating in New York, Calcutta, Manila, and 4 cities in China. Nature aided C. Itoh's expansion when an earthquake disrupted the operations of the company's Tokyo-based competitors in 1923. Although not one of the large industrial *zaibatsu* that flourished in Japan during the period between the world wars, C. Itoh benefited from the general increase in trade.

With the outbreak of WWII, C. Itoh was merged in 1941 with 2 other trading companies, Marubeni and Kishimoto, into a new company, Sanko Kabushiki Kaisha. C. Itoh and Marubeni were separated in 1949. When North Korea invaded South Korea the next year, C. Itoh used its international network of suppliers to supply UN forces with food, clothing, and other provisions. The company used its profits to diversify into petroleum, machinery, aircraft, and automobiles.

After the oil crisis of 1973 demonstrated Japan's vulnerability to oil import disruptions, C. Itoh actively participated in the development of petroleum production technology. To prevent the failure of Japan's 10th largest trading company, Ataka, the Japanese government arranged a merger in 1977, making C. Itoh the 3rd largest *sogo shosha*.

In 1985 C. Itoh established Japan Communications Satellite Company (JCSAT) with Mitsui and Hughes Communications. The company formed Japan Satellite Communications Network (with Mitsui, NEC, and Hughes Communications, 1986) and Japan Satellite Video (with NTT, Century Leasing Systems, and Hakuhodo, 1988) to lease JCSAT satellite transponders. JCSAT launched its first 2 satellites in 1989 and 1990.

In 1991 C. Itoh and Toshiba joined with Time Warner to form Time Warner Entertainment Company Limited Partnership to produce and distribute motion pictures and television programs and to supply and operate cable television systems in the US. In another joint venture with Time Warner, Time Warner Entertainment Japan, C. Itoh and Toshiba agreed to distribute Warner Bros. films and develop amusement parks in Japan.

C. Itoh changed its name to ITOCHU, a transliteration of its Japanese name, in 1992.

After sales dropped in 1993, ITOCHU began selling poorly performing subsidiaries and reduced its investment portfolio by over 1/3. In 1994 the company reached a licensing agreement to manufacture and sell Guess? products in Japan.

OTC symbol: ITO (ADR)
Fiscal year ends: March 31

WHO

Chairman: Isao Yonekura
VC: Teruo Hotta
President and CEO: Minoru Murofushi
EVP: Tadayoshi Nakazawa
EVP: Koya Mita
EVP: Junji Iwamoto
EVP: Takuya Yoshida
EVP; CEO, ITOCHU International (US): Jay W. Chai
Auditors: KPMG Peat Marwick

WHERE

HQ: 1-3, Kyutaromachi 4-chome, Chuo-ku, Osaka 541-77, Japan
Phone: +81-6-241-2121
Fax: +81-6-241-3220
US HQ: ITOCHU International Inc., 335 Madison Ave., New York, NY 10017
US Phone: 212-818-8000
US Fax: 212-818-8153

ITOCHU has 775 subsidiaries and associated companies operating worldwide.

	1994 Sales		1994 Trading Income	
	¥ bil.	% of total	¥ bil.	% of total
Japan	15,071	90	41	68
North America	412	2	14	23
Other countries	1,259	8	5	9
Total	**16,742**	**100**	**60**	**100**

WHAT

	1994 Sales	
	¥ bil.	% of total
Metals & ore	4,355	26
Machinery, aerospace & electronics	3,352	20
Energy & chemicals	2,725	16
Forest products, general merch., construction & other	2,411	14
Food & agricultural products	2,095	13
Textiles	1,804	11
Total	**16,742**	**100**

Selected Subsidiaries and Affiliated Companies
CENIBRA (wood pulp production, Brazil)
Chofu Cable Television (33.9%)
CSI Brewery Co., Ltd. (Hong Kong)
Daiken Corp. (fiberboard production)
Game Latin Inc. (Nintendo game distribution, US)
Guess? Inc. (licensing agreement, apparel, US)
Gwalia Consolidated Ltd. (mining, Australia)
SINAR MAS Group (brewing, Indonesia)
SINOPEC (plastics processing, China)
Time Warner Entertainment (11.2% with Toshiba, US)
Thai Telephone & Telegraph
TMI Europe SpA (textiles, Italy)
US Electricar Inc. (battery-operated vehicles)

KEY COMPETITORS

Anglo American	Mitsubishi
AT&T	Mitsui
BASF	Nippon Steel
Daewoo	Nissan
Hutchison Whampoa	RTZ
Hyundai	Samsung
Jardine Matheson	Sime Darby
Koor Industries	Sumitomo
Lucky-Goldstar	Swire Pacific
Marubeni	Toyota

HOW MUCH

$=¥112 (Dec. 31, 1993)	Annual Growth	1985	1986	1987	1988	1989	1990	1991	1992	1993	1994
Sales (¥ bil.)	1.6%	14,545	15,900	14,762	15,540	15,964	20,998	21,304	20,610	19,278	16,742
Net income (¥ bil.)	—	13	18	20	25	30	35	32	12	4	(14)
Income as % of sales	—	0.1%	0.1%	0.1%	0.2%	0.2%	0.2%	0.1%	0.1%	0.0%	—
Earnings per share (¥)	—	13	18	18	21	24	24	22	9	3	(10)
Stock price – high (¥)[1]	—	—	411	900	881	942	1,300	1,300	785	660	656
Stock price – low (¥)[1]	—	—	279	358	573	552	890	562	545	341	370
Stock price – close (¥)[1]	7.5%	281	375	713	573	942	1,300	645	615	415	537
P/E – high	—	—	23	50	41	39	53	59	87	220	—
P/E – low	—	—	16	20	27	23	37	25	61	114	—
Dividends per share (¥)	3.7%	4.33	4.55	4.76	4.76	4.76	5.00	6.00	6.00	6.00	6.00
Book value per share (¥)	6.9%	—	—	—	188	306	361	374	371	354	326
Employees[2]	0.2%	—	—	—	7,334	—	7,098	7,108	7,149	7,449	7,434

1994 Year-end:
Debt ratio: 90.1%
Return on equity: —
Cash (bil.): ¥628
Long-term debt (bil.): ¥2,115
No. of shares (mil.): 1,425
Dividends
 Yield: 1.1%
 Payout: —
Market value (mil.): $6,832
Sales (mil.): $149,482

Stock Price History[1]
High/Low 1986–94

[1] Stock prices are for the prior calendar year. [2] Parent company only

ITO-YOKADO CO., LTD.

Ito-Yokado, Japan's largest retailer, has held its own despite the continuation of Japan's worst recession since WWII. The company operates more than 11,000 convenience stores in Japan and North America, as well as superstores, men's and women's clothing stores, discount stores, supermarkets, and restaurants. Ito-Yokado has specialized in running the Japanese versions of such American chains as Robinson's department stores (The May Company), Oshman's sporting goods, and Denny's restaurants, and it was so successful with 7-Eleven that it was able to rescue 7-Eleven's parent, Southland Corporation, when it went bankrupt in 1990.

Ito-Yokado has taken a leaf from American retailing by emphasizing price points, which is counter to Japanese retailing tradition (primarily because 78% of the retail market is in the hands of mom-and-pop stores, which cannot afford to drive hard bargains with their suppliers). To get its price edge, the company buys its merchandise rather than follow the usual Japanese policy of perpetual return privileges. This gives the company an incentive to pay close attention to consumer buying patterns and helps it forge closer bonds with its vendors.

The company's founder, Masatoshi Ito, still holds 18% of the company's stock.

In the early 1940s Masatoshi Ito graduated from a commercial high school in Yokohama. After a stint at Mitsubishi, he left to fight for Japan in 1944. After WWII the 21-year-old joined his mother and brother in running a small family clothing shop (founded in 1913) in Tokyo. The small enterprise grew into a respectable department store, which Ito took over when his brother died in 1956. In 1958 the company was incorporated as Kabushiki Kaisha Yokado.

In 1961 Ito visited the US to see National Cash Register (NCR), a company interested in replacing Japanese retailers' abacuses with cash registers. Ito attended an NCR seminar on self-service retailing and visited such successful retailers as J. C. Penney, Sears, and Safeway. Confident that US-style retailing could be transplanted to Japan, Ito opened 2 superstores (low-priced food, clothing, and household products) in high-traffic areas of Tokyo. They were highly successful, and by 1965 Ito had opened 6 more. He changed the company's name to Ito-Yokado in 1965.

In 1972 the company launched Famil, a chain of family-style restaurants serving American, Japanese, and Chinese food. Then it opened several Denny's restaurants in Japan. Returning to the US in 1972 to meet with the Dallas-based Southland Corporation (7-Eleven convenience stores), Ito negotiated a royalty agreement and opened Japan's first 7-Eleven in 1974.

The 7-Elevens quickly stole much of the market from the small mom-and-pop stores that dominated Japanese retailing (the 7-Elevens were small enough to avoid triggering Japan's Large-Scale Retail Store Law, which was designed to protect the little family stores by establishing rigid controls over stores' sizes and hours). Ito capitalized on the predicaments of his fallen competitors by letting them become 7-Eleven franchisees. In 1975 the company established its York Mart subsidiary to open a chain of supermarkets in areas that could not support superstores.

In the 1980s Ito acquired Japanese rights to Robinson's department stores and Oshman's stores. In 1989 the company bought 58 7-Elevens in Hawaii. The next year Ito bought 70% of the struggling Southland Corporation for $430 million.

Since then, the company has closed more than 900 unprofitable stores and undertaken a major upgrading of the US 7-Elevens, which includes redecorating the stores, improving checkout and inventory systems, and improving the quality and selection of the stores' merchandise.

In 1992 it was revealed that Ito, along with several other heads of major corporations, had paid protection money to local mobsters, known as *sokaiya,* in order to ensure that the company's annual meetings would not be disrupted. Ito resigned and was replaced by Toshifumi Suzuki.

Sales have risen slowly in recent years, and earnings have been flat, reflecting consumer uncertainty. Although Ito-Yokado has made its fortune by underselling competition, the company is uneasy about getting into US-style pricing wars and would prefer to hold prices a little higher, making up the difference by precise customer targeting.

Nasdaq symbol: IYCOY (ADR)
Fiscal year ends: Last day of February

President and CEO: Toshifumi Suzuki
EVP Corporate Operations: Hyozo Morita
EVP Corporate Personnel: Hiroei Masukawa
Managing Director Finance: Tatsuhiro Sekine
CEO and CFO, The Southland Corporation (US): Clark J. Matthews II
VP Human Resources, The Southland Corporation (US): David Finley
Auditors: Coopers & Lybrand

HQ: 1-4, Shibakoen 4-chome, Minato-ku, Tokyo 105, Japan
Phone: +81-3-3459-2111
Fax: +81-3-3434-8378
US HQ: The Southland Corporation, 2711 N. Haskell Ave., Dallas, TX 75204-2906
US Phone: 214-828-7011
US Fax: 214-822-7848

The company has 6,666 retail stores in Japan and 5,796 convenience stores in the US and Canada.

	1994 Sales		1994 Pretax Income	
	$ mil.	% of total	$ mil.	% of total
Japan	20,505	74	1,862	99
North America	7,273	26	28	1
Adjustments	(43)	—	(104)	—
Total	**27,735**	**100**	**1,786**	**100**

	1994 Sales		1994 Pretax Income	
	$ mil.	% of total	$ mil.	% of total
Superstores & other retailing	17,586	63	889	47
Convenience stores	9,113	33	926	49
Restaurants	1,160	4	75	4
Other & adjustments	(124)	—	(104)	—
Total	**27,735**	**100**	**1,786**	**100**

Stores and Restaurants	No.
7-Eleven (convenience stores)	11,319
Denny's Japan (restaurants)	442
Famil (restaurants)	314
Ito Yokado (superstores)	147
Mary Ann (women's wear)	77
York Benimaru (supermarkets)	62
York Mart (supermarkets)	43
Steps (men's wear)	30
Daikuma (discount stores)	22
Oshman's (sporting goods)	4
Robinson's (department stores)	2
Total	**12,462**

Casey's General Stores
Circle K
Daiei
Daimaru
Dairy Mart
E Z Mart
Hankyu
Holiday Cos.
Isetan
Marui
Mitsukoshi
National Convenience
Nichii
Seiyu
Takashimaya
Uni-Marts
UNY

Stock prices are for ADRs ADR =4 shares	9-Year Growth	1985	1986	1987	1988	1989	1990	1991	1992	1993	1994
Sales ($ mil.)	14.3%	8,326	9,459	10,088	10,803	12,007	11,170	13,867	22,585	25,871	27,735
Net income ($ mil.)	11.7%	205	244	273	343	406	392	524	568	552	556
Income as % of sales	—	2.5%	2.6%	2.7%	3.2%	3.4%	3.5%	3.8%	2.5%	2.1%	2.0%
Earnings per share ($)	5.0%	2.16	2.52	2.76	3.40	4.00	3.84	5.16	5.57	5.41	1.36
Stock price – high ($)[1]	—	31.75	51.13	106.82	110.50	140.00	143.50	130.50	149.25	148.50	210.25
Stock price – low ($)[1]	—	20.50	28.75	47.83	75.25	100.00	100.00	85.00	104.75	110.75	108.00
Stock price – close ($)[1]	22.1%	30.50	49.81	92.25	108.63	130.46	131.00	103.88	139.50	119.00	184.25
P/E – high	—	15	20	39	33	35	37	25	27	27	155
P/E – low	—	9	11	17	22	25	26	16	19	21	79
Dividends per share ($)	17.1%	0.26	0.28	0.45	0.56	0.63	0.62	0.78	0.77	0.86	1.08
Book value per share ($)	15.1%	18.04	20.52	22.92	26.24	30.84	34.68	39.52	44.27	53.25	63.91
Employees	16.3%	24,116	25,406	26,685	28,142	29,780	30,666	31,110	32,076	95,797	93,529

1994 Year-end:
Debt ratio: 56.9%
Return on equity: 9.3%
Cash (mil.): $3,133
Current ratio: 1.18
Long-term debt (mil.): $2,842
No. of shares (mil.): 102
Dividends
  Yield: 0.6%
  Payout: 79.4%
Market value (mil.): $18,829

Stock Price History[1]
High/Low 1985–94

[1] Stock prices are for the prior calendar year.

OVERVIEW

Japan Airlines (JAL), familiar for its red crane logo, is the largest airline in Japan and #7 in the world. JAL planes carry 23 million passengers annually.

Since JAL went public in 1987, it has extended its travel industry interests to include hotels and restaurants, tour packages, air cargo services, and airline support services such as aircraft maintenance and ground support. JAL owns 25% of courier service DHL International. The company's AXESS network is Japan's primary computerized reservation system.

JAL and other Asian carriers have had a dismal decade so far, burdened by Japan's recession and falling passenger and cargo numbers. At the same time international

competition has been growing increasingly fierce. By 1994 JAL had incurred losses for 3 years in a row, creating a deficit totaling more than $750 million.

With help from extensive cost-cutting measures and a strong yen, which increased Japanese travel abroad, JAL is at least slowing its losses. Passenger counts were up in 1994, but JAL was forced to cut prices to meet the competition's lower fares. The 1994 opening of Osaka's new airport boosted JAL's overseas flights but increased competition by allowing more foreign flights into Japan.

JAL still has a modern fleet and a reputation for pampering passengers. This, plus proposed government subsidies, should help the airline weather its current fiscal storm.

WHEN

After WWII, foreign airlines, chiefly Northwest and Pan Am, provided air service to Japan, which was not allowed to form its own airline until the end of US occupation in 1951. That year a group of bankers, led by Seijiro Yanagito, founded Japanese Air Lines. The Allied Peace Treaty forbade the airline to use Japanese flight crews; therefore, in the early days, it leased pilots and equipment from Northwest. In 1953 the airline was reorganized as Japan Air Lines, with the government and the public owning equal shares. JAL was essentially a revival of the prewar Nihon Koku Kabushiki Kaisha (Japan Air Transport Company), the national airline created by the Japanese government in 1928 and dissolved by the Allies in 1945.

Under Yanagito, who ran the company until 1961, JAL expanded quickly, opening a transpacific route from Tokyo to San Francisco (1954) and extending regional service to Hong Kong (1955), Bangkok (1956), and Singapore (1958). The airline gained a foothold in Europe in 1961, after opening a polar route from Tokyo to London and Paris. Service from Tokyo to Moscow began in 1967. That year JAL formed Southwest Airlines (now Japan TransOcean Air) to serve the island of Japan and the Ryukyu Islands.

In 1974 JAL suspended flights to Taipei, mainstay of the Chinese anticommunist government, in favor of establishing service to Beijing and Shanghai. Japan Asia Airways, a new subsidiary, resumed flights to Taipei the next year. JAL ran into problems in the early

1980s: in 1982, when a mentally unstable JAL pilot crashed his plane into Tokyo Bay, killing 24, then in 1985 when a JAL 747 crashed into a mountainside, killing all but 4 of the 524 on board. Termed the worst single-plane accident in history, this disaster led to the resignation of most of JAL's top executives.

In 1985, with the dollar strong, JAL signed an 11-year fixed-rate contract for $3 billion worth of Boeing airliners — a deal that would haunt the company when the yen soared in the mid-1990s.

In 1987 the government sold its stake in JAL to the public. Since air transport was no longer nationalized, overseas routes were opened to the company's long-time domestic rival, All Nippon Airways (founded as Japan Helicopter and Aeroplane Transport, 1952).

In 1992 JAL reported its first loss ($100 million) since privatization, principally due to high labor costs and expansion of its fleet and facilities. With Japan falling into recession, JAL announced a 5-year, $4.8 billion cost-cutting program. Included in the cuts was one of the corporation's most costly sacred cows — hiring Japanese workers for life. New non-Japanese workers earn lower wages and fewer benefits.

After falling short of its cost-cutting goals, in 1993 JAL announced it would close half its North American offices, suspend employee recruitment, and freeze salaries. The company also signed an agreement with rival All Nippon Airways to share some aircraft maintenance costs.

Nasdaq symbol: JAPNY (ADR)
Fiscal year ends: March 31

Chairman: Susumu Yamaji, age 68
President: Matsuo Toshimitsu
EVP: Teiichi Kuribayashi
SVP Accounting, Finance, and Revenue Accounting: Osamu Igarashi
SVP and Managing Director (The Americas): Mitsuo Ando
Director Finance and Accounting (The Americas): Sadayoshi Noguchi
Director Administration (The Americas) (Human Resources): Junji Onose
Auditors: Showa Ota & Co.

HQ: Nippon Koku Kabushiki Kaisha, Tokyo Building, 7-3, Marunouchi 2-chome, Chiyoda-ku, Tokyo 100, Japan
Phone: +81-3-3284-2315
Fax: +81-3-3284-2316
US HQ: Japan Airlines, 655 Fifth Ave., New York, NY 10022
US Phone: 212-310-1318
US Fax: 212-310-1230
Reservations: 800-525-3663

JAL flies to over 70 cities in 26 countries.

	1994 Sales	
	$ mil.	% of total
International	4,863	51
Domestic	2,386	25
Adjustments	2,332	24
Total	**9,581**	**100**

	1994 Sales	
	$ mil.	% of total
Passenger	6,121	64
Cargo	1,128	12
Other	2,332	24
Total	**9,581**	**100**

Selected Major Airline Subsidiaries
Japan Air Charter Co., Ltd. (82.2%, charter services)
Japan Asia Airways Co., Ltd. (90.5%, regional services)
Japan TransOcean Air Co., Ltd. (51.1%, air transport)

Selected Major Nonairline Subsidiaries
AXESS International Network Inc. (computer reservation system)
DHL International, Ltd. (25%, courier service)
Hotel Nikko of New York, Inc. (hotels and restaurants)
JALPAK Co., Ltd. (75.1%, package tours)
Japan Airlines Development Co., Ltd. (67.1%, hotels)

Flight Equipment	No.
Boeing 747	81
Boeing 767	15
Douglas DC-10	14
Douglas MD-11	2
Total	**112**

Air Canada	Continental	Lufthansa
Air China	Airlines	Northwest Airlines
Air France	Delta	Philippine Airlines
Air India	EVA Airways	Qantas
All Nippon	Garuda	SAS
Airways	Indonesia	Singapore Airlines
America West	Airways	Swire Pacific
Ansett Australia	Hyatt	Thai International
British Airways	IRI	TWA
Carlson	KLM	UAL
Cathay Pacific	Korean Air	Virgin Group

	Annual Growth	1985	1986	1987	1988	1989	1990	1991	1992	1993	1994
Sales ($ mil.)	9.7%	—	—	—	—	—	6,627	7,794	8,202	11,178	9,581
Net income ($ mil.)	—	—	—	—	—	—	112	99	(100)	(417)	(247)
Income as % of sales	—	—	—	—	—	—	1.7%	1.3%	—	—	—
Earnings per share ($)	—	—	—	—	—	—	0.71	0.06	(0.06)	(0.23)	(0.14)
Stock price – high ($)[1]	—	—	—	—	—	—	26.83	26.43	19.00	16.75	16.00
Stock price – low ($)[1]	—	—	—	—	—	—	21.12	13.88	14.38	8.63	9.00
Stock price – close ($)[1]	(19.8%)	—	—	—	—	—	25.95	15.63	15.75	9.25	10.75
P/E – high	—	—	—	—	—	—	38	—	—	—	—
P/E – low	—	—	—	—	—	—	30	—	—	—	—
Dividends per share ($)	(100.0%)	—	—	—	—	—	0.06	0.05	0.05	0.06	0.00
Book value per share ($)	(42.2%)	—	—	—	—	—	15.98	1.77	1.68	1.66	1.78
Employees	0.5%	20,485	20,367	20,486	20,830	20,891	21,047	21,156	21,451	21,991	21,396

1994 Year-end:
Debt ratio: 80.8%
Return on equity: —
Cash (mil.): $1,027
Current ratio: 1.15
L-T debt (mil.): $8,653
No. of shares (mil.): 1,779
Dividends
    Yield: —
    Payout: —
Market value (mil.): $19,124

Stock Price History[1]
High/Low 1990–94

[1] Stock prices are for the prior calendar year.

JARDINE MATHESON HOLDINGS LIMITED

OVERVIEW

Based in Hong Kong, Jardine Matheson is one of the largest and oldest diversified trading companies in Asia. Although the basis of its wealth is the ownership of large tracts of prime business real estate in Hong Kong, its other interests include banking and financial services, insurance, retail establishments (car dealerships, supermarkets, and restaurants), shipping, and hotels.

Although the company is proud of its history in Hong Kong, Jardine retains a colonial outlook in that it has continued to define itself as European, rather than Asian. After building its business on receiving special concessions from China, Jardine has embarked upon a plan of reducing its risk vis-a-vis the Chinese takeover of Hong Kong in 1997. This program included moving its international headquarters to Bermuda in 1984, moving its primary stock listing to London in 1992, and transferring the stock listings for its subsidiaries from Hong Kong to Singapore in 1994. These actions, plus the its support of the efforts of Hong Kong's governor to democratize Hong Kong before China takes over, constitute a vote of no confidence that has not been lost on China.

The Keswick family, descendants of founder William Jardine, control the company through significant minority interests.

WHEN

Scotsmen William Jardine and James Matheson first met in Bombay in 1820. Twelve years later they established Jardine, Matheson in Canton, the only city in which China allowed foreigners to live. The company started shipping tea from China to Europe and smuggling opium from India to China. In 1839 Chinese authorities tried to stop the drug trade, seizing 20,000 chests of opium, 7,000 of them Jardine's. Jardine persuaded Britain to send gunboats to China, precipitating the First Opium War. China lost the war and signed an 1842 treaty opening 5 ports and ceding Hong Kong to Britain.

Jardine moved its headquarters to Hong Kong and resumed trading in opium. The Second Opium War resulted in the opening of 11 more ports and the legalization of opium imports. Jardine flourished. The company left the politically dangerous opium business and entered the brewing, silk and textiles, banking, insurance, and sugar businesses; formed Hongkong Land (HKL), a real estate company; introduced steamships to China; and built the country's first railroad line.

The Sino-Japanese War and WWII shut down Jardine. In 1945 the company reopened in Hong Kong with an airline, a brewery, textile mills, and real estate operations. Attempts to reestablish operations in China ended in 1954 after the Communist takeover. Proceeds from Jardine's 1961 public offering (oversubscribed 56 to 1) were used to expand into shipping.

In the 1970s the company embarked on a program of acquisitions throughout the world. As China emerged from the cultural revolution, Hong Kong's importance in trade decreased, hurting business, and by 1980 Jardine was a takeover target. *Taipan* (big boss) David Newbigging defended against takeovers by erecting a bulwark of cross-holdings of Jardine and HKL stock. The resulting debt pushed Jardine to the brink of bankruptcy, forcing it to sell assets.

Simon Keswick succeeded Newbigging in 1984 and proceeded to sell numerous businesses to lower debt. His investments in Mercedes-Benz distributorships and fast-food franchises turned Jardine around. In March 1984, as the UK and China negotiated the 1997 transfer of Hong Kong to Chinese control, Keswick announced the relocation of Jardine's legal headquarters to Bermuda. In a 1986 antitakeover transaction, the company created Jardine Strategic Holdings to hold interests in HKL and its spinoffs.

Jardine aborted an acquisition of 20% of Bear Stearns after the 1987 US stock market crash. This led to litigation that ended in 1991 with Jardine paying a $60 million settlement to Bear Stearns.

To increase its holdings outside Hong Kong, Jardine bought 26% of Trafalgar House, a British construction, shipping, and property company that owns the Cunard line, London's Ritz Hotel, and one of Europe's leading engineering and construction firms.

In 1994, after negotiations failed to exempt it from the Hong Kong stock exchange's trading rules (which make it easy to buy a controlling block of shares), Jardine Matheson delisted from Hong Kong.

OTC Symbol: JARLY (ADR)
Fiscal year ends: December 31

WHO

Chairman: Henry Keswick
Managing Director: Alasdair Morrison
Finance Director: C.I. Cowan
Personnel: Martin G. Barrow
President and CEO, Theo H. Davies (US):
Martin J. Juskot
CFO, Theo H. Davies (US): Mildred S. Hayden
SVP Human Resources, Theo H. Davies (US):
Beverly C. Nagy
Auditors: Price Waterhouse

WHERE

HQ: Jardine House, 33-35 Reid St., Hamilton,
Bermuda
Hong Kong HQ: Jardine Matheson Ltd., 48th Fl.,
Jardine House, GPO Box 70, Hong Kong
Phone: +852-843-8388
Fax: +852-845-9005
US HQ: Theo H. Davies & Co., Ltd., 841 Bishop
St., Ste. 2300, Honolulu, HI 96813
US Phone: 808-532-6500
US Fax: 808-532-6544

	1993 Sales		1993 Pretax Income	
	$ mil.	% of total	$ mil.	% of total
Australasia	3,068	36	86	10
Hong Kong & China	2,915	35	483	59
Europe	1,066	13	85	10
North America	449	5	41	5
Other Asia	927	11	129	16
Total	**8,425**	**100**	**824**	**100**

WHAT

	1993 Sales		1993 Pretax Income	
	$ mil.	% of total	$ mil.	% of total
Retail & distribution	6,822	81	396	47
Eng. & constr.	584	7	48	6
Transport services	446	5	41	5
Financial services	346	4	188	22
Property & hotels	227	3	173	20
Adjustments	—	—	(22)	—
Total	**8,425**	**100**	**824**	**100**

Selected Subsidiaries and Affiliates
Dairy Farm International Holdings (25%, supermarkets,
restaurants)
Hongkong Land Holdings (real estate, 17%)
Jardine Fleming Group Ltd.(50%)
    Corporate banking
    Investment management
    Stock brokerage
Jardine Pacific Holdings Ltd.
    Auto dealerships
    Engineering and construction
    Property
    Restaurants
    Shipping, security, and financial services
    Trading and distribution
Jardine Strategic (52%)
JIB Group, (61%, insurance, UK)
Mandarin Oriental (26%, hotels)

KEY COMPETITORS

Accor	Hutchison	Marubeni
Allied Group	Whampoa	McDonald's
Hang Lung	Hyatt	Mitsubishi
Development	Hyundai	Samsung
Hopewell	ITOCHU	Sime Darby
Holdings	Kumagai Gumi	Swire Pacific
HSBC	Marriott Intl.	

HOW MUCH

	Annual Growth	1984	1985	1986	1987	1988	1989	1990	1991	1992	1993
Sales ($ mil.)	16.4%	—	—	—	3,389	4,278	4,638	5,992	7,190	7,900	8,425
Net income ($ mil.)	20.3%	—	—	—	140	138	239	226	381	348	424
Income as % of sales	—	—	—	—	4.1%	3.2%	5.1%	3.8%	5.3%	4.4%	5.0%
Earnings per share (HK$)	47.6%	0.02	0.04	0.12	0.19	0.25	0.36	0.42	0.48	0.55	0.66
Stock price – high (HK$)	—	10.29	9.86	16.86	23.80	14.90	25.50	37.25	39.00	66.00	83.00
Stock price – low (HK$)	—	3.93	5.75	7.86	8.50	9.90	14.30	22.90	25.70	38.50	41.75
Stock price – close (HK$)	26.2%	6.21	9.79	16.07	10.30	14.60	24.40	28.10	38.50	42.75	50.50
P/E – high	—	—	—	—	—	—	—	—	—	—	—
P/E – low	—	—	—	—	—	—	—	—	—	—	—
Dividends per share ($)	41.0%	0.01	0.01	0.04	0.06	0.08	0.12	0.14	0.16	0.19	0.22
Book value per share ($)	20.8%	—	—	—	—	—	—	2.15	2.50	2.84	3.79
Employees	20.8%	—	—	—	—	—	94,000	120,000	120,000	200,000	200,000

1993 Year-end:
Debt ratio: 31.5%
Return on equity: 17.9%
Cash (mil.): $1,551
Current ratio: 1.06
Long-term debt (mil.): $676
No. of shares (mil.): 718
Dividends
    Yield: —
    Payout: 33.2%
Market value (mil.): US$4,696

**Stock Price History
High/Low 1984–93**

JOHN LABATT LIMITED

John Labatt, Canada's #2 beermaker (after Molson), is trying to redefine itself without causing a mutiny among shareholders. The company has sold most of its food (primarily dairy) segment. It now plans to sell 49% of its high-profile but low-earning broadcasting and sports interests as well.

Tension peaked between management and shareholders after Toronto-based holding company Brascan, Labatt's biggest shareholder, sold its stake in the company in 1993. Management moved to adopt a poison pill to avert unwanted takeover bids. But in 1994 shareholders vetoed the poison pill — the first such defeat in Canadian history.

Undeterred, CEO George Taylor continues to pursue Labatt's 2 primary segments: beer and broadcasting/sports. The company added the Toronto Argonauts (Canadian Football

League) and NTN Canada (35%, interactive media). The company also licensed The Discovery Channel in Canada and restructured several of its television and film production companies, creating Skyvision/Partners Film. Skyvision produces the *RoboCop* TV series.

Labatt raised eyebrows when it paid a generous $510 million for a 22% stake in Mexico's Femsa Cerveza, brewer of popular beers such as Dos Equis and Tecate. The move will increase debt in the short term but give the company a better position for the continuing international beer wars.

While the 1994 major league baseball strike dented Labatt's sports and broadcasting earnings, its concert promotion subsidiary, BCL Entertainment, benefited from big concert tours by the Rolling Stones and Pink Floyd.

John Labatt arrived in London, Ontario, from England in 1833. The farmer gained a reputation for the malting barley he sold to a local innkeeper's brewery. Labatt teamed up with master brewer Samuel Eccles and bought a stake in the innkeeper's brewery in 1847.

In the beginning the partners produced only 3 brands of beer (X, XX, XXX). In 1854 Labatt gained full control of the brewery. When the Great Western Railway came, he started shipping his products to nearby cities. Labatt died in 1866, leaving the brewery to his wife and son John II.

John II modernized the company and expanded operations as far as the Northwest Territories. He died in 1915, a year before Prohibition in Canada bankrupted all but 15 of Ontario's 65 breweries. Labatt survived because of a loophole in the law that allowed the production of alcohol for export.

During the 1920s and 1930s, Labatt became known for its generous employee benefits, including paid vacations and insurance.

After WWII Labatt went public and began a period of rapid expansion, acquiring Toronto-based Copland Brewing in 1946. Ten years later W. H. R. Jarvis became the first nonfamily president of the company.

By 1965 Labatt had a brewing capacity of 1.3 million barrels. Shortly thereafter the company began diversifying into food. Throughout this period Brascan acquired increasing interest in Labatt.

In 1980 the company made a deal with Anheuser-Busch to brew Budweiser in Canada, where it immediately captured about 8% of the market. With its leadership in beer intact, Labatt went on a decade-long shopping spree, acquiring an interest in the Toronto Blue Jays and several food and entertainment companies. Because Canada's antitrust laws threatened to block further Canadian expansion, Labatt began purchasing US businesses, including Johanna Farms (dairy, 1985) and Latrobe Brewing (Rolling Rock beer, 1987). The company bought 77.5% ownership of Birra Moretti and Prinz Brau (Italy, brewing, 1989). The food group acquired Black Diamond cheese (1990) and the Canadian license for Häagen-Dazs (1991).

In 1992 Labatt sold several food subsidiaries, including JLFoods, Miracle Feeds, and Everfresh. Archer-Daniels-Midland purchased the company's Ogilvie Mills (flour milling).

In 1992 and 1993 Labatt's Toronto Blue Jays won the World Series.

Labatt scored a coup in 1993 when it introduced "ice beer," made from a new patented process that it licenses to other brewers. Labatt has sued rival brewers Molson and Miller (US), alleging misuse of the term "ice beer."

In 1993 Canada and the US began talks to ease cross-border beer sales. Soon after, Labatt introduced its bargain beer, Wildcat, to protect its share of the Canadian market.

Principal exchange: Toronto
Fiscal year ends: April 30

Chairman: Samuel Pollock
VC; Group Chairman, Brewing: Sidney M. Oland
President and CEO: George S. Taylor, age 54,
C$875,000 pay
SVP Finance and Corporate Development:
Robert G. Vaux
SVP Corporate Resources (Human Resources):
Robert F. Dolan
President, Labatt's USA: Richard R. Fogarty
Auditors: Ernst & Young

HQ: Labatt House, BCE Place, 181 Bay St.,
Ste. 200, PO Box 811, Toronto, Ontario,
M5J 2T3 Canada
Phone: 416-865-6000
Fax: 416-865-6074
US HQ: Labatt's USA, 23 Old King's Hwy. South,
Darien, CT 06820
US Phone: 203-656-1876
US Fax: 203-656-0838

Labatt's interests include brewing, broadcasting,
entertainment, and professional sports.

	1994 Sales		1994 Operating Income	
	C$ mil.	% of total	C$ mil.	% of total
Canada	1,961	82	307	—
Other countries	438	18	(15)	—
Adjustments	571	—	(8)	—
Total	**2,970**	**100**	**284**	**—**

	1994 Sales		1994 Operating Income	
	C$ mil.	% of total	C$ mil.	% of total
Brewing	1,769	76	260	89
Broadcasting, sports & entertainment	630	27	32	11
Adjustments	571	(3)	(8)	—
Total	**2,970**	**100**	**284**	**100**

Selected Beer Brands
Birra Moretti (Italy)
Budweiser (Canadian license)
Carlsberg (Canadian license)
Clausthaler (non-alcoholic, Germany)
Guinness (Canadian license)
Labatt (Genuine Draft, Ice Beer, Maximum Ice)
Labatt's (Blue, Blue Light, Canadian Lager, Original Red, Strong)
President's Choice (Canadian license)
Red Stripe (Jamaica)
Rolling Rock (US, UK)
Sans Souci (Italy)

Broadcasting, Sports, and Entertainment
BCL Entertainment (75%, concert promotion)
International Talent Group (50%, artists' representative)
Labatt Communications Inc.
The Discovery Channel (80%, Canadian operation)
Dome Productions
Le Réseau des sports
NTN Canada (35%)
The Rep Shoppe
SkyDome (41.6%)
The Sports Network
The Toronto Argonauts
The Toronto Blue Jays (90%)
Viewers' Choice Canada (25%)
Skyvision/Partners Film

Adolph Coors
Allied Domecq
Big Rock Brewery
Capital Cities/ABC
Carlsberg
CBS
Cox
Danone
Foster's Brewing
General Electric
George Weston
Guinness
Heileman
Heineken
Iron City Brewing
Kirin
Molson
Moosehead Brewing
Philip Morris
S&P
San Miguel
Stroh

$=C$1.32 (Dec. 31, 1993)	9-Year Growth	1985	1986	1987	1988	1989	1990	1991	1992	1993	1994
Sales (C$ mil.)	2.3%	2,426	3,161	3,782	4,611	4,857	4,681	4,760	3,837	2,780	2,970
Net income (C$ mil.)[2]	7.3%	82	101	125	141	135	169	109	101	(70)	155
Income as % of sales	—	3.4%	3.2%	3.3%	3.0%	2.8%	3.6%	2.3%	2.6%	(2.5%)	5.2%
Earnings per share (C$)[2]	2.9%	1.18	1.38	1.55	1.68	1.60	1.78	1.03	0.98	—	1.53
Stock price – high (C$)[1]	—	12.63	16.06	25.00	29.75	26.25	27.50	24.88	27.75	30.38	28.63
Stock price – low (C$)[1]	—	8.75	10.88	14.31	20.13	20.50	21.13	18.38	20.00	24.13	21.75
Stock price – close (C$)[1]	8.5%	10.88	15.38	23.88	22.75	21.50	24.50	21.00	25.50	28.38	22.63
P/E – high	—	11	11	16	18	16	15	24	28	—	19
P/E – low	—	7	8	9	12	13	12	18	20	—	14
Dividends per share (C$)	6.4%	0.47	0.50	0.55	0.62	0.68	0.73	0.77	0.79	0.82	0.82
Book value per share (C$)	(0.1%)	8.52	9.41	10.60	11.76	12.85	14.08	14.42	15.23	11.37	8.44
Employees	(9.6%)	14,200	16,200	17,900	16,000	16,500	16,700	11,100	5,500	5,700	5,700

1994 Year-end:
Debt ratio: 43.9%
Return on equity: 15.4%
Cash (mil.): C$368
Long-term debt (mil.): C$701
No. of shares (mil.): 86
Dividends
  Yield: 3.6%
  Payout: 53.7%
Market value (mil.): $1,479
Sales (mil.): $2,250

Stock Price History[1]
High/Low 1985–94

[1] Stock prices are for the prior calendar year.   [2] Including extraordinary items

KIRIN BREWERY COMPANY, LIMITED

OVERVIEW

With a market share of nearly 50%, Kirin is Japan's largest brewer and the 4th largest beer maker in the world. The Tokyo-based company makes 2 of Japan's 3 most popular beers: Kirin Lager (Japan's #1 beer) and Ichiban Shibori.

While beer is what keeps Kirin buzzing, the company is involved in a variety of other operations. Kirin Beverage manufactures canned teas and coffees, carbonated drinks, and sports drinks. Through a joint venture with Seagram's Tropicana Products, it sells Tropicana 100% fruit juices. In another joint venture with Seagram, the company sells Chivas Regal whiskey, Mumm's champagne, and other wines and liquors.

Kirin has diversified into several other businesses. It sells dairy products and ground coffees, develops products for agricultural applications, provides engineering services, and operates several restaurant chains in Japan, including Shakey's Pizza. One of the company's fastest-growing businesses is its pharmaceuticals unit, which has developed 2 popular blood treatments.

The company's symbol, a half-horse, half-dragon creature called *kirin*, is said to bring good fortune to those lucky enough to see it. However, facing stiff competition in Japan, Kirin is not counting on just the mythical beast. It is refocusing on its best-selling Kirin Lager and continuing its diversification.

WHEN

American William Copeland came to Yokohama in 1864 and 5 years later established the Spring Valley Brewery, the first in Japan, to provide beer for the foreign nationals on the island. Lacking funds to continue the enterprise, Copeland closed the brewery in 1884. In 1885 a group of foreign and Japanese businessmen reopened it as Japan Brewery. The business created the Kirin label in 1888 and was soon turning a profit.

Initially, the company was predominantly operated by Americans and Europeans, but by 1907 the Japanese had filled the ranks and had adopted the Kirin name. During the early decades of the 20th century, the company expanded across Japan by establishing breweries and its own bottling plant.

Sales plummeted during WWII when the government set limits on brewing output. Nevertheless, Kirin established its R&D facilities, which are now a model for the industry.

After the war the US occupation forces inadvertently assisted Kirin when they split Dai Nippon Brewery (Kirin's main competitor) into 2 companies (Asahi and Sapporo) while leaving Kirin intact. Kirin pressed its new advantage and established itself as Japan's leading brewer during the 1950s.

The company made rapid technological advances in the 1960s (the decade when beer overtook sake as the nation's favorite drink) when it developed superior strains of malting barley and learned new ways to control the fermentation process.

During the 1970s Kirin introduced several new soft drinks to the market and in 1972 branched into liquor through a joint venture with Seagram (Kirin-Seagram). In 1976 Kirin established Kirin Australia to provide a steady supply of Australian malt to its breweries.

In the 1980s Kirin purchased several Coca-Cola bottling operations in New England and Japan. In 1988 the company entered the wine business by launching its Kirin Wine Club line and signed an agreement with Molson Companies to produce Kirin beer for the North American market. The company also created its information systems subsidiary.

In 1989 Kirin bought Napa Valley's Raymond Vineyards and began expanding its beer line, introducing, among others, Kirin Malt Dry, Ichiban Shibori, Kirin Premium Beer, and Akiaji, over the next few years.

In 1991 the company added imported beers from Czechoslovakia and Germany to its portfolio and formed a partnership with Seagram's Tropicana unit to market its drinks in Japan.

In 1993 Kirin chairman Hideyo Motoyama resigned after 4 company executives were arrested for allegedly paying about $300,000 to a group of racketeers who had threatened to disrupt Kirin's annual meeting by asking difficult and embarrassing questions. That same year Kirin signed a joint venture agreement with Anheuser-Busch to distribute Budweiser in Japan, and it signed an agreement with brewer Charles Wells to produce and market Kirin Lager in the UK.

In 1994 Kirin announced plans to import a new "ice" beer, made by Anheuser-Busch in Los Angeles under the Kirin name.

Nasdaq symbol: KNBWY (ADR)
Fiscal year ends: December 31

President: Keisaku Manabe
EVP: Yoshiomi Kimura
EVP: Takeshi Uekusa
Senior Managing Director: Seinosuke Furuya
Senior Managing Director: Kazuo Koide
Senior Managing Director: Toru Sasahara
Managing Director: Naoki Hashimoto
Managing Director: Kazunori Nakano
Managing Director: Yasuhiro Sato
Managing Director: Hiromi Murata
Managing Director: Kanoo Nakamura
President, Kirin USA: Hitoshi Oshima
Treasurer (CFO), Kirin USA: Takeshi Fujii
**General Manager Administration (Personnel),
 Kirin USA:** James Tate
Auditors: Asahi & Co.

HQ: 26-1, Jingumae 6-chome, Shibuya-ku, Tokyo
 150-11, Japan
Phone: +81-3-3499-6111
Fax: +81-3-3499-6151
US HQ: Kirin USA, Inc., 600 Third Ave., 21st Fl.,
 New York, NY 10016
US Phone: 212-687-1865
US Fax: 212-286-8065

Kirin has 15 breweries in Japan. It has
subsidiaries and affiliates in 11 countries.

	1993 Sales	
	¥ bil.	% of total
Beer	1,308	83
Soft drinks	211	13
Other	56	4
Total	**1,575**	**100**

Selected Beers
Akiaji
Beer Kojo
Fuyu Jitate
Ichiban Shibori
Kirin Draft
Kirin Golden Bitter
Kirin Lager

Selected Soft Drinks
Kirin Chassé
Kirin Gogono-kocha
Kirin Ho Oh Oolong Tea
Kirin Jive Coffee
Kirin Lemon Select
Kirin Postwater
Tropicana 100%

Other
Agricultural
 biotechnology
Engineering services
Foods, wines, and liquors
 Cafés Suavor (ground
 coffee)
Kirin Wine Club
Koiwai (dairy products)
Pharmaceuticals
Restaurants
 Giraffe restaurants/bars
 Kirin City pubs
 Shakey's Pizza (Japan)
Yeast products

Adolph Coors
Allied Domecq
Asahi Brewery
Bass
Bond
Cadbury Schweppes
Carlsberg
Chugai
 Pharmaceutical
Danone
Dole
Dr Pepper/7Up
Foster's Brewing

Gallo
Godo Shusei
Grand
 Metropolitan
Guinness
Heineken
Ito-Yokado
John Labatt
LVMH
Meiji Milk
Mercian
Molson
Nestlé

Nikka Whisky
PepsiCo
Philip Morris
Pokka
San Miguel
Sapporo
 Breweries
Seagram
Snow Brand Milk
Stroh
Sumitomo
Suntory
Tsingtao

$=¥112 (Dec. 31, 1993)	9-Year Growth	1984	1985	1986	1987	1988	1989	1990	1991	1992	1993
Sales (¥ bil.)	2.8%	1,226	1,290	1,296	1,302	1,357	1,257	1,428	1,530	1,602	1,575
Net income (¥ bil.)	8.9%	20	25	32	34	35	31	42	43	48	43
Income as % of sales	—	1.6%	1.9%	2.5%	2.6%	2.6%	2.5%	2.9%	2.8%	3.0%	2.7%
Earnings per share (¥)	5.6%	25	30	32	33	36	29	40	41	45	41
Stock price – high (¥)	—	574	717	1,587	2,803	2,268	2,000	1,943	1,620	1,390	1,490
Stock price – low (¥)	—	458	494	668	1,451	1,506	1,686	1,219	1,240	991	1,110
Stock price – close (¥)	9.4%	503	681	1,497	1,742	1,848	1,943	1,440	1,340	1,130	1,130
P/E – high	—	23	24	50	85	63	69	49	40	31	37
P/E – low	—	18	16	21	44	42	58	30	30	22	27
Dividends per share (¥)	4.4%	6.80	6.80	8.62	6.80	6.80	7.14	7.82	9.00	10.00	10.00
Book value per share (¥)	11.8%	227	251	277	307	335	491	503	537	590	620
Employees	1.0%	7,519	7,521	7,507	7,557	7,582	7,673	7,686	7,856	8,086	8,242

1993 Year-end:
Debt ratio: 13.3%
Return on equity: 6.7%
Cash (bil.): ¥241
Long-term debt (bil.): ¥82
No. of shares (mil.): 1,052
Dividends
 Yield: 0.9%
 Payout: 24.5%
Market value (mil.): $10,656
Sales (mil.): $14,061

**Stock Price History
High/Low 1984–93**

KLM ROYAL DUTCH AIRLINES

OVERVIEW

Celebrating its 75th anniversary in 1994, Amsterdam-based Koninklijke Luchtvaart Maatschappij (KLM Royal Dutch Airlines) is the world's oldest international airline. KLM is 38.2% owned by the Dutch government and is the #1 airline offering services between the Netherlands and the US.

Because demand for air service to Amsterdam has been low in comparison with other world capitals, KLM has developed into one of the most international of airlines. It has also diversified beyond international passenger traffic and has interests in a number of related businesses including computer reservation systems, helicopter ferrying, regional airlines, forwarding, and trucking.

In recent years KLM has taken on Federal Express and UPS with an aggressive cargo carrying strategy. The company was the 5th largest cargo carrier in the world in 1994, up from #8 in 1992.

KLM has also pursued various strategic airline alliances in an attempt to expand its share of the passenger market. It owns a 25% equity interest in debt-plagued Northwest Airlines and smaller shares in UK, Dutch, and Caribbean airlines. KLM and Northwest have combined some operations giving the Dutch carrier greater access to the North American market. KLM has also established a similar alliance with Singapore Airlines and Japan Airlines.

WHEN

Flight lieutenant Albert Plesman founded KLM in The Hague in 1919. A group of Dutch businessmen financed the venture, which had been granted the honorary title of Koninklijke or "royal" by Queen Wilhelmina.

Under Plesman's leadership KLM established service between Amsterdam and London (1920), Copenhagen (1920), Brussels (1922), and Paris (1923). The airline initiated the longest air route in the world (8,700 miles), from Amsterdam to Indonesia, in 1927 and extended its European network to Zurich (1928), Rome (1931), Prague (1935), Vienna (1936), and Oslo (1939). Hitler's occupation of Holland shut down KLM's European operations in 1940; the Germans imprisoned Plesman from 1940 to 1942.

After the war Plesman quickly reestablished commercial service, and by the mid-1950s KLM had expanded to Africa and the Americas. Service to Australia, first offered in 1938, was resumed in 1951. The company formed an aerial photography and survey subsidiary, KLM Aerocarto, in 1954, based on a department created by the airline in 1921. In 1957 KLM's stock began trading on the NYSE.

KLM formed KLM Helicopters to serve offshore drilling platforms in the North Sea in 1965. In 1966, to provide commuter services within the Netherlands, the airline established NLM Dutch Airlines, renaming it NLM CityHopper in 1976 after service had been expanded to adjoining countries.

Sergio Orlandini, KLM's president from 1973 to 1987, addressed the problems of overcapacity by converting the rear portions of KLM's 747s to cargo space. In 1988 the company bought 40% of Transavia, a Dutch charter airline, from Nedlloyd, a Dutch shipping and energy concern.

KLM started looking for partners in the late 1980s to help it compete in key markets. It bought 10% of Covia Partnership, owner and operator of United Airlines's Apollo computer reservation system (1988), and invested in Wings Holdings, a company established to buy Northwest Airlines in 1989.

In 1991 KLM raised its stake in Transavia to 80% and bought 35% of Air Littoral, a French regional airline, and 40% of ALM Antillean Airlines. Also during 1991 KLM sold a 49% interest in KLM Helikopters (renamed KLM ERA Helicopters) to Houston-based ROWAN Companies.

Airline deregulation in Europe has spawned numerous efforts to develop strategic relationships. A deal giving KLM and British Airways 20% each of Belgium's national airline, Sabena, fell apart in 1990. Then in 1991 it looked as though KLM and British Airways would unite. By early 1992, however, talks had collapsed.

KLM tied up an agreement with Northwest Airlines in 1992 to share operations, but KLM was hurt by Northwest's huge losses in 1992.

Following Northwest's return to profitability, KLM bought up brewer Foster's 5–6% stake in the airline in 1994 for $180 million, boosting its ownership in Northwest to nearly 25%.

NYSE symbol: KLM
Fiscal year ends: March 31

Chairman: C. J. Oort
President: Pieter Bouw
SVP and General Secretary (Principal Accounting Officer): J. J. T. Entzinger-Bennink
EVP Personnel and Organization: P. F. Hartman
VP North America and Mexico: Toon H. Woltman
Auditors: KPMG Klynveld

HQ: Koninklijke Luchtvaart Maatschappij N.V., Amsterdamseweg 55, Amstelveen, The Netherlands
Phone: +31-20-649-91-23
Fax: +31-20-648-80-69
US HQ: KLM Royal Dutch Airlines USA, 565 Taxter Rd., Elmsford, NY 10523
US Phone: 914-784-2000
US Fax: 914-784-2102

KLM serves 150 cities on 6 continents.

	1994 Sales	
	$ mil.	% of total
Europe	1,064	28
North America	921	25
Far East	718	19
Central & South America	431	12
Middle East	329	9
Africa	260	7
Adjustments	896	—
Total	**4,619**	**100**

	1994 Sales	
	$ mil.	% of total
Passengers	3,161	68
Cargo & mail	732	16
Other revenue	726	16
Total	**4,619**	**100**

Major Subsidiaries and Affiliates
Air UK Holdings Ltd. (14.9%, routes from UK to Amsterdam and other European cities)
ALM Antillean Airlines (40%, Caribbean airline)
Galileo International Partnership (12.1%, reservation system)
KLM Cityhopper (regional airline)
KLM ERA Helicopters (helicopter charters)
Koninklijke Frans Maas Groep (25%, trucking company)
Martinair Holland (minority stake, regional airline)
Northwest Airlines (25%, US)
Polygon Insurance Co., Ltd. (30.7%)
Transavia Airlines (80%, charters and scheduled service)

Flight Equipment	No.	Orders
Airbus A310	10	—
Boeing 737	36	1
Boeing 747	29	2
Boeing 757	2	4
Douglas DC-10	2	—
McDonnell Douglas MD-11	2	8
Other	32	—
Total	**113**	**15**

Air France	Continental	Lufthansa
Airborne Freight	Airlines	SAS
All Nippon Airways	Delta	Swire Pacific
AMR	DHL Worldwide	Swiss Air
British Airways	Express	Tower Air
Consolidated	FedEx	UAL
Freightways	IRI	UPS

	9-Year Growth	1985	1986	1987	1988	1989	1990	1991	1992	1993	1994
Sales ($ mil.)	12.4%	1,618	2,310	2,637	3,002	2,792	3,386	3,426	4,290	4,549	4,619
Net income ($ mil.)	(4.6%)	84	122	148	169	175	178	(330)	68	(311)	55
Income as % of sales	—	5.2%	5.3%	5.6%	5.6%	6.3%	5.3%	—	1.6%	—	1.2%
Earnings per share ($)	(9.7%)	2.16	3.13	2.91	3.20	3.32	3.22	(6.24)	1.18	(5.89)	0.86
Stock price – high ($)[1]	—	14.81	20.38	23.88	27.75	21.63	26.50	26.00	24.50	24.38	23.38
Stock price – low ($)[1]	—	9.41	12.75	17.50	13.25	15.00	19.88	11.00	11.13	12.50	13.13
Stock price – close ($)[1]	5.6%	12.88	18.75	18.13	15.75	21.00	25.38	11.50	23.50	13.88	21.00
P/E – high	—	7	7	8	9	7	8	—	21	—	27
P/E – low	—	4	4	6	4	5	6	—	9	—	15
Dividends per share ($)	—	0.00	0.51	0.69	0.75	0.75	0.69	0.86	0.00	0.52	0.00
Book value per share ($)	10.8%	11.79	19.65	26.65	32.06	29.26	32.35	26.62	28.19	22.74	29.79
Employees	2.8%	19,193	20,262	21,235	22,257	23,599	25,448	26,385	25,977	26,650	24,610

1994 Year-end:
Debt ratio: 77.6%
Return on equity: 3.5%
Cash (mil.): $974
Current ratio: 1.36
Long-term debt (mil.): $4,142
No. of shares (mil.): 85
Dividends
  Yield: —
  Payout: —
Market value (mil.): $1,341

Stock Price History[1]
High/Low 1985–94

[1] Stock prices are for the prior calendar year.

KOÇ HOLDING A.S.

Based in Istanbul, Koç (pronounced "coach") is Turkey's largest company. It is made up of a group of 106 companies and is controlled by the Koç family, Turkey's wealthiest clan (with a net worth estimated at $2.5 billion). The family holds 89% of the company's stock.

Koç's automotive businesses are its biggest revenue generator. Tofas, the company's joint venture with Fiat, produces 20 different passenger car models and has a 45% share of the Turkish market. Otosan is Turkey's leading maker of heavy trucks and minibuses, with 33% and 43% market shares, respectively. Türk Traktör, Turkey's #1 tractor manufacturer, holds 43% of the domestic market. In auto parts Koç's Döktas has 37% of the Turkish market for automotive castings.

Koç also has dominant positions in household appliances and consumer electronics in Turkey. Ardem is Turkey's leading maker of ranges and table-top cookers, and Bekoteknik is the #1 manufacturer of home electronics. Aygaz is the leading Turkish liquid petroleum gas seller. Koç also controls Turkey's largest insurance company, Sark Sigorta.

Koç's sales surged in 1993, thanks to increased demand for passenger cars and a greater availability of credit. Koç has worked to develop new export markets, including Central Asia, Russia, and Eastern Europe, and it is also entering the communications business. It joined a consortium that includes French media company Canal+, Time Warner's HBO, and Turkish publisher Milliyet to create Turkey's first pay TV service.

In 1917, 16-year-old Vehbi Koç and his father opened a small grocery store in Ankara, Turkey. With the fall of the Ottoman Empire after WWI, Turkey became a republic in 1923, and its capital was moved to Ankara, which was then only a village. Koç recognized an opportunity and expanded into construction and building supplies, winning a contract to repair the roof of the Turkish parliament building. By the age of 26, Koç was a millionaire.

Ford Motor made Koç its agent in 1928, and he set up Ford dealerships in Turkey. In 1931 Mobil Oil and Koç entered an exclusive agreement to search for oil inside Turkey.

Despite Turkey's neutrality in WWII, the fighting disrupted Koç's business. Turkey became isolationist after the war and restricted foreign concerns to selling through local agents, a practice from which Koç benefited by importing foreign products. General Electric and Koç entered a joint venture in 1946 to build Turkey's first electric bulb factory. In 1955 Koç set up Arçelik, the first Turkish producer of refrigerators, washing machines, and water heaters; Türk Demir Döküm, the first Turkish producer of radiators and, later, auto castings; and Türkay, the first private producer of matches. Another first came in 1959 with the construction of Turkey's first truck assembly plant (Otosan).

In 1962 Koç entered the LPG field with Aygaz (the first Turkish company to go public), and it opened Turkey's first tire factory with Uniroyal. In 1963 Koç assembled his

various businesses (28) into Koç Holding and sold stock to the public 3 years later. With Siemens, Koç built the first cable factory in Turkey in 1964. That same year Koç's Türk Traktör starting making tractors under a Fiat license. In a joint venture with General Electric, Koç set up the first Turkish producer of electric motors and compressors in 1965. The next year, using the Ford Cortina design, Koç's Otosan sold the Anadol, the first car to be made entirely in Turkey.

In 1971 Koç's Tofas, operating with a Fiat license, offered the Murat 124, Turkey's first steel-bodied car. In 1974 Koç bought Migros, Turkey's largest chain of supermarkets.

The Turkish military imposed martial law in 1980 and restricted foreign exchange payments, forcing Koç to limit its operations. In 1985, the first year in which foreign companies were allowed to directly export products to Turkey, Koç's Otosan and Ford Motor offered the Taunus, the first Ford car made in Turkey. The following year Koç and American Express started Koç-Amerikan Bank. In the late 1980s Vehbi's only son, Rahmi, assumed executive responsibilities at the company.

In 1991 Koç entered a joint venture with Prisunic, a French retailer, to open a chain of hypermarkets in Turkey. Tofas introduced 2 new vehicles in 1993, the Tempra station wagon and the Tipo hatchback.

In 1994 Rahmi Koç became chairman of a Turkish Marine Environment Protection Association, an antipollution organization.

Principal exchange: Istanbul
Fiscal year ends: December 31

Honorary Chairman: Vehbi Koç, age 93
Chairman: Rahmi M. Koç, age 62
CEO: Inan Kiraç
Executive Officer: Ugur Eksioglu
President, Finance Group: Tevfik Altinok
President, Durable Goods Group: Hasan Subasi
President, Otosan Group: Gökçe Bayindir
President, Foreign Trade Group: Tunç Ulug
President, Corporate Planning Group: Necati
Arikan
President Tofas Group: Temel Atay
VP Human Resources Management: Tamer
Sahinbas
General Manager, Ramerica International (US):
Davut Ökütçü
**CFO and Director HR, Ramerica International
(US):** Gunduz Yalcin
Auditor: Fazli Ayverdi

HQ: Nakkastepe, Azizbey Sok. No: 1, 81207
Kuzguncuk, Istanbul, Turkey
Phone: +90-216-341-46-50
Fax: +90-216-343-19-44
US HQ: Ramerica International, Inc.,
350 Fifth Ave., Ste. 4719, New York, NY 10118
US Phone: 212-971-9100
US Fax: 212-736-4958

Koç operates primarily in Turkey but conducts
international trading through offices in France,
Germany, Italy, the UK, and the US.

	1993 Sales	
	$ mil.	% of total
Turkey	13,842	96
Other countries	564	4
Total	**14,406**	**100**

	1993 Sales		1993 Pretax Income	
	$ mil.	% of total	$ mil.	% of total
Automotive	7,492	52	954	57
Industrial, commercial & energy	5,632	39	666	40
Finance & foreign trade	1,282	9	48	3
Total	**14,406**	**100**	**1,668**	**100**

Automotive
Döktas (41.1%, engine blocks and parts)
Mako (40%, electrical components for vehicles)
Otosan (27.2%, trucks, minibuses, and passenger cars
under Ford license)
Otoyol (40%, commercial vehicles and trucks)
Tofas (34.2%, passenger cars under Fiat license)
Türk Traktör (16.7%, farm tractors and agricultural
equipment)

Industrial, Commercial, and Energy
Arçelik (23.1%, household appliances and room air
conditioners)
Aygaz (31.2%, LPG)
Bekoteknik (20.8%, televisions and audio equipment)
Bozkurt (22.1%, textiles)
Izocam (24.9%, insulation materials)
Tat (34.8%, tomato paste and canned goods)
Türk Demir Döküm (34.6%, radiators, instant water
heaters, and boilers)

Finance and Foreign Trade
Koç Unisys (39.9%, Unisys computers and services)
Koç Yatirim (37.8%, financial management)
Marmaris Altinyunus (31.2%, hotel and restaurant
services)
Ram (17.1%, international trade)
Ramerica (33.3%, international trade)
Sark Sigorta (43.4%, insurance)
Simko (32.5%, Siemens products)

Case Equipment	Mannesmann
Caterpillar	Nokia
Chrysler	Philips
Daimler-Benz	Robert Bosch
Electrolux	Sabanci
Fiat	Turk Petrol
IBM	Volkswagen

	Annual Growth	1984	1985	1986	1987	1988	1989	1990	1991	1992	1993
Sales ($ mil.)	21.5%	—	3,043	3,587	4,911	5,570	6,430	9,430	9,905	11,458	14,406
Net income ($ mil.)	20.8%	—	—	—	—	208	222	360	226	320	536
Income as % of sales	—	—	—	—	—	3.7%	3.5%	3.8%	2.3%	3.0%	3.7%
Employees	4.2%	—	—	31,002	35,530	33,662	37,321	40,429	39,169	39,725	41,437

1993 Year-end:
Debt ratio: 31.8%
Return on equity: —
Cash (mil.): $691
Current ratio: 1.37
Long-term debt (mil.): $162

**Net Income
($ mil.) 1988–93**

KOMATSU LTD.

Komatsu can throw a lot of weight around. The Tokyo-based company is the world's 2nd largest construction equipment maker (after Caterpillar), manufacturing everything from bulldozers to wheel loaders to hydraulic shovels.

Komatsu also makes industrial machinery, such as presses and metal fabricating machines, semiconductor manufacturing equipment, generators, and diesel engines. The company provides services such as construction, civil engineering, and systems integration and makes computer systems and software. The company is partners in a 50/50 joint venture with Dresser Industries in US construction equipment manufacturer Komatsu Dresser.

Hurt by the strength of the yen against other currencies and by a Japanese recession, Komatsu has seen its sales shrink the last few years. In response it is restructuring, consolidating its production lines and reducing costs. Komatsu is also shifting procurement and production to overseas plants.

To get its business moving again, the company is looking for overseas expansion opportunities, particularly in China and Vietnam.

Komatsu traces its roots back to the Takeuchi Mining Company, founded in Japan in 1894. The company experienced major growth during WWI, and in 1917 it created its own in-house ironworks to make machine tools and mining equipment. In 1921 the company separated the ironworks from the mining business to create Komatsu Manufacturing.

The company grew to become one of Japan's major manufacturers of machine tools and pumps, consistently adding new products to its line. In 1924 it introduced its first metal press, and it expanded into agricultural equipment in 1931 when it introduced Japan's first crawler-type farm tractor. In 1935 it began producing high-grade casting and specialty steel materials.

WWII brought more business for Komatsu. The company made anti-artillery shells and bulldozers for the Japanese Navy. When the war ended, Komatsu's first major new product, introduced in 1947, was a bulldozer based on the one it had built for the navy. That same year it began making construction machinery and industrial vehicles as Japan rebuilt its infrastructure. In 1948 it began producing diesel engines.

Komatsu continued to expand during the 1950s. In 1952 it began producing motor graders, and in 1955 it made its first construction equipment exports, supplying motor graders to Argentina. Komatsu products were taken even farther afield in 1956 when the company produced snow vehicles for the Japanese Antarctic Expedition Team.

During the 1960s the company entered into a number of joint ventures with US manufacturers, including Cummins Engine (1961), Bucyrus Erie (1963), and International Harvester (1965). In 1967 Komatsu established its first overseas subsidiary, Komatsu Europe, in Belgium. That same year the company introduced the world's first radio-controlled bulldozer. In 1970 the company changed its name to Komatsu Limited.

The company continued to expand overseas during the 1970s, establishing subsidiaries in the US (Komatsu America), Brazil, and Germany in 1970, Singapore in 1971, and Panama in 1972. In 1976 Komatsu began producing bulldozers in Mexico, and it opened a subsidiary in Australia in 1978.

During the early 1980s Komatsu began a major push into the US, going head-to-head with Caterpillar, adopting the slogan "Maru C," meaning "encircle the cat." Thanks to a strong dollar in relation to the yen, Komatsu was able to undercut Caterpillar's prices by as much as 30%. The company continued to expand its US market share, and in 1986 the company began manufacturing construction equipment at a plant in Chattanooga, Tennessee, its first US factory.

In 1988 Komatsu signed a deal with Dresser Industries, merging the 2 companies' construction equipment manufacturing operations in the US, Canada, and Latin America under the name Komatsu Dresser.

In 1993 Komatsu signed a joint venture with Applied Materials, the world's largest maker of semiconductor manufacturing equipment.

Komatsu entered the PC LAN market in 1994, introducing a print server and 2 types of hubs.

OTC symbol: KMATY (ADR)
Fiscal year ends: March 31

WHO

Chairman: Ryoichi Kawai
President: Tetsuya Katada
Executive Managing Director; General Manager Industrial Machinery: Akihisa Minato
Executive Managing Director; General Manager Construction Equipment: Satoru Anazaki
Executive Managing Director; General Manager Finance and Accounting: Toshiro Nakaya
President, Komatsu Dresser (US): Norimichi Kitagawa
CFO and Controller, Komatsu Dresser (US): Robert J. Benson
VP Human Resources, Komatsu Dresser (US): Gary Aubry
Auditors: Deloitte Touche Tohmatsu

WHERE

HQ: 2-3-6 Akasaka, Minato-ku, Tokyo 107, Japan
Phone: +81-3-5561-2616
Fax: +81-3-3505-9662
US HQ: Komatsu Dresser Company, 200 Tri-State International, PO Box 1422, Lincolnshire, IL 60069-1422
US Phone: 708-831-6700
US Fax: 708-831-7211

	1994 Sales	
	¥ bil.	% of total
Japan	586	69
Other countries	260	31
Total	**846**	**100**

WHAT

	1994 Sales	
	¥ bil.	% of total
Construction equipment	537	64
Civil engineering & construction services	101	12
Electronics	54	6
Industrial machinery	50	6
Other	104	12
Total	**846**	**100**

Construction Equipment
Bulldozers
Cranes
Dump trucks
Hydraulic excavators
Loaders
Mobile debris crushers
Tunnel machinery

Civil Engineering and Construction Services
Contracting
Prefab housing construction
Public works projects

Electronics
Flat-panel display manufacturing equipment

Semiconductor manufacturing equipment

Industrial Machinery
Machine tools
Metal-fabricating machines
Presses
Robots

Other
Client/server systems
Compressors
Diesel engines
Generators
Hydraulic equipment
Iron and steel castings
Software

KEY COMPETITORS

AlliedSignal
Bechtel
Case
Caterpillar
Cooper Industries
Daewoo
Ford
Hino Motors

Hitachi
Hyundai
Isuzu
Kubota
McDermott
Mitsubishi
Mitsui
Navistar

Nikko
Peter Kiewit Sons'
Sakai
Sumitomo
Tenneco
Volvo

HOW MUCH

$=¥112 (Dec. 31, 1993)	Annual Growth	1985	1986	1987	1988	1989	1990	1991	1992	1993	1994
Sales (¥ bil.)	1.0%	796	789	—	—	—	887	989	920	870	846
Net income (¥ bil.)	(25.7%)	15	22	—	—	—	27	31	11	3	2
Income as % of sales	—	1.8%	2.8%	—	—	—	3.1%	3.2%	1.2%	0.3%	0.3%
Earnings per share (¥)	(28.2%)	26	17	16	—	—	27	31	11	3	3
Stock price – high (¥)[1]	—	545	610	561	795	925	1,460	1,380	1,020	790	910
Stock price – low (¥)[1]	—	480	433	450	474	566	892	910	706	532	625
Stock price – close (¥)[1]	5.3%	471	518	495	581	924	1,380	969	727	706	749
P/E – high	—	21	36	35	—	—	55	45	94	263	—
P/E – low	—	16	25	28	—	—	34	30	65	177	—
Dividends per share (¥)	0.0%	—	8.0	8.0	8.0	—	7.8	8.0	8.0	8.0	8.0
Book value per share (¥)	3.1%	—	459	—	432	—	—	—	—	515	504
Employees	2.4%	—	22,951	—	—	21,600	23,800	24,000	26,300	—	28,446

1994 Year-end:
Debt ratio: 50.9%
Return on equity: 0.5%
Cash (bil.): ¥237
Long-term debt (bil.): ¥143
No. of shares (mil.): 1,003
Dividends
  Yield: 1.1%
  Payout: 320.0%
Market value (mil.): $7,295
Sales (mil.): $8,212

**Stock Price History[1]
High/Low 1985–94**

[1] Stock prices are for the prior calendar year.

KOOR INDUSTRIES LTD.

OVERVIEW

"It's the politicians who have reached the agreement, but it will be the business communities on both sides who will have to cement it," says Koor CEO Ben Gaon of the Israel-PLO peace agreement. Gaon hopes to make Koor, Israel's largest industrial company, a major player in the Middle East.

Based in Tel Aviv, Koor is a holding company with interests that include construction, agrochemicals, food, telecommunications, steel, electronics, and international trade. Although bringing Arab and Israeli business interests together may seem like a tall order, Gaon and Koor have produced their share of miracles lately. A half decade of losses pushed the company to the brink of bankruptcy, but Koor has restructured and re-

bounded to become Israel's most profitable company.

To boost Middle East investment, Koor created Salam-2000, a partnership with Spain's Banesto Bank, Omnium Nord Africa (Morocco's largest company), and a group of Palestinian businessmen that plans to invest in the West Bank and Gaza Strip. However, Koor is not limiting its expansion to the Middle East. It hopes to boost exports by 40% by 1997. It is also working to diversify; plans include a chain of hotels, a Biblical amusement park, and a pharmaceutical company.

Israeli banks and Hevrat Haovdim, the business arm of the Histadrut Labour Federation, own 47.8% and 21.9% of the company, respectively.

WHEN

Koor Industries is an offshoot of Solel Boneh, a construction company established in 1924 in British Palestine by the Histadrut Labour Federation. Solel Boneh founded Koor as its manufacturing division in 1944 to provide employment for many of the Jews relocating to the area during and after WWII. Initially Koor made construction materials in Haifa. In 1951 the company took the first of many diversification steps by entering a telecommunications joint venture, Telrad.

An Arab attack on Israel quickly followed the nation's creation in 1948. Israel defeated its attackers, but the threat of future conflicts spurred the development of the country's defense industry. In 1952 Koor teamed with a Finnish firm to create Soltam, an Israeli artillery manufacturer.

Koor continued to expand and diversify through joint ventures, usually with foreign partners, creating a steel company in 1954 and Alliance Tire & Rubber in 1955. Koor and the Israeli government founded Tadiran (defense electronics, 1962), and Koor acquired chemical maker Makhteshim (1963) and food processor Hamashbir Lata (1970). The Sinai campaign (1956), Six-Day War (1967), and Yom Kippur War (1973) created opportunities for Tadiran, Soltam, and Telrad as Israeli defense spending increased. Koor and United Technologies set up a jet engine component venture in 1983.

With primary emphasis on employment, Koor never became very profitable. In 1983 it bought full control of Alliance after

investors threatened to force the liquidation of the unprofitable company. Koor was hurt in the 1980s by a government anti-inflation program that cut subsidies and lowered trade barriers for foreign competitors. Despite the program, inflation outstripped the rate of devaluation of the shekel, further damaging Koor's international cost competitiveness. The company received a temporary boost from Drexel Burnham Lambert junk bond guru Michael Milken, who arranged a $105 million bond issue in 1986.

Koor posted its first loss (excluding tax credits) in 20 years in 1986, and losses widened in 1987. Benjamin Gaon became CEO in 1988 and began restructuring the heavily indebted company. Alliance filed for bankruptcy, leading its former workers to demonstrate against Koor. Bankers Trust filed suit for Koor's liquidation after Koor missed a payment on its debt. Gaon kept closing plants, but the company incurred a loss in 1988 and a record $369 million deficit in 1989. Gaon negotiated a new arrangement with creditors in 1991, which included a restructuring that cut Hevrat Haovdim's holdings from 71% to under 26%.

In 1992 Koor and German partner Faktor Group sold 51% of Israel Edible Products to New Jersey–based CPC International for $40 million. Koor and Faktor will retain a minority interest in the company.

In 1994 Hevrat Haovdim began fielding offers for its remaining shares in Koor Industries.

Principal exchange: Tel Aviv
Fiscal year ends: December 31

Chairman: Eytan Sheshinski
President and CEO: Benjamin D. Gaon
VP Finance: Yehuda Milo
Legal Adviser: Ruth Guri
President and CEO, Tadiran Ltd.: Gurion
Meltzer
**President and CEO, Telrad Telecommunication
& Electronic Industries Ltd.:** Israel Zamir
**President and CEO, Merhav Ceramic & Building
Material Center Ltd.:** Uzi Merom
Manager, Koor 2000 (US): Dov Rochman
Auditors: Kost, Levary and Forer

HQ: 4 Koifman St., P.O. Box 1514, Tel Aviv
61014, Israel
Phone: +972-3-519-5201
Fax: +972-3-519-5353
US HQ: Koor 2000 Inc., 1270 Avenue of the
Americas, Ste. 2307, New York, NY 10020
US Phone: 212-765-5050
US Fax: 212-765-3375

Koor has offices in Australia, China, Germany,
Hong Kong, Israel, Italy, Japan, Mexico, the
Philippines, Singapore, South Africa, Spain,
Thailand, the US, and Vietnam.

	1993 Sales	
	$ mil.	% of total
Israel	1,634	67
North America	353	15
Europe	238	10
Asia & Australia	110	5
South America	68	3
Africa	9	0
Total	**2,412**	**100**

	1993 Sales		1993 Operating Income	
	NIS mil.	% of total	NIS mil.	% of total
Electronics	1,039	43	115	49
Building materials	582	24	77	33
Chemicals	343	14	41	18
Other	448	19	(8)	—
Total	**2,412**	**100**	**225**	**100**

Selected Subsidiaries

Electronics
Tadiran Electrical Appliances Industries Ltd. (85%)
Tadiran Ltd. (59.5%; batteries, military and paramilitary
communications equipment, telecommunications,
command, control, and intelligence systems)
Telrad Telecommunication & Electronic Industries Ltd.

Building Materials
Industries and Investments of Sefen Ltd. (63%,
laminates)
Merhav Ceramic and Building Materials Center Ltd.
(81.5%; ceramic tiles, faucets, and sanitary ware)
Nesher Israel Cement Industries Ltd.
Phoenicia Glass Works Ltd.

Chemicals
Agan Chemical Manufacturers Ltd. (45%; herbicides,
plant growth regulators, synthetic aromatic products)
Makhteshim Chemical Works Ltd. (69.32%; fungicides,
herbicides, insecticides, plant growth regulators)

Other
Gamda Trade Ltd. (supermarkets)
Israel Edible Products Ltd. (24.5%, processed food)
Koortrade (international marketing and trading)
Mega Shoe Industries Ltd.
Soltam Ltd. (mortars and artillery weapon systems)
United Steel Mills Ltd. (83%)

Alcatel Alsthom	BASF	Elron Electronic
AlliedSignal	DuPont	General Electric
American	ECI Telecom	Hoechst
Standard	Elbit	Loral
AT&T	Electrolux	St.-Gobain

	Annual Growth	1984	1985	1986	1987	1988	1989	1990	1991	1992	1993
Sales ($ mil.)	(4.1%)	—	—	—	—	—	2,849	2,692	2,190	2,336	2,412
Net income ($ mil.)	—	—	—	—	(339)	(278)	(369)	(52)	98	143	127
Income as % of sales	—	—	—	—	—	—	—	—	4.5%	6.1%	5.3%
Earnings per share ($)	—	—	—	—	—	—	(105.36)	(15.18)	3.21	11.13	9.48
Stock price – close (NIS)	109.8%	—	—	—	—	—	—	34	64	238	314
Dividends per share (NIS)	—	—	—	—	0.00	0.00	0.00	0.00	0.00	0.00	0.00
Employees	(8.1%)	—	33,700	—	—	—	24,344	18,450	16,000	16,337	17,184

1993 Year-end:
Debt ratio: 60.8%
Return on equity: 66.9%
Cash (mil.): NIS488
Long-term debt (mil.): NIS1,196
No. of shares (mil.): 26
Dividends
  Yield: —
  Payout: —
Market value (mil.): $2,797
Sales (mil.): $826

Net Income ($ mil.)
1987–93

Note: Historical figures are adjusted to December 1991 price levels.

KPMG

OVERVIEW

Once the world's largest accounting firm, Klynveld Peat Marwick Goerdeler (KPMG) is now in 2nd place (after Arthur Andersen). The company's US practice, KPMG Peat Marwick LLP, is the 4th largest accounting firm in the nation, after Arthur Andersen, Ernst & Young, and Deloitte & Touche.

KPMG blamed the drop on currency fluctuations, which lowered the value of its fees overseas, where it does 70% of its business. The firm continues to downsize; between

1990 and 1994 it cut more than 3,500 jobs, including those of more than 200 partners.

However, KPMG is expanding some of its services. In 1994, in an effort to increase its regulatory compliance business, it acquired Smith Banking Consultants, which helps financial institutions meet regulatory requirements such as the Community Reinvestment Act. KPMG also formed an alliance with Toshiba to provide hardware and software for sales force automation applications.

WHEN

KPMG was formed in 1987 when Peat, Marwick, Mitchell, & Copartners joined KMG, an international federation of accounting firms. The combined firms immediately jumped to #1 in worldwide revenues.

Peat Marwick traces its roots back to 1911, when William Peat, who had established a respected accounting practice in London, met James Marwick on a westbound crossing of the Atlantic. Marwick and fellow University of Glasgow alumnus S. Roger Mitchell had formed Marwick, Mitchell & Company in New York in 1897. Peat and Marwick agreed to join their firms, first under an agreement that terminated in 1919, and again in 1925 through a permanent merger to form Peat, Marwick, Mitchell, & Copartners.

In 1947 William Black became senior partner, a position he held until 1965. He guided the firm's 1950 merger with Barrow, Wade, Guthrie, the oldest and most prestigious US firm. He also built up the firm's management consulting practice. Peat Marwick restructured its international practice as PMM&Co. (International) in 1972 and reformed as Peat Marwick International in 1978.

In 1979 a group of European accounting firms led by the Netherlands's top-ranked Klynveld Kraayenhoff and Germany's 2nd-ranked Deutsche Treuhand discussed the formation of an international federation of accounting firms to aid in serving multinational companies. At that time 2 American firms that had been founded around the turn of the century, Main Lafrentz and Hurdman Cranstoun, agreed to merge in order to combat the growing reach of the Big 8. The Europeans needed an American member for their federation to succeed and had encouraged the formation of the new firm, Main

Hurdman & Cranstoun. By the end of 1979, Main Hurdman had joined the Europeans to form Klynveld Main Goerdeler (KMG), named after 2 of the member firms and the chairman of Deutsche Treuhand, Dr. Reinhard Goerdeler. Other members of the federation included C. Jespersen (Denmark), Thorne Riddel (Canada), Thomson McLintok (UK), and Fides Revision (Switzerland). KMG immediately became one of the world's largest accounting firms, muscling into the ranks of the Anglo-American firms.

In 1987 Peat Marwick, then the 2nd largest firm, merged with KMG to form Klynveld Peat Marwick Goerdeler (KPMG). Through the merger KPMG lost 10% of its business owing to the departure of competing companies that had formerly been clients of Peat Marwick or KMG; the firm nevertheless jumped into the #1 position worldwide, exceeding 2nd-ranked Arthur Andersen in total revenues in 1987.

In 1992 KPMG established the first joint accounting venture in China and opened an office in Estonia. In the same year the RTC sued KPMG for $100 million for alleged negligence and breach of contract in auditing Pennsylvania-based Hill Financial Savings Association. In 1993 the firm was named by the US Agency for International Development to head a consortium providing technical assistance to 12 countries of the former Soviet Union, as those countries attempt to privatize their economies.

In 1994 KPMG's Australian affiliate agreed to pay $97 million to settle a suit brought by the Australian state of Victoria. The state claimed that faulty audits were to blame in the collapse of Tricontinental Group, a subsidiary of the State Bank of Victoria.

International partnership
Fiscal year ends: September 30

Chairman: Hans Havermann
US Chairman and CEO: Jon C. Madonna
Administration and Finance Partner, KPMG Peat Marwick LLP: Joseph E. Heintz
General Counsel, KPMG Peat Marwick LLP: Ed Scott
Human Resources Partner, KPMG Peat Marwick LLP: Mary L. Dupont

HQ: KPMG, PO Box 74555, 1070 BC Amsterdam, The Netherlands
Phone: 011-31-20-656-7890
Fax: 011-31-20-656-7000
US HQ: KPMG Peat Marwick LLP, 767 Fifth Ave., New York, NY 10153
US Phone: 212-909-5000
US Fax: 212-909-5299

KPMG has offices in 131 countries. KPMG Peat Marwick LLP has 135 offices in the US.

	1994 Sales % of total
US	32
Other countries	68
Total	**100**

	1994 Sales % of total
Accounting & auditing	55
Management consulting/Tax	45
Total	**100**

Selected Services
Financial services
Health care and life sciences
Information, communications, and entertainment
Manufacturing, retailing, and distribution
Public Services

Representative Clients

Aetna	Nestlé
American Cyanamid	J. C. Penney
Apple Computer	PepsiCo
BMW	Pfizer
British Aerospace	Primerica
Citicorp	Revlon
Daimler-Benz	Saatchi & Saatchi Compton
Dr Pepper/Seven-Up	Siemens
General Mills	Tele-Communications
Gillette	Texaco
Hasbro	Union Carbide
Heineken	USAir
Kemper	Wells Fargo
Motorola	Xerox

Affiliated Firms
Century Audit Corp. (Japan)
KPMG Deutsche Treuhand-Gesellschaft (Germany)
KPMG Klynveld (Netherlands)
KPMG Peat Marwick (Belgium)
KPMG Peat Marwick (UK)
KPMG Peat Marwick (US)
KPMG Peat Marwick Huazhen (China)
KPMG Peat Marwick Thorne (Canada)
KPMG Reviconsult (Russia)

Arthur Andersen	Gemini Consulting
Bain & Co.	H&R Block
Booz, Allen & Hamilton	IBM
Boston Consulting Group	A. T. Kearney
Coopers & Lybrand	Marsh & McLennan
Deloitte & Touche	McKinsey & Co.
Delta Consulting	Perot Systems
Electronic Data Systems	Price Waterhouse
Ernst & Young	

	9-Year Growth	1985	1986	1987	1988	1989	1990	1991	1992	1993	1994
Sales ($ mil.)	17.3%	1,446	1,672	3,250	3,900	4,300	5,368	6,011	6,150	6,000	6,100
Offices	14.1%	335	342	620	637	700	800	820	819	1,100	1,100
Partners	10.4%	2,507	2,726	5,150	5,050	5,300	6,300	6,100	6,004	6,100	6,100
Employees	11.0%	29,864	32,183	60,000	63,700	68,000	77,300	75,000	73,488	76,200	76,200

1994 Year-end:
Sales per partner: $1,000,000

Sales ($ mil.) 1985–94

Note: Figures prior to 1987 are Peat Marwick only; 1987 through 1993 are total figures for postmerger KPMG Peat Marwick.

KUBOTA CORPORATION

OVERVIEW

Whether it's underground, on land, or over-head, Kubota is a leader in Japan. Based in Osaka, the company is Japan's largest maker of farm equipment (with a 40% market share of tractors), its largest maker of ductile iron pipe (for water supply and sewer systems), and Japan's #1 maker of roofing materials.

In addition, Kubota makes engines, construction machinery, industrial castings and machinery, environmental control facilities, and prefab housing. The company also has stakes in several US computer companies, including memory storage makers Maxoptix and Akashic Memories.

With its broad range of products, Kubota has weathered the recession in Japan. Since sales of iron pipe and environmental control systems rely heavily on government spending, the company is taking advantage of a stimulus package installed by the Japanese government to pump up its economy. It also could get help from heavy spending on infra-structure following the Kobe earthquake.

However, the strong yen has hurt Kubota's overseas operations. The company plans to move more of its production overseas to lower its costs and double its overseas procurements.

WHEN

The son of a poor farmer and coppersmith, Gonshiro Oode left home in 1885 at the age of 14 and moved to Osaka to find work. He began as an apprentice at the Kuro Casting Shop and spent several years learning about metal casting. He saved his money and in 1890 he opened Oode Casting.

Oode's new shop grew rapidly, thanks to the industrialization of the Japanese economy and the expansion of its iron and steel industries. One of Oode's customers, Toshiro Kubota, took a liking to the industri-ous young man and in 1897 Kubota adopted him. Oode changed his name to Kubota and changed the name of his company to Kubota Iron Works.

The newly christened Kubota made a number of technological breakthroughs during the early 1900s, including a new method of producing cast iron pipe he created in 1900. His company became the first to de-velop and make the pipe in Japan. It contin-ued to grow as Japan modernized its infrastructure.

In 1917 Kubota added mechanical parts and machinery, making steam engines, ma-chine tools, and agricultural engines. That same year the company began exporting products to other Southeast Asian countries. In 1930 the company restructured and incor-porated. Kubota continued to add product lines, including agricultural and industrial motors. Although WWII brought massive destruction to Japan, peacetime brought plenty of work for Kubota as the country re-built following the war.

The company continued to grow, becom-ing one of the most successful companies in post-war Japan. By 1960 it was Japan's largest maker of farm equipment, ductile iron pipe, and cement roofing materials. That same year Kubota introduced the first small-size agricultural tractor in Japan.

Kubota began expanding overseas during the 1960s and 1970s, creating subsidiaries in Taiwan (1961), the US (1972), Iran (1973), France (1974), and Thailand (1977).

The company made a major push into the US high tech industry during the 1980s. In 1985 it paid $64 million for 44% of super-computer graphics company Ardent. Two years later it bought disk company Akashic Memories for $22.4 million and 20% of mi-croprocessor and workstation maker Mips Computer Systems for $22.5 million (sold to Silicon Graphics in 1992). In 1989 it formed a joint venture with disk drive maker Maxtor to build optical storage products.

While it was loading up on high tech op-erations, Kubota also expanded its more low-tech, core businesses in the US. In 1989 it opened its first US manufacturing plant, in Gainesville, Georgia, to make front-end loader attachments, and in 1990 it bought a 5.4% interest in Cummins Engine.

In 1991 Kubota took over the operations of Stardent Computers, which had struggled since it was formed in a 1989 merger of Ar-dent and Stellar Computer.

However, the company was unable to re-vive its graphic workstation business, and in 1994 Kubota announced plans to withdraw from that market and dissolve its California-based Kubota Graphics subsidiary which had posted losses for 5 straight years.

NYSE symbol: KUB (ADR)
Fiscal year ends: March 31

WHO

Chairman: Shigekazu Mino
VC: Kazutaka Iseki
President: Kouhei Mitsui
EVP: Katsuzo Tomita
Executive Managing Director (Principal Financial and Accounting Officer): Osamu Okamoto
President, Kubota Manufacturing of America: Tetsuro Nomoto
VP and CFO, Kubota Manufacturing of America: Yuki Fujita
Personnel Manager, Kubota Manufacturing of America: Laura Vandiver
Auditors: Deloitte Touche Tohmatsu

WHERE

HQ: 2-47, Shikitsuhigashi 1-chome, Naniwa-ku, Osaka 556, Japan
Phone: +81-6-648-2111
Fax: +81-6-648-3862
US HQ: Kubota Manufacturing of America Corporation, Gainesville Industrial Park North, 2715 Ramsey Rd., Gainesville, GA 30501
US Phone: 404-532-0038
US Fax: 404-532-9057

	1994 Sales	
	$ mil.	% of total
Japan	7,997	84
Other countries	1,513	16
Total	**9,510**	**100**

WHAT

	1994 Sales	
	$ mil.	% of total
Industrial Products & Engineering	4,736	50
Internal Combustion Engine & Machinery	3,330	35
Building Materials & Housing	1,444	15
Total	**9,510**	**100**

Industrial Products and Engineering
Air conditioning equipment
Computers and peripherals
Ductile iron pipe
Electronic components
Filament winding pipe
Industrial castings
Pumps and valves
PVC pipe and fittings
Spiral welded steel pipe
Vending machines
Water and sewage treatment facilities
Weighing and measuring control systems

Internal Combustion Engine and Machinery
Combine harvesters
Engines for agricultural and industrial use
Farm tractors
Power tillers
Reaper binders
Rice transplanters
Small excavators and loaders

Building Materials and Housing
Bathtubs
Cement-based roofing material
Septic tanks
Unit bathrooms

KEY COMPETITORS

AGCO	Ford	Mitsubishi
American Standard	Formosa Plastics	NKK
Case	Hitachi	Premark
Caterpillar	Hyundai	Sintokogio
CKD	Inax	Sumitomo
Daewoo	Iseki & Co.	Takakita
Daimler-Benz	Isuzu	Tenneco
Deere	Komatsu	Volvo
Dresser	Kurimoto	Yanmar

HOW MUCH

Stock prices are for ADRs. 1 ADR=20 shares	9-Year Growth	1985	1986	1987	1988	1989	1990	1991	1992	1993	1994
Sales ($ mil.)	15.7%	2,567	3,918	4,594	5,212	5,408	5,195	6,350	6,849	8,468	9,510
Net income ($ mil.)	3.2%	60	46	89	142	138	48	51	32	50	80
Income as % of sales	—	2.3%	1.2%	1.9%	2.7%	2.6%	0.9%	0.8%	0.5%	0.6%	0.8%
Earnings per share ($)	2.7%	0.89	0.63	1.30	2.06	1.96	0.68	0.73	0.45	0.70	1.13
Stock price – high ($)[1]	—	31.00	38.25	55.00	95.00	155.00	195.00	163.25	120.00	108.50	125.25
Stock price – low ($)[1]	—	25.25	25.00	32.50	49.00	89.00	143.00	91.00	91.88	67.00	102.50
Stock price – close ($)[1]	16.9%	26.50	36.50	44.50	88.00	143.00	178.50	99.75	96.00	90.50	108.00
P/E – high		35	61	42	46	79	—	—	—	155	111
P/E – low		28	40	25	25	45	—	—	—	96	91
Dividends per share ($)	5.1%	0.60	0.70	0.52	0.95	1.62	0.69	0.78	0.73	0.82	0.94
Book value per share ($)	11.7%	15.82	23.51	28.73	34.82	33.32	28.50	32.12	33.78	39.95	42.81
Employees	(1.3%)	18,000	18,000	18,000	—	17,500	15,660	15,490	15,756	15,908	16,046

1994 Year-end:
Debt ratio: 74.1%
Return on equity: 2.7%
Cash (mil.): $655
Current ratio: 1.32
Long-term debt (mil.): $2,715
No. of shares (mil.): 70
Dividends
  Yield: 0.9%
  Payout: 83.2%
Market value (mil.): $7,607

Stock Price History[1]
High/Low 1985–94

[1] Stock prices are for the prior calendar year.

KYOCERA CORPORATION

OVERVIEW

Japan's Kyocera (named after its home city, Kyoto, and main product, ceramics) has cornered the market in the manufacture of semiconductor ceramic packages. In 1993 it held 60–65% of the $1.2 billion worldwide market in these integrated circuit (IC) packages (casings that provide electrical insulation and protect ICs from air, moisture, and physical shock). Despite the fact that the strong yen has hurt sales, Kyocera's leadership position has allowed it to lower production costs through increased volume capacity, undercutting competitors' prices.

Led by its founder and chairman, Kazuo Inamori, who owns 6.3% of the stock, Kyocera focuses on ceramic semiconductor products, which accounted for 24% of 1994 sales. Kyocera's superiority in this area is acknowledged; it played a major role in the design of the packages for Intel's Pentium chip and Motorola's Power PC. In addition the company's other ceramic products are used in everything from engine parts for industrial machinery to dental implants and artificial gemstones.

Faced with slow growth in the IC package business, Kyocera has diversified into communications, passive components, and systems. Kyocera is a leading maker of solar cells and thermal printheads. It also makes office equipment, cordless and cellular telephones, cameras, and camcorders.

WHEN

A rebel from his youth, Kazuo Inamori was born into a poor Japanese family in 1932. At age 23 he joined Shofu Industries, a Kyoto manufacturer of ceramic insulators, quitting 3 years later after an argument with supervisors. He and 7 colleagues then started Kyoto Ceramic in 1959.

Leaving an established company to start a new one was nearly unheard of in Japan, so the 8 men took a blood oath of loyalty to seal their commitment. Their first product was a ceramic insulator for cathode ray tubes. In the late 1960s the company developed the ceramic IC package that has made it a world-class supplier.

The company started manufacturing in the US in 1971 after buying Fairchild Camera & Instrument's failing plant. The company diversified into artificial gemstones (Crescent Vert, 1977) and dental implants (New Medical, 1978). In 1979 Inamori bought control of failing Cybernet Electronics (Japanese citizens-band radio maker), using it to move Kyoto Ceramic into the production of copiers and stereos, and with West Germany's Feldmühle (with whom it had already formed a European partnership) formed Kyocera Feldmühle (US producer of industrial ceramics and cutting tools).

In 1982 the company merged 5 subsidiaries, forming Kyocera Corporation. Another acquisition (Yashica) moved it into the production of cameras and other optical equipment in 1983.

In 1983 Kyocera ran into trouble. At that time NTT was the only legal supplier of telephones in Japan, but Inamori started marketing cordless telephones without the required approval. The government forced Kyocera to recall the telephones. In 1984 when the government abolished NTT's monopoly, Kyocera joined 24 other companies to form Daini-Denden (meaning "2nd phone company"), which later changed its name to DDI. That year Inamori established Inamori Foundation, which awards annual prizes for achievement in advanced technology, basic sciences, and creative arts.

More trouble with the government followed in 1985 when the overanxious Inamori marketed artificial bones without official approval. Kyocera got more bad press in 1986 when a deal to make hard disk drives for Silicon Valley's LaPine Technology fell apart, leaving LaPine out in the cold.

In 1988 Inamori reorganized Kyocera, setting up US, European, and Asian regional offices. Kyocera bought Elco (electronic connectors, US, 1989) and AVX (largest US multilayer ceramic capacitor maker, 1990).

Kyocera worked with Canon in 1992 to develop and produce video and electronic optical equipment. The company also worked with the Carl Zeiss Foundation (Germany) to make cameras and lenses.

In 1994 Kyocera signed a deal with Cirrus Logic for it to provide technology and integrated chips for a cordless phone project. Also that year the company announced that it would introduce a teleconferencing system for use with personal computers connected via a LAN.

NYSE symbol: KYO (ADR)
Fiscal year ends: March 31

Chairman: Kazuo Inamori, age 62
VC: Kinju Anjo, age 60
President: Kensuke Itoh, age 56
Senior Managing Director: Sadao Yamamoto, age 59
**Senior Managing Director; CEO, AVX
Corporation:** Marshall D. Butler, age 67
Managing Director and CFO: Yuji Itoh, age 57
**Managing Director; President, Kyocera
International, Inc.:** Rodney N. Lanthorne
VP Human Resources (US): George Woodworth
Auditors: Coopers & Lybrand

HQ: 5-22, Kitainoue-cho, Higashino,
Yamashina-ku, Kyoto 607, Japan
Phone: +81-75-592-3851
Fax: +81-75-501-6536
US HQ: Kyocera International, Inc.,
8611 Balboa Ave., San Diego, CA 92123-1580
US Phone: 619-576-2600
US Fax: 619-492-1456

Kyocera operates through 82 companies worldwide.

	1994 Sales		1994 Operating Income	
	$ mil.	% of total	$ mil.	% of total
Japan	3,146	58	395	80
US	1,041	19	65	13
Europe	654	12	2	1
Southeast Asia	574	11	31	6
Adjustments	(1,238)	—	—	—
Total	**4,177**	**100**	**493**	**100**

	1994 Sales		1994 Operating Income	
	$ mil.	% of total	$ mil.	% of total
Ceramic products	3,183	76	437	89
Electronic equip.	615	15	33	7
Optical instruments	379	9	23	4
Total	**4,177**	**100**	**493**	**100**

Ceramic Products
Consumer products
Electronic components
Fine ceramic parts
Semiconductor parts

Electronic Equipment
Cordless phones
Karaoke CD equipment
Laser printers
Videoconferencing units

Optical Instruments
Contax, Kyocera, and
Yashica cameras

**Selected Subsidiaries and
Affiliates**
AVX Corporation (US)
AVX/Kyocera (Singapore)
PTE Ltd.
DDI Corporation
Elco Corporation (US)
Kyocera Electronic
Equipment Co., Ltd.
Kyocera Finance Co., Ltd.
Kyocera Fineceramics S.A.
Taito Corporation
Universal Optical Industries,
Ltd. (Hong Kong)

ACX Technologies	Hitachi	Polaroid
Alcoa	IBM	Ricoh
AMP	Matsushita	St.-Gobain
AST	Minolta	Samsung
AT&T	Mitsubishi	Sanyo
Canon	Motorola	Seagate
Ceradyne	NEC	Seiko
Compaq	NGK Spark Plug	Sharp
Compression Labs	Nokia	Shure Brothers
Conner Peripherals	North American	Sony
DEC	Advanced Materials	Sumitomo
Dell	NTT	Thomson SA
Eastman Kodak	Oki	Toshiba
Ferro	Philips	Xerox
Fuji Photo	Pioneer	
Hewlett-Packard	Pitney Bowes	

Stock prices are for ADRs. ADR = 2 shares	Annual Growth	1985	1986	1987	1988	1989	1990	1991	1992	1993	1994
Sales ($ mil.)	13.8%	1,300	1,666	1,894	2,416	2,554	2,661	3,280	3,416	3,758	4,177
Net income ($ mil.)	10.0%	152	110	120	182	224	214	229	204	209	359
Income as % of sales	—	11.7%	6.6%	6.3%	7.5%	8.8%	8.0%	7.0%	6.0%	5.5%	8.6%
Earnings per share ($)	8.0%	1.92	1.39	1.56	2.16	2.62	2.31	2.44	2.18	2.23	3.84
Stock price – high ($)[1]	—	64.18	53.25	55.39	93.90	91.04	92.71	126.00	103.00	74.50	122.88
Stock price – low ($)[1]	—	42.67	27.10	37.68	45.64	67.87	66.80	74.00	60.00	51.00	64.50
Stock price – close ($)[1]	7.9%	53.01	43.74	48.02	80.59	79.40	75.00	84.75	63.50	70.13	105.50
P/E – high	—	33	38	36	44	35	40	52	47	33	32
P/E – low	—	22	20	24	21	26	29	30	28	23	17
Dividends per share ($)	11.2%	0.30	0.33	0.36	0.51	0.55	0.50	0.53	0.64	0.78	0.78
Book value per share ($)	16.3%	14.52	22.11	26.11	31.46	32.19	32.08	38.29	41.27	47.96	56.60
Employees	(3.5%)	—	—	17,300	12,397	—	—	14,031	14,473	10,682	13,470

1994 Year-end:
Debt ratio: 22.9%
Return on equity: 7.4%
Cash (mil.): $1,243
Current ratio: 4.19
Long-term debt (mil.): $461
No. of shares (mil.): 93
Dividends
  Yield: 0.7%
  Payout: 20.3%
Market value (mil.): $9,823

Stock Price History[1]
High/Low 1985–94

[1] Stock prices are for the prior calendar year.

LADBROKE GROUP PLC

UK betting concern Ladbroke took a gamble a few years ago when it purchased the exclusive rights to the Hilton Hotel name outside the US. The gamble is beginning to pay off; Ladbroke's Hilton International division, which operates 159 hotels in 47 countries, now accounts for over 20% of group revenues and nearly half of group profits.

Ladbroke Racing is the largest commercial off-track betting company in the world, with over 2,000 racing shops in the UK and Ireland. The company also operates betting shops in Argentina, Belgium, and the US. Its Vernon Pools subsidiary holds about 20% of the UK football pools market (a betting system based on professional soccer results).

Ladbroke sold home improvement retail chain Texas Homecare to J Sainsbury in 1995. The chain, the #2 retailer in the UK do-it-yourself market with 238 stores, had become less profitable and was struggling with low margins and fierce competition. Ladbroke's other business line, property, has been a drag on the company's momentum, barely moving into the black in 1993 after 2 years of losses. It owns commercial property in the UK and in the eastern US.

To reduce the company's long-term debt of around $1.7 billion, Ladbroke has been selling some of its real-estate assets. In 1994 Ladbroke sold $150 million of commercial property to Burford Holdings.

The Ladbroke Group has its origins in the late 1800s in the village of Ladbroke in central England, where a local racehorse trainer and his friend set up a partnership as commission agents to take bets on horse races. Although betting was illegal, it was allowed on an unofficial basis, and by 1900 the partnership had established itself in London's plush West End.

Ladbroke and Co. was sold to a business group, Beaver Holdings, in 1956. Cyril Stein, who later took charge of the company for over 3 decades, joined the consortium in 1956, and was soon appointed as managing director. He became chairman in 1966.

Due to the illegal nature of its business, the group kept a fairly low profile until the legalization of off-track betting gave the company impetus to expand. By the time Ladbroke Group went public in 1967 in an offering on the London Stock Exchange, it had 109 off-track betting shops in operation. By 1971 there were 660 licensed "Ladbrokes" betting shops around Britain.

Stein steered the company on a diversification course in the 1970s and 1980s. In 1972 Ladbroke acquired the London & Leeds Development Corporation, a real estate company with office projects in Amsterdam, Brussels, Paris, and the eastern US. It also established 4 real estate companies in the UK.

In 1973 Ladbroke ventured into the hotel business with the purchase of 3 British hotels, which formed the basis for a successful UK hotel chain. In the late 1970s the company suffered a major setback when its casino

ventures in London were closed down. Found guilty, in a highly publicized case, of violating government gaming laws, the firm abandoned the casino business in 1979.

In 1984 the company expanded its betting operations in Europe with the purchase of the Belgian Le Tiercé betting shop chain and a Dutch chain in 1986. In 1985 Ladbroke broke into the US market with the acquisition of the Detroit Race Course.

Ladbroke expanded into the UK do-it-yourself retail market in 1986 with the purchase of the Home Charm Group, operators of the Texas Homecare chain.

In a surprise move Ladbroke beat out competitors to purchase the 91-hotel Hilton International chain from Allegis Corporation for over $1 billion in 1987. The purchase of this prestigious chain made Ladbroke one of the top hotel operators in the world and gave it a presence in 44 countries. By 1993 Hilton International had 159 hotels in operation.

In 1989 the company expanded its gaming operations with the purchase of the Vernons football (soccer) pools concern, one of only 2 such operators in the UK market.

While Ladbroke's property and retail division suffered in the 1990s, the company's hotel chain expanded, opening 10 new hotels in 1992 and 7 more in 1993.

Ladbroke reentered the casino business in 1994, paying $75 million for 3 London casinos. Stein retired as chairman in 1994 after 37 years with the company. VC John Jackson was appointed to replace him.

OTC symbol: LADGY (ADR)
Fiscal year ends: December 31

Chairman: John B. H. Jackson, age 64
VC and Group CEO: Peter M. George, age 50
Group Finance Director: Brian Wallace
CEO, Hilton International (US): Tommaso
  Zanzotto, age 52
CFO, Hilton International (US): Alan Cornish
**Director Human Resources, Hilton
  International (US):** Dorie Finnegan
Auditors: Ernst & Young

HQ: 10 Cavendish Place, London W1M 9DJ, UK
Phone: +44-(01)71-323-5000
Fax: +44-(01)71-436-1300
US HQ: Hilton International Co.,
  One Wall Street Ct., New York, NY 10005
US Phone: 212-820-1700
US Fax: 212-809-7595

Ladbroke operates businesses worldwide.

	1993 Sales		1993 Operating Profit	
	£ mil.	% of total	£ mil.	% of total
UK	2,751	65	144	61
The Americas	682	16	22	9
Asia & Australasia	107	2	21	9
Other Europe	653	15	36	15
Other countries	76	2	14	6
Adjustments	—	—	(120)	—
Total	**4,269**	**100**	**118**	**100**

	1993 Sales		1993 Operating Profit	
	£ mil.	% of total	£ mil.	% of total
Betting & gaming	2,539	59	86	34
Hotels	894	21	118	47
Retail	692	16	8	3
Property	144	4	41	16
Adjustments	—	—	(135)	—
Total	**4,269**	**100**	**118**	**100**

Major Subsidiaries and Affiliates
Gable House Estates Ltd. (property)
Hampden Group PLC (29.86%, retail, Northern Ireland)
Hilton International Co. (hotels, US)
Hilton International Hotels (UK) Ltd.
Ladbroke & Co., Ltd. (betting)
Ladbroke City & County Land Co. Ltd. (property)
Ladbroke (Gibraltar) Ltd. (betting)
Ladbroke Group Finance (Jersey) Ltd.
Ladbroke Group Finance PLC
Ladbroke Group Properties Ltd.
Ladbroke Racing Corp. (US)
Satellite Information Services (Holdings) Ltd. (17.76%, TV racing coverage)
Tiercé Ladbroke SA (betting, Belgium)
Town and County Factors Ltd.
Vernon Pools Ltd. (betting)

Accor
Autotote
Bally Entertainment
Bass
Boots
Carlson
Forte
Four Seasons
Hilton
Hollywood Park
Hyatt
ITT
Littlewoods
Loews
Marriott Intl.
National Lottery
Penn National Gaming
Rank
Ritz-Carlton
Santa Anita Realty
W. H. Smith

£ = $1.48 (Dec. 31, 1993)	Annual Growth	1984	1985	1986	1987	1988	1989	1990	1991	1992	1993
Sales (£ mil.)	16.1%	1,116	1,343	1,766	2,135	2,848	3,660	3,801	3,786	4,167	4,269
Net income (£ mil.)	(1.2%)	29	43	84	140	196	208	206	154	1	26
Income as % of sales	—	2.6%	3.2%	4.8%	6.6%	6.9%	5.7%	5.4%	16.1%	0.0%	0.6%
Earnings per share (p)	(24.2%)	—	21.2	25.0	—	—	—	—	16.1	11.5	2.3
Stock price – high (p)	—	266	332	389	471	465	352	347	293	267	223
Stock price – low (p)	—	182	242	312	275	322	212	230	188	126	142
Stock price – close (p)	(3.9%)	262	319	334	322	434	341	248	232	183	183
P/E – high	—	—	16	16	—	—	—	—	18	23	96
P/E – low	—	—	11	12	—	—	—	—	12	11	61
Dividends per share (p)	(15.7%)	—	—	—	—	—	—	—	11.2	11.2	6.0
Book value per share (p)	(6.7%)	—	268	259	—	—	—	288	264	231	190
Employees	0.0%	—	—	—	—	—	—	—	78,000	77,000	78,000

1993 Year-end:
Debt ratio: 39.1%
Return on equity: 1.1%
Cash (mil.): £113
Long-term debt (mil.): £1,167
No. of shares (mil.): 1,141
Dividends
  Yield: 3.3%
  Payout: 258.6%
Market value (mil.): $3,081
Sales: (mil.) $6,318

Stock Price History
High/Low 1984–93

LAGARDÈRE GROUPE

Missiles (Matra) and magazines (Hachette) are only 2 of the ingredients of the heady Gallic cocktail of diversified businesses served up by Jean-Luc Lagardère. His other concerns range from automobile and transit systems to telecommunications, film broadcasting, banking, book publishing, and the space industry. Lagardère is both CEO of Matra Hachette and principal shareholder (5%) and managing partner of the Lagardère Groupe, a French limited partnership.

Lagardère tied the disparate companies together within the holding company that bears his name when it gained control of its primary operating company, Matra Hachette, in 1994. Matra Hachette, the combined

defense and magazine conglomerate that represents 90% of Lagardère's assets, was brought into the group fold via a stock swap approved by Matra Hachette shareholders that boosted the Lagardère Groupe's capital holdings from 37.6% to 93.4%.

Despite defense budget cuts, the Matra defense subsidiary (which makes air-to-air missiles and command systems) accounted for 10% of total sales in 1993. Matra also makes cars in collaboration with Renault.

On the communications front the Lagardère Groupe has made it a strategic priority to expand its services across print, CD-ROM, on-line, traditional TV, and interactive TV.

The Lagardère Groupe's flagship publishing business, Hachette, traces its origins back to 1826, when schoolteacher Louis Hachette bought a small book publishing and selling business in Paris. He published his first periodical, a journal for teachers, in 1827 and began buying rights to primary school texts in 1831. Business took off when France enacted a law in 1833 calling for free primary schooling. Librairie Hachette received an enormous order from the Ministry of Public Education, including orders for 500,000 alphabet primers.

An 1851 visit to W.H. Smith in London convinced Hachette that rail passengers would buy books from stores in stations. The next year he began signing contracts with French railroads and soon had a virtual monopoly on bookselling in French train stations. In 1853 Hachette started the Bibliothèque de Chemins de Fer (Railway Library) series of books and travel guides. In 1862 Emile Zola began a 4-year stint in press relations with Hachette.

Louis Hachette died in 1864. Around the turn of the century, Hachette bought France's leading newspaper distributors, and it acquired major French printing and binding companies in 1920. Hachette launched *Elle* in 1945, and the company acquired control of French publishers Grasset, Fayard, and Stock in the 1950s. In the 1970s Hachette diversified, with poor results.

Matra was founded in 1945 as a defense industry contractor and made aircraft armaments and missiles. Jean-Luc Lagardère took

over as Matra's director general in 1963 at the age of 35 and steered the company on a path of rapid diversification and growth. In the 1960s Matra entered the space systems market (satellites and space launchers) and also produced a series of Le Mans winning cars. In the 1970s Matra branched further into the civilian sector, developing transit systems and telecommunications products.

Lagardère gained control of Hachette in 1980 and launched international spinoffs of its magazines, including a successful US *Elle* (1985; by 1992 there were 19 international *Elles*) in partnership with Rupert Murdoch.

In the late 1980s Hachette bought an interest in the #2 French radio station, Europe 1; helped start another, Europe 2; purchased the 2nd largest magazine distributor in the US, Curtis Circulation; and bought Spanish encyclopedia publisher Salvat. In 1988 alone Hachette spent over $1.1 billion on Grolier (encyclopedias) and Diamandis Communications and bought out Murdoch's share of *Elle*. The company launched *Elle Décor* in the US in 1989 and purchased 25% of a money-losing French TV network, La Cinq, in 1990.

The La Cinq purchase was a disaster. The station collapsed a year later, causing Hachette to write off $643 million. To cover the huge debt, Lagardère merged Matra with Hachette in 1993; in 1994 the Lagardère Groupe took control of Matra Hachette.

The company acquired a London database specialist and an Austrian radio station in 1994 and increased its stake in Europe 1 Communication to 43.3%.

Principal exchange: Paris
Fiscal year ends: December 31

Chairman: Raymond H. Levy
**General Partner and Managing Partner;
Chairman and CEO, Matra Hachette:** Jean-Luc Lagardère
**Chairman of Group Finance Committee;
President, Matra Hachette:** Philippe Camus
**Special Advisor to the Chairman and EVP
Emerging Businesses:** Arnaud Lagardère
**President and CEO, Hachette Filipacchi
Magazines, Inc. (US):** David J. Pecker
**General Counsel and Secretary; Chairman,
Lagardère Sociétés:** Pierre Leroy
**Spokesman of the Managing Partner and EVP
Communications and Human Resources:**
Thierry Funck-Brentano
Auditors: Barbier Frinault et Autres (Arthur
Andersen & Co.)

HQ: 4, rue de Presbourg, 75116 Paris, France
Phone: +33-1-40-69-16-00
Fax: +33-1-47-23-01-92
US HQ: Hachette Filipacchi Magazines, Inc.,
1633 Broadway, New York, NY 10019
US Phone: 212-767-6000
US Fax: 212-767-5600

The Lagardère Groupe operates worldwide.

	1993 Sales	
	FF mil.	% of total
France	27,386	51
Other countries	26,595	49
Total	**53,981**	**100**

	1993 Sales	
	FF mil.	% of total
Distribution services	12,624	23
Print media	8,208	15
Telecommunications	7,476	14
Book publishing	6,258	12
Defense	5,510	10
Automobile	5,286	10
Space	5,123	9
Broadcast, film & display	2,406	4
Transit systems	1,020	3
Other	70	0
Total	**53,981**	**100**

Operating Companies
Hachette Distribution Services
Hachette Filipacchi Presse (66%, print media)
Matra Communication (69%), Matra Datavision (58%)
(telecommunications and CAD-CAM)
Hachette Livre (book publishing)
Matra Défense, Matra Cap Systèmes (50%)(defense)
Matra Automobile (in collaboration with Renault)
Matra Marconi Space (51%)
Europe 1 Communication (54%, broadcast, film, display)
Matra Transport (transit systems)

Others
Banque Arjil (investment bank)
Matra Hachette Multimedia (on-line and other media)
Matra Sécurité (access control systems)
Sicli (security systems)
Symah (TV image substitution system)

Advance	Capital Cities/ABC	News Corp.
Publications	Chrysler	Northrop
Alcatel Alsthom	Hearst	Grumman
Bertlesmann	Lockheed	Siemens
Bombardier	Martin	Thyssen
British Aerospace	New York	Time Warner
Canal+	Times	Viacom

$= 5.91 FF (Dec. 31, 1993)	Annual Growth	1984	1985	1986	1987	1988	1989	1990	1991	1992	1993
Sales (FF mil.)	—	—	—	—	—	—	36	19	53,112	55,102	53,981
Net income (FF mil.)	—	—	—	—	—	—	0	0	(448)	96	155
Income as % of sales	—	—	—	—	—	—	0.6%	2.0%	—	0.2%	0.3%
Earnings per share (FF)	—	—	—	—	—	—	0	0	(33)	3	5
Stock price – high (FF)	—	—	—	—	—	—	—	—	—	101	152
Stock price – low (FF)	—	—	—	—	—	—	—	—	—	67	84
Stock price – close (FF)	(7.8%)	—	—	—	—	—	206	78	71	83	149
P/E – high	—	—	—	—	—	—	—	—	—	30	32
P/E – low	—	—	—	—	—	—	—	—	—	20	18
Dividends per share (FF)	(1.9%)	—	—	—	—	—	2.7	3.0	1.5	2.2	2.5
Book value per share (FF)	15.9%	—	—	—	—	—	—	—	—	69	80
Employees	14.3%	12,400	12,500	14,200	16,200	24,640	30,550	31,210	28,460	44,394	41,394

1993 Year-end:
Debt ratio: 86.3%
Return on equity: 6.3%
Cash (mil.): FF13,726
Long-term debt (mil.): FF11,905
No. of shares (mil.): 33
Dividends
  Yield: 1.7%
  Payout: 53.3%
Market value (mil.): $832
Sales (mil.): $9,134

**Stock Price History
High/Low 1992–93**

(chart axis values: 160, 140, 120, 100, 80, 60, 40, 20, 0)

LG GROUP

OVERVIEW

Korea's 3rd largest *chaebol* (industrial group), after Samsung and Hyundai, LG Group (which changed its name from Lucky-Goldstar in 1995) consists of dozens of companies affiliated by cross-ownership. The group is involved principally in chemicals (Lucky, Ltd., the group's flagship and Korea's largest chemical company), electronics (Goldstar, one of the largest consumer electronics companies in Korea), financial services (Lucky Securities), and trading (Lucky-Goldstar International).

Lucky has moved into new business lines, including natural food seasonings, and is developing products for high-tech areas such as

genetic engineering. Goldstar continues to move into high-tech electronic goods, including high-definition television (HDTV) and thin-film transistor liquid crystal displays (LCDs) for laptop computers.

The group is looking to many of its Asian neighbors for growth opportunities, particularly China, where it has committed to invest $1 billion in areas such as electronics, chemicals, and communications.

With an order from the South Korean government for the country's *chaebol* to focus their operations, LG Group is streamlining by merging or selling off some of its subsidiaries.

WHEN

During WWII Koo In-Hwoi made tooth powder for Koreans to use in place of salt, then the common toothbrushing substance. Koo founded the Lucky Chemical Company in 1947 to make facial creams and, later, detergent, shampoo, and Lucky Toothpaste. The company soon became Korea's only plastics maker. Koo established a trading company in 1953.

Emulating Japanese exporters, Koo formed Goldstar Company in 1958 to make electric appliances. Goldstar initially made fans but later became the first company in Korea to make radios (1959), refrigerators (1965), televisions (1966), elevators and escalators (1968), and washing machines and air conditioners (1969). In 1967 Lucky collaborated with Caltex to build the Honam Oil Refinery, the first privately owned refinery in Korea. Both Lucky and Goldstar benefited from the *chaebol*'s cozy relationship with the government throughout the rule of Park Chung Hee (1962–79).

Koo died in 1969 and his eldest son, Koo Cha-Kyung, took control of the *chaebol* in 1970. Lucky Chemical changed its name to Lucky, Ltd., in 1974, began petrochemical production in 1977, entered a biotech venture with Chiron (US) in 1984, and built the world's largest single-unit petrochemical plant in Saudi Arabia in 1986.

In the 1970s and 1980s, Goldstar expanded rapidly as it established new electronics companies. Goldstar took advantage of cheap Korean labor to export private-label electronics items to customers, including J. C. Penney and Sears. In the late 1970s

Goldstar began investing heavily in semiconductor production in an effort to fulfill its own requirements for chips and to thrust itself into the high-tech world. To head off protectionism Goldstar set up a television factory in Huntsville, Alabama, in 1982. Goldstar companies entered several ventures with more technically advanced partners, including AT&T, NEC, Hitachi, and Siemens, and set out to capture office automation and higher-end consumer electronics markets with Goldstar brand goods.

Although revenue from electronic products grew rapidly, archrival Samsung sprinted past Goldstar in sales and profit (1984), as duplication of effort among group units and an inefficient organizational structure slowed progress. Goldstar reorganized in 1987. In the late 1980s the company suffered from rising wage rates, Korean currency appreciation, and severe labor unrest, but sales rebounded in 1990. Goldstar bought 5% of Zenith (US) in 1991. The deal included limited rights to Zenith's flat-screen and HDTV technology.

In 1992 Goldstar merged with sister Goldstar Electronic Devices, which manufactures parts for Goldstar's products. That same year, in an effort to increase overseas competitiveness and cut R&D costs, Goldstar and Samsung signed a patent-sharing agreement. Goldstar Cable signed a joint venture with Vietnam in 1993 to make fiber optic cable.

In 1994 Lucky Goldstar Trading signed an agreement with the local Saha government in Russia to develop the Elga, the world's largest coal field.

Principal exchange: Korea
Fiscal year ends: December 31

Group Chairman: Koo Cha-Kyung
President and CEO, Lucky, Ltd.: Sung Jae Kap
VC and CEO, Goldstar Co., Ltd.: Lee Hun Jo,
    age 62
President and CEO, Lucky-Goldstar
    International Corporation: Park Su-Whan
Senior Managing Director Finance and
    Accounting, Lucky, Ltd.: Yeo Seong-Koo
President, Goldstar USA: Woo Nam
Finance Manager, Goldstar USA: S. Huh
Auditors: Samil Accounting Corporation
    (Coopers & Lybrand)

WHERE

HQ: Lucky-Goldstar Twin Towers,
    20 Yoido-dong, Yongdungpo-gu, Seoul 150,
    South Korea
Phone: +82-2-787-5114
Fax: +82-2-787-7684
US HQ: LG Group, 1000 Sylvan Ave., Englewood
    Cliffs, NJ 07632
US Phone: 201-816-2000
US Fax: 201-816-0636

Lucky-Goldstar Group's companies operate in
more than 120 countries.

	Lucky, Ltd. 1993 Sales
	% of total
South Korea	72
Other countries	28
Total	**100**

WHAT

	Lucky, Ltd. 1993 Sales
	% of total
Precision chemicals	33
Industrial materials	32
Synthetic resins	32
Other	3
Total	**100**

Selected Member Companies

Goldstar Cable Co., Ltd.	Goldstar-Alps Electronics
Goldstar Co., Ltd.	Co., Ltd. (electronic
(consumer electronics)	components)
Goldstar Electric	Honam Oil Refinery Co., Ltd.
Machinery Co., Ltd.	(joint venture with Caltex)
Goldstar Electron Co.,	Kukje Electric Wire Co. Ltd.
Ltd. (semiconductors)	Lucky Development Co., Ltd.
Goldstar Information &	Lucky Engineering Co., Ltd.
Communications, Ltd.	Lucky, Ltd. (chemicals)
Goldstar Instrument &	Lucky Petrochemical Co.,
Electric Co., Ltd.	Ltd.
(industrial electric	Lucky Securities Co., Ltd.
equipment)	Lucky-Goldstar International
Goldstar Precision Co.,	Corp.
Ltd.	Lucky-Goldstar Trading
Goldstar Software, Ltd.	Sung Yo Co., Ltd. (consumer
Goldstar Telecommu-	electronics)
nication Co., Ltd.	

KEY COMPETITORS

Akzo Nobel	Hitachi	Motorola
BASF	Hoechst	Philips
Bayer	Hyundai	Samsung
Ciba-Geigy	IBM	Sharp
Daewoo	Intel	Sony
Dow Chemical	ITOCHU	Sumitomo
DuPont	Marubeni	Texas
Formosa Plastics	Matsushita	Instruments
General Electric	Mitsubishi	Toshiba
Hewlett-Packard	Mitsui	Union Carbide

HOW MUCH

$=Won808 (Dec. 31, 1993)	Annual Growth	1984	1985	1986	1987	1988	1989	1990	1991	1992	1993
Sales (Won bil.)	18.2%	—	602	723	928	1,210	1,285	1,585	1,838	2,096	2,281
Net income (Won bil.)	18.9%	—	11	16	29	64	64	62	44	31	45
Income as % of sales	—	—	1.8%	2.2%	3.1%	5.3%	5.0%	3.9%	2.4%	1.5%	2.0%
Earnings per share (Won)	(14.2%)	—	—	—	—	—	—	941	724	465	595
Stock price – high (Won)	—	—	—	—	14,179	22,103	26,765	27,353	27,353	19,500	17,000
Stock price – low (Won)	—	—	—	—	10,735	13,369	20,677	20,677	14,200	9,600	11,600
Stock price – close (Won)	3.1%	—	—	—	12,964	22,014	26,765	26,765	15,000	13,700	15,600
P/E – high	—	—	—	—	—	—	—	29	29	42	29
P/E – low	—	—	—	—	—	—	—	22	20	21	19
Dividends per share (Won)	(5.6%)	—	—	—	—	534	669	735	735	300	400
Book value per share (Won)	(2.7%)	—	—	—	—	—	—	13,723	13,294	12,799	12,626
Employees	6.0%	—	—	—	8,684	9,545	9,985	10,208	18,000	—	12,326

1993 Year-end:
Debt ratio: 63.3%
Return on equity: 4.7%
Cash (bil.): Won103
L-T debt (bil.): Won770
No. of shares (mil.): 67
Dividends
    Yield: 2.6%
    Payout: 67.2%
Market value (mil.): $1,294
Sales (mil.): $2,823

Stock Price History
High/Low 1987–93

30,000
25,000
20,000
15,000
10,000
5,000
0

Information presented for Lucky, Ltd., only

LLOYD'S OF LONDON

OVERVIEW

After 305 years Lloyd's of London has had to abandon some of its swashbuckling freedom and adopt the cautious, corporate discipline its members have traditionally scorned.

Since 1987 Lloyd's has been hit by an unprecedented string of disasters. In addition to claims on more natural disasters than had struck in a century, Lloyd's has been pummeled by US court decisions that made insurers liable for the unforeseen costs of cleaning up environmental contamination that happened decades ago.

These costs, along with antiquated (and some plain shady) business practices among many of the independent syndicates that write insurance under Lloyd's aegis, ruined many investors (known as Names) because of the custom of Names assuming unlimited personal liability in the case of a loss.

In 1993, with billions in claims and many Names refusing to pay or suing their syndicates for not informing them of risk, Lloyd's Corporation, which provides the trading venue, imposed new underwriting and reporting rules. It also assumed control of most syndicates' back-office functions, began setting up a reinsurance depositary for disposing of pre-1986 claims still pending, and, most radically of all, sought recapitalization by allowing corporate members.

WHEN

In 1688 Edward Lloyd opened Lloyd's Coffee House in London. Lloyd's provided maritime insurance brokers and underwriters with a place to meet and make deals. Underwriters did not assume risks jointly; rather, each was liable for only his own portion of the deal, but that personal liability was unlimited.

Lloyd's reputation for accurate shipping news made it the hub of London's maritime insurance industry. It began publishing *Lloyd's List*, a shipping newspaper, in 1734.

Lloyd's attracted people who used insurance as a cover for gambling. In one instance customers "insured" the gender of the Chevalier d'Eon, a transvestite, beginning Lloyd's tradition of writing wildly nonstandard insurance. Serious insurers persuaded a Lloyd's waiter to open the New Lloyd's Coffee House nearby in 1769. By 1774 the brokers and underwriters moved to the Royal Exchange.

In the 1800s Lloyd's began regulating its membership. Parliament passed the Lloyd's Act in 1871 to establish Lloyd's Corporation to oversee the activities of the underwriting syndicates. In the 1880s Lloyd's branched into nonmarine insurance. By 1900, Lloyd's wrote 50% of the world's nonlife insurance.

Prompt settlement of claims arising from the 1906 San Francisco earthquake boosted Lloyd's image in the US. Names (who provided the cash for claims) profited from war risk insurance in WWI. After the war Lloyd's entered automobile, credit, and aviation insurance. Hurricane Betsy, which hit the US Gulf Coast in 1965, inflicted severe losses on Lloyd's underwriters and reduced their insurance capacity.

In 1981 and 1982 a syndicate managed by Richard Outhwaite wrote contracts on the future liabilities of old insurance contracts with claims (many with asbestos exposure) still pending, in exchange for premium income. Questions were raised concerning Lloyd's disclosure requirements. Legal action ended in an out-of-court settlement.

But worse was to come. Investment at Lloyd's had traditionally attracted only the economic upper strata of British society, people who could afford to pay off in case of a claim. In the 1980s, however, Lloyd's attracted the newly well-off — highly paid people without great wealth — and allowed them to pledge property or other assets against claims reserves. Many of these assets were appraised at inflated values in the boom of the 1980s. In addition, Lloyd's exercised little oversight in continuing to allow the practice of insurance spiraling — permitting syndicates to close their books on pending claims by reinsuring them again and again. The 1980s were also a period of increased competition, which held down premiums.

The boom burst and threatened Lloyd's itself with ruin as Names, whose property was often reduced in value, revolted against the prospect of spending the rest of their lives working to pay Lloyd's. In 1992 new managers began a series of reforms aimed at standardizing reporting practices, limiting investor liability, and recapitalization.

Between 1991 and 1994 the number of syndicates decreased by half, premium rates increased as competition slowed, and interest by new corporate investors was high.

Insurance society
Fiscal year ends: December 31

Chairman: David Rowland, £450,000 pay
CEO: Sir Peter Middleton, £389,000 pay
Chairman, Regulatory Board: Sir Alan Hardcastle
Finance Director: Stephen Hall
Director Marketing and Public Affairs:
  Peter Lane
Managing Director, Central Services Unit: Joe
  Bradley
**Director Human Resources and Support
  Services:** Geoff Morgan
Director Systems and Operations: Andy Coppell
President, Lloyd's of London Press (US):
  Donald R. Wall
Auditors: Ernst & Young

HQ: One Lime St., London EC3M 7HA, UK
Phone: +44-(0)71-623-7100
Fax: +44-(0)71-626-2389
US HQ: Lloyd's of London Press, Inc., 611
  Broadway, Ste. 308, New York, NY 10012
US Phone: 212-529-9500
US Fax: 212-529-9826

	1993 Society Resources	
	£ mil.	% of total
Members' open year balances	19,650	72
Members' means	6,467	24
Central fund assets	904	3
Corporation of Lloyd's assets	252	1
High-level stop-loss fund assets	31	0
Total	**27, 304**	**100**

	1991[1] Premiums			
	Sales		Operating Income	
	£ mil.	% of total	£ mil.	% of total
Nonmarine ins.	3,393	56	(62)	—
Marine insurance	1,436	24	(452)	—
Motor	753	13	6	—
Aviation	432	7	(107)	—
Total	**6,014**	**100**	**(615)**	**—**

Affiliates
Lloyd's Corporation
  Additional Securities Ltd. (overseas insurance
    reserves)
  CentreWrite Ltd. (insurance)
  Lioncover Insurance Co. Ltd.
  Lloyd's of London Press Ltd.
  Lloyd's of London Press (Far East) Ltd. (Hong Kong)
  Lloyd's of London Press (Germany) GmbH
  Lloyd's of London Press, Inc. (publications, US)
  Lloyd's Maritime Information Services, Ltd. (50%,
    operation of information services)
  Sharedealer Ltd. (asset management)
  Syndicate Underwriting Management Ltd. (manager of
    Lioncover Insurance)

AIG
Allianz
Assurances Générales de France
AXA
Chubb
CIGNA
Colonia Konzern
Commerce Clearing House
Compagnie Financière et de Reassurance
Dun & Bradstreet
General Re
Hannover Re/Eisen und Stahl Re-Group
ITT
McGraw-Hill
Prudential
Reuters
Tokio Marine and Fire
Travelers
Union des Assurances de Paris
USF&G
Virgin Group

£=$1.48 (Dec. 31, 1993)	Annual Growth	1984	1985	1986	1987	1988	1989	1990	1991	1992	1993
Society Resources (£ mil.)[2]	11.1%	—	—	—	—	16,150	18,997	17,916	20,261	24,439	27,304
Net income(£ mil.)[1]	—	—	196	649	509	(510)	(2,063)	(2,319)	(2,047)	—	—
Income as % of resources	—	—	—	—	—	—	—	—	—	—	—
Employees	(0.1%)	—	—	—	2,247	2,278	2,157	2,147	2,136	2,574	2,227

**Society Resources[2]
1988-1993**

[Bar chart showing Society Resources from 1988 to 1993, y-axis from 0 to 30,000]

[1] Books are closed 3 years in arrears   [2] Total assets of the Names, corporation, and affiliates, including reserves provisions

HOOVER'S HANDBOOK OF WORLD BUSINESS 1995–1996   313

LONRHO PLC

OVERVIEW

Africa is the cradle of Lonrho's profits. Although the company is based in London, nearly 80% of its income comes from Africa. It is the largest motor-vehicle distributor in Africa and is the continent's #1 commercial food producer.

Lonrho is a holding company for a group of 640 subsidiaries with operations in 48 countries. The company's businesses span everything from gold and platinum mining to cotton and sugar production to manufacturing and insurance. Lonrho's African operations include agriculture, textile manufacturing, aircraft marketing, and the Mount Kenya Safari Club. In the UK its operations include car dealerships, printing (including

90% of the country's postage stamps), and building contracting. In the US Lonrho owns 39% of Hondo Oil & Gas and operates Princess Hotels.

Lonrho was long the domain of outspoken entrepreneur Roland "Tiny" Rowland, who lost control of the company to German developer Dieter Bock in 1994. The 2 men, who acted as co-managing directors, clashed over the direction of the company when Bock, who owns 18% of the company, wanted to sell off many of the company's assets, which Rowland had spent years accumulating. Bock plans to continue selling off pieces of the company and to focus on mining, hotels, and agriculture.

WHEN

The London & Rhodesian Mining & Land Company was founded in 1909 to acquire mining rights in Rhodesia. Through its first 50 years the company expanded into real estate, ranching, and agriculture but remained in relative obscurity. By 1961 it had only grown to $11 million in sales. That year Tiny Rowland traded his Rhodesian assets (gold mines, farms, and a Mercedes-Benz dealership) for a 48% interest in the company. When he joined London & Rhodesian as a managing director, Rowland, who speaks several African languages, began to expand the company throughout the continent, making long-lasting contacts with African leaders.

Also that year the company acquired the Beria oil pipeline running from Rhodesia to Mozambique. However, in 1965 the company, which shortened its name to Lonrho in 1963, shut down the pipeline when the British government began sanctions against Rhodesia following its declaration of independence.

Rowland continued to expand Lonrho operations during the 1970s. In 1973 a group of Lonrho's directors tried to oust Rowland, claiming, among other things, that he had paid off African leaders and had violated the Rhodesian sanctions. The British government began an inquiry and cleared him of violating the sanctions, although it did find that he had made some "questionable" payments, prompting Prime Minister Edward Heath to call Rowland "the unpleasant and unacceptable face of capitalism."

Rowland's face was still welcome in Africa, where he continued to expand Lonrho's

operations. Lonrho also expanded elsewhere. In 1975 it acquired Volkswagen and Audi distributors in Great Britain, and in 1979 it acquired Princess Hotels. In 1981 Rowland acquired the *Observer* newspaper (sold in 1993) and began a bid for retailer House of Fraser (owner of London department store Harrod's) but was blocked by the British government. Egypt's Al-Fayed brothers acquired House of Fraser in 1985, prompting Rowland to begin a decade-long lawsuit.

In 1987 Alan Bond made a bid to take over Lonrho. Rowland countered by releasing an account of Bond's shaky finances. Bond's company went bankrupt in 1991. However, with mounting debt and a recession, Lonrho had its own finances to worry about, and it began to sell off a number of assets to raise cash.

In 1992, in one of his most controversial moves, Rowland sold 1/3 of the Metropole Hotel chain to the Libyan government for $310 million. The deal sent Lonrho's stock plummeting, which caught the eye of Dieter Bock, who bought about 18% of the company with Rowland's blessing.

A year later Rowland continued to court controversy when he used Lonrho funds to bankroll a documentary that disputed British and US claims that Libya was behind the bombing of Pan Am Flight 103 over Lockerbie, Scotland.

In 1994, with Bock at the helm, Lonrho's pretax profit jumped 56% over the previous year. Sales were nearly $3.1 billion.

OTC symbol: LNRHY
Fiscal year ends: September 30

Chairman: Sir John Leahy, age 67
Managing Director and CEO: Dieter Bock, age 55
Deputy Managing Director: Nicholas Morrell,
  age 47
Finance Director: Robert Whitten, age 54
Associate Director and Group Secretary:
  M. J. Pearce
President, Princess Hotels (US): John F. Price
VP Finance, Princess Hotels (US): James Evans
VP Personnel, Princess Hotels (US): William
  Mullins
Auditors: KPMG Peat Marwick

WHERE

HQ: Cheapside House, 138 Cheapside, London
  EC2V 6BL, UK
Phone: +44-(01)71-606-9898
Fax: +44-(01)71-606-2285
US HQ: Princess Hotels International,
  805 Third Ave., 18th Fl., New York, NY 10022
Phone: 212-715-7000
Fax: 212-644-0293

| | 1993 Sales | |
	£ mil.	% of total
UK	719	38
Southern Africa	421	22
East, Central & West Africa	465	25
The Americas	179	10
Other countries	86	5
Adjustments	830	—
Total	**2,700**	**100**

WHAT

| | 1993 Sales | |
	£ mil.	% of total
Motor & equipment distribution	517	28
Manufacturing	401	21
Mineral extraction & refining	335	18
Hotels	260	14
General trade	196	11
Agriculture	118	6
Financial services	43	2
Adjustments	830	—
Total	**2,700**	**100**

Selected Subsidiaries and Affiliates
David Whitehead & Sons (Malawi) Ltd. (51%, textiles)
The Dutton-Forshaw Motor Group Ltd. (auto retailing)
Eastern Platinum Ltd. (73%, Bophuthatswana, mining)
EATEC Ltd. (Kenya, crop and livestock farming)
Greenaway Harrison Ltd. (financial, security, and
  commercial printers)
Hondo Oil & Gas Company (39%, US, oil and gas
  exploration)
Lusolanda S.A.R.L. (Angola, trading)
Metropole Hotels (Holdings) Ltd. (67%)
Mufindi Tea Co. Ltd. (75%, Tanzania)
National Airways and Finance Corporation Ltd. (South
  Africa, aircraft distribution)
Princess Properties International Ltd. (Bermuda, hotels
  and casinos)
Saville Tractors Ltd.
Zimoco Ltd. (Zimbabwe, motor vehicle distribution)

KEY COMPETITORS

Accor	Hilton
ADM	Hyatt
Anglo American	Kloof Gold Mining
Bass	Ladbroke Group
Broken Hill	Peninsula & Oriental
Club Med	Rank
De La Rue Company	Rustenberg Platinum
Hanson	Tate & Lyle

HOW MUCH

£=$1.48 (Dec. 31, 1993)	9-Year Growth	1984	1985	1986	1987	1988	1989	1990	1991	1992	1993
Sales (£ mil.)	(1.9%)	3,211	3,035	3,297	3,582	4,131	5,129	5,354	4,733	3,927	2,700
Net income (£ mil.)	17.6%	42	28	26	97	114	103	120	33	42	112
Income as % of sales	—	1.3%	0.9%	0.8%	2.7%	2.8%	2.0%	2.2%	0.7%	1.1%	4.1%
Earnings per share (p)	8.2%	11.6	7.4	6.9	24.4	26.1	22.0	24.8	6.6	8.3	15.1
Stock price – high (p)	—	111	131	166	245	331	295	296	277	181	114
Stock price – low (p)	—	68	95	110	132	127	206	182	148	57	70
Stock price – close (p)	2.0%	108	131	151	164	265	290	222	155	71	129
P/E – high	—	10	18	24	10	13	13	12	42	22	8
P/E – low	—	6	13	16	5	5	9	7	22	7	5
Dividends per share (p)	(8.1%)	7.9	8.6	9.5	11.2	13.1	18.5	20.4	16.9	5.2	4.0
Book value per share (p)	(12.5%)	—	—	—	—	—	—	273	—	206	210
Employees	(2.2%)	—	—	—	116,000	97,756	102,601	108,759	113,094	106,309	99,309

1993 Year-end:
Debt ratio: 28.5%
Return on equity: 8.4%
Cash (mil.): £193
Long-term debt (mil.): £307
No. of shares (mil.): 766
Dividends
  Yield: 3.1%
  Payout: 26.5%
Market value (mil.): $1,463
Sales (mil.): $3,996

Stock Price History
High/Low 1984–93

L'ORÉAL SA

OVERVIEW

L'Oréal is all dressed up and looking for places to go. Already the world's largest cosmetics company with a 12% market share, the Paris-based giant continues to expand geographically. CEO Lindsay Owen-Jones has his eye on emerging markets such as Thailand, South Korea, and Latin America, which he hopes can fuel growth.

L'Oréal makes a broad line of makeup, perfumes, and hair care, skin care, body care, and men's products. The company's brand names include general consumer products such as L'Oréal and Gemey-Paris; upscale products such as Lancôme, Biotherm, and Helena Rubinstein; and products sold to professional hair dressers, such as Redken.

L'Oréal's 56%-owned subsidiary, Synthélabo, makes pharmaceuticals, over-the-counter drugs, and medical devices. Other group interests include Marie-Claire (49% publishing) and Paravision International (film production).

Liliane Bettencourt, daughter of the company's founder and France's wealthiest individual, is L'Oréal's primary stockholder. She owns 51% of Gesparal, the holding company that controls 53.7% of L'Oréal (Nestlé controls the remaining shares of Gesparal).

WHEN

Parisian Eugène Schueller, a chemist by trade, developed the country's first synthetic hair dye in 1907. Schueller quickly found a market for his products with local hairdressers and in 1909 established L'Oréal to pursue his growing hair-products operations. The company's new name was a nonsensical word coined by Schueller because he liked the way it sounded.

L'Oréal expanded its line to include shampoos and soaps, all under the watchful direction of the energetic Schueller. Always the chemist, Schueller was known to taste hair creams to ensure that they were made up of the exact chemical composition that he required. In the 1920s L'Oréal became the first French company in the industry to advertise on radio.

After WWII, demand for L'Oréal's products intensified. When Schueller died in 1957, control of the company passed to his right-hand man, François Dalle. Dalle carried L'Oréal's hair care products into the consumer market and overseas and sold the company's soap operations in 1961. The next year Dalle launched Elnett, L'Oréal's popular hairspray.

In 1963 the company went public, although Eugène Schueller's daughter, Liliane Bettencourt, retained a majority interest. Diversification came in 1965 with the acquisition of Lancôme, a French maker of upscale cosmetics. Dalle followed the Lancôme purchase with a string of cosmetics acquisitions. L'Oréal entered the pharmaceutical business in 1973 by purchasing Synthélabo.

The company's interests became intertwined with those of the Swiss firm Nestlé in 1974, when Bettencourt traded nearly half of her L'Oréal stock for a 3% stake in Nestlé. Three years later the company bought a minority interest in the publisher of fashion magazine *Marie-Claire*.

During the 1980s L'Oréal vaulted from relative obscurity to become the world's leading cosmetics company, largely through such acquisitions as Metabio-Joullie (1980); Société d'Hygiene Dermatologique de Vichy (1980); and the cosmetics operations of Warner Communications (1984), which brought the company the Ralph Lauren and Gloria Vanderbilt brand names. In 1988 L'Oréal bought Laboratoires Pharmaceutiques Goupil (France's #1 toothpaste producer) and US beauty-products–maker Helena Rubinstein. In 1989 the company acquired a controlling interest in Laboratoires Pharmaceutiques Roche-Posay (skin care products) and the following year bought 47.5% of Jeanne Lanvin (perfumes).

In 1991 Jacques Corrèze, chairman of L'Oréal's US licensee (Cosmair), resigned after stories surfaced linking him to pro-Nazi activities during WWII. He died 2 weeks later. The same year L'Oréal purchased Delalande, a French drug company, and Dralle, a German beauty products business.

In 1993 L'Oréal announced it would no longer test cosmetics on animals, ending a 4-year battle with People for the Ethical Treatment of Animals. In order to strengthen its US presence, in 1994 L'Oréal bought control of Cosmair, its US licensee.

OTC symbol: ORE (ADR)
Fiscal year ends: December 31

WHO

Chairman and CEO: Lindsay Owen-Jones
VC: André Bettencourt
EVP: Guy Landon
VP Administration and Finance: Pascal Castres Saint-Martin
VP Consumer Division: Gérard Chouraqui
VP Production and Technology: Marcel Lafforgue
VP Human Resources: François Vachey
President and CEO, Cosmair (US): Guy Peyrelongue
CFO, Cosmair (US): Roger Dolden
SVP Human Resources, Cosmair (US): Dermot Flynn
Auditors: Pierre Feuillet; Albert Pavie

WHERE

HQ: 41, rue Martre, 92117 Clichy, France
Phone: +33-1-47-56-70-00
Fax: +33-1-47-56-80-02
US HQ: Cosmair Inc., 575 Fifth Ave., New York, NY 10017
US Phone: 212-818-1500
US Fax: 212-984-4999

	1993 Sales	
	FF mil.	% of total
France	13,562	34
Asia	3,059	7
Latin America	1,881	5
US	1,071	3
Other Europe	17,068	42
Other countries	3,522	9
Total	**40,163**	**100**

WHAT

	1993 Sales	
	FF mil.	% of total
Cosmetics	32,721	81
Pharmaceuticals & medical devices	7,124	18
Other	318	1
Total	**40,163**	**100**

Selected Cosmetics Brands	Pharmaceuticals and Medical Devices (Synthélabo, 56.6%)
Biotherm	Cardiovascular drugs
Cacharel	Central nervous system drugs
D'Anglas	Gastroenterological drugs
Gemey-Paris	Over-the-counter drugs
Helena Rubinstein	Pacemakers
Kérastase	Surgical instruments
Laboratoires Garnier	Urological drugs
Lancôme	
LaScad	**Other Operations**
L'Oréal	Artcurial (99%, art gallery)
Parfums Giorgio Armani	Laboratoires Galderma (50%, skin treatments)
Parfums Guy Laroche	
Parfums Lanvin	Le Club des Créateurs de Beauté (50%, mail order cosmetics)
Parfums Paloma Picasso	
Parfums Ralph Lauren	
Phas	Marie-Claire (49%, publishing)
Redken	
Roche-Posay	Paravision International (film production)
Vichy	

KEY COMPETITORS

Alberto-Culver	Gillette	Rhône-Poulenc
Amway	Helene Curtis	Roche
Avon	S.C. Johnson	Sandoz
Body Shop	LVMH	Shiseido
Ciba-Geigy	MacAndrews & Forbes	Unilever
Colgate-Palmolive		Yves Saint-Laurent
Elf Aquitaine	Mary Kay	
Estée Lauder	Procter & Gamble	

HOW MUCH

$=FF5.91 (Dec. 31, 1993)	9-Year Growth	1984	1985	1986	1987	1988	1989	1990	1991	1992	1993
Sales (FF mil.)	10.9%	15,804	16,430	18,130	20,095	24,445	27,170	30,360	33,445	37,568	40,163
Net income (FF mil.)	15.1%	729	775	898	1,090	1,315	1,542	1,828	2,155	2,298	2,585
Income as % of sales	—	4.6%	4.7%	5.0%	5.4%	5.4%	5.7%	6.0%	6.4%	6.1%	6.4%
Earnings per share (FF)	12.8%	15	17	14	18	21	25	29	35	40	44
Stock price – high (FF)	—	217	240	336	405	440	497	555	751	1,070	1,374
Stock price – low (FF)	—	175	185	234	207	230	392	420	447	716	980
Stock price – close (FF)	24.1%	187	238	320	254	440	497	471	751	1,067	1,305
P/E – high	—	14	14	23	22	21	20	19	21	27	31
P/E – low	—	11	11	16	11	11	16	14	13	18	22
Dividends per share (FF)	15.3%	3.00	3.30	3.70	5.00	6.00	6.00	7.00	8.40	9.60	10.80
Book value per share (FF)	10.7%	109	118	135	126	147	167	188	220	240	272
Employees	1.9%	27,117	26,402	26,700	26,860	27,570	28,401	29,286	29,877	31,908	32,261

1993 Year-end:
Debt ratio: 20.1%
Return on equity: 17.3%
Cash (mil.): FF3,660
Long-term debt (mil.): FF2,197
No. of shares (mil.): 58
Dividends
  Yield: 0.8%
  Payout: 24.3%
Market value (mil.): $12,849
Sales (mil.): $6,796

Stock Price History
High/Low 1984–93

DEUTSCHE LUFTHANSA AG

OVERVIEW

Lufthansa, the #2 airline in Europe (after British Airways) had been in an economic tailspin since 1991. European air travel decreased by 6% in 1991, the first decline in history, forcing Lufthansa into the red for the first time since 1973. The company was losing about $1.25 million a day in 1992. But firm management by Jürgen Weber (chairman since 1991) has pulled the jumbo company out of its nose dive. Although it is not yet soaring, Lufthansa was making a profit of $300,000 a month in 1994.

Weber took a no-nonsense approach. One of his first decisions was to announce layoffs; 1,800 workers lost jobs in 1992, and 6,000 more cuts were scheduled. His formula for the company's survival: "Our people have to work more for less money."

Lufthansa is 51.4%-owned by the German government, but in 1994 it planned to follow British Airways and KLM by dropping the state holdings to well below 50%.

Lufthansa is a leading cargo transporter and owns interests in other airlines (such as Lauda Air) and travel-related companies, including Amadeus, the European computer reservation system, and the Euro Lloyd travel agency.

In 1994 the company announced plans to restructure into new business units. The first of these — cargo, technical, and data systems — are expected to be operational by 1995.

WHEN

As a result of Dr. Kurt Weigelt's study, "Fusion in the Field of Air Traffic," the Weimar government created Deutsche Luft Hansa (DLH) in 1926 by merging 2 private German airlines, Deutscher Aero Lloyd (founded as Deutsche Luft Reederei in 1919) and Junkers Luftverkehr (formed in 1921 by aircraft manufacturer Junkers Flugzeugwerke).

With a core of routes emanating from Germany to Austria, Switzerland, England, Denmark, Sweden, Russia, and Hungary at the time of its founding, DLH went on to build what would become Europe's most comprehensive air route network by 1931. The company served the USSR through Deruluft, an airline (formed in 1921 and dissolved in 1941) jointly owned by DLH and the Soviet government. In 1930 DLH and the Chinese government formed a subsidiary at Nanking called Eurasia Aviation Corporation to develop air transport in China.

DLH established the world's first regular transatlantic airmail service from Berlin to Buenos Aires in 1934 and went on to develop air transport throughout South America. The outbreak of WWII ended operations in Europe, and the Chinese government seized Eurasia Aviation in 1941. In 1944 Dr. Klaus Bonhoeffer, head of DLH's legal department, led an unsuccessful coup against the Nazi leadership and was executed in 1945. Soon afterward all DLH operations ceased.

German airline service was not restored until 1954, when the Allies allowed the recapitalization of Deutsche Lufthansa. Starting with domestic routes (except to Berlin, which was reserved for Allied carriers), Lufthansa returned to London and Paris (1955) and then to South America (1956). In 1958 the airline made its first nonstop flight between Germany and New York and initiated service to Tokyo and Cairo. Lufthansa reported a $25,000 profit, its first ever, in 1963.

The airline opened a polar route from Frankfurt to Tokyo in 1964. Service behind the Iron Curtain resumed in 1966 when Lufthansa initiated flights to Prague. The stable West German economy helped Lufthansa maintain profitability through most of the 1970s, despite a world recession.

In 1988 Lufthansa bought 49% of Euro-Berlin France, a regional airline jointly owned by Air France, gaining, in a roundabout fashion, service to Berlin. The reunification of Germany in 1990 ended Allied control over Berlin airspace, allowing Lufthansa, which had bought Pan Am's Berlin routes for about $150 million, to fly there under its own colors for the first time since the end of WWII.

When Jürgen Weber became chairman in 1991, the company began seeking international partners and cutting staff. In 1992 Lufthansa also created a subsidiary, Lufthansa Express, to handle its domestic routes. This service then became a popular "no-frills" European shuttle service in 1993 aimed at the business market.

In 1994 Lufthansa finally made a profit after 3 loss years. Its passenger load factor was the highest in its history that year — 70%.

OTC symbol: DLH (ADR)
Fiscal year ends: December 31

Chairman: Jürgen Weber, age 53
Deputy Chairman and CFO: Klaus G. Schlede
Chief Executive Technical Services: Klaus
   Nittinger
SVP, The Americas: Frederick Reid
VP Human Relations, Lufthansa (US): David
   Buisch
Auditors: C&L Treuarbeit Deutsche Revision
   Aktiengesellschaft (Coopers & Lybrand)

WHERE

HQ: Von-Gablenz-Strasse 2-6,
   D-50679 Cologne 21, Germany
Phone: +49-221-8260
Fax: +49-69-696-6818 (Public Relations)
US HQ: Lufthansa German Airlines,
   680 Fifth Ave., New York, NY 10019
US Phone: 212-479-8801
US Fax: 212-479-0795 (Corporate Communications)
Reservations: 800-645-3880

	1993 Sales	
	DM mil.	% of total
Asia/Pacific	2,953	20
Germany	2,926	17
North America	2,418	16
Africa & Middle East	1,040	7
South America	689	5
Other Europe	5,326	35
Adjustments	2,379	—
Total	**17,731**	**100**

WHAT

	1993 Sales	
	DM mil.	% of total
Passenger	12,731	72
Freight	2,568	14
Mail	333	2
Other	2,099	12
Total	**17,731**	**100**

Major Subsidiaries and Affiliates
Amadeus Data Processing GmbH (50%, computer
   reservation system)
Cargolux Airlines International SA (25%)
Condor Flugdienst GmbH (air charters)
Delvag Luftfahrtversicherungs-AG (insurance)
Euro Lloyd Reisebüro GmbH (85%, travel agency)
Lauda Air Luftfahrt AG(26.5%, Austrian airline)
LSG Lufthansa Service GmbH (catering)
Lufthansa Airport- and Ground Services, GmbH
Lufthansa Cargo Airlines GmbH
Lufthansa Commercial Holding GmbH

Flight Equipment	No.	Orders
Airbus A300 & A310	23	—
Airbus A320 & A321	33	20
Airbus A340	9	5
Boeing 737	120	3
Boeing 747	39	—
Boeing 757	17	1
Boeing 767	6	3
DC 8-73	5	—
DC 10-30	11	—
Others	38	—
Total	**301**	**32**

KEY COMPETITORS

Air France	Dial	Qantas
AMR	IRI	SAS
British Airways	JAL	Singapore
Caterair International	KLM	Airlines
Continental Airlines	Northwest	Swiss Air
Delta	Airlines	USAir

HOW MUCH

$=DM1.74 (Dec. 31, 1993)	9-year Growth	1984	1985	1986	1987	1988	1989	1990	1991	1992	1993
Sales (DM mil.)	6.7%	9,856	10,726	10,384	10,960	11,845	13,055	14,447	16,101	17,239	17,731
Net income (DM mil.)	—	162	66	71	88	77	107	11	(436)	(394)	(101)
Income as % of sales	—	1.6%	0.6%	0.7%	0.8%	0.7%	0.8%	0.1%	(2.7%)	(2.3%)	(0.6%)
Earnings per share (DM)	—	9.31	3.81	4.06	4.10	3.60	3.84	0.40	(15.65)	(12.90)	(3.30)
Stock price – high (DM)	—	183	419	312	216	163	219	235	162	182	179
Stock price – low (DM)	—	133	180	155	106	130	145	101	99	84	97
Stock price – close (DM)	(0.2%)	182	225	180	136	148	200	112	160	105	178
P/E – high	—	20	110	77	53	45	57	—	—	—	—
P/E – low	—	14	47	38	26	36	38	—	—	—	—
Dividends per share (DM)[1]	(100.0%)	3.5	3.5	3.5	3.5	3.5	4.0	4.0	0.00	0.00	0.00
Book value per share (DM)	(0.8%)	75	74	75	100	100	114	106	90	75	70
Employees	2.4%	36,513	39,358	42,725	46,914	49,056	51,942	57,567	61,791	49,292	45,322

1993 Year-end:
Debt ratio: 74.1%
Return on equity: —
Cash (mil.): DM949
Long-term debt (mil.): DM5763
No. of shares (mil.): 31
Dividends
   Yield: 0.0%
   Payout: —
Market value (mil.): $3,120
Sales (mil.): $10,190

**Stock Price History
High/Low 1984–93**

[1] Not including rights issues

LVMH MOËT HENNESSY LOUIS VUITTON

OVERVIEW

Corks are popping at LVMH Moët Hennessy Louis Vuitton, the world's largest luxury goods conglomerate. Sales of champagne, which includes the Dom Pérignon and Pommery labels, have rebounded after dropping for 3 years in a row (1990–92). The firm's other 3 major segments, consisting of cognacs and spirits, luggage and leather goods, and perfumes and beauty products, have shown increasing kick since 1992.

LVMH is the world's leading producer of bubbly (43.8 million bottles of its prestigious brands were sold in 1993, giving the company a 19% share) and is also the world's largest producer of cognacs, with brands that sell for up to $300 a bottle. In addition to luggage, leather, and beauty products, LVMH produces sparkling and still wines in Australia, Europe, South America, and the US.

With sales rebounding in 1993 as the US and the UK began emerging from sluggish times, LVMH has also benefited from lower grape and eaux-de-vie (clear spirit distilled from fruit) prices for its champagnes and cognacs. To boost sales the firm intends to push its brands into new markets such as China, where cognac sales have expanded in recent years. LVMH is also reportedly looking to make a big acquisition with the $1.9 billion that landed in its treasury in 1994 when Guinness bought 34% of LVMH's subsidiary Moët Hennessy and sold its 24% of the parent company to Christian Dior, a separate entity controlled by LVMH CEO Bernard Arnault.

WHEN

Louis Vuitton opened his first store in Paris in 1854 to sell luggage and trunks. In 1896 the company introduced the LV monogram fabric that is still used on most of its products. By the turn of the century, Louis Vuitton had stores in the US and England.

The company operated primarily as a wholesaler until 1977 when Henry Racamier, a former steel executive who had married into the Vuitton family, took charge. Under Racamier sales soared from $20 million to nearly $2.5 billion within 10 years.

Concerned about being a takeover target, Racamier merged his company in 1987 with Moët Hennessy (a conglomerate that produced fine champagnes, cognacs, wines, and perfumes) and changed the company's name to LVMH Moët Hennessy Louis Vuitton. Moët Hennessy had been formed through the 1971 merger of Moët et Chandon (France's #1 champagne producer) and the Hennessy Cognac company. Perfume maker Christian Dior was acquired by Moët that same year.

Almost immediately, Racamier and Moët chairman Alain Chevalier found themselves in disagreement over the running of the company. To help consolidate his position within LVMH, Racamier invited outside investor Bernard Arnault to acquire stock in the company. Racamier expected a friendly and passive investor in Arnault but was quickly disillusioned. With the support of Guinness (a large shareholder of LVMH), Arnault managed to land a 43.5% controlling interest in LVMH. Chevalier stepped down, but former friend Racamier engaged Arnault in a battle for control of the company. After 18 months of legal fighting, with the courts usually favoring Arnault, Racamier left LVMH and set up Orcofi, a rival company that is in partnership with cosmetics giant L'Oréal. After the legal battle Arnault weeded out LVMH's top executives and began consolidating his empire.

In 1988 Arnault acquired a 12.4% interest in Guinness and bought the Givenchy Couture Group. In 1989 Arnault shocked the fashion world by replacing Dior's French artistic director Marc Bohan with Gianfranco Ferré, an Italian designer.

In 1990 LVMH acquired Lanson champagne from BSN for $620 million and kept its vineyards and the Pommery brand. It sold the Lanson brand in 1991. That same year LVMH launched the successful Dune and Amarige perfumes, acquired a majority interest in the J.G. Monnet cognac house from a subsidiary of Guinness, and bought an additional 2% of Guinness to maintain its 24% stake.

In 1993 the company sold its RoC skincare unit to Johnson & Johnson. That came after making 2 acquisitions that year, the Christian Lacroix fashion unit from the Au Bon Marché group, and Kenzo, another fashion house known for its youthful appeal. LVMH also acquired a 55% interest in Desfossés International, a French magazine publisher offering business and financial fare.

In 1994 LVMH had sales of just over $5 billion.

Nasdaq symbol: LVMHY (ADR)
Fiscal year ends: December 31

Chairman and CEO: Bernard Arnault
EVP and CFO: Patrick Houël
EVP Human Resources: Concetta Lanciaux
EVP: Daniel Piette
Chairman and CEO, Louis Vuitton: Jean Dromer
Chairman, LVMH (US): Evan Galbraith
Deputy CEO, Louis Vuitton: Robert Léon
President and CEO, Jas. Hennessy:
Henri de Pracomtal
CFO, LVMH (US): Bruce Ingram
Director Human Resources, LVMH (US):
Richard Pacheco
Auditors: Ernst & Young; Cogerco-Flipo

HQ: 30, avenue Hoche, 75008 Paris, France
Phone: +33-1-44-13-22-22
Fax: +33-1-44-13-21-19
US HQ: LVMH Moët Hennessy Louis Vuitton
Inc., 2 Park Ave., Ste. 1830, New York, NY
10016
US Phone: 212-340-7480
US Fax: 212-340-7620

	1993 Sales		1993 Operating Income	
	$ mil.	% of total	$ mil.	% of total
France	1,195	30	437	46
Far East	1,449	36	391	41
US	604	15	56	6
Other countries	776	19	64	7
Total	**4,024**	**100**	**948**	**100**

	1993 Sales		1993 Operating Income	
	$ mil.	% of total	$ mil.	% of total
Perfume & beauty	1,035	26	144	15
Cognac & spirits	988	24	323	33
Luggage & leather	957	24	391	39
Champagne & wines	920	23	131	13
Other	124	3	(41)	—
Total	**4,024**	**100**	**948**	**100**

Selected Brand Names

Perfumes and Beauty Products
Christian Dior
Diorissimo
Dune
Eau Sauvage
Poison
Christian Lacroix
C'est la Vie!
Givenchy
Xeryus
Kenzo

Luggage and Leather Goods
Christian Lacroix
Loewe
Louis Vuitton

Cognac and Spirits
Hennessy
Paradis
V.S.
V.S.O.P.
X.O.
Hine

Champagne and Wines
Canard-Duchêne
Chandon
Dom Pérignon
Mercier
Moët & Chandon
Pommery
Ruinart
Simi
Veuve Clicquot Ponsardin

Allied Domecq
Astrum
Bass
Benedictine
Benetton
Brown-Forman
Colgate-Palmolive
Dunhill
Estée Lauder

Financière Agache
Grand Metropolitan
Hermes
Kirin
L'Oréal
MacAndrews & Forbes
Piper-Heidsieck
Polo/Ralph Lauren
Remy Cointreau

Robert
Mondavi
Sara Lee
Seagram
Shiseido
Taittinger
Unilever

Stock prices are for ADRs. ADR = 1/5 share	Annual Growth	1984	1985	1986	1987	1988	1989	1990	1991	1992	1993
Sales ($ mil.)	4.3%	—	—	—	—	—	3,397	3,889	4,242	3,919	4,024
Net income ($ mil.)	4.5%	—	—	—	—	—	507	662	719	544	604
Income as % of sales	—	—	—	—	—	—	14.9%	17.0%	16.9%	13.9%	15.0%
Earnings per share ($)	2.9%	—	—	—	—	—	7.22	8.86	9.70	7.32	8.11
Stock price – high ($)	—	—	—	—	55.91	99.09	175.00	174.77	161.00	169.00	154.00
Stock price – low ($)	—	—	—	—	40.00	49.09	101.36	108.07	110.45	126.50	112.50
Stock price – close ($)	15.7%	—	—	—	53.18	98.07	172.73	118.41	160.00	131.50	127.75
P/E – high	—	—	—	—	—	—	24	20	17	23	19
P/E – low	—	—	—	—	—	—	14	12	11	17	14
Dividends per share ($)	17.3%	—	—	—	0.97	1.22	1.97	2.15	2.53	2.48	2.53
Book value per share ($)	4.1%	—	—	—	—	—	37.13	43.27	48.93	47.14	43.55
Employees	(1.7%)	—	—	—	16,511	15,555	16,930	14,272	14,650	15,501	14,874

1993 Year-end:
Debt ratio: 45.8%
Return on equity: 17.9%
Cash (mil.): $674
Current ratio: 1.69
Long-term debt (mil.): $2,076
No. of shares (mil.): 79
Dividends
  Yield: 2.0%
  Payout: 31.2%
Market value (mil.): $10,070

Stock Price History
High/Low 1987–93

(chart y-axis: 180, 160, 140, 120, 100, 80, 60, 40, 20, 0)

COMPAGNIE DES MACHINES BULL

OVERVIEW

No more bull! European computer rivals were up in arms over the 1994 decision of the French government to invest a further $2.1 billion into the troubled computer giant Compagnie des Machines Bull (commonly known as Groupe Bull) as it prepared for privatization. The company, which sells and leases computer equipment and data processing services worldwide through over 100 subsidiaries, is the 3rd largest Europe-based computer maker (after Siemens-Nixdorf and Olivetti) and has been bleeding cash for years.

Jean-Marie Descarpentries was chosen by the government as the new CEO in 1993 (the company's 3rd CEO in as many years) and faced the daunting task of reversing 5 consecutive years of losing money.

Descarpentries set about the task with a passion, halving the company's losses in the first half of 1994 compared to the previous year period, and putting the ax to the firm's bloated operations. He reduced Bull's Paris offices from 25 to 5 and reorganized the sprawling conglomerate into 7 product/service divisions and 4 geographic networks. Descarpentries plans further major cuts to the work force, already reduced to less than 32,000 from the 1988 high of over 45,000.

Bull's US-based PC division, Zenith Data Systems, the group's principal source of losses since 1989, reported a recovery in 1993. It beat out 22 rival companies to win a 3-year, $724 million contract to supply 300,000 PCs to the US government.

WHEN

Bull is named for Norwegian engineer Frederik Bull, who in 1919 invented a punch-card machine. Georges Vieillard, a French bank employee, bought the patents for Bull's machine in 1931. Vieillard, who wanted to develop a better adding machine, persuaded the owners of a punch-card supplier to finance his venture and Compagnie des Machines Bull was incorporated in Paris in 1933.

Bull started competing with IBM in 1935, after unveiling a tabulator capable of printing up to 150 lines a minute. Bull went on to confound its American rival by pioneering the use of germanium diodes (instead of electron tubes) in its first mainframe computer, the Gamma 3 (introduced in 1952). But the battle of one-upmanship proved to be costly. Bull defaulted on a $4 million loan payment in 1964 and, faced with financial ruin, jumped at the chance when General Electric (US) offered to buy a 50% stake (later increased to 66%). The company (renamed Bull-GE) continued to lose money until 1969. It became Honeywell Bull in 1970, when GE sold its computer businesses to Honeywell.

In the meantime the French government had formed Compagnie Internationale pour l'Informatique (CII) to ensure the survival of the French computer industry (1966). In 1975 CII merged with Honeywell Bull to form CII-Honeywell Bull (CII-HB). Initially, Honeywell owned a 47% minority stake in the company, but in 1982 it accepted a gradual buyout offer from the French

government. CII-HB then merged with 3 other French computer companies (Transac, Sems, and R2E) to form Groupe Bull in 1983.

Bull was on shaky financial ground in the early 1980s, posting sizable losses from 1981 through 1984, but it got back on track, at least temporarily, under the leadership of Jacques Stern. In 1987 Bull entered a US-based 3-way mainframe computer partnership (Honeywell Bull Inc.) with Honeywell and NEC. Originally owning 42.5% of the venture, Bull upped its share to 72.2% (reducing Honeywell's share from 42.5% to 12.8%) and renamed the venture Bull HN Information Systems. In 1989 Bull bought Zenith's computer businesses (Zenith Data Systems [ZDS], a leading US laptop computer and IBM-clone maker).

In 1991 Bull acquired the rest of Bull HN, buying out Honeywell (12.5%) and NEC (15%). Then in 1992 it forged a new alliance with IBM designed to provide an influx of both cash and technical expertise.

In 1992 the EC approved a state injection of $1.3 billion into debt-laden Bull. In 1993 Bull bought a 19.9% stake in Packard Bell, the #7 maker of PCs and the #1 supplier for the home market, and teamed it with Zenith Data Systems to jointly develop desktop PCs.

In 1994 AT&T and a French partner, Quadral SA, offered to buy 40% of Bull, on condition that the company, when privatized, would be licensed to compete in the French telecommunications market. Bull finished 1994 with $5.6 billion in sales.

Principal exchange: Paris
Fiscal year ends: December 31

Chairman and CEO: Jean-Marie Descarpentries
Deputy CEO: Hervé Mouren
Director Finance and Administration: Camille de Montalivet
President and CEO, Bull HN Information Systems (US): Axel Leblois
CFO, Bull HN Information Systems (US): Robert Kelly
VP Human Resources, Bull HN Information Systems (US): Kathleen McGirr
Auditors: Bernard Montagne, André Amic & Associés; Deloitte Touche Tohmatsu; B.D.A.

HQ: One Place Carpeaux, Tour Bull, Paris-la-Défense, 92800, Puteaux, France
Phone: +33-1-46-96-90-90
Fax: +33-1-46-96-90-92
US Address: Bull HN Information Systems, Inc., 300 Concord Rd., Billerica, MA 01821
US Phone: 508-294-6000
US Fax: 508-294-6440

	1993 Sales	
	FF mil.	% of total
Western Europe	19,994	71
North America	6,214	22
Other countries	2,042	7
Total	**28,250**	**100**

	1993 Sales
	% of total
Customer services	29
Enterprise servers	27
Personal computers	21
System integration services	10
Open systems & software	8
Other	5
Total	**100**

Selected Products and Services
DPS 9000/900 (Zeus) enterprise servers
FlowPATH (workflow management system)
IMAGEWorks (electronic documents management system)
MOSIC (multipartner management system)
Multivendor IT (information technology) services
Open systems and software
Personal computers
Z-NOTE notebook PC
Z-STOR personal server

Advanced Logic Research	Hyundai	Seagate
AMD	IBM	Siemens
Apple	Intel	Silicon
AST	LSI Logic	Graphics
AT&T	Lucky-Goldstar	Sony
BCE	Mitsubishi	Sun
Canon	Motorola	Microsystems
Compaq	National	Tandem
Computervision	Semiconductor	Texas
Cray Research	nCUBE	Instruments
DEC	NEC	Thinking
Dell	Oki	Machines
Gateway 2000	Philips	Toshiba
Hewlett-Packard	Samsung	Unisys
Hitachi	Sanyo	

$=FF5.91 (Dec. 31, 1993)	Annual Growth	1984	1985	1986	1987	1988	1989	1990	1991	1992	1993
Sales (FF mil.)	8.5%	13,596	16,109	17,796	18,701	31,546	32,721	34,580	33,450	30,187	28,250
Net income (FF mil.)	—	(489)	110	271	225	303	(267)	(6,790)	(3,301)	(4,724)	(5,068)
Income as % of sales	—	—	0.7%	1.5%	1.2%	1.0%	—	—	—	—	—
Earnings per share (FF)	(6.3%)	(170)	30	80	60	80	(60)	(1,410)	(22)	(238)	(95)
Stock price – high (FF)	—	1,550	2,450	3,800	2,810	1,380	1,250	900	520	475	310
Stock price – low (FF)	—	1,250	1,300	2,000	790	700	750	310	250	166	185
Stock price – close (FF)	(23.5%)	—	—	2,050	820	870	780	320	250	210	240
P/E – high	—	—	82	48	94	17	—	—	—	—	—
P/E – low	—	—	43	25	26	9	—	—	—	—	—
Dividends per share (FF)	—	0.0	0.0	0.0	0.0	0.0	0.0	0.0	0.0	0.0	0.0
Book value per share (FF)	(35.0%)	340	530	1,070	1,200	1,270	1,200	(220)	(58)	(138)	7
Employees	2.1%	26,435	26,403	26,804	26,337	45,557	43,617	44,476	39,878	35,175	31,735

1993 Year-end:
Debt ratio: 92.9%
Return on equity: —
Cash (mil.): FF1,336
Long-term debt (mil.): FF4,165
No. of shares (mil.): 53
Dividends
  Yield: —
  Payout: —
Market value (mil.): $2,166
Sales (mil.): $4,780

Stock Price History
High/Low 1984–93

MACMILLAN BLOEDEL LIMITED

OVERVIEW

MacMillan Bloedel (nicknamed "MacBlo") is Canada's largest forest products company. Headquartered in Vancouver, the company manufactures and markets a variety of products, including lumber, panelboards, engineered wood, newsprint, groundwood printing papers, containerboard, corrugated containers, and other packaging materials.

After posting losses 2 straight years, MacBlo has rebounded by chopping away at noncore assets and putting a buzz saw to costs. The company is focusing on expanding its packaging business and its building materials business (which has posted strong results recently, thanks to a surge in the building market). To pump up its paper business, MacBlo has announced plans to begin manufacturing magazine-quality paper by 1996.

The company continues to face difficulties from environmental protests. The construction of a California newsprint-recycling plant has been delayed by a number of environmental hurdles, and the UK subsidiaries of Kimberly-Clark and Scott Paper canceled pulp orders after Greenpeace threatened a European boycott to protest MacBlo's logging practices in an environmentally sensitive area of British Columbia.

WHEN

MacMillan Bloedel traces its roots back to several British Columbia timber companies formed in the early 1900s. In 1919, H. R. MacMillan founded the H. R. MacMillan Export Company, a lumber brokerage, with British lumber importer Montague Meyer. In the beginning it mainly sold railway ties to the UK, but soon expanded, competing by selling smaller parcels of lumber that its bigger competitors wouldn't bother with.

During the 1930s MacMillan Export bought timberlands, moved into milling, and became a vertically integrated lumber company. The company went public in 1945. In 1951, looking to expand its operations even further, MacMillan merged with lumber company Bloedel, Stewart & Welch.

Bloedel, Stewart & Welch was founded in 1911 by J. H. Bloedel, a manager of a Washington lumber company. The new company ran logging operations in British Columbia, and in 1924 it moved into manufacturing operations when it took over a debtor, the failed Shull Lumber & Shingle Company.

In 1935 Bloedel joined Seaboard Lumber Sales, a lumber cooperative whose main competitor was the H. R. MacMillan Export Company. Bloedel, Stewart & Welch rode a surge in lumber demand following WWII, thanks to a boom in the housing market.

In 1950 Bloedel and MacMillan began merger discussions. The 2 companies hoped that by combining operations they could better compete with larger US timber companies. The merger matched MacMillan's large marketing organization with Bloedel's large timber holdings. When the merger was completed, MacMillan's officers took charge of the company, with H. R. MacMillan named chairman.

In 1957 MacMillan Bloedel moved into newsprint. In 1960, looking to further build its newsprint and pulp business, the company merged with Powell River Company to create MacMillan, Bloedel & Powell River, the largest forest products company in Canada. Powell River had been founded in 1911, and by the mid-1940s it was the #1 newsprint producer in western Canada, operating the largest newsprint mill in the world.

The merger with Powell River created a clash between 2 corporate cultures: the tightly organized, hands-on approach used by MacMillan and the more laid-back approach used by Powell River. MacMillan's charges won out, and several former Powell River executives resigned. In 1966 the company changed its name to MacMillan Bloedel Limited.

MacBlo continued to expand through acquisitions and also began to diversify. However, an expansion of the company's shipping operation pushed it into the red in 1975, and the diversification plan was scaled back. In 1982 Noranda Mines acquired 49.8% of the company. During the 1980s MacBlo downsized its operations, cutting employment in half.

In 1991 MacBlo formed Trus Joist MacMillan with TJ International to manufacture specialty lumber. In 1993 Noranda sold its interest in MacBlo to investors in Canada and Europe.

In 1994 MacMillan Bloedel's sales were up 18% to $2.8 billion; profits tripled to just under $130 million.

Nasdaq symbol: MMBLF
Fiscal year ends: December 31

Chairman: Raymond V. Smith, age 67
President and CEO: Robert B. Findlay, age 60,
  C$414,000 pay
EVP Operations: R. Dale Tuckey, age 53,
  C$273,748 pay
SVP Finance and CFO: Glenn Ferguson, age 53
VP Human Resources: G. H. Johncox, age 53
**SVP Containerboard and Packaging; President,
  MacMillan Bloedel (US):** Frederick V. Ernst,
  age 55, C$213,516 pay
VP and CFO, MacMillan Bloedel (US): A. D.
  Fuller
VP Human Resources, MacMillan Bloedel (US):
  Charles F. Perkins
Auditors: Price Waterhouse

WHERE

HQ: 925 W. Georgia St., Vancouver, British
  Columbia V6C 3L2, Canada
Phone: 604-661-8000
Fax: 604-661-8377
US HQ: MacMillan Bloedel Inc.,
  PO Box 4840, Montgomery, AL 36103-4840
US Phone: 205-241-9100
US Fax: 205-263-1899

	1993 Sales $ mil.	1993 Sales % of total	1993 Operating Income $ mil.	1993 Operating Income % of total
US	1,300	46	15	10
Canada	1,188	42	119	85
Europe	59	2	0	0
Other countries	295	10	7	5
Total	**2,842**	**100**	**141**	**100**

WHAT

	1993 Sales $ mil.	1993 Sales % of total
Building materials	1,732	63
Pulp & paper	663	22
Containerboard & packaging	402	13
Other	45	2
Total	**2,842**	**100**

Pulp and Paper
Softwood kraft pulp — Telephone directory and
Standard newsprint — other specialty papers

Containerboard and Packaging
Corrugated containers
Corrugating medium
Linerboard

Building Materials
Cement-fiber roofing materials
Lumber
Particleboard
Plywood
Waferboard

Affiliates
N.V. Koninklijke KNP BT (17.1%, graphic paper and
  packaging products, The Netherlands)
MacMillan Bathurst (50%, corrugated containers)
Trus Joist MacMillan (49%, engineered lumber, US)

KEY COMPETITORS

Abitibi-Price	James River
Alco Standard	Kimberly-Clark
Boise Cascade	Louisiana-Pacific
Canadian Pacific	Manville
Canfor	Mead
Cascades	Noranda
Champion International	Scott
Domtar	Stone Container
Fletcher Challenge	Temple-Inland
Georgia-Pacific	Weyerhaeuser
International Paper	

HOW MUCH

$=C1.32 (Dec. 31, 1993)	Annual Growth	1984	1985	1986	1987	1988	1989	1990	1991	1992	1993
Sales ($ mil.)	6.6%	1,612	1,671	1,819	2,412	2,744	2,827	3,003	2,359	2,390	2,842
Net income ($ mil.)	11.9%	15	31	97	216	276	213	51	(81)	(38)	40
Income as % of sales	—	0.9%	1.8%	5.3%	9.0%	10.1%	7.5%	1.7%	—	—	1.4%
Earnings per share ($)	—	(0.05)	0.13	0.77	1.92	2.49	1.91	0.37	(0.85)	(0.41)	0.32
Stock price – high ($)	—	8.34	7.09	10.44	23.50	17.88	17.88	16.13	19.63	18.13	18.63
Stock price – low ($)	—	5.50	4.16	5.50	9.81	13.88	14.38	12.25	14.00	12.13	12.75
Stock price – close ($)	11.4%	6.16	5.91	9.81	17.63	15.13	15.63	14.38	16.13	13.25	16.25
P/E – high	—	—	55	14	12	7	9	44	—	—	58
P/E – low	—	—	32	7	5	6	8	33	—	—	40
Dividends per share ($)	—	0.00	0.00	0.25	0.82	0.90	0.68	0.68	0.52	0.49	—
Book value per share ($)	3.9%	—	—	7.25	8.97	10.86	12.69	14.39	11.57	9.44	9.49
Employees	(1.6%)	14,994	15,139	15,102	15,226	15,384	15,094	15,036	13,950	13,203	12,988

1993 Year-end:
Debt ratio: 58.9%
Return on equity: 3.6%
Cash (mil.): $197
Current ratio: 7.59
Long-term debt (mil.): $1,239
No. of shares (mil.): 124
Dividends
  Yield: 2.8%
  Payout: 143.8%
Market value (mil.): $2,011

Stock Price History
High/Low 1984–93

MANNESMANN AG

OVERVIEW

Mannesmann, a leading global producer of steel tubes, has developed into one of Germany's largest conglomerates, making systems and components for the automotive industry; telecommunications services; materials handling equipment for the construction industry; and compressed air equipment and compressors for oil, petrochemical, and transportation companies. It also builds plants for steel producers.

Mannesmann operates globally, with more than 127,000 employees working in 487 subsidiaries and affiliates in about 150 countries. Major businesses include Mobilfunk (51.3%-owned, which operates the first private mobile radio telephone network in Germany), Demag (a leading materials handling and metallurgical plant builder), Rexroth (drive controls), Mannesmannröhren-Werke (steel tubes), Mannesmann Anlagenbau (machinery and plant construction), VDO (auto control systems), and Fichtel & Sachs (clutches and suspensions).

In 1993 the conglomerate lost money in all of its divisions, with the steel tubes business being particularly hard hit. The flood of cheap steel from Eastern Europe and the collapse of its former Soviet market were blamed for the steep decline in orders. The company cut its work force by 9,000 in 1993.

WHEN

While working at their father's file factory in Remscheid, Germany, in 1885, Reinhard and Max Mannesmann devised the cross-rolling process, a means of manufacturing thick-walled seamless steel tubes. The 2 brothers started several tube mills using the process and by 1890 had perfected the manufacture of seamless steel tubes from a solid ingot. With financing from the Siemens family, the Mannesmanns merged their mills into the Deutsch-Österreichische Mannesmannröhren-Werke. The Mannesmanns left the board of management in 1893 and sold their stock in the company in 1900.

Backed by the Deutsche Bank, the company bought facilities in Austria, Silesia, Italy, and the UK. The company formed its first trading organization, Sociedad Tubos Mannesmann, in Buenos Aires in 1908.

Cartelization within the steel industry forced Mannesmann to vertically integrate its operations, acquiring iron ore and coal mines, a lime works, and raw steel factories. WWI disrupted exports (60% of sales) and cost the company its foreign assets. Following the war Mannesmann restructured to emphasize sales in central and southeastern Europe.

At the end of WWII, Mannesmann lost all of its foreign and East German plants, and most of its remaining facilities were destroyed. The Allies divided Mannesmann into 3 separate companies the same year, but the companies remerged in 1955. Mannesmann's rapid postwar recovery made it the largest German company by assets in 1953.

The company's pipe business benefited from increased demand for oil in the 1950s and 1960s. Faced with foreign government subsidized competition in world steel markets, Mannesmann became the first German coal and steel group to restructure. The company ceased mining operations in Germany and divested its coal mines. In 1968 Mannesmann purchased 50% of G. L. Rexroth, which it developed into a world leader in hydraulics. The company then bought Demag, a supplier of machinery in 1972 and the rest of Rexroth in 1975.

With its purchase in 1979 of Tally Corp., an American data systems engineering concern with European operations, Mannesmann moved into the information technology field. In 1981 Mannesmann bought Hartmann & Braun, which manufactures precision instruments and process-control systems for utility and chemical plants.

Mannesmann moved into automotive engineering in 1987 with the purchase of Fichtel & Sachs, a German supplier of clutches and suspensions. In 1988 the company acquired Buschman System Sales of Cincinnati, a machinery and plant construction firm. The next year Mannesmann established Mobilfunk, a cellular telephone consortium.

In 1992 Mannesmann's US subsidiary bought Rapistan to bolster its position in the US materials handling market.

In 1994 a news story broke alleging that the chairman, Werner Dieter, had committed fraud, sending the company's stock plummeting. Dieter retired in 1994, but German police stepped up their investigations, seizing various Mannesmann files.

OTC symbol: MNSMY (ADR)
Fiscal year ends: December 31

Chairman: Joachim Funk
VC: Klaus Czeguhn
Telecommunications Director: Peter Mihatsch
Member, Board of Management: Reinhold
  Schreiner
Member, Board of Management (US): Peter
  Prinz Wittgenstein
Financial Director: Klaus Esser
VP Finance, Mannesmann Capital (US):
  Reginald Shauder
**Director Human Resources, Mannesmann
  Capital (US):** Edward Zadravec
Auditors: KPMG Deutsche Treuhand-Gesellschaft

HQ: Mannesmannufer 2, Postfach 10 36 41,
  D-40027 Düsseldorf, Germany
Phone: +49-211-8-20-0
Fax: +49-211-8-20-21-63
US HQ: Mannesmann Capital Corporation,
  450 Park Ave., New York, NY 10022
US Phone: 212-826-6040
US Fax: 212-826-0074

	1993 Sales	
	DM mil.	% of total
Germany	11,896	43
North America	3,795	13
Asia	2,124	8
Latin America	1,122	4
Other countries	9,026	32
Total	**27,963**	**100**

	1993 Sales	
	DM mil.	% of total
Machinery & Plant Const.	12,383	44
Automotive Technology	6,009	21
Trading	4,196	15
Tubes & Pipes	2,691	10
Elec. & Electronic Eng.	1,290	5
Telecommunications	900	3
Corporate HQ & other	494	—
Total	**27,964**	**100**

Principal Subsidiaries and Affiliates

**Machinery and Plant
  Construction**
Krauss-Maffei AG (72%)
Mannesmann
  Anlagenbau AG
Mannesmann Demag AG
Mannesmann Demag
  Corporation (US)
Mannesmann Demag
  Ltd. (UK)
Mannesmann Rexroth
  GmbH

Automotive Technology
Boge GmbH
Fichtel & Sachs AG
VDO

Trading
Mannesmann Capital
  Corporation (US)
Mannesmann Handel AG

Tubes and Pipes
Mannesmannröhren-Werke
  AG (75%)

**Electrical and Electronic
  Engineering**
Hartmann & Braun AG
Mannesmann Tally
  Corporation (US)

Telecommunications
Mannesmann Mobilfunk
  GmbH (51%)

ABB	Fluor	Marubeni
AlliedSignal	FMC	Nippon Steel
Bechtel	Friedrich Krupp	Robert Bosch
Borg-Warner	General Electric	Rolls-Royce
Automotive	Illinois Tool Works	Siemens
Daimler-Benz	Ingersoll-Rand	Thyssen
Deutsche Telekom	Litton Industries	USX–U.S. Steel
Eaton	LTV	

$ = DM1.52 (Dec. 31, 1993)	Annual Growth	1984	1985	1986	1987	1988	1989	1990	1991	1992	1993
Sales (DM mil.)	6.6%	15,766	18,170	17,234	16,655	20,422	22,330	23,943	24,315	28,018	27,963
Net income (DM mil.)[1]	—	163	229	78	214	238	463	475	393	204	(344)
Income as % of sales	—	1.0%	1.3%	0.5%	1.3%	1.2%	2.1%	2.0%	1.6%	0.7%	(1.2%)
Earnings per share (DM)[1]	—	—	—	—	—	9	16	15	12	6	(9)
Stock price – high (DM)	—	—	—	—	190	217	368	408	302	313	429
Stock price – low (DM)	—	—	—	—	105	100	205	225	231	196	225
Stock price – close (DM)	25.9%	—	—	—	106	211	368	261	245	235	423
P/E – high	—	—	—	—	—	24	23	27	25	51	—
P/E – low	—	—	—	—	—	11	12	15	19	32	—
Dividends per share(DM)	(2.6%)	—	—	6.0	5.0	5.0	6.5	9.0	9.0	6.0	5.0
Book value per share (DM)	3.2%	—	—	—	—	145	159	175	179	173	170
Employees	2.3%	103,681	107,804	111,134	113,274	121,782	125,785	123,997	125,188	136,747	127,695

1993 Year-end:
Debt ratio: 20.6%
Return on equity: —
Cash (mil.): DM3,443
Long-term debt (mil.): DM925
No. of shares (mil.): 36
Dividends
  Yield: 1.2%
  Payout: —
Market value (mil.): $8,871
Sales (mil.): $16,071

**Stock Price History
High/Low 1987–93**

(chart y-axis: 450, 400, 350, 300, 250, 200, 150, 100, 50, 0)

[1] Including extraordinary items

MARKS AND SPENCER P.L.C.

OVERVIEW

Marks and Spencer is a global retailer of clothing, food items, and household goods, most of which are sold under its brand names St Michael and Marks & Spencer.

The company is something of an institution in the UK retail market. Referred to affectionately by the Cockney rhyming slang moniker "Marks and Sparks" by its British patrons, Marks and Spencer is the UK's leading retailer. It accounts for about 35% of the UK lingerie market and 10% of the women's shoe market. Of the men's underwear purchased in the UK, 35% is bought from Marks and Spencer's stores. Because the company works closely with suppliers and buys such a large quantity of clothing from them, it can afford to get tough and often comes away with the prices it demands. Marks and Spencer also offers customers a range of quality foodstuffs. It leads the UK market in sandwiches and ready-to-go meals.

The company has expanded internationally, with 56 stores in Europe outside of the UK, 40 in Canada, and 6 in Hong Kong. It also operates Brooks Brothers menswear stores in the US and Japan (its best selling foreign chain, accounting for 40% of revenues), Kings Super Markets (US), and D'Allaird's (retail, Canada).

The company has maintained its traditional format of combining apparel and food retailing and has retained a strong customer loyalty, its revenues climbing steadily despite the recent UK recession. It also has a high reputation among its peers; the company was voted as one of the most respected European companies in a 1994 *Financial Times* poll of European executives.

WHEN

Fleeing anti-Semitic persecution in Russian Poland, 19-year-old Michael Marks emigrated to England in 1882. Eventually settling in Leeds, Marks eked out a meager existence as a traveling peddler until 1884 when he opened a small stall at the town market.

Because he spoke little English, Marks laid out all of his merchandise and hung a sign that read "Don't Ask the Price, It's a Penny," unaware at the time that self-service and self-selection would eventually become the retailing standard. His methods were so successful that he had penny bazaars in 5 cities by 1890. Finding himself unable to single-handedly run the growing operation, Marks established an equal partnership with Englishman Tom Spencer, a cashier for a local distributor, forming Marks and Spencer in 1894. By the turn of the century, the company had 36 branches.

Following the deaths of Spencer (1905) and Marks (1907), management of the company did not return to family hands until 1917 when Marks's 28-year-old son Simon became chairman. In 1914 the company bought the London Penny Bazaar, an imitator of its original penny store idea.

During the 1920s Marks and Spencer broke with time-honored British retailing tradition by eliminating wholesalers and establishing links directly with manufacturers, a strategy at which the company still excels today. In 1927 Marks and Spencer went public and the following year launched its famous St Michael brand.

The company quickly turned its attention to pruning unprofitable departments to concentrate only on goods that had a rapid turnover. By the middle of the 1930s, Marks and Spencer was Europe's largest textile retailer.

The company sustained severe losses during WWII, when approximately half of its stores were damaged. Marks and Spencer rebuilt, and in 1965 Simon Marks's brother-in-law Israel Sieff became chairman.

During the early 1970s the company expanded to North America by buying 3 Canadian chains: Peoples (general merchandise), D'Allaird's (women's clothing), and Walker's (clothing shops, since converted to Marks & Spencer). The Canadian operations struggled to turn a profit.

In 1985 the company launched its long-overdue charge card and in 1988 entered the US retailing market by purchasing Kings Super Markets (New Jersey). It also acquired Brooks Brothers (upscale clothing stores) in 1988 for $750 million.

In 1992 it joined with a Viennese trading firm and a Hungarian retailer to open a clothing store in Hungary. In that same year Marks and Spencer sold Peoples.

The company opened new stores in Spain and Hong Kong in 1993 and in 1994 teamed with Turk Petrol to set up department stores in Turkey.

OTC symbol: MSL
Fiscal year ends: March 31

Chairman and CEO: Sir Richard Greenbury,
age 57, £688,938 pay
**Deputy Chairman and Managing Director,
Procurement:** J. Keith Oates, age 51
**Managing Director, Personnel, Store
Operations, Store Development, and Estates:**
Peter L. Salsbury, age 44
Executive Director, Financial Activities: Robert
W. C. Colvill, age 53
Executive Director, North American Operations:
Chris Littmoden, age 50
**Director Corporate Human Resources, North
American Operations:** Elizabeth Wood
Auditors: Coopers & Lybrand

WHERE

HQ: Michael House, 37-67 Baker St.,
London W1A 1DN, UK
Phone: +44-(01)71-935-4422
Fax: +44-(01)71-487-2679
US HQ: Marks and Spencer US Holdings Inc.,
346 Madison Ave., New York, NY 10017
US Phone: 212-697-3886
US Fax: 212-697-3857

	1994 Sales		1994 Operating Profit	
	£ mil.	% of total	£ mil.	% of total
UK & Ireland	5,685	87	810	93
Other Europe	247	4	27	3
Other countries	609	9	36	4
Total	**6,541**	**100**	**873**	**100**

WHAT

	1994 Sales	
	£ mil.	% of total
Retailing	6,418	98
Financial activities	123	2
Total	**6,541**	**100**

Stores
Brooks Brothers (US, Japan)
D'Allaird's (Canada)
Kings Super Markets (US)
Marks & Spencer (Europe, Hong Kong, Canada)

Selected Subsidiaries
Brooks Brothers Inc.
Brooks Brothers, (Japan) Ltd. (51%)
Kings Super Markets Inc (US)
Marks & Spencer Canada Inc
Marks and Spencer (France) SA
Marks and Spencer (Hong Kong) Ltd.
Marks and Spencer International Holdings Ltd.
Marks and Spencer US Holdings Inc
SA Marks and Spencer (Belgium) NV
St Michael Finance Ltd.

KEY COMPETITORS

Argyll	Hudson's Bay	Pathmark
Benetton	Ito-Yokado	J. C. Penney
Cadbury Schweppes	J Sainsbury	S&K Famous
Carrefour	John Lewis	Brands
Co-operative	Jos. A. Bank	Sears
Wholesale Society	Lane Crawford	Sincere
Dayton Hudson	The Limited	Swire Pacific
Edison Brothers	Liz Claiborne	Syms
Federated	May	Tenglemann
George Weston	Men's	Tesco
Grand Magasins	Wearhouse	Today's Man
Jelmoli SA	Montgomery	U.S. Shoe
Grand Union	Ward	Vacco
Great A&P	Nordstrom	Virgin Group

HOW MUCH

	9-Year Growth	1985	1986	1987	1988	1989	1990	1991	1992	1993[2]	1994
Sales (£ mil.)	8.2%	3,208	3,735	4,221	4,577	5,122	5,608	5,775	5,793	5,951	6,541
Net income (£ mil.)	13.8%	181	222	276	323	343	390	397	403	496	578
Income as % of sales	—	5.6%	5.9%	6.5%	7.1%	6.7%	7.0%	6.9%	6.9%	8.3%	8.8%
Earnings per share (p)	12.9%	7	8	10	12	13	15	15	15	18	21
Stock price – high (p)[1]	—	135	192	227	281	190	225	228	299	348	462
Stock price – low (p)[1]	—	99	115	167	160	140	149	181	219	268	311
Stock price – close (p)[1]	15.9%	120	176	180	183	154	201	223	279	330	454
P/E – high	—	19	24	23	23	15	15	15	20	19	22
P/E – low	—	14	14	18	13	11	10	12	15	15	15
Dividends per share (p)	11.7%	3.4	3.9	4.5	5.1	5.6	6.4	6.7	7.1	8.1	9.2
Book value per share (p)	10.2%	50	55	59	81	72	81	89	98	107	120
Employees	0.3%	60,252	63,144	66,704	68,450	76,313	75,144	74,528	67,894	62,080	62,120

1994 Year-end:
Debt ratio: 18.6%
Return on equity: 18.4%
Cash (mil.): £815
Long-term debt (mil.): £599
No. of shares (mil.): 2,779
Dividends
Yield: 2.0%
Payout: 44.0%
Market value (mil.): $18,664
Sales (mil.): $9,676

**Stock Price History[1]
High/Low 1985–94**
(chart, values 0–500)

[1] Stock prices are for the prior calendar year. [2] Accounting change

MARUBENI CORPORATION

Osaka-based Marubeni is one of Japan's largest *sogo shosha* (general trading companies), with sales of almost $140 billion in 1994. Marubeni trades in textiles, metals, machinery, agri-marine products, chemicals, fuels, minerals, foodstuffs, sporting goods, forest products, and general merchandise. The company is also involved in construction and civil engineering.

Marubeni is the entrepreneurial drive behind the Fuyo Group, a powerful assemblage of some 150 companies, including Canon, Hitachi, and Nissan. Functions of the Fuyo Group (Fuyo is another word for Mt. Fuji) include forming joint ventures and developing common think tanks.

Marubeni has been adversely affected in recent years by a downtrend in Japan's economy. Sluggish domestic demand has affected imports, and exports have suffered because of a strong yen. However, the company has remained profitable, due in large part to a 17% tax break it received in 1993. Like many Japanese companies, Marubeni has scaled down its operations. The company has cut the number of its subsidiaries by 38 through liquidation and mergers.

In cooperation with NTT, Hitachi, and ITOCHU, Marubeni is bidding on a computer contract for the People's Bank of China, which will connect the bank's offices and 80,000–100,000 of its branches.

Marubeni's origins are closely linked to another leading Japanese trading company. The man who started ITOCHU, Chubei Itoh, set up Marubeni Shoten K. K. in 1858 as an outlet in Osaka for his textile trading business. The symbol for the store was a circle (*maru*) drawn around the Japanese word for red (*beni*). As Itoh's global operations expanded, the Marubeni store served as headquarters.

C. Itoh & Co. prospered until excessive economic expansion forced it to reorganize in 1921. Marubeni was split off to trade textiles, although it soon expanded its operations to include industrial and consumer goods.

To mobilize for World War II, the Japanese government forced Marubeni to merge in 1941 with C. Itoh and another trading company, Kishimoto, into a new company, Sanko Kabushiki Kaisha. In 1944 Sanko, Daido Boeki, and Kureha Spinning were ordered to consolidate into a larger entity to be called the Daiken Company, but the war ended before all operations were fully integrated.

Marubeni was spun off from Daiken in 1949 and was authorized to conduct international trade, opening a New York office in 1951. Using its textile background, Marubeni diversified into food, metals, and machinery. During the Korean War Marubeni benefited from the UN's use of Japan as a supply base.

In 1955 Marubeni merged with Iida & Company and changed its name to Marubeni-Iida. The Japanese Ministry of International Trade and Industry granted Marubeni-Iida a concession to supply silicon steel and iron

sheets critical to the growing Japanese automobile and appliance industries. The company expanded into engineering by constructing factories, aircraft, and a nuclear reactor for the Japan Atomic Energy Research Institute. Other trading areas into which Marubeni-Iida expanded were petrochemicals, fertilizer, machinery, and rubber products.

Marubeni-Iida became part of the Fuyo Group of associated companies formed in the early 1960s. The company absorbed Totsu Company, a leading metal and steel trading operation.

In 1972 the company changed its name to Marubeni Corporation. The following year it bought Nanyo Bussan, another trading company. Also in 1973 Marubeni's image was tarnished by allegations that it had hoarded rice supplies on the Japanese black market. Marubeni's chairman was arrested 3 years later for violating Japanese foreign exchange control laws after disclosures that Marubeni had shared commissions from the sale of Lockheed aircraft with government officials.

In 1991 Marubeni established a joint venture with ICF International, a US engineering company, to construct, own, and operate a large-scale pulverized coal injection plant. In 1993 Marubeni teamed up with China National Petroleum Corp. to develop, refine, and market oil in Southeast and Central Asia.

In 1994 Marubeni became the first trading company to suspend automatic pay increases to its employees on the basis of seniority, in favor of a performance-based system.

OTC symbol: MAR (ADR)
Fiscal year ends: March 31

Chairman: Kazuo Haruna
VC: Mamoru Hashimoto
President: Iwao Toriumi
EVP Textile Group: Ryuhei Nakamura
Senior Managing Director, Corporate Accounting: Tetsuro Kitaoka
Senior Managing Director, Human Resources: Hiromasa Yamauchi
Chairman and CEO, Marubeni America: Haruro Watanabe
CFO, Marubeni America: S. Ichisaka
Auditors: Ernst & Young

HQ: 5-7, Hommachi 2-chome, Chuo-ku, Osaka 541-88, C.P.O. Box 1000, Osaka 530-91, Japan
Phone: +81-6-266-2111
Fax: +81-6-266-4280
US HQ: Marubeni America Corp., 450 Lexington Ave., New York, NY 10017
US Phone: 212-450-0100
US Fax: 212-450-0702

Marubeni operates more than 200 representative offices and nearly 650 affiliated companies in 90 countries.

	1994 Sales	
	¥ bil.	% of total
Japan	12,380	79
North America	1,272	8
Other countries	1,940	13
Total	**15,592**	**100**

	1994 Sales	
	¥ bil.	% of total
Machinery/Dev. & Const.	4,784	30
Metals	3,991	26
Energy/Chemicals	2,630	17
Textile	1,523	10
Agri-Marine Products	1,522	10
Forest Products/Other	1,142	7
Total	**15,592**	**100**

Selected US Subsidiaries and Affiliates

Archer Pipe and Tube Co., Inc. (steel pipe sales)
ATC Inc. (polypropylene compounds)
Clarino America Corp. (artificial leather)
Columbia Grain International, Inc. (grain trading)
Crest Steel Corp. (welded beams)
Energy U.S.A. Inc. (nuclear energy related business)
Fremont Beef Co. (meat processing)
Helena Chemical Co. (agrochemicals)
Kubota Tractor Corp. (development equipment)
MAC Fashion Inc. (apparel sales and importing)
Marubeni Plant Contractor, Inc. (plant construction)
Marubeni Real Estate Development Inc.
MIECO Inc. (petroleum trading)
National Power Development (construction of electricity generators)
Nissan Diesel America, Inc. (truck and bus sales)
ProCoil Corp. (steel sheet processing)
Trax Inc. (construction machinery)
Wateree Textile Corp. (taffeta weaving)
Yamakawa Manufacturing Corp. of America (auto parts)

Bechtel	Jardine Matheson	Nissho Iwai
Caterpillar	Lucky-Goldstar	PACCAR
Daewoo	Mannesmann	Rolls-Royce
Deere	Mitsubishi	Samsung
Friedrich Krupp	Mitsui	Sime Darby
Hyundai	Navistar	Sumitomo
ITOCHU	Nichimen	Tomen

$ = ¥112 (Dec. 31, 1993)	9-Year Growth	1985	1986	1987	1988	1989	1990	1991	1992	1993	1994
Sales (¥ bil.)	1.4%	13,706	14,313	13,246	13,762	14,678	18,765	19,565	18,731	17,626	15,592
Net income (¥ bil.)	(15.9%)	26	(15)	9	16	29	34	34	11	1	5
Income as % of sales	—	0.2%	(0.1%)	0.1%	0.1%	0.2%	0.2%	0.2%	0.1%	0.0%	0.0%
Earnings per share (¥)	(13.2%)	27	(15)	9	14	22	23	23	8	1	8
Stock price – high (¥)[1]	—	418	398	562	590	836	1,170	1,170	744	568	545
Stock price – low (¥)[1]	—	252	285	296	396	400	800	535	475	309	337
Stock price – close (¥)[1]	4.7%	293	322	446	396	836	1,170	660	550	371	443
P/E – high	—	15	—	65	41	38	52	51	93	768	72
P/E – low	—	9	—	34	28	18	35	24	59	418	45
Dividends per share (¥)	2.6%	4.76	4.76	4.76	4.88	5.00	5.00	6.00	6.00	6.00	6.00
Book value per share (¥)	2.6%	110	84	93	113	233	310	325	318	303	294
Employees	(0.3%)	10,250	10,170	10,118	10,008	9,987	9,905	9,935	9,949	—	10,006

1994 Year-end:
Debt ratio: 91.4%
Return on equity: 2.5%
Cash (bil.): ¥1,518
Long-term debt (bil.): ¥1,839
No. of shares (mil.): 1,493
Dividends
Yield: 1.4%
Payout: 79.7%
Market value (mil.): $5,905
Sales (mil.): $139,214

Stock Price History[1]
High/Low 1985–94

[1] Stock prices are for the prior calendar year.

MATSUSHITA ELECTRIC

Like the dinosaurs that strode across the sound studios in *Jurassic Park* (the money-spinning movie made by Matsushita's subsidiary, MCA), the lumbering electronics giant Matsushita is trying to make a big impression — in the multimedia industry. Matsushita acquired MCA for $6.6 billion in 1990. This purchase gave the company a US multimedia unit with holdings in film, theaters, TV, and publishing, i.e., the entertainment software to support the formats of its new hardware products: compact camcorders, digital audiotape, compact cassettes, and high-definition TV. Despite *Jurassic Park*'s success, entertainment brought in only 9% of 1994 sales, and the investment has yet to pay off. MCA executives have charged that Matsushita's conser-

vative management is too slow to cope with the fast-paced entertainment business.

Matsushita is the leading consumer electronics maker in the world and has built market share through low-cost, high-quality products. The company makes electronic and home appliances under the National, Panasonic, Quasar, and Technics brands and, through a controlling interest in Victor Company of Japan, the Victor and JVC brands.

Like archrival Sony, Matsushita has targeted the US and multimedia as fertile areas for growth. It has tied up a deal with 3DO to produce a high-end video game machine, hoping to produce an industry standard to best Sony, just as its VHS videos shellacked Sony's Beta videos in the 1980s.

Grade school dropout Konosuke Matsushita started in 1918 with $50 and built the largest consumer electronics company in the world. His fervent mission was to provide all households with high-quality appliances priced as low as possible and to support the greater social good. Revered as Japan's "god of business management," Matsushita formalized his ideas in 1932 with a 250-year corporate plan.

The company grew by developing inexpensive lamps, batteries, radios, and motors in the 1920s and 1930s. During WWII the Japanese government made the company build wood-laminate products for the military. Postwar occupation forces prevented Matsushita from working at his company for 4 years.

Matsushita rejoined his namesake company shortly before it entered into a joint venture, Matsushita Electronics, with Philips (The Netherlands) in 1952; it began producing televisions, refrigerators, and washing machines in 1953. Matsushita bought a majority stake in Victor Company of Japan (JVC, originally established by RCA Victor) in 1954. The 1959 opening of a subsidiary in New York began Matsushita's drive overseas.

By 1960 Matsushita had introduced vacuum cleaners, tape recorders, stereos, and color TVs. Marketed under the National, Panasonic, and Technics names, the company's products were usually not cutting edge but were always made efficiently in huge quantities and sold at low prices. Matsushita

became Japan's largest home appliance maker in the 1960s and continued to broaden its product lines, introducing air conditioners, microwave ovens, stereo components, and VCRs in the 1960s and 1970s. JVC developed the VHS format for VCRs. In 1974 the company bought Motorola's US TV plants, adding Quasar to its brand-name roster.

Under Akio Tanii's management (1986–1993), Matsushita expanded its semiconductor, office and factory automation, automobile electronics, audiovisual, housing, and air conditioning product offerings. In 1990 it paid $6.6 billion for MCA (the largest single purchase of a US company by a Japanese company to date). MCA had been founded in 1924 by Jules Stern, a Chicago ophthalmologist who had worked his way through medical school by organizing bands to play one-night stands. By 1937, when the company moved to Hollywood, MCA was handling talent for radio, TV, and motion pictures. In 1961 MCA bought Decca Records, which owned 87% of Universal Pictures. Under foreign ownership, MCA was forced to spin off its US TV stations.

In 1992 a Japanese loan-fraud scandal involving a Matsushita subsidiary led to the resignation of several executives, including Tanii himself, who stepped down in 1993.

In 1994 disgruntled MCA executives threatened to team up with the giants of the entertainment industry (David Geffen, Jeffrey Katzenberg, and Steven Spielberg) to buy back MCA.

NYSE symbol: MC (ADR)
Fiscal year ends: March 31

Chairman: Masaharu Matsushita
President: Yoichi Morishita, age 58
EVP: Tsuzo Murase
EVP: Hiroyuki Mizuno
Director of Finance: Masahiko Hirata, age 63
**Managing Director, Personnel Management and
General Affairs:** Hisao Tahara, age 63
**Chairman and CEO, Matsushita Electric
Corporation of America:** Kunio Nakamura
**CFO, Matsushita Electric Corporation of
America:** Ted Takahaski
Auditors: KPMG Peat Marwick

HQ: Matsushita Electric Industrial Co., Ltd.
(Matsushita Denki Sangyo Kabushiki Kaisha),
1006, Oaza Kadoma, Kadoma City, Osaka, Japan
Phone: +81-6-908-1121
Fax: +81-6-908-2351
US HQ: Matsushita Electric Corporation of
America, One Panasonic Way, Secaucus, NJ
07094-2917
US Phone: 201-348-7000
US Fax: 201-348-8378 (Personnel)

Matsushita has operations in 38 countries and
markets its products in over 160 countries.

	1994 Sales	
	$ mil.	% of total
Japan	43,535	68
Other countries	20,772	32
Total	**64,307**	**100**

	1994 Sales	
	$ mil.	% of total
Communication &
industrial equipment	15,926	25
Video equipment	12,683	20
Home appliances	8,132	13
Electronic components	8,051	12
Entertainment	5,697	9
Audio equipment	5,222	8
Batteries & appliances	3,366	5
Other products	5,230	8
Total	**64,307**	**100**

Major Products	
Audio products	Telephones
Batteries	TVs and VCRs
Camcorders	**Music Publishing**
Capacitors	MCA Music Entertainment
CD-ROM drives	Universal Amphitheater
Computers and PCs	**Book Publishing**
Copiers	Putnam Berkley
Displays and CRTs	**Retailing**
Fax machines	Spencer Gifts
Industrial robots	
Pagers	**Film Production/Distribution**
Semiconductors	MCA Inc.
	Universal Pictures

BASF	LG Group	Sharp
Bose	3M	Sony
Brother	Motorola	Thorn EMI
Compaq	NEC	Time Warner
Crédit Lyonnais	News Corp.	Toshiba
Daewoo	Oki	Turner Broadcasting
Fujitsu	Philips	Viacom
Hitachi	Pioneer	Virgin Group
IBM	Samsung	Walt Disney
Komatsu	Sanyo	Zenith

Stock prices are for ADRs. ADR = 10 shares	9-Year Growth	1985	1986	1987	1988	1989	1990	1991	1992	1993	1994
Sales ($ mil.)	14.5%	19,086	25,243	28,268	38,755	41,508	37,944	46,934	56,120	60,826	64,307
Net income ($ mil.)	(14.4%)	964	1,231	1,011	1,310	1,610	1,489	1,841	1,001	331	238
Income as % of sales	—	5.0%	4.9%	3.6%	3.4%	3.9%	3.9%	3.9%	1.8%	0.5%	0.4%
Earnings per share ($)	(15.8%)	5.16	6.28	5.24	6.45	7.60	6.85	8.33	4.57	1.60	1.10
Stock price – high ($)[1]	—	76.69	64.25	129.00	186.34	218.97	198.03	166.00	145.75	119.25	141.50
Stock price – low ($)[1]	—	49.31	46.19	57.13	88.78	159.22	153.75	115.50	105.00	83.00	87.00
Stock price – close ($)[1]	9.7%	58.56	61.28	120.66	160.28	197.53	164.00	118.00	116.50	93.00	135.00
P/E – high	—	15	10	25	29	29	29	20	32	75	129
P/E – low	—	10	7	11	14	21	22	14	23	52	79
Dividends per share ($)	7.1%	0.53	0.32	0.49	0.59	0.63	0.75	0.60	0.87	0.85	0.98
Book value per share ($)	16.0%	40.21	55.02	71.34	101.87	110.53	97.26	117.43	125.80	141.13	152.37
Employees	7.5%	132,814	133,963	135,881	134,186	193,088	198,299	210,848	242,246	252,075	254,059

1994 Year-end:
Debt ratio: 59.9%
Return on equity: 0.8%
Cash (mil.): $13,524
Current ratio: 1.58
Long-term debt (mil.): $12,237
No. of shares (mil.): 210
Dividends
  Yield: 0.7%
  Payout: 89.1%
Market value (mil.): $28,292

**Stock Price History[1]
High/Low 1985–94**

[1] Stock prices are for the prior calendar year.

MAZDA MOTOR CORPORATION

OVERVIEW

No one is singing, "It just feels right" around Mazda's headquarters these days. After 3 years of hammering by the strong yen; recessions in Japan, Europe, and the US; and the resurgent popularity of domestic cars in the US, Mazda slipped into the red in 1994.

In response Mazda (the smallest of Japan's large car makers) has let go more than 3,000 workers — mostly temporary contract workers — and redeployed other employees on the production line or out to sell cars door-to-door (a common sales practice there). It has also beefed up its overseas facilities, fleeing high domestic costs by exporting production to lower cost venues in Southeast Asia, China, and the US. It has no European production capacity, depending on Ford to produce some of its models for that market.

Mazda and Ford (which owns 25% of the company) have a relationship dating to 1969 (some have called Mazda Ford's small-car division). As Mazda's strategy of positioning itself as a niche maker of expensive, sporty cars has failed, the partnership with Ford has grown in importance. After 1994's loss, Ford increased its presence on Mazda's board to 7 members and, at the request of Sumitomo Bank, sent managerial assistance to Japan.

WHEN

Toyo Cork Kogyo was founded in 1920 in Hiroshima to produce cork. The company changed its name to Toyo Kogyo in 1927 and began producing machine tools in 1929. Impressed by Ford trucks used in earthquake relief efforts in 1923, founder and president Jugiro Matsuda had the company produce a 3-wheel motorcycle/truck hybrid (1931).

In the 1930s Toyo Kogyo expanded truck production, but the 2nd Sino-Japanese War forced it to cut truck output and make rifles. Although the company built a prototype passenger car in 1940, the outbreak of WWII refocused it on weapons.

The August 1945 atom bomb explosion in Hiroshima killed more than 400 Toyo Kogyo workers, but the devastated company persevered, producing 10 trucks in December. Four years later the company was turning out 800 per month. The Korean War boosted demand for the trucks in the early 1950s. In 1958 the company brought out a 4-wheeler.

The company launched the first Mazda, a 2-seat minicar, in 1960 (Mazda is derived either from a corruption of the founder's name, or from an ancient Japanese deity, or from a Zoroastrian deity). In 1961 Toyo Kogyo licensed the new, promising Wankel (rotary) engine technology from Audi. After releasing a string of models, Mazda became Japan's #3 automaker in 1964. In 1965 the company gained diesel technology in a licensing deal. In 1967 Toyo Kogyo introduced the first rotary engine Mazda, the Cosmo/110S, and followed with the Familia in 1968.

Exports to the US began in 1970, and the company grew rapidly, spending heavily on new production capacity. However, recession, high gas prices, and concern over the inefficiency of rotary engines led to a halt in growth and a massive inventory buildup in the mid-1970s. Sumitomo Bank stepped in to bail out Toyo Kogyo. The company shifted emphasis back to piston engines but managed to launch the rotary engine RX-7 in 1978.

Ford's need for small-car expertise and Sumitomo's desire for a large partner for its client led to Ford's purchase of 25% of Toyo Kogyo in 1979. Toyo Kogyo's GLC/323 and 626 models, introduced in the early 1980s, were sold as Fords in Asia, the Middle East, and Latin America. Later in the 1980s the company provided parts for the Ford Festiva, began assembling the Ford Probe, started supplying parts for the new Ford Escort, and began importing Fords (1988).

The company changed its name to Mazda in 1984 and established a US plant in 1985. Profits recovered until appreciation of the yen began to hurt margins in 1986. By 1988 the company had decided to focus on sporty niche cars, and it launched the hot-selling Miata and MPV in 1989 and the Ford-built Navajo in 1990.

In 1992 Mazda introduced the first Japanese vehicle, the 626, to be certified as having sufficient parts content (75%) to be classified as a US car under federal law. Mazda sold half its interest in its Flat Rock, Michigan, plant to Ford in 1992 and the next year reorganized Mazda of America, cutting staff drastically.

Although Mazda's management has been somewhat humiliated by the intervention, in which Ford has veto power over local decisions, the picture has improved somewhat.

Principal exchange: Tokyo
Fiscal year ends: March 31

Chairman: Norimasa Furuta, age 66
President: Yoshihiro Wada, age 63
CEO and President, Mazda Motor of America:
Kazuo Sonoguchi
**VP Human Resources, Finance, and
Administration, Mazda Motor of America:** Jeff
Badrtalei
Auditors: Asahi & Co.

HQ: 3-1, Shinchi, Fuchu-cho, Aki-gun,
Hiroshima 730-91, Japan
Phone: +81-82-282-1111
Fax: +81-82-287-5190
US HQ: Mazda Motor of America, Inc., 7755
Irvine Center Dr., Irvine, CA 97218
US Phone: 714-727-1990
US Fax: 714-727-6101

Mazda operates 2 manufacturing plants in Japan
and conducts assembly operations in 20 other
countries, including the US. The company's
vehicles are sold in over 130 countries.

	1994 Sales	
	¥ bil.	% of total
Japan	1,657	76
Other countries	531	24
Total	**2,188**	**100**

	1994 Sales	
	¥ bil.	% of total
Vehicles	1,187	67
Accessories & replacement parts	277	16
Parts & components	156	9
Other	148	8
Adjustments	420	—
Total	**2,188**	**100**

Passenger Car Models (US Markets)

626	MX-5 Miata
929	MX-6
B-series	Navajo
Millenia	Protegé
MPV	RX-7

Selected Subsidiaries and Affiliates
AutoAlliance International, Inc. (50-50 joint
venture with Ford)
Autozam Inc.
Eunos Inc.
Kurashiki Kako Co., Ltd.

BMW	
British Aerospace	Mitsubishi
Chrysler	Nissan
Daewoo	Peugeot
Daimler-Benz	Renault
Fiat	Saab-Scania
Ford	Suzuki
General Motors	Toyota
Honda	Volkswagen
Hyundai	Volvo
Isuzu	
Kia Motors	

$=¥112 (Dec. 31, 1993)	9-Year Growth	1985	1986	1987	1988[2]	1989	1990	1991	1992	1993	1994
Sales (¥ bil.)	4.1%	1,530	1,669	1,728	1,691	2,004	2,402	2,714	2,722	2,593	2,188
Net income (¥ bil.)	—	35	40	15	5	10	23	27	9	1	(49)
Income as % of sales	—	2.3%	0.9%	0.3%	0.5%	1.0%	1.0%	0.3%	0.3%	0.0%	—
Earnings per share (¥)	—	40	44	16	5	10	22	25	9	1	(46)
Stock price – high (¥)[1]	—	570	492	430	491	888	1,130	1,010	658	540	625
Stock price – low (¥)[1]	—	420	385	361	354	385	736	500	459	385	310
Stock price – close (¥)[1]	(0.7%)	435	390	372	395	745	1,010	568	520	406	409
P/E – high	—	14	11	27	106	86	49	41	73	—	—
P/E – low	—	11	9	23	76	37	33	20	51	—	—
Dividends per share (¥)	—	7.00	7.50	7.50	7.50	7.50	7.50	7.50	7.50	6.00	0.00
Book value per share (¥)	(3.4%)	281	323	329	326	331	365	373	374	383	205
Employees	0.7%	27,365	27,406	27,600	28,500	28,423	28,573	29,578	29,835	30,164	29,161

1994 Year-end:
Debt ratio: 68.1%
Return on equity: —
Cash (bil.): ¥218
Long-term debt (bil.): ¥468
No. of shares (mil.): 1,076
Dividends
  Yield: —
  Payout: —
Market value (mil.): $3,929
Sales (mil.): $19,536

**Stock Price History[1]
High/Low 1985–94**

[1] Stock prices are for the prior calendar year. [2] Accounting change

MICHELIN

OVERVIEW

Michelin has been bold in its pursuit of becoming the #1 tire maker in the world. The radial tire pioneer now dominates with a 20% world market share, but overexpansion and heavy debt has forced the company to restructure. Michelin makes 3,500 types of tires for vehicles ranging from automobiles and tractors to aircraft and earthmovers. It also manufactures tubes, wheels, steel cables, and Michelin maps. In addition, the company publishes Michelin Guide travel books. Michelin sells its products in 170 countries;

82% of its tires are sold outside France. It has 14 plants in North America.

The Michelin family controls and manages the company. Patriarch François Michelin has personally run the company for over 40 years, during which time the company developed a reputation for secrecy.

In a belated bid to modernize, Michelin began restructuring the company in 1993, doing away with supervisors, promoting employee innovation, and streamlining the once hierarchical decision-making process.

WHEN

After dabbling in the manufacture of rubber balls, Edouard Daubrée and Aristide Barbier formed a partnership in Clermont-Ferrand, France, in 1863 and entered the rubber business in earnest. Both founders died shortly afterward and the company struggled. In 1886 the Barbier family asked André Michelin, a successful businessman who had married into the family, to take over. Unable to devote full time to the venture, André persuaded his brother, Edouard, a Paris artist, to run the company, renamed Michelin in 1889.

In 1889 Edouard noticed the riding comfort afforded by air-filled tires. The tires were experimental, glued to the rims, and required several hours to replace. In 1891 Edouard made a bicycle tire with a detachable bolt that allowed replacement in 15 minutes.

The Michelin brothers promoted their removable tires by persuading cyclists to use them in long-distance races in which punctures were likely. The brothers demonstrated that pneumatic tires could work on cars in an auto race in 1895. In 1898 André commented that a stack of tires would look like a man if it had arms, a notion that led to Bib, the Michelin Man. André also launched the Michelin Guide for auto tourists in 1900.

Michelin opened a sales office in London (1905) and began production in Italy (1906) and New Jersey (1908). It made airplanes during WWI. Michelin inventions included detachable rims and spare tires (1906), tubeless tires (1930), treads (1934), and low-profile (squat, like today's) tires (1937). During the Great Depression Michelin closed the New Jersey plant and accepted a stake in Citroën, later converted into a minority interest in Peugeot, in lieu of payment for tires. André Michelin died in 1931, Edouard in 1940.

Michelin received a patent for radial tires in 1946. Expansion was largely confined to Europe in the 1950s. Michelin grew internationally in the 1960s, unchallenged in radials. In 1966 the company's US position was enhanced by Ford's decision to put Michelin radials on its 1968 Lincoln Continental Mark III and Sears's decision to sell Michelins.

Michelin enjoyed worldwide growth in radial sales in the 1970s. The company spent heavily on global expansion and started production in Greenville, South Carolina, in 1975. Michelin had become the #2 tire maker by 1980, but recession and expansion-related debt service induced losses of $1.5 billion between 1980 and 1984. Michelin rebounded and opened plants and sales companies in Asia. In 1990 the company paid $1.5 billion for Uniroyal Goodrich, the product of a merger of 2 US tire companies founded in the late 1800s.

Michelin successfully introduced a new-generation car tire, the MXT, in 1990 as an all-weather replacement to the MXL, the world's most popular tire. In 1991 the company offered the highest mileage passenger tire (80,000 miles) ever manufactured for the American market, the XH4. At the Detroit and Geneva Auto shows in 1992, Michelin presented its new "green" tires, which will contribute to greater fuel efficiency and cleaner air by having 35% less rolling resistance than standard tires.

In 1993 the company began a 2-year plan to rationalize production and reduce debt by about $600 million.

In a sign that Michelin was changing its ways, the company launched The Classic tire in 1994 at a price 15% below its standard tire price. The old Michelin never discounted.

Principal exchange: Paris
Fiscal year ends: December 31

Managing Partner: François Michelin, age 67
Managing Partner: Edouard Michelin, age 31
Managing Partner: René Zingraff
Finance Director: Eric Bourdais de Charbonnière
Director Human Resources, North America:
Jean-Louis Vincent
**Chairman, President, and CEO, Michelin Tire
(US):** Carlos Ghosn, age 40
**EVP Legal/Administrative (CFO), Michelin Tire
(US):** Jim Micali
Auditors: Paul-Carlos Mulquin, Dominique Paul,
and Gonzague Lauras, Compagnie Régionale
de Paris

WHERE

HQ: Compagnie Générale des Établissements
Michelin, 23 Place des Carmes-Déchaux,
63040 Clermont-Ferrand Cedex, France
Phone: +33-73-30-42-21
Fax: +33-73-30-22-02
US HQ: Michelin Tire Corporation,
PO Box 19001, Greenville, SC 29602-9001
US Phone: 803-458-5000
US Fax: 803-458-6359

	1993 Sales % of total
Americas	36
France	18
Other Europe	37
Other countries	9
Total	**100**

WHAT

	1993 Sales % of total
Tires & wheels	97
General rubber goods, maps, guidebooks & sundries	3
Total	**100**

Major Subsidiaries and Affiliates
Compagnie Financière Michelin (95.1%, holding
company)
Manufacture Française des Pneumatiques
Michelin (97.1%, French operations)
Michelin Aircraft Tire Corp. (92.8%, US)
Michelin Guides (travel books)
Michelin Korea Tire Co. Ltd. (95.1%)
Michelin Tire Corp. (95.1%, US)
Michelin Tires (Canada) Ltd. (95.1%)
Nihon Michelin Tire Co. Ltd. (95.1%, sales,
Japan)
Pneu Laurent (97.1%, retreading)
Pneumáticos Michelin Ltda. (95.1%, Brazil)
Pneumatiques Kléber (93.1%, tires)
Uniroyal Goodrich Tire Co. (95.1%, US)
Wolber (97.1%, bicycle tires)

Other Shareholdings
Banque Industrielle et Mobiliere Priveé (36.4%)
Peugeot SA (6.1%)

KEY COMPETITORS

Bandag	Goodyear
Big O Tires	Nokia
Brad Ragan	Pirelli
Bridgestone	Sears
Continental AG	Sime Darby
Cooper Tire & Rubber	Sumitomo

HOW MUCH

$=FF5.91 (Dec. 31, 1993)	Annual Growth	1984	1985	1986	1987	1988	1989	1990	1991	1992	1993
Sales (FF mil.)	4.0%	44,382	46,641	46,328	46,936	51,280	55,256	62,737	67,649	66,847	63,298
Net income (FF mil.)[1]	—	(2,242)	989	1,910	2,444	2,367	2,449	(4,811)	(699)	79	(3,670)
Income as % of sales	—	—	2.1%	4.1%	5.2%	4.6%	4.4%	—	—	0.1%	—
Earnings per share (FF)	—	(55)	19	28	34	29	24	(45)	(7)	1	(34)
Stock price – high (FF)	—	108	165	357	384	226	212	177	138	221	212
Stock price – low (FF)	—	73	74	173	169	136	152	58	63	120	131
Stock price – close (FF)	12.1%	75	165	255	178	197	168	63	122	182	210
P/E – high	—	—	9	13	11	8	9	—	—	—	—
P/E – low	—	—	4	6	5	5	6	—	—	—	—
Dividends per share (FF)	—	0.00	0.00	1.80	2.00	2.20	2.25	2.40	0.00	1.50	0.00
Book value per share (FF)	(7.7%)	140	140	138	165	173	168	104	105	104	68
Employees	(7.7%)	—	—	118,584	117,276	119,827	124,408	140,826	135,610	125,000	124,575

1993 Year-end:
Debt ratio: 83.7%
Return on equity: —
Cash (mil.): FF2,060
Long-term debt (mil.): FF26,754
No. of shares (mil.): 107
Dividends
  Yield: —
  Payout: —
Market value (mil.): $3,802
Sales (mil.): $10,710

**Stock Price History
High/Low 1984–93**

(chart: values 400, 350, 300, 250, 200, 150, 100, 50, 0)

Note: All share data pertain to "B" shares. [1] Including extraordinary items; including minority interests 1984

MINOLTA CO., LTD.

Reeling from a strong yen and a business slowdown in Japan, Minolta, a leading camera maker, is diversifying and pushing for more efficiency. As part of its continuing reorganization, the company in 1994 changed its name to Minolta Co., Ltd., from Minolta Camera Co., to reflect its broader product line. Once the leader in traditional single-lens reflex (SLR) cameras, Minolta redefined itself in the late 1980s as a processor of light and images when bested by lower-priced, more convenient cameras pioneered by Fuji Photo. Now Minolta is a producer of various office automation equipment — such as plain-paper copiers and fax machines, color copiers, microfilm

equipment, and laser printers — as well as optical precision instruments, which include SLR cameras, lenses, measuring instruments, binoculars, and planetariums. Office equipment represents 68% of total sales.

Minolta is boosting its product development, expanding manufacturing overseas, and streamlining its marketing operations to regain profits. Losses narrowed in 1994. The company also is developing office products for Japan like those in the US that combine imaging, fax, copying, and computing through systems management software. In late 1994 Minolta formed 2 joint ventures with Chinese companies to produce cameras and copy machines in China in 1995.

Kazuo Tashima, aided by German trader Wilhelm Heilemann and optical engineer Wilhelm Neumann, founded the Japanese-German Camera Company (Nichi-Doku Shashinki Shoten) in Osaka in 1928 to make quality optical equipment, introducing the Nifcalette bellows camera in 1929. Heilemann and Neumann left the company in 1931.

In 1933 Tashima coined the name Minolta for his expanding line of cameras. Similar in sound to the Japanese expression for ripening rice fields (*minoru-ta*), Minolta also is an English acronym for *M*achinery and *I*nstruments *O*ptica*l* by *Ta*shima.

In 1934 Tashima introduced the Minolta Vest, the camera that made Minolta a household word in Japan. Renamed Chiyoda Optics and Fine Engineering (Chiyoda Kogaku Seiko, 1937), the company made the first Japanese twin-lens camera in 1937 and during WWII made optical equipment such as binoculars and range finders for the Japanese military. Although its facilities were destroyed by Allied bombs in 1945, the company benefited from US postwar recovery loans.

The company expanded to the US and Europe in the 1950s and increased its presence in Southeast Asia in the 1960s. After astronaut John Glenn used a Minolta camera to take pictures from orbit in 1962, Tashima changed the company's name to Minolta Camera Company. In the meantime, the company diversified into office equipment, producing its first copier in the 1950s under

license from the Van der Grinten company of the Netherlands.

Minolta overtook Nikon as America's SLR leader in 1973. In 1974 it started producing the successful EG 101 copier. By 1975 exports made up about 80% of sales.

However, the company ran into some trouble in the late 1970s, when Canon's automated AE-1 outsold the SR-T 101. Not until 1985 did Minolta regain its leadership in the SLR market by introducing the fully automated Maxxum 7000.

In 1982 Tashima, who had directed Minolta for over 50 years, stepped into the chairmanship, allowing his son Hideo to replace him as president. The founder died in 1985.

Minolta reported a 41% drop in pretax profits in 1991, citing escalating R&D expenses and price competition as reasons for the decline. The company reorganized, giving its 5 operating managers full control over R&D to encourage faster, market-driven product development. Despite a cost-cutting program in 1992, Minolta skipped its 2nd-half dividend for the first time in 26 years. The company subsequently cut back on hiring and advertising, sold off some real estate assets, and cut directors' salaries by 10%.

In a continuing effort to diversify, Minolta announced in 1992 an agreement to establish retail sales outlets in Japan for Apple's Macintosh computers and to develop related products. In 1994 the company suspended production and sales of video cameras for the Japanese market.

Principal exchange: Tokyo
Fiscal year ends: March 31

Chairman: Hideo Tashima
President: Osamu Kanaya
Senior Executive Director: Tatsuro Doro
Executive Director Finance: Yoshihiko
  Higashiyama
Chairman, Minolta Corporation (U.S.A.):
  Sadahei Kusomoto
**President and CEO, Minolta Corporation
  (U.S.A.):** Hiroshi Fujii
**EVP and Treasurer, Minolta Corporation
  (U.S.A.):** Ko Ikeuchi
**Director Human Resources, Minolta Corporation
  (U.S.A.):** Thomas R. McVeigh
Auditors: Showa Ota & Co.

HQ: 3-13, Azuchi-machi 2-chome, Chuo-ku,
  Osaka 541, Japan
Phone: +81-6-271-2251
Fax: +81-6-266-1010
US HQ: Minolta Corporation (U.S.A.),
  101 Williams Dr., Ramsey, NJ 07446-1293
US Phone: 201-825-4000
US Fax: 201-934-4631 (Corporate
  Communications)

	1994 Sales	
	¥ bil.	% of total
Japan	126	39
Other countries	195	61
Adjustments	(110)	—
Total	**321**	**100**

	1994 Sales	
	¥ bil.	% of total
Copiers	162	50
Printers & other business		
equipment	59	18
Cameras	54	17
Camera accessories & other		
photographic equipment	28	9
Interchangeable lenses	12	4
Other	6	2
Total	**321**	**100**

Business Machines	**Other Products**
Copiers	Medical instruments
Fax machines	Optical systems
Laser printers	Planetariums
Microfilm equipment	Radiometric instruments
Word processors	

Cameras and Accessories
Binoculars
Cameras
Color analyzers
Compact cameras
Exposure meters
Interchangeable lenses
Spectrophotometers
Thermometers

Bausch & Lomb	IBM	Ricoh
Bell & Howell	Kyocera	Seiko
Brother	Matsushita	Sharp
Canon	3M	Sony
Eastman Kodak	NEC	Thomson SA
Fuji Photo	Océ	Toshiba
GEC	Oki	Xerox
Harris	Olivetti	Zenith
Hasler	Pitney Bowes	
Hewlett-Packard	Polaroid	

$=¥112 (Dec. 31, 1993)	Annual Growth	1985	1986	1987	1988	1989	1990	1991	1992	1993	1994
Sales (¥ bil.)	4.6%	214	245	309	309	291	306	371	356	348	321
Net income (¥ bil.)	—	4	7	11	7	3	2	(2)	(36)	(10)	(5)
Income as % of sales	—	2.0%	2.8%	3.6%	2.4%	0.9%	0.7%	—	—	—	—
Earnings per share (¥)	—	20	31	46	30	10	7	(8)	(69)	(371)	(17)
Stock price – high (¥)[1]	—	574	933	857	730	845	1,120	1,150	787	565	495
Stock price – low (¥)[1]	—	420	476	593	492	528	735	535	496	289	311
Stock price – close (¥)[1]	1.6%	492	867	639	519	753	1,070	608	545	339	427
P/E – high	—	29	20	29	73	121	80	—	—	—	—
P/E – low	—	21	10	20	49	75	53	—	—	—	—
Dividends per share (¥)	(100.0%)	7.14	7.14	7.87	7.87	8.50	8.50	8.50	4.25	0.00	0.00
Book value per share (¥)	2.4%	244	248	334	361	363	386	391	252	212	196
Employees	2.6%	—	—	—	6,687	—	6,537	6,608	6,741	6,826	5,701

1994 Year-end:
Debt ratio: 77.2%
Return on equity: (8.3%)
Cash (bil.): ¥55
Long-term debt (bil.): ¥39
No. of shares (mil.): 279
Dividends
  Yield: —
  Payout: —
Market value (mil.): $1,064
Sales (mil.): $2,866

**Stock Price History[1]
High/Low 1985–94**

[1] Stock prices are for the prior calendar year.

MITSUBISHI GROUP

If you can eat it, wear it, watch it, listen to it, or drive it, Mitsubishi makes it, and also gathered the raw materials and produced the machines that made it. Mitsubishi Group is Japan's 2nd largest *keiretsu* (a group of affiliated companies), with total group revenues of over $150 billion in 1994. A *keiretsu* has no legal identity.

At the center of the group of more than 150 companies are Mitsubishi Corporation (the group's chief trading company), Mitsubishi Bank (one of Japan's largest banks), and Mitsubishi Heavy Industries (Japan's largest heavy machinery maker). Other important companies include Mitsubishi Electric, which produces everything from satellite technology to home electronics to large-screen Diamond Vision TVs (*mitsubishi* means "3 diamonds" in Japanese), and Mitsubishi

Motors. Companies in the group also make foods, clothing, and shoes.

Until the Japanese recession hit, these interests played their part in the *keiretsu*'s structure by providing materials, supplies, and sales outlets for each other and diversifying income. But with much of Japan's economy in recession, diversity could not shield the group from declining sales and falling earnings (Mitsubishi Corp.'s were off 72% between 1991 and 1994).

Mitsubishi has wide international interests, which in theory should help stabilize results, but ecomomic problems in much of the world are putting this theory to the test.

Tokio Marine & Fire and Meiji Mutual Life Insurance each owns about 6% of Mitsubishi Corporation, and other Mitsubishi entities own 13%.

Yataro Iwasaki's close ties to the Japanese government (along with subsidies and monopoly rights) ensured the success of his shipping and trading company, Mitsubishi. Founded in 1870, Mitsubishi diversified into mining (1873), banking (1885), and shipbuilding (1887) and began withdrawing from shipping in the 1880s. In the 1890s it invested in Japanese railroads and property.

In 1918 the Mitsubishi *zaibatsu* (family-run conglomerate) spun off Mitsubishi Trading, its purchasing, sales, and central management arm. By WWII the Mitsubishi *zaibatsu* had become a huge amalgam of divisions and public companies. During WWII the group made warplanes (including the Zero fighter plane), ships, and explosives.

The *zaibatsu* were dissolved by order of the US occupation forces and Mitsubishi was split into 139 entities. After the occupation the Japanese government encouraged many former *zaibatsu* companies to reunite, chiefly as a means for capitalization, around the old *zaibatsu* banks. In 1954 Mitsubishi Trading reorganized as the leader of the Mitsubishi Group and established Mitsubishi International (New York), a trading subsidiary that became a leading exporter of US goods.

In the 1960s and 1970s Mitsubishi Trading exploited Japan's increasing need for raw materials by importing minerals and fuels. Renamed Mitsubishi Corporation in 1971, it was a leader of Japan's export drive.

The 1964 merger of 3 Mitsubishi companies created Mitsubishi Heavy Industries, Japan's leading producer of ships, power plants, heavy machinery, and aircraft. Mitsubishi Kasei, separated from its Asahi Glass (now the largest glass maker in Japan) and Mitsubishi Rayon (fibers) divisions by US fiat, became Japan's largest chemical concern. Mitsubishi Electric became one of Japan's leading electrical equipment and electronics manufacturers.

Throughout the 1980s the Japanese seemed economically invincible. A Japanese buying spree in the US brought calls for protectionism. (Mitsubishi bought a majority share of Rockefeller Center's management company.) Then the "bubble economy" burst, and with it went some of Mitsubishi's luster. The group fell behind in electronics and autos in the US, consumer demand dried up at home, and Mitsubishi Bank was left with a heavy burden of bad loans. The Heavy Industries unit was forced to cut its work force.

In 1993, in a loosening of old *keiretsu* ties, the company began importing sheet glass (formerly sourced from Asahi Glass) from the US. Also in that year Chrysler, a shareholder since 1971, announced that it would sell its interest in Mitsubishi Motors.

In 1994 Mitsubishi Electric began trying to revitalize its business by announcing a plan (with Hitachi) to challenge Intel in the flash-memory chip market.

OTC symbol: MTSBY (ADR)
Fiscal year ends: March 31

Chairman: Shinroku Morohashi
President: Minoru Makihara
Managing Director, Administration: Mitsutake
Okano
**President and CEO, Mitsubishi International
(US):** Mikio Sasaki
**EVP, Treasurer, and CFO, Mitsubishi
International (US):** Masatoshi Miyoshi
Auditors: Deloitte Touche Tohmatsu

WHERE

HQ: Mitsubishi Shoji Kabushiki Kaisha, 6-3,
Marunouchi 2-chome, Chiyoda-ku,
Tokyo 100-86, Japan
Phone: +81-3-3210-2121
Fax: +81-3-3210-8931
US HQ: Mitsubishi International Corporation,
520 Madison Ave., New York, NY 10022-4223
US Phone: 212-605-2000
US Fax: 212-605-2597

Mitsubishi has 190 offices worldwide.

	1994 Sales		1994 Operating Income	
	¥ bil.	% of total	¥ bil.	% of total
Japan	13,146	76	20	59
Europe	2,675	16	1	2
North America	1,060	6	6	17
Other regions	395	2	7	22
Adjustment	—	—	(1)	—
Total	**17,276**	**100**	**33**	**100**

WHAT

	1994 Sales	
	¥ bil.	% of total
Metals	6,394	37
Machinery/info. systems & services	4,268	25
Foods	2,195	13
Fuels	1,963	11
Chemicals, textiles & other	2,456	14
Total	**17,276**	**100**

Selected Affiliates

Asahi Glass Co., Ltd.
Kirin Brewery
The Meiji Mutual Life
 Insurance Co.
Mitsubishi Aluminum Co.,
 Ltd.
The Mitsubishi Bank, Ltd.
Mitsubishi Cable Industries,
 Ltd.
Mitsubishi Construction
 Co., Ltd.
Mitsubishi Electric Corp.
Mitsubishi Estate Co., Ltd.
Mitsubishi Gas Chemical
 Co., Inc.
Mitsubishi Heavy
 Industries, Ltd.
Mitsubishi Kakoki Kaisha,
 Ltd. (process equipment)
Mitsubishi Kasei Corp.
 (chemicals)

Mitsubishi Materials Corp.
Mitsubishi Motors Corp.
Mitsubishi Oil Co., Ltd.
Mitsubishi Paper Mills, Ltd.
Mitsubishi Petrochemical Co.,
 Ltd.
Mitsubishi Plastics Industries,
 Ltd.
Mitsubishi Rayon Co., Ltd.
Mitsubishi Steel Manufacturing
 Co., Ltd.
The Mitsubishi Trust and
 Banking Corp.
Mitsubishi Warehouse &
 Transportation Co., Ltd.
Nikon Corp. (cameras)
Nippon Yusen Kabushiki
 Kaisha (marine transport)
The Tokio Marine and Fire
 Insurance Co., Ltd.

KEY COMPETITORS

Daewoo
Hyundai
ITOCHU
LG Group
Marubeni

Mitsui
Nippon Steel
Samsung
Sime Darby
Sumitomo

HOW MUCH

$ = ¥112 (Dec. 31, 1993)	9-Year Growth	1985	1986	1987	1988	1989	1990	1991	1992	1993	1994
Sales (¥ bil.)	1.0%	15,815	17,221	17,095	12,660	13,365	15,644	19,727	18,122	17,793	17,276
Net income (¥ bil.)	(4.4%)	27	32	32	27	31	46	65	52	29	18
Income as % of sales	—	0.2%	0.2%	0.2%	0.2%	0.2%	0.2%	0.3%	0.3%	0.2%	0.1%
Earnings per share (¥)	(5.2%)	19	23	23	18	20	29	41	33	18	12
Stock price – high (¥)[1]	—	594	720	1,500	1,660	1,380	2,010	1,990	1,450	1,330	1,210
Stock price – low (¥)[1]	—	500	510	582	941	959	1,350	1,120	1,100	827	843
Stock price – close (¥)[1]	7.6%	555	624	990	989	1,330	2,010	1,370	1,300	854	1,070
P/E – high	—	31	31	81	83	47	53	49	44	73	103
P/E – low	—	26	23	32	48	33	35	27	33	46	72
Dividends per share (¥)	2.6%	6.36	6.68	7.00	7.00	7.00	7.00	8.00	8.00	8.00	8.00
Book value per share (¥)	4.4%	303	322	287	301	324	358	452	465	463	447
Employees	0.1%	13,865	14,125	13,925	13,932	13,690	13,237	13,629	13,602	—	10,297

1994 Year-end:
Debt ratio: 88.8%
Return on equity: 2.6%
Cash (bil.): ¥856
Long-term debt (bil.): ¥2,540
No. of shares (mil.): 1,565
Dividends
 Average yield: 0.7%
 Payout: 68.3%
Market value (mil.): $14,951
Sales (mil.): $154,250

**Stock Price History[1]
High/Low 1985–94**

Information is for Mitsubishi Corporation only. [1]Stock prices are for the prior calendar year.

MITSUI GROUP

OVERVIEW

Led by the world's oldest general trading concern, Mitsui & Co., the Mitsui Group is the largest business enterprise in the world and Japan's leading *keiretsu* (industrial group loosely connected through cross-ownership). It operates an empire of 742 companies, of which 333 are located outside Japan.

The group has major operations in construction, investment, finance, transportation, machinery, chemicals, nonferrous metals, and foodstuffs. Japan's largest LPG transport fleet is operated by a Mitsui company, and Mitsui & Co. dominates the Japanese import market for cigarettes and sports and hobby goods.

The economic slowdown in Japan and the strong yen have prompted Mitsui management to pursue a range of projects overseas, particularly around the Pacific Rim. In 1993 the company teamed up with DuPont to make and market chemicals across Asia.

China has emerged as a key market for Mitsui. By 1994 it was operating a wide spectrum of businesses there, from cement manufacturing to consumer products such as pocket pagers and foodstuffs. In that year it invested $85 million in 11 offices and 57 joint ventures and had 47 plants in operation. By the year 2000 Mitsui plans to have 100 joint ventures operating in China.

WHEN

Defeated by the Japanese shogun Nobunaga, the Mitsui family fled Omi Province in 1568. Unemployed samurai Sokubei Mitsui opened a sake and soy sauce brewery at the urging of his wife, Shuho, who eventually took over management of the business. Shuho encouraged her sons to enter business and the youngest, Hachirobei, went to Edo (now Tokyo) and opened a dry goods store (Mitsukoshi's predecessor) in 1673. Breaking with Japanese retailing tradition, the store offered merchandise at fixed prices on a cash-and-carry basis.

In 1683 Hachirobei started a currency exchange that evolved into Mitsui Bank. The business received a big boost in 1691 when it became the Osaka government's official money changer. Hachirobei's bank introduced money orders to Japan and profited by securing up to 90 days' float on funds transfers between Osaka, Edo, and Kyoto. Before he died in 1694, Hachirobei created a nontraditional succession scheme to pass control of the business to all related families, not just to the eldest son's family.

In the mid-1800s the government ordered Mitsui to help finance its war with rebels. The family hired Rizaemon Minomura, an outsider with government links, who managed to protect Mitsui from increasing demands for cash. Minomura then made a timely switch of support to the victorious rebel side and Mitsui became the bank of the Meiji government. The government's industrialization drive led Mitsui into paper, textiles, and a machinery business that was an antecedent of Toshiba. Minomura emphasized expansion in foreign trade and banking, formally creating Mitsui Bussan (now Mitsui & Co.) and Mitsui Bank in 1876. In the late 1800s the Mitsui *zaibatsu* (family-run conglomerate) profited from Japanese military activity, challenged Mitsubishi's shipping monopoly with its own line, and acquired coal mines. The Mitsui family withdrew from management of Mitsui Bussan in 1936, following a violent campaign by right-wing terrorists against the democratic capitalist establishment.

Prior to WWII the group benefited from the Japanese military buildup and helped fund Toyota. After the war, occupation forces split war-torn Mitsui into over 180 separate entities, but in 1950, 27 leaders of former Mitsui companies formed the Getsuyo-kai and the group began gathering itself together again. The larger Nimoku-kai was established in 1961. The group has expanded rapidly in petrochemicals and metals. Mitsui & Co. extended its overseas presence and bought 50% of AMAX's aluminum operations in 1974.

In 1990 Mitsui Bank and Taiyo Kobe Bank merged to form the world's 2nd largest bank, after Dai-Ichi Kangyo. Also in 1990 Mitsui & Co. terminated an ill-fated petrochemical venture in Iran, writing off a large portion of its $1.4 billion investment in the project.

In 1992 Mitsui joined up with Marathon Oil and McDermott International to conduct a feasibility study of oil and gas reserves off Sakhalin Island. Mitsui and other Japanese traders were enlisted by Oman in 1993 for a $9 billion LNG venture in 1994 Mitsui teamed up with National Media Corp. to launch a home-shopping network in Japan.

Nasdaq symbol: MITSY (ADR)
Fiscal year ends: March 31

Chairman: Koichiro Ejiri
President and CEO: Naohiko Kumagai
EVP: Akira Utsumi
EVP: Masaharu Takahashi
President and CEO, Mitsui & Co. (U.S.A.):
Goro Watanabe
EVP, Mitsui & Co. (U.S.A.): Yoshiyuki
Kawashima
Auditors: Deloitte Touche Tohmatsu

HQ: Mitsui Bussan Kabushiki Kaisha,
2-1, Ohtemachi 1-chome, Chiyoda-ku,
Tokyo 100, Japan
Phone: +81-3-3285-1111
Fax: +81-3-3285-9800
US HQ: Mitsui & Co. (U.S.A.), Inc., 200 Park
Ave., New York, NY 10166-0130
US Phone: 212-878-4000
US Fax: 212-878-4800

The Mitsui Group has offices in over 200 cities
worldwide.

	1994 Sales		1994 Operating Income	
	$ mil.	% of total	$ mil.	% of total
Japan	132,042	77	906	29
Europe	22,881	13	216	7
North America	9,738	6	932	30
Other regions	7,576	4	1,046	34
Adjustments	—	—	274	—
Total	**172,237**	**100**	**3,374**	**100**

	1994 Sales	
	$ mil.	% of total
Nonferrous metals	50,586	29
Machinery	36,221	21
Energy	18,857	11
Iron & steel	17,188	10
Foodstuffs	15,781	9
Chemicals	14,639	9
Other	18,965	11
Total	**172,237**	**100**

Principal Operating Groups

Communications and Transportation	Specialty Chemicals and Plastics
Electric Machinery	Textiles
Electronics and Information	Transportation Logistics
Energy	**Selected Affiliates**
Fertilizer and Inorganic Chemicals	Bussan Supply Co., Ltd.
Foods	Furukawa Electric Cables (Malaysia) Sdn. Bhd.
General Merchandise	Mitsui & Co., Overseas Steel Exploration Corp.
Industrial Machinery	Mitsui Bussan Construction Materials Co., Ltd.
Iron and Steel	
Nonferrous Metals	Mitsui Foods Inc.
Petrochemicals and Polymers	Mitsui Oil & Gas Co., Ltd.
Plant and Project	Nihon Unisys, Ltd.
Property and Service Business Development	Orient Marine Co., Ltd.
	Toyo Ship Machinery Co., Ltd.
	Toyota Canada Inc.

Daewoo	Mitsubishi
Hyundai	Nissho Iwai
ITOCHU	Samsung
Kanematsu	Sime Darby
LG Group	Sumitomo
Marubeni	Tomen

	9-Year Growth	1985	1986	1987	1988	1989	1990	1991	1992	1993	1994
Sales ($ mil.)	10.3%	71,135	102,841	98,839	128,158	126,346	123,675	148,264	134,163	149,315	172,237
Net income ($ mil.)	12.4%	40	66	105	187	304	231	292	203	116
Income as % of sales	—	0.1%	0.1%	0.1%	0.1%	0.2%	0.2%	0.2%	0.2%	0.1%	0.1%
Earnings per share ($)	8.4%	0.72	1.09	1.66	2.90	4.30	3.08	2.52	2.52	1.92	1.49
Stock price – high ($)[1]	—	29.35	39.72	91.35	126.46	159.13	205.50	192.00	134.00	128.50	157.25
Stock price – low ($)[1]	—	22.63	21.84	37.06	64.80	96.84	129.25	91.50	100.75	79.00	90.00
Stock price – close ($)[1]	20.2%	24.00	35.75	64.33	105.95	157.00	192.75	115.00	121.75	97.25	125.50
P/E – high	—	41	66	55	44	37	67	76	53	67	106
P/E – low	—	31	20	22	22	23	42	36	40	41	60
Dividends per share ($)	13.1%	0.36	0.41	0.61	0.71	0.95	0.72	0.84	0.89	0.96	1.09
Book value per share ($)	19.1%	15.03	19.13	25.14	34.74	42.01	49.96	57.12	60.57	67.35	72.71
Employees	0.4%	11,608	11,445	11,396	11,098	10,772	11,656	11,730	11,773	11,528	12,084

1994 Year-end:
Debt ratio: 92.2%
Return on equity: 2.1%
Cash (mil.): $9,990
Current ratio: 1.07
Long-term debt (mil.): $22,478
No. of shares (mil.): 78
Dividends
Yield: 0.9%
Payout: 73.2%
Market value (mil.): $9,779

Stock Price History[1]
High/Low 1985–94

Information is for Mitsui & Co., Ltd. only. [1] Stock prices are for the prior calendar year.

THE MOLSON COMPANIES LIMITED

OVERVIEW

The Molson name is most often associated with brewing, and for good reason — the company is the #1 brewer in Canada and the #2 beer exporter to the US. However, the Toronto-based company pours more than beer into its sales figures these days.

The company's biggest operation is not beer but cleaning. Diversey is the market leader in institutional cleaning and sanitizing, providing products and services to businesses in more than 100 countries. Through Beaver Lumber, Molson operates Canada's leading home improvement retailer, and it has a 25% interest in The Home Depot Canada. Molson also owns the most successful team in NHL history, the Montreal Canadiens. The company's brewing operations are run through Molson Breweries, a joint venture with Foster's and Miller Brewing in which it holds a 40% stake.

Although Diversey has struggled recently because of stiff competition, Molson is focusing on expanding that business and has announced plans to sell Beaver Lumber.

The Molson family owns 38.7% of the company's voting shares.

WHEN

John Molson founded North America's oldest brewery in Montreal in 1786. In order to ensure a steady supply of grain, Molson brought seeds from England and gave them to local farmers free of charge. Molson's brewery did a healthy business, thanks in large part to the lack of competition in this frontier city. With the brewery humming along, Molson began to diversify. In 1797 he added a lumberyard, and in 1809 he launched the *Accommodation,* Canada's first steamboat, to make runs between Montreal and Quebec City.

Beer production continued to grow at a rapid rate, and the company continued to modernize. However, the Molson family found interests outside the brewing business. Two of the founder's sons, William and John, founded Molsons Bank in 1854. During the 2nd half of the 1800s, the company's brewing sales remained relatively stagnant. In 1897 Fred and Herbert, the 4th generation of Molsons to run the brewery, took over and revitalized the company. By 1900 sales had increased by 40%. The pair embarked on a modernization of the company's facilities, adding electric lighting, refrigeration, and pasteurization equipment.

When a temperance movement swept through Canada during the 1910s, Molson and its fellow Quebec-based brewers started an anti-Prohibition campaign. In a referendum Quebec's citizens voted overwhelmingly against Prohibition. Molson got a boost from a surge in sales to Americans who came to drink in Montreal during the US Prohibition.

Sales took off following WWII, and by 1950 the company was making 1.5 million bottles of beer a day. Molson began an expansion into other provinces, opening a brewery in Toronto in 1955 and acquiring Sick's Brewery (5 breweries in Canada and 2 in the US, 1958), Fort Garry Brewery (Winnipeg, 1959), and Newfoundland Brewery (1962).

In 1971, as part of a diversification program, Molson acquired several home improvement retailers, including Aikenhead Hardware and Beaver Lumber. It diversified into chemical products when it made its first major US acquisition, Diversey Corp., in 1978. That same year the company acquired the Montreal Canadiens hockey team and a 30-year lease on the Montreal Forum.

Looking to increase its presence in the US beer market, where it was losing ground to imports such as Corona and Heineken, Molson formed the Masters Brewing Company with Coors to market Masters III, an upscale beer for the American market. However, the beer flopped in test marketing and the joint venture was abandoned in 1987.

In 1988, in a sign the company was moving beyond brewing, Molson hired Marshall Cohen, a lawyer and former civil servant with no brewing experience, to run the company. That same year Molson merged its brewing operations with Carling O'Keefe Breweries (a subsidiary of Australian brewer Elders IXL, which changed its name to Foster's in 1990) under the name Molson Breweries.

In 1991 Molson and Canadian Pacific announced plans to build a new arena in downtown Montreal.

Molson reduced its stake in Molson Breweries to 40% when Philip Morris's Miller Brewing bought a 20% interest in the company from Molson and Foster's in 1993. In 1994 Molson announced plans to export its Molson Ice beer to China.

Principal exchange: Toronto
Fiscal year ends: March 31

Chairman: Eric H. Molson
President and CEO; Executive Chairman, Diversey Corporation: Marshall Cohen, C$1,300,000 pay
President and CEO, Molson Breweries: J. Bruce Pope, C$499,183 pay
EVP and CFO: Stewart L. Hartley, C$423,133
SVP Personnel: D. H. Stanley
President, Diversey (US): Andrew Engleman
VP and CFO, Diversey (US): Peter Kenan
Director Human Resources, Diversey (US): Chris Millsap
Auditors: Coopers & Lybrand

HQ: Scotia Plaza, 40 King St. West, Ste. 3600, Toronto, Ontario M5H 3Z5, Canada
Phone: 416-360-1786
Fax: 416-360-4345
US HQ: Diversey Corp., 12025 Technical Ctr. Dr., Livonia, MI 48150
US Phone: 313-458-5000
US Fax: 313-458-3800

	1994 Sales	
	C$ mil.	% of total
Canada	1,706	57
US	552	19
Europe	484	16
Other countries	225	8
Total	**2,967**	**100**

	1994 Sales		1994 Operating Income	
	C$ mil.	% of total	C$ mil.	% of total
Cleaning & sanitizing	1,374	46	72	35
Brewing	854	29	118	57
Retailing	655	22	17	8
Other	84	3	(15)	—
Total	**2,967**	**100**	**192**	**100**

Major Group Companies and Segments
Beaver Lumber Co. Ltd. (home improvement retailing)
  Groupe Val Royal Inc. (44.5%, home improvement retailing)
  The Home Depot Canada (25%, home improvement warehouses)
Diversey Corp. (cleaning and sanitizing products and systems)
  Novamax Technologies Corp. (metal finishing)
Molson Breweries (40%)
Sports and Entertainment Segment (Montreal Canadiens hockey team, Montreal Forum arena)

Ace Hardware	Grand	Moosehead
Allied Domecq	Metropolitan	Brewing
Anchor Brewing	Guinness	Ogden
Anheuser-Busch	Heileman	Procter &
Aramark	Heineken	Gamble
Bass	Henkel	S&P
Big Rock Brewery	Home Hardware	Sears
Boston Beer	Stores	Servistar
Cott	D.H. Howden	Stroh
Cotter & Co.	Hudson's Bay	Tsingtao
Dial	John Labatt	Unilever
Ecolab	Kirin	Wal-Mart
	Kmart	

$=C$1.32 (Dec. 31, 1993)	9-Year Growth	1985	1986	1987	1988	1989	1990	1991	1992	1993	1994
Sales (C$ mil.)	5.3%	1,872	2,012	2,250	2,435	2,601	2,550	2,531	2,904	3,086	2,967
Net income (C$ mil.)	12.0%	45	36	52	79	87	118	(39)	126	165	126
Income as % of sales	—	2.4%	1.8%	2.3%	3.2%	3.3%	4.6%	—	4.3%	5.3%	4.2%
Earnings per share ($)	8.8%	1.00	0.81	1.09	1.60	1.77	2.39	(0.72)	2.25	2.76	2.13
Stock price – high ($)[1]	—	11.50	10.63	15.00	13.94	14.44	20.38	20.00	31.88	36.00	29.75
Stock price – low ($)[1]	—	7.88	7.25	9.44	9.63	11.31	13.63	14.19	21.75	28.13	22.13
Stock price – close ($)[1]	14.7%	8.31	9.56	11.31	11.50	13.75	19.75	16.38	29.63	28.75	28.63
P/E – high	—	12	13	14	9	8	9	—	14	13	14
P/E – low	—	8	9	9	6	6	6	—	10	10	10
Dividends per share ($)	3.4%	0.53	0.53	0.53	0.53	0.59	0.61	0.67	0.72	0.72	0.72
Book value per share ($)	10.1%	9.36	9.92	10.86	12.02	12.87	14.71	14.41	16.32	19.68	22.22
Employees	3.4%	10,900	11,000	11,400	11,400	11,600	13,900	13,800	15,800	16,400	14,700

1994 Year-end:
Debt ratio: 29.8%
Return on equity: 10.1%
Cash (mil.): $224
Long-term debt (mil.): $506
No. of shares (mil.): 59
Dividends
  Yield: 2.5%
  Payout: 33.8%
Market value (mil.): US$1,274
Sales (mil.): $2,241

Stock Price History[1]
High/Low 1985–94

[1] Stock prices are for the prior calendar year.

MOORE CORPORATION LIMITED

OVERVIEW

Canada's Moore Corporation is the world's #1 supplier of business forms and a leading provider of information management services. Moore's market has eroded as high-speed copiers and laser printers produce forms with greater clarity and lower costs. Its main product line, multipart paper forms, was developed before the computer revolution. Adding to its woes is a growing cultural aversion to paper and a sluggish worldwide economy.

With declining sales and a $78 million loss in 1993, Moore restructured its operations, cutting 3,000 jobs and closing several plants worldwide. It hired a new CEO, Reto Braun, who was credited with reviving Unisys. Moore also enthusiastically embraced the computer technology that was its biggest threat by buying companies that would give it an entreé into new markets: Computer Resources Trust (1993), Australia's largest business forms and services company and a supplier of bar coding and gaming tickets; Logidec Canada (1993, electronic publishing and printing services); and a 20% stake in JetForm (1994, software and electronics forms). The company also acquired 2 Canadian records management businesses.

In late 1994 Moore entered into 2, 10-year concurrent contracts, worth $1 billion, with Electronic Data Systems, which will revamp Moore's internal information systems while Moore takes charge of all EDS's business forms and commerical printing needs.

WHEN

In 1879 UK-born printer Samuel Moore and political cartoonist Thomas Bengough met in Toronto. Moore joined Bengough in publishing a conservative political newsletter called the *Grip*. He soon met John Carter, a sales-clerk trying to sell an innovative means of creating sales records. To end salespeople's fumbling with separate sets of forms and loose sheets of messy carbon paper, Carter proposed binding together multiple sets of customer and store receipts with a single sheet of carbon paper to be inserted between the forms as needed. Moore bought the idea, hired Carter, patented the product, and in 1882 formed Grip Printing and Publishing Company to produce The Paragon Black Leaf Counter Check Book. The next year Grip built a salesbook factory in Niagara Falls, New York. The product was a great success.

Moore and his associates set up the Paragon Check Book Company, a new UK operation, in 1886. Lamson Store Service Company, seeing synergies with its own product line, acquired the UK unit in 1889. Lamson sold retail cash-handling systems using hollow balls to carry currency down sloped tracks between salespeople and cashiers.

As the forms business grew, Moore bought Kidder Press (1899), maker of the printing presses he used, and created box and forms maker F.N. Burt (1909). In 1925 Moore bought Gilman Fanfold, whose owner purportedly had invented fanfolded paper after observing pleated skirts, in vogue at the time. In the same year Moore's organization began selling inexpensive, single-use carbon paper to be bound into sets of business forms, eliminating any handling of carbon paper. The product quickly proved popular and led to the development of snap-apart forms. The US government's use of carbon copies resulted in their use as legal documents in business, ultimately boosting sales. In 1929 Moore began consolidating his businesses into Moore Corporation Limited. Moore died in 1948.

By WWII all large, modern organizations were hooked on forms. During the war US Army paper-pushers sent a transport plane on an emergency mission to pick up Moore forms. After WWII Moore grew globally, initiating a slow-motion acquisition of Lamson in 1964 (culminating in 1977) and establishing Toppan Moore (Japan), a joint venture with Toppan Printing. Increased computer usage accelerated demand for Moore's forms.

In the 1970s and 1980s Moore entered direct marketing, image processing, and database management. Despite careful consideration Moore failed at its efforts to diversify into US computer supply retailing (MicroAge stores) and microcomputer systems.

In 1992 Moore appointed new presidents to head its US and European business forms divisions and sold off its Reid Dominion Packaging Division.

In 1993 Moore formed alliances with KoBel International (label company) and created a joint venture with an Italian state printing company.

NYSE symbol: MCL
Fiscal year ends: December 31

WHO

Chairman: M. Keith Goodrich, age 59,
$600,000 pay
President and CEO: Reto Braun, age 52
SVP and CFO: Stephen A. Holinski, age 47
**SVP; President and COO, North America
Operations:** John R. Anderluh, age 59,
$350,589 pay
VP Human Resources: Charles F. Canfield, age 44
CEO, Moore Business Forms (US): Patrick Allen
CFO, Moore Business Forms (US): Gary M.
Hubbard
**Director Human Resources, Moore Business
Forms (US):** Matthew R. Bove
Auditors: Price Waterhouse

WHERE

HQ: One First Canadian Place, PO Box 78,
Toronto, Ontario M5X 1G5, Canada
Phone: 416-364-2600
Fax: 416-364-1667
US HQ: Moore Business Forms & Systems, Inc.,
275 N. Field Dr., Lake Forest, IL 60045
US Phone: 708-615-6000
US Fax: 708-205-0648 (Corporate Communications)

Moore does business in 58 countries.

	1993 Sales	
	$ mil.	% of total
US	1,509	65
Europe	333	14
Canada	188	8
Other countries	299	13
Total	**2,329**	**100**

HOW MUCH

WHAT

	1993 Sales		1993 Operating Income	
	$ mil.	% of total	$ mil.	% of total
Business forms & systems	1,858	80	112	82
Direct marketing services	200	9	13	10
Database services	135	6	3	2
Business communication svcs.	126	5	8	6
Adjustment	10	—	(5)	—
Total	**2,329**	**100**	**131**	**100**

Selected Products and Services
Automated information management systems
Bar coding
Commercial printing
Database management
Direct marketing
Electronic publishing
Forms management software and equipment
Gaming tickets
Paper and electronic-based business forms
Records management

Selected Subsidiaries
Arcodex Records Manager Ltd. (records management)
Command Records Services Ltd. (records management)
Computer Resources Trust (business forms, Australia)
Data Repro Com Enterprises Ltd. (records management)
JetForm Corp. (20%, electronic forms)
Logidec Canada Inc. (electronic publishing and printing)

KEY COMPETITORS

ADP	R. R. Donnelley	Standard
American Business	Dun & Bradstreet	Register
Information	Equifax	TRW
Avery Dennison	Mead	United Stationers
Bell & Howell	Pitney Bowes	Young &
Deluxe	Scott	Rubicam

	9-Year Growth	1984	1985	1986	1987	1988	1989	1990	1991	1992	1993
Sales ($ mil.)	1.6%	2,021	2,068	2,114	2,282	2,544	2,708	2,770	2,492	2,433	2,329
Net income ($ mil.)	—	126	137	110	146	186	202	121	88	(2)	(78)
Income as % of sales	—	6.2%	6.6%	5.2%	6.4%	7.3%	7.4%	4.4%	3.5%	—	—
Earnings per share ($)	—	1.43	1.53	1.21	1.60	2.01	2.15	1.27	0.91	(0.02)	(0.78)
Stock price – high ($)	—	15.25	21.88	27.63	26.75	26.63	33.75	30.25	28.50	22.13	21.25
Stock price – low ($)	—	11.56	14.88	18.63	16.50	19.00	24.88	21.63	19.00	13.25	15.00
Stock price – close ($)	2.7%	15.06	20.25	20.63	20.00	25.25	28.88	22.75	21.25	17.13	19.13
P/E – high	—	11	14	23	17	13	16	24	31	—	—
P/E – low	—	8	10	15	10	10	12	17	21	—	—
Dividends per share ($)	3.8%	0.67	0.69	0.72	0.73	0.77	0.86	0.93	0.94	0.94	0.94
Book value per share ($)	4.4%	8.95	10.09	11.01	12.69	13.89	15.28	16.05	16.21	14.83	13.19
Employees	(1.9%)	26,256	27,331	27,070	26,480	25,943	26,359	25,021	23,556	23,124	22,014

1993 Year-end:
Debt ratio: 7.1%
Return on equity: —
Cash (mil.): $262
Current ratio: 2.24
Long-term debt (mil.): $68
No. of shares (mil.): 100
Dividends
  Yield: 4.9%
  Payout: —
Market value (mil.): $1,904

**Stock Price History
High/Low 1984–93**

An IRA bomb shook the headquarters foundations of international banking conglomerate National Westminster (NatWest) in London in 1991, but far more damaging to the bank has been its involvement in one of Britain's biggest financial controversies. The Blue Arrow scandal arose in the late 1980s out of NatWest's alleged violation of securities disclosure laws and forced CEO Tom Frost to resign in 1992 after he was connected with the case in court proceedings. To make matters worse, the bank's image was further tarnished by a large number of questionable loans authorized by the bank in 1991 and 1992, which forced it to allocate billions to cover bad debts.

NatWest is a leading international banking and financial services group with offices in 28 countries worldwide. One of Britain's Big 4 banks (along with Barclays, Lloyds, and HSBC's Midland), NatWest owns retail branches throughout the UK. Among its subsidiaries is Coutts & Co., a prestigious private international banking institution that caters to well-heeled customers.

In 1992 the bank streamlined its operations into 4 operational units, NatWest Markets (investment banking), International Businesses, US Retail Operations, and UK Branch Business. The group has been cutting staff to lower costs, axing some 15,000 jobs between 1990 and 1993.

The US is a growth market for the company with its New York–based US subsidiary, sharply increasing its asset base through a series of acquisitions.

National Westminster Bank is the descendant of 3 major UK banks dating back to the early 19th century: District Bank, National Provincial Bank, and Westminster Bank. The oldest of these banks, District Bank, was organized in 1829 as the Manchester and Liverpool District Banking Company to serve northwest England. By initially offering banking services to the textile trade, District Bank had built a UK banking network by the time it was acquired by National Provincial Bank in 1962. District Bank and National Provincial maintained separate identities and operations after the merger.

When National Provincial Bank was established in London as a joint stock company in 1833, the Bank of England had exclusive authority to issue bank notes within a 65-mile radius of London. National Provincial operated its banking offices in the provinces more than 65 miles from London so that it could issue its own notes. After WWI, National Provincial gradually acquired other banks, including Coutts & Company, Sheffield Banking Company, Northamptonshire Union Bank, and Guernsey Banking Company between 1919 and 1924; North Central Finance in 1958; and District Bank in 1962.

The stiff upper lip of the British banking community twitched when National Provincial announced in 1968 that it was merging with another large UK bank, Westminster Bank. Westminster was founded in 1834 as the London and Westminster Bank. In 1909 the bank merged with London and County Bank. Westminster expanded, opening offices in continental Europe and buying Ulster Bank in 1917 and Parr's Bank in 1918.

The principal operations of District Bank, National Provincial, and Westminster were consolidated between 1968 and 1970 into National Westminster Bank, creating the 5th largest bank in the world. NatWest bought Lombard Banking for £38 million in 1970, 31% of Creditwest (Italy) in 1972, and the National Bank of North America in 1977.

NatWest enlarged its American operations by buying First Jersey National in 1988 and Ultra Bancorp in 1989 but had to inject capital into its US subsidiary because of large real estate loan losses in the northeastern US.

In 1989 subsidiaries and former employees of NatWest were charged with criminal conspiracy to defraud, a charge arising out of the 1987 Blue Arrow rights offering in which County NatWest (CNW) acted as underwriter and financial advisor. CNW had failed to sell 13.5% of the offering and concealed that fact to avoid the embarrassment of a failed offering, a violation of UK disclosure laws.

In 1992 the company purchased Burns Fry Futures, a US-based futures and options broker (renamed NatWest Futures). In 1993 the US retail operations posted a profit of $273 million, up 107%. In a push to become a major force in the New York/New Jersey market, NatWest Bancorp acquired Citizens First Bancorp in 1994 for $500 million.

NYSE symbol: NW (ADR)
Fiscal year ends: December 31

Chairman: Lord Alexander of Weedon, age 57,
£304,532 pay
Group CEO: Derek Wanless, age 46
Deputy Group CEO: John W. Melbourn, age 56
Group CFO: Richard K. Goeltz, age 51
**Deputy CEO UK Branch Business; General
Manager, Human Resources and Strategic
Development:** Stuart R. Chandler, age 49
**Chairman and CEO, National Westminster Bank
(US):** John Tugwell, age 53
Auditors: KPMG Peat Marwick

WHERE

HQ: 41 Lothbury, London EC2P 2BP, UK
Phone: +44-(01)71-726-1000
Fax: +44-(01)71-726-1035
US HQ: National Westminster Bank Plc,
175 Water Street, New York, NY 10038-4924
Phone: 201-547-7000
Fax: 201-547-7791

NatWest has over 3,000 branch offices in the UK
and approximately 700 more worldwide.

	1993 Assets	
	£ mil.	% of total
UK	111,377	73
US	21,431	14
Other countries	20,054	13
Total	**152,862**	**100**

WHAT

	1993 Assets	
	£ mil.	$ of total
Cash & equivalents	1,289	1
Treasury & other bills	8,141	5
Debt securities	12,096	8
Equities	2,116	1
Loans & advances to customers	80,351	53
Loans & advances to banks	30,479	20
Other	18,390	12
Total	**152,862**	**100**

Selected Subsidiaries and Affiliates
Banco NatWest España SA (99.6%, Spain)
Centre-file Ltd. (computer services)
County NatWest Australia Ltd. (holding company)
County NatWest Ltd. (investment banking)
Coutts & Co. Group (private banking)
F van Lanschot Bankiers NV (80.6%, the Netherlands)
Isle of Man Bank Ltd.
Lombard North Central PLC
National Westminster Bancorp Plc (US)
National Westminster Bank AG (Germany)
National Westminister Bank of Canada
NatWest Estate Management and Development Ltd.
NatWest Futures Ltd. (brokerage)
NatWest Gilts Ltd. (securities)
Ulster Bank Ltd.

KEY COMPETITORS

H. F. Ahmanson	Dai-Ichi Kangyo
Bank of New York	Deutsche Bank
Bankers Trust	HSBC
Barclays	Industrial Bank of Japan
Canadian Imperial	Lloyds
Chase Manhattan	Midlantic Corp.
Chemical Banking	J.P. Morgan
Citicorp	Royal Bank of Scotland
Crédit Lyonnais	Standard Chartered
CS Holding	Union Bank of Switzerland

HOW MUCH

£=$1.48 (Dec. 31, 1993)	9-Year Growth	1984	1985	1986	1987	1988	1989	1990	1991	1992	1993
Assets (£ mil.)	8.8%	71,518	72,607	83,325	87,027	98,642	116,189	121,100	129,556	153,442	152,862
Net income (£ mil.)	8.1%	290	442	614	442	938	198	370	65	164	583
Income as % of sales	—	0.4%	0.6%	0.7%	0.5%	1.0%	0.2%	0.3%	0.1%	0.1%	0.4%
Earnings per share (p)	(2.5%)	44	61	47	29	62	15	13	4	10	35
Stock price – high (p)	—	310	361	288	397	470	365	368	358	423	634
Stock price – low (p)	—	202	284	218	249	255	255	227	246	251	398
Stock price – close (p)	8.4%	299	344	274	288	257	350	269	272	405	620
P/E – high	—	7	6	6	14	8	24	28	89	42	18
P/E – low	—	5	5	5	9	4	17	17	62	25	11
Dividends per share (p)	4.2%	12.8	14.1	10.3	12.0	14.1	16.7	17.5	17.5	17.5	18.5
Book value per share (p)	3.4%	233	261	309	324	381	377	365	324	317	315
Employees	0.2%	90,000	92,000	94,000	102,000	111,000	113,000	112,600	102,400	—	91,400

1993 Year-end:
Debt ratio: 95.8%
Return on equity: 11.1%
Equity as % of assets: 3.7%
No. of shares (mil.): 1,662
Dividends
  Yield: 3.0%
  Payout: 52.9%
Market value (mil.): $15,243
Assets (mil.): $103,285
Sales (mil.): $19,877

**Stock Price History
High/Low 1986–93**

NEC CORPORATION

OVERVIEW

NEC is #1 in Japan in PC sales and has been for years. But American rivals (e.g., Apple, IBM, Compaq, and clone makers) are snapping at NEC's heels and are beginning to take a bite out of its 49% market share.

The company is also the world's 2nd largest maker of semiconductors (behind Intel) and is a global supplier of computers, telecommunications, and other electronic products. NEC sells its products worldwide, but Japan remains the company's largest market. Revenues from Japan accounted for 76% of total sales in 1994. NEC's PCs sold in Japan use a proprietary operating system incompatible with US standards.

NEC has pushed the "C&C" concept, the integration of computers and communications, since 1977, but NEC by no means leads in this field; collaboration between different divisions in the giant company has been hesitant at best. New president Hisashi Kaneko, a former head of NEC's American operations, is trying to break down interdepartmental friction as well as inject more decentralized decision making into the Tokyo-tied management structure.

In a major policy shift in 1994, NEC made a grab for a larger share of the software market by agreeing to sell IBM-compatible PC servers in Japan.

WHEN

A group of Japanese investors led by Kunihiko Iwadare formed Nippon Electric Company (NEC) in a joint venture with Western Electric (US) in 1899. Starting as an importer of telephone equipment, NEC soon became a manufacturer and major supplier to Japan's Communications Ministry. Western Electric sold its stake in NEC in 1925. ITT (US) began acquiring shares and owned 59% of NEC before selling its stake in the 1960s. NEC became affiliated with the Sumitomo *zaibatsu* (conglomerate) in the 1930s.

After Nippon Telegraph and Telephone (NTT) was formed in 1952, NEC became one of its 4 leading suppliers. The postwar need to repair Japan's telephone systems and the country's continuing economic recovery resulted in strong demand from NTT. In the 1950s and 1960s, NTT business represented over 50% of sales, even though NEC had expanded overseas, diversified into home appliances, and formed a computer alliance with Honeywell (US). In 1968 NTT began working with NEC, Hitachi, and Fujitsu to develop computers for use in telecommunications.

In the 1970s Honeywell's lagging position in computers hurt NEC; the company recovered through in-house development efforts and a mainframe venture with Toshiba. In 1977 CEO Koji Kobayashi articulated his vision of NEC's future as an integrator of computers and communications through semiconductor technology. Now generally accepted, Kobayashi's thoughts were revolutionary at the time.

A joint effort between the Japanese government and private industry to develop VLSI chips took place in NEC's labs in the 1970s. NEC invested heavily in R&D and capacity expansion and became the world's largest independent semiconductor manufacturer in 1985. The company produced the world's first 4-megabit DRAM chip in 1986.

The company enjoyed great success in the Japanese PC market, garnering over 50% of the market in the 1980s despite a proprietary operating system. NEC's portable IBM clones were also well received internationally. NEC passed IBM to become Japan's #2 computer maker (after Fujitsu) in 1986 and entered into a mainframe computer partnership (now Bull HN Information Systems) with Honeywell and France's Machines Bull in 1987.

NEC has focused R&D spending on next-generation semiconductors (announcing joint development of advanced memory chips with AT&T in 1991), HDTVs, and supercomputers.

The company suffered embarrassment in 1991 when a 50.2%-owned affiliate (Japan Aviation Electronics Industry Company) admitted that it had illegally sold missile parts to Iran during the Iran-Iraq war. Attempting to make amends, NEC is promoting worldwide environmental conservation.

In 1992 NEC sold its 5 millionth PC-9800 series PC in Japan. In that same year Compaq challenged NEC with a cheap, Japanese-language PC that uses the IBM standard, forcing NEC to cut its PC prices. The rising yen and the sluggish Japanese economy also hurt NEC's income in 1992 and 1993.

In 1994 NEC announced plans to build an $800 million DRAM chip plant in Scotland.

Nasdaq symbol: NIPNY (ADR)
Fiscal year ends: March 31

Chairman: Tadahiro Sekimoto, age 67
President: Hisashi Kaneko, age 61
EVP (Finance): Yoshihiro Suzuki
SVP (Personnel): Hirokaru Akiyama
**Associate SVP; President and CEO, NEC
  America:** Mineo Sugiyama
Auditors: Price Waterhouse

WHERE

HQ: 7-1, Shiba 5-chome, Minato-ku,
  Tokyo 108-01, Japan
Phone: +81-3-3454-1111
Fax: +81-3-3798-1519
US HQ: NEC America, Inc., 8 Old Sod Farm Rd.,
  Melville, NY 11747-3112
US Phone: 516-753-7000
US Fax: 516-753-7041

In Japan NEC operates a network of 88
consolidated subsidiaries, 63 plants, and 370 sales
offices. Outside Japan the company operates 86
subsidiaries and affiliates in 30 countries.

	1994 Sales	
	$ mil.	% of total
Japan	26,556	76
North America	3,305	9
Asia	2,704	8
Europe	1,466	4
Other countries	1,065	3
Total	**35,096**	**100**

WHAT

	1994 Sales	
	$ mil.	% of total
Computers & industrial		
electronic systems	17,466	50
Communications sys. & equip.	9,500	27
Electron devices	6,435	18
Other	1,695	5
Total	**35,096**	**100**

**Computers and
Industrial Electronics
Systems**
Computers (PCs to
  supercomputers)
Engineering
  workstations
Industrial electronic
  systems

**Communications Systems
and Equipment**
Digital switching systems
Mobile communications
  systems
Radio transmission systems
Space electronics

Electron Devices
DRAMS
SRAMS

KEY COMPETITORS

Acer	Harris	Northern Telecom
Alcatel Alsthom	Hewlett-Packard	Novell
Apple	Hitachi	Oki
Artisoft	Honeywell	Packard Bell
AST	Hyundai	Philips
AT&T	IBM	Pioneer
Canon	Intel	Raytheon
Casio	Iomega	Samsung
Compaq	LG Group	Sanyo
Data General	Machines Bull	Sharp
Dell	Micron	Siemens
Ericsson	Technology	Silicon Graphics
Everex	Microsoft	Texas Instruments
Fujitsu	Mitsubishi	Toshiba
Gateway 2000	Motorola	TRW
GTE	Nokia	Unisys

HOW MUCH

Stock prices are ADRs ADR=5 shares	9-Year Growth	1985	1986	1987	1988	1989	1990	1991	1992	1993	1994
Sales ($ mil.)	16.3%	9,015	13,142	16,803	21,893	23,247	21,771	26,306	28,428	30,605	35,096
Net income ($ mil.)	(12.5%)	268	153	103	205	323	497	361	112	(407)	81
Income as % of sales	—	3.0%	1.2%	0.6%	0.9%	1.4%	2.3%	1.4%	0.4%	—	0.2%
Earnings per share ($)	(13.3%)	0.94	0.54	0.35	0.70	1.30	1.54	1.14	0.36	(1.06)	0.26
Stock price – high ($)[1]	—	32.63	33.63	78.50	89.88	90.50	80.75	71.50	62.75	50.00	50.50
Stock price – low ($)[1]	—	20.88	18.63	30.25	45.13	67.63	60.13	45.75	42.50	24.63	24.50
Stock price – close ($)[1]	5.2%	24.25	32.88	63.88	73.50	78.50	65.50	47.50	48.25	26.88	38.13
P/E – high	—	35	62	284	128	70	52	63	174	—	194
P/E – low	—	22	35	86	85	52	39	40	118	—	94
Dividends per share ($)	33.0%	0.03	0.05	0.06	0.28	0.30	0.26	0.30	0.32	0.34	0.39
Book value per share ($)	15.3%	6.93	10.11	11.97	16.29	17.41	16.75	20.36	21.49	22.79	24.90
Employees	5.7%	90,102	95,796	101,227	102,452	104,022	114,599	117,994	128,320	140,969	147,910

1994 Year-end:
Debt ratio: 80.6%
Return on equity: 1.1%
Cash (mil.): $3,839
Current ratio: 1.22
Long-term debt (mil.): $9,376
No. of shares (mil.): 308
Dividends
  Yield: 1.0%
  Payout: 150.0%
Market value (mil.): $11,740

**Stock Price History[1]
High/Low 1985–94**

[1] Stock prices are for the prior calendar year.

NESTLÉ LTD.

N-E-S-T-L-E-S/Nestlé makes the very best/ Choc...'late. This little ditty convinced a generation of American children that Nestlé was as American as apple pie. Or chocolate chip cookies (Toll House morsels), or evaporated milk (Carnation). And it is, but it is also French (Perrier), Italian (San Pellegrino), Chilean (La Lechera), Nigerian (Nutrend), and Japanese (MOM H.A.).

Nestlé, the world's largest food products company, has achieved this transnationalism by establishing largely autonomous operations throughout the world. Making international markets its own has been necessary

because the company would have no hope of building hefty sales in its home market, Switzerland, because of its small population.

Nestlé has traditionally grown through acquisitions, primarily in foods, but for a while into unrelated areas like hotels and restaurants (Stouffer, divestiture completed 1993). In 1994 the company rededicated itself to expanding by growing sales of its traditional specialties (milk products, candy, and beverages) in the burgeoning markets of Asia and Latin America and to gaining market share for its best-known brands in the mature markets of Europe and the US.

In the mid-19th century, as Europe's population became increasingly urban, safe dairy products became a memory for millions of people. In 1866 Charles Page, US consul in Zurich, and his brother, George, founded the Anglo-Swiss Condensed Milk Company in Cham, Switzerland, using Gail Borden's (founder of Borden, Inc.) technology for canning milk. In 1867 in Vevey, Switzerland, amid growing concern about infant mortality, Henri Nestlé tested his new concoction of concentrated milk, sugar, and cereal on a baby who refused his mother's milk. After 6 months the healthy boy was still drinking the formula. Nestlé introduced Farine Lactée Henri Nestlé (the company's name) commercially that year.

By 1874 both firms were prospering, and Nestlé, aged 61, sold his company, then doing business in 16 countries, to 3 local businessmen for one million francs in 1875. Nestlé and Anglo-Swiss each grew rapidly. In 1878, when Anglo-Swiss launched a milk-based infant food product, Nestlé's new owners responded by introducing a condensed milk product, beginning a battle that lasted until the companies merged in 1905 under the Nestlé name. In 1904 the company began selling Nestlé chocolate. In WWI, Nestlé was aided by Swiss neutrality but hampered by limited milk supplies so it expanded into regions less affected by the war, such as the US. In 1929 Nestlé acquired Cailler, the first company to mass-produce chocolate bars, and Swiss General, inventor of milk chocolate. Nestlé's 1920s investment in a Brazilian milk condensery paid an unexpected dividend when Brazilian coffee growers suggested that

Nestlé develop a water-soluble "coffee cube." Nescafé instant coffee was released in 1938 and though instant coffees proliferated in WWII, Nestlé could not enforce its patents on the process. The war also furthered the growth of its foreign operations.

After the war Nestlé continued its global expansion, entering new product categories through acquisition and internal product development. Important product introductions were its Crunch bar (1938), Quik drink mix (1948), and Taster's Choice coffee (1966). Most of the company's expansion came during the 1970s and 1980s with the acquisitions of Beringer Brothers wines, Stouffer, Libby, McNeill & Libby canned foods, Carnation, Hills Brothers and MJB coffees, Buitoni pastas, Rowntree candy, and Butterfinger and Baby Ruth candies.

In the 1980s Nestlé was one of a number of Western baby formula makers who became subject to boycotts by social activists for promoting the sale of baby formula in the 3rd world, where poor hygiene and maternal ignorance make formula a dangerous alternative to breast feeding. Agitation against Nestlé on this matter continues in the 1990s.

In 1992 Nestlé launched a hostile bid for Source Perrier. After much negotiation the purchase was completed, but EC regulators forced Nestlé to sell off some of Perrier's other water brands.

In 1993 and 1994 Nestlé prospered despite Europe's recession by streamlining operations, cutting unprofitable products, increasing sales in new markets, and aggressive marketing. In 1994 it acquired Alpo pet food from Grand Metropolitan.

OTC symbol: NSRGY (ADR)
Fiscal year ends: December 31

Chairman and CEO: Helmut O. Maucher
President and COO-Food: Ramón Masip
General Manager Finance, Control, Legal, Taxes, and Administration: Reto F. Domeniconi
General Manager; Chairman, Nestlé USA: Timm F. Crull
President and CEO, Nestlé USA: Joe Weller
EVP and CFO, Nestlé USA: Mario Corti
EVP Human Resources and Corporate Affairs, Nestlé USA: Cam Starrett
Auditors: KPMG Peat Marwick

HQ: Ave. Nestlé 55, CH-1800 Vevey, Switzerland
Phone: +41-21-924-2111
Fax: +41-21-921-1885
US HQ: Nestlé USA, Inc., 800 N. Brand Blvd., Glendale, CA 91203
US Phone: 818-549-6000
US Fax: 818-549-5884

Nestlé operates 489 factories in 69 countries.

	1993 Sales	
	SF mil.	% of total
US	12,776	22
France	7,051	13
Germany	6,487	11
UK	3,466	6
Other Europe	9,362	16
Other North America	2,997	5
Other countries	15,347	27
Total	**57,486**	**100**

	1993 Sales	
	SF mil.	% of total
Milk products & dietetics	15,951	28
Beverages	15,417	27
Prepared dishes & cooking aids	15,387	27
Chocolate & confectionery	8,650	14
Pharmaceuticals	2,081	4
Total	**57,486**	**100**

Major Brand Names (US Markets)

Milk Products and Dietetics	Quik	Baby Ruth
Carnation	Taster's Choice	Butterfinger
Coffee-Mate	Utopia	KitKat
Nestlé Sweet Success	**Prepared Dishes and Cooking Aids**	Nestlé Crunch
Beverages	Buitoni	Toll House
Arrowhead	Contadina	**Pharmaceuticals**
Berenger wines	Crosse & Blackwell	Alcon (opticals)
Hills Bros.	Libby	L'Oréal (25%)
Nescafé	Stouffer's	**Pet Foods**
Nestea	**Chocolate and Confections**	Alpo
Ozarka	After Eight	Fancy Feast
Perrier		Friskies
Poland Spring		Mighty Dog

Accor	Danone	Procter & Gamble
Allied Domecq	Eskimo Pie	Quaker Oats
Bausch & Lomb	General Mills	Ralston Purina
Borden	Grand	Group
Bristol-Myers Squibb	Metropolitan	RJR Nabisco
Brock Candy	Hartz	San Miguel
Cadbury Schweppes	Heinz	Sara Lee
Campbell Soup	Hershey	TLC Beatrice
ConAgra	Mars	Unilever
Dalgety	McKesson	Whitman
	Philip Morris	

$=SF1.49 (Dec. 31, 1993)	9-Year Growth	1984	1985	1986	1987	1988	1989	1990	1991	1992	1993
Sales (SF mil.)	7.0%	31,141	42,225	36,909	34,183	39,502	48,036	46,369	50,486	54,500	57,486
Net income (SF mil.)	7.7%	1,487	1,750	1,843	1,879	2,058	2,412	2,272	2,470	2,698	2,887
Income as % of sales	—	4.8%	4.1%	5.0%	5.5%	5.2%	5.0%	4.9%	4.9%	5.0%	5.0%
Earnings per share (SF)	5.4%	47	51	53	54	58	66	62	67	73	76
Stock price – high (SF)	—	550	903	970	1,124	886	893	924	893	1,160	1,294
Stock price – low (SF)	—	444	550	719	707	624	693	696	701	877	1,015
Stock price – close (SF)	9.6%	560	893	978	803	724	882	736	872	1,145	1,283
P/E – high	—	12	18	18	21	15	14	15	13	16	17
P/E – low	—	9	11	14	13	11	11	11	10	12	13
Dividends per share (SF)	7.2%	13.35	14.24	14.24	14.73	17.19	20.00	20.00	21.50	23.50	25.00
Book value per share (SF)	(0.8%)	417	337	456	456	319	379	365	435	359	388
Employees	4.8%	137,950	154,769	162,078	163,030	197,722	196,940	199,021	201,139	218,005	209,755

1993 Year-end:
Debt ratio: 45.5%
Return on equity: 20.2%
Cash (mil.): SF5,084
Long-term debt (mil.): SF4,073
No. of shares (thou.): 40
Dividends
  Yield: 1.9%
  Payout: 33.1%
Market value (mil.): $34,746
Sales (mil.): $38,581

**Stock Price History
High/Low 1984–93**

Note: Prior to 1993, all stock prices are for bearer shares.

THE NEWS CORPORATION LIMITED

OVERVIEW

Based in Sydney, The News Corporation is the world's largest newspaper publisher, but CEO Rupert Murdoch wants to conquer the world through another medium: television. To arm his company for the fight, Murdoch has been opening his wallet. He paid $1.6 billion for the rights to broadcast NFL games for 4 years on his Fox Broadcasting television network and invested $500 million in New World Television to persuade the company to switch its TV stations to Fox affiliates. Murdoch is also looking for expansion in other parts of the world. In 1993 he acquired 63% of Star Television, an Asian satellite TV network, from Hutchison Whampoa and the Li family.

News Corp. also owns 8 US TV stations, El Canal Fox (a Latin American cable TV chan-

nel), and interests in a TV network in Australia and a pay TV service in the UK. Its Twentieth Century Fox produces movies (*Mrs. Doubtfire, Speed*) and TV shows (*The Simpsons, NYPD Blue*).

Other holdings include the London *Times*; *TV Guide*, the most widely circulated US magazine, and book publisher HarperCollins. In Australia the company publishes 100 newspapers, including the *Australian*, and is involved in book publishing, commercial printing, and paper production. News Corp. also owns 50% of Ansett Australia (airline).

News Corp. posted record profits in 1994. Murdoch controls about 31.9% of the company through Cruden Investments, named for his boyhood home.

WHEN

Rupert Murdoch started in the newspaper business in 1952 when he inherited 2 Adelaide, Australia, newspapers from his father. After launching the *Australian*, the country's first national daily, in 1964, Murdoch bought *News of the World*, a London Sunday paper, in 1968. In 1969 he bought London's *Sun*, which he transformed into a sensationalist tabloid, featuring lurid headlines and topless women. In the US Murdoch created the supermarket tabloid *Star* in 1974 and bought the *New York Post* in 1976 (later sold), again using sensationalist tactics to boost circulation (one headline: "Headless Body Found in Topless Bar").

In 1981 Murdoch bought London's *Times* and a 40% stake in Collins Publishers, a London book publisher. After buying the *Chicago Sun-Times* in 1983 (sold in 1986), Murdoch bought 13 US travel, hotel, and aviation trade magazines from Ziff-Davis, as well as Twentieth Century Fox from Denver billionaire Marvin Davis in 1985. He became a US citizen to comply with FCC rules on broadcast ownership and in 1986 bought 6 Metromedia TV stations; Hong Kong's *South China Morning Post*; and Australia's #1 media company, the Herald & Weekly Times Group.

In 1986 Murdoch launched Fox Broadcasting, the first new US TV network since 1948. In 1987 he bought US book publisher Harper & Row and 20% of the UK's Pearson media group (since reduced to 4.9%). In 1988 News Corp. paid $2.8 billion for Triangle Publications, publisher of *TV Guide*, the

Daily Racing Form, and *Seventeen*, and bought religious publisher Zondervan. In 1989 it bought textbook publisher Scott, Foresman and the rest of Collins Publishers.

The company started Sky Television, a British satellite TV network, in 1989. After 18 months of intense competition, Sky joined with rival network British Satellite Broadcasting to form British Sky Broadcasting.

Murdoch bought 2 Hungarian dailies and 50% of Germany's Burda printing company in 1990. But after years of buying (and accumulating debt to do so), News Corp. began to put assets on the block and pay its debt and hoped for an upgraded credit rating.

In 1990 Murdoch sold the *Star* to *Enquirer* publisher G.P. Group for $200 million and an 80% stake in the newly formed Enquirer/Star Group. In 1991 he agreed to sell the *Daily Racing Form* and his US magazine holdings (except *Mirabella* and *TV Guide*) to K-III Holdings, a partnership controlled by Kohlberg Kravis Roberts. News Corp. sold its stake in Enquirer/Star Group to the public in 1991. That same year the company emerged from a financial restructuring involving almost 150 banks.

In 1992 Murdoch sold the *San Antonio Express-News* (his first US venture, bought in 1973) to Hearst for $185 million. The company acquired US on-line service Delphi Internet Services in 1993. In 1994 Star TV and Zee Telefilms formed an alliance to launch at least 3 satellite TV channels in India.

NYSE symbol: NWS (ADR)
Fiscal year ends: Sunday nearest June 30

**Chairman, Managing Director, and CEO; CEO,
News America:** Keith Rupert Murdoch, age 63
COO: August A. Fischer, age 55
CFO and Finance Director; CFO, News America:
David F. DeVoe, age 47
EVP: Richard A. Sarazen, age 61
EVP and Group General Counsel: Arthur M.
Siskind, age 55
**EVP Human Resources; EVP Human Resources,
News America:** William A. O'Neill
Chairman, Fox, Inc.: Chase Carey
Auditors: Arthur Andersen & Co.

HQ: 2 Holt St., Sydney, NSW 2010, Australia
Phone: +61-2-288-3000
Fax: +61-2-288-2300
US HQ: News America Holdings, Inc.,
1211 Avenue of the Americas, New York,
NY 10036
US Phone: 212-852-7000
US Fax: 212-852-7145

The News Corporation operates principally in the
US, the UK, Australia, and the Pacific Basin.

	1994 Sales
	% of total
US	69
Europe	17
Australia & Pacific Basin	14
Total	**100**

	1994 Sales
	% of total
Filmed entertainment	27
Newspapers	25
Television	18
Magazines/inserts	14
Books & other	16
Total	**100**

Filmed Entertainment
Twentieth Century Fox
Film Corp. (US)

Newspaper Publishing
The Australian and 100
other Australian
newspapers
Independent Newspapers
(50%, New Zealand)
New York Post
The Times and 4 other
UK newspapers

TV Broadcasting
British Sky Broadcasting
(40%, satellite service)
Fox Broadcasting Co.
(139 affiliates, US)
Fox TV (8 stations)

Star Television (63.6%,
Hong Kong)

Magazines/Inserts
Mirabella (US)
*The Times Educational
Supplement* (UK)
TV Guide (US)
Pacific Magazines and
Printing Ltd. (45%)

Book Publishing
HarperCollins Publishers

Selected Other Investments
Ansett Transport Industries
Ltd. (50%, air transport)
Australian Newsprint Mills
Ltd. (46.2%)
Sky Radio (71%, UK)

Advance
Publications
America Online
Bertelsmann
Capital Cities/ABC
CBS
Cox
Crédit Lyonnais
Dow Jones

Gannett
General Electric
H&R Block
Hearst
Knight-Ridder
Matsushita
McGraw-Hill
New York Times
Pearson

Prodigy
Publishing &
Broadcasting
Sony
Time Warner
Times Mirror
Turner Broadcasting
Viacom
Walt Disney

Stock prices are for ADRs. ADR=2 shares	Annual Growth	1985	1986	1987	1988	1989	1990	1991	1992	1993	1994
Sales ($ mil.)	14.8%	2,447	2,575	3,503	4,355	5,958	6,948	6,551	7,626	7,124	8,468
Net income ($ mil.)	22.4%	144	163	241	336	375	224	(211)	397	653	883
Income as % of sales	—	5.9%	6.3%	6.9%	7.7%	6.3%	3.2%	—	5.2%	9.2%	10.4%
Earnings per share ($)	20.0%	0.18	0.40	0.56	0.74	0.80	0.54	(0.87)	0.74	1.07	0.93
Stock price – high ($)[1]	—	—	—	8.05	11.90	7.28	9.03	7.78	8.62	14.15	21.06
Stock price – low ($)[1]	—	—	—	3.79	4.08	4.95	5.54	2.21	1.79	7.08	11.99
Stock price – close ($)[1]	12.2%	—	—	7.83	5.62	5.49	7.41	2.62	7.70	13.57	17.57
P/E – high	—	—	—	14	16	9	17	—	12	13	23
P/E – low	—	—	—	7	6	6	10	—	2	7	13
Dividends per share ($)	10.7%	0.02	0.00	0.02	0.03	0.09	0.05	0.03	0.07	0.05	0.05
Book value per share ($)	19.5%	2.10	2.65	5.01	8.89	6.30	19.00	4.30	14.11	13.98	10.46
Employees	2.0%	—	22,100	29,800	28,300	30,900	38,400	30,700	—	24,700	25,845

1994 Year-end:
Debt ratio: 49.4%
Return on equity: 9.8%
Cash (mil.): $316
Current ratio: 1.03%
Long-term debt (mil.): $5,679
No. of shares (mil.): 950
Dividends
Yield: 0.3%
Payout: 5.4%
Market value (mil.): $16,692

**Stock Price History[1]
High/Low 1987–94**

[1] Stock prices are for the prior calendar year.

NINTENDO CO., LTD.

OVERVIEW

Kyoto, Japan–based Nintendo is still the largest video game company in the world, but it has lost market share to its rival, Sega, and faces an increasing number of smaller competitors. In 1994 sales declined 23% after more than a decade of explosive growth.

Almost 40% of US (and a larger percentage of Japanese) households have Nintendo Entertainment Systems, stripped-down computers that demand constant feeding with new and more exciting games (the most popular are the Donkey Kong and Super Mario series) because selling game software is how the company makes its money. Unfortunately, there were no exciting new games in the early 1990s, and ho-hum marketing left Nintendo with a severe case of the uncools in its prime audience, males over 14 years old.

Part of the reason for Nintendo's decline has been its late entry into CD-ROM games. CD-ROMs, which run on PCs rather than requiring proprietary equipment, are an area much more open to competition. In 1994, however, Nintendo introduced a visually and aurally exciting product, Donkey Kong Country, for a new Super NES system. It also makes Game Boy, a hand-held game system.

The founding Yamauchi family controls Nintendo, holding the top spots in both Japan and the US, and owns 11% of the company.

WHEN

Nintendo (which means leave luck to heaven, or some close variant thereof) was founded in 1889 as the Marufuku Company to make and sell *hanafuda* (a Japanese game) cards. The company's success was furthered in the early 20th century when *hanafuda* became a major gambling pastime. In 1907 Nintendo began producing Western playing cards. It became the Nintendo Playing Card Company in 1951. It took its current name in 1963, 4 years after it began making theme cards under a licensing agreement with Disney.

In the 1950s and 1960s, Hiroshi Yamauchi, scion of the founding family, took the company public and diversified into new areas (including a "love hotel"). In the late 1970s Nintendo entered the budding field of video games by licensing Magnavox's Pong technology. Then it went into arcade games. In 1980 the company established its US subsidiary, Nintendo of America, whose first hit was Donkey Kong (meaning silly monkey). The next hit was Super Mario (named after Nintendo of America's warehouse landlord).

In 1983 the company released Famicom, a technologically advanced home video game system, in Japan. With its high-quality sound and graphics, Famicom was a smash, selling 15.2 million consoles and more than 183 million game cartridges in Japan alone.

In 1983–84 the US home game market crashed, sending pioneer Atari down in flames. Nintendo persevered, successfully launching Famicom in the US in 1986 as the Nintendo Entertainment System.

To prevent a barrage of independently produced, low-quality software (which had contributed to Atari's demise), the company established stringent licensing policies for its software developers: they needed approval of every game design, had to buy the blank cartridges from the company, and had to agree not to make the game for any of Nintendo's competitors, to pay development and marketing costs, and to pay Nintendo royalties for the honor of developing a game.

Designers chafed under these conditions, but they were part of Nintendo's strategy. The company minimizes its costs because its products, as discretionary purchases, are vulnerable to economic downturns (it is still suffering depressed sales due to the persistent recessions in Europe and Japan).

As the market became increasingly saturated, Nintendo sought new products, releasing Game Boy in 1989 and the Super Family Computer game system (Super NES in the US) in 1991. It also cross-marketed Super Mario with a movie based on the character.

In the 1990s Nintendo has been hit by the discovery that video games may induce seizures and an outcry against violent games. However, the company declined to participate in a ratings system devised by Sega because its own games were usually less violent (another reason for declining sales) than Sega's.

In 1994, in a quest for new and exciting games, Nintendo broke with tradition by making design alliances with companies like Silicon Graphics, and began giving other designers more favorable deals. One of the resulting products, a virtual reality game to be called Virtual Boy (created with Reflection Technology, Inc.), is set for sale in April 1995.

OTC symbol: NTDOY (ADR)
Fiscal year ends: March 31

	1994 Sales % of total
Japan	47
Other countries	53
Total	**100**

WHO

President: Hiroshi Yamauchi, age 67
Senior Managing Director: Katsunori Tanimoto
Senior Managing Director: Tokio Sotani
Senior Managing Director: Akio Tsuji
Managing Director: Hiroyuki Fukuda
Managing Director: Yasuhiro Onishi
Managing Director: Hiroshi Imanishi
Managing Director: Kimio Mariko
Managing Director; Chairman, Nintendo of America: Howard C. Lincoln, age 54
Managing Director; President, Nintendo of America: Minoru Arakawa, age 47
CFO, Nintendo of America: Bruce Holdren
VP Administration (Human Resources), Nintendo of America: John Bauer
Auditors: Chuo Audit Corporation

WHAT

Game Consoles
Famicom/Nintendo Entertainment System
Game Boy
Nintendo Ultra 64
Super Famicom/Super Nintendo Entertainment System

Selected Games
Donkey Kong Country
Sim City
Star Fox
Super Mario Bros. series
Tetris
Yoshi
Zelda series

WHERE

HQ: 60 Fukuine Kamitakamatsu-cho,
Higashiyama-ku, Kyoto 605, Japan
Phone: +81-75-541-6111
Fax: +81-75-531-9577
US HQ: Nintendo of America Inc., 4820 150th
Ave. NE, Redmond, WA 98052-9733
US Phone: 206-882-2040
US Fax: 206-882-3585

The company has offices and plants in Japan and major subsidiaries in Australia, Belgium, Canada, France, Germany, the Netherlands, the UK, and the US.

KEY COMPETITORS

3DO
7th Level
Acclaim
  Entertainment
Activision
Atari
Brøderbund
Cyan
Electronic Arts
Hasbro
Id Software
LucasArts
  Entertainment
Matsushita
Mattel
NEC
Pearson
Philips
Sega
Sony
Virgin Group
Walt Disney

HOW MUCH

$=¥112 (Dec. 31, 1993)	Annual Growth	1985	1986	1987	1988	1989	1990[2]	1991	1992	1993	1994
Sales (¥ bil.)	32.4%	68	81	123	145	203	240	471	562	635	486
Net income (¥ bil.)	28.7%	9	10	17	25	30	33	69	87	89	53
Income as % of sales	—	13.2%	12.3%	13.8%	17.2%	14.8%	13.7%	14.6%	15.5%	14.0%	10.8%
Earnings per share (¥)	27.2%	69	72	118	178	213	242	486	615	626	372
Stock price – high (¥)[1]	—	—	2,353	5,537	5,350	4,815	12,471	24,815	17,407	12,300	10,900
Stock price – low (¥)[1]	—	—	1,508	2,312	3,025	3,284	3,862	10,889	10,000	8,600	6,000
Stock price – close (¥)[1]	17.1%	2,016	2,353	4,564	3,210	4,612	11,111	14,000	11,700	10,600	7,100
P/E – high	—	—	33	47	30	23	54	51	28	20	29
P/E – low	—	—	21	20	17	15	17	22	16	14	16
Dividends per share (¥)	29.9%	11.2	11.2	15.0	17.4	21.7	30.9	43.5	60.0	70.0	70.0
Book value per share (¥)	36.6%	—	353	542	702	893	1,110	1,769	2,319	2,854	3,135
Employees	(3.6%)	—	—	—	—	684	730	777	825	943	568

1994 Year-end:
Debt ratio: 0.0%
Return on equity: 12.4%
Cash (bil.): ¥343
Long-term debt (bil.): ¥3.72
No. of shares (mil.): 142
Dividends
  Yield: 1.0%
  Payout: 18.8%
Market value (mil.): $9,766
Sales (mil.): $4,715

**Stock Price History[1]
High/Low 1986–94**

[1] Stock prices are for the prior calendar year. [2] 7-month fiscal year

NIPPON STEEL CORPORATION

OVERVIEW

Nippon Steel, the world's #1 steel producer, has been steeling itself for a downturn in demand for several years by diversifying into other industrial areas such as electronics and communications. Even so, the company is synonymous with steel, which still accounts for 70% of sales. A sluggish market and the rising yen have hurt the company; it reported a ¥54 billion loss in fiscal 1994 on sales that fell 7% below 1993 revenues.

The company has a substantial engineering and construction arm that is engaged in major civil engineering projects, including airports, bridges, harbors, highways, pipelines, and skyscrapers. A related service business division includes interests in restaurants, homes for the elderly, and the Space World education and amusement park in Yahata in the Kyushu prefecture in Japan.

Nippon Steel's electronics and information/communications division includes computer hardware, software, systems design, and telecommunications. Other areas of development include new materials such as silicon wafers and catalytic carriers.

A semiconductor division was organized in 1993 as part of the company's diversification strategy. Nippon Steel invests heavily in its research and engineering unit, which has over 2,000 researchers and technicians.

WHEN

Nippon Steel was forged in the first blast furnace in Japan, at Kamaishi, in 1857. Takato Oshima translated a Dutch manual to learn steelmaking technology.

In 1901 the Japanese government launched its Yawata Works on the island of Kyushu, and Japanese steelmaking again relied on Western teaching, this time in the form of foreign engineers who offered advice and counsel. Yawata grew and accounted for the bulk of Japanese steel production in the early years of the 20th century.

In the 1930s, as Japan prepared for war in the Pacific, the government merged the Yawata Works and other Japanese steel makers into the giant Japan Iron & Steel combine. During postwar occupation Japan Iron & Steel was ordered dissolved under the Excessive Economic Power Deconcentration Law of 1950. Yawata Iron & Steel and Fuji Iron & Steel emerged from the dissolution and, with the aid of Western training, the Japanese steel industry staggered to its feet . . . then took off running. In the late 1960s Fuji Steel bought Tokai Iron & Steel (1967), and Yawata Steel took over Yawata Steel Tube Company (1968).

Yawata and Fuji merged in 1970, over government objections, and became Nippon Steel, the largest steelmaker in the world. In the 1970s the Japanese steel industry was criticized in the US; American competitors complained that Japan was "dumping" low-cost exports. Nippon Steel aggressively courted China as another customer.

Nippon Steel began to diversify in the mid-1980s to wean itself from dependence on steel. It created a New Materials Projects Bureau in 1984 and retrained "redundant" steelworkers to make silicon wafers. It created an Electronics Division in 1986 and in 1988 began joint ventures with IBM Japan (small computers and software), Hitachi (office workstations), and C. Itoh (information systems for small- and medium-sized companies). It hopes to generate 20% of sales from electronics by 1995.

Nippon Steel opened a cold-rolled steel plant in Indiana (1990). The plant is the result of a $525 million joint venture, called I/N Tek, with Inland Steel of the US. A similar venture with Inland, the $450-million I/N Kote, churns out coated steel for the automotive industry.

California database software company Oracle signed a pact with Nippon Steel in late 1991. Nippon Steel agreed to sell Oracle's products in Japan and acquire as much as 25% of Oracle Japan. Nippon Steel's amusement park, Space World, opened in 1990; the company had to spend over ¥15 billon (more than 4 times its expected expense) to build a park worthy of competing with Tokyo Disneyland.

Nippon Steel teamed with Western Digital in 1992 to develop advanced disk drives and began a joint venture with Mazda to test hydrogen-powered engines. In 1993 Nippon Steel announced a ¥300 billion restructuring of its steelmaking operations, to be achieved primarily by cutting personnel.

In 1994 the company agreed to form an information systems venture with Electronic Data Systems to improve access to databases.

Principal exchange: Tokyo
Fiscal year ends: March 31

WHO

Chairman: Hiroshi Saito, age 74
President: Takashi Imai, age 65
EVP Sales: Yoshiro Sasaki, age 64
EVP Technical Admin.: Minoru Tanaka, age 62
EVP Corporate Planning: Toshio Miki, age 62
EVP Finance: Shigeru Omori, age 62
EVP Personnel: Takao Katsumata, age 64
President and CEO, Nippon Steel U.S.A.:
 Hiroshi Suetsugu, age 55
CFO, Nippon Steel U.S.A.: Kinya Akiyama
**Manager Human Resources, Nippon Steel
 U.S.A.:** Yasushi Aoki
Auditors: Chuo Audit Corporation

WHERE

HQ: Shin Nippon Seitetsu Kabushiki Kaisha,
 6-3, Otemachi 2-chome, Chiyoda-ku,
 Tokyo 100-71, Japan
Phone: +81-3-3242-4111
Fax: +81-3-3275-5607
US HQ: Nippon Steel U.S.A., Inc., 10 E. 50th St.,
 29th Fl., New York, NY 10022
US Phone: 212-486-7150
US Fax: 212-593-3049

Nippon Steel operates worldwide.

	1994 Sales
	% of total
Japan	81
Other countries	19
Total	**100**

WHAT

	1994 Sales	
	¥ bil.	% of total
Steel products	1,934	70
Engineering & construction	374	14
Chemicals, nonferrous		
metals & ceramics	219	8
Other	222	8
Total	**2,749**	**100**

Major Lines of Business

Steel
Plates and sheets
Rails
Stainless steel plates
Stainless steel tubing
Wire rods

**Engineering and
 Construction**
Major-project construction
Plant engineering
Service businesses (theme
 parks, restaurants)

Chemicals
Carbon materials
Cokes
Paint

New Materials
Semiconductor materials

**Electronics and
 Information/
 Communications**
Computers
Data processing services
Electronics devices

Titanium Products
Tube sheets and alloys

Aluminum Products
Sheet for automobiles

Semiconductors
High-speed DRAMS
Pattern designed wafers

KEY COMPETITORS

ABB	Inco	Mitsui
Alcan	IRI	NKK
Bechtel	Ito-Yokado	Rolls-Royce
Bethlehem Steel	Kawasaki Steel	RTZ
Broken Hill	Kobe Steel	Samsung
Fluor	LTV	Sumitomo
Friedrich Krupp	Mannesmann	Thyssen
Hitachi	Marubeni	USX–U.S. Steel
Hyundai	Mitsubishi	Walt Disney

HOW MUCH

$=¥112 (Dec. 31, 1993)	9-Year Growth	1985	1986	1987	1988	1989	1990	1991	1992	1993	1994
Sales (¥ bil.)	0.4%	2,660	2,860	2,685	2,178	2,147	2,973	3,209	3,230	2,951	2,749
Net income (¥ bil.)	—	3	42	37	(13)	32	117	91	78	2	(54)
Income as % of sales	—	0.1%	1.5%	1.4%	—	1.5%	3.9%	2.8%	2.4%	0.1%	—
Earnings per share (¥)	—	0	6	6	(2)	5	17	13	11	0	8
Stock price – high (¥)[1]	—	188	209	276	454	969	975	793	515	385	420
Stock price – low (¥)[1]	—	141	142	153	168	353	698	372	351	229	278
Stock price – close (¥)[1]	7.9%	155	155	169	362	870	793	448	375	292	307
P/E – high	—	—	33	50	—	202	56	60	47	—	54
P/E – low	—	—	23	28	—	74	40	28	32	—	35
Dividends per share (¥)	(7.4%)	5.00	5.00	5.00	3.00	3.00	6.00	6.00	6.00	6.00	2.50
Book value per share (¥)	5.0%	91	93	93	89	91	145	152	158	152	141
Employees	3.0%	66,549	65,001	64,060	61,423	58,186	55,863	54,062	53,290	51,897	50,458

1994 Year-end:
Debt ratio: 69.7%
Return on equity: 5.4%
Cash (bil.): ¥561
Long-term debt (bil.):¥1,365
No. of shares (mil.): 6,889
Dividends
 Yield: 0.8%
 Payout: 31.8%
Market value (mil.): $18,883
Sales (mil.): $24,545

**Stock Price History[1]
High/Low 1985–94**

[1]Stock prices are for the prior calendar year. [2]Note: All 1985–1988 data are unconsolidated.

NIPPON TELEGRAPH AND TELEPHONE

OVERVIEW

With 60 million phone lines and 1.3 million cellular customers, Nippon Telegraph and Telephone is the world's 2nd largest telecommunications company, after AT&T, and the world's most valuable company.

NTT's once-solid monopoly is being threatened. Inspired by the US phone industry's increased competitiveness following the AT&T breakup, Japan's telecommunications ministry has begun to gain ground in its decade-long effort to split NTT into several local and long distance companies. (NTT has already established 9 regional subsidiaries to support its wireless "personal handy phone.")

The Ministry of Finance hopes to stall the breakup until Japan's government sells part of its 65.6% share in NTT.

NTT's profits fell 68% from 1990 to 1994, but a hike in local phone rates, petitioned for in early 1994, should help ease the company's deficit. The hike would also allow NTT to cut its long distance rates, improving its share of that highly competitive market.

Meanwhile, NTT has joined with AT&T and Microsoft to commercialize computer-based multimedia technologies for use on its $391 billion fiber-optic network, which should have Japan fully "wired" by 2015.

WHEN

The Japanese Ministry of Communications began telephone service in 1889 and operated as a monopoly after 1900. After WWII the ministry reorganized and, in 1952, formed Nippon Telegraph and Telephone Public Corporation (NTT). Regulated by the Ministry of Posts and Telecommunications, NTT was charged with rebuilding and running Japan's war-ravaged phone system. The ministry created a separate company (KDD) to handle international telephone service in 1953. NTT owns 10% of KDD.

Japanese authorities created NTT in the image of AT&T but prohibited NTT from manufacturing, preferring to encourage competition among equipment suppliers. NTT bought most of its equipment from favored Japanese vendors. Four companies benefited most from this arrangement: NEC (the most favored), Hitachi, Fujitsu, and Oki Electric.

NTT expanded rapidly during the 1960s as Japan's economy surged. In the late 1960s NTT was installing 3 million lines per year. In 1968 NTT enlisted Hitachi, Fujitsu, and NEC to design and build computers for NTT's use, subsidizing critical R&D for Japan's future computer giants.

By the 1970s NTT had become a large, bureaucratic utility, and public suspicions of inefficiency and corruption led to political pressure to reform. In the late 1970s US trade representatives called for NTT to purchase non-Japanese equipment and were stunned when NTT president Tokuji Akikusa told them that the only items it would consider buying overseas were telephone poles and mops. But in 1981 the company entered into an agreement to open procurement to US companies.

NTT inaugurated a public fax network in 1981 and a videotex (reservation and order-processing) service in 1984. The company spent heavily in the 1980s on the nationwide installation of optical fiber for integrated systems digital networks (ISDN), capable of high-volume, high-speed data transmission.

In 1985 Japanese authorities began deregulating the telecommunications industry, opening NTT markets to competition (while maintaining price regulation) and selling NTT shares to the public. NTT became the world's most valuable public company at its initial public offering.

In 1990 NTT selected AT&T, Motorola, and Ericsson to develop a digital mobile telephone system. With increased competition and the constraints of regulation, company earnings began to slump.

In 1993 NTT began cutting its operating costs part of its ongoing battle to convince regulators that the company deserved approval of rate hikes in various business segments.

In 1993 and 1994 NTT began aggressively developing its high-tech communications capabilities, establishing alliances with several US companies, including General Magic, Oracle, and Silicon Graphics. The company is pursuing projects in interactive cable TV and advanced e-mail and facsimile transmissions.

In 1994 NTT began trading on the New York and London stock exchanges. Foreign ownership is limited to 20%. NTT's phone monopoly was further eroded in late 1994 when the government ordered it to allow certain competitors to connect to NTT's local phone lines.

NYSE: NTT (ADR)
Fiscal year ends: March 31

Chairman: Haruo Yamaguchi
President: Masashi Kojima
SEVP: Shigeo Sawada
SEVP: Jun-ichiro Miyazu
EVP: Muneo Ohashi
EVP: Morimasa Nishimura
EVP: Shunji Kaibuchi
EVP: Ko Ishii
EVP: Yutaka Hayashi
EVP: Noboru Miyawaki
EVP: Masakuni Asahara
EVP: Satoshi Hirose
VP Corporate Affairs and Public Relations (Human Relations): Toshihiro Inamura
President, NTT America: Koichiro Hayashi
Auditors: Price Waterhouse

WHERE

HQ: Nippon Denshin Denwa Kabushiki Kaisha (Nippon Telegraph and Telephone Corporation), 1-6, Uchisaiwai-cho 1-chome, Chiyoda-ku, Tokyo 100-19, Japan
Phone: +81-3-3509-5111
Fax: +81-3-3509-4598
US HQ: NTT America, Inc., 101 Park Ave., 41st Fl., New York, NY 10178
US Phone: 212-661-0810
US Fax: 212-661-1078

NTT operates principally in Japan but provides telecommunications consulting worldwide.

WHAT

	1994 Sales	
	¥ bil.	% of total
Telephone	4,880	73
Leased circuit	401	6
Sale of terminal equipment	309	5
Data communication facility	237	3
Telegraph	81	1
Other services	779	12
Total	**6,687**	**100**

Selected Services

Leased Circuit Services	**Other Services**
Conventional leased circuit services	Data communication facility services
High-speed digital circuit services	Digital data exchange services
Satellite communication services	F-Net (facsimile network) services
Video transmission services	ISDN services
	Multimedia
Telegraph Services	Pocket pager services
Telegram services	Telecommunications consulting
Telex services	Teleconferencing services
Telephone Services	Terminal equipment sales
Cellular telephone services	Videotex services
Public telephone services	
Telephone subscriber services	

KEY COMPETITORS

AT&T	Nippon Idou Tsushin
Cable & Wireless	Teleway Japan
Daini-Denden	Tokyo Digital Phone
Japan Telecom	Tu-ka Cellular Tokyo

HOW MUCH

$=¥112 (Dec. 31, 1993)	Annual Growth	1985	1986	1987	1988	1989	1990	1991	1992	1993	1994
Sales (¥ bil.)	3.9%	4,756	5,091	5,354	5,662	5,842	6,022	6,252	6,398	6,504	6,687
Net income (¥ bil.)	(16.7%)	428	186	193	267	264	261	261	221	153	83
Income as % of sales	—	9.0%	3.7%	3.6%	4.7%	4.5%	4.3%	4.2%	3.5%	2.4%	1.2%
Earnings per share (¥)	(9.5%)	—	11,903	12,350	17,127	16,898	16,737	16,740	14,144	9,825	5,346
Stock price – high (¥ thou.)[1]	—	—	—	—	3,180	2,530	1,930	1,470	1,130	760	1,000
Stock price – low (¥ thou.)[1]	—	—	—	—	1,600	1,700	1,350	720	720	453	606
Stock price – close (¥ thou.)[1]	(16.3%)	—	—	—	2,160	1,810	1,470	985	734	571	744
P/E – high	—	—	—	—	186	150	115	88	80	77	187
P/E – low	—	—	—	—	93	101	81	43	51	46	113
Dividends per share (¥)	—	—	—	—	5,000	5,000	5,000	5,000	5,000	5,000	5,000
Book value per share (¥ thou.)	4.1%	—	225	230	242	254	266	276	286	331	311
Employees	(2.6%)	314,000	304,000	297,596	291,142	283,294	272,903	264,908	257,663	242,303	248,000

1994 Year-end:
Debt ratio: 47.8%
Return on equity: 1.7%
Cash (bil.): ¥692
Long-term debt (bil.): ¥3,667
No. of shares (mil.): 16
Dividends
 Yield: 0.7%
 Payout: 0.1%
Market value (mil.): $103,629
Sales (mil.): $59,705

Stock Price History[1]
High/Low 1988–94

(chart y-axis: 3,500 / 3,000 / 2,500 / 2,000 / 1,500 / 1,000 / 500 / 0)

[1] Stock prices are for the prior calendar year.

NISSAN MOTOR CO., LTD.

OVERVIEW

Nissan, Japan's 2nd largest auto maker (after Toyota) and #4 in the world, hopes to find a detour around Japan's continuing economic woes. With the high yen and low sales slashing company profits, Nissan initiated a cost-cutting program in 1993 that includes plant closures, work slowdowns, standardized parts, and increased overseas production. The plan, designed to cut nearly $2 billion through 1996, is ahead of schedule.

Nissan sales in Japan are especially depressed, dropping more than 3.5% in 1994. While sales in most foreign markets are down,

US buyers took home more than 724,500 Nissans in 1993, an increase of 19.8%.

In 1994 Nissan and Korea's leading industrial group, Samsung, reached a $4.4 billion joint venture agreement to produce cars in Korea by 1998.

Meanwhile, a series of safety snafus has undermined Nissan's image. Several models were recalled in 1994, including Altimas, Maximas, and 240SX coupes. The company offered to buy back some models of its C22 minivans because of engine fires; the plan could cost Nissan as much as $200 million.

WHEN

In 1911 US-trained Hashimoto Masujiro established Tokyo-based Kwaishinsha Motor Car Works to repair, import, and produce automobiles. Using DAT ("fast rabbit" in Japanese) as its logo, Kwaishinsha made its first car in 1913. Renamed DAT Motors in 1925 and suffering from a strong domestic preference for American cars, the company consolidated its operations with ailing Jitsuyo Motors in 1926. In 1931 DAT introduced the son of DAT, the Datsun minicar (*son* means "damage" or "loss" in Japanese, hence the change in spelling).

Tobata Casting, a cast iron and auto parts maker, acquired Datsun's production facilities in 1933. Tobata's Yoshisuke Aikawa believed that a niche existed for small cars that did not compete directly with large US imports, and the car operations were spun off as Nissan Motors the same year. Aikawa imported US machinery and engineers, and in 1936 he bought and imported all the production equipment of a plant owned by financially troubled US carmaker Graham-Paige, creating Japan's first mass-producer of autos.

In WWII the Japanese government limited Nissan production to trucks and airplane engines, leaving its dealers with little to sell. Dealer defections gave Toyota a postwar advantage. During the occupation Nissan survived, in part, on US Army business.

A 1952 licensing agreement with Austin Motor (UK) put Nissan back in the car business. Adhering to US quality-control statistician William E. Deming's teachings, Nissan mass-produced reliable, inexpensive autos. A 40% import tax let Nissan compete in Japan despite the fact that it had higher costs than foreign makers.

Nissan elected to enter the US market in 1958 using the Datsun name and established Nissan Motor Corporation in Los Angeles in 1960. The company built an assembly plant in Mexico (1961) and introduced the popular Sunny in Japan (1966) and the 240Z in the US (1969). Exports rose during the 1960s as quality increased and unit costs declined as a result of just-in-time inventory management, factory automation, and higher volume.

In the 1970s Nissan expanded exports of fuel-efficient cars (e.g., Datsun B210) and diversified into rockets and motorboats.

In the 1980s the US name change from Datsun to Nissan confused customers and took 6 years (1981–1987) to complete. Nissan's high-end Infiniti line was launched in the US in 1989.

Nissan quietly took control of Fuji Heavy Industries, the troubled maker of Subaru autos, in 1990 with the approval of Fuji's banker, the Industrial Bank of Japan.

Nissan and DDI Corporation, an important Japanese telecommunications company, set up TU-KA Cellular Tokyo Inc. and TU-KA Kansai Inc. in 1991 and TU-KA Cellular Tokai Inc. in 1992 to provide digital mobile telecommunications.

Nissan reported a $450 million loss in 1993 — its first since going public in 1951. The loss was triggered by poor domestic sales caused by Japan's economic recession. The next year the company celebrated its 60th anniversary.

In 1994 Nissan became the UK's top auto exporter, shipping over 182,000 cars to 36 countries. That same year the company sold $200 million of its real estate holdings in an effort to reduce its deficit.

OTC symbol: NSANY (ADR)
Fiscal year ends: March 31

WHO

Chairman: Yutaka Kume
President: Yoshifumi Tsuji
Executive Managing Director, Accounting and Finance Group: Heiichi Hamaoka
President, Nissan North America: Robert J. Thomas, age 49
Director Finance, Nissan North America: Donald Westenhaver
Manager Human Resources, Nissan North America: Kathy Doi
Auditors: Showa Ota & Co.

WHERE

HQ: Nissan Jidosha, 17-1, Ginza 6-chome, Chuo-ku, Tokyo 104-23, Japan
Phone: +81-3-3543-5523
Fax: +81-3-3546-2669 (Corporate Communications)
US HQ: Nissan North America, Inc., 990 W. 190th St., Torrance, CA 90502
US Phone: 310-768-3700
US Fax: 310-327-2272

	1994 Unit Sales	
	No. of vehicles	% of total
Japan	1,087,987	40
North America	756,244	28
Europe	473,556	18
Latin America & Caribbean	178,614	7
Asia	88,438	3
Middle East	56,116	2
Oceania	34,746	1
Africa	15,314	1
Other regions	153	—
Total	**2,691,168**	**100**

WHAT

	1994 Sales	
	¥ bil.	% of total
Vehicles	4,145	71
Automotive parts & others	1,490	26
Production parts & components	72	1
Industrial machinery & marine equip.	43	1
Aerospace equipment	34	1
Textile machinery	17	—
Total	**5,801**	**100**

Automobile Models (US Markets)

Infiniti
  G20   M30
  I30   Q45
  J30
Nissan
  200SX
  240SX
  300ZX
  4x2 (trucks)
  4x4 (trucks)
  Altima
  Maxima
  Pathfinder
  Quest
  Sentra

Industrial Machinery and Marine Equipment

Automotive parts
Forklifts
Outboard motors
Pleasure boats
Trucks

Aerospace Equipment

Defense missiles
Rockets
Satellite launch vehicles

Nissan Texsys Co. Ltd.

Air Jet (textile looms)
LAN-Tex (PC-based automated systems for textile factories)

KEY COMPETITORS

BMW	Hyundai	Peugeot
Brunswick	Isuzu	Porsche
Caterpillar	Kia Motors	Reebok
Chrysler	Lockheed Martin	Renault
Daimler-Benz	MacAndrews &	Saab-Scania
Deere	Forbes	Suzuki
Fiat	Mazda	Thiokol
Ford	Mitsubishi	Toyota
General Electric	Navistar	Volkswagen
General Motors	Outboard	Volvo
Honda	Marine	Yamaha

HOW MUCH

$ = ¥112 (Dec. 31, 1993)	Annual Growth	1985	1986	1987	1988	1989	1990	1991	1992	1993	1994
Sales (¥ bil.)	3.4%	4,308	4,626	4,628	4,273	4,244	4,812	5,965	6,418	6,199	5,801
Net income (¥ bil.)	—	74	82	36	20	65	115	49	101	(56)	(87)
Income as % of sales	—	1.7%	1.8%	0.8%	0.5%	1.5%	2.4%	0.8%	1.6%	—	—
Earnings per share (¥)	—	39	16	9	29	48	46	19	40	(22)	(35)
Stock price – high (¥)[1]	—	695	668	717	875	1,380	1,650	1,500	826	694	860
Stock price – low (¥)[1]	—	575	569	529	550	705	1,250	690	628	529	550
Stock price – close (¥)[1]	6.5%	625	570	550	725	1,200	1,470	700	632	560	756
P/E – high	—	18	41	79	30	29	36	78	21	—	—
P/E – low	—	15	35	57	19	15	26	37	16	—	—
Dividends per share (¥)	(18.1%)	12.73	12.73	14.00	14.00	14.00	14.00	14.00	14.00	7.00	7.00
Book value per share (¥)	6.1%	526	629	627	616	628	666	709	722	685	629
Employees	3.1%	108,500	106,282	105,443	108,716	117,330	129,546	138,326	143,916	143,754	143,310

1994 Year-end:
Debt ratio: 71.9%
Return on equity: —
Cash (bil.): ¥170
Long-term debt (bil.): ¥2,368
No. of shares (mil.): 2,110
Dividends
  Yield: 0.9%
  Payout: —
Market value (mil.): $15,488
Sales (mil.): $56,319

**Stock Price History[1]
High/Low 1985–94**

(chart y-axis: 1,800 / 1,600 / 1,400 / 1,200 / 1,000 / 800 / 600 / 400 / 200 / 0)

[1] Stock prices are for the prior calendar year.

NOKIA GROUP

OVERVIEW

Nokia, one of Finland's largest companies, has emerged from more than a century of making basic industrial products, such as pulp, paper, and rubber goods, to be a major player in the global telecommunications market. Nokia only started making mobile phones in 1979, but by 1993 it had become the largest European mobile phone manufacturer and the 2nd largest in the US, after Motorola. It holds 20% of the highly competitive US mobile phone market.

The Nokia Group operates 5 divisions: Consumer Electronics (color TV sets, satellite receivers, monitors, and car audio systems), Mobile Phones (mobile phones and pagers), Telecommunications (public networks, mo-

bile phone networks, and dedicated networks), Cables and Machinery (cables, cable machinery, optical fiber, and aluminum products), and Tyres.

Run by a group of 40-something managers with international experience, the company is focusing on telecommunications and is exploring new markets around the world, including South Africa, Thailand, Ukraine, and the United Arab Emirates.

With telecommunications-related segments accounting for over 60% of Nokia's total revenues, 43-year-old president and CEO Jorma Ollila has set a course for divesting the company of its non-core assets. The company sold its power business in 1994.

WHEN

Nokia began in 1865 with the establishment of a groundwood mill to manufacture pulp and paper on the Nokia River in Finland.

Although Nokia flourished within Finland, the company was not well known to the rest of the world until it attempted to become a regional conglomerate in the early 1960s. The French computer firm Bull selected Nokia as its Finnish agent in 1962. In 1967, with the encouragement of the government of Finland, Nokia merged with Finnish Rubber Works, a tire and rubber footwear manufacturer formed in 1898, and Finnish Cable Works, a cable and electronics manufacturer formed in 1912, to form Nokia Corporation.

The oil crisis of 1973 created severe inflation and a large trade deficit for Finland. Nokia reassessed its heavy reliance on Soviet trade (39% of exports) and its growth strategies. In 1975 Nokia promoted the head of Nokia's Pulp, Paper & Power division, Kari Kairamo, to CEO. Since the company was already a world leader in mobile phone technology, Kairamo moved Nokia toward consumer and business electronics while improving Nokia's product line, its reputation for quality, and its production capacity. The company's basic industries — paper, chemicals, electricity, and machinery — were modernized and encouraged to expand into robotics, fiber optics, and high-grade tissues.

Sales, exports, and profits grew under Kairamo's leadership. In 1981 Nokia acquired a 51% interest in the state-owned Finnish telecommunications company, changing its name to Telenokia. The following year Nokia

custom designed and installed the first European digital telephone system in Finland. Also in 1982 Nokia bought Mobira, a Finnish mobile phone company, and Finnish Chemicals, a chlorine producer. Nokia next acquired an 18.3% interest in Salora, Scandinavia's largest color TV manufacturer, and Luxor, the Swedish state-owned electronics and computer firm. To compete in the wider European market, Nokia became an original equipment manufacturer for IBM in the UK, Hitachi in France, Ericsson in Sweden, and Northern Telecom in Canada.

The pace and size of acquisitions increased in the late 1980s. In 1986 Nokia acquired control of Sähköliikkeiden, Finland's largest electrical wholesaler. Nokia created the largest information technology group in Scandinavia, Nokia Data, by purchasing Ericsson Group's Data Division in 1988. Sales soared, but profits plunged because of stiff price competition in consumer electronics. Kairamo, a manic-depressive, committed suicide shortly before Christmas in 1988.

Nokia sold Nokia Data in 1991 to ICL to raise cash. That same year Nokia paid $57.8 million for Technophone, the UK mobile phone manufacturer, which had been #2 in Europe, after Nokia. Under the leadership of Jorma Ollila (appointed CEO in 1992), Nokia has focused on the telecommunications industry. In 1993 Nokia acquired Tandy's share in joint ventures making mobile phones in Texas and South Korea.

In 1994 Nokia sold its power company and announced plans to sell 80% of Nokia Tyres.

NYSE symbol: NOK Pr
Fiscal year ends: December 31

President, and CEO: Jorma Ollila, age 43
President, Nokia Consumer Electronics: Hannu
 Bergholm, age 44
President, Nokia Mobile Phones: Pekka
 Ala-Pietilä, age 37
President, Nokia Telecommunications: Matti
 Alahuhta, age 41
President, Nokia Cables and Machinery: Tapio
 Hintikka, age 51
CFO: Olli-Pekka Kallasvuo, age 40
Director Personnel: Kirsi-Marja Kuivalainen
President, Nokia Mobile Phones (US): Paul
 Chellgren
Auditors: KPMG; Coopers & Lybrand

HQ: Eteläesplanadi 12, PO Box 226, FIN-00101,
 Helsinki, Finland
Phone: +358-0-180-71
Fax: +358-0-656-388
US HQ: Nokia Mobile Phones Inc., 2300 Tall
 Pines Dr., PO Box 2930, Largo, Florida 34649
US Phone: 813-536-5553
US Fax: 813-530-7245

	1993 Sales	
	FIM mil.	**% of total**
Finland	3,547	15
Asia/Pacific	2,768	12
North America	1,985	8
Other West European	11,053	47
Other Nordic	2,394	10
Other countries	1,950	8
Total	**23,697**	**100**

	1993 Sales	
	FIM mil.	**% of total**
Nokia Consumer Electronics	6,938	29
Nokia Mobile Phones	6,314	26
Nokia Cables and Machinery	4,933	20
Nokia Telecommunications	4,578	19
Other operations	1,500	6
Adjustments	(566)	—
Total	**23,697**	**100**

Nokia Consumer Electronics
Luxor Electronics AB (Sweden)
Nokia Display Technics GmbH (Germany)
Nokia Electronics Bochum GmbH (Germany)
Nokia Unterhaltungselektronik GmbH (Germany)

Nokia Mobile Phones
Nokia Mobile Phones (UK) Ltd.
Nokia-Mobira AS (Denmark)

Nokia Cables and Machinery
NKF Kabel BV (56.95%, The Netherlands)
Nokia Kaapeli Oy/Nokia Cables Ltd.
Nokia-Maillefer Inc. (US)

Nokia Telecommunications
Nokia Telecommunications Inc. (US)
Nokia Telecommunications Ltd. (UK)

Other Operations
Nokia Tyres Ltd.

AT&T	GTE	Pirelli
BMW	Matsushita	Robert Bosch
Bose	Michelin	Sanyo
Bridgestone	Mitsubishi	Siemens
Continental AG	Motorola	Sony
Ericsson	NEC	Sumitomo
Fujitsu	Oki	Thomson SA
General Electric	Philips	Toshiba
Goodyear	Pioneer	Zenith

$=FIM5.78 (Dec. 31, 1993)	Annual Growth	1984	1985	1986	1987	1988	1989	1990	1991	1992	1993
Sales (FIM mil.)	10.9%	9,360	11,020	11,994	13,998	21,819	22,795	22,130	15,457	18,168	23,697
Net income (FIM mil.)	18.6%	165	550	531	843	815	274	344	(604)	(413)	767
Income as % of sales	—	1.8%	5.0%	4.4%	6.0%	3.7%	1.2%	1.6%	—	—	3.2%
Earnings per share (FIM)[1]	12.7%	4.2	12.0	10.6	15.32	13.67	4.36	5.47	(9.60)	(6.84)	12.29
Stock price – high (FIM)[1]	—	—	62	122	194	135	105	105	105	90	344
Stock price – low (FIM)[1]	—	—	34	54	84	78	60	45	45	38	82
Stock price – close (FIM)[1]	19.3%	59	54	90	112	82	95	55	47	82	289
P/E – high[1]	—	—	5	12	13	10	24	19	—	—	28
P/E – low[1]	—	—	3	5	5	6	14	8	—	—	7
Dividends per share (FIM)	8.0%	1.40	2.12	2.44	3.31	3.20	2.80	2.80	2.00	2.00	2.80
Book value per share (FIM)	3.7%	72	85	90	103	117	116	119	118	113	100
Employees	0.9%	27,874	27,619	28,509	29,276	44,588	41,326	37,336	29,167	26,700	25,800

1993 Year-end:
Debt ratio: 51.2%
Return on equity: 11.6%
Cash (mil.): FIM3,297
L-T debt (mil.): FIM3,397
No. of shares (mil.): 69
Dividends
 Yield: 1.0%
 Payout: 22.8%
Market value (mil.): $3,439
Sales (mil.): $4,093

**Stock Price History[1]
High/Low 1985–93**

[1] Free preferred shares 1984–1992, preferred shares 1993.

HOOVER'S HANDBOOK OF WORLD BUSINESS 1995–1996   365

THE NOMURA SECURITIES CO., LTD.

OVERVIEW

Nomura is the #1 brokerage house among the Big 4 in Japan, despite a sharp decline over the past few years in its core business. Nomura is a leading underwriter of bonds and is a major player in the equity-related issues in the Euromarket, but the firm's main business remains its Japanese stock brokerage. Nomura's profits have fallen sharply with the descent of the Japanese stock market and the resultant decline in commission and underwriting income.

Nomura's diversification into other financial instruments paid off in 1993 with strong returns from bond trading and mortgage-securities trading by its US subsidiary. The company is emphasizing local autonomy, with regional managers overseeing the sales of equity. It is also cutting unproductive offices and personnel.

To provide "one-stop" shopping for its customers, Nomura has restructured its equity sales division to include warrants, convertible bonds, and stocks.

Nomura executives have also indicated an interest in new overseas investments, especially in China and other Asian countries.

WHEN

Tokushichi Nomura started a currency exchange business in Osaka under the Nomura Shoten name in 1872. As money changing subsided with Japanese monetary reform, Nomura entered stock dealing. His business prospered and was taken over by his son Tokushichi II prior to the senior Nomura's death in 1907. In 1910 Tokushichi II formed Nomura's first syndicate to underwrite a portion of a government bond issue. As business grew, Nomura established the Osaka Nomura Bank (1918). The bond department became independent in 1925 and was named Nomura Securities.

The company opened a New York office (1927), entered stock brokerage (1938), and introduced its enormously successful stock investment trusts (1941).

Nomura rebuilt and aggressively expanded retail operations after WWII. The company encouraged stock market investing by promoting "million ryo (an old form of currency) savings chests," small boxes in which people were encouraged to save cash. When savings reached 5,000 yen, savers, usually women, would bring their boxes to Nomura and buy into investment trusts. Nomura distributed over one million chests in 10 years.

Nomura looked overseas for investment capital, helping to underwrite a US issue of Sony stock (1961) and opening a London office (1962). The company emerged as Japan's leading securities firm after a 1965 stock market crash left rival Yamaichi Securities near bankruptcy. When trade surpluses encouraged the Ministry of Finance to allow public ownership of foreign securities in 1971, Nomura began offering *samurai*

(yen-denominated foreign) bonds. The company grew rapidly in the 1970s, ushering investment capital in and out of Japan and competing with bank lending by issuing corporate debt securities.

Nomura expanded worldwide in the 1970s and 1980s, attained NYSE membership (1981), secured a seat on the London Stock Exchange (1986), opened Nomura Bank International in London (1986), became the world leader in Eurobonds (1987), and paid $100 million for 20% of merger and acquisition advisor Wasserstein Perella (1988). Nomura pursued retail business aggressively, hosting Tupperware-style investment parties in Japan.

With a sudden drop in the Tokyo stock market in 1990, Nomura stock toppled 70% from its 1987 peak. The company saw its equity underwritings fall from 1,201 in FY 1990 to 12 in the first 6 months of 1991.

As the Tokyo stock market continued to fall in 1991 and 1992, Japan's securities firms were rocked by public disclosure of *tobashi*, the Japanese practice of adjusting customer accounts so that some clients would avoid stock market losses. The chairman and president of Nomura resigned as the government investigated claims that Nomura had manipulated stock prices and improperly covered $114 million in losses suffered by wealthy clients. No charges were pressed.

In 1993 Nomura's US operations, led by Nomura Securities International, had pretax income of $120 million, the highest ever for a Japanese brokerage firm in the US.

In 1994 Nomura stocks began trading on the Singapore Stock Exchange.

OTC symbol: NOM (ADR)
Fiscal year ends: March 31

Chairman: Masashi Suzuki
President and CEO: Hideo Sakamaki
EVP: Kiichiro Iwasaki
EVP: Naotaka Murasumi
EVP: Tadashi Takubo
Co-chairman and CEO, Nomura Securities International (US): Max C. Chapman, Jr.
Chief Accounting Officer and CFO, Nomura Securities International (US): John Tofflon
Director Human Resources, Nomura Securities International (US): Charles Lomax
Auditors: Price Waterhouse

HQ: 1-9-1, Nihonbashi, Chuo-ku, Tokyo 103, Japan
Phone: +81-3-3211-1811
Fax: +81-3-3273-6376
US HQ: Nomura Securities International, Inc., 2 World Financial Center, Bldg. B, New York, NY 10281-1198
US Phone: 212-667-9300
US Fax: 212-667-1058

	1994 Sales	
	¥ bil.	% of total
Japan	414	61
Europe	132	19
Americas	114	17
Asia & Oceania	19	3
Total	**679**	**100**

	1994 Sales	
	¥ bil.	% of total
Interest & dividends	234	35
Commissions	221	32
Underwriting & distribution	103	15
Net gain on trading	95	14
Other	26	4
Total	**679**	**100**

Lines of Business

Securities	Financial Consulting
Brokerage	Asset management
Dealing	Banking
Distribution	Leveraged leasing
Underwriting	Mergers and acquisitions
	Real estate

US Affiliates
Babcock & Brown, Inc. (investment banking)
Nomura Rosenburg Investment Technology Institute
Wasserstein Perella Group, Inc. (investment banking)

BankAmerica	Kemper
Barclays	Lehman Brothers
Bear Stearns	Merrill Lynch
Canadian Imperial	J.P. Morgan
Charles Schwab	Morgan Stanley
Crédit Lyonnais	NatWest
CS Holding	Nikko Securities
Dai-Ichi Kangyo	Paine Webber
Daiwa Securities	Prudential
Deutsche Bank	Royal Bank
General Electric	Salomon
Goldman Sachs	Travelers
HSBC	Union Bank of
Imasco	Switzerland
Industrial Bank of Japan	Yamaichi Securities

$=¥103 (Dec. 31, 1993)	Annual Growth	1985	1986	1987	1988	1989	1990	1991	1992	1993	1994
Sales (¥ bil.)	5.3%	427	590	942	1,073	960	1,201	976	656	584	679
Net income (¥ bil.)	(4.1%)	73	111	221	268	214	276	123	20	(14)	50
Income as % of sales	—	17.1%	18.8%	23.5%	25.0%	22.3%	23.0%	12.6%	3.0%	—	7.4%
Earnings per share (¥)	(4.7%)	39	59	118	142	112	141	63	10	(7)	25
Stock price – high (¥)[1]	—	853	1,287	3,612	5,816	4,185	4,100	3,430	2,260	1,800	2,250
Stock price – low (¥)[1]	—	533	793	934	2,402	2,402	3,060	1,380	1,520	1,100	1,410
Stock price – close (¥)[1]	9.2%	809	980	2,835	2,583	3,750	3,440	1,770	1,620	1,490	1,790
P/E – high	—	22	22	31	41	37	29	55	—	—	89
P/E – low	—	14	13	8	17	21	22	22	—	—	56
Dividends per share (¥)	4.6%	6.67	7.25	9.71	12.14	13.11	15.00	15.00	15.00	10.00	10.00
Book value per share (¥)	14.6%	274	325	412	582	685	953	987	973	931	931
Employees	0.3%	—	—	—	—	—	16,000	16,000	16,800	16,200	16,200

1994 Year-end:
Debt ratio: 0.0%
Return on equity: 2.7%
Cash (bil.): ¥75
Long-term debt (bil.): $0
No. of shares (mil.): 1,962
Dividends
  Yield: 0.6%
  Payout: 39.6%
Market value (mil.): $31,364
Sales (mil.): $6,063

Stock Price History[1]
High/Low 1985–94

[1] Stock prices are for the prior calendar year.

NORSK HYDRO A.S

OVERVIEW

Norsk Hydro a.s is Norway's largest public industrial company. Fertilizer, the company's top product, accounts for 41% of revenues. Its North Sea–based oil and gas operations include interests in a Swedish refinery and gas stations throughout Scandinavia. Hydro's Petrochemicals Division produces 40% of Scandinavia's PVC pipe. Hydro also produces light metals (aluminum and magnesium).

Hydro has embarked on an ambitious plan to cut costs, increase production, and expand its product lines and markets. In 1994 it acquired Fison's NPK fertilizer business and agreed to combine operations at its French fertilizer plant with 2 Italian plants

owned by Enichem Agricoltura. Hydro has also expanded its fertilizer network with new offices in China, India, and Latin America.

Hydro plans to increase oil and gas production beyond the North Sea and will explore fields in Siberia and off Russia's coast. The company has joined a partnership that is building a gas pipeline in Germany. It has announced development of several efficient production technologies, including ways to reduce well drilling time.

Hydro's Petrochemicals Division, which owns 60% of Singapore Polymer Corporation, has expanded its Asian base by acquiring interest in a PVC maker near Shanghai.

WHEN

Norwegian entrepreneurs Sam Eyde and Kristian Birkeland began Norsk Hydro-Elektrisk Kvaelstofaktieselskap (Norwegian Hydro-Electric Nitrogen Corporation) in 1905. The company used electricity generated from waterfalls to extract nitrogen from the air for the production of fertilizer. The company sold most of its output in Scandinavia.

After WWII the Norwegian government seized German holdings in Hydro and took a 48% stake in the company. Hydro grew to be the largest chemical firm in Scandinavia, and in 1965, when Norway granted licenses for offshore petroleum exploration, Hydro was a Norwegian concessionaire, in partnership with foreign companies on many fields.

In 1969 the Phillips Petroleum–operated drilling rig Ocean Viking struck oil in the giant Ekofisk field and spurred the boom in the North Sea. Norsk Hydro owned a stake in the well's production. The Norwegian government, struggling to forge its petroleum policy, increased its share of Hydro to 51% and created Statoil, a completely state-owned company, in 1972. Hydro's North Sea success continued with the Elf Aquitaine–operated Frigg discovery in 1971.

Hydro had begun to branch out, with hydroelectric-powered aluminum processing at its KarmØy Works (1967) and with its fish-farming subsidiary Mowi (1969). During much of the 1970s, Hydro focused on oil and gas development, which has added to the treasury and helped finance growth, often through acquisitions.

Hydro pushed into the European fertilizer market with the acquisition of NSM (Nether-

lands, 1979), 75% of Supra (Sweden, 1981), Norsk Hydro Fertilizers Ltd. (UK, 1982), Ruhr Stickstoff AG (West Germany, 1985), and 80% of Cofaz (France, 1986). In petrochemicals it purchased 2 British PVC makers (Vinatex Ltd., 1981; BIP Vinyls Ltd.'s PVC business, 1982) to form Norsk Hydro Polymers. Hydro added aluminum extrusion plants in Europe, and in 1986 the Hydro-controlled Hydro Aluminum merged with ÅSV, another Norwegian aluminum company. Hydro consolidated its aluminum holdings in 1988.

Hydro served as operator in the Oseberg field, which began production in 1988 and grew rapidly to become a major source of oil and gas. In 1990 Hydro bought 330 Danish gasoline stations from UNO-X and in 1992 purchased Mobil Oil's Norwegian marketing and distribution system. These purchases boosted Hydro's distribution network to 1,063 gas stations.

In 1991 Hydro's agricultural segment acquired fertilizer facilities in Germany, the UK, and the US, plus W. R. Grace's ammonia plants in Trinidad and Tobago.

A weak world economy and increased competition limited Hydro's revenues in 1992 and 1993. The company countered slumping sales by lowering costs, increasing production, and selling noncore subsidiaries. In 1992 Hydro sold its pharmaceuticals subsidiary, Hydro Pharma a.s. In 1993 the company sold its interest in chocolate maker Freia Marabou. That sale, plus a sinking Norwegian Krone, gave the company an eightfold increase in pretax profits for the year.

NYSE symbol: NHY (ADR)
Fiscal year ends: December 31

Chairman: Torvild Aakvaag
President: Egil Myklebust, NOK1,813,000 pay
EVP and CFO: Leiv Lea Nergaard
EVP: Torstein Bergem
EVP: Thor Håkstad
EVP: Trygve Refvem
SVP and General Counsel: Odd Ivar Biller
SVP Human Resources: Hans Jørn Rønningen
President, Norsk Hydro USA: Bjorn H. Tretvoll
Auditors: Forum Touche Ross

WHERE

HQ: Bygdøy allè 2, N-0240, Oslo 2, Norway
Phone: +47-22- 43-21-00
Fax: +47-22-43-27-25
US HQ: Norsk Hydro USA Inc., 800 Third Ave.,
New York, NY 10022
US Phone: 212-688-6606
US Fax: 212-750-1252

Norsk Hydro sells its products worldwide.

	1993 Operating Income	
	$ mil.	% of total
EC countries	4,793	58
Norway	937	11
Other Europe	1,009	12
Other countries	1,554	19
Total	**8,293**	**100**

WHAT

	1993 Sales		1993 Operating Income	
	$ mil.	% of total	$ mil.	% of total
Agriculture	3,579	41	64	11
Light metals	2,167	25	60	10
Oil & gas	1,874	21	419	70
Petrochemicals	629	7	51	9
Other	507	6	(57)	—
Adjustments	(463)	—	—	—
Total	**8,293**	**100**	**537**	**100**

Selected Subsidiaries
Hydro Aluminum a.s (aluminum)
Hydro Chemicals Norge (industrial chemicals)
Hydro Czechoslovakia s.r.o. (agriculture)
Hydro Seafood a.s (salmon farming)
Hydrogas a.s (industrial chemicals)
Kirk Precision Ltd. (magnesium)
Mabo AS (petrochemicals)
Norsk Hydro (Far East) Ltd. (agriculture)
Pharmala a.s (biomedicine)
A/S Svælgfos (energy)

KEY COMPETITORS

Alcan	Continental	PDVSA
Alcoa	Grain	PEMEX
AMAX	Dalgety	Pennzoil
Amoco	Elf Aquitaine	Petrobrás
BASF	ENI	Petrofina
Bayer	Exxon	Phillips
BayWa	Formosa Plastics	Petroleum
British	George Weston	Reynolds Metals
Petroleum	Hoechst	Rhône-Poulenc
Broken Hill	Imperial Chemical	Royal Dutch/
Cargill	Inco	Shell
Chevron	Kemira	RTZ
Ciba-Geigy	Mitsui	Texaco
Coastal	Mobil	Thyssen
ConAgra	Occidental	USX–Marathon

HOW MUCH

Stock prices are for ADRs. ADR = 1 share	Annual Growth	1984	1985	1986	1987	1988	1989	1990	1991	1992	1993
Sales ($ mil.)	3.5%	—	6,282	7,367	8,748	9,160	10,062	10,365	9,987	8,373	8,293
Net income ($ mil.)	18.4%	—	104	(112)	294	524	408	493	(81)	(28)	399
Income as % of sales	—	—	1.6%	—	3.4%	5.7%	4.1%	4.8%	—	—	4.8%
Earnings per share ($)	1.7%	—	1.70	(0.30)	1.72	2.61	1.99	2.40	(0.39)	(0.13)	1.94
Stock price – high ($)	—	—	—	11.56	19.69	18.50	27.75	41.75	32.75	28.25	30.38
Stock price – low ($)	—	—	—	8.44	9.50	11.63	18.50	24.25	20.00	19.38	21.75
Stock price – close ($)	16.4%	—	—	9.69	11.75	18.00	25.25	30.75	23.25	22.00	28.00
P/E – high	—	—	—	—	11	7	14	17	—	—	16
P/E – low	—	—	—	—	6	5	9	10	—	—	11
Dividends per share ($)	7.3%	—	0.21	0.33	0.29	0.41	0.44	0.53	0.54	0.47	0.37
Book value per share ($)	21.3%	—	3.14	2.71	3.44	12.23	13.60	17.00	15.16	14.16	14.72
Employees	7.8%	—	26,000	43,122	39,139	39,000	32,782	33,042	34,957	34,000	32,500

1993 Year-end:
Debt ratio: 74.2%
Return on equity: 13.4%
Cash (mil.): $704
Current ratio: 1.42
Long-term debt (mil.): $3,258
No. of shares (mil.): 205
Dividends
  Yield: 1.3%
  Payout: 19.1%
Market value (mil.): $5,751

Stock Price History
High/Low 1986–93

NORTHERN TELECOM LIMITED

OVERVIEW

Canada-based Northern Telecom (NT) has global telecommunications wired. In 1994 alone NT, the world's 6th largest telecommunications manufacturer, signed deals to supply equipment for projects in the Cayman Islands, China, Colombia, Israel, Mexico, Switzerland, Taiwan, Tunisia, the UK, the US — and even undersea, for the British navy's submarines.

Core NT products include office telephone switching systems, PBXs, and mobile telecommunications equipment. But technology is NT's strong suit; 11% of revenues are spent on R&D. Recent innovations involve cutting-edge technologies such as multimedia and asynchronous transfer mode (ATM) formats.

Errors in NT's primary switching systems software created a company crisis in the early 1990s. Under CEO Jean Monty, recruited from 52.1%-owner BCE in 1993, the company has invested over $250 million to fix the glitches and restore customer confidence. Cost of the software rework and management realignment into 2 operating groups (Nortel North America and Nortel World Trade) gave NT a loss of nearly $900 million in 1993.

In 1994 NT won an order from Omnipoint (US) to supply equipment for the US's first Personal Communications Service (PCS), a radio frequency network to be centered around the New York City area.

WHEN

Northern Telecom traces its lineage to Bell Telephone Company of Canada, which was established in Montreal in 1880, just 4 years after the telephone's invention.

In 1882 the Northern Electric and Manufacturing Company was established to produce Bell Canada's mechanical equipment. By 1902 Northern Electric had grown to 250 employees and occupied a 48,000-square-foot manufacturing facility.

With the communications industry growing steadily, Northern Electric and Imperial Wire & Cable, an electrical wire manufacturer, decided to pool their resources to form the Northern Electric Company in 1914.

Northern Electric grew despite the Great Depression. During the 1930s the company created an electronics division, purchased a majority interest in Amalgamated Electric (1932), and established Dominion Sound Equipment (1935).

After spending WWII with nearly all its production supporting the Allied war effort, Northern Electric found itself ready to supply Canada's post-war economic boom. The company got a boost in the mid-1950s when the US Department of Justice forced majority shareholder Western Electric to sell its interest in Northern Electric. In 1957 Bell Canada purchased most of Western Electric's shares.

In 1958 Bell Canada and Northern Electric established Northern Electric Laboratories to push research and development. The laboratory eventually became Canada's largest research center. In 1965 researchers began developing the SP-1 switching system. This and other products were so successful

that in 1971 the laboratory spun off to become Bell-Northern Research Ltd.

During the 1960s Northern Electric began supplying switching gear overseas. It opened a joint venture manufacturing facility with the Turkish government in 1969. During the 1970s the company continued its international expansion, opening subsidiaries in the US (1971), Ireland (1973), and Hong Kong (1974), among others. In 1976 it purchased Cook Electric, a US company with Brazilian and Canadian subsidiaries.

Northern Electric remained wholly owned by Bell Canada until 1973, when Bell began selling off stock. In 1976 Northern Electric changed its name to Northern Telecom and introduced an innovative digital switch. When AT&T approved purchase of the switch in 1981, NT's growth took off.

In the 1980s NT pioneered the international services digital network (ISDN) switching system. In 1981 NT hired high-tech management veteran Paul Stern as chairman, CEO, and president. Stern shifted management, closed plants, and cut the work force. That year the company formed a joint venture company, called Telco, to assemble equipment in Mexico.

NT extended its global reach in 1991 when it bought STC PLC, a large British telecommunications company. Two NT operating divisions, Nortel North America and Nortel World Trade, were created in 1993 to oversee the company's global growth.

In 1994 NT sold part of its electronic components business to Siecor (US), raising $135 million.

NYSE symbol: NT
Fiscal year ends: December 31

WHO

Chairman: Donald J. Schuenke
President and CEO: Jean C. Monty, age 46,
$691,667 pay
CFO: Peter W. Currie
President, Nortel World Trade: James R. Long
President, Nortel North America: John A. Roth
SVP and General Counsel: Clive V. Allen
SVP Human Resources: Donald S. McCreesh
Auditors: Deloitte & Touche

WHERE

HQ: 3 Robert Speck Pkwy., Mississauga, Ontario
L4Z 3C8 Canada
Phone: 905-566-3000
Fax: 905-275-1143
US Operations: Northern Telecom,
2221 Lakeside Blvd., Richardson, TX 75082
US Phone: 214-684-1000
US Fax: 214-684-3733

Northern Telecom sells advanced telecommunications systems worldwide. US operations are located in Santa Clara, CA; Atlanta, GA; Raleigh, NC; Richardson, TX; and McLean, VA.

| | 1993 Sales | |
	$ mil.	% of total
US	4,842	48
Canada	3,118	31
Europe	1,693	17
Other countries	441	4
Adjustments	(1,946)	—
Total	**8,148**	**100**

WHAT

| | 1993 Sales | |
	$ mil.	% of total
Central office switching	3,875	47
Multimedia comm. systems	2,220	27
Transmission	1,111	14
Cable & outside plant	655	8
Other	287	4
Total	**8,148**	**100**

Selected Subsidiaries and Affiliates
Bell-Northern Research Ltd. (70%)
Netaş-Northern Electric Telekomünikasyon AS (51%, Turkey)
NorTel Australia Pty. Ltd.
Nortel Matra Cellular SCA (France)
Nortel Post and Telecommunications Technical Inc. (China)
Northern Telecom (Asia) Ltd. (Hong Kong)
Northern Telecom Canada Ltd.
Northern Telecom Europe Ltd.
Northern Telecom (Ireland) Ltd.
Northern Telecom Japan Inc.
Northern Telecom de México, SA de CV
Northern Telecom de España (50%, Spain)
Prism Systems Inc. (51%)

KEY COMPETITORS

Alcatel Alsthom	Hitachi
AT&T	Motorola
Australian Telecom	NEC
Bellcore	Oki
Canadian Pacific	Rogers Communications
Deutsche Telekom	Siemens
Ericsson	Compañía de Teléfonos
French Telecom	de Chile
Fujitsu	Toshiba
GTE	Unitel Communications

HOW MUCH

	Annual Growth	1984	1985	1986	1987	1988	1989	1990	1991	1992	1993
Sales ($ mil.)	7.1%	4,379	5,819	4,384	4,854	5,408	6,106	6,769	8,183	8,409	8,148
Net income ($ mil.)	—	334	411	313	347	183	377	460	515	548	(878)
Income as % of sales	—	7.6%	7.1%	7.1%	7.2%	3.4%	6.2%	6.8%	6.3%	6.5%	—
Earnings per share ($)	—	1.38	1.63	1.23	1.39	0.70	1.47	1.80	2.03	2.17	(3.54)
Stock price – high ($)	—	21.13	20.56	17.50	24.25	20.25	24.13	29.63	46.25	49.25	46.00
Stock price – low ($)	—	14.94	15.63	12.63	14.00	15.50	14.25	22.13	26.25	30.50	21.38
Stock price – close ($)	6.8%	17.06	17.50	15.81	17.13	16.63	23.13	28.25	45.00	43.00	30.88
P/E – high	—	15	13	14	17	29	16	17	23	23	—
P/E – low	—	11	10	10	10	22	10	12	13	14	—
Dividends per share ($)	6.7%	0.20	0.25	0.20	0.23	0.26	0.28	0.30	0.32	0.34	0.36
Book value per share ($)	4.8%	7.88	9.69	8.05	9.87	10.19	11.14	13.24	14.97	15.97	12.00
Employees	3.3%	—	46,549	46,202	48,778	—	47,572	49,039	57,059	57,955	60,293

1993 Year-end:
Debt ratio: 68.2%
Return on equity: —
Cash (mil.): $138
Current ratio: 1.16
Long-term debt (mil.):$1,512
No. of shares (mil.): 251
Dividends
Yield: 1.2%
Payout: —
Market value (mil.): $7,759

**Stock Price History
High/Low 1984–93**

NOVO NORDISK A/S

OVERVIEW

Novo Nordisk — the world's leading producer of insulin and industrial enzymes — is betting big on bugs. Although Novo lords over the world market for insulin with a 44% share and gets the bulk of its sales from insulin, profit margins on diabetic therapies are slipping as competition toughens. In response, Novo, which has about 50% of the $1 billion world enzyme market, is investing heavily in new enzymes (natural catalysts, often derived from microorganisms) that it hopes will take fat out of foods and sop up toxic spills. Novo, which is 25% owned by the Novo Nordisk Foundation, also makes vitamins and other nutritional products.

Novo, with an R&D budget of about 14% of sales, has developed more than 40 industrial enzymes. These biodegradable agents, which speed up chemical reactions, are used, for instance, in soft drinks to change starch to sugar and in detergents to remove protein stains. Now Novo is boosting efforts to find new enzymes so it can continue to dominate a global business growing at 10–15% a year. Novo also wants to broaden its pharmaceutical product line, which is dominated by insulin products. To those ends Novo started a new research unit for its health care group (1993) and spent $120 million (1994) to expand its North Carolina biotech operation.

WHEN

Danish engineer Harald Pedersen and his brother Thorvald, a pharmacist by trade, established Novo Industri in Harald's basement in 1925 to manufacture insulin.

Demand for the brothers' Insulin Novo prompted them to move to an old dairy factory in 1931, and within a decade Novo was selling its insulin in 40 countries. Using organs supplied by local slaughterhouses (insulin is produced from animal pancreases), Novo also began producing Catgut, a surgical thread made from sheep intestines, in 1938.

During WWII Novo started producing penicillin and trypsin, an animal enzyme that would lay the cornerstone for its eventual domination of the world enzyme market.

In the 1950s the company developed Heparin, a trypsin-based drug used to treat blood clots. Concerned with the future of the company, the founding Pedersen brothers formed the Novo Foundation late in the decade to assume primary control of the company. The company developed new technologies for the artificial synthesis of enzymes and during the 1960s unleashed several industrial enzymes on the market. Novo was dealt a severe blow in 1970 when its Alcalase enzyme (used in detergents) became targeted by environmentalists who claimed it was a health hazard. Sales plunged and the company was forced to lay off hundreds of workers before scientists deemed the product safe.

In the early 1980s Novo decided to introduce its insulin to the US market, traditionally the undisputed turf of Eli Lilly. In 1981 the company formed a joint venture with

E. R. Squibb (bought by Bristol-Myers in 1989) to sell the insulin in the US. Eli Lilly counterattacked by introducing its insulin into Novo's closely held European market. Both companies scored victories with the introduction of human insulin, but when the dust cleared, Eli Lilly still firmly held the US market and had taken European and Japanese market share as well.

In 1984 Novo bought Alfred Jorgensen Laboratory from Fermentation Ltd., and 2 years later acquired 75% of Ferrosan, a Danish producer of vitamins and health products, buying an additional 15% of Ferrosan in 1987.

Novo finally gained the lion's share of the world insulin market in 1989 when it merged with former competitor Nordisk Gentofte, a Danish insulin producer established in 1923. In 1990 Novo took over its US insulin marketing from Bristol-Meyers Squibb and quickly increased its market share from 18% to 23%. With its own marketing arm, Novo expects to make further gains in the US.

Novo Nordisk entered the 1990s with strategic alliances across the globe, including ventures with Abbott Labs and the US biotech concern Chiron. In 1991 Novo set up Novo Nordisk Engineering to provide consulting services to customers. In 1992 Novo invested $100 million in its enzyme plant in Franklinton, North Carolina.

In 1994 Novo acquired a site in China to further expand its enzyme supply capacity — the first stage in an investment that could climb to $210 million over the next decade.

NYSE symbol: NVO (ADR)
Fiscal year ends: December 31

President and CEO: Mads Øvlisen
EVP and CFO: Kurt Anker Nielsen
EVP Corporate Development: Sonnich Fryland
EVP Bioindustrial Group: Steen Riisgaard
EVP Health Care Research: Bruce L. A. Carter
President, Novo Nordisk of North America:
Henrik Aagaard
Treasurer, Novo Nordisk of North America:
Carsten Boess
Auditors: Revisionsfirmaet C Jespersen; Price
Waterhouse Denmark/Seier-Petersen

WHERE

HQ: Novo Allé, DK-2880 Bagsværd, Denmark
Phone: +45-44-42-6468
Fax: +45-44-98-03-27
US HQ: Novo Nordisk of North America, Inc.,
405 Lexington Ave., Ste. 6400, New York, NY
10017
US Phone: 212-867-0131
US Fax: 212-867-028

Novo Nordisk has offices in 51 countries and
sells its products in 130 countries.

	1993 Sales	
	$ mil.	% of total
EC	1,034	58
North America	295	16
Other Europe	122	7
Other countries	345	18
Adjustments	139	—
Total	**1,935**	**100**

WHAT

	1993 Sales	
	$ mil.	% of total
Health Care Group	1,214	68
Bioindustrial Group	494	28
Other products	88	4
Adjustments	139	—
Total	**1,935**	**100**

Bioindustrial Group
Bulk antibiotics
Industrial enzymes
Plant protection agents

Health Care Group
Animal source insulins
Antibiotics
Anticoagulants
Antidepressants
Bovine insulins
Central nervous system
drugs
Coagulation factors
Gastrointestinal drugs
Growth hormones
Gynecological products

Hematology products
Human insulins
Hypoglycemic agents
Insulin injection systems
Proteinase inhibitors

Other Products
Antioxidants
Cough medicines
Dietary fiber kits
Medical chewing gum
Minerals
Natural remedies
Nutrition products
Sponges
Vitamins

KEY COMPETITORS

Abbott Labs	Bristol-Myers	Gist-Brocades
Advanced Surface	Squibb	Glaxo
Technology	Carter-Wallace	Johnson &
Akzo Nobel	Ciba-Geigy	Johnson
American Home	Eastman Kodak	Merck
Products	Elf Aquitaine	Sandoz
Amgen	Eli Lilly	Schering-
C. R. Bard	Genencor	Plough
Baxter	International	SmithKline
Bayer	Genentech	Beecham

HOW MUCH

	9-Year Growth	1984	1985	1986	1987	1988	1989	1990	1991	1992	1993
Sales ($ mil.)	21.5%	335	464	570	825	819	1,153	1,443	1,662	1,701	1,935
Net income ($ mil.)	14.8%	61	68	71	79	93	113	132	157	203	211
Income as % of sales	—	18.2%	14.6%	12.4%	9.6%	11.3%	9.8%	9.1%	9.5%	11.9%	10.9%
Earnings per share ($)	9.9%	0.60	0.67	0.70	0.77	0.91	0.70	1.04	1.36	1.36	1.40
Stock price – high ($)	—	15.34	8.75	8.88	10.63	10.47	13.00	16.13	23.53	24.19	24.75
Stock price – low ($)	—	5.22	5.75	6.47	4.31	5.44	9.69	11.00	14.25	20.00	19.50
Stock price – close ($)	17.2%	5.94	7.34	8.22	5.34	9.69	12.53	15.59	22.38	22.19	24.75
P/E – high	—	26	13	13	14	12	19	16	17	18	18
P/E – low	—	9	9	9	6	6	14	11	11	15	14
Dividends per share ($)	8.0%	0.07	0.65	0.09	0.10	0.13	0.12	0.13	0.13	0.14	0.14
Book value per share ($)	13.0%	3.89	5.38	5.44	8.31	7.89	7.50	9.62	13.89	13.15	11.72
Employees	11.0%	4,570	4,828	5,758	5,873	6,002	8,094	8,742	9,627	10,733	11,648

1993 Year-end:
Debt ratio: 37.9%
Return on equity: 12.2%
Cash (mil.): $840
Current ratio: 2.49
Long-term debt (mil.): $492
No. of shares (mil.): 150
Dividends
  Yield: 0.6%
  Payout: 10.0%
Market value (mil.): $3,714

Stock Price History
High/Low 1984–93

OKI ELECTRIC

OVERVIEW

Things have not been okey-dokey at Oki Electric lately. One of Japan's leading communications equipment manufacturers, the Tokyo-based company has posted losses for 2 straight years. With a strong yen and a recession in Japan cutting into its sales, Oki has restructured by reorganizing production, reducing costs, and creating independent operations for its higher-volume products.

Oki is a major global supplier of telecommunications systems, electronic devices, and data processing systems. The company manufacturers everything from ATM machines and fax machines to underwater imaging systems and microprocessors. Most of its products are geared toward the corporate (rather than the consumer) marketplace. In the US the company's products include cellular phones and printers.

The company continues to invest heavily in research, with a particular emphasis on multimedia applications. It is currently working to develop a multimedia communications system. Oki is also increasing its presence in the Asia/Pacific region by boosting its marketing and servicing networks in the area.

WHEN

Oki dates back to 1881, when engineer Kibataro Oki, formerly of Japan's Department of Industry, founded Meikosha Company in Tokyo. Originally formed to manufacture and sell telephones, Meikosha was soon also producing telegraphs, bells, and medical equipment. The company's main manufacturing plant adopted the name Oki Electric Plant in 1889; the marketing division began operating under the name Oki & Company in 1896.

In 1907, a year after the death of Kibataro Oki, the Oki groups were united as a limited partnership, divided again in 1912, then ultimately recombined in 1917 as Oki Electric Company. Oki continued to expand its product line to include automatic switching equipment (1926) and electric clocks (1929).

Oki produced communications equipment for the Japanese military during WWII but shifted back to civil production after the war, starting work on the teleprinter and adding consumer goods, such as portable stoves. The company adopted its present name in 1949.

Oki entered the semiconductor and computer industries in the 1950s, joining Fujitsu, Hitachi, Toshiba, Nippon Electric Company, and Mitsubishi as one of Japan's Big 6 electronic makers by 1960. It started developing its overseas business, particularly in Latin America, where it built communications networks in Honduras (1962) and Bolivia (1966) and radio networks in Brazil (1971).

Oki formed a computer software division in 1970 and started building PCs in 1981. The company continued as a major supplier of telecommunications equipment to the Japanese government until the mid-1970s, when the government increased purchases from other companies. The loss of government business eroded both sales and profits for Oki, resulting in a $7 million loss in 1978. Former NTT executive Masao Miyake took over as Oki's president, initiating a dramatic reorganization of the company into 15 highly focused and profitable business units.

Oki later consolidated its US operations, forming Oki America (1984). But a new financial crisis followed in the mid-1980s, when the bottom fell out of the semiconductor market, and earnings plummeted into the red in 1986.

In 1987 Oki set up a division to provide oceanographic services (Oki Seataec). As a major provider of ATMs and bank computer systems, Oki enjoyed a ninefold increase in profits in 1989, sparked by growth in the Japanese financial industry. That same year Oki strengthened its position as one of the world's leading suppliers of computer systems and ATMs to the banking and financial sector by entering an agreement with Sun Microsystems that gives Oki access to Sun's financial software. In 1990 Oki and Hewlett-Packard formed a joint venture in Puerto Rico to build printed circuit boards.

In 1992 Oki signed an agreement with the French electronics firm Matra MHS to help develop computer chips. That same year Jun Jinguji was named president of the company, succeeding Nobumitsu Kosugi.

In 1994 Oki announced plans to build a semiconductor design facility in the US to study multimedia semiconductor technology. That same year Oki established a new subsidiary, Oki Data Corp., to handle its printer and fax machine operations.

Principal exchange: Tokyo
Fiscal year ends: March 31

President and CEO: Jun Jinguji, age 65
EVP: Shiko Sawamura
Senior Managing Director: Minoru Imai
Senior Managing Director: Tadao Higashi
Senior Managing Director: Masataka Yamamoto
President and CEO, Acting CFO, and Acting Director of Human Resources, Oki America (US): Hiroshi Yamazaki
SVP Business Development, Oki America (US): Tokihiko Shimomura
Auditors: Showa Ota & Co.

HQ: Oki Denki Kogyo Kabushiki Kaisha, 7-12, Toranomon 1-chome, Minato-ku, Tokyo 105, Japan
Phone: +81-3-3501-3111
Fax: +81-3-3581-5522
US HQ: Oki America, Inc., 3 University Plaza, Hackensack, NJ 07601
US Phone: 201-646-0011
US Fax: 201-646-9229

Oki has operations in 19 countries. Its products are sold worldwide.

	1994 Sales	
	¥ bil.	% of total
Japan	447	69
Other countries	205	31
Total	**652**	**100**

	1994 Sales	
	¥ bil.	% of total
Information processing sys.	280	45
Electronic devices	178	29
Telecommunications systems	163	26
Adjustments	31	
Total	**652**	**100**

Information Processing Systems
Automobile electronics
Banking systems (ATMs)
Data communication systems
OCR systems
Personal computers
POS systems
Printers
Traffic control systems
Underwater imaging systems
Workstations

Electronic Devices
Application-specific ICs
Memories
Microprocessors

Optoelectronic devices
Solid-state disk cards
Telecommunications and voice synthesis large-scale ICs

Telecommunications Systems
Cellular telephones
Fax machines
Fiber optics
Local area networks
Modems
Multimedia-multiplex systems
PBX systems
Radio equipment
Teleconferencing
Voice and fax mail systems

Alcatel Alsthom	IBM	Olivetti
AT&T	ITOCHU	Philips
Brother	Machines Bull	Pioneer
Canon	Mannesmann	Ricoh
Compression Labs	Matsushita	Sanyo
Diebold	Minolta	Seiko
Ericsson	Mitsubishi	Sharp
Fujitsu	Motorola	Siemens
Hewlett-Packard	NEC	Silicon Graphics
Hitachi	Nokia	Sony
Honeywell	Northern Telecom	Toshiba

$=¥ 112 (Dec. 31, 1993)	9-Year Growth	1985	1986	1987	1988	1989	1990	1991	1992	1993	1994
Sales (¥ bil.)	5.1%	418	393	407	451	556	630	661	681	640	652
Net income (¥ bil.)	—	9	(1)	2	4	36	38	10	0	(33)	(2)
Income as % of sales	—	2.2%	—	0.5%	0.8%	6.5%	6.0%	1.5%	0.0%	—	—
Earnings per share (¥)	—	19	(2)	4	6	28	28	16	(1)	(54)	(3)
Stock price – high (¥)[1]	—	894	719	835	879	1,153	1,260	1,260	870	606	573
Stock price – low (¥)[1]	—	572	463	539	468	625	936	582	530	290	316
Stock price – close (¥)[1]	(2.3%)	667	639	610	632	965	1200	695	600	338	540
P/E – high	—	47	—	209	147	41	45	79	—	—	—
P/E – low	—	30	—	135	78	22	34	37	—	—	—
Dividends per share (¥)	—	2.86	5.72	6.00	6.00	7.00	7.00	7.00	7.50	3.50	0.00
Book value per share (¥)	7.2%	136	156	175	196	218	259	317	312	255	254
Employees	2.5%	18,134	18,649	19,375	18,659	18,440	19,331	20,278	21,593	23,463	22,585

1994 Year-end:
Debt ratio: 76.0%
Return on equity: —
Cash (bil.): ¥157
Long-term debt (bil.): ¥259
No. of shares (mil.): 612
Dividends
 Yield: —
 Payout: —
Market value (mil.): $2,951
Sales (mil.): $5,821

Stock Price History[1] High/Low 1985–94

[1] Stock prices are for the prior calendar year.

OLIVETTI GROUP

OVERVIEW

Formerly the symbol of a successful modern management turnaround in Italy's parochial economy, Olivetti is now struggling to cope with turbulent computer markets and product price wars. It has not had a profit since 1990. In an efficiency effort, Olivetti made a divisional realignment and modified its operating processes, and the company work force has shed over 22,000 jobs since 1989.

Olivetti is the 2nd largest computer manufacturer in Europe after Siemens and makes everything from computer servers to typewriters. While most of its revenues currently come from hardware sales, the company is hoping to move more into such high-growth fields as computer services, telecommunications, and multimedia. On the systems side such efforts include designing, installing, and maintaining computer networks for companies such as Barclays Bank and McDonalds. In the telecommunications arena Olivetti is the biggest player in the consortium that received Italy's 2nd license for a cellular phone network (cellular phone popularity is growing in Italy) and is making plans for an Italian on-line service modeled after America Online. Chairman Carlo De Benedetti owns 38% of the company.

WHEN

Camillo Olivetti founded Olivetti in Ivrea in 1908 to produce the first Italian-made typewriter (introduced in 1911). The company later diversified into office furniture (1930), teleprinters (1938), and adding machines (1940). In 1933, a year after the company went public, Camillo's eldest son, Adriano, became general manager, leading Olivetti's diversification into computers, which resulted in Italy's first mainframe in 1959. That year Olivetti bought control of ailing US typewriter maker Underwood (founded by John Thomas Underwood, 1896), operating it as Olivetti Underwood until 1971, when it was restructured as Olivetti Corporation of America (OCA).

After Adriano's death in 1960, the Olivetti family sold most of its stake in the company to the Pirelli/Fiat syndicate in 1964. General Electric bought Olivetti's mainframe business that year. Because the company was slow to switch from mechanical to electric office equipment in the 1960s, earnings stagnated; Olivetti suspended its dividend in 1974.

Then in 1978 former Fiat executive Carlo De Benedetti invested $17 million in the company and, as CEO, slashed debt (and the payroll) while increasing R&D spending eightfold between 1978 and 1984. Olivetti introduced its first electronic typewriter in 1978 and bought Swiss typewriter maker Hermes Precisa International in 1981.

OCA, in the meantime, had suffered through more than a decade of losses. De Benedetti hoped to end this by selling OCA to Dallas-based Docutel (ATMs) in exchange for a 46% stake in the company in 1982. When the strategy failed and losses continued, Olivetti bought the rest of Docutel and used it to establish Olivetti USA (1985).

Olivetti unveiled its first PC in 1982, only one year after IBM had pioneered the industry. In 1983 AT&T bought a 25% stake in Olivetti. Toshiba bought 20% of its Japanese operations in 1985. De Benedetti hoped this would increase Olivetti's US and Japanese market shares. Sales in the US and Japan never met expectations, and AT&T later traded its stake in Olivetti to De Benedetti for 18.6% of his holding company, Compagnie Industriali Riunite (1989). Meanwhile, Olivetti bought 80% of the UK's Acorn Computers Group (1985) and Volkswagen's ailing office-products maker Triumph-Adler (1986). Olivetti boosted its stake in bank automation by buying Bunker Ramo (1986) and I.S.C. Systems Corporation (1989). World minicomputer demand softened in the late 1980s; in 1991 Olivetti posted its first loss in 13 years.

In 1992 Olivetti introduced the Quaderno, a subnotebook PC with voice recording capability. The announcement came soon after the introduction of a high-end workstation PC using RISC technology, all as part of a drive to restore Olivetti's reputation for innovative product development. Olivetti's reputation has been hurt by the 1992 conviction of De Benedetti for fraudulent bankruptcy in the scandal surrounding the 1982 Banco Ambrosiano collapse. The conviction is likely to be under appeal for years. In 1993 De Benedetti was arrested again on bribery charges. Experts suggest that another indication of company difficulties was DEC's 1994 sell-off of its 7.8% holdings in Olivetti.

OTC symbol: OLIVY (ADR)
Fiscal year ends: December 31

WHO

Chairman-CEO: Carlo De Benedetti
CEO: Corrado Passera
VC and CFO: Angelo Fornasari
VC: Elserino Piol
Secretary of the Board: Piera Rosiello
President, Olivetti USA: Salomon Suwalsky
CFO, Olivetti USA: Dave Frasier
Manager Human Resources, Olivetti USA:
Kelle Adams
Auditors: Coopers & Lybrand S.a.s.

WHERE

HQ: Olivetti S.p.A., Via Jervis 77, I-10015 Ivrea,
Italy
Phone: +39-125-522-639
Fax: +39-125-523-884
US HQ: Olivetti USA, Inc., 765 Hwy. 202 South,
Bridgewater, NJ 00807-6945
US Phone: 908-526-8200
US Fax: 908-526-8405

Olivetti has a direct sales and support
organization in 48 countries and a network of
more than 5,500 systems partners and dealers.
It operates through sales agents in 40 other
countries.

	1993 Sales	
	Lit bil.	% of total
Italy	2,922	34
Other Europe	3,966	46
Other countries	1,725	20
Total	**8,613**	**100**

WHAT

	1993 Sales	
	Lit bil.	% of total
Products	3,208	37
Systems	2,989	35
Services	2,416	28
Total	**8,613**	**100**

Selected Subsidiaries and Affiliates
Acorn Computer Group Plc (78.7%, UK)
Baltea SpA
Elea SpA
Olivetti Finanziaria Industriale SpA
Olivetti Mexicana SA
Olivetti USA, Inc.
Olivetti-Canon Industriale SpA (50%)
Opera Multimedia SpA
Syntax Processing SpA
Triumph-Adler Leasing GmbH (Germany)

Selected Products
Office products
Personal computers
M4-Modulo line
Multimedia personal computer
Philos and Echos notebook PCs
M6-Suprema line
Printers
Bubble inkjet and laser printers
Workstations

KEY COMPETITORS

Apple	Gateway 2000	Packard Bell
AST	GEC	Pitney Bowes
AT&T	Harris Corp.	Siemens
Compaqz	Hewlett-Packard	Sun Microsystems
CompUSA	Hitachi	Tandem
Data General	IBM	Silicon Graphics
DEC	Machines Bull	Unisys
Dell	NEC	
Fujitsu	Océ	

HOW MUCH

$=Lit1,713 (Dec. 31, 1993)	9-Year Growth	1984	1985	1986	1987	1988	1989	1990	1991	1992	1993
Sales (Lit bil.)	7.3%	4,578	6,141	7,317	7,376	8,407	9,031	9,037	8,607	8,026	8,613
Net income (Lit bil.)	—	356	504	566	402	356	203	60	(460)	(650)	(465)
Income as % of sales	—	7.8%	8.2%	7.7%	5.5%	4.2%	2.2%	0.7%	—	—	—
Earnings per share (Lit)	—	760	1,023	1,097	733	647	366	98	(760)	(1,294)	(400)
Stock price – high (Lit)	—	6,080	8,790	18,690	14,700	11,505	9,349	7,699	4,825	3,320	2,168
Stock price – low (Lit)	—	3,865	5,755	8,710	7,010	7,305	7,232	3,030	2,310	1,590	1,170
Stock price – close (Lit)	(10.6%)	5,875	8,780	13,650	7,480	9,000	7,395	3,220	2,445	1,790	2,149
P/E – high	—	8	9	17	20	18	26	79	—	—	—
P/E – low	—	5	6	8	10	11	20	31	—	—	—
Dividends per share (Lit)	—	240	275	320	340	340	340	270	0	0	0
Book value per share (Lit)	—	4,887	5,711	7,072	7,106	7,306	7,000	6,740	5,937	4,498	2,107
Employees	(8.9%)	47,613	48,944	59,091	58,087	57,560	56,937	53,679	46,484	40,401	35,171

1993 Year-end:
Debt ratio: 66.3%
Return on equity: —
Cash (bil.): Lit3,096
Long-term debt (bil.): Lit4,069
No. of shares (mil.): 1,162
Dividends
Yield: —
Payout: —
Market value (mil.): $1,458
Sales (mil.): $5,028

**Stock Price History
High/Low 1984–93**

PACIFIC DUNLOP LIMITED

OVERVIEW

Headquartered in Melbourne, Pacific Dunlop is a diversified manufacturing and marketing group. Among its subsidiaries are Ansell International, the world's largest manufacturer of latex and industrial gloves and of condoms; GNB Technologies, the world's #1 maker of industrial batteries; and Nucleus, the world's #1 maker of "bionic" ear implants.

Pacific Dunlop is one of Australia's largest companies, and each of its business units is the market leader in Australia and New Zealand. Its diversified roster of products includes tires, auto parts, clothing, shoes, sporting goods, electrical products, bedding, pacemakers, and packaged food products.

Pacific Dunlop is concentrating its geographic expansion on Asia and is already tasting sweet success in China, where it is the largest marketer and manufacturer of ice cream. However, the company's presence in China does not stop at dessert. Australia's most aggressive investor in China, it has operations in everything from underwear to industrial cables. In 1994 the company signed a joint venture to manufacture lead batteries in China.

WHEN

Pacific Dunlop's history begins with a veterinarian, a tricycle, and a bumpy road. In 1887 John Boyd Dunlop, a Belfast veterinarian, gave his son a tricycle for his birthday. When his son complained about the jolting ride on the rough country roads around Belfast, Dunlop came up with an air-filled tire that smoothed out the ride. Dunlop sold the rights to his tire to a pair of businessmen who founded the Pneumatic Tyre Company in 1889. By 1892 the new company had expanded into Continental Europe and North America, and in 1893 the company created a branch office and factory in Melbourne.

The company went public (as Dunlop Pneumatic Tyre Company of Australia) when its British parent sold its interests to the public in 1899. In 1903 Dunlop moved into a new market, automobile tires, and it grew as the automobile became more popular. In 1920 the company was incorporated as Dunlop Rubber Company of Australia. Unable to stay away, Dunlop U.K. bought a 25% interest in its Australian offspring in 1927. Two years later the company merged with Sydney-based Perdriau Rubber Company.

Dunlop concentrated on rubber-based products until the 1960s when the company began to diversify. It added clothing, textiles, and footwear, but it maintained its focus on rubber products. In 1969 it acquired rubber-gloves maker Ansell Rubber Company. During the 1970s Dunlop expanded outside Australia, establishing manufacturing plants in Malaysia, New Zealand, and the Philippines.

In 1980 Dunlop acquired its archrival, tire maker Olympic Consolidated Industries. Founded in 1922, Olympic began producing auto tires in 1934, engaging in heated competition with Dunlop. The acquisition also netted the company Olympic's cable manufacturing and wholesaling business. In 1984 Dunlop U.K. sold its shares in the company.

Led by John Gough, Dunlop continued to expand during the 1980s, with an emphasis on Asia and North America. In 1985 the company acquired British battery maker Chloride's North American operations, and in 1986 it signed a joint venture agreement to manufacture shoes in China. Also in 1986 the company signed a joint venture with Goodyear (South Pacific Tyres) to sell tires in Australia, New Zealand, and Papua New Guinea. That same year the company changed its name to Pacific Dunlop Limited.

In 1987 Pacific Dunlop expanded its battery operations when it paid $450 million for 60% of US-based GNB Holdings, maker of Champion batteries. The company moved into the health care business in 1988 with the acquisition of Nucleus & Telectronics, a maker of high-technology medical products, including pacemakers and "bionic" ear implants. That same year Philip Brass succeeded Gough as managing director.

Brass continued the company's diversification strategy. He added food to the company's business mix with the 1991 acquisition of Petersville Sleigh, one of Australia's largest food products companies. In 1993 Pacific Dunlop expanded its food operations with the acquisition of Plumrose, a maker of yogurt, pasta, and meat products.

In 1994 Telectronics recalled 3 models of pacemaker parts after failures led to the deaths of 2 patients.

Nasdaq symbol: PDLPY (ADR)
Fiscal year ends: June 30

Chairman: John B. Gough, age 66
Managing Director: Philip Brass, age 46
Executive General Manager Finance: Ian D. Veal
Group Managing Director, South Pacific Tyres:
Rodney L. Chadwick, age 48
Group Managing Director, GNB Technologies:
Graham G. Spurling, age 56
Group Managing Director, Ansell International:
Harry Boon
Treasurer: David M. Graham
VP Finance, Pacific Dunlop Holdings (US):
Michael McGetrick
Auditors: KPMG Peat Marwick

HQ: Level 41, 101 Collins St., Melbourne,
Victoria 3000, Australia
Phone: +61-03-270-7270
Fax: +61-03-270-7300
US HQ: Pacific Dunlop Holdings Inc., Ste. 4900,
3 First National Plaza, 70 W. Madison Ave,
Chicago, IL 60602
US Phone: 312-332-2878
US Fax: 312-332-5940

	1994 Sales	
	$ mil.	% of total
Australia	3,346	66
The Americas	1,162	23
Southeast Asia & New Zealand	345	7
Europe	224	4
Total	**5,077**	**100**

	1994 Sales	
	$ mil.	% of total
Consumer Products Group	1,342	27
Automotive Group	1,211	24
Distribution Group	912	18
Healthcare Group	778	15
Building & Construction Group	778	15
Other	56	1
Total	**5,077**	**100**

Consumer Products Group	Healthcare Group
Clothing	Condoms
Food	Ear implants
Footwear	Gloves
Sporting goods	Implantable cardiac pacemakers

Automotive Group
Batteries
Electric automobiles
Tires

Distribution Group
Automotive parts
Electrical products

Building and Construction Group
Bedding
Cables
Foam products
Industrial rubber goods
Project management

Alcatel Alsthom	Goodman Fielder	NIKE
Bandag	Goodyear	Nokia
Baxter	Johnson &	Philip Morris
Bridgestone	Johnson	Reebok
Carter-Wallace	Johnson Controls	RJR Nabisco
Continental AG	London	Safeskin
Cooper Industries	International	Siemens
Corning	Group	Sime Darby
Exide Corp.	Michelin	Sumitomo
Fruit of the Loom	Nestlé	Toyo

	Annual Growth	1985	1986	1987	1988	1989	1990	1991	1992	1993	1994
Sales ($ mil.)	9.7%	1,852	2,403	2,672	2,905	3,394	4,002	3,845	4,421	6,305	5,077
Net income ($ mil.)	6.9%	80	106	140	148	199	268	165	161	260	221
Income as % of sales	—	4.3%	4.4%	5.2%	5.1%	5.9%	6.7%	4.3%	3.6%	4.1%	4.4%
Earnings per share ($)	(3.3%)	—	—	—	1.03	1.39	1.76	0.84	0.69	1.03	0.84
Stock price – high ($)[1]	—	—	—	—	—	13.12	14.77	15.79	16.59	15.91	15.00
Stock price – low ($)[1]	—	—	—	—	—	8.47	11.25	11.93	12.61	10.68	11.48
Stock price – close ($)[1]	(2.7%)	—	—	—	—	12.70	14.77	13.75	15.57	12.27	14.88
P/E – high	—	—	—	—	—	9	8	19	24	15	18
P/E – low	—	—	—	—	—	6	6	14	18	10	17
Dividends per share ($)	1.4%	—	—	—	0.47	0.45	0.53	0.59	1.11	0.51	0.51
Book value per share ($)	5.7%	—	—	—	4.70	5.44	6.42	5.38	6.24	8.90	6.55
Employees	8.1%	24,452	25,886	29,774	36,605	44,753	41,013	40,504	48,252	47,071	49,449

1994 Year-end:
Debt ratio: 64.6%
Return on equity: 11.3%
Cash (mil.): $693
Current ratio: 1.04
Long-term debt (mil.): $711
No. of shares (mil.): 263
Dividends
  Yield: 4.7%
  Payout: 60.7%
Market value (mil.): $2,831

Stock Price History[1]
High/Low 1989–94

[1] Stock prices are for the prior calendar year.

PEARSON PLC

UK-based Pearson has spun off its china division (Royal Doulton) and sold its oil business (Camco) in the past 2 years and now is focusing its operations around its education, entertainment, and information businesses.

Pearson's primary revenues come from publishing. Its publications include the *Financial Times* business newspaper, Westminster Press regional newspapers, and *The Economist* magazine (50% ownership). Internationally, Pearson has 3 book publishers: Penguin, US-based Addison-Wesley, and Longman.

The company's television holdings are Thames Television and 14.2% of Yorkshire-Tyne Tees Television (regional UK TV companies), and 17.5% of British Sky Broadcasting (Rupert Murdoch's satellite TV company).

Pearson's Tussauds Group manages a number of visitor attractions in England, including Madame Tussaud's (wax museums), The London Planetarium, Warwick Castle, and theme parks.

The company also has a 50% stake in British investment bankers Lazard Brothers. Lazard Frères of Paris owns 8.7% of Pearson.

In 1844 Samuel Pearson became a partner in a small Yorkshire building firm. When he retired in 1879, his grandson Weetman took over, moving the company to London in 1884, 2 years after it had won its first London contract. The company enjoyed extraordinary success, winning numerous contracts, including one to build the first tunnel under New York's Hudson River and another to construct the main drainage system in Mexico City. By the 1890s the company (incorporated as S. Pearson & Son in 1897) was the world's #1 contractor. Weetman Pearson was knighted in 1894 and later received the titles of baron (1910) and viscount (1917).

In 1901 Weetman Pearson missed a railroad connection in Laredo, Texas, and, during his 9-hour wait, heard about the Spindletop oil gusher. Recalling reports of oil seepages in Mexico, he bought drilling rights to huge tracts of Mexican land. Pearson sank $25 million into his Mexican Eagle Oil Company. In turn, it made him a very wealthy man before he sold it to Shell Oil in 1919.

That year Pearson, by then Lord Cowdray, restructured S. Pearson & Son as a holding company separate from the construction business. In the 1920s the company bought newspapers and a stake in Lazard Brothers, and engaged in oil exploration (including the start-up and sale of US-based Amerada). Cowdray died in 1927 and, without him, so did the construction business. His heirs took over S. Pearson & Son and added unrelated businesses to a company that has since been called "a collection of rich men's toys."

In 1935 Pearson helped form British Airways (merged into British Overseas Airways Corporation, the predecessor of today's British Airways, in 1939). In 1957 Pearson bought control (it now owns 100%) of the *Financial Times* business newspaper and, with it, 50% of *The Economist* magazine. Pearson bought 54% of Château Latour (wine, 1963), 64% of Longman (1968), and, after going public in 1969, Penguin Books (1971), Royal Doulton (1971), Madame Tussaud's (1978), the rest of Longman (1982), and Camco (1987).

After a takeover scare in 1986, when Hong Kong's Hutchison Whampoa bought 4.9% of the company, Pearson's Lazard Frères affiliate bought a block of Pearson's stock to discourage the would-be suitor. Rupert Murdoch's News Corp. bought 20% of Pearson in 1987, rekindling rumors of a takeover.

Murdoch never took control and has since sold his stake in the company. In the meantime Pearson has taken steps to improve profitability. In 1988 and 1989 it sold Château Latour and its oil production businesses and bought Addison-Wesley (publisher, US), *Les Echos* (financial newspaper, France), 22.2% of Dutch scientific publisher Elsevier, and TRW's Reda Pump (oil services, US). The company bought Cuisenaire (teaching materials, US) in 1990. After a failed attempt to merge with Elsevier, in 1991 Pearson sold its Elsevier stake for $600 million.

Pearson in 1992 sold the 20.1% of Pickwick (music and video label) that it owned, realizing just over $20 million.

In 1993 Pearson bought London TV program maker Thames Television from Thorn EMI for around $150 million, and in 1994 the company entered the US educational software market with the purchase of Software Toolworks for $462 million.

Principal exchange: London
Fiscal year ends: December 31

Chairman: Viscount Michael Blakenham, age 56,
£403,000 pay
Managing Director and COO: Frank Barlow,
age 64
Finance Director: James Joll, age 57
Development Director: Mark Burrell, age 56
President, Pearson (US): David Veit, age 55
CFO, Pearson (US): David Greene
Director Human Resources, Pearson (US):
Randall Keller
Auditors: Coopers & Lybrand

HQ: Millbank Tower, London SW1P 4QZ, UK
Phone: +44-(0)71-411-2000
Fax: +44-(0)71-411-2390
US HQ: Pearson Inc., One Rockefeller Plaza,
New York, NY 10020
US Phone: 212-713-1919
US Fax: 212-315-4385

Pearson has worldwide interests in information,
education, and entertainment services.

	1993 Sales		1993 Operating Income	
	£ mil.	% of total	£ mil.	% of total
North America	508	38	77	40
UK	496	38	57	30
Other Europe	160	12	30	16
Asia/Pacific	122	9	19	10
Other countries	34	3	7	4
Total	**1,320**	**100**	**190**	**100**

	1993 Sales		1993 Operating Income	
	£ mil.	% of total	£ mil.	% of total
Books	819	62	102	47
Newspapers	384	29	48	22
Visitor attractions	79	6	16	7
Television	38	3	14	7
Investment banking	—	—	36	17
Adjustments	—	—	(26)	—
Total	**1,320**	**100**	**190**	**100**

Major Subsidiaries and Affiliates

Addison-Wesley Publishing
Co. Inc. (books, US)
British Sky Broadcasting
Ltd. (9.75%, satellite TV)
Les Echos SA (newspapers,
France)
The Economist Newspaper
Ltd. (50%)
The Financial Post Co.
(19.9%, Canada)
Financial Times Group Ltd.
Longman Group Ltd.
(books)
Penguin Books
USA Inc.

The Penguin Publishing Co.
Ltd.
Recoletos Compañia Editorial
SA (26.7%, newspapers,
Spain)
Software Toolworks
(educational software)
Thames Television Ltd.
The Tussauds Group Ltd.
(visitor attractions)
Westminster Press Ltd.
(newspapers)
Yorkshire-Tyne Tees
Television Holdings plc
(14.2%)

Advance
Publications
BBC
Bertelsmann
Brøderbund
Daily Mail Group
Davidson Associates
Dow Jones
Electronic Arts
K-III

Knowledge
Adventure
Lagardère
The Learning Co.
Matsushita
McGraw-Hill
News Corp.
Rank
Reed Elsevier

Reuters
Rogers
Communications
Thomson Corp.
Thorn EMI
Time Warner
Times Mirror
United Newspapers
Viacom

£=$1.48 (Dec. 31, 1993)	Annual Growth	1984	1985	1986	1987	1988	1989[1]	1990[1]	1991[1]	1992[1]	1993
Sales (£ mil.)	5.1%	843	970	953	952	1,195	991	1,045	1,078	1,145	1,320
Net income (£ mil.)	11.9%	54	58	74	98	127	233	88	134	105	148
Income as % of sales	—	6.4%	6.0%	7.8%	10.3%	10.6%	23.5%	8.4%	12.4%	9.2%	11.2%
Earnings per share (p)[2]	8.0%	14	15	19	24	26	29	25	18	17	28
Stock price – high (p)	—	148	217	309	507	398	415	403	379	459	614
Stock price – low (p)	—	101	144	192	262	310	310	299	295	302	356
Stock price – close (p)	17.2%	146	213	308	342	323	368	328	349	390	608
P/E – high	—	11	14	16	21	11	14	16	21	27	22
P/E – low	—	7	10	10	11	12	11	12	16	17	13
Dividends per share (p)[3]	13.2%	4.3	5.0	6.0	7.5	9.0	10.8	11.6	11.6	12.0	13.0
Book value per share (p)	(6.1%)	—	—	—	—	—	—	—	—	193	181
Employees	(16.3%)	27,872	30,158	27,800	23,250	26,017	27,915	29,410	28,492	27,966	15,514

1993 Year-end:
Debt ratio: 30.0%
Return on equity: 14.9%
Cash (mil.): £426
Long-term debt (mil.): £333
No. of shares (mil.): 550
Dividends
Yield: 2.1%
Payout: 46.6%
Market value (mil.): $4,949
Sales (mil.): $1,953

Stock Price History
High/Low 1984–93

[1] Restated [2] Excluding extraordinary items [3] Not including 1993 Royal Doulton spinoff

The 160-year-old Peninsular and Oriental Steam Navigation Company (P&O) is one of the world's most prestigious brand names, synonymous with ocean cruises. But the modern P&O is involved in a lot more than cruise lines. While it remains one of the world's largest shipowners with a fleet of cruise ships, ferries, bulk carriers, coastal tankers, container ships, Rhine barges, and offshore service vessels, its other interests are varied. They include port ownership, management, and stevedoring; property management and investment; road haulage, warehousing, and cold storage; construction and property development; exhibition halls; catering; and travel agencies.

Just under a quarter of P&O's revenues come from its shipping activity, while cruise lines, including the company's wholly owned Los Angeles–based Princess Cruise subsidiary, account for 43% of P&O's profits.

P&O's Bovis Construction subsidiary is a leading British building firm, responsible for a number of major UK buildings. Bovis has been expanding internationally in recent years and, with 14 projects on its books, is now the leading foreign construction firm in Moscow.

The rising tide of a global economic recovery is lifting P&O's sales as increased trade and consumer spending is placing increased demand on its shipping services.

In 1815 Scotsman Arthur Anderson joined the London office of shipbroker Brodie McGhie Willcox. They formed a partnership in 1822 and built a business based on trade between Britain and the Iberian Peninsula. With sailing ships and steamers they ran guns and shipped troops for the royalists during the Portuguese and Spanish civil wars of the 1830s.

In 1835 the 2 men teamed up with Irish shipowner Richard Bourne to establish the Peninsular Steam Navigation Company which offered a regular trading service between London, Spain, Portugal, and Gibraltar.

In 1837 Bourne won the first commercial contract to carry mail by sea between England and Spanish and Portuguese ports. The mail service became a bedrock of the company's revenues until WWII and the use of aircraft in international mail delivery. With the extension of the mail operation to the Mediterranean, the company expanded. In 1840 a contract for monthly mail deliveries to Alexandria, Egypt, allowed it to raise £1 million and to incorporate as a limited liability company, The Peninsular and Oriental Steam Navigation Company. Other routes followed: Suez/Calcutta (1843), Hong Kong (1845), and Sydney (1852). P&O's mail and passenger steamships provided a vital logistical support to the expansion of the British Empire.

Between 1914 and 1946 P&O expanded through the acquisition of several other shipping firms, including the British India Steam Navigation Company and the New Zealand Shipping Company. During the 1920s the P&O fleet reached its peak and the company operated nearly 500 ships.

During WWII P&O lost 182 ships that had been pressed into war service as troop carriers and cargo vessels.

After the war the company was forced to reorganize its business as aircraft took away its passenger and mail income. P&O diversified its shipping line into cruise ships and various forms of cargo ships, from containers to tankers. By the 1970s the company had involved itself in nearly every kind of merchant shipping except ice breakers.

In 1974 P&O diversified beyond shipping with the purchase of Britain's #4 construction company, Bovis. In 1985 the company acquired Sterling Guarantee Trust, owners of a diverse group of property and industrial service companies, whose assets included London's Earls Court and Olympia exhibition centers, and commercial properties in the US.

In the late 1980s and early 1990s chairman Jeffrey Sterling maintained the company on a course of international expansion, including the purchase of a German haulage and barge group and a stake in an Indonesian cruise line. In 1992 P&O formed P&O Asia and acquired interests in Chinese container terminals. The company sold 3 UK service businesses in 1993 for around $565 million.

P&O announced plans in 1994 to build the world's first 100,000-metric-ton cruise ship for its US cruise line subsidiary.

OTC symbol: PIA
Fiscal year ends: December 31

WHO

Chairman: Lord Sterling of Plaistow,
£534,000 pay
Managing Director: Sir Bruce D. MacPhail
Director Finance: D. E. A. Morris
Company Secretary: J. M. Crossman
Group Personnel Manager: K. M. Windsor
President, Princess Cruises (US): Peter G.
Ratcliffe
CFO, Princess Cruises (US): Colin Rumble
**SVP Fleet Personnel and Administration,
Princess Cruises (US):** Karl Wernett
Auditors: KPMG Peat Marwick

WHERE

HQ: The Peninsular and Oriental Steam
Navigation Company, 79 Pall Mall, London
SW1Y 5EJ, UK
Phone: +44-(0)71-930-4343
Fax: +44-(0)71-839-9338
US HQ: Princess Cruises Inc., 10100 Santa
Monica Blvd., Los Angeles, CA 90067-4189
US Phone: 310-553-1770
US Fax: 310-284-2833

	1993 Sales	
	£ mil.	% of total
UK & Ireland	2,124	37
US & Canada	1,681	29
Australasia, Far East		
& Pacific	946	17
Other Europe	868	15
Other countries	127	2
Total	**5,746**	**100**

WHAT

	1993 Sales		1993 Operating Profit	
	£ mil.	% of total	£ mil.	% of total
Housebuilding, construction & development	1,642	29	1	0
Cruises & ferries	1,384	24	169	43
Service businesses	1,281	22	83	21
Container & bulk shipping	1,261	22	31	8
Investment property	178	3	105	28
Total	**5,746**	**100**	**389**	**100**

Major Products and Services

Air freight	Housebuilding
Building contractors	Marine consultants
Bulk carriers	Offshore supply vessels
Business parks	Plant hire
Catering management	Port operations
Civil engineering	Property development
Cold storage	Resorts
Construction management	Rhine barges
Container depots	Road haulage
Container shipping	Ship management
Cruise lines	Stevedoring
Exhibition halls	Tankers
Ferries	Tours
Hotels	Warehousing

KEY COMPETITORS

Accor	Fluor
Alfred McAlpine	George Wimpey
American Classic Voyages	Hapag-Lloyd
American President	ITT
Carlson	Marriott Intl.
Carnival Corp.	Mitsui
Club Méditerranée	Royal Caribbean Cruise
Crowley Maritime	Royal Viking Line
Evergreen Marine	Thomas Cook

HOW MUCH

£=$1.48 (Dec. 31, 1993)	Annual Growth	1984	1985	1986	1987	1988	1989	1990	1991	1992	1993
Sales (£ mil.)	16.7%	1,894	1,629	1,952	2,920	3,376	4,578	5,036	4,897	5,528	5,746
Net income (£ mil.)	15.0%	60	88	152	204	259	271	179	174	192	403
Income as % of sales	—	3.2%	5.4%	7.8%	7.0%	7.7%	5.9%	3.5%	3.5%	3.5%	7.0%
Earnings per share (p)	8.3%	—	—	39.2	44.2	50.5	59.7	38.2	34.5	32.3	68.5
Stock price – high (p)	—	328	456	575	776	619	731	667	596	555	676
Stock price – low (p)	—	240	304	430	425	501	530	462	392	297	504
Stock price – close (p)	8.7%	306	455	525	501	530	631	536	424	505	646
P/E – high	—	—	—	15	18	12	12	17	17	17	10
P/E – low	—	—	—	11	10	10	9	12	11	9	7
Dividends per share (p)	8.0%	—	—	17.8	20.7	23.9	29.5	30.5	30.5	30.5	30.5
Book value per share (p)	11.5%	—	—	—	—	—	—	—	—	402	449
Employees	28.2%	—	31,505	—	—	—	75,034	—	—	71,133	51,755

1993 Year-end:
Debt ratio: 42.8%
Return on equity: 16.4%
Cash (mil.): £596
Long-term debt (mil.): £1,625
No. of shares (mil.): 597
Dividends
  Yield: 4.7%
  Payout: 44.5%
Market value (mil.): £5,705
Sales (mil.): $8,501

**Stock Price History
High/Low 1984–93**

PETROFINA S.A.

OVERVIEW

Petrofina — the oil, gas, and chemical conglomerate that is Belgium's largest industrial company — boosted its profitability in 1993, despite weak petrochemical earnings and the lowest crude oil prices in 7 years. The company credited efficiency gains from its restructuring with providing the spark, but the sale of over $270 million in assets no doubt played a sizable role.

Petrofina, through a network of 166 companies operating in 34 countries, explores for oil and natural gas; runs refineries; manages the FINA chain of gas stations in the US, Africa, and Europe; and produces chemical feedstocks, polymers, monomers, and paints. Most of its natural gas and oil are produced in Norway and the southern US. Its paints, which include lacquers and wood-protection coatings, are marketed under the Sigma label. It also controls Dallas-based FINA, Inc., a publicly traded, integrated petroleum company with 1993 sales of over $3 billion and 2,700 retail outlets in the midwestern, southeastern, and southwestern US.

Petrofina is streamlining operations by focusing its exploration on basins where it has expertise, investing heavily in improving its Antwerp refinery, and concentrating its petrochemical research on new polypropylene and high-density polyethylene products. In addition, the firm is cutting employment and continuing to sell off noncore assets.

WHEN

In 1920 a defeated Germany surrendered its interests in Rumanian oil. Belgian financiers formed the Compagnie Financière Belge des Pétrole, and this financial organization, later known as Petrofina, acquired the properties and began building an integrated petroleum company. The company's main investor was the wealthiest financial group in Belgium, Société Générale de Belgique.

In the years between WWI and WWII, Petrofina added refining and transportation, and its service stations sprang up throughout Europe. In the 1940s Petrofina suffered 2 blows — first, the invasion of Belgium by Hitler's armies, and second, the Communists' seizure of the Rumanian oil fields after the Iron Curtain dropped. To recover, Petrofina expanded abroad. In the 1950s Petrofina searched for crude oil in Africa and North America. American Petrofina, the company's main US subsidiary, was created in 1956. In 1971 the rich Norwegian North Sea field of Ekofisk began production, and Petrofina had a 30% stake in the field.

Petrofina flourished in the late 1970s and early 1980s, when its profits grew 15% a year. With those profits Petrofina bought Britain's Charterhouse Petroleum (1985) and oil and gas interests of US-based Williams Companies (1986). American Petrofina elbowed into the higher echelon of US oil companies, paying $600 million for Tenneco's southwestern exploration and production properties (1988).

In 1982 steel magnate–financier Albert Frère led a group of investors who took control of Groupe Bruxelles Lambert (GBL), the 2nd largest holding company in Belgium. Frère-led GBL and Société Générale joined forces in 1987 to lay siege to Petrofina. They sought control of Imperial Continental Gas (UK) to add its 7.2% stake in Petrofina to their 18% holding. Société Générale, though, became the target of an unsuccessful hostile takeover by Italian Carlo De Benedetti; then, in 1990, GBL had to face the fall of New York securities firm Drexel Burnham Lambert, in which the Belgian group was a major investor.

The Belgian holding companies returned their attention to Petrofina. With the 1990 retirement of CEO Jean-Pierre Amory, Frère became Petrofina's chairman, and Vicomte Etienne Davignon, chairman of Société Générale, became deputy chairman. The board was expanded to give half the seats to the 2 holding companies. Away from the boardroom, Petrofina in 1991 got authority to search 20,000 square kilometers in Russia for oil. Also in 1991 American Petrofina changed its name to FINA.

In 1992 Petrofina approved a 3-year, $1 billion addition to its Antwerp refinery for production of lighter, more environmentally safe oil products. Through its US subsidiary FINA, it also bought a high-density polyethylene plant in Bayport, Texas.

In 1994 the company sold its interest in a North Sea oil field to Union Texas Petroleum for $132 million. Also Elf Aquitaine, the French oil company rumored to be interested in a takeover in 1993, cut its stake in Petrofina from 4.9% to 2.15%

OTC symbol: PTRFY (ADR)
Fiscal year ends: December 31

Chairman: Albert Frère
VC, CEO, and Managing Director: François
Cornélis
VC: Vicomte Etienne Davignon
**Executive Director, Chemicals - Paints -
Research:** Axel de Broqueville
**Executive Director, Corporate Finance-
Insurance:** Michel-Marc Delcommune
Secretary Général, Legal: François Vincké
Director Human Resources: José G. Rebelo
President and CEO, FINA, Inc.: Ron W.
Haddock, age 53, $550,188 pay
VP and CFO, FINA, Inc.: Yves Bercy
Auditors: Klynveld, Peat Marwick, Goerdeler;
Tinnemans, Pourbaix, Vaes & Co.

HQ: 52, rue de l'Industrie, B-1040 Brussels,
Belgium
Phone: +32-2-288-9111
Fax: +32-2-288-3445
US HQ: FINA, Inc., FINA Plaza, 8350 N. Central
Expwy., Dallas, TX 75206
US Phone: 214-750-2400
US Fax: 214-750-2508

	1993 Sales	
	BF bil.	% of total
Europe	416	77
North America	125	23
Adjustments	(183)	—
Total	**358**	**100**

	1993 Sales		1993 Operating Income	
	BF bil.	% of total	BF bil.	% of total
Refining & marketing	450	75	8	30
Chemicals & paints	88	15	4	15
Exploration & prod.	55	9	15	55
Other	4	1	(1)	—
Adjustments	(239)	—	—	—
Total	**358**	**100**	**26**	**100**

Selected Subsidiaries and Affiliates
Cos-Mar, Inc. (50%, chemicals, US)
Fina Europe S.A. (marketing and holding company)
Fina France S.A. (marketing)
Fina Italiana SpA (marketing)
FINA, Inc. (petroleum and chemicals, US)
Fina plc (marketing, UK)
Norske Fina A/S (marketing, Norway)
Sigma Coatings B.V. (paints, The Netherlands)
U.I.C. Insurance Co. Ltd (66.7%, insurance, UK)

Akzo Nobel	Nobel
Amoco	Norsk Hydro
Ashland, Inc.	Occidental
Atlantic Richfield	Oryx
BASF	PDVSA
British Petroleum	PEMEX
Broken Hill	Pennzoil
Chevron	Petrobrás
Coastal	Phillips Petroleum
DuPont	PPG
Elf Aquitaine	Repsol
ENI	Royal Dutch/Shell
Exxon	Sherwin-Williams
Imperial Chemical	Sun Company
Imperial Oil	Total
Koch	Unocal
Mobil	USX–Marathon

$=BF36.2 (Dec. 31, 1993)	Annual Growth	1984	1985	1986	1987	1988	1989	1990	1991	1992	1993
Sales (BF bil.)	(3.7%)	500	584	351	319	364	444	435	430	377	358
Net income (BF bil.)	(7.9%)	15	17	18	18	20	22	22	16	5	7
Income as % of sales	—	3.0%	2.9%	5.1%	5.6%	5.6%	5.1%	5.3%	3.8%	1.2%	2.0%
Earnings per share (BF)	(10.3%)	821	895	919	879	1,002	1,007	981	701	199	307
Stock price – high (BF)	—	6,785	6,864	9,073	12,841	14,250	13,928	12,350	12,375	11,750	10,125
Stock price – low (BF)	—	4,515	5,055	5,500	7,300	7,545	11,525	9,770	9,230	7,010	7,200
Stock price – close (BF)	6.4%	5,669	6,136	9,073	7,745	13,675	12,050	9,820	10,775	7,490	9,870
P/E – high	—	8	8	10	15	14	14	13	18	59	33
P/E – low	—	5	6	6	8	8	11	10	13	35	23
Dividends per share (BF)	(11.2%)	—	—	—	—	507	533	555	561	280.0	280.0
Book value per share (BF)	3.6%	3,988	4,903	5,682	6,121	5,871	6,625	5,827	5,296	5,216	5,465
Employees	(4.6%)	22,500	22,700	22,200	22,100	23,000	23,600	23,800	17,069	15,490	14,696

1993 Year-end:
Debt ratio: 41.9%
Return on equity: 5.8%
Cash (mil.): BF2,812
Long-term debt (bil.): BF61
No. of shares (mil.): 23
Dividend
Yield: 2.8%
Payout: 91.1%
Market value (mil.): $6,340
Sales (mil.): $9,881

Stock Price History
High/Low 1984–93

PETRÓLEO BRASILEIRO S.A.

OVERVIEW

South America's largest industrial company, Petróleo Brasileiro (Petrobrás) is controlled by the Brazilian government, which holds 81.7% of the company's voting capital. Based in Rio de Janeiro, Petrobrás is an integrated oil and gas company.

Although most of Petrobrás's wells are onshore, most of its production comes from offshore. The company is recognized as a leader in offshore drilling technology, and it operates half of the world's deep-water wells. Petrobrás has invested heavily to increase its refining operations, and with 10 refineries and one asphalt plant the company is one of the world's largest petroleum refiners. The

company also controls 36% of Brazil's petroleum products market through a network of more than 7,000 service stations.

Since its founding, Petrobrás has held a monopoly on exploration and production in Brazil. However, the Brazilian Congress has been debating changes to the monopolistic status. Meanwhile, Petrobrás has begun looking for joint venture partners for 271 projects worth about $40 billion.

Petrobrás is also working to boost its natural gas operations. It is investing approximately $3.5 billion to build a pipeline from Bolivia to Brazil, which will begin pumping natural gas in 1997.

WHEN

"O petróleo é nosso!"
"The oil is ours!" proclaimed the nationalist slogan in 1953 Brazil, and Brazilian President Getúlio Vargas approved a bill creating a state-run monopoly on petroleum discovery, development, refining, and transport. The same year that Petróleo Brasileiro SA was created, a team led by American geologist Walter Link reported that prospects of finding petroleum in Brazil were slim. The report outraged Brazilian nationalists, who saw it as a ploy for foreign exploitation. Petrobrás proved it could find oil (one 1957 discovery prompted a week-long holiday for students), but Brazil continued to import crude oil and petroleum products. By 1973 Petrobrás produced about 10% of the nation's needs.

When crude oil prices soared during the Arab oil embargo, the government, instead of encouraging exploration for domestic oil, pushed Petrobrás into a program to promote alcohol fuels. Petrobrás was forced to raise its gasoline prices to make more costly gasohol attractive to consumers. A decision during the 1979 oil shock fixed the price of gasohol at 65% of gasoline, but, during the oil glut of the mid-1980s, Petrobrás's cost of making the alcohol fuel was twice that of gasoline.

In its search for oil, Petrobrás explored overseas. In 1980 it found an oilfield in Iraq, an important trading partner during the 1980s. Petrobrás drilled in Angola and, through a 1987 agreement with Texaco, in the Gulf of Mexico.

Domestically, Petrobrás plunged deeper into the thick Amazon jungle in 1986 to explore for oil. Since 1917, when petroleum

exploration began in the region, only 229 wells had been drilled because of the remote and hostile environment. By 1990 Amazon wells helped boost Petrobrás's total production for the year to a record high.

Also in the mid-1980s, Petrobrás began domestic production in the deepwater Campos basin off Rio de Janeiro state. Discoveries there in 1988, in the Marlim and Albacora fields, more than tripled its oil reserves.

In 1990, to ease dependence on imports, CEO Luis Octavio da Motta Veiga presented a 5-year, $16.9-billion plan to boost crude oil production to 71% of demand by 1995. That same year the company began liquidation of its mining and trading subsidiaries.

Before the invasion of Kuwait, Brazil relied heavily on Iraq, trading weapons for oil. After the invasion spawned increases in crude prices, Petrobrás raised pump prices, but, yielding to the government's anti-inflation program, still did not raise them enough to cover costs. It lost $13 million a day.

In 1993 the company sold 26% of distribution subsidiary Petrobrás Distribuidora to the public and also privatized several of its petrochemical and fertilizer subsidiaries.

A 1994 presidential order, bent on stabilizing Brazil's 40% per month inflation, cut the prices of oil products. Petrobrás claimed the cuts cost it $100 million per month in losses. Also in 1994 Brazil's Internal Revenue Service claimed the company owed $1 billion in back taxes. Despite its woes, the company managed to nearly triple profits to about $1.7 billion in 1994 on flat revenues.

Principal exchange: São Paulo
Fiscal year ends: December 31

Chairman and President: Joel Mendes Rennó
Financial Director: Orlando Galvão Filho
Director Exploration and Production: João Carlos França de Luca
Director Refining and Transportation: Aurílio Fernandes Lima
Human Resources: Clotário F. Cardoso
Legal Affairs: Helio Shiguenobu Fujikawa
President, Petrobrás America: Luiz Antonio Nascimento Reis
Planning and Financial Manager (CFO), Petrobrás America: Irlandi Alves
Administrative Assistant (Personnel), Petrobrás America: Regis Ferreira
Auditors: Ernst & Young, Auditores Independentes S/C

HQ: Av. República do Chile, 65, Rio de Janeiro CEP 20035-900, Brazil
Phone: +55-21-534-4477
Fax: +55-21-220-5052
US HQ: Petrobrás America Inc., 10777 Westheimer, Ste. 625, Houston, TX 77042
US Phone: 713-781-9799
US Fax: 713-781-9790

	1993 Oil and LNG Production	
	Bbls./day	% of total
Offshore	472,472	71
Onshore	195,819	29
Total	**668,291**	**100**

	1993 Natural Gas Production	
	Mil. cu. meters/day	% of total
Offshore	12.5	62
Onshore	7.7	38
Total	**20.2**	**100**

	1993 Sales		1993 Net Income	
	$ mil.	% of total	$ mil.	% of total
Petrobrás	16,546	69	666	84
Distribuidora–BR	6,461	27	102	13
Braspetro & subsidiaries	1,085	4	24	3
Petrofértil	5	—	(64)	—
Adjustments	(3,853)	—	(41)	—
Total	**20,244**	**100**	**687**	**100**

Selected Subsidiaries and Affiliates

Petrobrás Química SA (Petroquisa) (petrochemicals)
Petroquímica União SA (67.8%)
Companhia Petroquímica (CIQUINE, 31.4%)
Companhia Petroquímica Camaçari (CPC, 23.7%)
Companhia Petroquímica do Nordeste SA (COPENE, 36.2%)
Deten Química SA (DETEN, 33.2%)

Petrobrás Distribuidora SA (BR) (distribution and marketing of petroleum products, fuel alcohol, and natural gas)

Petrobrás Internacional SA (Braspetro) (overseas exploration and production, marketing, and services)
Brasoil UK Ltd.
Braspetro Angola
Braspetro Argentina
Braspetro Colombia
Braspetro Libya
Braspetro Oil Services Co. (Brasoil)
Petrobrás America Inc.

Amoco
Ashland, Inc.
Atlantic Richfield
British Petroleum
Broken Hill
Chevron
Coastal
DuPont
Elf Aquitaine
ENI
Exxon

Imperial Oil
Koch
Mobil
Norsk Hydro
Occidental
Oryx
PDVSA
PEMEX
Pennzoil
Petrofina

Phillips Petroleum
Repsol
Royal Dutch/ Shell
Sun Company
Texaco
TOTAL
Unocal
USX–Marathon
YPF

	Annual Growth	1984	1985	1986	1987	1988	1989	1990	1991[1]	1992	1993
Gross oper. rev. ($ mil.)	0.2%	19,804	18,595	17,476	19,882	14,500	18,788	20,448	16,996	18,095	20,244
Net income ($ mil.)	0.9%	634	1,056	1,895	94	265	128	511	(236)	5	687
Income as % of sales	—	3.2%	5.7%	10.8%	0.5%	1.8%	0.7%	2.5%	—	0.0%	3.4%
Employees	(4.2%)	—	—	—	—	—	67,676	55,569	53,857	56,209	56,900

1993 Year-end:
Debt ratio: 27.3%
Return on equity: 5.6%
Cash (mil.): $1,336
Current ratio: 0.98
Long-term debt (mil.): $1,867
No. of shares (mil.): 80,509

Net Income ($ mil.) 1984–93

[1] Excluding Petrobrás Química and Petrobrás Fertilizantes   [2] Excluding Petrobrás Fertilizantes

PETRÓLEOS DE VENEZUELA, S.A.

One of the largest oil companies in the world, Petróleos de Venezuela, also known as PDVSA (pronounced pay-day-VAY-suh), boasts the largest proved crude reserves outside the Middle East. The company is owned by the Republic of Venezuela, which depends heavily on oil revenues.

More than 60% of PDVSA's petroleum revenues come from abroad. The company has major downstream holdings overseas, including refining joint ventures in Germany, Sweden, and the US. It supplies more than 1.3 million barrels of crude oil and petroleum products a day to the US. Through its wholly owned subsidiary CITGO, it operates more than 12,500 gas stations in the US.

Although oil is the company's most important business, it also has operations in natural gas, coal, petrochemicals, and bitumen. The company's BITOR subsidiary continues to develop Venezuela's vast bitumen reserves on its Orinoco River. PDVSA's chemists have turned the tarlike ooze into a liquid called Orimulsion for use as fuel for electric generating plants.

In an effort to expand its oil production capacity from 2.3 to 4 million barrels a day by the year 2002, PDVSA is courting foreign investment. It is signing up foreign companies to profit-sharing and production-sharing agreements to help develop its vast oil deposits.

On invitation from dictator Juan Vicente Gómez, Royal Dutch/Shell explored for and produced oil in Venezuela just before WWI. After the war American companies, shying away from politically unstable Mexico, plunged into Venezuela. Standard Oil of Indiana (later Amoco) began Creole Petroleum in 1920 and sold it in 1928 to Standard of New Jersey (later Exxon). That year Venezuela became the world's largest exporter of oil, a position it would hold until 1970 when Iran took over the top spot.

In 1938 the Venezuelan government threatened nationalization of its oil industry. To avoid that fate the large foreign oil companies, at the encouragement of their war-wary home governments, agreed to pay more taxes and royalties. Venezuela set a pattern for the rest of the world's oil-rich nations when, in 1945, it decreed that it was a 50% partner in all oil operations. In 1960 Venezuela, through Oil Minister Juan Pablo Pérez Alfonzo, was a guiding force in the creation of OPEC, and in 1961 the Venezuelan government created the Venezuelan Petroleum Corporation (CVP). CVP was granted all unassigned petroleum reserves in the nation. By the early 1970s CVP produced about 2% of the nation's oil; international oil companies produced 70%.

In 1975 the first administration of President Carlos Andrés Pérez nationalized oil holdings, paid $1 billion for the assets of the oil companies, and created Petróleos de Venezuela (PDVSA) as the basket to hold its new properties. Instead of obliterating the oil companies, though, Venezuela formed stand-alone PDVSA subsidiaries similar to the old private structure. Shell operations became Maraven, Creole became Lagoven, and other smaller companies eventually combined into Corpoven. The oil companies operated their former possessions for a fee, and PDVSA took advantage of the expertise.

Free of debt and buoyed by high crude prices in the late 1970s and early 1980s, PDVSA formed joint ventures (Ruhr Oel) with Germany's Veba Oel and with AB Nynäs Petroleum in Sweden.

In the US, PDVSA bought 50% of CITGO, the former refining and marketing arm of Cities Service Company, from Southland (1986) and Champlin Refining from Union Pacific (1989). Mobil outbid PDVSA for Tenneco refineries, and the Saudi Arabian oil company snatched a joint venture refining-and-marketing deal with Texaco, but, undiscouraged, PDVSA bought a half interest in a Unocal refinery (1989) and purchased the remaining half of CITGO from flagging Southland (1990).

After the Gulf War of 1991, Venezuela pledged to support OPEC oil quotas while increasing its capacity. In mid-1992 the company opened some marginal fields to foreign investment for the first time since the oil industry's nationalization in 1975. That same year CITGO acquired part of Lyondell Petrochemical's Houston refinery to process PDVSA's heavy crude.

In 1994 Venezuelan President Rafael Caldera named Luis Giusti to succeed Gustavo Roosen as president of the company.

State-owned company
Fiscal year ends: December 31

President: Luis E. Giusti
Coordinator Control and Finances: Juan M.
Szabo
Coordinator Exploration and Production:
Francisco Pradas
Coordinator Human Resources: Nelson E.
Olmedillo
**Chairman, President, and CEO, PDV America
Corp.:** Alonso Velasco
Auditors: Espiñeira, Sheldon y Asociados (Price
Waterhouse)

WHERE

HQ: Edif. Petróleos de Venezuela, Torre Este, Av.
Libertador, La Campiña, Apartado Postal 169,
Caracas 1010-A, Venezuela
Phone: +58-2-708-4111
Fax: +58-2-708-4661
US HQ: PDV America Corp., 750 Lexington Ave.,
59th St., 10th Fl., New York, NY 10022
US Phone: 212-339-7944
US Fax: 212-339-7727

PDVSA operates in Belgium, the Caribbean,
Germany, Japan, the Netherlands, Sweden, the
UK, the US, and Venezuela.

	1993 Exports of Crude Oil	
	Thou. bbl./day	% of total
US & Canada	1,503	69
Central America/		
Caribbean	340	16
Europe	195	9
South America	80	4
Japan	8	0
Other countries	44	2
Total	**2,170**	**100**

WHAT

	1993 Sales	
	$ mil.	% of total
Petroleum	21,042	98
Petrochemicals	343	2
Coal	72	0
Adjustments	(182)	—
Total	**21,275**	**100**

Venezuelan Subsidiaries and Affiliates
Bariven (overseas purchasing)
Bitúmenes Orinoco (BITOR, bitumen)
Carbozulia (coal)
Corpoven (integrated petroleum)
Intevep (research and support)
Lagoven (integrated petroleum)
Maraven (integrated petroleum)
Palmaven (agricultural assistance and conservation
projects)
Pequiven (petrochemicals)

Overseas Subsidiaries and Affiliates
AB Nynäs Petroleum (50%, refining, Sweden)
Bahamas Oil Refining Co. (storage)
Bonaire Petroleum Corp., NV (storage)
CITGO Petroleum Corp. (refining, marketing, and
petrochemicals; US)
PDV America Corp. (investments management, US)
Petróleos de Venezuela UK, SA (marketing)
Refinería Isla (Curaçao refinery)
Ruhr Oel GmbH (50%, refining, Germany)
UNO-VEN Co. (50%, refining and marketing, US)

KEY COMPETITORS

Amoco	ENI	Petrobrás
Ashland Oil	Exxon	Petrofina
Atlantic Richfield	Imperial Oil	Phillips Petroleum
British Petroleum	Koch	Repsol
Broken Hill	Mobil	Royal Dutch/Shell
Chevron	National	Star Enterprise
Circle K	Convenience	Sun Company
Coastal	Norsk Hydro	Texaco
Diamond	Occidental	Total
Shamrock	Oryx	Unocal
DuPont	PEMEX	USX – Marathon
Elf Aquitaine	Pennzoil	

HOW MUCH

	Annual Growth	1984	1985	1986	1987	1988	1989	1990	1991	1992	1993
Sales ($ mil.)	(2.6%)	—	—	—	—	—	—	22,997	22,273	21,426	21,275
Net income ($ mil.)	(5.7%)	—	—	—	—	—	—	1,300	441	338	1,089
Income as % of sales	—	—	—	—	—	—	—	5.7%	5.7%	2.0%	1.6%
Petroleum											
reserves (mil. bbls.)	9.7%	28,034	29,326	55,521	58,084	58,504	59,041	60,055	62,650	63,330	64,447
Natural gas reserves (bcm)	16.1%	—	1,180	2,622	2,840	2,860	2,993	3,429	3,580	3,650	3,908
Employees	1.4%	43,553	44,851	44,674	44,203	45,069	46,940	51,883	50,137	50,506	49,218

1993 Year-end:
Debt ratio: 20.2%
Return on equity: 4.8%
Cash (mil.): $458
Current ratio: 1.49
Long-term debt (mil.):
$5,499

Net Income ($ mil.)
1990–93

PETRÓLEOS MEXICANOS

OVERVIEW

Petróleos Mexicanos (known as PEMEX) is bringing out the welcome wagon, but it only has a few seats. One of the world's largest oil companies, PEMEX is planning to allow increased foreign investment, but only on a limited scale. The state-owned company is an integrated petroleum business, with operations from exploration and production to refining and petrochemicals.

The company's push for foreign investment comes as Mexico has faced a currency crunch since the devaluation of the peso. PEMEX accounts for 30% of the country's

foreign exchange. However, don't make any plans to buy stock in this state-owned company. Long recognized as the tangible expression of Mexican nationalism, PEMEX has remained under government control while other national companies have been privatized.

Instead, PEMEX hopes the influx of outside investment will help improve efficiency. It plans to focus particularly on improving its ability to develop its huge natural gas fields to help expand Mexico's electricity generating capacity.

WHEN

Histories of Mexico recount the nation's first oil business. Natives along the Tampico coast gathered asphalt from naturally occurring deposits and traded with the Aztecs.

Just after the turn of the century, Americans Edward Doheny and Charles Canfield struck oil near Tampico, but their success was eclipsed in 1910 by a nearby well drilled by British engineer Weetman Pearson, leader of the company that became Pearson PLC. The legendary Potrero del Llano No. 4 gushed a plume of crude 35 stories high.

The discoveries opened Mexico's Golden Lane to development by foreign oil companies. President Porfirio Díaz had welcomed foreign ownership of Mexican resources, but revolution ousted Díaz, and the 1917 Constitution proclaimed that natural resources belonged to the nation. However, without legislation to enforce the provision, foreign oil companies continued to build Mexico into a leading world oil exporter. A 1925 act limited foreign companies' concessions.

During a bitter labor dispute in 1938, Mexican President Lázaro Cárdenas expropriated foreign oil holdings — the first-ever nationalization of oil holdings by a non-Communist state. Legislation followed that created Petróleos Mexicanos — PEMEX.

Without foreign capital and expertise, the new state-owned company struggled. Mexico became a net importer of petroleum and petroleum-based products in the early 1970s. For many Mexicans, though, PEMEX remained a symbol of pride, national identity, and economic independence, and that faith was rewarded in 1972 when a major oil discovery — on a scale with the Alaskan North Slope or North Sea — made PEMEX one of

the world's top oil producers again. The heady combination of ample domestic oil supplies and high world prices during the Iranian upheaval late in the 1970s fueled a boom and a government borrowing spree in Mexico. Between 1982 and 1985 PEMEX contributed more than 50% of government revenues. PEMEX profits serviced government debt, and corruption in the state-owned company was widespread.

When oil prices collapsed in 1985, Mexico cut investment in exploration, and production dropped. PEMEX also lowered investment in its oil refining and petrochemical facilities. To decrease its reliance on oil, Mexico began lowering trade barriers and encouraging manufacturing, even allowing foreigners stakes in some petrochemical processing, but not crude oil production.

Following his election in 1988, President Carlos Salinas de Gortari began to reform the company. In 1989 police captured Joaquin "La Quina" Hernandez Galicia, leader of the 200,000-member PEMEX union, after a violent gunbattle. He and 36 other leaders were jailed for charges ranging from corruption to stockpiling weapons, and the powerful union's grip was broken.

In 1992 a leaking PEMEX pipeline caused a disastrous explosion that killed over 200 people in Guadalajara, Mexico. The tragedy sent 4 PEMEX executives and several local officials to prison and galvanized public sentiment for company reform.

In 1994 Adrian Lajous Vargas was named head of PEMEX, succeeding Carlos Ruiz Sacristan, who was named Mexico's secretary of transport and communication.

State-owned company
Fiscal year ends: December 31

General Director: Adrian Lajous Vargas, age 51
Corporate Finance Director: Arturo Ortiz
Corporate Administration Director: Carlos F. Almada
Corporate Operations Director: Carlos Casasús
General Director Exploration and Production: Jaime M. Willars
General Director Gas and Basic Petrochemicals: Pedro Hass
General Director Petrochemicals: Luis Puig
General Comptroller: Javier Lozano
Auditors: Coopers & Lybrand; Despacho Roberto Casas Alatriste

WHERE

HQ: Marina Nacional 329, Col. Huasteca, C. P. 11320, México, D.F., Mexico
Phone: +52-5-531-6061
Fax: +52-5-726-1381

PEMEX operates throughout Mexico and maintains offices in Japan, Spain, and the UK.

	1993 Sales	
	$ mil.	% of total
Mexico	17,907	68
Other countries	8,331	32
Adjustments	448	—
Total	**26,686**	**100**

	1993 Crude Oil Production
	% of total
Offshore (Campeche Sound)	73
Chiapas & Tabasco	23
Other regions	4
Total	**100**

WHAT

	1993 Total Reserves	
	Barrels (mil.)	% of total
Crude oil	44,043	68
Natural gas (crude oil equivalent)	13,740	21
Gas liquids	6,733	11
Total	**64,516**	**100**

Divisions
Pemex Exploración y Producción (petroleum and natural gas exploration and production)
Pemex Gas y Petroquímica Básica (natural gas, liquids from natural gas, and ethane processing)
Pemex Petroquímica (petrochemical production)
Pemex Refinación (refining and marketing)
PMI Internacional (international marketing)

Subsidiaries and Affiliates
Cloro de Tehuantepec, SA de CV (CLOROTEC, 20%, chlorine and other chemicals)
Compañía Mexicana de Exploraciones, SA (COMESA, exploration support)
Compañía Operadora de Estaciones de Servicio, SA de CV (CODESSA, service station operations)
Distribuidora de Gas de Querétaro, SA (DIGAQRO, 96%, natural gas distribution)
Distribuidora de Gas Natural del Estado de México, SA (DIGANAMEX, 51%, natural gas distribution)
Instalaciones Inmobiliarias para Industrias, SA de CV (IIISA, construction)
Repsol, SA (integrated petroleum company, 5%, Spain)
Tetraetilo de México, SA (TEMSA, 60%, petrochemicals)

KEY COMPETITORS

Amoco	Exxon	Phillips
Ashland, Inc.	Imperial Oil	Petroleum
Atlantic Richfield	Koch	Repsol
British Petroleum	Mobil	Royal Dutch/
Broken Hill	Norsk Hydro	Shell
Chevron	Occidental	Sun Company
Coastal	PDVSA	Texaco
DuPont	Pennzoil	Total
Elf Aquitaine	Petrobrás	Unocal
ENI	Petrofina	USX–Marathon

HOW MUCH

	9-Year Growth	1984	1985	1986	1987	1988	1989	1990	1991	1992	1993
Sales ($ mil.)	3.6%	19,405	20,381	11,033	13,130	13,060	15,258	19,330	19,165	21,344	26,686
Net income ($ mil.)	72.7%	7	6	4	3,047	571	320	1,486	652	1,071	959
Income as % of sales	—	0.0%	0.0%	0.0%	23.2%	4.4%	2.1%	7.7%	3.4%	5.0%	3.6%
Employees	(5.3%)	175,420	183,179	155,907	178,745	170,766	164,744	167,952	166,896	125,000	106,951

1993 Year-end:
Debt ratio: 20.8%
Return on equity: 2.7%
Cash (mil.): $599
Current ratio: 1.51
Long-term debt (mil.): $5,650

Net Income ($ mil.) 1984–93

PSA PEUGEOT CITROËN

OVERVIEW

In a time of falling sales and an increasingly crowded market, French car manufacturer Peugeot, France's #1 automaker, recently overtook GM as the #2 automaker in Europe (VW is #1). The company manufactures cars under the Peugeot, Citroën, and Talbot nameplates; 2/3 of the cars are sold outside France. The company is also a leading manufacturer of mopeds, armored vehicles, and car parts.

The car company aims to nearly double its share of non-European sales by the year 2000, to over 25% of total sales. Among the places Peugeot is developing a presence are China, Egypt, India, Malaysia, and Poland. In 1991 Peugeot withdrew from the US market (reentry has been discussed, but no decision made) and updated its name (PSA Peugeot Citroën), image, and products.

Peugeot's CEO, Jacques Calvet, has kept Peugeot competitive by cutting costs and modernizing. Calvet remains critical of the number of Japanese car imports allowed under the 1992 EC/Japan accord.

WHEN

In 1810 Jean-Frédéric and Jean-Pierre Peugeot made a foundry out of the family textile mill in the Alsace region of France and invented the cold-roll process for producing spring steel. The brothers expanded by making saws, watch springs, and other metal products. Bicycle production began in 1885 at the behest of avid cyclist Armand Peugeot, Jean-Pierre's grandson.

Armand turned his interest to automobiles and built Peugeot's first car, a steam-powered 3-wheeler, in 1889. A gas-fueled Peugeot tied for first place in the 1894 Paris-Rouen Trials, the earliest auto race on record. In the same year Peugeot built the world's first station wagon, followed by the world's first compact, the 600-pound "Le Bébé," in 1905.

Peugeot built various factories in France, including one in Sochaux (1912) that remains the company's main factory. The company made the first diesel-powered passenger car in 1922. The 1929 introduction of the reliable 201 model was followed by a series of Peugeots featuring such innovations as synchromesh gears (1936). Despite heavy damage Peugeot bounced back quickly after WWII and began expanding overseas.

In 1954 CEO Roland Peugeot rebuffed a board proposal to rapidly expand Peugeot to global scale and push the company into head-to-head competition with US automakers. However, "bigger is better" thinking resurfaced in 1976 when the French government persuaded Peugeot to merge with Citroën.

André Citroën founded his company in 1915 and in 1919 became the first in Europe to mass-produce cars. Citroën hit the skids during the Depression and in 1934 handed Michelin a large block of stock in lieu of payment for tires. Although Citroën never fully recovered financially, by 1976 the company's line ranged from limousines to the deux chevaux minicar (discontinued in 1990).

In 1978, determined to become the "GM of Europe," Peugeot bought Chrysler's aging European plants and withering nameplates, including Simca (France) and Rootes (UK). Peugeot changed the nameplates to Talbot but failed to halt their sales slide. Peugeot lost nearly $1.2 billion in the 5 years ending in 1984. That year Jacques Calvet took over as CEO.

Calvet cut 30,000 jobs and spent heavily on modernization. Aided by the strong launch of the 205 superminicar, he returned Peugeot to profitability in 1985 and by 1989 had halved its production break-even point.

In the 1980s Peugeot inked production deals with Renault (industrial vehicles, motors, gearboxes) and Fiat (light trucks) and Japanese marketing deals with Suzuki, Austin Rover, and Mazda. In 1990 the company introduced a reasonably priced electric van.

In 1991, after 5 years of declining US sales, Peugeot decided to withdraw from the US; sales there had remained low despite excellent reviews. In 1992 Renault and Peugeot agreed to jointly develop electric cars and to set up battery recharging and servicing centers in at least 10 French cities. In 1993 Peugeot suffered its first loss ($239 million) since 1985. Company officials linked losses to an economic slump, unfavorable exchange rates, and high French interest rates.

In 1994 sales improved to $30.9 billion, due in part to a French government incentive for replacing cars over 10 years old. In early 1995 the company announced that it was considering reentering the US market.

OTC symbol: PGTRY (ADR)
Fiscal year ends: December 31

Chairman and CEO: Jacques Calvet
Managing Director: Pierre Peugeot
Managing Director: Jean Blondeau
Finance: Yann Delabrière
Human Resources: Michel Chanteclair
President, Peugeot Motors of America:
  Serge Banzet
Controller (CFO), Peugeot Motors of America:
  John Peles
Manager Human Resources, Peugeot Motors of America: Cheryl Sugalski
Auditors: Frinault Fiduciaire; Befec-Mulquin & Associés; Coopers & Lybrand

WHERE

HQ: 75 avenue de la Grande-Armée, 75116 Paris, France
Phone: +33-1-40-66-37-60
Fax: +33-1-40-66-51-99
US HQ: Peugeot Motors of America, Inc., One Peugeot Plaza, Lyndhurst, NJ 07071
US Phone: 201-935-8400
US Fax: 201-935-6425

	1993 Sales		1993 Pretax Income	
	FF mil.	% of total	FF mil.	% of total
France	79,690	55	(2,650)	—
Spain	11,853	8	(179)	—
UK	19,864	14	46	—
Other Europe	33,642	23	207	—
Other countries	382	0	(9)	—
Total	**145,431**	**100**	**(2,585)**	**—**

WHAT

	1993 Sales		1993 Net Income	
	FF mil.	% of total	FF mil.	% of total
Peugeot	80,099	55	(1,289)	—
Citroën	59,091	41	(2,257)	—
Engineering/Svcs.	5,868	4	546	—
Purchasing/R&D	366	0	(7)	—
Peugeot SA	7	0	958	—
Finance companies	—	—	742	—
Adjustments	—	—	(106)	—
Total	**145,431**	**100**	**(1,413)**	**—**

Selected Subsidiaries
Automobiles Citroën
Automobiles Peugeot
CycleEurope
Equipements et Composants pour l'Industrie Automobile (ECIA, 72%, automobile components)
GEFCO (transportation services)
Peugeot Motocycles (74%)
Peugeot Talbot Motor Co. Ltd. (UK)
PSA Finance Holding (financial services)
PSA International SA (financial services)
Société de Constructions Mecaniques Panhard & Levassor (SCMPL, military vehicles)

KEY COMPETITORS

BMW	Isuzu
Bridgestone	Kawasaki Motors
British Aerospace	Mazda
Caterpillar	Mitsubishi
Chrysler	Nissan
Cummins Engine	Renault
Daimler-Benz	Renco
Fiat	Saab-Scania
Ford	Suzuki
General Dynamics	Toyota
General Motors	Volkswagen
Harley-Davidson	Volvo
Honda	Yamaha
Hyundai	

HOW MUCH

$=FF5.91 (Dec. 31, 1993)	9-Year Growth	1984	1985	1986	1987	1988	1989	1990	1991	1992	1993
Sales (FF mil.)	5.3%	91,111	100,295	104,946	118,167	138,452	152,955	159,976	160,171	155,431	145,431
Net income (FF mil.)	—	(341)	314	2,269	4,916	8,848	10,301	9,258	5,526	3,372	(1,413)
Income as % of sales	—	—	0.3%	2.2%	4.2%	6.4%	6.7%	5.8%	3.5%	2.2%	—
Earnings per share (FF)	—	(14)	20	104	166	178	204	185	111	67	(28)
Stock price – high (FF)	—	129	254	626	839	700	979	919	640	802	797
Stock price – low (FF)	—	90	119	254	408	395	695	479	418	465	500
Stock price – close (FF)	23.4%	119	254	593	450	700	825	493	595	591	788
P/E – high	—	—	13	6	5	4	5	56	6	12	—
P/E – low	—	—	6	2	2	2	3	34	4	7	—
Dividends per share (FF)	—	0.00	0.00	5.00	8.50	14.00	16.00	16.00	13.00	10.00	0.00
Book value per share (FF)	18.9%	212	242	325	411	585	772	944	1,035	1,063	1,010
Employees	(2.9%)	187,500	176,800	165,000	160,600	158,100	159,100	159,100	156,800	150,800	143,900

1993 Year-end:
Debt ratio: 33.9%
Return on equity: —
Cash (mil.): FF5,407
Long-term debt (mil.): FF8,935
No. of shares (mil.): 50
Dividends
  Yield: —
  Payout: —
Market value (mil.): $6,667
Sales (mil.): $24,608

Stock Price History
High/Low 1984–93

PHILIPS ELECTRONICS N.V.

Philips, the world's 3rd largest electronics company, brought us cassette tapes, VCRs, and CD players. Now Philips is pinning its hopes on a new generation of personal gadgets to rev up the company's consumer electronics division, which accounts for over 35% of sales. Among Philips's next wave of high-tech toys are the interactive CD (CD-i), screen phones, digital compact cassettes (DCCs), multimedia, and flat panel displays. Some analysts say that despite heavy R&D investments, Philips has already missed its chance to grab big markets for CD-i and DCC.

Under Philips's R&D-driven strategy, even lighting is due for a high-tech makeover. The company continues to develop systems that combine lighting, security, telephone, environmental, and computer systems.

With European semiconductor sales rebounding, Philips has signed a cooperative agreement with IBM to develop semiconductors at a jointly owned plant in Germany.

In the US, Philips's new TriMedia division was formed to develop multifunctional digital signal processors for multimedia markets. The new processors, based on VLIW (very long instruction word) architecture, will be used by next-generation computers, including those under development through a Hewlett-Packard/Intel alliance.

In 1891 Gerard Philips (later joined by brother Anton) founded Philips & Co. in Eindhoven, Holland. Surviving an industry shakeout, Philips prospered as a result of Gerard's engineering and Anton's foreign sales efforts and had become Europe's 3rd largest light bulb maker by 1900. The company adopted the name Philips' Gloeilampen-fabrieken (light bulb factory) in 1912.

Dutch neutrality during WWI allowed Philips to expand and integrate into glass manufacturing (1915) and X-ray and radio tubes (1918). The company set up its first foreign sales office in Belgium in 1919; it started building plants abroad to avoid trade barriers and tariffs in the 1930s.

During WWII Philips created US and British trusts to hold majority interests in North American Philips (NAP) and in Philips's British operations. Philips repurchased its British businesses in 1955. NAP operated as an independent company until it was reacquired in 1987. After WWII Philips established hundreds of subsidiaries worldwide.

Philips started marketing televisions and appliances in the 1950s. It acquired a stake in Matsushita Electronics through a technology-licensing agreement in 1952. Philips introduced audiocassette, VCR, and laser disc technology in the 1960s but had limited success with computers and office equipment.

Despite its development of new technologies, Philips was unable to maintain market share against an onslaught of inexpensive goods from Japan in the 1970s. NAP acquired Magnavox (consumer electronics, US) in 1974 and a minority interest in Grundig in 1979.

NAP purchased GTE Television (Sylvania, US, 1981) and Westinghouse's lighting business (1983). Philips's successful PolyGram unit (formed in 1972) issued 20% of its stock to the public in 1989 and bought record companies A&M (US) and Island (UK) in 1990.

After incurring huge losses in 1990, Philips drafted Jan Timmer as president to return the company to profitability. Timmer immediately began cutting jobs and selling unprofitable subsidiaries.

In 1991 Philips adopted its present name and formed a partnership with Nintendo to develop CD-based video games. The company sold back its stake in Whirlpool (appliances), and DEC bought most of its computer business. In late 1991 Timmer hired former Hewlett-Packard executive Frank Carrubba as EVP to help revive the company.

In 1992 Philips and Grundig combined their VCR and camcorder operations. Philips also consolidated the accounts of faltering affiliate Grundig with its own (Philips owns 31.6% of the German consumer electronics manufacturer). Philips teamed with Motorola to build a design center to make video circuits for the new multimedia CD player. Philips lost almost $500 million in 1992, but by the end of 1993 the company had improved its financial outlook with sales of its Magnavox Electronic Systems unit and its interest in Matsushita Electronics. Also in 1993 Polygram added the revitalized Motown label to its stable of record companies.

In 1994 Philips wrote off most of its $175 million investment in failed media venture Whittle Communications.

NYSE symbol: PHG (ADR)
Fiscal year ends: December 31

Chairman of the Board of Management and President: Jan D. Timmer, age 61
EVP: Frank P. Carrubba, age 57
EVP and CFO: Dudley G. Eustace, age 58
President and CEO, North American Philips Corp.: Stephen C. Tumminello
Manager Human Relations, North American Philips Corp.: James R. Miller
Auditors: KPMG Klynveld

HQ: Groenewoudseweg 1, 5621 BA Eindhoven, The Netherlands
Phone: +31-40-786022
Fax: +31-40-785486
US HQ: North American Philips Corp., 100 E. 42nd St., New York, NY 10017-5699
US Phone: 212-850-5000
US Fax: 212-850-7314

Philips has organizations in 60 countries.

	1993 Sales		1993 Operating Income	
	$ mil.	% of total	$ mil.	% of total
The Netherlands	8,952	20	635	41
Asia	7,724	17	401	25
US & Canada	7,492	16	294	19
Latin America	1,783	4	143	9
Australia & New Zealand	518	1	21	1
Africa	180	0	5	0
Other Europe	19,012	42	84	5
Adjustments	(14,035)	—	—	—
Total	**31,626**	**100**	**1,583**	**100**

	1993 Sales		1993 Operating Income	
	$ mil.	% of total	$ mil.	% of total
Consumer prods.	17,867	51	523	28
Components & semiconductors	5,195	15	554	29
Professional prods.	5,068	15	95	5
Lighting	4,296	12	543	29
Miscellaneous	2,306	7	165	9
Adjustments	(3,106)	—	(297)	—
Total	**31,626**	**100**	**1,583**	**100**

Selected Consumer Brands	Major Products
A&M Records	Communication systems
Fine Arts	Consumer electronics
Magnavox	Domestic appliances
Marantz	Industrial electronics
Motown	Lighting
Norelco	Medical electronics
Philips	Recorded music
Polygram	Semiconductors

Alcatel Alsthom	Gillette	Sanyo
AMD	Hitachi	Sharp
AT&T	IBM	Siemens
Bell Atlantic	Intel	Sony
Bose	Lucky-	Texas
Canon	Goldstar	Instruments
Compaq	Matsushita	Thomson SA
Daewoo	3M	Thorn EMI
Dell	Mitsubishi	Time Warner
Deluxe Corp.	Motorola	Toshiba
Diebold	NEC	Tribune
Duracell	Nokia	U S WEST
Fujitsu	Oki	Viacom
Gateway 2000	Pioneer	Walt Disney
GEC	Ralston Purina	Xerox
General Electric	Group	Yamaha
	Samsung	Zenith

	9-Year Growth	1984	1985	1986	1987	1988	1989	1990	1991	1992	1993
Sales ($ mil.)	8.5%	15,199	21,677	25,328	29,874	27,933	29,991	33,074	33,382	32,172	31,626
Net income ($ mil.)	19.2%	281	309	467	306	265	415	(2,684)	575	(495)	1,050
Income as % of sales	—	1.8%	1.4%	1.8%	1.0%	0.9%	1.4%	—	1.7%	—	3.3%
Earnings per share ($)	10.0%	1.40	1.65	2.02	1.89	2.05	1.56	(8.83)	1.92	(1.60)	3.31
Stock price – high ($)	—	17.38	22.50	25.88	27.38	17.75	25.25	25.00	19.63	21.88	21.88
Stock price – low ($)	—	12.00	14.25	18.63	13.75	12.63	16.38	11.00	11.25	9.63	10.88
Stock price – close ($)	3.1%	15.63	22.38	19.88	14.50	17.13	25.00	11.75	17.50	10.75	20.63
P/E – high	—	12	14	13	15	9	16	—	10	—	6
P/E – low	—	9	9	9	7	6	11	—	6	—	3
Dividends per share ($)	(100%)	0.56	0.72	0.94	0.80	0.90	0.82	0.88	0.00	0.00	0.00
Book value per share ($)	(2.6%)	22.73	25.21	30.35	33.83	31.70	36.22	26.38	25.27	16.27	17.99
Employees	(3.4%)	343,961	345,604	344,200	336,700	310,258	304,798	272,787	240,001	257,671	252,214

1993 Year-end:
Debt ratio: 48.8%
Return on equity: 8.4%
Cash (mil.): $1,197
Current ratio: 1.68
Long-term debt (mil.): $4,028
No. of shares (mil.): 328
Dividends
  Yield: —
  Payout: —
Market value (mil.): $6,765

**Stock Price History
High/Low 1984–93**

PIONEER ELECTRONIC CORPORATION

OVERVIEW

Pioneer prides itself on its pioneering image. It has become a leading audio equipment maker and a world leader in audiovisual products and videodisc technology, as well as high-definition TV, laser karaoke, optical memory disk systems, VCRs, and particularly the laser disc (LD) player. Pioneer's recent emphasis has been on the new and expanding area of multimedia hardware and software, including advanced optical disc technology, car navigation systems, and cable TV systems.

But slack domestic demand and plummeting sales have forced Pioneer to pioneer in the human resources area too, attacking the Japanese sacred cow of lifelong corporate employment by laying off 35 middle managers in 1993. With nearly 2/3 of its sales coming from overseas, Pioneer has been hit harder than its more domestically focused rivals by the effects of the strong yen. But it is riding out the storm, hoping that its R&D investment in such cutting-edge technology as laser discs will pay off in the long term.

To stop the slide in its audio sales, the company plans to beef up the marketing of low-end audio models in the emerging markets of Asia, Eastern Europe, and Central and South America.

The Matsumoto family has controlled Pioneer since its founding in 1938.

WHEN

Nozomu Matsumoto, son of a Christian missionary, first listened to the high-fidelity sound of dynamic speakers in 1932. For audio quality, nothing made in Japan could compare, so he founded Fukuin Shokai Denki Seisakusho (Gospel Electric Works) in Osaka to develop Japan's first hi-fi loudspeaker, introduced in 1937. Matsumoto designed the company's trademark — a tuning fork overlaying the symbol for ohm (unit for measuring electrical resistance) — and chose the brand name Pioneer to reflect the company's spirit. The company moved to Tokyo in 1938. Pioneer turntables and amplifiers appeared in 1955, followed by hi-fi receivers in 1958. The growing success of its products led the company to adopt the name Pioneer Electronic Corporation in 1961.

Pioneer went on to emerge as Japan's #1 audio equipment maker in the 1960s, introducing the world's first stereo with its speakers separate from the control unit in 1962 and the world's first car stereo in 1963. Subsidiaries opened in the US and Europe in 1966, and the company's ADRs were listed on the NYSE in 1976.

Convinced that laser disc (LD) technology represented the audiovisual wave of the future, Pioneer started work on an LD video player in 1972, joining MCA in 1977 to form Universal Pioneer Corporation (UPC), which sold the first LD player to General Motors in 1979. Home LD players (under the LaserDisc name) appeared in the US in 1980 and in Japan in 1981. But consumers, particularly US consumers, wanted VCRs, not LD players. Demand for LDs remained sluggish through the early 1980s; so did Pioneer's earnings. The company lost money (about $12 million on $1.1 billion in sales) in 1982 but remained firm in its commitment to LD technology. A player for both LDs and CDs (compact discs) and the world's first car CD system appeared in 1984. Matsumoto's eldest son, Seiya, was appointed president in 1982.

Pioneer used its LD know-how to branch into office automation, introducing the Write-Once Read-Many (WORM) optical memory disk in 1985, and added a combination CD/CDV/LD (CDV is a CD with video) player to its LD product line in 1987. The company bought the IBM-MCA partnership, with over 1,400 laser-optical technology–related patents (Discovision Associates), and released the name *laser disc* for use by other manufacturers in 1989. LD players are now among the hottest consumer electronics products in the US and Japan.

Pioneer sold its interest in Warner-Pioneer (music software marketing) to its partner Warner (now Time Warner) in 1989. That same year Pioneer and US-based Trimble Navigation formed Pioneer Trimble to develop a computerized car navigation system. In 1990 Pioneer became 10% co-owner of Carolco Pictures and in 1991 released a Carolco-produced movie, *Terminator 2*. Also in 1991 the company agreed to supply stereos and CD players for BMW cars.

A rising yen and sluggish domestic demand in 1992 and 1993 hurt the company. In 1994 Pioneer teamed up with Oracle to jointly develop and market multimedia technology products.

NYSE symbol: PIO (ADR)
Fiscal year ends: March 31

WHO

President: Seiya Matsumoto
EVP: Kanya Matsumoto
EVP: Takeo Yamamoto
General Manager Finance and Accounting (Personnel): Masaaki Sono
Director and General Manager Industrial Relations: Katsuhiro Abe
President and CEO, Pioneer North America: Shoichi Yamada
Auditors: Price Waterhouse

WHERE

HQ: Pioneer Kabushiki Kaisha, 4-1, Meguro 1-chome, Meguro-ku, Tokyo 153, Japan
Phone: +81-3-3494-1111
Fax: +81-3-3495-4428
US HQ: Pioneer North America, Inc., 2265 E. 220th St., Long Beach, CA 90801
US Phone: 310-952-2210
US Fax: 310-952-2402

Pioneer has plants in Belgium, France, Japan, Malaysia, Mexico, Spain, the UK, and the US. Its products are sold worldwide.

	1994 Sales	
	$ mil.	% of total
Japan	1,890	38
North America	1,305	27
Europe	1,055	21
Other countries	700	14
Total	**4,950**	**100**

WHAT

	1994 Sales	
	$ mil.	% of total
Video products	1,669	34
Car electronics products	1,654	33
Audio products	1,300	26
Other	327	7
Total	**4,950**	**100**

Major Products

Cable TV converters	LD players
Car navigation systems	LD software
Car stereos	LD video jukebox systems
Cassette players	LD-ROMs
CD players	Multiscreen video systems
CD/CDV/LD combination players	Optical memory disks
CD-ROM changers	Satellite broadcast receivers
CDVs	Stereo components
Cordless telephones	Telecommunications systems
Digital audio players	Televisions
Factory automation systems	VCRs
Laser karaoke (sing-along) systems	

KEY COMPETITORS

Bose	Lucky-Goldstar	Scientific-Atlanta
Boston Acoustics	Matsushita	
Canon	Mitsubishi	Sharp
Casio	NEC	Sony
Fujitsu	Nokia	Tandy
General Electric	Oki	Thomson SA
General Instrument	Philips	Toshiba
Harman International	Polk Audio	Voyager
Hitachi	Robert Bosch	Yamaha
Ingersoll-Rand	Samsung	Zenith
International Jensen	Sanyo	

HOW MUCH

Stock prices are for ADRs ADR = 2 shares	9-Year Growth	1985	1986	1987	1988	1989	1990	1991	1992	1993	1994
Sales ($ mil.)	16.1%	1,302	1,572	2,249	2,496	3,015	3,235	4,265	4,618	5,135	4,973
Net income ($ mil.)	(5.4%)	28	(16)	26	69	125	186	244	215	77	17
Income as % of sales	—	2.2%	—	1.2%	2.8%	4.1%	5.8%	5.7%	4.6%	1.5%	0.3%
Earnings per share ($)	(7.4%)	0.18	(0.10)	0.16	0.42	0.75	1.11	1.36	1.19	0.43	0.09
Stock price – high ($)[1]	—	12.35	10.05	13.83	20.00	27.27	39.38	43.38	39.63	30.63	27.13
Stock price – low ($)[1]	—	7.04	5.58	6.61	9.19	18.92	21.14	26.50	23.00	20.38	17.18
Stock price – close ($)[1]	12.7%	8.63	7.33	13.22	18.19	26.36	39.09	29.25	27.75	22.00	25.38
P/E – high	—	70	—	86	48	36	36	32	33	71	—
P/E – low	—	40	—	41	22	25	19	20	19	47	—
Dividends per share ($)	10.1%	0.08	0.07	0.04	0.16	0.05	0.11	0.13	0.17	0.17	0.19
Book value per share ($)	19.3%	3.73	4.34	6.13	6.83	8.06	10.24	12.30	13.83	15.46	16.45
Employees	4.3%	11,961	12,522	12,437	12,745	12,942	13,898	15,307	16,574	17,340	18,341

1994 Year-end:
Debt ratio: 20.5%
Return on equity: 0.6%
Cash (mil.): $839
Current ratio: 2.01
Long-term debt (mil.): $292
No. of shares (mil.): 183
Dividends
  Yield: 0.7%
  Payout: —
Market value (mil.): $4,653

Stock Price History[1]
High/Low 1985–94

[1] Stock prices are for the prior calendar year.

PIRELLI S.P.A.

OVERVIEW

Pirelli's sales may have deflated recently, but the company has gained more traction. One of the world's largest tire makers, Pirelli has posted losses for 3 straight years, and in an effort to get back on the road to profitability, it has downsized, selling a variety of diversified businesses making everything from sneakers to conveyor belts. Pirelli is now focusing on 2 businesses: tires and cables.

Pirelli SpA is the holding company at the core of the complex ownership structure of the Pirelli group. The company's tire unit manufactures car, motorcycle, farm machin-

ery, and industrial tires. Its cable unit makes power cables, building wires, and telecommunications cables.

One of the world's largest makers of fiber optic cables, Pirelli is looking to build its telecommunications business. The company would like to buy a stake in Telecom Italia (a subsidiary of Italy's state-owned telecommunications company, STET), which the government is considering privatizing. However, fearing a monopoly, many Italian legislators have vowed to block any attempts by Pirelli to buy the company.

WHEN

After fighting for Italian unification with Garibaldi in the 1860s, Giovanni Battista Pirelli observed that France, not Italy, was providing rubber tubes for an Italian ship salvage attempt. The young patriot reacted by founding Pirelli & Co. in Milan in 1872 to manufacture rubber products. In 1879 Pirelli began making insulated cables for the rapidly growing telegraph industry and in 1890 started making bicycle tires. He introduced his first air-filled automobile tire in 1899.

Foreign expansion began in 1902 with a tire plant in Spain. In 1914 the company entered a British cable partnership with General Electric (UK). By 1929 Pirelli owned factories in Argentina, Brazil, and the UK. The company set up Société Internationale Pirelli (SIP) in Switzerland in 1937 and consolidated all non-Italian operations within it. After WWII the group expanded along with the worldwide growth in auto sales and began production in Turkey and Greece in 1962.

By the early 1970s Michelin's steel-belted radial tires had put other manufacturers on the defensive. Pirelli's entry into radials backfired when it became apparent that the tires wore out too quickly. In 1971 the company swapped stock with UK tiremaker Dunlop. Although the firms engaged in joint R&D, they never consolidated production. Soon after, Pirelli's Italian businesses incurred huge losses. A 1973 car crash knocked chairman Leopoldo Pirelli out of action for 7 months. Although the Italian operations survived, the 2 companies split in 1981 after bickering over accounting methods.

In 1982 Pirelli SpA, the Italian operating company, and SIP became holding companies by transferring their operating units into

jointly owned Pirelli Société Générale (Switzerland). Heavy spending on R&D and new equipment bolstered the newly unified tire business, and the 1986 purchase of Metzeler Kautscuk (Germany) made Pirelli one of the world's largest motorcycle tire makers.

In 1988, after buying SIP's Pirelli Société Générale holdings, Pirelli SpA became an operating company again and launched a hostile bid for Firestone through Pirelli Tyre. Outbid by Bridgestone, Pirelli settled for much smaller Armstrong Tire. In 1989 Pirelli sold 23.6% of Pirelli Tyre to the public to reduce debt from the Armstrong acquisition.

In 1990 Pirelli proposed an unusually complex and convoluted merger with Continental AG (Germany) that would have left Pirelli in control. When Continental declined, Pirelli recruited an investor group to buy its stock. Continental responded by allying itself with several leading German corporations (Daimler-Benz, Volkswagen, Allianz, and Deutsche Bank).

Negotiations continued throughout 1991, until Continental terminated the talks after learning of Pirelli's deteriorating financial condition. After repeated denials, Pirelli disclosed that it had agreed to reimburse its investor group for losses incurred in purchasing Continental stock. In 1992 Marco Tronchetti Provera succeeded his father-in-law Leopoldo Pirelli as managing director and began restructuring, selling assets, closing plants, and cutting employment.

In 1994 Pirelli sold its 50% interest in brokerage house Cabota Holding to Banco Ambrosiano Veneto. In early 1995 Pirelli agreed to cooperate with Continental on research projects involving truck tires.

OTC symbol: PIR (ADR)
Fiscal year ends: December 31

Chairman: Leopoldo Pirelli
Executive Deputy Chairman and Managing Director: Marco Tronchetti Provera, age 46
Deputy Chairman: Alberto Pirelli
Deputy Chairman: Filiberto Pittini
General Manager Finance and Administration: Carlo Buora
President and CEO, Pirelli Armstrong Tire (US): Paul Calvi, age 51
CFO, Pirelli Armstrong Tire (US): Romano Cateni
VP Human Resources, Pirelli Armstrong Tire (US): Russell Weymouth
Auditors: Reconta Ernst & Young S.a.s. di Bruno Gimpel

WHERE

HQ: Viale Sarca, 202, I-20126 Milan, Italy
Phone: +39-2-64421
Fax: +39-2-64423300
US HQ: Pirelli Armstrong Tire Corporation, 500 Sargent Dr., New Haven, CT 06536-0201
US Phone: 203-784-2200
US Fax: 203-784-2408

| | 1993 Sales | |
	Lit bil.	% of total
Italy	1,756	18
Central & South America	1,714	18
North America	1,440	16
Other Europe	3,439	38
Other regions	898	10
Total	**9,247**	**100**

WHAT

| | 1993 Sales | |
	Lit bil.	% of total
Tires	4,809	52
Cables	4,415	47
Other	23	1
Total	**9,247**	**100**

| | 1993 Tire Sales |
	% of total
Car tires	55
Industrial & commercial vehicle tires	26
Agricultural machinery tires	7
Motorcycle tires	5
Other	7
Total	**100**

| | 1993 Cable Sales |
	% of total
Power cables	31
Telecommunications cables	23
Building wires	14
Special cables	7
Enameled wires	6
Accessories, installation & other	19
Total	**100**

KEY COMPETITORS

Alcatel Alsthom	Nokia
Bandag	Northwestern
Barnes Group	Steel & Wire
Bridgestone	Pacific Dunlop
Continental AG	Phelps Dodge
Cooper Industries	Siemens
Corning	Sime Darby
Essex Group	Southwire
Goodyear	Sumitomo
Michelin	Toyo

HOW MUCH

$=Lit1713 (Dec. 31, 1993)	Annual Growth	1984	1985	1986	1987[1]	1988	1989	1990	1991	1992	1993
Sales (Lit bil.)	—	—	—	—	7,251	9,120	10,342	10,139	10,024	8,252	9,247
Net income (Lit bil.)[2]	—	33	48	51	97	224	239	139	(619)	(105)	(62)
Income as % of sales	—	—	—	—	1.3%	2.5%	2.3%	1.4%	—	—	—
Earnings per share (Lit)	—	—	—	—	—	267	282	140	(620)	69	41
Stock price – high (Lit)	—	1,795	3,383	5,918	5,227	3,055	4,054	3,125	2,072	2,260	1,484
Stock price – low (Lit)	—	1,290	1,751	3,064	2,609	1,700	2,760	1,505	1,047	1,076	988
Stock price – close (Lit)	(5.0%)	1,785	3,177	4,132	2,609	2,932	2,985	1,735	1,095	2,150	1,130
P/E – high	—	—	—	—	—	11	14	22	—	33	36
P/E – low	—	—	—	—	—	6	10	11	—	16	24
Dividends per share (Lit)[3]	(100%)	82	82	82	91	91	100	100	70	0	0
Book value per share (Lit)	—	—	—	—	—	—	—	—	—	1,670	1,717
Employees	(10.1%)	—	—	—	—	71,802	69,329	53,540	51,572	45,726	42,132

1993 Year-end:
Debt ratio: 51.6%
Return on equity: 2.4%
Cash (bil.): Lit628
L-T debt (bil.): Lit2,436
No. of shares (mil.): 1,517
Dividends
  Yield: —
  Payout: —
Market value (mil.): $1,000
Sales (mil.): $5,398

**Stock Price History
High/Low 1984–93**

[1] Pro forma, reorganization, fiscal year change   [2] Unconsolidated 1981–86   [3] Not including rights issues

PRICE WATERHOUSE LLP

OVERVIEW

Price Waterhouse (PW) is a global organization of management consultants, accountants, tax advisors, and auditors that provides advisory services to businesses, individuals, governments, and nonprofit entities.

Only a few years ago PW was the most prestigious of the Big 6 auditing firms and had a host of blue-chip clients. But its reputation has been tarnished lately by financial scandals, including a multibillion dollar damage suit brought by Touche Ross, liquidators of failed Bank of Credit & Commerce International. PW had acted as BCCI's auditor and,

plaintiffs claim, was in a position to blow the whistle on the bank's improper dealings but did not do so.

PW's information technology services have spurred recent growth. In 1994 the firm introduced TeamMate, Windows-based software that provides audit preparation, review, report generation, and storage capabilities.

Though the smallest of the Big 6, PW has retained its enviable list of clients. In 1994 PW converted itself to a limited-liability partnership, which protects the personal assets of partners not directly involved in a lawsuit.

WHEN

In 1850 Samuel Lowell Price founded an accounting firm in London, and in 1865 he took on Edwin Waterhouse as a partner. The firm quickly attracted several important accounts and a group of prestigious partners that included 4 Knights of the British Empire. Aided by the explosive industrial growth in Britain and the rest of the world, Price Waterhouse expanded rapidly (as did the accounting industry as a whole) and by the late 1800s had established itself as the most prestigious accounting firm in the world, providing its services in accounting, auditing, and business consulting.

By the 1890s the firm's dealings in America had grown sufficiently to warrant permanent representation, so Lewis Jones and William Caesar were sent to open offices in New York City and Chicago. United States Steel chose the firm as its auditors in 1902.

Through the next several decades, PW's London office initiated tremendous expansion into other countries. By the 1930s, 57 PW offices boasting 2,500 employees operated globally. The growth of PW in New York was largely due to the Herculean efforts of partner Joseph Sterrett, and PW, along with other accounting firms, benefited from SEC audit requirements. The firm's reputation was enhanced further in 1935 when it was chosen to handle the Academy Awards balloting. Its prestige attracted several important clients, notably large oil and steel interests.

During WWII PW recruited and trained women with college experience to fill its depleted ranks for the duration; some remained with the firm after the end of the hostilities. In 1946 the firm started a management consulting service.

While PW tried to coordinate and expand its international offices after the war, the firm lost its dominance in the 1960s, although by 1970 it still retained 100 of the *FORTUNE* 500 as clients. The company came to be viewed as the most traditional and formal of the major firms. PW tried to show more aggressiveness in the 1980s.

In 1989 the firm made plans to merge with Arthur Andersen, but the 2 managements were unable to agree on terms and style, and the merger was called off. When the deal fell through, the firm expanded internationally, merging with Swiss firm Revisuisse and opening an office in Budapest in that same year.

In 1992 PW lost a $338 million judgment in a suit brought by Standard Chartered PLC (UK). Standard Chartered had sued the firm for negligence in its audits of Arizona-based United Bank, which Standard Chartered had bought in 1987. However, the judgment was thrown out in late 1992 and a new trial was ordered.

In 1993 PW got into hot water with regulators when it was revealed that it had charged US thrift regulators 67 cents a page for copying more than 10 million documents in reviewing the assets of a failed S&L.

In 1994 the firm was sued by a Spanish shareholders' association that claimed that PW had failed to alert Banco Español de Crédito stockholders to the bank's financial troubles, and a $259 million lawsuit against PW's Hong Kong unit was settled out of court. In that same year the firm was granted a license to start up operations in Vietnam.

James Schiro was nominated to replace Shaun O'Malley as PW chairman in 1995.

Limited liability partnership
Fiscal year ends: June 30

WHO

World and US Chairman: Shaun F. O' Malley, age 59
Deputy World Chairman, and Europe Chairman: Jermyn Brooks
VC Human Resources: Richard P. Kearns
VC Management Consulting Services: Tom Beyer
General Counsel: Eldon Olson

WHERE

HQ: Southwark Towers, 32 London Bridge St., London SE1 9SY, UK
Phone: +44-(01)71-939-3000
Fax: +44-(01)71-378-0647
US HQ: 1251 Avenue of the Americas, New York, NY 10020
US Phone: 212-819-5000
US Fax: 212-790-6620

Price Waterhouse maintains 447 offices in 118 countries and territories.

	1994 Revenues	
	$ mil.	% of total
US	1,570	39
Other countries	2,410	61
Total	**3,980**	**100**

WHAT

	1994 US Revenues
	% of total
Auditing & accounting	43
Management consulting	32
Tax	25
Total	**100**

Selected Services
Audit and business advisory services
Employee benefits services
Government services
Industry services
International business development services
International trade services
Inventory services
Investment management and securities operations consulting
Litigation and reorganization consulting
Management consulting services
Merger and acquisition services
Partnership services
Personal financial services
Tax services
Valuation services

Representative Clients

AlliedSignal	Exxon
Amoco	Goodyear
Anheuser-Busch	W. R. Grace
Baxter	Hewlett-Packard
Borden	IBM
Bristol-Myers Squibb	Kellogg
Campbell Soup	Kmart
Caterpillar	J. P. Morgan
Chase Manhattan	NIKE
Chemical Banking	Ralston Purina
Chevron	Scott
CIGNA	United Technologies
Compaq	Walt Disney
Dresser	Warner-Lambert
DuPont	Washington Post
Eastman Kodak	Woolworth

KEY COMPETITORS

Arthur Andersen	Hewitt
Bain & Co.	IBM
Booz, Allen	A. T. Kearny
Boston Consulting Group	KPMG
Coopers & Lybrand	Marsh & McLennan
Deloitte & Touche	McKinsey & Co.
EDS	Perot Systems
Ernst & Young	SHL Systemhouse
Gemini Consulting	
H&R Block	

HOW MUCH

	9-Year Growth	1985	1986	1987	1988	1989	1990	1991	1992	1993	1994
Sales ($ mil.)	14.6%	1,170	1,488	1,804	2,097	2,468	2,900	3,603	3,781	3,890	3,980
Offices	2.4%	360	381	400	412	420	448	458	453	448	447
Partners	4.2%	2,100	2,300	2,297	2,526	2,680	3,007	3,227	3,221	3,242	3,045
Employees	5.7%	30,372	32,794	33,236	37,120	40,869	46,406	49,461	48,600	48,781	50,122

1994 Year-end:
Sales per partner:
$1,307,061

Sales ($ mil.)
1985–94

QANTAS AIRWAYS LIMITED

OVERVIEW

The koala is history, but the flying rat (as the airline's stylized kangaroo logo is called) is still on board at Qantas, Australia's #1 airline for domestic and international travel. After a rocky year in 1993, due in part to the costs of absorbing Australia Airlines, Qantas climbed back into the black in 1994, with a spiffed-up image, a new partner — British Airways — and the prospect of going public in 1995.

Aside from its domestic business, Qantas's primary service area is Asia and the Pacific, where many of the world's fastest-growing economies are located. Although about 30% of global air traffic is concentrated in Asia, price competition with other airlines is fierce.

Qantas also flies to Europe, where the partnership with BA provides greater access to European markets, and to the US, primarily to Los Angeles. Traffic to other US cities is handled through a variety of code-sharing agreements with US carriers. The company also runs catering operations and owns several resorts.

Qantas has trimmed jobs, streamlined facilities, and started a new advertising campaign whose theme is "I still call Australia home." These efforts will enhance its attractiveness to investors when the company's IPO (originally planned for 1994 but delayed because Australian privatizations deluged the stock exchange with issues) is announced.

WHEN

Ex-WWI pilots W. Hudson Fysh and Paul J. McGinness and stockman Fergus McMaster founded Queensland and Northern Territory Aerial Services (Qantas) in 1920 to provide an air link between Darwin in the Northern Territory and the railheads in Queensland. In 1922 Qantas started carrying airmail over a 577-mile route between Charleville and Cloncurry, and by 1930 it had blanketed northeastern Australia with air routes stretching from Darwin and Brisbane to the Coral Sea. Qantas moved its headquarters to Brisbane from Longreach (1930) and then to Sydney (1938).

In 1934 Qantas and Imperial Airways (predecessor of British Airways) formed Qantas Empire Airways to fly the last leg of a London-to-Australia mail route (Singapore to Brisbane). Qantas bought the British share of Qantas Empire in 1947 and was nationalized.

By 1950 the airline served almost every major city in the Pacific Rim. Qantas inaugurated the Wallaby route to Johannesburg (1952) and opened the Southern Cross route, previously operated by British Commonwealth Pacific Airlines, to San Francisco and Vancouver via Honolulu (1954).

In 1958 Qantas offered the world's first complete round-the-world service. (Pan Am had started a similar service in 1957 but was barred by the US government from crossing North America.) It bought a 29% stake in Malayan Airways in 1959. The company added several European destinations in the 1960s, including Frankfurt (1966) and Amsterdam (1967), and adopted its present name in 1967.

Tourism to Australia boomed in the 1970s. Initially the surge of competition from foreign (especially US) airlines hurt Qantas, contributing to its 2nd loss since 1924 ($4 million, 1971). But in 1973 annual boardings jumped 28% to exceed one million. Qantas's passengers flew about 4,217 miles per journey — the longest average trip length of any airline in the world.

In 1987 Qantas bought 20% (later reduced to 10%) of Fiji's Air Pacific, which it had owned from 1958 to 1978. Other acquisitions included Australia-Asia Airlines (1989) and 19.9% of Air New Zealand (1990).

Qantas enjoyed its most profitable year ever in 1989, but a strike by domestic pilots paralyzed Australia's tourist industry that year, bashing Qantas's earnings for fiscal 1990. Income for the next year remained low in part because of the Japanese recession.

In 1992 the Australian government sold British Airways a 25% stake in Qantas for about $450 million. The partnership improved business prospects for both airlines, but a 1994 application to allow the 2 airlines to fix prices and services was rejected by Australian authorities.

Qantas also became embroiled in a dispute with Northwest Airlines in 1993 over how many passengers Northwest was allowed to pick up in Japan. Australian and US aviation authorities entered the fray with mutual threats to cut the airlines' service between the US and Australia. The dispute was amicably resolved. In 1994 Qantas discontinued direct service to San Francisco.

State-owned company
Fiscal year ends: June 30

Chairman: Gary M. Pemberton, age 54
Managing Director: James A. Strong, age 50
Finance Director: Gary K. Toomey, age 39
Executive General Manager Marketing and Corporate Affairs: G. J. Dixon
Executive General Manager Sales: S. V. McPhee
Regional General Manager (US): Richard K. Porter
Financial Controller, Qantas (US): Janine Hoey
Manager Personnel Services, Qantas (US): Carl Feil
Auditors: KPMG Peat Marwick

WHERE

HQ: Qantas Centre, 203 Coward St., Mascot, N.S.W. 2020, Australia
Phone: +61-2-691-3636
Fax: +61-2-236-3339
US HQ: Qantas Airways Limited, 360 Post St., San Francisco, CA 94108
US Phone: 415-445-1400
US Fax: 415-981-1152
Reservations: 800-227-4500

Qantas flew to 86 cities in 24 countries in 1994, serving over 14 million passengers.

	1994 Sales	
	A$ mil.	% of total
Australia & Asia	3,618	55
UK & Europe	989	15
America & the Pacific	887	13
Other countries	262	4
Adjustments	846	13
Total	**6,602**	**100**

WHAT

	1994 Sales	
	A$ mil.	% of total
Passengers	4,926	75
Freight & mail	479	7
Tour & travel services	369	6
Other	828	12
Total	**6,602**	**100**

	1994 Jets (Long Haul)	
	No.	% of total
Boeing 737	34	37
Boeing 747	31	34
Boeing 767	22	24
Airbus	4	5
Total	**91**	**100**

Selected Subsidiaries and Affiliates
Australian Airlines Express Courier Pty. Ltd.
Australian Resorts Pty. Ltd.
First Brisbane Airport Pty. Ltd.
Qantair Ltd.
QH Tours Ltd.
TAA Aviation Pty. Ltd.
Thrinakia Pty. Ltd.

KEY COMPETITORS

Air China	KLM
Air France	Korean Air Lines
All Nippon Airways	Lufthansa
AMR	Northwest Airlines
Ansett	Philippine Air Line
Cathay Pacific	SAS
China Airlines	Singapore Airlines
Continental Airlines	Swire Pacific
Delta	Thai International
Garuda Indonesia	UAL
IRI	Virgin Group
JAL	

HOW MUCH

$=A$1.32 (Dec. 31, 1991)	9-Year Growth	1985	1986	1987	1988	1989	1990	1991	1992	1993	1994
Sales (A$ mil.)	17.3%	1,576	1,914	2,297	2,797	3,266	3,606	3,861	4,158	5,832	6,602
Net income (A$ mil.)	0.6%	148	23	64	131	177	12	44	138	(377)	156
Income as % of sales	—	9.4%	1.2%	2.8%	4.7%	5.4%	0.3%	1.1%	3.3%	—	2.4%
Passengers (thou.)	21.6%	2,450	2,587	3,021	4,329	4,001	4,233	4,143	4,534	12,223	14,252
Available seat km (mil.)	10.5%	26,553	28,641	32,095	45,502	39,222	41,469	43,563	43,559	58,611	65,292
Rev. passenger km (mil.)	12.2%	16,716	17,613	21,009	29,464	26,546	27,097	26,638	28,836	40,603	47,052
Passenger load factor	—	64.2%	63.3%	67.3%	69.7%	70.2%	69.1%	66.0%	66.2%	69.38	72.1%
Size of fleet	23.7%	23	24	30	32	40	42	50	—	122	126
Employees	9.6%	11,710	12,501	13,711	14,780	15,397	17,401	20,430	17,646	25,159	26,791

1994 Year-end:
Debt ratio: 67.9%
Return on equity: 7.4%
Cash (mil.): A$59
Current ratio: 0.71
Long-term debt (mil.): A$3,259
Sales (mil.): $4,806

Net Income (A$ mil.) 1985–94

QUEBECOR INC.

Pulp, fiction, and much more. Montreal-based Quebecor is a major player in the commercial printing, publishing, and paper production industries. The company's Quebecor Group subsidiary publishes a range of French-language magazines and newspapers, including *Le Journal de Montréal* and *Le Journal de Québec* (combined circulation of 1.3 million). Another subsidiary, Quebecor Printing, is the #2 printer in North America (behind R. R. Donnelley) and custom prints major circulation items in English, including the *National Enquirer, TV Guide, People, Sports Illustrated, Time,* and *Superman* comic books as well as around 24 regional editions of *Reader's Digest*. Other

custom printing lines include telephone books, catalogs, and bank notes. This book, *Hoover's Handbook of World Business 1995–1996*, was printed by Quebecor.

A 3rd subsidiary, Donohue, Inc., is a major pulp and paper producer, operates a newsprint plant with an annual capacity of 195,000 metric tons, and owns 2 sawmills.

Led by the flamboyant 69-year-old Pierre Péladeau, Quebecor has a reputation for aggressive acquisitions, having made over 100 mergers and buyouts since 1972. Quebecor has set its sights on European expansion, acquiring 70% of French printer Groupe Fécomme for around $12 million in 1993.

Insiders own about 27% of the company.

In 1950 Pierre Péladeau, a graduate of McGill University's law school, borrowed $1,500 from his mother so that he could buy a small Montreal newspaper called *Le Journal de Rosemont*. This became the base for Péladeau's publishing empire, and within a few years he had established 5 other weekly newspapers and his first printing firm.

In 1964 Péladeau seized the opportunity presented to him by a strike at the major Montreal paper *La Presse*. He assembled a team from his various weeklies and, according to company legend, had the tabloid *Le Journal,* which would become Quebecor's flagship, on the streets within 3 days.

Quebecor went public in 1972. By the late 1970s Péladeau expanded beyond Quebec and bought printing plants in Ontario. He also branched out into a variety of communications activities, including music publishing, photo finishing, and pay TV, but by the late 1980s had refocused the company on its core printing businesses.

In 1985 Quebecor got a foothold in the US with the purchase of printing plants in New Jersey and Michigan. Péladeau teamed up with Robert Maxwell in 1987 to form Mircor Inc. to buy a 55% share in forestry concern Donohue Inc. The company took a major step into the international arena when it purchased the printing group BCE PubliTech in 1988 for $161 million. The purchase catapulted the company to become the #1 commercial printer in Canada.

In 1990 Maxwell sold his US printing plants to Péladeau for $510 million. Péladeau

formed Quebecor Printing (USA) around the newly purchased printing assets. In addition to the printing plants, Quebecor had access to a customer list that was bringing in $744 million a year and to Maxwell's state-of-the-art rotogravure presses. Maxwell subsequently bought a 25.8% stake in the new company for $100 million.

Like his colleague and competitor Maxwell, Péladeau shared a reputation for flamboyance and controversy. In 1990 Péladeau was quoted as saying Jews take up "too much space" in Montreal's fashion district.

When the mysterious death of Robert Maxwell in 1991 was followed by revelations of deceptive finances and shady business dealings by the Maxwell empire, Péladeau was able to buy back all of Maxwell's shares in Quebecor at bargain basement prices.

Anticipating new opportunities with the passage of NAFTA, Quebecor expanded into Mexico with the 1991 purchase of Gráficas Monte Albán SA de CV, a specialist in book binding and publishing for the Mexican and South American markets.

In 1993 Quebecor acquired 3 printing plants in the US, from Arcata Corporation, as well as the only Canadian plant using the rotogravure process. Quebecor subsequently acquired Arcata in 1994.

In 1994 Quebecor's Donohue subsidiary acquired 49.9% of British Columbia–based Finlay Forest Industries from the Royal Bank of Canada. That same year, Quebecor had a net income of $63 million through $2.8 billion in sales.

AMEX symbol: PQB
Fiscal year ends: December 31

President and CEO: Pierre Péladeau, age 69,
C$620,589 pay
EVP: Raymond Lemay, C$222,705 pay
SVP Corporate Development: Daniel Paillé
VP Finance and Treasurer: François R. Roy
VP Human Resources, Quebecor Group: Yves
Dubuc
President and COO, Quebecor Printing (USA):
James A. Dawson, US$525,000 pay
VP and CFO, Quebecor Printing (USA): William
Glass
**VP Human Resources, Quebecor Printing
(USA):** Marc Shapiro
Auditors: KPMG Poissant Thibault-Peat Marwick
Thorne

WHERE

HQ: 612 Saint-Jacques St., Montreal, Quebec
H3C 4M8, Canada
Phone: 514-877-9777
Fax: 514-877-9757
US HQ: Quebecor Printing (USA) Corp.,
125 High St., Boston, MA 02110
US Phone: 617-346-7300
US Fax: 617-346-7361

| | 1993 Sales | |
	$ mil.	% of total
US	1,501	65
Canada	734	31
Other countries	89	4
Total	**2,324**	**100**

WHAT

| | 1993 Sales | |
	C$ mil.	% of total
Printing	1,682	72
Forest products	400	17
Publishing & distribution	242	11
Total	**2,324**	**100**

Major Products and Services	Selected Subsidiaries and
Advertising	Affiliates
Artistic weekly newspapers	Donohue Inc. (63.6%)
Books	Finlay Forest Industries
Daily newspapers	(49.9%)
De-inked pulp	Imprimeries Fécomme-
Lumber	Quebecor SA (70%,
Magazines	France)
Market pulp	Quebecor Printing Inc.
Newsprint	(75.4%)
Regional weekly	Quebecor Printing (USA)
newspapers	Corp.
Wood chips	Tej Quebecor Printing Ltd.
Woodlands management	(40%, India)

KEY COMPETITORS

Banta	Noranda
Boise Cascade	Pearson
Canadian Pacific	Quad/Graphics
Courier	Ringier
R. R. Donnelley	Southam
Fort Howard	Sullivan Graphics
Georgia-Pacific	Thomson Corp.
Graphic Industries	Toronto Sun
G.T.C. Transcontinental	Torstar
International Paper	Treasure Chest Advertising
James River	Valassis Communications
Kimberly-Clark	Wallace Computer
Lagardère	Webcraft
Mead	World Color Press

HOW MUCH

	Annual Growth	1984	1985	1986	1987	1988	1989	1990	1991	1992	1993
Sales ($ mil.)	30.5%	212	249	321	521	1,057	1,516	2,098	2,052	1,994	2,324
Net income ($ mil.)	23.1%	9	10	12	18	27	16	67	16	69	56
Income as % of sales	—	4.1%	3.9%	3.6%	3.4%	2.6%	1.1%	3.2%	0.8%	3.4%	2.4%
Earnings per share ($)	12.8%	0.28	0.31	0.38	0.48	0.67	0.34	1.32	0.30	1.05	0.83
Stock price – high ($)	—	3.25	5.33	7.19	8.38	8.69	9.13	6.81	9.50	13.50	16.13
Stock price – low ($)	—	1.67	3.00	4.31	4.25	5.00	6.19	4.75	6.56	8.88	13.25
Stock price – close ($)	17.8%	3.08	4.63	5.75	4.88	8.38	6.50	6.81	8.88	13.38	13.50
P/E – high	—	12	17	19	18	13	27	5	32	13	19
P/E – low	—	6	10	11	9	8	18	4	22	9	16
Dividends per share ($)	13.0%	0.05	0.06	0.04	0.08	0.10	0.12	0.11	0.11	0.12	0.15
Book value per share ($)	24.7%	1.26	1.76	2.07	3.10	3.87	4.98	6.23	11.58	16.32	11.41
Employees	12.1%	—	—	—	—	—	—	—	16,400	16,500	20,600

1993 Year-end:
Debt ratio: 75.1%
Return on equity: 10.6%
Cash (mil.): $2
Current ratio:1.71
Long-term debt (mil.): $469
No. of shares (mil.): 49
Dividends
  Yield: 1.1%
  Payout: 18.1%
Market value (mil.): $664

**Stock Price History
High/Low 1984–93**

THE RANK ORGANISATION PLC

UK-based The Rank Organisation is a diversified media and leisure-related conglomerate. It provides products and services to the movie and TV industries and owns casinos, nightclubs, resorts, and holiday package companies. Rank provides various travel services and operates holiday facilities, hotels, bingo parlors, and leisure centers, mostly in the UK. The company also offers video and film services and products, operates theaters, and finances movies in the UK. Rank owns 29% of business machines giant Rank Xerox (in tandem with Xerox Corporation) and 50% of the Universal Studios movies theme park in Orlando, Florida (a joint venture with MCA).

Other US businesses include several Hard Rock Cafes, the Kingston Plantation (resort development, Myrtle Beach, South Carolina), 15 Outdoor World caravan resorts on the Eastern Seaboard of the US, and timeshare and 2nd-home developments in the Pocono Mountains of Pennsylvania.

Video sales are picking up the slack caused by falling profits in Rank's leisure and recreation areas (especially its amusement centers and bingo halls) in 1994. The company managed to secure contracts for video duplication of the box office monster hits *Jurassic Park* and *Mrs. Doubtfire,* and the sleeper hit *Four Weddings and a Funeral.*

Joseph Arthur Rank, millionaire son of a founder of UK food giant Rank Hovis McDougall, entered moviemaking in 1934 by cofounding British National Films to produce religious movies. Rank quickly shifted emphasis. In 1935 he helped establish Pinewood Studios and General Film Distributors, which, following Rank's purchase of a stake in US-based Universal Pictures, became Universal's UK distributor.

Taking advantage of a depressed UK film industry, Rank bought 2 large studios, Denham (1938) and Amalgamated (1939). In 1941 Rank bought control of the Odeon and Gaumont-British theater chains, creating a huge, fully integrated film business.

In 1947 the British government slapped stiff tariffs on foreign films. When US filmmakers responded by cutting off movies to the UK, Rank's companies rushed in to fill the void, quickly producing as many movies as possible for UK distribution. The government rescinded the tariff the next year, and the UK was flooded with backlogged US films. Rank's companies reeled from the US onslaught.

The Rank empire suffered in the 1950s as television and other alternate entertainment forms flourished. But in 1956 the company's fortunes reversed when Rank chairman Sir John Davis struck a deal with the Haloid Company, now known as Xerox. In exchange for financing, Rank would receive about 1/3 of the profits of Rank Xerox. IBM and Gestetner had previously rejected the Haloid offer.

For 2 decades Rank Xerox registered better than 30% sales growth, and, after J. Arthur Rank's death in 1972, its profits

dwarfed those of Rank's operating units. Davis and his successors pumped the ever-increasing cash torrent into a diverse and perennially underperforming group of businesses, including bingo parlors, hotels, dance halls, and TV, appliance, and furniture manufacturing. The pitiful results of the diversification effort were exposed in the late 1970s as Rank Xerox's earnings receded under intensified competition in the copier market, particularly from Canon and Ricoh.

Disgruntled institutional investors installed Michael Gifford as chief executive in 1983. He immediately began cutting overhead and dumping businesses, at one point at a rate of one and a half per day. By focusing on leisure- and entertainment-related sectors, Gifford greatly improved Rank's operating profits. At the same time Rank Xerox's earnings improved through cost cutting and success with new document-related products.

In 1988 Rank joined with MCA, now a part of Matsushita, to create the Universal Studios theme park. Rank absorbed Mecca Leisure Group's bingo parlors, casinos, hotels, and clubs in a 1990 acquisition.

Rank Motorway Services (fuel stations and traveler lodging, UK) was sold in 1991 for $160 million. Six new Hard Rock Cafes were opened in 1993, bringing the total owned or franchised by Rank to 27 worldwide.

In 1994 Rank named ICI chief Sir Denys Henderson as its new chairman. That same year Rank announced it would change its fiscal year end from October 31 to December 31 in 1995. Rank reported 1994 revenues of $3.6 billion and profits of $465 million.

Nasdaq symbol: RANKY (ADR)
Fiscal year ends: December 31

Chairman: Sir Denys Henderson, age 61
Managing Director and CEO: Michael B. Gifford, age 58
Finance Director: Nigel V. Turnbull, age 51
Commercial Director: Douglas M. Yates, age 50
EVP and CFO, Rank America: John H. Watson
VP Human Resources, Rank America: Richard C. Snodgrass
Auditors: KPMG Peat Marwick

HQ: 6 Connaught Place, London W2 2EZ, UK
Phone: +44-(01)71-706-1111
Fax: +44-(01)71-262-9886
US HQ: Rank America Inc., 5 Concourse Pkwy., Ste. 2400, Atlanta, GA 30328-5350
US Phone: 404-392-9029
US Fax: 404-392-0585

The Rank Organisation operates entertainment, lodging, recreation, leisure, and other businesses in Canada, the UK, and the US.

	1993 Sales		1993 Operating Income	
	$ mil.	% of total	$ mil.	% of total
UK	2,166	69	209	70
US	782	25	60	20
Other Europe	86	3	12	4
Other countries	105	3	18	6
Total	**3,139**	**100**	**299**	**100**

	1993 Sales		1993 Operating Income	
	$ mil.	% of total	$ mil.	% of total
Recreation	1,031	33	94	32
Film & TV	940	30	54	18
Holidays	634	20	76	25
Leisure	401	13	75	25
Other	133	4	—	—
Total	**3,139**	**100**	**299**	**100**

Principal Subsidiaries

Associated Leisure Ltd. (gaming machines)
Butlin's Ltd. (Holiday World Centres)
Deluxe Laboratories Inc (film processing, US)
Film House Partnership (film processing, Canada)
Grosvenor Clubs Ltd. (casinos)
Hard Rock Cafe International Inc (restaurants, US)
Odeon Cinemas Ltd.
Pinewood Studios Ltd. (film production)
Rank Cintel Ltd. (broadcast equipment)
Rank Film Distributors Ltd. (feature film distribution)
Rank Holidays & Hotels Ltd.
Rank Leisure Ltd. (leisure centers and nightclubs)
Rank Orlando Inc (50%, Universal Studios Florida partnership, US)
Rank Xerox Ltd. (29%, business equipment)
Top Rank Ltd. (social and bingo clubs)

Accor
Anheuser-Busch
Bally Entertainment
Bass
Canon
Crédit Lyonnais
Forte
Jackpot Enterprises
Ladbroke Group
Littlewoods
Pearson
PepsiCo
Planet Hollywood
Samuel Goldwyn
Scottish and Newcastle Breweries
Sodak Gaming
Sony
Thomson Corp.
Time Warner
United Gaming
Virgin Group
Walt Disney
WMS Industries

	9-Year Growth	1984	1985	1986	1987	1988	1989	1990	1991	1992	1993
Sales ($ mil.)	15.1%	884	910	1,036	1,152	1,455	1,729	2,596	3,677	3,264	3,139
Net income ($ mil.)	13.7%	69	106	137	217	277	285	385	245	211	219
Income as % of sales	—	7.8%	11.6%	13.2%	18.9%	19.0%	16.5%	14.8%	6.7%	6.5%	7.0%
Earnings per share ($)	13.0%	0.23	0.35	0.53	0.80	1.02	1.05	1.09	0.54	0.47	0.09
Stock price – high ($)	—	3.05	5.55	7.20	10.80	11.00	13.80	12.00	11.70	11.00	11.00
Stock price – low ($)	—	2.08	2.63	4.75	6.10	8.30	10.00	7.50	7.80	6.60	7.60
Stock price – close ($)	18.2%	2.65	5.00	6.10	8.20	10.40	11.10	9.30	8.60	8.30	11.90
P/E – high	—	13	16	14	14	11	13	11	22	23	17
P/E – low	—	9	8	9	8	8	10	7	14	14	11
Dividends per share ($)	15.1%	0.13	0.14	0.28	0.28	0.00	0.42	0.80	0.50	0.49	0.46
Book value per share ($)	11.9%	2.54	3.02	3.14	3.98	5.52	6.43	1.10	5.41	5.57	6.99
Employees	9.6%	17,780	16,442	16,635	17,679	20,054	23,603	47,816	42,993	40,689	40,650

1993 Year-end:
Debt ratio: 40.2%
Return on equity: 10.3%
Cash (mil.): $487
Current ratio: 1.10
Long-term debt (mil.): $1,414
No. of shares (mil.): 317
Dividends
  Yield: 3.9%
  Payout: 66.7%
Market value (mil.): $3,772

Note: Financial information is for fiscal years ending October 31.

OVERVIEW

Reckitt & Colman is emptying its pantry and cleaning up. The London-based consumer products company signed a deal in late 1994 to acquire household products manufacturer L&F, whose products include Lysol disinfectant and Mop & Glo floor cleaner, from Kodak for $1.5 billion.

To pay for the acquisition and to increase its focus on household products, the company announced plans to sell its UK food business, including its flagship product, Colman's mustard, which it has manufactured for more than 180 years.

Reckitt & Colman still hopes to cut the mustard in the US, where it manufactures French's mustard. However, its big push is into household products. The company's newest members join its stable of products that includes Airwick Carpet Fresh, Woolite, Easy-Off, Saniflush, Black Flag, and Mr. Bubble. The company also sells pharmaceuticals and over-the-counter medicines in the UK, Australia, Asia, and South Africa.

Besides building its presence in the US, the company is also expanding elsewhere, including Southeast Asia and India.

WHEN

In 1804 Jeremiah Colman bought a flour mill near Norwich, England. Ten years later he moved his operations to a large mill in Stoke Holy Cross, where he milled flour and mustard seed. In 1823 his nephew, James, joined him and their business was incorporated as J. and J. Colman.

When Jeremiah died in 1851, James Colman's son, also named Jeremiah, became a partner in the company. In 1854 he took over the manufacturing operations when his father died. That same year the company began its move to larger headquarters at Carrow.

Jeremiah, who spent 24 years as a member of the House of Commons, worked to make the Carrow facilities as self-sufficient and waste-free as possible. The factory had its own foundry, print shop, paper mill (to make containers), and fire brigade. Byproducts from the milling process were sold to farmers for cattle feed and fertilizer, and mustard seed bags were converted to clothing. The company also had its own sawmill, providing timber both for construction and for employees' coffins. Jeremiah also became known for the benevolent treatment of his employees, opening a low-cost kitchen (1868), and hiring Britain's first industrial nurse (1878).

The company continued to expand, adding wheat flour, starch, and laundry bluing operations. In 1903 the company acquired Keen, Robinson & Co., a manufacturer of spices and infant and invalid foods, which had been founded in 1742. In 1912 J. and J. Colman got a stranglehold on British mustard sales when it acquired its only major competitor, Joseph Farrow & Company.

In 1913 J. and J. Colman joined another rival, starch manufacturer Reckitt & Sons, in a joint venture in South America. Reckitt & Sons traced its roots to a flour milling business started by Isaac Reckitt in England in 1819. The joint venture between Colman and Reckitt was a success, and in 1921 the 2 companies pooled all their overseas operations.

In 1938 the 2 companies created Reckitt & Colman Ltd. to manage their operations, although each company maintained a separate listing on the London Stock Exchange. In 1954 they formally merged into a single company. That same year the company acquired soap and polishes maker Chiswick Products.

The company formed its US subsidiary in 1977, and during the 1980s it made a number of acquisitions to build its presence in the US. Reckitt & Colman acquired Airwick Industries from Ciba-Geigy (1985, air fresheners), Durkee Famous Foods (1986, condiments), and Gold Seal (1986, bath products, including Mr. Bubble).

In 1990 the company picked up brands such as Black Flag insecticide and Easy-Off oven cleaner when it bought Boyle-Midway from American Home Products. After battling with US spicemaker McCormick, Reckitt Colman exited the US spice business in 1992, selling its Durkee-French US seasonings operations to Australia's Burns Philp & Co.

In 1993 Reckitt & Colman sold its Herb-Ox bouillon business to Hormel. In 1994 the company sold its ultramarine pigment business, Reckitt's Colors International, to Holiday Chemical Holdings.

Principal exchange: London
Fiscal year ends: First Saturday in January

Chairman: Sir Michael J. Colman, age 65
CEO: Vernon L. Sankey, age 44
Group Director Finance: Iain G. Dobbie, age 56
Group Director Europe: Colin C. C. Brown, age 53
Group Director Americas; Chairman and CEO, Reckitt & Colman Inc. (US): Michael F. Turrell, age 50
VP and CFO, Reckitt & Colman Inc. (US): Andrew Scott
VP Human Resources, Reckitt & Colman Inc. (US): John Alberto
Auditors: Price Waterhouse

HQ: One Burlington Ln., London W4 2RW, UK
Phone: +44-81-994-6464
Fax: +44-81-994-8920
US HQ: Reckitt & Colman Inc., 1655 Valley Rd., PO Box 943, Wayne, NJ 07474-0943
US Phone: 201-633-3600
US Fax: 201-633-3619

	1993 Sales	
	£ mil.	% of total
Europe	914	43
North America	553	26
Australasia & Asia	292	14
Latin America	242	12
Africa	95	5
Total	**2,096**	**100**

	1993 Sales		1993 Operating Income	
	£ mil.	% of total	£ mil.	% of total
Household & toiletry	1,436	69	206	65
Food	366	17	54	17
Pharmaceutical	211	10	46	15
Other	83	4	9	3
Total	**2,096**	**100**	**315**	**100**

Household and Toiletry
Air fresheners, deodorizers, and carpet fresheners
Denture and oral care products
Depilatories and body care products
Environmentally friendly cleaning products
Fine-fabric care and laundry aids
Hard-surface cleaners and furniture and floor care products
Insecticides
Lavatory cleaners and fresheners

Food
Condiments and flavor enhancers
Mustards
Sauces and savory mixes

Pharmaceutical
Analgesics
Antiseptics
Cough, cold, and flu remedies
Indigestion remedies and constipation treatments

Burns, Philip & Co.	Henkel	Philip Morris
Cadbury Schwepps	S.C. Johnson	Procter &
Clorox	Johnson &	Gamble
Coca-Cola	Johnson	RJR Nabisco
Colgate-Palmolive	London	SmithKline
CPC	International	Beecham
Danone	Nestlé	Unilever
Glaxo	PepsiCo	Upjohn

£=$1.48 (Dec. 31, 1993)	Annual Growth	1984	1985	1986	1987	1988	1989	1990	1991	1992	1993
Sales (£ mil.)	6.7%	—	1,267	1,329	—	1,394	1,566	1,764	1,987	1,904	2,096
Net income (£ mil.)	13.4%	—	62	86	—	128	123	130	141	94	169
Income as % of sales	—	—	4.9%	6.5%	—	9.2%	7.8%	7.4%	7.1%	4.9%	8.0%
Earnings per share (p)	7.7%	—	—	24.1	28.9	—	34.4	33.1	35.0	25.2	43.6
Stock price – high (p)	—	289	325	450	456	485	662	667	741	709	725
Stock price – low (p)	—	199	238	304	332	385	455	535	486	523	532
Stock price – close (p)	11.0%	283	325	433	392	455	639	645	623	623	722
P/E – high	—	—	13	16	—	14	20	19	20	28	17
P/E – low	—	—	10	10	—	11	14	15	13	21	12
Dividends per share (p)	11.9%	8.0	9.3	—	—	10.2	11.9	13.6	15.1	16.2	17.6
Book value per share (p)	13.9%	—	—	—	—	—	—	—	—	165	188
Employees	(6.0%)	—	34,500	—	—	—	22,000	23,800	22,500	21,000	21,000

1994 Year-end:
Debt ratio: 35.7%
Return on equity: 25.5%
Cash (mil.): £145
Long-term debt (mil.): £244
No. of shares (mil.): 375
Dividends
  Yield: 2.4%
  Payout: 40.3%
Market value (mil.): $4,007
Sales (mil.): $3,102

Stock Price History
High/Low 1984–93

One of the largest publishing companies in the world, Reed Elsevier is the marriage of 2 companies and 2 cultures. Britain's Reed International and the Netherlands's Elsevier each own 50% of the company. The 2 publishing giants share management of the company but have separate stock listings.

Reed Elsevier publishes consumer, trade, scientific, and professional journals and magazines; consumer, educational, and professional books; and regional newspapers. In the US its holdings include Cahners Publishing, whose titles include *Variety* and *Publishers Weekly,* and Reed Reference Publishing. UK holdings include *The Lancet,* a medical journal, and IPC Magazines. Amsterdam-based Elsevier Science publishes more than 1,000 English-language journals, including *Excerpta Medica* and *Nuclear Physics.* Reed Travel Group is a leading supplier of travel information and transactional services, and Reed Exhibition Companies is the world's #1 organizer of trade and public shows.

Looking to expand its presence in the US, the company acquired Mead's LEXIS/NEXIS on-line service for $1.5 billion in 1994.

The bicultural nature of the company's management has created some friction. In 1994 Reed's Peter Davis stepped down as co-chairman when the Dutch contingent pushed for (and won) management by a 4-person executive committee.

Named after the man who founded it as a newsprint manufacturing company in 1894, Albert E. Reed & Co. went public in 1903. For the next 50 years, Reed grew by buying UK pulp and paper mills. In the 1930s Reed began making packaging materials and in 1954 added building products. Reed expanded into New Zealand (1955), Canada and Australia (1960), and Norway (1962).

Chairman Sir Don Ryder radically altered the company in the 1960s and 1970s, leading Reed into other paper-based and paper-related products and into the wallpaper, paint, and interior-decorating and do-it-yourself markets. In 1970 Reed bought International Publishing Corp., Mirror Group Newspapers, and 29% of Cahners Publishing; Reed bought the rest of Cahners in 1977.

By 1978 Ryder's strategy proved flawed. Reed had difficulty coordinating its many companies and their independent business cycles. Strapped for cash, Reed dumped most of its Australian businesses.

Reed sold the Mirror Group to Robert Maxwell in 1984. Under CEO Peter Davis, a former grocery executive, Reed sold off the remainder of its nonpaper and nonpublishing companies by 1987 and focused on publishing. Reed bought Octopus Publishing, the UK's 2nd largest book publisher (1987), the UK *TV Times* (1989), News Corporation's Travel Information Group (electronic and printed guides, 1989), and Martindale-Hubbell (1990).

Maxwell's need to pay debts enabled Reed to buy his Macmillan directories (*Who's Who* books and *Standard Directory of Advertisers*) in 1991.

Davis, who had become chairman in 1990, announced in September 1992 that Reed would merge with Elsevier, the world's leading scholarly journal publisher, with which Reed had considered merging in 1987. Elsevier had been founded by 5 booksellers and publishers in Rotterdam in 1880 and had taken its name from a famous Dutch family publishing company, which had operated from the late 16th century to the early 18th century. Early successes for the company, which moved to Amsterdam in 1887, included Dutch versions of Jules Verne novels.

Elsevier entered the scientific publishing market in the 1930s, and following WWII it diversified into trade journals and consumer manuals and also continued to build its scientific publishing business. In 1979 the company merged with newspaper publisher Nederlandse Dagbladunie. That same year it made its first US acquisition when it acquired the Congressional Information Service.

In 1988 the company fended off a takeover from Maxwell by planning to merge with UK publisher Pearson; Maxwell was thwarted, the merger ultimately failed, and Elsevier later sold its Pearson stock. In 1991 Elsevier bought Maxwell's Pergamon Press.

In 1993 Reed Elsevier acquired Official Airlines Guides from bankrupt Maxwell for $425 million. In 1994, in an effort to increase US ownership, Reed International and Elsevier were both listed on the New York Stock Exchange.

NYSE symbol: RUK (Reed), ENL (Elsevier)
Fiscal year ends: December 31

WHO

Co-Chairman; Chairman, Elsevier NV: Pierre J. Vinken, age 66
Co-Chairman; Chairman, Reed International: Ian A. N. Irvine, age 57
CFO: Nigel J. Stapleton, age 47
Chairman and CEO, Reed Publishing (USA): Robert L. Krakoff, age 58
President, Elsevier Science (USA): Ron Schlosser
Auditors: Price Waterhouse (Reed); Coopers & Lybrand (Elsevier)

WHERE

HQ: 6 Chesterfield Gardens, London W1A 1EJ, UK
Phone: +44-(01)71-499-4020
Fax: +44-(01)71-491-8212
US HQ: Reed Publishing (USA),
275 Washington St., Newton, MA 02158
US Phone: 617-964-3030
US Fax: 617-558-4667
US HQ: Elsevier Science Publishing Co., 655 Avenue of the Americas, New York, NY 10010
US Phone: 212-989-5800
US Fax: 212-633-3990

	1993 Sales	
	£ mil.	% of total
North America	1,043	37
UK	786	28
The Netherlands	349	13
Other countries	618	22
Total	**2,796**	**100**

WHAT

	1993 Sales		1993 Operating Income	
	£ mil.	% of total	£ mil.	% of total
Business	1,011	36	185	33
Consumer	847	30	112	20
Scientific & Medical	499	18	154	28
Professional	439	16	107	19
Total	**2,796**	**100**	**558**	**100**

Business
Cahners Publishing Company (*Variety, Publishers Weekly*; US)
Misset (business publishing, the Netherlands)
Reed Business Publishing (*Computer Weekly*; UK)
Reed Exhibition Companies (trade shows)
Reed Travel Group (travel information and services)

Consumer
Bonaventura (magazines, *Elegance*; the Netherlands)
Cahners Consumer Magazines (*Modern Bride, Sail*; US)
Dagbladunie (newspapers, the Netherlands)
IPC Magazines (*Chat, Woman*; UK)
Reed Consumer Books (UK)

Scientific and Medical
Butterworth-Heinemann (books and journals, UK)
Elsevier Science (scientific journals, the Netherlands)

Professional
Butterworths (legal and tax publishing, UK)
Congressional Information Service (US)
Mead Data Central (LEXIS/NEXIS, US)
Reed Educational Publishing (UK)
Reed Reference Publishing (US)

KEY COMPETITORS

Advance Publications	Lagardère	Time Warner
Bertelsmann	Matsushita	Viacom
Dow Jones	McGraw-Hill	VNU
Dun & Bradstreet	News Corp.	West Publishing
H&R Block	Pearson	Wolters Kluwer
Knight-Ridder	Thomson Corp.	

HOW MUCH

£=$1.48 (Dec. 31, 1993)	Annual Growth	1984	1985	1986	1987	1988	1989	1990	1991[1]	1992[1]	1993
Sales (£ mil.)	11.2%	—	—	—	—	—	—	—	2,262	2,461	2,796
Net income (£ mil.)	23.0%	—	—	—	—	—	—	—	251	309	380
Income as % of sales	—	—	—	—	—	—	—	—	11.1%	12.6%	13.6%
Earnings per share (p)	11.0%	14	13	20	27	33	35	28	24	31	36
Stock price – high (p)[1]	—	136	185	308	633	471	471	475	529	655	912
Stock price – low (p)[1]	—	94	133	163	299	332	345	328	345	447	618
Stock price – close (p)[1]	23.3%	136	172	303	394	370	444	378	529	641	896
P/E – high	—	10	9	12	19	14	12	17	22	21	25
P/E – low	—	7	7	6	9	10	9	12	14	15	17
Dividends per share (p)	18.4%	4.1	4.6	5.6	8.0	10.0	14.0	15.0	15.8	16.8	18.8
Book value per share (p)	2.2%	130	136	132	145	180	267	236	—	255	157
Employees[2]	—	45,200	34,700	34,600	31,300	22,100	18,700	19,000	18,000	18,100	25,700

1993 Year-end:
Debt ratio: 38.6%
Return on equity: 17.4%
Cash (mil.): £503
Long-term debt (mil.): £579
No. of shares (mil.): —
Dividends
  Yield: 2.1%
  Payout: 52.4%
Market value (mil.): $13,981
Sales (mil.): $4,136

Stock Price History
High/Low 1984–93

[1] *Pro forma*   [2] Reed only 1984–1992

RENAULT

Just because Renault got dumped by Volvo after a 4-year courtship doesn't mean the French car maker isn't attractive. Despite the collapse of its proposed merger with the Swedish firm, Renault has performed well even in tough times, eking out profits for the last 7 years — a record matched only by Honda and Toyota. "Our strength is that our cars have personality," says Raymond Lévy, former CEO. Renault, once known for clunkers, is now the leading auto maker in France and has 11% of the EU market.

With the European Union opening up to international competition in the year 2000,

Renault wants to continue its assault on costs, hoping to maintain its profitability by being quick to get new products to market and by growing outside Europe. To those ends Renault expanded operations in Turkey and Latin America in 1993 and entered into a partnership to build vehicles in China.

In 1994 the French government, which owns 80% of the company, announced a plan to sell off 29% of Renault's shares, retaining a controlling interest of 51%. As part of the partial privatization effort, Volvo agreed to sell off about half of its 20% interest in the company.

In the Paris suburb of Billancourt in 1898, 21-year-old Louis Renault assembled a motorized vehicle with a transmission box of his own design. Louis and his brothers, Marcel and Fernand, established Renault Frères and produced the world's first sedan in 1899. Marcel died in a racing accident (1903) and Fernand left the business (1908), leaving Louis in sole possession of the company. He renamed it La Société Louis Renault in 1908.

Taxis soon became Renault's best-selling products. In 1914 a fleet of 600 Paris taxis shuttled French troops to fight the Germans in the Battle of the Marne. Renault also contributed to the war effort by building light tanks and airplane engines.

Between the wars Renault became increasingly self-sufficient, producing its own components and building foundries. The company expanded into trucks and tractors and became a major aircraft engine maker. Renault sustained heavy damage in WWII, but Louis Renault operated the remaining Paris facilities for the Germans during their occupation of France. After the liberation of Paris, he was accused of collaboration with the enemy and died in prison, awaiting trial, in 1944. The De Gaulle government nationalized Renault in 1945 and gave it its present name.

Worldwide economic growth aided Renault's postwar comeback in France and abroad. The company achieved its greatest success in high-volume, low-cost cars such as the 4 CV in the late 1940s and 1950s, the Renault 4 in the 1960s and 1970s, and the Renault 5 in the 1970s and 1980s.

In 1979 Renault acquired 46% of American Motors Corporation (AMC), expecting the purchase to help the company gain US market share. In the early 1980s AMC fared poorly, and Renault suffered from a worldwide slump in auto sales, an aging product line, and stiff competition from Japanese carmakers in the US. Decreasing sales revealed the company's unwieldy bureaucracy, low productivity, and above-average wages. In 1984 Renault lost over $1.5 billion.

Georges Besse took over management of Renault in 1985, trimmed employment by 20,000, and tried to reinstill the profit motive in the government-owned firm. When Besse was assassinated by terrorists in 1986, Raymond Lévy assumed his role and continued his policies, laying off 30,000 more workers and pulling out of the US by selling AMC to Chrysler (1987). Renault returned to profitability, aided by a booming car market and strong protectionist policies against Japanese carmakers in France, Italy, and Spain.

Renault and Volvo agreed to extensive cross-ownership and cooperation in international auto and truck operations in 1990. But the relationship, which was to have led to a merger, fell apart in 1993 when Volvo shareholders rejected the plan. Months later in early 1994, the 2 firms also agreed to dismantle their strategic partnership. As part of that agreement, Renault swapped its 25% stake in Volvo's car division for Volvo's 45% stake in Renault's troubled truck division. Also in 1994 Renault launched the Laguna, a sedan that would do well to be the hit that the Twingo has been since its 1993 debut.

State-owned company
Fiscal year ends: December 31

Chairman and CEO: Louis Schweitzer, age 51
President and CEO, Renault V.I.:
Jean-Pierre Capron
SVP and CFO: Christian Dor
SVP Human Resources: Georges Bouverot
President, Mack Trucks (US): Pierre Jacou
CFO, Mack Trucks (US): Guy Claveau
Auditors: Deloitte Touche Tohmatsu; Michel
Poisson; Ernst & Young

HQ: Régie Nationale des Usines Renault S.A.,
34, quai du Point-du-Jour, B.P. 103-
92109 Boulogne Billancourt Cedex, France
Phone: +33-1-41-04-50-50
Fax: +33-1-40-99-71-07 (Public relations)
US HQ.: Mack Trucks, Inc., 2100 Mack Blvd.,
Allentown, PA 18105
US Phone: 610-709-3011
US Fax: 610-709-3308

Renault does business in more than 100
countries.

	1993 Sales	
	FF mil.	% of total
France	80,451	48
North & South America	14,180	8
Asia/Pacific	8,925	5
Eastern Europe	3,175	2
Africa	2,363	1
Other EU	55,720	33
Other Western Europe	4,975	3
Total	**169,789**	**100**

	1993 Sales		1993 Pretax Income	
	FF mil.	% of total	FF mil.	% of total
Automobiles	130,179	77	1,548	—
Commercial vehicles	24,698	15	(2,010)	—
Financial services	10,098	6	1,335	—
Industrial companies	4,814	3	368	—
Adjustments	—	—	(147)	—
Total	**169,789**	**100**	**1,094**	**—**

Passenger Cars
Renault 4
Renault 5 and Superfive
Renault 9
Renault Alpine
Renault Clio
Renault Espace
Renault Express
Renault Fuego
Renault Laguna
Renault Safrane
Renault Twingo

Light Commercial Vehicles
Renault 4 Van
Renault Express
Renault Master
Renault Trafic

Major Finance Subsidiaries
Renault Crédit
International
Renault Finance
Sodechanges SA

Industrial Companies Division
Capital goods
Farm machinery
Industrial products
Transportation

US Subsidiary
Mack Trucks, Inc.

BMW	Kia Motors
British Aerospace	Kubota
Caterpillar	Mazda
Chrysler	Mitsubishi
Daewoo	Navistar
Daimler-Benz	Nissan
Deere	PACCAR
Dina	Peugeot
Fiat	Saab-Scania
Ford	Suzuki
General Motors	Tata
Hino Motors	Toyota
Honda	Volkswagen
Hyundai	Volvo
Isuzu	

$=FF5.91 (Dec. 31, 1993)	Annual Growth	1984	1985	1986	1987	1988	1989	1990	1991	1992	1993
Sales (FF mil.)	5.3%	106,911	111,382	122,317	147,510	161,438	174,477	163,620	165,974	184,252	169,789
Net income (FF mil.)	—	(12,721)	(10,897)	(5,874)	3,256	8,834	9,289	1,210	3,078	5,680	1,071
Income as % of sales	—	(11.9%)	(9.8%)	(4.8%)	2.2%	5.5%	5.3%	0.7%	1.9%	3.1%	0.6%
Employees	(4.8%)	—	—	196,731	188,936	178,665	174,573	157,378	147,185	146,604	139,733

1993 Year-end:
Debt ratio: 76.2%
Return on equity: 3.2%
Cash (mil.): FF8,744
Current ratio: 0.48
L-T debt (mil.): FF31,972
Sales (mil.): $28,734

Net Income (FF mil.) 1984–93

REPSOL, S.A.

OVERVIEW

Spain's largest industrial company, Repsol is a fully integrated oil and gas enterprise. Based in Madrid, the company controls 60% of the Spanish oil market and 90% of the liquefied petroleum gas market, a major source of fuel for Spanish households.

Repsol's exploration and production business produces about 25% of the company's crude oil requirements. The company is currently working to boost its crude oil production. Repsol operates 5 refineries in Spain and sells gasoline under the brand names Campsa, Petronor, and Repsol. The company is expanding its service station operations into other parts of Europe, including France,

Portugal, and the UK. Repsol's Petróleo and Química units produce basic and derivative petrochemicals such as propylene and polyethylene.

CEO Oscar Fanjul-Martin has been expanding his company's operations into natural gas for the past decade. The culmination of his strategy came when Repsol's 45%-owned subsidiary Gas Natural bought 91% of Enagas, Spain's state-owned natural gas company.

Instituto Nacional de Hidrocarburos (INH), a Spanish government agency, controls 40.5% of Repsol's stock, although it continues to sell its holdings.

WHEN

Repsol, officially created in 1987, is actually the result of efforts that began as early as the 1920s to organize Spain's fragmented energy industry.

Following an era of dependency on foreign investment during and prior to the period of Francisco Franco's dictatorship (1939–75), Spain began reorganizing its energy industry and in 1976 produced an unsuccessful First National Energy Plan. A better 2nd plan in 1979 established the Instituto Nacional de Hidrocarburos (INH), which in 1981 incorporated all public sector firms involved in gas and oil under one government agency.

Repsol was formed 6 years later to provide central management to a Spanish oil company that could compete in the unified European market. The government chose the name "Repsol," a well-known brand of Spanish lubricant products, for its name recognition within Spain and easy pronunciation for foreign customers. The company was charged with pursuing a global strategy that would bring together all levels of the industry, from exploration to extraction to sales at the gasoline pumps.

In May 1989 Repsol offered 26% of the company to public investors on the Madrid and New York stock exchanges. The highly successful offering raised over $1 billion and brought in 400,000 new shareholders to the company. In the same year Repsol increased its marine fleet with the purchase of Naviera Vizcaina shipping company and also bought Carless Refining & Marketing, a British

company, with its chain of 500 service stations operating mainly under the Anglo brand. Although Repsol was opening its doors to foreign investment, Spain maintained control over the country's energy industry, including a tightly guarded distribution network under government-controlled CAMPSA. CAMPSA oversaw a marketing/logistics system of pipelines, storage terminals, and sales outlets.

The Commission of the EC (Spain had entered the EC in 1986) demanded that Spain open its markets to other EC members. In 1991, under pressure from the EC, CAMPSA divided its 3,800 gasoline stations among its 4 major shareholders: Cepsa, Petromed, Ertoil, and Repsol. Repsol gained 66% of the logistical network and use of the CAMPSA brand name.

At present the Spanish energy industry is undergoing a liberalization marked by the dissolution of CAMPSA and the entrance of French oil giant Elf (with its purchase of part of Cepsa, Spain's largest private refiner) and British Petroleum (now controlling the small but efficient refiner, Petromed).

In early 1992 Repsol and the Spanish bank La Caixa merged their interests in natural gas to create Gas Natural, a new utility.

The Spanish government announced in June 1992 that it would reduce its majority holdings in Repsol through public sale of some of its stock. In 1993 the government reduced its stake to 40.5%, and in 1994 it announced plans to reduce its holdings to around 20% by mid-1995.

WHO

Chairman and CEO: Oscar Fanjul-Martin
VC: Guzmán Solana Gómez
President, Repsol Exploración: Antonio González-Adalid y García-Zozaya
President, Repsol Petróleo: Juan Sancho Rof
President, Repsol Comercial de Productos Petroliferos: Jose Luis Díaz Fernández
Director Finance: Carmelo de las Morenas López
Director Legal Affairs and Secretary of the Board: Francisco Carballo Cotanda
Director Human Resources: Jesús Fernández de la Vega Sanz
Auditors: Arthur Andersen & Co.

WHERE

HQ: Paseo de la Castellana, 278-28046 Madrid, Spain
Phone: +34-1-348-81-00
Fax: +34-1-314-28-21

Repsol has offices in 19 countries.

	1993 Sales	
	$ mil.	% of total
Spain	11,685	75
Other countries	3,800	25
Total	**15,485**	**100**

	1993 Net Crude Production	
	Thou. bbls./day	% of total
Near & Middle East	110	68
Spain	7	4
Other countries	45	28
Total	**162**	**100**

WHAT

	1993 Sales		1993 Operating Income	
	$ mil.	% of total	$ mil.	% of total
Refining & marketing	12,614	79	719	64
Gas	1,599	10	272	24
Exploration & production	964	6	133	12
Petrochemicals	789	5	(14)	—
Adjustments	(481)	—	(13)	—
Total	**15,485**	**100**	**1,097**	**100**

Selected Subsidiaries
Gas Natural (natural gas distribution, 45.3%)
Petronor EE. SS., SA (marketing, 86.58%)
Repsol Butano, SA (gas distribution)
Repsol Comercial de Productos Petroliferos SA (marketing, 96.93%)
Repsol Derivados, SA (specialty chemicals, 99.96%)
Repsol Distribución, SA (lubricants, 99.96%)
Repsol Exploración (exploration and production)
Repsol Naviera Vizcaína, SA (sea transport, 99.54%)
Repsol Oil International, LTD (crude oil and products trading, Channel Islands, 99.96%)
Repsol Petróleo (refining, 99.96%)
Repsol Química SA (chemicals)
Repsol International Finance BV (property holding, The Netherlands)

KEY COMPETITORS

Amoco	ENI	Pennzoil
Ashland, Inc.	Exxon	Petrobrás
Atlantic Richfield	Imperial Oil	Petrofina
British Petroleum	Koch	Phillips Petroleum
Broken Hill	Mobil	Royal Dutch/Shell
Caltex Petroleum	Norsk Hydro	Sun Company
Chevron	Occidental	Texaco
Coastal	Oryx	Total
DuPont	PDVSA	Unocal
Elf Aquitaine	PEMEX	USX–Marathon

HOW MUCH

	Annual Growth	1984	1985	1986	1987	1988	1989	1990	1991	1992	1993
Sales ($ mil.)	9.5%	—	—	—	8,972	8,709	9,746	15,435	17,974	17,047	15,485
Net income ($ mil.)	5.1%	—	—	—	415	494	589	709	727	626	560
Income as % of sales		—	—	—	4.6%	5.7%	6.0%	4.6%	4.0%	3.7%	3.6%
Earnings per share ($)	5.5%	—	—	—	1.38	1.65	1.96	2.37	2.42	2.09	1.90
Stock price – high ($)	—	—	—	—	—	—	24.88	30.38	27.25	30.75	31.38
Stock price – low ($)	—	—	—	—	—	—	16.25	20.13	20.75	20.88	22.25
Stock price – close ($)	7.6%	—	—	—	—	—	23.00	21.50	25.00	24.00	30.88
P/E – high	—	—	—	—	—	—	13	13	11	15	17
P/E – low	—	—	—	—	—	—	8	9	9	10	12
Dividends per share (Pta)	—	—	—	—	—	—	0.00	0.64	0.67	0.77	0.62
Book value per share (Pta)	2.2%	—	—	—	—	—	11.29	14.18	15.53	13.95	12.30
Employees	0.6%	—	—	—	—	19,077	19,171	21,284	20,848	19,632	18,797

1993 Year-end:
Debt ratio: 43.9%
Return on equity: 14.2%
Cash (mil.): $956
Current ratio: 0.99
Long-term debt (mil.): $1,320
No. of shares (mil.): 300
Dividends
 Yield: 2.0%
 Payout: 32.6%
Market value (mil.): $9,263

Stock Price History High/Low 1989–93

REUTERS HOLDINGS PLC

"How oft, as through the news we go,/When breakfast leaves an hour to loiter,/We quite forget the thanks we owe/To Reuter."

This 19th-century verse paid homage to the importance Reuters achieved as a general news agency. But the company began as a financial information distributor and in the 1990s is once more the premier source of financial news through its more than 220,000 computer terminals in 150 nations.

This network is also a trading venue — Instinet. Instinet offers an alternative to auction exchanges and is gaining market share against Nasdaq because it offers an unregulated anonymity that traders find attractive.

Reuters controls 95% of the electronic systems for spot foreign exchange trading with its Dealing 2000 foreign exchange system, which matches bids with asked currency prices and went on-line in 1992. Reuters also sponsors GLOBEX, an international after-hours futures exchange developed with the Chicago Board of Trade and the Chicago Mercantile Exchange.

Reuters went public in 1984 but remains controlled by the companies that bought into Reuters as a trust in the 1940s. These companies control the "Founders Share," which allows them to prevent anyone from gaining control of more than 30% of Reuters shares and to ensure that the company hews to the ideals embodied in the Reuter Trust Principles, which are intended to preserve the company's journalistic integrity, its tradition of dealing honorably with clients, and its leading position in the information business.

In 1850, as the Paris-Berlin telegraph line crept toward completion, Paul Julius Reuter, a former bookseller and sometime news correspondent, saw a chance to scoop his competitors. He first used carrier pigeons to bridge the telegraph gap between Aachen, Germany, and Brussels, Belgium. When the gap narrowed, he used gallopers on horseback. Reuter's business was briefly successful.

Moving to London in 1851, just as the first English Channel cable was laid, Reuter began telegraphing stock quotes between Paris and London and selling them to financial institutions. Coverage expanded to agricultural information and then general news, and the company grew with the British Empire. In 1865 Reuter's Telegram Co. was organized as a limited company in order to capitalize a proprietary North Sea cable to Germany. The Duke of Saxe-Coburg-Gotha (Germany; a relative of the British royal family) dubbed Reuter a baron in 1871.

Reuter ceded management to his son Herbert in 1878 and died in 1899. Herbert made the disastrous decision to establish Reuter's Bank (1913). In 1915, under pressure of anti-German feeling due to WWI, as well as the death of his wife and estrangement from his son, Herbert committed suicide.

Under successor Roderick Jones the company changed its name to Reuters Ltd. (1916) and sold the bank (1917). Following its founder's lead in exploiting new technology, Reuters started using radios and teleprinters in the 1920s. But the company suffered in the Depression, and its efforts to keep on top of the deteriorating international scene as WWII approached were insupportably expensive. After a managerial crisis that led Jones to resign, the UK government persuaded a British newspaper group to buy Reuters in 1941.

In the 1950s Reuters experienced problems as the empire broke up and it had to contend with the sometimes restrictive press rules of the new governments. It needed a new twist to remain profitable.

In 1964 Reuters gained non-US rights to Ultronic Systems Corporation's electronic stock reporting system, Stockmaster. The company's return to financial reporting had begun. In 1973, after currency exchange rates began to float, Reuters launched its Monitor electronic marketplace, which kept track of the foreign exchange market. Monitor Dealing, introduced in 1981, enabled dealers to trade currencies on-line.

With computer-based businesses dominating its general news services, Reuters went public in 1984 as Reuters Holdings PLC. Since then the company has acquired numerous on-line related services and gone into multimedia.

In this effort it has been so successful that in 1993 it unloaded some of its cash in a stock repurchase program and went on a buying spree that included Citicorp's Quotron. Reuters formed an agricultural information service with Farmland Industries in 1994.

Nasdaq symbol: RTRSY (ADR)
Fiscal year ends: December 31

Chairman: Sir Christopher A. Hogg, age 57,
£112,000 pay
CEO: Peter J. D. Job, age 52, £435,000 pay
Finance Director: Robert O. Rowley, age 44,
£267,000 pay
Editor-in-Chief: Mark W. Wood, age 41,
£250,000 pay
Director of Personnel and Quality Programmes:
Patrick A. V. Mannix
President, Reuters America: Brian M. D.
Vaughan
Auditors: Price Waterhouse

HQ: 85 Fleet St., London EC4P 4AJ, UK
Phone: +44-(0)71-250-1122
Fax: +44-(0)71-510-4064 (Corp. Relations)
US HQ: Reuters America Inc., 1700 Broadway,
New York, NY 10019
US Phone: 212-603-3300
US Fax: 212-247-0346

Reuters has more than 223,000 financial news
terminals in 150 countries.

	1993 Sales	
	$ mil.	% of total
Europe, Middle East & Africa	1,604	62
Asia/Pacific	570	22
Americas	422	16
Adjustments	177	—
Total	**2,773**	**100**

	1993 Sales	
	$ mil.	% of total
Information products	2,002	72
Transaction products	583	21
Media products	188	7
Total	**2,773**	**100**

Selected Products

Information
Commodities 2000
Decision 2000 (fixed-income securities market database)
Securities 2000 (market database)
Money 2000 (foreign exchange and money markets
information service)
Reuter Company Newsyear (equities news database)
Reuter East European Briefing
Reuter Technical Analysis (currency and commodities
market software)
The Reuter Terminal
Triarch 2000 (trading room system)

Transaction	**Media**
Dealing 2000	Reuter News Graphics Service
GLOBEX	Reuter World Service
Instinet	Reuters Televisions

ADP	McGraw-Hill
Agence France Press	Media General
Associated Press	Nasdaq
Bloomberg	New York Times
Dow Jones	NYSE
Dun & Bradstreet	Times Mirror
General Electric	Tribune
H&R Block	Turner Broadcasting
Knight-Ridder	United Press Intl.

Stock prices are for ADRs ADR = 3 shares	9-Year Growth	1984	1985	1986	1987	1988	1989	1990	1991	1992	1993
Sales ($ mil.)	23.6%	413	627	921	1,409	1,815	1,948	2,642	2,742	2,374	2,773
Net income ($ mil.)	26.1%	55	79	119	177	241	296	400	429	395	442
Income as % of sales	—	13.2%	12.5%	12.9%	12.6%	13.3%	15.2%	15.1%	15.7%	16.6%	16.0%
Earnings per share ($)	24.6%	0.19	0.29	0.44	0.21	0.88	1.19	1.44	1.54	1.41	1.38
Stock price – high ($)	—	5.31	8.09	12.72	22.72	15.31	26.13	35.56	29.06	34.56	42.56
Stock price – low ($)	—	4.22	4.97	7.56	10.44	11.56	14.13	16.06	17.88	27.19	27.69
Stock price – close ($)	25.7%	5.03	8.09	12.47	13.84	14.19	24.81	20.25	28.88	31.88	39.50
P/E – high	—	28	28	29	108	17	22	25	19	25	27
P/E – low	—	22	17	17	50	13	12	11	12	19	17
Dividends per share ($)	—	0.00	0.07	0.10	0.35	0.24	0.28	0.41	0.45	0.54	0.61
Book value per share ($)	20.5%	0.65	0.96	0.96	1.26	1.76	2.39	3.68	4.63	4.49	3.47
Employees	18.0%	50,300	71,500	103,100	141,300	169,100	194,800	200,900	201,800	207,600	223,700

1993 Year-end:
Debt ratio: 19.1%
Return on equity: 38.9%
Cash (mil.): $885
Current ratio: 1.24
Long-term debt (mil.): $59
No. of shares (mil.): 277
Dividends
  Yield: 1.4%
  Payout: 35.0%
Market value (mil.): $10,922

Stock Price History
High/Low 1984–93

RHÔNE-POULENC S.A.

When the French government decided to start selling off the family jewels (its state-owned conglomerates), Rhône-Poulenc was at the top of the list. France's #1 chemical company, and the 8th largest worldwide, was privatized in 1993. As a result, nearly all of the state's 43.4% stake was sold, bringing on board 2.9 million new shareholders. In 1994 about 54% of the company was owned by the public and institutions, 19% by a group of banks, 4% by employees, and 3% by the state.

The company has 5 core businesses: health, organic and inorganic intermediate products, specialty chemicals, fibers and polymers, and agrochemicals. Rhône-Poulenc operates in over 140 countries, and 59% of sales are derived from outside France.

The 1990 merger of its drug business with Rorer, creating Rhône-Poulenc Rorer (69% owned by Rhône-Poulenc), has played a key role in the company's sales growth. Health products accounted for about 41% of 1994 sales, up from 24% in 1989. Based in the US, Rhône-Poulenc Rorer reduced its nonprescription drug sector in 1993, selling Maalox antacid to Ciba-Geigy.

Rhône-Poulenc plans to market new anti-cancer drugs and to team up in joint ventures with DuPont and other drug firms in Asia. Still heavily saddled with debt, it planned to unload nearly $180 million worth of assets in 1994. Strapped for cash, the company had to pass on a tempting opportunity to buy American Cyanamid in that same year.

The product of a merger between Société Chimique des Usines du Rhône and Poulenc Frères, Rhône-Poulenc has continued to expand through mergers and acquisitions.

Etienne Poulenc, a pharmacist, had bought a Parisian apothecary in 1858. Poulenc began making pharmaceuticals and collaborated with drug company Comptoir des Textiles Artificielles (CTA).

Société Chimique des Usines du Rhône began producing dyes in Lyon in 1895. In 1919 Usines du Rhône launched Rhodia, a Brazilian arm that made perfumes for the famed carnival and grew to be Brazil's largest chemical company. Faced with German competition in Europe, Usines du Rhône switched to making specialty chemicals and then merged with CTA (1922) and Poulenc (1928).

Rhône-Poulenc developed new drugs, including antibiotics and antihistamines, and increased fiber production. Growth resumed after WWII, and the company acquired Theraplix (drugs, France, 1956), 50% of Institut Mérieux (drugs, France, 1968), and Progil and Pechiney–St. Gobain (basic and agricultural chemicals, France, 1969). By 1970 Rhône-Poulenc dominated the French chemical industry and was the 3rd largest chemical company in Europe.

In the 1970s protectionist-tariff lowering exposed Rhône-Poulenc to international competition at home. By licensing the US marketing rights of Thorazine, a tranquilizer, to SmithKline, the company failed to capitalize on the drug's success. Between 1980 and 1982 Rhône-Poulenc lost over FF3.1 billion. In 1982 the Mitterrand government nationalized the company.

The government turned to 39-year-old Loïk Le Floch-Prigent. Le Floch changed managers, eliminated poorly performing units, cut the payroll, and returned Rhône-Poulenc to profitability. In 1986 Jean-René Fourtou took over from Le Floch. Fourtou sold 20 businesses and bought more than 30, including Union Carbide's agricultural chemical operations (1986) and Stauffer's industrial chemical business (1987).

Rhône-Poulenc merged its drug businesses with Rorer in 1990 (pharmaceuticals, US), paying $2 billion for majority control. Also in 1990 the French government transferred to Rhône-Poulenc 35% of Roussel-Uclaf, France's 3rd largest drug producer.

In 1991 Rhône-Poulenc's vaccine division, Pasteur Mérieux, joined in partnership with Merck & Co. to develop multivaccines for children. The company also sold its media business, Rhône-Poulenc Systèmes, to Boeder AG and its health-food company, Diététique et Santé, to Sandoz. To boost its presence in the Far East, the company opened a plastics factory in Taiwan and a chemical factory in South Korea.

The newly privatized Rhône-Poulenc expanded into biotechnology in 1993 by buying 37% of Applied Immune Science as part of a cooperative research pact in cell and gene therapy. In 1994 the company took over Cooper, France's #2 OTC drug distributor.

NYSE symbol: RP (ADR)
Fiscal year ends: December 31

Chairman and CEO: Jean-René Fourtou, age 52
VC: Jean-Marc Bruel, age 56
SEVP and CFO: Jean-Pierre Tirouflet, age 41
Group SVP Human Resources: René Pénisson, age 50
President and COO, Rhône-Poulenc Inc. (US): Peter Neff
Auditors: Coopers & Lybrand

WHERE

HQ: 25, quai Paul Doumer, 92408 Courbevoie Cedex, France
Phone: +33-1-47-68-12-34
Fax: +33-1-47-68-19-11
US HQ: Rhône-Poulenc Inc., CN 5266, Princeton, NJ 08543-5266
US Phone: 610-454-8000
US Fax: 610-454-3573

Rhône-Poulenc operates more than 200 production and research facilities, principally in France, Austria, Brazil, Germany, Spain, Switzerland, the UK, and the US.

	1993 Sales	
	FF mil.	% of total
France	38,715	41
North America	21,732	23
Brazil	5,425	6
Other Europe	23,558	25
Other countries	5,103	5
Adjustments	(13,969)	—
Total	**80,564**	**100**

WHAT

	1993 Sales		1993 Operating Income	
	FF mil.	% of total	FF mil.	% of total
Health	33,720	41	5,694	83
Organic/inorganic intermediates	14,093	17	(78)	—
Specialty chemicals	12,822	15	559	8
Fibers & polymers	11,234	14	56	1
Agrochemicals	9,948	12	512	8
Other	945	1	(858)	—
Adjustments	(2,198)	—	28	—
Total	**80,564**	**100**	**5,913**	**100**

Health
Over-the-counter drugs
Plasma derivatives
Prescription drugs
Vaccines
Veterinary drugs

Organic and Inorganic Intermediates
Phenol and derivatives
Phosphates
Silicates

Specialty Chemicals
Fine organics

Food ingredients
Silicones

Fibers and Polymers
Engineering plastics
Films
Synthetic fibers and yarns

Agrochemicals
Herbicides
Insecticides
Seed protection and genetics

KEY COMPETITORS

Abbott Labs	Eastman	Monsanto
BASF	Chemical	Sandoz
Baxter	FMC	Sherwin-Williams
Bayer	Formosa Plastics	SmithKline
Bristol-Myers	Glaxo	Beecham
Squibb	W. R. Grace	Union Carbide
Ciba-Geigy	Hercules	Warner-Lambert
Dow Chemical	Hoechst	Wellcome
DuPont	Imperial Chemical	

HOW MUCH

$=FF5.90 (Dec. 31, 1993)	Annual Growth	1984	1985	1986	1987	1988	1989	1990	1991	1992	1993
Sales (FF mil.)	5.2%	51,207	56,102	52,694	56,160	65,334	73,068	78,810	83,817	81,709	80,564
Net income (FF mil.)	(6.5%)	1,755	2,058	1,912	2,193	2,878	3,016	1,097	1,227	1,516	962
Income as % of sales	—	3.4%	3.7%	3.6%	3.9%	4.4%	4.1%	1.4%	1.5%	1.9%	1.2%
Earnings per share (FF)	(15.5%)	—	—	—	11	15	15	5	5	6	4
Stock price – high (FF)[1]	—	—	—	159	118	135	155	122	124	168	169
Stock price – low (FF)[1]	—	—	—	86	70	64	112	48	58	116	125
Stock price – close (FF)[1]	6.8%	—	—	94	85	130	115	59	119	132	149
P/E – high	—	—	—	—	10	9	10	24	24	26	44
P/E – low	—	—	—	—	6	4	7	9	11	18	33
Dividends per share (FF)	(3.0%)	—	—	—	2.88	3.75	4.38	2.63	2.63	3.00	2.40
Book value per share (FF)	—	—	—	—	—	—	—	—	—	—	—
Employees	0.8%	—	—	77,166	82,500	79,670	86,024	91,571	89,051	83,283	81,678

1993 Year-end:
Debt ratio: 46.9%
Return on equity: 3.2%
Cash (bil.): FF6,579
Long-term debt (mil.): FF21,642
No. of shares (mil.): 252
Dividends
  Yield: 1.6%
  Payout: 63.2%
Market value (mil.): $6,337
Sales (mil.): $13,632

Stock Price History[1]
High/Low 1986–93

[1] Participation certificates, 1986-1992; "A" shares 1993

RICOH COMPANY, LTD.

OVERVIEW

Ricoh is one of the world's largest makers and suppliers of electronic office equipment, including copiers, facsimile machines, data processing equipment, and related supplies. It is also a leader in photographic equipment. The company has a 20% share of the facsimile market in Japan, ahead of rival Canon. Ricoh, since its inception, has been interested in the world market and has looked overseas for growth. It has subsidiaries and affiliates on 4 continents.

The company is committed to office automation R&D and was the first company to produce a high-speed office fax machine and multifunctional digital copier. It also produces an integrated office machine that can fax, photocopy, scan, edit, print — and do instant translation from English to Japanese.

Ricoh has also directed its innovational energy toward improving the environment. Its subsidiary, Ricoh UK Products, has developed a chlorofluorocarbon-free process to remove and recycle selenium coatings from copier drums. For this effort the company received a Queen's Award for Environmental Achievement in fiscal year 1994. Ricoh has also recently developed a toner-removal process that will allow copy paper reuse.

WHEN

Ricoh began in 1936 as the Riken Kankoshi Company to promote and produce positive sensitive paper used to develop film. With Kiyoshi Ichimura at the helm, the company soon became the leader in the sensitized-paper market in Japan. In 1938 the company changed its name to Riken Optical Company and began making cameras. In 1940 it produced its first camera under the Ricoh brand.

Following WWII the company was fortunate to be allowed to reconstitute itself with Ichimura still at its head. By 1954 Ricoh cameras were the leading sellers in Japan and were also popular abroad. In 1955 the company entered the office machine market with its compact mimeograph machine, the Ricopy 101. This was followed in 1960 by the Ricoh Offset duplicator. In 1962 the company established its US subsidiary, Ricoh Industries U.S.A. (which became Ricoh of America, Inc. in 1970 and in 1987 all US production subsidiaries became Ricoh Corporation), which began marketing cameras but found a more lucrative market with copiers. However, no office machines were sold under the company name in the US; rather they were sold under agreement with Pitney Bowes and Savin, with those names on the Japanese machines.

In 1963 the company name was changed to Ricoh. It entered the new field of office computers in 1965 with its data-processing system, the Ricoh Typer Standard. That same year it introduced the Ricopy BS-1, which was an electrostatic coated-paper copier.

During the 1970s Ricoh debuted the world's first high-speed fascimile machine, the Rifax 600S, and an information retrieval system, the Rinac 1000 (1974).

In 1973 Ricoh established a 2nd US subsidiary in California to assemble copier supplies and parts, becoming the first Japanese company to produce copiers in the US. Its first plain paper copier, the Ricopy DT1200, was released in 1975. In 1976 it introduced the Ricoh Printer 40, a daisy wheel printer, and its first word processor, the Ricoh WP-1. Rapicom was established in 1978 in Japan to develop facsimile products.

During the 1960s and 1970s Ricoh continued to sell its products in the US with the Savin and Pitney Bowes brand names; in the early 1980s Ricoh began marketing its products under its own brand.

Throughout the 1980s the company expanded. In 1983 it introduced a new PC and its first laser printer. By 1984 Ricoh had 7% of the US copier market. Other 1980s products included networking system products, a color copier, 2 minicomputers developed with AT&T, and the IMAGIO system (in Japan), which used a digital method to produce copies and could also be used as an input/output station for electronic filing systems. Despite the rising yen, in the late 1980s Ricoh's overseas sales continued to grow and in 1988 exceeded its domestic sales for the first time.

In 1990 Ricoh introduced the Artage 800, the world's fastest digital full-color copier. In 1991 the IMAGIO MF530, Ricoh's 6-function digital copier, was unveiled. The company increased its leading market share for plain paper copiers in Japan in 1993. Because of corporate consolidation and product introductions, 1994 was the first year in which net income increased despite a net sales decrease.

Principal exchange: Tokyo
Fiscal year ends: March 31

President: Hiroshi Hamada
EVP: Kenji Hiruma
EVP; Chairman, Ricoh Corp. (US): Hisahi Kubo
EVP: Shimpei Watanabe
Executive Managing Director: Takao Nawate
Executive Managing Director: Kazuhiro Sakai
Executive Managing Director: Tatsuo Hirakawa
VC and CEO, Ricoh Corp. (US): Hisao Yuasa
President and COO, Ricoh Corp. (US): Eric L.
Steenburgh
SVP and Treasurer, Ricoh Corp. (US): Etsuo
Kobayashi
**VP Administrative Support Group, Ricoh Corp.
(US):** Ted Graske
Auditors: Arthur Andersen & Co.

HQ: 15-5, Minami-Aoyama 1-chome, Minato-ku,
Tokyo 107, Japan
Phone: +81-3-3479-3111
Fax: +81-3-3403-1578
US HQ: Ricoh Corporation, 5 Dedrick Place,
West Caldwell, NJ 07006
Phone: 201-882-2000
Fax: 201-882-2506

	1994 Sales	
	¥ (mil.)	% of total
Japan	719	74
North America	114	12
Europe	95	10
Other	40	4
Total	**968**	**100**

	1994 Sales	
	¥ (mil.)	% of total
Copiers & related supplies	545	56
Communications & information systems	269	28
Other businesses	154	16
	968	**100**

Selected Products

Copiers	Data Processing
FT8800 Series	**Equipment**
IMAGIO MF Series	LP-M32
Preter 500 and 550	RIFILE 31
	IFS66
Fax Machines	
FAX3500L	**Cameras**
FAX2500L	SHOTMASTER ZOOM 105
FAX800	PLUS

Selected Subsidiaries and Affiliates

Ricoh Asia Industry Ltd. (China)	Ricoh Electronics, Inc. (US)
Ricoh Australia Pty., Ltd.	Ricoh Industries France SA
Ricoh Canada Ltd.	Ricoh Keiki Co., Ltd.
Ricoh Corporation (US)	Ricoh Micro-
Ricoh Creative	electronics Co., Ltd.
Development Co., Ltd.	Ricoh Seiki Co., Ltd.
	Ricoh UK Holdings Ltd.

Brother	Hitachi	Pitney Bowes
Canon	3M	Polaroid
Casio	Minolta	Sanyo
Eastman Kodak	NEC	Sharp
Fuji Photo	Nikon	Siemens
GEC	Océ	Toshiba
Harris Corp.	Oki	Xerox
Hewlett-Packard	Olivetti	

$=¥112 (Dec. 31, 1993)	Annual Growth	1985	1986	1987	1988	1989	1990	1991	1992	1993	1994
Sales (¥ bil.)	6.6%	546	594	592	674	729	835	1,003	1,017	1,022	968
Net income (¥ bil.)	(6.1%)	17	15	11	17	18	16	14	2	5	10
Income as % of sales	—	3.1%	2.6%	1.8%	2.5%	2.4%	1.9%	1.4%	0.2%	0.5%	1.0%
Earnings per share (¥)	(7.9%)	30.6	27.2	20.9	28.1	26.7	23.9	20.5	3.1	7.7	14.6
Stock price – high (¥) [1]	—	1,190	1,160	1,130	1,440	1,430	1,340	1,330	855	728	837
Stock price – low (¥) [1]	—	809	794	755	636	1,010	1,120	686	575	402	527
Stock price – close (¥)[1]	(2.8%)	931	1,080	1,020	1,130	1,220	1,280	715	640	607	719
P/E – high	—	39	43	54	51	54	56	65	—	95	57
P/E – low	—	26	29	36	23	38	47	33	—	52	36
Dividends per share (¥)	2.5%	8.0	8.0	8.7	9.5	9.5	9.5	10.0	10.0	10.0	10.0
Book value per share (¥)	—	—	—	—	—	—	—	—	—	—	—
Employees	17.8%	—	—	—	—	37,000	45,000	46,000	47,000	48,000	48,000

1994 Year-end:
Debt ratio: 61.7%
Return on equity: 2.7%
Cash (bil.): ¥233
Long-term debt (bil.): ¥338
No. of shares (mil.): 651
Dividends
  Yield: 1.4%
  Payout: 68.4%
Market value (mil.): $4,548
Sales (mil.): $9,401

Stock Price History[1]
High/Low 1985–94

[1] Stock prices are for the prior calendar year.

ROBERT BOSCH GMBH

It's stop and go at Robert Bosch, the world's leading maker of antilock braking and fuel injection systems. The Stuttgart-based company, the world's largest independent auto components maker, has not been able to get up to speed lately as demand in Western Europe and Japan has slowed. In 1993 its sales dropped for the first time since 1967.

In response Bosch has cut employment, reducing its work force by about 13,000 in 1993, with about 3/4 of the cuts occurring in Germany. The company has also taken a page out of its Japanese competitors' training manuals by instituting team-oriented work groups. In addition, it continues to invest heavily in R&D. It has unveiled Vehicle Dynamics Control, designed to improve road handling; United Airbag Systems, its joint venture with Morton International, is developing side-impact airbags.

Bosch also makes telecommunications equipment and owns 50% of Bosch-Siemens Hausgeräte, a European appliance leader. Bosch's Blaupunkt unit is a major car audio manufacturer.

The Robert Bosch Foundation, a charitable organization, owns 92% of the company, and the Bosch family owns 8%.

Self-taught electrical engineer Robert Bosch opened a Stuttgart workshop in 1886 and, in the next year, produced the world's first alternator for a stationary engine. In 1897 his company produced the world's first automobile alternator, beginning a series of electrical automotive product launches, including spark plugs (1902), starters (1912), and regulators (1913). Bosch believed in treating employees well and shortened their workday to 8 hours (extraordinary for 1906).

US operations begun in 1909 were confiscated in WWI as part of a trade embargo against Germany. Bosch survived the German depression of the 1920s, introduced power tools (1928) and appliances (1933), and bought Blaupunkt (car radios, 1933). Growth in German industrial and military demand for the company's products continued from the 1930s until WWII. Robert Bosch died in 1942, leaving 90% of his company to charity.

Bosch suffered severe damage in WWII, and its US operations were again confiscated. The company rebuilt its plants and enjoyed growing demand for its appliances and automotive products as postwar incomes increased worldwide. In 1963 Hans Merkle took control at Bosch. Because Merkle believed fuel efficiency and pollution control would be important issues in the future, Bosch invested large sums to develop electronic automotive components that raised gas mileage and lowered emissions. Bosch made the world's first electronic fuel injection system in 1967, equipping Volkswagen Beetles to satisfy California's new, stringent emission standards. In the same year Bosch and Siemens (West Germany) formed Bosch-Siemens Hausgeräte to manufacture appliances.

The oil crisis of the 1970s increased awareness of fuel efficiency, benefiting sales of Bosch's electronic fuel injection systems. In 1974 Bosch reentered the US, buying a plant in Charleston, South Carolina, to make fuel injection systems. That same year Bosch launched the first electronic ignition. The company introduced the first antilock braking system (ABS) in 1978.

A 1984 strike against Bosch in Germany disrupted automobile production throughout Europe and resulted in 38.5-hour workweeks for Bosch employees. By the end of the 1980s, electronic fuel injection was found in most new cars, and ABS was standard in most luxury cars. In the late 1980s the company developed a technology for multiplexing (employing one wire to replace many by using semiconductor controllers) in automobiles, established it as an industry standard, and licensed it to chipmakers Intel (US), Philips (the Netherlands), and Motorola (US). Throughout the 1980s and into the 1990s, Bosch acquired various telecommunications companies, including equipment and systems manufacturers.

In 1992 Bosch set up Diesel Technology with Penske Transportation (51% owned by Bosch) to develop and manufacture diesel injector equipment for heavy-duty commercial vehicles.

In 1994 Bosch joined a consortium (which includes Siemens, BMW, Daimler-Benz, and Volkswagen) that will build the infrastructure in Germany to support an interactive traffic guidance system.

Private company
Fiscal year ends: December 31

Chairman: Hermann Scholl
VC and CFO: Friedrich Schiefer
Chairman and CEO, Robert Bosch Corporation (US): Rainer Hahn
VP Human Resources, Robert Bosch Corporation (US): Alfred G. Koestler
Auditors: Schitag, Schwäbische Treuhand Aktiengesellschaft

HQ: Robert Bosch Platz 1, Postfach 10 60 50, D-70049 Stuttgart, Germany
Phone: +49-711-811-0
Fax: +49-711-811-6630
US HQ: Robert Bosch Corporation, 2800 S. 25th Ave., Broadview, IL 60153
US Phone: 708-865-5200
US Fax: 708-865-5203

Bosch has operations in 27 countries.

	1993 Sales	
	DM mil.	% of total
Europe	26,617	82
The Americas	3,947	12
Asia, Africa & Australia	1,905	6
Total	**32,469**	**100**

	1993 Sales	
	DM mil.	% of total
Automotive equipment	16,140	49
Communications technology	7,826	24
Consumer goods	6,719	21
Capital goods	1,784	6
Total	**32,469**	**100**

Automotive Equipment
Antilock braking, chassis, and safety systems
Bodywork electrics and electronics
Diesel fuel injection equipment
Lighting technology
Management systems for gasoline engines
Mobile communications
Semiconductors and electronic controls
Starters and alternators
Synthetic parts

Communications Technology
Car antennas
Mobile radio technology
Paging technology
Products and services for private communications networks
Space communication and satellite technology
Wireless and cable transmission technology

Consumer Goods
Heating technology
Household appliances and entertainment electronics (50% Bosch-Siemens Hausgeräte)
Power tools

Capital Goods
Assembly and handling equipment
Candy-making equipment
Hydraulic and pneumatic products
Industrial electronics
Packaging equipment

AlliedSignal	Fiat	Mannesmann
AT&T	Ford	Maytag
Black & Decker	GEC	Motorola
Borg-Warner	General	Navistar
Automotive	Electric	Nokia
Bose	General Motors	Pioneer
Breed	Giddings &	Rank
Chrysler	Lewis	Snap-on Tools
Cooper Industries	Ingersoll-Rand	Stanley Works
Cummins Engine	ITT	Tenneco
Dana	Koç	Textron
Eaton	Litton	Thomson SA
Electrolux	Industries	Whirlpool
Emerson	Loral	Yamaha

$=DM1.74 (Dec. 31, 1993)	9-Year Growth	1984	1985	1986	1987	1988	1989	1990	1991	1992	1993
Sales (DM mil.)	6.5%	18,373	21,223	23,807	25,365	27,675	30,588	31,824	33,600	34,432	32,469
Net income (DM mil.)[1]	(0.5%)	446	402	454	825	554	626	560	540	512	426
Income as % of sales	—	2.4%	1.9%	1.9%	3.3%	2.0%	2.0%	1.8%	1.6%	1.5%	1.3%
Employees	2.5%	131,882	140,374	158,142	161,343	165,732	174,742	179,636	181,498	177,183	164,506

1993 Year-end:
Debt ratio: 12.6%
Return on equity: 5.3%
Cash (mil.): DM6,761
Current ratio: 1.47
Long-term debt (mil.): DM1,201
Sales (mil.): $18,698

Net Income (DM mil.) 1984–93

[1] Includes minority interests

ROCHE GROUP

OVERVIEW

Swiss-based Roche is a leading pharmaceutical producer that also makes vitamins and supplies fragrances. Among the company's top products are 15 that each has annual sales of more than $100 million.

Once largely dependent on its drug Valium, the company continues to seek new drugs by investing in R&D (15% of sales in 1993), acquiring several companies, and entering into biotechnology partnerships.

Roche also owns 66% of Genentech, a leading California genetic engineering firm. Roche is providing Genentech with much-needed funding in exchange for access to a potentially prolific product pipeline. Until the end of June 1995, Roche has an option to buy the rest of Genentech at escalating prices.

In 1994, during a climate of cost-cutting and consolidation in the pharmaceutical industry, Roche agreed to purchase Syntex, a suffering US pharmaceutical company, for $5.3 billion, surprising a number of industry analysts. This moves creates the 4th largest drug company in the world and solidifies Roche's position in North America.

Roche was created in 1989 as a holding company for F. Hoffmann-La Roche and Sapac, which had been separate but linked companies. The Roche family has retained a controlling interest in the company for a century since its founding in 1894.

WHEN

Fritz Hoffmann-La Roche, backed by his family's wealth, began making pharmaceuticals in a lab in Basel, Switzerland, in 1894. At the time drug compounds were mixed at pharmacies, resulting in a lack of uniformity. Hoffmann was not a chemist but was committed to standardization for pharmaceuticals and their packaging. He saw the potential for mass-produced, branded drugs.

Just prior to WWI, after years of financial difficulty, Hoffmann was selling Thiocal (cough medicine), Digalen (digitalis extract), and other products on 4 continents under the Roche name. During WWI the Allies suspected that a Roche factory in Grenzach, Germany, was supporting the Germans. Concurrently, the Germans suspected the company of supplying the French. The Bolsheviks seized Roche's St. Petersburg facility. Devastated by the war, in 1919 Hoffmann sold company shares outside the family.

Between the wars Roche expanded, synthesizing vitamins C, A, and E, and eventually became the world's leading vitamin manufacturer. As volume grew, the company built plants and research centers internationally, including a facility in Nutley, New Jersey (1928). Expecting war, Roche had split in 2 in 1926, transferring its more distant operations into Sapac, a holding company.

Roche continued to develop successful drugs, including blockbuster tranquilizers Librium (1960) and Valium (1963). Valium was the world's best-selling drug until 1981, when SmithKline's Tagamet took the lead.

In the 1970s several governments accused Roche of Librium and Valium price gouging. Roche finally agreed to price restraints. In 1976 the company was found guilty of vitamin price fixing. In the same year a dioxin cloud escaped from a company factory in Italy, killing thousands of animals and forcing the evacuation of hundreds of families. Roche was criticized for its slow response.

When Valium went off patent in the US in 1985, Roche's pharmaceutical sales fell by nearly 50% in the next 2 years as cheaper imitations flooded the market. The company maintained its large US sales force by selling Glaxo's Zantac.

Roche purchased Fritzsche, Dodge & Olcott, a US flavorings company, in 1990 from BASF. In 1991 Roche paid $300 million to Cetus for its PCR (polymerase chain reaction) technology, which rapidly duplicates strands of genetic material.

By 1992 Roche's Nicholas company (purchased from Sara Lee in 1991) reported being one of the biggest over-the-counter drug businesses in Europe. Roche completed purchasing Fisons Consumer Health in the UK and Ireland in 1993, strengthening its move into the over-the-counter market.

Roche announced plans in 1995 to merge its clinical laboratory operations with those of National Health Laboratories Holdings. The resulting public company will have annual revenues of $1.7 billion and be the largest medical test lab operator in the US. Roche will retain a 49.9% stake in the company.

OTC symbol: ROHHY (ADR)
Fiscal year ends: December 31

WHO

Chairman and CEO: Fritz Gerber, age 65
COO and Head of Pharmaceuticals Division:
Armin M. Kessler
Finance and Accounting: Henri B. Meier
President and CEO, Hoffmann-La Roche (US):
Patrick J. Zenner
**SVP Finance, Human Resources and
Administration, Hoffmann-La Roche (US):**
Martin F. Spadler
Auditors: Price Waterhouse

WHERE

HQ: POB CH-4002, Basel, Switzerland
Phone: +41-61-688-8888
Fax: +41-61-691-0014
US HQ: Hoffmann-La Roche Inc.,
340 Kingsland St., Nutley, NJ 07110-1199
US Phone: 201-235-5000
US Fax: 201-562-2208

The company has operations in 54 countries.

	1993 Sales	
	SF mil.	% of total
North America	5,609	39
Asia	1,923	13
Latin America	1,208	8
Switzerland	315	2
Other Europe	4,775	33
Other countries	485	3
Total	**14,315**	**100**

WHAT

	1993 Sales	
	SF mil.	% of total
Pharmaceuticals	7,810	54
Vitamins & fine chemicals	3,270	23
Diagnostics	1,712	12
Fragrances & flavors	1,436	10
Other	87	1
Total	**14,315**	**100**

Pharmaceuticals
Anti-infectives
  Globocef
  Loceryl
  Quinodis
  Rocephin
Cardiovascular
  Inhibace
Central nervous system
  Aurorix
  Dormicum/Versed
  Valium
Dermatology
  Roaccutane
  Tigason
Oncology and virology
  Hivid
  Neupogen
  Roferon-A

Rheumatology and
  metabolic disorders
  Rocaltrol
  Tilcotil

**Vitamins and Fine
Chemicals**
Animal health products
Feed additives
Vitamins

Diagnostics
Analytical systems
Drug abuse testing

Fragrances and Flavors
Consumer and industrial
  goods
Flavorings and perfumes

KEY COMPETITORS

Abbott Labs	Corning	Novo Nordisk
American Home	DuPont	Pfizer
Products	Eli Lilly	Rhône Poulenc
Amgen	Glaxo	Sandoz
Bayer	Hoechst	Schering-Plough
BASF	IFF	SmithKline
Bristol-Myers	Johnson &	Beecham
Squibb	Johnson	Takeda
Chiron	Merck	Upjohn
Ciba Geigy		

HOW MUCH

$=SF1.49 (Dec. 31, 1993)	9-Year Growth	1984	1985	1986	1987	1988	1989	1990	1991	1992	1993
Sales (SF mil.)	6.3%	8,267	8,940	7,822	7,705	8,690	9,814	9,670	11,451	12,953	14,315
Net income (SF mil.)	23.2%	380	452	416	482	642	852	948	1,482	2,124	2,478
Income as % of sales	—	4.6%	5.1%	5.3%	6.3%	7.4%	8.7%	9.8%	12.9%	16.4%	17.3%
Earnings per share (SF)	22.3%	47	55	51	59	78	101	113	172	246	287
Stock price – high (SF)[1]	—	1,106	1,170	1,383	1,523	1,271	2,082	2,235	2,750	4,180	6,430
Stock price – low (SF)[1]	—	834	819	927	824	871	1,248	1,589	1,690	2,590	3,830
Stock price – close (SF)[1]	25.2%	834	1,170	1,104	903	1,248	1,761	1,854	2,610	4,170	6,310
P/E – high	—	24	21	27	26	16	21	20	16	17	22
P/E – low	—	18	15	18	14	11	16	14	10	11	13
Dividends per share (SF)	10.2%	20.0	12.6	12.6	13.0	15.0	18.6	20.6	28.0	37.0	48.0
Book value per share (SF)	9.3%	931	974	1,019	1,066	1,234	1,380	1,573	1,673	1,860	2,077
Employees	2.2%	46,199	45,477	46,513	47,498	49,671	50,203	52,685	55,134	56,335	56,082

1993 Year-end:
Debt ratio: 22.9%
Return on equity: 14.6%
Cash (mil.): SF14,588
Long-term debt (mil.): SF4,498
No. of shares (mil.): 9
Dividends
  Yield: 0.8%
  Payout: 16.7%
Market value (mil.): $36,530
Sales (mil.): $9,607

**Stock Price History
High/Low 1984–93**

[1] Participation certificates

ROGERS COMMUNICATIONS INC.

Mr. Rogers has a big neighborhood. Ted Rogers's telecommunications conglomerate, Rogers Communications, covers most of Canada. Its Rogers Cantel Mobile Communications subsidiary (80% owned) is the only firm with authorization to provide a national cellular telephone service, and it operates Canada's largest. It provides services to 24 million people (82% of the total population of Canada).

Rogers Cable Systems has 14 cable television systems with more than 1.8 million subscribers. This subsidiary also owns and operates services for pay television and pay-per-view and owns a chain of more than 70 video rental stores in Canada.

Rogers Broadcasting owns 10 AM and 6 FM radio stations in Alberta, British Columbia, Manitoba, and Ontario, as well as CFMT-TV in Toronto (Canada's only multilingual TV station), and shares control of YTV, a specialty TV network for young people.

The company's 4th major unit, Unitel (32% owned), is in the telecommunications business. It is 48% owned by Canadian Pacific and 20% by AT&T. Unitel provides public switched-voice long distance and public and private high-speed data services.

In a major move Rogers Communications acquired rival cable TV and publishing firm Maclean Hunter in 1994, creating Canada's largest communications company.

At the age of 21, Edward Rogers was the first Canadian to transmit a radio signal across the Atlantic, in 1921. In 1925 he invented the radio amplifying tube, an electronic device that revolutionized the home-receiver industry throughout the world by doing away with the need for batteries and making AC-powered home radios practical for the first time. The Rogers family has had a knack for getting involved in history. Rogers's ancestors included England's first Protestant martyr in the reign of Queen Mary (killed in 1555) and one of the Mayflower Pilgrims.

The son of a wealthy businessman, the hard-driving Rogers founded the Rogers Majestic Corp. in Toronto in the mid-1920s to manufacture his radio tubes and established several radio broadcasting companies. His CFRB ("Canada's First Rogers Batteryless") station grew to command the country's largest radio audience.

In 1931 he was granted the first license to broadcast experimental television, but Rogers died in 1939 of overwork and a bleeding ulcer, leaving his family and his company in poor financial condition. The family soon lost control of CFRB.

At the time of his father's death, Ted Rogers was only 5. But even as a youngster he showed some business acumen, buying up shares of Standard Broadcasting, the owner of CFRB.

Sharing the innovative business drive of his father, Ted bought CHFI, a 940-watt Toronto radio station for C$85,000 in 1960. This station pioneered FM broadcasting at a time when only 5% of the Toronto audience had FM receivers.

Rogers moved into the cable TV business in the mid-1960s and quickly expanded beyond his home base of Toronto. In the 1970s he bought out 2 larger competitors, Premier Cablevision and Canadian Cablevision. By 1981, with the takeover of UA-Columbia Cablevision, he became the CEO of the world's largest cable TV company with over 2 million subscribers. The media conglomerate adopted the name Rogers Communications Inc. for the group's holding company in 1986.

Rogers pushed the boundaries of another new technology, mobile telephones, through his Rogers Cantel subsidiary in the late 1980s and won a license for Canadian nationwide coverage in 1992.

Then, displaying an ambition that has him compared to the other Ted south of the border, Ted Turner, Rogers took on one of Canada's most entrenched monopolies, the long distance telephone service of Bell Canada. By teaming up with Canadian Pacific Ltd. of Montreal to create Unitel, Rogers's long distance telephone company has taken a big slice out of Bell Canada's market.

Rogers underwent bypass surgery in 1992, but shows little sign of slowing down. His Rogers Communications paid $2.1 billion for Canadian communications rival Maclean Hunter in 1994. Following this purchase, the latest in a series of acquisitions and new investments, Rogers Communications's long-term debt stood at over $2 billion.

Principal exchange: Toronto
Fiscal year ends: December 31

Chairman: H. Garfield Emerson
VC: Philip B. Lind, C$400,000 pay
VC: George A. Fierheller
President and CEO: Edward S. Rogers, age 61,
  C$610,000 pay
SVP Cable TV: Colin D. Watson, C$580,000 pay
SVP Wireless Communications: David S.
  Gergacz, C$482,538 pay
SVP Finance and CFO: Graham W. Savage,
  C$450,000 pay
VP and General Counsel: David P. Miller
VP Human Resources: Don Smith
Auditors: KPMG Peat Marwick Thorne

HQ: Scotia Plaza, Ste. 6400, 40 King St. West,
  Box 1007, Toronto M5H 3Y2, Canada
Phone: 416-864-2349
Fax: 416-864-2375

	1993 Cable Subscribers	
Location	No.	% of total
Toronto	597,653	32
Vancouver	292,703	16
Grand River	175,419	9
Surrey	144,840	8
Ottawa	129,457	7
Calgary	110,533	6
Victoria	88,559	5
London	79,882	4
Fraser	78,882	4
Oshawa	73,937	3
Others	107,218	6
Total	**1,879,083**	**100**

	1993 Sales		1993 Operating Income	
	C$ mil.	% of total	C$ mil.	% of total
Wireless comm.	606	45	199	43
Cable televison	593	45	252	54
Broadcasting	137	10	15	3
Adjustments	—	—	(16)	—
Total	**1,336**	**100**	**450**	**100**

Major Products and Services
Cable television
Cellular and other wireless communications
Radio and television broadcasting
Telecommunications
Video stores

Major Subsidiaries
Maclean Hunter Ltd.
Rogers Broadcasting Ltd.
Rogers Cable T.V. Ltd.
Rogers Cablesystems Ltd.
Rogers Canada Inc.
Rogers Cantel Mobile Communications Inc. (80%)
Rogers Cantel Mobile Inc.
Rogers Ottawa Ltd./Lte.
Rogers Telecom Ltd.
Unitel Communications Holdings Inc. (32%)
Unitel Communications Inc.

Baton Broadcasting	New Brunswick Telephone
BC Telecom	Newfoundland Telephone
BCE	Quebecor
GTE	Saskatchewan
The Island Telephone	Telecommunications
Manitoba Telephone	Shaw Communications
Maritime Telegraph and	Thomson Corp.
Telephone	Torstar Corp.
Moffat Communications	Viacom

$=C$1.32 (Dec. 31, 1993)	Annual Growth	1984	1985	1986	1987	1988	1989	1990[1]	1991	1992	1993
Sales (C$ mil.)	25.8%	169	190	238	274	362	606	906	1,011	1,172	1,336
Net income (C$ mil.)	—	(35)	(23)	12	(25)	85	—	(106)	(60)	(180)	(287)
Income as % of sales	—	—	—	5.0%	—	23.5%	—	—	—	—	—
Earnings per share (C$)	—	(0.24)	(0.16)	0.01	(0.21)	0.56	6.67	(1.32)	(0.76)	(1.30)	(1.89)
Stock price – high (C$)	—	—	—	—	—	—	19.07	19.71	16.38	16.00	25.63
Stock price – low (C$)	—	—	—	—	—	—	7.54	7.50	8.50	12.75	15.88
Stock price – close (C$)	8.2%	—	—	—	—	—	16.80	8.00	14.50	15.50	23.00
P/E – high	—	—	—	—	—	—	(12.2)	—	—	—	—
P/E – low	—	—	—	—	—	—	—	—	—	—	—
Dividends per share (C$)	—	—	—	—	—	—	0.00	0.00	0.00	0.00	0.00
Book value per share (C$)	(38.4%)	—	—	—	—	—	4.10	2.28	0.93	1.07	0.59
Employees	—	—	—	—	—	—	—	—	—	—	6,540

1993 Year-end:
Debt ratio: 72.8%
Return on equity: —
Cash (mil.): $266
Long-term debt (mil.): $2,767
No. of shares (mil.): 280
Dividends
  Yield: —
  Payout: —
Market value (mil.): $4,679
Sales (mil.): $971

Stock Price History
High/Low 1989–93

[1] 16-month year

ROLLS-ROYCE PLC

OVERVIEW

London-based Rolls-Royce plc, the 3rd largest gas turbine (jet engine) maker in the world, behind General Electric and United Technologies' Pratt & Whitney, shares its name with the luxury automaker, but the 2 have been separate entities since the British government split them in 1971.

Besides manufacturing jet engines for both commercial and military use, Rolls-Royce constructs power plants and power distribution systems (including nuclear installations) and manufactures marine and oil and gas pumping equipment. For the year 1993 more than 70% of the company's sales were made overseas.

In the early 1990s Rolls-Royce's aerospace market was hurt by military spending cutbacks and a slump in the airline industry; in 1991 Rolls-Royce posted an 82% drop in profits. The company cut over 7,000 jobs in 1991, 5,000 in 1992, and 6,000 in 1993. The top 3 engine makers are currently in a dog fight for shares in the shrinking market for more expensive engines for wider planes and the future spare parts markets associated with these new engines.

To counter aerospace industry difficulties, Rolls-Royce has created a number of successful alliances, including ones with BMW and Westinghouse.

WHEN

In 1906 automobile and aviation enthusiast Charles S. Rolls and engineer Frederick H. Royce unveiled the Silver Ghost, an automobile that soon earned their newly founded company, Rolls-Royce Ltd., a reputation as the maker of the best car in the world.

A year after Rolls's death in 1910, Royce (an inveterate workaholic) suffered a breakdown. He continued to design Rolls-Royce engines from his home, but management of the company fell to Claude Johnson, who remained chief executive until 1926.

During WWI the company started making aircraft engines but afterward returned primarily to making cars, buying Bentley Motor Company in 1931. Development of aircraft engines continued on a more limited basis, and in 1933 Rolls-Royce introduced the Merlin, which powered the Spitfire, Hurricane, and Mustang fighters of WWII.

Under Ernest Hives (chief executive from 1936 to 1957), Rolls-Royce assumed production of the Whittle turbojet engine in 1941. Renamed the Welland, this engine powered the Gloster Meteor, the only Allied jet fighter in active service during WWII. The company's Avon turbojet powered the world's first commercial jet airliner, de Havilland's Comet.

Hives's successor, Sir Denning Pearson, realized that Rolls-Royce had to break into the lucrative US airliner market to stay alive. The company bought its main British competitor, Bristol-Siddley Engines, in 1966, acquiring with it the contract to build the engine for the Anglo-French Concorde. But US engine makers General Electric and Pratt & Whitney kept Rolls-Royce out of the US market until 1966, when the company won the contract to build the engine for Boeing's 747. Lockheed ordered the company's RB211 for its TriStar in 1968, but Rolls-Royce underestimated the project's technical and financial challenges and entered bankruptcy in 1971. The British government stepped in and nationalized the aerospace division, spinning off the automobile division to the public. The RB211 entered service on the TriStar in 1972. Later versions now power Boeing's 747, 757, and 767 airliners.

As part of the Thatcher government's industry privatization, Rolls-Royce aerospace went public in 1987. In a diversification effort the company bought Northern Engineering Industries (mining and marine equipment, power plants) in 1989. However, the company remained busy in aerospace, entering into a joint venture with BMW to build an aircraft engine plant in eastern Germany in 1990.

In 1991 Rolls-Royce completed a 1,000-megawatt power station in Rihand, India. The Persian Gulf War hurt Rolls-Royce; civilian air travel decreased, which reduced spare parts orders, and the sale of 4 steam turbine generators to Iraq was suspended.

As part of a joint venture, Rolls-Royce and BMW signed a deal in 1992 to provide 200 engines for Gulfstream's GV business jets. In 1993 this joint effort launched the BR710 engine for Gulfstream and Canadair for their long-range business jets. In 1994 the company said it would buy competitor Alliance Engine for $525 million. Also in 1994 it had 25% of new civil engine orders worldwide.

OTC symbol: RYCEY
Fiscal year ends: December 31

Chairman: Sir Ralph Robins, age 61
CEO: Terence Harrison, age 60
Finance Director: Michael Townsend, age 52
President and CEO, Rolls-Royce (US):
John Sanford
Corporate Financial Controller, Rolls-Royce (US): Ken Patterson
VP Human Resource Administration and General Counsel, Rolls-Royce (US):
Tom Dale
Auditors: KMPG Peat Marwick

WHERE

HQ: 65 Buckingham Gate,
London SW1E 6AT, UK
Phone: +44-(01)71-222-9020
Fax: +44-(01)71-233-1733
US HQ: Rolls-Royce Inc., 11911 Freedom Dr.,
Reston, VA 22090-5602
US Phone: 703-834-1700
US Fax: 703-709-6086

	1993 Sales	
	£ mil.	% of total
United States	1,151	33
UK	997	28
Asia	558	16
Africa	165	6
Canada	137	3
Other Europe	379	11
Other countries	131	3
Total	**3,518**	**100**

WHAT

	1993 Sales		1993 Operating Income	
	£ mil.	% of total	£ mil.	% of total
Aerospace	2,139	61	20	23
Industrial power	1,379	39	68	77
Total	**3,518**	**100**	**88**	**100**

Aerospace

Civilian Aircraft Engines	Military Aircraft Engines
BR710	Adour
BR715	EJ200
RB211-524	Pegasus
RB211-535	
Tay	**Helicopter Engines**
Trent	Gem 42
V2500	RB211
	RTM322

Industrial Power

Industrial power plants	Nuclear power equipment
Gas turbine systems	and plants
Marine equipment	Oil and gas equipment
	Power station equipment

KEY COMPETITORS

ABB	Halliburton	RTZ
Alcatel	Hitachi	SCECorp
Alsthom	Ingersoll-Rand	Schumberger
Allison	Mannesmann	Siemens
Engine	McDermott	Textron
Bechtel	Mitsubishi	Thyssen
Cooper	Nippon Steel	Toshiba
Industries	Peter Kiewit	United
Dresser	Sons'	Technologies
Fluor	Reliance	Westinghouse
GEC	Electric	

HOW MUCH

£=$1.48 (Dec. 31, 1993)	Annual Growth	1984	1985	1986	1987	1988	1989	1990	1991	1992	1993
Sales (£ mil.)	10.7%	1,409	1,601	1,802	2,059	1,973	2,962	3,670	3,515	3,562	3,518
Net income (£ mil.)[1]	13.6%	20	77	120	134	145	192	134	24	(202)	63
Income as % of sales	—	1.4%	4.8%	6.7%	6.5%	7.3%	6.5%	3.7%	0.7%	—	1.8%
Earnings per share (p)[1]	(17.5)	—	—	—	19	22	22	19	8	7	6
Stock price – high (p)	—	—	—	—	240	148	203	233	177	176	177
Stock price – low (p)	—	—	—	—	96	108	132	149	121	89	97
Stock price – close (p)	5.4%	—	—	—	119	132	183	161	127	116	163
P/E – high	—	—	—	—	13	7	9	12	21	27	30
P/E – low	—	—	—	—	5	5	6	8	15	13	16
Dividends per share (p)	(1.0%)	—	—	—	5.3	6.3	7.0	7.3	7.3	5.0	5.0
Book value per share (p)	7.8%	51	64	83	107	118	117	121	117	91	100
Employees	1.3%	40,900	41,700	42,000	41,600	40,400	64,900	64,200	57,100	51,800	45,800

1993 Year-end:
Debt ratio: 25.4%
Return on equity: 6.2%
Cash (mil.): £891
Long-term debt (mil.): £360
No. of shares (mil.): 1,221
Dividends
 Yield: 3.1%
 Payout: 84.0%
Market value (mil.): $2,935
Sales (mil.): $5,204

**Stock Price History
High/Low 1987–93**

[1] Including extraordinary items in 1991

ROYAL AHOLD NV

OVERVIEW

Like its Dutch ancestors, Royal Ahold is taking to the high seas to do business in the New World. The company is one of the Netherlands's largest retailers, but lately it has been planting more flags in the US as it continues to expand its supermarket operations in America. Royal Ahold operates more than 2,100 supermarkets and specialty stores in the Netherlands, Belgium, the Czech Republic, Portugal, and the US.

In the Netherlands the company operates the Albert Heijn supermarket chain (that country's largest) as well as liquor stores, confectionery stores, and health and beauty and natural products retailers. It also owns

an institutional food supply company, a pharmaceutical distributor, and 73% of Schuitema, one of Holland's largest wholesale food distributors.

In the US the company operates nearly 600 supermarkets in 14 eastern states through 6 chains, including BI-LO, Giant, and Tops. Overall it is the 6th largest grocery retailer in the US.

Royal Ahold has expanded internationally to find new markets outside its small home market. The company plans to continue to acquire US supermarkets, with a goal of becoming the largest supermarket retailer in the eastern US.

WHEN

In 1887 Albert Heijn and his wife took over his father's grocery store in Ootzaan, the Netherlands. With the Dutch economy booming, thanks to the contributions of the country's extensive colonial network, Heijn's store prospered, and he began to expand.

By the end of WWI the company had a chain of 50 Albert Heijn grocery stores in Holland. It also began providing private label products, including coffee, tea, and chocolate. In 1923 the company expanded into restaurants. The company weathered both the Depression and the Nazi invasion of the Netherlands, and by the end of WWII it had almost 250 stores. In 1948 the company went public on the Amsterdam Stock Exchange.

As retailing changed, so did the company. In 1952 it opened its first self-service store and in 1955 its first supermarket. Through acquisitions and internal growth Albert Heijn became the #1 grocery retailer in the Netherlands. The company also continued to diversify, acquiring the Meester meat-packing plant (1966) and opening a chain of liquor stores (Alberto, 1969).

In 1973 the company changed its name to Ahold nv to reflect its development into a holding company with a range of food-related businesses. In 1976 the company expanded outside the Netherlands, founding a supermarket chain, Cadadia, in Spain.

In 1977 Ahold established a presence in the US when it paid $60 million for BI-LO, a supermarket chain with 98 stores in the Southeast. In 1981 Ahold continued its US expansion, acquiring Pennsylvania-based Giant Food Stores for $35 million.

After struggling in Spain, Ahold exited the supermarket business there in 1985 when it sold its chain of Cadadia stores to British Dee. In 1987, in commemoration of its 100th anniversary, Ahold was granted the title Koninklijke (Dutch for "royal") by the Queen of the Netherlands.

While it was being crowned at home, Royal Ahold continued to expand in the US. In 1988 it acquired 85% of First National Supermarkets, which now operates the Finast and Edwards supermarket chains. The deal doubled the size of Ahold's US operations. Also in 1988 the company began acquiring Dutch food wholesaler Schuitema. Ahold continued its US expansion in 1991 when it acquired New York–based Tops Markets.

However, the company did not confine its growth to the US. In 1991 it founded Euronova, a food retail and distribution company in the Czech Republic, and in 1992 it acquired 49% of J.M.R.-Gestâo de Empresas de Retalho (JMR), a Portuguese food retailer. That same year Ahold introduced a plan in Holland to allow shoppers to earn shares in the company by shopping in its stores.

In 1993 Ahold began listing its ADR shares on the NYSE in an effort to become more widely recognized by the US investment community. That same year JMR acquired 2 Portuguese supermarket chains, Inô Supermarkets and Modelo.

In 1994 Ahold paid about $125 million for Red Food Stores, a Chattanooga-based supermarket chain with 55 stores in the southeastern US.

NYSE symbol: AHO (ADR)
Fiscal year ends: First Sunday in January

Chairman: J. H. Choufoer, age 67
President: C. H. van der Hoeven, age 46
EVP Human Resources and Netherlands Food
   Retailing: P. J. van Dun, age 56
SVP Finance: A. M. Meurs
EVP; President and CEO, Ahold USA:
   Robert Zwartendijk, age 54
CFO, Ahold USA: Joseph Harber
Auditors: Deloitte & Touche

WHERE

HQ: Koninklijke Ahold nv, Albert Heijnweg 1,
   Zaandam, 1500 EA Zaandam, The Netherlands
Phone: +31-75-59-57-75
Fax: +31-75-59-83-62
US HQ: Ahold USA, Inc., Morris Corporate
   Center 1, Building C, 300 Interpace Pkwy.,
   Parsippany, NJ 07054
US Phone: 201-299-6590
US Fax: 201-299-6591

Royal Ahold's US grocery stores operate in
Connecticut, Georgia, Maryland, Massachusetts,
New Hampshire, New York, North Carolina, Ohio,
Pennsylvania, Rhode Island, South Carolina,
Tennessee, Virginia, and West Virginia.

	1993 Sales	
	Fl mil.	% of total
The Netherlands	13,422	50
US	12,310	45
Other countries	1,361	5
Total	**27,093**	**100**

WHAT

	1993 Sales	
	Fl mil.	% of total
Food retailing	22,714	84
Other	4,379	16
Total	**27,093**	**100**

Retail Stores
Albert Heijn (supermarkets)
BI-LO (supermarkets, US)
De Tuinen (natural products)
Edwards (supermarkets, US)
Etos (health and beauty, the Netherlands and Belgium)
Finast (supermarkets, US)
Gall & Gall (liquor stores)
Giant Food Stores (supermarkets, US)
Jamin (confectionery)
Jerónimo Martins Retail (49%, supermarkets, Portugal)
Mana (supermarkets, Czech Republic)
Ter Huurne (Dutch-German border stores)
Tops Markets (supermarkets, US)

Other
Grootverbruik Ahold (institutional food supply)
Pragmacare (pharmaceutical distributor)
Schuitema (73%, grocery wholesaler)
VACO (prepared meals, Belgium)

KEY COMPETITORS

Aldi	Red Apple Group
American Stores	Safeway
Delhaize	Spar International
Demoulas Super Markets	Star Market
Food Lion	Stop & Shop
Giant Food	Tengelmann
Grand Union	TLC Beatrice
Great A&P	Vendex
J Sainsbury	Wakefern Food
Kroger	Wegman's Food Markets
Pathmark	Winn-Dixie
Publix	

HOW MUCH

$=Fl1.92 (Dec. 31, 1993)	9-Year Growth	1985	1986	1987	1988	1989	1990	1991	1992	1993	1994
Sales (Fl)	11.0%	10,603	11,597	10,864	11,067	14,638	17,075	16,920	20,122	21,594	27,093
Net income (Fl)	13.6%	109	122	132	131	146	195	243	276	305	343
Income as % of sales	—	1.0%	1.1%	1.2%	1.2%	1.0%	1.1%	1.4%	1.4%	1.4%	1.3%
Earnings per share (Fl)	8.3%	1.44	1.60	1.53	1.51	1.68	2.03	2.42	2.72	2.94	2.95
Stock price – high (Fl)[1]	—	14.75	18.82	25.68	25.07	22.55	36.08	36.01	42.71	44.35	49.90
Stock price – low (Fl)[1]	—	10.53	10.11	14.83	13.48	14.60	22.35	27.04	29.60	35.08	42.30
Stock price – close (Fl)[1]	16.8%	11.62	17.13	28.75	14.75	22.43	33.93	33.25	38.90	43.31	46.90
P/E – high	—	10	12	17	17	13	18	15	16	15	17
P/E – low	—	7	6	10	9	9	11	11	11	12	14
Dividends per share (Fl)	13.5%	0.34	0.37	0.39	0.42	0.50	0.63	0.78	0.86	0.97	1.07
Book value per share (Fl)	5.7%	11.13	10.61	10.39	10.08	11.83	14.82	14.82	12.70	14.29	18.40
Employees	10.9%	47,052	50,566	55,150	61,217	80,284	83,968	87,978	103,069	110,654	119,027

1994 Year-end:
Debt ratio: 54.6%
Return on equity: 19.0%
Cash (mil.): Fl557
Long-term debt (mil.): Fl1,916
No. of shares (mil.): 116
Dividends
   Yield: 2.3%
   Payout: 36.2%
Market value (mil.): $2,817
Sales (mil.): $13,973

Stock Price History[1]
High/Low 1985–94

[1] Stock prices are for the prior calendar year.

ROYAL BANK OF CANADA

OVERVIEW

The 125-year-old Royal Bank (RBC) is Canada's largest financial institution. Known as "The Royal," RBC is one of 5 banks that dominate Canada's nationwide banking system, holding 28% of the country's personal deposits and residential mortgages and 27% of all consumer loans. RBC is also one of the 50 largest banks in the world, serving the US, Europe, Asia, Latin America, and the Caribbean.

In a country saturated with financial services, RBC made a shrewd move in 1993 by acquiring Royal Trustco Ltd., Canada's 2nd largest trust company, from the Edper-Bronfman conglomerate. Merging these 2 companies created the 4th largest bank in North America (after Citicorp, BankAmerica Corp., and Chemical Banking Corp.), boosted the bank's assets by 10%, and gave it an edge in one of the few fast-growing financial services areas: managing mutual funds and other investments. RBC also wants to expand its international banking operations, which already exist in 33 countries, into central Europe including the Czech Republic and may open more offices in such high-growth areas as Latin America and Asia. It is interested, too, in joint ventures in the US, like the 1994 agreement with Mellon Bank, which resulted in providing financial services to companies doing business on both sides of the US/Canada border.

RBC had a net income of approximately $866 million in 1994.

WHEN

Royal Bank of Canada has always had a southern exposure, ever since its creation as Merchants Bank in 1864. As the bank opened its doors in Halifax, the port city was bustling with trade spawned by the US Civil War raging below the border. After its incorporation in 1869 as Merchants Bank of Halifax, it added branches in other cities of eastern Canada. In 1882 Merchants opened a branch in Bermuda, turning south before it headed west. The gold strikes in Canada and Alaska in the late 1890s spurred Merchants to establish branches in western Canada.

At the same time, Merchants pushed into New York and, even farther south, into Cuba in 1899. Its success in Cuba led it to purchase 2 Cuban banks, Banco de Oriente (1903) and Banco del Comercio (1904).

The bank was on the move in other ways. To avoid confusion with another bank, it changed its name in 1901 to Royal Bank of Canada and transferred its headquarters from Halifax to Montreal in 1907.

RBC continued to acquire banks: Union Bank of Halifax (1910), Traders Bank of Canada (1912), Bank of British Honduras (1912), Quebec Bank (1917), and Northern Crown Bank (1918). Its largest acquisition was Union Bank of Canada (1925).

The bank stumbled, along with the rest of the economy, during the Depression but recovered its strength as war broke out in Europe in 1939. After WWII RBC aggressively financed expansion of the Canadian oil-and-gas and minerals industries.

When Castro seized power in Cuba, RBC tried to operate its branches under communist rule but sold its assets to Banco Nacional de Cuba in 1960. In the late 1970s and early 1980s, RBC aggressively grew overseas, with units in Britain (1979), West Germany (1980), Puerto Rico (1980), and the Bahamas (1980). Under CEO Rowland Frazee, the bank also beefed up its New York subsidiary, Royal Bank and Trust Company.

As Canada relaxed regulation on its banks, RBC acquired Dominion Securities in 1987. Allan Taylor, who started with the bank as a 16-year-old clerk and rose to the CEO post in 1986, turned his gaze south for expansion.

In 1991 the US Federal Reserve approved its brokerage arm, RBC Dominion, for participation in stock underwriting, but, on the other side of the world, Saudi Arabia blacklisted RBC for limiting activities in the region after Iraq invaded Kuwait. Also that year RBC acquired Quebec-based McNeil Mantha (investment banking) for $22 million.

In 1992 the bank faced a $650 million loss from having backed the Reichman family–owned Olympia & York, a troubled property developer gone under. In 1993 to diversify its operations, RBC bought Royal Trustco, Canada's 2nd largest trust company, and Voyageur Travel Insurance Ltd., the country's largest retail supplier of travel insurance.

A management shakeup in late 1994 created several new VC posts when heir-designate and RBC president John Cleghorn replaced Taylor as chairman and CEO.

Principal exchange: Toronto
Fiscal year ends: October 31

Chairman and CEO: John E. Cleghorn
VC: J. Emile Bolduc, age 55
VC: Gordon Feeney, age 53
VC: Bruce. C. Galloway, age 47
VC: Robert Sutherland
EVP Human Resources: W. J. McCartney
Auditors: Deloitte & Touche; Peat Marwick
Thorne; Price Waterhouse

HQ: One Place Ville Marie, PO Box 6001,
Montreal, Quebec H3C 3A9, Canada
Phone: 514-874-2110
Fax: 514-874-7197
US HQ: Financial Square
New York, NY 10005-3531
US Phone: 212-428-6200
US Fax: 212-968-1293

Royal Bank of Canada operates 1,731 branches in
Canada and more than 90 business units in 33
other countries.

	1993 Assets	
	C$ mil.	% of total
Canada	122,788	74
Europe	11,690	7
US	9,664	6
Latin America & Caribbean	5,094	3
Asia/Pacific	3,288	2
Adjustments	12,417	8
Total	**164,941**	**100**

	1993 Assets	
	C$ mil.	% of total
Cash & equivalents	10,874	7
Securities	29,315	18
Residential mortgages	42,654	26
Other loans	68,511	41
Other	13,587	8
Total	**164,941**	**100**

Major Subsidiaries and Affiliates
Atlantis Holdings Ltd. (Barbados)
Investment Holdings (Cayman) Ltd.
R.B.C. Holdings (Bahamas) Ltd.
RBC Dominion Securities Corp. (73%, US)
RBC Dominion Securities Ltd. (73%)
RBC Finance B.V.
RBC Holdings (USA) Inc.
Royal Bank Mortgage Corp.
Royal Bank of Canada Holdings (UK) Ltd.
Royal Trust Asia Ltd.
Royal Trustco Ltd.

Bank of Montreal	First Chicago
Bank of Nova Scotia	FMR
BankAmerica	Goldman Sachs
Bankers Trust	HSBC
Barclays	Imasco
BCE	Industrial Bank of Japan
Bear Stearns	Mellon
Canadian Imperial	Merrill Lynch
Chase Manhattan	J. P. Morgan
Chemical Banking	NatWest
Citicorp	Nomura Securities
Crédit Lyonnais	Paine Webber
CS Holding	Toronto-Dominion Bank
Deutsche Bank	Union Bank of Switzerland

$=C$1.32 (Dec. 31, 1993)	9-Year Growth	1984	1985	1986	1987	1988	1989	1990	1991	1992	1993
Assets (C$ mil.)	7.2%	88,003	96,017	99,607	102,170	110,054	114,660	125,938	132,352	138,293	164,941
Net income (C$ mil.)	(1.8%)	352	454	452	512	712	529	965	983	107	300
Income as % of assets	—	0.4%	0.5%	0.5%	0.5%	0.6%	0.5%	0.8%	0.7%	0.1%	0.2%
Earnings per share (C$)	(12.8%)	1.58	1.86	1.84	1.89	2.52	1.64	3.00	2.92	(0.05)	0.46
Stock price – high (C$)	—	17.69	16.19	17.63	19.44	18.25	24.38	25.69	28.50	29.00	29.25
Stock price – low (C$)	—	12.44	13.75	13.75	12.81	13.06	16.88	19.75	22.38	21.50	22.00
Stock price – close (C$)	8.2%	14.19	15.75	16.63	13.88	18.00	24.25	20.75	27.63	24.63	28.88
P/E – high	—	11	9	10	10	7	15	9	10	—	64
P/E – low	—	8	7	7	7	5	10	7	8	—	48
Dividends per share (C$)	1.7%	1.00	1.00	1.00	1.01	1.04	1.10	1.16	1.16	1.16	1.16
Book value per share (C$)	1.8%	15.43	16.55	17.07	14.20	15.58	16.16	18.10	19.91	18.82	18.09
Employees	3.7%	38,189	37,430	38,186	42,839	46,096	47,989	56,889	57,596	49,628	52,745

1993 Year-end:
Debt Ratio: 94.6%
Return on equity: 2.5%
Equity as % of assets: 4.7%
No. of shares (mil.): 314
Dividends
Yield: 4.0%
Payout: 252.2%
Market value (mil.): $6,873
Assets (mil.): $124,955
Sales (mil.): $8,845

**Stock Price History
High/Low 1984–93**

ROYAL DUTCH/SHELL GROUP

OVERVIEW

In terms of product sales, the Royal Dutch/ Shell Group has grown from a 1907 alliance between Royal Dutch Petroleum and British "Shell" Transport and Trading companies into the world's largest oil and gas conglomerate. As an oil refiner and seller, Royal Dutch/Shell edged ahead of Exxon in 1993 and outsells #3 Mobil by almost 2 to 1. Royal Dutch holds 60% and "Shell" Transport 40% of the group's 3 holding companies: The Shell Petroleum Company Ltd. (UK), Shell Petroleum Inc. (US), and Shell Petroleum N.V. (the Netherlands).

The group is engaged in oil and natural gas exploration and production, chemicals, polymers, crop protection products, and coal and metals businesses. The 3 holding compa-nies control operating and service companies that are active in over 100 countries. Royal Dutch/Shell maintains headquarters in The Hague and London and alternates the leader-ship roles between the 2 parent companies.

Its chief operational subsidiary in the US, Shell Oil, is one of the country's largest in-dustrial corporations and spends over $1 billion a year on oil field exploration. The company is a pioneer in the development of deep-sea oil fields in the Gulf of Mexico. Its Auger field is the deepest offshore well in the US (2,860 feet). The still deeper Mars project (2,933 feet) is scheduled to be operational in 1996.

A strike by Nigerian oil workers hurt the company's production output in 1994.

WHEN

In 1870 Marcus Samuel inherited an interest in his father's London-based company, a trad-ing business specializing in seashells from the Far East. Samuel expanded the business and, after securing a contract for Russian oil, began selling oil products in the Far East.

Standard Oil engaged in severe price-cutting to defend its Asian markets. Samuel secretly prepared his response and in 1892 unveiled the first of a fleet of tankers, all named after seashells. Specially designed to transport kerosene in bulk (Standard's was in cans), the ships pumped their cargo into stor-age tanks Samuel had built at key ports. Samuel's transportation cost advantage al-lowed him to compete with Standard while competitors went bankrupt. Rejecting acqui-sition overtures from Standard, Samuel cre-ated Shell Transport and Trading in 1897.

Concurrently, a Dutchman, Aeilko Zijlker, struck oil in Sumatra and formed Royal Dutch in 1890 to exploit the oil field. Young Henri Deterding joined the firm in 1896 and established a Far Eastern sales organization. Deterding became president of Royal Dutch in 1900 amid the battle for Asian mar-ket dominance. In 1903 Deterding, Samuel, and the Rothschilds created Asiatic Petro-leum, an oil marketing alliance in the Far East. In 1907, when Shell's non-Asian busi-ness was eroding, Deterding engineered a merger between Royal Dutch and Shell. The deal stipulated 60% control of the new com-pany by Royal Dutch shareholders, 40% by owners of Shell Transport and Trading stock.

Following the 1911 breakup of Standard Oil, Deterding entered the American market, building refineries and buying producers in the US. Shell products were available in every state by 1929. Royal Dutch joined the 1928 "As Is" cartel that fixed prices for most of 2 decades. Disturbed by Deterding's pro-Nazi sentiments, Shell management persuaded him to step down in 1936.

In its post-Deterding years, Shell profited from worldwide growth in consumption of oil-based products. It acquired 100% of its Houston-based subsidiary Shell Oil (US) in 1985, but shareholders sued, complaining that the US arm's assets were undervalued in the deal. A judge awarded the shareholders $110 million in 1990.

With the Persian Gulf crisis in 1990, the Royal Dutch/Shell Group saw margins fall, but, as postwar inventories swelled, pump prices fell more slowly than crude prices. That led to a 71% surge in the first quarter of 1991. Shell Oil, however, hurt by an explo-sion that crippled its Norco, Louisiana, refin-ery, saw a 39% drop in profits. In 1991 Shell sold a major California refinery to Unocal and launched a plan to cut 10–15% of its US work force. It sold its coal mining subsidiary to Ziegler Coal in 1992. In 1993 Shell and Nor-wegian oil company Saga teamed up to ex-plore Russian oil fields.

Union Carbide filed suit in 1994 to protest a plastics joint venture between Royal Dutch/ Shell and Montedison SpA of Italy, claiming antitrust violations.

NYSE symbols: RD (Royal Dutch);
SC (Shell) (ADR)
Fiscal year ends: December 31

WHO

Chairman; President, Royal Dutch Petroleum Company: Cornelius A. J. Herkströter
VC; Chairman of The "Shell" Transport and Trading Company: John S. Jennings
General Attorney: R. van der Vlist
President and CEO, Shell Oil (US): Philip J. Carroll
VP Finance and CFO, Shell Oil (US): P. G. Turberville
VP Human Resources, Shell Oil (US): B. W. Levan
Auditors: KPMG Klynveld (the Netherlands); Ernst & Young (UK); Price Waterhouse (US)

WHERE

HQ: Royal Dutch Petroleum Company (N.V. Koninklijke Nederlandsche Petroleum Maatschappij), 30 Carel van Bylandtlaan, 2596 HR The Hague, The Netherlands
Phone: +31-70-377-9111
Fax: +31-70-377-3115
HQ: The "Shell" Transport and Trading Company, public limited company, Shell Centre, London SE1 7NA, UK
Phone: +44-(01)71-934-1234
Fax: +44-(01)71-934-5252
US HQ: Shell Oil Company, One Shell Plaza, PO Box 2463, Houston, TX 77002
US Phone: 713-241-6161
US Fax: 713-241-4044

	1993 Sales	
	$ mil.	% of total
Europe	46,470	49
US	20,194	21
Other Eastern Hemisphere	17,306	18
Other Western Hemisphere	11,200	12
Adjustments	30,644	—
Total	**125,814**	**100**

WHAT

	1993 Sales		1993 Net Income	
	$ mil.	% of total	$ mil.	% of total
Oil & gas	83,057	87	5,641	100
Chemicals	9,464	10	(614)	—
Coal, metals& other	2,649	3	(72)	—
Adjustments	30,644	—	(458)	—
Total	**125,814**	**100**	**4,497**	**100**

KEY COMPETITORS

Amoco	Norsk Hydro
Ashland, Inc.	Occidental
Atlantic Richfield	Oryx
British Petroleum	PDVSA
Broken Hill	PEMEX
Chevron	Pennzoil
Coastal	Peter Kiewit Sons'
CONSOL Energy	Petrobrás
Diamond Shamrock	Petrofina
DuPont	Phillips Petroleum
Elf Aquitaine	Repsol
ENI	Saudi Aramco
Exxon	Shanghai Petrochemical
Hoescht	Sun Company
Horsham	Texaco
Huntsman Chemical	TOTAL
Imperial Chemical	Unocal
Imperial Oil	USX–Marathon
Koch	YPF
Mobil	

HOW MUCH

	9-Year Growth	1984	1985	1986	1987	1988	1989	1990	1991	1992	1993
Sales ($ mil.)	2.8%	97,831	94,569	81,404	98,026	99,445	106,090	132,414	131,529	128,420	125,814
Net income ($ mil.)	(0.9%)	4,883	3,876	4,500	4,649	5,234	6,537	6,533	4,288	5,369	4,497
Income as % of sales	—	5.0%	4.1%	5.5%	4.7%	5.3%	6.2%	4.9%	3.3%	4.2%	3.6%
Earnings per share ($)	0.8%	5.01	3.78	4.88	7.75	9.39	7.58	7.80	6.53	6.38	5.36
Stock price – high ($)	—	27.31	32.56	48.00	70.50	62.13	77.63	87.00	86.25	91.63	108.13
Stock price – low ($)	—	20.63	24.19	29.88	47.19	52.19	56.88	70.50	73.00	74.75	78.75
Stock price – close ($)	17.4%	24.69	31.50	47.75	55.94	57.00	77.50	78.63	86.25	81.00	104.38
P/E – high	—	6	9	10	9	7	16	11	13	14	20
P/E – low	—	4	6	6	6	6	8	9	11	12	15
Dividends per share ($)	11.7%	1.49	1.65	2.65	3.16	3.62	3.36	3.61	3.55	4.14	4.02
Book value per share ($)	6.4%	33.06	37.91	41.51	48.52	50.87	54.05	60.17	61.04	58.03	57.74
Employees	(2.7%)	149,000	142,000	138,000	136,000	134,000	135,000	137,000	133,000	127,000	117,000

1993 Year-end:
Debt ratio: 48.3%
Return on equity: 8.6%
Cash (mil.): $5,753
Current ratio: 1.27
Long-term debt (mil.): $3,675
No. of shares (mil.): 536
Dividends
  Yield: 3.9%
  Payout: 75.0%
Market value (mil.): $55,955

Stock Price History
High/Low 1984–93

Note: All share data are for Royal Dutch only.

THE RTZ CORPORATION PLC

OVERVIEW

RTZ is the world's largest mining and metals refining corporation. Copper and gold account for over 30% of RTZ revenues, industrial minerals (borax, silica, talc) nearly 27%, and coal and uranium 16%.

Although based in London, roughly half of RTZ's holdings are in North America. RTZ is the US's 3rd largest copper producer and 5th largest coal producer. Its Mojave Desert Boron Mine produces half the world's borax.

Diversity in location and product has helped RTZ weather recessions, political upheavals, and market gluts. Company management emphasizes the long view, both in the life of a producing mine and in project development. The company spends nearly $200 million a year looking for new mining opportunities.

Among RTZ's mine holdings are CRA (Australia; iron, coal, diamonds; 49%), Kennecott (US; copper, coal, gold; 100%), U.S. Borax (borates, silica; 100%), Palabora (South Africa; copper; 38.9%), and Corumba (Brazil; iron and manganese; 49%).

WHEN

RTZ was formed as Rio Tinto-Zinc Corporation, the result of the 1962 merger of the Rio Tinto Company and Consolidated Zinc. Rio Tinto, a British company, had begun mining in Spain in 1873. It sold most of its Spanish holdings in 1954 and branched out to Australia, southern Africa, and Canada. Consolidated Zinc had been founded as The Zinc Corporation in 1905 around the mineral-rich Broken Hill area of Australia. After The Zinc Corporation combined with New Broken Hill Consolidated and Imperial Smelting, the company discovered the world's largest deposit of bauxite (1955).

Rio Tinto-Zinc acquired U.S. Borax in 1968. U.S. Borax, with its 20 Mule Team trademark, had been built on one of the few great boron deposits. Boron use in cleansers became widespread in the late 19th century. Early California miners used 20-mule teams to haul huge wagons to meet the demand. A 1927 discovery in the Mojave Desert led to development of another huge boron mine.

U.S. Borax leaned heavily on its Western roots. Its detergent products sponsored *Death Valley Days*, an Old West TV series hosted for a time by Ronald Reagan. Until its Turkish mine was nationalized, RTZ controlled the world's boron supply. RTZ sold U.S. Borax's consumer products to Greyhound (later Dial Corporation) in 1988.

RTZ added a large copper mine at Bougainville in Papua New Guinea (1969). The company suffered through a slump in metals prices in the early 1980s. Derek Birkin, named CEO in 1985, solidified RTZ's minerals business with the $3.7 billion purchase of BP Minerals from British Petroleum in 1989. Among the booty from the purchase was Utah's Kennecott Corporation.

Kennecott was named for Robert Kennicott (a typographical error had altered the company's spelling), who died in Alaska while trying to establish an intercontinental telegraph line. In 1901 Alaskan prospectors in the area convinced Stephen Birch of copper mining's potential. Backed by J. P. Morgan and the Guggenheims, Birch built a railroad to haul the ore. Kennecott Copper joined railroad and mine operations in 1915.

Kennecott consolidated its hold on Chile's Braden copper mine (1925) and on the Utah Copper Company (1936) and other US mining properties. Among Utah's holdings is Bingham Canyon, the world's largest open-pit copper mine. British Petroleum–controlled SOHIO bought Kennecott in 1981. In 1989, the first year RTZ owned it, Kennecott was the largest single contributor to RTZ's bottom line. In 1991 RTZ committed $880 million to build a new smelter and upgrade the refinery at Bingham Canyon.

RTZ sold its chemicals business in 1989 and entered the 1990s with almost 30% of its assets in the US. In 1992 RTZ, citing conflict of interest with its other North American investments, sold its 51.5% share of the large Canadian mining operation Rio Algom Ltd.

After tribal feuding forced the shutdown of the Bougainville mine in 1991, RTZ wrote off $119 million. Kennecott prospectors had discovered a rich gold deposit in Papua New Guinea in 1982. But in 1993 RTZ said it would cut its share of the project to 20%, if approved by that government.

In 1993 RTZ sold its Pillar building products group, the last of its nonmining holdings. Through Kennecott it has purchased US coal mine operators Nerco, Cordero Mining Company, and Colowyo Coal Company.

NYSE symbol: RTZ (ADR)
Fiscal year ends: December 31

Chairman: Sir Derek Birkin, age 64, £588,681 pay
CEO: Robert P. Wilson, age 50
Deputy CEO: Ian C. Strachan, age 50
Finance Director: Christopher R. H. Bull, age 51
Mining Director: Leigh Clifford, age 47
President and CEO, Kennecott Corp. (US):
Robert Cooper, age 45
SVP Finance and Control, Kennecott Corp. (US): Tracy Stevenson
VP Human Resources, Kennecott Corp. (US):
Ron Skaer
Auditors: Coopers & Lybrand

HQ: 6 St. James's Square, London SW1Y 4LD, UK
Phone: +44-(01)71-930-2399
Fax: +44-(01)71-930-3249
US HQ: Kennecott Corporation, 10 E. South Temple, Salt Lake City, UT 84133
US Phone: 801-322-7000
US Fax: 801-322-8181

RTZ's assets are predominantly in North America and Australasia.

	1993 Sales		1993 Pretax Income	
	£ mil.	% of total	£ mil.	% of total
North America	1,426	39	233	35
Australasia	1,040	28	200	30
Africa	465	13	136	21
Europe	411	11	(9)	—
Other countries	318	9	94	14
Adjustments	1,162	—	(219)	—
Total	**4,822**	**100**	**435**	**100**

	1993 Sales		1993 Pretax Income	
	£ mil.	% of total	£ mil.	% of total
Mining & metals	2,659	73	562	72
Industrial minerals	1,001	27	220	28
Adjustments	1,162	—	(347)	—
Total	**4,822**	**100**	**435**	**100**

Selected Mines

Borates	**Gold**
Boron (US)	Bingham Canyon (US)
Tincalayu (Argentina)	Kelian (44%, Indonesia)
Coal	Morro do Ouro (51%, Brazil)
Cordero (US)	
Decker (50%, US)	**Iron Ore**
	Brockman (49%, Australia)
Copper	
Bingham Canyon (US)	**Silver**
Escondida (30%, Chile)	Bingham Canyon (US)
Neves Corvo (49%, Portugal)	**Talc**
	Talc de Luzenac (France)
Diamonds	**Titanium Dioxide**
Argyle (29%, Australia)	QIT's Lac Allard (Canada)

Alcoa	FirstMiss Gold	MIM Holdings
Alumax	FMC	Mitsubishi
Anglo American	Freeport-	Mitsui
Anschutz	McMoRan	Newmont
ASARCO	Gencor	Mining
Battle Mountain Gold	Industries	Penn Virginia
Brascan/Noranda	Hanson	Peter Kiewit
Broken Hill	Harnischfeger	Sons'
Codelco	Industries	Placer Dome
Coeur d'Alene	Homestake	Phelps Dodge
Mines	Mining	Reynolds Metals
Cyprus Amax	ITOCHU	Sumitomo
Echo Bay Mines	Kaiser Aluminum	United Co.
	Marubeni	Zambia Copper

£=$1.48 (Dec. 31, 1993)	9-Year Growth	1984	1985	1986	1987	1988	1989	1990	1991	1992	1993
Sales (£ mil.)	0.5%	4,602	4,647	4,345	4,527	4,928	6,156	5,078	4,885	4,613	4,822
Net income (£ mil.)	2.5%	230	286	244	284	425	588	507	308	239	287
Income as % of sales	—	5.0%	6.2%	5.6%	6.3%	8.6%	9.6%	10.0%	6.3%	5.2%	6.0%
Earnings per share (p)	2.1%	29	36	31	36	53	63	51	36	32	35
Stock price – high (p)	—	284	274	316	580	464	590	605	603	684	816
Stock price – low (p)	—	200	203	205	259	315	404	392	406	469	607
Stock price – close (p)	14.7%	237	207	282	350	421	581	392	472	684	812
P/E – high	—	10	8	10	16	9	9	12	17	21	23
P/E – low	—	7	6	7	7	6	6	8	11	15	17
Dividends per share (p)	11.0%	8.0	8.8	9.4	11.5	15.0	18.5	19.5	19.5	19.5	20.5
Book value per share (p)	3.3%	224	191	209	207	259	259	254	254	276	300
Employees	2.3%	74,004	75,197	82,551	78,705	84,149	82,492	73,612	73,495	68,298	59,975

1993 Year-end:
Debt ratio: 31.6%
Return on equity: 12.2%
Cash (mil.): £1,091
Long-term debt (mil.): £1,338
No. of shares (mil.): 1,064
Dividends
  Yield: 2.5%
  Payout: 58.4%
Market value (mil.): $12,781
Sales (mil.): $7,133

Stock Price History
High/Low 1984–93

RWE AKTIENGESELLSCHAFT

RWE is a holding company for Germany's largest electric company, RWE Energy, which serves more than 5 million residential customers, provides power to German industry, and distributes power to other utilities. However, the Essen-based company is involved in a variety of businesses other than power, including petroleum, mining, waste management, mechanical and plant engineering, and construction and civil engineering services.

RWE's utility business provides the most profits, but with the German government's opening up that country's utility industry to more competition, the company is losing its regional monopoly. In response, it is taking its expertise into new markets. A consortium that includes RWE has won a bid to buy a controlling interest in VEAG, an electric company in Berlin. RWE Energy has also bought stakes in power companines in the eastern German towns of Leipzig, Cottbus, and Chemnitz.

In addition, RWE is expanding into new businesses. The company has joined a consortium that includes Deutsche Bank and Mannesmann Eurokom that is building a nationwide digital communications network. It is also working to expand its waste management business, with a particular focus on building its recycling operations.

RWE's petroleum and chemicals division operates one of Germany's largest service station networks, and its construction and civil engineering unit is one of Europe's largest. In the US, RWE owns half of Consol Energy (with DuPont), the 2nd largest coal producer in the US (after Hanson's Peabody Holding).

Founded at the end of the 19th century, RWE mirrored the industrialization of Germany in its growth. The company was formed as Rheinisch-Westfälisches Elektrizitätswerk in 1898 by Erich Zweigert, the mayor of Essen, and Hugo Stinnes, an industrialist from Mülheim, to provide electricity to Essen and surrounding areas. On April 1, 1900, the company began supplying electricity.

To expand the company's base, Stinnes looked to bring in other cities, asking them to buy shares. In 1905 the cities of Gelsenkirchen and Mülheim bought shares in the company. In 1908 RWE and Vereinigte Elektrizitätswerke Westfalen (VEW) signed a contract to divide up the territories that each would supply.

In 1924 the company began construction of a network of powerlines connecting northern and southern Germany. The network was completed in 1930, linking the more populated North with the South.

In 1932 it acquired Rheinische Aktiengesellschaft für Braunkohlenbergbau, a coal producer. By 1939 as WWII began, RWE had plants extending over most of western Germany. However, the war brought massive destruction, and following the war the company began a massive rebuilding program. This program allowed the company to modernize many of its plants.

During the 1950s RWE continued to rely mainly on coal for its fuel needs, but in 1961 RWE and Bayern Atomkraft sponsored the construction of a light water demonstration nuclear reactor at Gundremmingen. The company became more involved in nuclear power, entering into several nuclear projects. In 1977 the Gundremmingen plant was shut down. To replace it RWE began construction of two 1,300-MW reactors which began operation in 1984. By 1985 more than 20% of the company's power came from nuclear energy.

While it continued to build its energy capabilites, RWE also was looking for diversification opportunities, and in 1988 it acquired Texaco's German petroleum and petrochemical subsidiary, Deutsche Texaco. RWE renamed the company RWE-DEA. By 1990 the company had operations in everything from energy to waste management to construction. It reorganized its operations, creating RWE Aktiengesellschaft as a holding company for group operations.

In 1991 RWE-DEA acquired the US's Vista Chemical for $590 million, and RWE's mining unit, Rheinbraun, paid DuPont $900 million for a 50% stake in Consolidated Coal (renamed Consol Energy).

In 1994 RWE signed a deal with the North Rhine-Westphalia government, giving RWE access to the Garzweiler 2 coal mine on the condition that the company invest $13.4 billion through 2030 to replace its older power stations with cleaner-burning ones.

OTC symbol: RWAGY (ADR)
Fiscal year ends: June 30

WHO

Chairman: Friedhelm Gieske
Member of the Board of Management, Group Finance Division: Wolfgang Ziemann
Member of the Board of Management, Petroleum and Chemicals Division: Peter Koch
Chairman, Vista Chemical (US): Dieter Dräger
President, Vista Chemical (US): W.C. Knodel
Manager Finance and Treasurer, Vista Chemical (US): Bob Whitlow
Manager Human Resources, Vista Chemical (US): Crystal Wright
Auditors: C&L Treuhand-Vereinigung Deutsche Revision (Coopers & Lybrand)

WHERE

HQ: Kruppstrasse 5, 45128, PO Box 103061, Essen, Germany
Phone: +49-201-18-50
Fax: +49-201-185-5199
US HQ: Vista Chemical Company, 900 Threadneedle, Houston, TX 77079
US Phone: 713-588-3000
US Fax: 713-588-3236

	1994 Sales	
	DM mil.	% of total
Germany	45,428	81
Other Europe	3,241	6
Other countries	7,081	13
Total	**55,750**	**100**

WHAT

	1994 Sales	
	DM mil.	% of total
Petroleum & Chemicals	22,751	41
Energy	18,806	34
Mechanical & Plant Engineering	6,189	11
Construction & Civil Engineering	4,571	8
Mining & Raw Materials	2,395	4
Waste Management	1,004	2
Other	34	—
Total	**55,750**	**100**

Petroleum and Chemicals
Chemicals
Crude oil production
Gas production
Petrochemicals
Petroleum products
Refining

Energy
Electricity
Gas
Heat
Steam
Water

Mechanical and Plant Engineering
Electrical plant engineering
Engineering services and special systems
Medical technology

Power systems and components
Printing machines

Construction and Civil Engineering
Commercial projects
Residential projects
Transport projects
Waste disposal projects

Mining and Raw Materials
Hard coal
Lignite
Uranium

Waste Management
Environmental consulting
Recycling management
Waste disposal
Waste water
Water management

KEY COMPETITORS

BASF
Bayer
British Petroleum
Exxon
Halliburton
Hanson
Hoechst
Royal Dutch/Shell
Siemens
VEBA
WMX Technologies

HOW MUCH

$=DM1.74 (Dec. 31, 1993)	Annual Growth	1985	1986	1987	1988	1989	1990	1991	1992	1993	1994
Sales (DM mil.)	7.8%	28,426	28,932	27,155	26,856	38,971	44,235	49,891	51,737	53,094	55,750
Net income (DM mil.)	8.3%	448	538	549	535	629	784	863	877	881	922
Income as % of sales	—	1.6%	1.9%	2.0%	2.0%	1.6%	1.8%	1.7%	1.7%	1.7%	1.7%
Earnings per share (DM)	2.3%	19	17	18	19	22	25	25	26	24	23
Stock price – high (DM)[1]	—	189	221	275	267	246	434	516	432	422	535
Stock price – low (DM)[1]	—	126	150	187	186	189	222	348	334	361	384
Stock price – close (DM)[1]	14.0%	165	193	241	210	227	434	370	386	403	535
P/E – high	—	10	13	15	14	11	18	21	17	17	24
P/E – low	—	7	9	10	10	8	9	14	13	15	17
Dividends per share (DM)	5.4%	12.5	12.5	12.5	12.5	14.1	15.6	17.2	18.8	17.1	20.0
Book value per share (DM)	4.3%	—	—	—	—	—	200	224	194	220	236
Employees	5.9%	70,249	71,883	72,785	72,127	78,162	97,596	102,190	105,572	113,642	117,958

1994 Year-end:
Debt ratio: 57.6%
Return on equity: 11.9%
Cash (mil.): DM17,841
Long-term debt (mil.): DM2,633
No. of shares (mil.): 33
Dividends
  Yield: 3.7%
  Payout: 88.1%
Market value (mil.): $11,154
Sales (mil.): $35,185

Stock Price History[1]
High/Low 1985–94

600
500
400
300
200
100
0

[1] Stock prices are for the prior calendar year.

SAAB-SCANIA HOLDINGS GROUP

OVERVIEW

Sweden-based Saab-Scania is an important aircraft and armaments producer (Saab), a global truck and bus manufacturer (Scania) with 11.4% of the 1993 European truck market, and a large importer of passenger cars (Volkswagen, Audi, SEAT, and Porsche). In 1991 Investor AB, an investment firm controlled by Peter Wallenberg, acquired full control of Saab-Scania at great expense and took the company private.

The European economic downturn in the early 1990s cut sales and net income significantly across the board for Saab-Scania. Saab Automobile, with a line of luxury cars (owned 50/50 with GM), has improved its manufacturing process and appears to be increasing its profitability. While the group's buses and trucks are doing well in Latin America, its luxury car company has a growing presence in Asia, especially in China and Hong Kong.

WHEN

In 1937 companies controlled by Axel Wenner-Gren, head of Electrolux, created Svenska Aeroplan AB (Saab) because the Swedish government needed a military aircraft producer. The government intended for Saab to cooperate with an aircraft manufacturer controlled by Marcus Wallenberg (Peter's father), but intercompany feuding slowed progress. Wallenberg joined the Saab board in 1939 when the government orchestrated Saab's acquisition of his enterprise. The first Saab-designed plane flew in 1940.

Swedish neutrality in WWII lessened the need for weaponry and, as the war's end approached, Saab management began planning to produce small cars. The basic styling of Saab autos remained unchanged from their introduction in 1947 until their redesign in 1967. In that period the cars became popular in Sweden but failed to catch on in the large US market. Saab benefited from massive Swedish rearmament in the 1960s and began building satellites, missiles, and computers. Wallenberg engineered the acquisition of Swedish truckmaker Scania in 1969.

Masinfabriks AB Scania began as a Swedish bicycle factory. Hilding Hessler and Anton Svensson took over in 1901 and used the company's experience in making a moped-like vehicle to produce autos (1901) and trucks (1902). After the 1911 merger with Swedish truck rival and railcar maker Vabis, Scania-Vabis entered bus production (1911) and exited the auto business in the 1920s.

Trucks dominated Scania-Vabis's output until WWII, when the company built tanks and other military vehicles. Scania-Vabis enjoyed strong postwar demand for trucks and buses, and in 1948 it became the Swedish Volkswagen importer, enabling it to recruit a national dealer network. Exports boomed through the 1960s.

Soon after the merger Saab-Scania acquired arms makers Malmö Flygindustri and Nordarmatur. The mid-1970s recession took its toll on the auto and computer segments, while détente dimmed prospects for the aerospace division. The company considered a merger with Volvo (which it rejected) in 1977. Saab-Scania finally did well in the US in the late 1970s with upscale autos.

In the 1980s Saab-Scania introduced a popular line of trucks, began developing commuter aircraft, and introduced the Saab 9000 series of cars. Seeking a prestigious European nameplate, General Motors bought 50% of Saab's passenger car business, Saab Automobile, for $600 million in 1989. After posting losses of over $800 million in 1990, Saab Automobile closed one of its factories, the lavish, 18-month-old plant in Malmö, Sweden.

That same year Saab-Scania experienced major cost overruns in its Gripen fighter aircraft program, and Swedish property developer Sven Olof Johansson acquired a 22% voting interest in Saab-Scania. Peter Wallenberg bought back the stock at a hefty premium and took his father's old company private in 1991 in a public bid for all shares and convertible debentures of Saab-Scania.

In 1992 Saab-Scania commissioned a new truck manufacturing facility near Angers, France, in anticipation of trucking deregulation and increased demand for truck transportation as a result of European economic unification. In 1993 the Group separated its commercial aircraft operations from its defense-related businesses.

In 1994 the new 9000 series car received the Swedish safest car award. In 1994 Saab Automobile received a 5-year contract from GM's US powertrain division to supply 40,000 car gearboxes annually, beginning in 1995.

Private company
Fiscal year ends: December 31

Chairman: Anders Scharp, age 60
President and CEO: Lars V. Kylberg, age 54
EVP and General Manager, Saab-Scania Finance: Bo G. Andréasson, age 50
EVP and Corporate Controller: Lars Ohlsson-Leijon, age 55
EVP Corporate Communications and Public Affairs: Kai Mammerich, age 51
EVP Passenger Car Activities: Rolf Sandberg, age 58
SVP Corporate Legal Staff and Secretary: Per Erlandsson, age 47
President and CEO, Saab Cars USA: James P. Crumlish
VP Finance and Administration, SAAB Cars USA: Ken Adams
Director Human Resources, SAAB Cars USA: Tom Reis
Auditors: SET-Svensson, Erikson & Tjus Revisionsbyrå; KPMG Bohlins; Ernst & Young

HQ: S-581 88 Linköping, Sweden
Phone: +46-13-18-00-00
Fax: +46-13-18-18-02
US HQ: Saab Cars USA, Inc., 4405A Saab Dr., PO Box 9000, Norcross, GA 30091
US Phone: 404-279-0100
US Fax: 404-279-6499

The company has operations in 21 countries.

	1993 Sales	
	SEK mil.	% of total
Europe, excluding Sweden	10,395	37
Sweden	8,227	30
Latin America	4,632	17
North America	1,500	5
Other countries	2,902	11
Total	**27,656**	**100**

	1993 Sales	
	SEK mil.	% of total
Scania Trucks & Buses	22,518	81
Saab Aircraft	3,220	12
Saab-Scania Combitech	2,032	7
Adjustments	(114)	—
Total	**27,656**	**100**

Operating Areas

Saab Aircraft AB (aircraft components, commercial aircraft)
Saab Combitech AB (automotive and industrial electronics, computers and systems for space vehicles, defense systems)
Saab Instruments AB
Saab Missiles AB
Saab Training Systems AB
Saab-Scania AB (military aircraft)
Saab-Scania Risk Management
Saab-Scania Treasury AB
Scania AB (buses, industrial and marine engines, trucks)

Associated Companies

Saab Automobile AB (50% joint venture with General Motors)
V.A.G Sverige AB (general agent for Audi, Porsche, SEAT, and Volkswagen)

BMW	Navistar
British Aerospace	Nissan
Daimler-Benz	PACCAR
Dina	Peugeot
Fiat	Renault
Ford	Renco
General Dynamics	Robert Bosch
General Motors	Siemens
Honda	Suzuki
Hyundai	Tata
Isuzu	Thomson SA
Mazda	Toyota
Mitsubishi	Volvo

$=SEK8.33 (Dec. 31,1993)	9-Year Growth	1984	1985	1986	1987	1988	1989	1990	1991	1992	1993
Sales (SEK mil.)	0.7%	25,956	31,840	35,222	41,403	42,488	44,905	29,035	29,299	26,992	27,656
Net income (SEK mil.)	(26.1%)	1,404	1,414	1,684	2,091	1,970	1,065	1,506	1,396	380	92
Income as % of sales	—	5.4%	4.4%	4.8%	5.1%	4.6%	2.4%	5.2%	4.8%	1.4%	0.3%
Employees	(5.3%)	43,055	46,807	48,980	50,373	50,001	48,708	29,388	29,329	28,759	26,497

1993 Year-end:
Debt ratio: 61.2%
Return on equity: 1.0%
Cash (mil.): SEK8,054
Current ratio: 1.06
Long-term debt (mil.): SEK11,130
Sales (mil.): $3,320

Net Income
(SEK mil.) 1984–93

SAATCHI & SAATCHI COMPANY PLC

OVERVIEW

The luster has long since faded from Saatchi & Saatchi, whose slick promotional work helped elect Margaret Thatcher and reposition British Airways as "the world's favorite airline." Once the largest ad agency in the world, Saatchi slipped to #5 in 1993, after WPP, Interpublic, Omnicom, and Dentsu.

Founding brothers Charles and Maurice Saatchi flourished in Thatcherite Britain, buying a host of disparate advertising and consulting firms. But by 1989 high debt and low returns from consulting businesses caused major losses. When Robert Louis-Dreyfus was appointed CEO in 1990, Saatchi was carrying debt of $1.2 billion.

Louis-Dreyfus (nicknamed "Jaws") set about cutting the fat from the company, selling off assets, slashing the work force by

1/3, and putting it through a life-saving recapitalization in 1991. He left the company to join Adidas in 1993 and was replaced by accountancy-trained Charles Scott. Charles Saatchi resigned in 1993, while Maurice Saatchi and Scott engaged in well-publicized disagreements about strategy.

Worse still was the underperformance of Saatchi's US operations (45% of its worldwide business). Sales declined in 1994, partly caused by the loss of the sales accounts of 2 major clients, Chrysler and Helene Curtis. After Maurice Saatchi was ousted by institutional stockholders in 1995, triggering an exodus of top executives and important clients (e.g., British Airways), he threatened to set up a competing firm using the Saatchi name.

WHEN

In 1947 Nathan Saatchi, a prosperous Jewish merchant, emigrated from Iraq to London with his wife and 3 sons, David, Charles, and Maurice. Charles left school at 17 and held a series of jobs before becoming a junior copywriter at an advertising agency. Feeling creatively confined, he opened his own consultancy in 1967. Younger brother Maurice finished university and went to work for a publisher that wrote about the advertising industry.

By 1970 Charles wanted to start his own ad agency and recruited the financially oriented Maurice. The agency opened in 1971 with a flashy campaign of self-promotion. It prospered, and in 1973, showing a profit of £90,000, it began to make acquisitions; one of the first failed when its liabilities turned out higher (and assets lower) than expected. Despite this setback and an industry recession, profits rose steadily. In 1975 the Saatchis completed the takeover of the much larger, publicly held Compton UK Partners, rising from 13th to 5th in size in the UK. Acquisitions and internal growth made Saatchi & Saatchi the largest agency in the UK by 1979.

In 1982 the Saatchis set their sights on another much larger firm — Compton Advertising in New York. Its purchase made Saatchi & Saatchi the 9th largest agency in the world. In 1985 the Saatchis acquired the Hay Group, a US consulting firm, for $125 million and the Howard Marlboro sales promotion company for $414 million. In 1986 the firm

bought Backer Spielvogel for $56 million and Ted Bates Worldwide for $450 million, vaulting the firm to #1 in the world. The Bates acquisition caused several key clients with over $250 million in billings to withdraw because of perceived client conflicts among the agencies now part of Saatchi.

In 1987 the company tried unsuccessfully to buy 2 UK banks, but by the end of the year high debt and the lower-than-expected profitability of many of the consulting groups acquired by the Saatchis caused financial problems that forced the agency to spend years on recovery.

In 1991 a recapitalization converted preferred shares to common, raised over $100 million, and diluted existing shareholdings by 84%. A 1-for-10 reverse stock split followed in 1992.

Selling off noncore assets has been a belated cost-cutting strategy, but Saatchi has unloaded its US law consultancy and its UK executive recruiting and financial communications businesses. It sold its Yankelovich Clancy Shulman market research firm in 1992 and its in-store marketing unit, Howard Marlboro Group, in 1993. It consolidated US-based Campbell Mithun Esty and UK-based KHBB into a worldwide network.

In 1994 Saatchi appointed Australian William Muirhead as North American CEO to breathe new life into its unprofitable US operations, but he resigned in 1995 after Maurice Saatchi's ouster.

NYSE symbol: SAA (ADR)
Fiscal year ends: December 31

WHO

President: J. K. Gill
CEO: Charles T. Scott, age 45, £365,537 pay (prior to promotion)
Finance Director: Wendy Smyth, age 40, £113,935 pay
Human Resources Director: Simon Goode
Auditors: KPMG Peat Marwick

WHERE

HQ: 83/89 Whitfield St., London W1A 4XA, UK
Phone: +44-(01)71-436-4000
Fax: +44-(01)71-436-1998
US HQ: Saatchi & Saatchi Holdings (USA) Inc., 375 Hudson St., New York, NY 10014-3620
US Phone: 212-463-2000
US Fax: 212-463-9855

The company has operations in 83 countries.

	1993 Sales		1993 Operating Income	
	$ mil.	% of total	$ mil.	% of total
US	540	45	31	60
UK	176	15	15	28
Other Europe	302	25	3	6
Other countries	185	15	3	6
Total	**1,203**	**100**	**52**	**100**

WHAT

Major Services and Operating Units

Advertising
Backer Spielvogel Bates Worldwide
Campbell Mithun Esty
Saatchi & Saatchi Advertising Worldwide

Direct Marketing
Kobs & Draft Worldwide

Media Services
Zenith Media Worldwide

Public Relations
Rowland Worldwide

Other Services
Albemarle Marketing Research
The Facilities Group
HP:ICM (face-to-face communications, UK)
National Research Group (market research, US)
Siegel & Gale (corporate identity and design, US)

Selected Major Advertising Clients

Avis	IBM
B.A.T	Johnson & Johnson
British Airways	Mars
BT	MasterCard
Campbell Soup	3M
Canon	Philip Morris
ConAgra	Procter & Gamble
DuPont	Renault
General Mills	Sara Lee
Heineken	Texaco
Hewlett-Packard	Toyota
Hyundai	Wendy's

KEY COMPETITORS

Bozell	Leo Burnett
D'Arcy Masius	NW Ayer
Dentsu	Omnicom
Foote, Cone & Belding	WPP
Interpublic Group	Young & Rubicam

HOW MUCH

	9-Year Growth	1984	1985	1986	1987	1988	1989	1990	1991	1992	1993
Sales ($ mil.)	22.2%	205	376	654	1,204	1,528	1,572	1,514	1,384	1,132	1,203
Net income ($ mil.)	(2.6%)	14	34	62	123	142	(30)	14	(162)	(929)	11
Income as % of sales	—	6.8%	9.0%	9.5%	10.2%	9.3%	—	0.9%	—	—	0.9%
Earnings per share ($)	(34.7%)	7.90	13.20	16.60	21.40	22.60	(11.20)	(2.50)	(5.10)	(17.59)	0.17
Stock price – high ($)	—	177.81	268.13	333.75	343.75	252.50	225.00	137.50	22.50	15.00	8.88
Stock price – low ($)	—	116.56	151.25	184.69	170.00	170.00	112.50	16.25	5.00	4.38	5.50
Stock price – close ($)	(31.3%)	171.56	268.13	242.81	232.50	178.75	127.50	20.00	6.25	7.00	5.88
P/E – high	—	23	20	20	16	11	—	—	—	—	52
P/E – low	—	15	12	11	8	8	—	—	—	—	32
Dividends per share ($)	(100.0%)	2.50	1.90	19.30	7.80	9.80	9.20	5.00	1.86	0.00	0.00
Book value per share ($)	—	48.75	92.00	(2.46)	12.56	(24.78)	(81.00)	(195.18)	(14.77)	(12.21)	(7.80)
Employees	13.4%	3,748	6,226	15,000	15,900	17,400	17,300	13,400	12,400	12,482	11,633

1993 Year-end:
Debt ratio: 100.0%
Return on equity: —
Cash (mil.): $228
Current ratio: 0.95
Long-term debt (mil.): $432
No. of shares (mil.): 73
Dividends
  Yield: —
  Payout: —
Market value (mil.): $431

Stock Price History
High/Low 1984–93

J SAINSBURY PLC

London-based J Sainsbury is one of the UK's big 3 food retailers (along with Tesco and Argyll Group). Sainsbury draws its strength from "Sainsbury's"-labeled products, which generate 2/3 of the company's sales. The company also sells cosmetics and personal care items under its label.

Most of the company's stores are located in the southern 2/3 of England. Sainsbury operates J Sainsbury supermarkets, Savacentres (the only dedicated superstores with both dry goods and food in the UK), Homebases (home and garden supplies), and, in the US, Shaw's supermarkets in New England.

The company is keenly aware of environmental issues and is the only UK retailer to have received an award from the US EPA because of its elimination of ozone-depleting refrigerants from its chillers.

In 1994 Sainsbury purchased a $325 million stake in Washington, DC–based Giant Food Inc. This stake includes the right to select 3 members of Giant's 7-member board. Analysts predict that Sainsbury will eventually take over the grocery company. Two members of the Sainsbury family alone (current chair David and former chair S. D.) control 23% of J Sainsbury's stock.

Newlyweds John James and Mary Ann Sainsbury established a small dairy shop in their London home in 1869, aiming to have one store to leave for each of their future sons. The store drew customers because it was clean and efficient, a far cry from most cluttered and dirty London shops.

A 2nd store opened in 1876, and other branches followed. The staid couple set up new stores meticulously, always ensuring order and quality. By 1914, 115 stores had been opened and the couple's sons had entered the business.

During WWI the company's stores established grocery departments to meet demand for preserved products, such as meat and jams, which were sold under the Sainsbury's label.

Mary died in 1927, and John followed the next year. Son John Benjamin, wholly devoted to the family business (he is reported to have said on his deathbed, "Keep the stores well lit"), took charge and in the 1930s engineered the company's first acquisition, the Thoroughgood stores.

Sales dropped by 50% during WWII, and some shops were destroyed by German bombs and rockets. The company opened its first self-service store in 1950 in Croydon. Sainsbury's 75,000-square-foot store in Lewisham, opened in 1955, was then considered to be the largest supermarket in Europe.

In 1961 the company became the first in the UK to computerize its distribution system. Sainsbury went public in 1973 and through the early 1970s increased nonfood merchandise sales. It established a joint venture with British Home Stores in 1975,

forming the Savacentre hypermarkets (which Sainsbury now wholly owns).

The company formed Breckland Farms, a joint venture with Pauls & Whites, to supply the needs of Sainsbury's meat departments. In 1979 Sainsbury partnered with Grand Bazaar Innovation Bon Marché of Belgium to establish high-end do-it-yourself stores. The 75%-Sainsbury-owned joint venture planned the first Homebase stores in 1981.

In 1983 most of Sainsbury's 229 stores were clustered in the south of England. A mature market and lots of competitors forced the company to look elsewhere. It began buying out Shaw's Supermarkets in New England and the next year opened its first store in Scotland, a hypermarket. By 1987 Sainsbury owned 100% of Shaw's 60 stores in Massachusetts, Maine, and New Hampshire.

In 1991 Sainsbury came under competitive pressure from Tesco and the Argyll Group, which also began building superstores.

In 1992 and 1993 Sainsbury and British Airways undertook a joint promotion; shoppers were allowed to trade Sainsbury receipts for flight coupons.

In April 1994 Sainsbury introduced its own version of classic cola in packaging similar to Coca-Cola's. Sales of the grocery store brand exploded. Subsequently, Coca-Cola threatened a lawsuit if the grocer did not change its look-alike packaging. Sainsbury agreed but also decreased Coca-Cola's shelf space in its stores.

In 1995 the company purchased the Texas Homecare home improvement retailer from Ladbroke.

OTC symbol: SAINY (ADR)
Fiscal year ends: Second Saturday in March

Chairman and CEO: David J. Sainsbury, age 53,
£303,000 pay
Joint Presidents: Lord Sainsbury of Drury Lane,
Sir Robert Sainsbury, and Lord Sainsbury of
Preston Candover KG
Joint Managing Director: D. A. Quarmby, age 52
Deputy Chairman and Joint Managing Director:
R. T. Vyner, age 57
Group Treasurer: D. N. Roberts
President and CEO, Shaw's Supermarkets (US):
Phil L. Francis
CFO, Shaw's Supermarkets (US): Scott Ramsey
Director Human Resources, Shaw's
Supermarkets (US): Dan Guilmette
Auditors: Clark Whitehill; Coopers & Lybrand

HQ: Stamford House, Stamford St.,
London SE1 9LL, UK
Phone: +44-(0)71-921-6000
Fax: +44-(0)71-921-6132
US HQ: Shaw's Supermarkets, Inc.,
140 Laurel St., E. Bridgewater, MA 02333
US Phone: 508-378-7211
US Fax: 508-378-3916

	1994 Sales		1994 Operating Profit	
	£ mil.	% of total	£ mil.	% of total
UK	9,280	88	765	96
US	1,303	12	31	4
Total	**10,583**	**100**	**796**	**100**

	1994 Sales		1994 Operating Profit	
	£ mil.	% of total	£ mil.	% of total
Retailing				
Food	10,246	97	766	96
Other	279	3	23	3
Property devel.	40	0	8	1
Food manufacturing	18	0	(1)	—
Total	**10,583**	**100**	**796**	**100**

1994 Stores	
	No.
Sainsbury's	341
Shaw's	87
Homebase	76
Savacentre	10
Total	**514**

Major Subsidiaries
Homebase Ltd. (home-improvement centers; 75%)
J Sainsbury (Channel Islands) Ltd.
J Sainsbury Developments Ltd.
NewMarket Foods Ltd.
Savacentre Ltd. (hypermarkets)
Shaw's Supermarkets, Inc. (US)

Aldi	L'Oréal
Argyll Group	Pathmark
Colgate-Palmolive	Procter & Gamble
Demoulas Super Markets	RMC Group
Grand Union	Royal Ahold
Great A&P	Schwarz Stiftung
Home Depot	Shoprite Group
Kmart	Star Market
Kwik Save Group	Tesco
Lidl	Unilever

£ = $1.48 (Dec. 31, 1993)	9-Year Growth	1985	1986	1987	1988	1989	1990	1991	1992	1993	1994
Sales (£ mil.)	15.0%	2,999	3,414	3,857	4,792	5,659	6,930	7,813	8,696	9,686	10,583
Net income (£ mil.)	3.1%	108	127	158	200	250	314	355	438	503	142
Income as % of sales	—	3.6%	3.7%	4.1%	4.2%	4.4%	4.5%	4.5%	5.0%	5.2%	1.3%
Earnings per share (p)	14.5%	8	9	10	13	15	18	22	25	28	27
Stock price – high (p)[1]	—	—	193	209	298	246	289	315	388	581	584
Stock price – low (p)[1]	—	—	141	170	207	187	196	244	302	337	360
Stock price – close (p)[1]	13.1%	147	184	1207	215	197	265	304	377	564	444
P/E – high	—	—	21	21	23	16	16	14	16	21	22
P/E – low	—	—	16	17	16	12	11	11	12	12	13
Dividends per share (p)	19.1%	2.2	2.7	3.5	4.2	5.0	6.0	7.3	8.8	10.0	10.6
Book value per share (p)	17.8%	39	46	54	68	77	92	108	150	171	170
Employees	8.0%	62,258	64,007	67,620	82,607	88,283	100,001	108,987	112,784	120,119	124,841

1994 Year-end:
Debt ratio: 23.1%
Return on equity: 15.8%
Cash (mil.): £224
Long-term debt (mil.): £611
No. of shares (mil.): 1,790
Dividends
  Yield: 2.4%
  Payout: 39.2%
Market value (mil.): $11,757
Sales (mil.): $15,656

Stock Price History[1]
High/Low 1986–94

[1] Stock prices are for the prior calendar year.

COMPAGNIE DE SAINT-GOBAIN SA

OVERVIEW

Materials giant Saint-Gobain is among Europe's oldest and largest industrial corporations. The Paris-based megagroup controls over 300 companies in 37 countries. Industrial subsidiaries are organized into 6 divisions: building materials; containers; flat glass, insulation, and reinforcements; industrial ceramics and abrasives; wood; and pipe.

Europe's recession has affected the construction and auto industries, cutting deeply into Gobain's business; income has dropped steadily since 1990 and was down 45% in 1993. Fiscal streamlining reduced debt and costs, leaving the company trim and healthy as markets began to recover.

Gobain has a tradition of aggressive acquisition that culminated in its purchase of US abrasives giant Norton in 1990. Purchases slowed during the early 1990s, but in 1994 the company sold its paper and packaging interests (10% of sales), raising over $1 billion for new acquisitions.

With sales spread across so many product lines and international markets, Gobain considers itself well defended against future economic and political uncertainties.

WHEN

Saint-Gobain (originally called Dunoyer) was founded in 1665, by order of Louis XIV, the Sun King. The company took its name from the town where its main factory was located. Louis needed mirrors to adorn his palaces; however, Venice had the monopoly on glass. Louis lured Venetian artisans to Paris. Some were poisoned by Italian assassins, but enough remained to teach Parisians their secrets. Gobain glass decorates Versailles.

Over the next century Gobain's fortunes fluctuated. With its decreed French glass monopoly, the company grew steadily yet suffered a bankruptcy. The Revolution interrupted company prosperity, but by the early 1800s Gobain was rolling again. It set up a sales office in New York in 1830 and its first foreign subsidiary in Germany in 1857. Under chemist Joseph Gay-Lussac, Gobain began dabbling in chemicals in the mid-1800s.

Gobain expanded to Italy (1889) and Spain (1904). By 1913 it was the leading European glassmaker. Glassmaking had changed little since the late 1600s, but in the 1920s Gobain workers pioneered the production of security glass by tempering.

Gobain diversified into glass fiber in the 1930s and set up operations in Brazil in 1937. In 1959 one of Gobain's competitors, Pilkington (UK), developed a glassmaking method that obviated the need for polishing by having a jet of hot gas shot over the glass. This new method cut production costs by 25% and capital expenditures in half. But to use the Pilkington method, Gobain had to pay $1.4 million up front and then a 6% royalty for the next 8 years. To keep its 50% EC market share, the company refit all of its factories to use the Pilkington method by 1965.

In 1968 BSN, 1/3 Gobain's size, tried to take over Gobain. The company was saved by the Suez Group, which forced Gobain to merge with Pont-à-Mousson, the world's leading iron pipe manufacturer. Called a "shotgun wedding" by *Forbes*, the merger forced much-needed restructuring upon crusty Gobain, which formed product-based units and sold its chemical interests.

In 1976 Gobain acquired a majority interest in US building materials maker CertainTeed. In 1982 Gobain was forced to divest some interests when it was nationalized by France's new Socialist government. Despite nationalization the company grew steadily during the 1980s, investing in Compagnie Générale des Eaux, the world's largest drinking water distributor.

In 1986, under a new French government, Gobain became the first company to be privatized. In 1989 the company purchased Générale Française de Céramique (clay tile), ISP (Yugoslavia, flat glass, 51%), and Vetri (Italy, glass containers, 79%). It bought Norton (US), the world's leader in abrasives, and Solaglas (UK) in 1990. German glassmakers GIAG and Oberland were purchased in 1991, and by 1992 Gobain was the world's leading glass manufacturer. In 1993 the company added Dutch glassmaker Veromco and Italian pipe manufacturer Tubi-Ghisa.

As Gobain's economic slump appeared to be ending in the mid-1990s, new trouble loomed on the horizon: CEO Jean-Louis Beffa was one of several French industrial leaders under investigation for corruption. Still, in 1994 Gobain posted net profits of $674 million through sales of $13.9 billion.

Principal exchange: Paris
Fiscal year ends: December 31

WHO

Chairman and CEO: Jean-Louis Beffa
SVP and General Delegate for the US and Canada; President and CEO, CertainTeed (US): Michel Besson
Finance Director: Jean-François Phélizon
VP Finance, CertainTeed (US): George B. Amoss
VP Human Resources, CertainTeed (US): Dennis Baker
Auditors: Befec, Mulquin & Associés; PSAUDIT (Price Waterhouse)

WHERE

HQ: Les Miroirs, 18, avenue d'Alsace, F-92400, Courbevoie, France; Cedex 27, F-92096 Paris–La Défense, France
Phone: +33-1-47-62-30-00
Fax: +33-1-47-78-45-03
US HQ: CertainTeed Corporation, 750 E. Swedesford Rd., Valley Forge, PA 19482
US Phone: 610-341-7000
US Fax: 610-341-7777

Saint-Gobain has roughly 300 subsidiaries and operates industrial units in 37 countries.

	1993 Sales		1993 Operating Income	
	FF mil.	% of total	FF mil.	% of total
France	27,048	37	1,435	29
Other Europe	27,628	37	934	19
Other countries	19,690	26	2,609	52
Adjustments	(2,827)	—	—	—
Total	**71,539**	**100**	**4,978**	**100**

WHAT

	1993 Sales		1993 Operating Income	
	FF mil.	% of total	FF mil.	% of total
Flat glass	11,735	16	799	15
Containers	11,326	16	975	18
Industrial ceramics & abrasives	11,190	16	733	13
Insulation	9,247	13	888	16
Pipe	7,942	11	865	16
Paperwood	7,935	11	(154)	—
Building materials	6,824	9	1,123	21
Fiber reinforcements	3,085	4	(316)	—
Other	2,650	4	65	1
Adjustments	(395)	—	—	—
Total	**71,539**	**100**	**4,978**	**100**

Selected Subsidiaries
CertainTeed (building materials, insulation, reinforcements; US)
Éverite SA (99.44%, building materials)
GIAG-Glasindustrie AG (99.66%, flat glass, Germany)
Isover SA (98.96%, insulation, Belgium)
Mexalit (49%, building materials, Mexico)
Norton Kabushiki Kaisha (industrial ceramics and abrasives, Japan)
Oberland Glas AG (59.92%, containers, Germany)
Pont-à-Mousson SA (98.92%, pipe)
Saint-Gobain Vitrage (flat glass)
Solaglas (99.16%, flat glass, UK)

KEY COMPETITORS

AFG Industries	Glaverbel	Mitsubishi
Armstrong	Guardian	Owens-Corning
World	Industries	Owens-Illinois
Asahi Glass	Hanson	Pilkington
Ball	Kyocera	PPG
Corning	Manville	Tetra Laval
Danone	3M	VIAG

HOW MUCH

$=FF 5.91 (Dec. 31, 1993)	Annual Growth	1984	1985	1986	1987	1988	1989	1990	1991	1992	1993
Sales (FF mil.)	1.7%	61,341	67,888	77,725	78,887	58,875	66,093	69,076	75,065	74,007	71,539
Net income (FF mil.)	16.9%	323	548	1,261	2,523	4,044	4,311	3,359	2,509	2,377	1,314
Income as % of sales	—	0.5%	0.8%	1.6%	3.2%	6.9%	6.5%	4.9%	3.3%	3.2%	1.8%
Earnings per share (FF)	(9.1%)	—	—	29	57	70	69	52	37	34	18
Stock price – high (FF)	—	—	—	—	523	625	715	670	498	614	605
Stock price – low (FF)	—	—	—	—	356	380	553	320	332	430	460
Stock price – close (FF)	5.9%	—	—	—	416	615	653	360	443	510	588
P/E – high	—	—	—	—	9	9	10	13	13	18	33
P/E – low	—	—	—	—	6	5	8	6	9	13	25
Dividends per share (FF)	2.2%	—	—	—	—	10.5	13.0	14.5	14.5	14.5	14.5
Book value per share (FF)	5.3%	—	—	312	283	356	409	431	455	461	447
Employees	(2.6%)	117,443	142,390	140,071	131,324	84,689	87,816	104,987	104,653	100,373	92,348

1993 Year-end:
Debt ratio: 46.2%
Return on equity: 4.0%
Cash (mil.): FF8,540
Long-term debt (mil.): FF17,338
No. of shares (bil.): 73
Dividends
  Yield: 2.5%
  Payout: 80.1%
Market value (mil.): $7,220
Sales (mil.): $12,105

**Stock Price History
High/Low 1987–93**

SAMSUNG GROUP

OVERVIEW

Samsung, South Korea's largest *chaebol* (industrial group), combines high-tech products and low-cost production to beat its competition. The $51 billion conglomerate's primary products are electronic, but it also manufactures machinery, petrochemicals, and ships. The mix even includes a professional baseball team, the Samsung Lions. The Lee family controls Samsung through interlocking ownership of its 33 component companies.

Samsung Electronics, which accounts for over 1/4 of company sales, is the world's #1 memory chip manufacturer, with 12.7% of the market in 1994.

Chairman Lee Kun-Hee has radically restructured management, emphasizing quality and individual responsibility. It's part of Lee's plan to make Samsung one of the world's top 5 technology firms with development of computer systems integration and software, environmental and energy systems, information systems, optics, and semiconductors.

In late 1994 Lee won a hard-fought campaign when Samsung received government permission to begin producing automobiles. The joint venture with Nissan, worth $4.5 billion, is expected to have cars on the market by 1997.

WHEN

In 1936 Japan-educated Lee Byung-Chull began operating a rice mill in Korea, then under Japanese rule. By 1938 Lee had begun trading in dried fish and had incorporated as Samsung (Korean for "Three Stars"). WWII did not inflict widespread destruction on Korea, and, by the end of the war, Samsung had transportation and real estate adjuncts.

The Korean War destroyed nearly all Samsung assets. Using the profits from a surviving brewery and importing goods for UN personnel, Lee reconstructed Samsung in South Korea. In 1953 he formed the highly profitable Cheil Sugar Company, at the time South Korea's only sugar refinery. Establishment of Cheil Wool Textile (1954) and banking and insurance ventures followed.

When a 1961 coup brought Park Chung Hee to power in South Korea, Lee, known for his wealth and ties to the former government, was accused of illegal profiteering. A 1966 smuggling scandal involving one of Lee's sons led to another scandal, but charges were dropped when Lee agreed to give the government an immense fertilizer plant he was building. Despite the setback Samsung continued to grow, diversifying into paper, department stores, and publishing. He established Samsung Electronics with help from Sanyo in 1969. The company grew rapidly as a result of the South Korean government's export drive and low wage rates. It gained engineering know-how by disassembling Western-designed electronic goods and producing inexpensive, private-label, black-and-white televisions and, later, color televisions, VCRs, and microwave ovens for General Electric, Sears, and others.

In concert with the government's industrialization push, the *chaebol* formed Samsung Shipbuilding (1974), Samsung Petrochemical (1977), and Samsung Precision Industries (aircraft engines and maintenance, 1977). Exports and a higher domestic standard of living helped group sales reach $3 billion in 1979. Samsung entered broadcasting, but, following the assassination of President Park, the new Chun regime took over all Samsung's broadcast properties.

In the 1980s Samsung began exporting electronic goods under its own name in an effort to increase margins. Success in low-end products encouraged Samsung to export up-market items.

When Lee died in 1987, his son Lee Kun-Hee assumed control. After years of importing technology and spending freely on R&D, in 1990 Samsung became a world leader in chip production. In 1991 Samsung Aerospace received a $2.5 billion contract to co-produce F-16 fighters with General Dynamics.

In 1992 Samsung and Motorola agreed to develop small, pen-based wireless computers. Also that year Samsung acquired Werk fur Fernschelektronik (of the former East Germany) and 20% of Kukje Securities (Korea). Encouraged by the Korean government, Samsung agreed to cooperate with fellow Korean *chaebol* Goldstar to obtain foreign technology to develop liquid crystal displays.

In 1994 Samsung announced it will globalize operations with new manufacturing facilities in China, Mexico, Thailand, the UK, and the US. It became the 2nd largest shareholder of the Chilean telecommunications company ENTEL.

Principal exchange: Korea
Fiscal year ends: December 31

Chairman: Lee Kun-Hee, age 52
VC: Soh Byong Hae
CEO: Song Bo Soon
President: Albert Kim
President and CEO, Samsung Electronics: Kim Kwang Ho
CEO, Samsung America: M. S. Lee
Treasurer, Samsung America: J. K. Kang
General Manager Human Resources, Samsung America: Robert Schachter
Auditors: Samil Accounting Corp.

HQ: CPO Box 1580, Seoul, Korea
Phone: +82-2-724-0361
Fax: +82-2-724-0198
US HQ: Samsung America, Inc., 105 Challenger Rd., PO Box 260, Ridgefield Park, NJ 07660
US Phone: 201-229-6050
US Fax: 201-229-6058

The Samsung Group has 254 subsidiaries and branch offices in 59 countries outside Korea.

	1993 Group Sales	
	$ mil.	% of total
Domestic sales	30,658	59
Export sales	20,873	41
Total	**51,531**	**100**

	1993 Group Sales	
	$ mil.	% of total
Financial & Information Svcs.	29,428	57
Electronics	13,438	26
Engineering	5,040	10
Consumer Prods. & Social Svcs.	2,779	5
Chemicals	846	2
Total	**51,531**	**100**

Principal Samsung Group Affiliates

Financial and Information Services
Samsung Corporation
Samsung Fire & Marine Insurance
Samsung Life Insurance
Samsung Securities
Samsung Winners Card

Electronics
Samsung Corning
Samsung Data Systems
Samsung Display Devices
Samsung Electro-Mechanics
Samsung Electronics
Samsung-GE Medical Systems
Samsung Hewlett-Packard

Engineering
Samsung Aerospace
Samsung Engineering & Construction
Samsung Heavy Industries
Samsung Watch

Consumer Products
Cheil Communications
Cheil Synthetics
Hotel Shilla Co.
Joong-Ang Daily News
Korea Secom
Samsung Lions

Chemicals
Samsung General Chemicals
Samsung Petrochemical

Daewoo
Hitachi
Hyundai
ITOCHU
Kia Motors
LG Group
Marubeni
Mitsubishi
Mitsui
NEC
Philips
Sumitomo
Toshiba

$=Won 808 (Dec. 31, 1993)	Annual Growth	1984	1985	1986	1987	1988	1989	1990	1991	1992	1993
Sales (Won bil.)	20.1%	2,568	3,802	4,275	5,670	6,811	7,613	7,952	10,199	12,055	13,321
Net income (Won bil.)	6.4%	7	6	7	8	11	11	13	15	16	12
Income as % of sales	—	0.3%	0.2%	0.2%	0.1%	0.2%	0.1%	0.2%	0.1%	0.1%	0.1%
Earnings per share (Won)	(5.5%)	—	1,162	1,028	1,258	1,397	1,018	1,031	1,033	1,089	738
Stock price – high (Won)	—	—	8,733	14,743	17,810	30,857	34,571	28,476	23,810	20,952	29,800
Stock price – low (Won)	—	—	6,333	6,476	9,524	16,095	22,286	21,238	18,571	11,714	15,700
Stock price – close (Won)	14.6%	—	—	10,905	17,238	30,857	30,857	6,123	19,905	17,905	28,300
P/E – high	—	—	8	14	14	22	34	28	23	19	40
P/E – low	—	—	5	6	8	12	22	21	18	11	21
Dividends per share (Won)	0.6%	—	476	476	571	571	571	571	571	571	500
Book value per share (Won)	—	—	—	11,162	12,661	13,301	14,010	15,466	16,128	—	—
Employees	(1.2%)	—	—	—	—	5,421	5,245	5,040	5,032	5,112	5,100

1993 Year-end:
Debt ratio: —
Return on equity: —
Cash (Won bil.): —
Long-term debt (Won bil.): —
No. of shares (mil.): 17
Dividends
  Yield: 1.8%
  Payout: 67.8%
Market value (mil.): $595
Sales (mil.): $16,486

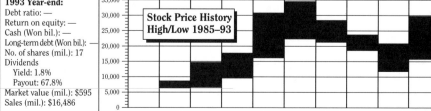

Stock Price History
High/Low 1985–93

Information presented for Samsung Corporation only

SAN MIGUEL CORPORATION

OVERVIEW

Manila-based San Miguel illustrates the problems of doing business in the developing world. San Miguel is the Philippines's largest goods-producing company (land development, commodity, and utility companies are its only competitors in size and sales), generating 4% of GNP and 7% of tax revenues, but its growth has been stymied by shortages of such basics as electricity. In 1993 power outages inhibited distribution and sales of perishables because of the lack of power for refrigeration in stores and homes. High ad valorem taxes (to help pay the nation's huge foreign debt) also cut into its alcohol sales.

Yet with its variety of products and interests, ranging from agricultural feeds to beer and other beverages to processed and fresh meats, ready-to-eat foods, and packaging, the company also illustrates the potential for profit inherent in doing business in the fast-growing Asia/Pacific area. And its home country has a large, yearning population whose economic prospects are improving.

San Miguel is in the midst of a program to upgrade its production and distribution facilities. It has also streamlined distribution within the Philippines and established brewing and bottling joint ventures to gain market share in other Asian regions. Another successful strategy is its network of international alliances (with Nestlé and Coca-Cola, among others).

WHEN

In 1890 Don Enrique Barretto y de Ycaza opened La Fabrica de Cerveza de San Miguel brewery in the San Miguel district of Manila. Don Pedro Pablo Roxas joined Don Enrique and, to ensure European-style brewing, hired German Ludwig Kiene as technical director. In 1895 the company's beer won its first prize at the Philippines Regional Exposition.

By 1900 San Miguel was outselling imported brands 5 to 1. Upon Don Pedro Roxas's death in 1913, the company became a corporation. By WWI San Miguel was selling beer in Hong Kong, Shanghai, and Guam.

Andrés Soriano y Roxas joined San Miguel in 1918 and in the 1920s established the Royal Soft Drinks Plant (1922), the Magnolia Ice Cream Plant (1925), and the first non-US national Coca-Cola bottling and distribution franchise (1927).

After the devastation of WWII, the company rebuilt and expanded, adding another brewery; more soft drink facilities; a power plant; a poultry and livestock feeds plant; and glass, carbon dioxide, and packaging plants.

In the 1960s the company changed its name to San Miguel Corporation. After the death of Andrés in 1964, his son Andrés Soriano, Jr., assumed the presidency. He modernized and decentralized operations into product segments. San Miguel continued to diversify in the 1970s.

A family feud erupted in 1983 when members of the 2 families controlling San Miguel (the Sorianos and their cousins, the Zobels) engaged in a proxy fight over control of the company. Enrique Zobel realized that he could not win the struggle and sold all of his shares (about 20% of San Miguel) to Eduardo Cojuangco, a Ferdinand Marcos crony and president of United Coconut Planters Bank. Upon Soriano's death in 1984, Cojuangco became chairman, thus securing the company under Marcos's sphere of influence.

During the 1986 election Cojuangco ordered all of the company's employees to vote for Marcos. When Aquino won, her government seized assets associated with Marcos and his followers, including Cojuangco's share of San Miguel. Cojuangco fled the country with Marcos, and Andrés Soriano III became CEO.

In 1989 Cojuangco returned to the Philippines. Two years later the Supreme Court effectively returned to Cojuangco his stake in San Miguel. That same year the company set up a joint venture with Yamamaura Glass (Japan) to manufacture containers for the Philippine market.

Also in 1991 the company, through its 60% owned Hong Kong subsidiary, reinforced its strong presence in China by establishing a joint venture, Guangzhou San Miguel Brewery. It also created Instafood, a packaged foods maker.

In 1992 San Miguel built a mineral water bottling plant and launched its Viva! and First brands and entered the Indonesian beer market, buying 49% of PT Delta Djakarta.

In 1994 the company continued to build new facilities and negotiated a joint venture agreement for a brewery in the increasingly popular market of Vietnam.

OTC symbol: SMGBY (ADR)
Fiscal year ends: December 31

Chairman and CEO: Andrés Soriano III
President and COO: Francisco C. Eizmendi, Jr.
SVP, CFO, and Treasurer: Delfin C. Gonzalez, Jr.
EVP San Miguel Brewing Group: Faustino F. Galang
SVP San Miguel Packaging Products: Raul C. Hernandez
Assistant VP, San Miguel (US): Jose Davila
Auditors: Joaquin Cunanan & Co. (Price Waterhouse)

HQ: 40 San Miguel Ave., Mandaluyong, Metropolitan Manila, 1501, PO Box 271, Manila Central Post Office, Philippines
Phone: +63-2-632-3000
Fax: +63-2-632-3099
US HQ: San Miguel Inc., 1900 South Norfolk, Ste. 270, San Mateo, CA 94404
US Phone: 415-345-1330
US Fax: 415-345-1481

San Miguel operates 4 breweries and one beer bottling plant in the Philippines, as well as breweries in China, Hong Kong, and Indonesia. In the Philippines San Miguel operates 21 soft drink bottling plants, 3 wine and spirits plants, one mineral water plant, and one distillery. It also operates 43 food production and processing facilities and 12 packaging manufacturing facilities.

	1993 Sales % of total	1993 Operating Income % of total
Beverages	65	77
Food & Agribusiness	27	17
Packaging	8	6
Total	**100**	**100**

Selected Beer
Anker
Cali Shandy
Gold Eagle
Red Horse
San Miguel NAB (nonalcoholic)
San Miguel Pale Pilsen

Selected Soft Drinks and Mineral Waters
Coca-Cola (Philippines)
Fanta
First
Royal
Sprite (Philippines)

Selected Wines and Spirits
Añejo Rum
Ginebra San Miguel
Vino Kulafu

Feeds and Livestock
B-Meg feed products

Cattle, hogs, and poultry

Foods
Aquaking (shrimp)
CampoCarne (processed meats)
Campofrio (processed meats)
Juices and drinks
Instafood Ready-to-Eat (prepared foods)
Magnolia (dairy products, poultry, juices)

Investments
Commodities
Insurance brokerage
Real estate

Packaging
Closures
Corrugated cartons
Glass
Plastic

Allied Domecq	Danone	Molson
Anheuser-Busch	Foster's Brewing	Nestlé
Bacardi	Guinness	PepsiCo
Bass	Heineken	Philip Morris
Cadbury Schweppes	John Labatt	Stroh
Carlsberg	Kirin	Tsingtao

$=P27.00 (Dec. 31, 1993)	9-Year Growth	1984	1985	1986	1987	1988	1989	1990	1991	1992	1993
Sales (P mil.)	21.7%	10,369	10,992	12,225	16,014	30,866	36,713	43,815	53,332	58,231	60,853
Net income (P mil.)	28.5%	422	364	1,111	1,758	2,052	2,431	1,796	2,812	3,585	4,029
Income as % of sales	—	4.1%	3.3%	9.1%	11.0%	6.6%	6.6%	4.1%	5.3%	6.2%	6.6%
Earnings per share (P)	27.7%	0.63	0.54	1.66	2.62	3.06	3.59	2.64	4.33	5.04	5.64
Stock price – high (P)[1]	—	3.15	2.29	13.67	25.69	28.79	73.87	32.13	49.63	68.75	143.00
Stock price – low (P)[1]	—	1.37	1.35	1.62	12.60	18.28	27.28	21.59	19.32	54.77	57.08
Stock price – close (P)[1]	66.8%	1.42	1.83	13.34	18.28	27.65	59.09	22.73	48.11	56.25	142.00
P/E – high	—	5	4	8	10	9	21	12	11	14	25
P/E – low	—	2	2	1	5	6	8	8	4	9	10
Dividends per share (P)	21.6%	0.20	0.20	0.22	0.36	0.53	0.59	0.61	0.61	0.65	1.16
Book value per share (P)	30.5%	2.64	3.05	3.70	4.86	12.00	15.14	17.47	20.89	24.11	28.96
Employees	17.3%	7,826	16,235	18,388	20,063	36,865	39,138	35,694	36,060	33,136	32,832

1993 Year-end:
Debt ratio: 48.0%
Return on equity: 21.3%
Cash (mil.): P10,749
L-Term debt (mil.): P12,526
No. of shares (mil.): 739
Dividends
Yield: 0.8%
Payout: 20.6%
Market value (mil.): $3,889
Sales (mil.): $2,254

**Stock Price History
High/Low 1984–93**

Note: Unconsolidated data 1984–87 [1] Class "A" shares

SANDOZ LTD.

OVERVIEW

Swiss pharmaceutical and chemical giant Sandoz, one of the country's Big 3 drug companies, shares its Basel home with competitors Ciba-Geigy and Roche.

Sandoz's 1994 purchase of Gerber baby foods was an effort to establish a 3rd dominant area, nutrition, along with its 2 traditionally dominant businesses, drugs and chemicals. Other segments include seeds, agrochemicals, and construction/environmental products.

The company's biggest business remains pharmaceuticals. Ranked #10 in the world, it produces a wide range of prescription drugs to treat everything from cardiovascular disease to mental illness. Sales solely of Sandimmun, a 1982 "wonder drug" that prevents the

body from rejecting transplanted organs, were about 18% of the drug division's 1993 revenue. Only 4% of Sandoz's sales come from Switerland.

Sandoz's chemicals division produces dyes, plastics, and chemicals for industrial use. Its seeds segment has a full line of vegetable, flower, and grain seed. The agrochemicals division makes a full line of herbicides, fungicides, and other biological pest control products. Sandoz's construction and environment unit makes everything from concrete corrosion inhibitors to flooring materials. The growing nutrition division, in addition to Gerber baby foods, produces Ovaltine (chocolate-flavored drinks), Wasa crispbreads, and Optifast (a liquid diet drink).

WHEN

In 1886 Alfred Kern and Edouard Sandoz established Kern und Sandoz to manufacture synthetic dyes in Basel. Kern died in 1893, and 2 years later the enterprise became a limited company with Sandoz as chairman.

The company expanded rapidly by introducing new dyes and gaining access to overseas markets. After weathering several difficult years, Sandoz grew through the end of WWI, when Germany's capitulation opened up the world chemical industry. To better compete in the world market, Sandoz joined with Basel neighbors Ciba and Geigy (which combined in 1970 to become Ciba-Geigy) to form the Basel AG cartel.

In the 1920s, a lean decade for the Swiss cartel, the company diversified into chemicals needed by the paper, textile, leather, and agricultural industries. Sandoz also established a pharmaceuticals division under Dr. Arthur Stoll, who created a way to commercially develop ergotamine, an alkaloid that would provide the basis for many of the company's pharmaceuticals.

During WWII Sandoz bought a Swiss coal mine to provide fuel for its operations, allowing the company to run unhindered by the war. After WWII Sandoz established operations in important global markets, went its own way when the Basel AG was dissolved in 1951, and by 1964 had annual sales of SF1 billion. During the postwar period the company's pharmaceutical division made significant inroads in developing psycho-

active drugs, including an experimental drug called Delysid (commonly known as LSD).

In 1967 Sandoz entered the nutrition field by buying the Berne-based Wander group of companies (dietetic products). In 1976 the company diversified into seeds, buying Minneapolis-based Northrup, King & Company and later Zaadunie B. V. (a Dutch seed company, 1980). During the 1980s the company added the Wasa Group (Swedish crispbread, 1982) and Master Builders from Martin Marietta (construction chemicals, 1985).

Catastrophe marred the company's 100th anniversary in 1986 when a warehouse fire spilled tons of chemicals into the Rhine River, killing fish and contaminating water as far away as the North Sea.

Diversification has continued in the 1990s. In late 1991 Sandoz bought shares in 2 US biotechnology companies, Genetic Therapy (6%) and SyStemix (60%). In 1992 the company made additional strides in research capacity by signing a long-term cooperative agreement with Scripps Research Institute in the US. In 1994 Marc Moret relinquished his CEO position; he remains chairman.

Many considered the company's 1994 purchase of Gerber, which sells 89% of baby food in North America, for $3.7 billion (53% over market price for shares) to be an unwise move. However, because of favorable exhange rates for the Swiss franc, Sandoz got a better deal than it first appeared and increased its nonpharmaceutical presence in the US.

OTC symbol: SDOZY (ADR)
Fiscal year ends: December 31

Chairman: Marc Moret, age 70
CEO: Rolf W. Schweizer, age 67
COO: Daniel C. Wagniere, age 57
Senior Financial Officer: Raymund Breu
Senior Officer in Charge of Management Resources and International Coordination: Alexandre F. Jetzer
CEO, Sandoz Corp. (US): Heinz Imhof
SVP Finance, Sandoz Corp. (US): Roland Lösser
VP Human Resources, Sandoz Corp. (US): Richard Bilotti
Auditors: Swiss Auditing and Fiduciary Company; Coopers & Lybrand SA

HQ: Lichtstrasse 35, CH-4002 Basel, Switzerland
Phone: +41-61-324-11-11
Fax: +41-61-324-80-01
US HQ: Sandoz Corp., 608 Fifth Ave., New York, NY 10020
US Phone: 212-307-1122
US Fax: 212-246-0185

	1993 Sales	
	SF mil.	% of total
Europe	6,401	42
US & Canada	4,643	31
Asia	2,760	18
Latin America	876	6
Africa & Australia	420	3
Total	**15,100**	**100**

	1993 Sales	
	SF mil.	% of total
Pharmaceuticals	7,348	49
Chemicals	2,500	17
Nutrition	1,722	11
Agro	1,315	9
Construction & environment	1,234	8
Seeds	981	6
Total	**15,100**	**100**

Selected Subsidiaries and Affiliates

Gerber Products Co.	Sandoz Chemicals Ltd.
Indústrias Químicas Resende SA (Brazil)	Sandoz Management Services SA (Belgium)
MBT Holding Ltd.	Sandoz Nutrition Ltd.
Master Builders, Inc. (US)	Sandoz Pharma Ltd.
Sandoz Agro Ltd.	Sandoz Overseas
Sandoz Corp. (US)	Finance Ltd. (British
Sandoz Industrial Chemicals Ltd. (Hong Kong)	Virgin Islands)
	Sandoz Seeds Ltd.

Abbott Labs	Heico	Ralcorp
ADM	Heinz	Rhône-
American Home Products	Hoechst	Poulenc
	Imperial	RJR Nabisco
Baxter	Chemical	Roche
Bristol-Myers Squibb	Johnson &	Schering-
Cargill	Johnson	Plough
Ciba-Geigy	Marion Merrell	Siemens
ConAgra	Dow	Slim-Fast
Dow Chemical	Merck	Nutritional
Eli Lilly	Monsanto	SmithKline
General Mill	Nestlé	Beecham
Glaxo	Philip Morris	Upjohn
Grand Metropolitan	Quaker Oats	Warner-Lambert

$=SF1.49 (Dec. 31, 1993)	9-Year Growth	1984	1985	1986	1987	1988	1989	1990	1991	1992[1]	1993
Sales (SF mil.)	8.2%	7,434	8,453	8,361	8,979	10,151	12,497	12,367	13,444	14,416	15,100
Net income (SF mil.)	17.1%	411	529	541	627	761	958	967	1,114	1,495	1,706
Income as % of sales	—	5.5%	6.3%	6.5%	7.0%	7.5%	7.7%	7.8%	8.3%	10.4%	11.3%
Earnings per share (SF)	13.3%	73	88	80	91	110	138	140	147	197	225
Stock price – high (SF)[2]	—	1,520	2,190	2,600	3,160	2,585	2,700	2,480	2,570	3,200	4,360
Stock price – low (SF)[2]	—	1,290	1,400	1,980	1,960	1,820	1,920	1,700	1,716	2,480	2,850
Stock price – close (SF)[2]	13.5%	1,400	2,190	2,200	2,360	1,915	2,305	1,800	2,460	3,140	4,360
P/E – high	—	21	25	33	35	24	20	18	17	16	19
P/E – low	—	18	16	25	22	17	14	12	12	13	13
Dividends per share (SF)	13.9%	18.00	20.00	21.00	22.00	24.00	30.00	30.00	35.00	47.00	58.00
Book value per share (SF)	7.3%	742	770	666	808	825	901	1,008	1,008	1,232	1,394
Employees	3.7%	38,036	40,166	42,627	43,996	48,079	50,655	52,640	53,400	53,360	52,550

1993 Year-end:
Debt ratio: 28.0%
Return on equity: 17.1%
Cash (mil.): SF6,180
Long-term debt (mil.): SF1,762
No. of shares (mil.): 8
Dividends
  Yield: 1.3%
  Payout: 25.8%
Market value (mil.): $22,163
Sales (mil.): $10,134

Stock Price History
High/Low 1984–93

[1] Accounting change [2] Bearer shares

SANYO ELECTRIC CO., LTD.

OVERVIEW

Sanyo Electric is one of Japan's and the world's largest industrial companies. Its 60 global manufacturing plants make a variety of electrical devices and appliances, including industrial and commercial equipment (refrigerated showcases, commercial air conditioners, and heating systems), video and audio equipment, semiconductors, information systems (calculators, computers, and telephone equipment), batteries, and home appliances (microwave ovens, air conditioners, and small appliances). The company also is a leading solar cell manufacturer and maker of CFC-free refrigerators.

With low-voltage sales of its consumer electronics and appliances, a strong yen, and 2 years of negative earnings, Sanyo ousted its president, cut staff, and shifted some of its manufacturing overseas. Despite increased sales Sanyo is having to focus on profits like never before. The company's long-term goals are to develop innovative products, buy manufactured parts for some of its consumer products, shift operations to more profitable products, and focus on specialized areas where it has an edge on its competitors, such as batteries, solar cells, and flat-screen liquid-crystal displays.

WHEN

Sanyo means "3 oceans" in Japanese. Toshio Iue, Sanyo's first CEO, had the Pacific, Atlantic, and Indian oceans in mind; he wanted to turn the company into an international enterprise. Sanyo was formed after WWII, when the Allies broke Matsushita Electric into 2 companies. Toshio, brother-in-law to Konosuke Matsushita, took charge of the company, which then made bicycle lamps.

By 1949 Sanyo was producing radios, in great demand in Japan. Sanyo outsold many of its competitors by offering very low prices and using plastic casings, introduced in 1952.

The company rapidly diversified in the 1950s and began making portable radios, refrigerators, fans, and washing machines. In 1953 a Japanese household appliances rush began and Sanyo led washing machine sales, having introduced an inexpensive whirlpool-action model. By the late 1950s Sanyo was Japan's leading exporter of transistor radios.

To raise money, in 1959 Sanyo created Tokyo Sanyo Electric, in which it took a 20% stake. In 1961 Sanyo established its first overseas factory in Hong Kong. That year Sanyo also created Cadnica, a rechargeable and durable battery. In 1968 Toshio's brother, Yuro Iue, took charge.

In 1973 Sanyo joined forces with Emerson Electric (US) to help bail out Emerson's Fisher, an electronics company. Sanyo began shifting its focus from appliances to high-tech products in the mid-1970s. The company began making color TVs in the US in 1976 and 2 years later bought Fisher from Emerson. Although sales slowed when Sanyo at first opted to develop VCRs using the ill-fated Betamax format, the company's sales rose tremendously in the 1970s, from $71 million in 1972 to $855 million in 1978.

The 1970s oil crisis drew the company into alternative energy development. Although demand waned at the passing of the crisis, Sanyo continued its energy research.

Taking the blame for deaths caused by faulty Sanyo kerosene heaters, CEO Kaoru Iue resigned in 1986, leaving the company to Toshio's son Satoshi. In 1986 Satoshi re-merged Sanyo and Tokyo Sanyo Electric. A high yen forced the company to manufacture increasingly outside of Japan; in 1986 Sanyo made more products offshore than any other Japanese company. Sanyo was Japan's leading TV maker that year and also formed a joint venture with Sears to manufacture TVs.

In 1987 Sanyo merged its 2 US operations, creating Sanyo Fisher (USA). Sales in the US subsequently increased, and by 1992 Sanyo had 20% of the CD boom box market. The company also developed the world's first CFC-free refrigeration system (Sanyo's CFC-free AC system is used at the Guggenheim Museum in New York).

Plummeting profits in 1992 forced out Satoshi, who was replaced by EVP Yasuaki Takano. Also that year Sanyo commissioned GE to produce air conditioning compressors and agreed to make semiconductors for high-definition TVs (HDTV) with LSI Logic (US). In 1993 Sanyo introduced a new management system that gave more responsibility to each business sector. Also that year the company set a world record for solar energy conversion efficiency. Sanyo finished 1994 with $115 million in net profits from $16.8 billion in sales.

Nasdaq symbol: SANYY(ADR)
Fiscal year ends: November 30

WHO

Chairman: Satoshi Iue
President: Yasuaki Takano
EVP: Seijo Takagi
EVP: Yutaka Kimoto
EVP: Muneo Arata
President, Sanyo North America: Motoharu Iue
SVP Accounting, Sanyo North America:
Mikio Ando
VP Human Resources, Sanyo North America:
Yoshinobu Nakatani
Auditors: Coopers & Lybrand

WHERE

HQ: 5-5 Keihan Hondori 2-chome,
Moriguchi City, Osaka 570, Japan
Phone: +81-6-991-1181
Fax: +81-6-991-6566 (Corporate
Communications)
US HQ: Sanyo North America Corporation,
666 Fifth Ave., New York, NY 10103
US Phone: 212-315-3232
US Fax: 212-315-3263

	1993 Sales	
	$ mil.	% of total
Japan	8,229	58
North America	2,080	15
Asia	2,015	14
Europe	1,176	8
Other countries	653	5
Total	**14,153**	**100**

WHAT

	1993 Sales	
	$ mil.	% of total
Info. systems & electronic devices	3,629	26
Home appliances	3,088	22
Industrial & commercial equipment	2,435	17
Video equipment	2,099	15
Audio equipment	1,325	9
Batteries & other	1,577	11
Total	**14,153**	**100**

Major Subsidiaries
Niigata SANYO Electronic Co., Ltd. (semiconductors)
SANYO Electric Credit Co., Ltd. (credit and leasing)
SANYO Electric Trading Co., Ltd. (import and exports)
SANYO Electronics (Singapore) Private Ltd. (cassette
recorders, radios, and color TVs)
SANYO FISHER (USA) Corp. (electronics)
SANYO Life Electronics Co., Ltd. (electric and electronic
equipment)
SANYO Manufacturing Corp. (TVs)
SANYO Semiconductor (H.K.) Co., Ltd.
Tottori SANYO Electric Co., Ltd. (audio equipment,
appliances, electronics, and information systems)

KEY COMPETITORS

ABB	Hitachi	Premark
Alcatel Alsthom	IBM	Ralston Purina
AMD	Intel	Group
Apple	Lucky-Goldstar	Samsung
AT&T	Mannesmann	Sharp
Black & Decker	Matsushita	Siemens
Chips and	Maytag	Silicon Graphics
Technologies	National	Sony
Compaq	Semiconductor	Thomson SA
Dell	NEC	Toshiba
Electrolux	Oki	Unisys
Fuji Photo	Olivetti	Wang
Fujitsu	Philips	Whirlpool
General Electric	Pioneer	Yamaha
Harris Corp.	Pitney Bowes	Zenith

HOW MUCH

	Annual Growth	1984	1985	1986	1987	1988	1989	1990	1991	1992	1993
Sales ($ mil.)	10.0%	6,010	6,271	6,915	9,124	10,332	9,727	11,282	12,444	12,559	14,153
Net income ($ mil.)	—	186	151	12	(133)	51	118	132	130	(10)	(14)
Income as % of sales	—	3.1%	2.4%	0.2%	—	0.5%	1.2%	1.2%	1.0%	—	—
Earnings per share ($)	—	0.90	0.71	0.05	(0.40)	0.14	0.31	0.34	0.33	(0.03)	(0.04)
Stock price – high ($)	—	—	10.13	14.25	19.75	33.00	35.63	36.88	25.25	21.25	22.00
Stock price – low ($)	—	—	7.88	9.38	11.88	16.38	28.50	19.75	16.75	13.25	13.88
Stock price – close ($)	(1.6%)	—	—	—	16.13	29.63	33.38	21.50	20.50	14.88	18.75
P/E – high	—	—	14	—	—	—	115	109	77	—	—
P/E – low	—	—	11	—	—	—	92	58	51	—	—
Dividends per share ($)	4.9%	0.15	0.17	0.23	0.20	0.24	0.24	0.24	0.21	0.24	0.23
Book value per share ($)	8.6%	7.98	9.21	11.12	13.74	15.05	13.23	14.44	14.77	15.06	16.73
Employees	12.8%	—	—	25,599	40,590	39,179	55,526	55,124	56,079	56,156	59,624

1993 Year-end:
Debt ratio: 53.8%
Return on equity: —
Cash (mil.): $4,866
Current ratio: 1.40
Long-term debt (mil.): $3,188
No. of shares (mil.): 388
Dividends
Yield: 1.2%
Payout: —
Market value (mil.): $7,266

**Stock Price History
High/Low 1985–93**

SCANDINAVIAN AIRLINES SYSTEM

OVERVIEW

Little known outside of Europe, the Scandinavian Airlines System (SAS) is a partnership of 3 companies representing the governments of Denmark (Det Danske Luftfartselskab/Danish Airlines), Norway (Det Norske Luftfartselskap/Norwegian Airlines), and Sweden (AB Aero-transport/Swedish Airlines). Denmark and Norway each owns 2/7 while the remainder is owned by Sweden and a few private investors.

SAS has suffered from a deep European recession, overcapacity, and a weak Swedish krone. Three years of red ink led SAS to try to merge with KLM, Swissair, and Austrian Airlines to create a new international carrier (Alcazar), but that venture failed in late 1993, leading to the replacement of its longtime CEO, Jan Carlzon. New CEO Jan Stenberg consolidated the group, which included shedding noncore businesses and cutting 2,900 jobs. By late 1994 SAS had sold its largest nonairline unit, SAS Service Partner (catering), Diners Club Nordic, and most of the SAS Leisure Group, Scandinavia's largest tour company. By spinning off its 42% stake in LanChile and creating a new Latvian airline with Baltic International, SAS has focused its air routes in Scandinavia, Western Europe, and the Baltic region.

SAS routes extend over 5 other continents through alliances with Austrian Airlines, Swissair, Continental Airlines, Icelandair, Thai Airways International, Varig, Qantas Airways, and Air New Zealand.

WHEN

Although SAS wasn't established until after WWII, the national airlines of Sweden (ABA), Norway (DNL), and Denmark (DDL) first met in 1938 to negotiate joint service to New York. The plan was delayed by the war but kept alive in Sweden, where banker Marcus Wallenberg founded Svensk Interkontinental Luftrafik (SILA), a private airline that later replaced ABA as Sweden's international carrier (1943). With SILA's financial backing, the yet-to-be-formed SAS obtained the necessary landing concessions to open a Stockholm–New York air route (1945). SAS was formed in 1946, with DDL and DNL each owning 2/7 and SILA/ABA owning 3/7.

After opening service to South America (1946), Southeast Asia (1949), and Africa (1953), SAS inaugurated the world's first commercial polar route in 1954. SAS bought 50% of the Swedish domestic airline Linjeflyg in 1957 (sold in 1990) and later formed the charter airline Scanair (1961) and the Danish domestic airline Danair (through a joint venture, 1971).

Deregulation of America's airlines (1978) signaled the demise of protectionist attitudes that had traditionally shielded the world's airlines from competition. SAS, born and raised in such a protected environment (and burdened by rising fuel costs), seemed ill-equipped to adapt, reporting its first loss in 18 years in 1980. Jan Carlzon, former head of Linjeflyg, became SAS's president in 1981. By targeting businessmen as the airline's most stable market and substituting an economy-rate business class for first-class service on European flights, Carlzon had turned SAS's losses into profits by the end of 1982.

Carlzon allied SAS with other airlines through marketing and ownership agreements. SAS bought about 25% of Airlines of Britain Holdings (ABH) in 1988, gaining a foothold at London's Heathrow Airport. Another purchase in 1988 brought SAS nearly 10% of Continental Airlines Holdings (raised to 16.8% in 1990). In 1989 SAS signed agreements that provided route coordination and hub-sharing with Swissair, Finnair, All Nippon Airways (terminated in 1993), LanChile, and Canadian Airlines International, and bought 40% of Saison Overseas Holdings (sold in 1991), owner of the Inter-Continental hotel chain. Continental Airlines's 1990 bankruptcy filing prompted SAS to write down its 16.8% interest in that airline by SEK780 million.

The company expanded service in 1991 and 1992, especially in Russia, Lithuania, and the Baltic States, and in Asia. Also in 1992 SAS acquired 51% of Linjeflyg, the Swedish airline, increased its stake in ABH to 35%, and introduced a frequent flyer program.

In 1994 the airline consortium folded the SAS trading subsidiary into the airline unit and through its hotel unit allied itself with Radisson Hotels to expand its presence in Europe, the Middle East, and Asia. In 1994 comparable revenue rose 7%, and the company posted over $200 million in net income, its first profit in 4 years.

Consortium
Fiscal year ends: December 31

Chairman: Tage Andersen, age 67
President and CEO: Jan Stenberg, age 55
Corporate Finance and Control: Gunnar Reitan
Human Resources: Bernhard Rikardsen
General Manager, SAS of North America: Owe
    Lowenborg
**Director Human Resources, SAS of North
    America:** Jerry Pinola
Auditors: KPMG; Deloitte & Touche

HQ: Frösundaviks Allé 1, Solna, S-195 87
    Stockholm, Sweden
Phone: +46-8-797-00-00
Fax: +46-8-85-82-87
US HQ: Scandinavian Airlines System of North
    America, Inc., 9 Polito Ave., Lyndhurst,
    NJ 07071
US Phone: 201-896-3600
US Fax: 201-896-3725
Reservations: 800-221-2350

SAS serves 103 cities in 33 countries. SAS also
has hotels in Austria, Belgium, China, Denmark,
Finland, Germany, Kuwait, the Netherlands,
Norway, Sweden, and Vietnam (opening 1996).

	1993 Passenger Miles (mil.)
Intercontinental	4,273
Europe	3,062
Iceland & Finland	1,354
Sweden	985
Norway	945
Denmark	263
Total	**7,882**

	1993 Sales	
	SEK mil.	% of total
Airline	27,538	66
Service Partner	4,816	12
Leisure	4,440	11
Trading	2,259	5
Hotels	1,853	5
Diners Club	517	1
Adjustments	(2,301)	—
Total	**39,122**	**100**

Major Subsidiaries
SAS Airline (global airline services)
    SAS Commuter (regional airline services)
SAS International Hotels AS

Selected Affiliates
Airlines of Britain Holdings PLC (ABH, 34.9%, owns
    British Midland, Loganair, and Manx Airlines)
Danair AS (57%, regional airline)
Grønlandsfly AS (37.5%, Greenland's domestic airline)
Linjeflyg AB (51%, regional airline services)

Flight Equipment	No.	Orders
Douglas MD-80 line	65	—
Fokker derivatives	41	—
Douglas DC-9	36	—
Boeing 767	15	2
Douglas MD-90	—	6
Boeing 737	13	3
SAAB	13	—
Total	**183**	**11**

Accor	Delta	Singapore
Aer Lingus	IRI	Airlines
Aeroflot	JAL	Swire Pacific
Air France	KLM	Tower Air
All Nippon Airways	LOT	UAL
AMR	Lufthansa	Virgin Group
British Airways	Northwest Airlines	

$=SEK8.33 (Dec. 31, 199)	9-Year Growth	1984	1985	1986	1987[1]	1988	1989	1990	1991	1992	1993
Sales (SEK mil.)	9.0%	18,005	19,790	21,585	24,288	27,556	28,786	31,883	32,286	34,445	39,122
Pretax income (SEK mil.)	—	829	892	1,322	1,445	3,262	1,977	(65)	(181)	(871)	(591)
Income as % of sales	—	4.6%	4.5%	6.1%	5.9%	11.8%	6.9%	—	—	—	—
Passengers (thou.)	7.1%	10,066	10,735	11,708	12,662	13,341	14,005	14,962	13,949	16,808	18,619
Available seat km (mil.)	5.7%	17,395	17,818	18,849	19,019	20,941	23,320	25,475	24,317	26,396	28,581
Rev. passenger km (mil.)	5.0%	11,681	11,966	12,471	13,207	14,027	15,229	16,493	15,416	16,554	18,138
Passenger load factor	—	67.2%	67.2%	66.2%	69.4%	67.0%	65.3%	64.7%	63.4%	62.7%	63.5%
Size of fleet	6.7%	85	87	104	102	109	119	132	135	158	153
Employees	3.0%	28,526	29,730	31,770	34,900	36,150	39,060	40,830	38,940	40,140	37,330

1993 Year-end:
Debt ratio: 73.7%
Return on Equity: (6.7%)
Cash (mil.): SEK9,318
Current ratio: 1.55
Long-term debt
    (mil.): SEK22,582
Sales (mil.): $4,696

Pretax Income
(SEK mil.) 1984–93

[1]15-month fiscal year

GROUPE SCHNEIDER

OVERVIEW

Paris-based Groupe Schneider is one of the world's largest electrical engineering companies, providing design and equipment for power transmission and control as well as heavy infrastructure construction services (through subsidiary Spie Batignolles). It is one of the few large French industrial concerns to escape nationalization. AXA, one of France's largest insurance groups, owns almost 8% of Schneider.

Schneider has been reorganizing since 1981. In 1993 this effort entered its final phase with a major recapitalization that saw the merger of its former parent company, Société Parisienne d'Entreprises et de Participations, with Schneider SA and the issue of new stock to existing stockholders. It also streamlined operations: Merlin Gerin and Telemecanique became Schneider Electric in Europe and their North American operations were merged into Square D (acquired 1991).

In 1994, after Schneider's takeover of 2 Belgian subsidiaries sparked protests (since settled for more money) by a minority of shareholders, the Belgian government issued arrest warrants against CEO Didier Pineau-Valencienne, for fraud in the valuation of stock. When Pineau-Valencienne entered Belgium to answer the charges, he was jailed for 12 days. After he jumped bail, a Belgian judge issued an international warrant for his arrest, making him a virtual prisoner in France.

WHEN

Schneider's roots go back to the dawn of the Industrial Revolution, when its predecessor company was founded in 1782 to produce industrial equipment. Then came the upheavals of the French Revolution and the Napoleonic Wars, which kept France's industrial development well behind that of England. In 1836 the company came under the control of 2 brothers named Schneider. Within 2 years they had built the first French locomotive (the country's first rail line had opened in 1832).

The company became one of France's most important heavy industrial companies, branching into a variety of heavy machinery and steel. But France's industrial development continued to trail that of Britain and Germany because of recurrent political upheavals (the violent revolutions of 1848 and the Franco-Prussian War, which saw the Germans occupying Paris in 1871). France also possessed less of the 2 natural resources most necessary for industrial development — coal and iron deposits — than did its rivals.

During WWI Schneider was an important part of France's war effort. After the war the company survived the postwar depression and regained its footing, only to be hit by the Great Depression. In the mid-1930s it was still under the control of the Schneider family, which foiled attempts to nationalize it.

The Blitzkrieg of 1939 brought much of France under Nazi occupation. Those Schneider factories that were not destroyed were commandeered to produce for the German war effort.

After the war the company rebuilt, helped along by generous aid and direction from the French government. Schneider was restructured as a holding company and its actual operating units were split into 3 subsidiaries, civil and electrical engineering, industrial manufacturing, and construction.

In 1963 Schneider concluded an alliance with the Empain Group of Belgium. At first the companies remained separate, but by 1969, 3 years after Schneider went public, they merged to become Empain-Schneider. Although the operating companies continued to be separate, there was a unified management. Also during this period and in the ensuing years, the company made numerous noncore acquisitions, entering such fields as ski equipment, fashion, publishing, and travel.

In 1980, as France took a turn to the left, the Empain family sold out. As the Mitterand socialist government threatened new nationalizations, Schneider's new management, under former Rhône-Poulenc executive Didier Pineau-Valencienne, re-engineered the company. Schneider not only shed its more exotic ventures but also turned its back decisively on its roots in heavy industry, choosing instead to concentrate on electrical controls and power systems, systems engineering, and infrastructure construction.

Pineau-Valencienne has given Schneider an international bent, ceding a great deal of autonomy to local managements and seeking to grow the company's non-European operations to more than half of sales.

Principal exchange: Paris
Fiscal year ends: December 31

Chairman and CEO: Didier Pineau-Valencienne
EVP European and International Divisions:
Jean-Louis Andreu
VP Finance: Jean de Courcel
VP and General Counsel: André Roquefeuil
VP Human Resources: Guy Lemarchand
President and CEO, North American Division:
Charles W. Denny
President and CEO, Square D (US): William P.
Brink
CFO and VP Human Resources, Square D (US):
Charles L. Hite
Auditors: Barbier, Finault et autres

HQ: 40, avenue André Morizet, F-92646
Boulogne-Billancourt Cedex
Phone: 33-1-46-05-38-20
Fax: 33-1-46-99-74-38
US HQ: Square D Company, 1415 S. Roselle Rd.,
Palatine, IL 60067
US Phone: 708-397-2600
US Fax: 708-397-8814

	1993 Sales	
	FF mil.	% of total
France	23,786	42
North America	11,628	21
Africa & Latin America	3,829	7
Asia	2,560	5
Middle East & other	3,449	6
Other Western Europe	11,125	19
Total	**56,377**	**100**

	1993 Sales		1993 Operating Income	
	FF mil.	% of total	FF mil.	% of total
Schneider Elect.	37,942	68	2,835	99
Spie Batignolles	18,300	32	35	1
Other	135	0	(75)	—
Total	**56,377**	**100**	**2,795**	**100**

Selected Services

Electrical Contracting and Construction

Industrial Control
Data acquisition and user-machine interfaces
Data processing
Power controls

Low-voltage Distribution
Building control systems (access, fire, and
intrusion alarms)
Communications networks
Distribution switchgear and protection devices
Installation equipment and systems

Power Transmission and Distribution
Power-grid protection and control
Safety and control/monitor equipment for
nuclear power plants

Uninterruptible Power Supplies

ABB	General	Peter Kiewit
Alcatel Alsthom	Electric	Sons'
American Power	Ingersoll-Rand	Raytheon
Conversion	Johnson	Rolls-Royce
Bechtel	Controls	Siemens
Coooper	Mitsubishi	Toshiba
Industries	Morrison	Westinghouse
Emerson	Knudsen	
Fluor	Omron	

$=FF5.91 (Dec. 31, 1993)	Annual Growth	1984	1985	1986	1987	1988	1989	1990	1991	1992	1993
Sales (FF mil.)	28.5%	5,888	7,660	25,751	29,294	40,493	45,236	49,884	50,022	61,441	56,377
Net income (FF mil.)	—	(15)	220	314	324	560	877	924	275	305	405
Income as % of sales	—	—	2.9%	1.2%	1.1%	1.4%	1.9%	1.9%	0.5%	0.5%	0.7%
Earnings per share (FF)	—	(5)	69	35	36	49	45	47	22	16	9
Stock price – high (FF)	—	—	171	413	355	323	483	590	406	391	479
Stock price – low (FF)	—	—	54	173	98	110	314	288	251	245	210
Stock price – close (FF)	6.4%	—	—	—	—	323	473	—	283	300	441
P/E – high	—	—	2	12	10	7	11	13	18	—	55
P/E – low	—	—	1	5	3	2	7	6	11	—	24
Dividends per share (FF)	4.9%	0.0	0.0	5.0	5.5	5.5	6.3	6.5	6.5	6.5	7.0
Book value per share (FF)	5.3%	172	141	144	153	183	241	265	271	230	273
Employees	(6.1%)	—	—	—	—	—	—	—	—	97,451	91,458

1993 Year-end:
Debt ratio: 51.0%
Return on equity: —
Cash (mil.): FF6,094
L-T debt (mil.): FF10,903
No. of shares (mil.): 60
Dividends
  Yield: 1.6%
  Payout: 80.4%
Market value (mil.): $4,485
Sales (mil.): $9,539

**Stock Price History
High/Low 1985–93**

SCITEX CORPORATION LTD.

OVERVIEW

Israel's Scitex is a leading manufacturer and distributor of electronic prepress systems, with more than a 40% share of the global market. Such global success is unusual for an Israeli company and all the more remarkable because its home market for such products is virtually nonexistent.

Scitex's success is based on aggressive R&D and marketing efforts (also rare among Israeli companies, which have generally emphasized R&D at the expense of marketing) that have resulted in the company's near lock on the high-end market for prepress equipment, with such customers as R.R. Donnelly, the New York Times, and National Geographic. In the mid-1990s, however, the

company has sought to expand its products into the middle range of the market, targeting smaller printers and in-house operations. Scitex has also introduced newer applications, such as the production of hard copy of images from medical diagnostic machines like CAT Scanners.

The company supports its products, which take graphic images from the layout stage to the preparation of 4-color illustrations, with a worldwide network of sales and service support personnel.

Scitex's largest shareholders, with about 12% each, are International Paper, CEI (Clal Electronics Industries Ltd.), and entities controlled by the Recanati family of Israel.

WHEN

Ephraim Arazi, an Israeli who had worked for Itek (optical systems) in the US, went back to Israel after the Six Day War. There he founded Scientific Technology (1968) to produce systems for the Israeli military. But he soon came to believe that the defense sphere, burdened with many controls and regulations, was not the field for success. Accordingly Arazi sought civilian applications and found one: automated scanners to design patterns for jacquard knits. With the help of Arthur Low, a Canadian, Arazi turned the company, Scitex (founded in 1971), into a success and opened a US distribution company. When the fad for patterned knits faded, around 1975, the company applied the same technology to developing prints for woven fabrics. Its first European office opened in 1974, and it began selling its products in Japan 2 years later.

With their North American backgrounds, Arazi and Low were more aware than most Israeli executives of the importance of marketing, and by the mid-1970s, marketing expenditures were keeping pace with R&D costs. They particularly emphasized the importance of elaborate exhibits at trade shows.

But fabric printing was a somewhat limited market, and in the late 1970s the company began to apply its technology to graphics and printing. Here at last was a true growth industry. Its first system, Response 300, was introduced in 1979. It was expensive, which meant that it could only pay for itself if used nearly continuously, and only major printing operations could use it

economically. And as they did, color illustrations improved and became less expensive.

Company sales exploded. In the early 1980s sales grew 100% every 2 years, and the work force doubled every 3 years. And they expected it to go on forever.

But it didn't, and by 1985 the company was in trouble. Scitex took in its belt a few notches. Although there were layoffs, across-the-board pay reductions minimized the number of people who lost their jobs. Major shareholders poured more money into the company, sales staff worked to prevent clients from being lured away by fearmongering competitors, and R&D continued hot and heavy. By 1987 the company was on track and returned to profitability in 1988.

By the next year Scitex had recovered enough to be attractive to a major investor like UK media magnate Robert Maxwell, who bought 27% of the company. He believed Scitex should become a major multinational company and that his new interest represented an attractive synergy with his printing holdings.

By 1991, however, Maxwell was overextended. Although Japanese investors sought his shares, he turned them down because of Japan's stance on trade with the Arab world. By then his share of Scitex was reduced to 19% and the company's 1991 US stock offering allowed him to dispose of his remaining interest in the company. The offering also left the company with a lot of cash, which it has used to fund an acquisitions program that continued in 1994 despite slow sales.

Nasdaq symbol: SCIXF (ADR)
Fiscal year ends: December 31

Chairman: Dov Tadmor, age 64
President and CEO: Arie Rosenfeld, age 50
EVP and CFO: Giora Bitan, age 39
EVP Marketing and Business Development: Yoav Z. Chelouche
Corporate VP Human Resources and Organization: Ilan Gonen
President, Scitex America: George S. Carlisle
VP Finance, Scitex America: Suzanne Rogers
VP Human Resources, Scitex America: John J. Whalen
Auditors: Kesselman & Kesselman

WHERE

HQ: Hamada St., Industrial Park, 46103 Herzlia B, Israel
Phone: 972-9-597-222
Fax: 972-9-502-922
US HQ: Scitex America Corp., 8 Oak Park Dr., Bedford, MA 01730
US Phone: 617-275-5150
US Fax: 617-275-3430

	1993 Sales	
	$ mil.	% of total
The Americas	341	55
Europe	209	34
Japan	45	7
Other countries	28	4
Total	**623**	**100**

WHAT

	1993 Sales	
	$ mil.	% of total
Sales	520	83
Service & supplies	103	17
Total	**623**	**100**

Selected Products
Design and layout software
Editing Systems
  PrisMagic (workstation)
  Prismax (workstation)
Image Input
  Leafscan (scanners)
  Lumina (camera scanners)
  Smart (scanners)
Imagesetting
  Dolev (drum imagesetters)
Management and Archiving Systems
Networking and Telecommunications
Proofing
  SmartJet
  Iris
Raystar CTP (computer-to-plate imagesetters)

Selected Subsidiaries
ImMIX
Iris Graphics, Inc.
Leaf Systems, Inc.
Nihon Scitex Ltd. (50%, Japan)
Scitex America Corp.
Scitex Asia Pacific (H.K.) Ltd.
Scitex Digital Printing, Inc.
Scitex Europe SA
Scitex Israel
Scitex Medical Systems, Inc.

KEY COMPETITORS

Agfa	DuPont	IBM
Barco Graphics	Fuji	Siemens
Dai Nippon	Hyphen	

HOW MUCH

	Annual Growth	1984	1985	1986	1987	1988	1989	1990	1991	1992	1993
Sales ($ mil.)	25.8%	—	—	133	159	192	238	352	430	550	663
Net income ($ mil.)	—	—	—	(34)	(5)	15	35	77	101	122	94
Income as % of sales	—	—	—	—	—	7.7%	14.9%	21.9%	23.4%	22.3%	14.2%
Earnings per share ($)	—	—	—	(1.54)	(0.21)	63.00	1.00	2.10	2.70	3.02	2.10
Stock price – high ($)	—	—	—	—	—	—	—	21.13	39.25	44.13	44.38
Stock price – low ($)	—	—	—	—	—	—	—	7.38	13.50	31.50	22.25
Stock price – close ($)	17.8%	—	—	—	—	—	—	15.13	35.50	42.75	24.75
P/E – high	—	—	—	—	—	—	—	10	15	15	21
P/E – low	—	—	—	—	—	—	—	4	5	10	11
Dividends per share ($)	14.0%	—	—	—	—	—	—	—	0.40	0.48	0.52
Book value per share ($)	29.9%	—	—	3.49	3.35	4.23	4.79	6.51	—	15.07	16.78
Employees	—	—	—	—	—	—	—	—	—	—	2,970

1993 Year-end:
Debt ratio: 0.2%
Return on equity: 13.9%
Cash (mil.): $273
Current ratio: 4.01
Long-term debt (mil.): $0
No. of shares (mil.): 43
Dividends
  Yield: 2.1%
  Payout: 24.8%
Market value (mil.): $1,057

Stock Price History
High/Low 1990–93

THE SEAGRAM COMPANY LTD.

The party may be winding down, but Seagram isn't waiting around for last call. Based in Montreal, the company is the 2nd largest distiller in the world (after Grand Metropolitan). However, with health-conscious consumers in the US (where it makes 43% of its sales) drinking less alcohol, in 1993 company sales dropped for the first time since the early 1980s.

In response the company continues to diversify. It owns 24.2% of DuPont and 14.2% of Time Warner and is expanding its Tropicana line, which has 31% of the world's chilled orange juice market.

Of course, Seagram can still mix potent potables. Its brands include 7 Crown, Crown Royal, and V.O. whiskeys; Chivas Regal scotch; Myers's rum; Martell cognac; and Mumm champagne. The company also sells wine, wine coolers, and mixers.

While Americans may be climbing on the wagon, Seagram still sees plenty of opportunities to set up another round in other parts of the world, with a particular focus on China and India. The Bronfman family (descendants of Sam Bronfman, the company's founder) owns approximately 36.4% of the total outstanding shares.

In 1916 Sam Bronfman bought the Bonaventure Liquor Store Company in Montreal and started selling liquor by mail order (the only legal way during Canadian Prohibition, which lasted from 1918 until the early 1920s). In 1924, with the help of his brother Allan, Bronfman opened the first family distillery in neighboring La Salle and took the name Distillers Corporation Limited. Bronfman, later known as "Mr. Sam," purchased the larger Joseph E. Seagram & Sons in 1928, went public, and changed his company name to Distillers Corporation–Seagrams Limited.

During the 1920s Bronfman established a lucrative bootlegging operation that smuggled whiskey into the "dry" US. The company may have accounted for half of the illegal liquor crossing the border. In 1928 Bronfman, expecting the end of Prohibition in the US, began stockpiling whiskey. When Prohibition ended in 1933, Bronfman had the world's largest supply of aged rye and sour mash whiskeys. To further meet US demand, he also purchased 3 US distilleries in quick succession in the 1930s.

Bootlegging had given whiskey a harsh image, which Bronfman sought to change by introducing his smooth, blended Seagram's 7 Crown in 1934. In 1939, after blending over 600 whiskey samples, Bronfman created Crown Royal in honor of the visit of King George VI and Queen Elizabeth to Canada.

During the 1940s Seagram expanded its liquor line. In 1942 it formed a partnership with Fromm and Sichel to buy Paul Masson (sold in 1987) and shortly thereafter purchased distilleries in the West Indies that would later produce the Captain Morgan and

Myers's brand rums. After WWII it acquired Mumm and Perrier-Jouët (champagne), Barton & Guestier and Augier Frères (wine), and Chivas Brothers (scotch).

Edgar Bronfman succeeded his father as company president in 1957, expanding the company's wine and spirits lines substantially. Beginning in the late 1950s, the Bronfman family diversified into everything from Israeli supermarkets to Texas gas fields. The company adopted its present name in 1975 and in 1980 acquired a major interest in DuPont when DuPont bought Seagram's interest in Conoco. In 1988 it acquired Martell SA (cognac) and Tropicana (fruit juices). In 1989 the company bought American Natural Beverages (ANB).

In 1990 Seagram bought Premium (maker of Seagram's mixers) and in 1991 realigned its businesses into spirits and nonspirits groups (they had previously been organized geographically). Seagram sold ANB (Soho Natural Soda) after failing to expand Soho across the US. Also in 1991 the company sold 7 of its spirit brands, including Wolfschmidt and Ronrico, to American Brands, Inc., in an effort to concentrate on its premium brands.

In 1993 it signed a deal with V&S Vin & Sprit to market the Swedish company's Absolut Vodka around the world. That same year the company, led by Edgar Bronfman, Jr., began buying up shares of Time Warner. (Time Warner officials claimed Bronfman was only interested in the glamorous Hollywood appeal of the media company.) Seagram says it will buy no more than 15% of Time Warner. In 1994 Edgar Jr. was tapped to succeed his father as CEO of the company.

NYSE symbol: VO
Fiscal year ends: January 31

Chairman: Edgar M. Bronfman, age 65,
$1,793,170 pay
Chairman of the Executive Committee: Charles
R. Bronfman, age 62, $1,228,400 pay
President and CEO: Edgar Bronfman, Jr., age 39,
$1,718,360 pay
SEVP (Principal Financial Officer): Stephen E.
Banner, age 55, $1,490,720 pay
SVP Human Resources: C. Richard Coffey, age 57
President, The House of Seagram (US): Steven
Kalagher
Auditors: Price Waterhouse

WHERE

HQ: 1430 Peel St., Montreal, Quebec H3A 1S9,
Canada
Phone: 514-849-5271
Fax: 514-933-5390 (Public Relations)
US HQ: The House of Seagram, 375 Park Ave.,
New York, NY 10152
US Phone: 212-572-7900
US Fax: 212-572-1080

Seagram has operations in 36 countries.

	1994 Sales		1994 Operating Income	
	$ mil.	% of total	$ mil.	% of total
US	2,575	43	108	14
Europe	2,188	36	411	55
Canada	146	2	152	20
Other countries	1,129	19	83	11
Total	**6,038**	**100**	**754**	**100**

WHAT

	1994 Sales	
	$ mil.	% of total
Spirits & wines	4,553	75
Fruit juices, coolers & mixers	1,485	25
Total	**6,038**	**100**

Major Owned and Distributed Brands

Whiskeys
100 Pipers
Blenders Pride
Boston Club (Japan)
Chivas Regal
Crown Royal
Four Roses
Glen Grant
The Glenlivet
Passport
Royal Citation
Royal Salute
Seagram's 7 Crown
Seagram's V.O.

Other Spirits
Absolut (vodka)
Captain Morgan (rum)
Mariachi (tequila)
Martell (cognac)
Myers's (rum)
Seagram's Extra Dry (gin)

Wines and Champagnes
Barton & Guestier
Charles Krug
Heidsieck-Monopole
C.K. Mondavi
The Monterey Vineyard
Mumm
Perrier-Jouët
Sandeman
Seagram's Wine Coolers
Sterling Vineyards

Fruit Juices and Mixers
2 Calorie Quest
Seagram's Mixers
Tropicana
100% Pure Juice
Pure Tropics
Season's Best
Tropicana Fruit Tea
Tropicana Twister

KEY COMPETITORS

Allied Domecq
American Brands
Anheuser-Busch
Bacardi
Bass
Brown-Forman
Cadbury Schweppes
Canandaigua Wine
Coca-Cola

Danone
Gallo
Grand
  Metropolitan
Guinness
Kirin
LVMH
Nestlé
Ocean Spray

PepsiCo
Pernod Ricard
Quaker Oats
Remy
  Cointreau
Sebastiani
  Vineyards
Taittinger
Whitman

HOW MUCH

	9-Year Growth	1985	1986	1987	1988	1989	1990	1991	1992	1993	1994
Sales ($ mil.)	8.8%	2,821	2,971	3,345	3,815	5,056	5,582	6,127	6,345	6,101	6,038
Net income ($ mil.)	(0.1%)	384	319	423	521	589	711	756	727	474	379
Income as % of sales	—	13.6%	10.7%	12.6%	13.7%	11.6%	12.7%	12.3%	11.5%	7.8%	6.3%
Earnings per share ($)	(0.4%)	1.06	0.86	1.11	1.36	1.53	1.84	2.01	1.92	1.26	1.02
Stock price – high ($)[1]	—	10.00	10.09	12.19	16.28	20.59	15.47	22.88	29.50	30.88	30.38
Stock price – low ($)[1]	—	6.00	7.50	9.34	10.69	12.25	12.50	15.06	20.41	25.13	24.50
Stock price – close ($)[1]	12.6%	9.00	10.06	12.00	15.19	13.63	15.34	22.00	28.50	25.38	26.13
P/E – high	—	9	12	11	12	13	8	11	15	25	30
P/E – low	—	6	9	8	8	8	7	7	11	20	24
Dividends per share ($)	12.1%	0.20	0.20	0.24	0.26	0.29	0.35	0.46	0.50	0.55	0.56
Book value per share ($)	5.5%	8.30	9.25	10.35	11.76	12.66	14.03	15.87	17.08	13.19	13.43
Employees	1.2%	14,200	14,300	14,400	13,400	16,200	17,600	17,700	16,800	15,800	15,800

1994 Year-end:
Debt ratio: 49.5%
Return on equity: 7.6%
Cash (mil.): $131
Current ratio: 1.27
Long-term debt (mil.): $3,053
No. of shares (mil.): 372
Dividends
  Yield: 2.1%
  Payout: 54.9%
Market value (mil.): $9,731

**Stock Price History[1]
High/Low 1985–94**

[1] Stock prices are for the prior calendar year.

SEGA ENTERPRISES, LTD.

OVERVIEW

SEGA's mascot, Sonic the Hedgehog, is king of the video game market's mountain. Sega leads the US market with a 55% share of system players. In the video-game war with Nintendo (with a US market share of 46%) SEGA has the "cooler" games to play and the faster 32-bit game player system. Both the faster system and the complicated, cool games appeal to the more sophisticated, older kids in the US (roughly 40% of all US households own game players).

The company has further changed the dynamics of the industry through its development of high-tech amusement parks found all over Japan. SEGA has over 1,100 such amusement centers in the country. Its first full-scale high-tech park, Joypolis in Yokohama, opened in July 1994. SEGA, through a partnership with Circus Circus, opened a small park, Virtua Land, in Las Vegas and is planning more in conjunction with Universal Studios. The company also makes portable video games and amusement machines for video arcades. It has started an interactive cable channel in the US that offers pay-for-play video games; players can access games through Compuserve.

SEGA plans to expand into other parts of Asia (including Taiwan and China) and increase its European sales. Products at various points in the planning stages include add-ons for exercise machines, interactive karaoke, and games for PCs on CD-ROM. CSK, a Japanese software company, owns 20% of SEGA.

WHO

One of the original founders of the Japanese electronic games industry was born in New York. David Rosen, who is still an advisor to SEGA, returned to Japan following a stint there in the military during the Korean War. He planned to marry his Japanese girlfriend and start an art export business.

However, the company, originally called Rosen Enterprises when founded in 1951, became more profitable in 1954 when it began importing instant photo booths made in the US. Rosen recognized the need for a quick method of making ID cards, which were used for numerous purposes in Japan. He modified the machines to improve the photo quality and they became quite successful. However, the Japanese became concerned about the US company and its advanced technology, and Rosen decided to offer licensing of his machines to Japanese operators — perhaps the first franchise operation in Japan.

As Japan's economy improved, Rosen, after much persistence, in 1957 imported coin-operated games into the country, later opening the first big bowling alley in Tokyo. In 1965, after becoming dissatisfied with US amusement game quality, he acquired a US company that made jukeboxes in Japan. The combined companies were renamed SEGA Enterprises (short for SErvice GAmes). It developed the popular game Periscope and began challenging US games. In 1970 Gulf+Western Industries acquired SEGA. The buyout led to Rosen's joining the board of Gulf & Western's Paramount Pictures.

In the early 1980s, as the video game industry floundered, Gulf+Western sold off SEGA's US operations. Rosen then assembled some Japanese investors, including CSK, a software firm, to buy SEGA's Japanese operation, which was a subsidiary of the US company. In 1984 SEGA again was a Japanese company; investors paid only $38 million.

Initially SEGA was eclipsed by Nintendo's 8-bit system released in 1985 in Japan. However, SEGA beat its rival to Europe with its own 8-bit game player. The rivalry continued in 1989 when SEGA introduced Genesis, the 16-bit game player. By 1991, when Nintendo finally came out with a 16-bit system, SEGA had already sold more than one million Genesis systems, and many games for Genesis were in their 2nd and 3rd generations. Also in 1991, SEGA came out with ads portraying the SEGA system as the one the "cool" guys in the neighborhood were playing. This coolness quotient grew when the Genesis version of the game Mortal Kombat, released in 1993, allowed players to rip off heads and pull out hearts. Nintendo's version was sanitized, and the SEGA version outsold Nintendo's 2 to 1. SEGA recalled the game, Night Trap, after its violence was examined in a congressional hearing in 1993.

In 1994 SEGA, with Time Warner and Tele-Communications, Inc. (TCI), launched its cable channel, providing Genesis owners with access to many game titles. The company's even faster 32-bit game system, Neptune, is debuting in late 1995.

OTC symbol: SEGNY
Fiscal year ends: March 31

Director and Chairman: Isao Okawa, age 65
Representative Director, President, and CEO:
Hayao Nakayama
Executive Managing Director: Tokuzo Komai
Executive Managing Director: Shoichiro Irimajiri
Executive Managing Director: Keizo Fujimoto
Managing Director, Accounting and Finance:
Tsuneo Naito
Managing Director, R&D: Hisashi Suzuki
President and CEO, SEGA of America:
Tom Kalinske
VP Treasurer, SEGA of America: Takaharu
Utsunoniya
Group Director Human Resources, SEGA of
America: Steve Goveia
Auditors: Chuo Audit Corporation

HQ: 2-12, Haneda 1-chome, Ohta-ku, Tokyo 144,
Japan
Phone: +81-3-5736-7034
Fax: +81--3-5736-7058
US HQ: SEGA of America, Inc., 255 Shoreline
Dr., Ste. 200, Redwood City, CA 94065
US Phone: 415-508-2800
US Fax: 415-802-3063

	1994 Sales	
	¥ mil.	% of total
Japan	181,320	44
Other countries	235,220	56
Total	**416,540**	**100**

	1994 Sales	
	$ mil.	% of total
Consumer products	2,287	67
Amusement centers	598	17
Amusement machines	506	15
Software royalties	41	1
Total	**3,432**	**100**

Selected Products

Video Game Players	Video Games
16-bit Mega Drive 2	Aladdin
Genesis 2 (US)	Garo Densetsu
Mega CD2 CD-ROM	Jurassic Park
SEGA CD2 (US)	Shining Force II

Selected Subsidiaries and Affiliates

Ado Electronic	SEGA Amusements
Industrial Co., Ltd.	Europe Ltd.
A-Wave Co., Ltd.	SEGA Amusements
Daio Shinko Co., Ltd.	Taiwan Ltd.
Deith Leisure Ltd.	SEGA Europe
G-SAT Inc.	Group Ltd.
Joytech Tokai, Ltd.	SEGA FALCOM Co., Ltd.
Light Printing Co., Ltd.	SEGA of America, Inc.
Nextech Co., Ltd.	SEGA Tech Co., Ltd.
S-AI Electronics Co., Ltd.	SONIC Co., Ltd.
	TREASURE Co., Ltd.

3DO	Mattel
Acclaim Entertainment	Nintendo
Activision	Sony
Atari	Virgin Group
General Magic	Walt Disney
Hasbro	WMS Industries

$=¥112 (Dec.31,1993)	9-Year Growth	1985[1]	1986	1987	1988	1989	1990	1991	1992	1993	1994
Sales ($ mil.)	48.3%	99	177	266	396	416	498	758	1,605	3,019	3,432
Net income ($ mil.)	60.2%	3	7	2	19	22	31	59	105	244	225
Income as % of sales	—	3.3%	3.9%	0.9%	4.7%	5.2%	6.2%	7.7%	6.6%	8.1%	6.6%
Earnings per share ($)	73.8%	—	—	—	—	—	—	—	—	0.33	0.57
Stock price – high ($)[2]	—	—	—	—	—	—	—	—	—	—	27.38
Stock price – low ($)[2]	—	—	—	—	—	—	—	—	—	—	17.50
Stock price – close ($)[2]	—	—	—	—	—	—	—	—	—	—	19.75
P/E – high	—	—	—	—	—	—	—	—	—	—	48
P/E – low	—	—	—	—	—	—	—	—	—	—	31
Dividends per share ($)	35.8%	—	—	—	—	0.02	0.01	0.02	0.03	0.06	0.09
Book value per share ($)	5.0%	—	—	—	2.74	2.66	2.20	2.54	2.23	3.20	3.68
Employees[3]	14.4%	1,043	1,071	1,199	1,343	1,454	1,695	1,786	2,324	3,034	3,492

1994 Year-end:
Debt ratio: 30.0%
Return on equity: 16.5%
Cash (mil.): $803
Current ratio: 2.71
Long-term debt (mil.): $688
No. of shares (mil.): 402
Dividends
 Yield: 0.5%
 Payout: 16.4%
Market value (mil.): $7,939

Stock Price History[2]
High/Low 1994

[1] Unconsolidated [2] Stock prices are for the prior calendar year. [3] Employee numbers do not include subsidiaries.

SEIKO CORPORATION

OVERVIEW

It's not quite Dick Tracy, but it's close. Seiko, one of the world's largest watchmakers, is bringing worldwide paging on a wristwatch. It hopes to expand into the highly competitive communications market by building on its reputation as one of the best-known watchmakers in the world. The company recently announced plans to introduce paging services in the US, Europe, and Asia. The announcement comes as Seiko's watch, clock, and jewelry sales have been hurt by a drop in consumer spending in Japan and a drop in watch sales overseas.

Seiko makes more than 5,000 different watch designs under such brand names as Lassale, Pulsar, Lorus, and Alba.

In addition to timepieces, the company markets quartz oscillators, IC chips, synthetic crystals, batteries, LCD pocket color TVs, PCs, ophthalmic frames and lenses, jewelry and accessories, contact lenses, semiconductors, printers, and robots.

Controlled by the Hattori family of Japan, the company is the marketing arm of the Seiko group, which includes manufacturers Seikosha, Seiko Instruments, and Seiko Epson. Seiko was the official timekeeper for the 1992 Olympics in Barcelona and the 1994 Lillehammer Winter Olympics. However, it was outbid by rival SMH, maker of Swatch watches, for the rights to time the 1996 Olympics.

WHEN

Kintaro Hattori started in the jewelry business at age 13. At the age of 21, in 1881, he set up K. Hattori & Co., in Tokyo's Ginza District to import clocks. As increasing railroad traffic created a demand for accurate timepieces, Hattori started manufacturing wall clocks at his Seikosha factory in 1892. Pocket watches followed in 1895, alarm clocks in 1899, and table clocks in 1902. Hattori began exporting clocks to China and opened his first foreign branch in Shanghai in 1913.

Hattori first used the name "Seiko" on a watch in 1924. "Seiko" means "precision" in Japanese. In 1930 the Seikosha plant started producing camera shutters. Daini Seikosha, the predecessor to Seiko Instruments, was set up as an independent watch manufacturer in 1937. Production shifted during WWII from timepieces to time fuses and ammunition. In 1942 Daiwa Kogyo, which later became Seiko Epson Corporation, was established.

By 1953 K. Hattori had restored itself to its prewar position in the Japanese watch market, with a 55% market share. The company attacked the US market in the 1960s by initially offering jewel-lever watches in the mid-range market with an average price of $50 and then expanding to the upper and lower ends of the market. This expansion was aided by K. Hattori's selection as the official timekeeper for the 1964 Tokyo Olympics. The company launched the world's first quartz wall clock in 1968 and the world's first quartz watch (the Seiko Astron) the following year.

During the 1970s K. Hattori expanded globally, establishing subsidiaries in Australia, the US, Canada, the UK, West Germany, Brazil, Panama, Switzerland, Sweden, and Hong Kong. The company broadened its quartz technology by offering the world's first lady's quartz watch in 1972 and the world's first digital watch with a liquid crystal display (LCD) in 1973.

K. Hattori introduced the world's first black-and-white TV watch in 1982. To promote its Seiko line of watches, the company changed its name to Hattori Seiko Co. the following year. In 1984 the company marketed the world's first computer wrist watches and the world's first LCD battery-operated, pocket color television.

The company changed its name from Hattori Seiko to Seiko Corporation in 1990. The following year it introduced the Seiko Perpetual Calendar capable of tracking dates for more than 1,000 years. Also in 1991 Seiko acquired joint venture partner American Telephone and Electronics (with which it developed the wristwatch pager) after AT&E filed for bankruptcy. In 1992 Seiko introduced a quartz watch powered by arm or wrist movements, dispensing with the need for batteries. That same year Seiko and DEC established a joint venture to market personal computers in Japan.

In 1994 the company joined a group funded by the US Department of Transportation to test systems designed to improve highway transportation.

Principal exchange: Tokyo
Fiscal year ends: March 31

Chairman: Reijiro Hattori
President: Masahiro Sekimoto
Senior Executive Director Watch and Clock Sales: Kazuo Yoshizaki
Senior Executive Director Consumer Products: Takayoshi Saito
Senior Executive Director Watch Operation: Hideo Matsukawa
President, Seiko Corporation of America: Takashi Wakuyama
SVP Finance, Seiko Corporation of America: Ron Luino
Manager Human Resources, Seiko Corporation of America: Janice DeKoning
Auditors: Asahi & Co.

WHERE

HQ: 6-21, Kyobashi 2-chome, Chuo-ku, Tokyo 104, Japan
Phone: +81-3-3563-2111
Fax: +81-3-5250-7065 (Public Relations)
US HQ: Seiko Corporation of America, 1111 MacArthur Blvd., Mahwah, NJ 07430
US Phone: 201-529-5730
US Fax: 201-529-2736

	1994 Sales	
	¥ bil.	% of total
Japan	254	76
Other countries	81	24
Total	**335**	**100**

WHAT

	1994 Sales	
	¥ bil.	% of total
Watches, clocks & jewelry	243	72
Ophthalmic products, personal care products & other	92	28
Total	**335**	**100**

Manufacturing Divisions

Seiko Epson Corporation (watches, computers, printers, semiconductors, liquid crystal displays)

Seiko Instruments Inc. (watches, computer graphic devices, CAE/CAD/CAM systems, electronic components, analytical and measuring instruments, intelligent robots)

Seikosha Co., Ltd. (clocks, time recorders, timing equipment for sports events, personal computers, printers, on-line systems, camera shutters, semiconductors)

KEY COMPETITORS

Apple	Hyundai	Pioneer
Bausch & Lomb	Intergraph	Premark
Canon	Kyocera	Roche
Casio	Lexmark	Samsung
Citizen	International	Sanyo
Compaq	Loews	Sharp
Eastman Kodak	Loral	Siemens
Electrolux	Lucky-Goldstar	SMH
Fossil	Machines Bull	Sony
Fuji Photo	Matsushita	Thomson SA
Fujitsu	Minolta	Thorn EMI
GEC	Mitsubishi	Three-Five
General Electric	Motorola	Systems
GM Hughes	NEC	Toshiba
Hanson	Oki	Xerox
Harris Corp.	Olivetti	Yamaha
Hewlett-Packard	Philips	Zenith
Hitachi		

HOW MUCH

$=¥112 (Dec. 31, 1993)	Annual Growth	1985	1986	1987	1988	1989	1990	1991	1992	1993	1994
Sales (¥ bil.)	(1.2%)	374	373	308	280	399	422	428	428	378	335
Net income (¥ bil.)	—	3	3	2	1	(3)	2	1	(2)	(5)	(6)
Income as % of sales	—	0.8%	0.7%	0.5%	0.5%	—	0.5%	0.2%	—	—	—
Earnings per share (¥)	—	27	29	17	13	(32)	18	7	(21)	(49)	(60)
Stock price – high (¥)[1]	—	—	1,330	2,140	1,700	2,390	4,600	6,080	4,290	1,650	1,450
Stock price – low (¥)[1]	—	—	846	960	990	1,190	1,970	4,040	1,510	770	800
Stock price – close (¥)[1]	(5.1%)	1,280	995	1,390	1,120	1,990	4,600	4,290	1,620	1,050	800
P/E – high	—	—	46	126	128	—	256	—	—	—	—
P/E – low	—	—	29	56	74	—	107	—	—	—	—
Dividends per share (¥)	0.0%	10.00	10.00	10.00	10.00	10.00	10.00	10.00	10.00	10.00	10.00
Book value per share (¥)	(8.4%)	—	—	—	—	—	—	314	292	279	241
Employees	(1.1%)	—	—	—	1,562	—	—	1,528	1,488	—	1,458

1994 Year-end:
Debt ratio: 92.4%
Return on equity: —
Cash (bil.): ¥82
Long-term debt (bil.): ¥86
No. of shares (mil.): 106
Dividends
Yield: 1.3%
Payout: —
Market value (mil.): $754
Sales (mil.): $2,989

Stock Price History High/Low 1985–94

[1] Stock prices are for the prior calendar year.

SHANGHAI PETROCHEMICAL

While most old factories in Communist and ex-Communist regimes are struggling to survive or to break even, China's state-run petrochemical company is making money hand over fist. Located in China's largest city and #1 port, Shanghai Petrochemical Company (SPC) is the 9th largest Chinese company and the largest petrochemical enterprise in China. It is the #1 producer of ethylene, a crucial ingredient in the manufacture of synthetic fibers, resins, and plastics, and also makes other intermediate petrochemicals such as benzene.

The booming Chinese economy, especially in the industrial centers on the eastern seaboard, has increased the demand for the firm's plastics, synthetic fibers, resins, and other "downstream" petrochemical products.

SPC is 64% owned by the Chinese government's China Petroleum Corp., or Sinopec. Sinopec is more than a major investor: it is also central planning under the guise of capitalism. Sinopec and the central government control 40% of SPC's output and provide it with almost all of its crude oil (at a 40% discount on world market prices).

Even so, SPC is attracting foreign investors. It was listed on the Hong Kong and NYSE stockmarkets in 1993 and on the Shanghai stock exchange in 1994.

SPC's top 20 executives and directors earn an aggregate salary of $24,551.

The Mao-inspired Cultural Revolution of the 1960s restored the aging leader's grip on political power but caused China to suffer immense political and economic disruptions and virtually closed down foreign trade.

In the early 1970s party reformists, led by Zhou Enlai and Deng Xiaoping (later to become "Paramount Leader"), advocated a policy of improved contact with the outside world and the restoration of foreign trade as a means of giving the Chinese economy access to much-needed advanced technology. In 1972, the year President Nixon's visit to China restored Sino-US ties, China launched a program to begin contracting for plant and equipment imports, especially in the petrochemical areas of chemical fertilizers for agriculture and artificial fibers for industrial use. In that same year Shanghai Petrochemical Complex was founded as China's first large petrochemical enterprise using imported equipment and technology.

Controlled by the ministry-level concern, China Petrochemical Corp. (Sinopec), the country's leading oil refiner, Shanghai Petrochemical grew to be the #1 petrochemical enterprise in the country. Part of the reason for this was that it fit squarely into the government's Four Modernizations policy, which, as expressed in party documents in 1978, envisaged "a powerful socialist country with modern agriculture, industry, national defense, and science and technology by the end of the century." The government introduced a series of ambitious 5-year plans in the late 1970s to achieve these goals and the additional aim of halving the economic gap between it and the industrialized nations of the West by 1985.

The other factor behind Shanghai Petroleum's growth was the booming economies of the coastal cities in the east and south, which were made possible by the economic liberalization policies that encouraged massive foreign investment. Guangdong Province in the south has led the way. Hong Kong industry migrated en masse to the province in the 1980s, seeking lower wages and lower overheads. Guangdong's exports jumped from $3 billion in 1985 to $10.5 billion in 1990. The expansion of industrial output here and in other Chinese cities resulted in greatly increased demand for Shanghai Petrochemical's products.

Emboldened by its growth and by further reforms in the oil industry in China in 1992, Sinopec restructured Shanghai Petrochemical Complex as Shanghai Petrochemical Company Limited (SPC) in 1993 and listed SPC on the Hong Kong and New York stock markets. SPC is the first People's Republic of China company to gain a listing on the New York Stock Exchange.

SPC chairman Wang Jiming sees overmanning as the chief problem faced by the company, although the unpredictability of central government policy is also a major issue. In 1994 the government imposed new import and price controls.

In that same year Sinopec assigned SPC to explore options for joint venture activities with Elf Aquitaine.

NYSE symbol: SHI (ADR)
Fiscal year ends: December 31

WHO

Chairman; VP, China Petrochemical Corp.
  (Sinopec): Wang Jiming, age 52
VC: Wang Mingshi, age 52
President: Wu Yixin, age 49
VP Production: Wang Guanze, age 57
VP Sales and Marketing: Gu Changji, age 51
VP Research and Development: Qu Guohua,
  age 57
VP Administration and Personnel: Zhou
  Yunnong, age 52
Executive Officer: Wang Chuanbo, age 58
Executive Officer: Xie Renjie, age 52
Auditors: KPMG Peat Marwick Huazhen and
  KPMG Peat Marwick

WHERE

HQ: Shanghai Petrochemical Company Limited,
  Jinshanwei, Shanghai 200540, China
Phone: +86-21-794-3143
Fax: +86-21-794-0050
US HQ: China Petrochemical Corporation
  (Sinopec), One World Trade Center, Ste. 4655,
  New York, NY 10036
Phone: 212-321-9460
Fax: 212-321-9467

Shanghai Petrochemical Company's products to
date are primarily for domestic consumption.
SPC's plants and operating subsidiaries are all
located within the borders of the People's
Republic of China.

WHAT

	1993 Sales
	% of total
Resins & plastics	30
Petroleum products	29
Synthetic fibers	27
Intermediate petrochemicals	12
Other	2
Total	**100**

Major Products	
Acrylic staple fiber	Polyester chips
Acrylic top	Polyester filament-DTY
Benzene	Polyester filament-POY
Butadiene	Polyester staple
Ethylene	PP resins
LDPE film	PVA fiber
LDPE resins	PVA granules
Naphtha oil	Residual oil
	VGO

KEY COMPETITORS

DuPont
Elf Aquitaine
Formosa Plastics
Hoescht
Imperial Chemical
Lyondell Petrochemical
Marubeni
Mitsubishi
Mitsui
Royal Dutch/Shell
Sinochem
Union Carbide

HOW MUCH

	Annual Growth	1984	1985	1986	1987	1988	1989	1990	1991	1992	1993
Sales ($ mil.)	26.7%	—	—	—	—	—	—	—	812	886	1,305
Net Income ($ mil.)	55.6%	—	—	—	—	—	—	—	10	12	24
Income as % of sales	—	—	—	—	—	—	—	—	1.2%	1.4%	1.8%
Earnings per share ($)	—	—	—	—	—	—	—	—	—	—	2.38
Stock price – high ($)	—	—	—	—	—	—	—	—	—	—	49.25
Stock price – low ($)	—	—	—	—	—	—	—	—	—	—	18.25
Stock price – close ($)	—	—	—	—	—	—	—	—	—	—	42.25
P/E – high	—	—	—	—	—	—	—	—	—	—	21
P/E – low	—	—	—	—	—	—	—	—	—	—	8
Dividends per share ($)	—	—	—	—	—	—	—	—	—	—	0.00
Book value per share ($)	—	—	—	—	—	—	—	—	—	—	14.37
Employees	—	—	—	—	—	—	—	—	—	—	39,000

1993 Year-end:	Stock Price History High/Low 1993
Debt ratio: 44.8%	
Return on equity: —	50
Cash (mil.): $310	45
Current ratio: 1.28	40
Long-term debt (mil.): $353	35
No. of shares (mil.): 62	30
Dividends	25
Yield: —	20
Payout: —	15
Market value (mil.): $2,632	10 / 5 / 0

SHARP CORPORATION

OVERVIEW

Haruo Tsuji, president of Sharp, is giving a hearty welcome to the Information Age because, he says, "Anywhere information exists there will be a display." That's good news for the Osaka-based company, because it is the world leader in liquid crystal displays (LCDs), with over 43% of the market. LCDs are used in everything from calculators to digital thermometers, but applications such as laptop computer screens and screens for the company's fast-selling ViewCam have been a major boost. Sharp continues to develop larger LCD screens, and many analysts believe LCDs will replace cathode ray tubes in TVs by the end of the century.

Tsuji is not putting all Sharp's eggs in one liquid crystal basket, though. The company is one of the world's leading makers of office automation products and home electronics, making TVs, VCRs, stereos, computers, and fax machines. Sharp also makes home appliances, such as refrigerators and microwaves, and produces integrated circuits (ICs) for its own products and customized ICs for others.

Sharp is spending heavily to build up its electronic parts business, where competition is not as stiff as in consumer products. To keep its consumer products business healthy, it is cutting costs by shifting both production and raw material procurement abroad.

WHEN

In 1912 Tokuji Hayakawa established a metal works in Tokyo to manufacture a type of belt buckle he had designed. Three years later he invented the first mechanical pencil, which he named the Ever-Sharp. The pencil was a commercial success, and eventually the company was named after it.

In 1923 an earthquake leveled much of Tokyo, including Hayakawa's business. Undaunted, Hayakawa moved to Osaka, built a new facility (which he financed by selling the rights to his pencil), and in 1925 introduced Japan's first crystal radio sets. Four years later he introduced a vacuum tube radio. In 1935 the company was incorporated.

After WWII the company developed an experimental TV, which it started to mass-produce in 1953 when Japan aired its first television broadcasts. Likewise Sharp was ready with color TVs when Japan initiated color broadcasts in 1960. During the 1960s the company saw tremendous growth and innovation, launching mass-produced microwave ovens (1962), mass-produced solar cells (1963), the first electronic desktop all-transistor-diode calculator (1964), and the first gallium arsenide light-emitting diode (LED, 1969). The company opened its first US office in 1962.

In 1970 Sharp built a factory to manufacture its own microchips, and in 1973 it began mass production of LCDs. The company continued to produce innovative electronic products, such as the first electronic calculator with a liquid crystal display (1973), solar-powered calculators (1976), and the first credit-card-sized calculator (1979).

In the early 1980s the company began producing VCRs and in 1984 released its color copier. That same year Sharp introduced a fax machine and concentrated its marketing efforts toward small businesses (while its competitors were scrambling for large corporate accounts).

In 1986 Haruo Tsuji became president, and in 1987 the company's profits fell more than 40% because of rising costs associated with the appreciation of the yen. Tsuji restructured the company and concentrated research on LCDs.

By the late 1980s Sharp was ready to blitz the market with a new line of creative products, including a high-definition LCD color TV (1987), a notebook-sized personal computer (1988), and an LCD projector capable of projecting TV or video pictures onto a large screen (1989). In 1990 the company released the first desktop color fax machine.

In 1992 Sharp introduced a cordless pocket telephone that operated continuously for over 5 hours and a simplified high-definition television (HDTV) priced under $8,000, less than 1/4 of competitors' prices. That same year the company announced strategic alliances with Intel (to develop flash memory chips), Apple (to build the Newton personal digital assistant), and The Shanghai Radio and Television (Group) Company (to make air conditioners, fax machines, copiers, and printers).

In 1994 the company announced plans to spend nearly $500 million to build an LCD plant in Taki-cho, Japan. Sharp plans to begin production at the plant in mid-1995.

OTC symbol: SHCAY (ADR)
Fiscal year ends: March 31

President: Haruo Tsuji, age 62
SEVP: Taizo Katsura
**SEVP and Group General Manager Creative
Lifestyle Planning Group:** Atsushi Asada
SEVP International Business: Yutaka Wada
**SEVP and Group General Manager Domestic
Sales and Marketing Group and Consumer
Electronics:** Kazuo Kubo
**Corporate Director and Group General Manager
Corporate Finance:** Yoshio Nagaike
President, Sharp Electronics (US): Toshiaka
Urushisako
VP Finance, Sharp Electronics (US): Barry Kay
VP Human Resources, Sharp Electronics (US):
Manfred Edelman
Auditors: Asahi & Co. (Arthur Andersen & Co.)

WHERE

HQ: 22-22 Nagaike-cho, Abeno-ku, Osaka 545,
Japan
Phone: +81-6-621-1221
Fax: +81-6-628-1667
US HQ: Sharp Electronics Corporation, Sharp
Plaza, Mahwah, NJ 07430-2135
US Phone: 201-529-8200
US Fax: 201-529-8425

	1994 Sales	
	¥ bil.	% of total
Japan	744	50
Other countries	746	50
Total	**1,490**	**100**

WHAT

	1994 Sales
	% of total
Electronic equipment	73
Electronic parts	27
Total	**100**

Selected Products

Air conditioners	Liquid crystal diode
Calculators	panels and units
Camcorders	Microwave ovens
Car audio systems	Optoelectric products
Cash registers	Printers
Cassette recorders	Refrigerators
Compact disc players	Stereos
Computers	Telephones
Copiers	Translation systems
Electronic organizers	Televisions
Fax machines	VCRs
Heaters	Vending machines
Integrated circuits	Video projectors
Karaoke machines	Washing machines

KEY COMPETITORS

AMD	Hitachi	Pioneer
Apple	Hyundai	Raytheon
Boston Acoustics	Insilco	Ricoh
Brother	Intel	Samsung
Canon	Lucky-Goldstar	Sanyo
Casio	Machines Bull	Seiko
Compaq	Matsushita	Siemens
Daewoo	Maytag	Sony
Dell	Minolta	Thomson SA
Electrolux	Mitsubishi	Thorn EMI
Fuji Photo	Motorola	Three-Five Systems
Fujitsu	NEC	Toshiba
GEC	Nokia	Whirlpool
General Electric	Oki	Xerox
Harris Corp.	Olivetti	Yamaha
Hewlett-Packard	Philips	Zenith

HOW MUCH

$=¥112 (Dec. 31, 1993)	9-Year Growth	1985	1986	1987	1988	1989	1990	1991	1992	1993	1994
Sales (¥ bil.)	2.8%	1,167	1,149	1,038	1,078	1,238	1,345	1,496	1,518	1,478	1,490
Net income (¥ bil.)	(2.5%)	40	36	21	20	29	42	47	39	30	32
Income as % of sales	—	3.4%	3.1%	2.0%	1.9%	2.4%	3.1%	3.1%	2.6%	2.0%	2.1%
Earnings per share (¥)	(5.4%)	48	49	44	25	23	31	44	37	28	29
Stock price – high (¥)[1]	—	1,286	1,027	1,071	1,223	1,350	1,880	1,980	1,630	1,440	1,580
Stock price – low (¥)[1]	—	866	656	723	728	901	1,110	1,070	1,110	850	928
Stock price – close (¥)[1]	5.0%	982	817	982	921	1,120	1,860	1,160	1,320	999	1,520
P/E – high	—	26	23	42	53	44	44	45	44	52	54
P/E – low	—	18	15	29	32	29	27	25	30	31	32
Dividends per share (¥)	1.3%	9.82	9.82	9.82	11.00	11.00	11.00	11.00	11.00	11.00	11.00
Book value per share (¥)	6.0%	437	462	473	526	563	680	683	708	718	740
Employees	4.8%	28,221	28,873	9,346	29,351	32,298	34,017	36,539	41,029	41,836	42,883

1994 Year-end:
Debt ratio: 43.8%
Return on equity: 4.0%
Cash (bil.): ¥688
Long-term debt (bil.): ¥223
No. of shares (mil.): 1,105
Dividends
  Yield: 0.7%
  Payout: 37.8%
Market value (mil.): $14,996
Sales (mil.): $13,304

**Stock Price History[1]
High/Low 1985–94**

[1]Stock prices are for the prior calendar year.

SHISEIDO COMPANY, LIMITED

OVERVIEW

Japan's largest cosmetics company, with a 27% share of that country's cosmetics market, Tokyo-based Shiseido is trying to put on a new face as its sales growth has slowed. The company's makeover includes a diversification away from cosmetics into some of its other businesses, including pharmaceuticals, where it has boosted R&D spending. The company also makes toiletries and runs health clubs and restaurants.

Shiseido rose to power in the 1920s when it franchised its retail outlets (now 25,000). These "mom-and-pop" cosmetics stores drew millions of loyal customers.

Shiseido has long focused on the high end of the market, but a slowdown in Japan's economy has sent customers looking for bargains rather than brand names. In response, the company is shifting to lower-priced, higher-volume products.

Shiseido is also looking to expand its overseas business by 50% by 1997. The company has a particular eye on China. It opened a factory in Bejing in 1993 and plans to open up to 150 stores in China in 1995. The company is also looking to boost sales in the US by concentrating heavily on skin care products.

WHEN

In 1872 Yushin Fukuhara, former head pharmacist for the Japanese admiralty, established Japan's first modern drugstore, Shiseido Pharmacy. "Shiseido," a name derived from Confucian philosophy, implies "richness of life." The store's customers were the nobility and the rich, attracted by the Western-style products and format of the store.

Shiseido manufactured Japan's first toothpaste in 1888 and pioneered, in 1897, the company's first cosmetics product, Eudermine, a skin lotion. In 1902 Fukuhara opened a Western-style soda fountain, importing everything from soda glasses to ice cream.

Yushin's 3rd son, Shinzo, aspired to be an artist, but, after studying in New York, he returned to Tokyo and began working for his father. Shinzo created Shiseido's first extensive makeup lines, introducing a flesh-toned face powder in 1906, a hair tonic in 1915, and a fragrance line 1918. When he brought a Western beautician to Tokyo, her *mimi-kakushi*, or "ear hiding," hairstyle created a sensation. Under Shinzo's influence, cosmetics replaced drugs as Shiseido's mainstay.

Shiseido began franchise operations in 1923 and its business boomed. It was listed on the Tokyo exchange the same year, and in 1927 Shinzo became president. In 1937 the mail-order Camelia Club was launched. During WWII the company couldn't make cosmetics, only medicines, and many of Shiseido's factories were destroyed. This led to near-bankruptcy in 1945, but Shiseido rebounded with a nail enamel in 1946.

In the 1950s and 1960s the company sparked fashion movements. In 1951 it introduced its "de Luxe" line of high-end

cosmetics and by 1956 had become Japan's #1 cosmetics concern. Shiseido began overseas operations in southeast Asia and steadily expanded its offshore businesses, setting up subsidiaries in Hawaii (1962), New York (1965), Milan (1968), Singapore (1970), Bangkok (1972), France (1980), Australia (1982), and the UK (1986).

In the 1970s Shiseido failed at marketing its broad line of products in the US. At home the company's market share was slipping. Shiseido was seen as out of touch with the young. Because of a law dating back to the 1880s when *kabuki* performers were poisoned by lead-based makeup, Japanese rules are strict regarding product development. It can take up to 2 years for a finished product to be marketed, making it lose its timeliness. The company segmented its cosmetics line into 5 age groups and began producing more lines but in smaller quantities in the early 1980s.

Shiseido developed a new, successful marketing strategy for the US in the mid-1980s. It began selling exclusive product lines in quality department stores like Macy's. The company acquired Carita (beauty salon, France, 1986), Zotos (hair products, US, 1988), and Davlyn (cosmetics, US, 1989).

The 1990s saw further market share slippage. In late 1991 the company formed a partnership with China's Beijing Liyuan Cosmetics to make high-end cosmetics. In 1993 Shiseido introduced its first ethical drug, an ophthalmological treatment used in certain types of cataract surgery and cornea transplants. In 1994 it announced plans to build a plant to make injectable preparations for the treatment of joint disease.

OTC symbol: SSDOY
Fiscal year ends: March 31

Chairman: Seiji Ishino
President and CEO: Yoshiharu Fukuhara
SEVP: Shozo Kozawa
SEVP: Kazuteru Matsuda
Senior Executive Director: Akira Genma
**Director and Chief Officer International
   Operations:** Sadao Abe
**President and CEO, Shiseido Cosmetics
   (America) Ltd.:** Yuji Kishida
Auditors: Chuo Shinko

WHERE

HQ: 7-5-5, Ginza, Chuo-ku, Tokyo 104-10,
   Japan
Phone: +81-3-3572-5111
Fax: +81-3-3289-4849
US HQ: Shiseido Cosmetics (America) Inc.,
   900 3rd Ave., New York, NY 10022
US Phone: 212-805-2300
US Fax: 212-688-0109

Shiseido markets its products in more than 40
countries.

| | 1994 Sales | |
	¥ bil.	% of total
Japan	512	93
Other countries	37	7
Total	**549**	**100**

WHAT

| | 1994 Sales | |
	¥ bil.	% of total
Cosmetics	390	71
Toiletries	102	19
Other	57	10
Total	**549**	**100**

Selected Brands

Cosmetics and Fragrances
Chant du Coeur
Clé-de-Peau
Elixir
Elserie
Ipsa
Revital
Saso
Shiseido
Uno
UV White
Vital Perfection
Whitess Essence N

Toiletries
Cellaid
Color Rinse Natural
Dungaree
Lustair

Moist Water
Richair
Savon d'Or
Shower Soap
Super Mild

Pharmaceuticals
Bibalance
Epiamart
Ferzea
Lookel

**Salon Products, Food
   Products, and Other**
Fine Rice
Fragrance Processor F-1
Infinite Color
Physemb
Qi

KEY COMPETITORS

Alberto-Culver
Allou
Amway
Avon
Benetton
Colgate-Palmolive
Estée Lauder
Gilette
IFF
Kao

Kirin
L'Oréal
LVMH
MacAndrews &
   Forbes
Mary Kay
Maybelline
Mochida
   Pharmaceutical
Nestlé

Neutrogena
Nippon Fine
   Chemical
Procter &
   Gamble
Sara Lee
SmithKline
   Beecham
Sunstar
Unilever

HOW MUCH

$=¥112 (Dec. 31, 1993)	Annual Growth	1985	1986	1987	1988	1989[2]	1990	1991	1992	1993	1994
Sales (¥ bil.)	4.5%	368	371	375	379	401	456	517	553	562	549
Net income (¥ bil.)	(0.2%)	15	15	14	9	10	11	16	16	13	15
Income as % of sales	—	4.1%	3.9%	3.6%	2.4%	2.4%	2.5%	3.1%	2.9%	2.4%	2.7%
Earnings per share (¥)	(2.2%)	45	42	38	25	26	30	42	42	34	37
Stock price – high (¥)[1]	—	—	984	1,555	1,766	1,488	1,901	1,901	1,745	1,609	2,010
Stock price – low (¥)[1]	—	—	710	895	992	1,037	1,210	1,315	1,371	1,290	1,190
Stock price – close (¥)[1]	5.6%	751	984	1,510	992	1,232	1,901	1,518	1,564	1,410	1,230
P/E – high	—	—	23	40	70	58	63	45	42	48	55
P/E – low	—	—	17	23	39	40	40	31	33	38	32
Dividends per share (¥)	6.2%	6.38	6.83	7.17	7.51	7.51	8.26	8.68	10.50	11.00	11.00
Book value per share (¥)	—	—	—	—	—	—	—	—	862	819	846
Employees	(1.0%)	—	—	—	—	—	—	3,641	3,605	—	3,897

1994 Year-end:
Debt ratio: 15.4%
Return on equity: 4.4%
Cash (¥ bil.): 79
Long-term debt (¥ bil.): 33
No. of shares (mil.): 400
Dividends
   Yield: 0.9%
   Payout: 29.9%
Market value (mil.): $4,393
Sales (mil.): $4,902

**Stock Price History[1]
High/Low 1985–94**

[1] Stock prices are for the prior calendar year.   [2] Fiscal year change

SIEMENS AG

Siemens is Germany's 2nd largest company, after Daimler-Benz AG, with sales of over $51 billion in 1994. The company supplies nearly all products, systems, and services used in converting fossil fuels, nuclear energy, and renewable energy sources into electricity. Siemens's other operations include telecommunications, medical engineering products, power plant engineering products, lighting, and transportation and automotive systems.

Siemens is feeling the effects of a recession plaguing Europe and especially Germany. In 1993 the company was unable to sustain growth in new orders for the first time in 7 years. Siemens Nixdorf Informationssysteme (SNI), a wholly owned subsidiary of Siemens

and one of the "Big Four" European computer makers, has lost money every year since it was acquired in 1990, including over $207 million in 1994. The division's broad product line (PCs, mainframes, software, and services) is thought to have impaired its ability to succeed in any one market. Siemens has restructured SNI into 9 business units and 4 system units to reflect market segmentation. Siemens has reduced its overall work force, with SNI bearing the brunt of the blow (5,000 jobs eliminated).

Siemens plans to make Asia/Pacific a major focal point of its global business. The company announced that it would invest up to $3.5 billion in the region by the year 2000.

In 1847 Werner von Siemens, an electrical engineer, teamed with a craftsman, Johann Halske, to make telegraphs as Siemens & Halske in Germany. Although Halske left the firm 20 years later, the company name was not shortened to Siemens until 1966. The firm's first major project linked Berlin and Frankfurt with the first long-distance telegraph system in Europe (1848). Siemens continued to string telegraph wires across Europe and in 1870 completed the 6,600-mile India Line running from London to Calcutta. The company made the first transatlantic cable, which connected Ireland to the US in 1874.

Siemens built Europe's first electric power transmission system (1876), the world's first electrified railway (1879), and one of the first elevators (1880). As a result of Werner von Siemens's discussions with Thomas Edison (1881), the company received a license to manufacture incandescent lights. Disagreement between the 2 inventors contributed to the different electrical voltage standards used by North America (110 volts) and Europe (220 volts). In 1896 the company patented the world's first X-ray tube and completed the first European subway, in Budapest.

Despite losses in WWI, Siemens recovered, forming Osram, a German light bulb cartel, with AEG and Auer (1919) and entering into a venture with Furukawa Electric called Fuji Electric (1923). Siemens developed radios and traffic lights in the 1920s and began production of electron microscopes in 1939.

Siemens suffered heavy losses in WWII but staged a quick recovery, developing silicates

for semiconductors, data processing equipment, and the world's first implantable pacemaker in the 1950s. Siemens formed joint ventures with Bosch (Bosch-Siemens Hausgeräte, appliances, 1967) and AEG (Kraftwerk Union, nuclear power, 1969), among others. The company profited from Germany's protectionist telecommunications policies, but its computer ventures with RCA and Philips in the 1960s and 1970s were disappointing.

In 1981 Karlheinz Kaske became the company's first CEO from outside the Siemens family. Under his direction Siemens entered into joint ventures with Philips, Intel, and Advanced Micro Devices.

In 1988 and 1989 it bought Bendix Electronics (US), Rolm Systems (manufacturing and development), 50% of Rolm Company (marketing and services, PBXs; US), and the telecommunications businesses of Plessey (UK). In 1990 Siemens and Nixdorf combined their computer businesses, forming SNI. Siemens bought the rest of SNI's shares for $474 million in 1991. In 1992 Siemens completed the purchase of Rolm Company.

In September 1992 Heinrich von Pierer took over from Kaske as CEO. In 1993 the company acquired Sylvania's lamp business from GTE and merged it with the former Osram companies in the US and Canada, forming a new company: Osram Sylvania. In 1994 Siemens entered into a $30 million joint venture with the China National Posts and Telecommunications Industry Corp. to produce fiber-optic cable. It is Siemens's 17th joint venture in China.

OTC symbol: SMAWY (ADR)
Fiscal year ends: September 30

WHO

Chairman: Hermann Franz
President and CEO: Heinrich von Pierer
Research and Development: Hans Günter Danielmeyer
Corporate Finance: Karl-Hermann Baumann
Corporate Human Resources: Werner Maly
President and CEO, Siemens Corp. (US): Albert Hoser
Treasurer, Siemens Corp. (US): Krister Winngren
Auditors: KPMG Deutsche Treuhand-Gesellschaft AG Wirtschaftsprüfungsgesellschaft

WHERE

HQ: Wittelsbacherplatz 2, D-80333 Munich, Germany
Phone: +49-89-2340
Fax: +49-89-234-4242
US HQ: Siemens Corporation, 1301 Avenue of the Americas, New York, NY 10019-6055
US Phone: 212-258-4000
US Fax: 212-767-0580

Siemens has operations worldwide.

	1993 Sales	
	DM mil.	% of total
Germany	59,206	60
North America	10,160	10
Other Europe	22,634	23
Other countries	6,150	7
Adjustments	(13,552)	—
Total	**84,598**	**100**

WHAT

	1993 Sales	
	DM mil.	% of total
Public communication sys.	13,549	14
Siemens Nixdorf Informations-systeme AG (SNI)	11,922	13
Industrial & building systems	8,946	10
Power generation	8,692	10
Medical engineering	7,905	9
Drives & standard products	6,538	7
Private communication sys.	6,267	7
Power trans. & distrib.	5,951	7
Automation	5,365	6
Transportation systems	3,580	4
Automotive systems	2,580	3
Semiconductors	2,145	2
Passive comp. & electron tubes	1,507	1
Defense electronics	1,238	1
Other products & services	5,422	6
Adjustments	(7,009)	—
Total	**84,598**	**100**

KEY COMPETITORS

ABB	General Electric	Oki
Alcatel Alsthom	Hewlett-Packard	Olivetti
Amdahl	Hitachi	Philips
AT&T	IBM	Raytheon
Bayer	Intel	Robert Bosch
British Aerospace	IRI	Rolls-Royce
Cooper Industries	ITT	Sagem
	Koor	Samsung
DEC	Machines Bull	Sanyo
Eastman Kodak	Mannesmann	Scitex
Electrolux	Matsushita	Sharp
Elscint	Maytag	Thomson SA
ENI	Motorola	Thorn EMI
Ericsson	NEC	Toshiba
Friedrich Krupp	Nokia	Westinghouse
Fujitsu	Northern	Whirlpool
GEC	Telecom	

HOW MUCH

$=DM1.74 (Dec. 31, 1993)	9-Year Growth	1985	1986	1987	1988	1989	1990	1991	1992	1993	1994
Sales (DM mil.)	5.0%	54,616	47,023	51,431	59,374	61,128	63,185	73,008	78,509	81,648	84,598
Net income (DM mil.)	1.8%	1,502	1,455	1,217	1,317	1,473	1,547	1,848	1,795	1,803	1,769
Income as % of sales	—	2.8%	3.1%	2.4%	2.2%	2.4%	2.4%	2.5%	2.3%	2.2%	2.1%
Earnings per share (DM)	0.0%	32	31	25	27	30	30	36	32	32	32
Stock price – high (DM)	—	935	920	790	569	843	816	673	817	850	800
Stock price – low (DM)	—	384	724	387	357	502	512	557	501	531	597
Stock price – close (DM)	(3.9%)	925	822	388	563	843	585	624	537	846	649
P/E – high	—	29	30	32	21	28	27	19	25	26	25
P/E – low	—	12	23	15	13	17	17	15	16	16	19
Dividends per share (DM)	5.5%	8.0	10.0	12.0	12.0	11.0	11.0	13.0	13.0	13.0	13.0
Book value per share (DM)	3.1%	280	317	324	344	358	322	333	322	342	369
Employees	2.3%	348,000	363,000	359,000	353,000	365,000	373,000	402,000	413,000	391,000	373,000

1993 Year-end:
Debt ratio: 18.2%
Return on equity: 9.0%
Cash (mil.): DM24,029
Long-term debt (mil.): DM1,665
No. of shares (mil.): 55
Dividends
  Yield: 2.0%
  Payout: 40.4%
Market value (mil.): $20,533
Sales (mil.): $48,620

Stock Price History High/Low 1985–94

SIME DARBY BERHAD

OVERVIEW

Sime Darby, Malaysia's largest conglomerate, is one of southeast Asia's biggest multinationals. It operates over 200 companies in 22 countries. Its core business activities include plantations (oil palm, rubber, cocoa, and fruit crops); property development; insurance; trading; heavy equipment (Caterpillar) and auto distribution (BMW, Ford, Land Rover, Scania); oil and gas services; and finished rubber products. About half of Sime Darby's revenues come from its operations in Hong Kong, Singapore, and Australia.

The company appointed a new group chief executive, Nik Mohamed bin Nik Yaacob, in 1993. Following this move Sime Darby announced that it will merge with its public subsidiary, Consolidated Plantations. This merger will give the company access to Consolidated's $190 million cash reserves and its vast land bank to help fund the company's long-term development plans.

Pemegang Amanah Raya owns 21.7% of Sime Darby, and the Hongkong and Shanghai Banking Corporation (HSBC), 16.6%.

WHEN

William Sime, a 37-year-old Scottish adventurer, convinced Henry Darby, a wealthy 50-year-old English banker, that money could be made in rubber, which had just been introduced to Malaya from Brazil. Together they established Sime, Darby & Co., Ltd. in 1910 to manage about 500 acres of rubber estates in the jungles of Malacca, Malaya. To overcome local hostility to their venture, the pair maintained close links with the Chinese business community, including Tan Cheng Lock, a leader of Malaya's independence movement, who was later made a Knight Commander of the British Empire and was awarded the highest Malaysian title, "Tun."

Riding a boom in rubber, Sime Darby became a managing agent for other plantations before moving into general trading. A branch office was set up in Singapore in 1915, and a London office was established for marketing.

To clear jungle to meet the growing demand for rubber, in 1929 Sime Darby bought Sarawak Trading, which held the franchise for Caterpillar heavy earth-moving equipment. Sime Darby moved its headquarters to Singapore in 1936.

In 1958 Sime Darby Holdings Ltd. was incorporated in England as successor to Sime, Darby & Co., Ltd. As demand for rubber softened in the late 1960s, Sime Darby was one of the first plantations to diversify into palm oil and cocoa. Sime Darby acquired the Seafield Estate and Consolidated Plantations Berhad in the early 1970s, becoming a dominant force in Malaysian plantations while it started processing crops into finished products. The success of the switch to oil palms allowed Sime Darby's autocratic British CEO, Denis Pinder, to gobble up numerous firms. In 1973 allegations appeared in newspapers about

improprieties at "Slime Darby." When Sime Darby's outside auditor was found stabbed to death in his bathtub, the Singapore police ruled it a suicide. Pinder ended up in Changi prison on misdemeanor charges.

After Pinder's successor upset Malaysians by investing in unsuccessful European ventures, Pernas, the Malaysian government trading corporation, bought Sime Darby shares on the London Stock Exchange and demanded that an Asian majority be placed on the board of directors. Outmaneuvered, the British lost control of Sime Darby in a midnight meeting on December 9, 1976. The only man acceptable as chairman to both the Asian and British board members was Tun Tan Siew Sin, a former Malaysian finance minister and the son of Tun Tan Cheng Lock. The company was reincorporated in Malaysia as Sime Darby Berhad in 1978, and in 1979 the head office was moved to Kuala Lumpur.

Sime Darby acquired the tiremaking operations of B. F. Goodrich Philippines in 1981 and the Apple Computer franchise for southeast Asia in 1982. It bought an interest in United Estates Berhad, a Malaysian property development company, in 1984. In 1989 Sime Darby bought Dur-A-Vend, a UK condom company, which markets a product called Jiffy with the slogan, "Do it in a Jiffy." In 1991 the company moved into tourism, acquiring the Sandestin resort in Florida for $45 million. It extended its Caterpillar franchise to both Papua New Guinea and the Solomon Islands in 1992. Subsidiary Consolidated Plantations opened a refinery in Egypt in 1993, and Sime Darby launched 3 new tire models in the Philippines in the same year.

In 1994 Sime Darby paid about $34 million for white-goods maker Lec Refrigeration.

OTC symbol: SIDBY (ADR)
Fiscal year ends: June 30

WHO

Chairman: Tun Ismail bin Mohamed Ali, age 75
Executive Deputy Chairman: Tunku Tan Sri
Dato' Seri Ahmad bin Tunku Yahaya, age 65
Group Chief Executive: Nik Mohamed bin Nik
Yaacob
Group Finance Director: Syed Fahkri Barakbah
President, Sandestin Resorts, Inc. (US):
Jim Rester
Auditors: Price Waterhouse

WHERE

HQ: 21st Fl., Wisma Sime Darby, Jalan Raja Laut,
50350 Kuala Lumpur, Malaysia
Phone: +60-3-291-4122
Fax: +60-3-298-7398
US HQ: Sandestin Resorts, Inc., 9300
Hwy. 98 East, Destin, FL 32541
US Phone: 904-267-8000
US Fax: 904-267-8097

Sime Darby operates around the world.

	1994 Sales		1994 Operating Income	
	M$ mil.	% of total	M$ mil.	% of total
Malaysia	3,564	42	378	48
Hong Kong	2,576	31	228	29
Singapore	1,104	13	76	10
Australia	599	7	52	7
Philippines	133	2	15	2
Other countries	417	5	32	4
Adjustments	(180)	—	—	—
Total	**8,213**	**100**	**781**	**100**

WHAT

	1994 Sales		1994 Operating Income	
	M$ mil.	% of total	M$ mil.	% of total
General trading	4,115	49	296	38
Heavy equipment	1,528	18	179	23
Manufacturing	1,424	17	156	20
Plantations	697	8	47	6
Property	408	5	90	11
Insurance	221	3	13	2
Adjustment	(180)	—	—	—
Total	**8,213**	**100**	**781**	**100**

Investment Holding
Sime Darby Commodities Inc. (US)

Heavy Equipment
AMIM Holdings Sdn. Bhd. (50.2%, Ford)
Land Rover (Malaysia) Sdn. Bhd. (43%)
Scandinavian Truck & Bus Sdn. Bhd. (71.7%, Scania)
Sime Darby Hong Kong Limited (74.9%, investments)
Tractors Malaysia (1982) Sdn. Bhd., (71.7%, Caterpillar)

Manufacturing
DMIB Berhad (25.6%, tires and mattresses)
Sime Darby Pilipinas, Inc. (55.6%; tires and other
rubber products, management of rubber plantations)

Plantations
Consolidated Plantations Berhad (50.1%; palm oil,
rubber, cocoa)

Property
Sime UEP Properties Berhad (51.2%; investment
holding and property services)
Sandestin Resorts, Inc. (US)

KEY COMPETITORS

Bridgestone	Michelin
Goodyear	Pirelli
W. R. Grace	Salomon
Jardine Matheson	Sumitomo

HOW MUCH

$=M$2.65 (Dec. 31, 1993)	Annual Growth	1985	1986	1987	1988	1989	1990	1991	1992	1993	1994
Sales (M$ mil.)	14.9%	2,346	2,248	2,528	3,367	4,420	4,977	5,575	6,198	7,041	8,213
Net income (M$ mil.)	20.0%	87	59	85	135	224	284	310	354	403	450
Income as % of sales	—	3.7%	2.6%	3.4%	4.0%	5.1%	5.7%	5.6%	5.7%	5.7%	5.5%
Earnings per share (M$)	17.0%	0.07	0.04	0.06	0.10	0.14	0.18	0.20	0.23	0.26	0.29
Stock price – high (M$)[1]	—	—	1.44	1.55	3.08	2.92	4.24	4.78	4.48	5.35	7.63
Stock price – low (M$)[1]	—	—	1.03	0.88	1.40	1.71	2.83	3.50	3.30	3.48	4.13
Stock price – close (M$)[1]	24.1%	—	1.33	1.53	1.79	2.85	4.08	4.12	3.86	4.78	7.50
P/E – high	—	—	36	26	31	20	23	24	20	21	27
P/E – low	—	—	26	15	14	12	16	18	15	14	14
Dividends per share (M$)	20.8%	—	—	0.04	0.05	0.08	0.10	0.10	0.12	0.14	0.15
Book value per share (M$)	7.8%	1.11	1.19	1.23	1.32	1.44	1.65	1.80	1.87	2.01	2.18
Employees	(1.8%)	—	—	—	—	35,000	30,000	30,000	30,000	30,000	32,000

1994 Year-end:
Debt ratio: 5.9%
Return on equity: 13.7%
Cash (mil.): M$1,372
Long-term debt (mil.): M$115
No. of shares (mil.): 1,567
Dividends
  Yield: 2.0%
  Payout: 51.2%
Market value (mil.): $4,370
Sales (mil.): $3,053

Stock Price History[1]
High/Low 1986–94

[1] Stock prices are for the prior calendar year.

SINGAPORE AIRLINES LIMITED

OVERVIEW

With service second to none, Singapore Airlines (SIA) is considered one of the world's best airlines. Renowned for gourmet meals, Dom Pérignon, and its sylphlike, sarong-clad cabin attendants (known as Singapore Girls), SIA consistently gets rave reviews from passengers and travel agents alike. Not only has SIA been profitable every year since it was founded in 1972, but it also has one of the youngest and most fuel-efficient jet fleets among international carriers; the average age of its jets is 5 years old.

Like other carriers SIA is suffering from a recent slump in air travel. But the elegant airline is positioning itself for a larger piece of the world's fastest-growing market — Asia. While other airlines are cutting costs, SIA is investing millions in new services, such as fax machines and satellite-linked telephones in its long-range jets.

To lure travelers, SIA cut first-class and business fares to Europe in 1993 (for the first time in 20 years) and to Asia, Africa, and the South Pacific one year later. Also in 1993 it created a frequent-flier program (Passages). SIA is integrating its schedules and undertaking joint marketing efforts with Swissair and Delta Airlines; pursuing more joint ventures (hotels, airport kitchens and ground handling equipment, regional airlines, aircraft leases, and maintenance facilities); and overall paring costs without sacrificing service. The government, as Temasek Holdings (Private) Ltd., owns 54% of SIA's stock.

WHEN

Singapore Airlines was formed as Malayan Airways in 1937 but did not begin scheduled service until 1947, when it was revived by the Mansfield & Co. shipping line to link Singapore with other Malayan cities. The airline added service to Vietnam and the Indonesian islands of Sumatra and Java by 1951, opening routes to Borneo, Brunei, Thailand, and Burma by 1958.

Meanwhile, British Overseas Airways Corporation (BOAC, predecessor of British Airways) bought 10% of Malayan (1948), raising its stake to 30% in 1959. That year Australia's flag carrier, Qantas Airways, bought 30% of Malayan. In 1962 the governments of Singapore, Malaya, Sarawak, and Sabah merged to form Malaysia, sparking Malayan to change its name to Malaysian Airways. Singapore then seceded from the federation (1965) but joined Malaysia to buy control of the airline from BOAC and Qantas (1966), changing the name to Malaysia-Singapore Airlines (1967).

The airline extended service to Bombay, Melbourne, Rome, and London (1971) and then to Osaka, Athens, Zurich, and Frankfurt (1972). But disagreements about the direction and objectives of the company led Malaysia and Singapore to dissolve it in 1972 in favor of 2 separate national airlines. The company's routes were divided, with the domestic network going to the Malaysian Airline System and international routes going to Singapore Airlines (SIA). Joe Pillay (of Singapore's Ministry of Finance) became SIA's first chairman. Ownership was divided chiefly between the government (82%) and the airline's employees (17%).

The airline was famous for its quality service by the mid-1970s, and its glamorous hostesses attracted about 3 million passengers a year. By 1974 SIA was serving 25 cities worldwide, adding flights to Auckland and Paris in 1976, Tehran and Copenhagen in 1977, and San Francisco, its first US destination, in 1978.

In 1985 the government reduced its holding in SIA to 63%. SIA joined Cathay Pacific and Thai International in 1988 to form Abacus, a computer reservation system for Asia- and Pacific-based carriers. In 1989 SIA formed an alliance with Delta Air Lines and Swissair, creating a coordinated route network of 288 cities in 82 countries, offering the others strength in a major world market: Delta in the US, Swissair in Europe, and SIA in the Pacific. In addition, in 1990 SIA bought a 5.1% stake in Delta and 2.8% of Swissair; Delta bought a 2.8% stake in SIA and Swissair bought 0.6% of SIA.

In 1993 SIA signed a letter of intent with the government of Cambodia for a 40% stake in Royal Air Cambodge. In 1994 SIA Engineering, a subsidiary, announced joint ventures with United Technologies' Pratt & Whitney and with Praxair to build a jet engine fan blade repair facility — the first of its type in the Asia Pacific region. Also that year SIA announced an order of up to 14 Boeing and 10 Airbus Industrie jets.

Principal exchange: Singapore
Fiscal year ends: March 31

Chairman: J. Y. Pillay
Managing Director: Cheong Choong Kong
Director of Finance: Tan Hui Boon
Director of Personnel: Syn Chung Wah
SVP North America: Teoh Tee Hooi
Manager Finance and Administration, North America: Michael Li
Manager Human Resources, North America: Jillian Madden
Auditors: Ernst & Young

HQ: Airline House, 25 Airline Rd.,
Singapore 1781
Phone: +65-542-3333
Fax: +65-545-5034
US HQ: Singapore Airlines, 5670 Wilshire Blvd.,
Ste. 1800, Los Angeles, CA 90036
US Phone: 213-934-8833
US Fax: 213-934-4482
Reservations: 800-742-3333

Singapore Airlines serves 69 cities in 40 countries.

	1994 Sales	
	S$ mil.	% of total
Asia	2,539	46
The Americas	1,263	23
Europe	1,147	21
Southwest Pacific	550	10
Adjustments	737	—
Total	**6,236**	**100**

	1994 Sales		1994 Pretax Profit	
	S$ mil.	% of total	S$ mil.	% of total
Airline operations	5,646	91	582	66
Engineering svcs.	313	5	127	15
Airport terminal svcs.	277	4	162	19
Total	**6,236**	**100**	**871**	**100**

Major Subsidiaries and Affiliates
SIA Engineering Co. Private Ltd(engine maintenance)
SIA Properties (Pte) Ltd (building services)
Singapore Airport Terminal Services Group
  SATS Airport Services Pte Ltd
  SATS Catering Pte Ltd
  SATS Security Services Private Ltd
Singapore Aviation and General Insurance Company
  (Pte) Ltd.
Singapore Flying College Pte Ltd (pilot training)

Computer Reservation System
Abacus Distribution Systems (with 12 partners)

1994 Flight Equipment	No.	Orders
Boeing 747	45	17
A310	19	2
A340	—	7
Total	**64**	**26**

All Nippon Airways	General Electric	Rolls-Royce
AMR	IRI	SAS
British Airways	JAL	Swire Pacific
China Airlines	KLM	Thai
Continental	Lufthansa	International
Airlines	Northwest	UAL
Delta	Airlines	Virgin Group
FlightSafety	Philippine	
Garuda Indonesia	Air Line	
Airlines	Qantas	

$=S$1.60 (Dec. 31, 1993)	Annual Growth	1985	1986	1987	1988	1989	1990	1991	1992	1993	1994
Sales (S$ mil.)	7.8%	3,166	3,175	3,483	4,011	4,566	5,093	4,948	5,421	5,648	6,236
Net income (S$ mil.)	18.0%	180	285	451	603	985	1,201	913	928	851	801
Income as % of sales	—	5.7%	9.0%	12.9%	15.0%	21.6%	23.6%	18.4%	17.1%	15.1%	12.8%
Earnings per share (S$)	14.8%	0.18	0.25	0.37	0.49	0.80	0.96	0.72	0.73	0.66	0.63
Stock price – high (S$)[1,2]	—	—	—	4.95	7.50	7.50	10.95	10.90	10.55	10.65	13.63
Stock price – low (S$)[1,2]	—	—	—	2.83	3.98	5.05	6.80	5.75	6.35	6.90	8.50
Stock price – close (S$)[1,2]	14.4%	—	—	4.60	4.98	7.35	10.15	6.55	10.30	9.25	13.50
P/E – high	—	—	—	13	15	9	11	15	15	16	22
P/E – low	—	—	—	8	8	6	7	8	9	10	14
Dividends per share (S$)	27.7%	0.03	0.05	0.07	0.08	0.12	0.18	0.20	0.23	0.23	0.23
Book value per share (S$)	17.9%	1.47	1.83	2.15	2.59	3.30	4.31	4.88	5.48	5.99	6.46
Employees	7.2%	—	—	—	16,063	17,168	18,894	20,592	21,891	23,117	24,377

1994 Year-end:
Debt ratio: 0.4%
Return on equity: 10.0%
Cash (mil.): S$1,047
Long-term debt (mil.): S$0
No. of shares (mil.): 1,283
Dividends
  Yield: 1.7%
  Payout: 36.0%
Market value (mil.): $10,821
Sales (mil.): $3,898

Stock Price History[1]
High/Low 1987–94

[1] Stock prices are for the prior calendar year.   [2] Foreign shares.

SMITHKLINE BEECHAM PLC

OVERVIEW

Despite the drug industry's ongoing merger mania, SmithKline Beecham is holding its position as the world's 5th largest drug company. It is #3 in over-the-counter sales. Company products include ulcer remedy Tagamet, whose patent expired in 1994, and such familiar OTC brands as Contac, Geritol, and Tums. The company also makes laboratory testing chemicals.

In 1994 SmithKline strengthened its OTC segment when it bought Sterling Winthrop's nonprescription business from Kodak. It then sold Sterling's North American OTC lines (including Bayer aspirin) to German drug maker Bayer A.G., allowing that company to regain North American rights to its brand name, which was appropriated during WWI. SmithKline also sold its animal health division to Pfizer in late 1994. Together the sales raised nearly $2.5 billion, which was used to cut acquisition-related debt.

Some of SmithKline's debt stems from the strategic acquisition of Diversified Pharmaceutical Services for $2.3 billion. DPS is one of the US's largest marketers of discount drugs to managed-care companies.

SmithKline is also investing in biotechnology, including underwriting Human Genome Sciences's project that has mapped 45,000 of the estimated 50,000–100,000 human genes. SmithKline plans to sell unspecified rights to the gene map as early as 1996.

WHEN

Thomas Beecham established an apothecary in England in 1847 and began newspaper advertising for Beecham's Pills, a laxative, in 1859. At one point in the late 1800s, 14,000 newspapers advertised Beecham's Pills. Sales soared in the UK and the US, where production had begun in 1888. Output surpassed one million pills per day in the early 1900s.

In 1924 land developer Philip Hill purchased the Beecham estate, including the pill business. In 1928 he registered the enterprise as Beecham's Pills Ltd. and began acquiring other consumer product lines, including Macleans (toothpaste, US, 1938), Eno Fruit Salt (laxatives, UK, 1938), and Brylcreem (men's hair care, UK, 1939).

Beecham's investment in pharmaceutical R&D paid off in 1959 when the company introduced the first partly synthetic penicillin and in 1961 when it developed the first broad-spectrum antibiotic. Amoxil became the most prescribed antibiotic in the US.

Beecham sought consumer goods companies with strong positions in markets outside the UK, acquiring Massengill (drugs, personal products; US; 1971), Calgon (bath products, US, 1977), Jovan (fragrances, US, 1979), Bovril (foods, UK, 1980; sold 1990), J.B. Williams (Aqua Velva, Sominex, Geritol; US; 1982), DAP (caulk, US, 1983; sold 1987 to USG), Germaine Monteil (Yardley, cosmetics; UK; 1984, sold 1990), and Norcliff Thayer (Tums, medications; US; 1985).

After years of poor earnings, Beecham changed CEOs in 1986, assigning American Robert Bauman the task of restructuring the company. Bauman sold nondrug companies between 1987 and 1990 and merged Beecham with troubled SmithKline Beckman in 1989.

Having started in 1830 as a small Philadelphia apothecary, SmithKline became a major pharmaceutical company, developing the Benzedrine Inhaler (1936), Dexedrine (1944), and Tagamet (1976). SmithKline's Contac cold medicine was a hit, but Tagamet transformed the company, becoming the world's best-selling drug in 1981. CEO Henry Wendt led SmithKline through the 1980s, but poor diversification results and low R&D productivity reversed the company's fortunes.

Although Tagamet's sales plummeted when the drug's patent expired, other drugs are boosting SmithKline's revenues. Sales are growing for the company's new #1 product, Augmentin (antibiotic, 1985). The FDA has approved Relafen (antiarthritis, 1992), Paxil (antidepressant, 1993), and Kytril (antiemetic, 1993). Although SmithKline has repeatedly failed to get FDA approval for an OTC version of Tagamet, its Hepatitis A vaccine, Havrix, is expected to win approval soon. The company is also conducting studies on newly developed drugs for angina, congestive heart failure, and prostate enlargement.

In 1994 SmithKline's animal health, consumer products, and clinical laboratories divisions all posted sales increases to further offset the loss of revenues from Tagamet.

SmithKline plans to continue selling noncore subsidiaries to reduce debt. Cadbury has expressed interest in its Ribena vitamin C drink and Lucozade energy drink business.

NYSE symbol: SBE (ADR)
Fiscal year ends: December 31

Chairman: Sir Peter Walters, age 63
CEO: Jan Leschly, age 54
Chairman, SmithKline Beecham Pharmaceuticals:
Jean-Pierre Garnier, age 47
CFO: Hugh R. Collum, age 54
Group Personnel Director: Dan Phelan, age 45
President, North American Pharmaceuticals:
Argeris Karabellas
Auditors: Price Waterhouse; Coopers & Lybrand

HQ: New Horizons Court, Brentford, Middlesex
TW8 9EP, UK
Phone: +44-(01)81-975-2000
Fax: +44-(01)81-975-2090
US HQ: SmithKline Beecham Corporation, One
Franklin Plaza, Philadelphia, PA 19101
US Phone: 215-751-4000
US Fax: 215-751-7655

	1993 Sales		1993 Operating Income	
	$ mil.	% of total	$ mil.	% of total
US	4,637	51	1,598	62
UK	725	8	146	6
Other Europe	2,072	23	474	18
Other countries	1,628	18	366	14
Adjustments	184	—	(814)	—
Total	**9,246**	**100**	**1,770**	**100**

	1993 Sales		1993 Operating Income	
	$ mil.	% of total	$ mil.	% of total
Pharmaceuticals	5,225	57	1,238	72
Consumer brands	1,996	22	245	14
Clinical labs	1,225	14	142	8
Animal health	614	7	96	6
Adjustments	186	—	49	—
Total	**9,246**	**100**	**1,770**	**100**

Selected Products (US Markets)

Consumer Products	Prescription Drugs
Aquafresh	Amoxil (antibiotic)
Contac	Augmentin (antibiotic)
Ecotrin	Dyazide (blood pressure)
Geritol	Eminase (blood clot
Horlicks	dissolver)
N'Ice	Havrix (hepatitis A vaccine)
Oxy	Kytril (nausea drug)
Sominex	Ornade (cold treatment)
Sucrets	Paxil (antidepressant)
Tums	Relafen (arthritis drug)
Vivarin	Stelazine (antidepressant)
	Tagamet (ulcer drug)
Diagnostic Tests	Thorazine (anxiety drug)
Antibody and antigen	Timentin (antibiotic)
testing	
Drug monitoring	
Toxicology	

Affiliated Foods	Glaxo	Pfizer
American Home	Hoechst	Rhône-Poulenc
Products	Johnson &	Sandoz
Bristol-Myers	Johnson	Schering-
Squibb	Marion	Plough
Ciba-Geigy	Merrell Dow	Upjohn
Eli Lilly	Merck	Wellcome

Stock prices are for ADRs. ADR = 5 shares	Annual Growth	1984	1985	1986	1987	1988	1989	1990	1991	1992	1993
Sales ($ mil.)	11.2%	—	—	4,395	4,688	4,233	7,906	9,195	8,761	9,133	9,246
Net income ($ mil.)	20.6%	—	—	329	453	509	769	1,050	1,193	1,274	1,220
Income as % of sales	—	—	—	7.5%	9.7%	12.0%	9.7%	11.4%	13.6%	13.9%	13.2%
Earnings per share ($)	26.5%	—	—	0.44	0.60	0.67	1.48	1.98	2.25	2.39	2.28
Stock price – high ($)	—	—	—	6.88	9.75	9.13	22.44	26.63	40.75	43.00	34.38
Stock price – low ($)	—	—	—	4.50	5.81	7.50	8.38	16.88	24.13	30.25	25.25
Stock price – close ($)	22.5%	—	—	6.63	8.19	8.38	21.56	26.38	39.81	33.13	27.38
P/E – high	—	—	—	16	16	14	15	13	18	18	15
P/E – low	—	—	—	10	10	11	6	9	11	13	11
Dividends per share ($)	23.0%	—	—	0.23	0.30	0.34	0.41	0.80	0.88	0.72	0.98
Book value per share ($)	—	—	—	2.70	3.73	2.81	(0.96)	1.36	2.61	—	—
Employees	5.0%	—	—	36,900	35,600	34,900	62,800	54,100	54,000	53,000	51,900

1993 Year-end:
Debt ratio: 47.7%
Return on equity: 76.2%
Cash (mil.): $1,746
Current ratio: 1.56
Long-term debt (mil.): $1,261
No. of shares (mil.): 536
Dividends
Yield: 3.6%
Payout: 43.1%
Market value (mil.): $14,675

Stock Price History
High/Low 1986–93

Note: All share data are for equity units.

SONY CORPORATION

OVERVIEW

From its earliest days electronics giant Sony has had a flair for selling innovation. Its first "pocket-size" radios were too big for normal shirt pockets and were sold by salesmen who had outsized pockets stitched on their shirts to hold the transistor radios. In the 1990s Sony is trying to sell another innovation that might not seem to fit, the merging of its main electronics manufacturing lines with its newly acquired entertainment businesses.

Although Sony's reason for getting into the entertainment business was to promote its "hardware" (CDs, cassette players, TVs, VCRs) by owning the "software" (records, tapes, films), the software lines have become substantial in their own right. Sony has investments in the US entertainment business on a par with its electronic manufacturing outlays in Japan. Its entertainment assets include Columbia and Tri-Star film studios, Loews cinemas, videogames, and Columbia and Epic records.

CEO Norio Ohga has stated that the future for Sony, whose electronic sales have floundered in recent years, lies in what is happening in the US, the home of both the major movie studios and the largest consumer electronics market in the world.

In 1993 Sony consolidated its US entertainment and electronics concerns into one organization with Michael Schulhof as its CEO. US sales accounted for $11.2 billion of the company's 1994 sales of $35 billion. And while the music side of the business has done well, expensive movie flops like *Last Action Hero* and *Wolf* have hurt sales, with little sign of the anticipated synergistic spinoff in increased hardware sales.

WHEN

Akio Morita, Masaru Ibuka, and Tamon Maeda, Ibuka's father-in-law, established Tokyo Telecommunications Engineering in 1946 with funding from Morita's father's sake business. Determined to innovate and create new markets, the company produced the first Japanese tape recorder (1950).

In 1953 Morita paid Western Electric (US) $25,000 for transistor technology licenses — a move that sparked a consumer electronics revolution in Japan. His company launched one of the first transistor radios in 1955, followed by the first Sony-trademarked product, a pocket-sized radio, in 1957. The company changed its name to Sony in 1958. It introduced the first transistor TV (1959) and the first solid-state videotape recorder (1961). Sony preempted the competition, becoming a leader in these newly emerging markets.

Morita moved to New York in 1960 to oversee US expansion. Sony launched the first home video recorder (1964), solid-state condenser microphone (1965), and integrated circuit–based radio (1966). Sony's 1968 introduction of the Trinitron color TV tube began another decade of explosive growth. Its Betamax VCR (1976) fell prey to products employing rival Matsushita's VHS technology. The Walkman (1979), in all its forms, was another Sony success.

By 1980 Sony faced an appreciating yen and intense price and quality competition, especially from developing Far Eastern countries. The company used its technology to diversify outside consumer electronics, and it began to move production to other countries to reduce the effects of currency fluctuations. In the 1980s Sony introduced Japan's first 32-bit workstation and became a major producer of computer chips and floppy disk drives. It also developed compact disc technology in partnership with Philips.

Sony acquired CBS Records from CBS for $2 billion in 1988 and Columbia Pictures from Coca-Cola in 1989 for $4.9 billion. The purchases made Sony a major force in the rapidly growing entertainment industry and gave the company a source of software material to sell with new hardware products.

Sony manufactures Apple's wildly successful PowerBook and the Data Discman, a portable CD player that displays text and audio from reference books. Data Discman was a hit in Japan in 1991 but failed to take off in the US. In 1992 Sony allied with Sega to develop CD video games and with Microsoft to make electronic audio/video/textbooks. Also in 1992 Sony launched a high-end CD player with a 90MHz High Density Linear Converter system, which minimizes distortion.

In 1993 Morita suffered a brain hemorrhage but recovered after surgery; he resigned in 1994. Earnings fell dramatically from 1992 to 1994.

NYSE symbol: SNE (ADR)
Fiscal year ends: March 31

Honorary Chairman: Akio Morita, age 73
President and CEO: Norio Ohga, age 64
Executive Deputy President (Finance and Personnel): Tsunao Hashimoto
President and CEO, Sony Corp. of America: Michael P. Schulhof, age 51
Chairman and CEO, Sony Pictures Entertainment: Peter Guber
Auditors: Price Waterhouse

WHERE

HQ: 7-35, Kitashinagawa 6-chome, Shinagawa-ku, Tokyo 141, Japan
Phone: +81-3-5448-2111
Fax: +81-3-5448-2244
US HQ: Sony Corp. of America, 9 W. 57th St., New York, NY 10019-2791
US Phone: 212-833-6849
US Fax: 212-833-6923
US HQ: Sony Electronics Inc., Sony Dr., Park Ridge, NJ 07565
US Phone: 201-930-1000
US Fax: 201-358-4058

	1994 Sales	
	$ mil.	% of total
US	11,208	31
Japan	9,939	27
Europe	8,085	22
Other countries	7,018	20
Total	**36,250**	**100**

WHAT

	1994 Sales	
	$ mil.	% of total
Audio equipment	8,162	22
Video equipment	6,491	18
Televisions	5,999	17
Music	4,483	12
Pictures	3,182	9
Other products	7,933	22
Total	**36,250**	**100**

Commercial/Industrial Products
CD-ROM drives
Charge-coupled devices
Components
Factory automation systems
Home video game software
Optical pickups
Semiconductors

Consumer Brands
Betamax
Discman
MiniDisc
Walkman

Consumer Products
Audio systems
Audiotapes
Camcorders
Car navigation systems
CD players
Laserdisc players
Still-image video cameras
TVs and VCRs
Videotapes

Entertainment
Sony Music Entertainment
Sony Pictures Entertainment

KEY COMPETITORS

AT&T	3M	Sanyo
BASF	Motorola	Sharp
Bertelsmann	NEC	Thomson SA
Blaupunkt	News Corp.	Thorn EMI
Bose	Nokia	Time Warner
Canon	Oki	Toshiba
Crédit Lyonnais	Olivetti	Trimble Navigation
Fuji Photo	Philips	Turner Broadcasting
Fujitsu	Pinnacle Micro	Viacom
Hitachi	Pioneer	Walt Disney
Lucky-Goldstar	Rank	Zenith
Matsushita	Samsung	

HOW MUCH

	9-Year Growth	1985	1986	1987	1988	1989	1990	1991	1992	1993	1994
Sales ($ mil.)	24.1%	5,196	5,806	8,246	11,655	16,678	18,617	26,249	29,495	34,766	36,250
Net income ($ mil.)	7.2%	291	345	257	268	549	650	832	905	316	149
Income as % of sales	—	5.6%	5.1%	3.1%	2.3%	3.3%	3.5%	3.2%	3.1%	0.9%	0.4%
Earnings per share ($)	(10.1%)	1.07	1.25	0.95	1.05	1.65	1.76	1.85	2.21	0.80	0.41
Stock price – high ($)[1]	—	15.79	19.43	21.36	36.59	53.18	59.77	55.90	49.88	38.00	50.63
Stock price – low ($)[1]	—	11.59	12.27	16.48	16.59	32.16	45.22	36.59	31.38	28.25	32.00
Stock price – close ($)[1]	16.4%	12.73	18.52	18.63	34.31	52.61	54.99	39.09	34.63	34.13	49.88
P/E – high	—	15	16	23	35	32	34	30	23	48	124
P/E – low	—	11	10	17	16	20	26	20	14	35	78
Dividends per share ($)	11.2%	0.15	0.14	0.19	0.25	0.27	0.25	0.27	0.29	0.34	0.39
Book value per share ($)	16.6%	8.69	11.14	14.60	19.81	22.22	24.75	28.19	31.03	33.33	34.54
Employees	12.8%	44,000	44,900	48,700	60,500	78,900	95,600	112,900	119,000	126,000	130,000

1994 Year-end:
Debt ratio: 50.4%
Return on equity: 1.2%
Cash (mil.): $5,486
Current ratio: 1.44
Long-term debt (mil.): $9,551
No. of shares (mil.): 374
Dividends
  Yield: 0.8%
  Payout: 95.1%
Market value (mil.): $18,642

Stock Price History[1]
High/Low 1985–94

[1] Stock prices are for the prior calendar year.

STET

OVERVIEW

STET is Italy's largest telecommunications company, a status that is meaningless because until recently it was the only telecommunications company and enjoyed the advantages of being a state monopoly.

STET is the telephone and telecommunications arm of IRI (the Italian state industrial holding company, which owns 53%) and includes telephone service companies and equipment manufacturers (as AT&T once controlled both of these areas in the US). But technological advances (which have broken communications monopolies) and the open-competition requirements of EC unification have propelled STET into the worldwide arena, and into a global struggle to the death.

In order to survive as anything but a local service carrier, STET is changing drastically. With privatization plans under way, IRI is pumping money into the company to upgrade its operations (Italy's phone service has been notoriously inefficient). STET is exploring new investments overseas and participating in joint ventures with such major players in communications systems and equipment as Siemens and Bell Atlantic.

WHEN

STET (Società Finanziaria Telefonica per Azioni) is a product of Benito Mussolini's vision of fascist statism. Mussolini believed that all of Italy's resources should serve the state's effort to recapture the glory of Rome. To this end, shortly after consolidating his hold on political power in Italy, Mussolini embarked on a program of nationalization, focusing first on 3 major banks and their equity portfolios (which, in the midst of the worldwide Depression, were large). Among the items in the banks' equity portfolios were 3 local phone services. These became the core of the company (STET) created in 1933 to handle IRI's phone services. As Italy modernized under Mussolini, phone services expanded, though the percentage of private households with phones was far lower than in the US. But STET did not gain total control over Italy's phone industry until after WWII.

Germany and Italy grew closer in the years leading up to WWII and Italian equipment makers entered into a joint venture with Siemens to make telephone equipment. STET came through the war relatively unscathed, with a high proportion of its infrastructure intact. After the war the Siemens properties, along with other equipment manufacturers, were taken over by another company, TETI, which was nationalized by IRI and put under the control of STET in 1958. This expanded STET's "natural" monopoly from service to equipment manufacturing.

During the 1950s and 1960s Italy's industries, particularly utilities and such "public" services as radio and television, were increasingly nationalized under IRI. Companies within the IRI family concluded alliances with each other and, as communications technology advanced, with independent companies, which were then frequently absorbed into STET.

During the 1960s and 1970s, STET's scope expanded to include satellite communications and data transmission.

But STET was on the brink of losing its monopoly because new technologies such as faxes, teleconferencing, and PCs were making STET's state-sponsored status irrelevant. In the race between equipment makers, STET is well behind the field, technologically. In addition, in a world in which individuals can buy satellite time its status as a necessary long distance carrier is threatened.

The communications revolution began in the US, where the struggle between computer and other communications equipment makers and AT&T as the keeper of the phone lines came to a head first. The monopoly lost in 1984 and the same process has happened in other countries, spurred on in Europe by the economic unification of the EC countries.

Change has not come easily to STET. Many Italians believe in the maintenance of state monopolies, not only on nationalistic grounds but also because of the strong anticompetitive stance of labor groups.

In 1994, in anticipation of STET's privatization, IRI reorganized STET and poured new capital into the company in the form of credits owed it by another IRI company, IRITEL. STET also began to think more globally, concluding an agreement to install and manage a communications system in China. In late 1994 US investment banker Morgan Stanley was chosen to advise on STET's privatization.

OTC symbol: STFEY (ADR)
Fiscal year ends: December 31

Chairman: Biagio Agnes
Deputy Chairman: Michele Savarese
Managing Director: Michele Tedeschi
EVP, Telecom Italia (US): Ettore Riccitelli
Controller, Telecom Italia (US): Joseph Rubino
Auditors: Arthur Andersen & Co.

WHERE

HQ: Società Finanziaria Telefonica p.a.,
Corso d'Italia, 41, 00198 Rome, Italy
Phone: 39-6-8589-1
Fax: 39-6-8589-434
US HQ: Telecom Italia, 499 Park Ave.,
New York, NY 10022
US Phone: 212-755-5280
US Fax: 212-755-5766

The company has telecommunications and
information operations primarily in Europe.

	1993 Sales	
	Lit bil.	% of total
Italy	28,013	94
Other EC countries	421	1
Other countries	1,348	5
Total	**29,782**	**100**

WHAT

	1993 Sales	
	Lit. bil.	% of total
Telecommunications svcs.	24,453	74
Manufacturing & installation	4,704	14
Publishing	2,153	7
Information processing	1,673	5
Adjustments	(3,201)	—
Total	**29,782**	**100**

Selected Subsidiaries
AET Telecomunicazioni S.p.A. (10%, systems
design and manufacture)
Finsiel (83%, technology investments)
ITALTEL - Società Italiana Telecomunicazione
S.p.A. (80%, telecommunications systems)
SIP - Società Italiana per l'esercizio delle
Telecomunicazioni, p.a. (58%, Italy's national
telephone company)
SIRTI S.p.A. (49%, design and installation of
communications and electrical systems)
STET International S.p.A. (51%, investments in
foreign communications companies)
Telecom Italia

KEY COMPETITORS

Alcatel Alsthom	Groupe Schneider
AT&T	International Cable Tel
BCE	MCI
BT	NTT
Cable & Wireless	Siemens
COMSAT	Sprint
Ericsson	TELEKOM
France Telecom	Telefónica de España

HOW MUCH

$=Lit1,713 (Dec. 31, 1993)	Annual Growth	1984	1985	1986	1987	1988	1989	1990	1991	1992	1993
Sales (Lit bil.)	13.8%	—	—	—	—	—	17,727	19,964	22,964	27,173	29,782
Net income (Lit bil.)	1.7%	—	—	—	—	—	949	958	971	965	1,014
Income as % of sales	—	—	—	—	—	—	5.4%	4.8%	4.2%	3.6%	3.4%
Earnings per share (Lit)	1.7%	—	—	—	—	—	205	207	210	209	219
Stock price – high (Lit)	—	—	—	—	—	—	—	—	2,390	2,410	4,480
Stock price – low (Lit)	—	—	—	—	—	—	—	—	1,690	1,035	1,735
Stock price – close (Lit)	22.8%	—	—	—	—	—	1,935	1,745	2,062	1,780	4,403
P/E – high	—	—	—	—	—	—	—	—	11	12	20
P/E – low	—	—	—	—	—	—	—	—	8	5	8
Dividends per share (Lit)	(15.9%)	—	—	—	—	200	200	100	100	100	100
Book value per share (Lit)	48.7%	—	—	—	—	—	570	1,663	1,992	2,668	2,785
Employees	1.5%	—	—	—	—	—	—	—	—	134,136	136,184

1993 Year-end:
Debt ratio: 48.5%
Return on equity: 8.0%
Cash (bil.): Lit352
L-T debt (bil.): Lit15,511
No. of shares (mil.): 4,600
Dividends
  Yield: 2.3%
  Payout: 45.7%
Market value (mil.): $11,824
Sales (mil.): $17,386

Stock Price History
High/Low 1991–93

SUMITOMO GROUP

OVERVIEW

The Sumitomo Group — including one of the world's leading trading companies, Sumitomo Corporation — distributes a broad array of commodities, industrial goods, and consumer products. It is also engaged in diverse enterprises ranging from coal mining to real estate. With the activities of its many affiliates centered around the Sumitomo Bank, the group is a *keiretsu,* or group of firms linked by cross ownership, with revenues of over $150 billion. Through Sumitomo Corporation it is Japan's top CATV operator.

The group's companies have been hurt by the slowing of the Japanese economy, resulting in declining sales and profits at Sumitomo Corporation every year since 1992. During 1994 only the corporation's metals products segment realized sales gains over weak results from the year before.

In the face of globalization, the Sumitomo Group is focusing on transforming itself from a general domestic trading house into a global investor in businesses that mesh with existing units and expand the group's reach.

WHEN

Around 1630 Masatomo Sumitomo, a Buddhist priest from the Kyoto area, opened a medicine shop/bookstore following the dissolution of his sect. His descendants have preserved his writings on business ethics and consider him the spiritual founder of the Sumitomo Group. The technological founder of the group was Riemon Soga, Sumitomo's brother-in-law, who researched and duplicated a Western copper smelting technique, enabling him to build a prosperous copper company. After Soga died in 1636, his son, Tomomochi, married Sumitomo's daughter and became the head of the Sumitomo family.

Tomomochi combined the families' businesses and moved to Osaka, where Sumitomo became Japan's dominant copper company. By 1693 the family had turned an old, dilapidated copper mine into one of Japan's top producers.

The family had earlier been tipped off to Besshi, a promising copper mining site. Besshi turned out to be a tremendous producer for over a century, but by the mid-1800s output had dropped. In the 1860s the government demanded funds from Sumitomo to quell a rebellion. Victorious rebels took over the family's businesses until Saihei Hirose, general manager of Besshi, convinced them that Sumitomo had been forced to contribute to the old regime.

Amid financial problems Hirose mortgaged the family's assets to modernize the mine, imported French technology, and bought ships for copper transport. Production soared and the grateful family appointed Hirose director general in 1878. His nephew, Teigo Iba, created Sumitomo Bank from existing family operations in 1895.

A copper wire business, founded in 1897, evolved into Sumitomo Electric and Sumitomo Metal Industries. The family formed Sumitomo Chemical in 1913 and in 1925 entered life insurance and established Sumitomo Trust.

Sumitomo managed Nippon Electric Company (NEC) from 1932 until occupation forces split the *zaibatsu* (family-run conglomerate) into numerous independent pieces following WWII. Employees of the old Sumitomo holding company migrated to a real estate and trading company, today's Sumitomo Corporation. Sumitomo companies regrouped, but much more loosely, in the 1950s. Sumitomo Corporation grew rapidly in concert with Japan's economic expansion and moved aggressively overseas.

Sumitomo Rubber bought control of Dunlop tire operations in Japan, the US, Canada, the UK, France, and Germany in the mid-1980s. Sumitomo Bank bought 12.5% of Goldman Sachs in 1986. In 1990 Sumitomo Bank chairman Ichiro Isoda was forced to resign in an illegal-loan scandal. In 1992 Sumitomo Metal Mining and the US's Phelps Dodge signed a contract giving Sumitomo 20% of a $1.5-billion project to develop copper and gold deposits in Chile's Candelaria mine, and Sumitomo Corporation bought a 33.5% share in Satellite Japan.

In 1993 Sumitomo Metal Industries invested $200 million in LTV to shore up its US supply of high-quality steel. The next year Sumitomo Corporation joined with Germany's Preussag AG in an oil deal in Kazakhstan, Sumitomo Bank director Kazufumi Hatanaka was slain gangland-style, and group companies agreed to build a $10 million wafer recycling plant in New Mexico.

Principal exchange: Tokyo
Fiscal year ends: March 31

Chairman: Tadashi Itoh
President: Tomiichi Akiyama
EVP Western Japan: Mutsumi Hashimoto
EVP: Hiro Kinoshita
General Manager, Personnel Division: Takashi Nomura
EVP, Sumitomo Corporation of America: Atsushi Nishijo
Auditors: Asahi & Co. (Arthur Andersen)

HQ: 2-2, Hitotsubashi 1-chome, Chiyoda-ku, Tokyo 100, Japan
Phone: +81-3-3217-5082
Fax: +81-3-3217-5128 (Corporate Communications)
US HQ: Sumitomo Corporation of America, 345 Park Ave., New York, NY 10154-0042
US Phone: 212-207-0700
US Fax: 212-207-0456

Sumitomo Corporation has offices in over 136 cities in 87 countries.

	1994 Sales	
	¥ bil.	% of total
Domestic	8,003	47
Import	2,183	13
Export	2,378	14
Offshore	4,436	26
Total	**17,000**	**100**

	1994 Sales	
	¥ bil.	% of total
Metals	6,116	36
Machinery	5,734	34
Chemicals & fuels	2,151	13
Foodstuffs	1,058	6
Textiles	416	2
General products, construction & real estate	1,526	9
Total	**17,000**	**100**

Principal Sumitomo Group Affiliates
Sumitomo Bakelite Co., Ltd.
The Sumitomo Bank, Ltd.
Sumitomo Cement Co., Ltd.
Sumitomo Chemical Co., Ltd.
Sumitomo Coal Mining Co., Ltd.
Sumitomo Construction Co., Ltd.
Sumitomo Corp.
Sumitomo Electric Industries, Ltd.
Sumitomo Forestry Co., Ltd.
Sumitomo Heavy Industries Ltd.
Sumitomo Life Insurance Co.
Sumitomo Light Metal Industries, Ltd.
The Sumitomo Marine & Fire Insurance Co., Ltd.
Sumitomo Metal Industries, Ltd.
Sumitomo Metal Mining Co., Ltd.
Sumitomo Precision Products Co., Ltd.
Sumitomo Realty & Development Co., Ltd.
Sumitomo Rubber Industries, Ltd.
The Sumitomo Trust & Banking Co., Ltd.

Hyundai	Mitsui
ITOCHU	Nisho Iwai
Kanematsu	Nittetsu Shoji
Kawasho	Sinochem
Marubeni	Tomen
Mitsubishi	Toyota

$=¥112 (Dec. 31, 1993)	9-Year Growth	1985	1986	1987	1988	1989	1990	1991	1992	1993	1994
Sales (¥ bil.)	4.2%	11,782	13,310	14,410	13,077	13,891	14,842	18,231	20,019	18,027	17,000
Net income (¥ bil.)	(13.9%)	28	34	29	28	29	35	47	47	20	7
Income as % of sales	—	0.2%	0.3%	0.2%	0.2%	0.2%	0.2%	0.2%	—	0.1%	0.0%
Earnings per share (¥)	(17.8%)	40	46	36	34	34	40	44	34	19	7
Stock price – high (¥)[1]	—	541	719	1,118	1,173	1,155	1,760	1,770	1,170	1,050	959
Stock price – low (¥)[1]	—	362	476	596	764	773	1,127	948	961	662	690
Stock price – close (¥)[1]	5.9%	520	628	886	806	1,136	1,750	1,020	1,040	761	868
P/E – high	—	14	16	31	34	34	44	39	34	55	140
P/E – low	—	9	10	17	22	23	28	22	28	34	101
Dividends per share (¥)	3.7%	5.79	5.79	6.36	6.36	8.18	8.00	8.00	8.00	8.00	8.00
Book value per share (¥)	9.9%	282	333	338	359	397	507	636	660	668	662
Employees	—	—	—	—	—	8,630	—	—	8,959	9,215	9,212

1994 Year-end:
Debt ratio: 79.8%
Return on equity: 1.0%
Cash (bil.): ¥1,319
Long-term debt (bil.): ¥1,054
No. of shares (mil.): 1,064
Dividends
  Yield: 0.9%
  Payout: 116.6%
Market value (mil.): $8,246
Sales (mil.): $151,786

Stock Price History High/Low 1985–94

Information presented is for Sumitomo Corp. only. [1] Stock prices are for the prior calendar year.

HOOVER'S HANDBOOK OF WORLD BUSINESS 1995–1996   487

SUZUKI MOTOR CORPORATION

OVERVIEW

"Four billion people live where cars are not used much yet. That is the market we are after," says Suzuki president Osamu Suzuki. A small player at home in Japan and in the US and Europe, Suzuki is the big kid on the block in the developing world. While its competitors are just beginning to see the potential of these countries, Suzuki has been there for years. Like most of its Japanese siblings, Suzuki has been hurt by the strong yen, but the company has avoided the hits some of its bigger competitors, such as Nissan and Honda, have taken.

Suzuki targets countries such as Cambodia, China, Egypt, Hungary, India, and Pakistan and then markets its minicars and motorcycles with a local partner. Suzuki concentrates on smaller vehicles (minicars and subcompact cars), sport-utility vehicles, and motorcycles. It is Japan's #1 maker of minicars and one of the world's largest motorcycle makers. Suzuki also makes marine engines and electric wheelchairs.

Fanatical about keeping costs down, the company works to standardize parts so they are interchangeable. It produces more of its cars outside Japan than its competitors, which helps keep prices low. General Motors, owner of 3.5% of Suzuki, sells Suzuki vehicles as GEO Metros and Trackers.

WHEN

In 1909 Michio Suzuki started Suzuki Loom Works in Hamamatsu, Japan. The company went public in 1920 and continued producing weaving equipment until, as WWII neared, it began manufacturing war-related products.

Following the war Suzuki moved its headquarters to the Shizuoka prefecture (1947) and turned its attention to the development of inexpensive motor vehicles. Suzuki first introduced a 36cc engine designed for motorizing bicycles in 1952. The company changed its name to Suzuki Motor in 1954, the same year Suzuki launched its first motorcycle. The unveiling of the 360cc Suzulight in 1955 marked the company's entry into minicars and was followed by the Suzumoped (1958), a delivery van (1959), and the Suzulight Carry FB small truck (1961).

Suzuki's triumph in the 1962 50cc-class Isle of Man TT motorcycle race started a long string of racing successes that propelled the Suzuki name to international prominence. The company expanded and established its first overseas plant in Thailand in 1967.

In the 1970s Suzuki accommodated market demand for motorcycles with large engines. A mid-1970s recession and the waning popularity of low-powered vehicles in increasingly affluent Japan hurt the company's domestic sales. The Japanese minicar industry produced 2/3 fewer cars in 1974 than in 1970. Suzuki responded by pushing overseas, beginning auto exports in 1974 and greatly expanding foreign distribution. In 1975 the company started motorcycle production in Taiwan, Thailand, and Indonesia.

Throughout the 1980s Suzuki boosted capacity internationally through joint ventures. In 1988 the company agreed to handle Japanese distribution of Peugeot cars. In Japan motorcycle sales peaked in 1982 but enjoyed a modest rebound in the late 1980s.

Suzuki's relationship with General Motors began in 1981 when it sold a stake to the US auto giant. Suzuki began producing Swift subcompacts in 1983 and sold them through GM as the Chevy Sprint and, later, the GEO Metro. In 1986 Suzuki and GM of Canada jointly formed CAMI Automotive to produce vehicles, including Sprints, Metros, and GEO Trackers (Suzuki Sidekicks), in Ontario. Production began in 1989.

Although sales through GM increased through 1990, US efforts with the Suzuki nameplate faltered shortly after the company formed its US subsidiary in Brea, California, in 1986. A 1988 *Consumer Reports* claim that the Samurai was prone to rolling over devastated US sales. The next year the company's top US executives quit, apparently questioning Suzuki's commitment to the US market.

In 1991 Suzuki established Magyar Suzuki, a joint venture with Hungarian automaker Autokonszern Rt., C. Itoh & Co., and International Finance Corporation, to begin producing the Swift sedan in Hungary.

In 1993 Suzuki expanded a licensing agreement with a Chinese government partner to become the first Japanese company to take an equity stake in a Chinese car-making venture. In 1994 Suzuki introduced the Alto van in Japan. At a price of $5,100, it is Japan's cheapest car.

Principal exchange: Tokyo
Fiscal year ends: March 31

Chairman: Hisao Uchiyama
President: Osamu Suzuki
VP: Makoto Oyama
VP: Yoshio Saito
Senior Managing Director: Shigeki Torii
Senior Managing Director: Masao Toda
Senior Managing Director: Masayuki Ikuma
President, American Suzuki Motor: Masao Nagura
Human Resource Manager, American Suzuki Motor: Ahmad Tarzi
Auditors: Seimei Audit Corporation

WHERE

HQ: 300 Takatsuka-cho, Hamamatsu, Shizuoka 432-91, Japan
Phone: +81-53-440-2061
Fax: +81-53-445-0040
US HQ: American Suzuki Motor Corporation, 3251 E. Imperial Hwy., Brea, CA 92621-6722
US Phone: 714-996-7040
US Fax: 714-524-2512

Suzuki operates manufacturing facilities in 28 countries and sells its products in 171 countries.

	1994 Sales	
	¥ bil.	% of total
Japan	1,035	84
Other countries	192	16
Total	**1,227**	**100**

WHAT

	1994 Sales	
	¥ bil.	% of total
Automobiles	711	58
Motorcycles	168	14
Other	348	28
Total	**1,227**	**100**

Products

Cars and Sport-Utility Vehicles (US Markets)	Other Vehicles
GEO Metro (sold by GM)	Motorcycles
GEO Tracker (sold by GM)	Motorized wheelchairs
Suzuki Samurai	**Other Products**
Suzuki Sidekick	General-purpose engines
Suzuki Swift	Generators
	Outboard motors
	Water pumps

Principal Overseas Subsidiaries and Affiliates

American Suzuki Motor Corp.
CAMI Automotive Inc. (joint venture with General Motors Canada)
Suzuki Australia Pty. Ltd.
Suzuki Canada Inc.
Suzuki France S.A.
Suzuki GB PLC
Suzuki Italia S.p.A.
Suzuki Motor de Colombia S.A.
Suzuki Motor España S.A.
Suzuki Motor GmbH, Deutschland
Suzuki New Zealand Ltd.
Suzuki Philippines Inc.

KEY COMPETITORS

B M W	Honda	Peugeot
British Aerospace	Hyundai	Renault
Brunswick	Isuzu	Saab-Scania
Chrysler	Kawasaki Kisen	Toyota
Fiat	Mazda	Vespa
Ford	Mitsubishi	Volkswagen
General Motors	Nissan	Volvo
Harley-Davidson	Outboard Marine	Yamaha

HOW MUCH

$=¥112 (Dec. 31, 1993)	9-Year Growth	1985	1986	1987	1988	1989	1990	1991	1992	1993	1994
Sales (¥ bil.)	6.8%	677	822	870	900	961	983	1,210	1,249	1,259	1,227
Net income (¥ bil.)	7.2%	8	6	10	11	7	6	16	20	19	15
Income as % of sales	—	1.2%	0.7%	1.1%	1.2%	0.7%	0.6%	1.3%	1.6%	1.5%	1.2%
Earnings per share (¥)	9.6%	28	21	32	35	17	14	39	48	45	64
Stock price – high (¥)[1]	—	540	635	778	705	829	1,010	1,040	758	882	1,080
Stock price – low (¥)[1]	—	400	475	470	500	586	700	520	580	580	800
Stock price – close (¥)[1]	8.0%	527	502	529	590	725	990	605	611	845	1,050
P/E – high	—	19	30	24	20	49	72	27	16	20	17
P/E – low	—	14	22	15	14	34	50	13	12	13	13
Dividends per share (¥)	1.6%	6.50	6.50	6.50	6.50	6.50	7.00	7.50	7.50	7.50	7.50
Book value per share (¥)	7.5%	325	345	367	407	453	466	500	538	579	624
Employees	0.8%	12,347	12,181	12,837	12,613	12,580	12,818	13,561	12,757	13,013	13,218

1994 Year-end:
Debt ratio: 39.6%
Return on equity: 10.6%
Cash (bil.): ¥173
Long-term debt (bil.): ¥76
No. of shares (mil.): 449
Dividends
  Yield: 0.7%
  Payout: 11.7%
Market value (mil.): $4,209
Sales (mil.): $10,955

**Stock Price History[1]
High/Low 1985–94**

[1] Stock prices are for the prior calendar year.

SWIRE PACIFIC LIMITED

OVERVIEW

For 10 years, as the reunification of Hong Kong and China nears, Swire Pacific has kept its head when all about it were losing theirs. The diversified holding company, still controlled by its founding family (through John Swire & Sons), brushed aside doubts about the future and cast its lot with China.

It could do little else, since the vast majority of its holdings are in Hong Kong. But unlike its competitor, Jardine Matheson, Swire has neither sought to hide its assets overseas nor to insulate itself from Chinese laws. It went so far as to eliminate the Union Jack painted on the planes of its most lucrative affiliate, Cathay Pacific Airways (of which it owns 51.8%). Cathay Pacific has grown along with the economies of the Pacific Rim, and 75% of passengers are Asian. The company also has an extensive real estate portfolio in Hong Kong, as well as holdings in Australia, Japan, Korea, Taiwan, and the US.

Swire has made many business contacts in China. It is an investor in many Chinese ventures, and in turn has welcomed Chinese investment in its own. The company has extensive bottling agreements with Coca-Cola and in 1994 concluded an agreement to bring its bottling operations to China.

WHEN

John Swire began a Liverpool trading company in 1816. When he died in 1847, the company, named John Swire & Sons, derived a large share of its business from the import of raw cotton from the US. Swire's son John redirected the company's focus to tea and textile trading in China when the US Civil War disrupted cotton shipments. Unhappy with his Far Eastern agents, Swire traveled to Shanghai and in 1866 formed a partnership with a customer, Richard Butterfield. The partnership, called Butterfield & Swire, took Taikoo ("great and ancient") as a Chinese name. Although Butterfield lasted only 2 years as a partner, the name lived on.

By 1868 Butterfield & Swire had established offices in New York and in Yokohama, where business subsequently benefited from the industrialization of Japan. In 1870 Butterfield & Swire opened an office in Hong Kong. John Swire & Sons entered the shipping business, creating China Navigation Company in 1872 to transport goods along the Yangtze River. The shipping line served all the major Pacific Rim ports by the late 1880s. The Hong Kong–based Tai-Koo Sugar Refinery began operations in 1884.

The 3rd John Swire took over in 1898 and built the Taikoo Dockyard in Hong Kong and other related facilities in China. The Japanese attack on China, WWII, and the Communist takeover devastated their Chinese operations. The company rebuilt in Hong Kong and in 1948 bought control of Cathay Pacific, a new Hong Kong airline with 6 DC-3s.

In the 1950s and 1960s, the Swires expanded the airline and established airport and aircraft service companies. Swire Pacific, the successor to Butterfield & Swire and holding company for most of the family's Hong Kong interests, went public in 1959. Swire Pacific picked up the Coca-Cola bottling franchise for hot, humid Hong Kong in 1965. The 5th generation of Swires, John and Adrian, rose to the top of the Swire Group in 1968. The Taikoo Dockyard merged its business with Hongkong & Whampoa Dockyard in 1972, and Swire Pacific began redeveloping the old site.

The 1984 agreement to return Hong Kong to Chinese control in 1997 plunged the colony into uncertainty. Capital flight and free-falling real estate values provided Swire with a great opportunity to pick up properties at bargain prices. When the economic policies of the Chinese government made people reasonably confident that property would not be expropriated, the real estate and building markets recovered, enriching Swire more.

Swire Pacific and Cathay Pacific have extended their links to China. In 1990 they purchased 35% of Hong Kong's Dragonair and gave it Cathay Pacific's Shanghai and Beijing routes. Dragonair (38% owned by the Chinese government) emphasizes mainland routes and has a better safety record than China's domestic airlines, making it the carrier of choice for foreigners doing business in China.

Swire Pacific profited well from the Pacific Rim boom, but in 1993 profits grew more slowly than they had recently because of the Japanese recession, which decreased the flow of Japanese business travelers, and a less frenzied real estate market. But the amount of money the company derives from rents has helped to stabilize its earnings.

OTC symbols: SWIRY (ADR)
Fiscal year ends: December 31

Chairman: Peter D. A. Sutch
Executive Director: H. J. Conybeare
Finance Director: Peter A. Johansen
President and CEO, Swire Pacific (US): Craig Taylor
VP and CFO, Swire Pacific (US): Brad Moore
Director Human Resources, Swire Pacific (US): Allison Johnson
Auditors: Price Waterhouse

WHERE

HQ: Swire House, 9 Connaught Rd., Central, Hong Kong
Phone: +852-840-8888
Fax: +852-810-6563
US HQ: Swire Pacific Holdings, Inc. 875 S. West Temple St., Salt Lake City, UT 84101
US Phone: 801-530-5300
US Fax: 801-530-5342

WHAT

	1993 Sales		1993 Operating Income	
	HK$ mil.	% of total	HK$ mil.	% of total
Aviation	26,315	62	3,057	51
Trading	6,569	15	203	3
Industries	4,941	12	261	4
Properties	3,856	9	2,417	41
Marine services	546	1	45	1
Insurance	235	1	(2)	—
Adjustments	(1,699)	—	488	—
Total	**40,763**	**100**	**6,469**	**100**

Selected Subsidiaries and Affiliates

Aviation
Cathay Pacific (51.8%)
Swire Aviation Ltd. (66.7%)

Trading
Swire & MacLaine Ltd.
Swire Loxley Ltd. (66.7%)
Reebok Hong Kong Ltd. (70.0%)
Carol Reed International Ltd. (70.0%)

Industries
German Hotel Experts Ltd. (90.0%)
Guangmei Foods Co. Ltd. (51.0%, China)
Swire Bottler Holdings Ltd.

Properties
Swire Properties Ltd.
Swire Properties Management Ltd.

Marine Services
Swire Pacific Ship Management Ltd.
Swire Pacific Offshore Maritime Ltd.

Insurance
Swire Insurance Holdings Ltd.

KEY COMPETITORS

Allied Group	The Limited
AMR	Marks and Spencer
Cadbury Schweppes	Mitsubishi
China Air	NIKE
The Gap	Northwest Airlines
Garuda Indonesia	PepsiCo
Hopewell Holding	Philippine Airways
HSBC	Qantas
Hutchison Whampoa	San Miguel
Hyundai	Sime Darby
ITOCHU	Singapore Airlines
JAL	Talbots
Jardine Matheson	UAL
Korean Airlines	US Shoe
Kumagai Gumi	Walgreen

HOW MUCH

$=HK$7.72 (Dec. 31, 1993)	Annual Growth	1984	1985	1986	1987	1988	1989	1990	1991	1992	1993
Sales (HK$ mil.)	14.6%	11,997	13,692	16,604	20,166	25,108	27,676	31,175	33,619	38,924	40,763
Net income (HK$ mil.)	18.0%	1,049	1,226	1,785	2,396	2,002	3,083	2,450	3,080	4,419	4,658
Income as % of sales	—	8.7%	9.0%	10.8%	11.9%	8.0%	11.1%	7.9%	9.2%	11.4%	11.4%
Earnings per share (HK$)	17.6%	0.68	0.81	1.16	1.54	1.90	1.94	1.54	1.94	2.78	2.93
Stock price – high (HK$)	—	5.38	8.47	16.92	28.90	19.30	23.20	22.40	24.20	39.00	70.50
Stock price – low (HK$)	—	3.26	5.13	8.25	12.20	14.80	13.20	14.10	14.80	23.00	28.75
Stock price – close (HK$)	32.9%	5.38	8.47	16.58	15.30	19.00	15.70	14.80	23.40	29.30	69.50
P/E – high	—	8	10	15	19	10	12	15	12	14	24
P/E – low	—	5	6	7	8	8	7	9	8	8	10
Dividends per share (HK$)	15.2%	0.32	0.39	0.52	0.62	0.76	0.80	0.80	0.89	1.03	1.14
Book value per share (HK$)	33.6%	2.83	4.01	5.78	9.49	14.42	17.04	17.96	21.94	28.86	38.48
Employees	2.3%	—	—	—	—	—	—	28,000	36,300	—	30,000

1993 Year-end:
Debt ratio: 33.8%
Return on equity: 8.7%
Cash (mil.): HK$627
Long-term debt (mil.): HK$26,569
No. of shares (mil.): 1,588
Dividends
  Yield: 1.6%
  Payout: 38.9%
Market value (mil.): $8,737
Sales (mil.): $5,270

**Stock Price History
High/Low 1984–93**

Note: Per share data presented for "A" shares only

TATA ENTERPRISES

OVERVIEW

The Tata Group, India's largest industrial conglomerate, comprises 90 companies. Its subsidiaries include holding company Tata Sons; Tata Iron and Steel (TISCO, 15%), India's largest company; Tata Engineering and Locomotive (TELCO), a major manufacturer of commercial vehicles; and Tata Consultancy Services (TCS), India's #1 software developer.

Strategic alliances are central to Tata's global growth strategy. In 1994 the company formed pacts with Daimler-Benz to assemble 20,000 cars annually; with Singapore Airlines to establish an Indian domestic carrier; and with Abacus Distribution Systems (US) to market Abacus's airline reservation system in India. Tata also joined with IBM to create

Tata Information Systems Limited (TISL). TISL's cutting edge Software Development Center is in Bangalore, India's Silicon Valley.

In 1995 Tata raised its equity in TISCO to 15% to ward off a hostile takeover. As India drops many of its import protections, TISCO is investing in a push to modernize productivity. Also in 1995 Tata joined with the Soros-Chatterjee Group (US) and the West Bengal state government to build a $1.25 billion petrochemical complex near Calcutta.

Among Tata's holdings is the Indian Hotels Company, also known as the Taj Group, a 54-hotel chain that includes the Lexington in New York City, the St. James Court in London, and the Taj Mahal Hotel in Bombay. The Taj Group has 21 hotels under development.

WHEN

Jamsetji Tata, a Parsee (Zoroastrian) from Bombay, started a textile trading company in 1868. He began manufacturing textiles, then embarked on a mission to industrialize India. Before his death in 1904, Tata had built the Taj Mahal Hotel in Bombay and set in motion plans to create a hydroelectric power plant, a forum for technical education and research in India, and a steel mill (and worker town) to supply rapidly expanding railroads.

Jamsetji's son, Dorabji, carried out the plans. Tata Hydro-Electric Power went online in 1910. The next year saw the creation of the Indian Institute of Science at Bangalore. Dorabji found a jungle site for the steel mill, renamed the area Jamshedpur after his father, and established Tata Iron and Steel in 1907, financed entirely by Indians. Doubtful that Indians could make steel rail, the British chairman of the Railway Board said he would "undertake to eat every pound of steel rail" Tata made. Dorabji would later comment on the man's probable indigestion after the mill shipped 1,500 miles of rail to British troops in Mesopotamia during WWI.

The steel company struggled after the war until British colonial powers enacted protective duties. After WWII and Indian independence, the government built a state-owned steel industry but allowed Tata's mills to operate through a grandfathering provision. Inefficient government operations led to high fixed prices for steel, and Tata profited.

Six years after Dorabji's death in 1932, the son of his cousin, 34-year-old J. R. D. Tata,

took over the family empire. India's first licensed pilot, J. R. D. had started Tata Airlines, later nationalized as part of Air India. He started Tata Chemicals in 1939. Tata Engineering and Locomotive, founded in 1945 to make steam locomotives, entered truck production in 1954 by collaborating with Daimler-Benz. With help from Volkart Brothers, a Swiss firm, the company started the Voltas manufacturing conglomerate in 1954. In 1962 Tata teamed with James Finlay of Scotland to create Tata-Finlay, now Tata Tea and 100% Indian-owned since 1982.

Until recently India's socialist government and unwieldy bureaucracy hampered Tata. The company was reluctant to pay bribes for licenses to enter new fields, and red tape and trade restrictions discouraged international expansion. A 1970 antitrust law ended the "managing agency" system through which Tata Sons held interests in subsidiary companies and Tata Industries managed them for a fee. The companies are now managed independently. Economic reform of the 1980s has allowed Tata to resume aggressive expansion.

After 38 years J. R. D. Tata retired as chairman in 1991. Infighting, including the forced retirement of some senior managers, landed Ratan Tata (J. R. D.'s nephew) in the top spot as head of Tata Group, TISCO, TELCO, and Tata Chemicals. J. R. D. died in 1993.

Engine maker Cummins (US) and TELCO formed a joint venture in 1993 to produce 60,000 engines annually by mid-1995.

Principal exchange: Bombay
Fiscal year ends: March 31

Chairman Tata Group, Tata Chemicals, Tata Engineering and Locomotive, Tata Iron and Steel: Ratan N. Tata
Managing Director, Tata Iron and Steel: J. J. Irani
Managing Director, Indian Hotels Co.: Ajit Kerkar
President, Tata Incorporated (US): Ashok Mehta

WHERE

HQ: Tata Sons Ltd., Bombay House, 24, Homi Mody St., Bombay 400 001, India
Phone: +91-22-204-9131
Fax: +91-22-204-8187
US HQ: Tata Incorporated, 101 Park Ave., New York, NY 10178
US Phone: 212-557-7979
US Fax: 212-557-7987

WHAT

Principal Member Companies
The Andhra Valley Power Supply Co. Ltd. (electric utility)
The Indian Hotels Co. Ltd. (Taj Group) (41 hotels in India; 49% of 13 non-Indian hotels run by Asian Resort and Restaurant Associates [ARRA], including Chicago's Executive Plaza, and Washington, DC's Hampshire Hotel)
National Radio and Electronics Co. Ltd. (consumer electronics)
Tata Chemicals Ltd.
The Tata Engineering and Locomotive Co. Ltd. (TELCO, commercial vehicles)
Tata Exports Ltd. (trading and manufacturing)

The Tata Hydro-Electric Power Supply Co. Ltd.
Tata Industries Ltd.
  Hitech Drilling Services India Ltd. (oil drilling)
  Tata Finance Ltd. (commercial and industrial equipment financing)
  Tata Honeywell Ltd. (manufacturing joint venture with Honeywell)
  Tata Information Systems (TISL, 50%, computer software and hardware joint venture with IBM)
  Tata Keltron Ltd. (telephone manufacturing in collaboration with Siemens)
  Tata Telecom Ltd. (PBX manufacturing in collaboration with Oki; Trans-India Network Systems, joint venture with AT&T)
The Tata Iron and Steel Co. Ltd. (TISCO, 15%)
The Tata Power Co. Ltd. (electric utility)
Tata Sons Ltd.
Tata Consultancy Services (TCS; computer systems/ software and management consulting)
Tata Tea Ltd.
Tata Unisys Ltd. (manufacturing and marketing joint venture with Unisys)
Voltas Ltd. (consumer and industrial products)

KEY COMPETITORS

Accor	Mitsubishi
Broken Hill	Mitsui
Cargill	MMTC
Carlson	National Organic
Computer Associates	Chemical Industries
DEC	New Otani
EDS	Nippon Steel
Fluor	Oberoi
Four Seasons	Oracle
Hilton	Perot Systems
Hindustan Motors	Ritz-Carlton
Hyatt	SHL Systemhouse
Imperial Chemical	Steel Authority of India
Inland Steel	Tea Trading Corp. of India
Mahindra and Mahindra	

HOW MUCH

$=Rs31.1 (Dec. 31, 1993)	Annual Growth	1985	1986	1987	1988	1989	1990	1991	1992	1993	1994
Tata Iron and Steel:											
Sales (Rs mil.)	12.8%	12,855	14,164	15,268	18,618	21,356	23,330	28,950	—	34,233	37,934
Net income (Rs mil.)	6.2%	871	584	922	1,543	1,485	1,601	—	—	1,270	1,800
Income as % of sales	—	6.8%	4.1%	6.0%	8.3%	7.0%	6.9%	—	—	3.7%	4.7%
Tata Engineering and Locomotive:											
Sales (Rs mil.)	14.0%	10,008	11,725	13,755	16,764	19,691	25,960	30,000	25,730	24,710	32,440
Net income (Rs mil.)	22.7%	162	29	270	633	1,280	1,420	—	1,370	300	1,020
Income as % of sales	—	1.6%	0.2%	2.0%	3.8%	6.5%	5.5%	—	5.3%	1.2%	3.1%
Employees	0.6 %	—	—	237,000	—	—	—	248,000	251,000	242,070	250,000

1994 Year-end:
Tata Iron and Steel
Sales (mil.): $1,219
Tata Engineering and Locomotive
Sales (mil.): $1,042

Tata Iron & Steel
Net Income (Rs mil.)
1985–94

TATE & LYLE PUBLIC LIMITED COMPANY

OVERVIEW

How sweet it is. Whether you are putting sugar in your coffee or sipping a soft drink, the company wants you to please your sweet tooth. Headquartered in London, Tate & Lyle is one of the largest sugar and corn refiners in the world, with operations in 32 countries.

Tate & Lyle's subsidiaries harvest beet and cane sugar and manufacture refined sugar, molasses, cereal sweeteners, and starches. The company is also involved in rum distillation, animal feeds, and specialty sweeteners. In the US its Domino subsidiary makes the #1 brand of grocery sugar. Another US subsidiary, A E Staley, makes Stellar, a corn-based fat substitute, and Krystar, a crystalline fructose sweetener.

Tate & Lyle has developed a low-calorie sweetener that is an altered form of sugar called sucralose. Marketed under the trade name Splenda, the sweetener has been approved in Canada, Russia, and Australia. Tate & Lyle and its US licensee, Johnson & Johnson subsidiary McNeil Specialty Products, are working to get FDA approval to sell the product in the US. In a bid to further tantalize the tastebuds, Tate & Lyle acquired 80% of Orsan, one of the world's largest producers of monosodium glutamate, in 1994.

WHEN

Tate & Lyle was created through the 1921 merger of 2 British sugar companies.

Henry Tate founded Henry Tate & Sons in 1869 and began building a sugar refinery in Liverpool in 1870. Tate was noted for his philanthropy, and in 1896 he provided the money to found the Tate Gallery. When he died in 1899, he left the business to his sons. In 1903 William Henry Tate took the company public, although only 17 investors, primarily family members, put up money for the company. Abram Lyle III founded his sugar company in 1881 when he bought Odam's and Plaistow Wharves, on the Thames River, to build a sugar refinery. While Tate focused on sugar cubes, Lyle concentrated on a sugary concoction called Golden Syrup.

Both companies were hit hard during WWI because they imported most of their raw beet sugar from Germany and Austria. In 1918 the 2 companies began to discuss a merger.

Although the 2 companies merged in 1921, it took longer for the 2 corporate cultures to come together, keeping separate sales organizations into the 1940s. In an effort to find new sources of sugar, Tate & Lyle began investing abroad. In 1937 it created the West Indies Sugar Company, which bought property in Jamaica and Trinidad and built a processing plant in Jamaica.

WWII brought hardships again for the company. Sugar rationing began in 1940 and both of its London factories were severely damaged by bombs. However, there was great demand for the company's inexpensive syrup. Following the war there was a movement to nationalize Tate & Lyle, but the company fought off the bid, thanks, in part, to a campaign featuring a cartoon character named "Mr. Cube" who spouted slogans such as "Only the State will make my price jump!"

In the 1950s Tate & Lyle continued to expand, buying Rhodesian Sugar Refineries (1953, now Zimbabwe Sugar Refineries) and Canada & Dominion Sugar Company (1959, now Redpath Industries). During the 1960s it diversified into other sweet-tasting businesses, buying United Molasses in 1965.

In 1976 Tate & Lyle acquired the only other independent British sugar refiner, Manbré and Garton. That same year it bought the US's Refined Sugars, giving Tate & Lyle its first entry into the US market. Because of a collapse in sugar prices, which cut into the company's earnings, the company closed its original Liverpool plant, laying off many 3rd-generation workers.

Neil Shaw became chairman in 1986 and began to search out new ways to satisfy the company's sweet tooth. In 1988 Tate & Lyle paid $1.9 billion for Staley Continental (now A E Staley), the US's 2nd largest corn refiner and major producer of high-fructose corn syrup. That same year it sold Staley's food service business to SYSCO for $700 million. Also in 1988 the company bought Amstar Sugar Corporation (name changed to Domino Sugar) for about $300 million.

In 1993 Staley formed a joint venture with ConAgra to make and market TrimChoice, an oat-based fat substitute.

In 1994 Shaw was knighted for service to the community and to the food industry. Tate & Lyle finished 1994 with $479 million in net income on $6.7 billion in sales.

OTC symbol: TATYY (ADR)
Fiscal year ends: Last Saturday in September

Chairman: Sir Neil M. Shaw, age 64
Deputy Chairman and Group Finance Director:
Paul S. Lewis, age 56
Managing Director European Sugar: John H. W.
Walker, age 49
Managing Director North American and
Australian Sugar: Paul J. Mirsky, age 47
Managing Director Cereal Sweeteners and
Starches North America: Larry G. Pillard
President and CEO, Domino Sugar (US):
Edward Makin
VP Human Resources, Domino Sugar (US):
John Anstedt
Auditors: Coopers & Lybrand

HQ: Sugar Quay, Lower Thames St., London
EC3R 6DQ, UK
Phone: +44-(01)71-626-6525
Fax: +44-(01)71-623-5213
US HQ: Domino Sugar Corporation, 1114
Avenue of the Americas, New York, NY 10036
US Phone: 212-789-9700
US Fax: 212-789-9746

	1993 Sales	
	£ mil.	% of total
US	1,562	41
UK	814	21
Other Europe	932	25
Other countries	509	13
Total	**3,817**	**100**

	1993 Sales	
	£ mil.	% of total
Cane & beet sugar	1,736	45
Cereal sweeteners & starches	1,279	34
Animal feed & bulk storage	439	12
Other	363	9
Total	**3,817**	**100**

Selected Subsidiaries, Affiliates, and Investments
Alcântara Sociedade de Empreendimentos Açucareiros,
SA (sugar refining, Portugal)
Amylum NV (66.3%, cereal sweeteners and starches,
Belgium)
Booker Tate Ltd. (50%, agribusiness)
Bundaberg Rum Co. (50%, Australia)
Bundaberg Sugar Co. Ltd. (raw sugar manufacture,
Australia)
Domino Sugar Corp. (sugar refining, US)
Orsan (80%, monosodium glutamate)
PM Ag Products Inc. (animal feeds and molasses, US)
Redpath Industries Ltd. (sugar refining, Canada)
Richards (Shipbuilders) Ltd.
A E Staley Manufacturing Co. (90%, cereal sweeteners
and starches, US)
Tate & Lyle Reinsurance Ltd. (Bermuda)
Tate & Lyle Sugars (sugar refining)
United Molasses (molasses and bulk storage)
The Western Sugar Co. (sugar beet processing, US)
Zimbabwe Sugar Refineries Ltd. (50.1%)

ADM	CPC
American Crystal Sugar	Imperial Holly
Bacardi	Monsanto
Cargill	Procter & Gamble
Connell Co.	Savannah Foods
Continental Grain	Spreckels Industries
Contran	Valhi

£=$1.48 (Dec. 31, 1993)	Annual Growth	1984	1985	1986	1987	1988	1989	1990	1991	1992	1993
Sales (£ mil.)	11.3%	—	1,627	1,645	1,701	2,088	3,466	3,445	3,263	3,366	3,817
Net income (£ mil.)	24.1%	—	27	27	70	70	111	166	144	116	149
Income as % of sales	—	—	1.6%	1.6%	4.1%	3.4%	3.2%	4.8%	4.4%	3.4%	3.9%
Earnings per share (p)	4.6%	—	—	—	25.0	32.3	26.4	29.1	33.0	26.2	32.7
Stock price – high (p)	—	150	197	219	315	296	301	320	409	443	439
Stock price – low (p)	—	103	139	173	187	247	204	233	263	285	256
Stock price – close (p)	11.7%	147	183	188	296	272	290	275	395	403	400
P/E – high	—	—	—	—	13	9	11	11	12	17	13
P/E – low	—	—	—	—	7	8	8	8	8	11	8
Dividends per share (p)	9.6%	—	—	—	—	—	9.0	10.0	11.2	12.0	13.0
Book value per share (p)	11.8%	—	—	—	—	—	—	—	—	177	198
Employees	17.4%	—	11,498	—	—	—	—	—	—	17,004	15,834

1993 Year-end:	
Debt ratio: 67.0%	
Return on equity: 22.3%	
Cash (mil.): £1,003	
Long-term debt (mil.): £523	
No. of shares (mil.): 358	
Dividends	
Yield: 3.3%	
Payout: 39.8%	
Market value (mil.): $2,119	
Sales (mil.): $5,650	

Stock Price History
High/Low 1984–93

TELEFÓNICA DE ESPAÑA, S.A.

With its phone service monopoly in Spain set to expire in 1998, Telefónica de España is buzzing over opportunities in South America. Since 1988 the firm, which is 32% owned by the Spanish government, has invested $5 billion in the region and seen sales of its international unit (Telefónica Internacional) soar, jumping tenfold in 1993 alone.

Nonetheless, the international unit accounts for only a tiny portion of the company's revenues (2% in 1993). As a result

Telefónica still relies on domestic growth to fuel total sales. But in a country with 36 lines per hundred residents (compared with about 51 in the US), the company, which operates about 14 million local lines, still has some room to expand at home. The firm also operates a mobile communications network with 150,000 subscribers, 1% of Spain's market.

In 1993, however, sales growth in Spain was anemic, as average usage fell 3% amid a weak domestic economy.

When a 1923 military coup brought General Miguel Primo de Rivera to power in Spain, the government-run telephone system was a shambles. Over half of the country's 90,000 lines did not work. With little cash in the government coffers, Primo de Rivera sought foreign assistance in running the Spanish telephone network. Several European telephone equipment manufacturers expressed interest, as did US-based telephone service company International Telephone and Telegraph (ITT).

Supported financially by National City Bank (now Citicorp), ITT bought 3 private Spanish telephone companies, later combining them to form Compañía Telefónica Nacional de España (Telefónica). After placing several influential Spaniards on Telefónica's board and getting help from the US ambassador to Spain, the ITT unit gained the telephone concession in 1924. ITT retained a controlling interest in Telefónica, and the government agreed not to try to reclaim the system for 20 years.

ITT purchased AT&T's European telephone equipment businesses and began operating a Spanish manufacturing subsidiary, the predecessor of Alcatel Standard Eléctrica. Modernization and expansion of the telephone network quickly followed.

When Franco came to power in 1939, he was thought to want to reward his German backers with the telephone franchise. US State Department pressure helped prevent expropriation, but Franco froze Telefónica's earnings and assets. ITT tried to sell Telefónica to German buyers in 1941 but backed out of the deal when the State Department objected. When the ITT franchise expired in 1945, the government bought ITT's

share of Telefónica. Telefónica grew with the Spanish economy, introducing long distance direct dialing in 1960, satellite communications in 1967, and international direct dialing in 1971.

In the 1980s Telefónica joined in several electronics and telecommunications partnerships with such companies as AT&T, Fiat, Fujitsu, and Electronic Data Systems. Spain's 1986 entry into the EC led to an explosion in demand for telephone services. Telefónica was unprepared, and complaints rose.

In 1990 Telefónica purchased a minority stake in Compañía de Teléfonos of Chile from Australian Alan Bond. In the same year a Telefónica-led consortium that included Citicorp won a bid to manage (with 60% control) the southern half of Argentina's formerly state-run telephone system.

Telefónica and AT&T agreed in 1991 to develop private international networks and, as part of a proposed fiber optic network, to construct a transatlantic cable, called the Columbus II, to link the US, Mexico, the Caribbean, Spain, and Italy.

Defying the European trend toward allowing more competition in telecommunications, the Spanish government extended Telefónica's monopoly over Spain's internal phone service for 30 years in 1991. But in 1994 the government announced it would be willing to meet the European Union's deadline of opening up to competition by 1998. In exchange Telefónica said it wanted to be allowed to enter new businesses such as cable TV. Also in 1994 the company acquired 35% stakes in 2 Peruvian phone companies (Compañía Peruana de Teléfonos and Empresa Nacional de Telecomunicaciones de Perú SA, or ENTEL) with a $2 billion bid — more than twice what US companies offered.

NYSE symbol: TEF (ADR)
Fiscal year ends: December 31

	1993 Sales % of total
Domestic automatic service	48
Subscriber service charges	23
International services	11
Data & image transmission	9
Mobile land & maritime services	3
Directories & yearbooks	1
Other	5
Total	**100**

WHO

Chairman: Cándido Velázquez-Gaztelu Ruiz, age 58
Managing Director and CEO: Germán Ancochea Soto, age 50
General Manager Telephone Service: Antonio López-Barajas y García-Valdecasas, age 55
General Manager Corporate Planning: Manuel A. Blanco Losada, age 51
Assistant General Manager Finance and Budgetary Control: Francisco Mochón Morcillo, age 46
Deputy General Manager Human Resources and Organization: Oscar Maraver Sánchez-Valdepeñas
Auditors: Price Waterhouse Auditores, S.A.; Audiberia

Selected Subsidiaries, Affiliates, and Investments
Amper, SA (15.35%, electronic components)
Cabinas Telefónicas, SA (public telephones)
Compañía de Teléfonos de Chile, SA (43.6%, local telephone service)
Compañía Peruana de Teléfonos (35%, telecommunications, Peru)
Compañía Publicitaria de Exclusivas Telefónicas, SA (97.3%, market research)
ENTEL (20%, telecommunications, Chile)
Eritel, SA (36.57%, software)
Hispasat, SA (25%, telecommunications satellite)
Industria Electrónica de Comunicaciones, SA (30%, portable and mobile communications equipment)
Sistemas e Instalaciones de Telecomunicación, SA (SINTEL; cable and installation)
Sistemas Técnicos de Loterías del Estado, SA (31.75%, lottery systems)
Telefónica Internacional de España, SA (76.22%, foreign investment)

WHERE

HQ: Gran Vía 28, 28013 Madrid, Spain
Phone: +34-1-556-8753 (Financial Department)
Fax: +34-1-584-7582
US HQ: Telefónica North America, Inc., 1209 Orange St., Wilmington, DE 19801
US Phone: 302-658-7581
US Fax: 302-655-5049

Telefónica's domestic telephone network extends throughout mainland Spain and to the Balearic and Canary Islands and the North African cities of Ceuta and Melilla.

KEY COMPETITORS

AirTouch	BT
Alcatel Alsthom	Ericsson
Ameritech	GTE
AT&T	MCI
BellSouth	Motorola

HOW MUCH

Stock prices are for ADRs. ADR = 3 shares	Annual Growth	1984	1985	1986	1987	1988	1989	1990	1991	1992	1993
Sales ($ mil.)	11.0%	—	—	—	—	5,513	6,607	9,048	11,115	10,724	9,293
Net income ($ mil.)	5.3%	—	—	—	495	555	629	792	1,086	703	673
Income as % of sales	—	—	—	—	—	10.1%	9.5%	8.8%	9.8%	6.6%	7.2%
Earnings per share ($)	3.2%	—	—	—	1.79	1.87	2.04	2.56	3.52	2.27	2.16
Stock price – high ($)		—	—	—	25.88	26.52	27.88	29.38	38.00	38.38	40.13
Stock price – low ($)		—	—	—	21.38	21.38	22.63	22.13	24.63	25.75	29.50
Stock price – close ($)	9.7%	—	—	—	22.38	23.63	24.63	26.38	37.50	29.50	39.00
P/E – high		—	—	—	14	14	14	11	11	17	19
P/E – low		—	—	—	12	11	11	9	7	11	14
Dividends per share ($)	3.2%	—	—	—	1.12	1.41	1.38	1.21	1.35	1.34	1.35
Book value per share ($)	(3.2%)	—	—	—	39.07	35.79	37.57	43.76	44.86	39.20	32.06
Employees	18%	—	—	65,766	63,300	66,000	71,155	75,350	75,499	74,437	74,340

1993 Year-end:
Debt ratio: 53.4%
Return on equity: 6.1%
Cash (mil.): $134
Current ratio: 0.53
Long-term debt (mil.): $9,712
No. of shares (mil.): 313
Dividends
  Yield: 3.5%
  Payout: 62.5%
Market value (mil.): $12,213

Stock Price History
High/Low 1987–93

COMPAÑÍA DE TELÉFONOS DE CHILE S.A.

Compañía de Teléfonos de Chile (CTC) is Chile's largest telecommunications company, with nearly 1.5 million lines reaching 92% of the population. In 1993 CTC even extended phone service to Antarctica, where Chile claims territory. The company offers local, domestic long distance, and international long distance service. It also provides cellular service in Santiago and the port city of Valparaíso. CTC has one of the world's 3 all-digital telephone networks.

In 1993 CTC realigned its operations, establishing 5 subsidiaries. CTC-Mundo was created to spearhead CTC's participation as a long distance carrier (finally allowed after a long legal battle). Before the court's anti-monopoly ruling, government regulations had required CTC to use long distance carrier ENTEL to route most nonlocal calls.

While deregulation increased competition and slashed the price of long distance calls in early 1994, other regulatory changes expanded CTC's protected local calling areas, allowing the company to increase local call prices as much as 70%.

With the backing of 43%-shareholder Telefónica de España, CTC hopes to expand beyond Chile's borders. The company has already sold cellular systems in Argentina and Brazil and has joined a consortium operating cellular services in 2 regions of Colombia.

The company also wants to be at the fore-front of South America's multimedia revolution. In 1994 it acquired 80% of Intercom, Chile's largest cable TV company, and plans to expand interactive offerings such as pay-per-view and home shopping.

Telecommunications in Chile began in 1880, 4 years after Alexander Graham Bell's invention of the telephone, with the establishment of Compañía de Teléfonos de Edison in Valparaíso, Chile.

The International Telephone and Telegraph Corporation (ITT) bought the company's 26,205 telephones in 1927. Three years later the Compañía de Teléfonos de Chile S.A. (CTC) was formed to acquire local telephone operating companies. CTC became ITT's largest telephone company in South America by controlling 92% of Chile's phones on a 50-year concession. About 12% of ITT's total 1962 profit came from revenues generated by CTC. By 1970 ITT's investment in CTC was valued at $153 million. CTC was ITT's last telephone property in South America to escape nationalization. Harold Geneen, the CEO of ITT, feared that the election of Marx-ist Salvador Allende in 1970 would lead to the nationalization of CTC and met clandestinely with officials of the CIA.

After Allende won the election, the Chil-ean government assumed management con-trol of CTC in 1971 but, to delay having to compensate ITT, did not formally expropriate CTC. During sensitive negotiations over com-pensation, internal ITT memos that discussed plans to prevent Allende's inauguration were leaked to the press. Allende offered a mere $12 million for CTC, or $141 million less than what it was worth.

Allende was killed in a 1973 coup led by General Augusto Pinochet, who was to run Chile under a cruel military dictatorship for the next 17 years. After Pinochet agreed to pay ITT's price for CTC, the Corporación de Fomento de la Producción (Corporation for the Promotion of Production or CORFO) bought in 1974 all of the Series A shares of CTC, which constituted the 80% of the company that had been owned by ITT.

After conducting an international open bid, CORFO sold 30% of its CTC shares to Bond Corporation Chile in 1988. Bond Chile increased its stake in CTC to 50%. Since CTC's bylaws and Chile's laws prohibited any shareholder from owning more than 45% of CTC stock, Bond Chile agreed to reduce own-ership to 45% by 1992.

A subsidiary of Telefónica de España, the Spanish telephone monopoly, purchased the stock of Bond Chile in 1990 and changed the company's name to Telefónica Internacional Chile. Later that year CTC became the first South American company to be listed on the NYSE, raising $92.5 million.

In 1993 CTC installed over 600,000 tele-phone lines and invested over $440 million in infrastructure, 80% of the total telecommu-nications investment in Chile.

CTC recorded significant paper gains in late 1994 because of the rapidly appreciating Chilean peso's impact on the company's dollar-dominated debt.

NYSE symbol: CTC (ADR)
Fiscal year ends: December 31

Chairman: Oscar Guillermo Garretón P., age 50,
P43,884,000 pay
Deputy Chairman: Nicolás Majluf S., age 49,
P34,036,000 pay
CEO: Jacinto Díaz Sanchez, age 44
**Senior Corporate VP Finance and
Administration:** Claudio García S., age 51
SEVP Corporate Communications: Christian
Chadwick D., age 44
SEVP Human Resources and Organization: José
Víctor Núñez U., age 51
Auditors: Langton Clarke Coopers & Lybrand

WHERE

HQ: San Martín 50, PO Box 16-D, Santiago, Chile
Phone: +56-2-691-2020
Fax: +56-2-699-1032

Compañía de Teléphonos de Chile serves 77% of
that country's territory with local, long distance,
and cellular telephone service.

Regions	1993 Lines in Service	
	No.	% of total
Santiago	835,930	58
Valparaíso	222,664	16
South	175,913	12
North	117,354	8
Central	85,277	6
Total	**1,437,138**	**100**

WHAT

	1993 Sales	
	$ mil.	% of total
Local service	322	37
Domestic long distance	166	19
International long distance	128	15
Line sales & connections	63	7
Equipment marketing	45	6
Cellular telephone service	41	5
Public telephones	40	5
Directory advertising	20	2
Other	36	4
Total	**861**	**100**

Subsidiaries
CTC-Celular SA (mobile telephone service)
CTC-Corp (private telecommunications services)
CTC-Equipos (sales, lease, and rental of commercial,
residential, and public telecommunications
equipment)
CTC-Istel SA (nonprofit health care for company
employees)
CTC-Mundo (domestic and international long distance
service)

KEY COMPETITORS

AT&T
Cable & Wireless
Chilesat
Compañía Telefónica Manquehue
ENTEL
Grupo Luksic
GTE
MCI
SBC Communications
Sprint
Telebrás
Telecom Argentina
Telefónica de Argentina
Telex-Chile

HOW MUCH

Stock prices are for ADRs ADR = 17 shares	Annual Growth	1984	1985	1986	1987	1988	1989	1990	1991	1992	1993
Sales ($ mil.)	22.8%	—	167	173	189	223	283	396	480	835	861
Net income ($ mil.)	—	—	(21)	52	37	68	127	114	138	231	210
Income as % of sales	—	—	—	30.1%	19.6%	30.5%	44.9%	28.8%	28.8%	27.7%	24.3%
Earnings per share ($)	—	—	(1.00)	2.43	1.62	2.63	3.17	2.53	2.74	0.25	0.23
Stock price – high ($)[1]	—	—	—	—	—	11.93	13.94	15.49	48.38	62.75	133.75
Stock price – low ($)[1]	—	—	—	—	—	7.97	9.75	10.88	15.50	37.00	75.00
Stock price – close ($)[1]	69.9%	—	—	—	—	—	—	16.00	39.75	59.50	78.50
P/E – high	—	—	—	—	—	5	4	6	18	—	—
P/E – low	—	—	—	—	—	3	3	4	6	—	—
Dividends per share ($)[1]	(6.3%)	—	—	—	2.28	2.94	2.95	2.02	1.73	1.47	1.54
Book value per share ($)[1]	(8.3%)	—	—	—	14.67	14.32	14.81	16.80	18.22	—	—
Employees	6.9%	—	—	—	—	—	7,366	7,530	7,994	7,991	9,000

1993 Year-end:
Debt ratio: 47.0%
Return on equity: 35.1%
Cash (mil.): $106
Current ratio: 1.07
Long-term debt (mil.): $921
No. of shares (mil.): 51
Dividends
  Yield: 2.0%
  Payout: —
Market value (mil.): $3,977

**Stock Price History
High/Low 1988–93**

(chart, vertical axis 0 to 140)

[1] Prior to July 1990, translated from Chilean pesos

TELÉFONOS DE MÉXICO, S.A. DE C.V.

That Teléfonos de México (Telmex) has brought phone service (at least a single phone) to 10,000 towns since 1990 indicates just how lousy service had been. That there are still only 8.8 lines per 100 residents (vs. roughly 51 in the US) indicates just how far the monopoly telephone service has to go. Yet it also demonstrates why Telmex, one of the most profitable companies in the world, has plenty of room for growth, why foreign firms have invested $18 billion in Telmex, and why MCI and Motorola are eager to plunge into Mexico's $1.5 billion long distance market.

Under a concession granted in 1990, Telmex will retain its nationwide long distance monopoly until 1997. In exchange, the company, which alone accounts for 26% of the entire Mexican stock market capitalization, agreed to increase lines by 12% a year and make other improvements. For instance, in 1994, as part of a $2.4 billion capital program, Telmex planned to install 1.5 million new lines, for a total of 8.3 million.

In preparation for the pending onslaught of competition, Telmex is cutting its long distance rates and hiking local call rates.

Mexican Telephone and Telegraph, backed by Boston interests allied with AT&T, received a government concession to operate in Mexico City in 1903. A similar concession was granted to a Swedish consortium, including equipment-maker Ericsson and the company operating Stockholm's phone system, in 1905. The consortium's interests were consolidated in Empresa de Teléfonos Ericsson in 1909. Mexico's phone system remained fragmented, though, because individual states could set up their own systems.

In 1915 Mexican Telephone and Telegraph was nationalized. The company languished after WWI, but the Ericsson enterprise thrived. In 1925 ITT's Sosthenes Behn won the concession to operate Mexican Telephone and Telegraph, and ITT quickly expanded the company's Mexico City operations nationwide. ITT linked the Mexican system to AT&T in the US and to other ITT operations in Latin America. In 1932 ITT won control of Ericsson and its subsidiaries. After WWII Telmex was created with the amalgamation of Mexican Telephone and the Ericsson subsidiary. Mexican investors bought Telmex in 1953, and the government closely regulated the company, then bought control of Telmex in 1972.

Mexico's phone service grew slowly while Telmex was part of the government. But the telecommunications revolution of the 1980s began to transform the once-sleepy monopoly. As early as 1982 Telmex engineers developed a plan to reconfigure Mexico City's often frustrating phone system.

Telmex, along with the rest of Mexico City, suffered devastation from 1985 earthquakes. The quakes affected more than 55,000 Telmex lines and severed long distance phone service.

Damage to Telmex facilities exceeded $25 million. The quakes, though, did offer the Mexican phone company the chance to rebuild and modernize. Telmex's capacity in the capital jumped 70% over its prequake network, and the new system included features such as 20 fiber-optic routes and digital microwave systems.

Mexican President Carlos Salinas announced in 1989 that Telmex would join the list of government entities to be privatized. In late 1990, after seeking bids from rival investment groups, the government awarded 51% voting control (20.4% of equity) of Telmex to a consortium that included SBC Communications, France Télécom, and Grupo Carso. SBC Communications and France Télécom each took 5% of equity, and Grupo Carso controlled 10.4% of equity. Grupo Carso, run by Telmex chairman Carlos Slim Helú, includes retailing, mining, manufacturing, and tobacco interests. State-run France Télécom is contributing skills in digital technology to modernize Telmex.

In 1991 Telmex joined with AT&T, Italcable, and Telefónica de España in developing a submarine fiber-optic cable to begin operation between Mexico, the US, and Europe in 1994. Later in 1991 Telmex began testing with AT&T and MCI a "Mexico Direct" service that uses an 800 number to handle collect or 3rd-party charge calls.

In 1994 the government announced that there would be no limit to the number of competitors that could enter the long distance market in 1997 when Telmex's national monopoly expires. That was viewed as a blow to Telmex and a boon to the likes of MCI and Motorola, who are eager to cross the border.

NYSE symbol: TMX (ADR)
Nasdaq symbol: TFONY (ADR)
Fiscal year ends: December 31

WHO

Chairman: Carlos Slim Helú
President: Juan Antonio Pérez Simón
Director Finance and Administration: Adolfo
  Cerezo Pérez
Director Operations: Jaime Pérez Bonilla
Director Long Distance: José A. Elguézabal
  Buchanan
Director Commercial: Carlos Kauachi Kauachi
Director Northern Telephone Operations: Jorge
  Casahonda Licea
Director Southern Telephone Operations:
  Leopoldo Muro Pico
Director Subsidiaries and Outside Plant: Javier
  Ramírez Otero
Director Human Resources and Labor Relations:
  Francisco Sánchez y García
Auditors: Ernst & Young

WHERE

HQ: Parque Vía 198, Oficina 508, Colonia
  Cuauhtémoc, 06599 México, D.F., Mexico
Phone: +52-5-703-3990
Fax: +52-5-254-5955

Telmex provides local and long distance service
in Mexico and also operates a cellular phone
service that covers 218 cities and 1,220 rural
communities.

WHAT

	1993 Long Distance Calls	
	mil.	% of total
Domestic long distance	1,358	81
International long distance	324	19
Total	**1,682**	**100**

	1993 Sales	
	$ mil.	% of total
Local service	3,686	42
Domestic long distance	2,904	34
International long distance	1,698	20
Other	324	4
Total	**8,612**	**100**

Telephone Services

800 service
Local service
National/international long distance
Pay phones (Ladatel)

Other Services

Telephone
Cellular telephone services (Radio Móvil Dipsa (Telcel))
Telephone services in Baja California and Northern
  Sonora (Telnor)
Construction
Building main pairs and secondary pairs
Yellow Pages
Phone directory production
Real Estate
Infrastructure construction
Real estate administration

KEY COMPETITORS

AT&T	GTE	Motorola
Bell Atlantic	MCI	Sprint
Grupo Iusacell		

HOW MUCH

Stock prices are for "L" ADRs 1 ADR = 20 shares	Annual Growth	1984	1985	1986	1987	1988	1989	1990	1991	1992	1993
Sales ($ mil.)	42.4%	—	—	—	—	—	2,094	4,097	5,230	6,644	8,612
Net income ($ mil.)	56.6%	—	—	—	—	—	482	1,087	1,877	2,559	2,900
Income as % of sales	—	—	—	—	—	—	23.0%	26.5%	35.9%	38.5%	33.7%
Earnings per share ($)	46.1%	—	—	—	—	—	1.20	2.20	4.20	4.80	5.46
Stock price – high ($)	—	—	—	—	—	—	—	—	48.25	60.13	67.88
Stock price – low ($)	—	—	—	—	—	—	—	—	24.25	40.38	43.63
Stock price – close ($)	20.2%	—	—	—	—	—	—	—	46.75	56.00	67.50
P/E – high	—	—	—	—	—	—	—	—	12	13	12
P/E – low	—	—	—	—	—	—	—	—	6	8	8
Dividends per share ($)	144.9%	—	—	—	—	—	—	—	0.16	0.48	0.96
Book value per share ($)	30.6%	—	—	—	—	—	0.90	1.16	1.58	2.18	2.62
Employees	0.7%	—	—	—	—	—	61,350	63,400	61,800	62,350	62,977

1993 Year-end:
Debt ratio: 30.0%
Return on equity: 26.5%
Cash (mil.): $1,789
Current ratio: 3.09
Long-term debt (mil.): $1,902
No. of shares (mil.): 531
Dividends
  Yield: 1.4%
  Payout: 17.6%
Market value (mil.): $35,845

Stock Price History
High/Low 1991–93

Note: Historic data reflect new peso.

In one of the biggest horse races of the decade, Teleglobe's CEO Charles Sirois would be happy to show. Sirois wants his company, the world's 7th largest telecommunications firm, to hit the homestretch hard to become the 3rd largest (after giants AT&T and British Telecom) in the next 5 years. Teleglobe is in a crowded field of companies that are jockeying to become the leading providers for the explosion of the oft-touted "information superhighway."

With a monopoly until 1997, Teleglobe is Canada's sole provider of international telecommunications services. It links Canadian phone users with every country in the world except the US. (Calls between the US and Canada are handled by US- and Canada-based carriers.) Teleglobe provides a variety of other services, including subsea cable installation, telecommunications consulting, and mobile communications. The company also provides software and services to insurance companies.

As part of its plan to expand its telecommunications business, Teleglobe signed a deal with TRW in late 1994 to build a global wireless phone system, called Odyssey, using low-flying satellites. The project is expected to cost $2.5 billion.

Sirois owns 20%, Canadian telephone company BCE owns 22%, and Ted Rogers, head of Rogers Communications, owns 4% of Teleglobe.

Created in 1958 to handle international telecommunications, Teleglobe was owned by the Canadian government until prime minister Brian Mulroney began a privatization program in the mid-1980s. Teleglobe, the most profitable of a group that included aircraft makers Canadair and de Havilland, was considered the most attractive of the companies on the block by analysts because it held a 5-year monopoly on Canada's international telecommunications services.

The bidding attracted some of Canada's largest companies, including Canadian Pacific and Bell Canada (a subsidiary of BCE). However, the winner of the auction was a little-known communications and data processing company named Memotec Data. It paid US$395 million to acquire Teleglobe in early 1987.

Memotec was founded in Montréal in 1977 to provide telecommunications products and services. Its first products were communication processors to link data networks. In 1979 Memotec was acquired by International Syscoms. The company expanded internationally, opening its first US sales office in 1981 and expanding into Asia and South America a year later.

In 1985 Eric Baker, former head of International Syscoms, and venture capital company Novacap Investments led a group that acquired a controlling interest in Memotec. The company grew rapidly, acquiring Real Time Datapro, an insurance services company, in 1985 and data communications products maker Infinet a year later.

In 1987 Memotec leapt to the forefront of the Canadian telecommunications industry with its acquisition, of Teleglobe. A few months after the acquisition, Canada's largest telephone company, BCE, bought a 1/3 stake in Memotec (since reduced to 22%).

Memotec continued to expand its services, creating Teleglobe International in 1988 to provide telecommunications consulting. In 1989 it expanded its insurance services business when it paid about $130 million for US-based ISI Systems. In 1990 it acquired 20% of satellite transmission company IDB Communications (acquired by LDDS in 1994) and entered a joint venture with IDB to provide mobile communication services for ships and aircraft. In 1991 the company changed its name to Teleglobe Inc.

In 1992 Charles Sirois, former head of BCE Mobile Communications, led a boardroom coup, buying part of BCE's stake in the company and leading a group of institutional investors to force chairman Eric Baker and CEO William McKenzie off the board. Sirois was named CEO. That same year the Canadian government extended Teleglobe's monopoly on overseas telecommunication services another 5 years.

Teleglobe spun off its communications products divsion in 1993 to focus on telecommunication services. In 1994 Telegobe joined a consortium, which include Mexico's Formento Radio Beep and US-based IXC Communications and Westel, to provide local and long- distance services in Mexico, once the market is opened to competition in 1997.

Principal exchange: Montreal
Fiscal year ends: December 31

Chairman and CEO: Charles Sirois,
C$480,000 pay
President and COO: André Lebel, C$350,325 pay
EVP Finance and CFO: Claude Séguin,
C$288,832 pay
**EVP Corporate Development and Corporate
Secretary:** Guthrie J. Stewart
President and CEO, ISI Systems (US): Simone
Garneau
VP Finance and Operations, ISI Systems (US):
Jack Carpenter
Director Human Resources, ISI Systems (US):
Lucia Valente
Auditors: Raymond, Chabot, Martin, Paré

HQ: 1000 de La Gauchetière St. West, Montréal,
Québec H3B 4X5, Canada
Phone: 514-868-8124
Fax: 514-868-7234
US HQ: ISI Systems, Inc., 2 Tech Dr., Andover,
MA 01810
US Phone: 508-682-5500
US Fax: 508-686-0130

	1993 Sales	
	C$ mil.	% of total
Canada	428	78
US	114	21
Europe	5	1
Adjustments	(3)	—
Total	**544**	**100**

	1993 Sales		1993 Operating Income	
	C$ mil.	% of total	C$mil.	% of total
Telecommunication services	435	80	128	93
Insurance systems	112	20	9	7
Adjustments	3	—	—	—
Total	**544**	**100**	**137**	**100**

	1993 Sales
	% of total
Switched voice & data services	79
Carrier services	8
Private network & mobile services	7
Message services	6
Total	**100**

Selected Telecommunication Services
Aerosat (aeronautical mobile service)
Globeaccess (international telephone service)
Globecall (audiotext message service)
Globesat (private network satellite service)
Globestream (private network submarine cable service)

Selected Subsidiaries
IDB Mobile Communications Inc. (50%, 2-way global
satellite communications)
ISI Systems, Inc. (insurance services, US)
Teleglobe Marine Inc. (submarine cable installation)
The Teleglobe International Group (telecommunications
systems construction, management, and consulting)

AT&T	Iridium
British Telecom	KDD
Cable & Wireless	Loral
COMSAT	MCI
EDS	Microsoft
France Telecom	SHL Systemhorse
GM Hughes	Sprint
Inmarsat	Teléfonos de Mexico

$=C$1.32 (Dec. 31, 1993)	Annual Growth	1984	1985	1986	1987	1988	1989	1990	1991	1992	1993
Sales (C$ mil.)	12.0%	—	—	—	276	300	294	333	376	438	544
Net income (C$ mil.)	7.8%	—	—	—	48	34	20	8	26	(51)	76
Income as % of sales	—	—	—	—	17.4%	11.2%	6.8%	2.4%	6.8%	—	13.9%
Earnings per share (C$)	(2.5%)	—	—	—	1.40	0.84	0.52	0.20	0.54	(1.19)	1.20
Stock price – high (C$)	—	—	—	—	20.00	15.38	11.82	10.75	11.00	13.94	20.63
Stock price – low (C$)	—	—	—	—	4.63	9.75	9.50	7.50	7.38	11.00	13.50
Stock price – close (C$)	7.0%	—	—	—	14.25	10.25	10.63	7.88	10.88	—	20.00
P/E – high	—	—	—	—	14	18	23	54	20	—	17
P/E – low	—	—	—	—	3	12	18	38	14	—	11
Dividends per share (C$)	—	—	—	—	0.00	0.10	0.24	0.28	0.28	0.28	0.31
Book value per share (C$)	2.2%	—	—	—	9.43	9.65	9.99	9.89	10.26	9.23	10.72
Employees	0.5%	—	—	—	2,060	2,075	2,497	2,500	2,340	2,082	2,128

1993 Year-end:
Debt ratio: 51.6%
Return on equity: 13.9%
Cash (mil.): C$15
Long-term debt (mil.): C$599
No. of shares (mil.): 57
Dividends
  Yield: 1.6%
  Payout: 25.8%
Market value (mil.): $857
Sales (mil.): $411

**Stock Price History
High/Low 1987–93**

THOMSON S.A.

OVERVIEW

Thomson is one of France's biggest industrial conglomerates. But, shrinking military budgets and a fragmented European market have stymied efforts to turn this state-controlled electronics giant into a French Intel.

In 1992 Thomson sold its home appliance subsidiary, Thomson Electroménager, to concentrate on its 2 core businesses: Thomson-CSF, the world's 3rd largest defense electronics company, is a maker of air defense systems, radar systems, weapons, and air traffic control systems (70% of 1993 revenues were from military sales); Thomson

Consumer Electronics (TCE) is the world's 4th largest maker of consumer electronics (audio and video products, TVs, and broadcast equipment). Through its ownership of the RCA and GE brands, TCE is also the US's #1 TV manufacturer.

Both the defense and consumer electronics companies have had to reorganize, cut jobs, and diversify through joint ventures. Mistakes in the past were masked by heavy public subsidies. In 1993 earnings plummeted and government officials began talking about privatization to reduce the red ink.

WHEN

In 1893, after buying patents from General Electric predecessor Thomson-Houston Electric (US), a group of French businessmen created Compagnie Française Thomson-Houston (CFTH) to make power generation equipment. CFTH diversified into electric railways and light bulbs, and, through 1920s and 1930s acquisitions, started making appliances, radio and X-ray equipment, and electrical cable. It created Alsthom (1928) to take over its electrical equipment manufacturing.

CFTH's consumer businesses prospered after WWII. In 1966 CFTH merged with Hotchkiss-Brandt (appliances, defense electronics, automobiles, and postal equipment) to form Thomson-Brandt. Thomson-Brandt formed Thomson-CSF in 1968 by merging its professional electronics businesses with Compagnie Générale de Telegraphie Sans Fil (electronics, communications).

In 1969 Thomson-Brandt transferred Alsthom to Compagnie Générale d'Electricité (CGE, now Alcatel Alsthom). In exchange CGE ceded the French appliance and data processing markets to Thomson-Brandt. In the 1970s the company continued acquiring and diversifying, but profits began to erode as "les barons," Thomson's senior executives, established fiefdoms and financial controls broke down. In 1982 the Mitterrand government nationalized the technically bankrupt company; Alain Gomez was chosen to run it.

Gomez soon discovered that the sprawling company had no treasury function. He hired Jean-François Henin as treasurer, cut costs and staffing, and focused Thomson-Brandt on consumer electronics and Thomson-CSF on defense electronics, fields in which he felt the company could compete globally.

In 1983 Gomez formed Thomson SA as a holding company for the firm's operating units and swapped the company's civil telecommunications business for CGE's military and consumer electronics units. Thomson-CSF bought most of the assets of Mostek (semiconductors, US, 1986) and merged its chipmaking businesses with SGS Microelettronica (semiconductors, Italy, 1987) to create SGS-Thomson. Gomez traded Thomson's medical division and $800 million for General Electric's GE and RCA consumer electronics concerns in 1987. Thomson-CSF and Aerospatiale formed Sextant Avionique, a joint flight electronics venture, in 1988.

Already the world leader in Airbus flight simulators, Thomson continued to grow, buying Link-Miles (Boeing and McDonnell Douglas simulators, UK, 1990) and trading control of its finance operations to Crédit Lyonnais for 15.5% of the bank's stock (in 1994 Thomson increased its stake to keep the bank solvent). Thomson-CSF bought 50% of Ferranti's (UK) sonar business and Philips's defense businesses. Philips and Thomson also participated in an unsuccessful effort to develop high-definition TV (HDTV).

In 1991 Thomson-CSF joined with GEC-Marconi (UK) to produce advanced radars, while Thomson bought 50% of Pilkington Optronics (laser and optical guidance systems, UK), MEL Communications (tactical radio, UK), and control of Atherton Technology (software engineering, US). In 1993 Thomson-CSF bought the radio and electron tubes unit of Asea Brown Boveri (ABB) and in 1994 combined its high-tech Syseca unit with French computer giant Groupe Bull to create Transtar (computer software).

Government-owned company
Fiscal year ends: December 31

Chairman and CEO, Chairman and President,
Thomson-CSF: Alain Gomez
SVP Finance: Alain Hagelauer
Director Human Resources: Paul Calandra
Chairman, Thomson Consumer Electronics:
Alain Prestat
Chairman and President, Thomson-CSF (US):
Benjamin Sandzer-Bell
Auditors: Arthur Andersen & Co.

HQ: 173, boulevard Haussmann
75415 Paris Cedex 08, France
Phone: +33-153-77-80-00
Fax: +33-153-77-83-00
US HQ: Thomson-CSF, Inc., 99 Canal Center
Plaza, Ste. 450, Arlington, VA 22314
US Phone: 703-838-9685
US Fax: 703-838-1686

Thomson has more than 180 companies in 40
countries.

	1993 Sales	
	FF mil.	% of total
North America	22,205	33
France	19,045	28
Western Europe	17,246	26
Middle East	2,924	4
Far East	2,712	4
Africa & Latin America	1,530	2
Other countries	1,843	3
Total	**67,505**	**100**

	1993 Sales	
	FF mil.	% of total
Civil & defense electronics	34,291	51
Consumer electronics	33,483	49
Adjustments	(269)	—
Total	**67,505**	**100**

Consumer Electronics Brands

Brandt	Nordmende	Saba
Ferguson	Proscan	Telefunken
General Electric	RCA	Thomson

Main Subsidiaries
Thomson Consumer Electronics (TCE)
Thomson-CSF (58.3%, defense and professional
electronics)

Major Joint Ventures
Crédit Lyonnais (21.6%, banking, with Caisse des Depots
& Consignations and the French government)
Ferranti-Thomson Sonar Systems UK Ltd. (30%; sonars,
with Ferranti)
Pilkington Optronics Ltd. (50%; optronics, with
Pilkington)
Sextant Avionique (66.3%; flight electronics, with
Aérospatiale)
SGS-Thomson Microelectronics NV (23.8%;
semiconductors, with IRI and Thorn EMI)
Short Brothers Plc (missile systems, Ireland)

Akzo Nobel	Koor	Raytheon
AlliedSignal	Litton Industries	Robert Bosch
AMD	Lockheed Martin	Rockwell
Black & Decker	LG Group	Samsung
British Aerospace	Loral	Sanyo
Daimler-Benz	Matsushita	Samsung
EG&G	McDonnell Douglas	Sharp
E-Systems	Mitsubishi	Siemens
GEC	NEC	Sony
General Dynamics	Northrop Grumman	Toshiba
GM Hughes	Philips	Yamaha
Intel	Pioneer	Zenith

$=FF5.91 (Dec. 31, 1993)	Annual Growth	1984	1985	1986	1987	1988	1989	1990	1991	1992	1993
Sales (FF mil.)	1.7%	57,895	59,883	62,650	60,182	74,834	76,663	75,228	71,277	70,989	67,505
Net income (FF mil.)	—	(21)	126	882	1,063	1,197	497	(2,474)	(702)	(544)	(3,030)
Income as % of sales	—	—	0.2%	1.4%	1.8%	1.6%	0.6%	—	—	—	—
Earnings per share (FF)	—	(2)	9	51	56	63	24	(97)	(26)	(20)	(114)
Dividends per share (FF)	—	0.00	0.00	0.00	8.44	7.20	0.00	0.00	13.90	0.00	0.00
Book value per share (FF)	(11.1%)	275	291	366	335	421	425	299	258	213	95
Employees	—	—	—	—	—	—	105,000	105,460	105,200	105,792	99,895

1993 Year-end:
Debt ratio: 90.5%
Return on equity: —
Cash (mil.): FF4,838
Long-term debt
(mil.): FF6,731
No. of shares (mil.): 27
Dividends
Yield: —
Payout: —
Sales (mil.): $11,422

Net Income
(FF mil.) 1984–93

THE THOMSON CORPORATION

The Thomson Corporation operates 3 major business lines: specialized information and publishing, newspaper publishing, and travel. The Thomson family owns 72% of stock.

Thomson publishes 39 Canadian dailies and 107 US dailies, mainly in regional markets, but it also owns the Toronto *Globe and Mail*, its flagship newspaper. Of these 146 dailies more than 90% are profitable and over 25% have operating margins of 25% or more. In the UK Thomson is #1 in regional newspapers, package tours (Thomson Tour Operations), and travel agencies (Lunn Poly), and it

owns Britannia Airways, a major UK charter airline.

Thomson Information/Publishing Group is a specialty publisher in such areas as reference (e.g., Gale Research, Van Nostrand Reinhold), law (e.g., Bancroft-Whitney, Carswell), and banking (Sheshunoff). Thomson offers 190 magazines, 200 on-line services, over 190 CD-ROM products, and books, directories, and other publications.

Thomson expanded into Latin America in 1993 with the acquisition of a Mexico City–based health care information business.

After failing at farming and auto parts distribution, Roy Thomson left Toronto for the hinterlands of Ontario and started a radio station in 1930. He began selling advertising and never stopped. Thomson entered the newspaper business when he bought the *Timmons Press*, a newspaper serving a gold-mining town, in 1934. Frugal and bottom-line oriented, Thomson started acquiring small-town newspapers.

Thomson made his first acquisition outside Ontario in 1949 and his first US purchase in 1952. In the 1950s Thomson Newspapers became the leader in number of newspapers published in Canada and began rapid expansion in the US. In 1953 Thomson personally bought the *Scotsman*, an Edinburgh-based newspaper, and moved to Scotland. When the UK opened the airways to commercial TV broadcasting, Thomson started Scottish Television Ltd. (1957) and merged it with the UK's Kemsley Newspapers, publisher of rural newspapers and the *Sunday Times*, to create International Thomson Organisation in 1959.

In the 1960s and 1970s, International Thomson entered holiday travel services and oil and gas production and bought the *Times* of London (1967). Meanwhile, in North America, the number of Thomson Newspapers' US dailies surpassed its Canadian total. Queen Elizabeth II conferred the title of Lord Thomson of Fleet upon Thomson, by this time a British subject, in 1970. J. Paul Getty invited International Thomson into a North Sea oil drilling venture in 1971. In 1973 the consortium struck oil. By the time of Lord Thomson's death in 1976, oil accounted for the bulk of International Thomson's profits.

Lord Kenneth Thomson, Roy's son, took over control of the family empire.

International Thomson management, foreseeing the ultimate depletion of its oil wells, began buying publishers in an effort to substitute publishing profits for oil earnings. After selling the *Times* to The News Corporation in 1981, International Thomson hunted for leading specialty publishers with subscription-based, rather than advertising-based, profitability, which lessened their vulnerability to recession. Purchases included *American Banker* and *Bond Buyer* (financial publications, 1983), Gale Research (library reference materials, 1985), South-Western Publishing (textbooks, 1986), Associated Book Publishers (legal information, textbooks; 1987), Lawyers Co-operative Publishing (1989), and several on-line information providers. The company completed the sale of its oil and gas holdings a year later.

In 1989 Thomson Newspapers and International Thomson merged to form The Thomson Corporation and in 1991 purchased Maxwell Macmillan Professional and Business Reference Publishing for $57 million. Thomson paid $210 million in 1992 for JPT Publishing (databases, including the Institute for Scientific Information — the world's #1 commercial scientific research database).

In 1994 Thomson failed in its bid for Mead's LEXIS/NEXIS on-line service but snared Information Access Company (a reference database service) from Ziff for $465 million. It also purchased a developer of medical information databases for $339 million. In 1995 Thomson announced the sale of 25 newspapers in the US and Canada.

Principal exchange: Toronto
Fiscal year ends: December 31

WHO

Chairman and CEO: Kenneth R. Thomson,
$1,034,091 pay
President: W. Michael Brown, $1,290,000 pay
**EVP; CEO, Thomson Information/Publishing
Group (TIPG):** Robert C. Hall, $786,500 pay
EVP; CEO, Thomson Newspapers: Richard J.
Harrington, $702,563 pay
EVP and CFO: Nigel R. Harrison, $650,000 pay
VP Administration/Human Resources TIPG:
Gerald D. Tenser
Auditors: Price Waterhouse

WHERE

HQ: Toronto Dominion Bank Tower, Ste. 2706,
PO Box 24, Toronto-Dominion Centre,
Toronto, Ontario M5K 1A1, Canada
Phone: 416-360-8700
Fax: 416-360-8812
US HQ: Thomson Information/Publishing
Group, The Metro Center, One Station Place,
6th Fl., Stamford, CT 06902
US Phone: 203-328-9400
US Fax: 203-328-9408

	1993 Sales		1993 Operating Income	
	$ mil.	% of total	$ mil.	% of total
UK	2,734	47	200	39
US	2,468	42	270	52
Canada	490	8	29	6
Other countries	157	3	19	3
Total	**5,849**	**100**	**518**	**100**

WHAT

	1993 Sales		1993 Operating Income	
	$ mil.	% of total	$ mil.	% of total
Info./publishing	2,701	46	440	60
Travel	2,040	35	117	16
Newspapers	1,108	19	174	24
Total	**5,849**	**100**	**731**	**100**

Thomson Information/Publishing Group
International Thomson Publishing (North America)
Thomson Business Information (North America)
Thomson Financial Services (North America)
Thomson Information Services (UK)
Thomson Professional Publishing (North America)
Thomson Regional Newspapers
(4 morning, 6 evening, 4 Sunday, and 20 weekly
newspapers; UK)

Thomson Travel Group
Britannia Airways (UK)
Lunn Poly (travel agencies, UK)
Thomson Tour Operations (UK)

Thomson Newspapers
39 daily newspapers in Canada, including the *Globe and
Mail* (Toronto); 17 weeklies in Canada, 26 in the US
107 daily newspapers in the US

KEY COMPETITORS

Accor	Dun &	Rank
American Business	Bradstreet	Reed Elsevier
Information	Gannett	E.W. Scripps
American Express	Hearst	Thomas Cook
Bloomberg	John Wiley	Times Mirror
Carlson	Knight-Ridder	Tribune
Commerce Clearing	Matsushita	Viacom
House	McGraw-Hill	West
Cox	News Corp.	Publishing
Dow Jones	Pearson	

HOW MUCH

$=C$1.32 (Dec. 31, 1993)	Annual Growth	1984	1985[1]	1986[1]	1987[1]	1988[1]	1989	1990	1991	1992	1993
Sales ($ mil.)	10.5%	—	2,634	3,946	3,940	4,726	5,112	5,364	5,980	5,980	5,849
Net income ($ mil.)	3.6%	—	208	258	304	380	420	385	166	166	277
Income as % of sales	—	—	7.9%	6.5%	7.7%	8.0%	8.2%	7.2%	2.8%	2.8%	4.7%
Earnings per share ($)	(1.5%)	—	0.54	0.53	0.66	0.80	0.78	0.70	0.53	0.30	0.48
Stock price – high (C$)[2]	—	—	14.45	19.31	20.81	17.96	20.00	17.00	18.25	17.63	16.88
Stock price – low (C$)[2]	—	—	9.96	13.17	13.55	15.12	15.75	13.00	14.00	12.13	13.75
Stock price – close (C$)[2]	6.7%	—	14.22	18.04	16.54	16.43	16.63	17.00	16.00	14.25	16.25
P/E – high	—	—	—	—	—	—	—	—	—	—	—
P/E – low	—	—	—	—	—	—	—	—	—	—	—
Dividends per share ($)	0.3%	—	—	—	—	—	0.21	0.44	0.45	0.45	0.45
Book value per share ($)	—	—	—	—	—	—	—	—	—	—	—
Employees	1.3%	—	—	—	—	—	44,000	44,800	45,800	46,000	46,400

1993 Year-end:
Debt ratio: 51.5%
Return on equity: —
Cash (mil.): $496
Current ratio: 1.07
Long-term debt (mil.): $2,993
No. of shares (mil.): —
Dividends
  Yield: —
  Payout: 93.8%
Market value (mil.): $9,775

Stock Price History
High/Low 1985–93

[1] Pro forma   [2] Adjusted prices of Thomson Newspapers, Ltd., common stock prior to 1989

Star-studded Thorn EMI is the world's 3rd largest music company (after Warner and Philips's Polygram); EMI artists include Frank Sinatra, the Rolling Stones, Janet Jackson, and Garth Brooks. The London-based company operates in 40 countries with 4 principal businesses: EMI Music (recording and music publishing), THORN Group (rental stores), HMV Group (retail music stores), and TSE (high-tech development). In the US about 12% of music sales come from EMI.

From 1992 through 1994, Thorn EMI sold several of its major nonentertainment subsid-

iaries and focused on its core sectors. Streamlining has paid off. Net profits have increased for the last 2 years, and in 1994 EMI music reported record results for the 6th consecutive year. HMV stores had strong sales in Australia, the US, and Japan; over 50% of HMV sales come from outside the UK.

In 1994 Thorn EMI continued to add to its growing roster of recording subsidiaries including US Christian label Star Song Communications. The company also expanded its share in a software development venture with Toshiba.

Jules Thorn founded the Electrical Lamp Service Company in London in 1928 to distribute electric lamps he had imported from other parts of Europe. He acquired several radio and lamp companies and combined these as Thorn Electrical Industries in 1936.

After WWII Thorn diversified into appliances, electronics, and TV manufacturing. By the 1960s the company was the UK's largest radio and TV maker. It became the largest global TV rental company when it acquired Robinson Radio Rentals in the late 1960s.

Diversification continued in the 1970s as Thorn picked up a host of small companies. In 1979 the company swallowed its biggest fish, electronics and entertainment concern Electric & Musical Industries (EMI). EMI, established in 1931 as a successor to a 19th-century gramophone producer, had gradually expanded its operations to produce everything from radar systems during WWII to the first television system for the BBC. In 1954 the company acquired Capitol Records in the US and became a major force in the entertainment industry, signing such artists as the Beatles in the 1960s and Pink Floyd in the 1970s. In 1972 EMI released its new scanning X-ray, which won global market leadership until it lost its technological edge and competitors' models made it obsolete. By the late 1970s the struggling company agreed to be purchased by Thorn for £165 million in 1979.

For the next several years, each of the constituent companies operated in isolation from the others. Colin Southgate became CEO in 1985 and refocused the company into 4 business sectors (music, technology, rental and retail, and lighting), selling all that did not fit.

In 1987 Thorn EMI purchased US-based Rent-A-Center for $594 million. It acquired 50% of Chrysalis Records, whose artists include Pat Benatar and Jethro Tull, in 1989.

In 1990 Thorn EMI added Filmtrax music publishing (UK) and the 50% it did not own of SBK Record Productions. Also in 1990 the company's HMV stores unit opened the US's largest music store in New York City.

In 1991 the company sold its European light bulb operations to General Electric for $138 million and received approval from the British government to buy control of UK broadcasting company Thames Television.

In 1992 Thorn EMI acquired Virgin Records, whose artists include Mick Jagger, Janet Jackson, and Phil Collins, for $960 million, placing itself with Warner and Polygram as one of the world's top music companies. It also purchased Sparrow, the US's largest Christian music company; Denmark's Medley Records; and the remaining 50% of Chrysalis.

In 1993 Thorn EMI sold its interest in Thames Television and its lighting division (upon which the company was founded). In late 1993 a *Wall Street Journal* article criticized practices of the company's Rent-A-Center stores. An investigation by former Senator Warren Rudman exonerated the company.

In 1994 the company's Central Research Laboratory subsidiary announced a "suspended image system" that projects a 3D-like image beyond a computer screen. CRL hopes to interest video game makers in the new technology.

The Rolling Stones' 1994 *Voodoo Lounge* album was that group's first release under a reported $40 million deal with Thorn EMI.

OTC symbol: THE (ADR)
Fiscal year ends: March 31

Chairman and CEO: Sir Colin Southgate, age 55, £584,977 pay
President and CEO, EMI Music: James Fifield, age 52, £7,200,000 pay
CEO, Thorn Group: Michael Metcalf, age 42
Group Finance Director: Simon Duffy, age 44
Director Human Relations: Anthe Siaslas
President, Capitol Industries–EMI (US): Charles Koppelmann
Auditors: Ernst & Young

WHERE

HQ: 4 Tenterden St., Hanover Square, London W1A 2AY, UK
Phone: +44-(01)71-355-4848
Fax: +44-(01)71-355-4494
US HQ: Thorn EMI Inc., Little Falls Center, Ste. 205, 2751 Centerville Rd., Wilmington, DE 19808
US Phone: 302-994-4100
US Fax: 302-994-4299

Thorn EMI has operations in 40 countries.

	1994 Sales		1994 Operating Income	
	£ mil.	% of total	£ mil.	% of total
UK	1,562	36	98	26
North America	1,237	29	97	25
Asia/Pacific	253	6	41	11
Other Europe	1,153	27	139	36
Other countries	87	2	8	2
Total	**4,292**	**100**	**383**	**100**

WHAT

	1994 Sales		1994 Operating Income	
	£ mil.	% of total	£ mil.	% of total
Music	1,760	41	246	62
Rental	1,512	35	130	33
TSE	408	10	(12)	—
HMV	404	9	6	2
Other	208	5	12	3
Total	**4,292**	**100**	**382**	**100**

Selected Subsidiaries

EMI Music
Capitol Records Inc. (US)
Chrysalis Records Ltd.
EMI Records Ltd.
EMI Music Publishing Ltd.
Toshiba-EMI (55%, Japan)
Virgin Records Ltd.

HMV Group
HMV retail music stores (179 stores in 6 countries)

THORN Group
Crazy George's
EasiOwn (Indonesia)
Fona (Denmark, UK)
Radio Rentals (Australia, UK)

Remco America Inc. (US)
Rent-A-Center (US)
Skala (Germany)
Visea (France)

TSE
Central Research Laboratory (technology R&D)
Malco (financial transaction cards)
Transit Systems (transit ticketing systems)

Other
Babcock Thorn (35%, dockyard management)

KEY COMPETITORS

Aaron Rents	Matsushita	Tandy
Bertelsmann	MTS	Time Warner
Best Buy	Musicland	Toshiba
Camelot Corp.	Philips	Trans World
Circuit City	Pioneer	Music
COMCOA	Samsung	Virgin Group
Good Guys	Sanyo	Warehouse
Hastings Books,	Sharp	Entertainment
Records & More	Sony	

HOW MUCH

£=$1.48 (Dec. 31, 1993)	9-Year Growth	1985	1986	1987	1988	1989	1990	1991	1992	1993[3]	1994
Sales (£ mil.)	3.2%	3,240	3,317	3,203	3,054	3,291	3,716	3,571	3,660	4,452	4,292
Net income (£ mil.)	14.7%	65	61	100	138	182	204	230	85	205	223
Income as % of sales	—	2.0%	1.9%	3.1%	4.5%	5.5%	5.5%	4.5%	4.0%	4.6%	5.2%
Earnings per share (p)[2]	6.8%	29	25	42	51	62	68	54	48	51	53
Stock price – high (p)[1]	—	671	464	506	796	646	859	790	793	888	1,017
Stock price – low (p)[1]	—	360	288	362	418	511	599	547	585	633	809
Stock price – close (p)[1]	9.3%	445	385	450	511	599	745	649	712	881	990
P/E – high	—	23	19	12	16	10	13	15	16	17	19
P/E – low	—	12	12	9	8	8	9	10	12	12	15
Dividends per share (p)	8.0%	17	17	18	21	26	29	29	30	32	34
Book value per share (p)	(4.1%)	251	231	249	201	182	205	189	160	111	172
Employees	(8.4%)	90,327	85,700	74,321	66,630	65,444	61,124	57,932	53,757	47,000	41,000

1994 Year-end:
Debt ratio: 41.3%
Return on equity: 37.1%
Cash (mil.): £114
Long-term debt (mil.): £348
No. of shares (mil.): 426
Dividends
  Yield: 3.4%
  Payout: 64.8%
Market value (mil.): $6,242
Sales (mil.): $6,349

**Stock Price History[1]
High/Low 1985–94**

[1] Stock prices are for the prior calendar year. [2] Not fully diluted 1985-1989 [3] Accounting change

THYSSEN AG

OVERVIEW

Thyssen — pronounced "TISS-in" — is hoping that improving auto sales will drive the conglomerate out of the major slump it fell into in fiscal 1993, when steel sales dropped 15%. Although the German conglomerate is a diversified company operating 310 consolidated businesses, steel accounts for about 1/3 of sales, and the recession in Germany, coupled with the decreased demand for steel, has hurt Thyssen's sales and income in recent years.

The company has 3 operating groups: capital goods and manufactured products (Thyssen Industrie, Budd, and the Wülfrath Group); trading and services (Thyssen Handelsunion); and steel (Thyssen Stahl).

Thyssen has begun laying off staff to cut costs and planned to ax 1,250 more in fiscal 1994, but the company's expected recovery faces 2 major obstacles. European governments are continuing to subsidize their loss-making steel industries (which has prompted the US to impose antidumping duties on European steel imports). In addition, small, efficient steelmakers (minimills) are beginning to enter the European market.

WHEN

August Thyssen founded a puddling and rolling mill near Mulheim on the Ruhr in 1871. Thyssen specialized in winning control of small factories and mines and, by WWI, was Germany's largest iron and steel company.

When August Thyssen died in 1926, son Fritz headed the company as it was amalgamated into a trust similar to the I. G. Farben chemical cartel. Called Vereinigte Stahl-werke, the trust assembled Germany's coal and steel producers under one structure. Fritz was an early, ardent supporter of the Nazis, but he bucked the party and fled to France at the beginning of WWII. His brother Heinrich escaped to Switzerland (Heinrich's son, Baron Heinrich Thyssen-Bornemisza, used his piece of the family fortune to build a world-renowned art collection). When Germany conquered France in 1940, Fritz was imprisoned in an insane asylum and, later, a concentration camp. When the Allies liberated France, he was arrested as a war criminal (1945). After he was acquitted, he and his wife moved to Argentina.

The Thyssen steel operation was carved up during the Allied occupation; it began anew in 1953, with its Bruckhausen complex as its only asset. As the German economy revived, Thyssen prospered and returned to its leadership in the steel industry.

Thyssen moved to diversify. In 1973 it acquired manufacturing giant Rheinstahl AG (later renamed Thyssen Industrie). Rheinstahl included everything from shipyards to Henschel locomotives, and integrating Rheinstahl's components proved difficult. Flamboyant CEO Dieter Spethmann (nicknamed Sun King of the Ruhr) rose to the challenge. Thyssen's shipyards retooled and began making offshore oil rigs just as the energy crises of the 1970s boosted demand. Thyssen also plunged into specialty steel markets and created Thyssen Handelsunion to wholesale other manufacturers' metal products.

In 1978 Thyssen acquired American automotive-components–maker Budd in its first overseas outing. Budd's railcar manufacturing operations proved a drag on profits. In 1985 Thyssen spun off Budd's railway car operations as Transit America.

Demand for steel dropped in the early 1980s, and European steelmakers cut work forces. In the meantime Thyssen's trading activity grew until it was the largest single contributor to sales in the late 1980s.

As Spethmann prepared to step down from the chairmanship, he received one vindication in 1989. The German government approved building track between Düsseldorf and Cologne/Bonn for Thyssen Henschel's high-speed train. The futuristic train, a Spethmann pet project, uses magnetic levitation to cut friction. Thyssen Industrie joined Siemens and Daimler-Benz in mid-1992 in a joint venture to promote Magnetschnellbahn, a high-speed magnetic railway system.

In late 1992 Thyssen Stahl cut its output by 300,000 metric tons (almost 1/4 of production) at its hot-rolling mills. Cost cutting continued in 1993 as Thyssen made plans to slash its steel labor force by about 1/3.

In 1994 Thyssen teamed up with Cookson Group, a British industrial materials company, to supply products to central and eastern European steel producers. Thyssen finished 1994 with a net profit of $58.1 million and sales of $22.5 billion.

OTC symbol: THY (ADR)
Fiscal year ends: September 30

Chairman Supervisory Board: Günter Vogelsang
Chairman Executive Board: Heinz Kriwet, age 63
VC: Dieter H. Vogel
CFO: Heinz-Gerd Stein
Chief Personnel Officer: Dieter Hennig
President, The Budd Co. (US): David P. Williams
Treasurer (CFO), The Budd Co. (US): Tom Stuart
VP Employee Relations, The Budd Co. (US): Robert Wangbichler
Auditors: KPMG Deutsche Treuhand-Gesellschaft

HQ: August-Thyssen-Strasse 1, PO Box 10 10 10, D-40001 Düsseldorf, Germany
Phone: +49-211-824-1
Fax: +49-211-824-36000
US HQ: The Budd Company, 3155 W. Big Beaver Rd., PO Box 2601, Troy, MI 48007-2601
US Phone: 810-643-3500
US Fax: 810-643-3593

Thyssen sells its products worldwide. While 48% of its sales are made outside Germany, 87% of its work force is employed in Germany.

	1993 Sales	
	DM mil.	% of total
Germany	17,564	52
North America	4,493	13
Asia	1,907	6
Other EU countries	6,533	20
Other Europe/CIS	1,780	5
Other countries	1,225	4
Total	**33,502**	**100**

	1993 Sales		1993 Pretax Income	
	DM mil.	% of total	DM mil.	% of total
Trading & services	14,096	39	167	—
Capital goods & manuf. prods.	11,659	32	164	—
Steel	10,621	29	(1,197)	—
Adjustments	(2,874)	—	2	—
Total	**33,502**	**100**	**(864)**	**—**

Major Subsidiaries and Affiliates

Trading and Services
Thyssen Handelsunion AG
Thyssen Sonneberg GmbH
Thyssen Sudamerica NV (Curaçao)

Capital Goods and Manufactured Products
The Budd Co. (auto components, US)
Thyssen Industrie AG (90%)
Wülfrath Group (building materials and products)

Steel
Rasselstein AG
Thyssen Stahl AG

Alcan	Eaton	Nucor
Alcatel Alsthom	Friedrich Krupp	Preussag
Anglo American	General Dynamics	Robert Bosch
Austrian Industries	Hyundai	Rolls-Royce
Bechtel	Inco	RTZ
Bombardier	Inland Steel	St.-Gobain
Borg-Warner	IRI	Tenneco
Automotive	Magna	TRW
Broken Hill	Mannesmann	Usinor-Sacilor
Cargill	Metallgesellschaft	VEBA
Cyprus Amax	Mitsui	Viag
Daewoo	Nippon Steel	USX–U.S. Steel

$=DM1.74 (Dec. 31, 1993)	Annual Growth	1984	1985	1986	1987	1988	1989	1990	1991	1992	1993
Sales (DM mil.)	0.4%	32,430	34,784	31,997	26,551	29,220	34,249	36,186	36,562	35,755	33,502
Net income (DM mil.)	—	163	449	348	283	648	764	636	479	319	(1,040)
Income as % of sales	—	0.5%	1.3%	1.1%	1.1%	2.2%	2.2%	1.8%	1.3%	0.9%	—
Earnings per share (DM)	—	—	14	11	9	21	24	20	15	10	(33)
Stock price – high (DM)	—	95	181	198	142	196	272	335	247	249	276
Stock price – low (DM)	—	65	86	122	98	98	189	178	177	148	158
Stock price – close (DM)	14.4%	82	170	124	105	191	272	185	200	162	276
P/E – high	—	—	13	18	16	9	11	17	16	24	—
P/E – low	—	—	6	11	11	5	8	9	12	15	—
Dividends per share (DM)	—	0.0	5.0	5.0	5.0	7.5	10.0	11.0	10.0	6.0	0.0
Book value per share (DM)	2.5%	91	104	109	111	129	145	152	156	154	113
Employees	0.8%	131,030	128,372	127,683	121,533	127,778	136,091	152,708	148,250	148,272	141,009

1993 Year-end:
Debt ratio: 61.6%
Return on equity: —
Cash (mil.): DM488
Long-term debt (mil.): DM3,391
No. of shares (mil.): 31
Dividend
  Yield: —
  Payout: —
Market value (mil.): $4,965
Sales (mil.): $19,254

Stock Price History
High/Low 1984–93

TOKIO MARINE AND FIRE

OVERVIEW

Tokio Marine and Fire is Japan's oldest and largest nonlife insurance company. Despite the adverse insurance conditions caused by Japan's sluggish growth and a spate of natural disasters, Tokio holds 18.2% of the Japanese property/casualty insurance market. Its nearest rival, Yasuda Fire, holds only 12.9%.

Tokio provides marine, fire and casualty, personal accident, auto, and other types of insurance in Japan through a force of 83,347 agents. Outside Japan Tokio has 46 offices and 14 underwriting agents. Its US operations include around 790 people, and the company operates under the names Tokio Marine Management and Houston General.

Tokio is tied in to the Mitsubishi Group, a network of Japanese companies that work closely together. Mitsubishi companies own about 14.5% of Tokio.

In addition to expanding its services to Japanese investors in China and Vietnam in 1993, the company also reorganized its database management systems. In 1994 it was planning to install one of the largest private client/server–based open systems networks in Japan. The network will connect 440 domestic offices and 3,300 terminals, allowing 14,500 staff members to exchange information. Tokio also made plans to enter life insurance and other new fields in Japan.

WHEN

Japan's first insurance company was founded with 11 employees in 1879 to insure cargo. The following year Tokio Marine and Fire began operations in London, Paris, and New York. During the 1880s the company began writing hull insurance and working through insurers in Marseilles, Liverpool, and Brussels.

In the late 1800s and early 1900s, the firm developed its foreign markets by appointing agents. Willis, Faber & Company, a London insurance broker, served as Tokio's agent in placing ship cargo and hull reinsurance. Tokio profited in marine insurance during the Russo-Japanese War (1904–05) and became one of the world's leading marine insurers. Tokio selected Appleton & Cox (New York) as the agent to develop its US operation.

The company began underwriting fire insurance in 1914 as a step toward becoming a full nonlife insurance company. In the period prior to WWII Tokio broadened its foreign operations through Cornhill Insurance of the UK and Assicurazioni Generali of Italy.

Tokio reorganized in 1944 by merging with Mitsubishi Marine Insurance and Meiji Fire Insurance. In 1956, 4 years after the end of the US occupation of Japan, Tokio resumed its overseas operation, which had been disrupted by WWII. The company became affiliated with Mitsubishi, one of the largest business groups in Japan. Other financial organizations in the group are Mitsubishi Trust & Banking (Japan's largest trust company), Mitsubishi Bank (Japan's 4th largest), and Meiji Mutual Life.

In 1980 Tokio bought Houston General Insurance (Fort Worth), a commercial property and casualty insurer, and established a property and casualty company in Malaysia. The company formed Tokio Reinsurance in Switzerland in 1982.

Tokio registered 3 million ADRs, each representing 5 shares of common stock, with the SEC in 1987. The company undertook the public securities offering to increase ownership of its shares in the US and to increase operating funds.

In the late 1980s Tokio continued its foreign expansion by acquiring a 10% interest in Sark Sigorta T.A.S., a Turkish insurance company. It also opened offices in Madrid (1988), Istanbul (1990), Milan (1990), and Santiago (1990). In 1989 the company paid $42 million for a 10% interest in Delaware Management Holdings, a Philadelphia-based investment counseling firm.

After restructuring the corporation in 1990, Tokio formed 7 regional headquarters and added branches. Also in 1990 a Tokio subsidiary invested $100 million to be partners in an investment firm run by former US treasury secretary William E. Simon and signed a cooperation agreement with Commercial Union Assurance Co. (UK), which was looking for opportunities in Japan.

In 1991 Tokio opened 2 overseas offices, and in 1992 it founded the Tokio Marine Research Institute as a think tank for insurance issues. Tokio set up a division in China to support Japanese investors there in 1993.

The company also gained permission in 1994 to open a branch office in Shanghai.

Nasdaq symbol: TKIOY (ADR)
Fiscal year ends: March 31

WHO

Chairman: Haruo Takeda
President: Shunji Kono
EVP: Shiro Horichi
EVP: Noboru Araki, age 60
Senior Managing Director: Yukihisa Hamaguchi, age 57
Senior Managing Director: Tsuneyasu Igarashi, age 58
Senior Managing Director Personnel: Masakazu Nakanishi
Managing Director Finance: Norihiko Tokunaga
Director and General Manager, Tokio Marine Management (US): Shinya Yoshikoshi
Auditors: KPMG Peat Marwick

WHERE

HQ: The Tokio Marine and Fire Insurance Co., Ltd., Tokio Kaijo Kasai Hoken Kabushiki Kaisha, 2-1, Marunouchi 1-chome, Chiyoda-ku, Tokyo 100, Japan
Phone: +81-3-3212-6211
Fax: +81-3-5223-3100
US HQ: Tokio Marine Management, Inc., 101 Park Ave., New York, NY 10178-0095
US Phone: 212-297-6600
US Fax: 212-297-6898

The Tokio Marine and Fire Insurance Co. operates 86 regional headquarters and branches and 465 subbranches in Japan, one branch in the US, and offices in the US and 43 other countries and territories.

WHAT

	1994 Assets	
	¥ bil.	% of total
Cash & equivalents	279	4
Equities	3,100	43
Bonds and other long-term investments	1,920	26
Other investments	801	11
Net premiums	153	2
Reinsurance	343	5
Other	674	9
Total	**7,270**	**100**

Selected Subsidiaries and Affiliates
América Latina Companhia de Seguros (São Paulo)
Berjaya General Insurance Sdn. Bhd. (Kuala Lumpur)
First Insurance Co. of Hawaii, Ltd. (Honolulu)
Houston General Insurance Co. (Fort Worth)
Pan-Malayan Insurance Corp. (Manila)
P.T. Asuransi Tokio Marine Indonesia (Jakarta)
Rural del Paraguay SA Paraguaya de Seguros (Asunción)
The Sri Muang Insurance Co., Ltd. (Bangkok)
Tokio Marine and Fire Insurance Co. (Singapore) Pte. Ltd.
Tokio Marine de Venezuela, CA (Caracas)
Tokio Marine Europe Ltd. (London)
Tokio Marine Internacional, SA (Mexico City)
Tokio Marine International Fund (Luxembourg) SA
Tokio Marine Management, Inc. (New York)
Tokio Re Corp. (New York)
Trans Pacific Insurance Co. (New York)
The Wuphoon Insurance Co. Ltd. (Hong Kong)

KEY COMPETITORS

AIG	General Re	Nichido Fire
Allianz	ITT	Nippon Fire
B.A.T	Kemper	Prudential
Chiyoda Fire	Lloyd's of London	State Farm
CIGNA	MetLife	Sumitomo
Dai-Tokyo Fire	Mitsui	Yasuda Fire

HOW MUCH

$=¥112 (Dec. 31, 1993)	Annual Growth	1985	1986	1987	1988	1989	1990	1991	1992	1993	1994
Assets (¥ bil.)	7.5%	3,786	3,833	5,263	6,241	7,676	7,650	7,614	6,675	6,833	7,270
Net income (¥ bil.)	20.9%	36	44	48	60	93	83	74	21	60	198
Income as % of assets	—	1.0%	1.1%	0.9%	1.0%	1.2%	1.1%	1.0%	0.5%	0.9%	2.7%
Earnings per share (¥)	(0.5%)	24	29	32	39	60	53	47	13	38	23
Stock price – high (¥)[1]	—	678	961	1,777	2,665	2,267	2,286	2,130	1,440	1,360	1,430
Stock price – low (¥)[1]	—	465	635	749	1,442	1,405	1,867	946	1,130	840	1,105
Stock price – close (¥)[1]	5.9%	626	786	1,571	1,442	2,152	2,076	1,320	1,290	1,210	1,050
P/E – high	—	28	33	56	68	38	43	45	111	36	62
P/E – low	—	19	22	23	37	23	35	20	87	22	48
Dividends per share (¥)	4.4%	5.44	5.89	5.89	6.35	7.12	7.12	8.00	8.00	8.00	8.00
Book value per share (¥)	(4.0%)	—	—	—	—	—	1,656	1,535	1,188	1,205	1,405
Employees	5.7%	—	—	—	10,683	11,131	12,000	12,995	14,054	14,500	14,900

1994 Year-end:
Debt ratio: 2.4%
Return on equity: 1.8%
Equity as % of assets: 29.9%
No. of shares: 1,547
Dividends
  Yield: 0.8%
  Payout: 34.8%
Market value ($ mil.): $14,503
Assets (mil.): $64,911
Sales (mil.): $11,900

Stock Price History[1]
High/Low 1985–94

[1] Stock prices are for the prior calendar year.

THE TOKYO ELECTRIC POWER CO., INC.

OVERVIEW

A sluggish economy and a cool summer meant a drop in demand for electricity from The Tokyo Electric Power Co. (TEPCO), the world's largest investor-owned electric utility company. It reported an increase in demand of only 0.7% in fiscal 1994, the lowest increase since fiscal 1980. TEPCO is one of 10 power companies operating in Japan and serves the 15,000-square-mile region in and around Tokyo. It is the world's #2 electric utility, after France's EDF. TEPCO supplies about 1/3 of Japan's electrical power.

TEPCO is weaning itself off oil and turning to nuclear power as the primary source of its power generation. In 1994 oil was only 19% of its fuel sources, down from nearly 40% in 1980. Nuclear power was the largest fuel source in 1994 at 37%. By the year 2003 nuclear power is expected to be 43% of its energy sources, and oil 8%. TEPCO also uses liquefied natural gas, liquefied petroleum gas, and coal as fuel sources. The company is dependent on fuel imports. Malaysia is TEPCO's #1 source for liquefied natural gas, and Canada is its top source for nuclear fuels.

Aside from its power generation business, TEPCO also has interests in construction and telecommunications. Kandenko Co., Ltd., Japan's largest electrical engineering company, is a TEPCO affiliate. TEPCO also has stakes in a TV company and a real estate concern.

WHEN

TEPCO traces its heritage to Tokyo Electric Light Co., Japan's first electric utility, formed in 1883. It switched on Japan's first power plant in 1887, a 25-kilowatt fossil fuel generator that supplied many businesses and factories with electric power for the first time. Fossil fuels continued as the primary source of electricity in Japan until 1912, when long-distance transmission techniques became more efficient, making hydroelectric power a cheaper source of energy.

In 1938 the Japanese government nationalized electric utilities, despite strong objections from Yasuzaemon Matsunaga, a leader in Japan's utility industry and former president of the Japan Electric Association. After WWII Matsunaga championed public ownership of Japan's electric utilities, helping to establish in 1951 the current system of 9 regional companies, each with a service monopoly. Of these, Tokyo Electric Power, which took over utilities operating in Tokyo and the surrounding districts, was the largest and that year was listed on the Tokyo exchange. Kazutaka Kikawada became TEPCO's president in 1961. Regulation of Japan's electric utilities has been entrusted to the Ministry of International Trade and Industry since 1965.

Fossil fuels made a comeback in Japan in the postwar era, since those plants could be built more economically than hydroelectric plants. When the OPEC oil embargo of the 1970s highlighted Japan's dependence on foreign oil as a fuel source, TEPCO responded by increasing its use of nuclear and LNG energy sources. In 1977 the company formed the Energy Conservation Center to promote conservation and conservation-related legislation and the following year opened an office in Washington, DC, to exchange data with the US government and utility industry.

In 1982 the company joined Toshiba, Texaco, SCEcorp, GE, and others to build a coal gasification plant in California's Mojave Desert, intending to use coal gasification technology to further shrink its dependence on foreign oil. In 1984 TEPCO announced that it would build its first coal-burning generator since the oil crisis. Since then TEPCO has set up Tokyo Telecommunication Network Company (a partnership that provides industrial and public telecommunications services, 1986) and TEPCO Cable TV (1989).

TEPCO established a global environment department in 1990 to conduct R&D on energy and the environment (e.g., global warming). The company grows beech trees for reforestation, develops electric cars, and demonstrates the use of phosphoric acid fuel cells as a battery-power alternative to standard fuel generation. Although electric sales were up in 1991, high fuel prices kept earnings down.

TEPCO takes an active interest in the development of alternative energy systems. In 1992 its R&D division was working on electrical vehicle prototypes. In 1993 TEPCO published a major report outlining the company's commitment to produce energy in ways that protect the environment.

In 1994 TEPCO announced plans to build 2 new nuclear units at its Fukushima-I plant.

Principal exchange: Tokyo
Fiscal year ends: March 31

Chairman: Shoh Nasu
President: Hiroshi Araki
EVP: Takeshi Abiru
EVP: Satoshi Hoshino
EVP: Ryo Ikegame
EVP: Katsumi Iwasaki
Managing Director: Kiyoshi Ishii
Managing Director: Yasuro Kawaji
Managing Director: Hiroshi Kawasaki
Managing Director: Nobuya Minami
Managing Director: Akinori Miyata
Managing Director: Tetsuo Takeuchi
General Manager (US): Konosuke Sugiura
Auditors: Showa Ota & Co.

HQ: Tokyo Denryoku Kabushiki Kaisha, 1-3,
Uchisaiwai-cho 1-chome, Chiyoda-ku,
Tokyo 100, Japan
Phone: +81-3-3501-8111
Fax: +81-3-5511-8436
US HQ: The Tokyo Electric Power Co., Inc., 1901
L St. NW, Ste. 720,
Washington, DC 20036
US Phone: 202-457-0790
US Fax: 202-457-0810

Tokyo Electric Power conducts business solely in
Japan but operates liaison offices in London and
Washington, DC.

Major Generating Facilities

Hydroelectric	Nuclear	Fossil Fuel
Azumi	Fukushima-I	Anegasaki
Imaichi	Fukushima-II	Hirono
Midono	Kashiwazaki	Kashima
Shin-Takasegawa	Kariwa	Sodegaura
Tamahara		Yogosuka
Yagisawa		

	1994 Sales	
	¥ bil.	% of total
Commercial & industrial	2,890	62
Residential	1,675	—
Other	156	3
Total	**4,721**	**100**

	Fuel Sources
	% of total
Nuclear	37
Coal/LNG/LPG	35
Oil	19
Hydroelectric	9
Total	**100**

Major Subsidiaries, Divisions, and Affiliates
Kandenko Co., Ltd.
London Office
The Tokyo Electric Power Real Estate
Maintenance Co.
Tokyo Telecommunication Network Co., Inc.
Washington, DC, Office

$= ¥112 (Dec. 31, 1993)	9-Year Growth	1985	1986	1987	1988	1989	1990	1991	1992	1993	1994
Sales (¥ bil.)	2.1%	3,915	4,189	3,906	3,940	3,938	4,087	4,384	4,597	4,700	4,721
Net income (¥ bil.)	(7.2%)	122	85	130	190	138	123	59	75	74	62
Income as % of sales	—	3.1%	2.2%	3.1%	4.9%	3.5%	3.1%	1.3%	1.6%	1.6%	1.3%
Earnings per share (¥)	(6.3%)	83	95	140	101	88	56	44	56	55	46
Stock price – high (¥)[1]	—	1,770	2,788	8,136	9,054	7,068	7,565	6,150	4,240	3,700	4,450
Stock price – low (¥)[1]	—	990	1,361	2,560	4,613	4,686	5,344	2,510	3,380	2,200	2,440
Stock price – close (¥)[1]	6.9%	1,694	2,711	7,593	4,950	6,776	5,950	3,650	3,540	2,600	3,080
P/E – high	—	21	29	58	90	80	135	139	76	67	97
P/E – low	—	12	14	18	46	53	95	43	60	40	53
Dividends per share (¥)	0.6%	47.56	47.56	47.56	49.02	49.02	49.02	50.00	50.00	50.00	50.00
Book value per share (¥)	3.2%	784	831	922	975	1,015	1,022	1,037	1,043	1,049	1,045
Employees	0.8%	39,195	39,058	39,334	39,570	39,552	39,404	39,640	40,081	40,789	41,967

1994 Year-end:
Debt ratio: 87.8%
Return on equity: 4.4%
Cash (bil.): ¥123
Long-term debt (bil.): ¥8,198
No. of shares (mil.): 1,339
Dividends
  Yield: 1.6%
  Payout: 108.7%
Market value (mil.): $36,823
Sales (mil.): $42,152

**Stock Price History[1]
High/Low 1985–94**

[1] Stock prices are for the prior calendar year.

HOOVER'S HANDBOOK OF WORLD BUSINESS 1995–1996   **515**

THE TORONTO–DOMINION BANK

OVERVIEW

The dominion that The Toronto-Dominion Bank (TD) rules in Canada is the securities business. Although only the 5th largest bank in Canada, TD has built up the country's biggest brokerage after ignoring the rush of its rivals (Royal Bank, Canadian Imperial Bank of Commerce, Bank of Nova Scotia, and Bank of Montreal) to acquire full service securities firms in the late 1980s following governmental deregulation of the securities industry.

The chartered bank serves individuals, businesses, financial institutions, and governments through a network of 975 branches across Canada. Internationally, the bank offers a broad range of financial and advisory services to businesses and governments worldwide. It operates offices in several major financial capitals including Hong Kong, London, New York, Singapore, Sydney, Taipei, and Tokyo.

Despite a weak economy, TD achieved Canada's largest credit card launch in 1993 with the TD/GM VISA Card, attracting over one million new accounts. The bank has also focused on building up its US operations and now ranks as the 8th largest among all banks operating in the US, measured in agenting syndications.

Outside North America the bank is developing a large network of correspondent banks to handle its domestic customers' offshore needs.

WHEN

The 1955 merger of 2 banks set up in the mid-19th century created The Toronto-Dominion Bank. The Bank of Toronto was the older bank, established in 1855 by a group of flour traders who wanted their own banking facilities to support their growing industry. The expanding volume of business in Ontario encouraged another group of businessmen to establish the Dominion Bank in 1869. The new bank emphasized the commercial aspects of banking and invested heavily in railways and construction.

Legislation set the stage for banking expansion in the mid-19th century. Lord Durham's Report of 1850 safeguarded competition in banking, and the Confederation of 1867 integrated the various Canadian colonies into a single country.

As railroads and other transportation connected settlements springing up in newly populated sections of Canada, the 2 banks established branches across the country to handle the booming growth in trade and other financial transactions.

Boom and bust years followed for both banks as they participated in the larger Canadian economy. Industries that would become Canada's mainstays — dairying, mining, oil, pulp, textiles — were being established. WWI and the demand for Canadian resources by the war effort transformed Canada from a debtor to a creditor nation. And true to the pioneering spirit of the nation, a Bank of Toronto official claimed to be the first to have set up a branch office with the help of aviation (in Manitoba in the 1920s).

Canada and its banks suffered in the bust times. Bank runs were a factor in the 1920s, and the Wall Street Crash of 1929 had a devastating effect on the banking industry. With the decrease of foreign trade and the closing of factories, the Bank of Toronto and Dominion Bank were both forced to close unprofitable branches.

To help coordinate the banking industry, the Bank of Canada was founded in 1934 to issue currency, set monetary policy, and control interest rates. After growing during and after World War II, both the Bank of Toronto and Dominion Bank decided to join forces in order to increase their capital base. In 1955 the 2 merged; on opening day the new bank had 450 branches in operation.

In the 1970s TD opened international branch offices in locations as diverse as Bangkok, Beirut, and Frankfurt. It also picked up a lot of developing nations' debt (as did other major Canadian banks). However, following the deregulation of the Canadian securities industry in 1987, CEO Richard Thomson (TD chairman since 1976) pulled back on international operations and focused on brokerage activities. In 1987 TD eked out a profit while its 4 rivals all lost money.

Maintaining the steady growth it had achieved in the 1980s, the bank had established 907 branches and had assets of C$74 billion by the end of 1992.

In 1993 TD acquired Central Guaranty Trust for around C$140 million. The bank followed its 1993 credit card launch by introducing a US dollar-based credit card in 1994.

Principal exchange: Toronto
Fiscal year ends: October 31

Chairman and CEO: Richard M. Thomson, age 60, C$1,825,548 pay
President: A. Charles Baillie, C$703,846 pay (prior to promotion)
VC: William T. Brock, C$615,986 pay
VC: J. Urban Joseph, C$615,548 pay
VC: Sydney R. McMorran, C$615,548 pay
EVP Finance: Robert P. Kelly
EVP: L. Arthur English
SVP, USA Division: Michael P. Mueller
SVP, General Counsel, and Secretary: R. Glenn Bumstead
SVP Human Resources: Allen W. Bell
Auditors: Ernst & Young, Price Waterhouse

HQ: Toronto-Dominion Centre, King St. W. and Bay St., Toronto, Ontario M5K 1A2, Canada
Phone: 416-982-8222
Fax: 416-982-5671
US HQ: Toronto-Dominion Holdings (USA), Inc., 31 W. 52nd St., New York, NY 10019-6101
US Phone: 212-468-0300
US Fax: 212-262-1923

| | 1994 Assets | |
	C$ mil.	% of total
Canada	75,948	76
US	17,974	18
Australia	1,759	2
UK	1,662	2
Other countries	2,416	2
Total	**99,759**	**100**

| | 1994 Assets | |
	C$ mil.	% of total
Cash	3,148	3
Securities	19,310	19
Business & other loans	35,117	35
Residential mort. loans	25,180	25
Personal loans	8,564	9
Customers' liability under acceptances	4,809	5
Other	3,631	4
Total	**99,759**	**100**

Major Subsidiaries

Business Windows Inc.
Green Line Investor Services Inc.
Penlim Investments Ltd.
TD Capital Group Ltd.
TD Evergreen Investment Services Inc.
TD Factors Ltd.
TD Finance Ltd.
TD Ireland
TD Mortgage Corp.
TD Nordique Inc.
TD Pacific Mortgage Corp.
TD Reinsurance (Barbados) Inc.
TD Trust Co.

Toronto Dominion Australia Ltd.
Toronto Dominion Bank (Europe) Ltd. (UK)
Toronto Dominion (Curaçao) NV (Barbados)
Toronto-Dominion Holdings (USA), Inc.
Toronto Dominion Investments BV (The Netherlands)
Toronto Dominion Securities
Toronto Dominion (South East Asia) Ltd. (Singapore)
Webb International Minerals Inc. (US)

B.C. Bancorp
Bank of Montreal
Bank of Nova Scotia
Canada Trustco Mortgage
Canadian General Investments

Canadian Imperial
Genecan Financial
Gentra
Hees Intl. Bancorp
Laurentian Bank

Montreal Trustco
National Bank of Canada
National Trustco
Royal Bank of Canada

$= C$1.40 (Dec. 31, 1994)	9-Year Growth	1985	1986	1987	1988	1989	1990	1991	1992	1993	1994
Assets (C$ mil.)	7.9%	50,218	51,447	54,525	59,285	63,069	66,900	68,905	74,133	85,011	99,759
Net income (C$ mil.)	6.4%	367	329	116	641	661	543	453	376	246	643
Income as % of assets	—	0.7%	0.6%	0.2%	1.1%	1.0%	0.8%	0.7%	0.5%	0.3%	0.6%
Earnings per share (C$)	5.2%	1.36	1.18	2.00	2.14	2.20	1.80	1.51	1.25	0.82	2.14
Stock price – high (C$)	—	12.88	14.19	19.06	19.25	23.00	20.63	19.75	19.75	21.88	23.63
Stock price – low (C$)	—	9.06	10.50	13.13	13.13	17.13	14.75	16.38	15.75	14.88	18.88
Stock price – close (C$)	5.8%	12.38	11.75	17.69	17.69	20.50	16.75	18.25	16.63	21.25	20.50
P/E – high	—	9	12	10	9	10	11	13	16	27	11
P/E – low	—	7	9	7	6	8	8	11	13	18	9
Dividends per share (C$)	7.9%	0.40	0.42	0.43	0.51	0.71	0.76	0.76	0.76	0.76	0.79
Book value per share (C$)	6.9%	9.21	10.08	10.25	11.33	12.76	13.82	14.55	15.14	15.30	16.74
Employees	2.6%	20,381	20,211	21,710	22,853	23,881	24,560	24,003	23,514	25,603	25,705

1994 Year-end:
Debt ratio: 75.4%
Return on equity: 13.3%
Equity as % of assets:5.4%
Long-term debt (mil.): C$2,510
No. of shares (mil.): 301
Dividends
  Yield: 3.9%
  Payout: 36.9%
Market value (mil.): $4,644
Sales (mil.): $5,283

Stock Price History High/Low 1985–94

OVERVIEW

Toshiba has one heck of a dance card. The #3 electronics firm in Japan (after Hitachi and Matsushita), Toshiba is engaged in over 2 dozen major partnerships or joint ventures, doing business with such heavyweights as IBM and Apple. And its strategy of lining up partners to share the risk of developing expensive new technologies, whether advanced chips or flat panel displays, has borne fruit. Toshiba is the world's #1 maker of large-scale memory chips (DRAMs) and a top supplier of color flat-panel displays for portable computers. Moreover, it is the world's #3 maker of all liquid crystal displays (LCDs), after Sharp and Seiko-Epson, and manufactures so many electrical products it's considered the General Electric of Japan.

Nonetheless, Toshiba has been battered in recent years by the Japanese recession and tougher global competition. In 1994 its profits fell for the 4th year in a row, off nearly 90% from 1990. To reverse the slide Toshiba wants to shorten its product development cycle and cut costs. It also is focusing on developing multimedia devices and LCDs (used in computers and video games). The market for LCDs alone is expected to quadru- ple, to $15 billion, by the year 2000.

WHEN

Two Japanese electrical equipment manufacturers came together in 1939 to create Toshiba. Tanaka Seizo-sha, Japan's first telegraph equipment manufacturer, was founded in 1875 by Hisashige Tanaka, the so-called Edison of Japan. In the 1890s the company started making heavier electrical equipment, such as transformers and electric motors, adopting the name Shibaura Seisakusho Works in 1893. Seisakusho went on to pioneer the making of hydroelectric generators (1894) and X-ray tubes (1915) in Japan.

The other half of Toshiba, Hakunetsusha & Company, was founded by Dr. Ichisuke Fujioka and Shoichi Miyoshi as Japan's first incandescent lamp maker (1890). Renamed Tokyo Electric Company (1899), the firm developed the coiled filament light bulb (1921) and the internally frosted glass light bulb (1925). It produced Japan's first radio receiver and cathode ray tube in 1924. In 1939 it merged with Shibaura Seisakusho to form Tokyo Shibaura Electric Company (Toshiba).

Toshiba was the first company in Japan to make fluorescent lamps (1940), radar (1942), broadcasting equipment (1952), and digital computers (1954). Production of black-and-white TVs began in 1949, the same year the company was listed on the Tokyo and Osaka exchanges. Even so, through the 1970s it was considered an also-ran, trailing other Japanese *keiretsu* (business groups) in size, market share, sales skills, and brand recognition. Part of the problem was a traditional and bureaucratic management that impeded technological innovation.

Then in 1980 electrical engineer Shoichi Saba became president. Saba invested heavily in Toshiba's information and communications segments. As a result the company became the first in the world to produce the powerful one-megabit DRAM chip (1985). In 1986 Toshiba unveiled the popular T3100 laptop computer. In the meantime Saba (named chairman in 1986) pushed Toshiba into joint ventures with Siemens (1985) and Motorola (1986) to exchange microcomputer and memory-chip technology.

But in 1987 Toshiba incurred the wrath of the US government. A subsidiary sold submarine sound-deadening equipment to the USSR, resulting in threats of US sanctions and a precipitous decline in US sales and its stock price. Chairman Saba and President Sugichiro Watari resigned in shame.

With Joichi Aoi at the helm, Toshiba has become a leader among Japanese companies in establishing a global presence. Toshiba and GE linked up in 1991 to promote cooperative business ventures in Asia in large home appliances. Easing years-long trade tensions between Japan, the US, and Europe, Toshiba, IBM, and Siemens inked an 8-year, $1 billion deal in early 1992. The companies hope to develop the first 256-megabit DRAM, likely to be a key component of future computers, by 1999. Also in 1992 Toshiba, IBM, and Apple announced a joint venture to make multimedia equipment and software. Toshiba followed Sony and Matsushita's leads, but in a smaller way, by investing in the US entertainment industry, buying a $500 million stake in Time Warner. In 1993 Toshiba sold its 69% stake in Onkyo, an audio product maker, and entered an alliance with NEC and MIPS Technologies to develop an advanced microprocessor.

Principal exchange: Tokyo
Fiscal year ends: March 31

Chairman: Joichi Aoi
President and CEO: Fumio Sato
SEVP: Keiichi Komiya
SEVP: Atsumi Uchiyama
SEVP: Hideharu Egawa
EVP: Yasuji Oku
EVP: Kunika Mizushima
VP Human Resources and Administration:
Takaaki Tanaka
CEO, Toshiba America: Takeshi Okatomi
Director Human Resources, Toshiba America:
Lynne Kennedy
Auditors: Price Waterhouse

WHERE

HQ: 1-1, Shibaura 1-chome, Minato-ku,
Tokyo 105-01, Japan
Phone: +81-3-3457-2105
Fax: +81-3-3456-4776
US HQ: Toshiba America, Inc., 1251 Ave. of the
Americas, 41st Fl., New York, NY 10020
US Phone: 212-596-0600
US Fax: 212-593-3875

	1994 Sales	
	¥ bil.	% of total
Japan	3,228	70
North America	519	11
Asia	470	10
Europe	302	7
Other countries	112	2
Total	**4,631**	**100**

WHAT

	1994 Sales	
	¥ bil.	% of total
Information/communication		
systems & electronic devices	2,438	50
Consumer products & other	1,314	26
Heavy electrical apparatus	1,232	24
Adjustments	(353)	—
Total	**4,631**	**100**

Selected Major Products

Batteries	Locomotives
Cameras	Nuclear power plants
Cellular telephones	Power plant systems
Color TVs and VCRs	Printed circuit boards
Computers	Radar and air traffic control
Electron tubes	Radio and TV systems
Elevators and escalators	Satellite communication
Home audio and video	systems
Household appliances	Semiconductors
Industrial equipment	Telecommunications systems
Lighting equipment	Workstations

KEY COMPETITORS

ABB	General Electric	Pioneer
Alcatel Alsthom	General Signal	Raytheon
AT&T	Harris	Ricoh
BCE	Hitachi	Rolls-Royce
Brother	Honeywell	Sanyo
Canon	Hyundai	Seiko
Casio	IBM	Sharp
Compaq	In Focus Systems	Siemens
Cooper Industries	Ingersoll-Rand	Silicon Graphics
Daewoo	Kyocera	Sony
Dell	Machines Bull	Sun
Electrolux	Matsushita	Microsystems
Emerson	Minolta	Thomson SA
Ericsson	NEC	Thorn EMI
Fuji Photo	Nokia	Westinghouse
Fujitsu	Oki	Yamaha
GEC	Philips	Zenith

HOW MUCH

$=¥112 (Dec. 31, 1993)	9-Year Growth	1985	1986	1987	1988	1989	1990	1991	1992	1993	1994
Sales (¥ bil.)	3.7%	3,343	3,373	3,308	3,572	3,801	4,252	4,695	4,722	4,628	4,631
Net income (¥ bil.)	(17.8%)	86	59	34	61	119	132	121	39	23	15
Income as % of sales	—	2.6%	1.8%	1.0%	1.7%	3.1%	3.1%	2.6%	0.8%	0.5%	0.3%
Earnings per share (¥)	(20.6%)	30	19	12	20	37	40	36	12	6	4
Stock price – high (¥)[1]	—	491	438	853	852	1,240	1,500	1,310	900	675	778
Stock price – low (¥)[1]	—	365	329	318	551	560	1,020	680	600	530	555
Stock price – close (¥)[1]	5.5%	420	370	350	580	1,010	1,270	706	635	635	680
P/E – high	—	16	23	71	43	34	38	37	75	105	—
P/E – low	—	12	17	27	28	15	26	19	50	83	—
Dividends per share (¥)	2.5%	8.00	8.00	8.00	8.00	8.00	10.00	10.00	10.00	10.00	10.00
Book value per share (¥)	6.1%	205	212	217	244	286	342	368	368	358	348
Employees	4.9%	114,000	120,000	121,000	122,000	125,000	142,000	162,000	168,000	173,000	175,000

1994 Year-end:
Debt ratio: 62.7%
Return on equity: 1.1%
Cash (bil.): ¥768
Long-term debt (bil.): ¥1,010
No. of shares (mil.): 3,214
Dividends
  Yield: 1.5%
  Payout: 264.6%
Market value (mil.): $19,514
Sales (mil.): $41,348

Stock Price History[1]
High/Low 1985–94

(chart y-axis: 1,600 / 1,400 / 1,200 / 1,000 / 800 / 600 / 400 / 200 / 0)

[1] Stock prices are for the prior calendar year.

TOTAL

OVERVIEW

TOTAL ranks 4th among Europe's oil and gas producers. Its operations span the industry from exploration and refining to distribution at more than 10,000 retail gas stations in Africa, Europe, and the US. TOTAL derives 11% of its revenues from specialty petrochemicals such as paints, inks, and adhesives.

The company operates in 80 countries and markets over 5,000 petroleum-based products. This diversity, plus a balance between its upstream (exploration and production) and downstream (refining and marketing)

segments, has helped it weather the industry's low crude prices, poor refining margins, and stagnating consumption.

TOTAL, which has 18 years worth of reserves, expects to increase production outside the Middle East by 40% by late 1995. The company continues to expand its reserves, with promising exploration projects in Nigeria and Yemen. Partnerships in Myanmar, Thailand, and Vietnam have gained the company a strategic presence in Southeast Asia's high-growth market.

WHEN

In 1924 a French consortium formed the Compagnie Française des Pétroles (CFP). The French government charged the group with developing an oil industry for the country. France, though lacking natural reserves within its borders, had a 23.75% stake in the Turkish Petroleum Company (TPC), acquired from Germany in 1920 as part of the spoils from WWI. When oil was discovered in Iraq (1927), the TPC partners (CFP; Anglo-Persian Oil, later British Petroleum; Royal Dutch/ Shell; and a consortium of 5 US oil companies) became major players in the oil game.

In 1929 France's government began its shareholding relationship with CFP, which gave the government a 25% stake (raised to 35% in 1931) but ensured the company's independence from government control. CFP began establishing refining and transporting capabilities, and by the start of WWII it was a vertically integrated petroleum company.

With France's defeat by Germany in WWII (1940), CFP was effectively blocked from any further expansion, and its stake in the Iraq Petroleum Company (formerly the TPC) was held by its partners until the end of the war. In 1948, over French protests, the US partners ended the "Red Line" agreement (a pact that limited members' competition within that Middle Eastern region).

After the end of WWII, CFP diversified its sources for crude, opening a supply in 1947 from the Venezuelan company Pantepec and making several major discoveries in colonial Algeria in 1956. Development of Algerian resources continued, with France providing technical and economic assistance in return for an assured supply of oil from a country that based its operations on the franc rather than the higher-valued pound sterling.

CFP began supplying crude to Japan, South Korea, and Taiwan in the 1950s. To market its products throughout northern Africa, France, and other European areas, the company introduced the brand name TOTAL in 1954. It entered the petrochemical market in 1956 and by the late 1960s consolidated those businesses under TOTAL Chimie.

In 1971 Algeria became the first major oil-producing country to nationalize its petroleum industry. This was not as dire a blow to CFP as it might have been earlier; by that time CFP was receiving only about 20% of its supplies from Algeria. Exploration had paid off, with discoveries in the 1960s in Indonesia and, in the early 1970s, in the North Sea.

In 1980 CFP joined Elf Aquitaine in a $200-million purchase of Rhône-Poulenc's petrochemical segment. In 1990 TOTAL purchased state-owned Orkem's coating business (inks, resins, paints, and adhesives).

TOTAL adopted its brand name as part of its title in 1985 (TOTAL Compagnie Française des Pétroles), and in 1991 it became simply TOTAL. That same year TOTAL was first listed on the NYSE.

In 1992 the French government lowered its stake in TOTAL to 5%, down from 34%. Despite the weak world economy, TOTAL's net income rose in 1993. The company continued to expand its reserves, including involvement in fields in Argentina, the Caspian Sea, and Colombia, where output at the Cusiana field is expected to double that country's oil production.

Also in 1993 TOTAL sponsored the record-setting team that flew a single-engine airplane around the world in less than 80 hours. In 1994 TOTAL posted net profits of $633 million on sales of $25.1 billion.

NYSE symbol: TOT (ADR)
Fiscal year ends: December 31

Chairman and CEO: Serge Tchuruk, age 54
SEVP; President, Exploration and Production:
Thierry Desmarest
EVP; President, Strategy and Finance: Alain
Madec
VP and CFO: Robert Castaigne
**Chairman, President, and CEO, TOTAL
Petroleum (North America):** Daniel Valot
Treasurer, TOTAL Petroleum (North America):
Douglas Kerner
**VP Human Resources, TOTAL Petroleum,
(North America):** Scott Topham
Auditors: Cabinet Cauvin, Angleys, Saint-Pierre
International; Arthur Andersen

WHERE

HQ: 24 Cours Michelet 92800 Puteaux, France
Phone: +33-1-41-35-40-00
Fax: +33-1-41-35-64-65
US Phone: 303-291-2271 (Investor Relations)
US HQ: TOTAL Petroleum (North America) Ltd.,
900 19th St., Denver, Colorado 80202
US Phone: (303) 291-2000
US Fax: (303) 291-2104 (Public Relations)

	1993 Sales	
	FF mil.	% of total
France	57,721	35
North & South America	19,164	12
Africa	8,957	5
Far East & other countries	41,312	25
Other Europe	37,759	23
Adjustments	(29,435)	—
Total	**135,478**	**100**

WHAT

	1993 Sales	
	FF mil.	% of total
Refining & marketing	75,576	47
Trading & Middle East	58,535	36
Chemicals	18,576	11
Exploration & production	9,874	6
Adjustments	(27,083)	—
Total	**135,478**	**100**

Selected Consolidated Subsidiaries

Refining/Marketing
Air Total Intl. (99%)
TOTAL Nigeria (60%)
TOTAL Petroleum North
America (TOPNA; 54%)
TOTALGAZ (99%)
TRD Total Raffinage
Distribution (99.8%)

Euridep (99.8%)
Hutchinson (99.8%)
TOTAL Chimie

Exploration/Production
TOTAL Angola
TOTAL Indonesie
TOTAL Norge
TOTAL Oil & Gas
Nederland
TOTAL Oil Marine

Trading and Middle East
TOTAL Intl. Ltd.
TOTAL Transport Corp.
TOTAL Transport
Maritime (99.7%)

Multiple Activities
Finalens (90.4%)
TOTAL America, Inc.
TOTAL Australia
TOTAL Deutschland
TOTAL Oil Holdings

Chemicals
Coates Brothers PLC
Cray Valley

KEY COMPETITORS

Amoco	ENI	Petrobrás
Anglo American	Exxon	Petrofina
Ashland, Inc.	Imperial Oil	Phillips
Atlantic Richfield	Koch	Petroleum
British Petroleum	Mobil	Repsol
Broken Hill	Norsk Hydro	Royal Dutch/Shell
Canadian Pacific	Occidental	Sun Company
Chevron	Oryx	Texaco
Coastal	PDVSA	Unocal
DuPont	PEMEX	USX–Marathon
Elf Aquitaine	Pennzoil	YPF

HOW MUCH

$=FF5.91 (Dec. 31, 1993)	Annual Growth	1984	1985	1986	1987	1988	1989	1990	1991	1992	1993
Sales (FF mil.)	(1.7%)	158,778	173,120	95,722	87,087	83,290	107,894	128,445	143,019	136,608	135,478
Net income (FFmil.)	6.3%	1,708	1,473	(471)	1,456	1,479	2,206	4,064	5,810	2,847	2,965
Income as % of sales	—	1.1%	0.9%	(0.5%)	1.7%	1.8%	2.0%	3.2%	4.1%	2.1%	2.2%
Earnings per share (FF)	(0.3%)	13.90	11.95	(3.27)	10.05	10.25	15.00	27.25	31.50	13.80	13.50
Stock price – high (FF)	—	—	82.25	121.25	139.50	96.25	144.25	182.50	280.00	277.00	335.38
Stock price – low (FF)	—	—	51.25	72.50	81.00	76.75	89.50	129.00	141.25	192.70	216.13
Stock price – close (FF)	20.2%	61.63	72.25	102.25	87.50	90.00	143.75	160.00	245.50	232.70	322.75
P/E – high	—	—	7	—	14	9	10	7	9	20	25
P/E – low	—	—	4	—	8	7	6	5	4	14	16
Dividends per share (FF)	7.2%	4.00	4.50	5.00	5.00	5.00	5.00	5.00	5.75	7.00	7.50
Book value per share (FF)	1.0%	205	194	158	161	161	164	182	211	215	225
Employees	1.1%	44,981	44,557	40,253	40,513	41,862	41,202	46,024	49,365	51,139	49,772

1993 Year-end:
Debt ratio: 39.7%
Return on equity: 6.1%
Cash (mil.): FF24,841
Long-term debt (mil.): FF23,540
No. of shares (mil.): 220
Dividends
  Yield: 2.3%
  Payout: 55.6%
Market value (mil.): $11,991
Sales: $22,924

Stock Price History
High/Low 1985–93

TOYOTA MOTOR CORPORATION

OVERVIEW

Japan's largest industrial concern, Toyota, has decided to take its business elsewhere. The largest automaker in Japan, with a 32% market share for cars and light trucks, is not abandoning its home country. However, the 3rd largest carmaker in the world (after General Motors and Ford), has been sideswiped by the strong yen, which has made exporting cars from Japan too expensive, so it is shifting much of its production overseas.

One place Toyota plans to move more production is the US. In 1994 it introduced the Avalon, a 6-seat sedan built at its Georgetown, Kentucky, plant. It plans to boost its US output and could possibly build another factory in the US. Toyota has also announced it will boost its purchases of US-made auto parts by 10% over the next few years. Toyota is not planting Japanese flags only in the US; it plans to build 150,000 cars in China by 1996. The company is also working to reduce expenses. Long known for its efficiency, it found a way to cut $1.5 billion in costs in 1994.

Toyota is associated with the Mitsui *keiretsu*, or business group, and owns stakes in its suppliers, including Daihatsu, Hino Motors (trucks), and Nippondenso (electronic auto parts).

WHEN

In 1926 Sakichi Toyoda established the Toyoda Automatic Loom Works in central Japan to produce a loom he had invented. Prior to his death in 1930, he sold the rights to his invention and gave the proceeds to his son Kiichiro Toyoda to begin an auto business. In 1933 Kiichiro opened an automotive department within the loom works and began copying US engine designs. When protectionist legislation (1936) improved prospects for Japanese automakers, Kiichiro split off the car department, took it public (1937), and, for clarity in spoken Japanese, changed its name to Toyota.

As Toyota began car production, the Japanese government forbade passenger vehicle manufacturing (1939) and forced the company to make trucks for the military.

The company suffered financial problems in the 5 years after WWII. In 1950 Toyota restructured by organizing Toyota Motor Sales, its marketing arm, as a separate company.

Toyota's postwar commitment to R&D, modernization, quality, and the Kanban system of synchronized parts delivery paid off with the successful introductions of the 4-wheel-drive Land Cruiser (1951); full-sized Crown (1955), sold mostly as a taxi; and the small, mass-market Corona (1957). Toyota Motor Sales doubled the number of Toyota franchises in 1957 but kept rivalry low by forcing dealers to specialize in segments of the Toyota line. In 1961 the sales company opened driving schools to broaden its market in increasingly prosperous Japan.

Toyota Motor Sales, U.S.A., launched the Toyopet Crown in the US in 1957. The small engine failed to bring the car up a hill to the showroom. After suspending exports to the US and studying the market, Toyota introduced the successful Corona (1965) and the Corolla subcompact (1968), now the best-selling car of all time. By 1970 Toyota was the 4th largest automaker in the world.

With efficient manufacturing systems and reliable products, Toyota continued to expand rapidly abroad through the 1970s and 1980s. In 1975 Toyota displaced Volkswagen as the #1 importer of autos into the US. After the oil crisis caused a shift in demand for fuel-efficient cars, Toyota developed systems for quickly retooling factories.

Toyota recombined with Toyota Motor Sales in 1982. US auto production began in 1984 with NUMMI, a joint venture with General Motors, and was augmented by output from Toyota Motor Manufacturing (Georgetown, Kentucky) in 1988. Toyota successfully launched its Lexus line in the US in 1989. By using customer satisfaction as a key measure for setting dealer compensation, Lexus has been able to outsell its competition in the US: BMW, Mercedes, and Infiniti.

Toyota's European expansion slowed as a result of an EC Commission decision to restrict Japanese auto imports until the year 2000. The company agreed in 1992 to distribute cars in Japan for Volkswagen. Toyota's full-size pickup, the T100, built by Hino Motors in Japan, was introduced to the US market in the fall of 1992. That same year production started at the company's new engine plant in the UK.

In 1994 Toyota introduced the RAV-4, a small sport utility vehicle designed to compete with the Suzuki Sidekick.

Nasdaq symbol: TOYOY (ADR)
Fiscal year ends: March 31

WHO

Chairman: Shoichiro Toyoda, age 68
VC: Masami Iwasaki
President: Tatsuro Toyoda
EVP: Toshimi Onishi
EVP: Masaharu Tanaka
EVP: Hiroshi Okuda
EVP: Iwao Isomura
EVP: Akihiro Wada
President and CEO, Toyota Motor Sales, U.S.A.:
  Shinji Sakai
EVP Group Finance and Administration, Toyota
  Motor Sales, U.S.A.: Robert Pitts
EVP Human Resources, Toyota Motor Sales,
  U.S.A.: Jim Lacy
Auditors: Itoh Audit Corporation

WHERE

HQ: Toyota Jidosha Kabushiki Kaisha,
  1, Toyota-cho, Toyota City,
  Aichi Prefecture 471, Japan
Phone: +81-565-28-2121
Fax: +81-565-23-5800
US HQ: Toyota Motor Sales, U.S.A., Inc.,
  19001 S. Western Ave., Torrance, CA 90509
US Phone: 310-618-4000
US Fax: 310-618-7800

Toyota operates approximately 50 manufacturing plants in more than 25 countries.

	1994 Sales % of total
Japan	57
Other countries	43
Total	**100**

WHAT

	1994 Vehicle Sales	
	No. of units	% of total
Passenger cars	3,293,550	80
Trucks & buses	837,296	20
Total	**4,130,846**	**100**

Automobile Models (US Markets)

4Runner	MR-2
Avalon	Paseo
Camry	Previa
Celica	Supra
Corolla	T100
Land Cruiser	Tercel
Lexus	

Other Products and Services
Automobile leasing and rental services
Aviation services
Cellular car telephone service
Factory automation equipment
Financial services
Forklifts and other industrial vehicles
Prefabricated houses

KEY COMPETITORS

BMW	Honda	Mitsubishi
Caterpillar	Hyundai	Nissan
Chrysler	Ingersoll-Rand	Peugeot
Daewoo	Isuzu	Renault
Daimler-Benz	Kia Motors	Saab-Scania
Fiat	Komatsu	Suzuki
Ford	Kubota	Volkswagen
General Motors	Mazda	Volvo

HOW MUCH

Stock prices are for ADRs ADR = 2 shares	9-Year Growth	1985	1986	1987	1988	1989	1990	1991	1992	1993	1994
Sales ($ mil.)	13.7%	29,986	37,113	47,852	58,670	55,835	60,461	71,598	80,809	95,338	95,032
Net income ($ mil.)	(3.7%)	1,797	1,929	1,869	2,528	2,410	2,902	3,135	1,891	1,648	1,277
Income as % of sales	—	6.0%	5.2%	3.9%	4.3%	4.3%	4.8%	4.4%	2.3%	1.7%	1.3%
Earnings per share ($)	(4.8%)	1.06	1.01	1.38	1.53	1.39	1.65	1.62	0.98	0.86	0.68
Stock price – high ($)[1]	—	9.25	21.65	24.65	33.85	32.53	29.44	25.91	24.75	34.88	45.13
Stock price – low ($)[1]	—	6.68	9.00	14.15	21.00	28.02	21.69	21.50	18.88	21.63	31.75
Stock price – close ($)[1]	18.4%	9.13	19.96	21.45	31.88	29.13	23.07	23.88	23.50	32.00	41.88
P/E – high		9	21	18	22	23	18	16	25	41	66
P/E – low		6	9	10	20	20	13	13	19	25	47
Dividends per share ($)	7.6%	0.15	0.19	0.23	0.23	0.19	0.17	0.19	0.21	0.24	0.29
Book value per share ($)	10.9%	10.28	12.22	14.53	14.91	16.43	16.54	19.69	20.17	23.90	26.10
Employees	3.7%	79,901	82,620	84,207	86,082	91,790	96,849	102,423	108,167	109,279	110,534

1994 Year-end:
Debt ratio: 50.0%
Return on equity: 2.7%
Cash (mil.): $9,591
Current ratio: 1.66
Long-term debt (mil.): $17,008
No. of shares (mil.): 1,878
Dividends
  Yield: 0.7%
  Payout: 42.6%
Market value (mil.): $78,648

Stock Price History[1]
High/Low 1985–94

[1] Stock prices are for the prior calendar year.

UNILEVER

OVERVIEW

Procter & Gamble's soap opera tactics in 1994 embarrassed Unilever with an exposé of the cloth-damaging potential of Unilever's new manganese-based laundry detergent. But for Anglo-Dutch Unilever, one of the world's largest packaged consumer goods companies, this soap suds skirmish was only one of many consumer product wars the beleaguered giant was fighting around the world. Other battles raged over ice cream, soap, margarine, shampoo, and sauces. Unilever's famous brands include Lipton, all, Dove, Vaseline, and Q-tips. Major product groups include margarine and oils, soap and detergents, fro-

zen foods, drinks, personal care products, and specialty chemicals.

Facing a slow-ending European recession and slow-growing populations in its main markets, Unilever has cast its eyes on Asia, Latin America, and Central Europe as areas for growth. Unilever has had longstanding success in India with its Hindustan Lever subsidiary. The Indian company boasts the world's best selling soap, Lifebuoy.

Unilever PLC (UK) and Unilever NV (the Netherlands), whose boards of directors are identical, operate as a single entity.

WHEN

After sharpening his sales skills in the family wholesale grocery business in England, William Hesketh Lever formed a new company in 1885 with his brother James. Lever Brothers introduced Sunlight, the world's first packaged, branded laundry soap. A proponent of large-scale advertising, Lever launched the product with a campaign that queried, "Why does a woman look old sooner than a man?" The answer: because she is aged by the "wash-day evil" of laundering without Sunlight soap. Sunlight was a success in Britain, and within 15 years Lever was selling soap in Europe, Australia, South Africa, and the US.

From 1906 through 1915 Lever acquired several soap companies in Britain, Australia, and South Africa and dominated those markets. Needing vegetable oil to make soap, Lever established plantations and trading companies around the world. Lever's United Africa Company was Africa's largest enterprise in the 20 years following its formation in 1929. During WWI Lever began using its vegetable oil to make margarine.

Rival Dutch buttermakers Jurgens and Van den Berghs were pioneers in margarine production. In 1927 they created the Margarine Union, a cartel that owned the European market. The Margarine Union and Lever Brothers merged in 1930 but for tax reasons formed 2 separate entities: Unilever PLC in London and Unilever NV in Rotterdam.

Despite the Depression, WWII, and efforts of archrival Procter & Gamble, Unilever expanded, acquiring American companies Thomas J. Lipton (1937) and Pepsodent (1944). However, Unilever's domination of the US market ended with P&G's 1946 introduction

of the first synthetic detergent, Tide. Backed by massive advertising, Tide quickly became America's leading detergent in the first of many marketing battles lost by Unilever's Lever Brothers subsidiary to P&G in the US.

Outside America, Unilever was more successful. Its businesses benefited from the postwar boom in Europe, increasing acceptance of margarine, new detergent technologies, and increasing use of personal care products.

Although internal product development fueled some growth, acquisitions (at one time running at the rate of one per week) have played a major role in shaping Unilever. Major acquisitions included Birds Eye Foods of the UK (1957) and, in the US, Good Humor (1961), National Starch (1978), Lawry's Foods (1979), Ragú (1986), Chesebrough-Pond's (1987), Calvin Klein Cosmetics (1989), and Fabergé/Elizabeth Arden (1989). Unilever is still buying businesses at a rapid rate. In 1991 the company acquired 27 businesses, including a detergent company, Lever Polska, in Poland, an ice cream company in Hungary, and others in Latin America and Europe.

In 1992 Michael Angus stepped down as chairman of Unilever PLC. He was replaced by Michael Perry, previously VC.

In 1993 Unilever acquired the Isaly Klondike Co. and Popsicle Industries Ltd., both ice cream businesses, for $155 million.

Unilever was exploring an ice cream joint venture in the Philippines with Ayala Corp. in 1994. That same year Unilever announced that it would cut its global work force by 7,500 to save around $342 million a year.

NYSE symbols: UL (Unilever PLC [ADR]);
UN (Unilever NV)
Fiscal year ends: December 31

WHO

Chairman (PLC)/VC (NV): Sir Michael Perry, age 60
Chairman (NV)/VC (PLC): Morris Tabaksblat, age 56
VC (PLC) and Detergents Coordinator: Niall FitzGerald, age 48
Financial Director: Hans Eggerstedt, age 56
President and CEO, Unilever US: Richard A. Goldstein
VP HR, Unilever US: T. Keith Rowland
Auditors: Coopers & Lybrand

WHERE

HQ: Unilever PLC, PO Box 68, Unilever House, Blackfriars, London EC4P 4BQ, UK; Unilever NV, PO Box 760, Rotterdam, The Netherlands
UK Phone: +44-(01)71-822-5252
UK Fax: +44-(01)71-822-5951
Netherlands Phone: +31-10-217-4000
Netherlands Fax: +31-10-217-4798 (press office)
US HQ: Unilever United States, Inc., 390 Park Ave., New York, NY 10022-4698
US Phone: 212-888-1260
US Fax: 212-906-4411

	1993 Sales		1993 Operating Income	
	$ mil.	% of total	$ mil.	% of total
Europe	22,809	55	2,004	55
North America	8,550	20	641	18
Other countries	10,519	25	1,004	27
Total	**41,878**	**100**	**3,649**	**100**

WHAT

	1993 Sales		1993 Operating Income	
	$ mil.	% of total	$ mil.	% of total
Food products	21,569	52	1,785	49
Detergents	9,785	23	736	20
Personal products	5,976	14	630	17
Specialty chemicals	3,517	8	416	12
Other	1,031	3	82	2
Total	**41,878**	**100**	**3,649**	**100**

Major Brand Names

Cosmetics/Perfume
Calvin Klein
Elizabeth Arden
Fabergé

Foods
Birds Eye
Boursin
Country Crock
Flora
Good Humor
I Can't Believe It's Not Butter!
Lipton

Peperami
Popsicle
Promise
Ragú
Stork

Personal Products
Aim
Close-Up
Cutex
Pepsodent
Pond's
Q-tips

Rexona
Signal
Timotei
Vaseline

Soap/Laundry
all
Dove
Lever 2000
Lifebuoy
Lux
Shield
Sunlight
Surf

KEY COMPETITORS

Amway	Eskimo Pie	Mars
Associated Milk Producers	Estée Lauder	Nestlé
Avon	George Weston	Philip Morris
Ben & Jerry's	Grand Metropolitan	Procter & Gamble
Benckiser	Henkel	RJR Nabisco
Campbell Soup	S. C. Johnson	Sara Lee
Carter-Wallace	Koor	Shiseido
Clorox	L'Oréal	SmithKline Beecham
Colgate-Palmolive	LVMH	TLC Beatrice
Danone	MacAndrews & Forbes	
Dial		

HOW MUCH

Stock prices are for ADRs. ADR=4 shares (PLC)	9-Year Growth	1984	1985	1986	1987	1988	1989	1990	1991	1992	1993
Sales ($ mil.)	9.3%	18,760	25,368	30,948	30,980	34,434	34,735	43,877	43,303	37,408	41,878
Net income ($ mil.)	16.3%	748	982	1,459	1,510	1,687	1,703	1,774	2,154	1,955	2,912
Income as % of sales	—	4.0%	3.9%	4.7%	4.9%	4.9%	4.9%	4.0%	5.0%	5.2%	7.0%
Earnings per share ($)	14.7%	1.22	1.90	1.76	3.04	3.60	3.51	4.24	4.61	4.19	4.18
Stock price – high ($)[1]	—	11.09	16.09	26.41	47.50	38.00	47.75	54.75	67.00	75.25	73.25
Stock price – low ($)[1]	—	9.00	9.59	15.19	25.69	29.25	33.00	40.50	47.25	61.63	56.00
Stock price – close ($)[1]	24.1%	10.16	16.09	26.41	35.25	33.00	47.75	53.25	66.75	67.50	70.75
P/E – high	—	9	9	15	16	11	14	13	15	18	18
P/E – low	—	7	5	9	9	8	9	10	10	15	13
Dividends per share ($)[1]	22.0%	0.27	0.42	0.60	0.84	0.72	1.02	1.67	1.04	1.93	1.62
Book value per share ($)[1]	10.1%	9.77	12.16	13.01	7.74	11.66	10.32	13.00	32.45	34.18	23.17
Employees	(0.9%)	319,000	304,000	298,000	294,000	291,000	300,000	304,000	298,000	287,000	294,000

1993 Year-end:
Debt ratio: 35.0%
Return on equity: 27.9%
Cash (mil.): $1,735
Current ratio: 1.29
Long-term debt (mil.): $2,180
No. of shares (mil.): 203
Dividends
  Yield: 2.3%
  Payout: 38.5%
Market value (mil.): $14,356

Stock Price History[1]
High/Low 1984–93

[1] All share data for 1984–1990 are for Unilever PLC.

In a country said to have more banks than dentists, Union Bank of Switzerland (UBS) has been one of the Big 3 bank companies of Switzerland (Swiss Bank Corporation and CS Holdings are the other 2) for over 50 years. Although slower to internationalize its operations than the others, its domestic dominance positions it as Switzerland's largest bank. UBS offers a comprehensive range of services including commercial banking, trade finance, foreign exchange, and precious metals trading.

In 1993 the foreign offices of UBS accounted for nearly 1/3 of the company's income. By contrast, Switzerland continued to languish in a recession and a number of financial institutions found themselves struggling for survival. In a structural reorganization UBS merged 3 subsidiaries. Bank Orca was merged with Bank Aufina, which then took over the consumer loan assets of Bank Rohner in 1994. Bank Aufina now controls all of the consumer credit activities of UBS. The bank's strategy is to increase its market share in Switzerland by increasing its sales efforts.

However, the focus of the company's expansion is its foreign markets, especially the fast-growing economies of East Asia, according to chairman and CEO Nikolaus Senn.

Prominent businessmen in Winterthur, Switzerland, formed the Bank of Winterthur in 1862 with an initial stock equity of 5 million Swiss francs. The bank catered to trading interests, operated a warehouse, and financed railroads.

In 1912 the Bank of Winterthur merged with the Bank of Toggenburg, formed in 1863, to create Schweizerische Bankgesellschaft, the Union Bank of Switzerland.

The bank expanded its reach in Switzerland through acquisition of smaller banks and by adding branches. Its assets nosed close to the SF1 billion mark but plunged — along with those of the rest of the world — during the Great Depression. With the acquisition of Eidgenössische Bank of Zurich after the end of WWII, UBS assets at last climbed over the SF1 billion mark.

UBS continued to build its business through acquisitions in the 1950s. In 1962 it could point to 81 branch offices. It purchased Interhandel, a cash-rich Swiss financial concern (1967) and 4 savings banks (1968). Although UBS had opened a New York office for representation in 1946, its first full-fledged foreign branch was opened in London in 1967. In the 1970s it created securities underwriting subsidiaries abroad.

International financial markets became supercharged in the 1980s, and UBS, which had started slowly, resolved to catch up quickly. As London prepared for the Big Bang of financial deregulation in 1986, UBS purchased Phillips & Drew, a brokerage house. Other international efforts in the late 1980s included purchasing a German bank (Deutsche Länderbank, 1986), opening a Tokyo office for Phillips & Drew (1986), and creating an Australian merchant-bank subsidiary (UBS Australia Ltd., 1987).

Lack of sophisticated electronic accounting systems at Phillips & Drew sparked losses on top of a $79 million loss in the 1987 stock market crash. Between 1987 and 1989 UBS lost $194 million on Phillips & Drew, merged Phillips & Drew with UBS Securities in London, and set a 5-year goal of turning UBS Phillips & Drew into a leading European investment bank as well as a profitable securities broker.

As the market for lending for highly leveraged transactions collapsed in 1990, UBS's North American operations went looking for deals. The bank underwrote the $313 million purchase of Great Northern Nekoosa by Georgia-Pacific.

In 1991 UBS Phillips & Drew absorbed UBS's London trading office. The company also set up offices in Paris, Singapore, and Hong Kong and took over Chase Manhattan's money-management unit in New York.

In 1991 the EC and the EFTA agreed in principle to establish a European Economic Area, which would have included Switzerland. However, in 1992 Switzerland refused to join, disappointing UBS president Robert Studer, who had supported the agreement.

In 1993 the Phillips & Drew name was dropped by UBS's UK securities arm. In 1994 UBS narrowly survived a challenge by Swiss financier Martin Ebner (UBS's largest stockholder with 18% of the bank's stock) to take control of the financial institution.

Principal exchange: Zurich
Fiscal year ends: December 31

Chairman: Nikolaus Senn
President: Robert Studer
EVP Corporate and Institutional Banking: Hans Heckmann
EVP Corporate Finance, Primary Markets, and Merchant Banking: Pierre de Weck
SVP Human Resources: Benno Stotz
EVP North America and CEO, UBS Securities Inc.: Markus Rohrbasser
Auditors: ATAG Ernst & Young SA

WHERE

HQ: Bahnhofstrasse 45, 8021 Zurich, Switzerland
Phone: +41-1-234-1111
Fax: +41-1-234-3415 (Investor Relations)
US HQ: UBS Securities Inc., 299 Park Ave., New York, NY 10171-0026
US Phone: 212-821-4000
US Fax: 212-715-3285

UBS operates in 289 locations in Switzerland and in 37 cities around the world.

	1993 Assets	
	SF mil.	% of total
Switzerland/Liechtenstein	111,369	36
EC countries	92,187	29
US	62,390	20
Japan	11,123	4
Other Europe	5,190	2
Other countries	28,996	9
Total	**311,255**	**100**

WHAT

	1993 Assets	
	SF mil.	% of total
Cash & equivalents	6,156	2
Balances due from banks	65,343	21
Trading securities	50,014	16
Investment securities	12,340	4
Mortgage loans	60,239	20
Other loans	97,223	31
Other	19,940	6
Total	**311,255**	**100**

Selected Swiss Subsidiaries and Affiliates
Bank Aufina AG
BDL Banco di Lugano
Cantrade Private Bank Ltd. (95%)
HYPOSWISS (99.6%)
Intrag (98%)
PBZ Finanzgesellschaft AG, Zurich
Saudi-Swiss Bank (51%)

Major Foreign Subsidiaries and Affiliates
SBG Beteiligungs-GmbH
UBS Australia Holdings Ltd.
UBS (Canada)
UBS France Holding SA
UBS Holdings Inc. (US)
UBS Securities Ltd. (UK)
UBS (Trust and Banking) Ltd. (Japan)

KEY COMPETITORS

BankAmerica	Dai-Ichi Kangyo
Barclays	Deutsche Bank
Canadian Imperial	HSBC
Chemical Banking	Industrial Bank of Japan
Citicorp	NatWest
Crédit Lyonnais	Royal Bank of Canada
CS Holding	Swiss Bank

HOW MUCH

$=SF1.49 (Dec. 31, 1993)	Annual Growth	1984	1985	1986	1987	1988	1989	1990	1991	1992	1993
Assets (SF mil.)	10.1%	131,031	139,453	152,167	160,416	166,583	216,430	233,983	249,291	266,753	311,255
Net income (SF mil.)	16.3%	584	692	776	753	778	989	897	1,216	1,343	2,268
Income as % of assets	—	0.4%	0.5%	0.5%	0.5%	0.5%	0.5%	0.4%	0.5%	0.5%	0.7%
Earnings per share (SF)	12.8%	—	35	38	36	37	45	39	53	58	92
Stock price – high (SF)	—	730	1,050	1,214	1,224	698	836	836	760	868	1,394
Stock price – low (SF)	—	630	716	970	595	564	596	516	490	660	845
Stock price – close (SF)	7.3%	716	1,036	1,200	604	640	820	546	722	862	1,354
P/E – high	—	—	30	32	34	19	18	22	14	15	15
P/E – low	—	—	20	25	17	15	13	13	9	11	9
Dividends per share (SF)	3.7%	23.0	24.0	40.0	24.0	24.0	27.0	27.0	27.0	29.0	32.0
Book value per share (SF)	9.5%	374	393	422	463	430	742	740	768	798	847
Employees	5.1%	17,647	18,667	19,990	20,881	20,872	17,539	27,470	27,677	27,280	27,500

1993 Year-end:
Debt ratio: 92.2%
Return on equity: 11.2%
Equity as a % of assets: 7.0%
No. of shares (mil.): 26
Dividends
  Yield: 2.4%
  Payout: 34.9%
Market value (mil.): $23,227
Assets (mil.): $208,896
Sales (mil.): $14,042

**Stock Price History
High/Low 1984–93**

(Chart y-axis: 0 to 1,400)

Note: Unconsolidated data 1984–88

The only reason that Vendex's 1994 financial results showed such great improvement is that it has been selling off its assets. After being hammered by recession and expansion-induced high debt, Vendex, the Netherlands's largest retailer (with $5 billion in sales) began shuffling group assets by reconfiguring its holding company structure, selling noncore and core assets (divesting large portions of its insurance operations and reducing its share in the US's Barnes & Noble from 32% to 11%), and downsizing stores.

Besides its 1,500 supermarkets and department and specialty stores, Vendex also operates cleaning and maintenance services (including commercial catering services), temporary-help agencies, coupon and trading stamp redemption companies, and a corporate training operation.

Vendex has streamlined its distribution operations, redecorated many stores, opened 3 new Vroom & Dreesmann stores in 1993 (its first in years), and made significant progress in reducing its debt load. And although stagnant employment in Europe has depressed the temporary-help industry, the outlook for the field is good.

Vendex is closely held, with 41% owned by Vede and the rest owned by the Dreesmann family and other investors.

In 1974 Anton Dreesmann, a doctor of economics and law and professor at the University of Amsterdam, assumed the leadership of Vroom & Dreesmann, a Dutch department store company founded by his grandfather.

Wanting to diversify from department stores, in the late 1970s Dreesmann started diversifying into commercial banking, temporary-help services, catering operations, office-cleaning services, and other retail operations, including photography and optical shops, jewelry stores, and electronics shops.

As the Netherlands turned to the left in the late 1970s, Dreesmann began looking for opportunities overseas, particularly in the US, Brazil, and Japan. He established Vendamerica, a US subsidiary to monitor retailing events in the US, and in 1978 met with William Dillard, founder of Dillard's department stores. Dreesmann paid $24 million for a 25% interest in Dillard's and took a place on its board of directors. Hard up for cash, Vendex sold this entire block in 1991.

In 1980 the company established a mail-order division (whose operations the company terminated in 1994) and made a bid for 50% of the retailing operations of W. R. Grace, but the 2 companies were unable to come to terms. Also in 1980 Dreesmann bought 3% of UNY, a leading Japanese retailer (superstores and a variety of smaller stores). In 1985 the company incorporated as Vendex International (although the Dreesmann family retained full control).

In 1987 Vendex strengthened its US retailing presence by buying a 50% stake in B. Dalton (bookstores) and a 32% share of Barnes & Noble's College Book Stores, both in partnership with Barnes & Noble CEO Leonard Riggio. At the same time the company continued to expand its European holdings, buying everything from a Dutch travel agency to a Belgian furniture store chain.

Focused on expansion in the late 1980s, Vendex failed to recognize changing trends in retailing at home and profits began to fall, all at a time when Dreesmann was falling victim to recurring strokes. In 1988 Dreesmann suffered a brain hemorrhage and appointed Arie Van der Zwan (another economics professor) as his successor. Van der Zwan laid off 18% of the company's department store employees and upgraded the stores. Dreesmann, known to his employees as "Uncle Anton," could not tolerate the layoffs and returned to sack Van der Zwan. In 1990 Dreesmann launched his own reorganization despite his failing health and remained involved in company management in 1994.

In 1991 Vendex began withdrawing from Brazil, and Mr. Goodbuys (another US investment) went bankrupt. In 1992 its 50% stake in Software, Etc. (another Riggio company, now NeoStar after a merger with Babbages), fell to 32% when that company went public.

The company's other US holding, Barnes & Noble, went public in 1993. The IPO was a success but the high stock price reduced the amount of shares warranted to Vendex, thus diluting the company more than anticipated, to 32% of Barnes & Noble. Although Vendex threatened to sue Barnes & Noble, the siren call of cash was strong and in 1994 Vendex sold more Barnes & Noble shares.

Private company
Fiscal year ends: January 31

WHO

Chairman Supervisory Board: H. Langman, age 63
VC Supervisory Board: Anton C. R. Dreesmann, age 71
Chairman Board of Management: J. M. Hessels, age 52
CFO: W. C. J. Angenent, age 54
Head of Personnel: J. A. H. Lempers
President, Vendamerica, Inc.: Arnold Becker
Auditors: KPMG Klynveld

WHERE

HQ: PO Box 7997, 1008 AD Amsterdam; De Klencke 6, 1083 HH Amsterdam, The Netherlands
Phone: +31-20-5490500
Fax: +31-20-6461954
US HQ: Vendamerica, Inc., 104 Field Point Rd., Greenwich, CT 06830
US Phone: 203-629-4676
US Fax: 203-629-2273

Vendex operates 1,559 retail clothing, food, and home furnishings stores in Belgium, France, Germany, Luxembourg, the Netherlands, Spain, and Switzerland. It also operates maintenance, security, and temporary employment agencies in Belgium, France, Germany, and the Netherlands and owns minority interests in Barnes & Noble and NeoStar in the US.

	1994 Sales	
	Fl mil.	% of total
Netherlands	7,774	79
Other countries	2,051	21
Total	**9,825**	**100**

WHAT

	1994 Sales		1994 Operating Income	
	Fl mil.	% of total	Fl mil.	% of total
Food	3,974	41	100	34
Department stores	1,685	17	60	20
Specialty stores	1,509	15	80	27
Maintenance svcs.	1,212	12	41	14
Temp. agencies	1,103	11	13	4
Other	342	4	2	1
Total	**9,825**	**100**	**296**	**100**

Selected Subsidiaries

Food Stores
Basismarkt (discount supermarkets)
Dagmarkt (supermarkets)
Eda (discount supermarkets)
Edah (supermarkets)
Edi (supermarkets)
Konmar (hypermarkets)
Torro (supermarkets)

Women's Fashions
Claudia Sträter
Hunkemöller
Kien
Kreymborg

Department Stores
Vroom & Dreesmann

Other Specialty Stores
Best-sellers (showroom retailing)
Dixons (photography and electronics)

Kijkshop (showroom retailing)
Klick (photography and electronics)
Luigi Lucardi (jewelry)
Perry Sport (sporting goods)
Pet's Place (pet products)
Royal Gold (jewelry)
Siebel (jewelry)
Stoutenbeek Wooncentrum (furniture)
Vedelectric (electric products and appliances)

Services
Financial services
Insurance
Maintenance services
Temporary-help services

Other Interests
Barnes & Noble (US, 11%)
NeoStar (US, 17%)

KEY COMPETITORS

Adia Services
Aldi
Allkauf SB-Warenhaus
Alsacienne de Supermarchés
Benetton
Carrefour
De Boer Winkelbedrijven
Ito-Yokado

Kmart
Macintosh N.V.
Mann Group
Marks and Spencer
Nanz Group
Otto Versand
Société au Bon Marché
Tenglemann
Woolworth

HOW MUCH

$=Fl1.94 (Dec. 31, 1993)	Annual Growth	1985	1986	1987	1988	1989	1990	1991	1992	1993	1994
Sales (Fl mil.)	7.3%	7,945	8,749	9,706	9,890	10,185	10,243	10,728	10,502	10,408	9,825
Net income (Fl mil.)	1.0%	236	265	302	226	172	96	90	146	124	258
Income as % of sales	—	3.0%	3.0%	3.1%	2.3%	1.7%	0.9%	0.8%	1.4%	1.2%	2.6%
Employees	1.5%	—	71,200	76,900	84,600	86,000	87,100	89,100	87,100	83,000	80,200
1994 Year-end:											
Debt ratio: 51.7%											
Return on equity: 20.6%											
Cash (mil.): Fl91											
Current ratio: 1.27											
Long-term debt (mil.): Fl1,279											
Sales (mil.): $5,058											

Net Income (Fl mil.) 1985–94

VICKERS P.L.C.

Although internationally recognized as an aviation pioneer (maker of the first plane to fly the Atlantic and the Spitfire), Vickers makes precision engineering equipment for a range of industries. The 166-year-old company makes and sells automobiles, armored fighting vehicles, medical instruments, marine equipment, and superalloys and precision components for aerospace industries.

The company has a reputation for top-of-the-line products, and its premium brands include Rolls-Royce and Bentley motor cars, Riva powerboats, Cosworth high-efficiency automotive engines, Challenger tanks, Air-Shields intensive-care medical equipment, and KaMeWa water jets.

Despite the high-profile names, Vickers's dependence on niche markets has made the company vulnerable to economic downturns. Rolls-Royce auto sales collapsed in 1991 in a depressed luxury-car market, plunging the group into the red. The long-term decline of the defense industry also threatens Vickers's military equipment sales. However, in the short term Vickers has bucked the downward trend in the defense industry by securing 2 big orders for Challenger 2 tanks, which will keep production going until 1996.

In 1828 Naylor, Hutchinson, Vickers & Company was established as a steel industry in the heart of England's steel production area in Sheffield. The company expanded and in 1836 opened up a sales office in New York. Vickers Sons & Company was incorporated in 1867, and Vickers Sons and Maxim Ltd. was set up in 1897.

Vickers provided arms and aircraft for the British forces during WWI and steadily gained a reputation as "armorer to the nation." It invented the first tank and the first effective machine gun. In 1919 John Alcock and Arthur Brown, flying a Vickers Vimy biplane bomber powered by Rolls-Royce engines, became the first men to fly the Atlantic. Vickers's engineering skills and innovation were responsible for several other notable aviation achievements in the next 2 decades, including the launch of the RICO airship in 1929 and the Spitfire in 1936.

In WWII Vickers became a major armaments supplier for air, sea, and land forces. Following the war, the Labour government nationalized Vickers's steel business in 1946 (later denationalized in 1954, then renationalized again in 1967). The company's attempts at diversification after the war into areas such as tractors, sewing machines, and copiers were largely unsuccessful.

In 1977 the government nationalized Vickers's shipbuilding and aerospace businesses, in essence taking away from Vickers the source of half of the company's sales and 2/3 of its profits.

In 1980 the struggling company acquired its long-time collaborator, Rolls-Royce Motors. Rolls-Royce itself had been in financial trouble and was still reeling from the loss of one of its major tank engine customers, the Shah of Iran.

David Plastow, former head of Rolls-Royce, became the CEO of the combined companies, and set about a major restructuring. Both companies were prestigious and had large market shares in the UK, but neither was a world player. Plastow launched a strategy aimed at making Vickers globally competitive by dropping noncore assets and businesses in declining markets. By 1985 Vickers had divested some 20 of its 50 subsidiaries, including its diesel division (to Massey-Ferguson) and its Australian heavy engineering concerns. During this period Vickers also began to acquire niche businesses in growth areas such as KaMeWa (1986), the world's #1 maker of pitch propellers; the Royal Ordnance tank factory at Leeds (1987) in the UK, a move which made Vickers the sole supplier of tanks in the country; and a number of specialized medical instrument companies.

In 1988 Vickers sold its furniture business, and in 1989 it sold its printing plate business, Howson-Algraphy, for $399 million.

Sir Colin Chandler was appointed managing director in 1990 (and promoted to CEO in 1992). In 1991 the British government signed a contract with Vickers for 127 Challenger 2 tanks. Also in 1991 Rolls-Royce launched the Bentley Continental R automobile to international acclaim. Vickers established a new division, Propulsion Technology, in 1993. In 1994 the British government ordered an additional 259 Challenger 2 tanks from the company. Vickers also signed a deal with BMW to jointly develop a line of luxury cars.

WHO

Chairman: Sir Robert Lloyd, age 65
CEO: Sir Colin Chandler, age 54
Chairman and CEO, Vickers Defence Systems: Gerald Boxall, age 57
CEO, Rolls-Royce Motor Cars: Chris J. Woodwark, age 47
Managing Director Finance and Planning: Roger Head, age 47
VP and Treasurer, Vickers America Holdings, Inc. (US): Dennis J. DeAngelis
Auditors: KPMG Peat Marwick

WHERE

HQ: Vickers House, Millbank Tower, Millbank, London SW1P 4RA, UK
UK Phone: +44-(01)71-828-7777
UK Fax: +44-(01)71-828-6585
US HQ: Vickers America Holdings, Inc., PO Box 387,120 Chubb Ave., Lyndhurst, NJ 07071
US Phone: 201-460-8854
US Fax: 201-460-7643

	1993 Sales	
	£ mil.	% of total
UK	241	35
Other Europe	137	20
North America	156	23
Asia	78	11
Africa	62	9
Other countries	16	2
Total	**690**	**100**

WHAT

	1993 Sales	
	£ mil.	% of total
Automotive	239	35
Defence	145	21
Propulsion Technology	136	20
Medical Equipment	130	19
Other	40	5
Total	**690**	**100**

Major Divisions and Operating Companies

Automotive
Cosworth Engineering
Rolls-Royce Motor Cars

Defence
Vickers Defence Systems

Propulsion Technology
Certified Alloy Products
Michell Bearings
Ross & Catherall
Stone Vickers
Trucast

Vickers Aerospace Components
Vickers Airmotive
Vickers Precision Machining

Medical Equipment
Air-Shields
Medelec
S & W Medico Teknik A/S
TECA Corp

KEY COMPETITORS

Acuson
Analogic
Becton, Dickinson
British Aerospace
Daimler-Benz
FMC
Ford
General Dynamics
General Motors
Lagardère Groupe
Olin
Porsche
Saab-Scania
TRW

HOW MUCH

£=$1.48 (Dec 31,1993)	Annual Growth	1984	1985	1986	1987	1988	1989	1990	1991	1992	1993
Sales (£ mil.)	1.5%	—	611	692	788	776	696	778	652	719	690
Net income (£ mil.)[1]	(8.0%)	—	42	31	—	—	179	63	(12)	(33)	26
Income as % of sales	—	—	6.9%	4.5%	—	—	25.8%	8.1%	—	—	3.7%
Earnings per share (p)	(12.8%)	—	18.2	20.4	21.8	24.1	29.1	33.2	—	—	8.0
Stock price – high (p)	—	109	171	270	244	190	258	246	245	188	176
Stock price – low (p)	—	63	106	148	123	144	157	172	146	60	96
Stock price – close (p)	5.6%	108	149	200	156	160	211	192	155	100	176
P/E – high	—	—	9	13	11	8	9	7	—	—	22
P/E – low	—	—	6	7	6	6	5	5	—	—	12
Dividends per share (p)	(5.5%)	5.0	6.2	7.5	8.4	9.4	11.1	12.4	7.5	1.9	3.0
Book value per share (p)	(3.6%)	—	—	94.9	—	—	—	—	85.0	126.6	85.0
Employees	(8.3%)	—	—	15,871	—	15,541	12,238	12,613	12,011	10,422	9,406

1993 Year-end:
Debt ratio: 25.5%
Return on equity: 8.4%
Cash (mil.): £115
Long-term debt (mil.): £34
No. of shares (mil.): 329
Dividends
  Yield: 1.7%
  Payout: 37.5%
Market value (mil.): $856
Sales (mil.): $1,021

**Stock Price History
High/Low 1984–93**

(Stock price history chart, values 0–300)

[1] 1989–1992 restated for accounting change.

VIRGIN GROUP PLC

OVERVIEW

London-based Virgin Group, founded by flamboyant entrepreneur Richard Branson, operates Virgin Atlantic Airways (VA), Virgin Retail Group, and Virgin Travel Group. It holds a 10% stake in computer game maker Virgin Interactive Entertainment (VIE).

VA, Britain's #2 airline, spent the last 2 years pursuing top dog British Airways for corporate "dirty tricks." In 1993 VA won a $935,000 libel judgment against its rival, but Branson ended negotiations over commercial damages to pursue the matter in court.

In 1993 VA doubled its fleet to 16 planes and added routes to San Francisco and Hong Kong. The next year it began franchising airline routes within Europe — the first time franchising had been tried in the airline industry. A deal that would allow Delta to book passengers into Heathrow on VA flights has been blocked because of a US-UK landing rights dispute.

Virgin Communications launched 1215 AM, Britain's first national commercial rock radio station in 1993; it won an FM franchise the next year. Also in 1994 Virgin Television opened its first Latin American facility in Mexico City.

Among Branson's most recent business surprises are joint ventures to market Virgin Cola, with Canadian beverage maker Cott; Virgin Vodka, with British whiskey distiller William Grant & Sons; and Virgin computers made by ICL, the UK's #2 computer maker.

Infamous as a prankster, Branson has flown the Pacific by hot-air balloon, water-skied while being towed by a blimp, and given an annual address in a rabbit suit. His fortune is the 4th largest in the UK.

WHEN

At 16 prankster Richard Branson dropped out of the prestigious Stowe School (where the headmaster told him he would end up rich or in jail) to start *Student,* a youth magazine. Despite his lack of publishing experience and capital, Branson lured such contributors as Jean-Paul Sartre and Alice Walker.

To keep his magazine above water, in 1970 Branson began a mail-order record business. A postal strike prompted Branson to open a record store in London, named "Virgin" because of his lack of experience in business and other things. He dropped *Student* and opened a recording studio in 1972. In 1973 he started the Virgin record label, which would record the Sex Pistols and Phil Collins.

Virgin Vision was formed in 1983 to distribute film and video products. Virgin Group sales reached £50 million that year. In 1984 Branson launched Virgin Atlantic Airways with only one plane and a London–New York route. VA offered 2 classes: upper class and an economy class Branson originally wanted to call "riff-raff class." Virgin Holidays, a tour operator, was formed in 1985, complementing the company's airline operations. The same year VA won a license to fly to Miami.

The next year Branson took the company public, selling about 35% of its stock. In 1987 Virgin leased another airplane and set up Virgin Records America; a subsidiary in Japan was also established. The company bought W. H. Allen, a publishing house, and 45% of Mastertronics Group, which then owned the UK distribution rights for Sega video games.

In 1988 Virgin opened 3 megastores outside of England and established Virgin Broadcasting and Olympic Recording Studios. VA became the UK's #2 long-haul airline (after BA) and began flying to LA and Tokyo, having acquired its 3rd and 4th planes. Also, Virgin Communications purchased a stake in Europe's Super Channel.

Branson bought back his company in 1988; the public had surprised analysts and never embraced the company's stock. Branson embarked on a selling spree, disposing of Virgin Vision, 25% of its Music Group, and 10% of Virgin Travel Holdings (all in 1989); 20% of Virgin Retail Europe (1990); and Mastertronics (1991).

In 1990 Virgin launched its 2nd record company, in New York, and linked up with Marui to establish megastores in Japan. In 1991 Virgin Publishing was formed, VA expanded service to Japan, and a joint venture with Sega to develop video games was begun.

Thorn EMI bought Virgin Music for almost $1 billion in 1992; per contract Branson was named president for life. That year Virgin Retail and Blockbuster Entertainment announced a joint venture to establish Virgin Megastores (retail music and entertainment) in Australia, Europe, and the US. In 1994 Blockbuster said it would open 50 new Virgin Megastores in the US by 1997.

Private company
Fiscal year end:
Virgin Atlantic Airways, October 31
Voyager Investments, October 31
Virgin Retail Group, October 31

Chairman: Richard Branson, age 44
Managing Director, Virgin Retail Group:
Simon Burke
Commercial Director: Paul Griffiths
EVP, Virgin Atlantic North America: David Tait
Personnel Manager, Virgin Group: Lily Lu

WHERE

HQ: 120 Campden Hill Rd., London W8 7AR, UK
Phone: +44-(01)71-229-1282
Fax: +44-(01)71-727-8200
US HQ: Virgin Atlantic, 96 Morton St.,
New York, NY 10014
US Phone: 212-206-6612
US Fax: 212-627-1494
Reservations: 1-800-862-8621

The Virgin Group's principal components include
an airline, package tours, hotels, retail
entertainment stores, consumer product
development and distribution, and video game
development and distribution.

	1993 Stores
Virgin Retail Goup	**No.**
UK & Ireland	24
Other Europe & Australia	19
Japan	8
US	2
Total	**53**

WHAT

	1994 Estimated Sales
	% of total
Virgin Retail Group	37
Virgin Travel Group	29
Virgin Communications	4
Other	30
Total	**100**

Selected Subsidiaries and Affiliates

Virgin Communications
  Virgin Publishing (book publishing)
  Virgin Radio (national radio franchise, UK)
  Virgin Television (post-production services)
Virgin Hotels Group
Virgin Retail Group (25%, with Blockbuster)
  Virgin Megastores (entertainment retail stores in
    Australia, Europe, Japan, and the US)
  Virgin Trading Company (consumer products,
    including mineral water, cola, computers,
    and vodka)
Virgin Travel Investments
  Virgin Atlantic Airways
Voyager Investments

KEY COMPETITORS

7th Level	Marriott Intl.
Accor	Mattel
Air France	MTS
All Nippon Airways	Musicland
AMR	NEC
Bertelsmann	Nintendo
British Airways	Northwest Airlines
Brøderbund	PepsiCo
Cadbury Schweppes	Rank
Carlson	Ritz-Carlton
Coca-Cola	SAS
Continental Airlines	Sierra On-Line
Cyan	Sony
Electronic Arts	Tandy
Hyatt	Thomson
Id Software	Time Warner
IRI	Tower Air
J Sainsbury	UAL
JAL	USAir
KLM	Voyager
Lagardère	Walt Disney
Lufthansa	

HOW MUCH

$=£1.57 (Dec. 31, 1994)	Annual Growth	1985	1986	1987	1988	1989	1990	1991	1992	1993	1994
Sales (£ mil.)	30.4%	138	240	279	475	625	780	1,063	1,000	1,200	1,500
Virgin Atlantic fleet size	37.0%	1	2	2	4	6	6	8	8	16	17
Employees	6.5%	—	—	—	—	—	—	7,450	—	—	9,000

1994 Year-end:
Sales (mil.): $2,220

Sales (£ mil.)
1985–94

NV VERENIGD BEZIT VNU

OVERVIEW

One of the largest publishers in Europe, VNU is the Netherlands's leading publisher of regional newspapers and mass-circulation women's magazines. Verenigd Bezit VNU acts as a holding company for VNU's 2 operating companies, VNU Verenigd Nederlandse Uitgeversbedrijven, which handles Dutch activities, and VNU International.

The company publishes more than 100 European consumer magazines, as well as newspapers, educational publications, and business and professional magazines. VNU also owns stakes in 3 television stations in the Netherlands and Belgium.

The company sold its printing operations in 1993 to concentrate on its publishing and television businesses. VNU plans to expand its consumer information business in Europe and is also working to build its business information operations. As part of that strategy, and to build its presence in the US, VNU acquired BPI Communications, publisher of *Billboard* and the *Hollywood Reporter*, for $220 million in 1994.

WHEN

VNU (United Dutch Publishing Companies) was formed through the 1964 merger of 2 of the Netherlands's largest mass-market consumer publishing companies, Cebema, based in 's-Hertogenbosch, and De Spaarnestad, headquartered in Haarlem. The new company added to its empire through a series of acquisitions during the late 1960s.

In 1967 it bought regional newspaper publisher Het Nieuwsblad van het Zuiden and book publisher Het Spectrum. Founded as a Roman Catholic printing house, Het Spectrum shifted its emphasis to nonreligious books following its acquisition. Spectrum began to publish Dutch translations of authors such as J. R. R. Tolkien, Somerset Maugham, Dorothy Sayers, and Ellery Queen. In 1968 VNU acquired magazine publisher NRM and Smeets, one of the largest offset printers in Europe.

The company's buying spree pumped up its sales and profits but also created an unwieldy organization. During the early 1970s VNU hired US management consultant McKinsey and Company to help it streamline its operations.

VNU continued to add more companies to the fold, including trade journal publisher Intermediair (1973), Belgian bookbinder Reliure Industrielle de Barchon (1974), and trade journal publisher Diligentia (1975). In the late 1970s the company began a move into professional publishing, and in 1980 VNU acquired the publishing portions of Computing Publications and of Business and Career Publications.

During the 1980s VNU began to focus on expanding its US business, primarily by building up its business information operations. In 1985 it acquired Disclosure, a provider of financial information on publicly owned companies. Through Disclosure, VNU focused on building its business information operations in the US. In 1986 VNU acquired New Jersey–based Hayden Publishing. The acquisition of Hayden, whose titles included computer and electronics magazines *Electronic Design*, *Computer Decisions*, and *Personal Computing,* proved to be a major debacle. Hayden's publications were hit by a decline in the computer business during the late 1980s, and the publishers also suffered through major turnovers in middle management. In 1989 VNU began selling off Hayden's assets.

While its prospects were not particularly rosy in the US, VNU continued to expand its operations elsewhere. Its 1988 acquisition of Audet made it the #1 publisher of regional newspapers in the Netherlands. In 1989 the company made its first foray into television when it bought an 11% stake in VTM, a new commercial Belgian TV station. That same year it acquired a 19% interest in Dutch TV station RTL 4.

In 1990 the company entered the Eastern European market, launching *Moscow Magazine*. In 1992 VNU increased its stake in RTL 4 to 38%. That same year the company acquired 50% of Spectra Marketing Systems (US) and entered a joint venture with Arbitron (US).

In 1993, as part of a plan to focus on its publishing operations, VNU sold its printing operations to Koninklijke De Boer Boekhoven, creating a new company, Roto Smeets De Boer, in which VNU holds a 30% interest.

In 1994 VNU acquired I/B/E/S (Institutional Brokers Estimate System), a financial information provider, from Citicorp.

OTC symbol: VNUNY (ADR)
Fiscal year ends: December 31

Chairman: J. L. Brentjens
Management and Organization Development:
K. de Best
Financial and Economic Affairs:
J. J. van der Rest
Secretary and General Affairs: L. C. A. M.
Schölvinck
CEO of VNU, USA: R. F. van den Bergh
VP and CFO, VNU, USA: Rosalee Lovett
Auditors: Moret Ernst & Young

WHERE

HQ: Ceylonpoort 5-25, 2037 AA Haarlem,
The Netherlands
Phone: +31-023-304-304
Fax: +31-023-304-754
US HQ: VNU, USA, Inc., 11 W. 42nd St.,
New York, NY 10036-8088
US Phone: 212-789-3680
US Fax: 212-789-3650

VNU has operations in Belgium, the Czech
Republic, France, Hungary, Italy, the
Netherlands, Spain, the UK, and the US.

	1993 Sales
	% of total
The Netherlands	64
Belgium	13
US	13
UK	6
Other countries	4
Total	**100**

WHAT

	1993 Sales	
	Fl mil.	% of total
Consumer magazines	1,146	50
Newspapers	561	24
Business information services	296	13
Business press	239	10
Educational publishing	68	3
Total	**2,310**	**100**

Consumer Magazines	**Business Press**
General interest	Career planning
Life style	Computer information
Puzzles	Electronics
Radio and television	Engineering
Self-made fashion	Environment
Special interest	Finance
Women's	Management
Youth	Seminars
	Textile industry
Newspapers	
Cable television newspapers	**Educational Publishing**
Free door-to-door	Classroom aids
Regional	Educational publications
	Magazines
Business Information	Software and micro
Services	computers
Chemical substance	
information	**Commercial Television**
Financial information	RTL 4/RTL 5 (38%,
Marketing and media	Luxembourg)
information	VTM (44%, Belgium)

KEY COMPETITORS

Advance	Knight-Ridder	Reader's Digest
Publications	Lagardère	Reed Elsevier
Bertelsmann	Market Guide	Reuters
CMP Publications	Matsushita	Thomson Corp.
Dow Jones	McGraw-Hill	Time Warner
Dun & Bradstreet	Morningstar	Wolters Kluwer
International Data	News Corp.	Viacom
Group	Pearson	Ziff-Davis

HOW MUCH

$=Fl1.79 (Dec. 31, 1993)	9-Year Growth	1984	1985	1986	1987	1988	1989	1990	1991	1992	1993
Sales (Fl mil.)	4.7%	1,524	1,591	1,735	1,972	2,504	2,612	2,718	2,735	2,737	2,310
Net income (Fl mil.)	11.9%	53	66	75	92	134	158	146	117	48	145
Income as % of sales	—	3.5%	4.1%	4.3%	4.7%	5.3%	6.0%	5.4%	4.3%	1.8%	6.3%
Earnings per share (Fl)	6.0%	5.59	6.04	6.41	7.88	9.41	11.11	10.29	8.22	3.11	9.43
Stock price – high (Fl)	—	51.13	78.75	89.08	97.50	97.00	115.00	113.50	99.70	92.00	177.00
Stock price – low (Fl)	—	34.25	49.05	67.63	45.30	53.50	87.00	73.70	68.20	68.70	87.70
Stock price – close (Fl)	14.6%	50.95	81.75	87.50	56.00	94.80	108.70	82.30	80.00	69.50	173.75
P/E – high	—	9	13	14	12	10	10	11	12	30	19
P/E – low	—	6	8	11	6	6	8	7	8	22	9
Dividends per share (Fl)	7.0%	1.95	2.13	2.31	2.75	3.20	3.60	3.60	3.60	3.60	3.60
Book value per share (Fl)	5.6%	24.24	28.83	21.28	25.23	25.75	45.81	47.83	52.25	41.98	39.44
Employees	0.4%	8,055	7,930	8,713	9,479	11,979	11,864	11,594	11,448	10,971	8,367

1993 Year-end:
Debt ratio: 35.4%
Return on equity: 23.1%
Cash (mil.): Fl149
Long-term debt (mil.): Fl303
No. of shares (mil.): 15
Dividends
  Yield: 2.1%
  Payout: 38.2%
Market value (mil.): $1,381
Sales (mil.): $1,191

Stock Price History
High/Low 1984–93

VOLKSWAGEN AG

OVERVIEW

Volkswagen — the #1 automaker in Europe — is radically remaking itself in an effort to regain profitability in the wake of its record $1.1 billion loss in 1993. Stung by the 15% auto sales decline in Europe in 1993 and huge losses at SEAT (Sociedad Española de Automóviles de Turismo), its Spanish subsidiary, Volkswagen is now being pushed hard by a new executive team to boost its productivity, cutting, for example, the time it takes to make a Golf from 30 hours to 8 hours by 1997.

Volkswagen, which makes about 3.3 million passenger cars annually, operates 23 plants, 10 of which are outside Europe. Its auto divisions include Audi along with SEAT and Volkswagen AG. The firm also has an interest in the Czech Republic's SKODA and offers consumer financing.

As part of the restructuring, in 1993 Ferdinand Piëch became chairman of the Board of Management, and the company reached an agreement with union workers to reduce the work week to 4 days.

WHEN

Since the early 1920s automotive engineer Ferdinand Porsche, whose son founded the Porsche car company, had wanted to make a small car for the masses. He found no financial backers for his idea until he met Adolf Hitler in 1934. Hitler formed the Gesellschaft zur Vorbereitung des Volkswagens (Company for the Development of People's Cars) in 1937 and built a factory and worker housing in Wolfsburg, Germany.

A German government agency instituted a savings plan in which workers regularly set aside small sums with the expectation of receiving a car in 3 years. During WWII, however, the plant produced military vehicles, and no cars were ever delivered.

Following WWII, British occupation forces oversaw the reconstruction of the bomb-damaged plant and initial production of the odd-looking "people's car" (1945). The British appointed Heinz Nordhoff, a tough but inspirational leader, to manage Volkswagen (1948) and turned the company over to the German government (1949).

In the 1950s Volkswagen launched the Microbus and built plants internationally. Although US sales began slowly, by the end of the decade acceptance of the unpretentious car had increased. Advertising carved VW's niche in the US, coining the name "Beetle" and featuring humorous slogans such as "ugly is only skin deep" and "think small."

In 1960 Volkswagen stock was sold to the German public. A year later the company settled with the 87,000 participants in Hitler's savings plan. Volkswagen purchased Auto Union (Audi) in 1966 from Daimler-Benz. In the 1960s the Beetle became a counterculture symbol, and US sales took off. By the time of Nordhoff's death in 1968, the VW Beetle had become the world's #1 selling car.

In the 1970s the outdated Beetle was discontinued in every country except Mexico. Volkswagen lost heavily during the model-changeover period, although its Brazilian unit was highly profitable. New models sold well in the late 1970s. Volkswagen opened America's first foreign-owned auto plant in Pennsylvania in 1978, but closed it in 1988.

Volkswagen agreed to several international deals in the 1980s, including a car venture in China (1984), the purchase of 75% of SEAT (Spain, 1986), and the merger of its suddenly faltering Brazilian unit with Ford's ailing Argentinian operations to form Autolatina (1987). The 2 automakers also agreed to jointly produce minivans in Portugal. In 1990 Volkswagen agreed to build China's largest auto plant and committed over $6 billion to buy and modernize SKODA. The next year Toyota agreed to begin selling Volkswagens and Audis in Japan in 1992.

In 1993 the company acquired V.A.G (UK), giving it control over all Volkswagen distribution activities in the UK. During that same year Clive Warrilow was named CEO of Volkswagen's sales operations in the US, where the company has about a 1% market share. José Ignacio López, the top purchasing executive at General Motors, joined the Volkswagen team in 1993 along with 7 former GM coworkers, touching off allegations that the group left with GM trade secrets. In late 1994 the company announced it would introduce an updated version of its classic Beetle in 1998. Built in Mexico, the car is geared for entry level US carbuyers. Also in 1994 CFO Werner Schmidt resigned over the large l993 loss the company incurred at SEAT.

OTC symbol: VLKAY (ADR)
Fiscal year ends: December 31

Chairman of the Board of Management:
Ferdinand Piëch, age 56
Member of the Board of Management,
Production Optimization and Procurement:
José Ignacio López de Arriortúa, age 53
CFO: Rutbert Reisch
Member of the Board of Management, Research
and Development: Ulricht Seiffert, age 52
Member of the Board of Management for Human
Resources: Peter Hartz, age 52
President and CEO, Volkswagen of America:
Clive B. Warrilow
Auditors: C & L Treuarbeit

HQ: D-38436 Wolfsburg, Germany
Phone: +49-53-61-90
Fax: +49-53-61-92-82-82
US HQ: Volkswagen of America, Inc., 3800
Hamlin Rd,, Auburn Hills, MI 48326
US Phone: 818-340-5000
US Fax: 818-340-5010

	1993 Sales	
	DM mil.	% of total
Germany	34,326	45
Latin America	9,051	12
Asia/Oceania	3,556	4
North America	3,469	4
Africa	1,315	2
Other Europe	24,869	33
Total	**76,586**	**100**

	1993 Sales
	% of total
Volkswagen	51
Audi	14
SEAT	9
Financial services	8
South America/Africa	8
North America	7
SKODA	3
Total	**100**

Selected Makes and Models

Audi	Volkswagen
80	Corrado
100	Golf
Convertible	Jetta
Coupé/quattro	Passat
V8	

Significant Manufacturing Subsidiaries
AUDI AG (98.99%, Germany)
AUTOGERMA SpA (Italy)
Autolatina Argentina SA (51%)
Autolatina Brasil SA (42.58%)
Shanghai-Volkswagen Automotive Co., Ltd. (50%,
China)
SKODA, automobilová as (31%, Czech Republic)
Sociedad Española de Automóviles de Turismo, SA
(SEAT, 99.99%, Spain)
V.A.G France SA
Volkswagen de México, SA de CV

BMW	Honda	Peugeot
Chrysler	Hyundai	Renault
Daewoo	Isuzu	Saab-Scania
Daimler-Benz	Kia Motors	Suzuki
Fiat	Mazda	Toyota
Ford	Mitsubishi	Volvo
General Motors	Nissan	

$=DM1.74 (Dec. 31, 1993)	9-Year Growth	1984	1985	1986[1]	1987	1988	1989	1990	1991	1992	1993
Sales (DM mil.)	5.9%	45,671	52,502	52,794	54,635	59,221	65,352	68,061	76,315	85,403	76,586
Net income (DM mil.)	—	245	665	621	598	738	984	1,054	1,103	78	(2,038)
Income as % of sales	—	0.5%	1.3%	1.2%	1.1%	1.2%	1.5%	1.5%	1.4%	0.1%	—
Earnings per share (DM)	—	10	28	21	20	25	33	33	34	2	(61)
Stock price – high (DM)	—	232	498	684	430	348	546	643	416	413	449
Stock price – low (DM)	—	163	189	424	218	202	308	332	283	234	241
Stock price – close (DM)	8.9%	205	498	427	225	348	540	337	303	243	440
P/E – high	—	23	18	33	22	14	17	19	12	—	—
P/E – low	—	16	7	20	11	8	9	10	8	—	—
Dividends per share (DM)	—	0	5	10	10	10	10	11	11	2	2
Book value per share (DM)	—	—	—	—	—	—	—	—	—	—	—
Employees	1.8%	238,353	259,047	281,718	267,125	258,528	257,561	267,997	267,009	259,696	280,137

1993 Year-end:
Debt ratio: 69.5%
Return on equity: —
Cash (mil.): DM12,276
Long-term debt (mil.): DM10,477
No. of shares (mil.): 33
Dividends
Yield: 0.5%
Payout: —
Market value (mil.): $8,446
Sales (mil.): $44,015

Stock Price History
High/Low 1984–93

[1] Accounting change

AB VOLVO

After driving indecisively in circles for much of the early 1990s, in 1993 Volvo finally asked for directions and found its way back to the main road. After a long detour into diversification, in 1994 the company rededicated itself to its core businesses: cars, trucks, buses, and commercial and aviation engines.

The catalyst for this move was a plan to merge with French automaker Renault that shocked many managers and enraged stockholders because of Renault's poor performance and government ownership. Within 3 months of the September announcement, the plan had been shot down; its architect, chairman Pehr Gyllenhammar, and other members of the board had resigned; and Volvo had announced its plans to refocus on its core businesses and divest by 1996 all the other businesses it had accumulated during Gyllenhammar's tenure.

After 2 years of losses, the gains realized from the first divestitures, which had begun in January 1994, vastly improved Volvo's financial position.

Swedish ball-bearing manufacturer SKF formed Volvo as a subsidiary in 1915. Volvo began assembling cars (1926), trucks (1928), and bus chassis (1932) in Göteborg, Sweden. Sweden's frigid winters made the company particularly attentive to engineering and safety, which remains a Volvo hallmark. The 1931 purchase of an engine maker marked Volvo's move from assembly into manufacturing. In 1935 Volvo became an independent company led by Assar Gabrielsson, a businessman, and Gustaf Larson, who attended to technical matters.

In the 1940s, while war raged through Europe, Sweden's neutrality allowed Volvo to continue growing, moving into component manufacture and tractor production (and the lack of imports from a world at war allowed it to dominate its home market). By 1949 vehicle output exceeded 100,000 units, 80% of which were sold in Sweden.

Volvo's acquisition of Bolinder-Munktell (farm machinery, diesel engines; Sweden; 1950) enhanced the company's position in the Swedish tractor market. During the 1950s Volvo introduced turbocharged diesel truck engines and windshield defrosters and washers. By 1956 car production had outstripped truck and bus output. European and North American sales helped push Volvo exports to nearly 50% of production in 1959.

Exports soared in the 1960s as Volvo's reputation for durability spread. Volvo began building production facilities internationally, the first in Belgium (1962).

In 1971, 36-year-old Pehr Gyllenhammar became Volvo's CEO. Aware that Volvo was too small to compete for long in its global markets, Gyllenhammar diversified and enlarged the company's business.

In 1981 Volvo bought Beijerinvest (energy, industrial products, food, finance, trading; Sweden) and White Motors' truck division (US) and in 1986 formed a North American truck venture with General Motors. A 1984 joint venture with Clark Equipment (US) created the world's 3rd largest construction equipment company. Volvo acquired Leyland Bus (UK) in 1988. During the 1980s Volvo steadily increased its holdings in Pharmacia (drugs, biotechnology; Sweden), Custos (investments, Sweden), and Park Ridge, among others. In 1990 the company consolidated its food and drug units with state-controlled holding company Procordia.

Also in 1990 Volvo was embarrassed by a faked ad in which a truck was shown running over a series of cars, crushing all but a Volvo.

In the largest industrial undertaking in Swedish history, Volvo spent over $2 billion to modernize its plants and develop the 800 series of performance-oriented family sedans, introduced in 1991.

In the same year Mitsubishi Motors joined the Dutch government and Volvo in NedCar, with each owning 1/3 of a joint venture to make and sell cars in the Netherlands. Volvo also began an alliance with Renault in anticipation of the unification of the EC economies, of which it was not a member. But by 1993 Sweden was tilting toward EC membership (its people voted for membership in late 1994) and a union with Renault was seen as a pointless and expensive loss of autonomy.

In 1993, with the breakup of Procordia, Volvo became the owner of 27% of Pharmacia and 74% of Branded Consumer Products (BCP). In order to sell its BCP assets (food, beverages, and matches), it must increase its holdings to 100%.

Nasdaq symbol: VOLVY (ADR)
Fiscal year ends: December 31

Chairman: Bert-Olof Svanholm, age 59
President and CEO: Sören Gyll, age 53
EVP: Sten Langenius, age 59
EVP: Lennart Jeansson, age 53
SVP and General Counsel: Fred Bodin, age 47
SVP and CFO: Jan Engström, age 43
President, Volvo North America: Albert R. Dowden
CFO, Volvo North America: Dave Korpics
VP Human Resources, Volvo North America: Keld Alstrup
Auditors: KPMG Bohlins AB; Coopers & Lybrand AB

WHERE

HQ: S-405 08 Göteborg, Sweden
Phone: +46-31-59-00-00
Fax: +46-31-54-79-59 (Volvo Car Corp.)
US HQ: Volvo North America Corporation, 535 Madison Ave., New York, NY 10022
US Phone: 212-754-3300
US Fax: 212-418-7435

Volvo markets and services its vehicles, engines, and aerospace products worldwide.

	1993 Sales	
	$ mil.	% of total
Europe, excluding Sweden	5,593	42
North America	3,805	28
Sweden	1,719	13
Other countries	2,222	17
Total	**13,339**	**100**

WHAT

	1993 Sales		1993 Operating Income	
	$ mil.	% of total	$ mil.	% of total
Car group	6,979	48	60	—
Truck group	4,733	32	92	—
Consumer products	475	3	54	—
Aerospace	435	3	15	—
Engines	358	2	14	—
Other operations	1,667	12	(48)	—
Adjustments	(1,309)	—	0	—
Total	**13,339**	**100**	**186**	**—**

	1993 Production
	No. of vehicles
Full-sized cars	210,500
Mid-sized cars	80,200
Trucks	50,900
Buses & bus chassis	5,040
Total	**346,640**

Cars (North American markets)
Volvo 850 series
Volvo 940 SE
Volvo 960

Trucks (North American markets)
Volvo FE
WHITEGMC

KEY COMPETITORS

BMW	General Motors	PACCAR
Brunswick	Honda	Peugeot
Chrysler	Hyundai	Renault
Cummins Engine	Isuzu	Rolls-Royce
Daewoo	Mazda	Saab-Scania
Daimler-Benz	Mitsubishi	Tata
Fiat	Navistar	Toyota
Ford	Nissan	Volkswagen
General Electric	Outboard Marine	Yamaha

HOW MUCH

Stock prices are for ADRs ADR = 1 share	Annual Growth	1984	1985	1986	1987	1988	1989	1990	1991	1992	1993
Sales ($ mil.)	2.7%	10,480	10,158	11,856	16,062	15,791	14,647	14,765	13,954	11,728	13,339
Net income ($ mil.)	—	188	300	360	571	544	771	(181)	254	(469)	(416)
Income as % of sales	—	1.8%	3.0%	3.0%	3.6%	3.4%	5.3%	—	1.8%	—	—
Earnings per share ($)	—	0.45	0.87	0.97	1.47	1.40	2.24	(0.01)	0.32	(1.21)	(1.07)
Stock price – high ($)	—	—	8.35	12.30	13.63	12.78	16.20	14.98	12.35	15.50	13.08
Stock price – low ($)	—	—	4.88	8.10	7.75	9.53	12.23	7.10	7.35	7.35	9.15
Stock price – close ($)	5.9%	—	8.20	10.00	9.45	12.60	14.43	7.45	11.38	9.80	12.93
P/E – high	—	—	10	13	9	9	7	—	39	—	—
P/E – low	—	—	6	8	5	7	6	—	22	—	—
Dividends per share ($)	4.6%	0.12	0.12	0.23	0.25	0.30	0.37	0.44	0.43	0.45	0.18
Book value per share ($)	16.6%	2.11	2.99	3.87	5.49	6.25	15.62	16.14	15.77	10.82	8.38
Employees	0.8%	68,586	67,857	73,147	75,340	78,614	78,690	68,797	63,582	60,115	73,641

1993 Year-end:
Debt ratio: 79.9%
Return on equity: —
Cash (mil.): $2,573
Current ratio: 0.94
Long-term debt (mil.): $1,698
No. of shares (mil.): 388
Dividends
  Yield: 1.4%
  Payout: —
Market value (mil.): $5,017

Stock Price History High/Low 1985–93

WATERFORD WEDGWOOD PLC

OVERVIEW

Not every company has a great-great-great-great-grandson of its founder sitting on the board of directors. Waterford Wedgwood does. As the company's illustrious name suggests, the firm has a long tradition to live up to. The merger of the Irish maker of the finest quality glassware, Waterford Crystal, and Josiah Wedgwood & Sons, the English fine china specialist, in 1986 brought together businesses that were both over 2 centuries old. But as the last several years of losses have shown, longevity and quality are only part of being a successful business.

In 1990 the company launched its first new brand of crystal in 200 years, Marquis by Waterford, and sold it at 20% below the traditional Waterford brand prices. The strategy paid off, and by 1993 the Marquis brand was the 6th largest-selling brand of premium glassware in the world. To date it has not hurt sales of its "Waterford" flagship brand.

The recent upturn in the US economy (with more consumer spending) and cost-cutting measures (including a 30% staff reduction at the Waterford plant and the contracting out of the Marquis production to makers in Germany and Slovenia) have also helped to put the company in the black.

The company is hoping that a similar innovation will boost Wedgwood china sales. In 1995 it plans to introduce a mid-priced china dinnerware set, the Wedgwood Embassy, and an even less expensive porcelain line, the Home Design.

Waterford Wedgwood's other lines include Coalport hand-painted figurines, Mason's ironstone lamps, and Johnson Brothers earthen tableware.

WHEN

Waterford dates back to 1783, when a glass manufacturer was established in the Irish port city of the same name. At the same time, across the Irish Sea, Josiah Wedgwood (1730-1795), a leading English artisan, was establishing a distinctive style of fine ceramic ware that incorporated neoclassical figures applied in a white cameo relief on a colored background. This style became the trademark of the products of Josiah Wedgwood and Sons (the name formally adopted in 1810). The company operated as a family business for the next 176 years and may have indirectly contributed to Darwin's theory of evolution. Charles Darwin married into the Wedgwood clan, which gave him the financial security to pursue his scientific research on a full-time basis. Wedgwood did not have a nonfamily director on its board until 1945.

The companies shared a reputation for quality and for the exquisite craftsmanship displayed in their glass and china products. However, both companies also experienced the vagaries of the market and financial difficulties. Waterford went bankrupt in 1851 and remained inactive until 1947, when the company was revived with the help of skilled artisans from Central Europe who were refugees from World War II. With this new base of skilled workers, the company started operations again and quickly reestablished the Waterford reputation for quality glassware, with its master/apprentice system and the painstaking, time-consuming processes required to produce handmade crystal. Waterford's profits rose steadily in the 1970s and early 1980s, with the US emerging as its primary market (75% of sales). In addition to consumer products, Waterford glassware has been used for the Boston Marathon Trophy and to hold President Reagan's jellybeans.

In 1986 Waterford borrowed heavily to acquire Wedgwood for $360 million, a move designed to allow both companies to cut costs by sharing marketing operations and by streamlining production. Strong union resistance to the deal, and to the cutting of 1,000 Waterford workers, led to a 14-week strike. This labor unrest and the falling dollar prompted a string of poor results in the late 1980s.

When Irish chairman and CEO of US-based H. J. Heinz Co. (and former Irish rugby star) Tony O'Reilly and Morgan Stanley took a 29.9% stake in Waterford Wedgwood in 1990 worth $125 million, the company was fighting for survival. Further job eliminations followed as the company struggled to reduce its break-even point.

By 1993 good sales of the Marquis mid-priced crystal line and increased US consumer spending heralded a return to profitability. In 1995 the company plans to sponsor a touring exhibition of its china to mark the 200th anniversary of Josiah Wedgwood's death.

Nasdaq symbol: WATFZ (ADR)
Fiscal year ends: December 31

WHO

Chairman: Anthony J.F. O'Reilly
Deputy Chairman: Donald P. Brennan
CEO, Wedgwood Group: Kneale H. Ashwell
Group Finance Director: Richard A. Barnes
Chairman and CEO, Waterford Crystal:
E. Patrick Galvin
Director Human Resources, Wedgwood Group:
George Stonier
Group Secretary and Group Corporate Counsel:
John B. Morgan
CEO, Waterford Wedgwood USA, Inc.:
Christopher J. McGillivary
Auditors: Price Waterhouse

WHERE

HQ: Kilbarry, Waterford, Ireland
Phone: +353-517-3311
Fax: +353-517-8539
US HQ: Waterford Wedgwood USA, Inc.,
1330 Campus Pkwy., Neptune, NJ 07753
US Phone: 908-938-5800
US Fax: 908-938-6915

	1993 Sales	
	Ir£ mil.	% of total
North America	140	44
Europe	119	37
Far East	41	13
Other countries	19	6
Total	**319**	**100**

WHAT

	1993 Sales	
	Ir£ mil.	% of total
Wedgwood Group (Wedgwood & Johnson Brothers)	193	60
Waterford Crystal	102	32
Other	24	8
Total	**319**	**100**

Wedgwood Products	Major Brands
Giftware	Adams
Earthenware	Alana
Fine bone china	Amherst
Porcelain	Coalport
Stoneware	Colleen
Tableware	Franciscan
Fine bone china table sets	Jasper
Hotelware	Johnson Brothers
Ironstone	Kildare
Johnson Brothers	Lismore
Cookware	Maeve
Giftware	Marquis
Tableware	Mason's Ironstone
Waterford Crystal Products	Queensware
Commemorative ware	Sheila
Giftware	Tall Colleen
Lightingware	Waterford
Studioware	Wedgwood

KEY COMPETITORS

Brown-Forman
Cie. des Cristalleries Baccarat
Corning
Hakon
Hoya
Mikasa
Noritake
Oneida
Pearson

HOW MUCH

$= (Ir£0.68 Dec. 31, 1993)	Annual Growth	1984	1985	1986	1987	1988	1989	1990	1991	1992	1993
Sales (Ir£ mil.)	2.8%	—	—	—	282	304	349	308	292	274	319
Net income (Ir£ mil.)	—	—	—	—	(18)	(5)	(30)	(28)	(5)	(19)	9
Income as % of sales	—	—	—	—	—	—	—	—	—	—	2.8%
Earnings per share (Ir£)	—	—	—	—	(0.04)	(0.01)	(0.07)	(0.05)	(0.01)	(0.03)	0.01
Stock price – high ($)[1]	—	—	—	—	21.75	19.75	14.88	9.13	6.75	6.50	6.38
Stock price – low ($)[1]	—	—	—	—	9.13	10.50	6.50	2.88	3.38	2.25	3.13
Stock price – close ($)	—	—	—	—	—	—	—	—	—	—	—
P/E – high	—	—	—	—	—	—	—	—	—	—	—
P/E – low	—	—	—	—	—	—	—	—	—	—	—
Dividends per share (Ir£)	—	—	—	—	0.03	0.01	0.00	0.00	0.00	0.00	0.00
Book value per share (Ir£)	(19.0%)	—	—	—	0.60	0.25	0.10	0.20	0.20	0.14	0.17
Employees	—	—	—	—	—	—	—	—	—	—	7,606

1993 Year-end:
Debt ratio: 56.2%
Return on equity: 8.4%
Cash (mil.): 36
Long-term debt (mil.): 92
No. of shares (mil.): 71
Dividends
Yield: —
Payout: —
Market value (mil.): $460
Sales (mil.): $450

**Stock Price History
High/Low 1987–93**

[1]ADRs representing 10 shares

YAMAHA CORPORATION

Production at Yamaha, the world's #1 manufacturer of musical instruments, has rarely been a problem. But getting the right strategy and the right marketing has. A recent illustration of bad marketing was the 200,000 wind instruments left unsold in 1990.

Until 1992 three successive generations of the Kawakami family had dominated Yamaha. They were preoccupied with trying to make a profit out of every skill the company developed. Consequently Yamaha meandered into a diverse range of businesses: archery equipment, golf clubs, audio equipment, music schools, kitchens, skis, electric bicycles, and others. After a failed attempt by heir apparent Hiroshi Kawakami to cut back Yamaha's work force through early retirement, the company's in-house labor union revolted and demanded his ouster. Kawakami resigned, and was replaced by Seisuke Ueshima, a

36-year Yamaha veteran, in 1992. He has set to work on a combination of product innovation and corporate restructuring. For instance, the Disklavier, an acoustic piano with a computer control that allows it to precisely replicate actual performances recorded on floppy disks, has opened a whole new market for this supposedly mature segment. The silent piano (an acoustic piano that produces sounds only through earphones) is another big seller. Thin-film magnetic heads for large-capacity disk drives are another successful niche for Yamaha, which has a 20% global market share.

Ueshima made a pact with the unions to keep most factory workers, lay off 30% of Japanese administrative staff, and cut overseas employees. Yamaha's marketing strategy involves pushing expensive musical instruments (like the Disklavier) to increase sales.

Torakusu Yamaha, a Japanese watchmaker and medical equipment repairman, tinkered with his first reed organ in 1885. Captivated, he decided to build one, completing it in 1887. He established Yamaha Organ Manufacturing Company in 1889 to manufacture reed organs and, as production intensified, incorporated the company as Nippon Gakki (Japan Musical Instruments) in 1897. Nippon Gakki began producing upright pianos in 1900 and grand pianos in 1902.

In 1920 the company diversified into the production of wooden airplane propellers (based on woodworking skills used in making pianos) and soon had added pipe organs (1932) and guitars (1946) to its line of musical instruments. Genichi Kawakami, whose father had managed the company since 1927, took over in 1950. He moved the company into motorcycle production in 1954, transferring the motorcycle business to Yamaha Motor, a separate but affiliated company, in 1955.

Kawakami established the Yamaha Music School System in 1954. Under his leadership Nippon Gakki became the world's largest producer of musical instruments, developing Japan's first electronic organ, the Electone, in 1959. Kawakami spearheaded the company's move into wind instruments (1965), stereos (1968), and microchips (1971). By 1982 musicians in

the Americas, Europe, and Asia could buy Yamaha brand products locally.

Yamaha Motor also diversified, starting with motorboats and outboard motors in 1960. By 1980 the company had added yachts (1965), automobile engines (1966), snowmobiles (1968), golf carts (1975), and all-terrain vehicles (1979). Motorcycle production continued to grow, and in 1982 Yamaha Motor claimed (prematurely) that it would surpass Honda as the world's #1 motorcycle maker. Honda responded with aggressive product introductions and price slashing that sent Yamaha Motor into red ink.

Nippon Gakki responded with a spate of diversification, particularly into customized chips for CD players. In 1983 Yamaha introduced a powerful synthesizer cheap enough to appeal to a mass market. The company changed its name to Yamaha Corporation in 1987. Yamaha emphasized exports of electronic instruments (a facility opened in China in 1989) and the mass production of integrated circuits. Meanwhile, Yamaha Motor's sales were revived in 1991, powered by demand for big bikes by aging baby boomers.

Yamaha's upscale Disklavier pianos accounted for 20% of the company's piano sales in 1992. In 1993 Yamaha Motor set up a motorcycle joint venture in China. In 1994 it also set up an office in Vietnam to explore challenging Honda's near monopoly there.

Principal exchange: Tokyo
Fiscal year ends: March 31

President: Seisuke Ueshima
Senior Managing Director: Teruo Hiyoshi
Managing Director: Kazukiyo Ishimura
Managing Director: Nobuo Sato
Managing Director: Shuji Ito
Chairman, Yamaha Motor Co.: Hideto Eguchi
President, Yamaha Corporation of America:
  Masahiko Arimoto
Division Manager Corporate Personnel, Yamaha
  Corporation of America: Don Patrick
Auditors: Masazumi Miyake

HQ: 10-1, Nakazawa-cho, Hamamatsu, Shizuoka
  Pref. 430, Japan
Phone: +81-53-460-2850
Fax: +81-53-456-1109
US HQ: Yamaha Corporation of America,
  6600 Orangethorpe Ave., Buena Park,
  CA 90620-1396
US Phone: 714-522-9011
US Fax: 714-522-9961

	1994 Sales	
	¥ bil.	% of total
Japan	323	72
Other countries	123	28
Total	**446**	**100**

	1994 Sales	
	¥ bil.	% of total
Musical instruments & audio products	286	64
Electronic equipment & metal products	67	15
Furniture & household products	49	11
Others	44	10
Total	**446**	**100**

Yamaha Corporation — Major Products and Services

Audio products	Percussion instruments
Bathroom fixtures	Pianos
Computer peripherals	Sound equipment
Digital musical instruments	Special metals
Electones	Sporting goods
Furniture	System kitchens
Large scale integration	Washstands
(LSI) microchips	Wind instruments
Music schools	

Yamaha Motor Products

All-terrain vehicles	Marine and auto engines
Boats and golf carts	Motorcycles
Electric bicycles	Snowmobiles

American Standard	Hyundai	Read-Rite
Arctco	Kawai	Robert Bosch
Baldwin Piano	Kohler	Samsung
Black & Decker	MacAndrews	Sanyo
BMW	& Forbes	Seiko
Brunswick	Matsushita	Sharp
Casio	Mitsubishi	Sony
Eljer Industries	NEC	Steinway
Fujitsu	Nissan	Suzuki
General Electric	Outboard Marine	Thomson SA
Harley-Davidson	Peugeot	Toshiba
Hitachi	Philips	Volvo
Honda	Pioneer	Zenith

$=¥112 (Dec. 31, 1993)	Annual Growth	1985	1986[2]	1987	1988	1989	1990	1991	1992	1993	1994
Sales (¥ bil.)	1.0%	407	426	413	436	467	487	509	513	483	446
Net income (¥ bil.)	—	(12)	6	9	11	8	4	8	6	2	(4)
Income as % of sales	—	—	1.3%	2.2%	2.5%	1.8%	0.8%	1.5%	1.2%	0.4%	—
Earnings per share (¥)	—	(61)	30	48	56	46	19	40	30	9	(21)
Stock price – high (¥)[1]	—	1,120	1,719	1,974	1,960	2,460	2,390	2,200	1,820	1,690	1,320
Stock price – low (¥)[1]	—	412	701	949	1,070	1,500	1,630	1,340	1,360	720	861
Stock price – close (¥)[1]	0.0%	945	1,265	1,357	1,670	1,860	2,080	1,690	1,590	900	948
P/E – high	—	—	58	41	35	54	124	55	61	180	—
P/E – low	—	—	24	20	19	33	85	34	53	77	—
Dividends per share (¥)	(1.5%)	6.87	6.87	7.91	8.70	10.00	10.00	10.00	10.00	6.00	6.00
Book value per share (¥)	4.5%	535	558	655	692	734	757	834	847	835	797
Employees	3.4%	—	—	—	13,108	—	12,423	12,241	11,647	11,000	10,676

1994 Year-end:
Debt ratio: 41.9%
Return on equity: —
Cash (bil.): ¥33
Long-term debt (bil.): ¥67
No. of shares (mil.): 194
Dividends
  Yield: 0.6%
  Payout: —
Market value (mil.): $1,642
Sales (mil.): $3,982

Stock Price History[1]
High/Low 1985–94

[1] Stock prices are for the prior calendar year.   [2] 11-month period

YPF SOCIEDAD ANÓNIMA

OVERVIEW

"Don't Cry for Me, Argentina" could be the theme song of YPF, Argentina's largest company, having survived over 70 years of economic and political upheaval. YPF is an integrated oil and gas company involved in the refining, marketing, transportation, and distribution of a wide range of oil and gas products. In 1994 the company had one billion barrels of oil reserves and 9.13 trillion cubic feet of gas, all located in Argentina.

A state-owned oil conglomerate for most of its life, the company was privatized in 1993 as part of President Carlos Menem's economic reform plans to privatize 50 state-owned companies. To help prepare the company for sale to the public, Menem brought in a former head of Baker Hughes, José Estenssoro, to draft a plan for privatization. The plan was so impressive that Menem gave him the job as CEO of the company in 1990.

Estenssoro drastically cut staff and sold off YPF's extraneous assets, including movie theaters, hospitals, and railroads.

Investors were impressed by the makeover, and the consequent privatization was a gusher with YPF shares selling at 21% above the $19-a-share asking price on the first day of trading. The offering of 45% of YPF raised $3 billion and is the largest single offering in the history of Latin America.

YPF invested about $1 billion in exploration and development in 1994, and in 1995 it hopes to produce 450,000 barrels a day, one and a half times the level of 1992. It plans to upgrade its work in the oil exporting business, primarily through neighboring Chile, and plans to enter into marketing operations with other neighboring countries as well. YPF is also developing its LPG and compressed natural gas markets.

WHEN

With the luck that attended many early oil discoveries, an Argentine government team discovered oil while drilling for water in 1907. The Argentine government was determined to keep domestic oil resources under the control of the national government and out of foreign hands. In 1922 a government oil supervisory body, Dirección Nacional de los Yacimientos Petrolíferos Fiscales (YPF), was formed to operate the newly discovered oil field in the south of the country, becoming the world's first state-owned oil company. But YPF was a poor performer in the 1920s, and imports from Standard Oil and other oil multinationals dominated most of the country's oil market. In the 1930s YPF made major oil discoveries across Argentina.

A major turning point came with the rise to power of Juan Perón in 1945. In the years that followed, Perón extended state control over broad sections of the economy, including oil. He nationalized British and American interests and greatly strengthened YPF's role in the oil sector, giving YPF a virtual monopoly of the oil business. In 1945 YPF produced 68% of the country's total oil production. By 1955 it produced 84%. In 1957 the company discovered a huge gas field in western Argentina, making YPF, and Argentina, a major gas producer. In 1958 YPF signed a contract with American oil giant Amoco to share production costs.

Despite the increase in resources, YPF's production failed to keep pace with the demands of the growing economy, and imports still dominated Argentina's oil market. Over the next 30 years, YPF experienced radical swings in government policy as ultra-nationalist military governments alternated with liberal, reformist governments. Overall, though, YPF grew as an underperforming, bloated, and inefficient conglomerate, protected from free market competition by government controls and contracts. For much of its existence, YPF did not subcontract to the private sector but built everything its workers needed itself, from hospitals to schools to supermarkets. Between 1982 and 1989, despite a World Bank–financed program to modernize YPF's refineries, the company lost over $6 billion.

Carlos Menem took over as Argentine president in 1989 and embarked on an aggressive liberalization and privatization plan. He brought in José Estenssoro to turn YPF around in 1990. By dumping $2 billion of noncore assets and 87% of its work force, the company emerged as a profitable concern and a hot IPO in 1993.

In 1994 the company began expanding beyond Argentina by shipping crude oil to Chile through a new 300-mile pipeline. YPF also plans to build natural gas pipelines to Brazil and to Chile.

NYSE: YPF (ADR)
Fiscal year ends: December 31

President and CEO: José A. Estenssoro, age 60
EVP and COO: Nells León
VP Refining and Marketing; Head of Restructuring Project: Eduardo Petazze
VP Exploration and Production: Marcelo Guiscardo
VP Engineering and Technology: Juan A. Rodríguez
VP Purchasing, Contracts, and Environmental Protection: Juan J. Garacija
VP Finance and Corporate Development: Cedric D. Bridger
VP and General Controller: Carlos A. Olivieri
VP Legal Affairs: Norberto Noblía
VP Human Resources: Raul H. Oreste
VP YPF - USA: Mateo Juan
Auditors: Pistrelli, Diaz & Asociados — Arthur Andersen & Co.

WHERE

HQ: Avenida Pte. R. Sáenz Peña 777-8 Piso, 1364 Buenos Aires, Argentina
Phone: +54-1-329-2000
Fax: +54-1-322-5639
US HQ: YPF - USA, Inc., 5 Greenway Plaza, Ste. 250, Houston, TX 77046
US Phone: 713-621-4850
US Fax: 713-621-4803

YPF's oil and gas operations are all located in Argentina.

WHAT

	1993 Sales	
	$ mil.	% of total
Downstream Strategic Business Unit (refining & marketing)	3,184	80
Upstream Strategic Business Unit (exploration & production)	776	20
Total	**3,960**	**100**

Major Products and Services

Downstream Strategic Business Unit
Marketing and transport
  Compressed natural gas
  Crude oil
  Liquid petroleum gas
  Petrochemical products
Refining
Service stations (2,700)

Upstream Strategic Business Unit
Natural gas sales
Oil and natural gas exploration
Oil and natural gas production
Storage
Transportation
Treatment

KEY COMPETITORS

British Petroleum	PDVSA
Broken Hill	Pemex
Caltex Petroleum	Petrobrás
Chevron	Petrofina
Coastal	Phillips Petroleum
Exxon	Royal Dutch/Shell
Imperial Oil	Texaco
Mobil	TOTAL
Occidental	Unocal

HOW MUCH

	Annual Growth	1984	1985	1986	1987	1988	1989	1990	1991	1992	1993
Sales ($ mil.)	(3.9%)	—	—	—	—	—	—	—	4,292	3,867	3,960
Net income ($ mil.)	64.5%	—	—	—	—	—	—	—	261	256	707
Income as % of sales	—	—	—	—	—	—	—	—	6.1%	6.6%	17.8%
Earnings per share ($)	64.1%	—	—	—	—	—	—	—	0.74	0.73	2.00
Stock price – high ($)	—	—	—	—	—	—	—	—	—	—	29.00
Stock price – low ($)	—	—	—	—	—	—	—	—	—	—	18.88
Stock price – close ($)	—	—	—	—	—	—	—	—	—	—	26.00
P/E – high	—	—	—	—	—	—	—	—	—	—	14
P/E – low	—	—	—	—	—	—	—	—	—	—	9
Dividends per share ($)	—	—	—	—	—	—	—	—	—	—	0.20
Book value per share ($)	—	—	—	—	—	—	—	—	—	—	14.08
Employees	(19.4%)	—	—	—	—	—	52,000	51,000	32,117	10,600	7,500

1993 Year-end:	
Debt ratio: 12.2%	
Return on equity: 14.9%	Stock Price History
Cash (mil.): $84	High/Low 1993
Current ratio: 1.13	
Long-term debt (mil.): $428	
No. of shares (mil.): 353	
Dividends	
Yield: 0.8%	
Payout: 10.0%	
Market value (mil.): $9,178	

ZAMBIA CONSOLIDATED COPPER MINES

OVERVIEW

Zambia Consolidated Copper Mines (ZCCM) may soon be swallowed by the "Jaws" of mining, Anglo American (South Africa). Or it may be cut up for bait . . . its mining and power subsidiaries "unbundled" and sold (Broken Hill, RTZ, Gencor, and Phelps Dodge have been mentioned as possible investors). Either way, Zambia intends to hook some much-needed capital by privatizing its largest company.

ZCCM, whose primary products are copper and cobalt, accounts for over 90% of Zambia's export revenues. Government-owned ZIMCO (Zambia Industrial and Mining Corporation) owns 60.3% of ZCCM, while the Bermuda-based Anglo American front company ZCI Holdings owns 27.3%.

ZCCM limped through the early 1990s, first as metals prices fell, then as production problems cut into its mining output.

But rising metal prices and cost-cutting measures may help stem sales declines.

As privatization looms, the company faces serious problems: An estimated 30% of ZCCM workers will be HIV-positive by the turn of the century. Less tragic but also costly, ZCCM's most productive mines are becoming exhausted, and development of new sources will require up to $700 million. To bring new sources on-line, development must begin soon, increasing pressure on Zambia's leaders to hurry privatization.

With all interested parties waiting to see if Japanese investment bank Nikko Securities will provide development funds to ZCCM and with potential investors trying to determine just how Anglo American will fit into ZCCM's future, Zambia President Frederick Chiluba could try to stall privatization until after the country's 1996 elections.

WHEN

Cecil Rhodes's British South Africa Company came to Central Africa in the 1890s in search of minerals. As demand for copper grew in the 1920s, spurred by the proliferation of electricity, 2 companies began developing copper deposits in the region: Zambian Anglo American Corporation and Roan Selection Trust (RST).

Zambia, formerly British protectorate Northern Rhodesia, has 1/5 of the world's known copper reserves. Revenues from copper mining provided the financial basis for much of the region's development, bringing in railroads and settlers. By 1952 the country earned 57.5% of its income from taxes on the sale of copper.

During the 1960s copper prices soared to record highs. Zambia gained its independence from Britain in 1964. It joined Chile, Peru, and the Congo in 1967 to form the International Council of Copper Producing Countries in an effort to stabilize prices.

In 1969 Zambia produced a record 700,000 tons of copper, 12% of the world's production and 96% of Zambia's export revenues. That year the country partially nationalized its 2 largest mining interests, those owned by Anglo American and RST (then a subsidiary of US-based AMAX). To oversee its mining interests, the government created ZIMCO (Zambia Industrial and Mining Corpo-

ration, incorporated in 1970). With nationalization ZIMCO became 51% owner of the mines, which were reorganized as Nchanga Consolidated Copper Mines and Roan Consolidated Mines Ltd.

Throughout the 1970s and 1980s, copper production fell as ore deposits played out and mines became delapidated. In 1981 the industry experienced its lowest production since independence. The next year the Nchanga and Roan holdings were merged to create ZCCM, with ZIMCO owning 60.3%, Zambia Copper Investments owning 27.3%, and RST owning 6.9%.

In the 1990s ZCCM began an aggressive program to save its copper industry by making it more efficient. It purchased a foundry, invested in regional transportation, and imported new mining technologies. Free market reforms began in 1991, with the country's first free elections. The reforms lead to fines for ecological damage and investigations into corruption among ZCCM executives. Determined to control expenses, in 1992 and 1993 ZCCM laid off nearly 10,000 workers. In 1994 ZCCM's Kabwe lead and zinc mine was closed due to losses.

With the 1994 announcement of plans to privatize ZCCM, Zambia — which depends so heavily on revenues from copper mining — was plunged into a heated political battle.

OTC symbol: ZAM (ADR)
Fiscal year ends: March 31

Chairman: R. L. Bwalya
CEO: Edward K. Shamutete
Director Operations: Pius H. Maambo
Technical Director: John M. D. Patterson
Director Corporate Planning: Edwin M. Koloko
Director Reorganization: Urban C. Chishimba
Secretary: Max Mukwakwa
Director Finance: M. Ijaz Ahmad
Director Human Resources: Bannie M. Lombe
Auditor: KPMG Peat Marwick

WHERE

HQ: Zambia Consolidated Copper Mines Limited,
5309 Dedan Kimathi Rd., PO Box 30048,
Lusaka 10101, Zambia
Phone: +260-1-229115
Fax: +260-1-221057

Zambia Consolidated Copper Mines operates 5
mining divisions and one power division.

	1994 Sales	
	$ mil.	% of sales
EEC	220	21
Japan	198	19
Thailand	100	10
Taiwan	80	8
Saudi Arabia	71	7
US	61	6
Malaysia	59	5
Singapore	52	5
Zambia	50	5
Other countries	150	14
Total	**1,041**	**100**

WHAT

	1994 Sales	
	$ mil.	% of total
Copper	889	86
Cobalt	144	14
Zinc	4	0
Zinc Sable 4	3	0
Lead	1	0
Total	**1,041**	**100**

	1994 Production	
	Metric tons	% of total
Copper	392,179	98
Cobalt	3,705	1
Zinc	3,446	1
Lead	2,002	0
Precious metals	43	0
Total	**401,375**	**100**

Principal Subsidiaries
Mines Air Services Ltd.
Mpelembe Drilling Co., Ltd.
Mulungushi Investments Ltd.
Ndola Lime Co. Ltd.
Scaw Ltd. (94%)
Zambia Detonators Ltd. (70%)
Zamcargo (Zambia) Ltd.

KEY COMPETITORS

Anglo American
ASARCO
Benguet
Broken Hill
Codelco
CRA
Cyprus Amax
Freeport-McMoRan
Homestake Mining
Inco

Industrial Minera
Metallgesellschaft
Noranda
Palabora Mining
Phelps Dodge
Placer Dome
Rio Algom
RTZ
Western Mining

HOW MUCH

	Annual Growth	1985	1986	1987	1988	1989	1990	1991	1992	1993	1994
Sales ($ mil.)	(4.4%)	—	—	—	1,362	1,931	1,943	1,917	1,521	1,385	1,041
Net income ($ mil.)	—	—	—	—	43	195	153	152	51	168	(174)
Income as % of sales	—	—	—	—	3.1%	10.1%	7.9%	7.9%	3.3%	12.1%	—
Earnings per share ($)	—	—	—	—	—	—	—	—	—	—	(1.40)
Stock price – high ($)[1]	—	—	—	—	—	—	—	—	—	—	4.66
Stock price – low ($)[1]	—	—	—	—	—	—	—	—	—	—	1.36
Stock price – close ($)[1]	—	—	—	—	—	—	—	—	—	—	—
P/E – high	—	—	—	—	—	—	—	—	—	—	—
P/E – low	—	—	—	—	—	—	—	—	—	—	—
Dividends per share ($)	—	—	—	—	—	—	—	—	—	—	0.00
Book value per share ($)	(6.4%)	—	—	—	—	—	—	—	—	30.49	28.53
Employees	(0.5%)	—	—	—	61,991	—	—	—	—	61,433	60,259

1994 Year-end:
Debt ratio: 20.1%
Return on equity: (6.6%)
Cash (mil.): $27
Current ratio: 1.03
Long-term debt (mil.): $454
No. of shares (mil.): 89
Dividends
　Yield: —
　Payout: —
Market value (mil.): —

Stock Price History[1]
High/Low 1994

[1] Stock prices are for the prior calendar year.

INDEXES

A

ARGENTINA

Buenos Aires
YPF Sociedad Anónima
544

AUSTRALIA

Mascot
Qantas Airways Limited
402

Melbourne
The Broken Hill
Proprietary Co. Limited
152
Pacific Dunlop Limited
378

South Yarra
Foster's Brewing Group
Limited 224

Sydney
The News Corporation
Limited 354

Tooronga
Coles Myer Ltd. 180

B

BELGIUM

Brussels
Petrofina S.A. 384

BERMUDA

Hamilton
Jardine Matheson
Holdings Ltd. 286

BRAZIL

Rio de Janeiro
Petróleo Brasileiro S.A.
386

C

CANADA

Mississauga
Northern Telecom
Limited 370

Montreal
Alcan Aluminium Limited
102
Bank of Montreal 116
BCE Inc. 130
Bombardier Inc. 138
Canadian Pacific Limited
162
Quebecor Inc. 404
Royal Bank of Canada
432
The Seagram Company
Ltd. 462
Teleglobe Inc. 502

Toronto
Canadian Imperial Bank of
Commerce 160
George Weston Limited
234
Hudson's Bay Company
262
Imperial Oil Limited 270
Inco Limited 272
John Labatt Limited 288
The Molson Companies
Limited 344
Moore Corporation
Limited 346
Rogers Communications
Inc. 426
The Thomson Corporation
506
The Toronto-Dominion
Bank 516

Vancouver
MacMillan Bloedel Limited
324

CHILE

Santiago
Compañía de Teléfonos de
Chile S.A. 498

CHINA

Shanghai
Shanghai Petrochemical
Co. Ltd. 468

D

DENMARK

Bagsværd
Novo Nordisk A/S 372

Copenhagen
Carlsberg A/S 168

F

FINLAND

Helsinki
Nokia Group 364

FRANCE

Blagnac
Airbus Industrie 98

Boulogne Billancourt
Régie Nationale des Usines
Renault S.A. 412

Clermont-Ferrand
Michelin 336

Clichy
L'Oréal SA 316

Courbevoie
Rhône-Poulenc S.A. 418
Compagnie de Saint-
Gobain SA 446

Évry
Accor SA 96

Neuilly-sur-Seine
Havas S.A. 244

Paris
Alcatel Alsthom 104
CANAL+ 164
Carrefour 170
Club Méditerranée SA
178
Crédit Lyonnais 184
Groupe Danone 196
Elf Aquitaine 206
Lagardère Groupe 308
LVMH Moët Hennessy
Louis Vuitton 320
PSA Peugeot Citroën 392
Groupe Schneider 458
Thomson S.A. 504

U

UK

Brentford
SmithKline Beecham plc **480**

Farnborough
British Aerospace PLC **144**

Hounslow
British Airways PLC **146**

Littlehampton
The Body Shop
International PLC **136**

London
Allied Domecq PLC **110**
Barclays PLC **118**
Bass PLC **122**
B.A.T Industries p.l.c. **124**
The British Petroleum
Company p.l.c. **148**
British
Telecommunications plc **150**
BTR plc **154**
Cable and Wireless PLC **156**
Cadbury Schweppes plc **158**
The General Electric
Company p.l.c. **232**
Glaxo p.l.c. **236**
Grand Metropolitan PLC **238**
Guinness PLC **240**
Hanson PLC **242**
HSBC Holdings plc **260**
Imperial Chemical
Industries PLC **268**
Ladbroke Group PLC **306**
Lloyd's of London **312**
Lonrho Plc **314**
Marks and Spencer p.l.c. **328**
National Westminster
Bank Plc **348**
Pearson PLC **380**
Peninsular and Oriental **382**
Price Waterhouse LLP **400**
The Rank Organisation
PLC **406**
Reckitt & Colman plc **408**

Reed Elsevier PLC **410**
Reuters Holdings PLC **416**
Rolls-Royce plc **428**
Royal Dutch/Shell Group **434**
The RTZ Corporation PLC **436**
Saatchi & Saatchi
Company PLC **442**
J Sainsbury plc **444**
Tate & Lyle Public Limited
Company **494**
Thorn EMI plc **508**
Unilever **524**
Vickers P.L.C. **530**
Virgin Group PLC **532**

Nottingham
The Boots Company PLC **140**

US

New York
Coopers & Lybrand L.L.P. **182**
Ernst & Young LLP **212**

Wilton
Deloitte & Touche LLP **198**

V

VENEZUELA

Caracas
Petróleos de Venezuela,
S.A. **388**

Z

ZAMBIA

Lusaka
Zambia Consolidated
Copper Mines **546**

S

S & W Medico Teknik A/S 531
S-AI Electronics Co., Ltd. 465
S. Pearson & Son 380
Saab Cars USA, Inc. 441
Saab-Scania Holdings Group **440–441**, 457
Saatchi & Saatchi Company PLC 200, 301, **442–443**
Saatchi, Charles 442
Saatchi, David 442
Saatchi, Maurice 442
Saatchi, Nathan 442
Saba 505
Saba, Shoichi 518
Sabena World Airlines 146, 292
Safari (liquor) 241
Safeway 282
Safrane automobile 413
Saft batteries 104, 105
Sahinbas, Tamer 295
Sähköliikkeiden electrical wholesaler 364
Saigne, Guy 245
Sail 411
J Sainsbury plc **444–445**
Sainsbury, David J. 444, 445
Sainsbury, John Benjamin 444
Sainsbury, John James 444
Sainsbury, of Drury Lane, Lord 445
Sainsbury, of Preston Candover, Lord 445
Sainsbury, Mary Ann 444
Sainsbury, Robert 445
Sainsbury, S. D. 444
Saint-Gobain SA, Compagnie de **446–447**
Saint-Martin, Pascal Castres 317
St Michael Finance Ltd. 328, 329
Saint-Gobain glass manufacturer 196
Saint-Gobain Vitrage 447
Saipem SpA 209
Saison Overseas Holdings 456
Saito, Hiroshi 359
Saito, Takayoshi 467

Saito, Yoshio 489
Saiwa biscuits 197
Sakai, Kazuhiro 421
Sakai, Shinji 523
Sakamaki, Hideo 367
Saks stores 124
Salam-2000 298
Salinas de Gortari, Carlos 390, 500
Salora TV manufacturer 364
Salsbury, Peter L. 329
Salvarsan (drug) 252
Salvat (publisher) 308
Samim 208
Sam's Club 177
Samsung Group 250, 310, 362, **448–449**
Samsung Lions 448, 449
Samuel, Marcus 434
San Antonio Express-News 354
San Miguel beer 196, 197, 451
San Miguel Corporation **450–451**
San Pellegrino 352
Sánchez y García, Francisco 501
Sánchez-Valdepeñas, Oscar Maravar 497
Sandberg, Rolf 441
Sandefur, Thomas E., Jr. 125
Sandeman wine 463
Sander, Dorothy E. 243
Sandestin Resorts, Inc. 476, 477
Sandimmun transplant drup 452
Sandoz, Edouard 452
Sandoz Ltd. 236, 418, **452–453**
Sandzer-Bell, Benjamin 505
Sanford, John 429
Saniflush 408
Sankey, Vernon L. 409
Sanko Kabushiki Kaisha 330
Sans Souci (beer) 289
Sanyo Electric Co., Ltd. 201, 448, **454–455**
Sapac 424
Sapporo brewery 290
Sara Lee 424, 443
Sarawak Trading 476
Sarazen, Richard A. 355

Sark Sigorta (insurance) 295, 512
Sarphati, Bernard 247
SAS International Hotels AS 457
Sasahara, Toru 291
Sasaki, Kanrad 191
Sasaki, Mikio 341
Sasaki, Yoshiro 359
Saso cosmetics 473
SAT (telephone company) 210
Satellite Information Services (Holdings) Ltd. 307
Satellite Japan 486
Satellite Service 165
Sato, Fumio 519
Sato, Nobuo 543
Sato, Toori 251
Sato, Yasuhiro 291
SATS Airport Services Pte Ltd 479
Saturn Corporation 142
Satzenbrau beer 241
The Saudi British Bank 261, 260
Saudi-Swiss Bank 527
Saunders, Ernest 240
Sauza tequila 110, 111
Savacentres Ltd. 444, 445
Savage, Graham W. 427
Savannah cigarettes 125
Savarese, Michele 485
Saville Tractors Ltd. 315
Savin 420
Savon d'Or toiletries 473
Sawada, Shigeo 361
Sawamura, Shiko 375
Sayers, Dorothy 534
SBC Communications 500
SBG Beteiligungs-GmbH 527
SBK Record Productions 508
Scalia, Frank V. 183
Scanair airline 456
Scandinavian Airlines System **456–457**
Scandinavian Truck & Bus Sdn. Bhd. 477
Scania 476
Scaw Ltd. 547
SCEcorp 514
Schachter, Robert 449
Scharp, Anders 205, 441
Schein Pharmaceutical 126
Schenley 240

INTRODUCING HOOVER'S COMPANY PROFILES ON DEMAND

A new fax delivery service that puts detailed company profiles from the

Hoover's Company Database at your fingertips

WHY WAIT? Get invaluable information immediately for such major public and private companies as Campbell Soup Co., Levi Strauss, Microsoft, and United Parcel Service.

The information is arranged in the same easy-to-use format as the company profiles found in *Hoover's Handbooks* and includes company overviews and histories, up to 10 years of key financial and employment data, lists of products and key competitors, names of key officers, addresses, and phone and fax numbers.

IT'S SIMPLE.

1. Choose any number of companies from the index on the following pages.*

2. Then call *800-510-4452*, 24 hours a day, 7 days a week to receive a detailed profile for only $2.95* for each company you choose. Have your fax number and the five-digit company code number ready.

3. A voice-automated system will guide you through your order, and you'll receive your company profiles via fax within minutes.

*American Express, MasterCard, and VISA accepted.

Index of Hoover's Company Profiles

MORE HOOVER'S COMPANY

Chipcom Corporation	11002	Cummins Engine Company, Inc.	10423	Eli Lilly and Company	10509
Chiquita Brands International, Inc.	11551	Cygne Designs Inc.	16293	EMC Corporation	10491
Chiron Corporation	12972	Cyprus Amax Minerals Company	10429	Emerson Electric Co.	10514
Chrysler Corporation	10334	Cyrix Corporation	16430	Enron Corporation	10521
The Chubb Corporation	10335	Cyrk Inc.	16222	Entergy Corporation	10524
CIDCO Incorporated	17123	Damark International, Inc.	14494	Equifax Inc.	10527
CIGNA Corporation	10259	Dana Corporation	10433	The Equitable Companies, Incorporated	13307
Circuit City Stores, Inc.	10343	Data General Corporation	10436	Ernst & Young LLP	40146
Circus Circus Enterprises, Inc.	10344	Day Runner, Inc.	10193	Express Scripts, Inc.	15773
Cirrus Logic, Inc.	12986	Dayton Hudson Corporation	10440	Exxon Corporation	10537
Cisco Systems, Inc.	13494	Dean Witter, Discover & Co.	15970	EZCORP, Inc.	13808
Citicorp	10345	Deckers Outdoor Corporation	16612	Federal Express Corporation	10552
The Clorox Company	10354	Deere & Company	10444	Federal National Mortgage Association	10553
CML Group, Inc.	10262	Dell Computer Corporation	13193	Federated Department Stores, Inc.	12493
The Coastal Corporation	10358	Deloitte & Touche	40120	Ferolito, Vultaggio & Sons	42106
Coastal Healthcare Group, Inc.	12837	Delta Air Lines, Inc.	10448	Fieldcrest Cannon, Inc.	10560
The Coca-Cola Company	10359	Deluxe Corporation	10451	First Chicago Corporation	10571
Cognex Corporation	13017	Destec Energy, Inc.	14008	First Fidelity Bancorporation	10573
Colgate-Palmolive Company	10363	The Dial Corp.	10680	First Financial Management Corporation	13440
The Columbia Gas System, Inc.	10369	Dialogic Corporation	42073	First Interstate Bancorp	10575
Columbia/HCA Healthcare Corporation	15237	Digi International Inc.	14110	First Union Corporation	10578
Compaq Computer Corporation	10381	Digidesign Inc.	16691	Flagstar Companies, Inc.	16962
Compression Labs, Incorporated	13057	Digital Equipment Corporation	10462	Fleet Financial Group, Inc.	10585
CompuCom Systems, Inc.	13060	Dillard Department Stores, Inc.	10463	Fleetwood Enterprises, Inc.	10586
CompUSA Inc.	15490	Discovery Zone, Inc.	16225	Fleming Companies, Inc.	10587
Computer Associates International, Inc.	10383	Dole Food Company, Inc.	10303	Fluor Corporation	10594
ConAgra, Inc.	10388	Domino's Pizza, Inc.	40131	FMC Corporation	10540
Conner Peripherals, Inc.	13081	DOVatron International Inc.	11577	Food Lion, Inc.	13499
Conrail, Inc.	10395	The Dow Chemical Company	10471	Ford Motor Company	10597
Consolidated Edison Company of		Dow Jones & Company, Inc.	10472	Forschner Group, Inc.	13503
New York, Inc.	10392	Dr Pepper/Seven-Up Companies, Inc.	15945	Fossil, Inc.	16093
Consolidated Freightways, Inc.	10393	Dresser Industries, Inc.	10476	Foundation Health Corporation	12909
Consolidated Graphics, Inc.	20099	Drypers Corporation	17143	FPL Group, Inc.	10542
Contel Cellular Inc.	13092	Duke Power Company	10481	Franklin Quest Co.	15674
Continental Airlines Holdings, Inc.	41903	The Dun & Bradstreet Corporation	10483	Fred Meyer, Inc.	13519
Continental Grain Company	40104	E.I. du Pont de Nemours and Company	10487	Fresh Choice, Inc.	12982
The Continuum Company, Inc.	11847	E. & J. Gallo Winery	40140	Fritz Companies, Inc.	12436
Cooper Industries, Inc.	10405	The E.W. Scripps Company	13254	Fruit of the Loom, Inc.	11960
Coopers & Lybrand L.L.P.	40107	Eagle Hardware & Garden, Inc.	15792	FTP Software, Inc.	16553
Copley Pharmaceutical, Inc.	15892	Eastman Chemical Company	16569	Funco Inc.	16963
Cornerstone Imaging Inc.	16506	Eastman Kodak Company	10500	The Future Now, Inc.	11008
Corning Incorporated	10409	Eaton Corporation	10501	Gannett Co., Inc.	10623
Cox Enterprises, Inc.	40110	Eckerd Corporation	16231	The Gap, Inc.	11469
CPC International Inc.	10268	Edison Brothers Stores, Inc.	10504	Gateway 2000 Inc.	16706
Cracker Barrel Old Country Store, Inc.	13128	EG&G, Inc.	10490	GEICO Corporation	10616
Cray Research, Inc.	10416	EIS International, Inc.	15796	Genentech, Inc.	10628
Crown Cork & Seal Company, Inc.	10419	Electronic Arts Inc.	14059	General Dynamics Corporation	10633
CSX Corporation	10274	Electronic Data Systems Corporation	41915	General Electric Company	10634
CUC International Inc.	12858	Electronics for Imaging, Inc.	15872	General Mills, Inc.	10639

PROFILES ON DEMAND

Company	No.
General Motors Corporation	10640
General Re Corporation	10643
General Signal Corporation	10644
Genzyme Corporation	13560
Georgia-Pacific Corporation	10648
Giant Food Inc.	11979
The Gillette Company	10655
Glenayre Technologies, Inc.	14179
Global Village Communication, Inc.	16980
GM Hughes Electronics Corporation	42070
The Goldman Sachs Group, LP	40176
The Good Guys, Inc.	14910
The Goodyear Tire & Rubber Company	10668
GranCare, Inc.	13710
Grand Casinos, Inc.	15382
The Great Atlantic & Pacific Tea Company, Inc.	10673
Great Western Financial Corporation	10677
The Green Bay Packers, Inc.	40994
Group Technologies Corporation	42003
Grow Biz International, Inc.	16366
GTE Corporation	10620
GTECH Holdings Corporation	15682
Gupta Corporation	14102
The Gymboree Corporation	16057
H. F. Ahmanson & Company	10691
H. J. Heinz Company	10693
H&R Block, Inc.	10689
Halliburton Company	10697
Hallmark Cards, Inc.	40196
Harcourt General, Inc.	10630
Harley-Davidson, Inc.	10706
Harris Corporation	10709
Hartmarx Corporation	10711
Hasbro, Inc.	12007
Healthwise of America, Inc.	16990
The Hearst Corporation	40209
Heartland Express, Inc.	13665
Heilig-Meyers Co.	10717
Herbalife International, Inc.	15594
Hercules Incorporated	10721
Herman Miller, Inc.	13676
Hershey Foods Corporation	10722
Hewlett-Packard Company	10723
Hillenbrand Industries, Inc.	10731
Hilton Hotels Corporation	10733
The Home Depot, Inc.	11470
Homecare Management, Inc.	15675
Honeywell Inc.	10742
Horizon Healthcare Corporation	10746
Hormel Foods Corporation	11977
Hospitality Franchise Systems, Inc.	10003
Host Marriott Corporation	10694
Household International, Inc.	10750
Houston Industries Incorporated	10751
Hyatt Corporation	40231
IBP, Inc.	10761
IDEXX Laboratories, Inc.	15304
Illinois Tool Works Inc.	10778
Immunex Corporation	13742
IMRS Inc.	15446
In Focus Systems, Inc.	10465
In Home Health, Inc.	16997
Information Resources, Inc.	13766
Informix Corporation	13768
Ingersoll-Rand Company	10785
Ingram Industries Inc.	40233
Inland Steel Industries, Inc.	10786
Insurance Auto Auctions, Inc.	15465
Intel Corporation	13787
Intelligent Electronics, Inc.	13790
INTERCO Incorporated	10768
Intergraph Corporation	13799
International Business Machines Corporation	10796
International Family Entertainment, Inc.	15628
International Flavors & Fragrances Inc.	10797
International Game Technology	13812
International Paper Company	10800
Intuit Inc.	16001
ITT Corporation	10773
J. C. Penney Company, Inc.	10810
J.P. Morgan & Co. Incorporated	10812
James River Corporation of Virginia	10817
Jean Philippe Fragrances, Inc.	15428
John Hancock Mutual Life Insurance Company	40248
Johnson Controls, Inc.	10825
Johnson & Johnson	10824
Kellogg Company	10841
Kelly Services, Inc.	13891
Kemper Corporation	10843
Kendall-Jackson Winery Ltd.	41123
Kent Electronics Corporation	12083
Kerr-McGee Corporation	10852
KeyCorp	10853
Kimberly-Clark Corporation	10856
King Ranch, Inc.	41129
Kmart Corporation	10830
Knight-Ridder, Inc.	10859
Koch Industries, Inc.	40267
KPMG Peat Marwick	40270
The Kroger Co.	10864
Lam Research Corporation	13941
Landry's Seafood Restaurants, Inc.	16351
Lands' End, Inc.	10883
LDDS Communications, Inc.	15160
Lehman Brothers Holdings Inc.	41936
Levi Strauss Associates Inc.	40278
The Limited, Inc.	11471
Litton Industries, Inc.	10902
Liz Claiborne, Inc.	13977
Lockheed Corporation	10903
Loews Corporation	10905
Lone Star Steakhouse & Saloon, Inc.	10372
Longs Drug Stores Corporation	10913
Loral Corporation	10915
Lotus Development Corporation	13985
Lowe's Companies, Inc.	10920
The LTV Corporation	10874
Lyondell Petrochemical Company	10924
MacAndrews & Forbes Holdings Inc.	40291
Magma Power Company	14011
Manville Corporation	10953
Marion Merrell Dow Inc.	10955
Mark IV Industries, Inc.	10957
Marriott International, Inc.	10958
Mars, Inc.	40297
Marsh & McLennan Companies, Inc.	10959
Martin Marietta Corporation	10961
Masco Corporation	10962
Massachusetts Mutual Life Insurance Company	40301
Mattel, Inc.	10966
Maxtor Corporation	14049
MAXXIM Medical, Inc.	14553
The May Department Stores Company	10969
Maytag Corporation	10970
McDermott International, Inc.	10972
McDonald's Corporation	10974
McDonnell Douglas Corporation	10975
McGraw-Hill, Inc.	10976
MCI Communications Corporation	13996
McKesson Corporation	10977
McKinsey & Company, Inc.	40304
The Mead Corporation	10978
Medaphis Corporation	15383
Medtronic, Inc.	10981

MORE HOOVER'S COMPANY

Meijer, Inc.	40307	NovaCare, Inc.	13749	Price Waterhouse LLP	40372
Mellon Bank Corporation	10983	Novell, Inc.	14287	Price/Costco, Inc.	17060
Melville Corporation	10984	Nucor Corporation	11098	The Procter & Gamble Company	11211
The Menís Wearhouse, Inc.	15603	NYCOR, Inc.	14188	The Promus Companies Incorporated	13861
Mercantile Stores Company, Inc.	10985	NYNEX Corporation	11044	The Prudential Insurance	
Merck & Co., Inc.	10986	Occidental Petroleum Corporation	11110	Company of America	40377
Merrill Corporation	14092	Octel Communications Corporation	14306	Public Service Enterprise Group Incorporated	11223
Merrill Lynch & Co., Inc.	10990	Office Depot, Inc.	14308	Publix Super Markets, Inc.	40378
Metropolitan Life Insurance Company	40313	Ogden Corporation	11112	Pyxis Corporation	16950
Michael Baker Corporation	12151	Oracle Systems Corporation	14337	Quad Systems Corporation	16037
Micro Warehouse, Inc.	13013	Oregon Steel Mills, Inc.	12208	The Quaker Oats Company	11237
Micron Technology, Inc.	14116	Oryx Energy Company	11128	Quantum Corporation	14521
Microsoft Corporation	14120	Outback Steakhouse, Inc.	13867	Quantum Health Resources, Inc.	11789
Midland Financial Group, Inc.	13916	Outboard Marine Corporation	11129	Quark, Inc.	42139
Minnesota Mining and Manufacturing		Owens-Corning Fiberglas Corporation	11132	R.R. Donnelley & Sons Company	11244
Company	11003	Owens-Illinois, Inc.	15483	RailTex, Inc.	41955
Mitek Surgical Products, Inc.	15435	Oxford Health Plans, Inc.	15344	Rallyís Hamburgers, Inc.	12479
Mobil Corporation	11006	PACCAR Inc.	14354	Ralston Continental Baking Group	16970
Mohawk Industries, Inc.	14105	Pacific Enterprises	11144	Ralston Purina Group	11254
Monro Muffler Brake, Inc.	15328	Pacific Gas and Electric Company	11145	Random Access, Inc.	13570
Monsanto Company	11010	Pacific Telesis Group	11147	Raymond James Financial, Inc.	11258
Montgomery Ward Holding Corp.	40322	PacifiCare Health Systems, Inc.	14364	Raytheon Company	11261
Morgan Stanley Group Inc.	11018	Paine Webber Group Inc.	11148	The Readerís Digest Association, Inc.	14377
Morton International, Inc.	11021	Panhandle Eastern Corporation	11150	Reebok International Ltd.	11266
Motorola, Inc.	11023	Papa Johnís International, Inc.	16241	Regal Cinemas, Inc.	16192
Mycogen Corporation	14178	Parametric Technology Corporation	14647	Reliance Electric Company	15234
Nabors Industries, Inc.	12173	ParcPlace Systems, Inc.	16769	REN Corporation - USA	14599
National Association of		Pathmark Stores, Inc.	40357	Reynolds Metals Company	11276
Securities Dealers, Inc.	41275	Paychex, Inc.	14388	Right Management Consultants, Inc.	14591
National Medical Enterprises, Inc.	11055	Pennzoil Company	11164	Rite Aid Corporation	11278
National Semiconductor Corporation	11058	PeopleSoft, Inc.	14838	River Oaks Furniture Inc.	14551
NationsBank Corporation	11036	PepsiCo, Inc.	11166	RJR Nabisco, Inc.	13122
Natural Wonders, Inc.	15658	PETsMART, Inc.	16273	Roadway Services, Inc.	14596
Natureís Sunshine Products, Inc.	14221	Pfizer Inc.	11175	Rockwell International Corporation	11283
Navistar International Corporation	11063	Phelps Dodge Corporation	11176	Roper Industries, Inc.	12127
NCI Building Systems, Inc.	14434	Philip Morris Companies Inc.	11179	Rubbermaid Incorporated	11294
NeoStar Retail Group, Inc.	12716	Phillips Petroleum Company	11182	Ryder System, Inc.	11298
Netframe Systems, Inc.	15712	Physician Corporation of America	16060	S.C. Johnson & Son, Inc.	40403
New York Life Insurance Company	40339	Physicians Clinical Laboratory, Inc.	15178	Safeguard Scientifics, Inc.	11311
New York Stock Exchange, Inc.	41286	PictureTel Corporation	13379	Safeskin Corporation	16603
The New York Times Company	12184	Pinnacle Micro Inc.	12424	Safety-Kleen Corporation	11312
Nextel Communications, Inc.	10950	Pinnacle West Capital Corporation	11188	Safeway Inc.	11308
NIKE, Inc.	14254	Pitney Bowes Inc.	11190	Salomon Inc	11315
Nordstrom, Inc.	14261	PLATINUM technology, inc.	10452	Sara Lee Corporation	11323
Norfolk Southern Corporation	11084	PNC Bank Corporation	11138	SBC Communications, Inc.	11379
Northrop Grumman Corporation	11093	Polaroid Corporation	11198	SCEcorp	11303
Northwest Airlines Corporation	17160	Powersoft Corporation	15962	Schering-Plough Corporation	11326
Northwestern Mutual Life		PPG Industries, Inc.	11139	Schlumberger NV	11327
Insurance Company	40344	Premark International, Inc.	11204	Schuler Homes, Inc.	15575

GET DETAILED INFORMATION ON AMERICA'S LARGEST AND

PROFILES ON DEMAND

Company	Code	Company	Code	Company	Code
SCI Systems, Inc.	14631	T. Rowe Price Associates, Inc.	41976	USA Waste Services, Inc.	15374
Scios Nova, Inc.	12874	Tandem Computers Incorporated	11440	USAA	40508
The Score Board, Inc.	12327	Tandy Corporation	11441	USAir Group, Inc.	11527
Scott Paper Company	11331	Tanger Factory Outlet Centers, Inc.	16200	USF&G Corporation	11528
Seagate Technology, Inc.	14678	Teachers Insurance and Annuity		USG Corporation	11529
Sears, Roebuck and Co.	11338	Association - College Retirement Equities Fund		USX Corporation - Marathon Group	11534
Sensormatic Electronics Corporation	14697		40457	USX Corporation - U.S. Steel Group	12969
Service Merchandise Company, Inc.	11342	Tech Data Corporation	14882	V. F. Corporation	11572
The Sherwin-Williams Company	11350	Tele-Communications, Inc.	14891	Value Health, Inc.	14234
Silicon Graphics, Inc.	11735	Teledyne, Inc.	11448	Ventritex, Inc.	14920
Skidmore, Owings & Merrill	41501	Telephone and Data Systems, Inc.	12376	Vertex Pharmaceuticals, Inc.	15321
Snap-on Incorporated	11362	Tenneco Inc.	11455	Vestar, Inc.	15071
Snyder Oil Corporation	11363	Texaco Inc.	11458	Viacom Inc.	12435
Sofamor Danek Group, Inc.	16492	Texas Instruments Incorporated	11462	Video Lottery Technologies, Inc.	15325
Software Spectrum, Inc.	15128	Texas Utilities Company	11464	Viking Office Products, Inc.	12076
Solectron Corporation	14296	Textron Inc.	11466	The Vons Companies, Inc.	11589
Sonic Corp.	13112	Thermedics Inc.	12383	Vulcan Materials Company	11591
Sotheby's Holdings, Inc.	12331	Thiokol Corporation	11474	W. R. Grace & Co.	11592
The Southern Company	11372	Thomas Nelson, Inc.	14915	Wabash National Corporation	15063
Southern Pacific Rail Corporation	16318	Three-Five Systems, Inc.	15949	Wal-Mart Stores, Inc.	11600
The Southland Corporation	41970	Time Warner Inc.	11482	Walgreen Co.	11601
Southwest Airlines Co.	11377	The Times Mirror Company	11483	Wall Data, Inc.	15996
Spartan Motors, Inc.	14767	The TJX Companies, Inc.	11432	The Walt Disney Company	11603
Spiegel, Inc.	14773	Toys "R" Us, Inc.	11495	Wang Laboratories, Inc.	12443
SportsTown, Inc.	15615	Trans World Airlines, Inc.	16885	Warner-Lambert Company	11606
Springs Industries, Inc.	11386	Transamerica Corporation	11500	The Washington Post Company	12444
Sprint Corporation	11560	The Travelers Inc.	16727	Watsco, Inc.	12446
Stac Electronics	15646	Tribune Company	11508	Wells Fargo & Company	11619
The Stanley Works	11397	TRW Inc.	11434	Wendy's International, Inc.	11621
Staples, Inc.	14790	Turner Broadcasting System, Inc.	12404	Westinghouse Electric Corporation	11627
Starbucks Corporation	15745	Tyco International Ltd.	11516	Weyerhaeuser Company	11630
State Farm Mutual Automobile		Tyson Foods, Inc.	14965	Whirlpool Corporation	11632
Insurance Company	40445	U.S. Long Distance Corporation	11840	Whitman Corporation	11634
STERIS Corporation	10740	U.S. Robotics, Inc.	15388	Whole Foods Market, Inc.	10952
Stone Container Corporation	11404	U S WEST, Inc.	11518	Winn-Dixie Stores, Inc.	11642
The Stop & Shop Companies, Inc.	15458	UAL Corporation	11520	Wm. Wrigley Jr. Company	11648
Storage Technology Corporation	11407	The Unicom Corporation	10376	WMX Technologies, Inc.	11610
Student Loan Marketing Association	11410	Union Carbide Corporation	11540	Woolworth Corporation	10538
Sturm, Ruger & Company, Inc.	14818	Union Pacific Corporation	11544	Xerox Corporation	11657
Sun Company, Inc.	11412	Unisys Corporation	11548	Xilinx, Inc.	15245
Sun Microsystems, Inc.	14833	United Parcel Service of America, Inc.	40483	Xircom, Inc.	14103
Sunrise Medical Inc.	14839	The United States Shoe Corporation	11557	Xpedite Systems, Inc.	16836
SunTrust Banks, Inc.	11416	United States Surgical Corporation	11558	Yellow Corporation	15192
Supercuts, Inc.	15444	United Technologies Corporation	11559	Young & Rubicam Inc.	40537
SUPERVALU Inc.	11419	United Video Satellite Group Inc.	16685	Zebra Technologies Corporation	15351
Sybase, Inc.	15350	United Waste Systems, Inc.	11221	Zenith Electronics Corporation	11660
Symantec Corporation	14850	Universal Corporation	11564	Zilog, Inc.	13211
Synopsys, Inc.	15534	Unocal Corporation	11569	Zoll Medical Corporation	15788
SYSCO Corporation	11423	The Upjohn Company	11570	Zoom Telephonics, Inc.	15365

FASTEST-GROWING COMPANIES IN SECONDS.